THE POLITICS

OF

UNITED STATES

FOREIGN POLICY

Third Edition

Jerel A. Rosati

University of South Carolina

WADSWORTH

™

THOMSON LEARNING

Australia • Canada • Mexico • Singapore • Spain
United Kingdom • United States

WADSWORTH

THOMSON LEARNING

Publisher	Clark Baxter	Production Service	UG / GGS Information Services, Inc.
Acquisitions Editor	David Tatom	Production Editor	Nancy Whelan
Editorial Assistant	Dianna Long	Copy Editor	Steven Baker
Technology Project Manager	Melinda Newfarmer	Cover Designer	Sue Hart
Marketing Manager	Janise Fry	Cover Image	Cameron Heryet/Getty Images
Marketing Assistant	Mary Ho	Compositor	UG / GGS Information Services, Inc.
Print/Media Buyer	Doreen Suruki	Cover and Text Printer	Webcom Limited
Permissions Editor	Kiely Sexton		

Printed in Canada

1 2 3 4 5 6 7 07 06 05 04 03

For more information about our products, contact us at:
Thomson Learning Academic Resource Center
1-800-423-0563
For permission to use material from this text, contact us by:
Phone: 1-800-730-2214
Fax: 1-800-730-2215
Web: http://www.thomsonrights.com

Library of Congress Control Number: 2003103162

ISBN 0155058843

Wadsworth/Thomson Learning
10 Davis Drive
Belmont, CA 94002-3098
USA

Asia
Thomson Learning
5 Shenton Way #01-01
UIC Building
Singapore 068808

Australia/New Zealand
Thomson Learning
102 Dodds Street
Southbank, Victoria 3006
Australia

Canada
Nelson
1120 Birchmount Road
Toronto, Ontario M1K 5G4
Canada

Europe/Middle East/Africa
Thomson Learning
High Holborn House
50/51 Bedford Row
London WC1R 4LR
United Kingdom

Latin America
Thomson Learning
Seneca, 53
Colonia Polanco
11560 Mexico D.F.
Mexico

Spain/Portugal
Paraninfo
Calle/Magallanes, 25
28015 Madrid, Spain

To my wife, family and friends, to all my students,
and to all those who strive to learn

PREFACE TO THE THIRD EDITION

I have been extremely pleased with the response to the first two editions of *The Politics of United States Foreign Policy*. It has been used at more than three hundred colleges and universities throughout the United States (including the National War College) and in over ten foreign countries, and has been translated into Mandarin Chinese. This has greatly exceeded my expectations and hopes. Here I would like to explain why I chose to write a textbook on the politics of U.S. foreign policy in the first place and what this book tries to accomplish, what is new to the third edition (and how instructors and students might benefit), why textbooks and works of synthesis are of underestimated value, and finally acknowledge the many people who made this all possible.

WHY A TEXTBOOK ON THE POLITICS OF U.S. FOREIGN POLICY?

Very simply, after receiving my education in political science and international studies, after living and working in Washington, D.C. for four years, and after teaching U.S. foreign policy (and engaging in research and scholarly writing) within academia for a decade, I was unhappy with the few textbooks and general surveys that existed on the topic for they did not capture the "politics" of United States Foreign Policy.

The politics of U.S. foreign policy is complex and messy and full of contradictions. It is very political and about the good, the bad, and the ugly. Politics is often boring and yet can also be interesting and sometimes fascinating. And politics is important and consequential (for the United States and the lives of Americans, as well as for the rest of the world and much of its citizens). Although it can easily seem to be confusing and a mystery to the outsider, U.S. foreign policy can and should be understandable to all despite the complicated and erudite discourse of the scholars and special-

ists, along with the simplistic political stereotypes and symbolism, that too often prevails among analysts, practitioners, journalists, and politicians. These were the reasons and the challenges that motivated me to write such a book.

Furthermore, numerous developments have occurred throughout the world and within American society over the last four decades that have made an understanding of the politics of U.S. foreign policy even more critical than before. The Vietnam War, the collapse of the gold standard, Watergate, détente, the oil embargo, the Iran hostage crisis, the Iran-contra affair, large federal budget and trade deficits, the collapse of the Soviet Union and communism in Eastern Europe, the end of the cold war, the Persian Gulf War, and most recently and obviously, September 11, 2001, and the subsequent war on terrorism—these are just some of the developments that suggest the need for an overview and understanding of how U.S. foreign policy is made. This book attempts to provide insight and understanding of the politics of U.S. foreign policy in light of recent history.

In this respect, *The Politics of United States Foreign Policy has been written with five general goals in mind:* to be accessible and interesting to the reader, to be comprehensive in topical and analytical coverage, to address central themes in U.S. foreign policy, to provide a strong sense of the actual workings of politics, and to integrate theory and practice so individuals can think theoretically and critically.

The first goal of *The Politics of United States Foreign Policy* is to provide information and knowledge that is accessible, interesting, and understandable to readers. Too many textbooks are plagued by an encyclopedic scope and excessive jargon. From a learning perspective this can be counterproductive, and this book addresses the problem by emphasizing the most pertinent information and significant patterns in the politics of U.S. foreign policy, as opposed to giving "equal time" to all potentially relevant information (which is also a problem for the increasingly popular

"condensed" editions). Such information and knowledge are organized in terms of three major perspectives
and consistently linked to the book's three central
themes, discussed below, so as to maximize understanding. Student interest and learning are also fur-
thered by an effort to describe and discuss the actual
dynamics of American politics in accessible and engaging prose.

The second goal of the book is to be comprehensive in topical and substantive coverage from three
broad analytical or theoretical perspectives. This book
provides a broad discussion of the government, the society, and the global and historical context, explaining
how they interact and affect the foreign policy process
of the United States. Beyond some familiarity with the
president and Congress, many students (undergraduates, graduates, everyday people, and even practitioners, including journalists) know little about the basic
institutions within the foreign policy bureaucracy, such
as the National Security Council, the State Department,
and the intelligence community. Hence, these institutions are discussed fully. *The Politics of United States
Foreign Policy* also discusses other important institutions that are often ignored, such as the military establishment, the foreign economic bureaucracy, the
courts, state and local government, and the political
culture of Washington, D.C. Because students may
similarly lack extensive knowledge of American society
and America's historical role within the global environment, these two perspectives merit coverage as well.
Most textbooks downplay the significance of public
opinion, political culture and ideology, the exercise of
civil liberties, electoral and group politics, and the impact of the media on the foreign policy process. They
also ignore ways in which the global environment and
changes in America's historic role within it affect domestic and governmental politics. Only by integrating
all three perspectives—the historical and global context, the government, and American society—can one
have the basis for developing a comprehensive understanding of the politics of U.S. foreign policy.

The book's third goal is to address three themes
that are central to the politics of U.S. foreign policy.
Many textbooks provide detailed information yet do
not address large questions that allow the student to
make sense of the material. This book synthesizes
what has been learned about how U.S. foreign policy
is made in order to maximize knowledge and under-

standing. It does this by posing three questions that
have been particularly significant in attracting the interest of scholars:

1. What have been the dominant historical patterns
   of continuity and change in the foreign policy
   process over time? What has been the impact of
   the end of the cold war and the September 11,
   2001, terrorist attacks?
2. To what extent has the president been able to
   manage and govern foreign policy?
3. How has the constant tension between democracy
   and national security evolved?

While a historical perspective is provided, the emphasis
is on the key patterns that have prevailed since World
War II. Students should learn that, while continuity has
been the norm in the short term, the foreign policy
process has undergone considerable change over time,
as experienced during the late 1940s and early 1950s
with World War II and the rise of the cold war and
then again since the late 1960s and early 1970s following the Vietnam War and Watergate. Compared to the
cold war years, for instance, the president has found it
much more difficult to govern foreign policy as the
tension between national security and democracy has
increased since Vietnam. Such patterns may be changing with the end of the cold war and the September 11
attacks as the United States navigates the twenty-first
century.

The fourth goal of the book is to provide a strong
sense of the politics involved in the making of U.S. foreign policy. Few textbooks capture the "reality" and dynamic nature of politics. In this respect, it is important
to acquire not only a basic knowledge of important institutions and the policymaking process but also an ap-
preciation of the ways in which they actually operate
within the political environment. To understand the
practice of U.S. foreign policy, students need to have a
feeling for and a comprehension of the politics involved—both within government and throughout society. They need to learn who the players are and how
they operate, interact, conflict, win, compromise, and
lose. Students must come to understand the beliefs and
the personalities that prevail in American politics as
well as the language of politics. This will hopefully capture their attention and interest and allow them to better understand the use of power and symbols in what is
a very political, complex, contradictory, and messy

process in a country like the United States with more than 270 million people.

The final goal is to integrate theory and practice throughout so as to encourage students to think analytically and theoretically. Different concepts and theoretical approaches (such as democratic peace theory) are introduced at various points in the book to help integrate and make sense of the material covered, as well as to emphasize the importance of conceptual thinking to further understanding. This is crucial to avoid the problem of presenting an excess of information without providing the necessary analytical tools that allow students to absorb and comprehend the material. Unlike many textbooks, I often discuss the major theoretical approaches after, not before, students are substantively grounded so they may better understand the value of theory for explaining foreign policy making. For example, the chapter on decisionmaking theory (highlighting group dynamics, as well as the role that individual perceptions and personality plays in policymaking) comes after the chapters on the president and the foreign policy bureaucracy. Thus, substantive knowledge, historical knowledge, and theoretical knowledge are woven together throughout the book to maximize understanding and critical thinking.

OTHER KEY FEATURES

In order to further these goals and provide a strong understanding of the politics of U.S. foreign policy, this book relies on a variety of additional pedagogical features:

- It integrates history and policy throughout. This includes, in addition to national security, coverage of international economics and foreign economic policy making, as well as issues typically ignored in foreign policy, such as foreign assistance and nation-building, gender and the role of women, and the war on drugs (among others). Background and illustrations are provided to supply perspective and information—something many students lack.
- Short essays (in boxes) are interspersed in each chapter to highlight significant illustrations, controversies, trends, key figures, and theoretical perspectives, to allow for more in-depth exploration of subjects related to the chapter, without detracting from the flow of the text.

- Each chapter ends with bibliographic essays under the subtitle "Suggested Sources" to guide students through the labyrinth of source materials available on any given topic as a starting point for further inquiry. More comprehensive than a list of recommended readings, each bibliographic essay highlights and comments on the best sources for additional information on the topic, including scholarly and policy-oriented books and articles, newspapers and journalistic accounts, government documents, and Websites.
- Selective and updated use of tables and figures are integrated in each chapter that are intended to be informative and promote critical thinking.
- There is a comprehensive index, constructed by the author, in the rear for quickly finding where topics are discussed throughout the book.
- Each chapter can stand on its own and be assigned out of order to reflect each instructor's organizational preferences.

NEW TO THE THIRD EDITION

Since so many have found the textbook of value, its basic integrity has been maintained. At the same time, a number of changes have been made that I believe have resulted in an even better and stronger textbook:

- It is completely updated and timely, integrating the implications of the end of the cold war, the George W. Bush administration, and the implications of September 11 and the war on terrorism in every chapter and throughout each chapter (not just an add-on at the end). This is a truly revised third edition.
- The chapters on the military and the intelligence community have been completely revised and updated.
- There is a chapter in which the tension between civil liberties versus national security, a topic not usually discussed in other textbooks, is highlighted in light of September 11.
- There is a chapter on elections and their impact on foreign policy, especially in light of the controversial 2000 presidential elections, which is typically ignored in other textbooks.
- There is now a chapter totally devoted to foreign economic policy making, which is very important

in U.S. foreign policy and usually ignored in other textbooks.

- There are now eighteen instead of twenty chapters, making the book more clearly organized and streamlined. The chapter on presidential power and leadership has been heavily revised and updated (and condensed from two chapters). The last two chapters have been integrated to provide an overall synthesis and conclusion about the making and future politics of U.S. foreign policy.
- Each chapter begins with a list of questions that lay out what the chapter will address and returns to them at the conclusion. Each chapter closes with key assessments, questions, and issues for further consideration, especially about the future.
- Key terms and concepts are **boldfaced** in the text and listed at the end of each chapter.
- *Italics* have been used throughout the text for highlighting major points.
- Three levels of subheadings are used and their titles have been refined to promote clarity and organization within each chapter.
- Appendix A provides an abridged version of those portions of the U.S. Constitution that are devoted and relevant to foreign affairs.
- Appendix B provides a brief, user friendly, guide on how to utilize electronic and print sources available on the internet and most libraries in order to conduct research and update information on U.S. foreign policy.
- With purchase of a new textbook, four months of free online access to InfoTrac® College Edition is available. This is probably the single best database available on international affairs, politics, and U.S. foreign policy with over 20 years worth of "full-text articles" from nearly 4000 scholarly, policy, and popular journals and magazines.

THE VALUE OF TEXTBOOKS AND THE NEED FOR SYNTHESIS

Let me offer a few thoughts about textbooks in general. The academic profession has increasingly come to regard the writing of textbooks as an unimportant and unscholarly effort of little value beyond the classroom. I find this to be a very disturbing and provincial view. A good textbook—Thomas Kuhn makes a distinction between an elementary and advanced textbook in *The*

Structure of Scientific Revolutions—provides critical information and knowledge about a given area of study. It engenders learning and interest and may even inspire further inquiry and learning. It reflects and may even help to define the field. But most likely, a good textbook provides a synthesis of the accumulated knowledge of a subject at a time when specialization and the overabundance of information and published material make the need for synthesis greater than ever.

This need for synthesis has begun to be recognized within the study of international relations and U.S. foreign policy. For example, in their statement of editorial philosophy for the journal *International Studies Review* begun a few years ago, Margaret Hermann and Robert Woyach point out that "the isolation of the different specialties in international studies limits the cross-fertilization that could lead to more integrative and synthetic perspectives." Bernard Cohen, one of the classic students of the field, noted the problem as early as 1956 in *The Political Process and Foreign Policy* when he wrote, "while there may be widespread recognition of the desirability of knowing more about how foreign policy is made, it is a far from simple task actually to build up a useful body of relevant knowledge about overall processes."

This textbook attempts to do just that. As I stated in the preface to the first edition, "I hope that this book not only serves as a worthwhile pedagogical tool but that it also contributes to a scholarly synthesis and understanding of the politics of U.S. foreign policy." I have been inspired to that task by the example of the classic texts I used as a student myself, whose breadth and depth of knowledge and rich and coherent understanding provide the foundation for my own.

This view has been reinforced by the positive and generous comments made by the book's many reviewers and users, who include professors in political science, international studies, and history, as well as practitioners. Here are a few:

- "It is really the best single source on all aspects of the policy process." Robert Soofer, Professor of National Security Strategy, National War College, Washington, D.C.
- "A valuable synthesis." Fred I. Greenstein, Princeton University
- "This is the most comprehensive, innovative and ideologically balanced text on American foreign

policy that I have even seen." George Clay Kiegh, Illinois Wesleyan University

- "It is a thoroughly stimulating, deeply engrossing analysis which I recommend highly to all students of U.S. foreign policy, young and old." Paul M. Kattenburg, former Foreign Service Officer and author of *The Vietnam Trauma in American Foreign Policy, 1945–1975*
- "In a unique blend of substance and theory that comprehensively examines U.S. foreign policy, Rosati has achieved that delicate balance between readability for undergraduates and theoretical relevance for both graduate students and specialists. This textbook clearly has no equal in the field!" Peter J. Schraeder, Loyola University, Chicago
- "He has woven a comprehensive fabric that contains institutional threads and political colors not ordinarily found in writings of U.S. foreign policy—certainly not in one book. It will be a valuable tool for the student and informative reading for the observer of America on the world scene." Frank K Sloan, former Deputy Assistant Secretary of Defense for International Security Affairs under President John F. Kennedy
- "This remains the best overall text on the Politics of United States Foreign Policy. . . . Rosati brings the complexity of the topic home to the average student but does so without the use of confusing language or overly professional jargon." Douglas A. Borer, Virginia Polytechnic Institute University
- "Professor Rosati has combined the intellectual courage to range beyond the conventional interpretations and sources with a rigorous scholarship of evenhandedness. This book has the potential to become a classic in the field." G. Lane Van Tassel, Georgia Southern University
- "This is an enormously rich book." Walter LaFeber, Cornell University
- "The best overview of this subject that I have ever read." Ralph Levering, Davidson College
- "Very comprehensive and quite impressive." Geir Lundestad, The Norwegian Nobel Institute
- "A comprehensive, topical and well-written examination of the U.S. foreign policy-making process . . . Rosati masterfully uses historical examples to explain conceptual and analytical approaches to the foreign policy-making process." *Millenium: Journal of International Studies* (published by the London School of Economics)

- "I love this book. Very sound approach that will only get better with each edition." Reviewer no. 1 (for the third edition)
- "I consider this the leading text. . . . No other text so thoroughly, effectively, and clearly focuses on the politics and policymaking of U.S. foreign policy." Reviewer no. 2

TO INSTRUCTORS AND STUDENTS

From the perspective of teaching and learning, I do not find having an instructor's manual, a test bank, and all the electronic software that often accompanies a textbook today to be all that helpful (although it appears impressive). I have tried to write this book so that all these features are within the text (or are unnecessary), as indicated above. But particularly helpful are the following:

- Overviews and summaries are provided in the introduction and concluding section of each chapter. A complete overview is provided in chapter 1 and a grand synthesis can be found in chapter 18.
- The creation of exams (and various assignments) by instructors and the preparation for exams by students also is aided by:

  The boldfacing and list of Key Terms

  The use of italicizing for identifying key points and patterns

  The use of three levels of subheadings within each chapter for organizing the material so that key aspects are presented to maximize clarity, depth and analysis, at the same time allowing one to integrate and synthesize each section into a coherent whole (for each chapter, for each Part, and for the entire book).

I do highly recommend making use of *InfoTrac* and Appendix B. It is a great database for conducting research and it is an easy way to keep the volume updated to the present day. Much of the information available in newspapers, magazines, policy journals and academic journals (such as those listed in Tables 17.4 and 17.5) can easily be found as full text (and can be downloaded as a text file or emailed to you and printed) to accompany the text.

ACKNOWLEDGMENTS

I am indebted to a large number of people who inspired me, from whom I have learned, and who took the time and effort to directly assist and support me in the writing of this book over the years. I would like to thank the following professors for having a large impact on my education: Bernard Brodie, David Sears, Steven Spiegel, Martin Weil, Sheldon Simon, Stephen Walker, Matt Bonham, Duncan Clarke, Stephen Cohen, Theodore Coloumbis, Nicholus Onuf, and Burton Sapin. I very much appreciate the comments of the various outside reviewers: Douglas Borer, Steve Chan, Larry Elowitz, John Gilbert, George Kieh, Martin Kyre, J. Patrice McSherry, Dean Minix, B. David Myers, Martin Sampson, James M. Scott, David Skidmore, Donald Sylvan, Lane Van Tassell, Larry Taulbee, David W. Thornton, and Walter F. Weiker. I remain grateful to my academic colleagues for providing valuable feedback: Earl Black, Ken Clements, Roger Coate, Betty Glad, Mal Hyman, Joe Hagan, Don Puchala, Zhou Qipeng, Dan Sabia, and Laura Woliver. And I remain grateful to numerous professional colleagues, including: Hal Birch (U.S. Army); James Davidson (U.S. Navy), Paul Kattenburg (Department of State), and Frank Sloan (Department of Defense).

Graduate students provided tremendous and valuable assistance, including Patrick Anderson (U.S. Army), Tony Bell, Jane Berthusen, John Cass (U.S. Army), Kemp Chester (U.S. Army), Dave Cohen, John Creed, Janine Davidson (former U.S. Air Force), Dwayne Fulmer, Rick Haeuber, Byongok Han, Steve Hook, Pamela Howard, Jack Lechelt, Bobby Phillips, Bret Traw, Steve Twing, Art Vanden Houten, Darin Van Tassell, Jennifer Willand, and Li Xinyu. I also have been fortunate enough to have had critical assistance from undergraduates: Teresa Brazell, Julie Close, Cody Lidge, Tina Morgan, Katherine Ray, Juli Sproules, and Adina Sigal.

I also would like to deeply thank David Tatom, a great editor and friend, who I have been fortunate to work with from the beginning through all three editions under four different publishers; and thank the many fine folks involved at Holt, Rinehart & Winston, Harcourt Brace Jovanovich, Harcourt Brace, and currently, Wadsworth, especially Dianna Long, Susan Alkana, Stephen Baker, Nancy Whelan, and Janise Fry for this edition. Finally, crucial psychological support has been essential and provided by my family, especially my wife, Karen, and my friends. Altogether, it has been an incredibly satisfying and taxing experience involving the help of many people that has produced a book on the politics of U.S. foreign policy for which I alone take complete responsibility.

I would love to hear any comments and receive feedback from instructors and students about the extent to which the book contributes to an understanding of the politics of United States foreign policy and about how I might further strengthen it in the future. My e-mail address is *rosati@sc.edu* (see *http://www.cla.sc.edu/GINT/facbio/rosati.html* for a biosketch).

Jerel Rosati
University of South Carolina
2003

CONTENTS

ESSAYS

FIGURES

TABLES

PART ONE

. . . .

INTRODUCTION

Chapter 1 discusses why United States foreign policy is significant to understand, introduces the concept of foreign policy and the underlying analytical framework used throughout the book for studying and understanding the complex politics of U.S. foreign policy, and begins to explore some of the major post–cold war developments since the collapse of communism in the Soviet Union and Eastern Europe and their impact on the making of U.S. foreign policy into the twenty-first century.

CHAPTER
1

. . . .

THE POLITICS OF U.S. FOREIGN POLICY

*T*he foreign policy of the United States has experienced important continuities and changes over time. Following World War II and with the rise of the cold war, United States foreign policy during the fifties and sixties revolved around the containment of Soviet and communist expansion throughout the world. The cold war years were also a time when the power of the presidency was preeminent in the making of U.S. foreign policy. Yet over the last thirty years numerous developments have occurred throughout the world and American society that have affected the conduct of U.S. foreign policy. Events such as the Vietnam War and Watergate challenged America's postwar containment policy and the power of the presidency. More recently, the end of the cold war brought about by the collapse of the Soviet Union and communism in Eastern Europe, and the September 11, 2001, terrorist attacks have opened up new opportunities and challenges for U.S. foreign policy.

Why did the United States pursue a policy of global containment following World War II and throughout the fifties and sixties? What impact did events such as the Vietnam War and Watergate have on U.S. foreign policy during the seventies and eighties? What impact does the

end of the cold war have on foreign policy as the United States enters the twenty-first century? What will be the impact of the September 11 attacks on U.S. foreign policy? Answers to these crucial questions can be found only upon examining the politics of U.S. foreign policy.

This chapter will provide a basic guide and overview to understand the politics of U.S. foreign policy for the rest of the book. *It will address the following questions:* What is foreign policy and the nature of the foreign policy process? How is U.S. foreign policy commonly studied? What analytical framework will be utilized to organize, discuss, and make sense of the politics of U.S. foreign policy? What are the three basic perspectives (or levels of analysis) and the three basic themes (or questions) that will be the basis for analyzing the material throughout the book? And we begin to raise the question, what are the implications of the end of the cold war and the September 11 attacks for the politics of U.S. foreign policy into the twenty-first century? But before addressing these questions, it is important to understand why United States foreign policy has a significant impact for Americans, and for individuals and people throughout the world.

THE RELEVANCE AND SIGNIFICANCE OF FOREIGN POLICY

Why should people care about the politics of United States foreign policy? Very simply, because it matters. *United States foreign policy has profound significance for the lives of people, both Americans and people abroad.* Americans in particular may be unaware of some of the important consequences that U.S. foreign policy may have because the impact on their everyday lives is so distant, indirect and often taken for granted.

For example, the standard of living of Americans is heavily affected by the state of the economy and America's role throughout the world economy, which is effected by foreign economic policies involving trade in goods and services, investment in companies and capital, monetary policies and currency fluctuations, and access to raw materials and energy. It is important to understand that the American economy has become more integral to, and dependent upon, the international political economy. At the turn of the twenty-first century, Americans export more than $1 trillion a year of merchandise goods and services and import more than $1.4 trillion a year from abroad. American investment abroad is approaching $7 trillion a year, while foreign investment within the United States is approaching $8 trillion per year. Monetary transactions valued at the equivalent of trillions of dollars are made almost everyday in American and global markets, which have significant impact on currency exchange rates—such as the value of the American dollar—investment, and trade. The United States imports roughly 50 percent of its domestic oil consumption, much of it from the Middle East, making it a vital area of the world, as demonstrated by the Persian Gulf War of 1991. All this is reinforced by the fact that the U.S. government spends and invests over $400 billion a year on the military and a scientific-industrial infrastructure to support the military—all impacting the economy and the standard of living of people within the military and throughout American society. Such economic transactions as discussed above have significant implications for the level of growth, inflation, and unemployment in the American economy in general, as well as for the jobs and incomes of individuals, including interest rate levels and taxes.

More direct and obvious is the impact of U.S. foreign policy on the security and health of the nation's citizens. Since the 1930s the United States has been engaged in numerous conflicts, including four major wars. World War II resulted in over 400,000 battle deaths; over 35,000 died during the Korean War; and over 55,000 died during the Vietnam War. It's also important to point out that, in addition to those who died, many more suffered from injuries in each of these major wars, including the Persian Gulf War. Furthermore, each of these wars required millions of personnel to serve in the military and potentially place their lives at risk. In fact, since the Korean War the United States has maintained a large permanent military in times of peace as well as war, deployed both at home and throughout the world. Times of war and national emergencies are also times of political tension at home when the demands of democracy are usually in conflict with the demands of national security. This impacts American individual freedom, premised on civil rights and liberties "for all" guaranteed in the Constitution of the United States. Despite the end of the cold war and the collapse of the Soviet Union, such concerns about security, physical well-being, and individual freedom are not likely to disappear, for the United States continues to maintain an active global presence and a large military that has been involved in numerous conflicts in different parts of the world in one capacity or another. Certainly the tragedy surrounding the events of September 11, 2001, brought all these issues very close to the lives of all Americans.

There are other important areas of foreign policy that impact Americans beyond economics and individual livelihood, security, and individual health and freedom. Some that come to mind involve immigration and population dynamics, the drug trade, the spread of AIDS, travel and tourism, and issues such as environmental protection, deforestation, and global warming. The point is that U.S. foreign policy is heavily involved in a myriad of activities and issues throughout the world that have implications—sometimes more immediate and direct, sometimes more indirect and underlying—for the everyday lives and futures of Americans.

It's also important to point out that not only does U.S. foreign policy have significance for Americans but it impacts the lives of people throughout the world. This may be more obvious to Americans even though it may not receive much attention. Such impact is mainly a function of the fact that the United States is much more powerful and much wealthier than the world's other societies and peoples. Therefore, U.S. foreign policies and behaviors abroad can have profound impact—sometimes for the better, sometimes for the worse—on people who live in other parts of the world.

One major illustration is the Persian Gulf War in 1991. In this particular case, although there were very few American (and allied) casualties, well over 100,000 Iranians—most of them civilians (relatively innocent men, women, and children)—were killed and injured from the massive bombing campaign, despite the shortness of the war. Clearly, Americans have to wrestle with these difficult moral and humanitarian questions involving U.S. foreign policy, but they also have to understand that America's role has an impact on the societies and lives of people throughout the world—which has subsequent potential security, political, economic, and social implications for the future of the United States and Americans in the twenty-first century. Certainly the September 11 attacks, President Bush's war on terrorism, and how that war is fought at home and abroad clearly highlights all of this.

Hence U.S. foreign policy is relevant and significant for the lives of people both within the United States and throughout the world. And it appears that the interdependencies and pace of interactions that exist across the globe are likely only to increase. Furthermore, it also appears likely that America's global presence and foreign policy will continue into the twenty-first century, though its particular foreign policy orientation and actions may not be easy to predict. Therefore, the relevance and significance of U.S. foreign policy on people's lives is likely to continue and possibly increase, which is why it is so important to study and to understand. And this can only be done by examining the politics of U.S. foreign policy.

UNDERSTANDING FOREIGN POLICY, ITS COMPLEXITY AND POLITICS

At this point it may be helpful to pause and ask, what is meant by foreign policy? This term is used all the time, and we probably know foreign policy when we see it.

But the concept is rarely if ever defined, and the lack of clarity concerning what it means contributes to ambiguity, confusion, and unnecessary disagreement. Very simply, foreign policy, or foreign relations, in this book refers to the scope of involvement abroad and the collection of goals, strategies, and instruments that are selected by governmental policymakers.[1]

In order to understand the foreign policy of a country, one needs to recognize who decides and acts. To say "the United States intervened" is part of our everyday language. But what do people mean when they use this phrase? In reality, countries do not act; people act. What is usually meant is that certain governmental officials, representing the state—that is, the United States—acted. A **state** is a legal concept that refers to the governmental institutions through which policymakers act in the name of the people of a given territory. The **foreign policy process,** or the **politics of foreign policy,** therefore, refers to how governmental decisions and policies are formulated and implemented. The focus in this book, then, is on examining the foreign policy process of the United States—how decisions and policies are made. The substance of policy, nevertheless, will be woven throughout in order to better understand the politics of U.S. foreign policy.

With this in mind, *two very important points must be understood about the nature of the foreign policy process* in the United States: that it is a very complex process and that it is a very political process. First, the U.S. foreign policy process is very complex and extremely messy. Many Americans tend initially to operate with a rather simple and straightforward view of the foreign policy process: that U.S. foreign policy is made and defined basically at the top of the political hierarchy, especially by the president. According to Roger Hilsman, former assistant secretary of state for Far Eastern affairs in the Kennedy administration, "As Americans, we think it only reasonable that the procedures for making national decisions should be orderly, with clear lines of responsibility and authority." We expect decisions to be made by "the proper, official, and authorized persons, and to know that the really big decisions will be made at the top . . . with each of the participants having roles and powers so well and precisely defined that they can be held accountable for their actions by their superiors and eventually by the electorate."[2]

Clearly, the president and his beliefs play a crucial role in the making of U.S. foreign policy. However, the president does not make U.S. foreign policy alone. According to Charles Maechling, Jr., "In propagating the delusion of a master hand and only one tiller, both the executive branch and the news media have collaborated as if in a silent conspiracy—the executive branch in order to enhance the prestige and image of its political leadership, and the news media to simplify the task of reporting and enlarge their audience by dramatizing a few personalities."[3]

The reality is that many other individuals and institutions are involved within the government and throughout the society in the foreign policy process: presidential advisers, high-level officials within the executive branch, the foreign policy bureaucracies, Congress, the courts, State and local governments, the public, political parties, interest groups and social movements, the media, and international actors. It is in this sense that the making of U.S. foreign policy is a complex process. It is also a messy process, for the variety of individuals and institutions that affect U.S. foreign policy do not stand still but constantly interact with and have an impact on one another. In other words, the policymaking process is not static but, as the word "process" implies, dynamic. If the process initially sounds confusing, don't be dismayed; given its overall complexity, the foreign policy process can easily be confusing.

Second, the foreign policy process in the United States is also very much a political process. We need to examine politics, for it is the essence of the foreign policy process. What is politics? In the minds of many Americans, politics is a dirty word that implies unsavory behavior in the political arena. Given such a negative connotation, there appears to be a widespread set of expectations and hopes that American politics should result in a rational process that is somehow "above politics." Let's turn to Roger Hilsman once again: "As Americans, with our flair for the mechanical and love of efficiency combined with a moralistic Puritan heritage, we would like to think not only that policymaking is a conscious and deliberate act, one of analyzing problems and systematically examining grand alternatives in all their implications, but also that the alternative chosen is aimed at achieving overarching ends that serve a high moral purpose. . . . And we feel that the entire decision-making process ought to be a dignified, even majestic [process]."[4] This, unfortunately, is a rather simple and unrealistic view of the nature of politics.

One common definition of politics is "who gets what, when, and how."[5] This definition emphasizes that politics is, as Hedrick Smith says in *The Power Game*, a "serious game with high stakes, one in which the winners and losers affect many lives—yours, mine, those of the people down the street, and of people all over the world."[6] Another definition of politics is the "competition for power and shared meaning." This simple but meaningful definition emphasizes the importance that ideas and symbolism play in the policy process. A final definition describes politics as "competition between different individuals and groups for control of the government, and for support of the public and influence throughout society, in order to promote certain ends." This is the broadest of the three definitions, emphasizing the role of different goal-oriented individuals and groups and the various arenas in which the political process takes place.

The three definitions are complementary and contribute to an understanding of what politics is all about. Together they illustrate that the politics of U.S. foreign policy involves competition among differently motivated individuals and groups, that politics involves the flow of power and symbolism throughout government and society, and that it involves winners and losers. Such politics defines the national interest—a concept that is supposed to represent what is best for the country. However, it is a very subjective concept, for different people will define what is best for the country differently. Not surprisingly, the term national interest is often invoked behind a particular policy view to garner support from government and society.[7] Ultimately, U.S. foreign policy (and the so-called national interest) tends to reflect the goals and priorities of those individuals and groups who are the most successful in influencing the political process within government and throughout society. Such a foreign policy process may be more or less moral depending on the type of value judgment made.

Clearly, the making of U.S. foreign policy is a complex process inseparable from politics. This has been a dominant theme that most of the early theorists—such as Gabriel Almond, Paul Hammond, Roger Hilsman, Stanley Hoffmann, Charles Lindblom, Richard Neustadt, Warner Schilling, Glenn Snyder, and Richard Snyder—emphasized throughout their work on the U.S. foreign policy-making process during the "high cold war" period of the 1950s and 1960s, when the world seemed simpler—a time when presidential power and the cold war consensus were at their apex.[8]

Since the Vietnam War, the complexity and political nature of the policy process has become more intense and increasingly visible. As we will see, it has become very difficult for a president to govern successfully and lead the country in foreign policy. In the words of I. M. Destler, Leslie H. Gelb, and Anthony Lake, in *Our Own Worst Enemy: The Unmaking of American Foreign Policy,* "The making of American foreign policy [has] entered a new and far more ideological and political phase."[9] Or as Hedrick Smith likewise observed in the eighties, "Presidents now have much greater difficulty marshaling governing coalitions" for "it is a much looser power game now, more wide open, harder to manage and manipulate than it was a quarter of a century ago when I came to town."[10] The complex politics of United States foreign policy, if anything, has been heightened with the collapse of the cold war.

THE STUDY OF
U.S. FOREIGN POLICY

The purpose of this book is to provide a strong understanding of the complex politics inherent in U.S. foreign policy. Clearly, most Americans, as indicated above, tend to have a rather simple and often naive view of American politics and the making of U.S. foreign policy. But such a simple view is not Americans' alone. Most non-Americans and observers of the American scene from abroad tend to simplify the American political process, as well—often equating "the president" with "United States foreign policy." Even the most educated and successful Americans often fail to fully appreciate the complexity and political essence of the policy process. As Hedrick Smith found, "Some of the most sophisticated people around the country often fail to understand the rules of the Washington power game.[11]

How does one study and understand the complex politics of U.S. foreign policy? *Three different approaches to the study of U.S. foreign policy have predominated* over the years: the policy approach, the historical approach, and the social science approach. Although these approaches are not mutually exclusive, Alexander George has argued over the years that different approaches to the study of U.S. foreign policy have produced different cultures, or communities of individuals who have been "socialized in quite different professional and intellectual worlds." This has created a gap in communication and understanding not only between academic scholars and practitioners but also among academic scholars who take different approaches to the study of U.S. foreign policy.[12]

The "policy approach" predominates among practitioners and those involved in politics and the policy world. Policy analysts tend to concern themselves primarily with contemporary affairs, emphasize the present and the near future, make policy recommendations, and write for policymakers and a broad, general audience. Policy analysts may use the tools of the historian or the social scientist. The "historical approach" to U.S. foreign policy comes out of the scholarly tradition of history and the humanities within academia. It tends to emphasize a historical understanding of U.S. foreign policy, attempts to recapture the specifics of the times, recognizes a wealth of factors influencing foreign policy, relies heavily on primary source documentation, and results often in well-written narratives for a scholarly and more general audience.[13] Finally, the "social science" approach to U.S. foreign policy reflects the rise of science within academia, as found in the disciplines of anthropology, economics, psychology, sociology, and in particular, political science. Social scientists tend to be concerned with explaining more limited facets of foreign policy in order to identify basic patterns. They attempt to understand these patterns through the use of concepts and the development of theory, employ more systematic research tools for collecting and analyzing information, and communicate their conclusions predominantly to fellow social scientists.

Each approach or orientation has something important to contribute, yet each cannot stand alone in furnishing a comprehensive understanding of the politics of U.S. foreign policy. Complementation and synthesis of the three approaches are key to acquiring breadth and depth of knowledge and understanding. In this respect, this work is sensitive to broad patterns and specific information about the politics of U.S. foreign policy, contemporary politics and past politics, a theoretical and historical understanding, competing policy recommendations, and a reliance on a variety of sources of information and studies from all three approaches. In other words, my orientation to the study of foreign policy is that of a social scientist who is sensitive to the importance of history and practice, thereby achieving a full understanding of the politics of U.S. foreign policy.

THE ANALYTICAL FRAMEWORK

How will we make sense of the complex politics of U.S. foreign policy? Through use of a general **analytical framework** that provides the basic structure or frame of reference for organizing and thinking about (that is, analyzing, conceptualizing, and synthesizing) the information and knowledge available so as to understand the politics of U.S. foreign policy. In other words, it lays out the key factors that are the basis for analysis and understanding. The analytical framework will consist of two key elements. First, we will examine the policy process from three different perspectives or levels. Second, we will address three themes that have been integral to the study of U.S. foreign policy since World War II. This analytical framework will not only make us aware of the complexity and politics of the foreign policy process but allow us to make sense of and understand the process of how American foreign policy is made.

THE THREE PERSPECTIVES

To make the complex politics of U.S. foreign policy fully understandable, this *book is organized into three basic parts, each reflecting a particular theoretical perspective* or **level of analysis:** (1) Part II discusses the historical and global context (Part I is the current introduction), (2) Part III focuses on the government and the policymaking process, and (3) Part IV concentrates on society and domestic politics.

Each part examines the key actors and forces involved and how they interact and impact the politics of U.S. foreign policy. As Burton Sapin argued over thirty years ago in his classic work, *The Making of United States Foreign Policy,* "While the characteristics of the contemporary international scene are of fundamental importance in shaping the contours of American foreign policy, they are not completely determining. . . . An important part of the explanation for American foreign policy actions lies in the nature of American society and the functioning of its political system and its national governmental machinery."[14] It is only by ex-

amining all three elements—the context, the government, and the society—that one can arrive at a comprehensive understanding of how American foreign policy is made (see **figure 1.1**).[15]

Historical and Global Context. We begin in Part II with the historical and global contexts—that is, the environment or setting in which the politics of U.S. foreign policy operates. The historical and global contexts tend to be the most indirect sources of influence on the policy process and hence are the most difficult to see, though the immediate situation can directly impact the political process, as well. The historical and global contexts set the stage and provide the foundation for the politics of U.S. foreign policy throughout government and society. Chapter 2 provides the historical context, a brief overview of the major patterns in the history of U.S. foreign policy, from its beginning to the present. Clearly, the present flows out of and is impacted by the past. Chapter 3 describes the global context. Since the end of World War II, the world has experienced considerable change, such as the rise and end of the cold war. Such changes in the global environment affect the nature of American power and the political process throughout society and the government, thus influencing U.S. foreign policy. In sum, both the historical and global contexts affect America's role in the world and impact the U.S. policymaking process. In fact, not only is a discussion of the historical context and global environment vital for understanding the current foreign policy process, the context—such as the end of the cold war and the September 11 attacks—has significant implications for the future politics of U.S. foreign policy, as well.

Government and the Policymaking Process. In Part III we delve into the center of the policymaking process with the government—beginning with the president, who has the most immediate and direct impact on policy and then moving outward. Chapter 4 examines presidential power and the president's ability to direct U.S. foreign policy. In many ways, chapter 4 provides an overview of the politics of U.S. foreign policy for the rest of the book. Chapter 5 discusses how the president attempts to manage foreign policy and makes use of the National Security Council within the executive branch. This sets the stage for examination of the major institutions of the foreign policy bureaucracy and their input in the policy process: the State Depart-

FIGURE **1.1**
THE THEORETICAL FOUNDATION FOR EXPLAINING FOREIGN POLICY

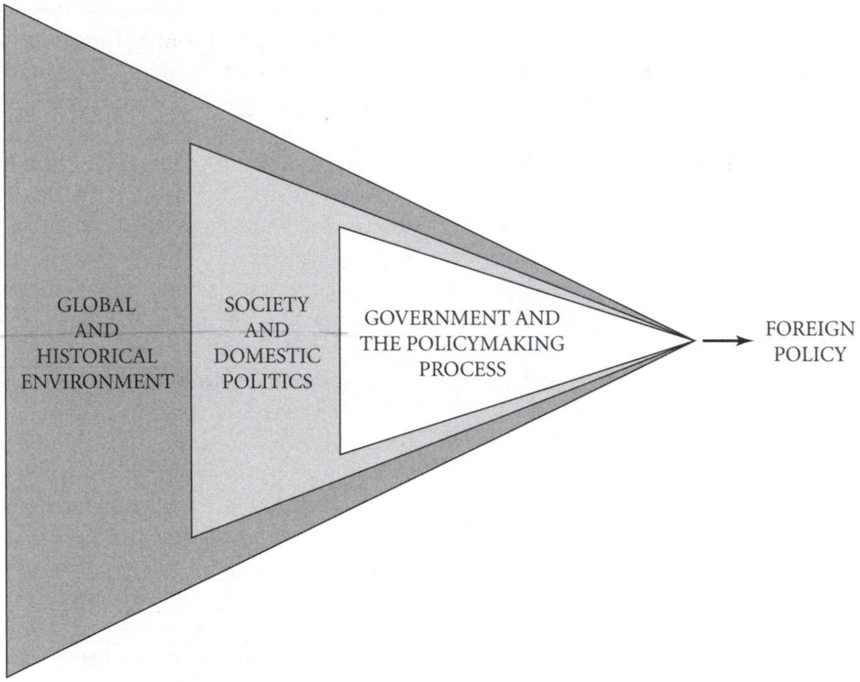

GLOBAL AND HISTORICAL ENVIRONMENT

SOCIETY AND DOMESTIC POLITICS

GOVERNMENT AND THE POLICYMAKING PROCESS

FOREIGN POLICY

ment in chapter 6, the military establishment in chapter 7, the intelligence community in chapter 8, the foreign economic bureaucracy in chapter 9. After a strong substantive foundation has been established, chapter 10 provides a summary overview and theoretical synthesis, employs different decisionmaking models to discuss the interaction of these institutions and explain the dynamics of the policymaking process within the executive branch, clarifying the nature of presidential power in foreign policy. Following coverage of the executive branch, chapter 11 examines the role of Congress in foreign policy and the nature of legislative-executive relations. Chapter 12 then briefly discusses the remaining governmental bodies involved in foreign policy making: the judiciary, State and local governments, and the unique political culture of the Washington, D.C., community. Although many of the institutions discussed above have not received much or any attention, much of the book focuses on the govern-

ment because a comprehensive understanding of the foreign policy process requires considerable knowledge of all the major governmental institutions and players involved in U.S. foreign policy.

Society and Domestic Politics. Relatively comprehensive coverage is also attempted in Part IV, which examines how the larger society and domestic politics affect the government and the foreign policy-making process. We begin in chapter 13 with the significant, and often underestimated, role of the public and its beliefs: public opinion, political ideology, and political culture on the making of U.S. foreign policy. This leads to an important, but usually ignored, discussion in chapter 14 of political participation and the exercise of civil liberties, especially during times of war and since September 11, in order to better understand the historical and future impact of participation on the politics of foreign policy. This allows us to examine the two most common and important forms of active participation that affect foreign policy: electoral politics in chapter 15 and group politics in chapter 16. The powerful effect of the media and the role of communications on the domestic and governmental political process is examined in chapter 17. Once again, some of these topics tend to be ignored or downplayed in the study of foreign policy, but this coverage and knowledge is absolutely essential to acquire a strong understanding of the making of foreign policy.

The book concludes in Part V with chapter 18, which provides a summary of all that we have covered, including a synthesis of how global, governmental, and societal factors interact. This is done by describing different conceptual models to provide varying theoretical and substantive interpretations of the overall foreign policy-making process since World War II, the Vietnam War, and the end of the cold war. The chapter also presents a model for understanding how continuity and change occur over time, with a discussion of the implications for the politics of United States foreign policy in the twenty-first century.

THE THREE THEMES

The information and knowledge presented in the following chapters is integrated around three themes. These themes are interrelated and address *three major questions* that have attracted the particular interest of scholars and are integral to understanding the foreign policy process, especially since World War II: ① What have been the dominant patterns of continuity and change in the foreign policy process over time? What has been the impact of the end of the cold war and the September 11 attacks? ② To what extent has the president been able to manage and govern foreign policy? and ③ How have the tensions between the demands of democracy and national security evolved?

Continuity and Change. It is important to identify major patterns of continuity and change in the foreign policy process over time in order to better understand U.S. foreign policy in the present and into the future. To identify major patterns of continuity and change, especially since World War II, a number of questions are addressed: What changes in the U.S. foreign policy process occurred following World War II?

What elements of the policy process have remained the same since the 1950s? What elements have changed especially during the post–Vietnam years? What are the current and future implications for the making of U.S. foreign policy since the end of the cold war and the September 11 attacks? Answers to these questions allow us to come to grips with the key patterns that have prevailed in the U.S. foreign policy process.

Whereas some analysts emphasize the prevalence of continuity—that is, little or incremental change over time—in the foreign policy process since World War II, other analysts emphasize change. In fact, three major patterns involving both continuity and change have predominated since the Second World War. First, World War II and the rise of the cold war resulted in major changes in the making of U.S. foreign policy, such as the dominance of American power throughout the world, an increase in presidential power, the establishment of a national security bureaucracy, and the rise of an anticommunist consensus in government and society. These foreign policy developments continued to affect foreign policy making throughout the fifties and sixties, until America's failure in Vietnam resulted in a second pattern of changes, including the decline of presidential power, the rise of the foreign economic bureaucracy, the collapse of the anticommunist consensus, and the relative decline of American power abroad. Not all has changed since the fifties, however, and this is reflected in a third pattern: the continuation, for example, of a large and significant national security bureaucracy within government tied closely to society since World War II. What has been the impact of the end of the cold war? To what extent have the September 11 attacks and President George W. Bush's war on terrorism changed things? It appears that the changes and continuities prevailing since the Vietnam War have intensified for the most part, though this will be explored throughout the book. Ultimately, the patterns of continuity and change identified allow us to make better sense of the policy process and the evolution of U.S. policy into the twenty-first century.

Presidential Governance of Foreign Policy. The second theme involves the president's ability to manage and govern U.S. foreign policy. When most Americans consider who makes foreign policy, they immediately think of the president as the commander in chief. The story, in fact, is much more complex than this, as discussed in chapter 4. In brief, prior to World War II the continuous struggle for power between the president and Congress in making U.S. foreign policy usually resulted in Congress dominating in times of peace and the president dominating in times of war. It was only with American involvement in World War II and, subsequently, the dawning of the cold war that power seemed to shift permanently to the president in foreign affairs, laying the basis for this popular perception.

Three patterns have, in fact, prevailed since World War II with regard to the president's role in foreign policy. During the cold war years from Harry Truman to Lyndon Johnson, the president and the executive branch dominated U.S. foreign policy making. However, in the post–Vietnam War years, the president's power has declined within government and in society, making it more difficult for the president to manage and govern foreign policy successfully. In other words, presidents are no longer as powerful as they once were in leading the country in foreign policy. With the collapse of the cold war, this post–Vietnam pattern has continued, but some changes have also occurred as we will explore—suggesting a possible third post–World War II pattern in presidential power. It appears that presidents now face greater opportunities to lead but also considerable political risks in doing so in attempting to govern foreign policy, as experienced by presidents George Bush (senior, who will be referred to as Bush Sr.), Bill Clinton, and George W. Bush (who will be referred to as Bush Jr. to avoid confusion). In addition to the collapse of the cold war, one of the interesting questions that will be consequential for the United States in the twenty-first century is the longer-term impact of September 11 and the war on terrorism on presidential power.

Tensions between Democracy and National Security. Another major theme that has confronted Americans, especially since World War II, is the constant tension between the demand for democracy and for national security. The democratic foundation of the United States, embodied in the Declaration of Independence and Bill of Rights, is premised on individual rights and the need to protect individual freedom and civil liberties from the central government. However, World War II and the cold war resulted in a massive expansion of the national security apparatus within the United States government. This has resulted in a classic contradiction. Democracy demands an informed and active citizenry, individual access to information, an open dialogue about the ends and means of society, and governmental accountability—often a cumbersome process. The demands of national security traditionally are quite the opposite: secrecy, distrust of enemies from without and within, unquestioning mass support, and an efficient process allowing quick responses to events abroad. Therefore, democracy and national security are in constant tension with each other.

Two patterns have prevailed in the tension between national security and democracy since World War II. First, during the cold war years, when most Americans perceived a major threat posed by Soviet communism, national security gained undisputed priority over democratic practice in the politics of U.S. foreign policy. Second, during the post–Vietnam years, democratic considerations have grown in importance due to changes in the foreign policy process in the wake of the Vietnam War. Therefore, the tension between democracy and national security has grown because both orientations lack sufficient political support from government and society to be ascendant. The Iran-Contra affair is symptomatic of the difficulty of balancing these contradictory demands. Despite the collapse of the cold war, this is a dilemma which, in all likelihood, will continue to confront Americans in the foreseeable future and will be addressed throughout the book. In fact, the September 11 attacks on the World Trade Center towers and the Pentagon and the subsequent war on terrorism have raised these tensions and contradictions to a new height that may result in a new pattern for the foreseeable future.

THE COLLAPSE OF THE COLD WAR, SEPTEMBER 11, AND POLITICS IN THE TWENTY-FIRST CENTURY

This book is organized in terms of the three perspectives discussed above, while the three themes will be discussed throughout the book. The analytical framework thus provides a meaningful way to make sense of the complexity and politics of U.S. foreign policy. The net result, I hope, will be the acquisition of a powerful understanding of United States foreign policy.

This is a particularly interesting time to examine the complex politics of U.S. foreign policy because the cold war has come to an end, the United States has recently entered the twenty-first century, and the nation experienced the September 11 terrorist attacks. What is the future of the politics of U.S. foreign policy? How will the interaction of context, government, and society affect continuity and change, presidential governance, and the tension between national security and democracy in the making of U.S. foreign policy? Obviously, no one really knows or can predict with any degree of certainty. Nevertheless, we can initially suggest some key trends and begin to discuss their possible implications, a discussion that will continue throughout the book.

The future implications for the foreign policy process of developments in the context, government, and society appear to be contradictory. Some developments seem to reinforce continuity, while others appear to promote change. Thus far, *two countervailing trends appear to be most important for the future politics of U.S. foreign policy:* (1) The end of the cold war abroad and at home; and (2) The maintenance of American power, interests, and involvement in the world.

One significant long-term development is the collapse of the Soviet empire, which appears to have reinforced and intensified the changes that have occurred in the politics of U.S. foreign policy since the Vietnam War. On the one hand, the decline of America's major adversary ended the cold war and, consequently, has reduced the demands of national security and further weakened the power of the presidency. On the other hand, the United States continues to exercise a powerful presence in pursuit of a variety of interests throughout a world of greater complexity and turbulence, as illustrated by the 1991 Persian Gulf War and the war on terrorism, which has reinforced concern with national security and the elements supporting strong presidential power in the foreign policy process. Ultimately, the politics of U.S. foreign policy is likely to experience continuity and change in the future in response to these two major trends as develop-

ments throughout government, society, and the global context interact over time, as discussed below and throughout the book.

The Collapse of the Cold War Abroad and at Home. First, with regard to the end of the cold war, the collapse of the Soviet empire is a momentous event in the twentieth century and world history. The rise of Soviet communism and the cold war was the principal justification for development of the American social and governmental institutions and beliefs that led to the policy of global containment and intervention, the preeminence of presidential power, and the demands of national security over the demands of democracy in the making of U.S. foreign policy. Although foreign policy changes occurred following the Vietnam War, much continuity prevailed in the national security process, especially in light of the growing Soviet buildup during the 1970s and 1980s.

With the end of the cold war, the major adversaries—the Soviet Union and communism—have declined or disappeared as a potent force in global affairs. Therefore, obvious questions arise: What national security threats does the United States face in this century? What are the major global issues facing the United States? How powerful a force and threat is terrorism? How large must the military be in order to protect American national security in the future? What is the proper role of the United States abroad?

Given the tremendous importance of communism and the Soviet threat to the politics of U.S. foreign policy from the late 1940s through the 1980s, their collapse may further reduce the demands of national security and presidential power that began in the late sixties and early seventies with the Vietnam War. Clearly, a sense of national emergency no longer exists in the post–cold war era—the perception of a cold war has been replaced with the perception of a time of relative peace abroad in the minds of most Americans. This could make national security-oriented institutions and beliefs throughout society and government less credible, raising serious questions concerning the extent to which they have become anachronistic and counterproductive as the United States enters the twenty-first century.

The end of the cold war initially seemed to imply that developments divorced from national security issues should gain in prominence in the politics of U.S.

foreign policy. Issues once low on the foreign policy agenda have become increasingly high-priority policy. This is most obvious with respect to the growing importance of the economic aspects of U.S. foreign policy but is also the case concerning international economics, immigration and refugees, public health, and environmental issues, among others. The growing prominence of these issues does not mean that they will be easy to address, only that they are more likely to make it onto the international political agenda and receive attention in the politics of U.S. foreign policy. In fact, many of these issues are very problematic and increasingly beyond the control of national governments in a world of growing complexity. This may further weaken the president's ability to govern foreign policy, for the key to presidential power has involved national security issues, especially when they have necessitated the use of force. Therefore, the logical portents for the future politics of U.S. foreign policy in a post–cold war world include the relative decline in the overwhelming importance of national security issues, a greater decline of presidential power, and a political process in which the demands of democracy prevail over the demands of national security.

No matter how logical and sound this scenario might seem given the end of the cold war, it ignores the role of politics in accounting for continuity and change. As we will see, it is very difficult to change the status quo in society or in government. In other words, the collapse of communism in Eastern Europe and the Soviet Union has not changed the fact that there are powerful political forces at work throughout American government and society that will resist change and promote continuity in the politics of U.S. foreign policy. The decline of the Soviet Union as the major adversary also has provided the United States with new opportunities to exercise global leadership and intervene abroad. Although the collapse of communism and the end of the cold war have provided unique opportunities for major changes in the politics of U.S. foreign policy, the overall political system tends to be resistant to change and operate with so much momentum that a crisis is frequently necessary to have a great impact on the politics of U.S. foreign policy, impacting presidential power and the tensions between democracy and national security. The most potent crisis has been the impact of the September 11 attacks, which have pro-

moted American power, interests, and involvement in the world.

The Maintenance of American Power, Interests, and Involvement in the World. The second major trend is that the United States continues to exercise a powerful presence in pursuit of a variety of interests throughout a world of greater complexity and turbulence. Today, with the collapse of the Soviet Union, the United States has become the preeminent power in a world of increasing complexity, interdependence, and turbulence. This reinforces the need for an infrastructure, institutions, and personnel throughout government and society that support America's global orientation into the twenty-first century, contributing to presidential power and the demands of national security.

In fact, it could be argued that the collapse of communism and the end of the cold war have given the United States greater opportunity to exercise leadership and force abroad. Now that the Soviet Union is no longer the major adversary of the United States, a major constraint has been eliminated with respect to U.S. ability to use political influence and, in particular, to exercise force abroad. With the end of the cold war, American policymakers have much greater flexibility in using force, as demonstrated in the Persian Gulf and the war in Kosovo. The successful outcome of the Persian Gulf War and the Bush Administration's pursuit of the war on terrorism in particular has reinforced the power of political forces in American society and government that prefer a large national security state despite the collapse of communism and the end of the cold war. In fact, some people have argued that recent changes in the global environment have allowed not only for the restoration of American power but also the potential to develop a "Pax Americana" if American leaders and U.S. foreign policy would seize "the unipolar moment."

The end of the cold war and the preeminence of the United States does not signal the end of conflict throughout the world, nor does it mean "peace is at hand," as many people initially argued. In fact, the end of the cold war may produce more conflict in a world of greater complexity where global issues proliferate and power is diffused. Although not on the scale of a U.S.-Soviet cold war, such conflicts have the potential to result in American involvement and trigger a crisis in American politics, thus dominating the political agenda. Certainly this has been the case thus far given the September 11 terrorist attacks. Furthermore, numerous issues occupy the global agenda and have implications for the United States, largely because of the United States' pervasive global presence—not only traditional security and diplomatic issues but those involving international economic and financial transactions, migration and refugees, drugs, human rights and other humanitarian concerns, the global environment, communications, and so on.

The Persian Gulf War, the Kosovo war, the war on terrorism, and other emerging conflicts in the post–cold war global environment have contradictory implications for American power, involvement, and interests abroad. In the short run, they appear to increase the opportunities the United States has to exercise force abroad while reinforcing presidential power and the demands of national security in the making of U.S. foreign policy. This has counteracted the effect that the collapse of the Soviet Union and the communist threat to America has in prompting changes to the politics of U.S. foreign policy. In the long run, however, this may further weaken American power and the president's ability to govern, if the United States is likely to be involved in, and have difficulty helping to resolve, the many issues that impact the world and the United States in a post–cold war world of ever greater complexity and uncertainty.

In the final analysis, the end of the cold war and the evolving post–cold war global environment have contradictory implications for the future politics of U.S. foreign policy. The end of the cold war has created increasing global complexity, posing both greater opportunities and constraints for the evolution and exercise of American power. The collapse of communism, the decline of the Soviet Union, and the rise of new issues on the political agenda suggest the likelihood of more foreign policy change heading away from cold war–era policies, further weakening the president's ability to govern foreign policy and increasing the demands of democracy. Yet the continued existence of instability and conflict throughout the world, including terrorist attacks—though on a smaller scale than a potential U.S.-Soviet war—reinforces the likelihood of an active U.S. presence in the world and the continued exercise of presidential power in the name of national security.

Although the boundaries or parameters of the future politics of U.S. foreign policy have been suggested, one cannot specify how politics will actually play out and affect U.S. foreign policy. The future implications may be limited or quite profound for the policy process and United States foreign policy, as we will explore throughout the book. But to fully grasp the present and to be able to look into the future, we must be grounded in the past. Therefore, we turn to Part II to examine the historical and global context of the politics of U.S. foreign policy. Although the focus of this volume is on the time period since the World War II, historical background will constantly be woven in along the way, beginning with chapter 2.

SUGGESTED SOURCES FOR MORE INFORMATION

The concept of foreign policy has received very little attention and inadequate treatment for the most part. The most helpful work that clarifies the meaning of foreign policy, the difference between process and policy, and its determinants is James N. Rosenau, "The Study of Foreign Policy," in James N. Rosenau, Gavin Boyd, and Kenneth W. Thompson, eds., *World Politics* (New York: Free Press, 1976), pp. 15–35. A strong sense of the complexity and politics of U.S. foreign policy is provided by Roger Hilsman, *To Move a Nation: The Politics of Foreign Policy in the Administration of John F. Kennedy* (New York: Delta, 1964), especially chapters 1 and 35; Stanley Hoffmann, *Gulliver's Troubles, or the Setting of American Foreign Policy* (New York: McGraw-Hill, 1968), especially Part III; and Hedrick Smith, *The Power Game: How Washington Works* (New York: Ballantine, 1988).

Two classic statements about analyzing foreign policy from an analytical perspective are Kenneth N. Waltz, *Man, the State, and War* (New York: Columbia University Press, 1959), and J. David Singer, "The Level-of-Analysis Problem in International Relations," in Klaus Knorr and Sidney Verba, eds., *The International System: Theoretical Essays* (Princeton: Princeton University Press, 1961), pp. 77–92. The classic work that synthesized different levels into a dynamic foreign policy framework is Richard C.

Snyder, H. W. Bruck, and Burton Sapin, "Decision-Making as an Approach to the Study of International Politics," in Richard C. Snyder, H. W. Bruck, and Burton Sapin, eds., *Foreign Policy Decision-Making* (Glencoe, Ill.: Free Press, 1962), pp. 14–185. For a more contemporary treatment, with a focus on the analysis of American foreign economic policy, see G. John Ikenberry, David A. Lake, and Michael Mastanduno, eds., "The State and American Foreign Economic Policy," *International Organization* 42 (winter 1988), special issue.

KEY TERMS

analytical framework
foreign policy
foreign policy process
level of analysis
national interest
politics
politics of foreign policy
state

PART TWO

. . . .

HISTORICAL AND GLOBAL CONTEXT

Part II provides the historical and global context—the environment or milieu—in which the politics of U.S. foreign policy operates. Chapter 2 provides an overview of the major patterns in the history of U.S. foreign policy, from its roots to the present. Chapter 3 discusses the evolution of world politics and American power, especially since World War II, and their implications for the politics of U.S. foreign policy in the past, present, and future.

CHAPTER 2

HISTORY OF UNITED STATES FOREIGN RELATIONS

*I*t is important to realize that an understanding of the foreign policy process provides the foundation for understanding the evolution of the substance of U.S. foreign policy. It provides the foundation for understanding why, for example, the United States fought a cold war and pursued a policy of containment around the world, why the United States intervened and Americanized the war in Vietnam that ultimately became a national tragedy, and to what extent the United States might continue to intervene and lead the world in a post–cold war environment as it enters the twenty-first century.

Familiarity with the evolution of the substance of U.S. foreign policy should, in turn, be valuable for better understanding the patterns of continuity and change that have occurred in the making of U.S. foreign policy over time. The history of U.S. foreign policy, in other words, influences the policymaking process over time. Clearly, both elements—policy and process—are closely linked, interact with each other, and are crucial for arriving at a full understanding of U.S. foreign policy. Therefore, an overview of the major patterns in the history of U.S. foreign relations is provided.

This chapter will address the following questions: Has U.S. foreign policy been isolationist, as many Americans are raised to believe? What were the European and colonial roots of U.S. foreign policy? How and why did U.S. foreign policy evolve after independence so as to become a global power after World War II? Can certain stages be identified in the history of U.S. foreign policy? How has the end of the cold war, as well as the terrorist attacks of September 11, 2001, impacted U.S. foreign policy, and what are its implications for the twenty-first century? Such historical context will help set the stage for better understanding the politics of U.S. foreign policy in the past and present and into the future.

MAJOR HISTORICAL PATTERNS

Many Americans have the perception that U.S. foreign policy was isolationist until World War II and internationalist thereafter. However, as any U.S. diplomatic historian knows, this simple breakdown of U.S. foreign policy over time distorts much more than it enlightens.

THE MYTH OF ISOLATIONISM

If one defines isolationism to mean uninvolvement abroad, clearly the United States has never been isolationist during its history. If one defines isolationism more loosely, as some people do, to mean uninvolvement in European political affairs, it would still be stretching reality to conclude that U.S. foreign policy was isolationist. The European powers, regardless of their geographic distance from the United States, were active in North America and throughout the Western Hemisphere after U.S. independence. Furthermore, the United States has never been able to avoid involvement in any of the major European wars since the rise of Napoleon in the early nineteenth century. But the question is moot, for one cannot speak of U.S. foreign policy solely in terms of U.S.-European relations as they do not capture the full scope of its involvement abroad.

As A. J. Bacevich recently stated, "Only by the loosest conceivable definition of the term, however, could 'isolation' be said to represent the reality of United States policy during the first century-and-a-half of American independence. A nation that by 1900 had quadrupled its land mass at the expense of other claimants, engaged in multiple wars of conquest, vigorously pursued access to markets in every quarter of the globe, and acquired by force an overseas empire could hardly be said to have been 'isolated' in any meaningful sense."[1] In fact, as early as 1940 historian Albert Weinberg observed that isolationism "was the coinage, not of advocates of reserve, but of opponents seeking to discredit them by exaggeration."[2]

A study by the United States Congress, in fact, makes clear the *long history of the use of U.S. armed force throughout the world since 1798* (see **table 2.1**). Before World War II, U.S. armed forces were used abroad 163 times. Before the Spanish-American War of 1898, there were 98 uses of U.S. armed forces abroad. Overall, the frequency of American armed intervention has remained pretty much the same over time—an average of about one armed intervention per year for over 140 years.

The extent of the use of now armed force throughout the world by the U.S. government since independence may come as a surprise to many Americans. Nevertheless, it serves to demonstrate the United States' internationalist orientation from the beginning.

Although the scope of armed intervention tended to be concentrated in the Western Hemisphere and Asia, the United States clearly intervened in other parts of the world as well.[3] Not only does such interventionist behavior indicate that the United States was quite active internationally and behaved similarly to other European powers abroad, but it inevitably made the United States a part of the evolving international political economy that was dominated by European states. It is important to point out that this congressional study excludes the use of U.S. armed forces against Native American people as the United States expanded westward during the nineteenth century. Clearly, throughout its history the United States has been anything but isolationist in its foreign policy.

EUROPEAN AND ENGLISH COLONIAL ROOTS

In fact, it is important to remember that *the original thirteen colonies were created as a result of European expansion in the world.* During the fifteenth and sixteenth centuries, Europe was emerging from a feudal age and becoming the most dynamic global force. This was the beginning of an age of European discovery and expansion that would last into the twentieth century. The rise of Europe, and so-called European great powers, would forever change the map of the world: initially by the rise of Spain and Portugal, followed by the Dutch, and then the English and the French. By the seventeenth century, following Christopher Columbus's historic voyage, most of present-day South America, Central America, and the Caribbean was colonized by Portugal and Spain (including the southern part of North America as far north as St. Augustine on the East Coast in present-day Florida). By this time, though, the power of Spain and Portugal were in decline, while that of England and France were on the rise.

England and France were actively expanding and colonizing in much of the world in search of power and wealth, including the "new world" of North America. The founding of Jamestown (in present-day Virginia) in 1607 and Plymouth (in present-day Massachusetts) in 1620 represented the beginnings of what was to become the thirteen English colonies. As Gregory Nobles writes, "Europeans did not come to North America just to explore, convert, and trade, of course; they came

TABLE 2.1
U.S. MILITARY INTERVENTIONS BEFORE WORLD WAR II

1798–1800—Undeclared naval war with France	1835–36—Peru	1860—Angola, Portuguese West Africa	1894–96—Korea
1801–05—Tripoli	1836—Mexico	1860—Colombia	1895—Colombia
1806—Mexico	1838–39—Sumatra	1863—Japan	1896—Nicaragua
1806–10—Gulf of Mexico	1840—Fiji Islands	1864—Japan	1898—Spain
1810—West Florida (Spanish Territory)	1841—Drummond Islands	1864—Japan	1898–99—China
1812—East Florida (Spanish Territory)	1841—Samoa	1865—Panama	1899—Nicaragua
1812–15—Great Britain	1842—Mexico	1866—Mexico	1899—Samoa
1813—West Florida (Spain)	1843—China	1866—China	1899–1901—Philippines
1813–15—Marquesas Islands	1843—Africa	1867—Nicaragua	1900—China
1814—Spanish Florida	1844—Mexico	1868—Japan	1901—Colombia
1814–25—Caribbean	1846–48—Mexico	1868—Uruguay	1902—Colombia
1815—Algiers	1849—Smyrna	1868—Colombia	1903—Honduras
1815—Tripoli	1851—Turkey	1870—Mexico	1903—Dominican Republic
1816—Spanish Florida	1851—Johanna Island	1870—Hawaiian Islands	1903—Syria
1816–18—Spanish Florida (First Seminole War)	1852–53—Argentina	1871—Korea	1903–04—Abyssinia
1817—Amelia Island (Spanish Territory)	1853—Nicaragua	1873—Colombia	1903–14—Panama
1818—Oregon	1853–54—Japan	1873—Mexico	1904—Dominican Republic
1820–23—Africa	1853–54—Ryukyu and Bonin Islands	1874—Hawaiian Islands	1904—Tangier, Morocco
1822—Cuba	1854—China	1876—Mexico	1904—Panama
1823—Cuba	1854—Nicaragua	1882—Egypt	1904–05—Korea
1824—Cuba	1855—China	1885—Panama	1906–09—Cuba
1824—Puerto Rico (Spanish Territory)	1855—Fiji Islands	1888—Korea	1907—Honduras
1825—Cuba	1855—Uruguay	1888—Haiti	1910—Nicaragua
1827—Greece	1856—Panama	1888–89—Samoa	1911—Honduras
1831–32—Falkland Islands	1856—China	1889—Hawaiian Islands	1911—China
1832—Sumatra	1857—Nicaragua	1890—Argentina	1912—Honduras
1833—Argentina	1858—Uruguay	1891—Haiti	1912—Panama
	1858—Fiji Islands	1891—Bering Sea	1912—Cuba
	1858–59—Turkey	1891—Chile	1912—China
	1859—Paraguay	1893—Hawaii	1912—Turkey
	1859—Mexico	1894—Brazil	1912–41—China
	1859—China	1894—Nicaragua	1913—Mexico
		1894–95—China	

TABLE **2.1**
(*cont.*)

1914—Haiti	1918–19—Mexico	1922–23—China	1940—Newfoundland, Bermuda, St. Lucia, Bahamas, Jamaica, Antigua, Trinidad, and British Guiana
1914—Dominican Republic	1918–20—Panama	1924—Honduras	
	1918–20—Soviet Russia	1924—China	
1914–17—Mexico	1919—Dalmatia	1925—Honduras	1941—Greenland
1915–34—Haiti	1919—Turkey	1925—Panama	1941—Dutch Guiana
1916—China	1919—Honduras	1926—China	1941—Iceland
1916–24—Dominican Republic	1920—China	1926–33—Nicaragua	1941—Germany
	1920—Guatemala	1927—China	1941–45—World War II
1917—China	1920–22—Russia	1932—China	
1917–18—World War I	1921—Panama-Costa Rica	1933—Cuba	
1917–22—Cuba	1922—Turkey	1934—China	

SOURCE: U.S. Congress, House, Committee on Foreign Relations, *Background Information on the Use of U.S. Armed Forces in Foreign Countries, 1975 Revision,* Committee Print (94th Cong., 1st Sess., 1975).

to stay. From their first footholds they extended their reach into the interior and planted permanent settlements. As they did so, the eastern half of North America became a patchwork of power bases, with European enclaves interspersed among traditional tribal territories."[4]

From a global and European perspective, such settlements resulted in the extension of the British empire into the eastern seaboard of North America and intensified European rivalry, especially between the French and British, for imperial control of the continent. As Nobles describes it,

> the struggle for control of North America embroiled European governments and their American colonists in a series of wide-scale wars for almost a century—the War of the League of Augsburg or, as it was known in the English colonies, King William's War (1688–97); the War of the Spanish Succession, or Queen Anne's War (1702–13); the War of the Quadruple Alliance (1719–21); the War of Jenkins' Ear (1739–42); the War of the Austrian Succession, or King George's War (1740–48), and the Seven Years' War (1756–63) [known to most Americans as the French and Indian War]. The fact that these wars acquired different names on different sides of the Atlantic underscores the two-

front nature of the conflict, with fighting in both Europe and America.[5]

Hence, the United States' historical roots can be found in the expansion and rivalry by which the fate of European empires was being determined in various parts of the world, including North America.[6]

By the latter part of the eighteenth century, what eventually resulted in the **American revolution** involved Englishmen fighting Englishmen for the future destiny of the Eastern seaboard and, with hindsight, much of the continent of North America. The issues that over time incited the American revolutionaries, formerly loyal British subjects, involved the nature of the imperial relationship with the "mother" country. From the perspective of the British crown, the thirteen colonies were an integral part of the British colonial and mercantile empire that increasingly spanned the globe. Therefore, the colonists rightfully were subjects of British imperial rule. From the perspective of the colonists, who increasingly saw themselves as possessing the rights of Englishmen, the British increasingly were abusing their power as they denied representation, taxed the colonies, and controlled trade with the rest of the world.

Eventually the political and economic conflicts escalated to the point of a formal **Declaration of**

Independence in 1776. The document begins by describing certain "truths" and natural rights (with which most Americans are familiar) and then lists the "history of repeated injuries and usurpations" by the king of Great Britain (with which most Americans are less familiar). It ends by declaring "that these United Colonies are, and of right ought to be, FREE AND INDEPENDENT STATES; that they are absolved from all allegiance to the British Crown, and that all political connection between them and the state of Great Britain

---

ESSAY 2.1

HISTORIOGRAPHY AND DIFFERING INTERPRETATIONS OF U.S. FOREIGN RELATIONS

The study of the conduct of United States foreign policy has always been characterized by disagreement and differing interpretations, or schools of thought. Usually, one interpretation tends to dominate or prevail among scholars of U.S. foreign policy—usually referred to as the "traditional" or **orthodox interpretation.** With time and new sources, other interpretations—known as **revisionism**—emerge that revise and challenge this orthodoxy. Sometimes a melding of orthodox and revisionist interpretations eventually occurs, producing a postrevisionist synthesis, or **postrevisionism.** Such is the nature of historiography.

As reflected in *American Diplomatic History,* an overview by Jerald Combs, there have been two centuries of changing interpretations of American diplomatic history. Given this penchant for interpretation and reevaluation, an understanding of the historiography and the differing interpretations produced over time becomes important for a full understanding of the evolution of U.S. foreign relations.

By the 1950s and the height of the cold war, it was popular for diplomatic historians to depict the Spanish-American War, of 1898, as "the" breaking point in United States foreign policy, where the United States was characterized as more isolationist before the war and then emerged as a world power with the war. This interpretation of "discontinuity" in U.S. foreign policy became the orthodox interpretation among American diplomatic historians, as represented by Dexter Perkins in *The American Approach to Foreign Policy.* But despite the use of a language of isolationism and the description of the growth among the mass public of isolationist sentiment toward European wars, U.S. foreign policy was still depicted as quite active abroad, though limited in geographic scope. Nevertheless, such an interpretation helped to propagate among the general public the notion that U.S. foreign policy was "isolationist" throughout much of its history, including after World War I—that is, until the cataclysmic events of World War II forced U.S. international involvement.

Eventually, throughout the sixties and seventies, revisionist interpretations grew in popularity and importance

among diplomatic historians, challenging the conventional understanding and its isolationist implications for U.S. foreign policy. Revisionists rejected the isolationist thesis and tended to depict the history of U.S. foreign policy as being much more continuous and expansive over its history. Such a perspective is reflected in such classic works as William Appleman Williams's *The Tragedy of American Diplomacy* and Richard Van Alstyne's *The Rising American Empire.*

As Thomas Bailey, one of America's preeminent diplomatic historians, basically confessed, "The embarrassing truth is that for eighteen years I further misled the youth of this land [about U.S. isolationism]. . . . By the time I became a graduate student I should have realized that cataclysmic changes, especially in the power position of a nation, seldom or never occur overnight. I should also have known that the very first obligation of the scholar is to examine critically all basic assumptions—the more basic the more critically."

The interpretation presented in this chapter represents more of a postrevisionist synthesis. Although U.S. foreign policy was never isolationist, it did experience both continuity and change over time. On one hand, the United States steadily grew in power and expanded throughout North America and the world. On the other hand, the United States experienced changes in its foreign policy; most important, the scope of its involvement abroad grew over time. Therefore, U.S. foreign policy can be said to have evolved through three major historical eras that reflected its steady rise over two hundred years to become the world power of its time.

SOURCES: Thomas A. Bailey, "America's Emergence as a World Power: The Myth and the Verity," *Pacific Historical Review* 30 (February 1961): 1–16; Jerald A. Combs, American Diplomatic History: Two Centuries of Changing Interpretations (Berkeley and Los Angeles: University of California Press, 1983); Dexter Perkins, *The American Approach to Foreign Policy* (New York: Atheneum, 1968); Richard W. Van Alstyne, *The Rising American Empire* (Chicago: Quadrangle Books, 1965); William Appleman Williams, *The Tragedy of American Diplomacy* (New York: Norton, 1959).

is, and ought to be, totally dissolved; and that, as free and independent states, they have full power to levy war, conclude peace, contract alliances, establish commerce, and do all other acts and things which independent states may of right do."

The British attempted unsuccessfully to put down the "rebellion," and the colonialists fought a "war of independence" for five long years. The outcome was far from preordained. American independence was finally won when British general Cornwallis surrendered at Yorktown in 1781, and the United States was officially recognized with the signing of the Treaty of Paris of 1783 (by England, France, Spain, and the United States). Ironically, the Treaty of Paris "gave the new American nation what England had fought for over a century to obtain: the vast interior region that reached westward to the Mississippi and ran from the upper Great Lakes almost to the Gulf of Mexico (Spain obtained all of Florida, which included the coastal region as far west as the Mississippi)."[7]

It is important to recall, despite the hard-fought effort of American troops under General George Washington (and other American colonists who supported the independence effort), that *other European powers were heavily involved in the war because of its implications for the European balance-of-power system and for the world.* Therefore, German (Hessian) troops fought alongside British troops. And the Americans (through the Continental Congress—the governing institution at the time) entered into a formal alliance with France, which supplied badly needed money and supplies (including arms) and a French fleet that was able to penetrate the British blockade and prevent General Cornwallis's escape. Furthermore, American merchants and traders secured guns and other essential items from other Europeans, especially the Dutch. As compellingly depicted by Barbara Tuchman in *The First Salute: A View of the American Revolution,* such European support and commerce, though typically underplayed in American history books, were absolutely essential to the success of the American war effort.[8] The creation of the United States, then, was a function of European power politics and expansion. And Europe and the larger global environment would continue to play an integral role in United States foreign policy after independence. Therefore, one way to think about the history of U.S. foreign policy is to divide it into *three major periods or eras since independence:* (1) The Continental Era, 1776–1860s; (2) The Regional Era, 1860s–1940s; and (3) The Global Era, 1940s–present.

U.S. foreign policy, in other words, represented both continuity and change over time. On one hand, it grew in power and expanded steadily throughout North America and the world. On the other hand, the United States over the same time experienced major changes in its foreign policy goals and the scope of its involvement abroad. Although dividing U.S. foreign policy into three periods runs the risk of simplifying the complex history of U.S. foreign relations, it should help the reader better understand the general patterns of continuity and change that have evolved throughout the history of U.S. foreign policy (see **essay 2.1** on the historiography and differing interpretations of U.S. foreign relations).[9]

THE CONTINENTAL ERA

The United States was never isolationist; from its earliest days as an independent state, the United States had an active foreign policy. In his famous "Farewell Address," George Washington, the first president of the United States, argued in favor of a foreign policy not of isolationism but of "nonalignment"—whereby the United States should avoid permanent alliances and entanglements. U.S. governmental officials followed his advice throughout this era, though most U.S. actions focused on the surrounding North American continent until the latter half of the nineteenth century. During this time, *two general goals preoccupied most American leaders:* nation building and continental expansion.

The United States was a new and relatively weak country at the turn of the nineteenth century. It had won its national independence from the global superpower of its time, England, but it faced many of the problems that any new country with a colonial history faces upon gaining independence. Although far from Europe, the former thirteen colonies were surrounded by territory that England, France, Spain, and Russia coveted and fought over. As Walter LaFeber has stated, "From the beginning of their history, Americans lived not in any splendid isolation, far from the turmoil and corruption of Europe many had hoped to escape. They instead had to live in settlements that were surrounded by great and ambitious European powers."[10]

The economy of the North American colonies also had been dependent on the English economy. Now the new country, in addition, was attempting to implement the first democratic experiment in the modern world. Given this environment, a priority for most Americans was "nation building": to build an independent country safe from its neighbors, construct a strong national economy, and establish a stable democratic polity. Therefore, much of the focus was on strengthening the internal situation in the United States.

The second goal, continental expansion, was closely linked to nation building. What better way to protect the nation from potentially hostile neighbors than to expand its territory and push the British, French, Spanish, and Russians (as well as the Mexicans and Native Americans) farther and farther away from the eastern seaboard, preferably off the North American continent and out of the Western Hemisphere? What better way to build a strong economy than through the acquisition of more land that could be put to work? Strengthening national security and the national economy also contributed to political stability. But this meant that "Americans—whether they liked it or not—were part of European power politics even as they moved into the forests and fertile lands beyond the Appalachian Mountains. They could not separate their destiny from the destiny of those they had left behind in Europe."[11]

Up to and including the purchase of Alaska from Russia in 1867, U.S. foreign policy was responsible for acquiring increasing amounts of territory throughout the North American continent that was eventually annexed to the United States. *Territory that was inhabited predominantly by Native Americans and claimed by European*

FIGURE 2.1

U.S. TERRITORIAL AND CONTINENTAL EXPANSION
BY THE MID-NINETEENTH CENTURY

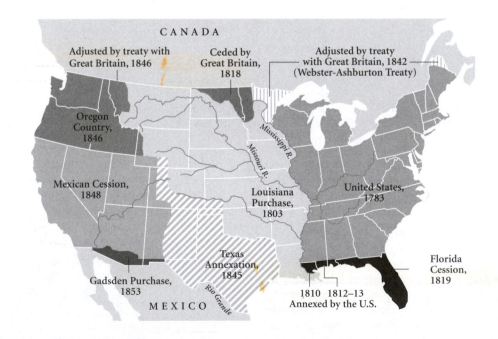

SOURCE: Walter LaFeber, *The American Age: United States Foreign Policy at Home and Abroad*, 2nd ed. (New York: W. W. Norton, 1994), p. 132.

states was acquired by the United States: from England in the North and Northwest, such as northern Maine and the Oregon territories; from France in Louisiana Territory to the west; from Spain in the Florida territories to the south; from Mexico in the Southwest, such as Texas and the southwestern territories (including California); and from Russia in the farthest reaches of the northwest, with Alaska (see **figure 2.1**).

Contrary to popular folklore, American continental expansion generated considerable involvement, diplomacy, and conflict with European states, Mexico, and Native Americans. Nevertheless, in Gregory Nobles's words in *American Frontiers: Cultural Encounters and Continental Conquest:*

> Often these stories are oversimplified and stereotypical, offering one-sided views that implicitly separate the world into "good guys" and "bad guys." Yet that simplicity is the source of their power: repeated over and over, the images and stories that permeate popular culture come together to form a more enduring American myth, what some historians call a "master narrative," which provides both an explanation for the past and a justification for the present.[12]

Much of the land, in fact, was sold to the United States as the weaker country in response to ongoing European power struggles or was literally taken by force. Americans, for example, during colonial times and after independence repeatedly attacked Canada, then a dominion of the British empire, in attempting to expand northward.

Shortly after independence, in fact, the U.S. government devised a plan annexing new territory to the United States—thereby allowing new states into the Union. The *Northwest Ordinance of 1787,* originally devised by a committee of the Continental Congress in New York (the first capital under the Articles of Confederation, the first constitution), chaired by Thomas Jefferson, called for dividing territory into a gridwork of townships. "Once the land had been surveyed, it could be sold to land companies or individuals, thus creating not just a source of revenue for the government but also a pattern of orderly settlement in the territory." Eventually, when the population reached sixty thousand, the territory could enter the Union "on an equal footing with the original states in all respects whatsoever." Hence, "while the delegates to the Consti-

tutional Convention in Philadelphia were hammering out a plan for a new national government, members of the Congress in New York [laid] out a plan for national expansion."[13]

Native American peoples, naturally, suffered the most from Western expansion. According to Walter LaFeber, "a central theme of American diplomatic history must be the clash between the European settlers and the Native Americans"—a population estimated to be between eight million and ten million inhabitants throughout North America by the time Christopher Columbus first arrived.[14] Clashes were constant with Indians as Americans expanded westward. Despite coexistence and the signing of treaties, the same pattern was repeated as Americans expanded farther and farther. "As usual with Indian treaties, [the] land was granted to them 'as long as the waters shall run and the grass shall grow.' And as usual, whites began to violate their own treaty." Ultimately, the fate of the Indians was sealed, given the growing power and technological superiority of the United States.[15]

The U.S. government "adopted a variety of distinct, sometimes seemingly contradictory strategies in dealing with the Indians who inhabited the interior. Soldiers and social reformers argued over appropriate policies for pacifying native people, and the government pursued two or more policies at once, making war or peace as best suited the situation." And like earlier European imperial powers, the U.S. government played "one Indian group against the other in military or diplomatic or economic alliances. But in the end United States Indian policy pointed in only one direction: toward the reservation." As further described by Nobles,

> government policy did not call for the extermination of Indians, only their cultural transformation. That is, in order to live peaceably in the United States, Indians would be pressured to give up their language, their way of life, and much of their land. In the minds of Jefferson and other leaders, such a policy was in the Indians' best interests, offering them incorporation into "civilized" society. Yet, as the government extended this open hand of philanthropy, it kept in the background the closed fist of force.[16]

The agents of U.S. continental expansion were not only the government, especially the army, but also thou-

sands of private and entrepreneurial Americans spilling westward in search of land, gold, profit, and freedom. "To be sure, the relationship between settlers and the state was often a troubled, even tumultuous one, and the desires of independent-minded people often clashed with the designs of government officials for 'orderly' settlement. Still, whatever the underlying uneasiness, common people and policymakers ultimately became allies in a process of conquest."[17] The net result was that by the 1860s the United States had grown from thirteen colonies on the eastern seaboard to a country that spanned the continent.

Richard Van Alstyne has referred to the United States as The *Rising American Empire*: "The early colonies were no sooner established in the seventeenth century than expansionist impulses began to register in each of them. Imperial patterns took shape, and before the middle of the eighteenth century the concept of an empire that would take in the whole continent was fully formed."[18] In the words of diplomatic historian Thomas Bailey, "The point is often missed that during the nineteenth century the United States practiced internal colonialism and imperialism on a continental scale." Given its strategic location in the new world, facing relatively weak indigenous peoples and European forces far from the center of Europe, the United States "from its birth . . . has been incomparably the luckiest of all the great nations—so far."[19]

According to Van Alstyne the United States was a creature of the British tradition and was conceived by American leaders in terms of empire—as an imperial republic. Thomas Jefferson, author of the Declaration of Independence and the third president of the United States—who dramatically increased the size of the United States with the Louisiana Purchase 1803 and sponsored the Lewis and Clark expedition to discover the West and search for a northwest passage to the Pacific (and the Orient)—communicated his expansive vision of an empire of liberty to James Monroe in 1801:

> However our present interests may restrain us within our limits, it is impossible not to look forward to distant times, when our rapid multiplication will expand it beyond those limits, and cover the whole northern if not the southern continent, with people speaking the same language, governed in similar forms, and by similar laws.[20]

Although Van Alstyne understood that his use of the language of **empire** was controversial, he argued nevertheless that the United States' "evolution from a group of small, disunited English colonies strung out on a long coastline to a world power with commitments on every sea and in every continent, has been a characteristically imperial type of growth." In other words, the United States was not different but quite similar to other European states, growing in power and expanding in influence abroad.

The United States was "active beyond the continent" as well, but this activity was more sporadic in nature. *American commerce and merchants were active in all areas of the globe,* especially Europe, the West Indies (i.e., the Caribbean), the Orient, and the slave trade of Africa. As Van Alstyne states,

> As a coastal country of the eighteenth century, the United States looked seaward as well as landward, and the paths of its growing empire in the nineteenth century stretched out to sea as well as across the continent. The United States was a commercial and seafaring state, as well as an agrarian state; and its mercantile and seafaring population was busily active in extending and developing long-distance sea routes even while the physical handicaps to transcontinental migration remained unsolved.[21]

In the tradition of European expansion and the search for wealth abroad, "China was the magnet which accounted for the path of empire into the Pacific broken by Yankee shipping in the 1780s. . . . From Portsmouth, New Hampshire, to Charleston, South Carolina, there was hardly a port on the Atlantic seaboard that did not have its China merchants." As Van Alstyne further explains:

> Sealskins from the Falkland Islands, sea-otter pelts from the Pacific northwest, natural sandalwood from the Sandwich Islands [Hawaiian Islands today], ginseng from the Pacific southwest, opium from Turkey and India, kegs of Spanish silver dollars, and finally cotton-piece goods from the new New England mill towns furnished the bulk of the cargoes with which the American China merchants maintained a balance of payments for their purchases [of such commodities as spices, silk, porcelain, and tea] in China.[22]

"During the eighteenth and nineteenth centuries," according to Alfred Eckes, "the founders of U.S. foreign policy pressed to open markets and attacked mercantilistic barriers abroad in order to bolster the domestic economy and secure independence."[23] Interruption of American commerce by the British during the Napoleonic War, for example, was a major cause of the War of 1812 between the United States and England.

Despite the "spirit of commerce" since colonial times, American merchants were unable to open up the mercantilist regulation of trade by the European powers and increasingly adopted a policy of economic nationalism, including the use of tariffs to encourage (and protect) the growth of domestic manufactures. Increasingly, tariff policy became trade policy in the nineteenth century. As Eckes found, "In practice the high-tariff position generally carried the day. Over a forty-year period from 1821 to 1861, the ratio of duties to total imports ranged from a low of 14.21 percent in 1861 to over 57 percent in 1832 under the Tariff of Abominations."[24]

The U.S. government, especially through the Navy, was also politically and militarily active beyond the continent (review table 2.1 again). The first diplomatic Consulate established overseas by the new government was in Canton, China, in 1789—one year after the approval of the Constitution of the United States. As early as 1821 "the navy began operating a squadron off the west coast of South America; and by 1835 intercourse with China and the East Indies reached the point where it justified the establishment of a separate East India squadron."[25]

Regarding Latin America, in 1823 the Monroe Doctrine was declared, stating that the new world in the Western Hemisphere was not open to colonization by Europeans. As early as 1850 the United States negotiated the Clayton-Bulwer Treaty for rights to build an interoceanic canal. And attempts also were made to annex Cuba and Santo Domingo (now known as the Dominican Republic) to the U.S. republic. In Asia, the United States, led by Daniel Webster, negotiated the 1844 Treaty of Wangxia, giving Americans "most favored nation" status (like other European countries) in trade and extraterritorial rights with China; Americans, led by Commodore Matthew C. Perry, forced Japan to open its ports to foreigners and commerce in 1854; and the Hawaiian and Midway Islands were occupied as transit points for American commerce with the Orient.

Unlike the thrust across the North American continent, these foreign policies beyond the continent were less integral and much more sporadic, lacking any consistent pattern over time. Thus, it is most helpful to view this era as a period of continentalism in U.S. foreign policy.

THE REGIONAL ERA

By the latter half of the nineteenth century, the United States had been quite successful in building an independent and transcontinental country that was growing more powerful. With steady continental expansion and the end of the Civil War, the United States no longer faced any immediate threats from its neighbors. The Civil War also settled the divisions between the North and South, allowing political stability at the national level. The national economy was vibrant and growing, and the transcontinental railroad was completed in 1869. In the words of Van Alstyne, "By all tests of pragmatism the United States emerged from that war more than ever an imperial state. It entered its period of consolidation and centralization, it began developing its internal economy intensively, and abroad it soon joined in the international scramble for material wealth and power."[26]

As the United States reached the limits of continental expansion, more and more Americans during the latter half of the nineteenth century were beginning to speak of the future of the United States in terms of a "manifest destiny." According to William Weeks, "Manifest Destiny was founded on the a priori conviction of the uniqueness of the American nation and the necessity of an American empire." Such an orientation reflected three key themes: "the special virtues of the American people and their institutions; their mission to redeem and remake the world in the image of America; and the American destiny under God to accomplish this sublime task. Under the aegis of virtue, mission, and destiny evolved a powerful nationalist mythology that was virtually impossible to oppose."[27]

In fact, the foundation for ideas of America's special virtue, mission, and destiny had existed from the time of the Puritan settlements in New England. They were popularized by John Winthrop's sermon in 1631, that the Puritan colony in Massachusetts Bay represented a "city upon a hill" from which the regeneration of the world might proceed. Many people came to view the United States as a special place where human society might begin anew, uncorrupted by Old World institutions and ideas, giving it a special mission and role in the world.

Such a nationalistic and expansive vision was clearly articulated in the language of the times as early as 1850 by William H. Seward, a U.S. senator from New York and later a prominent secretary of state under presidents Lincoln, Johnson, and Grant:

> The world contains no seat of empire so magnificent as this, which, while it embraces all the varying climates of the temperate zone, and is traversed by the wide-expanding lakes and long branching rivers, offers supplies on the Atlantic shores to the over-crowded nations of Europe, while on the Pacific coast it intercepts the commerce of the Indies. The nation thus situated, and enjoying forest, mineral, and agricultural resources unequalled . . . must command the empire of the seas, which alone is real empire. . . . The Atlantic States, through their commercial, social, and political affinities and sympathies, are steadily renovating the Governments and social constitutions of Europe and Africa; the Pacific States must necessarily perform the same sublime and beneficent functions in Asia. If, then, the American people shall remain an undivided nation, the ripening civilization of the West, after a separation growing wider and wider for four thousand years, will in its circuit of the world, meet again, and mingle with the declining civilization of the East on our own free soil, and a new and more perfect civilization will arise to bless the earth, under the sway of our own cherished and beneficent democratic institutions.[28]

Following the Civil War, in fact, *U.S. foreign policy actively promoted political stability and economic expansion abroad, especially in two regions of the world,* Latin America and Asia. U.S. foreign policy became increasingly a presence on the global stage, as best symbolized by the Spanish-American War, fought in 1898. "The Spanish-American War was an expression of two powerful historic drives: the pull to the south, and the pull across the Pacific toward Asia."[29]

The U.S. government and American business dramatically increased their "presence in Latin America," especially throughout Central America and the Caribbean. The presence of American business intensified with the rapid expansion of American trade, loans, and investment in the region. The U.S. government was also active in promoting friendly political regimes in the region that would be unresponsive to European involvement, open to American trade and investment, and stable enough to pay back their American bank loans.

Involvement of the U.S. government and American business in Latin America—a region which was experiencing decolonization, nation building by independent states, and considerable political instability—resulted in constant American military intervention and occupation, especially after the turn of the century. As Secretary of State Richard Olney proclaimed in 1895, "the United States is practically sovereign on this continent, and its fiat is law upon the subjects to which it confines its interposition." The "Olney Proclamation" reinforced the original purpose of the Monroe Doctrine, that the United States had the right, and now the power, to intervene and dominate its "own backyard"—foreshadowing what was to come with the Spanish-American War and after.

From President Theodore Roosevelt's "Big Stick" policies to William Howard Taft's "Dollar Diplomacy" and Woodrow Wilson's "New Freedom," through the Warren Harding, Calvin Coolidge, and Herbert Hoover administrations, the United States regularly sent the Marines to crush local rebellions, prop up old or new regimes, and restore political stability in virtually every major state in Central America and the Caribbean, often only to return again and again. Military intervention usually meant that the local customs houses were subsequently run by U.S. government officials to guarantee that revenues from tariffs and duties were collected to repay American loans. Financial supervision, for example, lasted thirteen years in Nicaragua (1911–1924), twenty-five years in Haiti (1916–1941), and thirty-six years in the Dominican Republic (1905–1941). American leaders so badly wanted a canal to connect the Atlantic and Pacific oceans, that in 1903 President Roosevelt actively supported and instigated Panamanian independence from Colombia. He then immediately recognized the new country and signed a treaty giving Panama $10 million, plus $250,000 a year for rights "in perpetuity" for a ten-mile-wide strip—which became the Panama Canal Zone—that cut the new country literally in half.

Clearly, American involvement and power had carved out a regional "sphere of influence." This was the period during which the United States acquired—primarily as a result of its diplomatic demands over Cuba, which triggered the so-called "splendid little war" with Spain (referring to the ease of the victory)—its earliest colonial possessions (and "protectorates") in the area, including Cuba, Puerto Rico, and the Virgin Islands. It wasn't until the 1920s and thirties, with Herbert Hoover and then Franklin Roosevelt's "Good Neighbor" policy, that direct intervention of American troops into the domestic affairs of U.S. neighbors was temporarily abandoned.

American foreign policy was in search of political stability and U.S. economic expansion in Asia as well, with China being the major prize. "Merchants, missionaries, adventurers, sea captains, naval officers, and consular officers crowded into the Pacific during the nineteenth century and spun a web whose strands extended to every part of the ocean."[30] Unlike Latin America, which was Christianized by the Spanish, there was a large American missionary presence in Asia, particularly in Japan and China. (It began as early as 1905 with over three thousand American missionaries in China.) And during the crisis with Spain over Cuba the U.S. navy, just before the Spanish-American War actually broke out, attacked the remnants of the Spanish empire in Asia, producing American Samoa, Guam, Wake Island, and most important, the Philippines as colonies of the United States.[31]

American involvement in Asia and the Pacific, however, (unlike that in Latin America) resulted in a much more limited use of force because of the region's distance from American shores and the strong military presence of England, France, Russia, and Japan. U.S. foreign policy in China, for example, emphasized an "Open Door" approach in order to maximize American involvement and trade.[32] Therefore, America's military and commercial involvement resulted in fewer costs as well as fewer gains. The United States, nevertheless, sent more than 120,000 American troops from 1899 to 1902 to fight its first counterinsurgency war and defeat a national independence movement in the Philippines to preserve its new colonial control.

Even though U.S. foreign policy was oriented toward the regions to its immediate south and distant west, it became *increasingly active in European affairs and on the world scene* in general. While officially neutral during the early part of World War I, the United States eventually became a major participant in bringing about the war's outcome. Woodrow Wilson was in fact highly instrumental in influencing the Treaty of Versailles, which officially ended the war and attempted to create a new liberal world order through the League of Nations. During 1918–1919, the United States even sent fourteen thousand troops—along with the British, Canadians, French, Czechs, and Japanese—to occupy part of the newly declared Soviet Union in an effort to aid the anti-Bolsheviks and reestablish a Russian front against Germany.

The twenties and thirties are popularly thought of as the height of isolationism in U.S. foreign policy. There is some truth to this, evidenced by the U.S. rejection of American participation in the League of Nations, the rise of isolationist sentiment among the American public and a strong peace movement, and American reluctance to become actively involved in European conflicts (especially during the Great Depression and the early years of World War II). As diplomatic historian William Cohen has argued, "rejection of the Treaty of Versailles and lack of membership in the League had little impact, however, on American involvement in world affairs in the decade that followed. In the 1920s the United States was more profoundly engaged in international matters than in any peacetime era in its history."[33]

Not only was U.S. foreign policy active in Latin America and Asia, but *the United States also took a number of important diplomatic initiatives* with the Europeans and Japanese. From November 1921 to February 1922, the United States hosted and actively promoted a major naval disarmament conference in Washington, D.C., that resulted in the first major arms control treaty in modern times (in addition, the same conference produced a Four Power Treaty and a Nine Power Treaty involving Pacific island possessions and the rivalry in China, signed by the United States). It was "an extraordinary event, symbolic of America's new role in world affairs."[34] In 1928 the United States and France jointly sponsored the Kellogg-Briand Pact in an effort to outlaw war. The United States also began to play an active, though unofficial, role relative to League activities.

Also, *the United States became increasingly important to the international political economy* following World War I, which was still dominated by the

Europeans. As a result of the debts and damage incurred by the war, European economies became increasingly dependent on the United States government and on American business as a source of trade and finance. "Demand for American capital was intense throughout the [1920s] despite high interest rates. Europeans needed dollars to purchase American goods needed for reconstruction, and they borrowed regardless of cost. The rest of the world, which traditionally turned to European bankers, had no alternative in the 1920s but to queue up in Wall Street."[35]

This foreshadowed the global leadership role that the United States would soon fully occupy but not until Europe once again rebuilt and launched a second world war. As Cohen has asserted, "Clearly, the impact of American trade, investments, and tourism on the world economy in the 1920s was enormous. No other nation even approximated the United States in economic importance. The British, who kept first place among importing nations, lost their preeminent investment role in Latin America and Canada, and were being challenged throughout Europe and the rest of the world, including their colonies, by American capitalists."[36]

By the 1920s, in Cohen's judgment, the United States had become a great power and acquired a "formal" and "informal" empire. As he stated in *Empire Without Tears*:

> It controlled an empire that included not only the Caribbean basin, but stretched across the Pacific, north and south, through Hawaii and Alaska, Midway, Wake, Guam, Samoa, and the Aleutians, to East Asia and the Philippines. Manufacturers nurtured markets and sired multinational corporations in Europe, while mining and lumber interests scoured North and South America. American entrepreneurs and missionaries wandered across the Middle East, South Asia, and Africa. It was the dawning of what Henry Luce would later call the "American century."[37]

Clearly, the United States was growing into a formidable power on the world stage while at the same time trying to maintain considerable independence of action. Nevertheless, outside of Latin America and Asia, U.S. foreign policy, especially in the national security area, lacked coherence and consistent involvement. Therefore, this era of U.S. foreign policy is best remembered as predominantly regionalist in orientation.

THE GLOBAL ERA

The Japanese attack on Pearl Harbor, on December 7, 1941, abruptly ended the regional era in U.S. foreign policy. The next four years saw the beginning of a new era of global involvement in which the United States, along with the Soviets, British, Chinese, French, and other allies, fought the Axis powers of Germany and Japan over the destiny of the globe. With the end of World War II, the United States became an active global power in the world and developed foreign policies of global consequence. Also during the global era the president increasingly was able to govern the making of foreign policy and lead the country.

WORLD WAR II AND IMMEDIATE POSTWAR FOREIGN POLICY

Consistent with U.S. foreign policy throughout its history, *the Roosevelt administration's postwar aims revolved around the two broad key issues of:*

1. economics, and
2. national security

But now the United States took an active leadership role in world affairs.

The first goal involved the need to restore economic stability and prosperity in the United States, as well as in Western Europe and throughout the world. This was deemed essential because the U.S. economy was heavily intertwined with the larger global capitalist economy, particularly the Western European economies—which were the core of the global economy and shattered by the Great Depression and World War II. Many Americans also feared that the end of the war would produce a massive recession in the U.S. economy.

The original strategy, arrived at in Bretton Woods, New Hampshire, in 1944, was to promote multilateral efforts with American allies to restore and manage an increasingly liberal, global market economy, based on a new system of fixed exchange rates and open, free trade. What came to be called the **Bretton Woods system** would provide necessary assistance and rules for economic transactions principally through the creation of three multilateral international organizations: the International Bank for Reconstruction and Development (IBRD, known as the World Bank) to make loans

[margin note: IMF GATT]

for economic recovery and development, the International Monetary Fund (IMF) to support the stability of national currencies based on gold, and the General Agreement on Tariffs and Trade (GATT) to promote and govern open trade. Success on the economic front in promoting a liberal capitalist world order was thought to be crucial for ensuring peace and minimizing threats to national security, as had occurred when the Great Depression led to the rise of Adolf Hitler.[38]

The second goal involved U.S. attempts to construct a new international political order that was stable and promoted the national security of the United States and its wartime allies, thereby preventing the outbreak of further wars. U.S. postwar involvement was deemed vital because of the collapse of Europe, which had dominated world politics for over two hundred years until the impact of the two world wars. In an effort to protect national security, President Franklin Roosevelt relied on a strategy of multilateral cooperation based on a sphere-of-influence approach and the creation of a new international organization to replace the League of Nations—the United Nations.

Roosevelt's strategy depended on global cooperation among members of the "Grand Alliance" during the war: the United States, Soviet Union, Great Britain, France, and China. The instrument for maintaining cooperation among the "big five" and preventing a challenge to the status quo, which could lead to the outbreak of a new war, was the creation of the United Nations, and especially the operation of the United Nations Security Council (a body in which each of the big five held veto power). Roosevelt also assumed that each of the five so-called great powers would exercise power over its regional sphere of influence: the United States in Latin America, the Soviet Union in Eastern Europe, Great Britain and France in Europe and their colonial possessions, and China in East Asia. This multilateral strategy of promoting global peace complemented the strategy of promoting global economic recovery and prosperity.

It should be pointed out that there is little scholarly consensus on the particular nature of the Roosevelt administration's postwar goals and strategy. Some scholars highlight President Roosevelt's idealism and commitment to democracy, human rights, and social welfare, emphasizing the role of the United Nations and other international organizations. Other scholars see Roosevelt as much more pragmatic and concerned with restoring political and economic stability, concen-

trating on the role of power and spheres of influence. President Roosevelt, and the foreign policy that emanated from his administration, was very complex and at times contradictory. In fact, it could be argued that he was both hopeful and pragmatic.[39]

Whatever the case, Roosevelt's overall strategy for restoring economic prosperity and national security quickly unraveled during the latter part of the 1940s. Before the war even came to an end, Roosevelt died and was succeeded as president by Harry Truman, who was unfamiliar with Roosevelt's postwar plans and lacked Roosevelt's considerable experience. The European economies were in much worse shape than most people had thought and were in need of assistance beyond that which the Bretton Woods–devised multilateral international organizations were capable of providing. Finally, any hope for lasting cooperation among members of the Grand Alliance to achieve national security quickly eroded as distrust, fear, and conflict between the United States and the Soviet Union escalated.

With the collapse of Roosevelt's grand strategy, U.S. foreign policy took a new course and can be seen as going through three periods or eras since the World War II: (1) the cold war era, late 1940s–1960s; (2) the post–Vietnam War era, late 1960s–1980s; and (3) the post–cold war era, 1990s–present. Familiarity with the dominant patterns in U.S. foreign policy that have prevailed since World War II is particularly important for giving the reader the historical context for better understanding how the politics of U.S. foreign policy has evolved over these same years.[40]

THE COLD WAR ERA *[margin note: national sec. + econ. prosperity]*

For roughly twenty years, *from the administration of President Truman through that of President Johnson, U.S. foreign policy experienced considerable continuity based upon the twin goals of national security and economic prosperity* that had remained unresolved following the war. The twin goals were based on the quest for global security and stability from a perception of the rising "threat" of Soviet communist expansionism and the promotion of a liberal international market economy based upon the principles of free, open trade and fixed exchange rates. This era also represented the height of the president's power to lead the country in the cold war.

Following the war, *for the first time since independence and the period of continentalism, Americans began to perceive an external threat to their national security:* the advance of Soviet communism. Because the fear of Soviet communism became the key problem for most Americans, national security concerns drove U.S. foreign policy during the cold war. U.S. national security was defined in terms of global security and stability, for the threat was perceived to be global and American leaders believed that, with the collapse of the British and French empires, only the United States had the power to respond. Although the United States and the Soviet Union never engaged in a "hot war" (that is, a direct military clash), the United States prepared for a direct military confrontation with the Soviet Union and engaged in a global **cold war.** Under American leadership a strategy of containment was developed that aimed to deter by the threat of coercion the spread of Soviet communism, first in Europe, then in Asia with the Korean War, and eventually throughout the world (see **essay 2.2** on **George Kennan,** father and critic of containment).[41]

ESSAY 2.2
GEORGE KENNAN, FATHER AND CRITIC OF CONTAINMENT

George Kennan has been one of the more influential individuals in the foreign policy-making community since World War II. An iconoclast throughout his foreign service and public career, he initially was the originator of containment and then became one of its leading critics.

George Kennan, born into a middle-class Wisconsin family, became a traditionalist and a romantic in the European aristocratic tradition. In foreign affairs he was both a Russophile, strongly anticommunist and fond of the Czarist past, and a believer in realpolitik. After joining the foreign service in the late 1920s, Kennan remained a relatively obscure European and Soviet specialist for the next two decades, especially once diplomatic relations between the United States and the Soviet Union were restored and the two countries became wartime allies.

With the end of World War II, however, and the increasing tension between the United States and the Soviet Union, Kennan suddenly rose to prominence in 1946 as a result of writing a "Long Telegram" from the American embassy in Moscow to the State Department. In this communiqué, he described the Soviet Union as a weak, cautious, and insecure yet ideological, dogmatic, and expansionist state that needed to be contained. A subsequent famous *Foreign Affairs* article published in 1947 and entitled "Sources of Soviet Conduct," authored by George Kennan under the pseudonym "Mr. X," was an expanded version of this telegram. In it he argued that "the main element of any United States policy toward the Soviet Union must be that of a long-term, patient but firm and vigilant containment of Russian expansive tendencies." This meant "the adroit and vigilant application of counterforce at a series of constantly shifting geographical and political points, corresponding to the shifts and maneuvers of Soviet policy." Clearly, Kennan was an early and powerful advocate for a strong American response to Soviet communist expansion, as well as the need to rebuild Western Europe (such as through the Marshall Plan).

Although Kennan is considered the "father" of containment, he soon became an early critic of the U.S. strategy. As the policy became increasingly globalized and militarized, his influence within the State Department and the U.S. government quickly eroded. Kennan resigned in 1953 and became a historian at Princeton University, where he went public with his criticism. He maintained that U.S. policymakers had turned his recommendations into a rigid doctrine much too reliant on the use of force and applied too indiscriminately abroad.

After the 1980s, Kennan, while always the realist, became a major proponent of a semi-isolationist position. Given developments in the global and domestic environment, he argued for major reductions in America's military establishment, reliance on nuclear weapons, and military presence abroad. In essence, he believed—as he had always argued—that U.S. foreign policy should revolve around its most vital interests: the geostrategic areas of North America, Western Europe, and Japan.

SOURCES: John Lewis Gaddis, *Strategies of Containment* (Oxford: Oxford University Press, 1982); George F. Kennan, *Around the Cragged Hill: A Personal and Political Philosophy* (New York: W. W. Norton, 1993); George F. Kennan, *At a Century's Ending: Reflections, 1982–1995* (New York: W. W. Norton, 1996); George F. Kennan, *Memoirs: 1925–1950* (Boston: Atlantic Monthly Press, 1967); George F. Kennan, *Sketches From a Life* (New York: Pantheon, 1989); David Mayers, *George Kennan and the Dilemmas of U.S. Foreign Policy* (New York: Oxford University Press, 1989); Anders Stephanson, *Kennan and the Art of Foreign Policy* (Boston: Harvard University Press, 1989); and Daniel Yergin, *Shattered Peace* (Boston: Houghton Mifflin, 1978); U.S. Department of State, *George F. Kennan's "Long Telegram"* (February 22, 1946); Mr. X, "The Sources of Soviet Conduct," *Foreign Affairs* (July 1947): 566–582.

The containment strategy was initially embodied in the Truman Doctrine, announced in 1947 and directed at containing Soviet expansion in the eastern Mediterranean countries of Greece and Turkey. In the words of one analyst, its future implications for U.S. foreign policy were to be global and quite profound:

> The Truman Doctrine contained the seeds of American aid, economic or military, to more than one hundred countries; of mutual defense treaties with more than forty of them; of the great regional pacts, alliances, and unilateral commitments: to NATO, to the Middle East, to the Western Hemisphere, and to Southeast Asia. It justified fleets of carriers patrolling the Mediterranean and the South China Sea, nuclear submarines under the polar icecap, air bases in the Thai jungle, and police advisers in Uruguay and Bolivia. In support of it, an average of a million soldiers were deployed for twenty-five years in some four thousand bases in thirty countries. It contained the seeds of a habit of intervention: clandestine in Iran, Guatemala, Cuba, the Philippines, Chile, and the CIA alone knows where else; overt in Korea, Lebanon, the Dominican Republic, Laos, Cambodia and Vietnam.[42]

The U.S. global strategy that developed during the late forties and fifties was to surround the Soviet Union and its allies in Eastern Europe and mainland Asia with American allies, alliances, and military forces in order to deter the Soviet Union from initiating a military strike and possibly triggering World War III. Containment of the Soviet Union and the People's Republic of China throughout the Eurasian continent was to be accomplished through the threat and use of conventional and, especially, nuclear military forces. In the Third World, where the U.S.-Soviet confrontation tended to be fought more indirectly over the "hearts and minds" of local elites and peoples, the United States relied on foreign assistance, counterinsurgency, and the use of covert paramilitary operations to promote friendly regimes. Containment of the Soviet Union was also pursued through the use of broad economic sanctions by the United States against it and its allies (such as in Eastern Europe and Cuba). Diplomacy and other noncoercive instruments of policy were put aside by the United States in East-West relations and superseded by the threat and use of coercion to deter and contain

what American leaders saw as major challenges to American national security commitments and national interests.[43]

Given the inability of Western European economies to recover from the Depression and the war, the United States also took the lead in unilaterally sustaining the Bretton Woods system—this was really **Bretton Woods II**—to promote a stable and prosperous international market economy. The original Bretton Woods system was to be based on a multilateral effort by the Europeans and Americans. However, the war-torn European economies were in need of recovery, which prevented the Bretton Woods system from operating as originally agreed. Instead, the strength of the American economy allowed the United States to unilaterally support the Bretton Woods system and focus on European economic recovery—hence Bretton Woods II.

The revival of the European economies was to be accomplished by providing massive capital outlays in the form of American assistance (such as the Marshall Plan), private investment and loans by U.S. multinational corporations, and trade based on opening the U.S. domestic market to foreign imports. Therefore, the Bretton Woods international economic system based on free trade and fixed exchange rates became dependent on the United States acting as the world's banker. Although primarily European-oriented, and later also Japanese-oriented, U.S. foreign economic policy was also active in promoting a market system in the Third World through its support of private investment and development abroad.[44]

With European economic recovery under way and America's growing prosperity during the fifties, national security policy became the predominant concern of most American leaders. Foreign economic policy often came to be referred to as "**low policy**" while national security policy was usually referred to as "**high policy**"—an indication of their level of significance for those engaged in making U.S. foreign policy during the cold war years.[45]

For twenty years American leaders, preoccupied with promoting national security throughout the globe, relied on a strategy of global containment and deterrence, trying to prevent Soviet communism from expanding its empire. American policymakers believed that protecting other countries from the Soviet threat indirectly protected the United States and enhanced its national security. Hence, lines were drawn, countries were labeled friend or foe, and national commitments to friendly regimes were made. And when foreign threats were perceived, the United States responded.

This policy of global containment inevitably led to American interventionism abroad and its tragic involvement in the Vietnam War. U.S. involvement began as a small assistance program to help the French maintain their colonial control of Indochina in order to prevent Vietnamese independence under Ho Chi Minh and Vietnamese communism. With the Korean War, the U.S. commitment escalated to the point that, by 1954 (the year of the battle of Dien Bien Phu and the Geneva Accords, which forced the French out of Vietnam), the U.S. government was paying for 85 percent of the French war effort. Under President Eisenhower, the U.S. assumed primary responsibility for supporting and maintaining the independence of South Vietnam. This policy led to increases in the number of "advisers" to the point that eighteen thousand American troops were in Vietnam by the time President John Kennedy was assassinated.

The steady and increasing American commitment to South Vietnam was never seriously challenged within the executive branch or by members of Congress. American policymakers, in both the executive branch and Congress, were operating within the cold war consensus. South Vietnam was seen as an independent state threatened by communist aggression from North Vietnam. For U.S. cold warriors, this represented the expansionist designs of a communist monolith that the United States could not afford to appease anywhere in the world for fear that this would feed the appetite of the aggressor. Therefore, it was believed to be vital for the United States to contain the communist threat in South Vietnam in order to prevent other Southeast Asian countries from falling to communism.

THE POST—VIETNAM WAR ERA

The Vietnam War was the first major war in the history of the United States that it lost. Simply put, after investing as much as $30 billion a year and over 500,000 troops during the height of American involvement in a war that lasted at least fifteen years, the United States' containment strategy was unsuccessful in keeping South Vietnam an independent, noncommunist country. As a result of America's failure in Vietnam, the pol-

icy of global containment of Soviet communism, which had prevailed since World War II, was challenged by competing foreign policy perspectives in American politics. U.S. foreign economic policy also changed in 1971 when President Richard Nixon discarded the convertibility of the U.S. dollar to gold and placed a 10 percent surcharge on Japanese imports, violating the principles of fixed exchange rates and free trade, which contributed to a situation in which the Bretton Woods system was no longer sustainable. This was a time when challenges to American power and the future of U.S. foreign policy were increasingly heard (see **essay 2.3** on Senator **J. William Fulbright** and the evolution of liberal internationalism).

Despite Vietnam, many scholars tend to see continuity in U.S. foreign policy since World War II. Most orthodox scholars tend to emphasize the permanence of containment as the basis of U.S. foreign policy since World War II; many revisionist scholars tend to emphasize the constant role of American economic expansion and management of the international political economy since the war. However, an increasing number of scholars and analysts have begun to conclude that the Vietnam War represented an important break in U.S. foreign policy in the post–World War II period.

The failure in Vietnam and the breakdown of the Bretton Woods system represented international and domestic changes that have resulted in *three new patterns in U.S. foreign policy during the post–Vietnam War era until the late 1980s.* First, with the growth of economic problems at home and abroad, foreign economic policy has become "high" policy again, becoming a major agenda item facing all presidents. Although most American leaders continue to see the need for a stable and liberal international market economy, they often are unsure over the particular strategy and means to promote economic stability. Second, with each new administration, there has been a modification in the direction of U.S. national security policy. Although a policy of containment continued to have its share of advocates, other policy orientations gained legitimacy and influenced the policymaking process. Third, in contrast to the cold war years, since the Vietnam War it has become very difficult for any president or administration to devise a foreign policy that has successfully responded to changes in the global environment and obtained substantial domestic support over time. This has forced every president to change or modify his foreign policy during his term, usually toward the political center. The result of these three patterns, which will be discussed throughout the rest of the book, is that the continuity in foreign policy experienced during the cold war years has been replaced by much less consistency and much more incoherence since Vietnam.

Although U.S. foreign economic policy became "high" policy with the breakdown of the Bretton Woods system in 1971, *foreign economic policy has lacked much coherence over time.* This is because of the increasing necessity for the government to address complex and intractable economic issues—such as inflation, unemployment, energy needs, deficits, and environmental concerns—in both the domestic and international arena. Presidents Nixon, Gerald Ford, and Jimmy Carter each have relied on different strategies at home and ad hoc approaches abroad to handle economic problems as they developed. Each attempted to maintain the stability of the international market economy by winning the multilateral support of the major allies—Western Europe, Canada, and Japan—for stopgap measures. In other words, U.S. foreign economic policy has lacked design and been defensive and reactive to domestic and international economic problems as they have arisen. The Reagan administration took a different approach, relying on a laissez-faire philosophy of minimal state intervention in the international political economy and emphasizing domestic economic growth as the key to expanding the global economy.

In the national security area, in some ways incoherence and inconsistency in U.S. foreign policy is even more visible. *The Nixon and Ford administrations represented the first real change in the global containment orientation* of U.S. cold war policy. National security policy changed from the cold war emphasis on containment of Soviet communism to ensure global security to a "realpolitik" focused on counterbalancing the Soviet Union as a traditional great power in order to promote global stability and order. For Henry Kissinger, who for a time was both the national security adviser and the secretary of state under Presidents Nixon and Ford, the major threat was not communist expansion and Soviet hegemony but global instability, which Soviet interventionism could only exacerbate. Therefore, the key was not just to contain the Soviet threat through force but also to encourage the Soviet Union to change from a revolutionary, expansionist

global actor into a legitimate status quo actor. This was to be done through a policy of détente based on the concept of "linkage": accommodation (such as the provision of prestige through summit meetings and economic assistance through trade, technology, and financing) when the Soviet Union was acting in accord with American desires; the threat and use of force when the Soviets were perceived as attempting to upset the existing balance of power.

There is disagreement over the extent to which U.S. foreign policy changed during the Nixon and Ford administrations. One school argues that the Kissinger years were a period of continuity with earlier cold war policies because attempts were still being made to contain the Soviet Union, though not only through the use of force. Another school argues that this was a time of discontinuity in U.S. foreign policy because Kissinger downplayed the threat of communism, emphasizing traditional great power politics. Both schools shed light on the question but tend to be incomplete. In fact, the Kissinger years appear to have represented a time of both continuity and change in U.S. foreign policy—a period of transition between the cold war policies of the past and the post–cold war policies of Jimmy Carter.[46]

Although U.S. foreign policy during the Nixon and Ford years of détente represented a change from the cold war policies of global containment, *the real break in the cold war came in 1977, when the Carter administration rejected containment* as the basis of its foreign policy. The people who initially staffed the Carter administration no longer saw a bipolar international system that pitted communism against the free world in a global cold war, or a traditional great power struggle between the Soviet Union and the United States. This cold war perception of international relations was replaced by the first truly post–cold war orientation in U.S. foreign policy since the end of World War II. The Carter administration saw a world of complex interdependence in which the United States would take the lead in the building of a cooperative global community. They downplayed the role of great powers, such as the Soviet Union; the utility of force; and preoccupations with traditional security issues. Instead, Carter pursued a foreign policy of adjustment to international change based on moral leadership, multilateralism, and preventive diplomacy, emphasizing human rights and negotiations instead of the use of force.

ESSAY 2.3
SENATOR J. WILLIAM FULBRIGHT AND THE EVOLUTION OF LIBERAL INTERNATIONALISM

Senator J. William Fulbright traveled a well-worn political path familiar to major political figures during the cold war and post–Vietnam War years. During the 1940s, Fulbright became an ardent liberal internationalist who was opposed to U.S. isolationism in world affairs; during the 1950s, he became a cold warrior in support of administration policy; and beginning in the mid-1960s, he became a critic of U.S. global containment, arguing in favor of a new liberal internationalism. As a member and then chairman of the Senate Foreign Relations Committee from 1944 to 1974, Senator Fulbright also played a leading role in the evolution of U.S. foreign policy. A brief examination of Fulbright's career should enhance an understanding of the evolution of the liberal internationalist orientation that has been so powerful in U.S. foreign policy over time.

J. William Fulbright was born in 1905. The son of a wealthy businessman, he was raised in Fayetteville, the site of the University of Arkansas. After quarterbacking the Razorbacks football team, he went to Oxford University as a Rhodes scholar in 1925. He became an admirer of Woodrow Wilson, who envisioned a peaceful and cooperative world order—often referred to as liberal internationalism or **Wilsonianism**—based on the spread of democracy and capitalism. After completing his studies at Oxford, Fulbright returned to the University of Arkansas to teach constitutional law. By 1939, at age thirty-four, he had become the youngest university president in the nation. Fulbright was elected to the U.S. House of Representatives in 1942 and gained a seat in the Senate two years later.

From the beginning of his political career, foreign affairs was his passion. As a freshman congressman, he authored the resolution that cleared the way for U.S. participation in the United Nations. This achievement gave him national prominence as an internationalist in a climate still dominated by isolationists. In 1946, as a member of the Senate Foreign Relations Committee, he steered a program through Congress that embodied his Wilsonian idealism—the Fulbright Scholar international exchange program. He championed American liberal internationalism and was a believer in the "American century"—that is, that America had the will and the power to make the world freer, more prosperous, and more just.

In the late forties and fifties, Fulbright began to reflect the more conservative political climate in the United States concerning foreign affairs. During the cold war, he became an ardent supporter of interventionist policies designed to contain the threat of communism. He backed all the major cold war initiatives, such as the Truman Doctrine and American intervention in the Korean War. And in 1954 his concern over Chinese expansionism prompted him to urge American intervention in Indochina in the event of a communist victory over the French.

In 1959 Fulbright became chairman of the Senate Foreign Relations Committee. In this powerful position, he remained highly supportive of America's global containment policies during the John Kennedy and Lyndon Johnson years. His 1963 book, *Prospects for the West*, rejoiced in the preeminence of American "world power and responsibility." In 1964 he not only voted for the Gulf of Tonkin resolution but introduced the resolution into the Senate for President Johnson and expedited its passage as a demonstration of support for the president and his policies in Vietnam.

Although a cold warrior, Fulbright occasionally strayed from the governmental line. He tended to see "imperialist Russia," rather than "communism," as America's principal enemy. Although Fulbright believed that the United States should contain Soviet and Chinese expansionism, he did not believe that ideological differences created an unbridgeable gap between the United States and the communist nations. Instead, he foresaw a gradual adjustment between West and East through negotiations. In *Old Myths and New Realities* in 1964, Fulbright argued that the Cuban missile crisis and the U.S.-Soviet negotiation of the Test Ban Treaty demonstrated that the cold war could be resolved. Toward this end, he called for recognition of China and further negotiations with the Soviet Union. Furthermore, he did not fear all global change, drawing a distinction between Third World nationalism and communism. This complex and optimistic view, which lay submerged in Fulbright's thought during the 1950s, became the foundation of his dissent in the 1960s.

Fulbright's first major break with Lyndon Johnson came when the president deployed Marines in the Dominican Republic in 1965. Fulbright publicly criticized the Dominican intervention as being counterproductive to American interests, which consisted of promoting stability and peace in the region. He believed that by stifling change and supporting the status quo, American policy actually promoted radicalism and revolution as the only means of change in Latin America. Fulbright continued to believe in the progress and hope that the United States represented; however, he now dissented from the means used to affect foreign policy and argued that the United States should support, rather than oppose, Third World nationalism.

His dissent over Vietnam finally led him to question the ends of U.S. cold war policy, as well. Fulbright refused to see the Vietnam War as part of a monolithic communist offensive. He suggested that a unified Vietnam under the nationalist rule of Ho Chi Minh and Vietnamese communism was compatible with American national interests, for it would restrain Chinese expansionism in Southeast Asia. He believed that U.S. refusal to recognize the new regime in China in 1949 had been a fateful mistake. In January 1966, Fulbright began a series of hearings that placed him outside administration policy by using the Senate Foreign Relations Committee to educate the American public about Vietnam and U.S. foreign policy.

In *The Arrogance of Power* in 1966, Fulbright took the argument a step further and entirely abandoned the cold war analytical framework. He argued that there were two Americas: one, generous, humane, and judicious, the other, narrowly egotistical and self-righteous. For Fulbright, cold war policies and U.S. interventionism abroad indicated that an aggressive and self-righteous America was prevailing in U.S. foreign policy:

> For the most part America has made good use of her blessings, especially in her internal life but also in her foreign relations. Having done so much and succeeded so well, America is now at that historical point at which a great nation is in danger of losing its perspective on what exactly is within the realm of its power and what is beyond it. Other great nations, reaching this critical juncture, have aspired to do too much, and by overextension of effort have declined and fallen.[A]

The United States, in other words, was beginning to suffer the fate of Rome, Britain, and other past imperial powers, in which "power tends to confuse itself with virtue and a great nation is peculiarly susceptible to the idea that its power is a sign of God's favor, conferring

upon it a special responsibility for other nations—to make them richer and happier and wise, to remake them, that is, in its own shining image."[B] Thus, U.S. foreign policy, especially as it was being executed in Vietnam, demonstrated an "arrogance of power" by acting as the world's policeman. "In so doing we are not living up to our capacity and promise as a civilized example for the world."[C]

The arrogance of U.S. foreign policy was a topic Fulbright continued to pursue in *The Crippled Giant* in 1972, discussing also its detrimental domestic consequences. Fulbright concluded that "having begun the postwar period with the idealism of the United Nations Charter, we retreated in disillusion to the cold war, to the Truman Doctrine and its consummation in Vietnam, easing the transition by telling ourselves that we were not really abandoning the old values at all but simply applying them in more practical ways. Now, having failed most shockingly and dismally [in Vietnam], we are beginning to cast about for a new set of values."[D] Fulbright's recommendation: "Perhaps we will settle for an old idealism—the one we conceived and commended to the world but have never tried"—the liberal internationalism of the 1940s.[E]

Fulbright was severely criticized by President Johnson, conservatives, and cold warriors. However, to liberals and members of the growing antiwar movement, Fulbright became something of a hero; he was the most prominent American leader to publicly criticize the administration's Vietnam policy and the containment policies that dominated the cold war. Fulbright was ultimately defeated for reelection in 1974. Yet, Fulbright and his liberal internationalist perspective helped to legitimize public dissent and promote a more open dialogue concerning the ends and means of U.S. foreign policy that has carried into the post–Vietnam War and post–cold war years.

B. Ibid.
C. Ibid., p. 22.
D. J. William Fulbright, *The Crippled Giant: American Foreign Policy and Its Domestic Consequences* (New York: Vintage, 1972), p. 177.
E. Ibid., p. 173.

SOURCES: J. William Fulbright, *Prospects for the West* (Cambridge, Mass.: Harvard University Press, 1963); J. William Fulbright, *Old Myths and New Realities* (New York: Random House, 1964); J. William Fulbright, *The Arrogance of Power* (New York: Vintage, 1966); J. William Fulbright, *The Crippled Giant: American Foreign Policy and Its Domestic Consequences* (New York: Vintage, 1972); and J. William Fulbright with Seth P. Tillman, *The Price of Empire* (New York: Pantheon, 1989).

A. J. William Fulbright, *The Arrogance of Power* (New York: Vintage, 1966), p. 3.

Although there was much disagreement during the early 1980s as to the nature of the Carter administration's foreign policy, a broad consensus has recently emerged that the administration entered office with a relatively optimistic vision of global change and a liberal internationalist orientation. Disagreement exists, however, concerning to what extent the administration's early foreign policy abandoned the containment strategy.[47]

In 1981 U.S. foreign policy under the Reagan administration fully returned to an emphasis on global containment of Soviet communism through the threat and use of force reminiscent of the cold war era of the 1950s and sixties, while retreating from multilateralism as well. The foreign policy was characterized by a large military buildup and the restoration of cold war policies in order to deter and challenge the Soviet Union in world politics. The Iran-Contra affair demonstrated the extent to which the Reagan administration was dedicated to fighting the cold war and "rolling back" Soviet-supported communism.[48]

Comparing the goals and strategies under Presidents Nixon and Ford, Carter, and Reagan demonstrates that, unlike the cold war years, the post–Vietnam War period has witnessed the initiation of different foreign policy orientations by each new administration. *Given existing international and domestic constraints, each administration has also been forced to moderate its initial policies with time.*

In the area of foreign economics, it was easy for the Nixon, Ford, and Carter administrations to modify their policies, since they had never actually devised a coherent strategy. However, the Reagan administration quickly found out that its unilateral supply-side and free market approach did not sit well among allies abroad or with many Americans at home, and it was forced to modify many of its policies during the latter part of the administration.

It is in national security policy, however, that changes in policy over time within the same administration were most obvious. For example, by the end of the Ford administration, the policy of détente was on the defensive. It was attacked by members of the Democratic party who were angry at American intervention in Angola and by members of Ford's own Republican party who perceived it as appeasement of the Soviet Union. President Carter came into office rejecting containment as the basis of his foreign policy, only

to reinstate it by the last year of his administration, following the Iran hostage crisis and the intervention of Soviet troops in Afghanistan. And although President Reagan came into office as a cold-warrior "hawk" ready to do battle with the "evil empire," he left office as an arms-control "dove," meeting four times with Mikhail Gorbachev, the general secretary of the Soviet Communist party, and signing the Intermediate Nuclear Forces Treaty.

Thus, the global era in U.S. foreign policy that began with American involvement in World War II has resulted in two globally oriented foreign policy periods separated by the Vietnam War. World War II and the rise of the cold war reflected international and domestic changes that produced twenty years of continuity in U.S. foreign policy. During this time, American national security policy was devoted to containing the threat of Soviet communism throughout the globe and was supported by a foreign economic policy based on American leadership of the international political economy. The Vietnam War and the breakdown of the Bretton Woods system represented international and domestic changes that put in question the viability of the United States to promote a global containment policy and to maintain economic prosperity at home. During the post–Vietnam War period, unlike the early cold war years, foreign economic policy has been restored to a significant place on the foreign policy agenda, different foreign policy initiatives have been taken by different administrations, and each administration has eventually been forced by circumstances outside its control to moderate its initial policies.

THE POST–COLD WAR ERA?

With the collapse of communism in Eastern Europe and the collapse of the Soviet Union, the United States appears to have entered a new era in foreign policy—a post–cold war era beginning in the 1990s. U.S. foreign policy may have entered a time when the contradictions between the legacy of America's expansive and cold war past, the implications of the tremendous changes that have enveloped the Soviet Union and Eastern Europe, and the uncertainty of domestic support need to be addressed and reconciled. In this respect, *the end of the cold war has provided current and future administrations with new opportunities and con-*

straints in their conduct of foreign policy. Such an environment predominated for President Bush Sr., President Clinton, and at the beginning of his term, President Bush Jr. However, the terrorist attacks of September 11 appear to have had a profound impact on the foreign policy of President Bush Jr., which may maintain a powerful legacy into the future.

The Bush Sr. Administration. Although accused of lacking global vision, Bush Sr.'s foreign policy in fact appeared to be heavily influenced by a realpolitik and power politics approach to world politics, leading to a strategy that remained heavily conditioned by the cold war legacy of containment. Its inclination, states political scientist Charles Kegley, was "to look to the future with a vision inspired by the past, and to postpone the awesome task of developing a comprehensive policy response to the profound changes that have recently transpired."[49]

As described by David Halberstam in *War in a Time of Peace,*

> the top civilians in the Bush administration were cautious in general, befitting men who had grown up and come to power during a prolonged period of relentless Cold War tensions, tensions made ever more dangerous by the mutual availability of nuclear weapons. They had come of age when you inherited a difficult, divided world, and if all went well during your tour of office, you handed off to your successor a difficult, divided world. The principal military men were cautious, too, but in a different way, befitting men who had experienced the full bitterness of the Vietnam War. Thus for all of the men around Bush, the geopolitical tensions in their lifetimes had been constant, the victories essentially incremental. Keeping things from getting worse was, in itself, a victory.... The irony was that the president and his most senior people had come to power in a period that was the exact opposite of what they had trained for.[50]

Not surprisingly, given the collapse of the Soviet Union and communism, no dominant and consistent foreign policy pattern prevailed during the Bush administration. Instead, the Bush administration displayed a "mixture of competence and drift, of tactical mastery set in a larger pattern of strategic indirection."[51] These contradictory patterns were best epitomized by its foreign policy toward the issues arising from the end of the cold war and toward the Persian Gulf conflict.

On the one hand, the Bush Sr. administration was very cautious and tentative in responding to global issues following the cold war. For example, the Bush administration elected to let Western European countries take the foreign policy initiative relative to the collapse of communism in Eastern Europe, the changes confronting the Soviet Union, the reunification of Germany, and the formal integration of the European Community.

On the other hand, the administration took the foreign policy initiative relative to international security issues more reminiscent of the past. For instance, the Bush administration's support for the People's Republic of China following Tiananmen Square, the American invasion of Panama, and the policy of brinksmanship and war in the Persian Gulf can best be understood from a power politics perspective in which American strategy remained heavily influenced by a reliance on the threat and use of force.

In other words, the Bush Sr. administration's foreign policy appeared to be caught between the strong legacy of the cold war past and the great uncertainty of a post–cold war future. This maybe was somewhat reminiscent of the Truman administration following World War II, in that the Bush administration was trying to cope with a postwar future of great uncertainty and conflict.

The Clinton Administration. After entering office in 1993, the Clinton administration was accused of considerable vacillation and hesitancy in the conduct of U.S. foreign policy. However, the administration in the beginning attempted to promote American leadership and a liberal international orientation abroad. The enlargement of democracy and of the international market economy was a dominant theme within the administration.[52]

Nevertheless, efforts to promote a more "multilateral-oriented" foreign policy faced early setbacks, especially in Somalia. At the same time, President Clinton did manage to initiate several significant foreign policy actions in Haiti, Mexico, Bosnia, and the Middle East. Also, the administration had great difficulty in responding to the continuing Yugoslavia crisis, and getting its NATO allies to work together multilaterally, until war resulted in Kosovo through a massive bombing campaign.

For the most part major foreign policy failures were avoided while the administration highlighted domestic policy and international economics. Most prominent in this regard were passage of the North American Free Trade Agreement (NAFTA) and the Uruguay round of the GATT agreement, which produced the World Trade Organization (WTO).

econ. for. policy

Overall, despite its liberal internationalist orientation, the Clinton administration, very much like the Bush Sr. administration, tended to become increasingly "reactive"—as opposed to "proactive"—abroad, and hence, U.S. foreign policy was somewhat incoherent and inconsistent. There is little doubt that the United States will continue to have a major impact throughout the world and have a globally oriented foreign policy. But in the complexity and uncertainty of the post–cold war period, presidents such as George Bush Sr. and Bill Clinton clearly have found it difficult to lead U.S. foreign policy for a sustained period of time, regardless of its internationalist orientation. It may simply be that the cold war era has been superseded by an increasingly complex and domestic environment in which the days of grand design have given way, despite the enormous power of the United States, to a more pragmatic time of muddling through.[53]

The Administration of George Bush, Jr. Such muddling through appears to have successfully captured the initial months of the new George Bush Jr. administration. Despite a seasoned national security team, it is very difficult to characterize the early Bush period. During the campaign, much of the foreign policy emphasis was on the need to lessen commitments, emphasize vital national interests, and exercise greater humility abroad (this was especially articulated during the second debate with Democratic candidate Al Gore, where foreign policy was the focus).

Once in office, Bush Jr.'s foreign policy orientation seemed to be somewhat reminiscent of his father's. There did not seem to be much of a global vision. Bush's foreign policy in fact appeared to be heavily influenced by a realpolitik and power politics approach to world politics, leading to a strategy that remained heavily conditioned by the cold war legacy, especially given his selection of so many foreign policy advisers

who had worked with his father. In the words of David Halberstam, "Bush Two was composed of men—and now women—who had dealt well with the final months and weeks of the Cold War, but had not been particularly deft in adapting to the very different circumstances in a changed post–Cold War world." Not surprisingly, no dominant and consistent foreign policy pattern prevailed early on in the administration.[54]

It was a very reactive administration, as illustrated by the U.S. spy airplane incident and initial crisis with China. Although the Bush administration initially took a very tough official position, it eventually had to soften its rhetoric, de-escalate the crisis, and even apologize (in diplomatic parlance) in order to have China return the American crew and eventually return the spy plane. But such a tentative and unclear foreign policy orientation all changed following the September 11 terrorist attacks on the World Trade Center in New York City and on the Pentagon in Washington, D.C.

A new Bush Jr. foreign policy has emerged in reaction to September 11. It is focused, it appears clear, and it is simple, revolving around a global war on terrorism. New enemies—Osama bin Laden and Al Qaeda, Saddam Hussein and Iraq, and terrorism—has replaced the old enemy of communism. The new foreign policy orientation is deterrence, containment, and destruction of terrorism and so-called terrorist threats throughout the world. This new emphasis is portrayed in the words of National Security Adviser Condoleezza Rice:

new Cold War

> I really think that this period is analogous to 1945 to 1947 in that the events so clearly demonstrated that there is a big global threat, and that it's a big global threat to a lot of countries that you would not have normally thought of as being in the coalition. That has started shifting the tectonic plates in international politics. And it's important to try to seize on that and position American interests and institutions and all of that before they harden again.[55]

As Michael Hirsh suggests, after September 11 in the minds of members of the Bush Jr. administration, "The United States was [now] faced with an irreconcilable enemy; the sort of black-and-white challenge that had supposedly been transcended in the post–Cold War period, when the great clash of ideologies [had] ended, [and] had now reappeared with shocking suddenness."[56] (see **essay 2.4** on the **Bush Doctrine**).

Bush's global war on terrorism has resulted in a major defense buildup, an emphasis on "homeland security," an effort to distinguish between friends and foes, a heavy reliance on the use of force abroad, especially in Afghanistan, and an increasing emphasis on the threat and use of preemptive strikes, especially relative to Iraq. The war on terrorism has become the core and the mantra of the Bush Jr. administration's foreign policy, to the neglect of numerous other foreign policy issues, in the minds of many. In the words of one critic, "The Bush Doctrine has been used to justify a new assertiveness abroad unprecedented since the early days of the Cold War—amounting nearly to the declaration of American hegemony—and it has redefined U.S. relationships around the world. . . . The truth, however, is that a year later there is still very little clarity about the real direction of U.S. foreign policy and the war on terror."[57]

This leads to numerous questions that are not easy to answer in a post–cold war world. What exactly is America's vital interests in a post–cold war and post–September 11 world? To what extent should U.S. foreign policy revolve around the threat of terrorism? How appropriate is the war on terrorism as the foundation and basis of U.S. foreign policy for the twenty-first century? What does it mean to conduct a war on terrorism? What should be the role of U.S. force? What role should other instruments of foreign policy play? Should the U.S. preemptively attack Saddam Hussein and Iraq? How important is the creation and maintenance of a global coalition? What other foreign policy issues of prominence are important, such as the Israeli-Palestinian conflict, the Indian-Pakistan conflict, international economics, and others? What role should the United States play in the world as the unchallenged superpower? To what extent should the United States be reactive or proactive? Should it emphasize unilateral or multilateral initiatives? None of these questions, or others, is easy to address, but they will be addressed in one way or another as the United States moves rapidly into the twenty-first century.

FROM THE PAST INTO THE TWENTY-FIRST CENTURY

Overall, an understanding of current U.S. foreign policy and its future requires grounding in a historical and global context. In other words, larger questions must be asked and addressed. What explains the dominant patterns and policies in the history of U.S. foreign relations? Why does the United States have a long history of international involvement and expansion despite the rise of isolationist sentiment? Why did cold war policies prevail for twenty years following World War II? In what ways did the cold war patterns in U.S. foreign policy change in the post–Vietnam War era and why? How will the end of the cold war and the September 11 attacks affect the future of U.S. foreign policy? To what extent will the United States' national security and economic goals abroad change or remain the same? Answers to these questions ultimately require an understanding of the politics of U.S. foreign policy.

But before we jump into the center of the policy-making process, it is important to look at the larger setting and global context in which the foreign policy process takes place. Changes in the global milieu often set the stage for changes in government and society. Therefore, the next chapter examines the impact that the evolution of American resources, the global context, and the U.S. role throughout the world have had on domestic politics and governmental policymaking. The impact of the end of the cold war, including the Persian Gulf and Kosovo wars, as well as the September 11 attacks, are also discussed. This will provide us with a better understanding of the history, and the possible future, of the complex politics of U.S. foreign policy.

SUGGESTED SOURCES FOR MORE INFORMATION

There is a massive amount of literature on the history of U.S. foreign policy. Valuable historical overviews are provided by Walter LaFeber, *The American Age: United States Foreign Policy at Home and Abroad Since 1750* (New York: W. W. Norton, 1989), and Richard W. Van Alstyne, *The Rising American Empire* (Chicago: Quadrangle Books, 1974). Gregory Nobles provides an excellent overview of American continental expansion in *American Frontiers: Cultural Encounters and Continental Conquest* (New York: Hill and Wang, 1997). A valuable general reference source is *The Encyclopedia of U.S. Foreign Relations*, edited by Bruce W. Jentleson and Thomas G. Paterson (New York: Oxford University Press, 1997). More generally, James MacGregor Burns has produced a three-volume modern classic on the history of the United States, *America: The Vineyard of Liberty* (New York: Knopf, 1982), *The Workshop of Democracy*

ESSAY 2.4
THE BUSH DOCTRINE

President Bush Jr.'s graduation speech at West Point presented on June 1, 2002 provides an overview and foundation for his administration's post–September 11 foreign policy, with an emphasis on fighting a global war on terrorism and engaging in preemptive strikes—which is commonly referred to as the Bush Doctrine. What follows is an abridged version of the speech.

"Our war on terrorism is only begun, but in Afghanistan it was begun well. . . .

This war will take many turns we cannot predict. Yet I am certain of this: Wherever we carry it, the American flag will stand not only for our power, but for freedom. Our nation's cause has always been larger than our nation's defense. We fight, as we always fight, for a just peace—a peace that favors human liberty. We will defend the peace against threats from terrorists and tyrants. We will preserve the peace by building good relations among the great powers. And we will extend the peace by encouraging free and open societies on every continent.

Building this just peace is America's opportunity, and America's duty. . . . America has no empire to extend or utopia to establish. We wish for others only what we wish for ourselves—safety from violence, the rewards of liberty, and the hope for a better life.

In defending the peace, we face a threat with no precedent. Enemies in the past needed great armies and great industrial capabilities to endanger the American people and our nation. The attacks of September the 11th required a few hundred thousand dollars in the hands of a few dozen evil and deluded men. . . .

The gravest danger to freedom lies at the perilous crossroads of radicalism and technology. When the spread of chemical and biological and nuclear weapons, along with ballistic missile technology—when that occurs, even weak states and small groups could attain a catastrophic power to strike great nations. Our enemies have declared this very intention, and have been caught seeking these terrible weapons. They want the capability to blackmail us, or to harm us, or to harm our friends—and we will oppose them with all our power.

For much of the last century, America's defense relied on the Cold War doctrines of deterrence and containment. In some cases, those strategies still apply. But new threats also require new thinking. Deterrence—the promise of massive retaliation against nations—means nothing against shadowy networks with no nation or citizens to defend. Containment is not possible when unbalanced dictators with weapons of mass destruction can deliver those weapons on missiles or secretly provide them to terrorist allies. . . .

Homeland defense and missile defense are part of stronger security, and they're essential priorities for America. Yet the war on terror will not be won on the defensive. We must take the battle to the enemy, disrupt his plans, and confront the worst threats before they emerge. In the world we have entered, the only path to safety is the path of action. And this nation will act.

Our security will require the best intelligence, to reveal threats hidden in caves and growing in laboratories. Our security will require modernizing domestic agencies such as the FBI, so they're prepared to act, and act quickly, against danger. Our security will require transforming the military you will lead—a military that must be ready to strike at a moment's notice in any dark corner of the world. And our security will require all Americans to be forward-looking and resolute, to be ready for preemptive action when necessary to defend our liberty and to defend our lives.

The work ahead is difficult. The choices we will face are complex. We must uncover terror cells in 60 or more

(New York: Knopf, 1985), and *The Crosswinds of Freedom* (New York: Knopf, 1989).

A good overview of America's growing internationalism following World War I can be found in William Cohen, *Empire Without Tears: America's Foreign Relations, 1921–1933* (New York: Knopf, 1987). Excellent discussions of the postwar aims of the Roosevelt administration and the origins of the cold war can be found in John Lewis Gaddis, *The United States and the Origins of the Cold War, 1941–1947* (New York: Columbia University Press, 1972); Daniel Yergin, *Shattered Peace: The Origins of the Cold War and the National Security State* (Boston: Houghton Mifflin, 1983); and Melvyn P. Leffler, *A Preponderance of Power: National Security, the Truman Administration, and the Cold War* (Stan-

countries, using every tool of finance, intelligence and law enforcement. Along with our friends and allies, we must oppose proliferation and confront regimes that sponsor terror, as each case requires. . . .

All nations that decide for aggression and terror will pay a price. We will not leave the safety of America and the peace of the planet at the mercy of a few mad terrorists and tyrants. We will lift this dark threat from our country and from the world.

Because the war on terror will require resolve and patience, it will also require firm moral purpose. In this way our struggle is similar to the Cold War. Now, as then, our enemies are totalitarians, holding a creed of power with no place for human dignity. Now, as then, they seek to impose a joyless conformity, to control every life and all of life.

America confronted imperial communism in many different ways—diplomatic, economic, and military. Yet moral clarity was essential to our victory in the Cold War. . . . Some worry that it is somehow undiplomatic or impolite to speak the language of right and wrong. I disagree. Different circumstances require different methods, but not different moralities. Moral truth is the same in every culture, in every time, and in every place. Targeting innocent civilians for murder is always and everywhere wrong. Brutality against women is always and everywhere wrong. There can be no neutrality between justice and cruelty, between the innocent and the guilty. We are in a conflict between good and evil, and America will call evil by its name. By confronting evil and lawless regimes, we do not create a problem, we reveal a problem. And we will lead the world in opposing it.

As we defend the peace, we also have an historic opportunity to preserve the peace. We have our best chance since the rise of the nation state in the 17th century to build a world where the great powers compete in peace instead of prepare for war. . . .

Competition between great nations is inevitable, but armed conflict in our world is not. More and more, civilized nations find ourselves on the same side—united by common dangers of terrorist violence and chaos. America has, and intends to keep, military strengths beyond challenge—thereby, making the destabilizing arms races of other eras pointless, and limiting rivalries to trade and other pursuits of peace. . . .

We must build strong and great power relations when times are good; to help manage crisis when times are bad. America needs partners to preserve the peace, and we will work with every nation that shares this noble goal.

And finally, America stands for more than the absence of war. We have a great opportunity to extend a just peace, by replacing poverty, repression, and resentment around the world with hope of a better day. Through most of history, poverty was persistent, inescapable, and almost universal. In the last few decades, we've seen nations from Chile to South Korea build modern economies and freer societies, lifting millions of people out of despair and want. And there's no mystery to this achievement.

The 20th century ended with a single surviving model of human progress, based on non-negotiable demands of human dignity, the rule of law, limits on the power of the state, respect for women and private property and free speech and equal justice and religious tolerance. America cannot impose this vision—yet we can support and reward governments that make the right choices for their own people. In our development aid, in our diplomatic efforts, in our international broadcasting, and in our educational assistance, the United States will promote moderation and tolerance and human rights. And we will defend the peace that makes all progress possible.

When it comes to the common rights and needs of men and women, there is no clash of civilizations. . . .

America has a greater objective than controlling threats and containing resentment. We will work for a just and peaceful world beyond the war on terror."

SOURCES: U.S., President, George W. Bush, "Graduation Speech at West Point," (June 1, 2002).

ford, Calif.: Stanford University Press, 1992). Richard A. Melanson, *Writing History and Making Policy: The Cold War, Vietnam, and Revisionism* (Lanham, Md.: University Press of America, 1983), provides an excellent overview of competing interpretations of the origins of the cold war.

Informative descriptions and assessments of U.S. foreign policy since World War II can be found in Richard J.

Barnet, *The Alliance: America-Europe-Japan, Makers of the Postwar World* (New York: Simon and Schuster, 1983); Seyom Brown, *The Faces of Power: Constancy and Change in Foreign Policy from Truman to Clinton* (New York: Columbia University Press, 1994); and Walter LaFeber, *America, Russia, and the Cold War, 1948–2002* (New York: McGraw-Hill, 2002).

David Halberstam provides a very informative understanding of the post–cold war foreign policies of presidents Bush Sr. and Clinton in *War in a Time of Peace: Bush, Clinton, and the Generals* (New York: Scribner, 2001). For the impact of September 11, 2001, on the Bush Jr. administration's foreign policy, see Michael Hirsh, "Bush and the World," *Foreign Affairs* (September–October 2002), pp. 18–43, and Nicholas Lemann, "The Next World Order: The Bush Administration May Have a Brand-New Doctrine of Power," *The New Yorker* (April 1, 2002), pp. 42–48.

KEY TERMS

American revolution
Bretton Woods II
Bretton Woods system
Bush Doctrine
cold war
containment
Declaration of Independence
détente
empire
George Kennan
high policy
isolationism
J. William Fulbright
Imperial republic
low policy
Open Door
orthodox interpretation
post–cold war orientation
postrevisionism
revisionism
sphere of influence
Truman Doctrine
Wilsonianism

$\mathcal{C}$HAPTER
3

. . . .

THE GLOBAL CONTEXT
AND AMERICAN POWER

$\mathcal{O}$ur understanding of the complex politics of U.S. foreign policy would be incomplete if it were limited to the two perspectives that are the focus of this book: the government and policymaking process, and the society and domestic politics. It is the interaction of the government, the society, and the larger context in which foreign policy is made that allows one to fully understand the complex politics of U.S. foreign policy. Consequently, it is necessary to examine the context of the global environment and American power in which domestic politics and the government policymaking process take place.

This chapter will address how the global context in general impacts American society and government, the impact of the rise of the cold war (and of the East-West conflict and American power) on world politics, the impact of the increase in greater global complexity since the 1960s, and the implications of the post–cold war era for world politics. Changes in the global environment and American power during the twentieth century set the stage for continuity and change in the politics of U.S. foreign policy throughout society and

government, affecting the president's ability to govern and the demands of national security versus democracy. Thus, the historical and global context plays a crucial role in affecting the complex politics of U.S. foreign policy and will continue to do so in the future.

INFLUENCE ON GOVERNMENT AND SOCIETY

The **global context**—or setting, environment, or milieu—refers to phenomena beyond or external to the institutions, beliefs, and processes of human interaction in government and society. The context therefore includes such elements as the country's resources, level of technology, and the larger global arena of which the United States is a part. Clearly, developments in the global environment and American power both directly and indirectly affect the societal and governmental political process of making U.S. foreign policy.

Although frequently obscure in the causal chain of events and hence difficult to ascertain, *the global environment plays a significant role in the politics of U.S. foreign policy in two principal ways.* First, global patterns set the "underlying" conditions or parameters of likely U.S. foreign policy. For example, the general patterns that prevail throughout the globe affect American power and the United States' international role, thus setting the context in which the politics of U.S. foreign policy operates in society and government.[1] Second, particular world events and relationships occurring often have an "immediate" impact on domestic politics and the U.S. policymaking process. International crises, for example, often play an influential role in the politics of U.S. foreign policy.[2] Specific events and relationships tend to be symptomatic of larger general patterns in world politics. Therefore, both general patterns and immediate events in the American context affect one another and are often mutually reinforcing.

The underlying and immediate impact of the global context on politics occurs in two ways: through the perceptions that people have of the world and by directly affecting the performance and outcome of foreign policy behavior. This distinction has been referred to by Harold and Margaret Sprout in *The Ecological Perspective on Human Affairs* as the difference between the psychological versus objective environment. As they explain it, "So far as we can determine, environmental factors (both nonhuman and social) can affect human activities in only two ways: such factors can be perceived, reacted to, and taken into account by the human individual or individuals under consideration. In this way, and in this way only . . . environmental factors can be said to 'influence,' or to 'condition,' or otherwise to 'affect' human values and preferences, moods, and attitudes, choices and decision." In contrast, environmental factors limit the execution of human undertakings. "Such limitations on performance, accomplishment, outcome, or operational result," the Sprouts assert, "may not—often do not—derive from or depend upon the individual's perception or other psychological behavior."[3]

The global context or environment, in other words, sets the parameters of opportunities and constraints that shape the perceptions of Americans in government and throughout society concerning the world, affecting probable courses of U.S. foreign policy action. The nature of the global environment and American power also determines the likelihood that the pursuit of U.S. foreign policy will be successful abroad. Under both circumstances, the context heavily circumscribes the politics of U.S. foreign policy.

Together, the interaction of the global context, government, and society is responsible for the politics of U.S. foreign policy. In this respect, the evolution of American power and the global environment set the stage or setting for the patterns in the politics of U.S. foreign policy that we discuss throughout this book. One cannot, therefore, fully understand continuity and change, the president's ability to govern, and the evolving tension between national security and democracy in the making of U.S. foreign policy, especially since World War II, without understanding the key patterns that have occurred in the evolution of American power and the global environment.

Although there are numerous ways to organize these larger contextual patterns, it is useful to speak of *three sets of developments, or major stages, in the evolution of the global environment and American power that were dominant since the Second World War:* (1) The rise of the cold war in world politics and American power, 1940s–1960s; (2) Increasing global complexity and the relative decline of American power, 1960s–1980s; and (3) The post–cold war era in world politics and American renewal, 1990s–present?

These developments in the global environment and American power have set the stage for continuity and change in the politics of U.S. foreign policy. The dawning of the cold war in world politics was instrumental in affecting the development of the foreign policy process following World War II. The subsequent rise of global complexity was consequential in stimulating the foreign policy changes that have occurred since Vietnam. The collapse of the cold war accompanied by a number of global forces and events has in turn set the context for the future politics of foreign policy as the United States enters the twenty-first century.

THE COLD WAR ERA IN WORLD POLITICS

A number of significant developments in the global context and American power have played important roles in the politics of U.S. foreign policy in the post–World War II years. Of these, *two major global developments stand out*: (1) The rise of the East-West conflict; and (2) The rise of American power. These developments precipitated a number of events and relationships throughout the globe that played a prominent role in the politics of U.S. foreign policy during the late 1940s and 1950s. Together, the interaction of these global developments, along with domestic developments within American society and government in the postwar years, produced what is often referred to as the cold war era in world politics.

THE RISE OF THE
EAST-WEST CONFLICT

The East-West conflict evolved following World War II with the increasing domination of the United States and the Soviet Union in world politics. This development coincided with the demise of the European empires, whose roots lay deep in the past.[4]

With the rise of technology and industrialization in Europe in the fifteenth century and after, European countries—especially Spain, Portugal, the Netherlands, France, and Great Britain—grew in power and came to dominate world politics. These countries were responsible for what has been called within Western civilization the "age of discovery and colonization." They extended their power throughout the planet, colonizing people and territory to form vast European empires (including the North American continent). Hence, European power rivalries and wars had profound consequences for world politics.

World Wars I and II represented the twentieth-century struggle for European and global hegemony. Entering the twentieth century, France and especially Great Britain were the two global powers that dominated the global status quo. At the same time, Japan and Germany rapidly grew in power and challenged Great Britain, France, and the status quo to acquire their "place in the sun." The result was war on a global scale. Ironically, rather than creating a new German and Japanese hegemony or restoring the old European hegemony, the two world wars contributed to the demise of Europe as the center of world politics.

With the decline of Europe, the Soviet Union and the United States filled the political vacuum. Actually, the Soviet Union and the United States grew in power throughout the nineteenth and twentieth centuries. As

we briefly discussed in chapter 2, the United States began as a new, liberal nation (gaining independence from the British empire), expanded westward to become a continental power by the mid-nineteenth century, attained regional power status by the turn of the twentieth century, and ultimately emerged as a global power by the mid-twentieth century. As the United States expanded westward and industrialized, a very similar process occurred in Russia (and the Soviet Union): It became a Eurasian power by expanding eastward (and southward) and industrializing (though at a less dynamic pace than the United States) under both the czars and then Bolshevism. Therefore, the decline of European power was accompanied by the rise of the Soviet Union and the United States in world affairs.

The ascendance of the Soviet Union and the United States in the wake of European collapse resulted in a global context in which an American-Soviet conflict of some type was virtually inevitable for a variety of reasons. In response to the rise of Adolf Hitler, the Soviet Union and the United States were cautious partners during World War II who found themselves in an alliance of convenience—an alliance that would have great difficulty surviving the postwar peace. For one thing, the war played out differently for each country: The United States focused its initial efforts in the Pacific and prospered tremendously from the war; in contrast, the Soviet Union bore the brunt of the European fighting and saw its country ravaged by the conflict. In addition, the fate of Europe—the world's industrial heartland over the previous centuries, whose economies were destroyed and social fabric was torn apart by the war—was determined by American and Soviet power. This set the stage for the territorial disputes that arose when American-led allied forces prevailed in Western Europe while Soviet-led forces occupied Eastern Europe, splitting Germany in two (as was the case with Korea in Asia). Finally, American and Soviet leaders came from societies with different histories, different value systems, and different postwar goals. U.S.-led efforts, for instance, to promote an international political economic order reflecting its liberal ideology contradicted Soviet postwar goals emphasizing spheres of influence, the imposition of so-called friendly communist neighboring regimes, and domestic reconstruction. With the end of war, therefore, near-perfect underlying conditions existed for the development of mutual suspicion and hostility, centered in Europe, between the Soviet Union and the United States.

Specific international events and crises reflecting these World War II and postwar developments impacted domestic politics and the government policy-making process in such a way that they spurred the rise of the cold war. Within the United States, for example, disputes over postwar economic reconstruction; the fate of Germany; the rise of communism in Eastern Europe; the Soviet-American conflict over Iran, Greece, and Turkey; the fall of Chiang Kai-shek and the Nationalist government in China; the North Korean attack on South Korea; and the Soviet explosion of an atomic bomb all contributed to the growing cold war environment both abroad and at home. With these events, the postwar debate over American foreign policy was soon dominated by a view of the Soviet Union as no longer an ally but an evil enemy attempting to achieve world empire.[5]

In response to these international developments and events, U.S. foreign policy became global in scope and increasingly oriented toward the perceived need to contain the threat posed by the Soviet Union and communism throughout the globe. These events and policies were accompanied by the governmental and societal patterns that will be discussed throughout the book, such as the rise of McCarthyism, the development of an anticommunist consensus, the rise of the national security bureaucracy and ethos, and the growth of presidential power.

These developments in global context, government, and domestic society were mutually reinforcing in the politics of U.S. foreign policy during the cold war years. Events during the 1950s and early 1960s—such as the Hungarian uprising; the rise of Third World nationalism and nonalignment; the rise of Fidel Castro in Cuba; the launching by the Soviet Union of the first satellite, Sputnik, to go around the world; the Cuban missile crisis; and the war in Indochina—fed American fears, influenced American politics, and promoted continuity in the cold war politics of U.S. foreign policy. Americans in both government and society saw a "free world" led by the United States pitted against a "totalitarian world" led by the Soviet Union in a global cold war throughout the 1950s and early 1960s. Hence the rise of the East-West conflict gave rise to presidential preeminence in the making of U.S. for-

eign policy, allowing the demands of national security to prevail over the demands of democracy.

THE RISE OF AMERICAN POWER

The politics of U.S. foreign policy also were affected heavily by the rise of American power in the world. As discussed in chapter 2, the United States had steadily grown more powerful since its independence, increasing the scope of its foreign involvement from a continental to a regional orientation. By the twentieth century, the United States clearly had become one of the world's "great powers." Yet it was not until the events of World War II that U.S. foreign policy fully entered the global era.

Following World War II the United States was able to pursue a policy of global containment because it was clearly the most powerful country in the world—possibly in the history of the world. While Europe, the Soviet Union, and Japan lost millions of people and saw their economies devastated by war, the United States suffered much less loss of human life. More important, however, the war effort lifted the American economy out of the Great Depression of the 1930s and catapulted it into unprecedented prosperity. Clearly, the United States was the global power, or superpower, of its time, setting the context for the politics of U.S. foreign policy that would prevail during the cold war era.

While the late 1940s and 1950s were the height of American power throughout the world, the power of the Soviet Union was much more limited throughout the globe. The Soviet Union both benefited and suffered from the war. Although the Soviet empire expanded to include much of Eastern Europe, the Soviet Union had to recover from the war's devastation—twenty million people died during the conflict and the economy was destroyed. The Soviet Union developed a formidable military as a result of the war, but it was predominantly a land army, limited to the continents of Europe and Asia. It has been argued that the Soviet Union's greatest asset was the ideological appeal of communism, which was potentially global. Ultimately, however, the economic, military, and political capabilities of the Soviet Union made it a Eurasian power during the cold war, especially during the period immediately following the war.[6]

United States economic, military, and political power, in contrast, was immense and far-reaching following the war and expanded in the 1950s. In the immediate postwar years, the American economy was the most powerful in the history of the world. American economic production was the key to Allied success in the war and was responsible for producing almost half the value of the world's goods and services following the conflict. As Godfrey Hodgson has observed:

> In 1945, the United States was bulging with an abundance of every resource that held the key to power in the modern world: with land, food, raw materials, industrial plant, monetary reserves, scientific talent, and trained manpower. It was in the war years that the United States shot ahead of all its rivals economically. In four years, national income, national wealth, and industrial production all doubled or more than doubled. In the same period, . . . every other industrial nation came out of the war poorer and weaker than when it went in.[7]

American multinational corporations and financial investment, which had been expanding since the turn of the century, came to dominate the postwar international marketplace.[8]

This allowed the United States to develop a large military and intelligence capability whose scope of activities was worldwide. Over half of the expanded federal budget, in fact, was devoted to the national security bureaucracy during the 1950s. Furthermore, a large portion of the American economy was placed on a war footing with the development of a military-industrial-scientific infrastructure supporting the demands of national security. These developments eventually provided the president and the executive branch with the capability to pursue and implement a global policy based on the strategy of containment.

The importance of the global context for the politics of U.S. foreign policy and American power can also be seen in areas traditionally considered domestic. The U.S. government, for example, also made major investments—in the name of national security—in transportation and education to strengthen American capabilities in support of an activist foreign policy. The United States experienced considerable transportation bottlenecks during World War II due to its dependence on an aging railroad system. Therefore, one of the major purposes behind the creation of the interstate highway system in the 1950s, with 90 percent of the

funding provided by the federal government, was to create the means to efficiently and reliably transport military troops and equipment across the country in times of national emergency or war.

Similarly, much of the expansion in higher education during the 1960s was fueled by Sputnik and the fear that the United States was falling behind the Soviet Union in science and technology. In response, the U.S. government made a major effort to support higher education by, for example, offering National Defense Student Loans (NDSLs), as they were first called, to increase college enrollments (especially in the hard sciences), thus laying the foundation for the financial aid system for students today.

Therefore, U.S. military and political clout following the war was considerably strengthened throughout the world and affected U.S. foreign policy. The U.S. government and American multinational corporations dominated the international political economy of the so-called free world. As the French and British empires collapsed, American power usually filled the vacuum and replaced European power, as occurred in Turkey, Iran, and Vietnam. The U.S. government, in fact, began to negotiate what became an extensive system of alliances and military bases to permanently deploy American troops overseas.

The development of international law and organizations in the postwar world was heavily influenced by the United States, as symbolized by the creation of the United Nations and Bretton Woods system. America's moral appeal as the victorious country promoting a liberal world order was also widespread following the war, especially in Western Europe.

The United States was so powerful following the war that it has been referred to not only as a great power or superpower but as the hegemonic power of its time.[9] In the more common language used by American leaders and the general public, the United States was considered the "world's policeman" and the "world's banker." American power was seen as so immense during the 1950s that the twentieth century was often referred to as the "American century." The consequence of these developments was that American power, as well as the perception of that power, provided the means to intervene throughout the world to contain Soviet communist aggression, defeat threats to the status quo arising from political instability and insurgency, and promote what has been called "nation building" in Third World countries in accordance with the American liberal model of political and economic development.

The immensity of American power, symbolized by its nuclear capability and its widespread military presence abroad, created incredibly high expectations of foreign policy success. Consequently, policy failure—such as the perceived "loss" of China and the stalemate in the Korean War—produced much political frustration, contributing to such developments as the rise of McCarthyism in American politics. For as powerful and hegemonic as the United States became during the postwar years, it nevertheless failed to fully control its destiny or those of others in world affairs.[10]

Despite the rise of the cold war as the overarching issue and the flowering of American power, the world remained vast and complex in many ways. Differences existed among American allies, nationalism was increasing throughout the world, international organizations gained a life of their own, the opposition of U.S. adversaries was often formidable, the complex politics of U.S. foreign policy compromised or constrained strategy and programs abroad, and there was always the role of chance or fortune in world politics. Therefore, U.S. foreign policy was pursued in the complex cold-war environment of world politics with no guarantees of success. But clearly, the 1950s represented the height of American power in both cold war politics at home and cold war policies abroad; although far from omnipotent, the United States at the apex of its global power was overwhelmingly the single most powerful actor on the global stage.

In sum, the major global-environmental developments during the cold war era in world politics discussed above set the underlying and immediate stage for the politics of U.S. foreign policy. The expansion of American power, coupled with the rise of the East-West conflict, contributed to the growth of presidential power and the prevalence of the demands of national security in American politics that became the foundation of a global policy of containment during the Truman, Eisenhower, Kennedy, and Johnson administrations. At the same time, developments in government and society in the politics of U.S. foreign policy contributed to the rise of the East-West conflict and the exercise of American power abroad. Therefore, a symbiotic process took place among government, society, and the global context that interacted to produce the

complex politics of U.S. foreign policy that came to dominate the cold war era.

GLOBAL COMPLEXITY AND AMERICAN DECLINE

During the 1960s, certain trends in the global environment and American power became increasingly consequential for the politics of U.S. foreign policy. *Two general global developments stand out in world politics:* (1) The rise of global pluralism and interdependence and (2) The relative decline of American power. These developments resulted in greater global complexity, deeply affecting domestic politics and the governmental policymaking process.

A more pluralistic and interdependent world, combined with the decline of American power, made it increasingly difficult for the United States to successfully pursue its cold war policies abroad—as best illustrated by the American failure in the Vietnam War and the ending of the Bretton Woods economic system, based on fixed currency rates and the gold standard. Thus, the rise of global complexity contributed to foreign policy failures and the changes in the politics of U.S. foreign policy that came about since the Vietnam War.

The Vietnam War represented both the height of the cold war era and the existence of much greater global complexity than before. From the late 1940s to the mid-1960s, the American effort to contain communism in Vietnam and Americanize the war was symptomatic of the rise of the East-West conflict and of American power. By the late 1960s, however, it was also becoming increasingly clear that U.S. failure to win the war reflected the advent of a more complex world and the decline of American power. The American failure in Vietnam, along with other events of the sixties and seventies, triggered the shift to a more pluralistic foreign policy process within the United States. This process has made it difficult for presidents to successfully govern foreign policy, as Richard Nixon, Gerald Ford, Jimmy Carter, and Ronald Reagan experienced (see chapter 4), and contributed to changes in the conduct of U.S. foreign policy between and within administrations, as discussed in chapter 2. Together, the rise of complexity abroad and pluralism at home have rein-

forced the dominant patterns in the politics of U.S. foreign policy prevailing since Vietnam.

THE RISE OF GLOBAL PLURALISM AND INTERDEPENDENCE

Since the end of World War II, the world also has
grown in complexity. Among the most important
global developments have been the economic recovery
and rise of Western Europe and Japan, the rise of
the Organization of Petroleum Exporting Countries
(OPEC), the arrival of new industrializing nations and
other actors in the international political economy, the
growth of Third World independence and nationalism,
and the diffusion of technology and armaments worldwide. As a consequence of these global developments, it
has become more difficult for the great powers to exercise influence abroad, especially through the use of
force, and economic issues have climbed to the top of
the global agenda alongside national security issues—
both impacting U.S. foreign policy. Therefore, the
East-West conflict between the United States and the
Soviet Union that once dominated world politics during the 1950s was joined by the rise of global pluralism
and interdependence. *These global developments did not
occur overnight, but evolved over time and have historical
roots.*[11]

The rise of global pluralism and interdependence
was heavily a function of the resurgence of Europe and
Japan in world affairs. Although the European and
Japanese economies were destroyed by the war, it was
only a matter of time before economic recovery took
place, given their technological know-how and previous level of economic development. The United States
fostered economic recovery by providing assistance
through the Marshall Plan, opening of the American
economy to foreign imports, and the bearing a disproportionate share of the defense burden, including the
stationing of American troops abroad. By the 1960s
Europe—especially West Germany—and Japan had
become prominent forces in the international political
economy. In fact, the European and Japanese
economies became so strong relative to the United
States' that the Bretton Woods system—the international economic system that had developed following
World War II, based on fixed exchange rates and free
trade—became unsustainable by the early 1970s.

Other developments contributed to the rise of pluralism and interdependence in the international political economy. Newly industrializing countries, such as
South Korea, Taiwan, Singapore, and Brazil, were becoming more competitive in the international economy. With oil as the basic source of energy in industrialized societies, OPEC also became more consequential
politically and financially due to its ability to periodically impact oil prices. Third World countries, in general, were becoming increasingly important to industrialized economies as a source of raw materials, as
export markets for finished goods, and as borrowers of
capital, resulting in large foreign debts. Also, with the
rise of détente, the Soviet Union, Eastern Europe, and
the People's Republic of China became more intertwined with the global capitalist economy. Furthermore, multinational corporations spread and expanded their influence throughout the globe, gaining
greater independence from government control. Finally, the breakdown of the Bretton Woods system increased the political and economic importance of international governmental organizations such as the
IMF, World Bank, and GATT on the workings of the
international political economy.

The growth of economic pluralism and interdependence made it more difficult for the United States to
successfully pursue its foreign economic policy abroad
and promote economic prosperity at home. In other
words, *the U.S. economy became increasingly dependent
upon and affected by forces beyond its borders*—similar to
the situation before World War II and as virtually all
other governments have been all too aware. Not surprisingly, economic problems at home and abroad grew
after the early 1960s and contributed to the metamor-
phosis of foreign economic policy from low to high priority in the politics of U.S. foreign policy.

Changes in the global context in which the United
States operated became more consequential for the
American economy. For example, the cyclical nature of
oil prices after the 1973 OPEC embargo and the demographic changes within the United States contributed to
both recession and growth in the American economy.
During the late 1970s, the American economy suffered
from double-digit inflation and unemployment, much
of which was fueled by the doubling of oil prices following the Iran-Iraq war and a bulge in the labor force
as the baby boomers of the 1950s flooded the job market. During the early 1980s, these same environmental

factors acted in reverse—oil prices and new entrants into the labor force declined dramatically, generating a decline in inflation and an economic expansion.

Clearly, the American economy was far beyond the control of the government and the president. As described by one journalist at the time, "Carter was battered by the same fundamental forces that bolstered Ronald Reagan. Yet neither had any real control over these forces. Nothing the White House has done, whether in style or in substance, has significantly affected the ebb and flow of our national economy in the past decade."[12] Although overstated, the point contains the valid implication that America's ability to control its own economy and destiny was becoming increasingly problematic in a world of greater complexity.

With the rise of global pluralism and interdependence, the United States by the 1960s experienced *similar constraints in exerting influence and control in national security affairs.* Europe, for example, not only recovered economically but began exercising greater political independence in world politics. France acted increasingly independent of U.S. foreign policy and withdrew from NATO, while West Germany initiated the "Ostpolitik" policy of building bridges with communist governments in Eastern Europe, thus stimulating the beginnings of détente. The development of nuclear weapons and the military competition between the United States and the Soviet Union produced a "balance of terror." In addition, the Soviet Union became a global military power during the late 1960s and 1970s, while simultaneously playing a more active political role through its involvement in the détente process. Furthermore, nuclear weapons capabilities spread to France, Great Britain, and the People's Republic of China. To complicate matters further, most colonies in the world had won their political independence by the 1960s, making Third World nationalism a growing force. Technology was diffusing throughout the world, especially sophisticated armaments, as a result of American, Soviet, and European exports. Conflicts, most of them civil and unconventional, proliferated and intensified throughout the world. Together, these developments in the global environment made it much more difficult for even a great power, such as the United States or the Soviet Union, to exercise political and military influence abroad—as each experienced, in Vietnam and Afghanistan.

The rise of global pluralism and interdependence made the world more complex, messier, and increas-

ingly consequential in affecting and constraining the foreign policies and domestic situations of all countries. The global environment had often acted to constrain the foreign policies of small countries, but the growth in global complexity now also constrained the foreign policy of the larger and more powerful countries as well, including the United States. In other words, the rise of global pluralism and interdependence meant a corresponding decline in American power throughout the world.

THE RELATIVE DECLINE OF AMERICAN POWER

As the world became noticeably more pluralistic and interdependent by the 1960s, the United States' economic and military ability to influence the world declined. The United States' decline was not in "absolute," or real, terms but was relative to changes occurring in the global environment. This relative decline of American power contributed to the U.S. defeat in Vietnam and the changes experienced by the Bretton Woods system. Ultimately, these dramatic events played an important role in the decline of presidential power in the making of U.S. foreign policy and the crisis of governance that has plagued American politics during the post–Vietnam War years.

In some respects, the decline of American power was inevitable. The immensity of American power in the late 1940s and early 1950s was clearly extraordinary—and temporary, given the devastation wrought by the war throughout most of the world. As Europe, Japan, and the Soviet Union recovered from the war, American power could only decline in comparison. Many of these changes were a function of the United States' success in promoting a liberal international economic order, reinforced further by the general growth in global pluralism and interdependence. Overall, these environmental changes resulting in the rise of global complexity contributed to American relative decline. This has led to a seeming contradiction in U.S. foreign policy that might be called the **paradox of American power:** the United States continued to be the most powerful country in the world but no longer was able to exercise the kind of economic, political, and military influence that it enjoyed at its height during the late 1940s and 1950s.

Although the United States remained the preeminent economic power, its economic influence nonetheless declined quite dramatically during the 1970s and 1980s from its post–World War II peak—the time period that provided the foundation for American global interventionism and the rise of presidential power in foreign policy. *A comparison of America's economic role in the world between 1950 and 1976 highlights its relative decline:* (1) The percentage of total world economic production produced within the United States declined from almost 50 percent to 24 percent; (2) The American share of world crude steel production fell from 45 percent to 17 percent; (3) American iron ore production shrank from 42 percent to 10 percent of the world total; (4) Crude petroleum production declined from 53 percent to 14 percent; (5) The percentage of international financial reserves decreased from 49 percent to 7 percent; (6) American exports fell from 18 percent to 11 percent of world trade; and (7) Even American wheat production as a percentage of global production declined from 17 percent to 14 percent.[13] Very simply, economic production in Europe and Japan and throughout the world had increased more rapidly than in the United States. In some cases, such as oil, there had actually been an absolute decline in American production.

The relative decline of the American economy was not simply quantitative but qualitative as well. In numerous areas, American companies lost the technological lead to foreign competitors, especially the Japanese. Whereas during the cold war years "Made in the U.S.A." had been considered the mark of excellence, during the 1970s and 1980s American products were no longer held in such high esteem either abroad or at home. Likewise, whereas "Made in Japan" had been an indication of cheap and unreliable goods as recently as the 1960s, it became the symbol of the highest quality available for manufactured and technological goods.

The relative decline of the American economy, especially in the manufacturing sector, can also be attributed to significant contextual developments at home. After the 1960s, inflation and federal deficits increased dramatically, hurting the American economy. American management styles became top-heavy in personnel, produced bloated salaries, and emphasized a short-term profit outlook. Moreover, rising affluence and mass consumption were accompanied by declining worker productivity. Also, the industrial, union, transportation, and educational infrastructures were aging

and becoming difficult and costly to revitalize. All of these factors and more contributed to the overall economic decline of the United States both at home and abroad during the 1970s and 1980s.[14]

A similar pattern occurred with respect to U.S. ability to threaten and use force successfully abroad after the Vietnam War. The U.S. government found it increasingly difficult to promote political stability and to exercise overt and covert military force. In Iran, for example, the United States was able to covertly overthrow the Iranian government with relative ease, installing the shah in 1953. Twenty-five years later, however, the United States could not stop the Iranian revolution and the rise of the Ayatollah Khomeini, triggering the Iran hostage crisis in American politics. Even in Central America, the traditional region of American hegemony, the United States faced new obstacles to the exercise of foreign policy influence. Small military or covert U.S. operations had determined the fate of Central American countries throughout most of the twentieth century; by the 1980s, however, the Reagan administration's covert war in Nicaragua involving over ten thousand contras was unable to defeat militarily the Sandinistas. Clearly, quick and easy military victories, such as in Grenada and Panama, were still possible, but they were becoming more costly politically and, with the rise of global complexity, becoming the exception to the rule.

The Vietnam War was symptomatic of the increased resistance that the United States found when attempting to exercise political and military force abroad. First, strong multilateral support for American military intervention abroad became less certain. Over fifteen allied countries had supplied combat troops in the Korean War; fewer than five did so in the Vietnam War. Europe not only refused to provide troops but criticized American involvement during the war. Second, beleaguered governments dependent on American support became more difficult to influence. As Lawrence Grinter demonstrated in his essay "Bargaining Between Saigon and Washington," the governments of South Vietnam and the United States continually worked at cross-purposes with each other. The South Vietnamese leadership aspired to maintain power and attract American assistance during the war, while the American leadership was preoccupied with containing communism and protecting American prestige. The net result was that the South Vietnamese government was not simply a "puppet on a string" but was able to resist and manipulate U.S. policy.[15] A third difficulty that the United States faced was nationalism, a force to be reckoned with. Vietnamese nationalism was the major asset of the Vietnamese communists in defeating the United States and the South Vietnamese. John Mueller demonstrated in "The Search for the 'Breaking Point' in Vietnam" that the Vietnamese communists were a most formidable enemy: over the centuries they had resisted and defeated the Chinese, Japanese, French, and finally the Americans.[16] The Soviet Union faced a similar problem in Afghanistan in the 1980s. Finally, the adversary was able to find sources of vital goods and supplies in order to carry out the war. The Vietnamese communists were able to take advantage of the East-West rivalry and the growing Sino-Soviet split to get Chinese and Soviet support.

The Vietnam War was indicative that the "good ole days" of simple power politics—in which great powers could easily dominate lesser powers through the threat of war, the use of force, and/or covert paramilitary action with minimal political costs—had disappeared. Richard Feinberg wrote in the 1980s:

> Compared to the situation that the colonial powers found in the heyday of imperialism, when a small flotilla of gunboats could manhandle an ancient civilization or conquer disorganized territories, many of today's Third World states wield much more formidable degrees of organized power. . . . While most Third World states may not yet be powerful enough to guarantee their own sovereignty, it has certainly become more problematical for foreign powers arbitrarily to impose their will upon them.[17]

In other words, the rise of global complexity weakened the likelihood of the successful application of military force. The American failure in Vietnam, most importantly, acted as a catalyst for the collapse of the anticommunist consensus, the reassertion of congressional power, and the more pluralistic domestic environment, all of which have multiplied the constraints on the president's ability to exercise force abroad, especially on a large scale over a prolonged period.

Overall during the 1970s and 1980s the United States was no longer the world's banker and found it increasingly difficult to act unilaterally as the world's policeman. The exercise of American power in the world remained formidable in comparison to any other single actor, but it was not what it once was. American power throughout the global arena, in other words, experienced relative decline since its height following World War II. This raised key questions and led to a major debate during the 1970s and 1980s: Is the United States in decline? Will the United States continue to decline? Can American power be renewed? Such questions were openly debated in American politics before the collapse of the Soviet Union and, though heard less often today, remain relevant (and will be addressed further below). Whatever the future of American power, however, its evolution will continue to play an integral role in the future politics of U.S. foreign policy.

In summary, the growth of global complexity has played a major role in the politics of U.S. foreign policy. The rise of global pluralism and interdependence has been accompanied by the decline of American power. These developments made it much more difficult for the United States to successfully pursue the foreign policies of the cold war years. The American failure in Vietnam and the changes in the Bretton Woods system were symptoms of these changes in American power and the global environment. These failures triggered political instability and a crisis of governance in American politics during the late 1960s and 1970s, resulting in important changes in the politics of U.S. foreign policy. As a result of the dynamic interaction of the government, the society, and the larger global environment, presidents have found it more difficult to govern foreign policy, while the contradictions between national security and democracy have grown since the Vietnam War.

THE POST–COLD WAR ERA AND AMERICAN RENEWAL?

The end of the cold war in 1989 and 1990 appears to have made the world an even more complex place, with contradictory implications for American power and United States foreign policy.

CONTRADICTORY POST–COLD WAR TENDENCIES

Some global developments seem to have reinforced continuity while others appear to have promoted change. Thus far, *two post–cold war global trends appear to be most important for the future politics of U.S. foreign policy:* ① The collapse of communism and other profound global changes and issues, and ② The continuation of global conflicts, crises, and wars.[18]

The Collapse of Communism and Other Complex Global Issues. The most significant long-term development in the global environment is the collapse of communism, which appears to have reinforced and intensified the changes that have occurred in the politics of U.S. foreign policy since the Vietnam War. The collapse of the Soviet empire was a momentous event in the twentieth century and world history, for it meant the end of the cold war and a world of even greater complexity.

The collapse of communism and the Soviet Union is consequential for the future politics of U.S. foreign policy for a very simple but fundamental reason. The rise of Soviet communism and the cold war following World War II was the principal justification for development of the institutions and beliefs in American society and government that led to the policy of global containment and intervention and the preeminence of presidential power in the making of U.S. foreign policy. Therefore, the collapse of communism and the Soviet Union should further reduce the demands of national security and presidential power.

On the other hand, with the collapse of the Soviet Union, the United States has become the preeminent power in the world—militarily, economically, and ideologically. Therefore, the United States is likely to continue to exercise a powerful presence in pursuit of a variety of interests in a world of greater complexity and turbulence. This is likely to reinforce the need for an infrastructure, institutions, and personnel throughout government and society who support America's global orientation into the twenty-first century, contributing to presidential power and the demands of national security. In fact, some people have argued that recent changes in the global environment have allowed not only for the restoration of American power but the potential to develop a "Pax Americana" if American leaders and U.S. foreign policy would seize the "unipolar moment."

The collapse of the cold war also allows for the possibility that American resources might be redirected toward revitalizing its economy. After all, the end of the Soviet communist threat reinforces the increasing importance of American foreign economic policy and

America's role within the international political economy. And the American economy did experience tremendous growth, restructuring, and competitiveness during the 1990s within the international political economy.

The collapse of communism in the Soviet Union and Eastern Europe has resulted in a single, integrated international political economy of growing interdependence and complexity. For at least forty years after World War II the Soviet Union attempted to withdraw and minimize its interaction with the larger, capitalist global economy dominated by the West and the United States—creating its own separate political economy made up of communist/socialist states. The collapse of communism in the Soviet Union and Eastern Europe, along with the economic transition within China since the death of Mao Tse-tung, has reintegrated these areas of the world within the larger international political economy. This means that all states and parts of the world, including the United States, are increasingly interdependent economically as the world has become a single international political economic system.

The international economic crises of the late 1990s, such as the collapse of the Mexican peso and of the "Asian tiger" economies, highlight the extent to which the United States is heavily interwoven in the fabric of the larger global economic system. This is reinforced by the tremendous rise of international economic transactions and trade with countries such as China as well as the development of the North American Free Trade Agreement (NAFTA) and the creation of the World Trade Organization (WTO). Such a world of global complexity and interdependence is only likely to grow and, thus, becomes increasingly important for U.S. foreign policy and for Americans as the United States enters the twenty-first century (see **essay 3.1** on the East Asian financial crisis and the role of international organizations such as the International Monetary Fund in U.S. foreign policy).

The end of the cold war would also seem to imply that developments divorced from national security should gain in prominence in the politics of U.S. foreign policy. Issues once "low" on the foreign policy agenda should become increasingly "high" policy as they become part of the international political agenda. This is most obvious with respect to the growing importance of the economic aspects of U.S. foreign policy but is also likely to affect North-South, immigration

ESSAY 3.1
INTERNATIONAL ORGANIZATIONS, THE ASIAN "ECONOMIC FLU," AND AMERICAN MULTILATERAL INTERVENTION

The U.S. government maintains official representation, missions, and leadership positions in a variety of international organizations (IOs). Among some of the more important are the United Nations (UN), United Nations Educational, Scientific, and Cultural Organization (UNESCO), North Atlantic Treaty Organization (NATO), Organization for Economic Cooperation and Development (OECD), European Union (EU), International Monetary Fund (IMF), World Bank, and World Trade Organization (WTO). As the world has grown in complexity, so has the role of international organizations and multilateral diplomacy. This is nicely illustrated by the economic crises that hit Asia in 1997–1999 and the U.S.-led multilateral response.

In the summer of 1997, the economy of Thailand began to go into a tailspin. Throughout the fall and winter of 1998, other Asian economies—including Indonesia, Malaysia, the Philippines, South Korea, and Taiwan—experienced a similar economic situation. These countries were referred to as the Asian "tigers" in the 1980s and 1990s because of their incredibly high rates of economic growth. But virtually overnight, their economies collapsed and investment capital fled the country to other economies, creating huge devaluations in their currencies (values dropping by as much as 80 percent) and triggering an international economic crisis.

The United States, along with Western European countries and Japan and the IMF, was quick to intervene to try to stabilize the international situation. Treasury Secretary Robert Rubin (previously President Clinton's national economic adviser and head of the newly created National Economic Council in 1993), explained in a speech on January 21, 1998, why the United States had intervened in the international economy to play such an active role, how the crisis affected the American economy and the lives of Americans, and why the nation must work multi-

laterally with other countries and international organizations, such as the IMF.

Today I would like to discuss the financial crisis in Asia; why the United States must protect its vital economic and national security interests by working to help restore financial stability and economic growth to that troubled region; and why acting promptly and effectively to do so protects the economic interests of every American.

To begin, I think it is important to place the recent events in Asia in the context of the emergence of the global financial system. Over the last several years, we have entered a new era for global financial markets and the global economy—an era of interdependence, complexity and opportunity. . . .

The countries in Asia are our customers, our competitors, and our security partners. Financial instability, economic distress, and depreciating currencies all have direct effects on the pace of our exports, the competitiveness of our companies, the growth of our economy and, ultimately, the well-being of American workers. Thirty percent of U.S. exports go to Asia, supporting millions of U.S. jobs, and we export more to Asia than Europe. In states like California, Oregon, and Washington, exports to Asia account for more than half of each state's total exports. . . . If the crisis were to spread more broadly to other emerging markets, then the impact on American workers and businesses could be much greater. Simply put, we cannot afford to stand back and gamble that the crisis will resolve itself. . . .

From the very beginning of this crisis, we at Treasury, in close cooperation with Chairman Greenspan and the staff of the Federal Reserve Board, have been

and refugee, public health, and environmental issues, among others. In this respect, the collapse of communism and the Soviet Union is reinforced by other significant global developments, such as the reunification of Germany, the growing integration of Western Europe, the expansion and intensification of the marketplace throughout the world, the growth of Third World debt, the global spread of AIDS, and the destruction of the environment in much of the world. Most of these

issues are very problematic and increasingly beyond the control of national governments in a world of growing complexity, which may exacerbate the difficulty the U.S. government and society have in adjusting to global change and the post–cold war era.

Continuation of Global Conflicts, Crises and Wars. The end of the cold war, however, does not signal the end of conflict in the world, nor does it mean

deeply involved in crafting an international response involving the countries of the region, the G-7 [the Group of Seven, which includes Canada, France, Great Britain, Germany, Italy, and Japan, along with the United States], the World Bank, and the Asian Development Bank—all working with the International Monetary Fund. The president's national security team including Secretary [of State] Albright, Secretary [of Defense] Cohen, and National Security Advisor Berger, have been integrally and critically involved in this effort. . . .

The central provider of this financial assistance (involving the equivalent of billions of dollars) is the International Monetary Fund, with additional support from the World Bank and the Asian Development Bank. In addition, the United States has joined other industrial countries in indicating its willingness to provide supplementary financial resources in some situations if a country fully adheres to the reform program and further resources become necessary. . . .

The IMF is the right institution to be at the center of these support programs. This institution, which was established at the initiative of the United States fifty years ago, has long benefited Americans. The core mission of the IMF has always remained the same—to promote financial stability, trade, and economic growth.

The United States has worked forcefully to help the IMF meet the new challenges of the modern financial system, and there is simply no other institution capable of performing its mission. With tremendous expertise and technical resources, the IMF has the ability to shape effective reform programs. As a multinational organization, it is able to require an economically distressed country to accept conditions that no contributing nation could require on its own. Finally—and critically important—the IMF internationalizes the burden during a global financial crisis by using its pool of capital

instead of the United States having to bear that burden alone. . . .

Some say that doing nothing would be best, because markets would ultimately solve the problem on their own. Let me say as someone who spent twenty-six years on Wall Street and who has an enormous belief in markets, there are problems that markets alone cannot solve. In this country, we recognized that long ago, with measures such as the Federal Reserve System, the Securities and Exchange Commission, and deposit insurance. Laws and institutions support healthy free market activity by dealing with issues beyond the ability of unfettered markets to handle. There is simply too much risk that markets alone will not resolve these problems of financial instability, and therefore given our stakes in Asia we must try to help get these countries back on track. . . .

Much of what Rubin says may go against the grain of many Americans' understanding of the so-called free market. He describes a very complex, and confusing, international political economy vulnerable to rapid change. Nevertheless, it should shed light on why the United States—with the world's largest and strongest economy—has played such a vital role and intervened in the past, such as when Russia's market economy was emerging after the collapse of communism or when the Mexican economy and peso collapsed precipitously in 1995. Although initially reluctant, the administration of George Bush Jr. participated in a multibillion-dollar multilateral financial loan through the IMF in response to Argentina's and Brazil's collapsing economy and financial crisis in 2001. This discussion should shed light on the complexity of globalization and why the United States is likely to intervene multilaterally and through the use of international organizations like the IMF in the future as the world enters the twenty-first century.

SOURCE: U.S. Treasury, Office of Public Affairs, "Treasury Secretary Robert E. Rubin Address on the Asian Financial Situation to Georgetown University" (Washington, D.C., January 21, 1998).

"peace is at hand." In fact, the cold war's end in a world of greater complexity, where global issues proliferate and power is diffuse, may produce more conflict and crises. Although not on the scale of the U.S.-Soviet conflict, such conflicts have the potential to trigger American intervention in the world.

The Persian Gulf crisis and war of 1991 demonstrates that the collapse of communism and the end of the cold war have given the United States greater opportunity to exercise leadership and force abroad. Now that the Soviet Union is no longer the United States' major adversary, a major constraint has been eliminated with respect to U.S. ability to use political influence and, in particular, exercise force abroad. During the Bush Sr. and Clinton administration, the most significant short-term developments in this regard have been the Persian Gulf and Kosovo wars, which have reinforced both concern with national security and the elements supporting strong presidential power in the foreign policy process. As the Persian Gulf War in particular made clear, the United States is the lone superpower in the world, which increases the nation's opportunities to exercise force abroad. The immediate result of the Persian Gulf and Kosovo wars, hence, has been to counteract the changes within American government and society prompted by the collapse of the Soviet Union and the communist threat to America as they adapt to the future of a post–cold war world.

Since taking office, the Bush Jr. Administration has been forced to respond to numerous international crises, including the EP-3 airplane incident with China, the financial crises in South America, the nuclear weapons crisis with North Korea, the continuing crisis in the Middle East between Israel and the Palestinians, and the terrorist crises generated by September 11.

Although the issues and problems surrounding terrorism have been around for some time throughout the world and in the United States, they became particularly salient for most Americans in the wake of the tragedy and scope of the casualties caused by the direct attacks on important American symbols on American soil—the World Trade Center towers in New York City, which were completely destroyed, and the Pentagon, in Washington, D.C. But as President Bush Jr. and his advisers have so often said, unlike the Persian Gulf or Kosovo wars, the war on terrorism will not be an easy war, against an easily identifiable enemy, that can be accomplished quickly and convincingly.

An equally important point is that many other types of conflicts exist and are likely throughout the world: disputes arising from traditional rivalries and state boundaries, such as in the Middle East and between India and Pakistan; concerning changes in the power and influence of state actors, such as China, Russia, and the European Union; involving ethnic groups and loyalties, over and within state boundaries; concerning the demands and needs for scarce resources such as water; resulting from the movements and migration of peoples, demographic changes, and growth of refugee populations; originating in economic competition and growing inequality between rich and poor, around the globe and within regions and states; and concerning the environment and pollution, such as deforestation and global warming; and more. The list is potentially endless and open to the imagination, especially in a world of greater interdependence and complexity in which technology and time seem to be evolving faster and faster as planet earth proceeds into the future.

Although the collapse of the Soviet Union and ensuing post–cold war global environment have increased the opportunities for the United States to exercise leadership and force abroad in the short term, going to war and relying on force in the long term may contribute to a further weakening of American power at home and abroad. Important to remember is that the relatively easy military victory over Iraq in 1991 required the use of over half a million American troops—a massive military intervention, on the scale of the Korean and Vietnam Wars. In this respect the victory was not a repeat of the simple victories in Grenada and Panama. As the world has grown in complexity, military success may require the use of greater force and more flexible (military and nonmilitary) strategies than in the past, with no guarantees of rapid and relatively painless success. This is reinforced by the possibility that the use of military force may not be as relevant and productive for the myriad of global conflicts that the world and the United States face. This may very well be the case with the post–September 11 war on terrorism—a new type of war for the United States and most Americans.

Clearly, the end of the cold war and the evolving post–cold war global environment have contradictory implications for the future politics of U.S. foreign policy. The end of the cold war has created increasing global complexity, posing both greater opportunities and constraints for the evolution and exercise of American power. And whatever the consequences, it is also quite clear that the United States will continue to be the global power, pursuing interests throughout the world and a globally oriented foreign policy for the foreseeable future.

IS THE TWENTY-FIRST CENTURY THE AMERICAN CENTURY?

Most scholars and analysts of world politics and U.S. foreign policy agree that the relative power of the United States has declined from its immediate post–World War II peak. Following the war's devastation, the United States found itself in an extraordinary period of world history that could not last forever.

However, since the 1970s and 1980s, there has been considerable disagreement over **American decline or revival**—the extent of the decline in American power and whether it will continue to decline or is likely to be renewed. With the collapse of the cold war and the Soviet Union and since the September 11 attacks, the United States may have entered another extraordinary period of potential power, which has generated new controversies about the future of the United States (and the West). This is no mere academic debate, for the evolution of American power has serious implications for the future of U.S. foreign policy and Americans' standard of living.

Declinists tend to emphasize that the United States has experienced relative economic and military decline in global affairs, that this trend is continuing, and that its reversal is unlikely over time. This position gained notoriety with the publication of *The Rise and Fall of the Great Powers* in 1987 by Paul Kennedy and has been the focal point of the debate ever since. Kennedy's book is "about national and international power in the modern—that is, post-Renaissance—period. It seeks to trace and to explain how the various Great Powers have risen and fallen, relative to each other, over the five centuries since the formation of the new monarchies of Western Europe and the beginnings of the transoceanic, global system of states."[19]

Kennedy believes that the power of all societies throughout history has been dynamic—that great powers pass through "cycles of rise and decline." "The relative strengths of the leading nations in world affairs," he argues, "never remain constant, principally because of the uneven rate of growth among different societies and of the technological and organizational breakthroughs which bring a greater advantage to one society than to another." These are the sources of a country's economic and military power and determine its relative rise and decline in world affairs. Furthermore, "wealth," states Kennedy, "is usually needed to underpin military power, and military power is usually needed to acquire and protect wealth." However, if "too large a proportion of the state's resources is diverted from wealth creation and allocated instead to military purposes, then that is likely to lead to a weakening of national power over the long term." Furthermore, "if a state overextends itself strategically—by, say, the conquest of extensive territories or the waging of costly wars—it runs the risk that the potential bene-

fits from external expansion may be outweighed by the great expense of it all—a dilemma which becomes acute if the nation concerned has entered a period of relative economic decline."[20]

Thus, great powers that have risen to global prominence as a result of gains in economic and military power eventually experience decline in world affairs when their economies weaken and they engage in **imperial overstretch.** In other words, decline occurs if the gap widens between a great power's ends and means—between its foreign policy goals and its ability to carry them out. This means that a country must either expand its economic capabilities in order to slow and avoid decline, limit its foreign policy goals and curtail its national security commitments in order to adjust to decline, or experience further decline.

Kennedy found that the great powers of modern Western history—Spain, the Netherlands, France, and Great Britain—usually failed to recognize decline and responded with too little, too late. "Like all other civilizations at the top of the wheel of fortune," Kennedy contends, "the British could believe that their position was both natural and destined to continue. And just like all those other civilizations, they were in for a rude shock."[21] Kennedy argues that the United States during the 1960s was in a situation similar to those Great Britain and other previous great powers once faced.

For Kennedy, the United States confronts the "two key tests" of being "number one" in a situation of relative decline. First, "whether, in the military/strategical realm, it can preserve a reasonable balance between the nation's perceived defense requirements and the means it possesses to maintain those commitments." Second, whether "it can preserve the technological and economic bases of its power from relative erosion in the face of the ever-shifting patterns of global production."[22] Overall, Kennedy is pessimistic concerning the ability of the United States to reverse its downward course, given changes in the global environment beyond American control and the political obstacles posed to internal change within American government and society.[23]

Although pessimistic, Kennedy is not predicting collapse or that the United States is absolutely declining or severely declining relative to others. Instead, he concludes, "what we are witnessing at the moment is the early decades of the ebbing" of America's extraordinary economic power following World War II to its more natural state. "That decline is being masked by the country's enormous military capabilities at present, and also by its success in internationalizing American capitalism and culture." Kennedy points out, however, that even when the United States "declines to occupy its natural share of the world's wealth and power, a long time into the future, the United States will still be a very significant power in a multipolar world, simply because of its size." Therefore, the task facing American political leaders into the twenty-first century "is to recognize that broad trends are under way, and that there is a need to manage affairs so that the relative erosion of the United States' position takes place slowly and smoothly, and is not accelerated by policies which bring merely short-term advantage but longer-term disadvantage."[24]

Revivalists tend to argue that the United States has not declined as rapidly as the declinists claim and that the revival of American power in the future is likely. Samuel Huntington is among the most optimistic proponents of revivalism. In his essay "The U.S.—Decline or Renewal?" He argues that claims about American decline are widely exaggerated, that they have occurred frequently in the past, and that there is a "self-renewing genius" to American society (though, somewhat ironically, with the collapse of the cold war, Huntington has become more pessimistic about America's future given the coming "clash of civilizations"). In *Bound to Lead*, Joseph Nye acknowledges that the United States has experienced decline but emphasizes that the nation was not as powerful following World War II as declinists often suggest, has not declined as precipitously as the declinists argue, and faces no rival that can replace it as the global power "bound to lead" in world affairs in the future. Furthermore, the United States continues to enjoy certain advantages, such as the power of ideas, financial flows, and mass communications—what he calls "**soft power**"—that will allow it to exercise global leadership in the future.[25]

Henry Nau, in *The Myth of America's Decline*, emphasizes the increasing convergence toward democracy and freer markets among industrialized countries since World War II (somewhat similar to Francis Fukuyama's argument about "the end of history" due to the globalization and triumph of liberalism). From this perspective, a decline in relative American power may actually translate into an overall increase in America's position in the world community if the nation's economy is strengthened. Richard Rosecrance, in *America's Economic Resurgence*, discusses the preconditions necessary for making the United States into a "trading state," allowing for the revival of American power, such as the need to reduce the federal deficit, improve the quality of education, increase savings and investment in research and development, cut bureaucracy, curb the preoccupation of American business and finance with short-term profits at the cost of long-term market shares, and divert resources from external military requirements to internal needs. Although optimistic, Rosecrance recognizes that these necessary changes are likely to be forced upon the United States as it becomes more fully integrated within the international political economy and faces international crises.[26]

By the turn of the twenty-first century, with the collapse of the Soviet Union, the triumph of the Gulf War, and the economic recovery and boom of the 1990s, it appeared that the revivalists have prevailed. Yet as Michael Cox summarizes and assesses the debate, "of course it is easy to be wise after the event. It is easier still to forget how few analysts failed to predict what happened in the 1990s. Even the revivalists did not get it right. The United States, they argued, possessed structural advantages that meant that it was not in decline. But that was not the same as anticipating the great changes that then occurred. And there was a good reason for this: like nearly everybody else, they never entertained the possibility of the Cold War coming to an end, followed two years later by the disintegration of the Soviet Union. This was critical." Therefore, Cox continues, "after one of the more extraordinary decades of the postwar period, the United States presented a picture of itself to the world that would have been difficult to envisage ten years earlier, unimaginable in the 1970s." "Indeed, if we were to take the longer view, and compare America's position in 2000 with that which it held in 1945, a very strong case could be made that it was actually in a far more favorable situation at the end of the century than it was just after the war."[27]

In fact, according to some of the nation's most notable commentators and scholars, today "America is no mere superpower or hegemon but a full-blown empire in the Roman and British sense." According to one conservative commentator, "People are now coming out of the closest on the word empire. The fact is no country has been as dominant culturally, economically, technologically and militarily in the history of the world since the Roman Empire." What is most astonishing is that, whereas the term **empire** has traditionally been avoided by Americans given its negative and imperial connotation, now "from the isolationist right to the imperialist-bashing left, a growing number of experts are issuing stirring paeans to American empire."[28] In fact, Michael Cox refers to the 1990s and the United States as a time of "empire strikes back."

In assessing this debate and considering America's future in the global community, *a number of important points must be kept in mind*. First, the United States remains the most powerful single actor on the global stage; it is the only complete superpower. Second, while the (hard) military power and the (soft) economic power of the United States may have declined from their height just after World War II, they are still quite formidable. Furthermore, the soft power of American ideas, science and technology, the English language, and popular culture—has actually grown throughout the world, providing the U.S. government with new opportunities in world affairs. Third, the chief strength of a market-oriented political economic system is the dynamism of capitalism. The American market-oriented system has demonstrated that it has the potential to adapt and recover and even strengthen America's economy, as best demonstrated during the 1990s. Finally, the United States has been a major beneficiary of the collapse of the Soviet empire and any threat it may have posed. The decline of its major adversary increases American power, allowing policymakers to exercise leadership and exert more force abroad for a period of time. At the beginning of the twenty-first century, America's armed forces and military expenditures are second to none and, along with those of its closest allies, represent roughly three-fourths of the world's military expenditures. Furthermore, the end of the cold war buys time for the United States to adjust to developments abroad and promote renewal at home.

At the same time, it is likely that the United States may find it very difficult to adjust its slowly evolving position in global affairs. First, most of the key global developments are simply beyond American control, especially in the long run. Even though the collapse of communism has made the United the preeminent military power (possibly in world history) without a great power challenger, the use of force is not guaranteed to succeed or be easy or to avoid negative consequences at home and abroad. Furthermore, the international political economy remains complex and difficult to control in a world of greater globalization, interdependence, technological change, and uneven development (all of which may benefit many other people, states, and transnational forces throughout the world). Second, as will be discussed throughout this book, continuity tends to prevail over change in the complex politics of the United States. Established social and governmental groups and institutions tend to be status quo oriented and have the power to resist change; and peoples' beliefs are usually more a function of lessons derived from the past than a response to the needs of the future. The maintenance and resurgence of the U.S. military on a global scale reflects considerable continuity with the cold war years. Third, the collapse of communism and the Soviet Union may produce a false sense of optimism concerning the future, prompting deferment of needed changes within society and government—reinforced by the successful military outcome in the Persian Gulf and Kosovo wars. The cold war's end also has reinforced the collapse of the foreign policy consensus, as well as made it more difficult to build a new one. Fourth, governments and societies tend to be "reactive," requiring crises to produce change, as the attacks of September 11 made clear. Long-term planning, for example, plays little role in American government or in the private sector.[29] Fifth, if changes do occur in American society and government, there is little guarantee that they will address, let alone arrest, international and domestic developments. Change can take many forms and have different consequences; the most likely development prevailing in American politics is a Band-Aid approach to problems—responding to the immediate symptoms, rather than the underlying causes, of domestic and international changes. For example, is America's global war on terrorism going to increase or decrease America's domestic cohesion and its global power, prestige, and legitimacy in the future? Finally, the concepts of "decline" and "revival" may be too simplistic, reflecting either too much of a downward fall or an upward surge instead of the complexity and contradictory patterns of evolutionary change.

In sum, the American people have the opportunity to adapt to changes in their environment and move in new directions, but they will have great difficulty in doing so. Much of the success of their efforts will depend on U.S. leadership and the nation's domestic political environment and their impact on foreign policy—a focus of the rest of the book. This will not only impact the future of world politics, but will affect the politics of U.S. foreign policy, as well as impact people's standard of living and quality of life in the United States and throughout the world. One likely consequence, for example, is increasing inequality and stratification in the United States and other parts of the world, a potentially ominous trend for the future of both domestic and international politics.

As Torbjorn L. Knutsen emphasizes in *The Rise and Fall of World Orders,* one of the critical ingredients of global power that has not received sufficient attention is that much may depend on the extent to which global changes and U.S. foreign policy impact the nation's international prestige and legitimacy among other great and rising powers, as well as among people throughout the world. Such normative power maximizes international support of a hegemon's foreign policy and world order orientation, requiring less use of coercion. This is why international law and the international community are so important.

Therefore, as Knutsen argues, "if a new world order is to be established under American aegis, then the United States must appear as a just and trustworthy leader." Given the world's complexity and diversity and the United States' tendency to act unilaterally (usually in the name of liberalism, democracy, and human rights), it is likely that the United States will not only remain the most powerful country in the world but may slowly, but inevitably, experience greater challenges to its power and foreign policy in the future. Such may be the paradoxical nature of American power in the contemporary and future world. Or as Knutsen states, "Because they confuse their own political mythology with the natural state of affairs, hegemons regularly express a remarkable inability to understand the seething mix of hatred, admiration and ridicule that they inspire abroad. They are not in the habit of examining closely their own myths, rules, laws and values. They simply take them for granted" (see **essay 3.2** on American unilateralism and the importance of international law).[30]

According to Richard Betts, in an article entitled "The Soft Underbelly of American Primacy," "September 11 reminded those Americans with a rosy view that not all the world sees U.S. primacy as benign, that pri-

macy does not guarantee security, and that security may now entail some retreats from the economic globalization that some had identified with American leadership. Primacy has two edges—dominance and provocation." In fact, for Betts,

> American global primacy is one of the causes of this war. It animates both the terrorists' purposes and their choice of tactics. To groups like al Qaeda, the United States is the enemy because American military power dominates their world, supports corrupt governments in their countries, and backs Israelis against Muslims; American cultural power insults their religion and pollutes their societies; and American economic power makes all these intrusions and desecrations possible. Japan, in contrast, is not high on al Qaeda's list of targets, because Japan's economic power does not make it a political, military, and cultural behemoth that penetrates their societies.[31]

The vastness and pervasiveness of American power, in other words, have complex and contradictory implications.

In the case of the United States, as Reinhold Niebuhr wrote as far back as 1953, the illusion of American omnipotence "is a natural mistake of a commercial community which knows that American hegemony is based upon our technical-economic power but does not understand the vast complexities of ethnic loyalties, of social forces in a decaying agrarian world, of the resentments which a mere display of military power creates among those who are not committed to us." This is especially the case when it comes to American, Western, and so-called cosmopolitan values of liberalism toward non-Western people and cultures, especially in Asia and the Middle East. As Edward Said asserts in *Orientalism,* people construct and acquire a "political vision of reality whose structure [promotes] the difference between the familiar (Europe, the West, 'us') and the strange (the Orient, the East, 'them')." Or as Don Puchala has found in his work on the comparison of historical empires, states, and civilizations, the values of past empires and hegemons are often resisted or only partially assimilated by different peoples and cultures in different ways over time.[32]

Yet, since all hegemons are the most powerful and see themselves as the most progressive societies of their

ESSAY 3.2
AMERICAN UNILATERALISM AND THE IMPORTANCE OF INTERNATIONAL LAW

The development of international law and organizations in the post-World War II world was heavily influenced by the United States, as symbolized by the creation of the United Nations (and Bretton Woods system), including the Security Council, General Assembly, International Bank for Reconstruction and Development (the World Bank), International Monetary Fund (IMF), and the General Agreement on Tariffs and Trade (GATT). Yet, over the years the United States government and the American people appear to have developed a love-hate relationship with the existence of international law (and international organizations such as the United Nations). Nowhere is this dichotomy more visible than under the Bush Jr. administration.

Why is international law so important? As Christopher Joyner, a scholar of international law, indicates, "American history confirms that the function of international law and U.S. foreign policy are inextricably intertwined. The rules of modern international law are in great part products of negotiations in which U.S. diplomats played important roles and U.S. foreign policy is in part dependent on the rules of international law for its operation."

Why is this the case? As Joyner explains, "International order depends on a framework of agreed presumptions, customs, commitments, expectations, and sanctions that all states, including the United States, accept to regulate international society. International law furnishes the rules for relations between states, sets standards for the conduct of governments within this international system, and facilitates establishment of multilateral institutions [such as the United Nations] toward these ends." In other words, the United States "has become the chief state architect and purveyor of international legal rules in the twenty-first century."

And being the most powerful country in the world with interests in maintaining much of the status quo, the United States is also the major beneficiary of international law. "Legal rules keep international society functional, contribute to economic order and political stability, and provide a basis for common ventures and mutual intercourse. Given that international law serves to limit the actions of all governments, it therefore enhances the security and independence of the United States in its dealings with other states."

But this also means that the United States "is not free to be disorderly or promote changes on its own whim"—to both use international law to enhance its interests when it wants as well as to ignore international law when it wants in the name of national interests and security. "To foster the security and independence of its own territory and limit the conduct of other governments, the United States must accept corresponding limitations on its own behavior. To secure the confidence accrued from law, the United States must consent to being restricted in its ability to frustrate the expectations of other states." To do otherwise—as the powerful can, especially the United States—is to argue in favor of "the ends justifies the means" despite the law; is to engage in American unilateralism in foreign dealings; and is to put American credibility, prestige, and legitimacy as the global leader at risk as discussed by Knudsen and others.

Despite being the major creator of international law since World War II, the United States has a mixed record in getting Senate consent to numerous international treaties despite presidential support. What makes the Bush Jr. administration relatively unique is its regular unwillingness to make or facilitate international agreements to resolve legal issues—in fact, to be quite obstructionist—which has provoked great consternation throughout the international community.

Numerous illustrations are briefly chronicled as contributing to this impression of unilateralism during the first two years of the Bush Jr. administration alone:

1. In December 2001, the United States officially gave notice of withdrawal from the 1972 Anti-Ballistic Missile Treaty, essentially killing the landmark agreement. The ABM pact, negotiated with the former Soviet Union during the cold war, specifically forbids testing and deployment of a ballistic missile defense system.
2. In July 2001, the United States walked out of a London conference convened to discuss a 1994 protocol intended to strengthen the 1972 Biological and Toxin Weapons Convention (which is ratified by 144 states, including the United States.). This would permit the United States (and other countries) to continue work on a number of biological weapons under development.

3. In July 2001, the United States was the only state in the General Assembly to oppose the United Nations Agreement to Curb the Illicit Trade in Small Arms and Light Weapons. The Bush administration, in sympathy with the views of the National Rifle Association, claimed that international curbs on small-arms trafficking represent an attempt by the United Nations to interfere with American domestic firearms policy.

4. In April 2001 the United States was not re-elected to the United Nations Human Rights Commission. Within the commission, the United States stood virtually alone in opposing resolutions that supported lower cost access to HIV/AIDS drugs, acknowledged a basic human right to adequate food, and called for a moratorium on the death penalty.

5. Historically a core supporter for the United Nations Convention for an International Criminal Court (ICC), the United States was one of seven governments that voted in opposition to the statute while 120 other states approved it. Eventually, the United States got the United Nations to agree to exempt American military forces from prosecution within the ICC.

6. In December 1997, the Land Mine Convention was signed by 122 states. The United States refused to sign, along with Russia, China, India, Pakistan, Iran, Iraq, Vietnam, Egypt, and Turkey. The Clinton Administration's rationale was the need to protect South Korea from North Korea, with the caveat that the United States would eventually comply by 2006. The Bush Jr. Administration disavowed the caveat in August 2001.

7. President Bush declared the Kyoto Protocol to the Climate Change Convention, signed by the United States in 1998, "dead" in March 2001. The treaty, negotiated by more than 100 states over a decade, calls for the 38 largest industrial nations to reduce their emissions of greenhouse gases, especially in response to global warming.

8. In July 2002, the United States ended the U.S. contribution to the United Nations Population Fund, which helps poorer countries with family planning and advice on population control, health, and sexual matters.

9. In September 2002 the United States withdrew from the International Conference on Racism in South Africa. The conference brought together 163 governments to address issues involving racism and xenophobia including the growing problem of human trafficking, gender concerns, migration and racism, racism against indigenous peoples, and how to ensure minority rights in multi-ethnic states.

Such a record did not stop the Bush Jr. administration from pressuring the United Nations Security Council in 2002 to support a resolution—U.N. Resolution 1441—demanding Iraq to comply with an unlimited weapons inspection process and furnish information about the development of weapons of mass destruction, or face the necessary consequences. Clearly, in this case the U.N. resolution was a means by the Bush Jr. administration to indicate that it has the support of the international community and international law in order to rally political support at home and abroad for disarming Iraq and removing Saddam Hussein, by U.S. military force if necessary. But the above record concerning American unilateralism and international law may help to explain the considerable criticism the Bush Jr. administration has received both at home and especially abroad.

For Chris Joyner, "The conclusion is clear: international law is far from being an idealist pipe dream. International legal means are in fact realistic policy instruments that the United States must increasingly exercise if multilateral agreements are to be secured on common solutions and approaches for dealing with common global problems. In a world of intensifying interdependence and globalization, the United States needs international law to protect its fundamental national interests. Similarly, American foreign policy must be formulated in such a way that the United States accepts the norm of state responsibility to uphold its international legal obligations. To do otherwise is to ignore the lessons of U.S. diplomatic history and, more perturbing, to render the world an even more politically, economically, and ecologically complicated place in which to live."

SOURCES: Quotes are from Christopher C. Joyner, "International Law," in Alexander DeConde, Richard Dean Burns, and Fredrik Loevall, eds., *Encyclopedia of American Foreign Policy, Volume 2* (New York: Charles Scribner's Sons, 2002): 259–281. See also, "Our Law, Your Law," *The Economist* (June 29, 2002): 20–25.

age, they are highly susceptible to simplistic images built around an inflated self-concept and fear of others. As Knutsen found, "this fear of the other worked to constrain the liberties which the hegemons, in their fits of self-congratulatory arrogance, flaunted to the world—and which the world after a while interpreted as inconsistency at best or hypocrisy at worst."[33] Senator J. William Fulbright at the height of the Vietnam War described the result in his book *The Arrogance of Power.*

> the tendency of great nations to equate power with virtue and major responsibilities with a universal mission. The dilemmas involved are pre-eminently American dilemmas, not because America has weaknesses that others do not have but because America is powerful as no nation has ever been before, and the discrepancy between her power and the power of others appears to be increasing. One may hope that America, with her vast resources and democratic traditions, will find the wisdom to match her power; but one can hardly be confident because the wisdom required is greater wisdom than any great nation has ever shown before.[34]

Clearly, at the turn of the twenty-first century, much remains uncertain. World events and patterns of rise and decline (and possible renewal) always become clearer, though still open to debate, with time. So what of the future of the United States and the world? Will the twenty-first century be the "American century?" To what extent will the forces of globalization and liberalism prevail? What will be the impact of the U.S. global war on terrorism?

What also will be the future of other peoples, cultures, and indigenous forces? To what extent will a world of greater interdependence and complexity affect the future of nation-states? Of transnational forces? Of terrorism? Will it be easier or more difficult in the future world for any great power, hegemonic power, or empire—including the United States—to navigate, impact, and maintain global legitimacy?

Although the future of the United States is both promising and full of challenges, it clearly remains uncertain. No one has a crystal ball. But one thing seems relatively clear: We may have entered a time of world history where the future of the United States will probably be unlike that experienced by any other previous great power. Throughout history, great powers in decline have traditionally faced a great power war that accelerated their fall—a most unlikely future scenario for the United States, given the existence and lethality of nuclear weapons and the collapse of the Soviet Union in the cold war. Therefore, the United States is in somewhat of a fortunate situation, allowing the society and government to adapt to and probably muddle through the twenty-first century as an extremely formidable global power facing an increasingly complex and multifaceted global environment. Yet only time will tell whether the future of U.S. foreign policy and the war on terrorism will promote or damage the development of a new American century. And the controversy about the future of America and the world will continue.

BEYOND GLOBAL CONTEXT AND POWER

In sum, contemporary patterns in the global environment and the evolution of American power have played a significant role in the politics of U.S. foreign policy and will continue to do so in the twenty-first century. Ultimately, it is the dynamic interaction between the government, society, and global context that will determine the complexity and direction of the future politics of U.S. foreign policy, as is explored at greater length throughout the book and in the concluding chapter. Yet, it is to the government and the policymaking process that we now turn, beginning at the center of the policy process by addressing presidential power and the president's ability to govern U.S. foreign policy.

SUGGESTED SOURCES FOR MORE INFORMATION

Much has been written about recent international developments and the evolution of world politics. Geoffrey Barraclough, in *An Introduction to Contemporary History* (Middlesex, England: Penguin, 1964), provides a classic statement of the decline of Europe and the rise of the Soviet Union and the United States in world politics, as does Eric Hobsbawm in his more recent *The Age of Extremes: A History of the World, 1914–1991* (New York: Vintage, 1994).

General theoretical implications of these global changes, emphasizing the rise of pluralism and interdependence, for the making of foreign policy are discussed in Edward L. Morse, *Foreign Policy in Gaullist France* (Princeton: Princeton University Press, 1973). Torbjorn L. Knutsen provides an excellent history of the rise of the West and the evolution of liberal, conservative-realist, and radical theoretical perspectives for understanding world politics in *A History of International Relations Theory* (Manchester, England: Manchester University Press, 1997).

The evolution of the international political economy since World War II, and the role of the United States within it, are described by Thomas L. Friedman, *The Lexus and the Olive Tree: Understanding Globalization* (New York: Knopf, 2000); Robert Kuttner, *The End of Laissez-Faire: National Purpose and the Global Economy After the Cold War* (New York: Knopf, 1991); and Daniel Yergin and Joseph Stanislaw, *The Commanding Heights: The Battle Between Government and the Marketplace That Is Remaking the Modern World* (New York: Simon and Schuster, 1998). For a more critical, Third World perspective, see Paul Harrison, *Inside the Third World* (New York: Penguin, 1993), and Helen Epstein, "Time of Indifference," *New York Review of Books* (April 12, 2001), pp. 33–38.

Occasionally, efforts are made down the uncertain and treacherous path of predicting broad future trends in world politics and their implications for the future of U.S. foreign policy. Some of the more interesting and provocative efforts include Daniel Bell, "The Future World Disorder," *Foreign Policy* 27 (summer 1977): 109–35; Seyom Brown, *New Forces, Old Forces, and the Future of World Politics* (New York: Addison-Wesley, 1997); Zbigniew Brzezinski, *Global Turmoil on the Eve of the 21st Century* (New York: Scribner, 1992); Paul Kennedy, *Preparing for the Twenty-First Century* (New York: Random House, 1993); Nicholas X. Rizopoulos, ed., *Sea-Changes: American Foreign Policy in a World Transformed* (New York: Council on Foreign Relations Press, 1990); and Richard Rosecrance, "The Rise of the Virtual State," *Foreign Affairs* (July–August 1996): 45–61.

A proliferation of work has been published that focuses on the rise and decline of American power in world affairs. The classic statement on American decline remains Paul Kennedy's *The Rise and Fall of the Great Powers: Economic Change and Military Conflict from 1500 to 2000* (New York: Random House, 1987). A more optimistic picture of America's future can be found in Joseph S. Nye, Jr., *Bound to Lead: The Changing Nature of American Power* (New York: Basic Books, 1990). See also the excellent study by Torbjorn L, Knutsen, *The Rise and Fall of World Orders* (Manchester, England: Manchester University Press, 1999). Michael Cox provides a very good summary of the literature and discusses future implications in "September 11th and U.S. Hegemony—Or Will the 21st Century Be American Too?" *International Studies Perspective* (February 2002): 53–70. Richard K. Betts specifically analyzes the relationship between American power and September 11 in "The Soft Underbelly of American Primacy: Tactical Advantages of Terror," *Political Science Quarterly* (spring 2002): 19–36. An excellent job of placing the rise and decline of great powers and empires in historical context can be found in Donald J. Puchala, "The History of the Future of International Relations," *Ethics & International Affairs* 8 (1994): 177–202.

KEY TERMS

American decline or revival
declinists
empire
global context
hegemonic power
imperial overstretch
international crises
paradox of American power
psychological versus objective environment
revivalists
soft power
Sputnik

PART THREE

· · · · · · · · · · · · · ·

GOVERNMENT AND THE POLICYMAKING PROCESS

Part III examines the center of the policymaking process, beginning with the president and moving outward to the bureaucracy of the executive branch, Congress, and then the rest of government. Chapter 4 discusses the paradox of presidential power, the difficulty of governing in foreign policy, and the importance of presidential leadership. Chapter 5 discusses the significance of presidential management of the bureaucracy, focusing on the National Security Council process. Chapters 6, 7, and 8 discuss the important bureaucratic roles of the State Department, the military establishment, and the intelligence community in the making of foreign policy. Chapter 9 focuses on the growing role of the foreign economic bureaucracy and the development of the National Economic Council. Chapter 10 provides a synthesis of the overall policymaking process throughout the executive branch by summarizing the major models of decisionmaking theory and discussing important theoretical elements for better understanding policymaking. We then discuss the critical role of Congress and the nature of legislative-executive relations in Chapter 11. Finally, Chapter 12 briefly discusses the judiciary, state and local governments, and the Washington political community.

CHAPTER
4

. . . .

PRESIDENTIAL POWER AND LEADERSHIP

Most Americans are raised to believe that the president is the most powerful figure in the United States. In fact, many of us acquire an image of an omnipotent president. At a very young age, we are taught that the president is a very benevolent father figure who controls the government and represents the American people. As Stanley Hoffmann observed thirty years ago, "The American system of government seems unable to prevent a kind of hand-wringing, starry-eyed, and slightly embarrassing deification of the man in the White House, a doleful celebration of his solitude and his burdens." Naturally, Hoffmann added parenthetically, "when things go badly, there is, of course, a tendency to besmirch the fallen idol."[1]

In this chapter, we examine the following major questions: To what extent is this popular image of a nearly omnipotent president accurate? How much power does the president really have? What implications does this power have for presidential governance, especially in the area of foreign affairs? How can presidents exercise leadership so as to maximize their power and success? What has been the impact of World War II, the Vietnam War, the collapse of the cold war, and

the September 11 terrorist attacks? We begin with the post–cold war presidency thesis in the making of U.S. foreign policy.

THE POST–COLD WAR PRESIDENCY THESIS

During the cold war the president was supreme in the making of foreign policy. But this began to change during the 1970s and 1980s with the decline of the intensity of the cold war as a result of the Vietnam War and the rise of détente between the United States and the Soviet Union. Ultimately, the Soviet Union collapsed and the cold war ended, over a decade ago now. How have the decline and collapse of the cold war impacted the ability of the president to govern and lead U.S. foreign policy? Has the making of U.S. foreign policy changed?

Ultimately, it is very difficult for post–cold war presidents to govern foreign policy, lead the country, and manage the executive branch so as to produce a consistent and coherent foreign policy. I refer to such ideas about limitations on contemporary presidential power as the **post–cold war presidency thesis.** The end of the cold war has created new opportunities for U.S. foreign policy, but it has also exacerbated the difficulties that a president faces in exercising power in general and in the area of foreign policy.

The global environment remains quite complex; most presidents have demonstrated limited leadership and management skills relative to domestic and bureaucratic politics; and presidents have been incomplete in their backgrounds, interests, and knowledge about both national security and foreign economic policy. Hence, presidents have had great difficulty in governing foreign policy since the decline of the cold war, as we will see with the presidents during the 1970s and 1980s and those since the end of the cold war.

The major exception appears to be crises, such as the Persian Gulf crisis and those triggered by the September 11, 2001, terrorist attacks on the World Trade Center, in New York, and the Pentagon, in Washington, D.C. Presidential supremacy developed in foreign policy making during the cold war because the superpower conflict was perceived as a permanent time of crisis and national emergency for two decades following World War II. But the cold war and the existence of a permanent crisis state actually has been an anomaly throughout the history of U.S. foreign policy. Certainly, this sense of permanent crisis declined with the tragedy of Vietnam and disappeared with the collapse of the Soviet Union and the cold war.

Crises still occur and allow presidents to be extremely powerful, but this tends to be only temporary and for limited foreign-policy scope. This is certainly what President Bush Sr. experienced with the Persian Gulf War—all-time highest public approval ratings in 1991 only to be followed by defeated for reelection in 1992. Have the terrorist attacks of September 11 created a new period of permanent crisis and national emergency? Has it made President Bush Jr. supreme in the making of foreign policy like former cold war presidents? Or has the overwhelming political support that President Bush Jr. experienced begun to decline with time? Despite September 11, does Bush Jr. also face numerous global and domestic constraints as well as opportunities? What are the implications for the future of the Bush presidency in particular and presidential power in general in the long run?

This chapter will begin to address these questions and provide an initial overview of presidential power. We begin by discussing the general elements of presidential power, their implications for the paradox of presidential power and presidential governance, and how presidential power has played out in foreign policy, especially since World War II. We will then talk about the importance of presidential leadership for presidential power, especially since the time of Franklin Roosevelt. And we will discuss the post–cold war opportunities, risks, and challenges that presidents must face in the foreseeable future, including the implications of September 11 and the war on terrorism. This will provide us with an introduction and overview of presidential power and the post–cold war presidency thesis for better understanding the politics and the future conduct of U.S. foreign policy in the twenty-first century.

The Elements of Presidential Power

The president is the most powerful political actor in the United States. He occupies many constitutional roles and has many capabilities that contribute to his power. However, the president also faces many constraints and uncertainties that limit his power. Therefore, the president, though powerful, is not nearly as powerful as the popular stereotype held by many Americans.

CONSTITUTIONAL ROLES AND STRENGTHS

The president occupies many different roles, or wears many different hats, that provide him with the capability to exercise considerable power. Among the *roles that are most important in contributing to presidential power are the following:* (1) Commander in chief; (2) Chief diplomat; (3) Chief administrator; (4) Chief of state; (5) Chief legislator; (6) Voice of the people; and (7) Chief judicial officer.

These roles have their origins in Article II of the U.S. Constitution and have evolved throughout the history of the United States through constitutional amendments, legislation, judicial rulings, and changes in custom.[2]

Commander in Chief. The president is the commander in chief, which means that he has ultimate authority over the military. According to the Constitution, the military is under the authority of the elected civilian leadership. In theory, then, the president controls the U.S. military, meaning that, when the president gives an order, members of the military and the Department of Defense comply. By virtue of his position as president, he is to be treated like a six-star general. This gives the president considerable power because, as commander in chief, he dictates the use of American armed forces abroad.

Since World War II the president has exercised his powers as commander in chief very broadly. It was President Harry Truman who decided to send American troops to Korea in 1950 to fight in America's first war since World War II. American escalation and use of armed force in Vietnam throughout the 1950s, 1960s, and 1970s was a result of decisions made by presidents Dwight Eisenhower, John Kennedy, Lyndon Johnson, and Richard Nixon. The decision to secretly support the contras in their effort to overthrow the Sandinistas in Nicaragua was made by President Ronald Reagan. President George Bush Sr. invaded Panama and ordered over 500,000 American troops to fight the war in the Persian Gulf. President Clinton led a major NATO bombing campaign in the war in Kosovo, and President George Bush Jr. has led a global war on terrorism. These examples represent presidential decisions in which there was little, if any, involvement by the U.S. Congress. Although only Congress has the constitutional right to declare war, these were presidential initiatives and presidential wars.

Chief Diplomat. The president is also often referred to as the chief diplomat, or chief negotiator representing the United States. This role originates with the president's constitutional duty to nominate the secretary of state and ambassadors to countries abroad, to receive foreign ambassadors, and to negotiate treaties. Although the secretary of state and ambassadors have traditionally been responsible for the day-to-day practice of diplomacy abroad, the appointive power helps to ensure that their actions represent presidential wishes and presidential decisions. Presidents also have the right to offer, or withdraw, official U.S. diplomatic relations with foreign governments.

More recently, the president has begun to exercise his right to act as an actual negotiator himself by heading American diplomatic delegations, something that has increased in frequency over the last three decades with the rise of "summitry." President Nixon led the American delegation to Moscow in 1972 to complete the first Strategic Arms Limitation Talks (SALT) with the Soviet Union. President Carter spent thirteen days negotiating with President Anwar Sadat of Egypt and Prime Minister Menachem Begin of Israel in 1978 to produce the Camp David Accords. President Reagan had more major summits than any previous president since Franklin Roosevelt—four with Soviet leader Mikhail Gorbachev between 1985 and 1989, emphasizing arms control and the Strategic Arms Reduction Talks (START). President Clinton led the American delegation that attempted to bring a settlement to the Israeli-Palestinian conflict. Also, U.S. presidents participate every year with leaders from the major industrialized democracies in a summit to discuss measures to contribute to the stability and growth of the international political economy.

Chief Administrator. The president is also the chief administrator, which means he has authority over the executive branch. So in theory, all the governmental agencies within the executive branch, all the cabinet secretaries, and all the bureaucrats respond to presidential wishes and decisions. One of the major ways the president exercises this administrative power is through appointments. The president selects his personal staff, nominates cabinet secretaries, and appoints most of the high-level officials in each of the departments and agencies that make up the executive branch. This important aspect of presidential power reinforces his roles as commander in chief and chief diplomat. In foreign policy, this means that the president has authority and considerable power over the foreign policy apparatus within the executive branch. Thus he relies on the National Security Council, National Economic Council, State Department, Defense Department, the intelligence community, and other bureaucratic agencies to assist him in formulating and implementing U.S. foreign policy decisions.

Chief of State. The president is not only the chief administrator, or official **head of the government,** but is also the **chief of state.** This means that the president, through the office of the presidency, represents the state of the United States of America and thus is the symbolic political leader of the United States. In many countries throughout the world, the person at the head of the government is not the same person who is the chief of state. For example, governments of Great Britain and Japan are headed by prime ministers while the chief of state is a monarch or emperor. In the United States, these two roles are combined in the single office of the presidency.

Although primarily symbolic, the role of chief of state is another ingredient of presidential power. The importance of symbolism should not be downplayed, for the outcomes of politics are heavily a function of its successful use. To compare Great Britain and the United States again, when a foreign head of state arrives in Great Britain, the first, official visit, according to the diplomatic protocols of international behavior, is with the queen, for she represents the state. In contrast, the same foreign leader coming to the United States will pay official respects first to the president. This indicates the additional status that the president has in his role as head of state, which translates into another element of his power.

Chief Legislator.   Although the president is not a member of Congress, he does occupy the role of de facto chief legislator. In the modern relationship between the legislative and executive branches, much of the legislation before Congress originates in the executive branch and is submitted by the president—such as the budget of the U.S. government, as well as programs for defense spending and foreign assistance. Therefore, Congress often responds to the president's agenda, thereby giving him a political advantage in gaining Congress's acceptance of his programs.

The other technique that contributes to the president's legislative powers is his constitutional right to veto legislation. Not only does he initiate much legislation, he can prevent legislation from becoming law if he so chooses. Congress may override a presidential veto with a two-thirds affirmative vote for the legislation in the House of Representatives and in the Senate, but this happens infrequently. Therefore, the president can stop legislation he does not like or, by threatening a veto, force members of Congress to modify legislation to conform with his desires—an important exercise of presidential power in the legislative area.

Voice of the People.   The president is often referred to as the "voice of the people" because, along with the vice president, he is the only public official who is elected (albeit indirectly) by the entire American populace. A member of Congress represents a district

of roughly a half-million people. A senator represents a state, which may represent only a few million Nevadans or as many as thirty million Californians. But only the president can argue that he has a "national electoral mandate" and represents all of the American people, reinforcing his role as chief of state. Each candidate who has been successful in gaining the presidency has claimed the possession of an electoral mandate because his majority vote demonstrates that his goals represent the wishes of the American people. Therefore, most presidents act as if they have a mandate to promote and implement those policies that were promised and discussed during the presidential campaign. Although a majority of the presidential vote was never achieved by Bill Clinton (because of three major presidential candidates) or George W. Bush (Al Gore had a plurality of the popular vote, while Bush had a majority in the electoral college), each claimed an electoral mandate and public consensus behind him and his vision of America—another important symbolic way to exercise presidential power.

Chief Judicial Officer.   The president also enjoys important judicial powers in two areas. First, the president has the authority to pardon any individual guilty of a crime. For example, President Ford pardoned former president Nixon before he could be indicted for breaking the law in the Watergate affair. Second, all of the judges who serve on federal district courts, the federal courts of appeals, and the United States Supreme Court are nominated by the president. This can be a very important source of presidential power since federal judges, unlike state and local judges, are appointed for life and can be the final arbiters of the law of the land. As presidents appoint new judges to the courts, judicial decisions may change over time, thus effecting public policy. For example, the Supreme Court was considered a liberal court during the 1950s and 1960s. However, during the seventies and eighties the Court changed and adopted a much more conservative orientation due to Republican presidential appointees. President Clinton was the first Democratic president in over twenty-five years to make appointments to the Supreme Court. The nomination of federal judges, however, may be the power of least significance to the president in exercising control over foreign policy for, as we will see in chapter 12, the judiciary typically tends to play a relatively passive role in the making of U.S. foreign policy.

LIMITS AND CONSTRAINTS

The president occupies a number of important roles that allow him to exercise considerable power. At the same time, it is important not to overestimate this power, which often occurs given most Americans' popular conception. The president faces *a number of limitations and constraints in exercising power, including:* (1) Time, (2), Information, (3) The bureaucracy, (4) Congress, (5) State and local governments, (6) Political parties, and (7). Interest groups and social movements.

These limitations and constraints mean that on many occasions the president finds that, regardless of his wishes, he has great difficulty in getting his way. The limits and constraints on presidential power tend to be strongest when it comes to domestic policy, but they exist for foreign policy as well.

Time. The president's first major problem is insufficient time to complete all the tasks necessary to govern successfully. The president has one of the most demanding jobs imaginable: He is trying to govern a very complex society of over 280 million people and is responsible for representing the United States abroad in all of its international interactions. This means that the president is responsible for dealing with hundreds of individuals and issues every day. And more people and issues are trying to get his attention all the time. The president is also generally interested in implementing a program in accordance with his own vision of America and the world.

The president, however, like any human being, has only so much time to devote to people and issues. Beyond eating and sleeping and attending to a few other personal needs, the presidency is a full-time occupation seven days a week. The job of president is actually much more complicated than the simple picture popularly portrayed. Much of his day is occupied with staff meetings and performing ceremonial duties, such as entertaining foreign dignitaries, publicly signing new pieces of legislation, or responding to national issues and disasters. Although each president has his own style, the job demands a great deal of time and energy, especially if the president wants to govern successfully. (See **essay 4.1** for more on the president's schedule.)

The president's time is limited not only from a daily perspective but in terms of his time in office as well. The president may have as little as four years and certainly no more than eight years (according to the **Twenty-Second Amendment** to the Constitution) to accomplish all that he has set his sights on. Therefore, presidents are forced to be selective as to how they will occupy their time. For those issues on which the president is extremely attentive, he may exercise considerable power. However, for the remaining issues on which he lacks interest or time, the president may find that he is the president in name only.

Information. Another limitation on presidential power involves information problems. Most presidents are politicians who possess, at best, only general knowledge of the world around them and how the political policymaking process works at the national and international levels. Despite having previously been a governor or member of Congress, much of their knowledge is acquired through on-the-job training because, unfortunately, there is no existing occupation that can adequately prepare one for becoming president of the United States. This means that presidents must use valuable time and require much staff support for information and advice.

The president faces two problems in terms of information: scarcity and overabundance. A president may find that he does not have enough information. This is quite common, especially in the area of foreign policy. Presidents often have great difficulty getting sufficient information about international events, particularly during crises, when time becomes even more limited and important. Unfortunately, even without adequate information, a president may have no choice but to make decisions. The other problem is that the president often gets too much information in dealing with an issue. The problem here is that, given his pressing schedule, he doesn't have enough time to digest all the available information or he may be provided with contradictory information. Nevertheless, decisions must be made. Having too little or too much information makes it that much more difficult for the president to successfully exercise power.

The Bureaucracy. The third major constraint is the bureaucracy. As discussed above, the president is the chief administrator, and in theory, the bureaucracy responds to his desires. However, the bureaucracy has also become so large and entrenched that it is often unresponsive to the president and his personal staff and policy advisers. Thus the development of a large bureaucracy has had contradictory consequences for presidential power: It can be of great value for the president in his roles as commander in chief, chief diplomat, chief administrator, or chief legislator yet can also be extremely unresponsive to presidential requests or commands. *Bureaucratic organizations have a number of advantages* that allow them to remain relatively autonomous and free of presidential control.

First, a new president enters office with a set of policies and programs administered by the bureaucracy already in place. Each bureaucratic organization, therefore, tends to develop its own goals, subculture, and tasks over time that may be at odds with the policies preferred by the president. Second, the president is heavily dependent on the bureaucracy for information. The bureaucracy determines not only the quantity of information available to the president but also its quality—its level of comprehensiveness, the interpretation of reality embedded in the language, and the range of viable options for presidential consideration (often protecting and reflecting the agency's position). Another advantage that members of the bureaucracy have is time. The president and his personal staff are there for only four, perhaps eight, years, whereas many bureaucrats occupy positions of importance for ten, twenty, or thirty years (and as members of the civil service they have tenure or other rights that make it very difficult for presidents to fire them—even for incompetence).[3] A fourth advantage is that bureaucrats often have close relationships with members of Congress, who ultimately must approve the programs and funding for the executive branch bureaucracy. Therefore, it is not unusual for networks to develop between executive branch employees and members of Congress around various issues, with each group dependent on the other.

The final advantage that bureaucratic organizations enjoy is official independence from presidential authority. Many organizations, such as the Federal Reserve Board, are independent of presidential authority, at least in daily operations. This situation has arisen because of congressional decisions in the creation of these organizations, granting them legal autonomy to ensure that they would be more responsive to Congress than to the president. These officially autonomous organizations not only can resist the president's exercise of power by taking advantage of their information and

close relationships with members of Congress but also have the legal right to ignore presidential requests. Therefore, the president, though he is chief administrator, faces considerable bureaucratic constraints on the exercise of his power. The importance of the bureaucracy in foreign policy necessitates my devoting the next six chapters to it.

Congress. The president and Congress share power. Therefore, while the president initiates and can veto legislation, Congress is often a major constraint on the exercise of presidential power. When the president first enters office, he usually enjoys a brief honeymoon with Congress, during which members are more likely to be responsive to presidential requests in light of the president's recent victory. However, the honeymoon rarely lasts more than a few months, and then it's back to business as usual in presidential-congressional relations. Given the constitutional foundations of congressional power and the contemporary dynamics of the two chambers, to be discussed in chapter 11, the president quickly finds that Congress is often extremely unresponsive to his requests and can at times be quite obstructionist.

Traditionally, members of Congress have actively influenced domestic policies, much to the president's chagrin. Although more responsive and less obstructionist in the area of foreign policy since World War II, Congress became much more independent and assertive in this area as well following the Vietnam War and Watergate. Many members of Congress also have agendas of their own that may be incompatible with the president's agenda. Furthermore, since the Vietnam War and continuing into the post–cold war years, the U.S. government has usually been divided (with a Republican president and a Democrat-run Congress, or vice versa) making it that much more difficult for the president to be effective. In sum, the fact that the legislature is an independent branch with independent power means that Congress and the president will be involved in a constant power struggle.

State and Local Governments. Another constraint on the president's ability to exercise power is the independence of state and local governments. The president may be the commander in chief, the chief of state, and the chief administrator; however, he has no legal authority over state and local governments. State

ESSAY 4.1
TIME CONSTRAINTS AND THE PRESIDENT'S DAILY SCHEDULE

The presidency may be the most demanding job in the world. The president is heavily dependent on his staff to assist him in arranging his schedule and getting him through the numerous items and issues he must attend to during a day. Some presidents tend to be more active and involved than others. The schedule below records *the actual life of a president for a typical day,* in this case for President Carter on Friday, November 16, 1979.

5:00 A.M.	President received a wake up call from White House operator.
5:29	The president went to the Oval Office.
7:15–7:25	The president met with his assistant for National Security Affairs, Zbigniew Brzezinski.
7:30	The president went to Cabinet Room to participate in a breakfast meeting to discuss foreign policy issues with Walter F. Mondale, vice president; Cyrus R. Vance, secretary of state; Harold Brown, secretary of defense; Lloyd N. Cutler, counsel; Hedley W. Donovan, senior adviser; Hamilton Jordan, chief of staff.
8:22	The president returned to the Oval Office, accompanied by and met with Vice President Mondale, Secretary of State Vance, and National Security Adviser Brzezinski.
8:55–9:12	The president met with Secretary of Defense Brown.
9:27	The president went to the South Grounds.
9:28	The president motored from the south grounds to the Washington Hilton Hotel where he participated in the White House Conference on Libraries and Information Services.
9:31	The president was greeted by Charles Benton, chairman, and Marilyn K. Gell, director of the White House Conference on Libraries and Information Services.

9:35	The president went to the off-stage announcement area, then to the podium in the International Ballroom and was introduced by Mr. Benton.
9:39–9:52	The president addressed approximately 1,200 guests attending the conference, with members of the press present.
9:55	The president returned to his motorcade and returned to the south grounds of the White House.
10:02	The president returned to the Oval Office.
10:06–10:08	The president placed a call to Senator Howard W. Cannon (D-Nevada).
10:30–11:00	The president met with Vice President Mondale; Hamilton Jordan, staff aide; Joseph L. "Jody" Powell, press secretary; Alonzo L. McDonald, Jr., White House staff director; Frank B. Moore, assistant for Congressional Liaison; Ray Jenkins, special assistant, Press Office; Stuart E. Eizenstat, assistant for Domestic Affairs and Policy; Counsel Cutler; and National Security Adviser Brzezinski.
11:30	The president met with Neil Hartigan, lt. governor (D-Illinois) and Robert S. Strauss, ambassador at large designate.
11:35–12:10	The president met with Hedley Donovan, senior presidential adviser.
11:35	The president received a call by Representative Eligio "Kika" de la Garza (D-Texas).
11:46–11:51	The president received a call from Representative James Wright (D-Texas).
12:16	The president participated in a photo opportunity with Charles Richard Stanton, mayor (D-Manchester, New Hampshire); John Hoben, coordinator of Resources and Development, Manchester, New Hampshire;

governments in the United States have their own power bases, embodied in the fifty state constitutions. The framers of the Constitution created a federal system of government in which two sets of governments, each with its own sovereignty and authority, were es-

tablished: a central government, usually referred to as the federal government by Americans, and state governments. Although state and local governments are most active in the domestic area, chapter 12 reviews how the role of state and local governments has grown

and Bruce Kirschenbaum, associate for Intergovernmental Affairs.

12:19   The president participated in a photo opportunity with James Whitmore, actor; Mrs. James (Mary) Whitmore; and Alan G. Raymond, staff assistant, Office of Communications.

12:20–12:23 The president participated in a farewell photo opportunity with Doris Brenner, departing administrative assistant, Office of Congressional Liaison, and Danny C. Tate, deputy assistant for Congressional Liaison.

12:27   The president returned to the second floor residence.

12:30   The president and the first lady had lunch.

12:47   The president returned to the Oval Office.

1:03   The president participated in a briefing for state governors to discuss the Iranian situation and the energy supply, with members of the press present.

1:39   The president returned to the Oval Office.

1:45–1:50   The president met with his speech-writer, Achsah P. Nesmith.

2:22   The president met with Timothy E. Kraft, campaign manager, Carter-Mondale Presidential Committee, Inc.

2:25   The president met with Press Secretary Powell.

2:31   The president met with Ed Kelly, commissioner of Parks and Recreation for the city of Chicago, Illinois, and Campaign Manager Kraft.

2:40–2:50   The president met with Secretary of State Vance and National Security Adviser Brzezinski.

2:52–5:00   The president returned to the Cabinet Room and participated in a meeting to discuss defense appropriations for the 1981 U.S. budget with James McIntyre, director of the Office of Management and Budget, and other officials.

3:06–3:13   The president received a call from Senator Robert C. Byrd (D-West Virginia), Majority Leader of the Senate.

4:31   The president received a call from Robert Krueger, ambassador at large and coordinator for Mexican Affairs.

5:00   The president returned to the Oval Office.

5:05   The president met with Jack Watson, Jr., assistant for Intergovernmental Affairs and Cabinet secretary.

5:07–5:22   The president met with Luther H. Hodges, Jr., under secretary of Commerce.

5:45   The president and the first lady hosted a reception for members of the National Council of Negro Women on the State Floor.

6:07–6:30   The president addressed approximately 485 guests attending the reception, with members of the press present.

6:30   The president returned to the second floor residence.

7:01–7:14   The president received a call from Benjamin R. Civiletti, attorney general.

7:08–7:11   The president placed a call to Counsel Cutler.

7:10   The president had dinner with the first lady; Amy Carter; Joanne and Paloma Kressman of Portsmouth, New Hampshire. Paloma Kressman was an elementary school student who asked a question at the president's town meeting in Portsmouth.

7:49   The presidential party went to the family theater where they watched the movie, If I Had a Million

8:57   The president returned to the second floor residence.

10:09   The president went to the south grounds and went jogging.

10:28   The president returned to the second floor residence.

11:45 P.M.   The president retired.

in foreign affairs, most notably relative to foreign economic policy.

Political Parties. The president is the head of his party. However, in the United States, being party leader does not translate into great political influence in governing and electoral politics. Unlike those in most other countries, parties in the United States are weak. Hence, the Democratic and Republican parties are weak tools of presidential power. For example, presidents cannot force members of their own party to support them in Congress, for congressional members have independent power bases. Nor can the president dictate to the party his heir for the presidential nomination. Therefore, although electoral politics is important, as we will discuss in chapter 15, the weakness of American parties makes it that much more difficult for the president to exercise power successfully.

Interest Groups and Social Movements. A final impediment to the exercise of presidential power is the impact of interest groups and social movements on domestic politics and the governmental process. The United States contains thousands and thousands of groups organized to promote their own goals and interests, regardless of what the president believes or wants. These groups utilize all avenues available to them in making their views known and promoting their interests, including influencing Congress, members of the executive branch bureaucracy, the media, and the American public.

Presidents who attempt to change aspects of public policy find resistance not only within the federal bureaucracy and Congress but throughout society from groups that are quite comfortable with the status quo. At the same time, many social movements and groups demand changes in governmental policy that, if opposed by the president, may result in the creation of political antagonists or enemies. Interest groups and social movements tend to be more visible when it comes to domestic issues, but as discussed in chapter 16, they have grown in importance in the area of foreign policy as well, thus complicating the lives of presidents even further.

UNCERTAIN ELEMENTS

In addition to the strengths presidents possess and the limitations they face in the exercise of power, a number of uncertain elements that a president cannot control affect his ability to govern. Sometimes these elements may work for him, enhancing his power; other times they work against him, acting as another constraint on presidential power. These *uncertain elements in the makeup of presidential power include:* (1) The courts, (2) Public opinion, (3) The media, and (4) The global context.

The Courts. Although the president nominates all federal judges and the Senate tends to approve, with an occasional exception, all of these nominations, this does not guarantee that judges' rulings will support presidential policies. The classic example of an appointment run amok, at least from the president's perspective, was President Eisenhower's appointment of Earl Warren as chief justice of the Supreme Court. Eisenhower thought he was appointing a political moderate, but Earl Warren led the Supreme Court in a liberal direction over the course of the next two decades. The uncertainty of predicting the political views of judicial appointees is reinforced by the fact that most judicial rulings are made by federal judges who were appointed by previous presidents. Therefore, while the courts generally tend to play a passive role in the area of foreign policy, the impact of judicial rulings on presidential power varies.

Public Opinion. The public is an important source of presidential power, as we will find in chapter 13. Yet, public opinion can also turn against a sitting president, as Johnson, Nixon, Ford, Carter, and Bush Sr., in particular, discovered. Public opinion tends to be most supportive of the president when he enters office (and during crises) to decline over time. Initially, there is a honeymoon during which the public thinks highly of the new president and gives him the benefit of the doubt. During times of crisis the public also tends to rally around the president. However, public approval of the president and his policies tends to diminish the longer he stays in office. Therefore, public opinion strengthens a president's power early in office but increasingly constrains presidential power through his tenure.

The Media. The media represent another source of great uncertainty in the exercise of presidential power. In order to better understand media coverage and its impact, discussed in chapter 17, it is important to remember that different individuals and groups, within government and throughout society, try to influence the media and the power they have over the communications process to gain control of the government and influence domestic politics. Presidents, in particular, are heavily dependent on the media to help them promote a positive image. Overall, there is a cyclical pattern in the media's impact on presidential power. The media are a crucial source of presidential power early on for gaining the presidential nomination, winning the election, and exercising power in a new administration. However, they are also a source of much of the difficulty that presidents face later in office, regardless of who is in office or his party affiliation, which contributes to the negative impact of the other constraints and uncertainties on presidential power discussed above.

The Global Context. The final element that has an inconsistent impact on presidential power is the global context, as already discussed in chapter 3. Although presidents make decisions that impact the global environment, presidents often react to events and developments as they occur abroad. President Nixon, for example, was forced to respond to the dramatic rise in oil prices precipitated by the Arab oil embargo of 1973. President Ford had little time to pull out the remaining Americans from the chaos of South Vietnam after the collapse of the South Vietnamese military in 1975. President Carter had no choice but to deal with the fall of the shah in Iran and the taking of American hostages in 1979. President Reagan had to respond to Mikhail Gorbachev, a new Soviet leader in 1985, who proposed numerous initiatives toward further arms control and disarmament. President Bush Sr. faced an environment where, on one hand, the cold war had ended with the collapse of communism in Eastern Europe and the Soviet Union and, on the other hand, Iraq invaded Kuwait. President Clinton came into office just as the state of Yugoslavia broke up, resulting in new states and the outbreak of violent conflicts. President Bush Jr. faced a Chinese-American crisis shortly after taking office when an American spy plane collided with a Chinese fighter and was forced to land on Chinese soil; more important, months later he had to react to terrorist attacks on U.S. soil. Sometimes international events and developments strengthen the president's exercise of power; sometimes they create problems.

Not only are presidents unable to control the particular international situation with which they are faced, but they have little control over America's global position, which reflects a set of underlying, long-term trends within the international system. Truman, Eisenhower, Kennedy, and Johnson each had the good fortune to be president during a period in which the

United States was clearly the global superpower in every dimension. However, subsequent presidents beginning with Nixon came to office during a time of relative decline of U.S. power, as reflected in the military challenge of the Soviet Union and the economic challenges posed by Europe, Japan, and the Pacific Rim countries. Although the end of the cold war has provided new opportunities for U.S. foreign policy, presidents Bush Sr., Clinton, and Bush Jr. have the disadvantage of exercising power in an increasingly complex world.

THE PARADOX OF PRESIDENTIAL POWER

How do we make sense of the nature of presidential power given all the elements discussed above? The president has important constitutional roles and strengths that make him a powerful player in the political arena but at the same time faces limits and constraints on his ability to exercise power. The successful exercise of presidential power becomes even more problematic when one considers uncertain elements that impact on the president with little regularity, sometimes strengthening his hand and other times weakening it. When all is said and done, presidents face a **paradox of presidential power:** On one hand, the president is a powerful actor; on the other hand—relative to the rest of government, the society, and the global context—he faces many constraints in successfully exercising power.[4]

The president is not nearly as powerful as most Americans believe. While at times he is able to successfully influence the policy process, at other times he has very little impact on that process, regardless of his best efforts to exercise power. As President John F. Kennedy understood, the president "is rightly described as a man of extraordinary powers. Yet it is also true that he must wield those powers under extraordinary limitations."[5] One of Harry Truman's more famous remarks was in reference to presidential power after meeting his successor, General Eisenhower: "He'll sit right here and he'll say, 'Do this. Do that!' And nothing will happen. Poor Ike—it won't be a bit like the army. He'll find it very frustrating."[6]

The notion of paradox provides us with a general understanding of the nature of presidential power. Much more must be said, however, about when and where the president is most able, and least able, to exercise power. Specifically, we need a better understanding of the concept of power and how it is exercised. We must also be aware of different domains or areas in which it is possible to exercise power.

Power, very simply, is the ability to influence the surrounding environment in ways one prefers. *The exercise of power can be accomplished in one of two ways:* First, there is the "positive" exercise of power—that is, the ability to initiate, to implement, to make something happen. This is what most people think of when it comes to the exercise of power: making others do something that they are reluctant or opposed to doing. A second way to exercise power, which may be called "negative" power, is the ability to negate, to prevent others from doing something against one's wishes. The use of negative power is typically ignored, yet is important in the overall exercise of power.[7]

Does a president generally have the upper hand in exercising positive or negative power? On the one hand, to initiate and implement policy, he usually needs the support of others—a tall order to fill given the constraints and uncertainties he faces. He needs to build political coalitions to support his initiatives and, at a minimum, convince others not to oppose his policies. The exercise of negative power, on the other hand, is less demanding. It is easier for a president to stifle or negate something. This does not require building and maintaining extensive political coalitions in support of policy initiatives as they evolve over time. Rather, negation is more a question of preventing an initiative from surfacing on the political agenda or stopping it after it has surfaced—a much simpler task. The president, for example, has the unique ability to stifle virtually any piece of legislation he chooses through his use of the veto, which is rarely overridden. Although there is no guarantee that the president will succeed in exercising negative power, the odds are much higher than in his efforts to exercise positive power.

To have a clearer understanding of presidential power, we also need to discuss the domain, or **issue area,** in which power is exercised. For some issues the president is likely to be a powerful political figure, while on other issues he may lack power. But which issues? Issues may be classified in a variety of ways, but a *breakdown into two traditional issue areas is helpful:* domestic policy and foreign policy. Although distinctions between policies that are primarily domestic or primar-

ily global are increasingly difficult to make, this traditional division serves the purpose of clarifying the paradox of presidential power.[8]

The president has greater strengths and fewer weaknesses in the exercise of power in foreign policy as opposed to domestic policy. Three of the constitutional roles contributing to presidential power really involve only foreign affairs: commander in chief, chief diplomat, and chief of state. These roles allow the president to exercise much more power, both positive and negative, in the foreign policy area, especially during crises. Furthermore, many of the constraints that he faces tend to be weaker in the area of foreign policy. The bureaucracy, Congress, the courts, state and local governments, the public, political parties, the media, and interest groups all play independent roles in the making of U.S. foreign policy. However, they tend to be more active and influential concerning domestic policies. When it comes to formulating policies to cope with domestic economic issues, for instance, everyone gets into the act and attempts to obtain a piece of the pie.

By combining the two ways power can be exercised with the two types of issue areas, we can develop a simple yet valuable, two-by-two classification scheme for making better sense of the paradox of presidential power (see **figure 4.1**). What we find is that the president is most powerful in influencing U.S. foreign policy, especially if he is opposed to an initiative or decides to do nothing—that is, not to act. The president still enjoys considerable power in initiating foreign policies, but since Vietnam he has had to face more constraints. His greatest influence on domestic policy lies in his ability to oppose policy initiatives taken by others. He is least powerful when he attempts to influence domestic policy positively, especially if he is attempting to initiate policy, whether it involves the budget, welfare, or the economy.

In sum, the question of presidential power does not allow for a simple, black-or-white answer. Instead, there exists a paradox of presidential power. A variety of factors influence presidential power, and the net result is that the president is both the most powerful political figure in the United States and at the same time extremely constrained. He is most powerful in areas of foreign policy and least powerful in the domestic policy arena. He is most successful in exercising power when he opposes the initiatives of others but requires more skill and luck to promote successfully policies of his

FIGURE **4.1**
CATEGORIZING PRESIDENTIAL POWER

The Exercise of Power

	Positive	Negative
Foreign policy	Moderate	High
Domestic policy	Low	Moderate

Issue Area

own. These are the patterns or trends that make up the paradox of presidential power, making it difficult for a president to govern successfully and, consequently, fulfill the high expectations most Americans have of him.

THE PROBLEM OF PRESIDENTIAL GOVERNANCE

The paradox of presidential power makes it extremely difficult for a president to govern successfully today. *Two patterns seem to affect the president's ability to govern and lead the country:* (1) A president tends to go through a presidential life cycle in which presidents are strongest when they enter office and then their power tends to decline over time; and (2) A crisis of governance (or of leadership) now seems to exist in American politics in which no individual or organization, including the presidency, is able to lead the government and country.

These patterns have become increasingly visible since the Vietnam War and have important consequences for the foreign policy-making process.[9]

THE PRESIDENTIAL LIFE CYCLE

The paradox of presidential power has important consequences for the way the political process works and for the president's ability to influence that process over time. Most presidents find that their ability to exercise power tends to go through a cyclical process over the course of their term of office: They enter office near the peak of their power, and by the end of their term they are considerably weaker. To explain this **presidential life cycle,** one must understand how the paradox of presidential power impacts the president's ability to govern over time.

A president enters office with all of his constitutional roles fully available to him, constraints at their weakest, and with most of the uncertain elements working in his favor. Newly elected presidents, as discussed above, proclaim an **electoral mandate** for themselves and their policies. During the first few months in office, the president enjoys a **honeymoon** not only with the Congress but with the media and the public as well.[10] This begins with the president's inauguration, celebrated as a triumph of American democracy in action. People tend to be hopeful and interested in the new president, the first lady, their personal characteristics, and his style of governing, and the president enters a relatively hospitable political environment in which he is provided the leeway to initiate new policies. This makes it a most inopportune time for individuals and groups to be critical of the new leader of the United States.

Within a short period of time, however, the honeymoon with Congress and the media is over. Congress begins to act independently of presidential wishes, especially if the majority party is different from the president's party—a common occurrence since Vietnam. Members of the media soon spend more time addressing the issues and critically analyzing presidential policies. Interest groups and social movements make concerted efforts to influence the policymaking process. Under such conditions a president quickly finds he is no longer operating with a clean slate in an optimistic political environment. In fact, the longer the president is in office, the more likely that critical judgments will be made by individuals and groups throughout government and society concerning how well the president is doing and who benefits from his policies. As the political environment becomes more critical and uncontrollable, the president finds that his public approval rating also tends to decline.

Both presidents Jimmy Carter and Bill Clinton experienced very short honeymoons. Lyndon Johnson, a former majority leader in the U.S. Senate and a shrewd observer of American politics, once gave the following portrayal of the presidential life cycle after a landslide victory:

> When you win big you can have anything you want for a time. You come home with that big landslide and there isn't a one of them [in Congress] who'll stand in your way. No, they'll be glad to be aboard and to have their photograph taken with you and be part of all that victory. They'll come along and they'll give you almost everything you want for a while and then they'll turn on you. They always do. They'll lay in waiting, waiting for you to make a slip and you will. They'll give you almost everything and then they'll make you pay for it. They'll get tired of all those columnists writing how smart you are and how weak they are and then the pendulum will swing back.[11]

The president's ability to exercise power successfully usually declines significantly within a few years. During this period, his strengths diminish, his constraints intensify, and the uncertain elements tend to work more often against than with him. The decline of public support follows not a linear pattern but that of a bumpy road, with peaks and valleys. The major exception to this pattern occurs during times of national emergency and crisis, when the constraints on presidential power are temporarily reduced as the public turns to the pres-

ident for leadership and crisis resolution. These spurts of public approval during crises are reinforced by congressional deference to the president, especially in foreign policy, and his tendency to dominate communications and the media. However, once the crisis subsides, normal politics resurface and the downward pattern tends to continue. Eventually, the constraints multiply to the point that the president has considerable difficulty exercising power over most issues. By the end of his term, he may be so weak that he is referred to as a **lame-duck** president.

Figure 4.2 demonstrates the overall decline in public approval that every contemporary president has faced through the life cycle of his presidency—with President Bill Clinton the major exception to the rule.[12] Lyndon Johnson had an instinctive feel for the rhythm of the presidency, especially in terms of the president's relationship with Congress. "You've got to give it all you can, that first year," Johnson told Harry McPherson, a top aide. "Doesn't matter what kind of majority you come in with. You've got just one year when they treat you right and before they start worrying about themselves. The third year, you lose votes. . . . The fourth's all politics. You can't put anything through when half the Congress is thinking how to beat you."[13]

This cyclical pattern is largely a function of presidential promises and expectations—in the minds of political leaders, the politically involved and active, and especially members of the general public.[14] During the presidential nomination and general election campaigns, all candidates promise the American people that, if elected, they will improve the quality of voters' lives. They promise to clean up the environment, improve the quality of education, prevent American men and women from dying abroad, and keep America free and strong. These promises are particularly important when it comes to bread-and-butter issues, which tend to interest Americans the most and affect them most directly. Candidates promise to restore or maintain economic prosperity, to reduce inflation and unemployment, to improve the economy so that all Americans will have a better chance of attaining the "American Dream."

These promises, certainly a normal part of any election process, create expectations among the public that presidents are simply unable to fulfill. Regardless of how many issues presidents actually addressed, however, most of the problems do not go away. In fact,

FIGURE 4.2

PUBLIC APPROVAL OF PRESIDENTIAL PERFORMANCE, 1945–2003

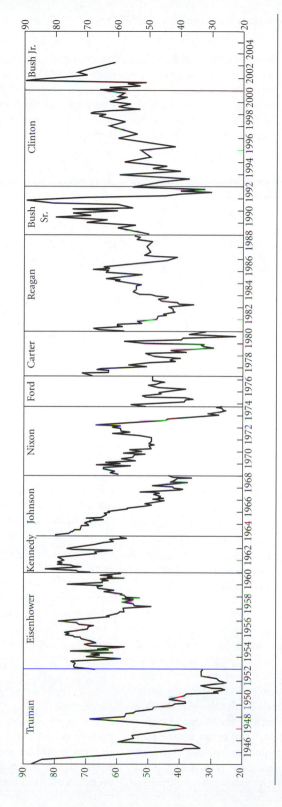

SOURCE: The Gallup Opinion Index; The Gallup Report.

79

many get worse and new ones arise constantly. Why? Very simply, presidents are not powerful enough, nor do they serve long enough, to fulfill the promises and high expectations they have created. David Halberstam, in *The Best and the Brightest*, described the problem of high expectations that President Kennedy encountered:

> As President, Kennedy was faced with that great gap of any modern politician, but perhaps greatest in contemporary America: the gap between the new unbelievable velocity of modern life which can send information and images hurtling through the air onto the television screen, exciting desires and appetites, changing mores almost overnight, and the slowness of traditional governmental institutions produced by ideas and laws of another era, bound in normal bureaucratic red tape and traditional seniority.[15]

The process of promoting expectations that are likely to remain unfulfilled reinforces the vicious life cycle of presidential power. By the end of his term in office, therefore, it is not unusual for the president to be much weaker than when he took the oath of office. The presidential life cycle makes it very difficult for him to implement his preferred policies. The inability to fulfill the optimism and high expectations created early on also means that much of the American public will grow disenchanted with the incumbent president (a feeling reinforced by the last three presidential elections, which failed to deliver the winner a majority of the vote) and impatient to see a new individual as president. This sets the stage for a repeat performance of the presidential life cycle for the new president—early optimism eventually replaced by pessimism and frustration.

AMERICAN POLITICS AND THE CRISIS OF GOVERNANCE

The paradox and life cycle of presidential power have led to a **crisis of governance (or leadership)** in American politics that has heightened since the Vietnam War and the end of the cold war. Presidents are elected to govern and lead the country, but they are unable to do so, for political power is dispersed throughout government and society and the president faces major limitations and constraints in the exercise of his power. This means that, even when the problems facing the country

are growing in severity, not only are presidents unable to govern and lead, but their administrations are often seen as failures in the public eye. The crisis of governance actually has intensified over the years as a result of the rise of divided government, in which the president and Congress are led by people of opposing political parties.[16]

Given the popular image of presidential power, presidents receive credit when things are perceived as going well and are blamed when things go badly. Unfortunately, American politics and the policy process are incredibly complex and beyond considerable presidential control. With so many complex issues and problems to address—the debt problem, the economy, energy, welfare, education, the environment, foreign policy—this is a very demanding time to be president. As long as presidential promises and public expectations remain high, the president's job becomes virtually an impossible task.

Should success occur, given the lack of presidential power, it is probably not by the president's own design. Nonetheless, the president—the person perceived to be the leader of the country—will be rewarded in terms of public prestige, greater power, and reelection (for him or his successor). However, if the president is perceived as unsuccessful—a failure—this results not only in a weakened president but one the public wants replaced, creating the opportunity to challenge an incumbent president or his heir as presidential nominee. It also reinforces the imperative that the new president, from whichever party, will distance himself from many of the policies of his predecessor. This contributes to change, as opposed to continuity, in the types of public policies pursued by presidents, making it very difficult for the U.S. government to form a coherent long-term program for governing and leading the country into the twenty-first century.

PRESIDENTIAL POWER IN FOREIGN POLICY: AN OVERVIEW

To what extent do the paradox of presidential power and the presidential life cycle affect the president's ability to govern U.S. foreign policy? To what extent does a crisis of governance exist in the foreign policy-making process? Although they are not nearly as powerful as the popular stereotype assumes, the president has greater strengths and fewer weaknesses in the exercise of power in foreign, as opposed to domestic, policy. In fact, it was during the cold war that presidential power in the making of foreign policy reached its height. Since the Vietnam War, however, the president's ability to govern and lead foreign policy has declined and become much more complex. Such a state of presidential power has intensified with the end of the cold war.

SOME HISTORICAL CONTEXT

The president has not consistently dominated the foreign policy process throughout American history. As will be discussed in greater depth in chapter 12, the U.S. Constitution produced a central government with "separate institutions sharing powers," resulting in an "invitation to struggle" between the executive and legislative branches. In fact, executive-legislative relations in foreign policy have been fluid and dynamic, and have fluctuated with changes in the political environment.

As described by Arthur Schlesinger, Jr., in *The Imperial Presidency*, executive-legislative relations have been characterized by a kind of "pendulum or cyclical effect."[17] In times of national emergency, particularly war, power tends to flow toward the president and the executive branch. During times of peace, when conflict has subsided, power tends to flow back to Congress. Yet while Congress tends to reassert its constitutional authority and power following war, increases in presidential power during periods of conflict tend to be so extensive that it seldom returns to prewar levels. Thus, the cyclical ebb and flow in executive-legislative relations in foreign policy has enabled a president to accumulate greater power over time.

PRESIDENTIAL SUPREMACY DURING THE COLD WAR

As a result of World War II and the rise of the cold war, the president became supreme in the making of foreign policy. Aaron Wildavsky wrote an influential article four decades ago defending the **two presidencies thesis.**[18] He argued that there were really two presidencies: a powerful presidency in foreign policy and a weak presidency in domestic policy. Examining the legislative-executive relationship during the 1950s and 1960s, he found that presidents were much more successful in influencing foreign policy legislation than in affecting the outcome of domestic legislation. According to the two presidencies thesis, the paradox and life cycle of presidential power were operative only in the realm of domestic policy, but the president was able to govern and lead the country when it came to foreign policy.

This was a powerful analysis and gained much popularity. In the fifties and sixties—the high cold war era—presidents were extremely powerful political actors in the making of U.S. foreign policy. Constraints were relatively weak, and the uncertain elements tended to be supportive of presidential efforts to contain the threat of communism. The foreign policy bureaucracy, for example, expanded and became an important tool for implementing the president's containment policies. Congress largely was acquiescent and supportive of most presidential initiatives during the cold war years of globalism in U.S. foreign policy. A strong anticommunist consensus developed among the American citizenry and foreign policy elite, resulting in strong public, media, and interest group support of a policy of containment and presidential actions abroad. This was also a period in which political party differences were minimal and state and local governments and the courts were inactive in foreign policy. This supportive domestic climate also existed at a time when the United States was the world's preeminent power. The preference for a strong presidency, especially in foreign policy, was strong not only in the country generally but particularly in liberal, academic, and intellectual circles.[19]

It is important to recall that before World War II few governmental institutions were oriented toward foreign affairs and national security. The policymaking elite was extremely small and centered in the State Department. World War II changed this dramatically. Overnight, the U.S. government was redirected to devote itself to fighting a global war: The military expanded enormously, and civilian agencies grew to assist the president in fighting the war. The governmental war effort, in turn, put the economy and society on a war footing to provide the necessary personnel, equipment, and services to achieve U.S. victory. However, unlike previous wars in American history, the United States demobilized only for a short time following that victory. With the rise of anticommunism, the United States quickly remobilized and expanded its resources in order to fight a global cold war. The power of the presidency and the foreign policy bureaucracy thus continued to grow during the cold war years, becoming what appeared to be a permanent part of the American landscape.[20]

The fifties and sixties were perceived to be a time when communism directly threatened the security of the United States. During such times of perceived national emergency, the president could exert considerable powers as commander in chief, head of state, chief diplomat, and chief administrator, with Congress increasingly acquiescent to presidential initiatives. In fact, by the mid-fifties a bipartisan consensus developed between Democrats and Republicans in support of the president and U.S. foreign policy.

The cold war years of American globalism were thus a time of extraordinary presidential power in foreign affairs—certainly not the norm in the history of U.S. foreign policy. This is not to say that the president faced no opposition or that he controlled all foreign policy issues. Nonetheless, the president was clearly the dominant political figure and exercised a disproportionate amount of influence over U.S. foreign policy. Presidents had the ability to formulate and implement policies in accordance with their cold war beliefs.[21]

THE DECLINE OF PRESIDENTIAL POWER SINCE VIETNAM AND THE COLD WAR

The tragedies of Vietnam and Watergate symbolized the end of global containment as the basis of U.S. foreign policy and signified the end of the extraordinary power that presidents enjoyed in making foreign policy. The president retains the ability to exercise considerable power in foreign affairs; however, the constraints and uncertainties he faces have increased during the post-Vietnam years, making it much more difficult for the president to dominate foreign policy. With the end of the cold war, the constraints and uncertainties in the making of foreign policy have continued to multiply.

The anticommunist consensus that existed in government and society could not survive the Vietnam War. Its collapse produced a reassertive Congress, new and varied interest groups and social movements, more critical media, and a cynical public. The post-Vietnam years also symbolized and accelerated the weakening of American power relative to other world actors in the international political economy. Foreign economics,

and other so-called "low policy" and "intermestic" issues (i.e., issues that span both domestic and foreign policy), likewise rose in significance and increasingly became a part of the foreign policy agenda.[22] Therefore, a president entered office facing constraints and uncertainties that hampered his ability to utilize the sources of presidential power described above. In fact, all presidents since Vietnam have experienced considerable problems in governing and leading the country in foreign policy.

In the past, given the strength of anticommunism and the national security state, the president could lead the country, but only in the direction of fervent anticommunism, containment, and interventionism. Since Vietnam, with the collapse of the anticommunist consensus and the rise of pluralist politics, the president—and in reality, the political system—has a difficult time generating leadership in any direction for a sustained period of time. Every post-Vietnam president has failed to generate a new consensus or sustain much support for his policies for any length of time.

Whereas the president's positive and negative power in foreign affairs was quite high during the cold war, his power today has diminished, especially his ability to exercise positive power in foreign policy. During the cold war the paradox and life cycle of presidential power did not seem to affect presidents much in the area of foreign policy; however, in the wake of Vietnam and Watergate, presidents must now contend with these patterns. The era of two presidencies and extraordinary presidential power in foreign policy appears to be over. Presidents are still the most powerful individual actors, but they no longer automatically govern and dominate the making of U.S. foreign policy. Rather, it may be more appropriate to discuss a post–cold war presidency thesis.[23] This also raises the question, discussed below, whether the September 11 attacks and President Bush Jr.'s global war on terrorism has changed the essence of presidential power in foreign policy.

THE IMPORTANCE OF PRESIDENTIAL LEADERSHIP

How do presidents maximize their power and success? How can they overcome or minimize the crisis of governance in American politics? How can they increase their ability to govern foreign policy? The key is presidential **leadership.**[24] Strong leaders, on the one hand, are able to maximize their strengths and capabilities, minimize the constraints they face, and force the uncertain elements to work better and longer in their favor. Strong presidents are more able to exercise power and govern. Weak leaders, on the other hand, have great difficulty exercising power and governing, for they operate in a world dominated by insurmountable obstacles and constraints. Although this is particularly the case in domestic policy, presidential leadership is also important for presidential power and governance in foreign policy.

The classic statement on presidential leadership is *Presidential Power: The Politics of Leadership* by Richard Neustadt.[25] Neustadt's basic argument is that the key to presidential power is the **power to persuade,** which is a function of political leadership. Presidents who enter office and expect to "command" are quickly disappointed and frustrated. Barking orders may get results for military leaders, but it does not work within the government. Because of the paradox of presidential power and the existence of the presidential life cycle, presidents cannot command. In fact, as Neustadt points out, efforts at exerting presidential power through command are an indication of presidential weakness, for presidents should rely on their legal and formal authority only as a last resort. The command model of governing may be consistent with the way most Americans are raised to think of presidential power, but the key for presidential governance is to persuade others that it is in their best interest to do what the president prefers.

Neustadt understood the problem of presidential governance in the American system. The only way to overcome the constraints and uncertainties that a president faces is through the power of persuasion, which depends on the qualities of political leadership that the individual brings to the office and develops as president. Neustadt identified *three crucial elements of political leadership and presidential power:* (1) Professional reputation, (2) Public prestige, and (3) Presidential choices.

Professional reputation refers to how other political actors inside and outside Washington, D.C., judge the president's ability to get things accomplished. Presidents with a reputation for being very skillful in exercising power and for having to be reckoned with when opposed are most persuasive. **Public prestige** refers to how other political actors—whether in the bureaucracy, Congress, interest groups, or the media—perceive the level of public support for the president. Presidents with a positive public image are more powerful, for high credibility and popular support throughout the country are important political assets in Washington. Strong presidents who are able to persuade are those with high levels of professional reputation and public prestige.

This emphasis on professional reputation and prestige underscores the importance of perceptions and images. A president exercises leadership and political power by influencing the image others have of him. Leadership involves the ability to create the illusion of being powerful. According to Hedrick Smith in *The Power Game,* "Presidents—past, present, and future—have less power than the country imagines, but the successful ones convey the impression of power and get reputations as strong presidents by playing down their problems and trumpeting their few clear victories."[26]

Perceptions and images have always been important in politics, but with the rise of the electronic media, the importance of **symbolism and symbolic politics** has grown. People and groups interact politically based on the images they hold of each other and the images they have of what is possible, whether or not those images closely correspond to reality. Thus, the power to persuade depends on how a president and his administration are perceived by others.

Much of a president's professional reputation and public prestige is a function of his personal characteristics—his personality and particular style of operating and presenting himself.[27] The impact of a president's personality varies, contributing to or hindering his professional reputation and public prestige depending upon how his personal characteristics affect his leadership style. It is important to remember that no individual can easily alter his personal characteristics and habits, for they have been learned since childhood. But as George Reedy stated, the presidency "provides a stage upon which all of his personality traits are magnified and accentuated."[28] Therefore, since images and symbolism are so crucial to professional reputation and public prestige, a president can try to mold a more positive image of himself (within the limitations of his personality). Presidents who want to exercise power successfully and govern need to be aware of these aspects of leadership long before they decide to run for the office.

The third important element of presidential leadership is **presidential choices.** A president's ability to lead and persuade is a function of the choices he makes, for which only he is responsible. The choices a president makes affect his professional reputation and public prestige. Such choices may allow a president to take advantage of later opportunities as they arise, exercising power when little opportunity seems available given existing constraints. Ultimately, this requires that *the president and his staff need to be skillful in three areas:*

1. Managing the executive branch and the decision-making process,
2. Building coalitions and politically interacting with other players in and out of Washington, D.C., and
3. Symbolically communicating his priorities and preferences to society and the world.

These are political requirements involving important choices for successful presidential leadership.

According to Neustadt, "passive" presidents tend to be little more than clerks who merely occupy the office. To lead and govern, presidents must be "active"—actively involved in becoming informed, making decisions, and supervising their implementation. They must know who they can and cannot rely on in the government and beyond. They must be aware of the political implications of what they say and do. In other words, a president's choices are the means by which he exercises leadership and power in the complex politics of U.S. foreign policy.

Richard Pious, in *The American Presidency,* has added important insights into the impact of presidential choice and activism on presidential leadership. He argues that the paradox of presidential power has become so constraining that a president must exercise **prerogative government** if he wants to govern and lead the country. By prerogative government, Pious means that presidents must be very active and arrive at decisions that push the Constitution to its limits in exercising presidential power. Presidents are more likely to exercise presidential power and prerogative government during times of crisis. "The president justifies his decisions on constitutional grounds, on powers enumerated, or on those claimed. . . . When his expansive interpretation is challenged, he appeals to the public for support by defining his actions in terms of 'national security' or 'the national interest.'"[29]

Those presidents who have a more expansive view of presidential power tend to be the most successful in governing and go down in history as the best presidents. However, activist presidents who exercise prerogative government also run the political risk of abusing their power, which can damage or destroy them. This is because the Constitution is an ambiguous document, and it is often unclear whether a president is exercising power legitimately or abusing it. Presidents have the greatest opportunity to exercise prerogative government during crises and national emergencies. However, the final determinant of the legitimate exercise of presidential power is politics.

Pious found that, throughout American history, *three political outcomes have occurred when presidents have exercised prerogative government.* First, presidents are most successful in exercising prerogative government in the area of foreign affairs during a time of national emergency, such as war. During such times, the president is able to legitimately exercise extraordinary powers because of the urgency of the situation. This is what happened under presidents Abraham Lincoln and Franklin Roosevelt as they exercised prerogative government in the face of the greatest of all national emergencies, a civil war and a world war. The worst that presidents can expect under such circumstances is what Pious calls "frontlash" after the emergency has subsided. That is, presidents can expect Congress and domestic politics to reassert their primacy during times of normalcy, again constraining presidential power.

Second, presidents may experience political "backlash" if they exercise prerogative government over domestic policy, even during a national emergency. In domestic policy, unlike foreign policy, presidents are not given much leeway or flexibility to respond to crises. Bureaucrats, members of Congress, and other political players are very protective of their positions and roles in the domestic policy-making process. Such was the case with President Harry Truman's seizure of steel mills in 1951 in the name of national security, in response to a strike during the Korean War. The political response was very critical of Truman for his exercise of emergency national security powers involving a labor-management dispute—clearly a domestic issue. Presidents with an expansive view of the Constitution during domestic emergencies will eventually be perceived as abusing power and may expect to suffer severe political setbacks.

Presidents also run the risk of "overshoot and collapse" when exercising prerogative government, resulting in a president's fall from power. This risk is most likely to occur when there is no perception of emergency in society, and is especially acute if domestic affairs are involved. A president exercising prerogative government under these conditions will be widely perceived as abusing his power and oath of office. The domestic political resistance is likely to be so severe that the president may have to fight for his political life. President Reagan faced this possibility with the Iran-contra affair and survived, and President Clinton was able to survive the Monica Lewinsky affair. However, President Nixon suffered from overshoot and collapse as a result of Watergate.

PATTERNS IN FOREIGN POLICY LEADERSHIP AND GOVERNANCE

The concepts of professional reputation, public prestige, and prerogative government are helpful for understanding the president's ability to lead and govern in general and in foreign affairs. These three elements of presidential leadership explain why Franklin Roosevelt was the most successful president in modern times, why presidents Truman, Eisenhower, and Kennedy were able to dominate foreign policy during the cold war, why the situation began to change under President Johnson, and why it has been so difficult for presidents to govern in foreign affairs since Vietnam and the end of the cold war.

THE ROOSEVELT PRESIDENCY

Regardless of whether one liked the direction in which he led the country, Franklin Delano Roosevelt was one of America's greatest presidents if greatness is measured by ability to govern and lead. He was elected president an unprecedented four times and occupied the office for thirteen years. Why? Because he was a politician with tremendous leadership skills and he became president at a unique time in American history.

Roosevelt entered office in 1933, when the United States was experiencing the full force of the Great Depression, the greatest national emergency to confront the United States since the Civil War. As a newly elected Democratic president, replacing Republican Herbert Hoover, he represented a change and hope for the future—two things for which people were looking, given the severity of the economic collapse. As an activist president, he took advantage of the extraordinary situation to move his New Deal legislation through Congress as he presided over the most active first hundred days in the history of legislative-executive relations. Roosevelt was also a consummate politician who personally ran the White House and restored the faith of the American people through his famous "fireside chats" over the radio. Moreover, the Japanese attack on Pearl Harbor in 1941 presented the president and the country with another national emergency, which gave Roosevelt extraordinary powers to wage war as commander in chief.

Roosevelt was an extremely powerful president and successful political leader—to students of the presidency he is often considered the model presidential leader in modern American politics. Not surprisingly, it has been virtually impossible for subsequent presidents to match his feat, for not only did Roosevelt enjoy a strong professional reputation and high public prestige, he operated during times of domestic and international emergency allowing him to exercise prerogative government.[30]

THE COLD WAR YEARS

U.S. involvement in World War II took the country out of the Depression, but it did not produce lasting peace. Instead, escalation of mutual suspicion and fear between the United States and the Soviet Union led to the rise of the cold war—another time of national emergency in the minds of most Americans. This sense of national emergency gave presidents during the 1950s and 1960s extraordinary powers over national security and foreign policy, accounting for the two presidencies thesis formulated by Aaron Wildavsky.

It is not that Truman, Eisenhower, and Kennedy had great leadership skills stemming from professional reputation and public prestige—the personal situation varied from president to president. The consequential factor was public perception that the cold war represented a contest that the United States and the free world could not afford to lose. It was fought through the strategy of containment, which emphasized the threat and use of force. These cold war beliefs and policies required a strong president who was able to combat the enemy quickly and secretly with public support and little opposition. To respond to the threat of communism, therefore, the demands of national security took precedence. Presidents were able to exercise prerogative government in foreign policy as the norm for twenty years. Their power was virtually undisputed on questions of war and peace, as demonstrated by the long history of presidential decisions taken by Truman, Eisenhower, Kennedy, and finally Johnson, resulting in the Americanization of the war in Vietnam.

THE TRANSITION YEARS

Ironically, the Vietnam War represented not only the height of presidential power but also the beginning of the end of the extraordinary exercise of prerogative power in foreign affairs. Because of Vietnam, presidents were challenged about their conduct in foreign policy for the first time in over twenty years. What had been accepted as a legitimate exercise of presidential power in the political climate of the cold war years became increasingly considered presidential abuse of power in the political climate of the post-Vietnam years. The uncertainties and constraints on presidential power, either silent or supportive of the president during the cold war, resurfaced.

President Lyndon Johnson represented both the height and decline of what became referred to as the **imperial presidency.**[31] He was the first victim of the changed political environment facing the president. Since his days as Senate majority leader, he had been known for his ability to wheel and deal in Washington's corridors of power. His very high professional reputation was a result of his overall aggressiveness and strong style of personal interaction. Johnson became president after the assassination of President John F. Kennedy in 1963, but he was very uncomfortable before the general public. He lacked charisma and was unable to display a sense of confidence in public appearances, such as on national television. Therefore, his public prestige, though quite high following the 1964 electoral landslide, lacked a strong bedrock of public support and declined severely as his administration's handling of the Vietnam War was increasingly challenged.

Operating with cold war beliefs emphasizing the need to contain communist aggression, presidential de-

cisions were made that resulted in the escalation of American intervention in Vietnam, which increased from 18,000 American troops under President Kennedy in 1963 to over 500,000 troops by 1966 under President Johnson. The Vietnam War had thus become Americanized. While the American role escalated and the war continued, President Johnson and other military and administrative leaders told the American people that it was only a matter of time until the Vietnam War would be won—that there was "light at the end of the tunnel." Then in February of 1968, during the Vietnamese holiday Tet, the North Vietnamese army and Vietcong guerrillas launched a major offensive in which most of the country, including cities throughout the south and the U.S. Embassy in Saigon, came under enemy occupation or siege. Although it was repulsed by American and South Vietnamese forces, the **Tet offensive** indicated that the Johnson administration's public optimism was unjustified, and his credibility with the American people was destroyed.

Although Johnson was in many ways a master of the political smoke-filled room, his weak skills at building public prestige made it impossible for him to overcome the crisis of governance that he experienced over the Vietnam War. The president, the American war effort in Vietnam, and the cold war beliefs on which the containment strategy was founded were increasingly challenged both within the government and throughout the domestic arena by a growing antiwar movement and public disenchantment. Johnson was so deeply affected by his loss of support that, rather than fight the political changes that were taking place around him, he declined to seek the Democratic presidential nomination for the 1968 election and withdrew from public life—the first post-World War II presidential casualty of a failed major U.S. foreign policy initiative.

THE POST–VIETNAM WAR YEARS

By the late 1960s, presidents attempted to govern and lead in a new political environment that was no longer automatically hospitable to the exercise of presidential power in foreign affairs. The issues the country faced were of greater complexity and scope than ever before. Consequently, presidential governance in foreign affairs became increasingly dependent on the presidential leadership skills that involved professional reputation, public prestige, and presidential choices. Yet if we examine recent presidents, *strong and durable political leadership is not a common commodity.*

Neither Johnson, Nixon, Ford, nor Carter had strong leadership skills overall. Consequently, these presidents were perceived as failures by the end of their term of office. Only President Reagan was able to buck the trend, yet even he was politically damaged and considered a lame duck at the close of his term. President Reagan seemed to have maintained high levels of professional reputation and public prestige, which may explain why he has been the most successful of contemporary presidents, even while suffering from the Iran-contra affair.

The Nixon Presidency. President Nixon, like Johnson before him, was also known for exercising power better within Washington than among the general public. Nixon's professional reputation was not so strong as Johnson's, nor his public prestige so weak. President Nixon was able to build a strong staff that centralized and exercised power in the White House. Although not a strong orator, he was better able to communicate to what he called the "silent majority" and, given all his years in public life, he had strong support among more conservative segments of the public.

Nixon's downfall came because he did not fully understand (or accept) the extent to which the domestic political environment was changing. As his predecessors had, Nixon tried to govern foreign policy with a free hand, while more and more Americans doubted the validity of communism as the major threat to the United States and questioned the basis of twenty years of containment policies and of presidential prerogative government in foreign affairs. From Nixon's perspective, the traditional authority of presidential power in national security affairs was being challenged. His reaction was to set in motion activities to fight the domestic political opposition, leading to Watergate and the abuse of presidential power.

The key to understanding the fate of President Nixon was his policy toward the war in Vietnam. He had told the American public in 1968 that he had a "secret plan" to end the Vietnam War, which would restore peace while maintaining American honor. The secret plan consisted of a strategy involving simultaneous de-escalation, escalation, and negotiations. De-escalation meant that U.S. troops were slowly phased out through a process of "Vietnamization."[32] Escalation entailed stepped-up American bombing of Indochina, as well as invading guerrilla sanctuaries in Cambodia and Laos. De-escalation and escalation, reinforced by détente initiatives with the Soviet Union and the People's Republic of China, were intended to elicit a negotiated agreement with the North Vietnamese, producing "peace with honor" and buying South Vietnam a "decent interval" for survival.

However, with the escalation the antiwar movement reached its height. Antiwar activists called for the immediate withdrawal of all U.S. forces from Indochina and challenged American interventionism abroad. Nixon, a scrappy fighter from his earliest political days, responded by attacking the domestic opposition as if it were the enemy. This led to a number of illegal and unconstitutional activities by the Nixon White House. Revelations about Nixon's abuse of presidential power, known as **Watergate,** led to his downfall. First, a Senate committee held hearings, followed by House Judiciary Committee hearings, which voted three counts of impeachment. This led President Nixon to resign in 1974, fearing a House of Representatives vote in favor of impeachment and conviction in the Senate. Therefore, soon after his triumphant reelection in 1972, Nixon was forced to leave office in disgrace.

The impact of the Vietnam War and Watergate on the Nixon administration illustrates the incredible tension that can develop between the demands of national security and democracy. Many of the difficulties President Nixon faced were of his own making, for he had failed to understand the limitations and constraints on the exercise of presidential power generated by events such as the Vietnam War. Watergate resulted from President Nixon's efforts, in the name of national security, to implement his secret plan to provide peace with honor in Vietnam and win reelection while simultaneously using his office to thwart the rise of a legitimate political opposition. President Nixon, acting as if he had the ultimate authority over foreign policy, was unwilling to accept democratic challenges to his exercise of power. Very simply, Richard Nixon's downfall was a result of his abuse of presidential power. He was only the second president in American history to face impeachment for "high crimes and misdemeanors," and the second presidential casualty of U.S. foreign policy in Vietnam.[33] (For an overview on what Watergate was all about, see **essay 4.2.**)

ESSAY 4.2
A CRISIS OF GOVERNANCE FACES THE PRESIDENCY: WHAT WATERGATE WAS ALL ABOUT

The origins of Watergate began with President Nixon's Vietnam policy. In 1969 the president decided to secretly order the U.S. military to bomb enemy forces along the Ho Chi Minh Trail in Cambodia, a country which was officially a neutral party in the Vietnam War. On September 6, the story broke on the front page of the *New York Times*, triggering massive antiwar demonstrations throughout the country. Nixon and National Security Adviser Kissinger were furious, to say the least. At Kissinger's request, Nixon agreed to allow the Federal Bureau of Investigation (FBI) to wiretap, illegally, members of Kissinger's National Security Council staff and a number of journalists in an effort to determine who was leaking information to the media. As the leaks continued, President Nixon turned to members of the White House staff—such as H. R. Haldeman, John Erlichman, Charles Colson, and G. Gordon Liddy, who came to be known as the "plumbers"—to plug White House leaks (all were later criminally indicted, found guilty, and sentenced to prison).

Throughout 1970, in response to intensified American bombing in Indochina and the invasion of Cambodia, the antiwar movement grew larger and louder, threatening Nixon's Vietnam policy. The White House responded by treating the antiwar movement as the enemy and devising a campaign to damage its credibility and destroy Nixon's critics, which included students, academics, journalists, and members of what Nixon often referred to as the liberal establishment.

The "enemies project" resulted in a wide range of illegal activities, such as the surveillance of activist groups and sabotage of demonstrations, use of the Federal Communications Commission to coerce the news media into providing less negative coverage of the administration, and threatening individuals with tax audits by the Internal Revenue Service. The most infamous exploit of the plumbers involved the burglary of Daniel Ellsberg's psychiatrist's office in an effort to find scandalous information that would discredit Ellsberg, who had been responsible for leaking the explosive *Pentagon Papers* to the media (which had exposed the government's Vietnam policy process in the 1960s).

By 1971 President Nixon had begun to worry about the outcome of the 1972 presidential election. The economy was overheating, the policy of détente had yet to produce any great accomplishment, the North Vietnamese were completely unresponsive at the negotiating table (while American troops were withdrawing from Vietnam), and domestic opposition was increasingly vocal. Nixon's reelection fears turned the attention of the White House to the upcoming presidential campaign. The Nixon White House came up with a number of dirty tricks and illegal activities designed to "ensure the president's reelection." This included illegally spying on the leading Democratic contenders, especially Senator Edward Kennedy. Millions of dollars were also covertly solicited from wealthy individuals and large corporations by the Committee to Reelect the President (CREEP), directed by Attorney General John Mitchell—a direct violation of a new 1972 federal campaign law requiring public disclosure.

Taking no chances, the Nixon White House also attempted to "sabotage" the campaigns of the political opposition. Its most notorious effort involved the manufacture of a fictitious letter slandering Senator Edmund Muskie's wife. Printed in the *Manchester Union Leader* just prior to the New Hampshire primary, the episode ruined Muskie's hopes for gaining the Democratic nomination. It was this type of activity that led to the burglary of the Democratic party headquarters in the Watergate Hotel in Washington, D.C., which gave the ensuing scandal its name and publicly exposed the wide-ranging illegalities and subsequent cover-up by President Nixon.

From wiretapping, to the "enemies project," to efforts to ensure the reelection of the president, and finally to the cover-up, the legacy of these illegal and unconstitutional activities was a destroyed president and the long-term diminution of presidential power.

SOURCES: Carl Bernstein and Bob Woodward, *All the President's Men* (New York: Warner, 1974); John Dean, *Blind Ambition* (New York: Pocket Books, 1977); J. Anthony Lukas, *Nightmare: The Underside of the Nixon Years* (New York: Penguin, 1973); Jonathan Schell, *The Time of Illusion* (New York: Vintage, 1975).

The overshoot and collapse of the Nixon presidency came not only from changes in the political environment that had new negative consequences for presidential exercise of prerogative government but also from the fragility of Nixon's public prestige (he was not particularly admired or well liked by either his political peers or the general public). He had been in the public limelight since the late forties, usually attacking others politically, as with the Alger Hiss affair, or defending his record, as he did as vice president under Eisenhower and after his unsuccessful race for the presidency in 1960. He created political enemies along the way and developed a reputation among much of the public as a mean-spirited politician (symbolized by the popular nickname "Tricky Dick"). The weak foundation of Nixon's public prestige, therefore, made him politically vulnerable during Watergate.

The Ford Presidency. Ford was a relatively passive president who had low levels of professional reputation and public prestige. Gerald Ford was a likable person but never would have become president on his own. Nixon had picked him as vice president to replace Spiro T. Agnew, who had been forced to resign on charges of corruption. Not only was Ford catapulted overnight into the presidency after having been minority leader in the House of Representatives, but he also possessed no election mandate. These circumstances were reinforced by his passivity in managing the government and the general public perception that he was not a particularly "presidential" individual.

President Ford was unable to overcome the stigma of Watergate and his pardon of President Nixon. He continued to pursue many of the policies emphasized during the Nixon administration, as reflected in his retaining Henry Kissinger as secretary of state. However, many of these policies were now under attack. American intervention in Angola was cut off by liberal opponents who feared another Vietnam. Détente with the Soviet Union and efforts to normalize relations with the People's Republic of China were attacked for being too "soft" by conservative anticommunists within his own party. In fact, Ford barely survived a challenge by Ronald Reagan for the Republican presidential nomination. The situation got so bad that Ford and Kissinger no longer used the word *détente* when discussing U.S. foreign policy. Given his low levels of pro-

fessional reputation and public prestige, it was not surprising that Ford was voted out of office in 1976 after having been president only three years—another failed president.

The Carter Presidency. Jimmy Carter attempted to put the tragic episodes of Vietnam and Watergate behind the country by instilling in the office a new spirit of honesty and idealism, represented by his commitment to human rights and peace. Carter was the first person to gain the presidency by running against Washington, pledging that he would clean up governmental corruption and discard the politics-as-usual approach. Carter was also the first president who was a true "outsider" to national politics. His political experience had been as governor of Georgia, not in Washington, D.C. He entered office resistant to the politics of Washington and with few political friends. Nevertheless, although not a great orator, Carter had a public presence that instilled hope and high public expectations about the future, especially among the more liberal segments of the population.

He entered office an activist president with relatively high public prestige and very low professional reputation. Yet, though extremely intelligent, President Carter was naive about the importance of presidential leadership and the difficulties of exercising political power. Early on, he antagonized members of Congress and the bureaucracy, thus destroying his honeymoon and his professional reputation. Despite the popularity of his human rights campaign and his ability to bring peace to Egypt and Israel with the Camp David Accords, by the end of his administration the economy went into a tailspin with double-digit inflation and unemployment. Moreover, the public's perception of his mishandling of U.S. foreign policy abroad haunted him as it had his predecessors, especially the Iran **hostage crisis.**

After years of U.S. support since the 1950s, the shah of Iran fell from power in 1979. Ayatollah Khomeini, a prominent religious figure, became Iran's new leader, and in the political turmoil fifty-two American diplomatic personnel were taken hostage in Teheran. For 444 days, the hostage crisis was the lead story in American politics. This initially resulted in a rise in public support for the president, but Carter's inability to free the American hostages destroyed the earlier optimism that had surrounded his presidency. Americans became frustrated, which intensified when the Soviet Union invaded neighboring Afghanistan to prop up their allied regime in Kabul. President Carter was never able to recover politically from the economy and the events in Iran and Afghanistan—he became another victim of the crisis of governance, written off by most of the public as a failure.

Surprisingly, since he left office, popular approval and admiration have grown for Jimmy Carter—which is quite unique among **ex-presidents.** Unlike most former presidents, Jimmy Carter has not disappeared into retirement and private life. Instead, Carter has chosen to remain involved in world affairs through his activities with the Carter Center in Atlanta. He has committed himself to the pursuit of good works such as promoting human rights, overseeing foreign democratic elections, negotiating regional conflicts, and assisting human development abroad and at home—recently receiving the Nobel Peace Prize for his efforts.[34]

The Reagan Presidency. Ronald Reagan has been the only president since Vietnam and before the collapse of the cold war able to overcome the crisis of governance that is part of the paradox and life cycle of presidential power. But even Reagan experienced a major crisis of governance during his administration— the Iran-contra affair. After months of great uncertainty, he was able to overcome the crisis, though his public approval and his ability to govern were damaged considerably. In fact, during the height of the crisis in 1987, it was unclear whether President Reagan would survive politically.

President Reagan assumed office prepared to initiate a new conservative agenda: to strengthen American defense forces and resolve overseas while unleashing the market to restore economic prosperity at home and abroad. He pledged to renew and strengthen America's efforts to combat terrorism and communism abroad. The Reagan administration dramatized the threat of terrorism to Americans and U.S. national security. The administration's other high priority was to defeat and contain the communist threat posed by the Soviet Union, especially in Central America. The goal of U.S. foreign policy was to defeat the Marxist-Leninist-led guerrillas in El Salvador and to overthrow the Sandinista revolutionary regime in Nicaragua through the threat and use of force. The U.S. government provided financial and military support to friendly regimes in the region, such as El Salvador, Guatemala, and Honduras, to help them in their fight. Covertly, the Central Intelligence Agency (CIA) became responsible for creating, arming, and supporting a counterrevolutionary group to overthrow the Sandinistas known as the contras.

To finance his Central American policy, President Reagan requested large amounts of assistance, over $200 million a year, from Congress. Despite Reagan's efforts to raise public consciousness about the gravity of the situation, the threat of communism in Central America never became a high-priority issue among the majority of the public, and there was much public criticism of his policies. Members of Congress granted the Reagan administration only a portion of the assistance it wanted during the first few years, with the biggest political battles fought over covert assistance to the contras. The issue became so politicized that Congress prohibited the U.S. government from providing any support or assistance to the contras at all during 1985 and 1986. This set the stage for the **Iran-contra affair.**

Regardless of the congressional ban, Reagan decided that the threat of communism and the future of Nicaragua required that the administration continue covert support to the contras (these operations are discussed in greater depth in chapter 8, on the intelligence community). President Reagan also decided that he was willing to covertly sell arms to Iran in exchange for American hostages.

It was not long before White House operations in support of the contras leaked to the press. The revelation that really came to haunt the Reagan presidency, however, involved the story that the United States was trading arms for hostages with Iran. After being told by Reagan that he would never negotiate secretly with terrorists and that they only understood force, most Americans could not believe that the president had agreed to negotiate with the so-called leading terrorist of them all, the Ayatollah Khomeini. President Reagan's denials only made the political situation worse for him and his administration. Then the public learned that some of the money the administration had received from the Iranian arms deal had been illegally diverted from the U.S. Treasury to the contras.

As with Watergate, a congressional investigation proceeded to determine the level of presidential abuse of power, and members of the Reagan administration were indicted. For almost a year, President Reagan and his administration were badly shaken and on the defensive about Iran-contra. Ultimately, President Reagan was able to survive the crisis and complete his term, though he was considerably diminished in power and public prestige. (See **essay 4.3** on the stress presidents face in office and the toll it takes on them.)

As the only contemporary president who has enjoyed high levels of both public prestige and professional reputation, Ronald Reagan was able to overcome the constraints and uncertainties that a president faces throughout his term of office. Reagan actually entered politics with low levels of both public prestige and professional reputation. When he assumed the governorship of California, he had been written off as a conservative ideologue and two-bit actor. He proved the political pundits wrong then and would do so again. It may be that these initially low expectations about a Reagan presidency worked to his advantage.

Reagan was, in fact, a complex man of many contradictions. While he rarely immersed himself in the

---

ESSAY 4.3
The Stress and Toll of the Office

Modern presidents have experienced considerable problems in governing and leading the country. Presidents Johnson, Nixon, Carter, Reagan, and Clinton all experienced a crisis of governance in foreign policy that gave rise to a domestic political crisis. In fact, the crises became so severe that each president became overwhelmed by them. He found little time and energy to respond to other issues and presidential responsibilities, which were either put on hold or carried out by subordinates with little presidential supervision. Clearly, the stress and toll of the office is immense, causing many presidents to noticeably age during their presidencies.

President Johnson was constantly preoccupied by the Vietnam quagmire during the last three years of his administration, to the point that it was difficult for his advisers and staff to get his attention on other matters. As President Nixon's cover-up of Watergate unraveled, he devoted himself to "damage control." As Congress came closer to impeaching him, his moods would swing from tenacious defense of his office to incredible despair, hopelessness, and obsession with little else but the future of his presidency (to the point that Henry Kissinger, who now enjoyed the roles of both national security adviser and secretary of state, was virtually in charge of U.S. foreign policy). Jimmy Carter became preoccupied with the release of the hostages. And for one year the Monica Lewinsky affair dominated Clinton's presidency and all of American politics.

In some ways, Ronald Reagan may have been affected the most by his political crisis. Reagan was completely "shocked" by the political damage that the Iran-contra revelations produced. Here was an individual who had beat the odds all his life—first as an actor in Hollywood, then in the California governorship, and finally with the

U.S. presidency. Even though he was heavily criticized throughout his tenure, President Reagan was extremely popular with the American people, was very successful in exercising power, and won a landslide reelection in 1984.

Then, all of a sudden, the world turned upside down. Such is the contemporary nature of presidential politics. When Americans learned that President Reagan had sold arms to and negotiated with the Khomeini regime, they couldn't believe it. When Reagan denied any involvement, his credibility was questioned for the first time, and the so-called **Teflon presidency** collapsed. And when it was learned that some of the money received in the arms-for-hostages deals had gone to the contras, in direct opposition to a congressional ban on all contra aid, congressional investigations were triggered to examine Iran-contra and determine whether the president had abused the powers of his office.

President Reagan, who had appeared at the height of his power, was now on the defensive, trying to minimize the political damage. Reagan, never one to be too heavily involved in the day-to-day details of governing, was so badly shaken that for a time he became virtually paralyzed as president. It was reported that the situation became so bad at one point that his advisers began to discuss seriously whether they should invoke the Twenty-Fifth Amendment, which allows the vice president to temporarily act as president if the sitting president becomes physically or emotionally disabled. Although badly shaken and damaged politically, Reagan ultimately survived and recovered to some extent to complete his term of office.

SOURCE: Jane Mayer and Doyle McManus, *Landslide: The Unmaking of the President, 1984–1988* (Boston: Houghton Mifflin, 1988), prologue.

issues, he entered office with a very active agenda. Although he was relatively uninvolved in the daily operations of presidential governance, he recruited a strong presidential staff that was capable of pursuing his policies. This played to his greatest strength: his ability to communicate to the general public. Reagan, as an individual, became well liked by the American people, especially after his assassination attempt. He had the ability to speak to them and gain their support by using language and symbols that most Americans understood and to which they responded. It was as if the more the American people became familiar with Reagan, the more they liked him. Not only was Reagan good at being the "great communicator," he actually was most comfortable when in the public limelight. It was his rise in public prestige, reinforced by his growing professional reputation, that was the key to his ability to govern, lead, and survive.

Iran-contra demonstrates that Reagan was also a president willing to exercise prerogative government in support of foreign policy goals that he deemed vital. Like Nixon before him, he acted as if the political environment had not changed since the 1950s. He felt that the president, as commander in chief, possessed the same right as presidents before him during the earlier cold war—to conduct U.S. foreign policy as he saw fit. As long as the operations involving Nicaragua and Iran remained covert or were kept off the public agenda, Reagan was a formidable president. However, once the stories broke, Reagan experienced a crisis of governance that damaged both his professional reputation and public prestige. Unlike Nixon's, Reagan's presidential abuse of power was not considered as severe, limited as it was to the conduct of foreign policy, and his high level of public prestige allowed him to weather the political storm and leave office with a general reputation as a successful president.

POST–COLD WAR
OPPORTUNITIES AND RISKS

It would appear that these same presidential leadership skills, including the occasional resort to prerogative government, are still necessary for presidents to successfully govern in the post–cold war era. If anything, strong and judicious presidential leadership has be-

come increasingly important for the conduct of U.S. foreign policy, and will continue to be so unless a new sense of national emergency—so crucial for presidential power—arises to rival the cold war. Obviously, a critical question is whether the terrorist attacks of September 11 and the U.S. war on terrorism have generated a new permanent sense of national emergency reminiscent of the cold war.[35]

To be able to govern in foreign policy, therefore, presidents must not only exercise prerogative government while avoiding being perceived as abusing power but also make the kind of presidential choices that maximize political leadership and support—throughout the country and inside the Washington beltway—for their policies and result in electoral success. Unfortunately, most individuals elected as president of the United States have not been viewed as particularly strong and successful leaders—such leadership skills may be quite uncommon.

Due to changes in the domestic environment since Vietnam and the end of the cold war, a crisis of leadership for the presidency and the country exists. The president, the only person capable of providing sustained national leadership, has a very difficult time leading the country. The fragmented nature of American beliefs, as well as competing domestic interests and institutions, has constrained presidential action. Regardless of what the president has promised in either domestic or foreign policy, he has been unable to fulfill expectations for long. The complexity of the domestic environment, reinforced by the complexity of the global system, with increasing interdependence and globalization, simply no longer allows much latitude for presidential success. This has been reinforced by the complex and multifaceted nature of contemporary foreign policy: The differences between foreign and domestic policy are less clear, and the foreign policy agenda has expanded beyond the cold war focus on national security issues to include many other foreign policy and global issues, as best illustrated by the prominence of economic issues at home and abroad.

This complexity has produced what can be called a post–cold war presidency thesis, according to which presidents find it very difficult to lead and manage foreign policy for a sustained period of time, whether in an internationalist direction or not. The net result of this crisis of leadership has been that with each new administration, as well as over the course of the same administration, U.S. foreign policy has tended to become increasingly *reactive—as opposed to proactive—*and hence incoherent and inconsistent over time. This is likely to continue into the twenty-first century, making it very difficult for the United States to exercise the kind of sustained global leadership that so many seem to hope for, or fear.

The collapse of the cold war has produced an interesting paradox for presidential leadership relative to the future of U.S. foreign policy: It gives the president great opportunities but also creates great risks. Unlike those of the 1950s, contemporary presidents are no longer driven to pursue only an anticommunist containment policy. They now have more flexibility to pursue a wider range of foreign policy options abroad. Yet it is unclear how far a president may go in pursuing any policy before losing public and governmental support.[36]

As Destler, Gelb, and Lake argue, "The making of American foreign policy has been growing far more political—or more precisely, far more partisan and ideological."[37] Hence, according to Alexander George, "the necessity for ad hoc day-to-day building of consensus under these circumstances makes it virtually impossible for the President to conduct long-range foreign policy in a coherent, effective manner."[38] This has meant that each administration since the end of Vietnam has been forced to modify its initial policies abroad, usually toward the ideological center, in response to domestic political challenges. This pattern helps to account for why U.S. foreign policy often appeared to lack coherence and consistency after the end of the cold war under presidents Bush Sr. and Clinton, whose foreign policies are discussed below. I will then discuss to what extent the September 11 attacks and President Bush Jr.'s focus on a global war on terrorism have fundamentally altered presidential power, especially in the making of foreign policy.

THE BUSH SR. PRESIDENCY

George H. Bush became president at a time when the world would soon witness the collapse of the Soviet Union and communism in Eastern Europe. These momentous events have, if anything, intensified the rise of diversity and pluralist politics in the making of U.S. foreign policy that began with the Vietnam War, complicating the president's ability to govern. Bush, who

was widely considered to be a strong president in the realm of foreign policy, was unable to take advantage of the post–cold war environment and a tremendously successful and popular war in the Persian Gulf to win reelection in 1992.

Bush entered office pledging to use his considerable governmental experience to continue most of the policies of his predecessor, but with a "kinder and gentler" style. Bush's leadership style was quite different from Reagan's: more informal and low-keyed, more active and hands-on, less ideological, and more politically sensitive. The most common criticisms of President Bush were that he attempted to govern without a vision or an agenda, that his presidency was too reactive and cautious, and that he was too sensitive to public relations and politics. Yet early on, Bush's leadership style paid off. His public approval ratings into his third year were over 70 percent, an all-time high for post–World War II presidents.

However, as we have learned, to begin office strong is not unusual. Although his public approval was high, Bush, unlike Reagan and many of his predecessors, lacked truly strong political support. Also, he was not a particularly good public speaker and, moreover, did not develop an active domestic agenda and faced an economic recession. Nor did he inspire confidence in a foreign policy based on a realpolitik vision of the world, in which his administration was highly reactive to events and initiatives taken by others, such as Soviet leader Mikhail Gorbachev and Iraq's Saddam Hussein.

There is no doubt that George Bush was shocked to discover that, despite his great victory in the Persian Gulf War and public approval ratings approaching 90 percent, he was soon voted out of office, largely due to perceptions that he did little to address the nation's domestic ills. President Bush clearly made the crucial mistake of underestimating the softness of presidential support and the volatility of the domestic political environment since Vietnam.

THE CLINTON PRESIDENCY

President Bill Clinton experienced considerable difficulty in governing throughout his tenure both at home and abroad. According to one analysis, "No president since World War II has faced such relentless and vitriolic criticism in the beginning of his term." Yet Clinton managed to escape the presidential life cycle, won reelection against a weak Republican candidate, and completed his second term of office with more popularity—despite the Monica Lewinsky affair—than he enjoyed when he started his first term. In fact, he is the first president to serve two full terms in the post–cold war era and the first Democratic president to be reelected since FDR, over fifty years ago.

Clinton was commonly perceived as trying to do too much too quickly, to the point that it was difficult for people to acquire a positive image of the man and the direction he wanted to take the country. He was also handicapped early on by a very tough Democratic primary race and by questions of personal and financial infidelity that have continued to surround him and his aides. All this was reinforced by the "Hillary factor," having a very strong and capable woman as first lady who was a lawyer and accustomed to being active in her professional life—which resonated well with some people but not with others.

Clinton suffered early political defeats, such as with appointments and, in particular, over his effort to legitimize "gays in the military"—which really hurt his public prestige and professional reputation. During his first two years he failed even to get major parts of his legislative program (such as his first budget and his major initiative to reform health care) through a Congress controlled by his own party. And then, in 1994, the Democratic party suffered a huge electoral defeat, the Republican party gaining control of both the Senate and the House of Representatives—for the first time since 1954—producing divided government once again. But he was able to rebound politically when he won a major showdown with the Republican-led Congress in late 1995 and early 1996 over the budget—which included two government shutdowns.

President Clinton was also accused of considerable vacillation and hesitancy in the conduct of U.S. foreign policy. Efforts to promote a more multilateral foreign policy faced early setbacks, especially in Somalia. At the same time, President Clinton did manage to initiate several significant foreign policy actions in Haiti, Mexico, and Bosnia-Kosovo in spite of public and congressional opposition. Major foreign policy failures were avoided while the administration chose to emphasize domestic policy and international economics. Most prominent in this regard were passage of the North American Free Trade Agreement (NAFTA); the Uruguay round of the GATT, producing the World Trade Organization; and normalized trade relations with China.[39]

And then Clinton and the country went through and survived a yearlong crisis of governance over the **Monica Lewinsky affair**—involving the president's sexual relations with a former White House intern. Against the wishes of a majority of the American public (who opposed Clinton's personal behavior but deemed it to be more of a private matter), a Republican special prosecutor and Congress conducted numerous and intensive investigations of the Clintons, eventually voting articles of impeachment for presidential abuse of power. The articles of impeachment were voted down in the Senate on a highly politicized and partisan vote (all Democrats voting against impeachment, almost all Republicans voting in favor).

Clinton very easily could have been another failed president, but he not only survived politically but was able to maintain an active agenda until the end of his term, and he left office with greater public approval than when he entered. Bill Clinton has demonstrated throughout his political career that he is a political survivor. Back in the 1992 presidential campaign, he was often referred to as "Slick Willy" and the "comeback kid" because he was able to rebound when he appeared close to defeat, and he has had the uncanny ability to occupy the political center. Somewhat like Ronald Reagan's Teflon presidency, but for very different reasons, nothing seems to politically damage Clinton too much or for too long.

Bill Clinton's political success may have been in part due to most Americans' lowered expectations, at least relative to him and his presidency. He was elected, after all, with only 43 percent of the vote as a result of a three-way race in 1992. And while most Americans did not seem to particularly admire the man, especially concerning his personal character and charges of womanizing, they appeared to have found him and his policies more acceptable than any of the viable alternatives. Most important, Bill Clinton was the beneficiary of an economy that not only avoided going into recession but actually grew strongly throughout his presidency.[40]

Bill Clinton appears to be a very complex man who seemed to have *contradictory leadership styles*. On one hand, he had a strong interest and concern for both policy and politics. His verbal facility and intelligence is formidable, and he brought energy and optimism to the White House. In the words of Jack Watson, a former White House chief of staff, he was "exuberant, informal, interactive, non-hierarchical, and indefatigable."[41] On the other hand, Clinton often got himself into trouble by lacking self-discipline and not focusing on a set of specific goals. He is amiable to the point of being ingratiating with friends as well as foes. He is very articulate, but his ability to communicate in public was counteracted by his tendency to become too long-winded and mired in detailed lists.

Fred Greenstein wrote, "I have been particularly struck by the diversity of the qualities Clinton brings to his leadership, the extent to which they seem at times to be warring with one another, and the novelty of their combination in a single individual."[42] Sometimes these traits came together to make him a relatively strong leader, but much of the time they coalesced to hinder his ability to lead and govern—But clearly he was a "natural-born politician."

In foreign policy some of Bill Clinton's initiatives—such as the military interventions in Haiti and Kosovo, as well as the bailouts of the Mexican peso and Asian financial crisis—may be considered exercises of prerogative government. In each case the administration was faced with considerable public and congressional opposition to the initiative and proceeded nonetheless. In each case there were many in Congress who argued that the president did not have the authority to act alone, and yet he did so. Furthermore, each of these instances of prerogative government occurred in the absence of any semblance of national emergency in the post–cold war environment. And yet in none of the cases did the Clinton administration suffer from "backlash" or "overshoot and collapse."

Perhaps political backlash was avoided in each case because the policies, for the most part, were successful—or at least they weren't seen as failures—and seemed distant from most Americans' vital concerns. Whatever the case, the political risks taken by the Clinton administration for his major foreign policy initiatives seem to have paid off to the extent that Haiti, Kosovo, Mexico, and the Asian financial crisis all ceased being potentially damaging foreign policy problems for Clinton. Hence, the continued importance of prerogative government to presidential leadership and power in the post–cold war era.

THE BUSH JR. PRESIDENCY

George W. Bush had a very inauspicious beginning as president. He was elected in 2000 with a smaller popular vote than Al Gore, the Democratic candidate. The

electoral votes and electoral college were under challenge, especially in Florida, where Bush's brother was governor. And ultimately his election as the forty-third president of the United States was decided by a 5–4 U.S. Supreme Court decision. So President Bush Jr. began his term of office with a rather low sense of national legitimacy.

Although George Bush was previously governor of Texas and ran for president as a "compassionate conservative," he was not widely respected or admired for his political focus, background, or knowledge— especially in the area of foreign policy. The conventional wisdom was that he picked a seasoned foreign policy team that would make up for what he lacked in knowledge about U.S. foreign policy and world politics. No grand vision was initially offered and his first few months in office were rather uneventful, with the exception of a minicrisis with China and some criticism over his energy and environmental policies. Most of the President's focus seemed to be on domestic politics—in particular, successfully passing a large tax cut. Overall, within a year of entering office, the American public had relatively low expectations of Bush Jr., he seemed an agreeable man but lacking prominent stature, his public prestige was just beyond a majority, but he had a respectable professional reputation given his domestic tax cut and the experience of his foreign policy team.

And then came September 11, 2001. The twin towers of the World Trade Center in New York City were attacked by two airplanes driven by terrorists, reducing them both to rubble. And another plane flown by terrorists hit the Pentagon. There were thousands of dead and wounded, prominent American symbols on United States soil were attacked, and most Americans were in a state of shock and disbelief. Quickly reacting to the disaster and ensuing crisis, President Bush seemed to become a new man and a new president over the course of the next few weeks. Ultimately, he went before the American people and declared a global war on terrorism.

The immediate response was that the country (and much of the world) rallied around the flag and the president. For the next few months public approval of presidential behavior hovered around 90 percent. Overnight, Bush Jr. had become the "war president" whose principal focus would be to fight the global war on terrorism. Numerous policies and programs were announced (which will be discussed at greater length in other chapters) and enacted in the name of national emergency and prerogative government. According to the Bush administration, the United States has entered a new era of national emergency and permanent crisis, similar to what President Truman faced following World War II, in which the United States would have to respond with all its energy and might to eradicate the new global threat.

This was best symbolized by Bush's State of the Union address on January 29, 2002—what has also been referred to as his "Axis of Evil" speech. The speech promoted and reinforced evil images of the enemy–which were automatically conjured up in the minds of most Americans at the mere mention of the names Osama Bin Laden or Saddam Hussein or the countries Iraq, Iran, and North Korea. Somewhat reminiscent of John F. Kennedy's inaugural address in 1961 focusing on the cold war, President Bush's called Americans to war, to patriotism, and to duty and reminded them of their innocence and exceptionalism:

> All nations should know: Americans will do what is necessary to ensure our nation's security.... Our war on terror is well begun, but it is only begun. This campaign may not be finished on our watch, yet it must be and it will be waged on our watch.... History has called America and our allies to action, and it is both our responsibility and our privilege to fight freedom's fight.... We want to be a nation that serves goals larger than self. We have been offered a unique opportunity, and we must not let this moment pass.... We have a great opportunity during this time of war to lead the world toward the values that will bring lasting peace.

The speech ended: "Steadfast in our purpose, we now press on. We have known freedom's price. We have shown freedom's power. And in this great conflict, my fellow Americans, we will see freedom's victory."

Virtually the entire speech revolved around foreign policy and the war on terrorism. Bush highlighted three major themes: "national security," "homeland security," and "economic security." Clearly, the president was trying, and for the most part succeeding, to rally the country behind his presidency in declaring a war on terrorism in response to the national crisis triggered by September 11. *Which leads us to a number of key political questions that will impact the future of presidential power and the politics of U.S. foreign policy:* To what extent will September 11,

the new enemy of terrorism, and the war on terrorism resonate in the twenty-first century in comparison to images of communists and the war on communism following World War II? Will the American people feel like it's a time of war and national emergency? Or will people feel like it is more of a war during a time of relative peace? Through the metaphor and call for war, can President Bush sustain political support into the presidential election of 2004 and beyond? To what extent will the demands of the war on terrorism begin to infringe on the values of democracy and the demands of individual rights and liberties?

Until the spring of 2002, it appeared that maybe this was another time of permanent national emergency, now requiring a global war on terrorism with implications similar to the cold war's for the politics of U.S. foreign policy. But then President Bush and his administration began to receive criticism about the declining state of the economy; about corporate scandals, some of which affected members of the administration; and about his inability to pass additional domestic legislation and deal with other pressing domestic issues. This criticism even carried over into the area of foreign policy, regarding the initial American neglect of and then reaction to the Israeli-Palestinian conflict, the India-Pakistan conflict, and the collapse of the economies in South America, especially Argentina and Brazil.

And despite the initial success in Afghanistan, questions and criticisms have been raised about the war on terrorism, about the implications for civil rights and liberties at home, about the success of the war on terrorism at home and abroad, and about whether the United States should preemptively attack Saddam Hussein and Iraq. And growing criticism was heard throughout the global community as well as within American politics. In fact, by spring of 2003 President Bush Jr.'s public approval rating remained high but had declined from 90 percent down into the fifties (review figure 4.2). Furthermore, criticism was coming not only from the Democratic party but increasingly from within the Republican party. And whereas the Bush administration initially appeared to be united, divisions within it and the foreign policy team became increasingly obvious. In fact, talk about attacking Iraq generated so much international and domestic criticism that President Bush politically capitulated to the need for a national debate and for ultimately going to Congress and the United Nations for support, very much like his father did before the Persian Gulf War.[43]

This suggests that the post–cold war presidency thesis is still quite powerful, even in a political environment in which the president has been able to exercise considerable prerogative government and engage in a global war on terrorism. Ultimately, it is too early to tell or forecast the implications of September 11 and the war on terrorism, given the limited time that has passed since the Bush administration and the war on terrorism began, as well as the volatility of the domestic and international political climates. Therefore, additional time and analysis are necessary to determine the implications of September 11 and the war on terrorism for the future of the Bush administration and the politics of U.S. foreign policy.

It is possible that we may have entered a new political environment, reminiscent of the national emergency and crisis of the cold war, thus maximizing the president's ability to exercise leadership and power. At the same time, the shift from what appeared to be total overwhelming national support for President Bush and the war on terrorism to the decline of overall public approval within one year suggests that, though the president may have become more powerful in the area of national security in general and the war on terrorism in particular, the paradox of presidential power and the post–cold war presidency thesis continues to operate in the general domain of foreign policy. Ultimately, it will be the complex interaction of the policymakers, presidential leadership, domestic politics, the global environment, and events that will determine the future trajectory of presidential power and the politics of U.S. foreign policy.

SUMMARY AND CHALLENGES OF THE POST–COLD WAR WORLD

This important chapter *provides an overview of the politics of U.S. foreign policy.* We began by introducing the major elements within government, society, and the global environment that make an impact on presidential power. We found that, while most Americans have high expectations of presidential power, in reality, these elements produce a paradox of presidential power. Although presidents possess significant constitutional roles and strengths, they also face important constraints and uncertainties. Presidents usually go through a presidential life cycle in which they leave office much weaker than they were when they entered. Together, the paradox of presidential power and the presidential life cycle reflect a crisis of governance (or leadership), making it difficult for any president to govern successfully and lead the country in a direction consistent with his beliefs. Although these patterns of presidential power are strongest in the area of domestic policy, they have also impacted foreign policy in the years since the Vietnam War and the end of the cold war. The two presidencies thesis of the cold war years appears to have been replaced by a post–cold war presidency thesis. Therefore, the best way for a president to exercise power and govern is through strong presidential leadership, realizing at the same time that there are no guarantees of success in the complex politics of U.S. foreign policy.

The discussion of presidential power and governance provides an initial *overview of the three foreign policy–making themes*—continuity and change, the president's ability to govern, and the tension between democracy and national security—addressed throughout this book. First, the foreign policy process has become more complex because of the changes that have occurred in the wake of the Vietnam War and the end of the cold war. Presidents now face more constraints and opposition throughout government, society, and the global environment in the conduct of foreign policy. Second, presidents have had a difficult time governing and leading the nation since Vietnam and the cold war's end, even in the area of foreign policy. Given the extraordinary powers suggested by the two presidencies thesis, the president was able to govern foreign policy with minimal difficulty during the cold war years. Since the mid-1960s, however, the paradox of presidential power and the presidential life cycle have made presidential governance of foreign policy much more problematic—a post–cold war presidency appears to exist. Third, whenever presidents have exerted prerogative government and pressed assertive foreign policies since Vietnam, tensions between democracy and national security have produced political crises for both the president and the political system. The tension between democracy and national security peaked during Watergate, destroying President Nixon and damaging the presidency. Tension rose again during the Iran-contra affair, but President Reagan and his presidency survived. And tensions have also arisen due to President Bush Jr.'s war on terrorism abroad and at home.

The events of Watergate and Iran-contra illustrate the changes that have occurred in the foreign policy–making process since Vietnam and the difficulty that presidents now have in governing foreign policy. They also demonstrate that the foreign policy process has become increasingly democratic and that presidents are now commonly challenged in their conduct of foreign policy. In sum, presidents must realize that they can no longer exercise power and prerogative government in the name of national security, as commonly occurred during the cold war, without risking considerable political backlash and possible overshoot and collapse. Not even Ronald Reagan, with his tremendous symbolic skills and prestige with the American people, was able to rise above the paradox of presidential power. And if Reagan was unable to avoid a crisis of governance and the presidential life cycle, what is the omen for presidents with lesser leadership skills?

What about the implications of the end of the cold war and of September 11? So far the impact is contradictory for presidential power: On one hand, they provide unique opportunities for more foreign policy change away from the cold war policies of the past; on the other hand, the events have also further weakened the president's ability to govern foreign policy into the future. It was the sense of national emergency associated with the cold war during the fifties and sixties, after all, that was the ultimate source of presidential power and American global leadership following World War II. This means that the fragmented and pluralist political environment that has prevailed since Vietnam will likely continue in the post–cold war future, posing greater foreign policy opportunities and political risks for presidents and American leadership abroad. And as the American public focuses its concern increasingly on "intermestic" (and especially economic) issues, presidents who are perceived as dealing successfully with those issues are likely to enjoy an increase in their popularity and ability to govern in foreign policy and in general. But much will depend on the image that Americans have of a president's policies and of their relative success, at home and abroad—a function of the turn of events and the strength of presidential leadership.

Until September 11 it was difficult to envision a strong, proactive global leadership role for the United States across different administrations navigating the challenges of the twenty-first century over a sustained period of time. It appeared that the cold war era had been superseded by an increasingly complex global and domestic environment in which the days of presidential supremacy and grand design in foreign policy had given way to a time of a U.S. foreign policy more likely to be reactive—to muddle through. This may not be what most people mean by American leadership in the world, but it appears to have been the case under George Bush Sr. and Bill Clinton—the first two post–cold war presidents. Only time will tell whether September 11 and President Bush Jr.'s war on terrorism will resonate throughout the international community, the domestic political environment, and the American people, producing a new permanent crisis and sense of national emergency that transcends the post–cold war presidency thesis. Clearly, since the end of the cold war the quality of leadership has remained consequential with respect to the president's ability to govern, and we can only speculate as to how the future will unfold. This will certainly be the case under President Bush Jr. In order to get a stronger understanding, we now turn to one of the most significant sources that a president has to exercise leadership and power—his efforts to manage the executive branch and the foreign policy bureaucracy.

SUGGESTED SOURCES FOR MORE INFORMATION

The classic statement on presidential power and presidential leadership is Richard E. Neustadt's *Presidential Power: The Politics of Leadership* (New York: John Wiley, 1960). Other fine works addressing the paradox of presidential power and its consequences for governance are James MacGregor Burns, *The Power to Lead: The Crisis of the American Presidency* (New York: Simon and Schuster, 1984); Godfrey Hodgson, *All Things to All Men: The False Promise of the Modern American Presidency* (New York: Touchstone, 1980); and Michael Nelson, ed., *The Presidency and the Political System* (Washington, D.C.: Congressional Quarterly Press, 2000). Hedrick Smith, in *The Power Game: How Washington Really Works* (New York: Ballantine, 1988), provides an excellent discussion and feel for the realities of presidential power and American politics through examining the Reagan years.

Arthur M. Schlesinger, Jr., in *The Imperial Presidency* (New York: Houghton Mifflin, 1989), provides an excellent history of the evolution of executive-legislative relations in foreign affairs by describing the growth of presidential power leading up to Watergate. For other historical works, see Stephen Skowronek, *The Politics Presidents Make: Leadership from John Adams to Bill Clinton* (Cambridge, Mass.: Harvard University Press, 1997).

For a general assessment of the two presidencies thesis during the post-World War II era, see Steven A. Shull, ed., *The Two Presidencies: A Quarter Century Assessment* (Chicago: Nelson-Hall, 1991). The changes affecting presidential power and governance in foreign policy since Vietnam are impressively captured by Thomas E. Mann in "Making Foreign Policy: President and Congress," Thomas E. Mann, ed., *A Question of Balance: The President, The Congress and Foreign Policy* (Washington, D.C.: Brookings Institution Press, 1990), pp. 1–34, and I. M. Destler, Leslie H. Gelb, and Anthony Lake, *Our Own Worst Enemy: The Unmaking of American Foreign Policy* (New York: Simon and Schuster, 1984). Jerel Rosati addresses the future implications of the end of the cold war on presidential power and U.S. leadership abroad in "United States Leadership Into the Next Millennium: A Question of Politics," *International Journal* (spring 1997): 297–315.

Another excellent work on presidential power and leadership is Richard M. Pious's *The American Presidency* (New York: Basic Books, 1996), especially his discussion of the exercise of prerogative government. For a general overview of the significance and basis of leadership in political affairs, see James MacGregor Burns, *Leadership* (New York: Harper Torchbooks, 1978); Alexander L. George and Juliette L. George, *Presidential Personality and Performance* (Boulder, Colo.: Westview Press, 1998); and Fred I. Greenstein, *The Presidential Difference: Leadership Style from FDR to Clinton* (New York: Free Press, 2000).

The following sources provide strong discussions of different administrations and presidential leadership styles: Doris Kearns, in *Lyndon Johnson and the American Dream* (New York: New American Library, 1976), does a fascinating job of explaining Johnson's life and presidency in terms of his personality, his role in American politics, and his place in America's political culture. Gary Wills, in *Nixon Agonistes: The Crisis of the Self-Made Man* (New York: Houghton Mifflin, 1969), has written a very interesting political biography of Richard Nixon in the context of American history. Two revealing insights into Jimmy Carter and his presidency are Hamilton Jordan's memoir, *Crisis: The Last Year of the Carter Presidency* (New York: G. P. Putnam's Sons, 1982), and the psychobiography by

Betty Glad, *Jimmy Carter* (New York: W. W. Norton, 1980). An excellent account of the Reagan presidency can be found in Lou Cannon, *President Reagan: The Role of a Lifetime* (New York: Simon and Schuster), while Gary Wills has written a powerful analysis of the life of Ronald Reagan and his place in American history entitled *Reagan's America* (New York: Penguin, 1988). For thoughtful insights into President Clinton's background, personality, and leadership styles, see Fred Greenstein, "The Two Leadership Styles of William Jefferson Clinton," *Political Psychology* 15 (June 1994): 351–62; David Maranis, *First in His Class: A Biography of Bill Clinton* (New York: Simon and Schuster, 1995); and Stanley A. Renshon, "After the Fall: The Clinton Presidency in Psychological Perspective, *Political Science Quarterly* (spring 2000): 41–65. For President Bush Jr., especially after September 11, see Bob Woodward, *Bush at War* (New York: Simon and Schuster, 2002).

KEY TERMS

chief of state
crisis of governance (or leadership)
electoral mandate
ex-president
head of the government
honeymoon
hostage crisis
imperial presidency
Iran-contra affair
issue area
lame duck
leadership
Monica Lewinsky affair
paradox of presidential power
post–cold war presidency thesis
power
power to persuade
prerogative government
presidential choices
presidential life cycle
professional reputation
public prestige
symbolism and symbolic politics
Teflon presidency
Tet offensive
Twenty-Second Amendment
two presidencies thesis
Watergate

CHAPTER 5

. . . .

THE BUREAUCRACY, PRESIDENTIAL MANAGEMENT AND THE NATIONAL SECURITY COUNCIL

The president's beliefs about the nature of the world and America's role within it are a very important guide to the type of foreign policy that will be pursued under his administration. Setting the general direction and tone of an administration, however, does not guarantee that a president's vision and priorities will prevail. The previous chapters emphasize the powers and actions of the president, yet he does not and cannot operate alone. In fact, much of the government's foreign policy is made and carried out by the bureaucracy. This creates a significant paradox: The president's ability to govern is heavily dependent on the foreign policy bureaucracy, yet the bureaucracy is so large and complex that it is very difficult to control. Presidential governance, therefore, requires that presidents be not only strong political leaders but strong managers as well.

In this chapter, we will address the following major questions: How large and complex is the foreign policy bureaucracy? How do presidents manage the bureaucracy? What role does the National Security Council play to assist the president in managing and governing foreign policy? As we will see, a president's success in managing the bureaucracy, given its enormous size and complexity, is very much a function of his choices concerning his personal agenda and level of involvement, the personnel who staff his administration, and how he organizes the foreign policy–making process, in particular the operations of the White House and the National Security Council (NSC). The more successful he is in this management task, the more he will be able to exercise presidential power in accordance with his roles as commander in chief, chief diplomat, chief administrator, and chief legislator. In other words, presidential management of the foreign policy bureaucracy is a key determinant of the extent to which the president will be able to govern U.S. foreign policy.

A HUGE AND COMPLEX FOREIGN POLICY BUREAUCRACY

The president is the chief administrator, but much of the bureaucracy is beyond presidential control. This means that *the bureaucracy is both a source of and a constraint on presidential power*. The more successful a president is in managing the bureaucracy, the fewer the bureaucratic constraints and the greater his ability to exercise power. Strong presidential management indicates strong leadership skills, for it provides an important indication of a president's professional reputation and his ability to make important presidential choices.

Presidential management was significant throughout the cold war years and has become of greater importance since the decline of presidential power following the Vietnam War and the end of the cold war. If the president is to exercise much power in his efforts to govern, whether in foreign or domestic policy, he must attempt to manage and control the federal bureaucracy. Yet presidential management of the executive branch is not an easy task. *Three major aspects of the bureaucracy complicate the president's task of its management and administration:* (1) Size, (2) Complexity, and (3), Historical development.[1]

BUREAUCRATIC SIZE

The U.S. executive branch bureaucracy has become huge. The president presides over five million personnel, located in thirteen major departments and hundreds of other organizations and agencies, who spend well over $1 trillion a year on thousands of programs and policies throughout the United States and the world. The executive branch involves so many people, agencies, funds, and programs that the president's job as chief administrator is simply an impossible task. However, he has no choice but to try to manage and control as many areas as possible if he is to exercise any power over the bureaucracy.

The foreign policy bureaucracy itself is quite large. The Department of Defense (DOD) is the largest of all executive branch organizations; it employs over three million civilian and military personnel (including re-

serves) throughout the world and spends over $300 billion a year. In addition, many other agencies, such as the Department of State, the Agency for International Development (AID), and the Central Intelligence Agency (CIA), are devoted to foreign affairs. In fact, it would not be an exaggeration to say that virtually every department and agency in the executive branch contains an international component. Clearly, the scope of government with which a president must deal in his effort to manage the foreign policy bureaucracy is staggering (see **table 5.1** for an overview of the more active agencies involved).

As table 5.1 reveals, there are many agencies that most people have probably never heard about or do not realize are involved in foreign policy. For example, within the Office of the White House, the Office of Science and Technology Policy advises the president on scientific and technological considerations involving national security, foreign relations, and other national concerns. The Office of National Drug Control Policy was established under President Reagan to coordinate and add coherence to the myriad executive branch agencies that have become involved in the war on drugs.

Many presidential cabinet departments have units with selective but important international roles. The Department of Transportation, in addition to housing the U.S. Coast Guard, is responsible for the government's policy on international aviation and maritime issues through the Office of the Assistant Secretary for Aviation and International Affairs, the Federal Aviation Administration, and the Maritime Administration. The Department of Justice contains, besides the Federal Bureau of Investigation (FBI), the Drug Enforcement Agency, the lead agency in actually fighting the drug war, with offices in over fifty countries. Also within the Justice Department, the Immigration and Naturalization Service is very important to immigration policy.

There are also a number of independent agencies and governmental corporations involved in global affairs. The Environmental Protection Agency is heavily responsible for international environmental issues within the executive branch. The Federal Maritime Commission is an independent agency that regulates the waterborne domestic and foreign offshore commerce of the United States. The African Development Foundation and the Inter-American Foundation are

TABLE 5.1
THE FOREIGN POLICY BUREAUCRACY

	INTERNATIONALLY ORIENTED AGENCIES	DOMESTICALLY ORIENTED AGENCIES
EXECUTIVE OFFICE OF THE PRESIDENT	National Security Council National Economic Council Office of the U.S. Trade Representative	White House Office Office of Management and Budget Office of Science and Technology Policy Office of National Drug Control Policy
PRESIDENTIAL DEPARTMENTS AND AGENCIES	Department of State Department of Defense Department of Energy Department of Homeland Security Central Intelligence Agency Agency for International Development Peace Corps	Department of Treasury Department of Agriculture Department of Commerce Department of Labor Department of Justice Department of Veterans Affairs Department of Transportation
INDEPENDENT AGENCIES	International Trade Commission Export-Import Bank Overseas Protection Investment Corporation Trade and Development Agency Board for International Broadcasting National Endowment for Democracy African Development Foundation Inter-American Foundation Panama Canal Commission U.S. Institute for Peace	Federal Reserve Board National Aeronautics and Space Administration Environmental Protection Agency Federal Maritime Commission

SOURCE: *United States Government Manual.*

nonprofit government corporations that provide grants and loans to local private groups in the region that promote development. The U.S. Institute for Peace is an independent nonprofit government corporation whose purpose is to develop and disseminate knowledge about the peaceful resolution of international conflict.

The reality is that virtually every executive branch department and agency has responsibility and involvement in international affairs in some way. For example, the Department of the Interior's Office of Insular Affairs coordinates and oversees federal policy toward the territories of American Samoa, Guam, the U.S. Virgin Islands, the Commonwealth of the Northern Mariana Islands, the Republic of the Marshall Islands, the Federal States of Micronesia, and the Republic of Palau—all part of the United States' colonial acquisitions from earlier days. The Center for International

Education is part of the Department of Education, and the Department of Health and Human Services is involved in issues of international health through its Office of International and Refugee Health. The Federal Communications Commission regulates foreign communications by Americans, and the Federal Emergency Management Agency (FEMA) develops and coordinates national programs to respond to any national security emergency. Even the Department of Housing and Urban Development has an assistant to the secretary for international affairs.

The president (and/or Congress) also has created numerous governmental boards, committees, and commissions whose activities, usually symbolic, involve international affairs. Among these are the Committee on Foreign Investment in the United States, the Japan–United States Friendship Commission, the president's Foreign Intelligence Advisory Board, the Textile Trade Policy Group, and the Trade Policy Committee. All together, we're talking about a huge foreign policy bureaucracy.

BUREAUCRATIC COMPLEXITY

Not only is the bureaucracy immense, it is also incredibly complex. Some organizations like the Department of Defense are quite large; others are tiny, like the Peace Corps. Each organization has its own set of goals and missions. Some organizations, like DOD, have multiple goals and missions; others, like the Peace Corps, have very few functions. Many times the tasks of different organizations overlap. For instance, the intelligence community, discussed in chapter 8, is made up of many executive branch organizations that contribute information and analyses to high-level policymakers, thereby performing functions that often force them to compete with each other.

Another component of bureaucratic complexity is the degree to which various organizations have *different levels of autonomy* from presidential authority. The president has legal authority within the executive branch over those organizations located in the Executive Office of the Presidency, classified as cabinet departments, or presidential agencies. Most of the organizations classified as independent agencies in table 5.1 are independent of presidential authority. Fortunately, from a presidential perspective, most, but by no means

all, of the traditional foreign affairs organizations are legally under the president's authority.

Adding to the complexity of the foreign policy bureaucracy is the *fading distinction between foreign and domestic policy bureaucracies.* Traditional national security bureaucracies were easy to identify, such as the State Department, the military, and the intelligence community. With the collapse of the foreign policy consensus behind containment during the 1960s and the growth of global interdependence, these distinctions have lost much of their meaning. U.S. foreign policy is now much more than just national security policy. It also involves policies in such areas as economics, immigration, the environment, transportation and communications, technology, and narcotics. As explained by Edward Morse, in *Foreign Policy and Interdependence,* the spread of technology, modernization, and global interdependence has led to the breakdown in the separation between foreign and domestic policy as well as between high and low politics.[2]

In fact, many of the agencies responsible for these areas of policy were generally considered domestically oriented in the past. Today these agencies have an important international dimension—an indication of the increasing complexity and "internationalization" of the bureaucracy over time. Raymond Hopkins was one of the earliest scholars to highlight the **internationalization of domestic bureaucracies** and the development of global networks of bureaucratic (personnel) interaction, especially in the "principal areas of food, energy, finance, communication, environment, economic growth, and the spread of technology."[3] This has contributed to the relative independence and autonomy of much of the bureaucracy from presidential authority.

As Edward Morse pointed out in the early 1970s, "Most of the departments and ministries of modern governments associated with predominantly domestic areas have some kind of international bureau. The proliferation of these international bureaus severely undercuts the ability of one foreign ministry or department to control the external policies of its government, thus severely restricting the coordination of foreign policies."[4] Such complexity, internationalization, and independence in the governmental bureaucracy has made the president's management task increasingly complicated and impossible.

BUREAUCRATIC HISTORICAL DEVELOPMENT

Two hundred years ago the U.S. government was tiny compared to what it is today; it was composed of the president, the vice president, a small personal staff, and four small departments: State, Treasury, War, and Justice. Although the federal bureaucracy has expanded in the last two centuries, most of the growth in the bureaucracy's size and complexity has occurred during the twentieth century.

Bureaucratic growth has taken place in three successive waves. The first major expansion of the federal bureaucracy resulted from the New Deal legislation of the 1930s under President Franklin Roosevelt; the second took place in national security and foreign affairs during World War II and the cold war under presidents Roosevelt, Harry Truman, and Dwight Eisenhower; and the last occurred with President Lyndon Johnson's Great Society programs of the 1960s.

The expansion of the bureaucracy came from government's responses to the urgency of events and the times. Government did not grow by design but in response to situations perceived to be so dire and widespread that only the federal government, as opposed to state and local governments (or private initiatives), had the capability to address them. New bureaucratic agencies with new organizational goals and missions were created to respond to new problems. Governmental bureaucracy and programs grew during the 1930s to respond to the economic woes of the Great Depression; the bureaucracy further increased during the 1940s and 1950s in response to the national security challenges posed by international fascism and communism; and it grew again during the 1960s to address the problems of poverty and inequality raised by the social movements and events of that decade.

A primary reason for lack of foresight and design in bureaucratic growth is that such growth can only occur if approved by Congress. Members of Congress were aware that creating new executive agencies would bolster presidential power in executive-legislative relations. Because of congressional reluctance to place new agencies under presidential authority, many of these agencies were created through political compromise in order to retain congressional influence in the executive branch. Furthermore, although the political will can often be found to create a new agency and new jobs, it rarely surfaces to eliminate an old, outdated agency and superfluous jobs. These political actions help to explain how bureaucratic growth occurs. Adding one bureaucratic layer on top of another, with differing degrees of autonomy given to different agencies, has created the bureaucratic complexity that makes it so difficult for presidents to act as chief executives.

With respect to the conduct of U.S. foreign policy, the foreign affairs bureaucracy was relatively small in the years before World War II. As Charles Maechling, Jr., has explained:

> Before World War II, the foreign policy decision apparatus—to the extent that it existed at all— consisted of the president and secretary of state; a handful of administration appointees in the Department of State and major embassies; the senior diplomats of a tiny but adequate Foreign Service; a few military and naval officers serving in important commands or as attaches; and a constellation of influential lawyers and bankers, involved in the Council of Foreign Relations and largely residing on the East Coast.[5]

The bureaucracy's tremendous expansion in foreign policy took place over two decades in response to two major conflicts, World War II and the cold war. The key law that was the basis for the permanent expansion of the foreign policy bureaucracy was the **National Security Act of 1947**. It was one of the most important acts ever passed by Congress and signed by the president, because it laid the foundation for the modern foreign policy bureaucracy. The act *restructured the national security process in three major areas:*

1. The military, by creating the National Military Establishment (forerunner to the Department of Defense), consisting of the secretary of defense, the Joint Chiefs of Staff, and the Departments of Army, Navy, and Air Force;
2. Intelligence, by creating the Central Intelligence Agency and the director of central intelligence; and
3. National security advice to the president, by creating the National Security Council.

The genesis of this restructuring was "the British War Cabinet and chiefs of staff committee system, later modified to conform to American notions of command responsibility and staff function."[6] The major intent behind the restructuring was to produce a more efficient national security process that would be more valuable to the president in his conduct of foreign policy. At first, during the early cold war years, the foreign policy bureaucracy was a major source of additional presidential power, for the president was chiefly responsible for influencing the early goals and missions of the new bureaucratic organizations in support of his foreign policies. However, the foreign policy bureaucracy soon became so large, so complex, and so entrenched that presidents have had to be increasingly concerned with management of the bureaucracy in order to maximize their ability to govern foreign policy.

The most recent expansion of the national security bureaucracy has come in response to the September 11, 2001, terrorist attacks. In addition to providing large budgetary increases for the military and the intelligence community, President Bush Jr. created the Office of Homeland Security by executive order to coordinate the government's counterterrorist efforts. In 2002 President Bush decided to ask Congress to turn the office into a full-fledged Department of Homeland Security in order to reorganize numerous executive branch agencies involved in counterterrorism under the new department and give it greater stature to help coordinate and lead the counterterrorism effort. As is discussed in greater depth in chapter 8, on the intelligence community, members of Congress agreed to the new department, but it does not fully reflect President Bush's wishes. Much of the intelligence community, especially the FBI and the CIA, will remain untouched, and many relevant agencies will remain outside the new cabinet agency. Therefore, even though establishment of an Office, and then Department, of Homeland Security might bring some improvement in cooperation, decentralization and coordination problems will continue to prevail in the government's war on terrorism, reinforcing the importance of presidential management of the foreign policy bureaucracy as a critical source of presidential power in the conduct of U.S. foreign policy.

PRESIDENTIAL MANAGEMENT

Given that the bureaucracy has become so large and complex, how can a president manage the bureaucracy and make it work for him? *Three sets of presidential*

choices are vital in determining the president's ability to manage the foreign policy bureaucracy. They involve: (1) The president's foreign policy orientation, agenda, and level of involvement; (2) The appointment of executive branch personnel; and (3) The organization of the foreign policy–making process.[7]

These choices must be made early and are so important that the candidate who has been newly elected in November will have made many of these decisions even before he officially assumes office in January. The three-month **presidential transition period** is when the president-elect determines his agenda, the personnel he will appoint to work for him, and how the various foreign policy makers and organizations throughout the executive branch will interact. These decisions are critical if a president wants to enter office ready to exercise power and govern, poised to take advantage of the honeymoon period and early optimism that surrounds the start of a new administration.[8]

THE PRESIDENT'S ORIENTATION, AGENDA, AND LEVEL OF INVOLVEMENT

The president's beliefs and worldview set the general direction and foreign policy orientation for the administration. Different presidents have different foreign policy orientations and, consequently, establish different policy agendas as to what issues and policies should receive priority and attention. The foreign policy orientations and agendas of successive presidents, especially since World War II, have been briefly described in chapter 2 (on the history of U.S. foreign relations) and chapter 4 (on presidential governance of foreign policy).

Presidents try to set goals and promote policies that reflect their foreign policy orientation and agenda. This is critical because the role of the bureaucracy is too important to be left to chance; a president must be attentive to and actively involved in the bureaucracy's operations so as to ensure that U.S. foreign policy during his administration accords with his preferences. The more a president is attentive to and involved in what goes on throughout the executive branch, the more likely he will influence and manage the bureaucracy in accordance with a foreign policy orientation and agenda of his choosing.

Because the bureaucracy is so large and complex, a president must be selective as to the issues most important to him and the agenda he decides to promote, given the time and information constraints he faces. He must understand that, while he can never gain complete mastery over the entire bureaucracy, the bureaucracy will be most responsive to those issues and agenda items that he most prizes and is most active in promoting. General policy reviews, especially at the beginning of a new administration; involvement in the policymaking process; and presidential speeches offer unique opportunities for the president to gain control over the bureaucracy and foreign policy.

But ultimately, the president must rely on others to assist him in governing, in exercising presidential leadership, and in managing the bureaucracy. Hence, presidential staff and advisers, and the policymaking process, are absolutely critical in affecting the bureaucracy's response to the president's orientation and agenda.

APPOINTMENT OF STAFF AND ADVISERS

To this point we have emphasized what the president can do as an "individual" through his use of presidential power and governance, leadership, and management of the bureaucracy. However, the president is not alone and is dependent on others in efforts to manage the bureaucracy and govern. This is why the term **presidency** has been used in this book to refer to the institution or office of the presidency, composed of the president and other individuals and organizations who represent, work for, and act in the president's name. Therefore, presidential choices about who to appoint for his staff and advisers are quite critical.

In deciding who will serve in his administration, the president must make *three general sets of appointments:*

1. Personal presidential staff;
2. Major policy advisers; and
3. High-level officials responsible for other cabinet departments and executive agencies.

The president must rely on these people to manage the bureaucracy and exercise presidential leadership and power. Their performance affects his ability to govern for-

eign policy. Presidential dependence on appointees also means that with each new president, there will be considerable change in top-level personnel, most of which come from outside the executive branch—a uniquely American system of governmental management.

As Bill Quandt has found regarding U.S. foreign policy, especially towards the Middle East, the last seven presidents—from Johnson to Clinton—to occupy the Oval Office before George W. Bush have

appointed 10 Secretaries of State, 9 Directors of Central Intelligence, 11 Secretaries of Defense, and 12 national security advisers. During this same period 9 different Assistant Secretaries for Near Eastern and South Asian Affairs have served, as have 9 directors of the Middle East office of the National Security Council. On average, then, the top personnel in charge of Middle East policy changes about every three or four years.[9]

Franklin Roosevelt was the first modern president to expand his personal staff by creating the **Executive Office of the Presidency (EOP)** as a means to manage and cope with a bureaucracy that was rapidly growing in size and complexity beyond the president's control. Today, the EOP contains the people and organizations that a president tends to rely on most in managing the bureaucracy and governing: the White House Office (WHO), Office of Management and Budget (OMB), National Security Council (NSC), and National Economic Council (NEC) (see **figure 5.1**).

The president's personal staff works directly for him in such places as the **White House Office (WHO).** These are the people who act as the eyes and ears of the president and who are preoccupied with protecting and promoting his professional reputation, public prestige, and presidential choices. They are responsible for the president's daily activities and help him to prepare for public appearances. Given their proximity and importance to the presidency, they have also become more involved in the making of U.S. foreign policy.[10]

The **chief of staff** is the most significant of the president's personal staff and interacts with the president more frequently than anyone else. The chief of staff is responsible for the president's daily schedule and oversees the rest of the White House staff. This is a very consequential position because the chief of staff

FIGURE **5.1**
THE EXECUTIVE BRANCH

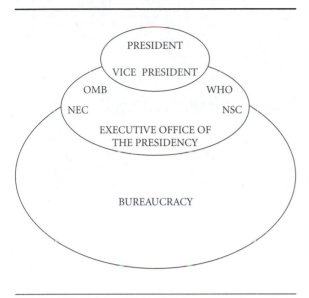

These officials are responsible for the most important foreign policy organizations within the executive branch: the National Security Council, the Department of State, the Department of Defense, the Central Intelligence Agency, the National Economic Council, and the Department of the Treasury. They are the people with whom the president interacts most on a daily basis in making foreign policy, with the national economic adviser and secretary of the treasury most instrumental for foreign economic policy and the other officials more consequential in the national security area.

The president also appoints hundreds of other high-level officials to fill positions throughout the executive branch. *For most agencies, he appoints the head or director and the positions at the next three or four hierarchical levels* within the agency. In the State Department, the president has the authority to make appointments at the five highest hierarchical levels: the secretary of state, deputy secretary of state, undersecretaries of state, assistant secretaries of state, and deputy assistant secretaries of state. These appointments do not guarantee presidential control, as we will see in greater depth in the next few chapters, for the bureaucracy has a life of its own and often "captures" appointees to reflect bureaucratic interests. Yet these appointments are one of the key means available for a president to manage and control as much of the bureaucracy as possible in support of his agenda and worldview.[11]

Certain *selection criteria* tend to influence presidential appointments. Presidents try to appoint people who are knowledgeable and who share their ideological outlook and worldview. They also select people with whom they are comfortable and whom they believe to be loyal. Most members of the White House staff, for example, usually consist of people with whom the president has grown familiar and comfortable, often recruited from his campaign team. Quite commonly the chief of staff, and maybe one or two others on the White House staff, are the president's close personal friends and, consequently, may also act as trusted policy advisers as well. The people during the campaign who acted as his advisers (for both domestic and foreign policy), briefed him, and wrote his foreign policy speeches often are appointed to key positions and become major policy advisers. For other high-level officials, the president must rely on his personal staff for

usually acts as the intermediary between the president and all staff and advisers who interact with him. Some of the other important White House staff would include positions such as chief political strategist, communications director, press secretary, and White House counsel. Another position that has become increasingly valuable to presidents of late is that of vice president (see **essay 5.1** on transforming the vice presidency and the roles of Al Gore and Dick Cheney).

The president must also decide who will occupy major policy positions in the U.S. government and act as his policy advisers. Of the many appointments a president makes, *six key foreign policy appointments stand out:*

1. Special assistant to the president for national security affairs (better known as the national security adviser or NSC adviser);
2. Secretary of state;
3. Secretary of defense;
4. Director of central intelligence;
5. Special assistant to the president for economic affairs (called the national economic adviser or NEC adviser); and
6. Secretary of the treasury.

ESSAY 5.1
TRANSFORMING THE VICE PRESIDENCY

THE PROMINENT ROLES OF AL GORE
AND DICK CHENEY

The office of the **vice president** has been in transition over the last two decades. Throughout much of American history, the vice president has been a relatively insignificant player in the policymaking process, unless the president died or resigned (which since World War II has been responsible for Harry Truman, Lyndon Johnson, and Gerald Ford becoming president). It also has been an important stepping stone for eventually gaining the party's nomination to run for president (after the president's term of office ended). Nevertheless, people have been chosen as vice president predominantly for political purposes, such as to "balance" the ticket within the party for the upcoming presidential election (to win over voters of certain geographical areas or ideological orientations). Not being a trusted adviser or friend, the vice president was usually relegated to symbolic and unimportant activities (such as to preside over the Senate as stipulated in the Constitution). Thomas Marshall, vice president under Woodrow Wilson, described the job by saying, "The only business of the vice president is to ring the White House bell every morning and ask what is the state of health of the president."

This began to change in the late 1970s under President Jimmy Carter, who turned increasingly to Vice President Walter Mondale for counsel and political support. The importance of the role of the vice president continued to increase, though more selectively, with George H. Bush under President Ronald Reagan and Dan Quayle under President Bush Sr. However, with the election of Bill Clinton and then George W. Bush as president and Al Gore and then Dick Cheney as vice president, the office of the vice president has become a much enhanced position of power and respect.

Born March 31, 1948, in Carthage, Tennessee, Albert Gore, Jr., was the son of a U.S. senator. A member of the baby boom generation, **Al Gore** graduated from Harvard in 1969, served in the army during the Vietnam War as a journalist, and was eventually elected to the U.S. House and then the Senate from the state of Tennessee, following in his father's footsteps. Unlike past running mates, Gore wasn't asked to be the vice presidential candidate in 1992 by Clinton merely for the sake of party balance. Gore, who is in the same age group and born in the same geographic region as Clinton, was chosen more because he made a reputation for himself as a deep thinker committed to several issues and as a politically savvy individual who seemed to be above politics.

Within Clinton's White House, Gore became an active participant and trusted adviser, including in the area of national security affairs—an area that Gore has dealt with for many years and in which Clinton was much more of a novice. Perhaps Gore's most defining issue was his commitment to the environment. He also pushed to "reinvent government" by lessening red tape and making governmental bodies more efficient. Gore was one of the first vice presidents to effectively promote high-profile national issues.

Dick Cheney may be an even more powerful vice president under President Bush Jr., given Cheney's vast experience and contacts. Born in Nebraska in 1941, Cheney grew up in Casper, Wyoming, and then headed east to attend Yale University before returning to Wyoming to earn a political science graduate degree at the University of Wyoming in 1965. Cheney took his first government job in the Nixon administration as a special assistant to Donald Rumsfeld, who was then director of the Office of Economic Opportunity. In August 1974, after President Nixon resigned from office, Rumsfeld was asked to join the White House staff as an assistant to President Gerald Ford, and Cheney moved with Rumsfeld. From 1975 to 1977 Dick Cheney was President Ford's chief of staff.

After Ford's defeat to Jimmy Carter in 1976, Cheney successfully ran for office as congressman from Wyoming in 1978. He left Congress in March 1989, when President Bush Sr. asked him to be secretary of defense, after John Tower, Bush's first choice for the position, was rejected by the Senate. Although Cheney never served in the Vietnam War (receiving deferments), he became part of President Bush Sr.'s inner circle in the making of U.S. national security policy and in prosecuting the Persian Gulf War. After Bush Sr.'s defeat to Bill Clinton in 1992, Cheney moved into private business, becoming chief executive of Halliburton—the largest oil-drilling, engineering, and construction services firm in the world.

Like Gore, Dick Cheney was selected as the Republican vice presidential candidate to compliment George Bush Jr., given his younger age and limited foreign policy background. Vice President Cheney joined a foreign policy team of officials who he had considerable experience with under former presidents, especially Secretary of Defense Donald Rumsfeld and Secretary of State Colin Powell.

Given President Bush Jr.'s' lack of foreign policy experience and expertise, it appears that Vice President Cheney has become a major foreign policy player and confidant to the president. Although he may be just one major official among equals, some analysts believe that, given his previous experience and his personal relationship with and close proximity to the president, Cheney may be the most prominent foreign policy voice within the Bush Jr. administration. He has clearly been a very visible and outspoken vice president, especially when it comes to national security policy. In any event, Dick Cheney and Al Gore serve as prominent illustrations of

the increasing importance of the vice presidency—which includes the vice president and his personal staff.

SOURCES: Howard Fineman, "Gore's World," *Newsweek* (December 23, 1996), pp. 22–25; Paul Kengor, *Wreath Layer or Policy Player: The Vice President's Role in Foreign Policy* (Lexington, Mass.: Lexington Books, 2002); Paul C. Light, *Vice Presidential Power: Advice and Influence in the White House* (Baltimore: Johns Hopkins University Press, 1984); Eric Schmitt, "For Cheney, A Low Profile and a Major Role," *New York Times* (October 11, 2001); Elaine Sciolino and Todd S. Purdum, "Al Gore, One Vice President Who Is Eluding the Shadows," *New York Times* (February 19, 1995), pp. 1, 32; Barbara Slavin and Susan Page, "Cheney Rewrites Roles in Foreign Policy, *USA Today* (July 29, 2002).

information and recommendations (see **essay 5.2** on the selection and background of major presidential staff and advisers, as well as the importance of their offices' location in proximity to the president).

Time also affects these decisions and presidential management, for many are made by the president-elect during the brief transition period. And there is no guarantee that people will accept when asked—President Clinton repeatedly struggled to find a director of central intelligence. All of these factors affect the president's success in selecting competent bureaucratic managers to carry out his agenda.

Presidential management in the Bush Sr. administration, for example, was hindered by the slow rate of presidential appointments. Five months after President Bush took office, 80 percent of the senior positions in

government departments and agencies remained unfilled, leaving most of the bureaucracy to be run and managed by President Reagan's appointees. President Clinton's and President Bush Jr.'s rate of appointments were also slow.[12]

Another important issue is senatorial approval. Appointments to staff agencies within the Executive Office of the Presidency, such as the White House Office and the National Security Council, do not require Senate approval. From a constitutional perspective, these personnel and agencies are considered the president's personal staff. Most other high-level appointments in the executive branch require the **advice and consent** of the Senate. A president tries to nominate people who will gain Senate approval as soon as possible, thereby getting his people in position to help him manage the bureaucracy.

ESSAY 5.2
MAJOR PRESIDENTIAL STAFF AND FOREIGN POLICY ADVISERS

IMPORTANCE OF BACKGROUND AND LOCATION

The American system of governmental management is unique among modern industrialized societies. With each new president, there is considerable change in top-level personnel throughout the executive branch, and there is usually turnover in major staff and advisers during a president's term of office, especially after reelection. On the one hand, this gives the president the opportunity to better control and manage the executive branch. On the other hand, the lack of stability and expertise at the top can also be a major disadvantage as well, especially in the conduct of foreign policy.

Clearly, it is important to understand how a president selects his staff and advisers, and where they tend to come from. Some may be his friends or individuals he has known; many will be new to him. Also, most major appointments tend to consist of white males (though this is no longer exclusively the case) who are highly educated and *come from prominent institutions throughout the country, especially the following professions:*

1. Law
2. Business
3. Politics and government
4. Academia and research institutes

President Clinton's major staff members and advisers—probably the most diverse in American history—were drawn primarily from Arkansas and the campaign team. The vast majority of his major advisers and officials possessed law degrees or doctorates, many from Harvard, Yale, or Georgetown—the schools attended by Clinton and Vice President Gore. There were at least fifteen Rhodes scholars, like Clinton, in the administration. As one analyst stated, "It is education, more than birth, wealth, or previous experience in government, that defines the people Mr. Clinton has chosen to serve with him."[A] But education, experience, and connections made by crossing Clinton's career path also figured, for "they all seem[ed] to know each other. . . . Friendships formed at elite colleges and law schools have been sustained through an archipelago of think tanks, foundations, councils, and associations."[B]

President Bush Jr.'s major staff and advisers were selected in a fashion similar to Clinton's. Many came from Texas and/or worked for him while he was governor of Texas and then on the presidential campaign team. President Bush also appointed and surrounded himself with foreign policy advisers who previously worked for his father, George H. Bush, as president and also have worked for the Ford and Reagan administrations, including Dick Cheney, Donald Rumsfeld, Colin Powell, Condoleezza Rice, and Larry Lindsey (see **table 5.2** for President Bush Jr.'s major staff and foreign policy advisers).

The major staff and advisers to the president tend to get, and often fight for, the largest, nicest, most promi-

A. Jack H. Watson, Jr. "The Clinton White House," *Presidential Studies Quarterly* 23 (1993): 433.

B. David Ignatius, "The Curse of the Merit Class," *Washington Post* (February 27, 1994), p. C1.

TABLE **5.2**
PRESIDENT BUSH JR.'S MAJOR STAFF AND FOREIGN POLICY ADVISERS, 2001

POSITION	NAME	BACKGROUND
VICE PRESIDENT	Richard "Dick" Cheney	Politics, government, and business
CHIEF OF STAFF	Andrew Card	Campaign team, politics, business, family friend
SENIOR ADVISER AND ASSISTANT TO THE PRESIDENT	Karl Rove	Campaign team and Texas public affairs
WHITE HOUSE COUNSELOR	Karen Hughes	Campaign team, Texas politics, communications, close personal friend
PRESS SECRETARY	Ari Fleischer	Politics
NATIONAL SECURITY ADVISER	Condoleezza Rice	Campaign team, academia, and government
NATIONAL ECONOMIC ADVISER	Larry Lindsey	Campaign team, government, and Bush family friend
SECRETARY OF STATE	Colin Powell	Military and government
SECRETARY OF DEFENSE	Donald Henry Rumsfeld	Politics and government
CHAIRMAN OF JOINT CHIEFS OF STAFF	Richard Myers	Military
DIRECTOR OF CENTRAL INTELLIGENCE	George Tenet	Government
SECRETARY OF THE TREASURY	Paul O'Neill	Business and government

FIGURE 5.2
WHITE HOUSE STAFF AND OFFICES IN THE WEST WING, 2001

FIRST FLOOR:
1. **President Bush**
2. **Linda Gambatesa**, director, Oval Office operations
3. **Ashley Estes**, personal secretary to the president
4. **Ari Fleischer**, press secretary
5. **Jennifer Millerwise**, assistant press secretary
6. **Anne Womack**, assistant press secretary
7. **Steve Hadley**, deputy national security adviser
8. **Condoleeza Rice**, national security adviser
9. **Dick Cheney**, vice president
10. **Andrew H. Card**, chief of staff
11. **Joshua Bolten**, deputy chief of staff (policy)
12. **Joseph Hagin**, deputy chief of staff (operations)

SECOND FLOOR:
13. **Margaret La Montagne**, domestic policy adviser
14. **Lawrence Lindsey**, economic policy adviser
15. **Marc Sumerlin**, deputy economic adviser
16. **Karen Hughes**, counselor
17. **Margaret Tutwiler**, adviser to the president and special consultant for communications
18. **Nicholas E. Calio**, legislative affairs director
19. **Dan Bartlett**, deputy to the counselor
20. **David Hobbs**, legislative affairs deputy (House)
    Ziad Ojakli, legislative affairs deputy (Senate)
21. **Clay Johnson**, presidential personnel
22. **Timothy E. Flanigan**, deputy counsel
23. **Alberto R. Gonzalez**, counsel
24. Deputy to senior adviser
25. **Karl Rove**, senior adviser
26. **John Bridgeland**, deputy domestic policy adviser

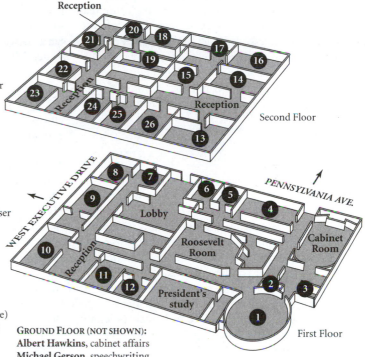

GROUND FLOOR (NOT SHOWN):
Albert Hawkins, cabinet affairs
Michael Gerson, speechwriting
Harriet Miers, staff secretary
Hector F. Irastorza Jr., management & administration
Brad Blakeman, appointments & scheduling
GROUND FLOOR LOWER PRESS OFFICE:
Claire Buchan, deputy press secretary
Scott McClellan, deputy press secretary

SOURCE: National Journal (January 27, 2001), p. 248. Staff information from the White House West Wing floor plan from *Time* magazine.

nent, and closest offices to the president within the White House. Figure 5.2 shows the location of White House staff and offices in the West Wing at the beginning of President Bush Jr.'s presidency. Notice the location of the offices of the most prominent personal staff and foreign policy advisers to the president listed in Table 5.2. Naturally, cabinet secretaries and the chair of the JCS have the most prominent offices within their main departmental buildings separate from the White House.

SOURCES: Richard Barnet, *Roots of War: Men and Institutions Behind U.S. Foreign Policy* (New York: Penguin, 1972); David Ignatius, "The Curse of the Merit Class," *Washington Post* (February 27, 1994); Charles Maechling, Jr., "Foreign Policy-Makers: The Weakest Link?" *Virginia Quarterly Review* 52 (winter 1976): 1–23.

Usually a president's nomination to a governmental position eventually gains Senate approval. However, every now and then a presidential appointment can become controversial. President Clinton suffered politically early on from some ill-fated appointments, such as Zoe Baird's nomination as head of the Justice Department (which was withdrawn upon disclosure that she did not pay taxes for her home domestic help). And following his successful reelection in 1996, President Clinton nominated his national security adviser, Anthony Lake, to be director of central intelligence only to see the Senate confirmation hearings become controversial and politicized, leading to Lake's withdrawal.

ORGANIZING THE POLICYMAKING PROCESS

The president must decide not only who will staff his administration but how they will interact so that he is kept informed and able to make decisions and implement them according to his wishes. The president cannot assume when he takes office that the policymaking system in place will automatically do these things for him, allowing him to manage the bureaucracy. On the contrary, if a president wants to manage the bureaucracy, as opposed to responding to bureaucratic momentum, he must initiate a policy process that responds to his demands.

Important questions about how to organize the policymaking process that a president must address include whether the process should be:

1. White House centered, State Department centered, or mixed/ad hoc?
2. Centralized or decentralized?
3. Open or closed to staff and advisers?

The president must decide whether to rely on a lead agency to be responsible for coordinating the foreign policy process; whether to have only a few individuals who are allowed to act in the president's name responsible for the overall conduct of foreign policy or to have power more decentralized throughout the foreign policy bureaucracy; and what level of access to grant different policymaking officials in the process, especially at the presidential level.

Decisions about these issues determine how the foreign policy–making process will operate. These are decisions that presidents-elect must make before they enter office. If the president, or his personal staff, is reluctant to be involved in influencing the policymaking process, answers will soon develop by fait accompli without presidential input, thereby weakening the president's ability to manage the foreign policy bureaucracy. As Richard Neustadt in *Presidential Power* would say, unless the president is willing and able to make hard choices, he is more likely to act as a clerk than a leader. These are crucial decisions, for how the policy process operates determines the extent to which information and policy alternatives flow to the president, whether the bureaucracy is responsive to his agenda, and whether policies are implemented in accordance with his decisions.

It is not unusual for presidents to enter office claiming that they will rely on **cabinet government** as their principal means of managing the bureaucracy. This means that the president plans to rely heavily on his cabinet secretaries and departments for information and advice. Under cabinet government, the president meets periodically with all members of his cabinet to discuss various issues and arrive at policy decisions. Such a policymaking process tends to be highly decentralized and open, often allowing the State Department to act as the lead agency responsible for coordinating the conduct of U.S. foreign policy. In this scenario, the secretary of state is the principal spokesperson for U.S. foreign policy, acting as the major adviser to the president, and the State Department is responsible for coordinating the policy process within the rest of the foreign policy bureaucracy.

Cabinet government and a **State Department–centered system** constitute the popular perception of presidential power and executive branch operation: The president meets with all of his major advisers around a big table and arrives at policy decisions. Unfortunately, a president who attempts to operate this way quickly discovers that the bureaucracy, including the cabinet departments and many of the cabinet secretaries whom he appointed himself, are not very responsive to him. Presidents cannot afford to assume that, simply because they occupy the Oval Office, the bureaucracy will respond to them—it is too big, complex, and set in its ways.

Despite the early optimism that may exist about cabinet government, a strong State Department, and a decentralized and open policy process, presidents quickly learn that this is not the way to manage effectively the foreign policy bureaucracy and maximize presidential power. In fact, *three general patterns have prevailed in the foreign policy process* for most presidents since World War II:

1. Presidents tend to rely on a White House–centered system.
2. The policymaking process tends to become more centralized with time.
3. The level of participation in the process tends to narrow and close over time.

Presidents quickly turn to relying on those they trust most, who tend to be the White House staff and agencies within the Executive Office of the Presidency. Within a short time, the president usually begins to rely on a small number of advisers. This occurs because of time constraints on the president and increasing familiarity among the president and his advisers. Hence, the predominance of a **White House–centered system.**

At first, the president does not know many of his appointees well. Then, as the president begins to interact with his advisers, he begins to learn more about their policy views, personalities, and operating styles and makes judgments about the value of their advice, trust, and friendship. With time the president tends to become more selective as to whom he interacts with and relies on for advice. This often tends to "close" the policymaking process and narrow the range of information and opinions that come before the president, because the presidency is such an "awesome office . . . where no one really stands up to the president, where there is no equality, where no one tells the president he is wrong." In other words, inevitably the office "tends by its nature to inhibit dissent and opposition."[13]

In managing the foreign policy–making process, presidents have increasingly relied on the national security adviser and the National Security Council. Unlike much of the established and entrenched bureaucracy, including the Department of State and the Department of Defense, members of the White House Office and the National Security Council are most responsive to the president. They lack an independent base of power, working only for him and under his complete authority. Bureaucratic autonomy also tends to promote a more centralized process that limits presidential access to those policymakers in whom the

president has greatest confidence and with whom he is most comfortable.

To sum up, the key to presidential management of the foreign policy bureaucracy involves the choices the president makes concerning his foreign policy orientation and personal agenda, his level of involvement, his executive-level appointments, and the dynamics of the policymaking process. These presidential choices determine the extent to which the president will manage the bureaucracy and make it responsive to him. However, what works for one president may not work for others. *These presidential choices are very much a function of a president's personal characteristics*—his beliefs, personality, and operating style.[14]

Over the years there have been numerous commissions created and studies conducted that have called for governmental reform and a restructuring of the foreign policy process. Some scholars once maintained that a State Department–centered foreign policy system was preferable.[15] However, it has become increasingly understood that what counts is what the president prefers and finds most comfortable given his orientation and personality. Therefore, it is not surprising that presidential management of foreign policy tends to revolve around a White House–centered system that becomes more centralized and closed over time, for it is most responsive to presidents and their personal characteristics. To better understand presidential management of the foreign policy bureaucracy and the operations of a White House–centered system, especially in the area of national security, we must examine the National Security Council in some detail and the process by which it operates.

THE NATIONAL SECURITY COUNCIL

The **National Security Council (NSC),** within the Executive Office of the Presidency, is the key organization the president has relied on since World War II to manage the foreign policy bureaucracy. The national security adviser usually is the single most important appointment the president makes. He is often the most important policy adviser to the president and is responsible for coordinating the foreign policy–making process within the executive branch. Therefore, one cannot really understand how the president manages

American foreign policy unless one understands the operations of the National Security Council, especially its origins and evolution and the actual process under different presidents.[16]

ORIGINS

As discussed above, the National Security Council came into existence in 1947 with the passage of the National Security Act, which restructured the policy process in the areas of defense, intelligence, and national security advice to the president. The NSC was *created to serve three principal functions:*

1. Advise the president,
2. Act as a vehicle for long-range planning, and
3. Promote the coordination and integration of the national security process.

The NSC was originally intended to be the major group to provide foreign policy advice to the president.

The *structure of the National Security Council consisted of two elements:*

1. A formal decisionmaking council composed of high-level foreign policy officials, and
2. A small support staff headed by an executive secretary.

The "original statutory members" of the NSC included the president, secretary of state, secretary of defense, secretary of the Army, secretary of the Navy, secretary of the Air Force, and the chairman of the National Security Resources Board (responsible for emergency planning and civil defense). A small staff, headed by a civilian executive secretary, provided support for the formal council advisory meetings, helped coordinate the policy process, and conducted long-range planning.

The purpose of the National Security Act was to rationalize the national security process and force the president to be more responsive to formal lines of authority in the foreign policy bureaucracy, especially within the military. The act's formulation and passage was a response to what many people, in both Congress and the executive branch, thought was a chaotic national security policy–making process during World War II. Within months of the attack on Pearl Harbor, the United States was transformed from an officially neutral country with a tiny foreign policy bureaucracy to a participant in the war with a rapidly growing na-

tional security bureaucracy. The expansion of U.S. armed forces, and the bureaucracy to support and implement the use of troops in both theaters of the war, was so massive and so rapid that the policy process within the military became chaotic.

Not only was the U.S. government frustrated in administering a large wartime bureaucracy, but many people were unhappy with President **Roosevelt's management style.** Roosevelt avoided formal channels of communication and instead relied on an informal, ad hoc managerial style. He oversaw the bureaucracy and made policy by relying on a variety of individuals of different ranks located throughout the bureaucracy. This managerial style served Roosevelt well as president, but displeased many high-level officials, especially within the military, whom Roosevelt bypassed in the formal chain of command. This concern with a chaotic process and informal managerial style was reinforced by the rise to the presidency of Harry Truman, a man who lacked considerable knowledge and experience in foreign policy.

These perceptions provided the original incentive behind the National Security Act of 1947. The desire to provide the U.S. government with a policymaking apparatus that would promote greater efficiency and preparedness in the national security process accounts for the NSC's advice, long-term planning, and coordination functions. At the same time, to force the president to comply with a more formal process and adhere to the chain of command, the membership of the NSC was set by law and composed largely of members of the newly created National Military Establishment (forerunner to the Department of Defense). Modeled after the British war cabinet, it was a means of imposing a cabinet government on the president when national security decisions were involved. The only legal flexibility that the original act gave the president was the ability to invite officials to NSC meetings in addition to the statutory members.[17]

CHANGING PATTERNS IN THE NSC

Presidents have found the NSC, as originally designed, to be both a potentially useful tool for and a source of frustration in managing foreign policy. It should not be surprising to learn that presidents have used those aspects of the NSC they have found useful while ignoring or circumventing those aspects they have found constraining—using the NSC in ways that were unintended by those who drafted the 1947 act. *Two major changes to the original NSC under postwar presidents are evident:*

1. Providing policy advice and coordinating the policy process for the president have become the NSC's two major functions, while long-term planning has become unimportant.
2. The NSC staff (and the NSC adviser) has become more significant over time, while the National Security Council as a decisionmaking body has declined in importance.

Advising the president and coordinating the foreign policy machinery remain the NSC's two major functions. However, the third function, **long-term planning,** has almost never been implemented. The one possible exception involved the Truman administration and the development of **NSC-68.** National Security Council memorandum no. 68 was a staff document approved by the president in 1950. It represented a concerted effort by members of the NSC staff to predict U.S.-Soviet relations into the 1950s and recommend U.S. foreign policy alternatives for presidential consideration. NSC-68 provided the official justification of the policy of global containment of Soviet communism and, through the institutionalization of this policy due to the Korean War, influenced the foreign policies of subsequent administrations during the cold war.

The National Security Council has not developed any important long-term planning since NSC-68. This may not serve the country's best interests, for as the United States enters the twenty-first century, the lack of a long-term strategy may hamper the conduct of U.S. foreign policy. The absence of long-term planning, however, is not unique to the NSC nor difficult to understand. The NSC staff is small compared to other governmental organizations and incredibly overworked. The staff responds to the needs of the national security adviser and the president, who are primarily occupied with responding to immediate events and day-to-day governing. Consequently, there is little time, interest, or reward involved in long-term planning.

Although the National Security Council has grown in significance for the president, the National Security Act legally defined whom the president must accept as his major foreign advisers. Clearly, this is not acceptable to most presidents. If a president wants to exercise

power, as opposed to being a clerk, he must be allowed to determine whom he will rely on for foreign policy advice. Changes in the law have been made reflecting this concern—the current statutory members of the council are the president, vice president, national security adviser, secretary of state, secretary of defense, and chair of the Joint Chiefs of Staff. The president can invite other individuals to participate as he sees fit. Very simply, presidents will interact with those policymakers they trust the most and will avoid officials with whom they have policy disagreements or personality conflicts. The president is the key figure in affecting the dynamics of the policy process, at least at the presidential level, and he will manage the bureaucracy in ways that are consistent with his operating style.

Each president has used the NSC as it has suited him. This has ultimately resulted in the decline of the council's significance as a formal decisionmaking body. Therefore, the foreign policy process has gradually become White House centered as the president has increasingly relied on the national security adviser and the NSC staff to manage the process and provide him with an independent source of information and advice (see **table 5.3** for a list of national security advisers and their backgrounds).

PRESIDENTIAL MANAGEMENT STYLES AND THE ROLE OF THE NSC

Presidential management styles have differed with each president and have evolved over time. According to I. M. Destler, Leslie H. Gelb, and Anthony Lake, in *Our Own Worst Enemy: The Unmaking of American Foreign Policy,* there have been *three major stages in the evolution of the National Security Council* and the foreign policy process at the presidential level: (1) Presidents Truman and Eisenhower used the NSC Council as an advisory body with a staff to support their reliance on cabinet secretaries and their departments. (2) Under presidents Kennedy and Johnson, the NSC Council was eclipsed, and the traditional role of the cabinet, especially the State Department, was challenged by the rise of the national security adviser and staff. (3) Beginning with President Nixon, the national security adviser and staff became ascendant in the policymaking process.[18]

TABLE **5.3**
NATIONAL SECURITY ADVISERS

	YEAR APPOINTED	PRESIDENT	BACKGROUND
Sidney W. Souers	1947	Truman	Business and Navy
James S. Lay, Jr.	1950	Truman	Business and Army
Robert Cutler	1953	Eisenhower	Law and Army
Dillon Anderson	1955	Eisenhower	Law and Army
William Jackson	1953	Eisenhower	Law, business, and Army
Robert Cutler	1957	Eisenhower	Law and Army
Gordon Gray	1958	Eisenhower	Law and Army
McGeorge Bundy	1961	Johnson	Law, Army, and journalism
Walt W. Rostow	1966	Johnson	Academia
Henry A. Kissinger	1969	Nixon	Academia and government
Brent Scowcroft	1975	Ford	Academia and Army
Zbigniew Brzezinski	1977	Carter	Academia
Richard V. Allen	1981	Reagan	Academia and government
William P. Clark	1982	Reagan	Law
Robert C. McFarlane	1983	Reagan	Army and government
John M. Poindexter	1985	Reagan	Navy
Frank C. Carlucci	1987	Reagan	Business and government
Colin L. Powell	1987	Reagan	Army
Brent Scowcroft	1989	Bush Sr.	Army and academia
Anthony Lake	1993	Clinton	Academia and government
Samuel "Sandy" Berger	1997	Clinton	Law and government
Condoleezza Rice	2001	Bush Jr.	Academia and government

THE EARLY NSC AS ADVISORY BODY

During the 1950s, the National Security Council was used as an advisory body to assist the president in making foreign policy. This worked well with the management styles of presidents Truman and Eisenhower, who relied on strong cabinet officers, such as the secretary of state, for information and advice. Even though the NSC provided information and advice to the president, the secretary of state remained the chief foreign policy spokesperson and adviser to the president, and the State Department often acted as the lead organization in formulating and implementing foreign policy.

Truman's Management Style. Harry Truman was president during the difficult time between the end of World War II and the escalation of the cold war. Truman lacked the international experience and expertise requisite to deal with the unfolding transition in America's global role. As president, he relied on the secretary of state, Dean Acheson, and the secretary of defense, General George C. Marshall, for counsel and to carry out presidential policy. Along with his White House presidential counselor, Clark Clifford, an informal advisory process developed between President Truman and these officials.

Truman initially was hesitant to compromise his independence by relying on the NSC, but following the North Korean attack on South Korea in 1950, it became a regular forum for discussion. The NSC staff was kept very small, consisting of roughly twenty people under an executive director who organized and provided support for the council meetings. As the council's use as an advisory body increased, President Truman came to rely on two major channels for information and advice: the formal advisory process, through use of the council, and an informal process of personal interaction between the president and his closest advisers.

Eisenhower's Management Style. Under President Eisenhower, the U.S. policy of global containment became institutionalized through the expanded national security bureaucracy. Eisenhower was more comfortable utilizing the NSC, for he was accustomed to such formal mechanisms in the military and it fit well with his particular style. The National Security Council was relied upon heavily as an advisory body to President Eisenhower. And the position of **special assistant to the president for national security affairs** (referred to as the **national security adviser**) was created to supervise the staff.

In eight years, the NSC held 346 meetings, roughly one each week, as compared to 128 meetings in over five years under President Truman. Most of the meetings lasted two and a half hours, with President Eisenhower usually presiding.[19] Two interagency committees, both managed by the national security adviser, were created to assist in the preparation of the formal meetings and to oversee policy implementation. The NSC staff tripled in size and became the major vehicle for coordinating the information and advice provided to the president by the national security departments and agencies.

President Eisenhower did not rely solely on the formal NSC process for information and advice. John Foster Dulles, the secretary of state, was the major foreign policy spokesperson throughout the administration and acted as a major adviser to the president.

Furthermore, because the National Security Council process tended to be slow and cumbersome, President Eisenhower also relied on more informal channels of interaction. When it came to fast-moving developments and crises, President Eisenhower, as President Truman had before him and presidents would after him, arrived at policy decisions after informally consulting the most trusted members of his administration.

THE RISE OF THE NSC ADVISER AND STAFF

Changes during the Eisenhower administration set the stage for the decline of the NSC as a formal advisory body and the rise of the national security adviser and staff as independent sources of information and advice for the president. It was not, however, until the Kennedy administration that the national security adviser and staff occupied these new roles, eclipsing the role of the National Security Council and challenging traditional cabinet organizations such as the State Department. By the early 1960s, the modern NSC process was in place and *three contemporary characteristics have become commonplace for presidential management:*

1. The formal National Security Council as advisory body was replaced by interagency groups whose membership was determined by the president;
2. The NSC staff became the personal staff to the president for foreign policy; and
3. The national security adviser became the key official responsible for managing the interagency groups and coordinating the policy process, as well as for providing information and advice to the president.

Presidential management of the foreign policy–making process, in other words, has come to rely increasingly on a White House–centered system that emphasizes the use of the national security adviser and staff.

JFK's Management Style. John Kennedy entered office as an activist president eager to get the country moving and lead the free world. However, he had no clear strategy for managing the foreign policy process. His personal management style tended to be very informal and akin to the ad hoc style used by Franklin

Roosevelt. He was uncomfortable relying on a large advisory body such as the National Security Council and quickly scrapped Eisenhower's formal foreign policy apparatus. With this decision, the National Security Council—as a formal advisory body whose membership is stipulated by law—ceased to be influential. However, Kennedy offered no alternative decisionmaking structure. The initial policymaking process under Kennedy resulted in ad hoc interaction among his foreign policy advisers, the creation of informal interagency groups whose membership was decided by the president, and considerable leeway for departments and agencies.

This ad hoc management style lasted only a few months—until the **Bay of Pigs fiasco.** The covert effort to train a Cuban military force and overthrow Castro by invading Cuba, which began under President Eisenhower, failed miserably when Kennedy allowed it to go forward in April 1961. Much of the blame was attributed to the decentralized and chaotic nature of the decisionmaking process that had first developed under Kennedy. To address the problem, the decisionmaking process became more centralized through the national security adviser, who ensured that all information and advice reached the president. The interagency groups were now managed by National Security Adviser McGeorge Bundy.

In this climate, the national security adviser increasingly came to act as a personal adviser to the president, as well as a manager. This advisory role was reinforced by the substantial growth in foreign policy expertise and specialization in the NSC staff, providing the president with an independent source of information and advice. Such White House activism was reinforced by President Kennedy's low regard for the competence of the State Department and his appointment of Dean Rusk as secretary of state. An indication of the growing status and influence of the national security adviser and staff was the location of their offices. They moved from the basement of the Executive Office Building (across from the White House) to the basement of the White House—much closer to the president. A "situation room" for crisis management was also set up in the White House basement, enabling the president to receive and transmit international communications as well as hold meetings and manage interagency coordination.

Given popular notions about the significance of the National Security Council as a decisionmaking body, presidents feel compelled to act symbolically as if they rely on the NSC in order to comply with the law and maintain legitimacy with the public. For example, even though President Kennedy was the first to scrap use of the formal National Security Council, the deliberating body he relied upon during the Cuban Missile Crisis was called **Excomm,** which stood for "Executive Committee to the National Security Council."

LBJ's Management Style. This pattern of growing White House management continued under President Lyndon Johnson, although Johnson's particular management style was quite different from his predecessor's. Johnson initially decided to work with Kennedy's appointees to maintain continuity and promote legitimacy for his presidency, even though as vice president he had never been comfortable and felt like an outsider with Kennedy's people. The relationship between Johnson and in particular Robert Kennedy, John Kennedy's younger brother and attorney general, was quite hostile.

While Kennedy had preferred to appoint the "best and the brightest," drawn from such elite universities as Harvard, and actively engage them for information and advice, Johnson preferred men who were loyal and supportive, especially after he had arrived at a decision. With time, President Johnson came to rely on his own group of advisers and replaced many of Kennedy's appointees, such as McGeorge Bundy, who was replaced as national security adviser by Walt Rostow in March 1966.

Johnson was neither knowledgeable about nor interested in foreign policy. He was much more interested and involved in domestic policy. As a Texas politician and former majority leader in the U.S. Senate, he loved to be "in the know" and to wheel and deal in politics. He also became president just prior to the 1964 presidential elections, so he was preoccupied quite early with winning election and acquiring a mandate for his Great Society agenda. Johnson's management style in foreign policy reflected all of these factors.

For most foreign policy issues, Johnson remained uninvolved, except when he had to respond to a crisis, such as the revolution in the Dominican Republic in 1965 or, increasingly, the Vietnam War. He preferred to delegate authority to people with whom he was impressed and could trust, such as Robert McNamara at the Defense Department and Dean Rusk at the State Department. When he wanted additional advice, he did not turn to his young staff, as Kennedy had, but rather to those senior political figures he knew well, such as former advisers Dean Acheson and Clark Clifford.

Although interagency groups did operate through the NSC, key presidential decisions were made in informal sessions with his closest advisers. Many of his most important decisions involving Vietnam, for instance, were made during his "Tuesday Lunch group," composed of senior advisers Clifford, McNamara, Rostow, and Rusk. When he did get highly involved, he tended to dominate the policy process. Therefore, Johnson's tendency was either to delegate authority and let the bureaucracy develop a consensus position or to be highly involved in promoting consensus behind him.

THE NSC ADVISER AND STAFF ASCENDANT

Beginning with President Nixon, the national security adviser and staff became ascendant over the cabinet officers and departments for information, advice, and management of the foreign policy process for the president. As presidents began to rely more on their national security advisers, the position gained prominence and power. The national security adviser also began to act as a spokesperson for the president and became active in the actual operations and conduct of U.S. foreign policy. The national security adviser became first among equals relative to other key foreign policy officials. To assist the national security adviser, the staff grew in size and influence as well.

The height of White House centralization of the policymaking process was reached under President Nixon with Henry Kissinger as national security adviser. In contrast to earlier administrations, in which the national security adviser and staff coordinated and managed the foreign policy bureaucracy, Nixon and Kissinger attempted to control the bureaucracy by using it or circumventing it. The level of centralization was modified under President Ford and moreso under President Carter, so that other cabinet officers and departments were able to play a greater role. Nevertheless, the policy process remained White House cen-

tered, with the national security adviser and NSC staff responsible for managing the system and operating as the president's personal foreign policy staff. President Reagan, a believer in delegation and cabinet government, attempted to reverse these trends but had little success.

Overall, the *policymaking process at the presidential level has tended to operate at two overlapping levels:*

1. An informal process among the president's closest advisers, and
2. A formal NSC interagency process through use of the national security adviser and the NSC staff.

The informal process usually involves the president meeting with his closest advisers in person or speaking with them over the phone. Ultimately, as described by Charles Maechling, Jr.,

> no important decision in the area of national security or foreign policy is made by a president . . . without in some degree being shaped and formulated by an interdepartmental decision process. Even the information and advice on which a decision is based filters through to the highest authority in a form that consciously or unconsciously reflects the assumptions and viewpoints of key subordinates and second-level decision-makers.[20]

Post–cold war administrations have continued to rely on an informal advisory process and a formal NSC interagency process. In this respect, not much has changed since the end of the cold war. Presidents Bush Sr., Clinton, and Bush Jr. have continued along the lines of presidents Ford and Carter of having strong cabinet officials operating within a White House–centered foreign policy system. To better understand how contemporary presidents have managed the executive branch, a more detailed look at the actual operation of the foreign policy–making process is needed.

The Nixon-Kissinger System. Nixon came to the presidency with a strong interest in foreign affairs. He also had a great distrust of the bureaucracy, which he felt tended to limit information and options available to the president. President Nixon's management strategy was to use the White House as the major instrument in foreign policymaking. This resulted in a very centralized decision-making structure that relied not on the National Security Council as an advisory body but the national security adviser, Henry Kissinger.[21]

The NSC system that Nixon and Kissinger set up attempted to use the bureaucracy to provide a broad array of information and options to the president on those issues he considered important. This was to be done through the creation of numerous interagency committees, whose membership was decided by the president and national security adviser. Although some of the committees met more frequently than others, all were chaired by Kissinger. President Nixon, always the loner, rarely attended, preferring to consider the products of the committees by himself and personally consult with his closest advisers, who increasingly became Henry Kissinger for foreign policy. (See **figure 5.3** for an overview of the Nixon-Kissinger policy process.)

Nixon and Kissinger activated the bureaucracy by issuing a national security study memorandum (NSSM), which laid out the issue to be addressed, the agencies involved, and presented deadlines for agency submission of policy recommendations. Once the studies and recommendations were complete, interagency meetings chaired by Kissinger would be convened to consider policy options and make recommendations for transmittal to the president. Once the president decided on a particular course of action, often in consultation with Kissinger, a national security decision memorandum (NSDM) would be issued describing the president's decision and instructing the bureaucracy on the policy's implementation. Henry Kissinger's staff oversaw this complex policy process, serving as an independent source of information and options for Kissinger and Nixon.

Initially, this policy process worked by forcing the bureaucracy to provide information and advice

FIGURE **5.3**

THE NIXON-KISSINGER SYSTEM

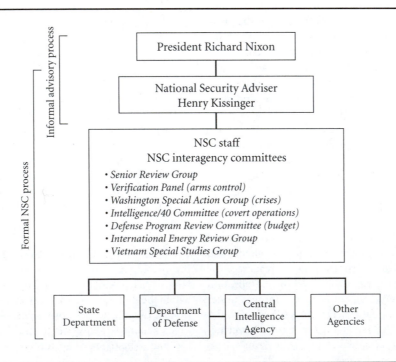

to the president and allowing him to arrive at decisions that would be communicated to the bureaucracy for implementation. By the second year in office, however, President Nixon had a stronger sense of the foreign policy goals and strategy he wanted to pursue and formed a special relationship with Henry Kissinger. Thus, Nixon and Kissinger were no longer as interested in information and advice but concentrated on policy initiatives and implementation. The result was that Kissinger and the NSC system were increasingly used as a means to control and circumvent the bureaucracy.

Kissinger became the president's manager, major adviser, spokesman, and, in some cases, implementer of foreign policy. Kissinger's power was symbolized by his movement from the basement of the White House to a prestigious office on the main floor of the West Wing, down the hall from the Oval Office. Kissinger came to act as Nixon's alter ego in foreign policy, especially once Watergate began to break. The policy process became so centralized in Kissinger's hands, usually with Nixon's blessing, that the ability of many traditional foreign policy agencies and high-level officials to influence the process dwindled. Kissinger and his staff, nevertheless, did develop important contacts and networks with trusted lower-level officials throughout the bureaucracy. Given Kissinger's crucial role, the size of the NSC staff reached its height of over one hundred staffers during this period.

Nixon and Kissinger did not trust the bureaucracy to implement major policy initiatives, perceiving it as too resistant, cumbersome, and leaky and therefore relying increasingly on what has been called the **back channel.** During negotiations over the SALT I arms control treaty, for example, while the official American and Soviet delegations met formally—"the front channel"—Henry Kissinger often met with the Soviet ambassador to the United States in secret to present the administration's position. This also occurred when the Nixon White House made the surprise announcement that Kissinger was in Peking negotiating the normalization of relations with the People's Republic of China, altering thirty years of U.S. foreign policy and shocking most foreign policy officials. Therefore, the national security adviser, rather than the secretary of state, came to act as the chief negotiator in the name of the president.

Henry Kissinger, and thus the office of national security adviser, reached a pinnacle of power under President Nixon that no single policymaker had experienced before or since. When William Rogers eventually resigned in 1973, Nixon appointed Kissinger as secretary of state as well, and one man held the two most important foreign policy positions in the U.S. government. Such a centralized policy process was responsive to Nixon and Kissinger for those issues in which the president was most interested. However, few policy alternatives tended to be considered, and there was considerable internal dissent throughout the executive branch. The system's major weakness was that Kissinger was a single individual, able only to accomplish so much. Consequently, the Nixon-Kissinger system was unable to control or heavily influence dozens of other foreign policy issues in which the U.S. government remained constantly involved. (See **essay 5.3** for more discussion of Kissinger's unique role in the foreign policy–making process.)

This White House–centered system under Henry Kissinger continued to operate after Nixon's resignation because of **President Ford's management style,** though with some modifications. New appointments made by Ford opened up the policy process to other officials, such as Donald Rumsfeld as secretary of defense. In 1975, Lieutenant General Brent Scowcroft, Kissinger's deputy national security assistant since 1973, became the national security adviser and managed the day-to-day NSC process. Nonetheless, Gerald Ford, who had minimal exposure to foreign affairs, developed a close working relationship with Henry Kissinger and remained dependent on his secretary of state throughout his term of office.

Carter's Management Style. Although Carter's worldview was very different from Nixon's, the Carter administration's foreign policy–making apparatus was very similar to that which existed early in the Nixon administration. While the Carter foreign policy system was centralized within the White House, it was still relatively open to input by cabinet officials and departments. President Carter managed U.S. foreign policy by relying upon a formal NSC process and an informal advisory process dependent on his national security adviser and secretary of state.[22]

ESSAY 5.3
HENRY KISSINGER

SCHOLAR, STATESMAN, REALPOLITICIAN, MANIPULATOR, SPOKESPERSON, CELEBRITY

Henry Kissinger, who was born in Germany but became a naturalized U.S. citizen, achieved the pinnacle of power within his profession. Following World War II, he became a professor of government at Harvard University and was a well-respected scholar and author on international politics, U.S. foreign policy, and political-military strategy. During the cold war, he also became a member of the prestigious Council on Foreign Relations, which was composed of prominent experts in the area of foreign affairs and was often referred to as the "foreign policy establishment." Before his appointment as national security adviser by Richard Nixon, Kissinger had been in and out of government and had acted as a close adviser to presidential hopeful, and Nixon rival, Nelson Rockefeller. Kissinger stands out because he embodied the realpolitik tradition in foreign policy and made the national security adviser ascendant in the making of U.S. foreign policy.

Kissinger is often remembered as a policymaker because of his distinctive worldview, which heavily influenced the Nixon administration's foreign policy. Kissinger, unlike many other American policymakers, came from the **realpolitik tradition** of understanding world politics. He was not really interested in morality or reforming the world, as was the "Wilsonian" liberal internationalist tradition. Instead of fighting an "ideological" cold war between the free world and communist totalitarianism, Kissinger believed in the overriding importance of maintaining "stability" between the two great powers, the United States and the Soviet Union, through the exercise of "power" and force abroad. Thus, he was a key actor in initiating détente with the Soviet Union and normalizing relations with the People's Republic of China.

What is less well-known about Kissinger was his ability to acquire and maintain power within the policymaking process. Kissinger dominated the NSC process and drove the staff members relentlessly. They worked for him, not the president. He was extremely demanding and, when staff work did not meet his standards, it was not unusual for him to explode and berate staffers for their shoddy work. Kissinger came to rely on a staff-within-the-staff, those he found to be most capable and trustworthy, and became suspicious of much of his staff. For example,

when word leaked out to the press about America's secret bombing of Cambodia in 1969, Kissinger was furious and requested that Nixon wiretap members of the NSC staff—the earliest use of the tactics that led to Watergate. His autocratic style resulted in much discontent among his staff, many of whom resigned (later to appear as advisers to Democratic presidential hopefuls, such as Jimmy Carter). He operated the same way as secretary of state in that he avoided utilizing the State Department as an institution, preferring to act as a "lone ranger" with the support of a small, loyal staff.

Kissinger was a master at maximizing his position and influence within the Nixon and Ford administrations. Like Nixon, he deeply distrusted the bureaucracy and had a passion for secrecy and manipulation. His rise to power and special status with presidents came at others' expense. This was most blatant with Secretary of State William Rogers, a personal friend and confidant of Richard Nixon, whom Kissinger publicly and repeatedly humiliated. Yet President Nixon rarely objected to Kissinger's maneuvers, because he often saw his cabinet officers as lightweights, like Rogers, or as bureaucratic impediments to conducting foreign policy.

Kissinger eventually became the major foreign policy spokesman for the president. Initially, this was done behind the scenes in **background briefings** to journalists who attributed their information to a "senior official." Kissinger was truly a master at feeding (and leaking) information to the media to promote the president's policies. He worked the media like no foreign policy official before him or since. By 1973 Kissinger came out in the open as the public spokesman for foreign policy. Over the next two years he became a media star and celebrity. This caused conflict with Nixon's personal White House staff, because they feared that Kissinger's publicity was detracting from the president's public prestige. However, with President Nixon soon fighting for his political life over Watergate, Kissinger was perceived as one of the few shining lights within the administration.

Kissinger had a very large and, at the same time, fragile ego. His unfinished two-volume memoirs, already over two thousand pages, is indicative of this. Kissinger loved to exercise power, yet he was extremely jealous and protective of his policy views. When his position was challenged or he did not come out on top in the policy process, it was not unusual for him to become extremely upset. Kissinger submitted his resignation numerous times, yet it was never accepted. Instead, he was soothed and, in the end, often got his way.

Although Kissinger has not had an official governmental position since President Ford left office, he has continued to enjoy great stature and influence within the Washington political community. Kissinger has remained visible in the national media and has built a prestigious consulting firm, Kissinger Associates, and two of his clos-est associates, Brent Scowcroft and Lawrence Eagleberger, were appointed national security adviser and secretary of state, respectively, by President George Bush Sr.

SOURCES: Seymour H. Hersh, *The Price of Power: Kissinger in the Nixon White House* (New York: Summit Books, 1983); Marvin Kalb and Bernard Kalb, *Kissinger* (New York: Dell, 1974); Roger Morris, *Uncertain Greatness: Henry Kissinger and American Foreign Policy* (New York: Harper and Row, 1977); John Newhouse, *Cold Dawn: The Story of SALT* (New York: Holt, Rinehart and Winston, 1973); and Bob Woodward and Carl Bernstein, *The Final Days* (New York: Avon, 1986).

Although the National Security Council was again intended to be used as the main decisionmaking body, it fell into disuse relatively early in the Carter administration. Two formal interagency groups within the NSC system became primarily responsible for the working operations of the foreign policy process. The Policy Review Committee (PRC) was established to develop policy at the secretarial level on issues for which one department had been designated as the lead agency by the president. The Special Coordinating Committee (SCC) was established to deal with crosscutting issues, such as arms control and crisis management, and was chaired by National Security Adviser Zbigniew Brzezinski. At the lowest level of the NSC system were two groups at the assistant secretary level that did much of the legwork for the PRC and SCC and were also responsible for issues of lesser significance: interdepartmental groups (geographically oriented) and ad hoc groups.

As with the Nixon administration, the formal foreign policy process was activated when the president issued a presidential review memorandum (PRM) identifying the issue and requiring policy research by the appropriate committees and agencies. Once the study was completed and transmitted to the president, he would decide on a particular course of action. At this point, a presidential directive (PD) was issued describing the president's decision and instructing the bureaucracy on the procedures for implementation. Obviously, the process was much more confusing and cumbersome than this simplistic portrayal. (See **figure 5.4** for an overview of the process as it existed in the Carter administration.)

President Carter relied principally upon two individuals he respected and admired, **Zbigniew Brzezinski** and **Cyrus Vance,** in making the foreign policy process viable and effective. Brzezinski, as national security adviser and head of the NSC staff, was primarily responsible for coordinating the interagency operations of the NSC system, while Secretary of State Vance was the chief negotiator and major spokesperson for the president. Both individuals were key advisers to the president in foreign affairs, staying in close contact with the president and each other throughout the course of the day. Brzezinski usually briefed the president in the morning concerning major world developments and their effect on U.S. foreign policy. In the evening, Vance often sent a report directly to the president summarizing his views for the day. Important issues were discussed during President Carter's weekly "foreign policy breakfasts" on Fridays with Brzezinski, Vance, and other presidential advisers such as Secretary of Defense Harold Brown, Vice President Walter Mondale, and Chief of Staff Hamilton Jordan. Brzezinski also presided over a weekly luncheon with Vance and Brown. The informal advisory process did not end there, however, for President Carter was usually available in the Oval Office to see his advisers or discuss policy with them over the phone.

The foreign policy system worked fairly well during the first two years. It was White House centered, yet open and flexible, providing the president with a wide array of information and advice. Carter lacked considerable experience and knowledge of foreign affairs, but he was very active in learning about world politics and was involved in daily decisionmaking. Carter, Brzezinski, and Vance got along together for the most part and shared a sense of optimism about the future of U.S. foreign policy. The main problem that President Carter experienced during this period was that he pressed too many initiatives too quickly.

FIGURE **5.4**
CARTER'S FOREIGN POLICY SYSTEM

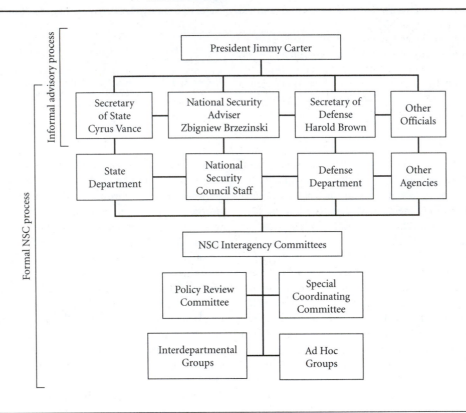

By the third year the foreign policy process began to break down due to Brzezinski's growing hard-line views concerning the need to contain Soviet interventionism abroad, reinforced by the president's growing indecisiveness regarding the utility of force in dealing with situations such as the shah's unstable regime in Iran. Not only did Brzezinski and Vance increasingly differ over proper policy, but their personal styles of action exacerbated the situation. Vance had risen through the ranks of the foreign policy establishment during the cold war years, when one operated in a gentlemanly, nonpartisan, and quiet fashion; Brzezinski represented the new type of ambitious, partisan, and activist foreign policy professional. The growing conflict over policy and personal style resulted in considerable bureaucratic infighting, especially between the staffs of Brzezinski and Vance.

With the taking of American hostages in Iran and the Soviet intervention in Afghanistan in late 1979, President Carter supported Brzezinski over Vance, reinstating the containment strategy as the cornerstone of U.S. foreign policy. President Carter also decided to attempt a military rescue of the hostages, a decision arrived at while Vance, the lone dissenter, was vacationing in Florida. With Vance no longer enjoying the president's confidence and his policy views increasingly isolated within the administration, he resigned, thus becoming the first secretary of state to resign voluntarily on a matter of principle in over sixty years.[23] Consequently, Zbigniew Brzezinski and his NSC staff had clearly become ascendant within the foreign policy process by the end of Carter's term of office.

Reagan's Management Style. President Reagan entered office committed to reversing the Carter trend toward a strong national security adviser and NSC staff. Reagan preferred to rely on his foreign policy officials and their agencies for information and advice. It was much more of a cabinet government that, nonetheless, remained White House centered because of the dominant role played by Reagan's White House staff. As with previous presidents, a two-tiered system developed: a formal NSC process and a more important informal advisory process. However, unlike other recent presidents, Reagan's national security adviser and staff were supposed to act as little more than custodians responsible for coordinating the process, reminiscent of their role during the early NSC days.[24]

Three major interagency committees, referred to as Senior Interdepartmental Groups (SIGs), were created within the NSC as the means to generate information and advice to the president. One SIG covered intelligence matters and was chaired by the director of central intelligence; another, chaired by the secretary of defense, involved defense policy; the third was chaired by the secretary of state and dealt with more traditional foreign policy matters. As under President Carter, the interagency process was triggered by the issue of a presidential review memorandum (PRM) that ultimately led to a presidential decision (PD). Eventually, a Crisis Management Group was also created, chaired by Vice President George Bush. Each of these committees reported to the president through his White House staff. (See **figure 5.5** for an overview of the process.)

Unlike Kissinger, who chaired all the interagency committees, or Brzezinski, who chaired some, the national security adviser in the Reagan administration

FIGURE **5.5**
REAGAN'S EARLY FOREIGN POLICY SYSTEM

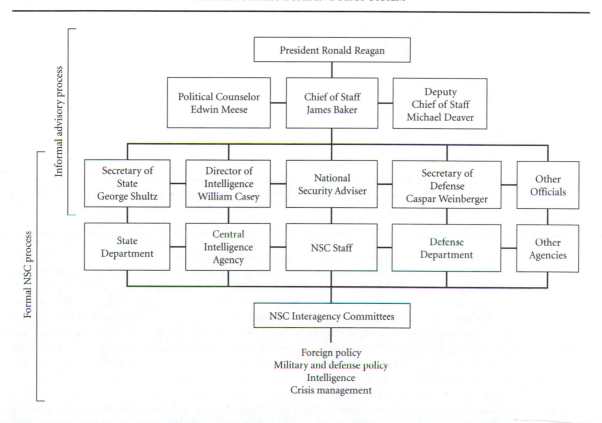

chaired no committees. The national security adviser's job was to supervise the staff and provide support for the formal NSC process described above. Nor did Reagan's first appointee as national security adviser, Richard Allen, act as a major adviser or spokesperson for the president. President Reagan, unlike his predecessors, had the national security adviser report to him through the White House staff. As an indication of the decline in the national security adviser's stature and influence within the Reagan administration, his office was moved away from the president into the White House basement.

President Reagan relied on a much larger informal advisory process than his predecessors. Reagan preferred to delegate authority, tended to remain uninvolved in daily operations, and lacked considerable experience and knowledge of foreign affairs. The principal foreign policy officials on which Reagan depended for information and advice were Secretary of State Alexander Haig (later George Shultz), Secretary of Defense Caspar Weinberger, and Director of Central Intelligence William Casey. Unlike his immediate predecessors, however, Reagan also relied heavily upon his White House staff—James Baker, Michael Deaver, and Edwin Meese during his first term and Donald Regan, then Howard Baker, during his second term. The "triumvirate" of Baker as chief of staff, Deaver as deputy chief of staff, and Edwin Meese as political counselor enabled President Reagan to be effective in exercising presidential power. They not only were among his closest confidants but also acted as intermediaries between the president and the formal NSC system.

From the beginning, however, the foreign policy–making process failed to function smoothly. The first major problem involved the secretary of state's role within the system. **Alexander Haig** thought that he was going to be responsible for developing a State Department–centered system for the president. Haig had the greatest amount of governmental experience in foreign affairs, previously acting as Kissinger's deputy national security adviser, Nixon's chief of staff, and supreme commander of allied forces in Europe under Ford. He believed that he was to be the key foreign policy spokesperson, major foreign policy adviser, and foreign policy manager—the "vicar" of the Reagan administration's foreign policy. Haig could not understand that, even though Reagan had de-emphasized the role of the national security adviser and staff, he pre-

ferred a White House–centered system that relied on his personal staff. President Reagan, who preferred a collegial atmosphere of interaction with his advisers, also was uncomfortable with Haig's strong and intense personality. The result was constant political infighting between Haig and the White House staff. Haig threatened to resign numerous times and was flabbergasted when President Reagan finally accepted his resignation in 1982.

The second major problem involved frequent turnover of key personnel under President Reagan. Reagan had six national security advisers, each one lasting little more than a year. Even though the national security adviser's role was downplayed, the adviser still had an important position to play in coordinating the policy process; and given the size and complexity of the foreign policy bureaucracy, it took time to master the workings of the executive branch and devise a proper strategy for managing the bureaucracy. National security advisers, like presidents, have to learn on the job. They have to mold a close working relationship with the president and other foreign policy officials. The problem under President Reagan was that, after months of learning, adjusting to, and tinkering with the policymaking process, the national security adviser was replaced by a different individual. Richard Allen was replaced by William Clark, then by Robert McFarlane, John Poindexter, Frank Carlucci, and finally Colin Powell.

These constant changes of crucial personnel created havoc in the foreign policy process. They reduced the national security adviser's clout within the executive branch even further than originally intended by the president; the major exception was William Clark, who, though knowing little about foreign policy, was personally close to the president.[25] Consequently, the national security adviser was often unable, through insufficient influence or lack of experience, to manage the process. Power moved to other officials in the policy process, such as Baker, Meese, George Shultz (who replaced Haig as secretary of state), and Weinberger.

After winning reelection in 1984, Reagan oversaw major changes in the White House staff that he had relied on so much. Deaver left the White House to become a political consultant, Meese was appointed attorney general, and James Baker switched positions with Donald Regan to become secretary of the treasury. President Reagan approved these major changes nonchalantly, yet this presidential choice may not have served him well, for the old team of Baker, Deaver, and Meese might have been much more protective of the president and critical of the activities that produced the Iran-contra affair.

Another problem was the political infighting among Reagan's principal advisers, which became legendary. The national security adviser was unable to either stop it or channel it in more productive directions, and President Reagan had great difficulty facing such confrontations and disciplining his subordinates. Major political battles regularly were fought over who would become the next national security adviser.[26] The disarray in the policymaking process only got worse when Reagan's personal aides—Baker, Deaver, and Meese—left the White House.

There was so little management of the policy process by the middle years of the Reagan administration that informal coalitions between officials and groups developed over different issues. For example, despite a consensus within the administration in support of the contras and their effort to overthrow the Sandinistas in Nicaragua, even after American assistance was banned by Congress, there was considerable disagreement among Reagan's advisers over exchanging arms for hostages with Iran. Secretary of State George Shultz and Secretary of Defense Caspar Weinberger fought the initiative. President Reagan, however, was committed to the Iran venture, and consequently, the circle of participants within the policy process narrowed: the White House, NSC, and CIA remained involved, while the secretary of state and the secretary of defense were eliminated or circumvented. The actual implementation of both these initiatives was taken by the NSC staff. Thus, the **operational NSC staff,** begun under Kissinger, reached its height under the Reagan administration and contributed to the NSC's ascendance during Reagan's second term.

For a number of reasons, success in managing the bureaucracy in the name of the president was greater by the latter part of the administration. First, Frank Carlucci and then Colin Powell were brought in as national security adviser. These were two able men with considerable foreign policy experience who restored the stature of the national security adviser and staff and increased their influence over the policy process. Two of the dominant personalities and foreign policy officials within the Reagan administration also departed:

Secretary of Defense Weinberger returned to private life and Director of Central Intelligence Casey died in office. Finally, former senator Howard Baker replaced Donald Regan as chief of staff, helping to make the policy process work more efficiently for the president. Hence, President Reagan left office with a White House–centered system under the able management of a strengthened national security adviser and staff.

Bush Sr.'s Management Style. The initial foreign policy process in the Bush Sr. administration was similar to what transpired under President Ford, the early Carter years, and late in the Reagan administration—a White House–centered system revolving around an NSC process in which cabinet officials and departments played a prominent role. President Bush was comfortable with such a White House–centered policymaking process because of the foreign policy expertise and policymaking experience he acquired during the Nixon, Ford, and Reagan years, especially as director of central intelligence, U.S. ambassador to the United Nations, and vice president.[27]

Bush personally relied most on a "small, informal advisory process" that usually included National Security Adviser Brent Scowcroft, the White House chief of staff (initially John Sununu, then Samuel Skinner), Secretary of State James Baker, Secretary of Defense Richard Cheney, and Chairman of the Joint Chiefs of Staff Colin Powell. Emphasis was with loyalty and quiet teamwork, "in marked contrast to the public feuds over policy and bureaucratic turf in previous administrations—the Shultz-Weinberger, Vance-Brzezinski, or Rogers-Kissinger battles."[28] President Bush, for example, relied heavily on this small group of officials for information and advice in formulating the decisions following Iraq's August 2, 1990, invasion of Kuwait to respond forcefully in defense of Saudi Arabia, to pursue a policy of brinksmanship to compel Iraq to withdraw from Kuwait, and then, when that failed, to go to war.

President Bush also relied on a "formal interagency policy process" dependent on the NSC staff and the coordination of National Security Adviser Scowcroft, who had held the position under President Ford. Interagency groups operated at different levels: the interaction of senior governmental officials for more significant and general issues and, for lesser issues, the involvement of groups of lower-level officials representing the foreign policy bureaucracy, organized along more specific geographical and functional lines (see **figure 5.6** for an overview of the Bush Sr. process).

Specifically, Scowcroft and his deputy national security adviser served as chairs of the two key NSC committees coordinating the Bush administration's foreign policy machinery—the NSC Principals Committee (PC, a secretary-level group) and the NSC Deputies Committee (DC, a deputy secretary-level group). Below these committees, the Bush White House established a series of NSC interagency working groups, or policy coordinating committees (PCC) established by the national security adviser or the two lead NSC committees. In the Bush administration's system, these interagency PCCs did most of the work to formulate policy options for higher-level consideration and also to supervise and coordinate the implementation of policy choices. Organized into various regional (e.g., Europe, Soviet Union, Latin America) and functional units

(e.g., arms control, defense, intelligence), these working groups were chaired by assistant secretaries of state for the regional units, and assistant secretaries (or their equivalents) from Defense, Treasury, the CIA, and elsewhere for functional units. However, an NSC staff member served as executive secretary for each working group so as to increase White House control and policy coordination.

The Deputies Committee and the Principals Committee process helped to further centralize policy control by the White House, national security adviser, and NSC staff. The DC, through the deputy national security adviser and the NSC staff, reviewed all work from the coordinating committees and made recommendations to the PC, under the leadership of the national security adviser. Effectively, the Principals Committee served as a White House-led center for considering all national security questions along with President Bush's all important informal sessions with his principal ad-

FIGURE **5.6**
BUSH SR.'S FOREIGN POLICY SYSTEM

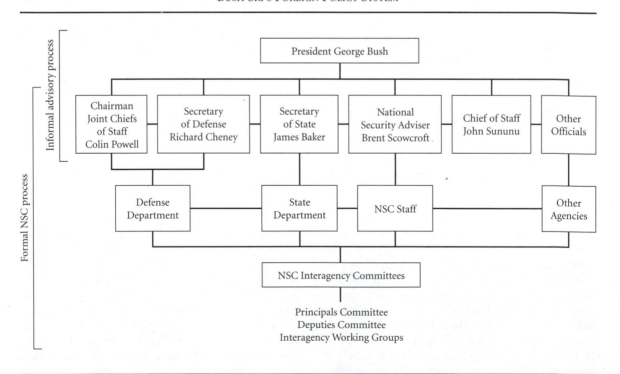

visers. In this way, the Bush Sr. administration attempted to coordinate foreign policy across bureaucratic agencies and place the White House at the center of foreign policy making.

CLINTON'S MANAGEMENT STYLE AND NSC

Like his predecessor, President Clinton supplemented a formal NSC interagency process with a heavy reliance upon informal meetings among his principal foreign policy advisers. However, Clinton, as a politician and former governor, was a relative newcomer to foreign, especially national security, affairs. Domestic policy and (domestic and international) economics were never far from his mind. Consequently, much of his time, especially early on, was spent on foreign policy cramming to get up to speed. Clinton's preference was to set broad guidelines and pay spasmodic attention to different issues as they arose. As Secretary of State Warren Christopher delicately put it, President Clinton laid down "the broad guidelines of foreign policy, expecting his State Department and national security advisers to implement them as a team, working together, and holding them accountable if they don't carry it out in a fairly straightforward way."[29]

In his first term Clinton showed a strong preference for informal meetings with his closest advisers, especially Secretary of State Christopher, National Security Adviser Anthony Lake, and Defense Secretary Les Aspin and, later, Aspin's successor, William Perry. Three informal settings were particularly important: the president's early-morning foreign policy briefing by the national security adviser; discussions with top aides after meetings with foreign leaders; and the weekly Wednesday lunch among Clinton's foreign policy principals in the West Wing. In fact, early on in the administration, Clinton's apparent unwillingness to establish more frequent formal meetings on foreign policy created concern among advisers like Secretary of State Christopher.

Clinton's "formal NSC interagency process" was actually closely modeled on Bush Sr.'s NSC system. At the top was the Principals Committee (PC), which served as the senior interagency committee and was chaired by the national security adviser. One new development, reflecting the importance of economic is-

sues and the post–cold war world under President Clinton, was that he broadened the circle of principal members to include the secretary of the treasury, the U.S. ambassador to the United Nations, the special assistant to the president for economic policy, and the White House chief of staff. Below the Principals Committee was the Deputies Committee (DC), which was chaired by the deputy national security adviser and which carried out much of the work of the interagency process, supervising policy implementation and reviewing issue papers to be used by the PC. The Deputies Committee was also charged with setting up and supervising a series of Interagency Working Groups (IWGs) at the assistant secretary level to help prepare policy studies and to help facilitate implementation of decisions within bureaucratic agencies (see **figure 5.7** for an overview of the process under Clinton).

The Clinton administration did bring some reorganization to the NSC staff, dividing up the European Affairs office into an Office for Western Europe and another for Russia, Ukraine, and Eurasian Affairs, and creating offices for Non-Proliferation Policy, Environmental Affairs, and Democracy Affairs, reflecting new post–cold war policy concerns. At the same time the size of the NSC staff was cut from approximately 180 in the Bush administration to 150 people (of which 90 were detailees from other executive branch agencies).

The person responsible for coordinating the national security machinery was National Security Adviser Anthony Lake. Very much like National Security Adviser Brent Scowcroft under President Bush, Lake entered office determined to keep a lower public profile, believing that it would not only enhance his role as coordinator of the policy process but also prevent much of the bitter infighting that occurred between national security advisers and secretaries of state in past administrations.

Despite a relatively high degree of collegiality among the principal members of the foreign policy team, both Lake and his deputy, Sandy Berger, were initially criticized by observers for putting too much emphasis on presenting consensus positions to the president, which both slowed the advisory process and watered down the final product. Lake and Berger were also criticized for not being proactive enough in the important tasks of managing the NSC staff and interagency process.

FIGURE 5.7
CLINTON'S FOREIGN POLICY SYSTEM

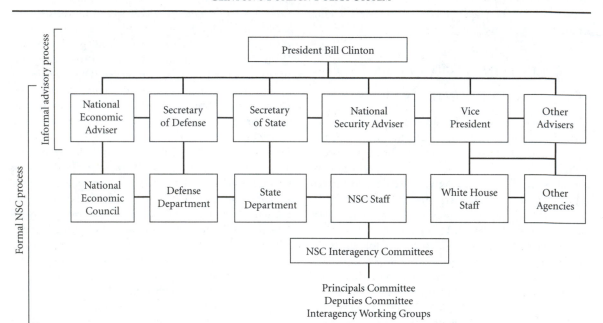

This made it very difficult for the administration to formulate any consistent policy whenever there were divisions between the principals and because President Clinton himself was often not focused on issues of national security. The key change, according to David Halberstam, "among the main figures in national security was the president himself. For Bush, foreign policy had been his raison d'etre. For Clinton, it was an inconvenience, something that might pull him away from his primary job at hand–domestic issues, above all the economy." In fact, Clinton from the very beginning "had little interest in meeting foreign leaders." Many of these problems were most visible in the Clinton administration's policy toward the former Yugoslavia.[30]

Observers of the administration generally agree that the shortcomings described above were largely worked out during the second half of the president's first term, with the result being a much more efficient and effective process primarily due to key personnel changes, especially when Sandy Berger (who had a much closer relationship with President Clinton than Lake and had known him for a long time) became national security adviser); Madeline Albright, former ambassador to the United Nations, became secretary of state; and William Cohen (a former senator from Maine and the only major Clinton appointee from the Republican party) became secretary of defense. And Clinton was often forced to pay more attention to national security issues in reaction to international events and crises. This may have been reinforced by his concern with his presidential legacy during his last year in office, following the Monica Lewinsky affair, as best illustrated by his personal efforts to bring about an Israeli-Palestinian peace.

Unlike traditional national security policy, however, Clinton from the very beginning took an active interest in, and was extremely knowledgeable about, domestic and international economics—a relatively unique phenomenon among modern presidents. Given its importance to him, and in order to better coordinate and centralize the administration's economic policy, both domestic and foreign, President Clinton created the National Economic Council, modeled on the NSC. The role of the foreign economic policy–making process in general, and the NEC and the national economic adviser under Bill Clinton will be discussed at much greater length in chapter 9.

BUSH JR.'S MANAGEMENT STYLE AND NSC

Like his two predecessors, President George W. Bush supplements a formal NSC interagency process with a heavy reliance upon informal meetings among his principal foreign policy advisers. President Bush Jr., especially since the attacks of September 11, appears to have a strong preference for informal meetings with his closest advisers, including Condoleezza Rice as national security adviser, Colin Powell as secretary of state, Donald Rumsfeld as secretary of defense, General Richard Myers as chairman of the Joint Chiefs of Staff (JCS), George Tenet as director of central intelligence, and Dick Cheney as vice president.

His formal NSC interagency process is actually closely modeled on that of President Bush Sr.'s and President Clinton's NSC systems. At the top is the Principals Committee (PC), which serves as the senior interagency committee and is chaired by the national security adviser. Below the Principals Committee is the Deputies Committee (DC), which is chaired by the deputy national security adviser and carries out much of the work of the interagency process, supervising policy implementation and reviewing issue papers to be used by the NSC principals. The Deputies Committee also relies on a series of Interagency Working Groups (IWGs) at the assistant secretary level to help prepare policy studies and to help facilitate implementation of decisions within bureaucratic agencies (see **figure 5.8** for an overview of the Bush Jr. process).

Since George W. Bush was declared the winner of the 2000 presidential election, there has been considerable speculation about the nature of the foreign policy process and the foreign policy orientation that will emanate from Washington, D.C. Some initial observations can be made from what has transpired since President Bush Jr. took office and has had to react to the September 11 attacks, based on the open record and limited sources available, as well as knowledge about

the general workings of U.S. foreign policy making. But it needs to be understood that this is an initial and tentative analysis that must remain open to change and revision as time and events unfold.[31]

First, there seems to be a general consensus that George W. Bush entered office relatively inexperienced and lacking in knowledge about national security and international affairs. Second, what little knowledge and experience Bush had appears to involve international trade and other so-called "low policy" issues (such as economics and immigration), principally from his previous role as Texas governor. But even here it must be acknowledged that this experience and knowledge overwhelmingly involved state and local politics, with the exception of Mexico. Furthermore, in Texas the governor's office is a relatively weak one (as compared to states with stronger governors such as California), and much of Bush's role appears to have been as much symbolic as substantive.

Third, Bush has appointed and surrounded himself with national security people who previously worked for his father as president, George H. Bush, and/or who worked for the Ford and Reagan Administrations. Most of these individuals have considerable experience and knowledge about national security affairs, and many of the most prominent among them are from the older, cold war generation, as opposed to the younger, post–cold war generation. Fourth, very few of the higher-level advisers and policymakers within the administration have much experience in international economics. This is especially the case with his major foreign policy and national security advisers.

Fifth, despite the fact that the higher-level personnel share a general conservative ideology and a general realist approach toward international politics, there are different and competing foreign policy views within the administration. Secretary of Defense Donald Rumsfeld (former ambassador to NATO under Nixon and chief of staff and defense secretary under Ford) and Vice President Dick Cheney (former secretary of defense under Bush Sr. and member of the Nixon and Ford administrations, in which Rumsfeld was somewhat instrumental) appear to reflect a more aggressive realist orientation favoring a strong U.S. leadership role abroad. Secretary of State Colin Powell (former chair of the Joint Chiefs of Staff under Bush Sr. and national security adviser under Reagan) appears to reflect a more selective and prudent realist orientation. These

FIGURE **5.8**
BUSH JR.'S FOREIGN POLICY SYSTEM

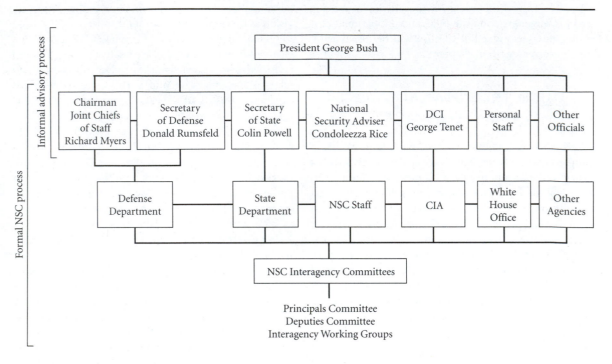

differences have particularly emerged over how to implement the war on terrorism and whether to preemptively invade Iraq. And then there are more unknown
or unclear policymakers, such as National Security Adviser Condoleezza Rice (former NSC staff member
under Bush Sr. and major foreign policy adviser to
Bush Jr. during the campaign), JCS chairman Richard
Meyers, and especially, George W. Bush himself. So the
administration appears to be composed of major foreign policy makers of different conservative internationalist stripes.

Sixth, somewhat reminiscent of the Reagan administration, President Bush Jr. also appears to rely
heavily on his personal White House staff. In particular, Bush relies on Chief of Staff Andrew Card, Senior
Advisor to the President Karl Rove, and Karen Hughes
(the initial White House counselor who subsequently
resigned but still acts as informal adviser and consultant). These personal advisers are often present during
informal sessions with the president and his major national security advisers in order to provide domestic

political as well as general advise. It is important to remember that Card, Rove, and Hughes have been very
close to Bush Jr. since his days as governor of Texas.

Seventh, Bush's initial management style (and
knowledge and experience) was very different than his
father's and more reminiscent of Reagan. Bush Jr. is
much more of a delegator, a novice who is less interested in foreign policy, and appears to be more conservative politically than his father in general. Reagan also
liked to delegate and was a relative foreign-policy
novice, despite a strong anticommunist orientation.
The initial NSC process and role of the national security adviser as coordinator were downplayed and kept
at very low profile, Therefore, the possibility strongly
existed for considerable infighting and turf warfare
among policymakers, making presidential access consequential for presidential foreign policy decisions
under Bush as it was for Reagan.

Since September 11, Bush has become much more
hands-on when it comes to the war on terrorism and
has come to rely increasingly on an informal advisory

process of trusted principals, supported by the more formal NSC Principals and Deputies Committees. This may have provided bureaucracies and agencies with much leeway in pursuing and implementing policies, especially for other issues that receive little presidential attention. This could be a formula for a very problematic policymaking process under President Bush Jr. that ultimately he must resolve.

Finally, the above observations raise the question as to how well prepared this administration is for addressing future, post–cold war international issues into the twenty-first century, as opposed to issues more reminiscent of the cold war past. Since the September 11 terrorist attacks, the Bush administration's foreign policy has completely revolved around pursuing a war on terrorism and deterring states from acquiring weapons of mass destruction, especially in the case of Iraq. So in some ways new foes—terrorists, Osama bin Laden and Al Qaeda, Saddam Hussein and Iraq—have apparently replaced the Soviet Union and communism as the new enemy providing the foundation and basic orientation of U.S. foreign policy. As depicted by Bob Woodward in *Bush at War,* Bush has been transformed by September 11 into the war president, approaches the war on terrorism as a personal crusade, and tends to be very proactive and dominate his informal advisory process.[32]

In less than one year after September 11, beginning in the summer of 2002, controversy already has developed throughout the international community and within American domestic politics as to the adequacy of President Bush Jr.'s war on terrorism and whether Iraq should be invaded and Saddam Hussein overthrown. Furthermore, questions have also been raised as to whether or not the Bush administration has been focusing too much of its time, attention, and energy on the war on terrorism, to the neglect of numerous other foreign policy and global issues that need to be addressed, including the Israeli-Palestinian conflict, the India-Pakistan conflict, the financial collapse of the South American economies, the recovery of the American and international political economy, and energy policy and the environment, to name a few.

This may mean that the Bush administration quite likely will tend to be more reactive than proactive toward international issues and events, with the possible exception of the war on terrorism; to be better able to deal with more traditional issues of national security policy than other, global issues; to be more likely to pursue unilateral than multilateral, consultative policies; and to be forced to adjust many of its policies in the face of complex obstacles and constraints, domestic and international, that are beyond its control (and to which it is likely to give insufficient attention and thought). This more reactive approach is certainly not unique to the Bush Jr. administration but reflects the likelihood that the post–cold war presidency thesis continues to operate even in a post–September 11 political environment.

THE NSC AND PRESIDENTIAL MANAGEMENT TYPES IN PERSPECTIVE

All post–World War II presidents have had mixed success in managing the foreign policy bureaucracy. Presidential management depends on the important choices a president makes about his foreign policy orientation, his political agenda and level of involvement therein, his presidential appointments, and the organization of the decisionmaking process. As the bureaucracy has grown in size and complexity, the National Security Council has come to be the major institution involved in managing the foreign policy bureaucracy, though not as originally intended. The president has come to rely increasingly on a White House–centered foreign policy process managed by the national security adviser and staff.

These developments do not guarantee that the formal NSC process will run as smoothly or that the informal advisory process will be as collegial as presidents would like. In fact, many observers of U.S. foreign policy believe that the national security adviser has become too prominent as a foreign policy adviser and spokesman, to the detriment of his more important role as coordinator of the policymaking process. Nevertheless, successful management of the foreign policy–making process depends largely on the president's choices and particular style of interaction.

From the perspective of the years since World War II, there have been both continuity and change in the overall making of U.S. foreign policy. There has been considerable continuity in the national security process and reliance on the NSC. The major change has been in the area of foreign economic policy making, which no longer takes a backseat to national security policy making, as it did during the cold war.

The National Security Council was created to address and evolved around national security issues. The NSC process has not been very helpful to the president in areas that once were considered "low policy" during the cold war. Issues such as foreign economic policy have grown in importance for American society and U.S. foreign policy over the last few decades. The national security adviser and the NSC staff, however, tend to lack interest and expertise in these "nontraditional" areas and generally interact more with the national security bureaucracy. Thus, issues that do not easily come under the purview of the national security bureaucracy have been very problematic in presidential management of foreign policy.

Therefore, under President Clinton the National Economic Council was created and has been relied upon since to coordinate much of the process, indicating the growing importance of economics in U.S. foreign policy. At the same time, as will be discussed in greater depth in chapter 9, the NEC symbolizes the continued trend toward White House–centered policymaking in response to presidential efforts to better manage and govern foreign policy.

In sum, it appears that there are *three types of foreign policy presidents or presidential management styles*:

1. A national security president
2. A foreign economic president
3. A foreign policy novice

At least since World War II, presidents, and their closest advisers, appear to be stronger in experience and knowledge in national security policy, or foreign economics, or neither, but not both.

The **national security president** is represented by most presidents since World War II; George Bush, Sr. fits the mold perfectly. The **foreign economic president** has been rare since World War II, Bill Clinton arguably being the only example. The **foreign policy novice** has little experience and knowledge in either national security or foreign economic affairs, most recently reflected by the early presidencies of Jimmy Carter and George Bush Jr. With September 11, Bush Jr. has become a national security president focused on the global war on terrorism.

What the post–cold war world probably needs is a fourth type of "well-rounded foreign policy president," one with background, interest, and knowledge in both national security and foreign economic affairs. This is

increasingly important because, despite the development of a strong NSC, the creation of the NEC, and a much more White House–centered policymaking process giving the president greater ability to manage U.S. foreign policy, the post–cold war presidency thesis and a foreign policy agenda reflecting a variety of issues are likely to continue into the foreseeable future.

To conclude, the National Security Council process is best equipped for assisting the president in managing the bureaucracy on more traditional issues of national security, such as the use of force or diplomacy in support of foreign policy. For these issues the State Department, the military, and the intelligence community have a history and a bureaucratic life of their own that has complicated the president's management task. Therefore, as we will see in the next three chapters, the national security bureaucracy has evolved to be both an important tool and constraint on the exercise of presidential power in foreign policy.

SUGGESTED SOURCES FOR MORE INFORMATION

For a brief and official overview of the entire bureaucracy, see the most current edition of the *United States Government Manual* (Washington, D.C.: U.S. Government Printing Office). An excellent overview of how bureaucracies work is provided by James Q. Wilson, *Bureaucracy: What Government Agencies Do and Why They Do It* (New York: Basic Books, 1989). For excellent overviews of the rise of the foreign policy bureaucracy and foreign policy managers, see Charles Maechling, Jr., "Foreign Policy-Makers: The Weakest Link?" *Virginia Quarterly Review* 52 (winter 1976): 1–23, and Richard Barnet, *Roots of War: Men and Institutions Behind U.S. Foreign Policy* (New York: Penguin, 1972), part I. Raymond F. Hopkins provides valuable insights about recent bureaucratic developments in "Global Management Networks: The Internationalization of Domestic Bureaucracies," *International Social Science Journal* 30 (1978): 31–45.

An extensive literature has developed on presidential management of the policymaking process and the role of the National Security Council. I. M. Destler, Leslie H. Gelb, and Anthony Lake, in *Our Own Worst Enemy: The Unmaking of American Foreign Policy* (New York: Simon and Schuster, 1984), provide an excellent overview of the evolution of the policy process and the NSC. Karl F. Inderfurth and Loch K. Johnson, eds., *Decisions of the Highest Order: Perspectives on the National Security Council* (Pacific Grove, Calif.: Brooks/Cole, 1988), and U.S. Congress, Senate, Committee on Foreign Relations, *The National Security Adviser: Role and Accountability,* Hearings (96th Cong., 2nd sess., April 17, 1980), also provide a good historical overview of the NSC.

Alexander L. George, in *Presidential Decisionmaking: The Effective Use of Information and Advice* (Boulder, Colo.: Westview Press, 1980), provides not only a good overview of presidential management styles and models, but an excellent discussion of the major impediments to a rational policy process and means to improve presidential management based on the major findings of social science. For a helpful typology of the national security advisory system, see Kevin V. Mulcahy and Harold F. Kendrick, "The National Security Adviser: A Presidential Perspective," in Colin Campbell and Margaret Jane Wyszomirsky, eds., *Executive Leadership in Anglo-American Systems* (Pittsburgh: University of Pittsburgh Press, 1991), pp. 259–79.

On developments and implications of the post-cold war era, see Randall B. Ripley and James M. Lindsay, eds., *U.S. Foreign Policy After the Cold War: Processes, Structures, and Decisions* (Pittsburgh: University of Pittsburgh Press, 1997), and James M. Scott, ed., *After the End: Making U.S. Foreign Policy in the Post-Cold War Environment* (Durham, N.C.: Duke University Press, 1998). David Halberstam does a particularly good job of describing the foreign policy dynamics, divisions, and personalities involved during the administrations of presidents Bush Sr. and Clinton in *War in a Time of Peace: Bush, Clinton, and the Generals* (New York: Scribner, 2001), as does Bob Woodward on the Bush Jr. administration in *Bush at War* (New York: Simon and Schuster, 2002).

KEY TERMS

advice and consent
back channel
background briefings
Bay of Pigs fiasco
Zbigniew Brzezinski
cabinet government
Dick Cheney
chief of staff
Excomm
Executive Office of the Presidency (EOP)
Al Gore
Alexander Haig
internationalization of domestic bureaucracies
Henry Kissinger
long-term planning
National Security Act of 1947
national security adviser
National Security Council (NSC)
national security president versus foreign economic
      president versus foreign policy novice
NSC-68
operational NSC staff
presidency
President ford's management style
presidential transition period
realpolitik tradition
Roosevelt's management style
special assistant to the president for national security
      affairs
State Department–centered system
Cyrus Vance
vice president
White House–centered system
White House Office (WHO)

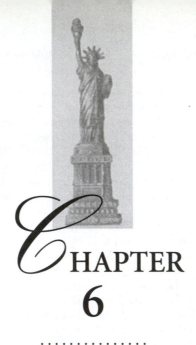

CHAPTER 6

· · · · · · · · · · · · · ·

UNDERSTANDING BUREAUCRACY: THE STATE DEPARTMENT AT HOME AND ABROAD

The Department of State is one of the most important organizations involved in the making of U.S. foreign policy in the executive branch. The State Department was one of four original cabinet departments created as part of the new government of the United States in 1789. Throughout most of American history, the State Department was the lead organization responsible for the conduct of U.S. foreign policy. However, with the rise of the cold war, the containment strategy, and the president's effort to manage foreign policy, the State Department's influence declined. Although the policymaking process is no longer State Department–centered, the department remains an important bureaucratic institution involved in foreign policy.

This chapter will address the following questions: Why has the State Department's influence declined since World War II? How is the department organized and how does it operate? What role do the secretary of state and the State Department play in a post–cold war environment? The chapter also addresses the larger question of how bureaucracy works in general.

A CONCEPTUAL APPROACH FOR UNDERSTANDING BUREAUCRACY

As should be clear from the previous chapter, understanding the foreign policy bureaucracy is absolutely essential for comprehending the policymaking process and U.S. foreign policy. It is important for students of U.S. foreign policy to understand how a bureaucracy works in order to fully appreciate the roles that institutions like the Department of State, Department of Defense, and intelligence community play in the policy process. It is the bureaucracy, after all, that actually implements governmental policies and is responsible for most governmental behavior.

A **bureaucracy,** whether public or private, consists of an organization with the following characteristics: (1) hierarchy (of authority and status), (2) specialization, and (3) routinization.

Bureaucratic organizations usually are hierarchically structured with divisions of authority and labor specified throughout. Hierarchy involves a top-down division of authority in which every official occupies a particular authority role. People in positions near the top of the organization not only enjoy more authority, they also require more general knowledge and skills since they deal with large questions and the "bigger picture." As one moves down the bureaucratic hierarchy, positions become increasingly specialized and routinized with individuals having less and less authority to act independently of superiors and increasingly likely to repeatedly perform the same tasks that involves a tiny facet of the organization's operation.

To elucidate the workings and nature of bureaucracy, a more specific analytical framework (or conceptual approach) is introduced that lays out the key factors as the basis for analysis and understanding that will be utilized in the rest of the book. In particular, *four basic elements or characteristics need to be examined* to provide a relatively comprehensive understanding of any bureaucratic organization: (1) the historical context, (2) the functions (or mission or tasks), (3) the structure (or organization), and (4) the subculture (see **figure 6.1** for a visual summary).[1]

The Department of State is the first of a number of important bureaucratic organizations we will examine that play a critical role in the making of U.S. foreign policy. By examining its broad historical context, purpose, bureaucratic organization, and subculture, we will gain a better understanding of the evolution and role of the Department of State in the making of U.S. foreign policy. Examining the State Department in some detail will not only allow us to learn more about how that department in particular operates but also enhance our understanding of how bureaucracies operate in general and their implications for presidential governance of U.S. foreign policy.

THE CONTEXT OF THE DECLINE OF STATE'S HISTORIC ROLE

The historical context is important for understanding the role of a bureaucracy. For more than 150 years, until World War II, the State Department was the major organization responsible for foreign affairs. U.S. foreign policy was made within the State Department, managed by its members, and carried out by ambassadors and other department members abroad. Other organizations within the government, such as the Treasury Department and especially the military, were involved in the conduct of U.S. foreign policy, but the State Department was the dominant foreign policy agency. During the twentieth century, however, power in the conduct of U.S. foreign policy began to flow to other agencies in the governmental bureaucracy and to the White House. Thus, the State Department has experienced a real decline in its overall influence in the conduct of U.S. foreign policy.

Four global and historical patterns account for the decline of the State Department's central importance in the making of U.S. foreign policy: (1) the growing importance of international affairs for the United States, (2) the growing power of the United States in the world, (3) the global communications revolution, and (4) the rise in the use of force in U.S. foreign policy.

These broad patterns of change throughout the world and within the United States set the stage for the rise of the presidency and other foreign policy agencies at the expense of the State Department.

Increasing Importance of International Affairs. During the twentieth century, international affairs became increasingly important for the United States. From its inception and throughout the nineteenth

FIGURE **6.1**
EXPLAINING BUREAUCRATIC ORGANIZATIONS

Historical Context

Functions (or mission or tasks)

Structure (or organization)   Bureaucracy

Subculture

century, the U.S. government had the good fortune to be surrounded by two oceans and weak neighbors, which allowed the government to concentrate on internal development and expansion across the North American continent with minimal opposition. However, with World War I, the global depression of the 1930s, the global war of the 1940s, the cold war of the 1950s and 1960s, and the increasing interdependence of the international political economy, events far beyond American borders became increasingly important. The U.S. government, including the president, can no longer afford to concentrate solely on domestic affairs and be unresponsive to the international scene. As discussed in the previous chapter, the governmental bureaucracy has grown in size and complexity to respond to these international changes and events. With the creation and expansion of the National Security Council, Department of Defense, intelligence community, Department of the Treasury, and other foreign affairs agencies, the State Department was no longer the only organization within the executive branch with major responsibilities for the conduct of foreign affairs.

Rise of American Power. The United States also became more powerful throughout this period. A regional power at the turn of the twentieth century, by World War II the United States had become the most powerful country in the history of the world. Therefore, not only was the United States increasingly impacted by the international system, but U.S. foreign policy was also increasingly affecting the workings of that system. America's growing global role during World War II and the cold war increased presidential power in the making of foreign policy. The United States was now so powerful and the implications of its actions abroad were seen as so important, that the conduct of foreign policy could no longer be left to the State Department. Instead, presidents now attempted to directly govern foreign policy and manage the growing foreign policy bureaucracy. With the growth in presidential interest and involvement, therefore, presidential management of the foreign policy system increasingly revolved around a White House–centered system using the national security adviser and National Security Council staff.

The Global Communications Revolution. The third major reason for the decline in the influence of

the State Department was the communications revolution. Before the existence of the airplane and telephone, it took months for American officials in different parts of the world to travel or communicate with each other. The president was dependent on the State Department and its members located abroad to officially represent the U.S. government. American ambassadors and other State Department employees consequently had wide latitude in influencing negotiating positions or other important aspects of U.S. foreign policy. Changes in technology and the development of instant communications have allowed the president to become less dependent on the State Department in his day-to-day management of foreign policy.

Increasing Reliance on Force. The final reason for the State Department's fall from its leading position in the policymaking process has been the reliance on force as a major instrument in U.S. foreign policy. With the rise of the cold war, U.S. foreign policy focused on the need to contain the threat of Soviet communism throughout the globe. The basis of the containment strategy—the effort to confine the Soviet empire to Eastern Europe and China—was to deter a Soviet challenge to the international status quo through the threat of force and, if this failed, to use force to roll back Soviet gains. The containment policy resulted in the expansion of America's military capabilities through the development of nuclear weapons, a large standing conventional military force, counterinsurgency forces, and covert operations. This meant not only the growth of the military and the Central Intelligence Agency (CIA) as bureaucratic organizations, but the president's increasing use of these organizations as the means of conducting U.S. foreign policy. Diplomacy, the strength of the State Department, was superseded by the threat and use of force during the cold war years. Hence, the rise of force as the major instrument in U.S. policy reinforced the decline of the State Department relative to other parts of the foreign policy bureaucracy.

STATE'S FUNCTIONS OVER TIME

Each bureaucracy develops its own set of functions or missions or tasks over time. Although the State Department has declined in overall importance, it remains oriented to fulfilling the *five major purposes or missions* for which it was originally created: (1) to represent the government overseas, (2) to present the views of foreigners to the U.S. government, (3) to engage in diplomacy and negotiations, (4) to analyze and report on events abroad, and (5) to provide policy advice.[2]

One of the most important purposes of the State Department is to represent the U.S. government overseas, usually to foreign governments. The members of the State Department who are part of the foreign service (known as **foreign service officers,** or **FSOs**) serve abroad in embassies in the capital cities of foreign countries, in consulates in major cities of foreign countries, in other missions abroad, and in international governmental organizations such as the United Nations. In this role, the U.S. ambassador and the foreign service officer act in the name of the U.S. government and communicate the official foreign policy of the United States to people abroad. Given the primitive nature of transportation and communications fifty years ago, this was a crucial role because the FSO was the principal channel through which governments communicated. Today, with more and more organizations of the U.S. government employing official representatives overseas, this unique role of the foreign service officer has declined in importance. Also, with the technological revolution in transportation and instant communications, the U.S. president and foreign leaders no longer are dependent on foreign service officers to communicate official governmental policy.

A second major State Department purpose is to represent the views of foreigners, usually foreign governments, to the U.S. government. Almost two hundred foreign governments maintain embassies in Washington, D.C., staffed principally by members of their foreign ministries (equivalents of the State Department). An important job of the foreign service is to interact with foreign government officials in the United States and abroad, learn their official positions on international issues, and communicate their views to other parts of the U.S. government. The fact that the State Department represents the views of a certain constituency is not unique within the bureaucracy. It is quite common, for example, for the Department of Labor to represent the views of unions, the Department of Commerce to represent business, the Department of Agriculture to represent farmers, and so on. However,

the fact that the State Department represents the views of foreign governments, as opposed to organized domestic interests, is unique within the bureaucracy, possibly making it more difficult for foreign service officers to understand domestic politics and influence the policymaking process. Also, with the rise of other bureaucratic agencies and the mass media, contemporary presidents are no longer as dependent on the State Department for learning the foreign policies of other governments.

The third major purpose of the State Department is to conduct diplomacy and negotiations abroad. In the past, if the president wanted to conclude a treaty or come to some common understanding with an adversary or friend, he had to rely on ambassadors and foreign service officers to negotiate in the name of the U.S. government. Communications were so slow that the president had little choice but to entrust considerable authority to his ambassadors and subordinates abroad, who were not only the primary international representatives of the U.S. government but also the major negotiators and diplomats. This is no longer the case. The speed of communications now gives presidents the ability to control negotiations on those issues they deem most important. President Richard Nixon believed that opening relations with the People's Republic of China and concluding the first SALT treaty with the Soviet Union were too important to entrust to the bureaucracy, so he relied instead on the personal diplomacy of National Security Adviser Henry Kissinger. Nor is it unusual for the president to appoint a special envoy to represent the U.S. government in his name for a particular foreign policy issue, or for the president, or his closest advisers, to pick up the phone and communicate directly with international leaders.

The State Department's fourth major purpose is to analyze and report on foreign events. Most foreign service officers located abroad spend the bulk of their time analyzing events and transmitting these analyses through cables back to the State Department in Washington, D.C. Most of the FSOs in Washington spend much of their time reading the cables, using them as the principal source of information for communicating with their superiors—ultimately the secretary of state—and fulfilling their foreign policy functions. Decisions and directions for implementing and representing U.S. foreign policy abroad are subsequently communicated via cable to the embassies, consulates, and missions in the field. In some ways, the **cable traffic** remains the heart and soul of the contemporary State Department—consisting of over 2.5 million cables and 25 million e-mail messages a year.[3] Yet, whereas past presidents may have relied to a considerable extent on reports and analyses of foreign events provided by the State Department, they now also tend to rely on their own staff through the national security adviser, have a large bureaucracy at their disposal (including the intelligence community), and consult the mass media to keep informed about world politics.

State's final major function is to provide policy advice to the president. The foreign policy process tended to be State Department centered before World War II but has become increasingly White House centered since the 1940s. Since passage of the National Security Act in 1947 the president has come to rely increasingly on the NSC adviser and staff for the information and policy advice essential to day-to-day management of foreign policy, and to rely less on the State Department. Whatever information and advice does seep up to the White House from the State Department must work its way through the formal NSC process used by the president for managing U.S. foreign policy. The president also tends to rely on a small informal circle of major advisers, one of which may be the secretary of state. Thus, the overall policy influence of State may heavily depend on the working relationship between the president and the secretary of state.

Overall, the State Department continues to play an important role in U.S. foreign policy—this is important to understand—but the State Department as an institution within the executive branch has suffered a decline of influence from its once leading role in the foreign policy process. The expansion of the bureaucracy since the 1940s has made the State Department one of a number of important institutions in foreign policy and has made the president less dependent on it. Although no longer dominant, the State Department continues to perform its primary functions and continues to play a major role in the politics of U.S. foreign policy.

BUREAUCRATIC ORGANIZATION AND STRUCTURE

In addition to historical context and functions, it is important to understand how a bureaucracy is structured

or organized. The State Department began in 1789 with a staff of six, a budget of $7,961, and two diplomatic missions. Over two hundred years later, at the turn of the twenty-first century, the State Department has a budget of almost $6 billion and operates more than 250 diplomatic missions overseas.[4] Of its twenty-four thousand employees, only about thirty-five hundred are foreign service officers. Other employees are basically support personnel: doctors, security officers, secretaries, drivers, and other workers who assist the FSOs, who have primary responsibility for fulfilling the State Department's major functions. Roughly two-thirds of all department employees are located in its home office in **"Foggy Bottom"** in Washington, D.C., and the remaining third are located abroad. For foreign service officers within the department, the reverse is true; roughly one-third of all FSOs are located in Washington, D.C., while the other two-thirds are located at missions abroad.

In comparison to most contemporary bureaucracies within the U.S. government, the *State Department is actually relatively small.* If one considers the State Department as an organization consisting of thirty-five hundred people with a large support staff, for a total of over twenty-four thousand employees, it is among the smaller organizations in the U.S. government. At the same time, the State Department is a very complex organization because it is a global bureaucracy and most of its foreign service officers are located abroad. In fact, because of its geographic scope and the foreign service subculture (to be discussed later), the State Department has come to operate as if it were a very large bureaucratic organization both at home and abroad.

AT HOME

The State Department shares the common elements found in any government or private sector bureaucracy: hierarchy, specialization, and routinization. **Figure 6.2** shows that there are five major hierarchical levels within the State Department: the secretary of state, deputy secretary of state, undersecretaries of state, assistant secretaries of state, and deputy assistant secretaries of state. The top three levels of officials are referred to as the "seventh floor principals," because their offices are on the top, or seventh, floor of the State Department building in Washington, D.C. The **secretary of state** is the chief officer responsible for governing

FIGURE 6.2
OVERVIEW OF STATE DEPARTMENT ORGANIZATION

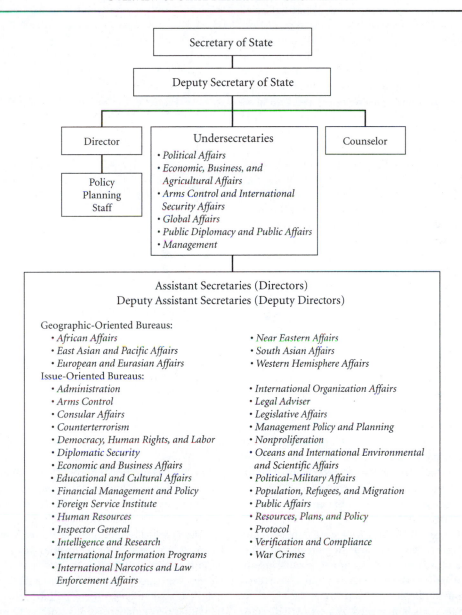

SOURCE: U.S. Department of State, *Atlas of United States Foreign Relations, United States Government Manual.*

and managing the State Department for the president. The **deputy secretary of state** runs the State Department when the secretary is absent, for example, on a foreign trip, and often acts as the secretary's alter ego. The department underwent reorganization in 1999 so that now the secretary and deputy secretary have the support of six **undersecretaries,** each responsible with a support staff for supervising one of the following broad areas: political affairs; economic, business, and agricultural affairs; arms control and international security affairs; global affairs (including the environment, human rights, and health issues); public diplomacy and public affairs; and management (including budget and personnel). The counselor and the Policy Planning Council also may be of value to the secretary of state; both were created after World War II to assist the secretary in providing a broader long-term perspective. However, the counselor, director of policy planning, and the policy planning staff have been used in various ways by the secretary, depending largely on the personalities involved.

The highest-ranking officials in the State Department, the seventh-floor principals tend to be generalists and are responsible for the department's overall conduct. Most of the specialized work of the department, however, occurs at the **bureau** level. The State Department, like other bureaucracies involved in foreign policy, is organized into geographic and issue-oriented bureaus. There are six geographic bureaus: African Affairs, East Asian and Pacific Affairs, European and Eurasian Affairs (including Russia), Near Eastern Affairs, South Asian Affairs, and Western Hemisphere Affairs. The bureaus are run by **assistant secretaries** and **deputy assistant secretaries** (or directors and deputy directors)—referred to as "bureau principals"—the fourth and fifth hierarchical levels in the State Department.

Within a geographic bureau, the assistant secretary has one or more deputies, and the bureau's regional focus is subdivided into single countries or small groupings of countries (see the organization of the Near Eastern Affairs Bureau depicted in **figure 6.3.** Each of these country subdivisions is managed by a **country director** who reports to one of the deputy assistant secretaries responsible for that part of the region, who in turn reports to the assistant secretary. Thus, the assistant secretary and the deputy assistant secretaries develop expertise and have responsibilities at the regional level. The assistant secretary for Near Eastern Affairs, for example, is likely to be a principal adviser to the undersec-

FIGURE **6.3**
ORGANIZATION OF NEAR EASTERN AFFAIRS BUREAU

SOURCE: U.S. Congress, *Congressional Directory.*

retary of state and possibly the secretary of state (and his or her deputy) on Middle East issues. The country director within the bureau is the specialist, the expert, on the current situation in a particular country and the key link in all of the information and decisions communicated—through the cable traffic—between his superiors at home and those in the field.

ABROAD

In the State Department abroad, more than 280 diplomatic missions are operated internationally. About 170 of these are embassy missions (usually called **embassies**) in countries with which the United States maintains official diplomatic relations. The remaining hundred or so missions are **consular posts** that provide various services for Americans and issue visas to foreigners for travel to the United States, support the main embassy in larger metropolitan areas, and maintain other permanent missions, such as to international organizations like the United Nations or Organization of American States. In the few special cases where it does not have full diplomatic relations with a country (such as Cuba), the United States usually is represented by a U.S. Liaison Office or U.S. Interests Section.

The State Department employs over eight thousand people in its missions abroad, and roughly two-thirds of its foreign service officers, about twenty-three hundred members, are also stationed abroad. The size and complexity of embassies vary enormously, though they are all organized in a similar bureaucratic fashion. The largest embassy is in London with a staff approaching three hundred; one of the smallest embassies is in Brazzaville, People's Republic of the Congo, with a staff of only a few people.

Figure 6.4 gives a brief idea of how an overseas mission, such as an embassy, is organized. The common bureaucratic elements are evident: hierarchy, specialization, and routinization. The **ambassador** is the chief of mission, the highest representative of the United States stationed abroad, with responsibility over those individuals employed by the embassy. He has the assistance of a deputy chief of mission and a country team, composed of foreign service officers from the State Department and other governmental agencies with more specific areas of responsibility.[5]

An interesting aspect of figure 6.4 is the *overseas presence of personnel of agencies* other than the State Department. Until World War II, most officials stationed abroad as representatives of the U.S. government were from the State Department. This is no longer the case, symbolizing the decline of the State Department's role in the overall conduct of U.S. foreign policy. The U.S. government has at least thirty thousand employees abroad (not counting American troops in military bases or CIA personnel). Of these, State Department personnel comprise roughly 30 percent of the total, a sizable segment but not as dominant as in the past. In addition to the State Department, most government personnel abroad work for the Agency for International Development (about 20 percent), Department of Defense (about 25 percent, excluding troops), and Peace Corps (about 20 percent). In 1999 the public affairs counselor and the United States Information Agency (with about 5 percent of overseas personnel) became officially part of the Department of State through the creation of an undersecretary for public diplomacy and public affairs. The presence of some of these agencies is so large that they may have their own facilities separate from the main embassy, although the ambassador remains the senior U.S. governmental official within the country.

One agency that is not depicted in figure 6.4 is the Central Intelligence Agency. It does have a major presence abroad but is officially kept secret. The **CIA station chief,** for instance, is likely to have an official posi-tion attached to the embassy in order to provide "cover" and diplomatic immunity. Other CIA personnel and operatives will either be attached to the embassy or occupy private roles within the country (such as working for a multinational corporation).

As discussed in the previous chapter, almost every department and agency within the executive branch is internationally involved in some way and has representatives overseas. Examining the government's official presence abroad reinforces the conclusions drawn above concerning changes in the foreign policy bureaucracy over time; while the State Department's influence has declined, the influence of other agencies, such as the Defense Department and the CIA, has increased tremendously.

AID AND USIA: AFFILIATED YET AUTONOMOUS

Two important agencies that have not received much attention but are loosely affiliated with the State Department are the Agency for International Development (AID), which provides developmental assistance abroad, and the United States Information Agency (USIA), the main agency responsible for international communications and cultural programs abroad.

AID and Foreign Assistance. AID is the governmental agency with the principal responsibility to administer economic assistance and supervise economic development policy abroad. Although associated with the Department of State, it is basically an autonomous and independent agency. AID's mission has been part of a larger governmental effort to provide foreign assistance abroad (see **essay 6.1** for an overview of U.S. foreign assistance).[6]

The Agency for International Development was established in 1961 by President John F. Kennedy (along with the Peace Corps) to help Third World countries develop and to counter the expansion of Soviet influence around the world. AID provides loans, grants, and technical assistance to developing countries to spur economic and political development. The agency administers its bilateral assistance programs through a central headquarters and overseas offices, with a workforce composed of direct hires and personal services contractors (both U.S. and foreign national personnel). As discussed above, AID often has a larger overseas presence than the foreign service in a developing country.

FIGURE **6.4**

A U.S. MISSION IN A FOREIGN COUNTRY—VENEZUELA

Chief of Mission
Ambassador
Personal Representative of the President

Deputy Chief of Mission
Minister–Counselor

COUNTRY TEAM

Mission Unit	Agricultural Trade Office	Agricultural Counselor	Public Affairs Counselor	Commercial Counselor	Political Counselor	Economic Counselor	Admin- istrative Counselor	Consul General	Defense Attaché	Head Military Group (advisory)	Other Agencies Present: Drug Enforce- ment Agency Federal Aviation Admin- istration Inter- American Geodetic Survey Internal Revenue Service	U.S. Consulate in Maracaibo, U.S. staff: 3 State 1 USIA
Home Agency	Agriculture	Agriculture	USIA	Commerce	Department of State				Defense	Defense		

SOURCE: U.S. Department of State, *Atlas of United States Foreign Relations* (December 1985), p. 9.

ESSAY 6.1
U.S. FOREIGN ASSISTANCE

Following World War II the U.S. government began to engage in the practice of **foreign assistance.** Most of this assistance in the post–war years went to Western Europe in the form of the **Marshall Plan** to help those countries reconstruct their economies and stabilize their political systems. As Western Europe recovered from the war and the cold war began, more and more of American foreign assistance was directed to other areas of the world as part of the United States' larger strategy to contain the Soviet Union and communism.

Foreign assistance involves a variety of aid programs and government agencies. *Security-related assistance*—that is, programs that are targeted to stabilize foreign governments and strengthen police and military forces—is provided covertly by the Central Intelligence Agency (CIA) and, principally, by the Department of Defense. *Economic developmental assistance*—programs to promote human welfare, economic development, and political stability in other societies—is provided by the Department of Agriculture (Food for Peace Program), the Department of the Treasury (through multilateral assistance to international governmental organizations such as the World Bank, African Development Bank, Asian Development Bank, Inter-American Development Bank, and other United Nations agencies), the **Peace Corps** (created by President John Kennedy) to help people of developing countries—there are over six thousand volunteers today in more than seventy countries—meet basic needs for health, food, shelter, and education), and most importantly, the Agency for International Development (AID).

Since the 1990s, U.S. foreign assistance has fluctuated around $15 billion a year, with security-related and developmental aid to other countries around $9 billion and $6 billion, respectively. Most of the foreign assistance goes to countries considered strategically important and friendly to the United States. The largest recipients over the past two decades have been Egypt (about $2 billion) and in particular Israel (about $3 billion), which together have received over one-third of American assistance since the

signing of the Camp David Accords brought peace between the two countries. Since the September 11 attacks, assistance has increased to countries in the Middle East and South Asia—Pakistan has been given over $1 billion a year to support the U.S. war on terrorism.

In the cold war era, foreign aid was partly justified as a way to counter Soviet influence. However, in today's political environment foreign aid is a particularly difficult sell. Questions continue to be raised about the effectiveness and purpose of foreign assistance. Members of Congress, who heavily influence foreign assistance legislation and budgets, do not believe that foreign aid is a salient issue with voters, and public opinion on foreign aid often gives policymakers contradictory signals: Americans believe in helping those in need but are much more concerned with the needs of American society at home than of societies abroad.

Most Americans actually tend to greatly overestimate the amount the United States spends on foreign assistance. They would be surprised to know that the foreign assistance budget is less than one-fourth of 1 percent of the total federal budget and that it has not grown in constant dollars in over a decade (thus actually declining quite a bit in real dollars). And in addition to providing assistance for strategic motives, many of the foreign assistance laws require donor countries to purchase American products. Yet Americans typically see foreign assistance as "charity," which makes such programs vulnerable to domestic politics. Nevertheless, foreign assistance, especially from the presidential and bureaucratic perspective, continues to be a vital part of U.S. foreign policy.

SOURCES: Robert A. Packenham, *Liberal America and the Third World: Political Development Ideas in Foreign Aid and Social Science* (Princeton: Princeton University Press, 1973); Vernon W. Ruttan, *United States Development Assistance Policy: The Domestic Politics of Foreign Economic Aid* (Baltimore: Johns Hopkins University Press, 1996); U.S. Congress, Congressional Budget Office, *Enhancing U.S. Security Through Foreign Aid* (April 1994); U.S. Congress, Congressional Budget Office, *The Role of Foreign Aid in Development* (May 1997).

Much of the economic assistance has been directed to support countries of special political or security interest to the United States—that is, allied governments. For example, large amounts of developmental assistance went to Vietnam during the 1960s and to El

Salvador during the 1980s—countries perceived to be directly threatened by communist movements internally and communist powers externally. The goal of developmental assistance, especially during the cold war, was to help states develop mature market economies and stable, effective governments so as to resist these threats. In other words, the U.S. government and AID in particular have been engaged in the very difficult and controversial task of **nation building** and modernizing societies abroad in the promotion of U.S. foreign policy. Recent interventions in Panama, Somalia, Haiti, and Afghanistan suggest that the American effort to build stable and modernizing nations, even in a post–cold war environment, continues to be problematic at best.

Beginning with the rise of East-West détente in the 1970s, but especially with the collapse of the Soviet Union, AID's policies have been redirected increasingly away from security concerns. The agency's officially stated objectives today include: (1) advancing democracy, (2) promoting economic growth, (3) protecting public health and family planning, (4) providing humanitarian assistance, and (5) protecting the environment.

AID has a budget of about $7 billion and is active in over one hundred countries, with personnel in over ninety countries. AID's methods include providing technical assistance and financial support for various in-country projects, although much of the money has been used to provide economic support for the balance-of-payments deficits that most Third World countries have to finance.

AID's small piece of the budget pie has been shrinking. It has responded by embarking on an ambitious reform plan and found ways to cut over eighteen hundred staff and dozens of organization units. The agency has attempted to shed programs that are not clearly related to development and has reevaluated the countries and programs receiving aid. In addition to organizational reform, AID has attempted to reform a scandal-ridden procurement process (for purchasing technical and material support) and respond to criticisms that its policies were helping American business locate overseas at the expense of American jobs. These may have saved the agency from further budget cuts and threats to AID's organizational existence, especially from Congress and, in particular, Republican senator Jesse Helms of North Carolina, who was chair of the Foreign Relations Committee. Hence, AID is likely to continue to play a vital role in foreign assistance and U.S. foreign policy around the world.

USIA: Culture and Communications. The U.S. government, especially with the rise of the cold war,

has been involved in disseminating information about the United States and in promoting U.S. cultural activities abroad. This has resulted in the presence of a small yet important bureaucracy involved in communications and international broadcasting.[7]

The **United States Information Agency (USIA),** known abroad as the United States Information Service (USIS), has been the major cultural and communications agency of the U.S. government. It is engaged in a variety of informational, educational, and cultural activities in more than two hundred overseas posts in more than 120 countries. These activities include international broadcasting and press releases; the publication of magazines; the development and release of film, television, and videotape programs; the maintenance of libraries and book programs; lectures and cultural presentations; and English instruction.[8]

USIA also administers a number of **international exchange programs,** such as the Fulbright program, involving over twenty thousand students, scholars, and practitioners from America and abroad (this is actually one large part of over seventy international exchange and training programs administered in more then fifteen federal departments and agencies involving over sixty thousand people). These programs and activities are most visible in the world's developing countries. The purpose behind USIA's activities is to promote cross-cultural knowledge and understanding that, it is argued, will promote a more supportive environment for U.S. foreign policy.[9]

Voice of America (VOA), which operates under USIA auspices, is the major broadcasting arm and official voice of the U.S. government (see **essay 6.2** for a brief discussion of Radio Free Europe and Radio Liberty). Begun during World War II as part of the war effort, VOA broadcasts a mixture of general news, public affairs programs, music, and entertainment throughout the world in over forty languages (through a global network of shortwave and medium-wave "AM band" transmitters) to an estimated audience of over 100 million people. It maintains a staff of over two thousand, the vast majority of whom work in the United States. The broadcasts originate in Washington, D.C., and are transmitted overseas via relay stations and commercial satellite circuits.

Since its creation, the nature of VOA's broadcast format and content has been debated. Some advocate that VOA should serve purely as a propaganda outlet in

ESSAY 6.2
RADIO FREE EUROPE AND RADIO LIBERTY

Radio Free Europe (RFE) and **Radio Liberty (RL),** in addition to VOA, are the two other major agencies involved in international broadcasting (The Department of Defense maintains the U.S. Armed Forces Radio and Television Service, aimed at American personnel on U.S. military bases and ships around the world). They were created in 1950 and 1953, respectively, by the U.S. government to broadcast anticommunist propaganda to the peoples of Eastern Europe and the Soviet Union. RFE and RL were set up to appear as private entities, staffed by emigrés from Eastern Europe and the Soviet Union, while covertly funded by the CIA. Broadcasts attempted to foment domestic unrest and instability based on the assumption that people in mass society are vulnerable to simple and aggressive "persuasive communications."

After the CIA's covert role became public in the early 1970s, RFE and RL became independent of the CIA and were supervised by an independent Board for International Broadcasting. Nevertheless, their bureaucratic structures and subcultures have not fundamentally altered, and they continued to broadcast propaganda to create unrest within the Soviet Union and Eastern Europe. As a response to the Soviet invasion of Afghanistan in 1979, Radio Liberty began to operate Radio Free Afghanistan. During the 1980s, Radio Free Europe and Radio Liberty broadcast throughout the day in six languages to Eastern Europe and in fifteen languages to the Soviet Union, employed over seventeen hundred people, and spent an annual budget of more than $100 million.

The collapse of the Stalinist regimes in the Soviet Union and Eastern Europe has deeply affected Radio Liberty and Radio Free Europe. Until recently, information for their propaganda broadcasts was heavily dependent on third-party sources due to their limited access to the Soviet Union and Eastern Europe. Today, the content of the broadcasts is much more positive about internal developments. The stations' editors and reporters have access to the countries to which they broadcast and increasingly rely on their own reporting. As of the early nineties, Radio Free Europe and Radio Liberty operated bureaus in Eastern Europe and the former Soviet Union.

The dramatic changes throughout Europe raise questions concerning the future and ultimate purpose of Radio Liberty and Radio Free Europe. They have moved their operations from Munich, Germany, to Prague, in the Czech Republic, while experiencing considerable downsizing in staff and budget. Some people have argued that Radio Liberty and Radio Free Europe can be abandoned completely now that communism has collapsed in Eastern Europe and the Soviet Union has declined as a threat. Others have argued that the two stations should serve a new mission to provide an alternative domestic medium of communications that promotes democracy in the region. Clearly, they are seeking a new role in the twenty-first century.

SOURCES: Kim Andrew Elliott, "Too Many Voices of America," *Foreign Policy* 77 (winter 1989–1990): 113–31; Sig Mickelson, *America's Other Voice: The Story of Radio Free Europe and Radio Liberty* (New York: Praeger, 1983); Lars-Erick Nelson, "Dateline Washington: Anti-Semitism and the Airwaves," *Foreign Policy* 61 (winter 1985–1986): 180–96; John Spicer Nichols, "Wasting the Propaganda Dollar," *Foreign Policy* 56 (fall 1984): 129–40; Christopher Simpson, *Science of Coercion: Communication Research and Psychological Warfare, 1945–1960* (New York: Oxford University Press, 1994); U.S. Congress, General Accounting Office, *International Broadcasting: Downsizing and Relocating Radio Free Europe/Radio Liberty* (April 1995); and U.S. Congress, General Accounting Office, *Improved Oversight Can Reduce Broadcast Violations at Radio Free Europe/Radio Liberty* (June 24, 1985).

which the United States is portrayed in a positive light while American adversaries are portrayed negatively. Others feel that it should operate more subtly, reflecting some of the norms of the journalism profession and the American national media.

Given this debate, the nature of Voice of America's programming has fluctuated under different administrations. During the Reagan administration, for example, VOA became much more propaganda oriented, as seen through the development of **Radio Martí** and **Television Martí** to propagandize the virtues of the American way of life to the people of Cuba. **Radio Free Afghanistan** was created as part of President Bush Jr.'s war on terrorism. The Bush administration would also like to create Middle East Radio Network (as well as contract out through the Pentagon to a public relations firm to present the U.S. side of the war to over seventy countries). Part of the reasoning behind this is that, according to one report, the Voice of America's Arabic service reaches only a paltry 2 percent of the Arab population. Clearly, with the collapse of the Soviet Union and communism in Eastern Europe, VOA (and other broadcasting outlets) has been having difficulties adjusting to a post–cold war world and modernizing its facilities.[10]

Unlike the national security and foreign economic bureaucracy, the communications and cultural bureaucracy is quite small. Furthermore, it remains a low priority in the eyes of most policymakers, for communications and cultural policies are considered peripheral instruments of U.S. foreign policy. A simple illustration of this is USIA's total operating budget, which is less than 0.25 of 1 percent of total military spending.[11] This has resulted in a continuous debate about the importance of the role of culture and communications in U.S. foreign policy, as well as about how to use the limited resources available. In this respect, the collapse of communism in Eastern Europe and the decline of the Soviet Union represent an opportunity to rethink the priority and purpose of U.S. cultural and communications policy.

Many people argue that cultural and communications policy is a powerful instrument and should play a more vital role in U.S. foreign policy. But they often disagree over priorities and the form it should take. Some, as within the Reagan administration, have advocated greater reliance on the power of international broadcasting and propaganda to support U.S. foreign policy. Others have supported a greater commitment to educational and cultural programs to promote mutual understanding and friendship as an important basis of U.S. foreign policy.

Nevertheless, most policymakers give cultural and communications policy little notice. In 1999 USIA became officially part of the Department of State through the creation of an undersecretary for public diplomacy and public affairs and was organized into three bureaus: Public Affairs, Educational and Cultural Affairs, and International Information Programs. Nevertheless, it remains semi-independent and located at the same southeast Washington, D.C., site—distant from the State Department, in Foggy Bottom in northwest D.C. Therefore, with little effort by the president and his major advisers to centralize and bring coherence to cultural and communications policy, the bureaucratic agencies involved are permitted to act with relative autonomy with whatever resources they have.

BUREAUCRATIC PATTERNS

Three patterns concerning bureaucratic structure within the State Department must be kept in mind:

1. It is a hierarchical organization.
2. The policy process is complex and issue dependent.
3. The presidential appointment process has produced controversy.

These patterns are not unique to the State Department but apply to other organizations within the foreign policy bureaucracy, as well.

First, the State Department is hierarchically organized and structured. Not only is there a top-to-bottom hierarchy of authority and labor, but a pecking order also exists within each level. For example, at the undersecretary level, Management is considered the least significant and prestigious of the six positions, while the undersecretary for political affairs is considered the most significant and prestigious by members of the foreign service because it is a policy position involving the essence of State Department activity. A similar pecking order exists at the bureau level and abroad. The geographic bureaus are considered more important and prestigious than those that involve cross-cutting issues, with the European Bureau traditionally the most prestigious (given its focus on Western Europe, Eastern Europe, and now Russia) and the African Bureau the least prestigious (rarely an important area in U.S. foreign policy). The issue-oriented bureaus that are involved in political matters, such as the Political-Military Bureau, also are considered more important.

Abroad, large embassies in industrialized countries, as in London, England, are more desirable and prestigious than small embassies in Third World countries, as in Brazzaville, Congo. Likewise, the political counselor position is most preferable abroad. These patterns of hierarchy and prestige tend to hold generally, but the rise of "hot" issues will temporarily enhance one bureau or position over another, as when the Vietnam War increased the importance of the East Asian and Pacific Bureau and the Southeast Asia embassies during the 1960s, the conflicts in El Salvador and Nicaragua increased the importance of the Western Hemisphere Bureau and the regional embassies during the 1980s, and since 2001, the war on terrorism and conflicts in the Middle East and between Pakistan and India have made the Near Eastern and South Asian Bureaus more prominent.

Second, the nature of the policy process within the State Department is heavily dependent on the importance of the foreign policy issue involved. To understand this process, it is helpful to see the department as a complex bureaucracy addressing numerous issues that determine who will be involved and at what level. The secretary of state, like the president, is most influential for those issues in which he is most interested and involved. Yet most issues are routine (involving visas, a report, or a local incident abroad) and can be handled by a few people in the appropriate bureau at home and in the field abroad. In these cases, a bureaucratic process exists in which information and decisions routinely flow up and down within the department at home as well as through regularized channels between Washington, D.C., and the field offices.

Those issues perceived to be more significant for U.S. foreign policy involve a much larger process, including higher-level officials within and beyond the State Department. This can be illustrated by the U.S. government's repeated efforts to further a comprehensive settlement of the Arab-Israeli conflict. The issue falls within the immediate jurisdiction of the Bureau for Near Eastern Affairs and involves the most relevant assistant secretary and country directors (Israel, Jordan, Egypt, Syria, and Lebanon) and relevant embassies in the field. But the importance of the issue often increases the scope of the participants. The Near Eastern Affairs Bureau principals and many of the seventh-floor principals, possibly including the secretary of state, are likely to be involved and kept abreast of matters. Currently, the Middle East has important implications for other country directors within the bureau and for other bureaus—such as European Affairs (given their dependency on Arab oil); Political-Military Affairs (since it is the site of a major military conflict); Democracy, Human Rights, and Labor as well as Population, Refugees, and Migration (given the Palestinian refugee status and violence in the West Bank and Gaza Strip); Legal Affairs (for questions involving international law); Congressional Relations (given the interest of certain members and committees); and Public Affairs (given the interest of the media and the public). Nor is the issue restricted to the State Department; the president (especially through the NSC adviser and process) and other elements of the foreign policy bu-

reaucracy are likely to be involved. Therefore, the more an issue is perceived as significant, the more likely a variety of bureaus will be involved, the higher up the issue will go within the department, and the more likely other elements of the foreign policy bureaucracy will also be involved, resulting in a larger, more complex policy process.

The third important point concerns the controversy over the appointment process and personnel. The president technically appoints all ambassadors and major officials within the State Department down to the deputy assistant secretary. Since the president is not likely to have much foreign policy expertise, he relies on his personal staff and the secretary of state for selecting appropriate people. Remaining policy positions, such as country directors at home or members of the embassies abroad, are staffed by foreign service officers who are placed through a long-standing personnel system administered by the director general of the foreign service under the undersecretary for management. As with the civil and military services, the president has very little, if any, influence over personnel decisions within the foreign service.

Controversy has always surrounded presidential appointments. Members of the foreign service tend to believe that appointments to ambassadorships and high-level positions below the secretary of state should go to foreign service officers, for they have the greatest expertise and understand the workings of the State Department. Some presidents have appointed more FSOs to important policy positions than others, but non-FSOs have been increasingly appointed at the assistant secretary and deputy assistant secretary levels as well as to ambassadorships. FSOs have been getting fewer significant appointments at home and often become ambassadors to smaller, less important countries. Outside appointees tend to be from business, academia and research institutes, or government, and they may be knowledgeable about foreign affairs but not about the foreign service or the operations of the department.

Particularly irksome to the foreign service are presidential **political appointments.** This refers to those individuals nominated, such as ambassadors, who are basically unqualified for the job—they are friends or, more often, major contributors to the president's campaign who possess little foreign policy interest or knowledge. In these cases, the prestige of being appointed ambassador, a title that reverts to the individual for life, is thought to be a personal thank-you for friendship and political support, not a request for commitment and hard work.

Under President Bush Sr. roughly one-third of the ambassadors were non-foreign-service-career appointees, and more than 50 percent of those ambassadorships were considered political appointments. One example should suffice to provide the flavor of the more controversial ambassadorial appointments by a president: Peter Secchia, a multimillionaire lumber tycoon who was crucial in Bush's victory in the Michigan Republican party caucus over presidential challenger Pat Robertson, was appointed ambassador to Italy. Ambassador Secchia created controversy in Italy by his tendency to use profanity and make sexist remarks in public. Although political appointees can sometimes cause controversy and diplomatic faux pas abroad, they can also breathe fresh air into an embassy abroad and make constructive use of their personal connections with the president (and the presence of a capable foreign service officer as the deputy chief of mission can make a strong team abroad.)

Bush Sr. actually continued a tradition that extended back to President Andrew Jackson in the early nineteenth century. Regardless of the merits of and objections from the foreign service and elsewhere, the tradition of political ambassadors has continued under Presidents Clinton and Bush Jr. and is bound to continue into the future (with the blessing of the U.S. Senate, which usually approves presidential appointments with little or no dissent).[12]

In sum, the bureaucratic patterns found in the State Department are common to bureaucracies in general, including other foreign policy agencies within the executive branch. Bureaucracies like the State Department are complex institutions of hierarchy, specialization, and routinization in which the policymaking process is affected by the nature of the issue. This often produces political tension between bureaucratic **insiders**—members of the permanent bureaucracy—and bureaucratic outsiders—presidential appointees, who are often referred to as **in-outers** since they tend to go back and forth between the government and private sectors and from one government position to another. Insiders, such as the foreign service in the State Department, tend to be part of a particular subculture and loyal to the institution where they have worked for years. In-

outers tend to have little understanding or allegiance to the particular bureaucracy for which they work. How this tension between insiders and in-outers plays itself out has important ramifications for the policymaking process in general, including the particular role of the State Department and the foreign service.[13]

THE FOREIGN SERVICE SUBCULTURE

To fully understand the behavior of a bureaucracy like the State Department, it is vital that we examine a fourth basic characteristic: its **organizational subculture.** Every organization or bureaucracy eventually develops a subculture, or a number of subcultures. Subculture refers to the common set of goals and norms acquired by individuals within a group or organization, such as the State Department's foreign service. These beliefs and norms result in certain incentives and disincentives that influence the behavior of individuals within the organization. The subculture, according to James Q. Wilson in *Bureaucracy,* produces "a persistent, patterned way of thinking about the central tasks of and human relationships within an organization. Culture is to an organization what personality is to an individual. Like human culture generally, it is passed on from one generation to the next. It changes slowly, if at all."[14]

New members quickly discover they are expected to learn and absorb the rules and norms that pervade the organization. These rules and norms are formally or officially communicated and enforced (for example, by disseminating departmental guidelines on appropriate "professional" behavior or by affecting career advancement through the personnel evaluation and promotion system) and informally enforced (such as through peer interaction). People quickly learn how to play by the rules of the game if they want to be accepted by their peers and be professionally successful within the organization. This produces conformity in the behavior of most individuals, thereby reinforcing and promoting the organizational subculture. The subculture of the foreign service is particularly strong because of its small size—only thirty-five hundred FSOs—relative to other bureaucratic organizations. Together, the structure and subculture of the State Department bureaucracy determine how well the department fulfills its primary functions and influences the overall policymaking process.

Identifying and describing a subculture is no simple feat. Discussing the major beliefs and norms that prevail in a group or organization necessarily results in broad generalizations that oversimplify the organization's complexity and are unlikely to apply to any one individual. Despite these complications, much work has been done on the subculture of the foreign service and a strong consensus exists on its major attributes. It is commonly argued that *five key characteristics comprise the subculture of the foreign service officer.*[15]

1. A tendency to be elitist or exclusivist,
2. A preference for overseas experience and to identify with foreign viewpoints,
3. An emphasis on the policy instruments of diplomacy and negotiation,
4. A tendency to be generalists,
5. A tendency to be loyal and cautious.

The foreign service is commonly considered an elitist or exclusivist group. This elitism takes two forms. First, the foreign service is elitist in the sense that it is difficult to become a foreign service officer and FSOs consider themselves to be the crème de la crème of the government in foreign policy expertise. There is much truth to this, for the demand to join the foreign service is extraordinarily high and the job openings are few. The Foreign Service Exam also is extremely demanding. Few applicants do well, and those who score high have no guarantee that a position will be found for them.

The foreign service is also considered elitist in another sense: Throughout most of its history, membership in the foreign service consisted of men who were white Anglo-Saxon Protestants (WASPs) from wealthy, urbane families who often attended Ivy League schools. In other words, the foreign service consisted of a very exclusive **old boy network.** Entrance into the foreign service was based on anything but merit. Instead, the key was an individual's "pedigree"—family, background, education—and his connections. This exclusiveness resulted in an air of superiority among foreign service officers relative to other government employees, especially as other foreign policy bureaucracies expanded during World War II and the cold war.[16]

Much has changed within the State Department, especially over the last thirty years. The old boy system has opened up to new entrants. Connections and pedigrees have been replaced by a more demanding merit system based upon the Foreign Service Exam. Women, minorities, and individuals who are not from the Northeast, nor Protestant, nor upper- or upper-middle class, have become part of the foreign service. Nonetheless, the process of change has been a slow one and the foreign service continues to be dominated by white men from affluent segments of society. (See **essay 6.3** on gender and race discrimination in hiring and personnel systems).

A second characteristic of the foreign service subculture is that FSOs usually prefer to be stationed abroad and tend to identify with foreign viewpoints. For a foreign service officer, to be abroad rather than in Washington, D.C. is to be where the action and excitement is—in the field. It is also the way to see and experience the world, often a key motivating factor among foreign service applicants. This is reinforced by a foreign service officer's privileged lifestyle abroad and constant interaction with foreign elites. The preference is not only for overseas experience but also for choice assignments, such as London, Paris, or Rome. This orientation toward overseas experience and identifying with foreign countries is reinforced by the foreign service personnel system, in which career advancement is based on service abroad. To be posted in Washington, D.C., too often or too long hurts career opportunities. In fact, the ultimate career goal of a foreign service officer is to become an ambassador, not secretary of state or another major policymaking official close to the president.

This emphasis on overseas experience and identifying with foreign viewpoints often is detrimental to the ability of FSOs to operate successfully in the foreign policy maze at home. Because FSOs are more interested and knowledgeable about what is happening abroad than at home, they may not be motivated or equipped to influence the policymaking process outside the State Department. Since they are perceived as identifying with foreign viewpoints, they often are accused of "going native," and other officials in the policymaking process may not take an FSO's policy positions seriously. Although the foreign service has produced some top policymakers, governmental politics tends to be an

ESSAY 6.3
GENDER AND RACE DISCRIMINATION IN HIRING AND PERSONNEL SYSTEMS

Considerable controversy has existed over the composition of the foreign service. Even though personnel selection and promotion is currently based on a merit system, most foreign service officers are white men from more privileged backgrounds. More women and minorities have gained entry to the foreign service in the last few decades, but they remain completely underrepresented in comparison to their numbers in society. This pattern becomes even more noticeable as one moves up the career ladder to more senior positions in the foreign service.

In a 1989 class action suit, a U.S. Court of Appeals found the State Department guilty of sex discrimination against women in its hiring and promotion practices and ordered that such promotion practices be remedied and the Foreign Service Exam revised. Yet some people remain frustrated with the gradual nature of the changing composition and emphasize the need to make the foreign service more democratic and more representative, arguing that diversity can be a source of strength to the department's international efforts in a world of great heterogeneity. Other people tend to emphasize the importance of tradition or competence as the service's supreme goals.

Controversy over gender and race is not unique to the foreign service. Unrepresentative personnel patterns have dominated both governmental and private organizations throughout most of American history. Nor has the exclusivist bias been the exclusive monopoly of the State Department. It also existed in the Office of Strategic Services (OSS), for example, during World War II. But since

that time, most government organizations have experienced a leveling process as they have expanded in size and as American society has become more open. Yet some organizations, like the Federal Bureau of Investigation under the domineering leadership of J. Edgar Hoover and subsequent directors, have resisted to the present day. The State Department falls somewhere between these two extremes.

Although slow to change, the State Department's personnel system is becoming more merit oriented. Yet because the Foreign Service Exam is so demanding, those from more advantaged backgrounds are likely to perform better. Also, because of the foreign service's small size, job openings are few and the rate of turnover is slow. New personnel problems are also arising. Where once the spouse (and children) accompanied the foreign service officer from post to post and played the important role of host, the rise of professional careers for both the husband and the wife has generated much frustration with the rotation tradition of "worldwide availability." As always, controversies over personnel are likely to plague the State Department, and other governmental organizations, into the future.

SOURCES: Judith Havemann, "State Department Acknowledges Sex Bias," *Washington Post* (April 20, 1989), pp. A1, A20; Philip Shenon, "F.B.I. Orders 11 Hispanic Agents to Be Promoted After Bias Suit," *New York Times* (September 20, 1990), p. A11; Philip Shenon, "F.B.I. Settles Suit by Black Workers on Discrimination," *New York Times* (January 12, 1990), pp. 1, 12; U.S. Congress, General Accounting Office, *State Department: Minorities and Women Are Underrepresented in the Foreign Service* (June 1989).

FSO's weakest suit. These subcultural traits make it difficult for the State Department as an organization to influence strongly the foreign policy–making process.[17]

The third major characteristic of the foreign service is its emphasis on diplomacy as the principal tool of U.S. foreign policy. Foreign service officers see themselves as diplomats—a long-honored profession in the history of world politics. And the ability to engage in diplomacy and conduct negotiations is an art. Diplomacy is not something one learns in a book but something acquired through field experience overseas (or in earlier times, it was part of an elitist subculture into which one was born). The problem with the foreign service's focus on diplomacy is that, with the rise

of the cold war, the United States de-emphasized the role of diplomacy as an instrument of its foreign policy. It was superseded by increased reliance on the military, economic, and cultural instruments of foreign policy: force, covert operations, assistance, trade, economic sanctions, cultural programs, and international broadcasting. Despite the collapse of the cold war, as the instruments to support America's global policy have multiplied, the foreign service's emphasis on the role of diplomacy has contributed to the decline of the State Department.

Fourth, foreign service officers tend to be generalists. Although the foreign service prides itself on its foreign policy expertise, most FSOs are not specialists.

This is a function of the foreign service personnel system. Not only is there an emphasis on overseas service, as discussed above, but a rotation system operates based usually on three-year tours. This means that every three years an FSO is stationed in a new post abroad (though every third or fourth tour may be at home), often in a new region of the world. It is not unusual, for example, to find a new FSO with a degree in East Asian studies posted first in Haiti, then maybe in Somalia, then in Washington, D.C., in the Western Hemisphere bureau, abroad again in Cameroon, and so on, maybe never getting the opportunity to use his or her original East Asian training. The little specialized training that does take place occurs within the State Department (no bureaucratic incentives exist to obtain, for example, graduate degrees). The emphasis, rather, is to produce well-rounded experts with wide-ranging experience and intuitive understanding, able to fulfill any foreign policy position. Those individuals who prefer to stay within a region and specialize do so at the risk of career advancement. The major exception to this pattern is when an FSO begins to gain considerable seniority; at that point an area of specialization may be carved out. But the ideal goal for most FSOs remains to be stationed in Europe and to achieve an ambassadorship.[18]

This emphasis on the creation of well-rounded, generalist diplomats runs counter to the expansion of bureaucracy, which emphasizes the development of specialists. On the one hand, the development of personnel with general knowledge and a broader perspective allows for the integration of context and history in policy analysis, something that has eroded with the growth of specialization on top of specialization. On the other hand, FSOs are often at a disadvantage with their counterparts from other bureaucracies because they may lack detailed knowledge vital to an issue making its way through the policy process. This also produces problems of competency abroad. The rotation system provides little incentive for learning the local language and culture, for each posting tends to be a way station toward career advancement. In those few cases when an FSO has begun to learn about Somalia and speak Somali, for example, he or she has been sent to a new post.[19]

The fifth characteristic common to FSOs is their tendency to be loyal and cautious. Foreign service officers are loyal to the foreign service and identify closely with the State Department as an institution. Such loyalty is easy to understand, for most FSOs spend their adult careers within the foreign service and the State Department. Given the limited number of foreign service officers, an FSO ends up working and interacting with familiar colleagues over fifteen or twenty years. Informal networks of relationships that build up with time are reinforced by the formal personnel process in which one's immediate superiors regularly evaluate his or her performance. These factors help to explain why the foreign service subculture is so pervasive and institutional loyalty so strong.

FSOs are also known for being cautious. They not only are hesitant about bucking the dominant beliefs and norms of the foreign service but often provide "low-risk" advice and are reluctant to take individual policy initiatives. As discussed above, the State Department, though a small bureaucracy, operates like a very large one. Before a request or decision is cabled abroad, for instance, the desk officer with primary jurisdiction must make sure it has been cleared (approved) by all other officials interested in the issue. If an issue triggers the participation of officials from seven or eight bureaus, no matter how distant their involvement, all the participants are kept apprised of the process and sign off on any decisions, even if they are quite minor and routine. These overlapping jurisdictions result in a cautious, cumbersome process built around compromise and consensus among the parties involved.

Why so loyal and cautious? These traits can be found in the history of the State Department from its beginning, but they intensified during the late 1940s and 1950s. The end of World War II and the coming of the cold war brought in the rise of anticommunism and McCarthyism in the country and the government, especially in Congress (McCarthyism is discussed in greater depth in the chapters on Congress, the public, and civil liberties). McCarthyism resulted in political charges of un-Americanism and communism against individuals and institutions, especially the State Department for "losing the cold war and selling out America to communism." **Alger Hiss,** a high-level State Department official, was accused in 1948 of being a traitor for his activities during World War II and was convicted of perjury (resulting in the rise of Congressman Richard Nixon, who led the political attack against Hiss). With the "fall" of China in 1949, senior officials of the Far Eastern bureau who predicted that the Chinese Nationalists, given their corruption and brutal authoritarian behavior, would lose the civil war to the Chinese Communists became scapegoats and were forced out of the department and their careers destroyed.

By the early 1950s, McCarthyism became so powerful and reckless that high-level officials within the Harry Truman administration were attacked for being "appeasers" and "fellow travelers" of communism. The secretary of state and the department were, for example, referred to as the "Dean Acheson College for Cowardly Containment of Communism" by Congressman Richard Nixon. With the attacks continuing under Truman and after the election of Dwight Eisenhower as a Republican president, loyalty oaths and loyalty programs were instituted throughout the government, and the practice developed of expanding the scope of classified information, making it unavailable to the public in the name of national security.

In this political climate, many officials were purged from the State Department for not having sufficiently "hard-line" anticommunist views. Journalist David Halberstam described the situation among the East Asian specialists: "The best had been destroyed and the new experts were different, lesser men who had learned their lessons, and who were first and foremost good anti-communists."[20] Survivors of the political attacks and purges within the State Department—such as Dean Rusk, who was in the Far Eastern bureau at the time and later became secretary of state under presidents Kennedy and Johnson—drew the obvious lesson that to take the initiative and stand out from the pack in foreign policy was a major risk to one's career. Those who attempted to operate as policy entrepreneurs and buck the status quo, such as former State Department official George Kennan (see essay 2.2), were pushed to peripheral positions, if they remained in the foreign service at all. Thus, cautiousness and secrecy increased within the foreign service, and an extensive clearance procedure was instituted within the State Department to ensure that an individual was not alone in approving decisions that might become politically controversial.[21]

This portrait of the foreign service subculture is not particularly complimentary. Many FSOs are likely to disagree with what they might consider to be a caricature of the foreign service. However, this is the consensus position within the foreign policy literature, and this perspective also tends to be shared by other members of the foreign policy bureaucracy, including the White House, as we will discuss in the next section. Such perceptions have important implications for State's role in the policymaking process.

CONSEQUENCES FOR PRESIDENTIAL RELIANCE ON STATE

Presidents and their closest advisers have generally had a negative perception of the State Department's performance in the last few decades. John Kennedy, for example, referred to the State Department as a "bowl of jelly." Lyndon Johnson considered members of the foreign service to be "sissies, snobs, and lightweights who sacrificed too little and thought themselves better than their country." Richard Nixon declared in the 1968 campaign that "I want a secretary of state who will join me in cleaning house in the State Department."[22] These negative images of and experiences in working with the State Department have contributed to presidents' increasing reliance on a White House–centered policymaking process.

From a presidential perspective, *six complaints are often voiced* about the State Department's performance:[23]

1. Inefficient and slow,
2. Poor staff work,
3. Unresponsive,
4. Resistant to change,
5. Incapable of putting its house in order,
6. Unable to lead.

It is often argued that the State Department is inefficient and slow. As discussed above, the State Department operates as a very large, cumbersome bureaucracy with an extended clearance procedure that involves numerous officials and bureaus for any issue. The president and other major foreign policy officials have often found that the State Department moves too slowly, especially if there is a pressing issue at hand. When the State Department does respond, another complaint is that the staff work is often poor. National

Security Adviser Kissinger, after issuing a National Security Study Memorandum directing the bureaucracy to provide information, analyses, and policy alternatives, was often frustrated with the work produced by the State Department and forced them to prepare new studies.

Another complaint is that the State Department is unresponsive to the president. Presidents and their advisers say not only that staff work is slow and inadequate but that staff are unable to follow orders well. The State Department is perceived as being unresponsive since foreign service officers are permanent members of the bureaucracy who will outlive the short political life of any president. Furthermore, given the foreign service's particular subculture, FSOs often seem to act as if they know what is best for U.S. foreign policy. A closely related complaint often heard is that the State Department resists change. Bureaucratic resistance to change is not unique to the State Department; all bureaucracies develop patterns and policies over time, making them resistant to changes the president may want to initiate.

The fifth common complaint is that the State Department is incapable of putting its own house in order. In other words, the State Department has not been successful in reforming its structure and subculture so that it operates more efficiently, produces higher quality staff work, and is more responsive to presidential orders and initiatives. Endless studies of the operations of the State Department have been conducted, and a number of efforts at reorganization have occurred since World War II. The net result has been superficial change in the formal organizational chart while the foreign service subculture and day-to-day bureaucratic operations of the State Department remain intact. The difficulty in changing a bureaucratic organization, from without or within, is not limited to the State Department. The subculture of any organization tends to produce bureaucrats—foreign service officers in the case of the State Department—who believe that they are performing their jobs properly, helping to fulfill the functions of the organization, and making a contribution to the public policy of the U.S. government.

Considering these complaints, it is not surprising that presidents have found the State Department unable to lead U.S. foreign policy—the final complaint commonly heard. No matter how much a president may want to rely on the State Department for the conduct of U.S. foreign policy, he soon finds that State is unable to lead, for it has resisted change in the internal workings of the department and the foreign service. This is why the roles of the national security adviser and staff have grown tremendously over time to the detriment of the State Department.

THE SECRETARY OF STATE AND OTHER KEY OFFICIALS

Despite the decline of the State Department as an institution, individual State Department officials have played influential roles in the making of U.S. foreign policy for the president and within the policymaking process. The *distinction between the State Department as an institution and individuals within the State Department* is very important to understand. Secretaries of state often act as major spokespersons for the administration in foreign policy and major advisers to the president, as was discussed in the previous chapter, about presidential management of the foreign policy process. And lower-level State Department officials may also play important roles depending on the people involved and the issue.

Table 6.1 details the secretaries of state since the Roosevelt years. Many of the people who have served as secretary of state have been consequential in the making of U.S. foreign policy. Henry Kissinger, Cyrus Vance, George Shultz, James Baker, Warren Christopher, Madeline Albright, and Colin Powell are all examples of strong and powerful secretaries of state in U.S. foreign policy who have had good relationships with the president since the ascendancy of a White House–centered system.

Strong and powerful secretaries of state, in turn, rely heavily on many officials within the State Department (some of which are in-outers) for the information and advice in formulating their policy positions. Hence, the decline of the State Department as an institution in the formal policymaking process has not foreclosed key State Department officials from exercising influence in the foreign policy–making process. The case of **Madeline Albright** under President Clinton is particularly interesting since she is the first woman to

TABLE **6.1**
SECRETARIES OF STATE

NAME	YEAR	PRESIDENT	BACKGROUND
Edward R. Stettinius	1944	Truman	Business and government
James F. Byrnes	1945	Truman	Law, Congress, and Supreme Court
George C. Marshall	1947	Truman	Army
Dean Acheson	1949	Truman	Law and government
John Foster Dulles	1953	Eisenhower	Law and government
Christian A. Herter	1959	Eisenhower	Congress and government
Dean Rusk	1961	Kennedy	Foundation and government
William P. Rogers	1969	Nixon	Law and government
Henry Kissinger	1973	Nixon	Academia and government
Cyrus R. Vance	1977	Carter	Law and government
Edmund S. Muskie	1980	Carter	Law, Congress, and government
Alexander M. Haig	1981	Reagan	Army and government
George P. Shultz	1982	Reagan	Academia, business, and government
James A. Baker, III	1989	Bush, Sr.	Law and government
Lawrence S. Eagleburger	1992	Bush, Sr.	Government
Warren M. Christopher	1993	Clinton	Law and government
Madeline K. Albright	1997	Clinton	Academia and government
Colin Powell	2001	Bush, Jr.	Army and government

become secretary of state in the history of the United States (see **essay 6.4**).

THE FUTURE?

With the end of the cold war, it would be logical to conclude that the State Department as an institution should play a more prominent role in the making of U.S. foreign policy. The functions of the State Department would appear to be in greater demand in a post–cold war environment. Yet, it must be pointed out that the negative perceptions of the department's competency shared by political leaders and the continued likelihood of global conflict, such as the Persian Gulf and Kosovo wars as well as the war on terrorism, suggest that the department's status is not likely to change dramatically.[24]

This is the conclusion of a management task force commissioned by the Department of State to examine its own role and needs into the future given the collapse of the cold war. Entitled *State 2000: A New Model for Managing Foreign Affairs,* the study concluded that "this report puts a particular premium on leadership of the Department of State that is open to new ideas and that promotes a new culture in the institution. It is time to forge a new mind-set." Yet, they explicitly acknowledged that it will be "a difficult adaptation for an institution bound in tradition" and "there are, of course, limits to what the leadership of the Department can do about the culture of the institution." The report ended on this striking note: "The Cold War is over. . . . If we cannot change now—as a nation, as a government and as an institution—when can we?"[25]

Therefore, it should no longer be surprising that, although the State Department will remain a key

ESSAY 6.4
MADELINE ALBRIGHT

THE FIRST WOMAN AT THE TOP OF FOGGY BOTTOM

Madeline K. Albright secured her place in history as the first woman to be secretary of state in February 1997. *Throughout American history, the making of U.S. foreign policy has been fundamentally a male affair.* However, since the 1960s and the Vietnam War, more and more women have become involved in international affairs and have begun to occupy more foreign policy positions and more prominent roles. Jeane Kirkpatrick became the first female American ambassador to the United Nations under President Reagan. Laura Tyson was President Clinton's national economic adviser. Condoleezza Rice became the first woman to occupy the prominent position of national security adviser under President Bush Jr. But the appointment of Albright is the most significant because of the secretary of state's special, prominent role in U.S. foreign policy.

Her rise is a great success story for an immigrant and a woman. Born in Czechoslovakia in 1937, Albright had to flee from her home country when it was taken over by communists in 1948. She and her family eventually immigrated to the United States, where she was educated at Wellesley, a women's college. She got involved in politics during her college years as a volunteer for presidential candidate Adlai Stevenson. Her marriage from 1959 to 1982 to Joseph Albright saw her through the raising of three daughters, a Ph.D. in political science, and a budding political career with the Democratic party. Strangely, it wasn't until she was appointed secretary of state that she publicly acknowledged that she had just become aware—at age sixty—of her Jewish heritage.

Her appointment as U.S. ambassador to the United Nations secured her a prominent position in the arena of foreign policy. From 1993 to 1996, Albright firmly asserted President Clinton's wishes for tough stands on issues ranging from Bosnia to Haiti. In her early years at the UN, she promoted the practice of "assertive multilateralism." When Secretary of State Warren Christopher made it clear to President Clinton that he wanted to leave government service, Albright finally got the call she had been longing for—although, as with most major presidential appointments, the choice was far from unanimous among Clinton's inner circle.

An advocate of American activism and assertiveness, Secretary Albright was likely to take a more proactive approach to foreign policy and was often successful in getting the support of the president and Congress (such as concerning Kosovo). She also proved to be a relatively strong foreign policy voice, especially in comparison to her predecessor. Albright was able to project an image of strength complemented with enough femininity to win her the respect of top foreign leaders.

In a society where women are highly underrepresented throughout government, particularly at the higher levels, even the image of breaking into top positions offers encouragement to the ranks of women and minorities hoping to garner employment in foreign policy. Fittingly, one journalist has written of Albright's appointment as secretary of state: "The image of a woman leading American diplomacy makes a statement that no slogan can."

SOURCES: Matthew Cooper, "The Lady Is a Hawk," *Newsweek* (December 16, 1996), pp. 24–28; Matthew Cooper and Melinda Liu, "Bright Light," *Newsweek* (February 10, 1997), pp. 22–29; Nancy Gibbs, "The Many Lives of Madeline," *Time* (February 17, 1997), pp. 52–61; Jacob Heilbrunn, "Albright's Mission," *New Republic* (August 22 & 29, 1994), pp. 19–25.

agency in the foreign policy bureaucracy and individual officials within the department will continue to play significant roles, the president has turned to other agencies within the government for information, advice, and management of the national security process, such as the Department of Defense and the intelligence community in addition to the National Security Council. Yet, as we will see in the next two chapters, the president has had problems in managing these bureaucratic organizations as well.

SOURCES FOR MORE INFORMATION

The State Department and the foreign service have not received the kind of attention that other elements of the national security bureaucracy such as the NSC, the military establishment, and the CIA have received. Nevertheless, for a good history and overview of the State Department in U.S. foreign policy, see Barry Rubin, *Secrets of State: The State Department and the Struggle Over U.S.*

Foreign Policy (New York: Oxford University Press, 1985). A strong analysis of the tension between insiders and in-outers and its impact on the State Department and the NSC in the policymaking process is given by Bert A. Rockman in "America's Department of State: Irregular and Regular Syndromes of Policy Making," *American Political Science Review* (December 1981): 911–27. Anthony Lake, director of policy planning under President Carter, provides an informative illustration of the dynamics of the State Department's policymaking process toward Nicaragua in *Somoza Falling* (Boston: Houghton Mifflin, 1989).

An excellent discussion of the foreign service subculture and its impact on the State Department's role in the policy process that is still quite relevant is supplied by Duncan Clarke, "Why State Can't Lead," *Foreign Policy* (spring 1987): 128–42. Although dated, Charlton Ogburn, Jr., provides a realistic description of the typical day-to-day bureaucratic flow of activity and cable traffic within the Department of State in "The Flow of Policy Making in the Department of State," in H. Field Haviland, Jr., and Associates, *The Formulation and Administration of United States Foreign Policy, a Report for the Committee on Foreign Relations of the United States Senate* (Washington, D.C.: Brookings Institution, 1960): 172–77. For a look inside the workings of an embassy abroad, see Robert Hopkins Miller, *Inside an Embassy: The Political Role of Diplomats Abroad* (Washington, D.C.: Congressional Quarterly Press, 1992).

The opportunities and challenges that the end of the cold war has posed for the State Department as an institution are discussed by John Owens, "The U.S. Foreign Service: An Institution in Crisis," *Mediterranean Quarterly* (summer 1991): 27–50; Strobe Talbott, "Globalization and Diplomacy: A Practitioner's Perspective," *Foreign Policy* (fall 1997): 69–83; and U.S. Department of State, *State 2000: A New Model for Managing Foreign Affairs* (December 1992).

KEY TERMS

Alger Hiss
ambassador
assistant secretary
bureaucracy
bureaus
cable traffic
CIA station chief
consular posts
country director
deputy assistant secretary
deputy secretary of state
embassies
Foggy Bottom
foreign assistance
foreign service officer (FSO)
insiders versus in-outers
international exchange programs
Madeline Albright
Marshall Plan
nation building
old boy network
organizational subculture
Peace Corps
Radio Free Afghanistan
Radio Free Europe
Radio Liberty
Radio and Television Martí
secretary of state
undersecretary
United States Information Agency (USIA)
Voice of America (VOA)

CHAPTER 7

. . . .

THE MILITARY ESTABLISHMENT

The U.S. military is a governmental institution that experienced tremendous growth in the twentieth century. Throughout most of its history until World War II, the United States had a modestly sized military that was distant from much of American society. But with the war and rise of the cold war, the military grew to be the largest bureaucratic institution in the United States and a major force in American foreign policy. Since the end of the cold war, the military has continued to be a very significant bureaucracy despite some downsizing. Yet surprisingly, the military has not received much attention in works that attempt to understand the politics of U.S. foreign policy.

This chapter will examine the historical evolution, functions, organizational structure, and subcultures of the military establishment—relying on the same framework described in the previous chapter for examining the bureaucracy—and discuss their effects upon the policymaking process and the use of force in the conduct of U.S. foreign policy. The chapter will also address the following questions: What has been the impact of the Goldwater-Nichols Act of 1986, the end of the cold war, and the global war on terrorism in light of

September 11, 2001, within the military establishment and for the politics of U.S. foreign policy?

HISTORICAL TRENDS AND OVERVIEW

Two very different militaries have existed since the beginning of the United States: a small professional military during the country's first 150 years and an immense military establishment since World War II.[1]

THE OLD U.S. MILITARY

Three characteristics prevailed during much of American military history to World War II. First, the United States generally maintained only a small career military. During times of conflict—such as the War of 1812, the Mexican-American War, the Civil War, and World War I—the U.S. government recruited a "citizen militia," forming a large military to fight the war and then quickly demobilizing it when hostilities ceased. Much of this can be explained by the limited threats to the U.S. government and its citizens, given its fortunate geographic location and the relative weakness of its two neighbors. This policy was reinforced by a popular distrust of the large professional military establishments that existed in the Old World.

The second characteristic of the military was that it was extremely fragmented and decentralized. Instead of a unified military with different services responsible for different missions, the United States government maintained two separate military departments: a **Department of the Navy** (including the Marines) and a **War Department** (consisting of the army and later an army air corps—the embryo of today's separate air force). These were two of the four original departments included in the executive branch, and they were separate and autonomous. Overall direction and coordination were the responsibility not of the military but of a civilian commander in chief, the president of the United States.

The third important characteristic of the pre-World War II military was that it was an important source of political recruitment. Many of America's major political leaders were once generals in the U.S. Army. For example, presidents George Washington, Andrew Jackson, Ulysses S. Grant, and Dwight Eisenhower, to name a few, were prominent generals in the army. Their prowess as warriors was responsible for their later recruitment and success as politicians. The role of military experience and a war record in political recruitment and success has not been restricted to the presidency but has been apparent at all levels of America's political system throughout its history. With America's trying experience in the Vietnam War the issue of military experience lost much of its value in the recruitment of candidates and in political campaigning, but it can occasionally become an issue, as it did during the 1992 presidential campaign over the question of Bill Clinton's avoidance of the draft.

Although the professional U.S. military has been small, structurally fragmented, and a source of political recruitment throughout much of its history, one should not conclude that it has not been an active force in U.S. foreign policy. In addition to protecting the territorial integrity of the United States before World War II, the U.S. military was actively used to support westward expansion (for example, to defeat and control the

Native Americans), as well as American commerce and interests abroad. As discussed in chapter 2, from 1798 to *before* the beginning of World War II there were 162 instances of the use of U.S. armed forces abroad (review **table 2.1**).[2] This figure excludes the use of U.S. armed forces against Native Americans. Thus, the military has played an active part in the history of U.S. foreign policy as it evolved from a continental power to a regional power. With World War II and the cold war, however, the United States became a global power and the military was greatly transformed.

THE MODERN MILITARY ESTABLISHMENT

America's entry into World War II and its efforts to contain the threat of Soviet communism during the subsequent cold war resulted in a set of major changes in the U.S. military. *Three modern patterns have prevailed:* (1) greater centralization and specialization, (2) emergence of a large, permanent professional military, and (3) tremendous expansion in bureaucratic size and scope. With these changes, the old military was transformed into a modern military establishment that has had a major impact on American society and the conduct of U.S. foreign policy.

Efforts at Greater Unification and Specialization. The experience of World War II created concern for the need to unify the military, as symbolized by the passage of the National Security Act of 1947. There was concern not only over the policymaking process at the presidential level during World War II, prompting the creation of the National Security Council, but also about the fragmentation, lack of coordination, and infighting among the different services supporting the war effort. Nowhere was this more noticeable than in the Pacific theater, where the military lacked an overall commander of American armed forces. Jurisdiction was divided between the Army and the Navy: General Douglas MacArthur was in charge of American forces in the Southeastern Asian theater (with General Joseph W. Stilwell in charge of the China-Burma-India theater), while Admiral Chester Nimitz was responsible for military operations throughout the northern and central Pacific. This division of authority resulted in two major, and not always complementary, military strategies being implemented by the United States in the Pacific.

The war experience of a fragmented and decentralized military triggered efforts to address this problem. A major debate ensued within the military and the political environment. The Army favored a highly integrated military system, but the Navy strongly opposed this. The National Security Act reflected a compromise: The old War and Navy departments were replaced by a single Department of Defense (DOD) (after the creation initially of the National Military Establishment), composed of a loose confederation of four services: the Army, Navy, Marines, and Air Force. Coordination of service activities was to be accomplished by the Joint Chiefs of Staff, and the Office of the Secretary of Defense was created to make the military more responsive to the president as the commander in chief. However, as will be discussed below, while the military may be less organizationally fragmented than it once was, it remains among the most decentralized bureaucracies in the U.S. government.

Large, Permanent Military. The second major change was the development of a large, permanent military, replacing the small career force that temporarily grew in size during wartime. Although the U.S. military did begin to demobilize after World War II, the rise of the cold war resulted in a reinstitution of the **draft** in 1947 in order to maintain a large military force that received extensive training even in peacetime (that is, when a major "hot war" did not exist).

This revolutionary transformation in the American military did not come easily and was bitterly fought over in Congress during the late 1940s, until the Korean War resulted in American military intervention. This change occurred because, for the first time in their history, most Americans feared for the security of their country and believed that the threat of communism required the development of a large, permanent, professional military to keep the peace.

Expansion in Size and Scope. Following World War II, the **Department of Defense (DOD)** became the *largest bureaucracy in the U.S. government* and American society. In 1989—the year the Berlin Wall came down—the DOD spent almost $300 billion per year and employed over 4 million people: about 2 million full-time soldiers, 1.5 million troops in the reserves

and National Guard, and 1 million civilians. Military spending represented roughly 30 percent of total expenditures by the U.S. government (this percentage was much higher during the 1950s and 1960s); DOD also employed roughly 60 percent of all full-time U.S. government employees (not including members of the reserves and the National Guard) and one-third of all federal civil servants.

This was the largest American bureaucracy not only in numbers but also in the geographic scope of its *deployment at home and abroad.* In 1989, DOD personnel were located on over one thousand military bases and other properties in every state of the Union (representing more than twenty-four million acres, equivalent to the territories of Connecticut, Massachusetts, New Hampshire, Rhode Island, Vermont, and two Delawares). Some 500,000 troops were permanently stationed throughout the world in over three thousand installations, including over 330 military bases in over twenty countries and twenty-five U.S. overseas territories (such as the Panama Canal Zone), predominantly in Europe, Asia, and the Pacific.[3] With military personnel in over 130 countries, "the United States provide[d] military training, in one form or another, to 75 percent of the world's armed forces."[4] In other words, the Department of Defense had developed into a massive, global bureaucracy.

Since the collapse of the Soviet Union, the Department of Defense has experienced some **downsizing** (or in military jargon, there has been a **drawdown**). Military spending has declined during the 1990s in current dollars but remains over $300 billion per year. The biggest cuts have been in active military personnel. Overall, currently there are over 3 million DOD personnel: about 1.4 million active full-time soldiers; almost 1.3 million in the reserves and the National Guard; and about 600,000 civilians. The number of military bases in the United States and abroad has also been reduced somewhat, but almost 300,000 active-duty personnel remain stationed abroad.[5] Although smaller, the Department of Defense remains huge in size and scope and is still the largest bureaucracy.

The military actually consists of a *society within American society.* The military has its own system of laws, courts, and military police (MP). Most military bases are relatively urban complexes that maintain barracks and residential facilities for families, medical (for example, hospitals) and educational facilities (from kindergarten to adult extension college classes), commissaries and PXs (military supermarkets and department stores), and recreational facilities (bowling alleys, movie theaters, and country clubs). The military has made an effort to provide its personnel at home and abroad with every amenity of modern life, at least in terms of material comfort.[6]

In addition to the Army, Navy, and Air Force academies, the military operates its own system of graduate colleges and universities for preparing its middle officers for senior staff and command positions, including the Army War College, Naval War College, Air University, Armed Forces Staff College, Defense Systems Management School, and the National Defense University, which consists of the National War College and Industrial College of the Armed Forces. The military services, individually and jointly, also maintain a number of colleges and research institutes in the health sciences as well as a **Reserve Officer Training Corps (ROTC)** program located in many public colleges and universities in the country. DOD also owns more than seventy industrial plants and facilities, many dating back to World War II.

The Department of Defense and the military services expanded so much in the 1940s and 1950s and in so many areas of everyday life that they have become the major "socialist"—that is, government-supported—sector in American society. Given both its tremendous size and scope, the DOD may well be the single largest bureaucracy in the world.

Furthermore, the military is considerably more than the Department of Defense. For example, the Department of Transportation includes the Coast Guard (with over thirty-five thousand personnel), which has important military functions. The Department of Veterans Affairs (VA) was created to assist wounded war veterans and maintains an extensive system of VA hospitals throughout the country. The space program within the National Aeronautics and Space Administration (NASA), originally a civilian-run organization to promote a nonmilitary space mission, supports more military than civilian missions today. The Department of Energy is responsible for the research and development of nuclear weapons. (See **essay 7.1** for an overview of the nuclear weapons acquisitions process.) In sum, the modern military has developed into such

an immense bureaucracy in comparison to the military of the past that it is more accurate and helpful to speak of the **military establishment.**

FUNCTIONS OF THE MILITARY

Since the early 1950s the military has become somewhat less fragmented; has developed into a large, permanent, professional force during peacetime; and has grown enormously in size and scope. What has not changed are the functions or purposes the military serves. The primary purpose of the military is to defend and protect the government and the state. A second function is to fight and destroy (and for the individual soldier, be willing to give up one's life) in support of the country. This is the soldier's ultimate mission and is such a unique function, in comparison to any other organization within the government or society, that it requires unique training to "resocialize" individuals to accept and engage in mass killing. A third important function of the American military is to conduct military operations at the direction of the political and civilian leadership, as stipulated in the U.S. Constitution.

The maintenance and use of military force became the foundation for the U.S. policy of containment during the cold war, which tended to revolve around a "threat-based" orientation and foreign policy. American troops were sent abroad in conflict situations during the Korean War, in Lebanon in 1958 and the Dominican Republic in 1965, and during the Vietnam War. Barry Blechman and Stephen Kaplan, in *Force Without War: U.S. Armed Forces as a Political Instrument,* found that in the thirty-year period between 1946 and 1975, American policymakers used the armed forces as a political instrument to influence the actions of other countries 215 times.[7] The threat and use of military force has continued since the Vietnam War and end of the cold war, most visibly in Grenada, Panama, the Persian Gulf, Bosnia and Kosovo, and Afghanistan. Knowledge of the bureaucratic organization and subcultures of the Department of Defense is needed to better understand the role of the military establishment in the making and conduct of U.S. foreign policy given the environment and threats that may exist in the twenty-first century.

ESSAY 7.1
THE DEPARTMENT OF ENERGY, THE NUCLEAR WEAPONS PRODUCTIONS PROCESS, AND THE ENVIRONMENTAL THREAT

The Department of Energy has responsibility for the design, manufacture, testing, and retirement of nuclear weapons for the U.S. government. This practice originated with the **Manhattan Project,** which developed the atomic bomb during World War II. The rise of the cold war necessitated increasing production of nuclear bombs and warheads, providing America with a military arsenal to contain the threat of Soviet communism. During the 1940s and 1950s, an extensive network of government-owned plants was built to produce nuclear weapons and, later, fuel for nuclear submarines. These were operated by private industry and universities under contract and supervised by the **Atomic Energy Commission**, which became subsumed under the Department of Energy in the 1970s.

The nuclear weapons production process demonstrates the role of the permanent military establishment and its presence in American society following World War II. For over forty years, this large governmental industrial infrastructure has existed to produce nuclear weapons for the U.S. military, thereby contributing to the formation of a close relationship among the military, civilians within the government (such as the Departments of Defense and Energy, as well as Congress), private industry, the scientific community, and local communities involved in the defense process. The government's production system for nuclear weapons included the following *major facilities and activities:*

Los Alamos Scientific Laboratory, Los Alamos, New Mexico (operated by the University of California). Home of the first atomic bombs; designs nuclear weapons.

Lawrence Livermore Laboratory, Livermore, California (operated by the University of California). Designs nuclear weapons.

Sandia National Laboratories, Albuquerque, New Mexico (operated by Sandia Corporation). Conducts research, development, and engineering of nuclear weapons systems.

Argonne National Laboratory, Argonne, Illinois (operated by the University of Chicago). Conducts research and development on nuclear fuel cycle systems.

Oak Ridge Reservation, Oak Ridge, Tennessee (operated by Martin Marietta Energy Systems). Enriches uranium.

Paducah Gaseous Diffusion Plant, Paducah, Kentucky (operated by Martin Marietta Energy Systems). Enriches uranium.

Portsmouth Gaseous Diffusion Plant, Piketon, Ohio (operated by Goodyear Corporation). Enriches uranium.

Feed Materials Production Center, Fernald, Ohio (operated by Westinghouse Materials Company). Processes uranium for use in nuclear warheads.

Ashtabula Extrusion Plant, Ashtabula, Ohio (owned and operated by Reactive Metals). Processes uranium for use in nuclear warheads.

Hanford Production Operations, Richland, Washington (operated by Westinghouse Electric and other corporations). Conducts nuclear research and development; makes plutonium from uranium; stores high-level radioactive waste.

Savannah River Plant, Aiken, South Carolina (operated by DuPont Corporation). Makes plutonium and tritium from uranium; stores high-level radioactive waste.

Rocky Flats Plant, Golden, Colorado (operated by Rockwell International). Processes plutonium for use in nuclear warheads.

Kansas City Plant, Kansas City, Missouri (operated by Allied Corporation). Produces nonnuclear components for nuclear warheads.

Mound Facility, Miamisburg, Ohio (operated by Monsanto Chemical Corporation). Makes detonators and timers for nuclear warheads.

Pinellas Plant, St. Petersburg, Florida (operated by General Electric Company). Produces components for nuclear warheads and measuring devices for nuclear weapons testing.

Pantex Plant, Amarillo, Texas (operated by Mason and Hanger-Silas Mason Company). Final nuclear warhead assembly point for new nuclear warheads; disassembly for old nuclear warheads.

Nevada Test Site, about sixty-five miles northwest of Las Vegas, Nevada (operated by a consortium of corporations). Tests nuclear warheads underground.

Tonopah Test Range, Tonopah, Nevada (operated by Sandia National Laboratories). Tests the ballistics of nuclear weapons above ground.

These government-owned facilities covered thirty-nine hundred square miles and employ some ninety thousand people. Since much of the work was subcontracted out by the Department of Energy, the overall production of nuclear weapons—at its height during the eighties—involved over 140,000 workers in over 120 (public and private) facilities scattered across twenty-three states. The complicated route from nuclear weapons conception to governmental approval and then to actual testing and production took five to ten years. The stockpile life of a completed nuclear warhead, for which the Department of Energy is also responsible, is fifteen to twenty years.

With the growing pursuit of arms control (such as the Test Ban Treaty), the end of the cold war, and the collapse of the Soviet Union, many of the nuclear production facilities, though still owned by the U.S. government, have been mothballed. Much of the nuclear material that has been produced is, in fact, reusable in nuclear weaponry. However, questions have now been raised as to what to do with these facilities—including the storage, reuse, and transportation of such dangerous materials—and how to address the vast environmental problems that have accumulated and largely been neglected over the years.

Vast resources are needed to dispose of twenty-seven hundred tons of spent fuel, 10,500 hazardous substances, and 100 million gallons of high-level waste over 2.3 million acres of land, involving 120 million square feet of buildings on 120 sites. Some of the deadly radioactive waste must be stored for thousands of years. Estimates of environmental cleanup costs range anywhere from $175 billion to $500 billion and probably involves decades.

SOURCES: Thomas B. Cochran, William M. Arkin, Robert S. Norris, and Milton M. Hoenig, *Nuclear Weapons Databook:* Volume II, *U.S. Nuclear Warhead Production,* and Volume III, *U.S. Nuclear Warhead Facility Profiles* (Cambridge, Mass.: Ballinger, 1987); U.S. Congress, Congressional Budget Office, *Cleaning Up the Department of Energy's Nuclear Weapons Complex* (May 1994).

DOD's Organizational Ideal versus Political Reality

The Department of Defense has expanded into an enormous national and global bureaucracy characterized by hierarchy, specialization, and routinization (or standard operating procedures). To better understand the dynamics of the defense process, one has to compare the formal organizational model to political reality. According to the formal organization chart and the ideal bureaucratic model, the Department of Defense operates very rationally within *a pyramid-like structure composed of three levels:* The individual services implement and carry out the plans and policies of their superiors—the Joint Chiefs of Staff, who consist of the senior military officers, and the Office of the Secretary of Defense, which represents the president and the civilian control dictated by the Constitution. Unfortunately, the political reality of the policymaking process within the Defense Department has been far removed from the ideal since World War II.

The process and workings of the Department of Defense are among the most complex of any governmental bureaucracy. The 1947 National Security Act did not centralize or streamline the civil-military relationship. The actual result was the development of military services that possessed their own missions, standard operating procedures, and subcultures over which the president has been able to exercise only limited control, producing a particular American way of war.[8] The Goldwater-Nichols Act of 1986 intended to fix the civil-military relationship problems, providing a more efficient organization of DOD and a more effective fighting force, as will be discussed below.

CIVIL-MILITARY STRUCTURE AND PROCESS

The military became so enormous and remained so decentralized during the cold war that it was literally impossible for the president to oversee, even with the support of the Office of the Secretary of Defense. Once a program or activity was in place, like the production of a weapons system or the establishment of a military base with facilities and employees, it became very difficult to change because of the economic and political costs involved. If a president had no complaints concerning the services as they were, he was probably pleased with their performance. However, if a president wanted to fine-tune the military or a particular operation, or wanted to reform the overall structure, he was likely to find that the military services and the Joint Chiefs of Staff were often unresponsive to him as commander in chief.

The **services** are the implementers of United States defense policy. The Army, Navy, Marines, and

Air Force each have specialized responsibilities in preparing for and engaging in war. Each service operates bases throughout the country and the world where the troops are stationed and weapons kept. "Strategic nuclear forces" (that is, long-range nuclear strike forces) are operated by the Air Force (such as the Minuteman and MX intercontinental ballistic missiles and the B-52, FB-111, B-1, and B-2 bombers) and the Navy (the Poseidon and Trident submarine-launched ballistic missiles). All four services (and the reserve and guard components of each) are also a part of the military's "general purpose forces"—the classic combat forces trained and equipped for conventional war. The Army is primarily responsible for land warfare. The Navy maintains over five hundred ships, including twelve aircraft carriers with hundreds of aircraft, for sea and coastal warfare. The Marine Corps is as an assault force, maintaining its own air and landing craft. The Air Force operates over two thousand aircraft in support of its air warfare mission. Day-to-day military operations are based on clearly defined divisions of labor (between and within services) and rank (from general down to army private).

The **Office of the Secretary of Defense (OSD)** was created to provide better civilian control of the military and to advise the president. OSD is the predominantly civilian side of the Department of Defense and is bureaucratically organized similar to the State Department. The major hierarchy of administrative officers are the secretary of defense, a deputy secretary, undersecretaries, assistant secretaries, and deputy assistant secretaries, all nominated by the president. Most of the routine day-to-day activity within OSD takes place in organizational units or bureaus that specialize in certain defense subjects and issues. The Defense Department's structure allows for the military through the Office of the Secretary of Defense to be responsive to the president in accordance with his constitutional role as commander in chief.

The **Joint Chiefs of Staff (JCS)** was created to coordinate military strategy among the services and represent the entire military in advising the secretary of defense and the president. The JCS originally consisted of the five highest military officers: the chair, vice chair, chief of staff of the Army, chief of naval operations, chief of staff of the Air Force, and commandant of the Marine Corps.[9] The chair of the JCS is appointed by the president for up to four years, while the other posi-

tions are a function of the personnel systems within the individual services. A joint staff, no larger than four hundred military officers on loan from the individual services for a limited term, exists to support the JCS's work and mission.

The Joint Chiefs of Staff has actually been a weak body for much of its history, unable to enforce a coherent military policy and coordinate the individual services. The chairman of the JCS, the only presidential appointment representing the entire military, had until recently only one vote and no power to force the other members to support him. Each of the other four members represented the interests of their individual services. Decisions over issues tended to produce competing interests that were resolved through compromise and consensus within the JCS, and each service tended to get most but not all of its demands met. In this way, the JCS was able to symbolically present a unified military position that the civilians in the Office of the Secretary of Defense and the president found difficult to combat.[10]

The Office of the Secretary of Defense has had little legal authority to influence the operations of the JCS or the individual services. To illustrate the fragmentation within the Department of Defense and the independent autonomy of the individual services, official U.S. governmental publications, such as the *United States Government Manual* and the *Congressional Directory,* list the Army, Navy, and Air Force (the Marine Corps is an autonomous part of the Navy) as separate "departments" within the executive branch even though they are officially a part of the Department of Defense. The individual services tended to have almost autonomous power within the Department of Defense, making it very difficult for the president through the secretary of defense to formulate a comprehensive and coherent military policy. (See **table 7.1** for the secretaries of defense since DOD was created).

The key to understanding the decentralized process of the Department of Defense since World War II is to examine who controls the **budget and personnel systems,** for they determine how any organization actually operates. Decisions about the military budget (how to spend the money available) and military personnel (tours of duty and promotions) are made within each of the services. Furthermore, the budgetary and personnel practices within each service have become institutionalized and standardized, making them

TABLE 7.1
SECRETARIES OF DEFENSE

NAME	YEAR	PRESIDENT	BACKGROUND
James V. Forrestal	1947	Truman	Wall Street and government
Louis A. Johnson	1949	Truman	Law and government
George C. Marshall	1950	Truman	Army
Robert A. Lovett	1951	Eisenhower	Wall Street and government
Charles E. Wilson	1953	Eisenhower	Business
Neil H. McElroy	1957	Eisenhower	Business
Thomas S. Gates, Jr.	1959	Eisenhower	Business and government
Robert S. McNamara	1961	Kennedy	Academia and business
Clark M. Clifford	1968	Johnson	Law and government
Melvin R. Laird	1969	Nixon	Congress
Elliot L. Richardson	1973	Nixon	Law and government
James R. Schlesinger	1973	Ford	Academia and government
Donald Rumsfeld	1975	Ford	Congress and government
Harold Brown	1977	Carter	Academia and government
Caspar W. Weinberger	1981	Reagan	Law and government
Frank C. Carlucci	1987	Reagan	Business and government
Richard B. Cheney	1989	Bush	Congress and government
Les Aspin, Jr.	1993	Clinton	Academia and Congress
William J. Perry	1994	Clinton	Academia and business
William Cohen	1997	Clinton	Law and Congress
Donald Rumsfeld	2001	Bush, Jr.	Congress and government

very resistant to change. As General David C. Jones, former chairman of the JCS, has stated, "He who controls dollars, promotions and assignments controls the organization—and the services so control, especially with regard to personnel actions."[11]

Decisions over which weapons to build, where to deploy them, and how to use them in combat are typically made within an individual service, validated by the JCS, and usually approved by OSD—all within the constraints of the overall military budget. The president and the secretary of defense might exercise influence on those issues in which they are most interested and attentive. Otherwise, the Joint Chiefs of Staff, the Office of the Secretary of Defense, and the president have limited impact on the actual operations of the services—the heart and soul of the military.

One more complexity deserves mention. In addition to the military services, the JCS, and the OSD, a fourth bureaucratic element exists within the Department of Defense. Each of the services is officially under an Office of the Secretary of the Army, Navy, and Air Force, respectively, to provide additional civilian control of the military. Each of these offices encompasses a full-scale bureaucracy (like the Office of the Secretary of Defense) for administering each service under the authority of the secretary of defense and the president. The reality, however, is that the secretaries of the Army, Navy, and Air Force tend to be civilian spokespersons and promoters of the individual services. Therefore, these offices "water down" the secretary of defense's role and further complicate the president's constitutional role of commander in chief.

With the dramatic expansion, enormous bureaucratic size at home and abroad, and relative decentralization of the military establishment brought about by the rise of the cold war, *numerous problematic trends have developed including* (1) difficulty of military coordination, (2) information problems, and (3) duplication and overlapping of activities. These are problems common to all complex bureaucracies. However, with regard to the military, they have remained unknown to most Americans given the unquestioning patriotism toward the armed forces, the popular folklore about American military prowess, and the Pentagon's public relations campaign to promote the military, for example, through television commercials. Overall, the U.S. military "war machine" has been big and powerful since World War II, yet a close examination demonstrates that it has not been nearly as effective a fighting force or as fine-tuned an organization during war or peace as many Americans commonly believe.

Coordination Problems. Within the military establishment there is general consensus on goals and official national military strategy. However, lack of coordination among the services has made it difficult to develop a truly unified and mutually reinforcing military orientation that coheres overall. Each service has tended to pursue its own mission and tactical orientation largely independent of the others. Thus, the United States has maintained a patchwork military strategy representing the different missions and orientations of the various services, which together may or may not have promoted the overriding goals of U.S. foreign policy.

Why is coordination within the military so difficult? The tremendous size, decentralization, specialization, and strength of the subcultures of the bureaucracy allow minimal military as well as civilian control. This has often led to considerable **interservice rivalry.** The Army, Navy, Marines, and Air Force all compete with each other for resources, control, and preeminence. Even though the military has enjoyed substantial financial support from the president, Congress, and the public at large throughout most of the post–World War II period, competition has been severe among the services for resources, roles, and missions—the ultimate indicators of success and the main tools for building a modern force. Leaders of the services typically deal with this problem by agreeing to roughly equal shares, with the Air Force usually the most favored (given its responsibility for nuclear strategic forces and technologically sophisticated warplanes) and the Army least favored (given its reliance on manpower). This has allowed the services to staple together their individual requests for resources and present a generally unified position to the president, the Congress, and the country, thereby maximizing their political chances of success.[12]

The same lack of real coordination often existed in military operations. Once American forces are engaged in combat abroad, every service expected to get a piece of the action. In the Vietnam War not only were the army, navy, marines, and air force all involved, but the U.S. Coast Guard patrolled the inland waterways along the Mekong Delta. The Iran hostage rescue mission in 1980 involved a mixed military team from the different services with specialized Air Force helicopter pilots who trained to fly U.S. Army Delta Force soldiers for the night mission. The Navy balked at the idea of Air Force helicopters flying from Navy aircraft carriers. To appease the Navy a last minute change substituted Marine Corps helicopters and pilots not properly trained for the night flying resulting in the fiery end to the mission.[13]

In addition to the strong interservice rivalry (between services), much **intraservice rivalry** (within a service) exists as well. Each service is organized into different commands (and units) that develop particular subcultures, with which individual soldiers tend to identify strongly, and compete for resources. As with the State Department, a pecking order of prestige exists within the services. For example, because the aircraft carrier is considered the mainstay of the U.S. Navy, aviators are more revered than surface sailors and submariners, and officers with flight backgrounds are more likely to reach top command positions.

This intraservice rivalry has important implications for America's ability to conduct war successfully, as was the case in Vietnam. Under President John F. Kennedy most of the eighteen thousand troops sent were **Army Special Forces** (or **Green Berets**). Although originally organized in the late 1950s to conduct behind-the-lines training of partisan forces against the United States' cold war enemies, during the early 1960s

Green Berets became specially trained to perform counterinsurgency operations. These operations required certain political, economic, and cultural skills (such as language training), in addition to military skills, to help the population defend itself. However, by the mid-sixties more and more conventionally trained soldiers became involved, pushing counterinsurgency into the background. This was reinforced by the dominant Army view that Green Berets, though held in high regard for their prowess, are the service's deviants or "ugly ducklings" since they are not trained to do things the conventional army way. Hence, as the war became Americanized, Army leaders operating within the dominant subculture pushed the Green Berets to more peripheral roles, such as helping local Indochinese who were off the beaten path in mountain or border regions. The conventional Army, instead, came to rely on the helicopter and the air cavalry—the latest technologies for concentrating firepower by quickly moving personnel and equipment in support of "search and destroy" operations. Such special forces continue to make up only a small number and percentage of the overall military personnel, which has important implications in a post–cold war and post–September 11 global environment.[14]

Problems of Information. Beyond the difficulty of communicating within such an enormous bureaucracy, other information problems plague the military. The first is a heavy reliance on obtaining measurable indicators of military capabilities and operations, while de-emphasizing the more intangible or human dimensions of warfare. Second is a tendency to inflate or deflate the information in accordance with service interests.

In Vietnam, for example, under General William Westmoreland and Secretary of Defense Robert McNamara, **body counts** became the ultimate "objective" indicator of how well or poorly the United States was performing in the war. Thus, if enemy body counts went up, this was used as an indication to the Department of Defense and the country that the United States was winning. Not surprisingly, after a firefight, soldiers on the ground made estimates of body counts from a distance (as opposed to risking ambush) and sent them up the chain of command. Furthermore, soldiers and officers learned to err on the side of higher body counts to please their superiors and advance their careers, resulting in the overreporting of enemy-killed-in-action figures.

At the same time, there were also incentives to deflate the number of North Vietnamese Army (NVA) troops coming down the Ho Chi Minh Trail into South Vietnam. Political battles were fought over the "order of battle"—that is, the size of enemy forces in South Vietnam—with CIA estimates much higher than the military's throughout 1967. The military won the political fight in Washington, but historical hindsight supports the CIA position. Not only did General Westmoreland and the military leadership of the Military Assistance Command in Vietnam (MACV) knowingly deflate and cover up evidence of larger North Vietnamese troop infiltration southward, but the Joint Chiefs of Staff and the civilian leadership, including President Johnson, were aware of the accuracy of the larger enemy numbers. They simply found the lower estimates more politically appealing for boosting public optimism and combating the antiwar demonstrations that were increasing on the home front. Thus, the reporting system from the ground to the military and civilian leadership in Washington reinforced overreporting of enemy body counts and underreporting of enemy forces, giving a false impression to the American people of "light at the end of the tunnel" that was overwhelmed by the Tet Offensive.[15]

Such information problems are not unique to the Vietnam War. They continue to the present day, as illustrated by the Kosovo War, where the number of military casualties inflicted by the NATO bombing were highly inflated as initially reported by the military and civilian leaders. In fact, one of the major lessons of the Vietnam War that continues to have a major impact is that, during wartime, information needs to be closely controlled by the military and the Department of Defense.

Duplication and Overlap of Activities. Given the size and autonomy of and competition between the services, considerable duplication and overlap of activities have resulted. Although most Americans believe that there is but one Air Force, the U.S. military in fact has at least four major air forces: the Air Force itself; the Army Air Force (consisting primarily of helicopters to support the Army's land mission), which maintains more aircraft than the Air Force; the naval air arm, involving a large carrier air force to defend the Navy fleet and undertake air strikes; and the Marine Air Force to support its own mission.

Why does each service have its own air force and fly its own missions? The absence of dependable support from the other services—such as air support from the Air Force for Army troops—forced each service to fend for itself, promoting duplication. Some duplication may be helpful to ensure the success of a mission, but the military services have been so decentralized and autonomous that excessive duplication has been more often the norm.

In Vietnam each of the services flew its own sorties (air missions) against the enemy, often with little coordination between the services. The **air war in Vietnam** was in fact more complex than this because, while the services ran their own air wars in the south, President Johnson and his foreign policy advisers controlled the air war over North Vietnam. Furthermore, the CIA maintained its own air force in support of its covert missions. Thus, the United States not only controlled the skies over Indochina but fought numerous air wars at the same time. In fact, the best way to understand the Americanization of the war in Vietnam is not as a unified military effort under a single commander but as a number of different wars fought by different components of the U.S. government.

Such is also the case with America's strategic nuclear forces, in which a **nuclear triad** is maintained. The United States has had three major ways to deliver nuclear warheads on Soviet (or other foreign) territory since the 1960s: bombers, from air to land; intercontinental ballistic missiles (ICBMs), from land to land; and submarine-launched ballistic missiles (SLBMs), from sea to land. Although Secretary of Defense McNamara concluded during the 1960s that it would take only roughly two hundred one-megaton warheads to destroy the Soviet Union as a functioning society, the U.S. military has maintained thousands of nuclear warheads for over thirty years, since long before the Soviet nuclear buildup achieved rough parity with the United States in the early 1970s. With offensive nuclear weaponry still dominated by the Air Force and the Navy, the Army has been active in promoting an antiballistic missile system since the late 1950s.

THE AMERICAN WAY OF WAR

Due to the Defense Department's structure, some of the problematic trends discussed above, and the orien-

tation of the military subculture (to be discussed below), *a tremendous military paradox exists:* The U.S. military has become a very powerful force over time, yet it is limited in what it is able to perform. The military primarily is organized and trained to fight nuclear and conventional wars—the American way of war—with only limited elements devoted to subconventional or "low-intensity" warfare. Examining the military's record in warfare since World War II, the quality of its performance prior to Goldwater-Nichols was unimpressive, except for those few occasions involving more classic conventional warfare.

Warfare Before and After World War II. Throughout its history, the U.S. military has been organized and trained for classic conventional warfare. The great military strategists and wars that have influenced the U.S. military historically have been European, the British military being the main model for emulation. World Wars I and II, the greatest conventional military clashes in world history, demonstrated the need to organize and train for massive, general conventional war and called for a strategy of concentration of forces and attrition to defeat the enemy.

This was reinforced by the **Korean War.** On one hand, the U.S. military was successful in stopping the North Korean invasion of South Korea after the peninsula was divided following World War II. On the other hand, the United States unsuccessfully tried to militarily reunify the entire peninsula, only to trigger massive Chinese military participation that produced prolonged military stalemate until a cease fire was agreed to in 1953. The three-year war resulted in over 35,000 American soldiers dead (and over 100,000 wounded). The Korean War was both a "limited" war and the only "major" traditional conventional war the United States has fought since World War II—until the war in the Persian Gulf in 1991.

The atomic bombing of Hiroshima and Nagasaki did not change this strategy initially; nuclear weapons merely became a part of the general arsenal in support of the conventional strategy of attrition. The development of nuclear deterrence theory, the increasing destructiveness of nuclear weapons, and advances in missile technology during the 1950s resulted in the military also being organized and trained for a new, nuclear form of war. Since World War II, therefore, the *U.S. military has been prepared to fight principally two types of wars:* most important, a conventional war, and also a nuclear war.

For forty years, U.S. military plans focused on conventional and nuclear war with the Soviet Union. This preparation was the foundation of containment and the deterrence strategy, to stop Soviet expansionism through the threat and use of military force. Such a strategy presupposed a conventional war most likely occurring in central Europe and then on the Korean Peninsula in Asia. It has been based on a nuclear battle to be predominantly fought on the territories of the United States and the Soviet Union. Refinements have been made to these general strategies, such as a concern with limited nuclear war, limited conventional war, and the creation of a Rapid Deployment Force, not all directed solely at the Soviet Union. Nevertheless, the bulk of America's military has been organized, equipped, trained, and deployed to fight first in a general, conventional war and then a nuclear war.

In actuality, the U.S. military also has had difficulty performing well in more conventional conflicts. As General David Jones, former chairman of the Joint Chiefs of Staff, explained, the U.S. military always has been slow to get on track and perform well. Most Americans remember World War II as a great military victory, and it was. But as General Jones points out, the key to American success was time and industrial production: time to get industry mobilized for war production and to get the equipment and troops to the field. It took two years for the military to organize and equip itself in order to really damage and wear down the enemy.[16] And the Korean War was ultimately a military stalemate (which successfully contained but did not liberate North Korea).

Historically, reliance on a conventionally trained military did not pose a problem for dealing with uprisings or guerrilla war. Such conflicts were not widespread and were easily subdued by sending American marines to restore stability in places like Nicaragua, as was often done during the early part of the twentieth century. However, since World War II, in addition to the rise of the United States and the Soviet Union after the destruction of the European empires, there has been an explosion of nationalism, an increase in new state and nonstate actors, and a proliferation of weaponry throughout the globe.

Post–World War II conflicts have had major implications for contemporary warfare. First, Third World states have become better able to resist militarily the projection of great-power military force abroad. Second, most of the actual low-intensity conflicts throughout the world, such as civil wars, guerrilla wars, and terrorism, began to directly involve the great powers. This has meant that use of conventional force has become less appropriate with time and has had greater difficulty succeeding. This situation is not unique to the United States but confronts all conventionally oriented military forces (as illustrated by the Soviet experience in Afghanistan in the 1980s and 1990s).

The Vietnam War. The United States first faced this new environment in Vietnam. Most American leaders, and the public, operated under the assumption that the projection of American military force into Vietnam would quickly contain the enemy and stabilize the situation. Yet the United States and the American military were poorly prepared for a war where there were no front lines, where distinguishing between friend and foe was nearly impossible, where a peasant by day could be a Viet Cong guerrilla by night, and where the enemy's will to resist was greater than the American will to win. Thus, a conventionally trained military was thrown into a most unconventional war. The military attempted to adapt its conventional strategy as the situation evolved, but even a half million troops and $35 billion a year were not enough to defeat the enemy and obtain the objectives of the political leadership. Instead, the military and the United States suffered its first major defeat in war.

The **military lessons of Vietnam** have been hotly debated. Some have emphasized that in future wars the U.S. military must emphasize the ability to deliver massive conventional force more quickly with greater freedom of action from the political leadership. Others have emphasized the need for military reform in order to have a more efficient and flexible military that can adapt to changing war environments and respond to the president's goals.

On Strategy by Harry Summers, a retired colonel in the U.S. Army, was the first major analysis of American's military experience in Vietnam to be well received within the military. Summers argued that the U.S. military mistakenly tried to adapt its strategy and tactics to fight a counterinsurgency war, when in fact the enemy by the mid-1960s was engaged predominantly in conventional combat. He argued the United States should have allowed the Army of the Republic of Vietnam (ARVN) to pursue counterinsurgency in South Vietnam while the U.S. military formed a conventional front along the demilitarized zone between North and South Vietnam (the DMZ) and, by invading Laos, extend it across Laos to the Thai border to prevent North Vietnamese infiltration into South Vietnam.[17]

Besides overlooking the difficulty of training the South Vietnamese Army in counterinsurgency warfare, for which the American military was ill equipped, Summers's analysis has been severely criticized as misconstruing the nature of the Vietnam War. According to Major Andrew Krepinevich, in *The Army and Vietnam*, the enemy relied on an unconventional strategy until the latter years of the war. Despite tactical modifications, the U.S. military was ill equipped and ill trained for the war throughout both the "advisory" and intervention periods that lasted from 1954 to 1973. One quote by an Army general is particularly telling:

> General Williams agreed that "if you really want to be cost-effective, you have to fight the war the way the VC [Vietcong] fought it. You have to fight it down in the muck and in the mud and at night, and on a day-to-day basis." Yet, the general told the correspondent, "that's not the American way, and you are not going to get the American soldier to fight that way."[18]

In *The Limits of Air Power*, Mark Clodfelter, an Air Force major, found that, although the United States dropped more bombs in Indochina than all the allies dropped during World War II, the conventional use of air power failed to deter the enemy.[19] From this perspective, the lesson of Vietnam is that, unless the U.S. military acquires a real counterinsurgency and low-intensity military capability, it may continue to experience major problems when conflicts do not fit the conventional mold.

After Vietnam to the 1980s. The Vietnam War, for the most part, has reinforced the bureaucratic structure and subculture of the military in support of the principle of concentration—to overwhelm the enemy with a quick delivery of massive firepower—along with a new interest in force mobility. Although American society and government have been constantly mobilized for war since World War II, military performance since Vietnam, especially throughout the 1970s and 1980s, has been often found lacking. As military strategist Edward Luttwak concluded in *The Pentagon and the Art of War*:

> Irrefutable facts overwhelm the patriotic impulse to overlook our failures in war—from Vietnam in its most varied and prolonged entirety; to the clumsy Mayaguez raid of 1975, in which forty-one died to save forty; to the Iran rescue attempt in 1980, which ended in bitter humiliation, with eight dead and none rescued; to the avoidable tragedy of Beirut, which took the lives of 241 Marines and other servicemen in October 1983; to the Grenada operation of the same month, in which the high heroism of the troops had to redeem gross failure of planning and command; to the Lebanon bombing raid of December 4, 1983, in which the Navy lost two costly aircraft, where others bombed day after day losing no aircraft at all.[20]

American military incompetence after the Vietnam War reached its peak during the Grenada invasion, as described in **essay 7.2**, prompting military reforms such as the Goldwater-Nichols Act.

Knowledge of the U.S. military's actual performance, however, largely has remained hidden from the American public. One of the factors that has contributed to this is the Pentagon's effort to strengthen public support by controlling the information communicated through the media when American troops are engaged abroad. This was the major lesson the military learned from the Vietnam War—that the press contributed to the military's failure and needed to be controlled. A policy of **media censorship** by the government, in fact, has prevailed in war since the Grenada invasion, when President Reagan proclaimed it a great triumph. By the time the press learned and reported the real story, most Americans were no longer paying much attention (this will be discussed in greater depth in chapter 17, on the media and the communications process).

The problems of military strategy and coordination, information, and duplicating and overlapping of activities in the Post–world War II period were serious by the early 1980s. The additional problems JCS had in fulfilling its advisory role to the president and secretary of defense, along with the military fiascos of the seventies and eighties spurred debate on reform of the military and JCS. The discussion of reform was initiated in February 1982 by then JCS chairman General David Jones at a closed-door session of the House

ESSAY 7.2
The Grenada Victory as Military Fiasco

Many Americans and the Reagan administration celebrated the American invasion of Grenada as a great victory. Much of the excitement created by the invasion was due to the fact that it occurred immediately after the killing of over two hundred American soldiers in Beirut and, more important, it represented America's first military victory since the loss in Vietnam. On closer inspection, however, the Grenada invasion could not have failed, despite the fact that U.S. military operations were often incredibly inept from beginning to end.

What should have been a quick military advance and mopping-up exercise became an incredibly slow, cumbersome, and inefficient military operation. Consider the mission: to defeat a token force of 679 Cubans, most of whom were construction workers, and a few Grenadians on an island that was only 133 square miles (twice the size of the District of Columbia). Yet Operation Urgent Fury required three days and over seven thousand Marines, rangers, paratroopers, and independent commando teams from all the services, backed up by the aircraft carrier *Independence*'s task force, to subdue the enemy and occupy the island—all for the official purpose of rescuing predominantly American medical students who were never in danger.

The problems were endless. First, intelligence was poor. The intelligence community did not know the number of enemy troops or how well they were equipped. When the military operations bogged down after the first day, estimates escalated to as high as several thousand Cuban troops. The military did not have maps of the island, requiring many of the invading troops to rely on tourist maps from Exxon during the three-day operation. And the invading troops were never briefed about a second medical school campus with American students.

Second, the command structure was inappropriate for the task. Although this was a land operation, the military strategy was planned and commanded by naval officers for the simple reason that Grenada is geographically located within the boundaries of the Navy—dominated Atlantic Command headquartered in Norfolk, Virginia. Thus, the operational commander was a vice admiral on the aircraft carrier *Independence*, while there was never any agreement concerning the existence of a single commander for the ground forces and every service naturally had to play a role in the invasion.

Third, the military operations were slow and inefficient. Army rangers (the Army's elite conventional troops)

invaded from the north, while the Marines invaded from the south. Yet, advances were repeatedly stalled by sporadic enemy fire and overinflated reports of enemy strength. The rangers and Marines had to be reinforced by paratroopers from the Army's 82nd Airborne Division on the second and third days. A team of the Navy's elite troops, the SEALs, was dispatched to rescue the governor-general of Grenada but became trapped with the governor and his family in the governor's residence. A secret Delta Force of elite army commandos failed in its mission to rescue political prisoners. Both the SEALs and the Delta Force eventually were rescued by the Marines.

Fourth, units from the various services had difficulty communicating with one another. In one case, it was reported that a ranger unit was unable to call in an air strike to the Navy command. To overcome this obstacle an ingenious soldier slipped into a nearby phone booth and used his AT&T long-distance card to reach Fort Bragg, North Carolina, which relayed the request through the Pentagon to the *Independence* for the air strike.

In the end, U.S. forces suffered eighteen killed (and one hundred sixteen wounded) as opposed to twenty-five Cubans killed. Accidents also occurred: Twenty-one Grenadian civilians were killed by a bombing error, fourteen American soldiers were wounded by an errant U.S. air strike, several rangers were killed when two helicopters collided, and four Navy SEALs drowned in an overturned boat. The operation was so slow in rescuing the American students that 224 of them may have been placed at greater risk by the operation itself, since they were completely at the mercy of the Cubans and Grenadians. However sloppy the military operation, it was ultimately successful and was claimed a great military victory by the Reagan administration. The military response was to issue over sixteen hundred medals for meritorious service and heroism, even though only seven thousand American troops set foot on the island and a much smaller number were actually involved in combat.

SOURCES: Major Mark Adkin, *Urgent Fury: The Battle for Grenada* (Lexington, Mass.: Lexington Books, 1989); Drummond Ayres, Jr., "Grenada Invasion: A Series of Surprises," *New York Times* (November 14, 1983), pp. A1, A6; James Coates and Michael Kilian, *Heavy Losses: The Dangerous Decline of American Defense* (New York: Penguin, 1985); Edward N. Luttwak, *The Pentagon and the Art of War* (New York: Touchstone, 1985); and Stuart Taylor, Jr., "In Wake of Invasion, Much Official Misinformation by U.S. Comes to Light," *New York Times* (November 6, 1983), p. A20.

Armed Services Committee. Jones argued that the ability of the chair of the JCS to advise the president had become watered down by the power that the service chiefs wielded. Additionally, he argued that command and control of forces needed to go through the joint chair with the power to decide force structure and employment options left to the regional commanders once they were given the mission. The legitimacy of his arguments was enhanced in 1983 by the debacle in Grenada and the bombing of the U.S. Marine barracks in Beirut (and reinforced by later events in Somalia). The debate and calls for reform were taken up by Congress and eventually resulted in the Goldwater-Nichols Act of 1986.[21]

GOLDWATER-NICHOLS AND AFTER

The **Goldwater-Nichols Act,** passed in 1986, addressed four specific issues within the military establishment. First, the act redefined the role of the chair of the JCS (CJCS), making him the sole adviser to the president and requiring him to inform the president only of dissenting service chief opinion. This removed the old corporate system of advisory consensus. Second, the act increased the power of the CJCS by providing him with a vice chair and a joint staff responsive to him, further solidifying his role as preeminent adviser to the president on military affairs. Third, the act clarified the operational chain of command of the commander in chiefs and made them directly responsible to the secretary of defense and the president, removing service competition and duplication of effort in a theater of operation. Lastly, the act made Joint service or "Joint Time" mandatory for all officers who wished to be promoted to General, thus removing any stigma associated with service on the Joint Staff. Officers now seek out Joint Staff service, with only the "best and the brightest" receiving such assignments, which mark them for continued service and potential to rise to the very top of the military hierarchy. Ultimately, the Goldwater-Nichols Act had a major impact on the military and its role in U.S. foreign policy.[22]

The initial results of the changes in the CJCS's role were not clearly apparent. Admiral William Crowe implemented the changes, focusing on gradually and quietly consolidating the power of the CJCS. It is said that

Crowe planted the vineyard of the CJCS and General Colin Powell reaped the harvest of grapes.[23] The appointment of **General Colin Powell** in 1989 increased the power of the JCS chair because of his considerable political skills in operating within the military and as a presidential adviser. This has made the presidential appointment of the CJCS even more important and "politicized" (see **table 7.2** for a list of the chairmen of the Joint Chiefs of Staff).

A trend, in fact, has begun to develop wherein the appointment of a chair to the JCS increasingly represents the presidential desires of the time (rather than seniority and JCS successor norms). John Shalikashvilli replaced Powell in part because of his support for the Clinton administration's use of force in Bosnia. General Henry Shelton received his appointment in part because of his squeaky-clean record as compared to the Clinton administration's first appointment, who had a history of adulterous affairs. Most recently, the Bush Jr. administration appointed Air Force general Richard Myers, who has a history with space technology and supports the development of a missile defense system.

At the tactical level, the services used to dominate military operations through the unified commands. Unified commands contain forces from two or more services (the Navy and Marine Corps are considered within the same department) and are regional or functional in orientation. However, the unified **commander in chief (CINC)** no longer is responsive to the head of his service (such as the Army chief of staff or the chief of naval operations). Goldwater-Nichols changed the operational chain of command so that the CINC reports directly to the secretary of defense and the president, usually through the chair of the JCS. This has not only increased the power of the civilians and the CJCS but has made each CINC extremely powerful. During a time of mobilization or war, the relevant CINC now has the authority and power to call up and deploy forces from the different services. In conducting military operations, the world is divided up into five major regions and five major functional areas, each led by a CINC (see **table 7.3** for an overview of the unified commands). One journalist has described the CINCs as the "modern-day equivalent of the Roman Empire's proconsuls," exerting more influence then most civilian diplomats and extremely "well-funded, semi-autonomous centers of U.S. foreign policy."[24]

TABLE 7.2
CHAIRMEN OF THE JOINT CHIEFS OF STAFF

NAME	YEAR	PRESIDENT	BACKGROUND
Omar N. Bradley	1949	Truman	Army
Arthur W. Radford	1953	Eisenhower	Navy
Nathan F. Twining	1957	Eisenhower	Air Force
Lyman L. Lemnitzer	1960	Eisenhower	Army
Maxwell D. Taylor	1962	Kennedy	Army
Earle G. Wheeler	1964	Johnson	Army
Thomas H. Moorer	1970	Nixon	Navy
George S. Brown	1974	Nixon	Air Force
David C. Jones	1978	Carter	Air Force
John W. Vessey	1982	Reagan	Army
William J. Crowe, Jr.	1985	Reagan	Navy
Colin Powell	1989	Bush	Army
John M. Shalikashvili	1993	Clinton	Army
Henry Shelton	1997	Clinton	Army
Richard Myers	2001	Bush, Jr.	Air Force

Although the rivalry between and within the services continues, since the Goldwater-Nichols Act, there has developed a new military emphasis on **jointness.** This may be especially the case at the operational level, with stronger unified commands and a stronger chair of the JCS providing military advice. The military subculture also may be incorporating more of a joint orientation, especially at the more senior levels. All senior officers are now expected to complete at least two years of "Joint Duty"; those who get the opportunity to go to the war colleges (and rise to the top) often attend a war college of another service; and the joint staff of the JCS is now considered a significant duty and an important stepping stone to career advancement.

WAR, LOW-INTENSITY CONFLICT, AND OOTW

Goldwater-Nichols has had a major impact on the military's conduct, helping to alleviate (but not eliminate) coordination, information, and duplication problems. It has also helped to make the military more successful during the use of troops and force especially in post–cold war conflicts.

The U.S. military has experienced important military successes in Panama, the Gulf War, and Kosovo, certain problems notwithstanding. The December 1989 **invasion of Panama** was successful in overthrowing General Manuel Noriega—perhaps an inevitable outcome. Nevertheless, many problems existed with the invasion, and Panama may have been an exceptional case given its location and unique history. The U.S. military enjoyed extremely close proximity, with twelve thousand troops stationed in the Panama Canal Zone, and began to plan for the operation as early as October. Furthermore, the military's Southern Command for the region was based in Panama City, the capital of Panama, and Americans were highly familiar with the country. Even with these advantages, the invasion force was so large—twenty-four thousand troops—that it failed to surprise the poorly trained twelve-thousand-man Panamanian Defense Forces, intelligence on the whereabouts of Noriega and the

TABLE 7.3
THE MILITARY'S UNIFIED COMMAND STRUCTURE

COMMANDS	AREA OF RESPONSIBILITY	TRADITIONAL COMMANDER IN CHIEF (CINC)
REGIONAL		
European Command (EUCOM)	Europe, sub-Saharan Africa, and Israel	Army or Air Force general
Pacific Command (PACOM)	The Pacific, Asia, and the Indian Ocean	Navy admiral
Central Command (CENTCOM)	Mideast and North Africa	Army or Marine general
Southern Command (SOUTHCOM)	Central and South America	Army general
Northern Command (NORTHCOM)	North America, the Caribbean, and coastal waters	Marine general or Navy admiral
FUNCTIONAL		
Strategic Command (STRATCOM)	Nuclear Forces	Air Force General
Transportation Command (TRANSCOM)	Movement of forces and material	Air Force general
Space Command (SPACECOM)	Space operations and satellites	Air Force general
Special Operations Command (SOCOM)	Special-purpose forces of all services	Army general
Joint Forces Command (JFCOM)	Force provider to the CINCs to fulfill future Joint Vision 2020	Army general

level of armed resistance was faulty, the military did not attempt to control or destroy the government's communications center for almost a full day (allowing Noriega to broadcast nationally), and widespread looting was allowed to occur. Much of this was due to the fact that, as the *New York Times* reported, "the main part of the Panama attack was a virtual replay of a World War II battle, with paratroops dropping from the sky and tanks blasting through a city to overwhelm the opposition."[25] The victory came at the cost of twenty-five American soldiers killed and hundreds wounded (many due to friendly fire), thousands of Panamanian civilian casualties (and displaced persons) through indiscriminate bombing and shelling, the maintenance of a large American military occupation force, the provision of millions of dollars in reconstruction aid to the new government, which quickly resorted to old, corrupt ways, and widespread global condemnation for American gunboat diplomacy, especially given its twelve previous invasions of Panama.[26]

The strategy of overwhelming force and mobile concentration of firepower was applied to the **Persian Gulf War** with much greater success. Clearly, the movement of over 500,000 American troops to the Persian Gulf following Iraq's invasion of Kuwait on August 2, 1990, was an impressive feat. No country other than the United States (including the Soviet Union before its collapse) has the capability to move and maintain such a massive force so far and for so long. This was followed by quick military success in a war led by the air campaign, followed by a quick land campaign. In fact, one major military innovation in the wake of the Vietnam War, in particular, was the Army's adoption of the **air-land battle doctrine.** As opposed to the more conventional technique of directing massive firepower at the heart of the enemy, the air-land battle orientation emphasizes mobility and flexibility in the concentration and application of firepower on the ground with the support of the other services in the air to attack the enemy where they might be most vulnerable. The famous "left hook" ground attack by American and allied forces was tremendously successful against the Iraqi forces, and there was considerable air support by the Air Force and Navy.

This stunning success in light of past performances raises the question, *Why did the U.S. military perform so successfully in the Persian Gulf War?* Principally because this was the kind of conventional war that the American military is best trained and equipped to fight. The U.S. military, and its allies, was able to control the skies and deliver massive firepower in Kuwait and Iraq to damage and wear down a predominantly conventionally trained and equipped land army with low morale operating away from home. In addition, according to military strategist Eliot Cohen, "the United States fought in a theater ideally suited to our military strengths, an empty desert. . . . We had half a year to mass and train troops, and to prepare elaborate plans to attack. . . . We also had the luxury of one of the best port, road, and air base networks in the world, including military facilities built by our engineers, and the support of a wealthy and cooperative host nation." Also, with Iraq facing economic sanctions and isolated from the world, the United States "could bring to bear the weight of our cold war–rich armed forces without fear of Soviet opposition in the theater or aggression elsewhere."[27] The Persian Gulf War, in other words, represented a classic conventional confrontation that the U.S. military had not seen since World War II and in which the conditions were optimal for a compelling American military victory.

As successful as the military operation was, Iraq was not an easy military target like Grenada or Panama. The military defeat of Iraq, a country with a gross national product of only $40 billion, was a costly venture that required over a half million American and allied troops in a massive and prolonged military buildup resulting in mass destruction and thousands of casualties. Such a large American military force had been fielded only two previous times since World War II—the Korean and Vietnam wars. The success of the air war was so overwhelming that the Army and Marines, given the shortness of the ground war and the rout of the Iraqi army, were never really tested. Yet equipment and training problems affected the ground campaign. Secretary of Defense Richard Cheney, for example, criticized the National Guard for its lack of short-term readiness—it was activated, but only the noncombat units were deployed.[28] And questions per-

sist about strange illnesses afflicting many of the veterans, referred to as "Gulf War syndrome."

The Persian Gulf War, therefore, was without a doubt an American military triumph but one which must be placed in perspective. This was somewhat similar to the successful **Kosovo War** under President Clinton. Although the physical environment of the former Yugoslavia was not nearly as ideal as the desert, Serbia was a weaker (and more overextended) conventional military adversary than Iraq. Regardless, the American-led NATO attack and massive bombing of Kosovo and Serbia, reinforced by the threat of a ground invasion, was very successful in persuading Serbia's leadership to capitulate and withdraw its forces within weeks. What makes this victory particularly unique was that it was accomplished purely through an air war without the use of any ground troops—a military first. This raises questions that go back decades, and which have been mulled over for years by military strategists, about the superiority of air power and whether advances in technology are sufficient to win wars. How successful was the air war in Kosovo, why did it succeed, and what are its future military implications?[29]

In responding to the challenges of the 1990s and the turn of the century, the military also has placed a somewhat greater emphasis on money, resources, personnel, and training for low-intensity conflict. The Army Special Forces, or Green Berets, deal specifically with training indigenous guerilla forces. The Army's Delta Force and the Navy SEALS (sea, air, land) specialize in counterterrorism. Furthermore, the contemporary military focuses its light and airborne army units specifically on low-intensity conflict. These forces are tailored and designed to operate independently or as part of a larger conventional mission.

The military has also begun to be better prepared to respond to what they call "operations other than war," or **OOTW** (pronounced "ootwah"). OOTW focuses on less conventional military/civilian operations that developed in the 1990s such as humanitarian, peacekeeping and peace enforcement missions. For example, U.S. Army light and airborne units now routinely train with other services at the Joint Readiness Training Center (JRTC) at Fort Polk, Louisiana, where most conceivable low-intensity conflicts and OOTW scenarios are fought against a permanent opposing forces (OPFOR) unit that trains to fight as a guerilla

Stop!

army. Civilian role players augment the scenarios, providing the confusion and fog of war that often occurs in an OOTW situation. The emphasis on reality, including such details as civilian role players who don't speak English, civilian media intervention, and an elusive and lethal OPFOR, push the limits of the joint military in training. The effectiveness of this institution should not be underestimated as many units deploying overseas will train at the JRTC with a mission-specific scenario played out for them that better prepares the unit for execution abroad.

THE PREVAILING MILITARY SUBCULTURE

To fully understand the workings of the military and civil-military relations within the Department of Defense, one has to examine the department's organizational subculture in addition to its bureaucratic structure, functions, and historical development. It would be a mistake to speak of a single subculture for the entire department. The DOD bureaucracy is not only enormous but also diverse, composed of many different elements. DOD contains both civilian and military personnel, with the military component organized into four different services. Additional distinctions also exist within the military, as between officers and enlisted personnel. Thus, one should speak of multiple subcultures within the Department of Defense.

Diversity notwithstanding, there has been a growing consensus among scholars and analysts of the U.S. military that a number of general characteristics have pervaded the military over the years. *Most members of the military, especially career officers, tend to share five characteristics:*

1. A managerial style,
2. Pursuit of procurement and high technology,
3. Preoccupation with careerism,
4. Promotion of the principal of concentration in warfare strategy, and
5. Belief in the separation of politics and military combat.

Many of these characteristics are shared by the permanent civilian bureaucracy within the military establishment, as well, but the focus here is on the military subculture. Goldwater-Nichols may be having an impact on some of these characteristics (as indicated above).[30]

It is commonly argued that the military no longer produces warriors, but rather a "managerial class" of military leaders. The primary purpose of the military is to prepare and engage in war and, historically, carrying out this function required the development of a warrior class in society. In the United States, the military has been the institution where this warrior tradition was fostered. However, the manager has become ascendant over the warrior since modern bureaucratic warfare demands the ability of officers to become "managers of violence." Or maybe to be more accurate, officers are now expected to be both warriors and administrators.

Given the enormous expansion of the military bureaucracy in size, scope, and complexity, this is a natural development. The warrior is most appropriate for command positions in the field, not for administering a large bureaucracy. The skills that have increasingly been in demand as the bureaucracy has grown in size have been administrative. This natural bureaucratic development has been reinforced by the civilian leadership of the Department of Defense, especially beginning with Secretary of Defense **Robert McNamara.**

McNamara entered office committed to seizing control of the Department of Defense and making it more efficient and responsive to the president. McNamara's background was in the corporate world, and he had gained a reputation as an excellent manager while chief executive officer of the Ford Corporation. During the Kennedy and Johnson administrations, McNamara appointed numerous "whiz kids" to positions in the Office of the Secretary of Defense in his effort to restructure the department as well as streamline and improve the flow of information and the budgetary process. Although the basic military missions of the services continued, McNamara was successful in having his managerial approach penetrate throughout the military.

The most successful military officers in the military today are those with administrative skills. Symptomatic of this change are the postgraduate degrees and curriculum pursued by senior officers. Where degrees and courses in history and military strategy were once the norm, today the emphasis is on business administration, public administration, and engineering. Even at U.S. military colleges, knowledge of military history, international conflict, and military strategy is no longer dominant (except at the Army War College, Naval War College, Air University, and National War College for senior officers). The emphasis is not on the art of war but on learning how to administer a large bureaucracy.[31] This has been accompanied by the rise of "bureaucratese" within the military—the development of a technical language among a select group of professionals and bureaucrats (including academics). Acronyms and jargon, such as *MAD* (mutual assured destruction), *KIA* (killed in action), and collateral damage (civilian injuries and fatalities and property damage), have proliferated, distancing the military and civilian managers from the brutality of war.[32]

The rise of "managerialism" has been reinforced by a second characteristic of the military subculture, the quest for more procurement and high technology. A strong norm has developed that a modern military requires expensive "hardware" (weaponry and support facilities). This means not only a large quantity of hardware but the best and most technologically sophisticated hardware available. For years there has been tremendous pressure within the Air Force, for example, to replace the aging B-52 with the B-1 and the B-2 Stealth bombers. Not unique to the military, this pursuit of high technology is shared by most civilians within the Department of Defense (and Congress), as well. Much of American society has an abiding faith in the promise of technology. The goal is not only to deter and win wars but to gain the symbolic value and prestige conferred by state-of-the-art weapons. This pursuit of high technology has intensified with cuts in personnel that the military has experienced since the Vietnam War and, especially, the end of the cold war.

This "materialist" bias for more weapons, particularly those that are state of the art, reinforces a decline in the importance of the soldier-warrior, requires more expert personnel to maintain and administer the hardware, and de-emphasizes the importance of intangibles—such as leadership and will—during time of conflict. It also has led the upper echelons of the military to take a much more active political role in civil-military relations: influencing the president, lobbying Congress (along with civilian cohorts in the defense industry), using the media, and campaigning to build public support for more procurement and high technology (and obviously, challenging those who oppose military requests or want defense cuts). Thus, the military, along with its supporters, has become a potent political force

in the politics of national defense, reducing military accountability to civilian leadership and exacerbating the difficulties the president faces as commander in chief.

A third characteristic of the military subculture is the rise of **careerism.** Many junior officers deplore the paper pushing, the high-tech syndrome, and the politicking as contributing little to mission readiness, but they are understandably reluctant to buck the power of bureaucracy. A personnel system has developed within each of the services that promotes individual conformity to the dominant norms and status quo and places a premium on individual preoccupation with career advancement. There is an "up or out" expectation according to which either an officer is regularly promoted within the service, requiring very high evaluations from his or her superiors, or his career will suffer. Furthermore, officers are expected to "punch their tickets"—that is, serve in a variety of positions and roles throughout their service. This normally includes a combat record, which is usually crucial to high career advancement. As many observers have pointed out, the military career ladder is now little different from the governmental or corporate career ladder, typical of any large bureaucracy. Its effect is also quite similar: to develop an "organization man or woman." In each of the services, the end product is a military officer who learns organizational norms and is able to contribute to the performance of the individual services' missions as they currently exist.

A fourth characteristic is part of the socialization or conditioning of military personnel: the belief in the principal of concentration of forces and firepower as the most effective strategy to deter, weaken, exhaust, and ultimately defeat the enemy. This is what the U.S. military has been fundamentally organized, equipped, and trained to do. Given the different responsibilities and missions of each service, this emphasis has resulted in the historical development of three different warfare strategies. The army emphasizes control of land through the destruction of the enemy's army and occupation of its territory (for the Marines preferably through amphibious landings); the Navy emphasizes a maritime strategy of control of the sea by decisive defeat of the enemy's fleet; and the Air Force asserts the primacy of airpower over every other form of combat for defeating the enemy.[33]

After World War II, warfare strategies of concentration of forces were oriented toward containing and, if need be, fighting the Soviet Union. Hence the development of large general-purpose forces, many of which were stationed on military bases in allied countries, intended to prevent the Soviet Union from militarily expanding beyond the Eurasian continent. This conventional military force was reinforced by the development of large nuclear forces to deter a Soviet attack by the threat of total destruction. Implementing this basic approach to war reinforced the need for a high-technology military administered by a large bureaucratic apparatus. It also has had implications, as discussed above. Since the Vietnam War there has been a greater emphasis on the importance of mobility as well as concentration of forces, especially within the Army. And with the collapse of the Soviet empire, the military has had to redirect its warfare strategy toward new adversaries and areas of the world.

The final characteristic of the military's subculture is a belief in the separation of politics and military combat. Given the nature of the American Constitution, the military perspective is that the civilian leadership, symbolized by the president and the Congress, decide when and where to go to war; but once the decision has been made, it is time for the politicians and civilians to stand aside and let the military do what it does best: fight wars. Some within the military also have concluded, therefore, that the services should control the administrative and operational process during peace as well as war, since peace is a time in which to prepare for war. Presidents and other civilians see the nature of **civil-military relations** quite differently. They believe that the president is the commander in chief before, during, and after a war, and as stipulated in the U.S. Constitution, the military should be responsive to civilian leadership and presidential orders.

Given the opposing interpretations, the military and civilian leadership often have found themselves in political battles during times of peace and war. For example, during the Korean War President Harry Truman relieved General **Douglas MacArthur** from his command of the United Nations forces for insubordination, triggering a national controversy over the conduct of the war and the containment policy. The American failure in the Vietnam War fueled a similar debate, for many attributed the loss of the war to civilian interference with the military's ability to perform its mission, while others blamed the military's inability to succeed within the appropriately described limitations set by the civilian leadership. Civil-military differences

continue to exist and be consequential in light of the legacy of Vietnam and the greater role of the chair of the JCS, especially when it comes to the use of force, as will be discussed further below.[34]

CONTINUING AND NEW MILITARY ISSUES

Because of the military's post–World War II history, its enormous size and scope, and its prevailing subculture despite the changes produced by Goldwater-Nichols, *a number of patterns have continued or arisen in some basic areas* that deserve attention and thought, including (1) waste and military readiness, (2) leadership and morale, and (3) the rise of the all-volunteer military.

Waste, Military Readiness, and Human Error. Most Americans are raised to be distrustful of large bureaucracies as wasteful and inefficient. There is enough truth in this claim to nourish this unfavorable stereotype. Because the largest American bureaucracy of all is the military establishment, it is not surprising to find a large amount of waste and inefficiency within the military that impacts military readiness and the safety of military personnel.

Nowhere is waste more visible than in the weapons procurement process. The Department of Defense contracts with private industry to produce the weapons and equipment agreed to by the Congress and the president in the budget. The defense contract process is supervised by the Office of the Secretary of Defense and the civilian offices of the individual services to ensure that private competition, quality production, and fair prices are maintained. However, the weapons acquisition process has rarely, if ever, operated according to this ideal. Instead, during the 1950s and 1960s, a time of tremendous expansion of the military's bureaucracy and budget, a network of relationships developed among the military, civilians within DOD, members of Congress, and private industry (supported by much of the scientific community) in which everyone benefits from the procurement of weaponry and other defense products (this will be discussed at greater length in chapter 16, where I examine the extent to which a military-industrial complex exists).[35]

"High prices" and "cost overruns" have become the norm. Although there has never been enough money to please everyone involved, the military has been the favored institution within the U.S. government: over half of the budget of the U.S. government went to DOD in the fifties (it declined during the sixties and has held steady at roughly one-fourth of the budget since the seventies). Consequently, little incentive has been given to produce an efficient and cost-effective budgetary and weapons acquisition process, especially as DOD has become increasingly dependent on a small core of private corporations engaged predominantly in defense production, inflation has increased, and weapons have become more technologically sophisticated (with the military often engaged in what has been called "goldplating"—demanding every type of technological gadgetry be added to its weapons systems).

The net result is that, unless the government cancels a project—an unlikely prospect—costs commonly have been considerably higher than the original projection. These cost-plus factors are most noticeable in big-ticket military items, such as bombers, fighters, missiles, aircraft carriers and other large surface ships, submarines, and tanks, but they exist for almost all military purchases, including simple spare parts (such as hammers and washers bought in huge bulk). Probably the most notorious of all the military costs were coffeemakers for warplanes that the military purchased for about $3,000 each. In an effort to defend its exorbitant cost, the company spokesman insisted that "what you have here is a very complicated device. . . . There are some people who would rather go down to the supermarket and buy these items for an airplane. But I wouldn't particularly want to be on that airplane."[36] Robert Costello, an undersecretary of defense for acquisition in the Reagan administration, publicly stated that up to 30 percent of the $150 billion spent yearly by the Pentagon on procurement probably is squandered.[37]

These high costs and constant overruns are a function not simply of economics and politics but serious lobbying and corruption as well. This has been pervasive in the military procurement establishment for decades and well-known to insiders. Yet, the general public has been kept in the dark because few insiders speak up publicly, and those who become whistleblowers are harshly treated by the individuals and organizations involved in the military establishment (usually careers are destroyed and credibility is lost).[38] Besides, for twenty years an anticommunist consensus

in the country considered it unpatriotic to question the American military. In recent years, however, the media and the public have become more receptive to charges of waste and corruption in the military at the taxpayers' expense, and the military has attempted to reform its defense procurement process and make it more efficient.

Unfortunately, it is a question not only of cost and waste but of **military readiness** and performance. Weapons have become so expensive that the military can afford fewer items, such as tanks or fighters. Many important weapons have not only declined in numbers over time but have become more sophisticated, increasing the likelihood of flaws in design and production cost increases. Weapons are now so technologically sophisticated that they require much more expertise to use, tend to be less reliable especially in combat, and require more time and skill to repair. Therefore, becoming dependent on fewer and more technologically sophisticated weapons, though ones with greater potential to deliver firepower, may have in some ways reduced the military's overall combat readiness and effectiveness.[39]

Weapons may be deployed with great fanfare by the military and defense industry, but they often promise much more than the weapon can deliver. Problems produced by a technologically sophisticated weapon can also threaten lives beyond the normal risks of war, which are well-known to the soldier in the field. The anti-tank TOW missile has great accuracy but requires the soldier to remain immobile until the missile hits the tank hundreds of yards away. The Bradley Fighting Vehicle was developed for the Army to rapidly move infantry around the battlefield while providing protection from enemy fire, but initial tests demonstrated it easily exploded on contact, killing everyone inside.[40]

Critics say some of these weapons should never have been built or should have been redesigned according to realistic performance and reliability standards and with the safety of the soldier in mind. Supporters emphasize the genuine technical difficulties of weapons development. However, once a decision is made, usually years before a weapon is actually produced for deployment by the military, the tendency is to turn a blind eye to any and all criticism and proceed full speed ahead—although occasionally a weapons system has been axed. In the case of the Bradley Fighting Vehicle, civilian and military personnel in the Department of Defense, along with the defense contractor, went so far as to rig the tests to cover up fatal design flaws—which caused a public furor once exposed and led to the development of an improved "A2 Bradley model." In fact, most major weapons systems have undergone significant adjustments after being in the field.[41]

When weapons systems do not perform as promised and American soldiers die in the process, the official military position is usually **human error**—that individuals screwed up. For example, in 1987 in the Persian Gulf, the U.S.S. *Stark*'s radar was unable to see an incoming Iraqi missile that struck the *Stark*, killing thirty-seven people. A year later, the U.S.S. *Vincennes*, with the most sophisticated Aegis air-defense system available, shot down an Iranian civilian jetliner that it mistook for an F-14 warplane, killing 290 people. In both cases, the official Navy report cited human error as the culprit. However, the U.S.S. *Stark* was badly designed and its sophisticated electronic surveillance equipment failed to see the Iraqi missile approaching (it was finally spotted by a sailor on board just before it hit). The sophisticated command and communications center of the U.S.S. *Vincennes* not only was unable to distinguish between a civilian jetliner and a fighter but also was extremely complex and difficult to operate, contributing to the likelihood of human error during a time of great stress, such as combat.[42] However, if the military takes an official position other than "human error," both the military and the defense industry are potentially subject to criticism and libel, threatening the cozy network of relationships that have developed in the military procurement process.

At the same time, it is important that the American public acquires a more realistic understanding that wars are—by definition—times of great danger, when there is much confusion and human suffering. Unfortunately, the incredible American success of the Persian Gulf and Kosovo wars (with images of pin-point-accurate, so-called smart bombs, despite large numbers of civilian casualties) has not contributed to an increased understanding of what the great Prussian military strategist Carl von Clausewitz referred to as "the fog of war."[43] The war on terrorism and the war in Afghanistan, despite its ultimate success against the Taliban regime, have unfortunately resulted in unintended casualties and collateral damage, better reflecting the complexities and difficulties of the fog of war.

Leadership and Morale. As the military has become increasingly bureaucratic and managerial, strong leadership, especially on the battlefield, and the morale of the combat soldier have suffered, especially with the Vietnam War. During the early phases of American military intervention in Vietnam, from the early 1960s to 1968, morale was quite high. When it became clear that the United States was not winning the war, morale and leadership in the military suffered, especially among foot soldiers. Failure to succeed was the major cause for declining morale, but the bureaucratic structure and military procedure reinforced this trend.

For example, within the U.S. Army, the combat tour of duty was six months for officers but one year for enlisted personnel. This created many problems in the field. To grasp this, it is important to understand that the American soldier, trained for conventional war, was transported within days from the States into an alien world where the war was unconventional and the local people were from very different cultures. A soldier who became a "grunt" on the ground quickly learned that the army handbook had not prepared him for Vietnam. Hence, new recruits "in country" had to learn what Vietnam was all about, adapt, and acquire new skills while on the march. Within a few months, they became hardened soldiers who had learned how to fight the enemy and stay alive. Unfortunately, the hardened soldier in the field was often commanded by officers who were completely new to Vietnam and tried to command by the book.

From a bureaucratic perspective, the six-month command tour allowed most of the officer corps to "punch their ticket" and acquire combat experience to promote their careers before serving out their one-year tour in a staff position. To a youthful, largely draftee army—increasingly with new, inexperienced officers and fated to spend a full year in the bush unless wounded or killed—the practice often produced internal conflict among the troops. This situation spread in the late 1960s as American troops were slowly withdrawn from the war as part of the "Vietnamization" process. Where those officers proved inept or uncaring, dissatisfaction spread and some soldiers engaged in minor mutinies and "fragging" incidents—assassination attempts against the officer in command.

Much of the bitterness that developed among combat soldiers was reinforced by the fact that, of the half million troops stationed in Vietnam at the height of the war, no more than 200,000 were actually engaged in combat (others were in support roles such as logistics and administration). This was a function of the military's administrative orientation and its effort to Americanize the war by building military bases, supporting the latest technological weapons, and providing American personnel with the best shelter, food, clothing, and rest and recreation available. Much can be said for efforts to make overseas combat situations as endurable as possible, but this goal requires large numbers of personnel to support the soldier in the field.

The problems of leadership and morale were reinforced by events at home. With the installation of the draft and availability of deferments to college students, Army enlisted personnel became disproportionately working class and minority. Black soldiers, in particular, had a hard time reconciling fighting for the "white man's country" abroad, while their brothers were fighting for black civil rights at home. Morale sank so low that drug use among American personnel became common, especially the use of marijuana and heroin, which were readily available in the "Golden Triangle" of Indochina (where Burma, Laos, and Thailand meet).

To add insult to injury, after their tour of duty, soldiers were immediately flown back to the States. Unfortunately, many were poorly prepared and received little guidance from the military for coping with reentry into American society and civilian life given their stressful combat roles. Their "homecoming" was often quite a shock, for they tended to receive two responses from their fellow citizens: Many within the antiwar movement demonstrated against them (for they represented the military), and the mass public ignored them, preferring to forget about a war that America was losing. There were no homecoming parades. Uniforms quickly were discarded, and the **Vietnam veterans** had to deal on their own with the war and personal problems they might have developed. Little support for the Vietnam veteran was forthcoming from society (even among existing veterans' organizations, whose membership was overwhelmingly composed of World War II and Korean War veterans) or government (including the military and the Veterans Administration).[44]

The negative legacy of Vietnam still lingers for the U.S. military. It required a decade for Americans to begin to cope with the experience of Vietnam. Yet, the completion of the **Vietnam War Memorial** in Washington, D.C., helped to heal some of the wounds of war, especially for the Vietnam veteran. President Reagan's commitment to a large defense budget and praise for the American military rebuilt morale within the military. Most importantly, the military triumph in the Persian Gulf War and the "welcome home" to the troops contributed to the restoration of morale within the military and throughout American society.

An All-Volunteer and Diverse Military. The military has not only become "civilianized" by bureaucratic development over time but also become an all-volunteer and much more diverse organization with time. The peacetime draft was abolished in 1973 in reaction to the Vietnam War, and polls indicate that most Americans remain strongly opposed to a draft. However, the all-volunteer force presents new problems for the U.S. military and its foreign policy.

The armed services, particularly the Army, has had difficulty recruiting sufficient numbers of skilled individuals. **Military recruitment** tends to be less a problem when unemployment increases, for the services become a more attractive option for the unemployed. The military has made a concerted effort to attract recruits through a major marketing campaign, especially concentrating on television advertising. However, the recruitment emphasis since Vietnam has not marketed the warrior aspect of military service (with the possible exception of the Marines) but has concentrated on the excitement of visiting exotic lands and acquiring technical skills that will be helpful in obtaining jobs in the civilian economy.

The rise of a volunteer, civilianized military has resulted in a debate over the quality of the armed services, especially in the Army. Some observers argue that the caliber of the military soldier is, on the whole, higher today than ever before. They point to overall higher levels of education to illustrate their position. However, other observers argue that the skill potential of new recruits has increased little, an especially troubling situation in an era of increasingly sophisticated weaponry. Furthermore, retention rates (that is, reenlistments) have declined or have been denied due to downsizing with the end of the cold war, reducing know-how in the ranks.

Another issue that has been raised is the overall **diversity and representativeness** of the military in a democratic society. With the all-volunteer military, fewer whites and fewer people from the middle and upper classes are serving, especially in the Army and Marines. In many ways the military has become a vehicle for promoting opportunity for individuals from disadvantaged backgrounds. However, the fairness of a situation in which the least advantaged should bear the burden of defending all Americans has raised questions about the value of a national draft of young Americans and mandatory national service (military and civilian). Other important questions also have been raised about the proper role of women, the situation that families face, and about gays in the military (which are only likely to increase, as discussed in **essay 7.3**).

This also raises a related issue: the decline of a knowledgeable public when it comes to the military and use of force. Important public policy decisions over defense spending and military force are increasingly made and influenced by civilian leaders and people with little experience in and knowledge of the military or war. There are no easy answers to these issues, but having a universal service requirement versus an all-volunteer military clearly has implications for the composition of the military, its conduct on the field, and the future of U.S. foreign policy. This may have even greater implications given the increases in military technology and changes in the global environment that the military may face in the twenty-first century.

ESSAY 7.3
THE NEW FACE OF THE AMERICAN MILITARY

MINORITIES, WOMEN, GAYS, AND FAMILIES

The last few decades have witnessed a considerable change in the makeup of the American military. According to Martin Binkin, "Once peopled mostly by young, unmarried, white males, today's armed forces are composed of unprecedented proportions of minorities, women, married couples, and single parents and are dependent more than ever before on part-time reservists." Such changes parallel changes within American society, but special problems may exist given the military subculture and the unique function of the military to engage in war.

Minorities, especially African Americans, have succeeded in joining all areas of the American armed forces since the 1970s. Not until the 1940s under President Truman did the military become integrated. The debates were rancorous, such as over the impact on military cohesion and combat effectiveness, and the transition was difficult over the years, but for the most part blacks have become accepted members of the American military. In fact, African Americans currently constitute about 20 percent of the U.S. military—with over 30 percent of these in the Army—and constituted 25 percent of the troops who served in the Gulf War. In addition, African Americans are more likely than whites to make a lifelong career out of the military. Moreover, advancement opportunities are opening up for African American men in the military, as seen with the rise of General Colin Powell to chairman of the Joint Chiefs of Staff. Nevertheless, a number of sensitive issues have been raised about "economic" conscription, the likelihood of a disproportionate number of black casualties in a future war, and interracial strife within the military—all of which were evident during the Vietnam War but were avoided by the overwhelming speed and triumph of the Persian Gulf War.

Women now make up about 15 percent of the armed forces—over 200,000 soldiers (as opposed to 2 percent in the early 1970s). According to Binkin, "The transition, however, has been anything but smooth. The armed services, traditionally one of the most male-dominated institutions in American society, has had great difficulty adapting to the wider role of women." Major debates have surfaced over the role of women in the military, including basic training, accommodations, and involvement in combat. When the U.S. military first opened its doors to women on active duty, they were limited to "noncombat" roles, which eventually was defined as exclusion from "direct-combat" positions. However, women have increasingly been allowed in combat positions, as the definition of what is combat has become blurred, and in combat environments, as occurred in the Persian Gulf War. "Especially in today's unconventional and dangerous assignments like Afghanistan, women are serving as helicopter crews, fighter pilots, forward logistics specialists, medics, and military police." Within the Army, "jobs closed to women are small units of infantry, armor, field artillery, and Special Forces. Seventy percent of all Army jobs are open to women."

Another major issue of increasing concern involves the question of **sexual harassment**. Incidents, like the 1991 Tailhook scandal, involving a convention of naval aviators where women were often abused and in some cases raped, have become increasingly evident and public over the years. What Gregory Vistica, in *Fall From Glory*, says about the Navy is true about the military in general: "Sexual abuse is difficult to root out because it is now so embedded in the Navy's day-to-day culture. Over the last 30 years, an attitude of contempt toward women has become routine not only below decks but also in the officers' quarters." And with more issues of sexual harassment becoming public, advancement within the military has been hampered and careers have been ruined—for both men and women. This has become a huge and very difficult issue to address, in which even the "top brass" are increasingly concerned about the repercussions of sexual harassment.

Gays in the military also have become a prominent issue. Homosexuals (including lesbians) have always been a part of the military throughout history, but only recently has the issue of gays and lesbians become public. And given the "male, macho, and homophobic" orientation of the prevailing military subculture, this issue has been as controversial and emotional as the issue of the proper role of women in the military—maybe even more so. President Clinton's effort to legitimize the role of gays in the military shortly after he took office created a huge furor within the military and throughout American society, which severely damaged his public prestige and destroyed his honeymoon early on in his administration, making it much more difficult for him to govern.

One issue that has not received much attention given the changing nature of the military, is the issue of the family in the military. Over 100,000 members of the military are single parents (including about 40,000 men) and "dual-service parents" (where both the father and mother are in active or reserve military units). This has been a growing trend, with now over 50 percent of the services' enlisted members married (in 1971 only 20 percent were married). This has produced inevitable problems of assignment and deployment, as well as about who'll take care of the kids during a national emergency or war? Another issue that needs to be addressed is the relatively high rate of domestic abuse, especially in light of the four wives murdered by their husbands at Fort Bragg, North Carolina, in 2002.

Clearly, the changing nature of the military, of combat, and of American society has produced a transformation the American armed forces must now confront. Issues about minorities, women, gays, families, and more are here to stay and may never be resolvable. Many of them go to the heart of the military as an institution and to its unique function of preparing people to fight and possibly die. Nevertheless, as Binkin concludes,

with the quick end to Operation Desert Storm, these issues failed to develop into real problems. Understandably, the inclination now is to ignore them. But left unattended, they will return to haunt future military conflicts. Their unpredictable, but potentially damaging, military, political, and social implications argue strongly that they be resolved now, while memories are still fresh and while a fundamental rethinking of the post–cold war U.S. military establishment is already under way.

SOURCES: Martin Binkin, "The New Face of the American Military," *Brookings Review* (summer 1991): 7–13; Charles C. Moskos and John Sibley Butler, *All That We Can Be: Black Leadership and Racial Integration the Army Way* (New York: Basic Books, 1996); Randy Shilts, *Conduct Unbecoming: Lesbians and Gays in the U.S. Military* (New York: St. Martin's Press, 1993); Gregory Vistica, *Fall From Glory* (New York: Simon and Schuster, 1995); David Wood, "In Afghanistan, Women Are on the Front Lines," *Army Times* (March 11, 2002), p. 18.

SUMMARIZING THE DIFFERENT BUT OVERLAPPING SYSTEMS

In sum, the Department of Defense has become such an enormous, complex, and confusing enterprise that probably no one really understands how the entire process operates. Nevertheless, it is possible to identify general patterns of behavior within DOD. Rather than a simple top-down, centralized civilian-controlled process, the workings of the Department of Defense can be better understood if seen as *three independent but overlapping systems or processes* involving:

1. Administration (the military's basic infrastructure);
2. Advice (small in terms of organizations and personnel); and
3. Operations (the meat of the military).

This simplifies the complex policy process within the department yet provides a means for making sense of the basic operating patterns and understanding the implications for presidential governance of foreign policy. **Figure 7.1** visually summarizes how the dynamics of military establishment in each of these three critical areas has evolved since World War II and since Goldwater-Nichols, especially in comparison to the formal ideal laid out at the beginning of the chapter.

The least exciting but very important process within the Department of Defense is the *administrative process.* This involves day-to-day management of the military and is controlled by the individual services. Personnel decisions about recruiting, training, tours, and promotion are individual service affairs, as are the daily routines and activities concerning health, schooling, provisions, recreation, security, and so on. Requests for weaponry are also heavily influenced within each of the services, ultimately through the chief of staff and the JCS.

In the *advisory process* concerning decisions of war and peace, the Office of the Secretary of Defense and the Joint Chiefs of Staff—especially the chair—are the most important organizational elements in the Department of Defense. The president is the commander in chief and determines when and where to use armed force abroad. Most presidents rely on their most trusted foreign policy advisers, including the secretary of defense, when it comes to such important decisions. The advisory role of the JCS depends on the particular president's relationship with his senior military officers. Usually, the chair of the JCS has the greatest authority and credibility with the president because he is the only member not representing the interests of a particular service. Since Goldwater-Nichols, the relevant CINC may also play an important advisory role, directly to the civilians or indirectly through the CJCS, because he is ultimately responsible for implementing military strategy and the use of force.

The *operational process* includes the military strategy and tactics employed by the armed forces and involves both the individual services, the Office of the Secretary of Defense, and since the Goldwater-Nichols Act, the chair of the Joint Chiefs of Staff and the relevant CINC. The secretary of defense and OSD clearly have their greatest independent impact, when they have any impact at all, at the strategic level. A president may be able to affect war preparations, national military strategy, and overall force structure (such as the overall number of Navy ships, as well as the development of one of the larger weapons programs), but this will largely be a function of past strategy and current service policies. Much of OSD's strategic influence naturally will be a function of politics, depending on the level of interest and attention displayed by the president, the secretary of defense, the secretary's immediate subordinates (as well as their working relationship with the JCS, especially the chair), and naturally, Congress. Even then, OSD has to contend with a military strategy and infrastructure that is already in place and service requests for more resources, such as weaponry and money, to promote their mission as they see it.

At the tactical level, once a presidential decision is made to go to war or to intervene militarily, the president has little control over the existing command structure and set of bureaucratic standard operating procedures for implementing the decision within each of the services. During the Vietnam War, President Johnson made certain operations off limits, such as attacking Cambodia, Laos, or North Vietnam, for fear of triggering the military intervention of the People's Republic of China (as occurred during the Korean War when American troops pushed up the Korean Peninsula approaching the Chinese border). Although certain political restrictions have always been imposed by civilian leaders during war, actual military operations have been conducted by the unified commands and the services. Thus, the basic tactical strategy of "search and destroy" was selected by General William Westmoreland, the commander in chief of American forces in Vietnam.[45] A president, through the secretary of defense and OSD and the advice of the chair of the JCS, may be able to fine-tune specific military tactics, but more than this is beyond his competence and control. Since Goldwater-Nichols, the commander in chief, usually the regional CINC, is the main military official responsible for employing the forces of the different services and has considerable leeway in doing so.

In sum, decisions to use American armed forces are dominated by the civilian leadership, while decisions concerning basic operations and administration of the armed forces are made within the military. With the tremendous expansion of the military since World War II, a system has evolved in which the president determines when and where to use armed force, but the military tends to dominate the actual conduct of the war. In other words, presidents can begin and end wars, but the military fights them. This is the kind of

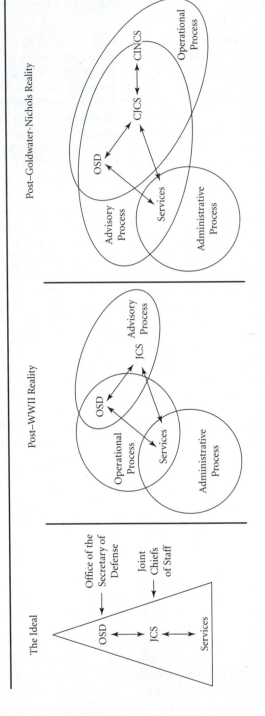

FIGURE 7.1
DEPARTMENT OF DEFENSE POLICY DYNAMICS

NOTE: CINCs, commander in chiefs; CJCS, chair of the Joint Chiefs of Staff; JCS, Joint Chiefs of Staff; OSD, Office of the Secretary of Defense.

division of labor that is preferred by most within the military but that often frustrates presidents who want to control and govern U.S. foreign policy.

THE VALUE OF MILITARY ADVICE

Many Americans do not realize that since the Korean War the civilian leadership, including the secretary of defense and the president, have often been skeptical of military advice. The chair of the JCS tends to have the greatest credibility, for he is the only high-ranking military officer who does not represent individual service interests. Ultimately, the value of military advice will depend on personalities and working relationships. With Goldwater-Nichols and the increased prominence of the CJCS as military adviser, the credibility of military advice appears to have improved under Presidents Reagan, Bush Sr., and Clinton, but less so under Bush Jr.

The common stereotype portrays the military as always recommending the use of force to deal with international crises. In fact, studies of military advice during crises suggest that the military tends to be reluctant to initiate the use of force. In *Soldiers, Statesmen, and Cold War Crises*, Richard Betts found the Army to be the most cautious in recommending force (since it takes the brunt of the casualties), while the Air Force tends to be most optimistic about force, especially the use of air power. He also found that the military has its greatest impact on civilian leadership when military advice opposes the use of force (since this is the unexpected position), while it is least credible when it recommends force. The military may be eager to expand its capabilities through more sophisticated weaponry and more personnel, but it tends to be reluctant to put them at risk. However, once a decision to use force has been made, the military aggressively argues that civilians should stand aside and allow the military to do whatever is necessary to succeed, which may require escalation.[46]

Through most of the cold war years, in fact, the *civilians were more hard-line,* quicker to recommend force and take a inflexible stance to impress military leaders, as occurred during the Vietnam War.[47] This trend has continued to the present and was evident during the Reagan administration, in which major internal battles ensued over the use of force. Secretary of State George Shultz was the major advocate of military force, while Secretary of Defense Caspar Weinberger, representing the military, was reluctant to use force unless it had the full support of the American public. Concerning U.S. foreign policy toward Central America, Secretary of State Alexander Haig and later Assistant Secretary of State for Inter-American Affairs Elliott Abrams were vocal proponents of the threat and use of force, as opposed to the more skeptical position of chairman of the JCS Admiral William Crowe. Likewise in the Bush Sr. administration, Bob Woodward in *The Commanders* reports that President Bush and National Security Adviser Brent Scowcroft were the most vehement in support of a major military response to the Iraqi invasion of Kuwait and the need to take Saddam Hussein to the brink of war to compel his withdrawal, while Secretary of State James Baker and the Joint Chiefs of Staff, particularly Chairman Colin Powell, were much more cautious, preferring economic sanctions over force. A similar situation arose between military and civilian leaders over Bosnia and Kosovo during the Clinton administration, according to David Halberstam in *War in a Time of Peace.* The civilian leadership in the Bush Jr. administration, especially President Bush and Secretary of Defense Donald Rumsfeld, were the most vocal for a quick military response after September 11 and quite unhappy with the initial war plans for Afghanistan and Iraq provided by the military.[48] Clearly, one of the major lessons learned by the military from the Vietnam War, especially within the Army, is to avoid the use of troops unless overwhelming force will be used and there is strong and visible public backing. This has led to what is commonly referred to as the **Weinberger-Powell Doctrine** (see **essay 7.4**).

Some analysts fear that the chair of the JCS and military leaders have grown too powerful, especially relative to the civilian leadership, since Goldwater-Nichols. This is debatable. What is has changed is that the advisory voice of the CJCS now is being heard and the CINCs have much greater operational effectiveness in terms of command and control. The role of General Colin Powell as advisor in Panama, the Gulf War, Bosnia, and Somalia clearly helped shape U.S. policy in those regions. In all these operations the CINCs decided when and how their forces would be employed with little participation of the service chiefs.

ESSAY 7.4
THE DEVELOPMENT OF THE WEINBERGER-POWELL DOCTRINE

The mid-1980s was a time for not only reorganizing the military command structure through the Goldwater-Nichols Act but also questioning the role and doctrine of the military. Military failures in Vietnam, Beirut, and Grenada cast doubt on the way the U.S. conducted war and how it should respond in times of crisis. In response to this debate, what became the Powell Doctrine, named after Chairman of the Joint Chiefs of Staff General Colin Powell, became the popular military paradigm for the employment of U.S. forces abroad.

The keys to this doctrine were spelled out first by Secretary of Defense Caspar Weinberger in Washington, D.C., on November 28, 1984, at an address to the Washington Press Club. In this address he defined six criteria for the use of force: (1) The United States should not commit forces to combat overseas unless the particular engagement or occasion is deemed vital to its national interests or its allies' interests, and the conflict should be declared before the United States takes action. (2) Once ground troops are committed, they should be supported wholeheartedly. (3) If the United States decides to commit forces overseas, it should have clearly defined political and military objectives. (4) The relationship between U.S. objectives and the forces committed must be continually reassessed and adjusted if necessary. (5) Before the United States commits forces to combat abroad, support must be assured by the American people and Congress. And (6) the commitment of U.S. forces should be a last resort. These criteria were aimed at defining the role of the U.S. military in the future to ensure another Vietnam did not occur.

Some took these criteria as a checklist for deciding whether to commit forces to combat. Les Aspin in congressional testimony on September 21, 1992, just prior to his becoming secretary of defense, disputed what had become known as the Weinberger-Powell Doctrine—now more commonly referred to as the Powell Doctrine. In his congressional testimony Aspin called for a more flexible response to war fighting and asserted that no checklist to commit troops could be devised. He sited situations in Bosnia and Somalia that did not fit the

traditional sense of war making. In sum he refuted the Weinberger-Powell Doctrine and called for more open-ended criteria in determining the use of U.S. forces in combat.

In response to Les Aspin's flexible approach to the employment of troops, General Powell published an article in *Foreign Affairs* titled "U.S. Forces and the Challenges Ahead" in which he redefined the checklist approach to committing U.S. troops, citing the success of U.S. forces in Panama and the Gulf War, which were tailored in both cases to meet the threats presented. He highlighted that Weinberger's six points be used only as a guide to the commitment of troops. Overall, he espoused the use of decisive force to overcome a threat, clearly defined rules of engagement (RUE), and an exit strategy to avoid mission creep (i.e., the adding of extra tasks and goals) and excessive casualties. In short, the military should not be placed in a situation where it cannot utilize overwhelming force, win, and come home swiftly with strong public support. General Powell and the thinking behind the so-called Powell Doctrine played an integral role on U.S. policy in the 1990s. For example, in Bosnia, ground troops were not employed until after Powell retired because of the lack of a clear exit strategy and obtainable political goals. And the United States did not engage in war until Kosovo and relied on bombing from a high altitude, fearing that the loss of American lives would endanger U.S. support.

Although the United States has used force abroad and will continue to do so, the Powell Doctrine continues to exercise a powerful presence, especially within the U.S. military.

SOURCES: David Halberstam, *War in a Time of Peace: Bush, Clinton, and the Generals* (New York: Scribner, 2001); Richard N. Haas, *Intervention: The Use of American Military Force in the Post–Cold War World* (Washington, D.C.: Carnegie Endowment for International Peace, 1994); F. G. Hoffman, *Decisive Force: The New American Way of War* (Westport, Conn.: Preager, 1996), Colin Powell, "U.S. Forces: the Challenges Ahead," *Foreign Affairs* (winter 1992–93).

Overall, *the president is faced with certain limitations in his choices regarding the use of force.* First, the president has limited viable military options from which to choose: principally some type of nuclear strike or conventional strike in a world where nuclear war has been avoided and major conventional battles appear to be relatively infrequent. As Eliot Cohen has concluded, "The most substantial constraints on America's ability to conduct small wars result from the resistance of the American defense establishment to the very notion of engaging in such conflicts, and from the unsuitability of that establishment for fighting such wars."[49] Second, changes in the international environment, such as nationalism and the proliferation of weaponry, make it increasingly costly and difficult for a great power to exercise force successfully abroad even with the collapse of the Soviet Union. Third, when the military has exercised force abroad, its performance, especially in low-intensity conflict, has been mixed. Clearly, despite the Powell Doctrine, since the end of the cold war the military has been forced to adapt to different types of low-intensity conflict and to become more involved in OOTW (operations other than war). And since September 11, 2001, civilian leaders within the Bush Sr. administration, especially Secretary of Defense Rumsfeld, have been trying to make major and controversial changes in the force structure, strategy, and tactics of the military establishment which has triggered considerable military resentment.

The president's decisions to use force and the military's implementation are also heavily a function of politics. Presidents have to be much more cautious than they were during the cold war, because of the breakdown of consensus and the fact that Americans have high expectations for quick success. It is important to remember that President Bush Sr. took a divided country to war in the Persian Gulf on January 17, 1991, and President Clinton exercised prerogative government as commander in chief to launch a war in Kosovo that was a low priority in the minds of most Americans. Although quickly forgotten in victory, at the time these were difficult and politically risky decisions made by presidents concerning the use of force, and there were no guarantees of military success with minimal American casualties. Both wars highly exceeded expectations (among the leadership of the military as well as civilian military strategists) despite their conventional nature, and both were quick success stories with very few "Americans" killed in action (KIAs) and wounded. Such are the military and political constraints that face President Bush Jr's administration as it engages in the war on terrorism and decides about the use of force in such places as Afghanistan and Iraq.

REFORM AND HOW MUCH IS ENOUGH IN LIGHT OF THE END OF THE COLD WAR AND SEPTEMBER 11

Many of the bureaucratic problems discussed in this chapter are inevitable functions of the size of modern society. Large populations require large bureaucracies, which do not easily adapt to changes in the environment. In actuality, the U.S. military is relatively efficient in pursuing the missions and norms that have prevailed within the individual services, especially given the fact that the military establishment is a huge, institutional, bureaucratic juggernaut. However, the key questions remain: How relevant are the missions and norms of the military establishment for confronting the problems facing U.S. foreign policy and national security in the post–cold war era and in the twenty-first century? And how much reform is enough? Real reform requires change in the organizational structure and subculture which is difficult under the best of conditions.[50]

The Department of Defense, nevertheless, has undergone changes over the years, especially since the Vietnam War and the end of the cold war. The U.S. Army has moved toward a form of air-land maneuver warfare; Congress passed the Goldwater-Nichols bill, giving the chair of the Joint Chiefs of Staff more power and creating greater jointness in military operations; President Reagan appointed a presidential commission that phased out numerous military bases; and the military has been experiencing some downsizing and operational changes in the past decade. But are these changes sufficient as the United States moves into the twenty-first century?

Many argue that the military remains so large and complex that these have not fundamentally changed the military's basic orientation. The disaster of the Vietnam War and other faulty military performances simply have not led to much reform within the military establishment. For forty years the U.S. military expanded and focused on fighting the Soviet Union throughout the world. With the collapse of the Soviet Union and much of communism, Americans have much less to fear. The post–cold war environment may be a unique opportunity to achieve real reform within the military establishment for the world of the twenty-first century. Yet the U.S. military is an institution that remains very much the same and is still essentially organized to fight conventional wars.

At the same time, the decline of communism and the Soviet empire have triggered the search for new military missions away from Europe, toward low-intensity conflicts, and involving military OOTW—such as the drug war, antiterrorism, peacekeeping, and humanitarian intervention. In fact, despite the end of the cold war and because of the September 11 attacks, the military has become more active in a variety of missions and has seen its military budget increasing substantially. Which leads to a critical generic question: How big does the military establishment need to be? This was a question raised and debated endlessly during the cold war, and this will probably be the case in the foreseeable future as the questions below suggest.

How large should the military budget be at the beginning of the twenty-first century? The U.S. DOD budget is around $300 billion (and this excludes military spending for such departments as Energy, the Coast Guard, and NASA) and is increasing at a time when no major adversary like the Soviet Union exists. To place this in comparative context, the U.S. government accounts for about 36 percent of the world's military expenditures (see **table 7.4**). Members of NATO, including the United States, account for about 57 percent of the world's military expenditures. Adding traditional U.S. allies that are not part of NATO, such as Japan, Taiwan, South Korea, and Australia, brings the portion to over two-thirds of the world's military expenditures. And President Bush requested that the U.S. military budget for fiscal year 2003 increase by $48 billion—which is virtually the size of the military budgets of the next three largest countries in Table 7.4, Russia, Japan, and China. And what are the most appropriate types of weapons systems and force structures for the future? Throwing money to the military to address the

complexity of the post–cold war environment and the war on terrorism appears to be a major part of U.S. foreign policy, but how much is enough?

How much is enough also needs to be asked in terms of the frequency and variety of military missions. The end of the cold war did not produce global peace. The U.S. military has been used with as much frequency following the cold war as it did during the cold war. Military OOTW has incrementally grown and now represents the most frequent use of military force in the post–cold war world. This has been reinforced and supplemented with the U.S. global war on terrorism, which involves many new and subtle forms of low-intensity conflict. Such operations, nevertheless, do not reflect the core mission and essence of the American military. Once again, how much is enough, especially given the traditions and subcultures of the military? And what other organizations can the U.S. government turn to that have the resources and organizational ability to even attempt to perform such missions?[51]

And then there is the question of how much is enough in terms of military personnel in a post–cold war and post–September 11 environment? Many argue that the military does not have sufficient manpower to perform all these missions and that constant activation has hurt military readiness. Officially, the Department of Defense has experienced some downsizing, with the biggest cuts, around 30 percent in the 1980s and 1990s, in active military personnel. There are currently around 1.4 million active full-time soldiers (about 500,000 in the Army, 370,000 in the Navy, 170,000 Marines, and 350,000 in the Air Force). But there are also about 750,000 personnel in the reserves and 500,000 in the National Guard. What is not well-known is that since the Persian Gulf War the reserves and the National Guard have constantly been activated and engaged in all variety of military missions abroad. Unlike the Vietnam War, the reserves and National Guard are no longer a way to avoid the active military but are an integral part of the overall military that is on constant call and is regularly activated (and at a lower cost since reserve and Guard members are employed only part-time until activated). This means that the total U.S. military force is actually composed of about 2.65 million troops, reflecting minimal downsizing since the end of the cold war and a different organizational, administrative, and operational orientation.

MILITARY EXPENDITURES BY THE WORLD'S NATIONS, 2000 (IN US$ MILLIONS)

US$M	COUNTRY	US$M	COUNTRY	US$M	COUNTRY
294,695	United States	1,081	Ukraine	93	Honduras
58,810	Russia	931	Vietnam	87	Mauritius
44,417	Japan	862	Sri Lanka	85	Mozambique
41,167	China	861	Peru	84	Costa Rica
34,292	France	809	Romania	80	Tajikistan
33,894	United Kingdom	788	New Zealand	79	Estonia
28,229	Germany	777	Hungary	76	FYROM
20,561	Italy	760	Syria	72	Congo
18,321	Saudi Arabia	735	Cuba	70	Latvia
17,545	Brazil	684	Ireland	68	Burkina Faso
17,248	Taiwan	670	Bangladesh	68	Senegal
14,472	India	568	Sudan	65	Burundi
12,496	South Korea	553	Lebanon	65	Zambia
10,609	Turkey	510	Jordan	57	Guinea
9,373	Israel	509	Croatia	55	Papua New Guinea
7,456	Canada	489	Yemen	49	Jamaica
7,329	Iran	453	Cyprus	49	Nepal
7,053	Spain	448	Ethiopia	48	Haiti
6,952	Australia	435	Bahrain	47	Chad
6,392	The Netherlands	394	Zimbabwe	44	Maldives
5,457	Greece	392	DROC	43	Central Africa Republic
5,559	Mexico	366	Belarus	41	Madagascar
5,190	Sweden	357	Kazakstan	39	Somali Republic
4,658	Argentina	356	Uruguay	36	Benin
4,707	Singapore	350	Tunisia	35	Trinidad and Tobago
3,579	Pakistan	348	Brunei	32	Fiji
3,338	United Arab Emirates	347	Bulgaria	21	Kyrgyzstan
3,335	Belgium	340	Slovakia	30	Togo
3,210	Kuwait	314	Ecuador	29	Lesotho
3,191	Poland	307	Kenya	29	Mali
2,930	Algeria	247	Uganda	26	Malawi
2,900	Switzerland	245	Afghanistan	26	Malta
2,891	Chile	245	Botswana	26	Nicaragua
2,856	Norway	223	Slovenia	26	Niger
2,821	Egypt	213	Azerbaijan	25	Bahamas
2,708	Malaysia	206	Eritrea	25	Liberia
2,464	Thailand	195	Lithuania	23	Djibouti
2,401	Denmark	192	Cambodia	23	Mauritania
2,340	Nigeria	183	Bosnia	21	Moldova
2,197	Portugal	173	Turkmenistan	20	Bhutan
2,058	Myanmar	168	El Salvador	19	Laos
1,995	Columbia	154	Cameroon	19	Mongolia
1,912	South Africa	149	Armenia	17	Belize
1,790	FRY	141	Tanzania	15	The Gambia
1,733	Oman	132	Côte d'Ivoire	13	Barbados
1,680	Morocco	128	Bolivia	11	Suriname
1,609	Austria	127	Panama	10	Seychelles
1,522	Finland	126	Luxemburg	9	Sierra Leone
1,479	Philippines	123	Gabon	7	Cape Verde
1,493	Indonesia	121	Paraguay	7	Guyana
1,481	Uzbekistan	116	Georgia	6	Guinea Bissau
1,470	Iraq	115	Guatemala	4	Antigua and Barbuda
1,427	Qatar	112	Dominican Republic		
1,377	Venezuela	111	Albania		
1,250	Angola	109	Rwanda		
1,176	Libya	103	Namibia	811,452	Global Total
1,133	Czech Republic	95	Ghana	464,654	NATO Total

SOURCE: International Institute for Strategic Studies, *The Military Balance, 2001–2002* (New York: Oxford University Press, 2002).

FIGURE 7.2
U.S. MILITARY PERSONNEL ON
ACTIVE DUTY ABROAD, 2000

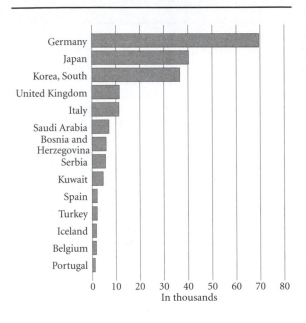

Peninsula) contemplated in the June 2001 *Quadrennial Defense Review* (QDR, conducted every four years) drives the official post–cold war national military strategy, justifying the force requirements for each of the services as well as for maintaining the U.S. government's global military primacy and preventing the rise of any new, major adversaries.[53] The September 11 attacks and the Bush administration's global war on terrorism have both reinforced and changed some of these orientations. The 2001 QDR and the overall national military strategy have since been amended in light of September 11, where the two-major-regional-conflicts strategy has been replaced by the following general strategy: "Our challenge is to win the war on terrorism while we remain ready to sustain our other global commitments, maintain the quality of the Joint Force, and transform [our armed forces] to ensure military superiority to deal with the threats of the 21st century."[54] This is quite an expansive and enormous undertaking. Is it enough? Is it appropriate? Does it respond to the global issues and complexity of the twenty-first century? What does this mean for the future of the military and its use both at home and abroad?

Clearly, there are no simple solutions concerning appropriate military force structure, military strategy, and the use of the military in a post–cold war environment of great complexity. Some critics argue, including Secretary of Defense Donald Rumsfeld, that if U.S. foreign policy is to continue to rely on the threat and use of force, the military must be reformed to improve its conventional performance and gain a real capability in low-intensity warfare. Others argue that the U.S. government and military should continue to rely on its principal nuclear and conventional missions. But there is little consensus and much disagreement at both the strategic and tactical levels, including the implications of high technology weaponry and precision firepower. According to Stephen Biddle, in "Afghanistan and the Future of Warfare," the stunning success of the combination of special operation forces, precision weapons, and indigenous allies was not as revolutionary as some people think. "Contrary to popular belief, there was plenty of close combat in Afghanistan. . . . What the Aghan war ultimately shows is that even today, continuity in the nature of war is at least as important as change."[55]

Therefore, the end of the cold war and the success in the Persian Gulf and Kosovo wars have contradic-

And how much of a permanent military presence should the U.S. have abroad? The number of military bases in the United States and abroad has also been reduced somewhat, but almost 300,000 active-duty personnel remain stationed abroad.[52] **Figure 7.2** provides an idea of where most of the active-duty military are stationed abroad. Altogether, the United States maintains over two hundred military bases in thirty-five different countries and territories (see **table 7.5**) and is busy acquiring basing rights and building military bases abroad, especially in the Near East. Furthermore, about fifty thousand active-duty military are regularly stationed "afloat" (such as on aircraft carriers). And thousands of active-duty military, reserve, and National Guard units are temporarily stationed abroad on a rotational basis, which gives the U.S. military a considerable "footprint" throughout the world.

Finally, what should be the national military strategy agreed to by civilians and the military? In fact, the assumption of the possibility of "two major regional conflicts" (such as in the Persian Gulf and the Korean

tory implications for the future of the military establishment. And President Bush's global war on terrorism has only complicated and clouded the difficulties in addressing these questions. Much depends on the bureaucratic functions, structures, and subcultures as they evolve. In the final analysis, the extent to which change and reform in the future military will occur depends on the politics and outcome of the military establishment and U.S. foreign policy, especially in reaction to events abroad and at home.

SUGGESTED SOURCES FOR MORE INFORMATION

A wealth of material has been written in the last two decades on the military, much of it taking a critical perspective. The more critical analyses in the post–World War II years have come from the liberal and left political perspectives. Today, however, the military establishment is commonly critiqued from all sides. Excellent overviews and analyses of the military, for example, have been provided by liberal journalist James Fallows in *National Defense* (New York: Vintage, 1981); conservative journalists James Coates and Michael Kilian in *Heavy Losses: The Dangerous Decline of American Defense* (New York: Penguin, 1985); a military strategist Edward N. Luttwak in *The Pentagon and the Art of War* (New York: Touchstone, 1985); and former chairman of the JCS General David C. Jones in "What's Wrong With Our Defense Establishment," *New York Times Magazine* (November 7, 1982), pp. 38–42, 70–83. Lawrence J. Korb provides an assessment of the military's budget and strategy in a post–cold war environment in "Our Overstuffed Armed Forces," *Foreign Affairs* (November–December 1995): 22–34. An excellent contemporary overview is provided by Peter L. Hays, Brenda J. Vallance, and Alan R. Van Tassel, *American Defense Policy* (Baltimore: Johns Hopkins University Press, 1997). A wide-ranging discussion of the theory and use of force throughout modern American history is conducted by Bernard Brodie, one of the original modern civilian strategists, in *War and Politics* (New York: Macmillan, 1973).

Andrew F. Krepinevich, Jr., in *The Army and Vietnam* (Baltimore: Johns Hopkins University Press, 1986), provides a good discussion of the Army's conventional strategy of attrition and how it affected the military conduct of the Vietnam War. Neil Sheehan tells a powerful story of the history of American participation in the Viet-

nam War in *A Bright Shining Lie: John Paul Vann and America in Vietnam* (New York: Vintage, 1988), while David Halberstam provides an excellent portrayal of the policymaking process responsible for the Americanization of the war in *The Best and the Brightest* (New York: Random House, 1969). Three books conveying a strong sense of the war as it took place in Vietnam are a novel by Tim O'Brien, *Going After Cacciato* (New York: Dell, 1975); *Dispatches* (New York: Avon, 1968) by journalist Michael Herr; and *The Real War* (New York: Pantheon, 1987) by journalist Jonathan Schell. Myra MacPherson illuminates the effect of the Vietnam War on the generation asked to fight it in *Long Time Passing: Vietnam and the Haunted Generation* (New York: New American Library, 1984).

Eliot A. Cohen provides a good overview in the "Constraints on America's Conduct of Small Wars," *International Security* 9 (fall 1984): 151–81, and an assessment of the Persian Gulf War in "After the Battle," *New Republic* (April 1, 1991), 19–26. To better understand the impact of the Goldwater-Nichols Act, see Peter J. Roman and David W. Tarr, "The Joint Chiefs of Staff: From Service Parochialism to Jointness," *Political Science Quarterly* (spring 1998): 91–122; and Dana Priest, "The Proconsuls" *Washington Post*, four-part series (September 28, 29, & 30, 2000). An informative account of civil-military relations and military advice on the use of force can be found in Richard K. Betts, *Soldiers, Statesmen, and Cold War Crises* (Cambridge, Mass.: Harvard University Press, 1977). David Halberstam uses the policies under presidents Bush Sr. and Clinton toward the aftermath of the breakup of Yugoslavia to illustrate civil-military relations, the Powell Doctrine, the utility of force, and the critical role of individuals and institutions to better understand the contemporary dynamics of U.S. foreign and military policy in *War in a Time of Peace: Bush, Clinton, and the Generals* (New York: Scribner, 2001).

Finally, on the important issue about the changing composition of the military, including the controversies over women and gays, see Martin Binkin, "The New Face of the American Military," *Brookings Review* (summer 1991): 7–13; Gerald J. Garvey and John J. DiLulio, Jr., "Only Connect? Cohesion vs. Combat Effectiveness," *New Republic* (April 26, 1993), pp. 18–21; Stephanie Gutmann, "Sex and the Soldier," *New Republic* (February 24, 1997), pp. 18–22; Randy Shilts, *Conduct Unbecoming: Lesbians and Gays in the U.S. Military* (New York: St. Martin's Press, 1993); and Gregory Vistica, *Fall From Glory* (New York: Simon and Schuster, 1995).

TABLE 7.5

AMERICAN MILITARY BASES AND INSTALLATIONS OUTSIDE THE UNITED STATES

AUSTRALIA(2)
AIR FORCE
Joint Defense Facility
    Nurrungar
Joint Geological and
    Geophysical Research
    Station

BAHAMAS (1)
NAVY
Naval Undersea Warfare Center

BAHRAIN (1)
NAVY
Administrative Support Unit

BELGIUM (5)
AIR FORCE
Kleine Brogel Air Base

ARMY
16th Combat Equipment
    Company
80th Area Support Group
    Chievres Air Base
Northern Law Center

CANADA (1)
AIR FORCE
22nd Wing

CUBA (1)
NAVY
Guantanamo Bay, Naval
    Base

DIEGO GARCIA (1)
NAVY
Diego Garcia, Naval Support

EGYPT (3)
AIR FORCE
Cairo West AFB
Cairo (East)

MULTINATIONAL BASE
Mulitnational Force and
    Observers

FRANCE (1)
AIR FORCE
Istres Air Base

GERMANY (54)
AIR FORCE
Bitburg Annex
Kaiserslautern Military
    Community
Kisling NCO Academy

Ramstein Air Base
Rhein-Main Air Base
Sembach Air Base
Spangdahlem Air Base
USAFE Air Postal Squadron
    Det 1

ARMY
6th Area Support Group,
    Garmish
6th Area Support Group,
    Stuttgart
67th Combat Support
    Hospital/USAMEDDAC
98th Area Support Group
100th Area Support Group
221st Base Support Battalion
223rd Base Support Battalion
280th Base Support Battalion
282nd Base Support Battalion
293rd Base Support Battalion
414th Base Support Battalion
Anderson Barracks
Army Postal Group Europe,
    Rheinau
Augsburg Military
    Community
Babenhausen Area Support
    Team
Bamberg Military
    Community
Barton Barracks, Ansbach
Baumholder Military
    Community
Campbell Barracks
Coleman Barracks
Faulenberg Kaserne, Wurzburg
Friedberg Area Support
    Team
Funari Barracks
Germersheim Sub-
    Community
Giebelstadt Army Airfield
Heidelberg Military
    Community
Johnson Barracks
Kaiserslauten Military
    Community
Kapaun Air Station
Katterbach Air Field/Kaserne
Kitzingen Military
    Community
Kleber Kaserne

Kleber Kaserne (Kaiserslautern
    Law Center)
Landstuhl Regional Medical
    Center
Patton Barracks
Ray Baracks
Rose Barracks
Rose Barracks, Vilseck
Storck Barracks, Illesheim
Sullivan Barracks
Taylor Barracks
US Army Corps of Engineers

JOINT SERVICE
    INSTALLATION
NATO School (SHAPE),
    Oberammergau
Stars and Stripes Kaserne

GREECE (2)
AIR FORCE
Araxos Air Base

NAVY
Souda Bay, Naval Support
    Activity

GREENLAND (1)
AIR FORCE
Thule Air Base

GUAM (6)
AIR FORCE
Anderson Air Force Base

ARMY NATIONAL GUARD
Adjutant General of Guam

NAVY
Guam Naval Magazine
Guam US Naval Hospital
Naval Computer &
    Telecommunications Area
Naval Station, Guam

HONDURAS (3)
AIR FORCE
Joint Task Force—Bravo

ARMY
Joint Task Force—Bravo

JOINT SERVICE
    INSTALLATION
Joint Task Force—Bravo

ICELAND (1)
NAVY
Keflavik Naval Air Station,
    Keflavik

ITALY (11)
AIR FORCE
Aviano Air Base
Ghedi Air Base
San Vito dei Normanni Air
    Station

ARMY
22nd Area Support Group
Camp Darby, Livorno
    Military Community
Caserma Ederle/Vicenza
    Military Community

NAVY
La Maddalena Navy Support
    Office
Naples (Capodichino) Naval
    Support Activity
Naval Computer &
    Telecommunications Area
Naval Regional Contracting
    Sigonella Naval Air
    Station

JAPAN (28)
AIR FORCE
Asian Office of Aerospace
    Research & Development,
    Tokyo
Kadena Air Base
Yokota Air Base

ARMY
35th Supply & Service
    Battalion
Army Corps of Engineers,
    Japan district
Asian Office of Aerospace
    Research & Development,
    Tokyo, Camp Zama
Torii Station

DOD
Pacific Stars and Stripes

JOINT SERVICE
    INSTALLATION
Misawa Air Base
Misawa, Naval Air Facility

MARINE CORPS
Camp Smedly D. Butler, MC
Camp Courtney
Camp Foster
Camp Hansen
Camp Kinser

Camp Lester
Camp Schwab
Futenma, Marine Corps Air
    Station
Iwakuni Marine Corps Air
    Station

NAVY
Asian Office of Aerospace
    Research & Development,
    Tokyo
Atsugi Naval Air Facility
Kadena Naval Air Facility
New Sanno Hotel, US Naval
    Joint Services Activity
Sasebo, US Fleet Activities
Yokosuka, Fleet Activities
Yokosuka, US Naval Hospital

UNITED NATIONS
Futenma, Marine Corps
    Air Station

JOHNSTON ATOLL (1)
ARMY
Army Chemical Activity Pacific

**KOREA, REPUBLIC OF
    (37)**
AIR FORCE
6005th Air Postal Squadron,
    OL-D, Det 1
Kimpo Military Mail
    Terminal
Kunsan Air Base
Osan Air Base

ARMY
Camp Carroll
Camp Casey
Camp Castle
Camp Colbern
Camp Edwards
Camp Essayons
Camp Garry Owen
Camp George
Camp Giant
Camp Greaves
Camp Henry
Camp Hialeah
Camp Hovey
Camp Howze
Camp Humphreys
Camp LaGuardia

Camp Long
Camp MacNab (Cheju Do)
Camp Mobile
Camp Nimble
Camp Page
Camp Red Cloud
Camp Sears
Camp Stanley
Camp Stanton
Camp Walker
K-16 (Army Airfield)
Kimpo Military Mail
    Terminal
Pusan Storage Facility
US Army Corps of Engineers,
    Far East District
Yongsan Army Garrison
Zoeckler Station

NAVY
Chinhae Fleet Activities

LUXEMBOURG
ARMY
23rd Combat Equipment
    Company

**MARSHALL ISLANDS
    (1)**
ARMY
Kwajalein Missle Range

NETHERLANDS (7)
AIR FORCE
Volkel Air Base

ARMY
18th Combat Equipment
    Company
19th Combat Equipment
    Company
254th Base Support Battalion
Combat Equipment Group-
    Europe, HQ
Military Traffic Management
    Command, Europe
Netherlands Law Center

NORWAY (1)
AIR FORCE
426th Air Base Squadron

PANAMA (5)
AIR FORCE
Howard Air Force Base

ARMY
Fort Clayton
Fort Davis
Fort Sherman

NAVY
Panama Canal Naval Station

PORTUGAL (1)
**JOINT SERVICE
    INSTALLATION**
Lajes Field

PUERTO RICO (6)
ARMY
Fort Buchanan Army
    Garrison

ARMY NATIONAL GUARD
Adjutant General of
    Puerto Rico
Camp Santiago

NAVAL RESERVE
Roosevelt Roads Naval
    Reserve Center

NAVY
Roosevelt Roads Naval
    Station
Sabana Seca, US Naval
    Security Group Activity

SAUDI ARABIA (2)
AIR FORCE
Eskan Village
Prince Sultan Air Base

SINGAPORE (1)
NAVY
Logistics Group Western
    Pacific

SPAIN (2)
AIR FORCE
Moron Air Base

NAVY
Rota Naval Station

THAILAND (1)
AIR FORCE
Air Force Technical
    Applications Center,
    Det 415

TURKEY (4)
AIR FORCE
Balikesir Air Field

Incirlick Air Base
Izmir Air Station

NATO
Vecini Akin Garrison

**UNITED KINGDOM
    (16)**
AIR FORCE
424nd Air Base Squadron,
    RAF, Fairford
Alconbury RAF Base
Croughton RAF Base
European Office of Aerospace
    Research & Development,
    London
Feltwell RAF Base
Fylingdales-Moor RAF Base
Lakenheath RAF Base
Mildenhall RAF Base
Molesworth RAF Base
Research & Development
    Liaison Office London
    (USAF), London

ARMY
Army Research, Development
    & Standardization Group,
    UK
Hythe Depot Activity

DOD
Menwith Hill

NAVY
Office of Naval Research
    Europe, London
Upwood RAF Base
West Ruislip RAF Base

VIRGIN ISLANDS (1)
ARMY NATIONAL GUARD
Adjutant General of the
    Virgin Islands

WAKE ISLAND (1)
ARMY
Wake Island Missile Launch
    Facility

TOTAL = 209 in 35 Countries and Territories

SOURCE: William R. Evinger, ed. *Directory of U.S. Military Bases Worldwide,* 3rd ed (Oryx Press, 1998).

KEY TERMS

air-land battle doctrine
air war in Vietnam
Army Special Forces (Green Berets)
Atomic Energy Commission
body counts
budget and personnel systems
careerism
civil-military relations
commander in chief (CINC)
Department of Defense (DOD)
Department of the Navy
deterrence strategy
diversity and representativeness of the military
downsizing or drawdown
draft
gays in the military
Goldwater-Nichols Act
Grenada invasion
human error
interservice rivalry
intraservice rivalry
invasion of Panama
Joint Chiefs of Staff (JCS)
jointness

Korean War
Kosovo war
low-intensity conflict
General Douglas MacArthur
Manhattan Project
Robert McNamara
media censorship
military establishment
military lessons of Vietnam
military readiness
military recruitment
nuclear triad
Offices of the Secretary of the Army, Navy, and Air Force
OOTW (operations other than war)
Persian Gulf War
General Colin Powell
Reserve Officer Training Corps (ROTC)
services
sexual harassment
source of political recruitment
Vietnam War Memorial
War Department
weapons procurement process
Weinberger/Powell Doctrine

CHAPTER 8

. . . .

THE INTELLIGENCE COMMUNITY

An important development affecting U.S. foreign policy in the post–World War II period has been the rise of an extensive intelligence community within the executive branch. As with the presidency and the military, before the war, the United States intelligence community had only a limited capability. With the onset of the cold war and the U.S. policy of containment, however, a number of bureaucratic organizations developed with intelligence responsibilities.

In this chapter we will address the following questions: What are the major purpose and primary activities associated with the intelligence community? What are the various roles and missions of the major intelligence organizations? What are some of the major issues affecting the quality of intelligence? What role has the Central Intelligence Agency and covert operations played in U.S. foreign policy since World War II? In addition to addressing the implications for continuity and change in the foreign policymaking process and the president's ability to govern, this chapter also reviews the significant tensions that have developed between the demands of national security and of democracy since the rise of the intelligence community and a

national security ethos throughout the government into the post–cold war era.

All of theses questions and issues are of particular importance in light of the September 11, 2001, terrorist attacks and the Bush administration's subsequent war on terrorism. According to one intelligence specialist, "On September 11, 2001, Americans were reminded that the overweening power that they had taken for granted over the past dozen years is not the same as omnipotence. What is less obvious but equally important is that the power is itself part of the cause of terrorist enmity and even a source of U.S. vulnerability."[1]

PURPOSE AND ACTIVITIES OF INTELLIGENCE

The meaning of the term **intelligence** has become quite elastic over the years.[2] During the early part of the twentieth century, intelligence simply referred to information or news. By the 1940s, the word meant information that had been processed and made useful to decisionmakers at the various levels of the government and military. Since the 1950s, however, *intelligence has come to represent three broad sets of activities managed* by organizations within the U.S. government (as will be discussed in the next section):

1. Data collection and analysis,
2. Counterintelligence, and
3. Political and paramilitary intervention.[3]

The primary purpose of the intelligence community is to provide timely and accurate information to policymakers—this is what most intelligence is all about. This activity is referred to by the community as the "**intelligence cycle** or process." Most intelligence organizations are engaged in collecting and analyzing information for military and civilian policymakers in the executive branch. As discussed in earlier chapters, the president requires information to make decisions and govern U.S. foreign policy. Thus, the management

of intelligence is both an important source of presidential power and constraint on its exercise.

The intelligence cycle is comprised of five activities that occur concurrently, generating a continuous process of interaction between intelligence collectors, producers, and consumers: (1) planning and direction, (2) collection, (3) processing, (4) analysis and production, and (5) dissemination (see **figure 8.1**). The United States currently possesses many technologically advanced methods of gathering intelligence. The systems used in the gathering (or collecting) of intelligence are, however, a finite resource. The intelligence community requires direction (or stated requirements) in order to accurately meet the consumers' needs. These requirements are the beginning of the "intelligence process." Often, however, policymakers are reluctant to clearly state their needs due to the obvious political consequences of being wrong.

FIGURE **8.1**
THE INTELLIGENCE CYCLE

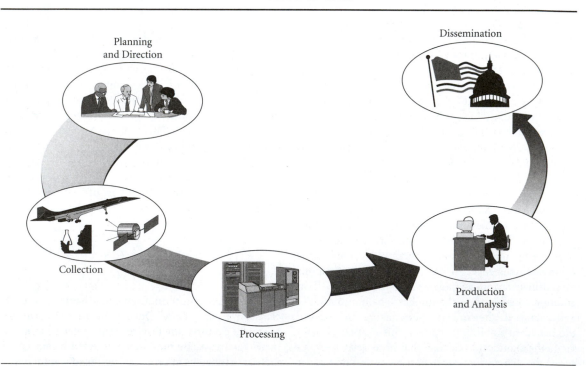

SOURCE: Office of Public Affairs, Central Intelligence Agency, *Fact Book on Intelligence* (April 1983).

In 1995 President Clinton signed Presidential Decision Directive (PDD) 35 which clearly stated his administration's collection priorities for the intelligence community. Such directives provide needed focus to the efforts of the intelligence community. However, counterterrorism was a relatively low priority under President Clinton, as it was for President Bush Sr. before him and President Bush Jr. after him—until the September 11, 2001, terrorist attacks.

Once requirements are received, collection techniques are then allocated to gathering the data. Inevitably, some requirements will be covered better than others, based on the capabilities and access available to the various collection methods. The United States has developed a very large array of methods for collecting intelligence ranging from the simple to the extremely complex. *Four of the most common methods of collection are:* information derived from electronic signals (SIGINT), from photography (PHOTINT or IMINT), from human sources (HUMINT), and from "open-sources" publicly available appearing in print or electronic form (such as radio, television, and newspapers).

Once collected, the raw information is processed. Because material gathered in the collection stage is almost never useful in its raw form, processing is required to render complex data into useful elements that an analyst can then use to piece together an intelligence picture. A complete intelligence picture is ideally constructed from several different sources and methods (for example, information gathered through human sources is confirmed or denied by electronic and photography methods).

During the analysis and production stage, pieces of information from various sources are pulled together to paint a complete intelligence picture. The people who do this are called **source analysts.** Source analysts synthesize information from the various collection means and methods that they have access to within the intelligence community. For the intelligence community, the analysis stage is when true intelligence is created. Therefore, the community makes a clear distinction between raw information and intelligence. The products that have been through this cycle and disseminated to policymakers are referred to as "finished intelligence."

Finished intelligence products are then disseminated to the policymakers in various forms. One of the most important finished intelligence products is the National Intelligence Estimate (NIE). An NIE provides a synthesis of the most authoritative judgments of the intelligence community on subjects of highest concern to U.S. policymakers. On the surface the process appears simple. However, the intelligence process has experienced several systemic problems (which will be discussed later) that have consistently frustrated its execution.

Another important function of intelligence is counterintelligence, that is, protecting intelligence information, personnel, and national security organizations from eavesdroppers, spies, and double agents. For forty years, American counterintelligence focused on protecting the national security bureaucracy from penetration by its major adversary, the Soviet Union, and its allies. The need to insulate the intelligence community and national security bureaucracy has resulted in the development of an extensive security and secrecy system throughout the government. Although all organizations that are engaged in intelligence gathering need to protect their information and have a narrow counterintelligence mission, some agencies have a broader counterintelligence mission that affects the larger intelligence community and U.S. foreign policy.

In addition to the two traditional intelligence functions discussed above, American intelligence agencies also have been tasked with covert political and paramilitary operations in support of U.S. foreign policy. These involve governmental acts, such as propaganda campaigns, psychological warfare, secret financial assistance, destabilization campaigns, partisan resistance movements, assassinations, and coups d'etat. The Central Intelligence Agency (CIA) is the organization most involved in this area and has developed a certain notoriety for its covert operations over the years, as will be discussed in the chapter's second half.

THE MAJOR INTELLIGENCE ORGANIZATIONS

Much of the public equates governmental intelligence activity with the Central Intelligence Agency; however, the intelligence community is much more than just the CIA. Since the 1940s, a large and complex intelligence community has developed within the executive branch of the U.S. government. The expansion of the community is in part due to the development of specific technologically sophisticated intelligence capabilities. The growing management needs of these capabilities have resulted in the expansion of several intelligence organizations and are associated with the major methods of collection—imagery intelligence (IMINT or PHOTINT), signals intelligence (SIGINT), and human intelligence (HUMINT).

The major intelligence organizations are (1) the National Security Agency (NSA); (2) Army, Navy, and Air Force intelligence; (3) the National Reconnaissance Office and the National Imagery and Mapping Agency; (4) the Defense Intelligence Agency; (5) the State Department's Intelligence and Research Bureau; (6) the Federal Bureau of Investigation; (7) other agencies in the executive branch, such as the Departments of Energy and Commerce, that are engaged in intelligence activities; and (8) the Central Intelligence Agency.[4] These organizations fall within three general categories based on their principle function in the intelligence process.

First, the producers are those that analyze and disseminate finished intelligence products to consumers. These products take many forms, from daily summaries to detailed research studies, but it is through these products that the intelligence community primarily interacts with policymakers. Second are the organizations that focus on collection and processing (remember, processing refers to the rendering of complex raw data, such as imagery and signals, into information products the analyst can then use in the development of a finished intelligence product). This is the largest grouping, where most of the growth in the intelligence community has taken place. Thirdly, some organizations also conduct an additional function in the research and development of equipment (or collection platforms). For example, the National Reconnaissance Office (NRO), while producing imagery products, is also engaged in the development of new, more technologically advanced imagery systems. In addition to collection and analysis of intelligence, these organizations may also have major counterintelligence and political and paramilitary intervention missions.

INTELLIGENCE ORGANIZATIONS OF THE DEFENSE DEPARTMENT

Most intelligence organizations, including personnel and budget, are officially a part of the Department of Defense. The Pentagon spends eighty-five cents of every intelligence dollar, with the big accounts being those of the NSA and NRO, America's technical collection services.[5]

The National Security Agency. The National Security Agency (NSA) was created in 1952 within the Department of Defense, though its origins go back to World War I and the army's Signal Corps. It has grown to become the largest and, along with the CIA, most important intelligence agency. Unlike the CIA, the NSA has been successful in keeping its existence and operations hidden from the public.

The major function of the National Security Agency is the collection and exploitation of SIGINT (communication, radar, and telemetry intelligence). NSA maintains "listening posts" around the world, equipped with sophisticated electronics for intercepting communications messages, for example, via telephone or microwave. Most of these listening posts are located in U.S. governmental facilities abroad, including U.S. embassies and particularly American military bases. The intercepted messages are relayed to NSA's Fort Meade, Maryland, headquarters, where an extensive and sophisticated array of computers process the information, making it useful for further evaluation by intelligence analysts.

NSA also has special responsibility in **cryptology,** the study of making and breaking codes. Because everyone in the intelligence business is conditioned to be extremely security conscious and aware of eavesdropping by other governments, many of the messages communicated between governmental officials are sent in code (or encryption) to protect their contents if intercepted. The National Security Agency devises the codes for the U.S. government, performing an important counterintelligence function.

Since much of the information that NSA intercepts is in code, efforts are made to break the codes of other countries and decipher the messages, unbeknownst to the original source. More and more people have come to realize the importance of breaking enemy codes, especially in times of war. During World War II, much of the Allies' early success against the Axis powers was a result of British and American efforts to break German and Japanese codes. In fact, the Battle of Midway, crucial for gaining naval control of the Pacific, was an American triumph largely because of knowledge of the Japanese fleet's general destination, gained as a result of the Japanese code being broken. During the Falkland Islands War of 1982, although the U.S. government officially proclaimed a position of neutrality, the NSA had broken the military code used by Argentina and shared the information with Great Britain—which played a crucial part in helping the British win the war.

The National Reconnaissance Office and the National Imagery and Mapping Agency. The National Reconnaissance Office (NRO) and the National Imagery and Mapping Agency (NIMA) are additional important intelligence organizations within the Department of Defense. Neither organization is well-known to the American public. Both elements are involved in the imagery subfield of intelligence, which since the end of World War II, has experienced tremendous growth in the techniques and sophistication of intelligence collection. As a result, over time many organizations have evolved to deal with the expansion of imagery collection. In the 1990s management and coordination of these organizations was recognized to be lacking. Therefore, NIMA was created in 1996 to centralize the management of imagery. It was formed by the consolidation of four different independent governmental organizations and several departmental activities all dealing with the management of imagery.

The NRO was created during the cold war to help centralize the management of reconnaissance flights. Information provided by aerial surveillance has played an important role in the conduct of U.S. foreign policy since the late 1950s, especially in defense policy and arms control. Today, the NRO is responsible for the development as well as the supervision (via the Air Force and NASA) of high-altitude surveillance mechanisms (e.g., imagery-based intelligence, or IMINT). NIMA then processes the raw data acquired from the airborne platforms into imagery products used by the source analysts.

In the 1950s, U.S. governmental knowledge of the Soviet Union was very sparse, yet important national security decisions had to be made. "Sovietology" was a new field within the United States, and the Soviet Union remained a closed society. NSA's capabilities in communications intelligence were primitive, and the CIA had difficulty penetrating the Soviet system

through espionage at a time when a very intense anti-communist climate permeated American society. Not surprisingly, Americans initially came to fear a "bomber gap" and then a "missile gap" when the Soviet Union successfully launched Sputnik in 1958—the first satellite placed in global orbit. In this environment, the U.S. government made important national security decisions to expand its military capabilities and nuclear strategic forces in accordance with its containment policy based on a worst-case scenario of the military threat and capabilities posed by the Soviet Union.

In the late 1950s, a major technological development occurred that helped to address this information problem. The United States developed the U-2 spy plane, a fast high-altitude plane designed to fly long distances over the Soviet Union and equipped with photographic equipment for taking detailed ground pictures. The U-2 became an important source of early information on Soviet military forces and demonstrated, among other things, that the bomber and missile gaps were in favor of the United States. U-2 flights by the CIA and Air Force intelligence also helped to verify the existence of Soviet intermediate-range missiles in Cuba during the early days of the Cuban Missile Crisis in 1962.

The public first became aware of the supersecret spy plane when pilot Gary Powers and his U-2 were shot down and captured by the Soviet Union in 1960. In response to this event, and to better coordinate aerial reconnaissance, the National Reconnaissance Office was created in 1960. During the Cuban missile crisis, a U-2 was actually shot down over Cuba. As the U-2 became increasingly vulnerable to surface-to-air missiles, the NRO began to rely on a new spy plane—the SR-71—and the use of satellites to obtain military information about the Soviet Union. Over the years, major advances have been made in the capabilities of satellites to see tremendous detail on the ground (though the precision and timeliness of the detail has been overblown by too many Hollywood movies). **Satellite reconnaissance** has become the major means available to the U.S. government for verifying compliance with arms control treaties (as well as one important source of intelligence, including the war on terrorism).

As one can imagine, the use of imagery in painting the intelligence picture is extremely valuable to intelligence analysts. In recent years, however, the continuing reliance on imagery has been called into question. Over the years flight paths and orbits of satellites have been compromised. As a result, it is not too difficult for those wishing to keep their activities secret to limit their activities when imagery assists are known to be overhead. Two examples highlight the contemporary limits of imagery: the 1994 Rwandan genocide and the 1998 Indian nuclear tests. During the Rwandan conflict, imagery assets were unable to give policymakers a clear picture of the situation on the ground, for they were unable to overcome the restrictions of the tropical environment to show the movements of refugees and combatants. In 1998 the United States was surprised by nuclear weapons tests conducted by the Indian government, and a congressional inquiry concluded the failure was in part due to the overreliance on imagery assets.

The Defense Intelligence Agency. The Defense Intelligence Agency (DIA) was created in 1961 in response to the Bay of Pigs fiasco, where the Central Intelligence Agency trained Cuban expatriates to invade Cuba and overthrow Fidel Castro—an operation that failed miserably and led to the condemnation of the United States throughout the globe. The DIA's purpose is to better coordinate the many intelligence activities undertaken by the Department of Defense in the hope of giving the military a single and more influential voice in the government's intelligence process.

The DIA has played an increasingly important role in the post–Goldwater-Nichols Act, joint military structure (discussed in the previous chapter). The DIA provides the military services and the regional commanders in chief (CINCs) with finished intelligence products focused on their requirements. These requirements are usually tactical in nature, focusing on the composition, disposition, and capabilities of potential military adversaries.

Although it made sense to create a new organization to coordinate and meet military intelligence needs, it has not always worked so smoothly in practice. Many of the problems that afflict the military establishment also plague the Defense Intelligence Agency. Staff consists of military and civilian analysts drawn from the individual services and the Office of the Secretary of Defense, requiring that the different subcultures and divided loyalties within the organizations be overcome.

The Intelligence Organizations of the Military Services. Each of the military services maintains its own intelligence capability. American military intelligence consists primarily of service efforts to collect and process tactical military information, including the force structures, tactics employed, and operational capabilities of other military forces—especially those of the Soviet Union after World War II. Recently, the Army and Air Force have developed unmanned aerial vehicles (UAVs), which seem to be playing a more important role in intelligence collection. Several UAVs were shot down during U.S. military actions in Afghanistan.

Army intelligence (G-2) is one of the oldest of the nation's intelligence operations. In addition to its focus on military tactical intelligence, G-2 has a counterintelligence function and an extensive history of involvement in preventing treason, espionage, sabotage, gambling, prostitution, and black marketeering at home and abroad.

Many of the personnel who work for military intelligence also work for the National Security Agency. Most of NSA's listening posts for intercepting communications are located on U.S. military bases and facilities operated by military intelligence personnel, as well as other means or platforms, such as airborne systems. For example, shortly after George W. Bush was inaugurated in 2001, there was a collision between a Chinese jet fighter and an American EP-3 spy plane along the border of China (the EP-3 was loaded with electronics equipment that enabled the U.S. military to eavesdrop on China). The Chinese jet fighter crashed, and the American spy plane was able to land in China. The plane and crew were seized and held by the Chinese government, triggering an early crisis in Chinese-American relations for the new Bush administration. With around fifteen hundred military installations throughout the world and American forces on constant patrol, it should be clear that the military and NSA have a tremendous capacity for intercepting global communications.

As discussed in the previous chapter, the Goldwater-Nichols Defense Reorganization Act of 1986 forced the services into a joint operational environment. As a result the primary customers of military intelligence are currently the commanders in chief (CINCs) of the unified commands. Each CINC has his own joint intelligence center (JIC) that responds to his own needs and makes requests for particular intelligence collection, usually through the DIA.

NON-DOD ORGANIZATIONS

Compared to the regional or tactical focus of much of the DOD intelligence activities, the Central Intelligence Agency is the principle intelligence organization responsible for national or strategic needs. The CIA is supposed to exert coordinating control over the whole community. This authority also includes "tasking authority" over the intelligence-collecting assets of the entire community to meet national security needs. The difficulties of this herculean task will be discussed later; for now it is important to understand the CIA's main customers are the National Security Council and the president. Other cabinet-level departments have their own intelligence activities. Although the most important are under the Departments of State (the Bureau of Intelligence and Research, or INR) and Justice (the FBI), other executive branch agencies, such as the Departments of Energy and Commerce, also conduct intelligence activities related to their own areas of interest.

The Bureau of Intelligence and Research. The State Department is involved in intelligence work, predominantly in analysis through its Bureau of Intelligence and Research (INR). INR analyzes the department's cable traffic from abroad and information from other agencies in the intelligence community. As one of the producers of finished intelligence, it is actively involved in the process that produces communitywide intelligence estimates (NIEs) and provides advice to the secretary of state and State Department personnel on intelligence matters. Because the INR is so much smaller than the other two producers of finished intelligence (CIA and DIA), it is often thought to be the weakest. However, INR's influence is often a function of the secretary of state. For example, Secretary of State George Shultz (1982–1989) met regularly with the assistant secretary who ran the bureau, whereas James Baker (1989–1992) rarely did.

The FBI. The Federal Bureau of Investigation (FBI) is a part of the Department of Justice. It began as the Bureau of Investigation in 1908 and is the oldest governmental organization developed solely for the purpose of intelligence. Although the FBI is now the intelligence organization with primary responsibility for U.S. domestic counterintelligence and internal security, it had a more varied life in its earlier days.

During World War II and before the creation of the CIA, the FBI was active throughout Latin America—a region of the world where the United States was the major financial and military power, particularly in the Caribbean and Central America. As the U.S. government became involved in World War II, President Franklin Roosevelt instructed the FBI to develop an intelligence capability for collecting information and conducting counterintelligence and political action in the region.

Since the creation of the CIA, the FBI's legal jurisdiction has been limited to activities within the United States. The FBI is unique not only in its geographic focus on the United States but in its performance of both domestic-oriented and foreign policy functions, including federal law enforcement, foreign counterintelligence, and internal security against threats to the U.S. government. From 1924 to 1972 the FBI was run by one man—**J. Edgar Hoover.** (See **essay 8.1** on Hoover and the FBI's pursuit of security.)

The FBI's structure, subculture, and actions were heavily influenced by Hoover and continue to reflect his reign, though to a lesser extent today.[6] The historic law-enforcement and anticommunist counterintelligence orientation have been particularly problematic in having the FBI respond and adapt to a post–cold war and post–September 11 environment, especially where the emphasis has been on intelligence activities against terrorism. In light of its poor anti-terrorism performance, the FBI is undergoing a major reorganization. Only time will tell whether a major reorganization will in fact actually lead to major, successful reform. It is very difficult to change the long-standing patterns of a law enforcement–oriented agency into an efficient and responsive law enforcement and anti-terrorism agency.

The Departments of Energy and Commerce. Although a very small part of the intelligence community, the Departments of Energy and Commerce control intelligence activities focused on their needs. The Energy Department's intelligence concerns are primarily centered on issues of nuclear weapons and related research. Its ability to manage national security concerns in this area were recently called into question with the Win Ho Lee spy case (discussed in chapter 14, on civil liberties). While evidence against Lee remains suspect, the incident did reveal security concerns relating to some of the United States' most sensitive secrets. The Department of Commerce conducts overt intelligence activities through its commercial attachés assigned to embassies around the world.

ESSAY 8.1
J. Edgar Hoover and the Pursuit of Security

J. Edgar Hoover was one of the most powerful figures in the U.S. government through much of the twentieth century. He served in the Department of Justice under nineteen attorneys general, including forty-eight years as director of the FBI. In the minds of most Americans at the time, his name and agency were synonymous with the defense of American security against threats to law and order. With Hoover's death, however, new information has appeared that documents a much more sordid history. Recent works, such as *Secrecy and Power: The Life of J. Edgar Hoover* by Richard Powers, demonstrate that Hoover ran the national police force with an iron grip. He regularly violated people's civil liberties and rights in order to destroy perceived threats to national security. Examining the life of Hoover allows one to better understand the rise of the FBI as an important intelligence organization, the history of American anticommunism, and the contradictions that have developed between democratic practice and the pursuit of national security.

Hoover was born in Washington, D.C., in 1895, the fourth child in the family. He never married and resided in his parents' house near the Capitol until his mother died in 1938. He never joined a political party nor voted. Yet according to Powers, Hoover developed very strong political and moral beliefs that were shaped by his upbringing in turn-of-the-century Washington and his formative experience in the Justice Department during World War I.

During the early years of the twentieth century, Washington, D.C., was very much a small southern company town. Hoover was raised in a family, neighborhood, and city that was overwhelmingly middle class, white, Christian, and Protestant. Between 1900 and 1920 the District systematically institutionalized "Jim Crow" laws segregating the races. In this environment, J. Edgar Hoover acquired a "turn-of-the-century vision of America as a small community of like-minded neighbors, proud of their achievements, resentful of criticism, fiercely opposed to change."[A]

During the late nineteenth century and early twentieth century, the United States was undergoing massive and rapid change as a result of industrialization and im-

migration. Nativist (anti-foreigner) sentiments grew in response to changes symbolized by alien ideas and habits that threatened native-born Americans' way of life. Hoover shared these concerns and devoted his life to eradicating these threats to America, rising to prominence in the process. "As twentieth century standards of the mass society swept over traditional America, subverting old values, disrupting old customs, and dislodging old leaders," states Powers, "Americans who were frightened by the loss of their community saw in Hoover a man who understood their concerns and shared their anger, a powerful defender who would guard their America of memory against a world of alien forces, strange people, and dangerous ideas."[B]

Hoover was literally born into the federal government, for most of his family and relatives were its employees. He went to work for the Library of Congress in 1913, received a law degree from George Washington University, and joined the Justice Department as a clerk in 1917. He won quick promotion to "attorney," and helped to administer the department's supervision of German aliens in the Alien Enemy Bureau during World War I. This is where Hoover first witnessed the country's growing hysteria over German spies, traitors, and saboteurs and the government's campaign to destroy political dissent.

Near the end of the war, a new hysteria developed over bolshevism with the Bolshevik Revolution in 1917 and the rise of business-labor disputes at home. The Justice Department, under Attorney General A. Mitchell Palmer, dealt with this "Red Scare" by conducting mass roundups and deportations of alien radicals. Hoover was promoted to special assistant to the attorney general in charge of the Radical Division's campaign against communism. Although Palmer and Hoover did not succeed in using the Red Scare raids to pass a peacetime sedition law to set strict legal limits on political dissent, they severely damaged the communist, socialist, and labor movements. As part of the antiradical campaign, Hoover relied on the assistance of private anticommunist organizations and devised a public relations campaign to promote anticommunism through the media and among the public.

The antiradical campaign ended when excesses against innocent victims and violations of civil liberties

A. Richard Gid Powers, *Secrecy and Power: The Life of J. Edgar Hoover* (New York: Free Press, 1987), p. 3.

B. Ibid., pp. 3–4.

and rights were exposed. Nevertheless, the campaign gave Hoover "and his Bureau a claim to be the government's official authority on anything involving communist activities. Hoover's 1919 studies of communism were, with little exaggeration, fundamental texts in the evolution of the anticommunism that was American orthodoxy for the next fifty years."[C] And starting in 1924 as director of the Bureau of Investigation (which became the FBI in 1934), Hoover used the same strategy and methods to destroy threats to national security that he had utilized during the World War I antisedition campaign and Red Scare.

In the 1920s and 1930s, Hoover transformed the FBI into a modern and professional bureaucracy under his control. Through his authoritarian rule, he molded the FBI to represent the legal and moral guardian of the nation. Much of this period was spent improving the FBI's criminal intelligence capabilities and fighting a war on gangsters and crime, symbolized by the triumphs (often fictionalized) and celebrity of Hoover and his G-men— the government men in the FBI.

World War II and the cold war fed new fears and hysteria concerning what Hoover had always believed to be the greatest threat to national security: subversion and communism. During the late 1930s, under the direction of President Franklin Roosevelt, "the Bureau was once again creating indexes of dangerous citizens and aliens, infiltrating political groups to gather general intelligence, and tapping phones, but by then Hoover had become such a reassuring symbol of security and stability to Americans that any protests were drowned out in the applause for Public Hero Number One."[D]

World War II and the cold war eliminated all restraints from Hoover's surveillance and involvement in America's political scene. For the next thirty years, Hoover and the FBI targeted political dissenters in a renewed antiradical campaign against communism. During the late 1940s and early 1950s, Hoover fed the growing anticommunist hysteria and the McCarthy movement. According to Powers, "throughout the fifties, despite the total collapse of American communism, Hoover never slackened in his efforts to persuade the president and the public that, all appearances to the contrary, the threat from communism was greater than ever."[E] In fact, in 1956, **Operation Cointelpro** was instigated to employ illegal and unconstitutional means to sabotage and destroy communists, communist sympathizers, and fellow travelers. This paranoia with subversion and treason led Hoover to extend Operation Cointelpro to the civil rights, black nationalist, and antiwar movements during the 1960s, for Hoover saw them as vulnerable to communism and a threat to American security. His nemesis became Martin Luther King, Jr., whom Hoover believed to be a communist and a personal threat to the small-town traditional values that Hoover was determined to uphold.

J. Edgar Hoover became so powerful that no president dared to replace him, even after he reached retirement age. He died in office in 1972 at the age of seventy-seven, a controversial figure who had directed the Bureau of Investigation for forty-eight years. Hoover's legacy was a profound impact on the FBI, the U.S. government's quest for national security, and American politics. In the end, as Powers concludes, "he achieved his life's goal by destroying American communism, and was a powerful supporter for traditional values; however, those values supported racial and other injustices, and his covert attacks on personal and public enemies violated principles of constitutional limits on governmental power."[F]

C. Ibid., p. 97.
D. Ibid., p. 227.

E. Ibid., p. 337.
F. Ibid., p. 492.

SOURCES: William Keller, *The Liberals and J. Edgar Hoover: Rise and Fall of a Domestic Intelligence State* (Princeton: Princeton University Press, 1989); Kenneth O'Reilly, *Hoover and the Un-Americans: The FBI, HUAC, and the Red Menace* (Philadelphia: Temple University Press, 1983); and Richard Gid Powers, *Secrecy and Power: The Life of J. Edgar Hoover* (New York: Free Press, 1987).

The CIA. Created by the National Security Act of 1947, the Central Intelligence Agency soon became the single most important agency responsible for intelligence abroad. The CIA has played an important role in the collection and analysis of data, is the primary intelligence organization responsible for counterintelligence outside the United States, and has become the major intelligence organization engaged in political and paramilitary action abroad. In addition to these three intelligence functions, the director of central intelligence (DCI) is responsible for coordinating the entire intelligence community for the president of the United States.

Since its beginnings, the CIA has developed into *a large bureaucratic organization composed of four general divisions or directorates:* intelligence, science and technology, administration, and operations. Most current CIA personnel are involved in the basic intelligence functions of data collection and analysis. The intelligence directorate (DI) is responsible for producing the CIA's own intelligence assessments (IAs) for the policymaking community and participating in the development of national intelligence estimates (NIEs), which are a product of the entire intelligence community. The science and technology directorate (DS&T) is responsible for developing mechanisms and gadgets used in the type of intelligence activities made most famous in the 007 James Bond movies (though these have always been more science fiction than reality). The DS&T, for instance, developed the U-2 and SR-71 spy planes. The administration directorate (DA) engages in personnel decisions and manages the paperwork throughout the CIA bureaucracy. The personnel within intelligence, science and technology, and administration occupy traditional professional roles; only those within the operations directorate (DO) are involved in covert operations. Further analysis of the CIA's intelligence activity and its covert role in U.S. foreign policy is provided below.

HISTORICAL DEVELOPMENT OF A LARGE, COMPLEX COMMUNITY

The historical development of modern intelligence began at the beginning of the twentieth century in Great Britain. During the 1920s and 1930s, intelligence functions developed in most European states. In the United States, modern intelligence developed more slowly. A common attitude toward intelligence held by many American policymakers up to World War II was symbolized by Secretary of State Henry Stimson during a 1929 discussion of the need for intelligence, when he proclaimed that "gentlemen do not read each other's mail."[7] This attitude was consistent with the political culture of the American public, who believed that the United States represented democratic ideals and principles, as opposed to the warlike attitudes and balance-of-power politics that prevailed in Europe, based on the assumption that individual freedom and rights

were something to uphold while big government spying abroad and at home was something to fear.

Nevertheless, "although most Americans believe the United States did not become deeply involved in intelligence operations until the creation of the Office of Strategic Services (OSS) during World War II," Nathan Miller demonstrates in *Spying for America: The Hidden History of U.S. Intelligence* that the U.S. government has "participated in such activities—with varying degrees of success—since the Revolution."[8] The U.S. government had a very limited intelligence capability during the nineteenth century, relying on the Secret Service, the military, and the State Department. American intelligence became more professional and grew during the first half of the twentieth century with the establishment of military intelligence, the FBI, and during World War II, the Office of Strategic Services (OSS), the precursor of the CIA.

With the passage of the National Security Act of 1947 and the advent of the cold war, intelligence expanded into a large, complex, modern community. Each major intelligence organization (except the State Department's INR) has evolved into a large bureaucracy. Although the information is classified, it has been estimated that during the 1980s the American intelligence community employed over 150,000 people and spent close to $40 billion annually to implement its intelligence missions.[9] Since the collapse of the Soviet Union, the intelligence budget and staff likely have experienced some downsizing, followed by a significant increase due to the September 11 attacks and President Bush's war on terrorism.

The intelligence community not only grew over the twentieth century, especially after World War II, but also became much more complex. Numerous bureaucratic organizations inside and outside DOD are involved in intelligence in the traditional security area. And many other executive agencies have intelligence roles in foreign policy, as well, each with a unique intelligence purpose and mission—which may grow in a post–cold war environment, especially in nontraditional areas such as economics. This complexity has been reinforced by the development of different subcultures, since these intelligence organizations were created at different times, evolved under different conditions and leadership, and performed different intelligence functions.

FIGURE **8.2**
THE INTELLIGENCE COMMUNITY: AN ORGANIZATIONAL VIEW

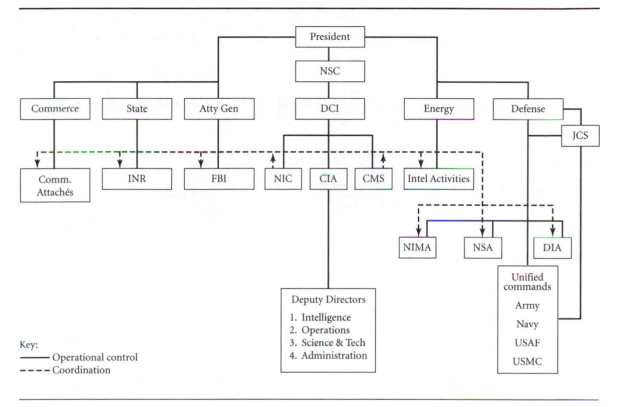

NOTE: See the text for meanings of acronyms

PATTERNS IN THE INTELLIGENCE PROCESS

The rise of a large and complex intelligence community has affected both the intelligence cycle and product. **Figure 8.2** places the organizations into their formal relationships as described above and emphasizes the hierarchical relations between the organizations. **Figure 8.3,** in contrast, is a better way to see how the intelligence agencies actually function and interact.[10] This function-oriented approach emphasizes the roles and missions performed by each organization and allows one to understand *the three dominant (systemic or reoccurring) patterns that have developed affecting the collection, analysis, and dis-*

semination of intelligence: (1) difficulties in achieving coordination, (2) producer-consumer problems, and (3) variations in intelligence success.[11]

COORDINATION PROBLEMS

The intelligence community has become so large and complex that coordinating the organizations' work in support of the president's foreign policy is very difficult. This is a recurring theme in the executive branch, as was noted concerning presidential management of foreign policy in chapter 5 and the military establishment in chapter 7.

The **director of central intelligence (DCI)** is charged to coordinate the intelligence process and act

FIGURE **8.3**
THE INTELLIGENCE COMMUNITY: A FUNCTIONAL VIEW

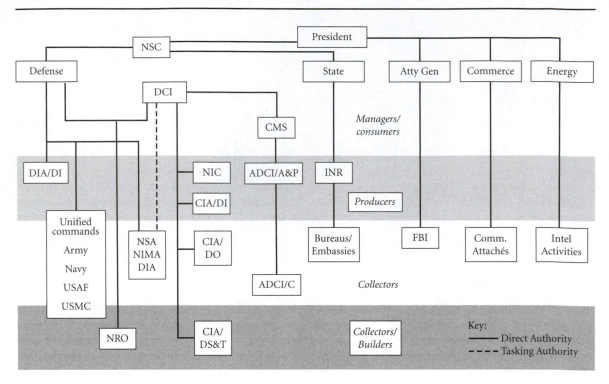

NOTE: See the text for meanings of acronyms.

as the principal intelligence officer and adviser to the president (see **table 8.1** for a list of the directors of central intelligence). The functional view graphically demonstrates the limited control the DCI has over day-to-day intelligence activities. This is perhaps one reason for the CIA's apparent attraction to covert operations—the DCI can directly affect them. With so much of the intelligence community operating under the Department of Defense, it is inevitable that the people executing the missions within the intelligence community will be more responsive to the DOD's institutional incentives and pressures. However, this does not detract from the DCI's lawful responsibility to manage the entire intelligence community. As head of the community, he has been given broad powers and a good deal of money to exercise them. The DCI was also given a deputy director (DDCI), responsible for managing the daily re-

quirements of running the CIA, in order to free up the director to better manage the entire community.

The Community Management Staff (CMS) and the National Intelligence Council (NIC) are the two principle tools through which the director is to coordinate the community. The CMS was vastly enlarged in the 1997 intelligence authorization bill by its funding of several new high-level positions (called assistant directors, ADs). Assistant directorships were created over collection (ADCI-C) and analysis and production (ADCI-A&P). The DCI through this apparatus currently has a greater ability to manage the community than ever before, but it remains to be seen whether the community will be responsive to the new level of direction.

Beyond managing the CIA and targeting certain intelligence priorities, the DCI appears to continue to

TABLE **8.1**
DIRECTORS OF CENTRAL INTELLIGENCE

NAME	YEAR	PRESIDENT	BACKGROUND
Sidney W. Souers	1946	Truman	Business and Navy
Hoyt S. Vandenburg	1946	Truman	Air Force
Roscoe H. Hillenkoetter	1947	Truman	Navy
Walter Bedell Smith	1950	Truman	Army and diplomacy
Allen Welsh Dulles	1953	Eisenhower	Law and government
John A. McCone	1961	Kennedy	Business and government
William F. Raborn, Jr.	1965	Johnson	Navy and business
Richard M. Helms	1966	Johnson	Journalism and government
James R. Schlesinger	1972	Nixon	Academia and government
William E. Colby	1973	Nixon	Law and government
George H. Bush	1975	Ford	Business, Congress, government
Stansfield Turner	1977	Carter	Navy
William J. Casey	1981	Reagan	Law and business
William H. Webster	1987	Reagan	Law and government
Robert M. Gates	1991	Bush Sr.	Government
R. James Woolsey	1993	Clinton	Law and government
John M. Deutsch	1995	Clinton	Academia and government
George J. Tenet	1997	Clinton	Government
George J. Tenet		Bush Jr.	

have limited actual authority to govern the larger intelligence community. The National Security Agency; Army, Navy and Air Force intelligence; National Reconnaissance Office and NIMA; and the Defense Intelligence Agency are part of the Department of Defense and most of the personnel operate within the military chain of command. The Intelligence and Research Bureau is responsive to the structure and norms of the State Department. And the FBI is a semiautonomous agency within the Department of Justice.

Recent events such as the nuclear tests conducted by India and the bombing of the Chinese embassy in Belgrade indicate that the community is still very fragmented in the execution of its efforts. As figure 8.3 shows, the Community Management Staff has no legal authority over the members of the intelligence community it is supposed to coordinate. It appears that the

traditional hierarchical relationships remain the most influential in the day-to-day management of the intelligence process.

While the CMS is supposed to help coordinate the collection effort, the National Intelligence Council (NIC) is supposed to assist in the dissemination stage of the intelligence process. The NIC is an interagency organization composed of senior analysts from the various members of the intelligence community. NIC produces the **National Intelligence Estimates (NIEs)**, intended to be an important product of the intelligence community. The NIE is one of the few products the intelligence community produces jointly. Yet policymakers often criticize NIEs because they are said to reflect the lowest common denominator agreed upon by the various members of the NIC. Such compromised intelligence assessments tend to be the order of the day, given the intelligence agencies' different subcultures and perspectives.

The functional model (in comparison to the formal organizational view) shows visually the channels through which intelligence is collected, produced, and managed. It also shows just how little of the intelligence community the director of central intelligence actually controls on a day-to-day basis. The lines running from top to bottom are often referred to as "stovepipes" by the community. Rather than bringing different means of collection together and having a coherent intelligence cycle, each stovepipe is created as intelligence passes through various agencies depending on the stage of the intelligence process and the particular means of collecting information (reflecting the different functions of collectors, collectors/builders, and producers, as depicted in figure 8.3). These separate stovepipes demonstrate the "subcommunities" within the larger intelligence community. These subcommunities have often behaved as competitors, with each responding to the same intelligence requests or requirements on its own.

The decentralized bureaucratic nature of the intelligence community means that considerable independent action is performed by the various intelligence agencies, and when they do interact, the policymaking process experiences infighting and compromise. During the Cuban missile crisis, for example, when the president was trying to verify whether intermediate-range strategic missiles capable of delivering nuclear warheads on the United States were stationed in Cuba, the National Reconnaissance Office and the CIA were feuding over which bureaucracy had responsibility for the U-2 flights. U-2 flights were deferred for two days, until the NRO and the CIA agreed that they would each be responsible for alternate flights. Thus crucial information was delayed during a period when the United States and the Soviet Union faced their greatest crisis.[12]

Coordination in counterintelligence has been an area of particular historic contention between the FBI and the CIA. The cultures of intelligence and law enforcement are vastly different. For the intelligence-oriented CIA, the purpose is policy. For the law enforcement-oriented FBI, the purpose is to convict criminals. Various spy cases have highlighted the lack of coordination between the two organizations. The lack of coordination probably delayed the detection and arrest of CIA double agent Aldrich Ames for years until 1995. In the aftermath of the Ames case, the FBI and CIA created a jointly staffed counterintelligence office to try to correct the mistakes.

The events of September 11, 2001, however, show there is still much to be worked out. Despite the initial emphasis by the Bush administration and the media on the lack of warning and complete surprise of the terrorist attacks, it is now known that the intelligence community actually had many different pieces of information, but there was very poor communication, coordination, and cooperation among a variety of intelligence organizations, especially within the FBI.

One of President Bush Jr.'s initial responses was to issue an executive order creating an Office of Homeland Security (OHS) within the Executive Office of the Presidency, with former Pennsylvania governor Tom Ridge as its first director. What is particularly interesting is how centralized the process was that led to the creation of the Office of Homeland Security for it was devised by President Bush's White House staff, especially at the suggestion of Andrew Card, the Chief of Staff. "No department heads were asked to join the clique of senior White House aides who planned the redesign. Cabinet secretaries didn't know about the plan until the last minute," including most major foreign policy advisers.[13]

The purpose of OHS is to coordinate and centralize intelligence among the numerous organizations involved (which include literally dozens of different governmental departments and agencies, plus their interaction with state and local governments) to prevent and respond to security threats against the United States. According to former national security adviser Anthony Lake, if the Office of Homeland Security is to be effective, Ridge will have to "take powers away from various different agencies that now have them. There is nothing harder in the federal government than doing that."[14]

Despite the authority given to Director Ridge and his ability to report directly to the president, the Office of Homeland Security has struggled in gaining some control over the highly decentralized and sprawling intelligence community. If one places the Office of Homeland Security in the figures 8.2 and 8.3, according to figure 8.2 it would look very centralized and very hierarchical. However, the reality is that creating OHS has produced another intelligence organization, another bureaucratic layer, and another stovepipe within the intelligence community.

In June 2002 President Bush Jr. asked Congress to increase the prestige and visibility of OHS by approving its change to a **Department of Homeland Security (DHS)**—giving it cabinet-level status. In order to accomplish this, Congress had considerable say to the final composition since it must approve any new department. Ultimately, the White House and Congress consolidated 22 federal agencies and 177,000 employees to form a new department—transferring the Customs Service from Treasury, most of the Immigration and Naturalization Service from Justice, the Transportation Security Administration from Transportation, the Federal Emergency Management Agency, the Coast Guard from Transportation, and the U.S. Secret Service from Treasury (along with smaller agencies from other departments). With a budget request of about $35 billion for 2003, this represented the most ambitious effort to reorganize and expand the federal government in the area of foreign policy since 1947.

It is unclear to what extent this may help (or hurt) Secretary Ridge in what may be a very difficult if not impossible mission. The DHS, unlike the Office of Homeland Security which was part of the Executive Office of the Presidency, is now part of the larger executive branch bureaucracy. Under the legislation, despite some reorganization and transfer of some agencies to the new department, the most important intelligence agencies involved in anti-terrorism—the FBI and CIA, as well as those in DOD—maintain their independence and jurisdictional autonomy. Furthermore, NSC Adviser Condoleeza Rice (with President Bush Jr.'s approval) has also made it very clear that the national security adviser and NSC staff (and interagency process) will not report to the homeland security secretary, and in response to September 11, she has beefed up the NSC's anti-terrorism unit and staff. Therefore, although there might be some potential improvement in cooperation through the existence of a Department of Homeland Security, decentralization and coordination problems will probably continue to prevail involving the functions of homeland security and the governmental apparatus that exists to fight the war on terrorism (see **table 8.2** for an overview of the elaborate bureaucratic war on terrorism).

PRODUCER-CONSUMER PROBLEMS

The vast array of intelligence gathering methods and their effectiveness have resulted in an explosion of data available to the consumer (i.e., the policymaker), resulting in the "vacuum cleaner problem," as the community refers to it. The community now has the ability to easily overwhelm consumers with reams of information. The growing task presented to the community by the technology and information age is the challenge of sorting through the volumes of information to find what is relevant at any given moment. Despite the coordination problems, a large number of finished products are disseminated to policymakers in various forms (see **essay 8.2** for an overview). The problem is not a shortage of assessments but their production and consumption.

Problems have developed between the intelligence "producers"—analysts within the intelligence community—and "consumers"—the policymakers, especially the president and other high-level officials, who use this information to make decisions and justify their policies. The problem is that the president often finds that the intelligence community does not provide him with useful information, while members of the intelligence community often get ambiguous and contradictory guidelines from their superiors and the president.

The president and other policymakers and members of the intelligence bureaucracy occupy different roles, and different motivations influence their behavior. Consequently, it should not be too surprising that a producer-consumer problem has arisen and become a common part of the intelligence process. Presidents are always sensitive to the domestic political implications of their policies as they try to gain control of the bureaucracy, govern foreign policy, and lead the country.

When they have not already made up their minds or when they are not strongly leaning in a particular direction, presidents often want relevant information and honest intelligence appraisals to better understand the issue and arrive at an optimal decision. However, when a course of action has been already decided or if a president is ideologically predisposed, he is likely to want information that reinforces his views. Under either of these circumstances, a president may become frustrated with the intelligence product that comes across his desk, especially if it is a result of infighting and compromise.

TABLE 8.2
MAJOR FEDERAL AGENCIES INVOLVED IN THE WAR ON TERRORISM

Although the federal government appears monolithic to many, in the area of terrorism prevention and response (as in so many other areas), it has been anything but. Over forty federal agencies are involved in the war on terrorism (and more than twenty federal entities in bioterroism alone). The war on terrorism, especially at home, also involves the role of 50 states and hundreds of local governments as well (and their corresponding officials and agencies). The official list is classified, but here is a partial list of the major national bureaucratic players and their roles:

NATIONAL POLICY

National Security Council (White House)—coordinates foreign strategy

Department of Homeland Security —coordinates domestic defense

Council of Economic Advisers (White House)—coordinates economic recovery

INTELLIGENCE

Central Intelligence Agency— coordinates all foreign intelligence, deploys spies

National Security Agency— (Defense) intercepts foreign communications

National Reconaissance Office (Defense)—runs spy satellites

Defense Intelligence Agency (Defense)—coordinates military intelligence

Special Operations Command (Defense)—scouts hostile territory

State Department—negotiates with foreign governments

Federal Bureau of Investigation (Justice)—investigates attacks

Treasury Department—monitors suspicious financial activity

Securities and Exchange Commission—monitors suspicious trades

PREEMPTION AND RETALIATION

Defense Department—stages military strikes

FBI—arrests terrorists

Drug Enforcement Administration (Justice)—attacks e.g., Afghan opium trade

Treasury Department—freezes terrorist accounts

BORDER SECURITY

Coast Guard (DHS in peacetime, Defense in wartime)—patrols coasts and waterways

Immigration and Naturalization Service (DHS)—monitors people entering U.S.

Customs Service (DHS)—monitors goods entering U.S.

North American Aerospace Defense Command (Defense/Canada)— monitors aircraft and missiles

DISASTER PREPAREDNESS AND RESPONSE

FBI—coordinates crisis response

Office for Domestic Preparedness (Justice)—trains and equips local agencies

Federal Emergency Management Agency—supports, trains, and equips local fire, medical personnel

Bureau of Alcohol, Tobacco, and Firearms (Treasury)—trains locals in explosives handling

National Guard (Defense)— provides disaster relief, security

Joint Task Force, Civil Support (Defense)—coordinates other military assistance

Health and Human Services Department—assists locals with bioterrorism, mass casualties

Centers for Disease Control and Prevention (HHS)—detects disease outbreaks

Environmental Protection Agency—responds to chemical attacks

Energy Department—responds to radioactive and nuclear attacks

Agriculture Department— responds to attacks on food supply, crops, and livestock

Food and Drug Administration— monitors food supply

Veterans Affairs Department— provides extra hospital space

Transportation Department— protects transportation infrastructure

National Infrastructure Protection Center (FBI)— protects computer networks

Critical Infrastructure Assurance Office (Commerce)—protects computer networks

SOURCE: Sydney Freedberg, Jr. "Shoring Up America," *National Journal* (October 20, 2001), p. 3243; U.S., General Accounting Office, *Combating Terrorism: Intergovernmental Partnership in a National Strategy to Enhance State and Local Preparedness* (March 22, 2002).

ESSAY 8.2
SELECTED PRODUCTS OF THE INTELLIGENCE COMMUNITY

Finished intelligence products are categorized by the community as current, estimative, warning, and research. For each of these, the term national may appear in the title. This generally indicates that the product is intended for use at the highest national levels. Also, the contents of the product are reviewed and coordinated within the intelligence community (time permitting in the case of current intelligence), and significant dissenting views are usually noted.

The following does not represent an exhaustive list of the products of the intelligence community but is only a sample of the voluminous amount of information that the community puts out. The intent is to provide an overview of the types of products and the major customers that the intelligence community serves. Changes may have been made in light of the September 11 attacks.

CURRENT INTELLIGENCE PRODUCTS

President's Daily Brief. A compilation of current intelligence items of high significance to national policy concerns prepared six days a week by the CIA. It is tailored to meet daily intelligence needs as defined by the president and is distributed only to the president, vice president, and a few senior executive branch officials designated by the president.

Secretary's Morning Summary. A product prepared by the INR for the secretary of state seven days a week. Distribution is made within the department, White House, NSC, and selected ambassadors overseas.

National Intelligence Daily. A compilation of key current intelligence items published six days a week by CIA's DI, in consultation with DIA, INR, and NSA. This product can vary in classification and is tailored to specific interests. Dissemination is limited based on classification and topics. Versions of this publication are cabled to major U.S. military commands and selected U.S. posts overseas.

Daily Economic Intelligence Brief. A compilation of articles on current significant economic issues prepared five days a week by CIA. It is tailored to meet the needs of senior economic policy officials at the Cabinet or deputy level.

Military Intelligence Digest. This product is a compilation in magazine format produced five days a week from DIA, service intelligence, and major military commands inputs. It provides intelligence of current interest to national-level policymakers on military or military-related topics (e.g., regional security, nuclear security and proliferation,

strategy, and resources). Distribution is to policymakers and military commanders worldwide.

Executive Highlights. Published five days a week with inputs from DIA and NSA, this product presents articles on crisis or near-crisis situations. It is designed to keep the secretary of defense, chair of the Joint Chiefs of Staff, and other top decisionmakers informed of developments that might require immediate action by the United States. Distribution is made in hardcopy in the Washington area and in softcopy and electronic message to military commanders elsewhere.

Defense Intelligence Terrorism Summary. This product is a compilation produced five days a week presenting information and analyses on terrorism threats and developments that could affect DOD personnel, facilities, and interests. It also includes a monthly terrorism review by combatant commands. It is produced in a hardcopy version for the Washington area and an electronic message version for military commands overseas.

WEEKLIES/PERIODICALS/
AD HOC PUBLICATIONS

Defense Intelligence Report. This ad hoc product is produced by DIA to address a single policy-relevant event, situation, or development. The report is brief, one to eight pages, and is produced very quickly. It is targeted at executive-level consumers, with distribution to other appropriate customers.

Economic Intelligence Weekly. This product contains analyses of major foreign economic developments and trends published weekly by CIA's Directorate of Intelligence for top and midlevel policymakers.

CIA Regional Reviews. These are periodic assessments (from weekly to monthly) of foreign political, economic, military, and social events relevant to U.S. interests. These publications, produced by the regional analytic offices of the Directorate of Intelligence, cover regional and national events in Africa, Europe, Latin America, the Middle East, East Asia, South Asia, and the newly formed states of the former Soviet Union.

Terrorism Review. A monthly publication of the CIA's Counter-Terrorist Center. The publication addresses current trends in international terrorism activity and methods. It also tracks international terrorist incidents.

Peacekeeping Perspectives. A biweekly journal produced by the State Department's INR on multilateral conflict management and humanitarian operations. It provides the only comprehensive review of current or projected peacekeeping operations or humanitarian issues.

ESTIMATIVE INTELLIGENCE PRODUCTS

National Intelligence Estimates (NIEs). NIEs are produced by the National Intelligence Council. Therefore, they provide the most authoritative judgments of the intelligence community on subjects of highest concern to U.S. policymakers. Unlike current intelligence products, which describe the present, NIEs examine future scenarios and their implications for U.S. policy. Based on input from all parts of the intelligence community, NIEs must be approved by the heads of the major intelligence agencies. Other products of the NIC which are not as in-depth include:

Special Estimates—very short policy-relevant analysis provided on short notice.
Update Memorandums—produced when new evidence, analysis, or perspective is made available.
NIC Memorandums—provides greater analysis than the Special Estimates but not the in-dept analysis of the NIE.

Defense Intelligence Assessment. Developed by DIA, it responds to broad consumer interest by presenting comprehensive analysis on a policy-relevant event, situation, issue, or development in five to twenty-five pages. The report is thematic, with evaluative and judgmental exposition. This document is targeted at planning and policy staffs at various levels.

WARNING INTELLIGENCE

The Warning Watchlist. This weekly report tracks and assigns probabilities to potential threats to U.S. security or

policy interests that may develop within a six-month time frame; it also occasionally issues "special warning notices."

Warning Memorandum. Initiated either by the NIC for Warning or through that office by any element of the intelligence community, this special warning notice focuses on a potential development of particularly high significance to U.S. interests. The Warning Memorandum is forwarded to the DCI and simultaneously to the National Foreign Intelligence Board principals for their telephonic concurrence; the process must be completed within several hours. The DCI then decides whether to disseminate the Warning Memorandum to policy officials, to order an NIE on the topic, or both.

Defense Warning System Warning Reports and *Watch Condition Changes.* These ad hoc DIA messages are the most important products of the Defense Warning System. They provide immediate warning of developing high-threat situations and issues to system members and other decisionmakers.

RESEARCH AND SCIENTIFIC AND TECHNOLOGICAL INTELLIGENCE

Standard research aids produced annually by CIA's Office of Current Production and Analytic Support are *The World Factbook* and the *Handbook of Economic Statistics (HES).* Classified and unclassified editions of the *Factbook* contain basic information on 248 countries and other entities. The *HES* contains data on selected economic topics and commodities.

SOURCE: U.S. Director of Central Intelligence, *A Consumer's Guide to Intelligence.*

In the bureaucratic and political environment in which the intelligence community operates, it is easy to see how analysts can also become frustrated with the intelligence process. The ideal mission of intelligence officers involved in data collection and analysis is to provide a comprehensive and honest assessment of available information. Yet, they operate within a bureaucratic setting and must be cognizant of how their work affects their careers. Furthermore, they have to be very attuned to the policy inclinations and personal perspectives of higher-level officials, such as the president and his political appointees.

The producer-consumer problem affected intelligence estimates in Vietnam. According to John

Huizenga, chief of intelligence estimates for Soviet affairs during the Lyndon Johnson administration, "In doing estimates about Vietnam, the problem was that if you believed that the policy being pursued was going to be a flat failure, and you said so, you were going to be out of business."[15] Anticommunist beliefs and faith in the invincibility of American power were so firmly embedded in the minds of American officials that only certain narrow interpretations of the data in conformity with governmental policy were allowed. Ironically, as described by Daniel Ellsberg, a former Department of Defense official and eventual critic of the war, "there has never been an official of Deputy Assistant Secretary rank or higher (including myself) who could have passed in office a midterm freshman exam in modern Vietnamese history, if such a course existed in this country."[16]

The same pattern of the **politicization of intelligence** plagued the process in the Reagan administration. Reagan officials ignored National Security Agency information indicating that the Soviet generals who ordered the destruction of a South Korean jetliner in 1983 had genuinely believed that it was a spy plane, pressured the CIA to produce studies concluding that El Salvadoran guerrillas and the Nicaraguan government posed a threat to U.S. security, and compelled the CIA to bring its estimates of Soviet military expenditures and production into accordance with the more pessimistic assessments made by military intelligence.[17]

In other words, the intense anticommunism of President Reagan and other administration high-level officials, such as Director of Central Intelligence William Casey, was said to have slanted and tainted the honesty of the process responsible for intelligence information and assessments. One of the few times such producer-consumer problems as took place under Director Casey were publicly aired occurred in the fall of 1991 during the nomination hearings of Robert Gates, Casey's former deputy director of intelligence whom President Bush Sr. appointed to be director of central intelligence. Gates's nomination was withdrawn after the acrimonious hearings. Clearly, members of the intelligence community often must respond to cross-cutting pressures, and this affects the intelligence process and often contributes to producer-consumer problems.[18]

Such problems affected U.S. policy against terrorism in the post–cold war years. Terrorism is not a new global and foreign policy issue for the United States: "It took 267 attacks in the United States to kill 23 people in the 1980s. The 10 years that followed saw many fewer attacks—only 60—but nearly nine times the casualties—182. A single bombing on April 19, 1995, . . . in Oklahoma City accounted for 168 dead. The same trend held overseas: fewer attacks, more lives lost." And in 1995 President Clinton signed Presidential Decision Directive 35, which clearly stated his administrations' collection priorities for the intelligence community, including the importance of terrorism. In fact, "by any measure available, Clinton left office having given greater priority to terrorism than any president before him" and provided the executive branch with considerable resources to fight terrorism. After the August 1998

bombings of two U.S. embassies in Kenya and Tanzania, the CIA began to send teams to Afghanistan to help capture and perhaps kill Osama bin Laden.[19]

Anti-terrorism, however, was not a relatively high foreign policy priority under President Clinton, nor was it for presidents Bush Sr. or Bush Jr.—until the September 11 terrorist attacks. In the words of Richard Betts, following the end of the cold war and collapse of the Soviet Union, "for many, [American] primacy was confused with invulnerability. American experts warned regularly of the danger of catastrophic terrorism—and Osama bin Laden explicitly declared war on the United States in his *fatwa* of February 1998. But the warnings did not register seriously in the consciousness of most people. Even some national security experts felt stunned when the attacks occurred on September 11."[20]

VARIATION IN INTELLIGENCE SUCCESS

In an ideal setting, the intelligence community is engaged in a very precarious business. Even without problems in the producer-consumer relationship and coordination difficulties due to the intelligence community's large size, bureaucratic nature, and complexity, the success of intelligence is not guaranteed. The world is simply too big, too complex, and constantly evolving for information ever to be complete or adequate, while predictions about future behavior and trends can never be more than probabilities. For example, the incredible changes that took place in the Soviet Union and Eastern Europe during the late 1980s and early 1990s understandably surprised and shocked the Western intelligence community.

In fact, ever since the surprise attack on Pearl Harbor in 1941, scholars and analysts have pointed out that there will always be a major **signal-to-noise problem**—in other words, given the vast amount of stimuli and potential information available, it is very difficult to sort out the truly relevant information and signals that need to be highlighted, collected, processed, and analyzed.[21] And the environmental and noise problems have grown tremendously over the years. According to Director of NSA, Lt. General Michael V. Hayden, "Forty years ago there were 5,000 stand-alone computers, no fax machines and not one cellular phone. Today there are over 180 million computers—most of them networked. There are roughly 14 million fax machines and 40 million cellphones, and those numbers continue to grow."[22]

When one adds the size and complexity of the intelligence community, difficulties in coordination, and producer-consumer problems, a considerable amount of *intelligence failure is inevitable* in actual practice. The ambiguity of the phenomena to be explained and predicted, the intelligence community's bureaucratic structure, and major policymakers' personalities and beliefs together determine the nature of the intelligence process and the value of the end product. Along with intelligence successes, such as the Cuban missile crisis, there will be intelligence failures.[23]

During the Vietnam War, key questions involved the strength of the enemy's forces and the ability of the U.S. military to weaken enemy will by destroying enemy personnel and supplies getting into South Vietnam. Yet uncertainty is always the norm in war, especially a war fought in an unconventional way and far from home. Nevertheless, as noted in the previous chapter, the military and the CIA constantly fought over these intelligence estimates during the mid-1960s, while President Johnson and his closest military and civilian advisers supported the more optimistic military assessments. Therefore, the Tet Offensive represented a critical intelligence failure that led to the fall of President Johnson and the defeat of the United States in Vietnam.

The size and scope of the Iranian Revolution against the shah of Iran in 1979, as well as the failure of the shah to repress it, was a surprise to members of the U.S. government. Although it is impossible to predict the time and intensity of any domestic instability, one of the reasons why developments in Iran came as such a surprise was that the intelligence information relied upon by American policymakers had come from sources close to the shah's regime. The American intelligence community did not have access to Iranians who were critical of the shah. After the close relationship between the U.S. and Iranian governments began in 1953, the American intelligence community relied increasingly on official Iranian sources and on Savak, Iran's intelligence agency, for information about Iran's domestic situation. The information Savak provided portrayed a stable and vibrant shah regime, even though the domestic opposition was slowly building over the years.[24]

Iraq's attack on Kuwait on August 2, 1990, represented both intelligence failure and success. First, the U.S. intelligence community and policymakers showed little foresight concerning any threat that Iraq posed to American interests. On the contrary, after the rise of Ayatollah Khomeini in Iran, the Reagan and Bush Sr. administrations supported and sided with President Saddam Hussein in the 1980s. Second, although there was little intelligence foresight, as Saddam Hussein's threats against Kuwait increased and he began to mass Iraqi troops along the Kuwaiti border in July of 1990, the CIA warned administration policymakers of a possible invasion and predicted that one was imminent twenty-four to forty-eight hours before it occurred. Third, despite this warning, President Bush and his close advisers chose to discount and ignore the warning as unlikely—a classic example of the producer-consumer problem with intelligence estimates. Hence, when the Iraqi invasion occurred on August 2, President Bush and his advisers were initially shocked and caught by surprise. It has been reported that the national intelligence officer responsible for the warnings about the impending Iraqi attack was subsequently demoted and that President Bush's decision to double the American military presence in the Persian Gulf to over 500,000 troops for a possible offensive may have been based on intelligence reports that overestimated the Iraqi military in and around Kuwait by as much as 300,000 troops.[25]

On August 18, 1991, President Bush and other high-level officials of his administration were shocked to learn of the overthrow of Mikhail Gorbachev, the president of the Soviet Union. Yet "for nearly a year the CIA and the Pentagon's DIA had peppered the Bush administration with a series of increasingly dire warnings that Mikhail Gorbachev's days were numbered. The problem was getting anyone to pay attention." In fact, on August 17, the day before the coup, "the CIA's *National Intelligence Daily (NID)*, which circulates among top administration officials, said Kremlin conservatives were prepared to move against the Soviet president." Nevertheless, "until tanks rolled in the streets of Moscow, the White House and the State Department insisted that Gorbachev could weather any challenge."[26] One of the problems was that the State Department's Bureau of Intelligence and Research maintained that Gorbachev's future was safe. More important, however, it appears that President Bush's commitment and reliance on Gorbachev in American-Soviet relations, shared by his senior advisers, colored his optimism. Thus, what could have been a great intelligence success ended in intelligence failure.

Intelligence estimates are both a vital part of the policymaking process and a very difficult process for maximizing the success of U.S. foreign policy. Yet the patterns of coordination problems, consumer-producer problems, and variations in intelligence success are not well known or understood among the general public. Americans are brought up with such great faith in science, learning, technological know-how, and American ingenuity that they do not appreciate the global complexity, uncertainty, and unpredictability that presidents and governments must cope with in formulating and implementing policy. Intelligence failures are inevitable, and future events are often unpredictable and uncontrollable. Thus, it is a worthwhile exercise to examine the role of intelligence in policymaking and develop proper expectations of the intelligence community.

The collapse of communism in Eastern Europe, symbolized by the fall of the Berlin Wall and the collapse of the Soviet Union in the late eighties and early nineties, are the ultimate illustrations of this unpredictability, for it came as a shock and a surprise to virtually everyone within the intelligence community and throughout the world.[27] Nevertheless, the politics of U.S. foreign policy are such that presidents are heavily judged on how they respond to such unpredictable events and, more important, on their outcomes, thus impacting their future ability to govern.

The terrorist attacks of September 11 fanned anew the debate over intelligence failures. The events clearly force the United States to come to grips with what it should expect from its intelligence community. They also highlight the difference between **strategic versus tactical intelligence warning,** especially in dealing with such crude attacks. The intelligence community had significant indicators that large-scale attacks were being planned—allowing for strategic intelligence warnings. However, knowing the exact time and place that suicide attackers will strike may prove to be too much to ask (especially in an open society), making tactical intelligence warning very problematic.[28]

The details of the attacks are still in the process of investigation. But in hindsight, "it is becoming clear that the CIA, FBI and other agencies had significant fragments of information that, under ideal circumstances, could have provided some warning if they had all been pieced together and shared rapidly."[29] Among some of the most important facts that are known thus far are the following: after tracking two identified terrorists abroad and living in the United States for one year and nine months, the CIA did not notify other government agencies until August 23, 2001 (after one of their visas expired the State Department, not knowing any better, issued a new one; in another instance after being warned by the CIA, the FBI lost track of two suspected terrorists after their arrival in the country and processing by the Immigration and Naturalization Service (INS); in January 2001 the Federal Aviation Administration (FAA) issued fifteen memos to the aviation industry warning of possibly imminent hijacking of airliners inside the United States, with two naming Osama bin Laden as a suspect; on July 5 in a White House meeting, counterterrorism officials warned the FBI, FAA, INS, and other agencies that a major attack on the United States was coming soon; on July 10 the FBI's Phoenix office warned that an unusual number of Middle Eastern men were enrolling in U.S. flight schools and speculated that they may have been part of an Osama bin Laden plot—but the report was ignored at FBI headquarters; on August 6 President Bush was warned about the possibility of Al Qaeda strikes, including the hijacking of airplanes; on August 17 an FBI field office in Minnesota warned that Zacarias Moussaoui might be planning to "fly something into the World Trade Center"—he was arrested, but there was no follow-up FBI investigation; on the day before September 11 the National Security Agency intercepted two cryptic communications that referred to a major event scheduled for the next day but analysts at the secret eavesdropping agency did not read the messages until September 12. Whether these warnings could have led to a successful tactical warning is still unlikely—the quote above does state under "ideal" conditions. But there is no doubt that the intelligence community and the intelligence cycle could have performed much better.[30] And this realization has led to a major shake-up of the intelligence community and other governmental organizations, especially involving the FBI and homeland security.

Stop!

THE CENTRAL INTELLIGENCE AGENCY

According to Theodore Draper, "Of all the organizations that miss having the Soviet Union as an enemy, the CIA has undoubtedly been hit the hardest. The reason is that the CIA was specifically established in 1947 to struggle with the Soviet enemy.... But now the enemy has vanished. Its most dedicated American antagonist has been deprived of its mission." Now, "the CIA wanders about in a wilderness of self-doubt and recrimination."[31] It will be interesting to see what impact the war on terrorism will have on its future.

The *origins of the CIA* lie with the operations of the **Office of Strategic Services (OSS),** which was created on June 13, 1942, under the authority of the armed services chiefs of staff in support of U.S. efforts in World War II. Although the OSS is often remembered for some daring (and usually unsuccessful) covert operations behind enemy lines under Director "Wild Bill" Donovan, the office was also engaged in analyzing the enemy using bright, young minds of all ages and diverse backgrounds. The OSS utilized civilians and members of all branches of the armed forces in gathering and evaluating information from the major theaters of operations as well as from underground groups in enemy-occupied territory. The OSS was disbanded following the war, and many of its intelligence activities and personnel were lodged temporarily with the Central Intelligence Group, until passage of the National Security Act of 1947 created the CIA.

The National Security Act, which made the Central Intelligence Agency the major agency responsible for intelligence abroad, was the product of political compromise. Many perceived a need for a foreign intelligence capability during peacetime and supported an agency that could centralize the intelligence process. However, others argued against the rise of a super spy agency reminiscent of the German gestapo, and some saw the power of centralization as a threat to those agencies already involved in intelligence. Therefore, a new intelligence agency was created but placed under "civilian leadership." At least one of the two leadership positions, the director of central intelligence (DCI) and deputy director, had to be occupied by a civilian. Both positions had to be confirmed by the Senate, and the DCI reported directly to the president. While the DCI

was given authority to coordinate the intelligence process throughout the government and to act as the major adviser to the president on intelligence matters, the other intelligence agencies retained their autonomy. The act also attempted to clarify jurisdictional boundaries and disputes, restricting the FBI to domestic activities and limiting the CIA's legal role to areas outside U.S. borders.

When most people think of the CIA, they think of covert operations and "dirty tricks." As essay 8.1 on Hoover and the FBI shows, the CIA is not the only intelligence agency involved in covert operations. Although the CIA is the intelligence organization primarily engaged in political and paramilitary covert operations abroad, these are not the agency's only functions and activities. The CIA is heavily involved in all three basic intelligence functions and bears the additional responsibility of coordinating the intelligence community, making it a unique intelligence agency.[32]

The **Directorate of Operations (DO)** is responsible for the CIA's most renowned activities—covert operations. *Operations actually involve two types of activities:* espionage and political and paramilitary intervention. **Espionage** involves human intelligence and counterintelligence, such as running spies and double agents abroad in order to access information and preventing foreign intelligence agencies from penetrating the CIA. Political and paramilitary action involve covert operations, where so-called dirty tricks are most commonly practiced.

The CIA, in other words, operates as a large bureaucracy with a significant division of labor. Given its size and complexity, the agency is composed of different subcultures. The intelligence and the science and technology directorates tend to employ analysts and scientists who often hold Ph.D.'s and are research and scholarly oriented, paralleling what one might find in a research institute or university. Operations, in contrast, is composed of two different subcultures because espionage and political-paramilitary intervention are two different activities and require different kinds of skills. Espionage agents act as spies and tend to be secretive, cautious, and loyal. Their style of operation is most realistically depicted in the novels of John Le Carré, such as *The Spy Who Came in From the Cold*. CIA operatives involved in political and paramilitary activities tend to be much more action oriented, adventuristic, bold, and often flamboyant. In fact, the upper echelon in operations and throughout the CIA, going back to the days of the OSS, have been charged with elitism since they predominantly come from the most prominent universities and socioeconomic backgrounds.[33]

EVOLUTION OF THE CIA AND COVERT OPERATIONS

The CIA is much more than a group of covert operatives who spy abroad and manipulate others in the name of U.S. national security. Nevertheless, it is *important to understand the evolution of the CIA and its covert operations for two reasons,* especially as they pertain to political and paramilitary action. First, operations and action types—often referred to as "cowboys"—have dominated CIA leadership through most of its history. Directors of central intelligence, for example, have tended to come from the operations side of intelligence within the government and military, as indicated in table 8.1 (many of the earlier DCIs were originally with the OSS). Second, American policymakers have relied upon CIA covert operations as a major U.S. foreign policy instrument since World War II. While the U.S. government attempted to deter Soviet expansion through the threat of nuclear and conventional war, it relied on political and paramilitary intervention to fight communism covertly throughout the globe during the cold war. Theodore Shackley, a senior covert operations specialist who spent twenty-eight years with the CIA, has referred to political and paramilitary action as "the third option," superior to diplomacy and war.[34]

To fully understand the intelligence community and U.S. foreign policy since World War II, it is crucial to go beyond the government's overt behavior and examine its **covert action** as well. The CIA is the major government organization responsible for covert foreign policy behavior. Most Americans, however, do not understand the individuals, alliances, and activities that pervade the global underworld and so underestimate the important role the secret world of covert operations played in the U.S. government's effort to fight the cold war for over forty years and its potential new covert role in the war on terrorism. Given the CIA's secrecy and preoccupation with manipulation, we can never know everything about covert operations and

must remain skeptical of new information as it arises. Nonetheless, since the 1970s a growing body of information has painted a consistent picture of CIA covert operations in pursuit of American national security.[35] *From its creation until the collapse of the Soviet Union, the CIA and its covert operations evolved through three stages:* (1) the "good ol' days," 1947 through the early 1970s; (2) the "fall" and reform, early 1970s to 1979; and (3) the resurgence, since the 1980s.

THE "GOOD OL' DAYS"

As with most of the national security bureaucracy, the late 1940s and 1950s represented a time when the *CIA quickly grew in budget, personnel, and missions.* All the agency's bureaucratic directorates and functions expanded, but none more so than the operations directorate. Estimates are that the vast majority of the CIA's budget and personnel throughout the cold war were devoted to operations. The president used the CIA to perform certain covert political and paramilitary actions that no other agency performed and that were officially denied in public. CIA covert operations became the "hidden hand" of U.S. foreign policy.

The CIA was allowed considerable independence in running its covert operations under presidential supervision. New presidents often retained the previous DCI and, when making a new appointment, chose an individual who had risen within the CIA and the operations division. This maximized the CIA's continuity and power over the years. The heyday of covert operations occurred under Director **Allen Dulles** from 1952 to 1961, a time when his brother, John Foster Dulles, also served as secretary of state.[36] Even though the president often remained distant from the details of an operation, the DCI responded to presidential initiative and choice. Also, no real oversight existed outside the executive branch. The CIA had considerable leeway in its covert operations because during the cold war the president and the executive branch were dominant in national security policy and an anticommunist consensus existed in government and society.

Such a permissive attitude toward the CIA did not exist at its creation. According to the **CIA's charter** in the National Security Act of 1947, no political and paramilitary role was envisioned. The CIA was created to provide the president with an intelligence capability to engage in data collection and analysis as well as to coordinate the larger intelligence community existing at the time. In fact, "in spite of the anticommunist tenor of the Truman Doctrine, and in spite of the presence of anticommunists in Congress, nobody mentioned the Soviet Union or its clandestine services in the congressional debate on the CIA provision of the National Security Act. Congressmen were introspectively concerned with gestapo-like tendencies at home."[37] However, one clause of the CIA charter allowed it to "perform such other functions and duties related to intelligence affecting the national security as the National Security Council may from time to time direct," and this provided the later legal justification for involving the CIA in cloak-and-dagger operations.[38] Thus, the CIA soon became the major governmental organization responsible for covert actions abroad in support of the policy of containment.

One can better understand the vital role that political and paramilitary intervention was to play in U.S. foreign policy if one imagines the post–World War II world that most American leaders saw. It was a world perceived to be divided between the forces of good and evil—the free world represented by the United States, democracy, freedom, and Christianity against the communist bloc represented by the Soviet Union, communism, totalitarianism, and atheism. It was a world of great-power rivalry where the Soviet Union was seen as aggressive, expanding its territorial control, and directly threatening American interests and the status quo. American policymakers were preoccupied with rearming and creating alliances to deter Soviet expansionism and, if deterrence failed, to fighting a "hot" war. At the same time, American policymakers increasingly came to rely on covert operations to fight the "cold" war. Reliance on covert operations intensified as American public opinion turned sour toward America's military stalemate in the Korean War, where no end was in sight and American troops increasingly came home injured and dead.

The CIA became an important tool of U.S. foreign policy immediately after its creation in 1947. The cases discussed below highlight but a few of the *important covert activities abroad, which include:*

Manipulating foreign democratic elections;

Organizing partisan resistance movements;

Overthrowing foreign governments;

Participating in foreign assassinations;

Supporting friendly, often authoritarian, governments;

Training foreign military, intelligence, and police personnel; and

Pursuing various covert actions at home against American citizens.

It has been reported that by 1953 the CIA had major covert operations in progress in forty-eight countries, while three-fourths of the agency's budget and two-thirds of its employees were devoted to espionage and political intervention.[39] A U.S. Senate select committee investigating foreign and military intelligence in 1975 found that the CIA had "conducted some 900 major or sensitive covert action projects plus several thousand smaller projects since 1961."[40] In other words, the CIA, in its heyday, was engaged in covert operations all over the world, with as much as one-third of its interventions taking place in "pro-Western" democracies.[41] **Table 8.3** highlights some of the major covert operations during the "good ol' days" that have come to light. The nature of covert operations and the secrecy involved means much CIA covert activity remains unknown.

One of the agency's earliest actions involved the effort to manipulate the 1948 Italian and French national elections through a propaganda campaign. World War II had destroyed the economies of the European states and created political instability throughout Europe. Legal communist parties were flourishing in France and Italy. In Italy, American policymakers feared that a victory by the Italian Communist party in the 1948 elections would result in the fall of Italian democracy and provide an important strategic ally to the Soviet bloc. The CIA intervened to fund and support the Christian Democratic party. Intervention included efforts to discredit the Italian Communist party election campaign by distributing propaganda and disinformation through a network of Italian media "assets" (paid agents) employed throughout the print and electronic media—newspaper, magazine, and radio reporters and editors. The Christian Democrats won the election, although it remains unclear whether the CIA played a decisive role. The irony of the covert Italian and French campaigns was that U.S. foreign policy manipulated a democratic election abroad while publicly committed to the promotion of democratic practice. The success of the Italian and French covert campaigns set the stage for future CIA intervention in democratic politics in Italy, other European nations, and wherever a threat to American interests was perceived.

TABLE 8.3
MAJOR CIA COVERT OPERATIONS DURING THE "GOOD OL' DAYS"

1947–48	Propaganda campaign during the 1948 Italian national elections
1947–48	Propaganda campaign during the 1948 French national elections
1948–52	Partisan resistance movements in Eastern Europe and Soviet Union
1949	Anglo-American effort to overthrow the Albanian government
1950–70s	Propaganda campaigns through Radio Liberty and Radio Free Europe
1952–60	Kuomintang (KMT) Chinese partisan resistance movement on Sino-Burmese border
1953	Anglo-American overthrow of Prime Minister Mohammed Mossadegh of Iran
1953–54	Campaign to support Ramon Magsaysay's presidential candidacy and counter Huk insurgency in Philippines
1954	Overthrow of President Jacobo Arbenz of Guatemala
1950s–70s	Subsidization of domestic and foreign groups and publications
1953–70s	Drug testing and mind-control program
1954–70s	Effort to overthrow leader Ho Chi Minh and the North Vietnamese government
1955	Effort to destabilize President José Figueres's government of Costa Rica
1958	Support of Tibetan partisan resistance movement in China
1958–65	Effort to destabilize President Sukarno of Indonesia
1960	Alleged effort to assassinate General Abdul Kassem, leader of Iraq
1960	Alleged effort to assassinate President Abdul Nasser of Egypt
1960	Alleged effort to assassinate political leader Patrice Lumumba of Congo
1961	Effort to overthrow Fidel Castro, leader of Cuba
1961	Effort to assassinate Rafael Trujillo, leader of Dominican Republic
1961	Effort to destabilize President Kwame Nkrumah of Ghana
1960s	Effort to assassinate Fidel Castro of Cuba
1960s	Fought secret war in Laos
1962–63	Destabilized the Ecuadorean governments of Ibarra and Arosemena
1963	Destabilized Prime Minister Cheddi Jagan's government of British Guiana
1963	Supported overthrow of President Ngo Dinh Diem of South Vietnam
1960s	Conducted pacification and Phoenix programs in Vietnam
1964	Campaign in support of President Eduardo Frei in 1964 Chilean elections
1964	Supported military coup against President Joao Goulart of Brazil
1967	Supported military coup in Greece
1967–70s	Domestic campaign against antiwar movement and political dissent
1970–73	Destabilized Chilean government of President Salvador Allende

SOURCES: Rhodri Jeffreys-Jones, *The CIA and American Democracy* (New Haven: Yale University Press, 1989); Jonathan Kwitny, *Endless Enemies* (New York: Penguin, 1984); Thomas Powers, *The Man Who Kept the Secrets* (New York: Pocket Books, 1979); John Prados, *President's Secret Wars* (New York: William Morrow, 1986); John Ranelagh, *The Agency* (New York: Simon and Schuster, 1986); David Wise and Thomas B. Ross, *The Invisible Government* (New York: Vintage, 1974); U.S. Congress, Senate, *Alleged Assassination Plots Involving Foreign Leaders*, Congressional Report (94th Cong., 1st sess., November 18, 1975); and U.S. Congress, Senate, *Final Report of the Select Committee to Study Governmental Operations with Respect to Intelligence Activities*, Books 1–6, Congressional Report (94th Cong., 2nd sess., April 14, 1976).

In the late 1940s and 1950s, the CIA also supported partisan resistance movements in communist countries to promote internal instability and domestic uprisings. The CIA trained emigrés and secretly transported them into Albania, Poland, Yugoslavia, the Baltic states, Soviet Georgia, and the Ukraine. After the nationalist supporters of Chiang Kai-shek were driven out of mainland China and established a new Taiwan government on the island of Formosa, the CIA set up a partisan movement in Burma, where many of the nationalist forces had fled. These partisan resistance efforts made very little headway; in fact, in most cases they were quick and complete failures.

Under President Dwight Eisenhower, the CIA became involved in its *first successful overthrow of a foreign government*—the Iranian coup of 1953. Historically, Iran had been ruled by the Pahlavi dynasty, headed by the shah, in a region of the world traditionally dominated by Great Britain. World War II, however, unleashed Third World nationalism, which gained strength in Iran until the shah and the Pahlavi dynasty collapsed in 1953. The leader of the Iranian nationalists, Mohammed Mossadegh, proclaimed an independent and neutralist state in the growing cold war and demanded that Great Britain renegotiate its most favorable contract for Iranian oil. The British, whose empire was in eclipse at this time, asked for U.S. assistance to oust the new nationalist regime. U.S. policymakers feared that Mossadegh was playing into the hands of the communists and the Soviet Union. Thus, the CIA and the British MI6 (their CIA equivalent) staged a military coup in which Mossadegh was overthrown and the shah's regime was restored. The shah subsequently awarded Gulf, Standard of New Jersey, Texaco, and Socony-Mobil a 40 percent share of Iranian oil rights.[42]

The **1954 coup in Guatemala** is one of the CIA's more important actions, for it became the model for many of the agency's subsequent actions. Guatemala had a history of dictatorial rule. In 1950 the nation experienced its first taste of democracy with the election of Jacobo Arbenz Guzmán as president. However, relations between Guatemala and the United States faltered when Arbenz promoted agrarian reform to improve the situation of the impoverished masses. These reforms alienated both the oligarchy that dominated the Guatemalan economy and American policymaker preferences for U.S. foreign investment and reliance on the market as the path to economic development. The situation deteriorated further when Arbenz expropriated 234,000 acres of uncultivated land owned by the United Fruit Company, an American company that owned over 40 percent of Guatemalan territory. By late summer of 1953 American policymakers, including President Eisenhower and Secretary of State Dulles, concluded that the Arbenz regime was becoming increasingly communistic and posed a threat to American national security. A shipment of Soviet bloc (Czechoslovakian) arms to the Guatemalan military in May 1954, in response to American governmental cuts in ties, served to confirm and justify the need for a covert overthrow of the Arbenz government.

Unlike the Iranian case, this was a "CIA-controlled" operation from beginning to end, for Central America was a region that the United States had traditionally dominated. The CIA trained several hundred Guatemalans on a United Fruit Company plantation in neighboring Honduras and chose Colonel Carlos Castillo Armas to lead the attack. On June 18 the small military force led by Colonel Castillo Armas crossed into Guatemala toward Guatemala City, the capital. Actually, President Arbenz could have easily defeated the small invading army. However, the invasion force appeared much larger and closer, in part due to the CIA's psychological warfare campaign. Psychological covert operations were reinforced when several small planes piloted by CIA operatives bombed Guatemala City and other key towns. Arbenz lost his nerve and fled the country, and Castillo Armas became the new military dictator. Democracy in Guatemala, thus, was overthrown by the CIA, and Guatemala would not experience another move towards constitutional democracy until the 1990s.[43]

The most unsavory type of CIA covert operation was foreign assassinations. During the 1960 independence crisis in the Congo (later known as Zaire), it is alleged that the CIA attempted to assassinate the first prime minister and nationalist African leader, Patrice Lumumba, who was perceived as being too independent of American interests and open to communist subversion. The CIA was supposedly unsuccessful in its assassination attempts. However, Lumumba was assassinated eventually, although it remains unclear who was the culprit. With Lumumba and others out of the way, the CIA and the U.S. government backed the rise to power of Mobutu Sese Seko, general of the army, who ruled a corrupt regime for thirty years and impoverished the country.[44]

In addition to destabilizing, overthrowing, and eliminating so-called unfriendly regimes and leaders, the CIA was active in supporting the stability of foreign governments allied to the United States and bolstering the status quo. Such support often included participating in an allied government's violent repression of its own people. As George Kennan, in a report to Secretary of State Dean Acheson, stated as early as 1950:

> We cannot be too dogmatic about the methods by which local communists can be dealt with. . . . Where the concepts and the traditions of popular government are too weak to absorb successfully the intensity of communist attack, then we must concede that harsh governmental measures of repression may be the only answer; that these measures may have to proceed from regimes whose origins and methods would not stand the test of American concepts of democratic procedure; and that such regimes and such methods may be preferable alternatives, and indeed the only alternatives, to further communist successes.[45]

In Indonesia, for example, the U.S. government and the CIA, beginning in 1958, actively tried to destabilize President Sukarno, a prominent leader of the Third World nonaligned movement (like many Indonesians, he had only one name). After his overthrow in 1965, American intelligence assisted the new government of General Suharto in eliminating Indonesian Communist party (PKI) members and repressing all internal dissent, which included providing the Indonesian army with lists of people to be arrested and killed. As one former U.S. embassy official put it, "It was a big help to the army. They probably killed a lot of people, and I probably have a lot of blood on my hands, but that's not all bad. There's a time when you have to strike hard at the decisive moment." Estimates of the number of Indonesians killed in the ruthless campaign range from 300,000 to as many as one million, with hundreds of thousands jailed without trial. Within the agency, the **Indonesian campaign** was considered another model for future operations.[46] U.S. governmental support for brutal dictatorial regimes throughout the world, in fact, was common, including the Mobutu government in Zaire, the shah of Iran, and the Somoza government in Nicaragua.

Not only was the CIA active in supporting allied governments, but foreign leaders were often on the CIA payroll, and the CIA frequently engaged in training of foreign intelligence personnel, including those engaged in covert operations. The armed forces and the national police of many governments allied with the United States also were trained by U.S. military and government personnel. Thus, the U.S. government was heavily engaged in providing overt and covert support with billions of dollars of foreign assistance to friendly governments to ensure their security as part of America's larger campaign to fight the cold war.

In what CIA officers at the time considered to be one of their "greatest coups," a tip from a "deep cover" CIA agent in South Africa led to the August 5, 1962, arrest of Nelson Mandela, the underground leader of the African National Congress (ANC), the major force opposing the Afrikaner government and the system of apartheid.[47] Nelson Mandela remained imprisoned by the South African government until February 1990, and ironically, after the transition to black majority rule he became the first president of South Africa.

A variety of covert operations begun under the Eisenhower administration were used in the U.S. government's effort to be rid of Fidel Castro in Cuba. The initial operation was designed and implemented very much like the 1954 Guatemalan operation. Hundreds of Cubans who had left Cuba and were living in Miami were recruited and trained by the CIA in Honduras as an invasion force. In 1961 President John Kennedy supported the **Bay of Pigs operation,** and the Cubans invaded with limited air cover provided by the CIA. Unlike the Guatemalan operation, however, the Bay of Pigs invasion was a complete failure. The actual invasion strategy was flawed to begin with, and Castro did not flee but used the Cuban military to destroy and capture the invading force. The Bay of Pigs fiasco was the first major CIA covert operation that became public, embarrassing the U.S. government and President Kennedy.[48]

From that point on President John Kennedy and his brother, Attorney General Robert Kennedy, mounted a vendetta against Fidel Castro, authorizing the CIA to use all means available to destabilize and assassinate Castro. The CIA went so far as to turn to the Mafia for assistance, for the Mafia maintained connections in Cuba forged in the days when they ran gambling casinos, before Castro took power. Yet the covert plans to assassinate Castro failed. Most were harebrained schemes that only James Bond could have pulled off, such as attempts to slip Castro the hallucinogen LSD via a cigar, to give him a pen with a poison tip, to explode clamshells while he dove in the Caribbean, and to sprinkle his shoes with an agent to make his beard fall out and with it, according to the psychological warfare experts, his Latin machismo.[49] Many people think that all the intrigue and activities involving the CIA, the Cubans, the Mafia, and the intelligence underworld had something to do with the events surrounding Lee Harvey Oswald and the assassination of President John F. Kennedy.

Failures did not deter the CIA's involvement in covert operations, nor the president from relying on such operations as a major instrument of U.S. foreign policy. The early successes of the Italian elections and the Iranian and Guatemalan coups reinforced an optimism that pervaded the world of covert operations. Thus the United States' Americanization of the war in Vietnam not only led to a major overt military effort to keep South Vietnam independent of North Vietnamese communism but included major covert efforts in Vietnam, as well. The U.S. government, with the use of the CIA, supported President Ngo Dinh Diem beginning in 1954. When Diem became less effective and lost credibility as an independent leader of South Vietnam, the U.S. government backed a military coup against Diem in 1963. From that point on, South Vietnam experienced a revolving-door government, as one military general after another became president, with U.S. government support crucial for each leader's rise and fall. The CIA was also active in training members of the Meo and Hmong tribes to conduct military operations in support of the American war effort, including a secret war in Laos. The Vietnam-era program for which the CIA was most notorious was the **Phoenix program,** which resulted in the development of a massive internal security apparatus for identifying and "neutralizing" thousands of suspected Vietcong and communist supporters. Not only were many innocent individuals jailed, but torture, terrorism, and political assassination were also used as part of the Phoenix operation.

Beginning with the Bay of Pigs fiasco through the 1960s, the CIA started to decline in influence and effectiveness. CIA intelligence estimates lost credibility in the White House, especially under presidents Johnson and Nixon. Operations were less successful than in the 1950s and were being exposed in the media, creating embarrassment and controversy for the U.S. govern-

ment and the American people at home and abroad. Nonetheless, even though the CIA's political fortunes declined, the president felt that he had little choice but to rely on the CIA and its covert operations to support U.S. global commitments and the containment strategy designed to eradicate threats to American national security.

The last major covert operation during the "good ol' days" occurred in the **Chilean coup d'etat** during the Nixon administration. Chile had been operating as a democracy since the early 1960s. However, the popularity of the Christian Democratic leader, Eduardo Frei, was declining by the late 1960s. The major challenger in the 1970 national elections was Salvador Allende, an avowed Marxist who believed in socialist democracy. Although the CIA intervened heavily in the elections, Allende received a plurality and became the president of Chile. Allende's economic policies angered American multinational companies, such as ITT and the copper industry, and the U.S. government imposed economic sanctions on the new government. Covertly, the CIA under President Nixon led a campaign to destabilize the Chilean economy and persuaded the Chilean military to stage a coup. The military coup came in 1973 and installed Augusto Pinochet as the dictator of Chile for the next sixteen years.

The CIA was also active at home, although such activity was in violation of the National Security Act of 1947. The CIA spent millions of dollars funding hundreds of private individuals and groups active in business, labor, journalism, education, philanthropy, religion, and the arts as a means to promote the anticommunist message and stifle dissent against the U.S. policy of containment. Hundreds of academics located in over one hundred American colleges and universities contributed to CIA-funded projects, while the National Students Association, the largest student organization in the country, was funded primarily by the CIA from 1952 to 1967. Although those who were directly supported agreed to work and front for the CIA, thousands of others unknowingly and indirectly aided the CIA by joining organizations it sponsored.[50]

With the growing movement against the Vietnam War in the mid-1960s, the CIA under presidents Johnson and Nixon conducted **Operation Chaos** "to find out [the] extent to which Soviets, Chicoms [Chinese communists] and Cubans are exploiting our domestic problems in terms of espionage and subversion."[51] This resulted in CIA attempts to infiltrate the antiwar movement and undermine its credibility and impact. No evidence was ever found that the mounting unrest was anything other than indigenous and democratic. Yet a computerized list was developed, naming over 300,000 citizens and organizations that the CIA deemed to be potential security threats. Not only did the president and the CIA violate the intelligence legal charter, Operation Chaos violated the constitutional right of American citizens to freely voice their opinions and participate in democratic politics (this will be discussed at greater length in chapter 14, on the impact of national security on civil liberties).

THE "FALL" AND REFORM

The failure of Vietnam politicized segments of American society and contributed to the collapse of the anticommunist consensus. The domestic political environment became even more critical when the revelations of Watergate uncovered abuses of presidential power. These abuses included the use of current and former CIA operatives, such as E. Howard Hunt and a number of Cubans from Miami who were a part of the original Bay of Pigs operation, in illegal and unconstitutional activities. In this new political climate, charges were made that the president had become too powerful and abused his office in the name of national security. The CIA was a special focus of attention and was accused of activities which were immoral, illegal, and counterproductive to the long-term interests of the American people.

President Gerald Ford appointed the Rockefeller Commission in 1975 to investigate the intelligence community and recommend reforms. But, as with many presidential commissions, the Rockefeller Commission had little credibility. It was seen as a means for removing the issue of covert operations from the national spotlight and minimizing the demands for reform. From the president's perspective, covert operations were a useful instrument of foreign policy. In fact, while the Rockefeller Commission was operating, President Ford and Secretary of State Henry Kissinger were supervising a major CIA covert operation in Angola. This involved funding, training, and equipping two independence forces that were battling a Soviet-backed independence force for control of Angola following the end of Portuguese colonialism. Ford and Kissinger

tried to keep the operation secret from Congress at a time when members of Congress were reasserting their authority in foreign affairs. When word of the Angolan operation leaked, Congress voted to abort it and began its own investigation of intelligence.[52]

The House and Senate each conducted major investigations of the intelligence community and covert operations. The **Pike and Church Committee investigations** (named after the chairman of each chamber's Foreign Relations Committee) led to the first public knowledge of the scale of covert operations conducted by the CIA. Most Americans were, to put it mildly, shocked to discover the degree to which their government was in the business of overthrowing democracies, conducting coups d'etat, and performing political assassinations. The exposés were responsible for the negative image that most Americans now hold of the CIA as the supersecret cloak-and-dagger arm of the U.S. government. The exposés also led to the "fall" of the CIA and the call for intelligence reform.

In this political climate, the intelligence community, especially the CIA and covert operations, experienced a major decline. Under President Ford, and to a greater extent under President Jimmy Carter, the CIA budget and personnel were cut, while greater emphasis was placed on the intelligence side of the agency and its technological capabilities. During this time, DCIs, such as George Bush under President Ford and Admiral Stansfield Turner under President Carter, were recruited from outside the intelligence community. Nowhere were the cuts greater than in the operations directorate, for both espionage and political action. During this time, over eighteen hundred covert operatives were fired or forced to take early retirement, and most covert operations were cut, including major political and paramilitary programs. Presidential executive orders were issued that limited the kinds of covert operations the CIA could conduct, such as forbidding U.S. governmental personnel from becoming involved in political assassinations.

Where members of Congress had previously supported presidential foreign policies, preferring to remain uninvolved and, for the most part, uninformed about the CIA's covert activities, they now became actively involved in overseeing covert operations by creating new, permanent **intelligence committees** in both chambers. Furthermore, the **Freedom of Information Act**, passed in 1967, was strengthened to allow public access to classified information. The net impact was that the use of covert operations as a tool of U.S. foreign policy, and morale among covert operatives, reached its nadir by the end of the 1970s.[53]

RESURGENCE

Beginning in 1980 the CIA and covert operations got a new lease on life. The resurgence of the CIA began during the last year of the Carter administration, reflecting the rise of political conservatism and growing concern with the threat of the Soviet Union after its invasion of Afghanistan in December 1979. President Carter approved a major covert operation to send money and arms to the Afghan resistance forces through U.S.-controlled sources and agents in Pakistan. Support to the Afghan resistance escalated under presidents Reagan and Bush Sr. So began U.S. and CIA support for the Islamic jihad and war by various extremist groups that would eventually be directed against the United States *after* the Soviets were defeated.

It was under the Reagan administration, however, that the CIA and the use of covert operations became a major force in U.S. foreign policy reminiscent of the cold war days. **William Casey**, a personal friend of President Reagan, a self-made businessman and millionaire, a strident anticommunist, and a former member of the OSS during World War II, was selected as the director of central intelligence. Under Casey, the CIA rejuvenated its operations division and rehired many former covert operatives. Although the CIA's budget remained secret, experts believe that it may have grown over 20 percent a year—a faster rate of growth than that experienced by the military in its buildup and at a time when efforts were made to impose domestic spending cuts.[54]

Although he succeeded in winning Congress's approval of the defense buildup, President Reagan was unable to convince most Americans of the critical and immediate nature of the communist threat, even in nearby Central America. Given the political environment and the administration's commitment to defeating communism, Reagan policymakers felt they had no choice but to rely on covert operations, and the CIA under Casey became active in combating communism abroad. The CIA launched over a dozen "major" covert operations (defined by the congressional intelligence committees as an operation costing over $5 million or designed to overthrow a foreign government) in places such as Central America, Afghanistan, Angola, Iran, Libya, Ethiopia, Mauritius, and Cambodia. The most important of these operations involved creating the contra resistance force in an attempt to destabilize and overthrow the new Nicaraguan Sandinista regime—the most significant covert operation during the Reagan administration.[55]

The **contra covert war** was eventually outlawed by Congress in 1985 and 1986. Nevertheless, the Reagan administration circumvented the law by pursuing the contra operation through the NSC staff and relying on private operatives and groups. President Reagan chose to exercise prerogative government at a time when most Americans were not convinced that the threat of communism constituted a national emergency. And in the post–Vietnam War environment it is extremely difficult to keep covert operations covert for long. Therefore, the lack of political support in the country for a return to the cold war guaranteed a crisis of governance for the Reagan presidency when the true nature of the contra covert operations became exposed. (See **essay 8.3** for an overview of the secret contra war.)

One plot that has received virtually no attention was the CIA plan to destabilize the Marxist regime in Grenada as early as summer of 1981. Although the 1983 American invasion of Grenada was officially justified to the American public as a humanitarian effort to save Americans whose lives were endangered, the story is much more complex. The tiny West Indies island of Grenada had a Marxist government, led by Prime Minister Maurice Bishop, that was receiving assistance from Cuba. Soon after President Reagan took office, the CIA presented to the congressional intelligence committees a covert plan to destabilize the Grenadan economy and the Bishop government. The reception by members of the intelligence committees was negative, and the plans were shelved. In 1983, however, a power struggle ensued within the ruling Marxist leadership, and Prime Minister Bishop was deposed by his more radical adversary. The bloody coup gave the Reagan administration the justification for doing overtly what it had originally wanted to do covertly. The U.S. military was called upon to invade and occupy the island to overthrow the Marxist government, send a signal to the Sandinistas and Fidel Castro (the longtime American adversary who was supporting the Nicaraguan government) that the United States meant business, and "rescue" American medical students, who were never threatened by the coup in the first place.[56]

ESSAY 8.3
THE SECRET CONTRA WAR

Nowhere was the threat of communism perceived to be greater during the Reagan administration than in Central America, especially in Nicaragua, where the administration attempted to destabilize the country and overthrow the government. The U.S. "rollback" policy consisted of overt action and covert war. The U.S. government imposed economic sanctions and cut off trade to damage the Nicaraguan economy (historically dependent on American trade). The U.S. military threatened the use of force against Nicaragua by regularly conducting military exercises off the Nicaraguan coasts and in Honduras near the northern border of Nicaragua (where American military bases and airstrips were built). The ultimate means employed by the Reagan administration to overthrow the Sandinistas, however, was reliance on covert war. Under DCI William Casey, a major covert operation was devised by the CIA to develop, train, and equip a counterrevolutionary force of Nicaraguans, known as the contras. By the mid-1980s, the contras had been molded into a ten thousand- to fifteen thousand-strong military force and were conducting military operations in Nicaragua.

The government engaged in a public relations campaign, including the use of political propaganda and disinformation, to maximize support and minimize dissent. Nevertheless, most of the public was unresponsive, and Congress never gave President Reagan all that he wanted and often imposed restrictions on the conduct of policy. In fact, domestic opposition grew to the point that Congress passed the Boland Amendments beginning in 1982, prohibiting U.S. attempts to overthrow the Nicaraguan government and, in 1985 and 1986, making it illegal for the U.S. government to directly or indirectly assist the contras.

In the minds of most Reagan administration officials, however, the urgency of the communist threat outweighed congressional restrictions imposed by law under the Constitution. President Reagan decided in the name of national security to pursue the contra war and attempted to keep it secret from Congress and the American public. The covert contra war not only became a major part of the Iran-contra scandal for President Reagan but also led to considerable CIA excesses reminiscent of the "good ol' days."

Beginning in 1981, virtually all high-level foreign policy officials within the Reagan administration—including President Reagan, Vice President Bush, Director Casey, and Secretary of State George Shultz—were involved in a broad variety of covert activities in support of the contras, implemented through the intelligence community and the national security bureaucracy—thus circumventing the law long before Congress cut off assistance to the contras through the Boland Amendments. These activities included CIA—rather than contra—attacks on Nicaraguan oil installations and mining of Nicaraguan harbors; the secret channeling of military equipment to the contras from the Pentagon or cooperative third countries (such as Honduras and Panama); CIA advocacy of terrorist strategies, including assassination, in a training manual it produced for the contras; and efforts to pressure Costa Rica (which was officially neutral) to support the creation of a southern front for the contras (such as the CIA staging phony Sandinista raids on the Costa Rican border).

The Reagan administration tried to disassociate the CIA and the government officially from its covert contra war. In the early years, efforts were made to create new intelligence units within DOD for conducting covert political and paramilitary operations. More important, White House operatives created a secret network of private individuals and groups, including former intelligence and covert operators (such as General Richard Secord and numerous Cubans from the Bay of Pigs days) and staunch anticommunists (such as General John Singlaub and Carl "Spitz" Channel), to assist the contras in Central America and to raise money and equipment.

These private efforts intensified after the Boland Amendments were passed, cutting off assistance. Supervision of the covert operations was transferred to the NSC (under national security advisers Robert McFarlane and John Poindexter and NSC staffer Colonel Oliver North) in an effort to observe the letter of the law. However, the Reagan administration remained actively involved: The CIA continued to employ agents on the ground in Central America (such as Felix Rodriguez); and administration officials, including President Reagan, Assistant Secretary of State for Inter-American Affairs Elliott Abrams, and Colonel Oliver North, personally solicited millions of dollars from private Americans and foreign countries (such as Saudi Arabia, Brunei, Israel, South Africa, South Korea, and Taiwan).

As news of these activities leaked out, the administration tried to cover them up. Administration officials, including McFarlane, Casey, and Abrams, misled and lied to Congress. The attorney general, Edwin Meese, obstructed FBI investigations in Miami that involved gun-running operations to the contras (Miami was the major transit point for the contras in the United States). When the diversion of money to the contras from the Iranian arms-for-hostages swap was revealed, Colonel North was busy shredding official governmental documents while Department of Justice officials were sitting outside his office.

The Reagan preoccupation with eradicating communism at all costs resulted in other unconstitutional and antidemocratic excesses. In 1983 an administration proposal was developed, originating in the NSC under Colonel North, to devise a plan to declare martial law and suspend the Constitution if domestic dissent occurred after U.S. military intervention in a foreign conflict. The FBI, under Director William Webster (who became the DCI after Casey's death), conducted a surveillance and harassment campaign against domestic dissenters to Reagan's Central American policies. In another action, money raised by Channel and North for the contras was diverted to support pro-contra Republican candidates in 1986 congressional races against Democratic candidates critical of the administration's policies.

The anticommunist, ends-justify-the-means mindset that prevailed throughout the intelligence community, especially within the CIA and its covert operatives, allowed other excesses, such as personal corruption and profiteering among those involved in the secret private networks. General Secord and his financial associate, Albert Hakim, charged exorbitant prices for the guns they transported,

accumulating millions of dollars in Swiss bank accounts (some of which went to Colonel North). Many of the contras, as well as covert operatives recruited by the CIA to support them, were selling weapons and supplies on the black market, laundering money, and smuggling drugs into the United States. Although CIA and NSC officials were aware of this behavior, they chose to ignore it for the larger goal of overthrowing the Sandinistas and rolling back communism.

Clearly, the secret contra war raises significant questions about acting above the law and the Constitution, highlighting the contradictions between the demands of national security and democracy. It also helps to provide an understanding why, when many of these activities were publicly exposed, they triggered a constitutional crisis for the country and the presidency of Ronald Reagan.

SOURCES: Leslie Cockburn, *Out of Control: The Story of the Reagan Administration's Secret War in Nicaragua, the Illegal Arms Pipeline, and the Contra Drug Connection* (New York: Atlantic Monthly Press, 1987); Theodore Draper, *A Very Thin Line: The Iran-Contra Affairs* (New York: Hill and Wang, 1991); Steven Emerson, *Secret Warriors: Inside the Covert Military Operations of the Reagan Era* (New York: G. P. Putnam's Sons, 1988); Jane Hunter, Jonathan Marshall, and Peter Dale Scott, *The Iran-Contra Connection: Secret Teams and Covert Operations in the Reagan Era* (Boston: South End Press, 1987); Robert Parry and Peter Kornbluh, "Iran-Contra's Untold Story," *Foreign Policy* (fall 1988): 3–30; U.S. Congress, *Report of the Congressional Committees Investigating the Iran-Contra Affairs: With Supplemental, Minority, and Additional Views* (Washington, D.C.: U.S. Government Printing Office, 1987); and Bob Woodward, *Veil: The Secret War of the CIA* (New York: Simon and Schuster, 1987).

Not only did the CIA become more active in political and paramilitary operations, but President Reagan and DCI Casey waived or ignored many of the restrictions imposed on such operations by presidents Ford and Carter. Surveillance by the intelligence community of Americans abroad, restricted during the 1970s, was again allowed. Intelligence agencies could also open U.S. mail with the approval of the attorney general—a court order had been necessary under Presidents Ford and Carter. President Reagan also eased restrictions on the conduct of intelligence operations within the United States.[57]

President Reagan also tightened the security and secrecy system that had developed throughout the intelligence community and the government. It became much more difficult for the public to gain access to information under the Freedom of Information Act. Reagan tried to institute a lie detector program not only for members of the intelligence community but for all

civilian employees of the U.S. government. The president had to tone down most of these efforts in response to the dissent and opposition it created (his own secretary of state, George Shultz, threatened to resign over it), but the intelligence community and the government became much more security conscious during the Reagan administration. Ironically, American intelligence suffered more breaches of security and spy scandals during the 1980s than ever before.

To pursue its covert operations, the Reagan administration resisted and circumvented congressional oversight of the intelligence community. Administration officials regularly misled and lied to members of Congress. Director Casey, for example, was extremely reluctant to share information with the two congressional intelligence committees; he was notorious for evading questions and mumbling answers. Yet administration officials were not reluctant to leak and manipulate classified information for political ends.

Under President Bush Sr. the growth in the CIA budget slowed, but covert operations continued to play an active role in foreign policy. The case of Panama best illustrates this. President Bush ordered the invasion of Panama with twenty-four thousand troops in December 1989 to topple General Manuel Noriega, who was said to pose a threat to the Panama Canal and American lives. To maximize public support for the operation, following Noriega's capture, the Bush administration portrayed Noriega as a petty dictator, common criminal, and drug addict who was also involved in the practice of voodoo. Although there is much truth to this, the story is more complex and has a longer history than most Americans are aware.

President Bush Sr. seems to have had a fixation on the need for the **overthrow of General Manuel Noriega** since the closing days of his vice presidency. Bush perceived Noriega as a constant thorn in his side—similar to the way the Kennedys felt about Castro or President Reagan perceived Gadhafi. Before the American invasion, at least five covert plans under presidents Reagan and Bush were implemented to overthrow Noriega. When the failure of the October 1989 coup attempt—the fourth such attempt—became public, political accusations of incompetence and failure of nerve were leveled against President Bush.

The story gets much more complex and bizarre. Noriega actually had a long history of involvement with American intelligence operatives, including George Bush. Noriega became a CIA asset as early as 1960, when he was first recruited by American intelligence as an officer in training at Peru's military academy. He was also trained by the American military in the School of the Americas in Panama, where he excelled in three courses on espionage. He continued on the CIA payroll during his rise as Panama's intelligence chief and as president of Panama.

While George Bush was director of central intelligence in 1976, Noriega is reported to have received more than $100,000 a year for his cooperation and intelligence information. DCI Stansfield Turner, under President Carter, cut the relationship between Noriega and the CIA (though he was still used as a liaison for U.S. agencies). However, it was renewed in 1981 to the reported tune of $200,000 per year when William Casey became the new DCI under President Reagan. In 1984, although Noriega rigged the Panamanian presidential election against the popular opposition candi-

date, he continued to receive the support of the U.S. government.

If Noriega understood anything, it was wealth and power. Not only was he employed by the CIA, he was also working for Fidel Castro, the Colombian Medellin drug cartel, and the Sandinistas, and making a great deal of money in the process. Although the CIA was aware of Noriega's duplicity and double-dealing, including his involvement with the drug trade since 1971, it chose to protect him, for he had occasionally provided information that enabled the Drug Enforcement Administration to intercept drug traffickers (though he protected the major drug players in the trade). Most important, Noriega was helping the Reagan administration and CIA to support the contras with guns, money, and training in its covert war against the Sandinistas.

Noriega's relationship with the Reagan administration eventually turned sour. In 1986, when he was approached by Reagan administration officials, including Colonel Oliver North and National Security Adviser John Poindexter, to pressure Costa Rica to provide assistance for a southern front against the Sandinistas, Noriega refused. Panama under Noriega also became one of four key Latin American states to push the Contadora process, an effort to promote peace in Central America through diplomacy. Noriega was also becoming an embarrassment for the U.S. government as his longtime connection to American intelligence and involvement in the drug trade began to leak out in the American press. It appears that it was the reversal of Noriega's Nicaraguan policy, reinforced by the potential security risk and public embarrassment that he now posed, that led the Reagan and Bush administrations to seek to topple him through economic sanctions, covert overthrow efforts, and finally, the American invasion of Panama.[58]

The end of the cold war gave pause to a resurgence in covert activities and even triggered a public debate about downsizing and reforming intelligence community activities, especially the role of covert action involving espionage and paramilitary operations. But by the mid-1990s under President Bill Clinton, especially after the August 1998 bombings of two U.S. embassies in Kenya and Tanzania, the CIA began to experience additional resurgence. With the September 11 attacks and President Bush Jr.'s global war on terrorism, the CIA and covert action have been given a whole new lease on life that has generated a new set tensions between the demands of national security and democracy.

THE TENSIONS BETWEEN NATIONAL SECURITY AND DEMOCRACY

The American cold war preoccupation with threats to American national security, and the development of a large and complex intelligence community, has resulted in the *existence of an extensive security and secrecy system in government.* This development has created a dilemma for the United States and its citizens, for the demands of national security and the demands of democracy are often incompatible. *Tensions between national security and democracy are particularly significant in three areas:*

1. Independence versus accountability,
2. Secrecy versus availability of information, and
3. The legitimacy of covert operations.

On one hand, democracy requires that governmental agencies be held accountable to elected leaders and the public. Accountability requires a public that is informed, watchful, and politically active. Such a democratic process is often slow and cumbersome. The practice of democracy at home and its emphasis on civil liberties and human rights also tend to lead citizens to question the legitimacy of unsavory and ruthless covert operations, such as manipulating elections, promoting coups, and engaging in political assassinations in the name of freedom and democracy abroad.

The demands of national security, on the other hand, often require a quick and efficient foreign policy response. A premium is placed on the independence and secrecy of governmental operations to keep the enemy at bay. The use of all means available to protect and further national security is considered a necessity in a world where morality is seen to have little relevance. Consequently, the interests of national security require that the public be supportive of the government's foreign policy.

As we have seen, tensions between the requirements of national security and democracy have fluctuated over time. According to Harry Howe Ransom,

American threat perceptions are a crucial factor in explaining the changing tensions between national security and democracy and the evolution of intelligence and covert operations. When perceptions of enemy threat are high, the demands of national security tend to prevail, resulting in the rise of intelligence activities, particularly covert operations. When threat perceptions decline, democratic considerations tend to rise, and the legitimacy of intelligence functions, especially covert operations, is often questioned.[59]

This explains *the two major patterns that have prevailed since the end of World War II:* (1) During the cold war years of high threat perceptions, the demands of national security prevailed over democracy, and a national security ethos grew, whereas (2) after the Vietnam War, low threat perceptions prevailed and democratic norms grew in importance while the demands of national security have lost much of their legitimacy outside the government, although the national security ethos continues to prevail within government. The September 11 attacks and the war on terrorism may result in a new and different pattern, depending on the threat perceptions that exist within the government and American society.

THE PREVALENCE OF A NATIONAL SECURITY ETHOS

During the cold war, most Americans felt that the security of the United States was greatly threatened by the Soviet Union and communism. This produced a large and complex intelligence community with minimal democratic accountability and maximal independence in which most information was classified, secrecy became the norm, and an "anything goes" attitude toward covert operations developed. Thus, power moved to the president, and the CIA's covert operations became a major foreign policy tool. These practices resulted in the rise of a **national security ethos** in which the values of power politics, independence, and secrecy permeated the minds and subcultures of the individuals and organizations who were part of the national security community. Such an orientation emphasizes a preoccupation with great-power rivalry, the maintenance of stability and order, and the exercise of force and power independent of domestic and democratic politics in the name of national security.[60]

The overwhelming preoccupation with national security and power politics during the cold war and the "good ol' days" of the CIA led to considerable excess. No real oversight, for example, of the intelligence community and CIA operations ever took place. The so-called "independent" oversight boards within the executive branch were active only infrequently and staffed by kindred spirits who shared the national security ethos. Intelligence spending was hidden in the Department of Defense budget. With the prevailing anticommunist consensus and the president's commitment to containment, the CIA had wide leeway in acting abroad. For the most part, the Congress, judiciary, media, and public went along with what they were told in the name of national security.

The national security ethos first developed out of concern with protecting American security from foreign enemies but soon resulted in a preoccupation with secrecy and a growing distrust of the American public. Although a **secrecy and classification system** did not formally exist within the government until 1951, the norm quickly developed of labeling virtually all government documents and information that involved national security as classified.[61] Restriction of information also allowed the president and members of the national security bureaucracy to monopolize information and control the foreign policy process. The public was kept uninformed and forced to accept official policies at face value, creating contempt among public officials about the ignorance and fickleness of the American people.

The preoccupation with secrecy integral to the national security ethos legitimized in officials' minds the practices of misleading and lying to the public. Incredibly, the government officially denied not only its involvement in covert operations but even the existence of the CIA for a while. Such half-truths or lies were always justified in terms of the ultimate goal of national security. As explained by Assistant Secretary of Defense Arthur Sylvester in 1963, "when the nation's security is at stake, the government has the right, indeed the duty, to lie if necessary to mislead an enemy and protect the people it represents."[62] Therefore, presidential directives, such as NSC 5412/I on March 12, 1955, called for covert operations "so planned and executed that any U.S. Government responsibility for them is not evident to unauthorized persons and that if uncovered the U.S. Government can plausibly disclaim any responsibility for them."[63]

The secrecy system allowed the president and the national security bureaucracy to use classified information to hide incompetence and garner political support from American society. Furthermore, secrecy and deception protected officials from the political and public backlash that they feared might result if some of the information was made public, for intelligence activities were often inconsistent with public rhetoric about democracy, human rights, and freedom.

For example, immediately following World War II, most Americans would have found it difficult to understand that Nazi (including gestapo and SS) intelligence officers were recruited by American intelligence. Even though some were known to have committed war crimes and crimes against humanity, their knowledge of the Soviet military and Eastern Europe and access to anticommunist spy networks was considered invaluable for U.S. intelligence. The Army's Counter Intelligence Corps was the U.S. military's primary group for finding, arresting, and recruiting Nazis. Klaus Barbie, the "butcher of Lyons," was recruited by the Counter Intelligence Corps, which protected him from extradition to France, where he was wanted for war crimes, and helped him to escape to South America in 1951.[64]

In covert operations, no effort was made to discriminate between types of undercover activities. Morality, higher principles, and international law were not allowed to get in the way of power politics and fighting a cold war in which the security of the United States was perceived to be at stake. As NSC 5412/I stipulated, everything and anything was allowed:

> Propaganda, political action; economic warfare; escape and evasion and evacuation measures; subversion against hostile states or groups including assistance to underground movements, guerrillas and refugee liberation groups; support of indigenous and anticommunist elements in threatened countries of the free world; deception plans and operations; and all activities compatible with this directive necessary to accomplish the foregoing.[65]

Such measures were justified in terms of an anticommunist philosophy and a power-politics, ends-justifies-the-means strategy that became the basis of the national security ethos. As explained by the top secret report of the General James Doolittle Committee to the 1954 Hoover Commission on government organization:

> It is now clear that we are facing an implacable enemy whose avowed objective is world domination by whatever means at whatever cost. There are no rules in such a game. Hitherto acceptable norms of human conduct do not apply. If the U.S. is to survive, long-standing American concepts of "fair play" must be reconsidered. We must develop effective espionage and counterespionage services. We must learn to subvert, sabotage and destroy our enemies by more clever, more sophisticated and more effective methods than those used against us. It may become necessary that the American people will be made acquainted with, understand and support this fundamentally repugnant philosophy.[66]

Many of these covert operations were so incompatible with the American political culture of liberal democracy that secrecy was of the essence. Often the goal was not really to maintain secrets from enemies abroad; the existence of an operation was often exposed, sometimes deliberately, on the assumption that knowledge of a CIA operation invoked sufficient fear to promote its success (recall the 1954 Guatemalan coup). Instead, it was imperative to maintain secrecy at home for fear that leaks would trigger domestic opposition that would place the future of covert operations at risk. The exercise of power to combat communism preoccupied U.S. officials above all else, to the extent that they were willing to interact with anyone—including Nazis and the criminal underworld—in the name of national security.

A preoccupation with national security and secrecy also bred distrust of democracy and constitutional rights at home. The fear of communism was so great that the president and the intelligence agencies saw any domestic dissent as an internal threat and acted to repress it. Domestic covert operations included the CIA's Operation Chaos, the FBI's Operation Cointelpro, and large spying operations by the National Security Agency and Army intelligence. The CIA opened the mail of American citizens, kept over 1.5 million names on file, and infiltrated religious, media, and academic organizations; the FBI carried out more than 500,000 investigations of so-called subversives without a single court conviction and created files on over one million Americans; the National Security Agency monitored cables sent overseas or received by Americans from 1947 to 1975; Army intelligence investigated over 100,000 American citizens during the Vietnam War era; and the Internal Revenue Service allowed tax information to be misused by intelligence agencies for political purposes.[67]

In other words, a wide-ranging set of domestic covert operations were performed that broke the law and violated the civil rights and liberties of American citizens in the name of the protection of American democracy. National security and politics became completely interwoven, and democratic practice suffered the consequences. The president and the intelligence community took the law and the Constitution into their own hands to silence and destroy those individuals and organizations that were challenging their political goals and interests. Recalling the argument of Richard Pious, discussed in chapter 4, the 1950s and 1960s represented a time when the president exercised prerogative government over the conduct of foreign policy (the impact on civil rights and liberties will be discussed in chapter 14).

The national security and power politics mindset was such that virtually any kind of activity, no matter how bizarre, was deemed necessary to fight the cold war, regardless of the law, ethics, or the rights and safety of human beings. Paranoia about threats to security in the late 1950s was so great that **Project MKULTRA** was created. Its purpose was to acquire "brainwashing" techniques that the U.S. intelligence community was convinced were used by the Chinese, North Korean, and Eastern European governments. Project MKULTRA consisted of Frankenstein-like projects that involved mind-control experiments on human beings. One CIA-funded project involved work by a Canadian psychiatrist designed to wipe the human mind clean through extensive electroshocks, LSD injections, and weeks of drug-induced suspended animation. Following this process of "depatterning," the patient was exposed to a series of positive messages designed to replace the negative ones supposedly destroyed. Over one hundred Canadians used as guinea pigs in this project suffered severely. The U.S. government was sued in the name of many of these Canadians once these activities became public, and the U.S. government subsequently paid them $750,000 in an out-of-court settlement. Yet the United States admitted no fault or wrongdoing.

From 1953 to 1963 the CIA was responsible under Project MKULTRA for funding over two hundred mind-control projects on Americans and Canadians in universities and institutions throughout the United States and Canada.[68]

The excesses of the national security ethos, as demonstrated by CIA covert operations, *damaged the reputation of the U.S. government* and its foreign policy. The independence and secrecy required by the CIA was supposed to help defeat communism while promoting security and democracy for America and its allies. Instead, American excesses played into the hands of U.S. critics and made the U.S. government and the CIA the personification of evil to many abroad. In Iran, for example, the U.S. government overthrew a nationalist leader, installed the shah of Iran on the throne, and backed his ruthless and brutal dictatorship for over twenty-five years. This knowledge should allow Americans to better understand the hatred that so many Iranians felt toward the U.S. government and why the United States was portrayed by many Iranians as the "Great Satan" since the 1970s, especially under Ayatollah Khomeini. CIA excess has also bred mistrust among U.S. allies, whose secrets have been compromised and whose involvement risks considerable political embarrassment. It also has made it difficult for the CIA to recruit quality personnel. Finally, it has bred distrust and cynicism among the American public about their government.[69]

THE RISE OF DEMOCRATIC NORMS

The American failure in Vietnam, the normalization of relations with the People's Republic of China, and the détente policies of the early and mid-1970s resulted in a political climate in which many Americans no longer saw the Soviet Union or international communism as a threat to U.S. national security. Other problems competed for attention, such as the strength of the American economy at home and abroad. In this political environment, presidential and covert foreign policy activities typical of the cold war were now seen as unnecessary, immoral, and illegal. In the post–Vietnam War era, covert activities were judged by more democratic norms of behavior, resulting in Watergate, the fall of the CIA, and efforts at intelligence reform.

Excesses were experienced in this period as well, as the political pendulum swung from one extreme to another. Revelations concerning the CIA and its covert operations produced such a domestic political uproar that an intelligent debate about the purpose and need for intelligence never resulted. Instead, political leaders, especially in Congress, rushed to find blame and castigate the intelligence community in response to the new political climate. Not only did the CIA's covert operations suffer, but the credibility of its intelligence estimates were questioned as well.

Changes were made concerning intelligence information and activities, but *little real reform was accomplished*. The president and Congress were unable to agree on an intelligence charter that set legal guidelines on the intelligence community in a way that balanced the demands of national security and democracy. Rather, the CIA and, in particular, the operations directorate suffered from severe cuts, personnel changes, and a decline in morale. Yet despite such decline and limitations, the CIA's organizational structure and subcultures remained in place, and a national security ethos continued to prevail throughout much of the government.

AN UNEASY COEXISTENCE OF NATIONAL SECURITY AND DEMOCRACY

The presidency of Ronald Reagan retriggered the tension between the quest for national security and democracy, as symbolized by the Iran-contra affair, which represented the old cold war policies of the past operating in a post–cold war political environment. The lack of real, permanent intelligence reform during the 1970s and the Iran-contra affair of the 1980s indicate that the national security ethos pervading the government and intelligence operations had not diminished over the years. And although Iran-contra produced a political and constitutional crisis, it resulted in no new reforms. Unlike the 1975 congressional revelations about CIA activities, the **Tower Commission and joint congressional committee reports** treated the covert and questionable activities associated with Iran-contra as an aberration due to faulty leadership, as opposed to a long-standing institutional and historical pattern in U.S. national security policy.[70]

The national security bureaucracy continued to be large and extensive in the 1980s. What altered was the domestic political environment, which became much more receptive to democratic standards during the post–Vietnam War era. Thus, a national security ethos continued to prevail in the executive branch at a time when many Americans increasingly questioned the intelligence community's nonaccountability, secrecy, and covert operations. As journalist Tim Weiner revealed, government spending for covert intelligence activities remained buried and hidden in the Department of Defense's "black budget," which grew to over $36 billion by 1989, making such activities difficult if not impossible to hold accountable in accordance with democratic practice.[71]

The existence of a national security bureaucracy and ethos operating in a post–Vietnam domestic environment produced a political situation open to excess, abuse, and scandal. Covert operatives, for example, continued to be heavily involved in an underworld where criminals abound and are called upon to support covert activities in the name of national security. For example, the CIA's connections with the Mafia, General Noriega, and the contras illustrate that it relied upon individuals and organizations who were involved in the **illegal narcotics trade.** According to a report by the U.S. Senate Subcommittee on Terrorism, Narcotics, and International Operations of the Committee on Foreign Relations, "Instances in which foreign policy considerations took precedence over the war on drugs included . . . law enforcement investigations into illegal activities associated with the contras on the Southern Front, a narcotics sting operation directed at a high Bahamian government official, the intervention of U.S. officials on behalf of the Honduran General convicted in a narco-terrorism plot, and the handling of Panama's General Manuel Antonio Noriega."[72] Such covert operations were in direct contradiction of the U.S. government's overt rhetoric concerning the "war on drugs."

Abuse was not limited to the CIA but continued to exist throughout the intelligence community and national security bureaucracy. For example, following the failed Iran hostage rescue attempt in 1980 and in response to frustration over interservice rivalry and CIA ineptitude, the Joint Chiefs of Staff created a number of supersecret military intelligence units (secret even to most members of the intelligence community). With capabilities similar to the CIA, the task of these units was to conduct antiterrorist missions and carry out covert operations throughout the world. As information about these supersecret operations began to leak

throughout the national security bureaucracy, bureaucratic rivalry and charges of improprieties led to a series of secret court-martials during the mid-1980s in which the units were disbanded. DCI William Casey used these secret intelligence units to support the contras and circumvent Congress.[73]

Activities by the FBI demonstrated that the legacy of Hoover lived on. During the 1980s, agents from fifty-two of the FBI's fifty-nine national offices conducted investigations of over twenty-three hundred individuals and thirteen hundred groups opposed to President Reagan's Central American policies, including such organizations as the National Council of Churches, the Maryknoll Sisters, the United Automobile Workers, and the National Education Association. Although no criminal activity was ever uncovered, only six FBI agents were disciplined, and the director of the FBI during that time, William Webster, was later selected as director of central intelligence by President Ronald Reagan.[74]

Another illustration is the controversy that arose during the late 1980s over the FBI's "Library Awareness Program" designed to persuade librarians to help the bureau identify Soviet spies—four years after the rise of Soviet leader Mikhail Gorbachev and just months before the initial collapse of communism in Eastern Europe. Librarians who resisted and criticized the program were placed under surveillance by the FBI in order, according to a February 6, 1989, memo to Director William S. Sessions, "to determine whether a Soviet active-measures campaign had been initiated to discredit the Library Awareness Program.[75]

These illustrations indicate that old habits die hard while the unresolved contradictions between national security and democracy continue to intensify. And the September 11 attacks on the World Trade Center in New York and the Pentagon in Washington, D.C., have reinforced theses habits while also triggering a major response and war on terrorism by the United States and the intelligence community.

A POST–COLD WAR, POST–SEPTEMBER 11 ERA OF INTELLIGENCE UNCERTAINTY?

The collapse of the Soviet Union and the end of the cold war represented a historic opportunity for some serious rethinking of the role of intelligence in American society and U.S. foreign policy. For example, how large and what kind of an intelligence community is required as the United States enters the twenty-first century? How much accountability and independence should intelligence agencies possess? How much information should be made available to the public, and how much secrecy does the government need? What type of information and intelligence does the government require? What types of counterintelligence and covert operations are necessary and legitimate, given the United States' commitment to democracy at home and abroad? What is the proper relationship between the demands of national security and democracy?

Americans need to give these crucial questions much thought. Americans must also consider their country's proper role in the world since it is the foreign policy of global containment that exacerbated the tremendous tensions between national security and democracy. Unfortunately, there are no easy, simple answers. If anything, the September 11, 2001, attacks and the war on terrorism reinforce the importance of airing and addressing these questions.

In the post–World War II years, when the intelligence community first fully developed, answers to these questions appeared overwhelmingly simple and were in favor of the demands of national security. Since Vietnam there has been little agreement within the political system. Demands for both national security and for greater concern with democracy are heard. Yet despite the end of the cold war, few public efforts have been made to seriously explore and discuss these contradictory demands in a world of great complexity. Unfortunately, what efforts were made quickly dissipated in post–September 11 politics.

The reality appears to be that even before September 11, little if any intelligence reform had been accomplished. Despite cutbacks and downsizing, estimates of the intelligence budget during the 1990s remain around $28 billion (over $3 billion for the CIA, over $13 billion for the major Pentagon intelligence agencies, and over $10 billion for Army, Navy, and Air Force intelligence).[76] Many of the CIA's basic intelligence functions suffered with the end of the cold war. The agency cut back on recruiting agents and closed down many stations abroad, including most of those throughout Africa. CIA analysts, like many throughout the intelligence community, increasingly relied on technical sources of information, like communication-,

radar-, telemetry-, and image-based intelligence (SIGINT and IMMINT), instead of human intelligence (HUMINT). "Once operators had prided themselves on their grasp of local language and culture." In the last few decades, in contrast, "the CIA has long been wary of letting officers become too closely identified with any single country, language, or region." And the region that has suffered the most in terms of lack of language expertise, area study skills, and limited human intelligence resources has been North Africa, the Middle East, and Central Asia. In fact, it's possible that there is not a single CIA agent today operating inside Islamic fundamentalist circles.[77]

The FBI and especially the CIA were wracked by problems and scandal over the 1990s.[78] With the collapse of the Soviet Union, the CIA became an organization in search of a mission. Its budget and staff underwent major cuts. Leadership experienced continuous turnover with presidents having great difficulty in finding people willing to serve. Morale within the agency appeared to be extremely low. Nowhere have the problems of the CIA been more evident than in the area of counterintelligence, where the agency has had a sordid history and has recently been struck by scandal after scandal in which American spies have turned traitor. Recently the FBI has faced major spy scandals, as well (see **essay 8.4** on spies gone bad.)

In addition to the issue of what is the appropriate future for covert operations within a democratic society and the role of counterintelligence, intelligence collection, analysis, and assessments are quite significant. According to Stansfield Turner, director of central intelligence from 1977 to 1981, "It is difficult to exaggerate how thoroughly the gathering of information on the Soviet Union, and especially its military power, has dominated U.S. intelligence operations since the Cold War began. Today . . . it is difficult to see how anyone could argue that a substantial adjustment by the intelligence community is not in order."[79] Turner suggested that the 1990s required a shift toward economic intelligence, political intelligence on Third World countries, and intelligence about growing global problems such as terrorism, drug trafficking, and the environment. Yet as Turner acknowledged, change away from traditional national security concerns and issues are not easy to accomplish "where the Cold War ethos runs very deep" and "will be opposed by the various military intelligence agencies when, after all, that threat is their raison d'etre."[80]

ESSAY 8.4
SPIES GONE BAD: COUNTERINTELLIGENCE, JAMES ANGLETON, AND ALDRICH AMES

Within the field of U.S. intelligence, there lies the insular and secretive world of counterintelligence. Those assigned to this area are responsible for the protection of secrets from the prying eyes and ears of foreign intelligence agencies, both at home and abroad. The duties of the men and women of **counterintelligence (CI)** range widely and include the prevention and investigation of espionage, subversion, and sabotage against American targets. In order to perform these tasks, CI agents utilize skills in surveillance, investigation, interviewing, and interrogation. The functions performed by CI are of the highest priority, for they are intended to protect American secrets from those who would use such information to harm the United States. Counterintelligence also provides for the self-inspection and self-regulation of the intelligence community. It is in this last area that the field of counterintelligence has recently come under particular scrutiny and criticism. Revelations of "moles" within the U.S. intelligence community, especially within the CIA, have brought about much talk about the need for intelligence reform and major restructuring.

World War I provided an environment ripe for the emergence of what could be called America's first counterintelligence organ. Due to the widespread hysteria spreading throughout the country over pro-German spies, traitors, and saboteurs, the fledgling Bureau of Investigation was assigned the task of supervising German aliens in the United States, giving J. Edgar Hoover the chance to rise quickly to prominence, as discussed in essay 8.1. Until World War II, and the wartime creation of the OSS, the FBI had the corner on the CI market. But with the passage of the National Security Act of 1947, the CIA was born and made responsible for counterintelligence abroad, with the FBI its domestic counterpart.

Counterintelligence within the CIA was dominated throughout much of the cold war by one man, the legendary **James J. Angleton**. In 1943, after graduating from Yale University and completing more than a year at Harvard Law School, Angleton enlisted in the Army as a private. He served with the OSS counterintelligence arm (X-2) in London, eventually managing the Italian desk. After the war, Angleton served briefly as personal assistant to DCI Admiral Roscoe Hillenkoetter, then was promoted into the directorate of operations (DO), where he was chief of the CI staff from 1954 until 1974.

Throughout his reign, Angleton was obsessed with ferreting out "moles"—members of the American intelligence community who were acting as double agents and betraying their country—and ensuring that defectors from foreign intelligence services, such as the Soviet KGB, were authentic (not fakes trying to penetrate and manipulate American intelligence). At the time it was thought that, if an American citizen was to betray his or her country, it would be for reasons of ideology—the turncoat would have secret sympathies for the Soviet Union and communism.

Angleton's tenure as head of CI was marked by paranoia and an obsessive preoccupation with giant conspiracies and elaborate schemes of deception. Angleton constantly searched for a master mole—a senior American official secretly controlled by the Kremlin, burrowed deep inside the inner sanctum of the CIA. This led to countless mole hunts, most of which were fruitless—ruining the careers of a number of his loyal colleagues (especially within the CIA's important Soviet division) and treating Soviet defectors as if they were all deceptive. Much of Angleton's paranoia may have been a function of his friendship with Kim Philby in the early fifties, a British agent, who actually was a Soviet mole who later escaped to Moscow in 1963. Whatever the explanation, not only was Angleton feared, but his excessive paranoia and mole hunts damaged the agency and led to an oppressive, overly suspicious atmosphere at CIA headquarters in Langley, Virginia. In fact, according to Joseph Finder, Angleton was "an extreme manifestation of the collective psychosis that gripped the intelligence community during the fevered years of the cold war. He was the purest distillation of cold war theology, or pathology."

Eventually Angleton's paranoia and witch-hunts for American traitors led to his downfall, given the public revelations about the CIA in the wake of the Vietnam War and the congressional, especially Senate Church Committee, investigations of the CIA in 1974. In Angleton's absence and with the general breakdown of governmental trust common in the post-Vietnam era, a less vigilant counterintelligence environment prevailed at the CIA. Ironically, beginning in the 1980s, American intelligence suffered numerous breaches of security and treasonous behavior that it had never experienced before, symbolized by the Walker family, Pollard, and Ames spy scandals. In all of these spy cases, the culprit was not so much ideology as money and personal greed.

The 1990s **Ames spy scandal** was particularly egregious. Rick Ames joined the CIA in 1962 and was engaged in espionage activity throughout his CIA career. But something seemed to happen to his life and his work in the early 1980s, when he was stationed in Mexico City, where he was recruiting defectors and running double agents as part of the cold war. In 1985 Ames began to meet secretly with Soviet officials and provide them with secret information. At one point he became chief of the Soviet counterintelligence branch of the Soviet/East Europe Division of the CIA. For nearly ten years he sold Moscow nearly every secret he had about American espionage activities in Russia. In return, Ames was paid somewhere between $1 million and $3 million. In fact, in 1989 Ames paid $540,000 in cash for a home in a Washington, D.C., suburb.

Even though Ames had a history of heavy drinking, had worked in the CIA's Soviet division, and began to spend far more money than his salary allowed, it took the CIA eight years to identify him as a mole. Counterintelligence within the CIA had become careless, and it was almost as if the CIA as an institution did not want to face the possibility that it had been penetrated by one of its own agents.

James Angleton's search for the master mole finally ended in 1995. Although Ames was convicted and sentenced to life imprisonment, the Ames case was an intelligence disaster for the United States, especially for the CIA. Ames betrayed dozens of Soviets whom the CIA had recruited and revealed hundreds of American intelligence operations to the Soviet KGB. Within the CIA, no one was dismissed or demoted—eleven officers were reprimanded—despite the systematic failure to weed out Ames. The FBI has experienced similar spy scandals since, as when, in May 2002, former FBI agent Robert Hanssen was sentenced to life in prison for spying for Moscow since 1979. Such spy scandals serve as a reminder that although the cold war is over, the intelligence business and the spy war go on.

SOURCES: Brian Duffy, "The Cold War's Last Spy," *U.S. News & World Report* (March 6, 1995), pp. 48–57; Joseph Finder, "The Life and Strange Career of a Mole Hunter," *New York Times Book Review* (June 30, 1991), pp. 11–12; Tom Mangold, *Cold Warrior: James Angleton, The CIA's Master Spy Hunter* (New York: Simon and Schuster, 1991); Tim Weiner, David Johnston, and Neil A. Lewis, *Betrayal: The Story of Aldrich Ames, An American Spy* (New York: Random House, 1995); Robin W. Winks, *Cloak and Gown: Scholars in the Secret War* (New York: William Morrow, 1987); David Wise, *Molehunt: The Secret Search for Traitors That Shattered the CIA* (New York: Random House, 1995).

A demand for intelligence collection and analysis to help policymakers steer the ship of state in the future will continue. Data collection and intelligence assessments have broadened, but the bulk of the community, especially within DOD, remains narrowly focused on more traditional national security issues. A preoccupation with secrecy continues to drive the national security bureaucracy and policymakers. According to *Secrecy: A Report of the Commission on Protecting and Reducing Government Secrecy,* chaired by senators Daniel Patrick Moynihan and Larry Combest, as recently as 1995 there were an estimated 3.6 million classification actions, of which about 400,000 were labelled "Top Secret." Some two million civilian and military federal officials (along with another one million people in industry) can classify information.[81]

Despite regular calls and reports for intelligence reform, while the intelligence community has undergone some change, little real reform is evident. Clearly, the community is a creature of the past, and old habits tend to prevail. Such limited changes and, most important, limited reform are indicative of an intelligence community that remains heavily influenced by powerful bureaucratic functions, structures, and subcultures that have developed over time as it attempts to adapt and seek new missions now that the cold war is over.[82]

That new mission appears to be the war on terrorism. Changes are being rapidly made by the president and the political environment to respond to the urgency of the attacks and prevent future terrorism. Terrorism has become the major priority of President Bush Jr. and other intelligence consumers. The defense budget is being increased tremendously, turning money over to the Department of Defense and the intelligence community. Strong anti-terrorism laws—such as the USA Patriot Act—have been and are being passed, and the intelligence community is undergoing some restructuring. Government secrecy has increased, reflecting the persistent national security ethos. A variety of intelligence activities popular during the cold war have resurfaced, and many of the restrictions on paramilitary intervention have been lifted, including the possibility of assassinations (especially of Saddam Hussein by the Bush administration). This raises questions and concerns about the civil rights and liberties embedded in a democratic polity (which will be discussed at greater length in chapter 14).

How well prepared and equipped is the intelligence community for fighting the war on terrorism and aiding U.S. foreign policy throughout the twenty-first century? Although most scholars and analysts seem to agree that the intelligence community is not very well prepared or equipped in its current form, there is much disagreement about what should be done, what changes and reforms need to be attempted, and to what extent the intelligence community should focus on terrorism in comparison to a myriad of other issues that must be dealt with in the twenty-first century. As Gregory Treverton states, "Sept. 11 drove home the fact that terrorism is an old world problem but in new world circumstances. . . . The required reshaping of the clandestine service goes well beyond what is imaginable in today's political climate. Indeed, today's first answer—more money—is exactly what is not required."[83]

In sum, until the proper role of intelligence, counterintelligence, and paramilitary action within a democracy in a post–cold war era are publicly aired and debated, the tension between national security and democracy is likely to pose a basic dilemma for the United States into the foreseeable future. This tension will also impact the future of U.S. foreign policy and how well the United States adapts to the world around it. In the final analysis, the future of the intelligence community and the working out of the tension between national security and democracy ultimately will depend on the interplay of international developments and the complex politics of U.S. foreign policy.

Suggested Sources
for More Information

The 1960s marked the beginning of a growing body of literature on intelligence, especially with regard to the CIA and its covert operations. Many of the earlier books were written by insiders who were either promoters and apologists for the agency or severe critics. However, the last decade has produced a spate of books that have a more analytical and scholarly orientation. Nathan Miller, in *Spying for America: The Hidden History of U.S. Intelligence* (New York: Paragon House, 1989), provides a very informative history of the evolution of American intelligence, its professionalization and bureaucratization, since the founding of the republic. Loch Johnson, in *America's Secret Power: The CIA in a Democratic Society* (New York: Oxford University Press, 1991), and Mark M. Lowenthal, in *Intelligence: From Secrets to Policy* (Washington, D.C.:

Congressional Quarterly Press, 2002), provide an excellent overview of the modern intelligence community, the intelligence process, and the CIA. Richard K. Betts explains the likelihood of intelligence failures from a more theoretical perspective, in "Analysis, War, and Decision: Why Intelligence Failures Are Inevitable," *World Politics* 31 (October 1978): 61–90.

The Man Who Kept the Secrets: Richard Helms and the CIA (New York: Pocket Books, 1979) by Thomas Powers, *Gentleman Spy: The Life of Allen Dulles* (Houghton Mifflin, 1995) by Peter Grose, and *The Agency: The Rise and Decline of the CIA* (New York: Simon and Schuster, 1986) by John Ranelagh provide excellent overviews of the history of the CIA. A good analytical treatment, emphasizing the impact of politics on the CIA's evolution can be found in Rhodri Jeffreys-Jones, *The CIA and American Democracy* (New Haven: Yale University Press, 2003). An excellent discussion of the policymaking process involving covert action, the growth of democratic accountability, and the potential for abuse is provided by Loch Johnson in "Covert Action and Accountability: Decision-Making for America's Secret Foreign Policy," *International Studies Quarterly* 33 (March 1989): 81–109. Theodore Draper, in *A Very Thin Line: The Iran-Contra Affairs* (New York: Hill and Wang, 1991), provides the best, though somewhat incomplete, overview of Iran-contra.

One of the best biographies of J. Edgar Hoover and discussions of the FBI is *Secrecy and Power: The Life of J. Edgar Hoover* (New York: Free Press, 1987) by Richard Powers. The rest of the intelligence community has not received the attention it deserves. For example, little was known or written about the National Security Agency until *The Puzzle Palace: A Report on America's Most Secret Agency* (New York: Penguin, 1982) was published by James Bamford. In addition to those cited above, for a disturbing but fascinating look into the rise of the national security ethos within the intelligence community and the U.S. government, and its contrariness to the demands of democracy, see Christopher Simpson, *Blowback: America's Recruitment of Nazis and Its Effects on the Cold War* (New York: Macmillan, 1988).

The implications of the end of the cold war for the future of intelligence and the CIA are addressed by Peter Andreas and Richard Price, "From War Fighting to Crime Fighting: Transforming the American National Security State," *International Studies Review* (fall 2001): 31–52; Richard K. Betts, "Fixing Intelligence," *Foreign Affairs* (January–February 2002): 43–59. Loch K. Johnson, *Secret Agencies: U.S. Intelligence in a Hostile World* (New Haven: Yale University Press, 1996); John Prados, "No Reform

Here: A Blue-Ribbon Panel Proved Once Again That 'Intelligence Reform' Is Something of an Oxymoron," *Bulletin of Atomic Scientists* (September–October 1996); and Tim Weiner, "The CIA's Most Important Mission: Itself," *New York Times Magazine* (December 10, 1995), pp. 62–76, 80–82, 104–105.

The nature of the intelligence process relative to the tragedy of the September 11 attacks is discussed by Seymour M. Hersh, "What Went Wrong: The CIA and the Failure of American Intelligence," *The New Yorker* (October 8, 2001), and Michael Hirsh and Michael Isikoff, "What Went Wrong," *Newsweek* (May 27, 2002), pp. 28–35. The implications of September 11 and the war on terrorism are addressed by Richard K. Betts, "The Soft Underbelly of American Primacy: Tactical Advantages of Terror," *Political Science Quarterly* (spring 2002); 19–36; Grenville Byford, "The Wrong War," *Foreign Affairs* (July–August 2002): 34–43; Gregory F. Treverton, "Intelligence Crisis, " GovExec.com (November 1, 2001).

KEY TERMS

1954 coup in Guatemala
Ames spy scandal
Bay of Pigs operation
William Casey
Chilean coup d'etat
CIA's charter
contra covert war

counterintelligence (CI)
covert action
cryptology
Department of Homeland Security (DHS)
director of central intelligence (DCI)
directorate of operations (DO)
Allen Dulles
espionage
Freedom of Information Act
Illegal narcotics trade
Indonesian campaign
intelligence
intelligence committees
intelligence cycle
James J. Angleton
J. Edgar Hoover
National Intelligence Estimate (NIEs)
National security ethos
Office of Strategic Services (OSS)
Operation Chaos
Operation Cointelpro
Overthrow of General Manuel Noriega
Phoenix program
Pike and Church Committee investigations
politicization of intelligence
Project MKULTRA
satellite reconnaissance
security and classification system
signal to noise problem
source analysts
strategic versus tactical intelligence warning
Tower Commission and joint congressional committee
   reports

CHAPTER 9

....

THE FOREIGN ECONOMIC BUREAUCRACY AND THE NEC

Previous chapters have reviewed the presidency and certain executive branch agencies that are most important in the making of American national security policy. The foreign policy bureaucracy, however, includes numerous less visible agencies that play a vital role in the making of U.S. foreign economic policy—a topic that deserves, though it often does not receive, much attention. It is only by understanding the complexity and scope of the foreign policy bureaucracy for both national security and international economic policy that one can begin to fully comprehend the role of the executive branch in the making and conduct of U.S. foreign policy.

The foreign economic bureaucracy expanded in size and importance in the twentieth century as a result of a number of factors, including industrialization at home and American economic expansion abroad during the late nineteenth and early twentieth century, the onset of the Great Depression, American global economic ascen-

dance with World War II and the cold war, and changes in America's economy and its role in the international political economy since the breakdown of the Bretton Woods system from the early 1970s to the present.

This chapter provides an overview of the foreign economic bureaucracy and policymaking process in their historical and contemporary contexts—especially the key governmental institutions involved, presidential efforts at coordination, the prevailing free market economic subculture, and the new role of the National Economic Council. We will see that, as with national security policy, the foreign economic bureaucracy is quite large, the policymaking process is quite complex, and presidential interest and efforts to centralize and manage the process have grown over the years, culminating in the creation of the National Economic Council under President Clinton. In order to better understand the significance of economics for U.S. foreign policy, some historical background is necessary.

U.S. FOREIGN ECONOMIC POLICY IN HISTORICAL CONTEXT

For most of America's history, foreign policy heavily revolved around foreign economic policy—especially involving trade. Trade policy, in fact, played an important role in the movement for independence from Britain. Even policies that are traditionally thought of as security issues were couched mainly in economic terms. For example, America's first attempt to project military power beyond its shores in the battles against the Barbary pirates were motivated by attacks on commercial shipping and the high costs and risks of sailing the Mediterranean Sea. Even after World War I, Americans still believed that their interests in the rest of the world were largely commercial. American foreign economic policy since the United States' inception has focused on internal economic development, the protection of domestic industry from foreign competition and investment, and the expansion of American commerce abroad, especially in Latin America and Asia (see chapter 2 for an overview).[1]

This pattern in U.S. foreign economic policy was deeply affected by the collapse of the international economy accompanying the Great Depression and the onset of World War II. After the war with Germany and Japan, Americans realized that "open door" policies, "dollar diplomacy," and world trade depended on global peace and stability, which in turn depended upon America's military strength and determination to maintain international order. This eventually resulted in the United States becoming economically ascendant throughout the world and actively involved in efforts to restore a new stability and prosperity to the international political economy. As briefly discussed in chapter 2, these efforts led to the creation of the Bretton Woods international economic system, founded on the principles of free trade, fixed exchange rates based on the gold standard, reconstruction and development aid, and the development of international economic organizations (such as the General Agreement on Tariffs and Trade, the International Monetary Fund, and the World Bank). These developments reinforced the great importance of foreign economics in U.S. foreign policy and contributed to the expansion of the foreign economic bureaucracy.

With the preeminence of the American economy in the international political economy *during the cold war years, the president was able to subordinate foreign economic policy to the pursuit of national security* and the containment of Soviet communism. During the 1950s and 1960s the American economy, now recovered from the Great Depression, prospered; American business expanded its multinational presence throughout the world; European economies recovered and the international economy grew, with the United States occupying the role of global banker and consumer; and economic sanctions were imposed on the Soviet Union and its close allies in support of the containment strategy. Thus, foreign economic policy was typically considered "low" policy, requiring little attention and expertise by most policymakers involved in the "high" policy of national security affairs. This meant that there was much delegation of responsibility to senior and lower-level officials within agencies involved in foreign economics. Responsibility, therefore, for the conduct of U.S. foreign economic policy resided with the bureaucracy throughout the cold war era. Although this arrangement is still conventional wisdom in the minds of many Americans, subordinating foreign economic policy to national security policy was an aberration in the history of U.S. foreign policy and remains one of the powerful legacies of the cold war era.

Foreign economic policy is now "high" policy once again in the post–cold war era. Beginning in the 1960s the international economic system experienced increasing instability while American economic strength declined. As an indicator of a weakening of the American economy, in 1968 exports of American cars abroad were surpassed for the first time by imports of foreign cars into the United States. By 1971 the Bretton Woods system no longer could be sustained: President Nixon removed a weakened dollar from the gold standard and allowed its value to float relative to other major currencies; a surcharge was placed on Japanese imports to offset growing deficits in the balance of payments and the rise of protectionist sentiment at home; and wage and price controls were imposed on the American economy to arrest the growth of domestic inflation. Beginning in 1973, America's energy costs also began to escalate with the rise of the ability of the Organization of Petroleum Exporting Countries (OPEC) to influence the supply of oil.

These changes in the international economic environment have intensified many of the problems of inflation, unemployment, and deficits experienced by the economy and Americans at all levels—national, state, and local. Such conditions have forced international economic issues onto the government and public agendas, making foreign economic policy and the foreign economic bureaucracy part of "high" U.S. foreign policy. The signing and passage of the North American Free Trade Agreement (NAFTA), as well as the creation of and American participation in the World Trade Organization (WTO) under Presidents Bush Sr. and Clinton are indicative of the high priority of U.S. foreign economic policy.[2]

CONTEMPORARY U.S. ECONOMIC INVOLVEMENT AND INTERDEPENDENCE

American ascendance in the international political economy has experienced relative decline since its height during the 1950s, as discussed in chapter 3. Today, the U.S. economy has become more inter-twined with the workings of the international economy. American economic transactions have proliferated abroad and continue to have considerable impact on the evolution of the international political economy. At the same time, economic transactions emanating from abroad have increasingly penetrated and impacted the workings of the American economy. Thus, the American economy has become a larger part of, and more dependent upon, the international political economy, thereby increasing the importance of foreign economic policy and policymaking. As the patterns in trade, energy, and investment discussed below indicate, these trends are likely to continue in the future. This profoundly affects employment, wage, and other economic patterns that impact American society and Americans' standard of living and quality of life.

U.S. international trade has both increased and deteriorated over the years. American exports of merchandise goods and services climbed to more than $1 trillion by 2000. Likewise foreign imports of goods and services exploded to more than $1.4 trillion the same year (see **table 9.1** for the growth in U.S. international

TABLE **9.1**
U.S. INTERNATIONAL TRADE (BILLIONS OF DOLLARS)

YEAR	EXPORTS	IMPORTS	TRADE BALANCE
1960	25.9	22.4	3.5
1965	35.3	30.6	4.7
1970	56.6	54.4	2.3
1975	132.6	120.2	12.4
1980	271.8	291.2	−19.4
1985	288.8	410.9	−122.1
1990	537.2	618.4	−81.1
1995	794.4	890.8	−96.4
1996	852.1	954.0	−101.8
1997	935.0	1,042.7	−107.8
1998	932.7	1,099.5	−166.8
1999	957.4	1,219.2	−261.8
2000	1,065.7	1,441.4	−375.7
2001	1,004.5	1,352.4	−347.9
2002*	—	—	−435.2

*Initial estimate.

SOURCE: U.S. Department of Commerce, Bureau of Economic Analysis.

trade). Whereas the United States typically ran small merchandise trade surpluses in the 1950s and 1960s (exporting more than importing), annual trade deficits began in 1971 and have been the norm since, as indicated in table 9.1. The trade deficits have grown quite large since 1985, especially in the areas of merchandise goods, running consistently between $100 billion and $200 billion a year and then increasing even more in the last few years. The trade deficit for 2002 reached an all-time high of $435 billion.

Figure 9.1 shows that the leading countries for U.S. trade exports and imports are in North America, Asia, and Europe. At the same time, billions of dollars' worth of exports and imports involve countries of the developing world as well. The figure also clearly shows the large trade deficits that the United States has with such countries as Canada, Mexico, Japan, England, Germany, and especially China. Thus, the American economy and the standard of living of Americans have become increasingly affected by the flows of international trade.

American international investment has also proliferated dramatically, while the American economy has become more heavily affected by foreign investment. American (governmental and private) investment assets abroad, once $85.6 billion in 1960, totaled $1.25 trillion in 1988, and was over $6 trillion in 2000. Total foreign investment assets within the United States also exploded from $40.9 billion in 1960 to $1.79 trillion in 1988, and was over $8 trillion as of 2000 (see **table 9.2**). Many of these foreign assets are investments in securities and other liabilities to finance U.S. corporate spending and government deficits that have ballooned since the 1980s. Most of the American investment abroad—as much as 90 percent—represents private assets. Direct foreign investment by American companies abroad was $327 billion in 1988, a year in which it was surpassed for the first time since World War II by direct investment by foreign companies in the United States, totaling $329 billion. American foreign investment abroad surpassed $1.4 trillion in 2000, while foreign direct investment in the United States approached $1.4 trillion. Although three-quarters of direct American investment abroad is made within developed countries, over $300 billion was made in developing countries, especially in Latin America and Asia.

During the 1970s and especially during the 1980s, the U.S. government also began to experience huge

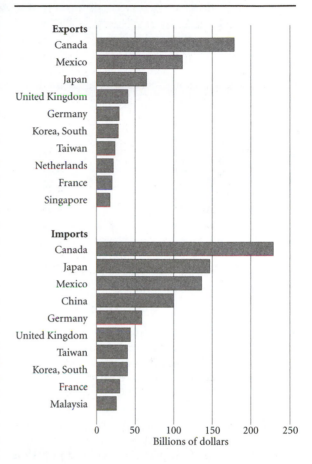

FIGURE **9.1**
U.S. TRADE WITH LEADING COUNTRIES
(BILLIONS OF DOLLARS)

SOURCE: U.S. Census Bureau, *Statistical Abstract of the United States: 2001.*

budget deficits. During the Reagan administration the total national debt of the U.S. government almost tripled, from $900 billion in 1980 to $2.6 trillion in 1988. As the size of the debt increased, the interest that the government had to pay to finance the debt also grew, from 9 percent of the federal budget in 1980 to 14 percent by 1988 and over 15 percent by 1995. Such budget deficits impact interest rates, currency exchange rates, and international transactions such as the trade balance—eating away, many people argue, at the fabric

TABLE 9.2
FOREIGN INVESTMENT (BILLIONS OF DOLLARS)

YEAR	U.S. INTERNATIONAL INVESTMENT	FOREIGN INVESTMENT IN THE U.S.
1960	86	41
1965	120	59
1970	165	107
1975	295	221
1980	607	501
1985	949	1,061
1990	2,179	2,424
1995	3,452	3,967
1996	4,009	4,605
1997	4,558	5,528
1998	5,080	6,191
1999	5,889	6,972
2000	6,167	8,010

SOURCE: U.S. Census Bureau, *Statistical Abstract of the United States: 2002.*

of America's economic strength. After reaching a height of over $200 billion of debt per year and over $4 billion of total debt in the early 1990s, the federal budget began to experience surpluses for the first time in decades during the Clinton administration, some of which went to pay down the total national debt—setting the stage, according to many people, for the economic boom of the nineties. This contributed to a steady decreasing of the percentage devoted to pay off the interest on the national debt. However, as a result of the recession at the turn of the century and the massive tax cuts under President Bush Jr., the federal budget went into deficit again beginning in 2002, and the total federal debt is approaching $6 trillion. The federal budget deficit for 2003 is estimated to be between $200 and $300 billion, exacerbated by the large increases in defense spending and the growing wars on terrorism and especially with Iraq. Such growing deficits also mean that the interest payments on the debt will be growing again as a percentage of the federal budget (see **table 9.3**).

Deficits, economic transactions, and currency exchange rates in other countries also impact the United States and the overall international political economy.

The best examples of this in recent years are probably the collapse of the Mexican peso and economy in 1995 and the Asian financial crises during the late 1990s. In both cases, the United States actively intervened in order to prevent the financial instability from spreading to the United States and the rest of the world, as well as restore financial stability to the immediate countries of concern. As was discussed in chapter 3, such economic instability is illustrative of the growing interdependence among the economies of the world. And such interdependencies are only growing, as indicated by daily foreign exchange trading: In the early 1990s, the equivalent of about $800 billion in currency transactions took place in a day; by 2000, currency transactions and trading were approaching the equivalent of $2 trillion dollars every single day. Such transactions are only likely to grow, intensify, and quicken as markets grow and technology spreads and accelerates.

Beginning in the 1970s, the American economy could no longer rely on the reliable flow of cheap oil. American production had declined at home while American and Western multinational oil companies increasingly lost control of production abroad after

TABLE **9.3**
U.S. GOVERNMENT BUDGET (MILLIONS OF DOLLARS)

YEAR	TOTAL BUDGET	DEFICIT (SURPLUS)	TOTAL NATIONAL DEBT	% OF BUDGET DEVOTED TO PAYING INTEREST ON DEBT
1960	92,191	301	290,525	—
1965	118,228	−1,411	322,318	—
1970	195,649	−2,842	380,921	—
1975	332,332	−53,242	541,925	—
1980	590,947	−73,835	909,050	8.9
1985	946,423	−212,334	1,817,521	13.7
1990	1,253,198	−221,229	3,206,564	14.7
1995	1,515,837	−164,007	4,921,005	15.3
1996	1,560,572	−107,510	5,181,921	—
1997	1,601,282	−21,990	5,369,694	15.2
1998	1,652,611	69,187	5,478,711	14.5
1999	1,703,040	124,414	5,606,087	13.4
2000	1,789,562	236,292	5,686,338	12.5
2001	1,863,926	127,104	5,807,463	10.9
2002*	2,052,320	−106,184	5,854,990	8.7

*Estimated by U.S. Congressional Budget Office.

SOURCES: U.S. Census Bureau, *Statistical Abstract of the United States: 2002;* Office of Management and Budget; U.S. Department of the Treasury.

1973, with the OPEC embargo of Arab oil exports following the outbreak of the Arab-Israeli Yom Kippur War. Steps were taken to slow the rate of energy consumption in the 1980s. There were considerable improvements in energy consumption and the fuel efficiency of motor vehicles, with a corresponding decline in the oil consumed and the percentage of oil imported. In the early 1980s the United States was becoming more efficient in its energy and oil consumption, but these positive trends reversed in the 1990s (see **table 9.4**).

Overall, while the United States represents 5 percent of the world's population, it consumes roughly 25 percent of the world's energy. The United States remains highly dependent on the importation of foreign oil—the key source of energy in industrialized societies—for over 60 percent of its oil consumption. Foreign oil imports are now approaching ten thousand barrels a day (one barrel equals forty-two gallons). American energy dependence on foreign oil plays a critical role in making the Middle East region of great strategic importance, as demonstrated in the Persian Gulf War of 1991 and the war on terrorism and Iraq following September 11, 2001.

This brief overview of American foreign economic transactions should illuminate the increasing importance of the international political economy for the American economy. It should also help to explain the return of economic issues to the realm of "high" U.S. foreign policy as well as the need to review the relevant governmental institutions involved in the foreign economic policy–making process.

TABLE 9.4
U.S. OIL CONSUMPTION AND IMPORTS (QUADRILLION BRITISH THERMAL UNITS)

YEAR	OIL CONSUMED	OIL IMPORTED	% OF OIL IMPORTED
1970	29.52	7.47	25.3
1975	32.73	12.95	39.6
1980	34.20	14.66	42.9
1985	30.92	10.61	34.3
1990	33.55	17.12	51.0
1995	34.55	18.86	54.6
1996	35.76	20.27	56.7
1997	36.27	21.74	60.0
1998	36.93	22.91	62.0
1999	37.71	23.13	61.3
2000	37.96	23.78	62.6

SOURCE: U.S. Census Bureau, *Statistical Abstract of the United States: 2002.*

RELEVANT GOVERNMENTAL INSTITUTIONS

The government's involvement in the politics of U.S. foreign economic policy has grown, resulting in an expanded bureaucratic structure. Since the 1950s, small departmental advisory staffs with international responsibilities have turned into full-fledged bureaus, while agencies within the Executive Office of the Presidency have become more active in international economic matters. Furthermore, the jurisdictional lines between those governmental institutions that have primary responsibility for domestic economic policy, as opposed to foreign economic policy, have become blurred, for domestic and international economics have become much more intertwined.

Therefore, *numerous governmental institutions play a role—large or small—in the making of U.S. foreign economic policy.*[3] Among those most directly involved are (1) the Department of the Treasury, (2) Department of State, (3) Department of Agriculture, (4) Department of Commerce, (5) Department of Energy, (6) Federal Reserve Board, (7) Department of Labor,

(8) International Trade Commission, (9) Export-Import Bank, (10) Overseas Private Investment Corporation, (11) Trade and Development Agency, (12) Council of Economic Advisers, (13) Agency for International Development (and the Peace Corps), (14) Office of Management and Budget, and (15) Office of the United States Trade Representative. Some organizations are more significant than others for U.S. foreign economic policy, and some are located within the Executive Office of the Presidency (EOP) and occupy more of a consultative or coordinating role, as indicated in **table 9.5.**

Major Departments and Agencies. The *Treasury Department is probably the most important agency* in areas of international economics, such as trade and monetary issues, and it has often taken the lead on questions of foreign economic policy in general. The **secretary of the treasury** acts as a major policy adviser to the president, with responsibilities involving domestic and international financial, economic, and tax policy. The *treasury secretary also officially represents the U.S. government in key international economic organizations* such as the International Monetary Fund (IMF),

TABLE **9.5**
EXECUTIVE BRANCH ORGANIZATIONS SHAPING ECONOMIC POLICY TODAY

ORGANIZATION	OFFICES, BUREAUS, AND AGENCIES
MAJOR DEPARTMENTS AND AGENCIES	
Treasury Department	Office of International Economic Affairs
State Department	Bureaus of Economic, Business, and Agricultural Affairs; International Organizations; and Oceans and International Environmental and Scientific Affairs
Agriculture Department	Office of International Cooperation and Development, Foreign Agriculture Service, and Commodity Credit Corporation
Commerce Department	International Trade Administration; Bureaus of Export Administration and Foreign Commercial Service; and U.S. Travel and Tourism Administration
Energy Department	Office of the Assistant Secretary for International Affairs and of Energy Emergencies
Federal Reserve System	Board of Governors and twelve Federal Reserve Banks
OTHER DEPARTMENTS AND AGENCIES	
Labor Department	Bureau of International Labor Affairs
U.S. International Trade Commission	
Export-Import Bank	
Overseas Private Investment Corporation	
Trade and Development Agency	
Agency for International Development	
EXECUTIVE OFFICE OF THE PRESIDENCY AGENCIES	
Council of Economic Advisers	
Office of Management and Budget	
Office of the U.S. Trade Representative	

SOURCE: Chris Dolan, "Striking a Balance: Presidential Power and the National Economic Council" (Ph.D. diss., University of South Carolina, 2001); *U.S. Government Manual 2001–02.*

the World Bank, the Inter-American Development Bank, and the African Development Bank (see **table 9.6** for a list of the names and backgrounds of the secretaries of the treasury since the Roosevelt administration).

The secretary heads a large, complex bureaucratic department of which the undersecretary for international economic affairs and the Office of the Assistant Secretary for International Economic Affairs has primary departmental responsibility over international monetary, financial, commercial, energy, and trade policies and programs. The office plays an important role in diplomatic negotiations concerning international economic matters and oversees U.S. participation in the multilateral development banks, such as the World Bank, to which the U.S. government contributes over $9 billion in grants and credits on an annual basis—which helps to explain why the United States has such a major voice in the World Bank and the IMF.

TABLE **9.6**
SECRETARIES OF THE TREASURY

NAME	YEAR	PRESIDENT	BACKGROUND
Henry Morganthau, Jr.	1934	Roosevelt	Law, agriculture, and government
Fred M. Vinson	1945	Truman	Law, business, and government
John W. Snyder	1946	Truman	Banking and government
George M. Humphrey	1953	Eisenhower	Law and business
Robert B. Anderson	1957	Eisenhower	Law, education, and government
C. Douglas Anderson	1961	Kennedy	Business and government
Henry H. Fowler	1965	Johnson	Law and government
Joseph W. Barr	1968	Johnson	Law, business, and government
David M. Kenney	1969	Nixon	Law, business, and government
John B. Connally	1971	Nixon	Law and government
George P. Shultz	1972	Nixon	Academia, business, and government
William E. Simon	1974	Nixon	Business and government
W. Michael Blumenthal	1977	Carter	Academia, business, and government
G. William Miller	1979	Carter	Law, business, and government
Donald T. Regan	1981	Reagan	Wall Street
James A. Baker III	1985	Reagan	Law and government
Nicholas F. Brady	1988	Reagan	Business and government
Nicholas F. Brady		Bush Sr.	
Lloyd Bentsen	1993	Clinton	Law and Congress
Robert Rubin	1995	Clinton	Law and Wall Street
Paul O'Neill	2001	Bush Jr.	Business and government
John W. Snow	2003	Bush Jr.	Law, government, and business

The Department of State also plays a prominent role in all areas of U.S. foreign economic policy. Although the State Department has had a long history of managing U.S. external relations, it has declined relative to the Treasury Department in influence on U.S. international economic policy. At the senior official level, the undersecretary for economic, business, and agricultural affairs acts as principal adviser to the secretary concerning international trade, agriculture, energy, finance, and transportation and relations with developing countries.

At the lower bureaucratic level, the Bureau for Economic and Business Affairs has primary day-to-day departmental responsibility for formulating and implementing policy with regard to foreign economic matters. Other bureaus share some major responsibilities in international economic issues, as well, such as the Bureau of International Organizations and the Bureau of Oceans and International Environmental and Scientific Affairs. The Department of State and, increasingly, the Department of the Treasury are the two major bureaucratic institutions involved in all aspects of foreign economic policy making.

The Department of Agriculture plays a major role in the area of agricultural trade. The Office of International Cooperation and Development works with international food and agricultural organizations and provides technical assistance and training in agriculture to other countries, particularly in the developing world. The Foreign Agricultural Service was created in 1953 to stimulate overseas markets for U.S. agricultural products, principally through its network of agricultural counselors, attachés, and trade officers stationed overseas and reinforced by a support staff abroad and at home.

The Foreign Agricultural Service, like the State Department's foreign service, has its own organizational structure and subculture. It maintains a worldwide agricultural intelligence and reporting system and plays an active role in U.S. governmental trade policy and trade negotiations. The Foreign Agricultural Service also supervises and participates in the Food for Peace Program (Public Law 480 Program) and the Commodity Credit Corporation, which provides grants and credits to foreign governments and purchasers both as economic assistance and to encourage the development and expansion of overseas markets for U.S. agricultural commodities.

The Department of Commerce has important international responsibilities in the area of trade. The department's International Trade Administration has the primary responsibility for the importation of foreign products, international economic policy, and trade promotion, especially nonagricultural. The Foreign Commercial Service is stationed overseas to provide services to the U.S. exporting and international business community. A major effort to more aggressively promote American exports abroad was made under the Clinton administration, especially when Ron Brown was the secretary of commerce.

The United States Travel and Tourism Administration is the bureaucratic agency within the Commerce Department that attempts to promote foreign **tourism** in the United States. The number of foreign visitors to the United States has steadily grown from over ten million in 1970 to over twenty million by 1980 and over forty million during the 1990s. Foreign visitors exceeded fifty million by 2000 and spent over $90 billion.[4] The Bureau of Export Administration directs the government's export control policy, which includes processing license applications and enforcing U.S. export control laws.

Export controls have been used heavily for national security purposes since World War II. Through-

out the cold war, the United States, in coordination with U.S. western allies through CoCom (the Coordinating Committee for Export Controls), restricted exports to the Soviet Union and its allies—engaging in "economic containment" as part of the larger containment strategy. The United States advocated a strict and wide embargo, with its allies preferring a narrower, strategic embargo. Although controls for national security purposes have loosened considerably, especially during détente and since 1991 with the profound changes in Eastern Europe and the former Soviet Union (with the major exception of the continued economic embargo directed at Cuba), certain U.S. export controls continue for such goods as high-technology items.[5]

The Department of Energy has the major responsibility for energy policies, plans, and programs. The Office of the Assistant Secretary for International Affairs and Energy Emergencies manages programs and activities relating to the international aspects of overall energy policy. These activities include energy preparedness and plans in case of national emergency, involvement in international energy negotiations, and coordination of international energy programs with foreign governments and such international organizations as the International Energy Agency and the International Atomic Energy Agency.

Similar to other agencies with specialized missions, the involvement of the **Federal Reserve Board (the Fed)** in the international economic sphere flows from its mission of monetary management within the domestic economy. The Fed is an independent agency that determines and executes the general monetary, credit, and operating principles of the U.S. Federal Reserve System, serving as the government's central bank. It is headed by a Board of Governors that makes the key financial decisions and oversees the Fed system as a whole, including the twelve Federal Reserve Banks and their twenty-five branches and other facilities located throughout the country. The Fed's role in international monetary issues and its ties with other international organizations (such as the International Monetary Fund) has expanded over the years.

By influencing the lending and investing activities of American commercial banks, such as the cost and availability of money and credit, the Federal Reserve Board affects not only the state of the American economy but the country's international balance-of-payments position and the government's foreign economic policy as well. Fed policies not only impact the American and international political economy by directly influencing the American banking system but influence the activities of other major banking systems as well, such as in Europe and Japan.[6]

The president appoints the seven members of the Fed's Board of Governors, with the advice and consent of the Senate, and designates the chair. But as an independent agency, and unlike the cabinet departments or agencies discussed above, the Fed and in particular its chair are not "officially" under presidential control. **Alan Greenspan** has been head of the Federal Reserve for over ten years—the longest reign of any Fed chair in its history. The Fed through Alan Greenspan has become very prominent in affecting U.S. economic policy at home and abroad under presidents Bush Sr., Clinton, and Bush Jr.

Other Departments and Agencies. Agencies with narrower responsibilities also affect U.S. foreign economic policy. The Department of Labor handles questions concerning domestic and international labor. The department's Bureau of International Labor Affairs assists in formulating international economic and trade policies that affect American workers, represents the United States in international bodies such as the International Labor Organization, and engages in technical assistance abroad and trade union exchange programs.

The U.S. International Trade Commission (ITC) is an independent agency with broad powers of investigation relating to customs laws, export and import trade, and foreign competition. For example, the commission often adjudicates disputes between American industry and international corporations within the United States over charges of unfair trading practices. The ITC is made up of six commissioners appointed for nine-year terms by the president with the advice and consent of the Senate.

The **Export-Import Bank (Eximbank)** is a government corporation that subsidizes American company exports abroad. Although established in 1934 to promote trade with the Soviet Union, during most of its history it has not been employed for that purpose. Instead, it provides grants and credits to aid the export financing of U.S. goods and services but is prohibited from competing with private financing. Outstanding

credits of the Export-Import Bank authorized by Congress in 1995 were $12 billion and not to exceed $75 billion in total.[7]

The Eximbank also guarantees the Foreign Credit Insurance Association, an association of U.S. insurance companies organized by the bank in 1961 to ensure export transactions against risk of default. Supporters maintain that Eximbank assistance is an important tool for generating employment and income in the domestic economy and strengthening U.S. foreign trade. Opposition has ranged from charges that government participation in export financing is inequitable and an unnecessary intrusion into the private sector to complaints about Eximbank's emphasis on nuclear power and commercial aircraft exports.[8]

The Overseas Private Investment Corporation (OPIC) is an independent agency that stimulates foreign investment, predominantly in developing countries. It offers U.S. exporters assistance in finding investment opportunities, insurance to protect their investments, and loans and loan guaranties to help finance their projects. OPIC insures American companies against the political risks of foreign investment, such as expropriation and damage from war, revolution, insurrection, or civil strife. With the collapse of Stalinist regimes, OPIC has begun to actively support American investment in the economies of Eastern Europe.

The Trade and Development Agency, as of 1992 another independent agency, was designed to assist in the creation of jobs for Americans by helping U.S. companies export and pursue other overseas business opportunities. It tries to work closely with industrializing and developing countries abroad.

The Agency for International Development (AID) is principally responsible for administering economic assistance and supervising economic development policy abroad. Although officially associated with the Department of State, it is basically an autonomous and independent agency. AID's mission has been part of a larger governmental effort to provide foreign assistance abroad, in part to contain the expansion of the Soviet Union and communism during the cold war and in part to engage in Third World political, economic, and social nation building, which is now its principal post–cold war orientation (see chapter 6 for an overview of AID, the Peace Corps and American foreign assistance).

EOP Agencies. Agencies within the Executive Office of the Presidency also have become more active in the making of U.S. foreign economic policy—especially the Council of Economic Advisers, Office of Management and Budget, Office of the United States Trade Representative, and National Economic Council.

The **Council of Economic Advisers (CEA)**, with three members and a small staff, was created in 1946 to assess the state of the American economy and advise the president on economic matters. One of the three CEA members is assigned international responsibilities and participates in official delegations to the Organization for Economic Cooperation and Development (OECD) countries—Western Europe, Canada, and Japan. CEA members are usually academics in economics and often do not have much of a role in day-to-day economic advice. The major exception has been Laura Tyson, who as head of the CEA and later as a member of the new National Economic Council, acted as a prominent adviser to President Clinton.

In addition, the Office of Management and Budget and the Office of the United States Trade Representative, which are discussed in greater detail below, have major responsibilities concerning budgetary and trade matters and play important roles in the president's effort to coordinate and manage U.S. foreign policy as it affects economic policy.

ECONOMIC CULTURE AND THE FREE MARKET ETHOS

So many agencies are involved in U.S. foreign economic policy that a major problem of governmental coordination has arisen within the executive branch. Even though a vast decentralized structure of competing interests permeates the foreign economic bureaucracy, where authority was broadly delegated during the cold war, there has also existed an underlying consensus or subculture, or what sometimes has been referred to as an **economic culture,** of shared values that has provided a certain degree of cooperation and common direction in U.S. foreign economic policy since World War II. *An economic culture premised on a strong* **free market ethos** *based on a classical liberal economic paradigm* prevails throughout much of the foreign economic bureaucracy and American society. The free

market ethos rests on the faith in the power of the private market to promote growth and prosperity with minimal governmental intervention.[9]

Throughout American history, a strong faith in the free market in the evolution of capitalism and the workings of the domestic economy has developed. However, given America's economic nationalist and protectionist past, the free market ethos did not undergird thinking about U.S. foreign economic policy until after World War II—when the United States became the world's economic superpower. Today, these beliefs have become so firmly embedded in American culture that the free market ethos provides the common understanding on which most Americans base their belief in the benefits of "free trade" and the proper path of economic development. As Herbert McClosky and John Zaller found in their study *The American Ethos*, alongside a strong belief in democracy, a faith in capitalism and the free market was the foundation of American cultural identity.[10] This certainly appears to reflect much of the thinking of members of the Bush Jr. administration.

The free market ethos is held by most American policymakers. Officials throughout the foreign economic bureaucracy, such as former assistant secretary of international affairs Gerald L. Parsky in the Treasury Department in the 1980s, consistently proclaimed the free market ethos as the basis of policy: "It is our firm conviction that the market mechanism is on the whole the most efficient method of assuring that supply and demand of commodities are kept in balance in a dynamic world. Although markets do not always operate efficiently, the appropriate remedy is to strengthen their functioning, not intervene, or further impede market operations."[11]

Although presidents and other high-level officials may lack knowledge and confidence in matters of international economics in comparison to specialists, their understanding of the world and their policy inclinations as well have tended to be heavily informed from a free market perspective. The free market ethos that permeates government does not eliminate the political and bureaucratic infighting that runs rampant but does allow for compromise and provides a relatively consistent general orientation to U.S. foreign economic policy.

Differences in policy orientations between and within administrations over international economics have grown over the years, but they still tend to be more a matter of degree, involving priorities and tactics of policy as opposed to basic goals. Some American officials (often considered more conservative) emphasize the need for minimal cooperation and intervention by governments in the international political economy to allow the magic of the marketplace to work, while others (often considered more liberal) advocate greater multilateral management in order to minimize instability and maximize economic growth in a global economy of growing interdependence. But both positions are market oriented and reside within the free market ethos.

As analyst Stephen Cohen illustrates, "No agency has openly argued in the post–World War II period for a permanent shift in the essentially **open-door policy** for U.S. companies wishing to invest overseas or for foreign companies wishing to invest in the United States. There has been a general agreement in the executive branch that the burden of proof is on the advocates of utilizing governmental restrictions or subsidies to affect the global flow of goods, services, and capital."[12] Thus, although the principles and institutions supporting free trade have come under criticism, scholar Judith Goldstein found that "liberalism still holds a social position not unlike a 'sacred cow' in the policymaking community."[13]

This common free market ethos in American government and society may help to explain why presidents have not felt the same urgency to coordinate and centralize the foreign economic policy machinery within the White House as they have in the national security area—that is, until Bill Clinton and the National Economic Council.

COORDINATION EFFORTS AND PROBLEMS FROM ABOVE

Historically, the State Department was the lead agency responsible for coordinating U.S. foreign economic policy (except during war, when the White House usually became more prominent), while the foreign economic bureaucracy was much smaller and less complex and bureaucratic.

This began to change during the twentieth century, especially after World War II and since the 1950s. The foreign economic bureaucracy expanded in size and complexity and has become more important for overall U.S. foreign policy. Meanwhile, the State Department's role as lead agency has declined in foreign economic policy, as well as in national security affairs (as discussed in chapter 6). The Treasury Department, in contrast, has grown in prominence, but not to the point of being powerful enough or able to coordinate foreign economic policy–the department is like "a first among equals," with the secretary of treasury usually serving as the president's official economic spokesperson.

Power therefore is extremely decentralized within the foreign economic bureaucracy, making it very difficult for the president to manage economic aspects of foreign policy. *Presidents have used different strategies to coordinate the foreign economic policy–making process over the years,* including relying on (1) the Office of Management and Budget, (2) the United States Trade Representative, and most often, (3) interagency committees usually coordinated within the Executive Office of the Presidency.[14]

An early effort at coordination involved the government's budgetary process. The Bureau of the Budget was created in 1921 and placed within the Executive Office of the Presidency by President Franklin Roosevelt in 1939 in order to coordinate and streamline the budgetary process of an expanding government. The Bureau of the Budget was the precursor of the **Office of Management and Budget (OMB),** created in 1970 to coordinate and supervise the government's budget and fiscal program for the president. The formulation of the budget of the U.S. government is of great importance because if affects the activities of all bureaucratic agencies and represents the fiscal and spending policies of the federal government, currently to the tune of $2 trillion per year, heavily influencing the American economy and foreign economic policy. One analyst has stated, "Although the politics of the budget is often considered an internal concern, no external issue is as critical to foreign and national security strategy."[15]

According to journalist Hedrick Smith, during the Reagan years the OMB apparatus was "the second most powerful staff in Washington, almost rivaling the top White House staff. . . . Its staff of six hundred included some of the very best career professionals in government, experts on every field."[16] Although the president's ability to coordinate and manage the government's budget and fiscal policies has improved with the assistance of OMB, this has not allowed the president to develop a coherent governmental policy with respect to issues involving international monetary matters, trade, investment, energy, and assistance.

The late 1970s witnessed the growing prominence of the **Office of the United States Trade Representative (USTR)** as a coordinator of U.S. trade policy. Created by Congress in 1962 as part of the Executive Office of the Presidency, beginning under President Carter the United States trade representative, a cabinet-level official with the rank of ambassador, has acted as a major presidential adviser, public spokesperson, and often the chief representative of the U.S. government on trade matters. Overall, despite the importance of the USTR, it has had limited success in directing and managing U.S. trade policy for the president, much of which has depended on the strength of the individual trade representative, his or her relationship with the president, and the quality of the USTR staff.

Most presidents have come to rely on the creation of different "interagency committees" at the cabinet and subcabinet levels to promote interaction and coordination of foreign economic policy. These agencies are often coordinated within the Executive Office of the Presidency or are chaired by a lead agency, most often the Treasury Department. These efforts have had mixed success, and none of the interagency groups has gained the kind of permanence and prestige that the National Security Council (NSC) system has come to enjoy in national security policy. Yet the NSC system, as discussed in chapter 5, has rarely played more than a peripheral role in foreign economic policy, being more oriented toward political and military affairs. As journalist John Leacacos put it, "The Achilles' heel of the NSC system has been international economics."[17] A brief overview of presidential coordination efforts is provided below.[18]

A BRIEF OVERVIEW OF PRESIDENTIAL COORDINATION

An effort at policy coordination first emerged under President Dwight Eisenhower, who created the Council on Foreign Economic Policy in 1954 with the intention of providing coordination of foreign and domestic economic policies and integrating various foreign economic policies. The chair was involved in most of the important issues, but the State Department, Treasury

Department, and National Security Council retained responsibilities for most areas. The council had no authority over agencies and usually worked on an ad hoc basis close to the president. The cabinet-level group rarely met and was written off as ineffective by a 1961 budget review.

President Kennedy preferred an even more ad hoc management style and discontinued both the Advisory Board of Economic Growth and Stability and the Council on Foreign Economic Policy. In their place, Kennedy created individual interagency committees to deal with domestic economic issues and separated foreign economic policy from domestic policy. The Interdepartmental Committee of Under Secretaries on Foreign Economic Policy and the deputy assistant for national security affairs (Carl Kaysen) were largely responsible for international economic issues. Although the NSC, through Kaysen, had responsibility for policy coordination (with the Bureau of the Budget, the Council of Economic Advisers, the Federal Reserve, and a trade adviser), the State Department dominated international economic issues during this time.

Under President Johnson the NSC still coordinated major foreign economic policy, under Francis M. Bator, the deputy assistant. Informality made it effective, and NSC staffers were given substantial power and direct access to Johnson when necessary. In addition to the NSC, other White House staff was involved, especially the special counsel to the president. Interagency committees were also important, especially on foreign aid and defense procurement. The Trade Expansion Act Advisory Committee (and subcommittees) handled trade issues, but outcomes were often appealed to the president. While the informal NSC mechanism continued under Johnson, by 1967–1968 it became less effective; the title of assistant deputy was abolished and the function divided between two senior staffers. President Johnson eventually opted for a more centralized process and increasingly came to depend on Secretary of Heath, Education, and Welfare Joseph Califano for domestic and economic policy.

President Nixon attempted to utilize both a multiple advocacy and a centralized decisionmaking approach. Secretary of the Treasury John Connally, then George Shultz, coordinated domestic economic policy but channeled it through White House Domestic Adviser John D. Ehrlichman. Kissinger's NSC played a centralized role in making (rather than coordinating) foreign policy, but Kissinger was more interested in security than economic issues. To handle foreign economic policy, Nixon therefore created the Council on International Economic Policy (CIEP) on the advice of the Advisory Council on Executive Organization (the Ash Council) in 1971.

This cabinet committee was chaired by Nixon and run by an executive director holding the title assistant to the president (held by Peter G. Peterson and later Peter M. Flanigan) and his small staff. The CIEP was sometimes compared to the NSC and its executive director, but it never approached the level of influence of Kissinger's NSC. The creation of the CIEP was supported by most agencies (with the notable exception of the State Department) and White House staff. The council attempted to pacify the State Department, allowing the secretary of state to chair meetings in the president's absence and also to chair the Operations Committee, which handled day to day responsibilities. In addition to the council's struggle with the State Department, CIEP's relationship with Treasury and the special trade representative (STR—the forerunner to the USTR) was problematic. Treasury Secretary John Connally's "economic nationalism" stole much of the CIEP's thunder. Treasury jealously guarded international monetary decisions, and the STR sought to retain trade policy—two trends that would continue into the 1990s.

In Nixon's second term, the CIEP's position was further compromised when the president created the Council on Economic Policy (CEP), with jurisdiction over both domestic and foreign economic policy. Secretary of the Treasury George Shultz was designated "special assistant to the president for economic affairs" and chaired both the CIEP and CEP, relying on a small White House staff (under Kenneth W. Dam) to manage the CEP. Whereas the CEP attempted to facilitate coordination among the CIEP, Treasury, and the STR, the CIEP did not play a major role in policymaking except on a few trade issues. Competition between the STR and the NSC eventually lead to the CIEP's demise. Although Shultz's CEP was less visible than the CIEP, it was considered more effective.

President Gerald Ford created a multiple-advocacy body to coordinate both domestic and international economic policy making out of the White House—the Economic Policy Board (EPB). Although nominally chaired by the treasury secretary, in practice the EPB was directed by Executive Director L. William Seidman from within the White House. The EPB shared advisory responsibilities with the OMB, the Domestic Council, and the Energy Resources Council. Effective communication and good relationships among the participants led to adequate coordination and a pragmatic division of labor. The EPB met daily and held additional meetings to deal with specific problems. The board was also involved in long-range projects. EPB's experience demonstrated the strength of a centralized, multiple-advocacy structure but also indicates the critical importance of key individuals.

Nixon's and Ford's efforts to respond to the collapse of the Bretton Woods system symbolize the beginning of serious presidential efforts to centralize the economic policy–making process. For the first time, domestic and foreign economic policy making was integrated through the CEP and then the EPB. Also, the position of special assistant to the president for economic affairs was created and occupied by first Schultz and then Seidman.

President Jimmy Carter's administration coordinated economic policy with a mix of centralized, multiple-advocacy, and ad hoc mechanisms. Carter created a body similar to but less formal than the CEP called the Economic Policy Group (EPG), chaired by the treasury secretary. The EPG was intended to manage both domestic and international policy but in practice handled only domestic issues. As with other policy areas in the Carter administration, international economic policy was fractured by the constant infighting within the administration. For example, the OMB was opposed to adding Treasury as a statutory member of the NSC. Even though the NSC had agreed to share foreign economic policy and play a primary role only when security issues were involved, National Security Adviser Zbigniew Brzezinski skillfully usurped control over most issues, and foreign economic policy was once again funneled through the NSC. Brzezinski was successful in placing NSC staffer Henry Owen as the coordinator of most foreign economic policy decisions, especially on economic summits. As a result of the disarray and conflict in the Carter White House, the EPG remained informal and weak.

President Ronald Reagan demonstrated aspects of both a centralized and a multiple-advocacy model. Instead of a single body to coordinate economic policy, Reagan created various cabinet councils, directed by

Political Counselor Edwin Meese III. The Economic Policy Council (EPC), headed by Treasury Secretary Donald Regan, dealt with most economic issues. But Chief of Staff James Baker formed the Legislative Strategy Group (LSG), that could rework EPC decisions. The LSG did not focus on international economic issues, leaving these to Treasury, the EPC, and the NSC.

In Reagan's second term, when James Baker and Donald Regan switched positions, EPC was managed by Treasury Secretary Baker and was responsible for foreign economic policy, while Chief of Staff Regan dominated domestic economic policy making. The EPC was considered active and effective in managing trade policy, and the NSC participated in EPC meetings when international issues were involved. Reagan's EPC might have facilitated the president's decision-making process on high-priority issues, but it was staffed by only three or four people. Since, the EPC—like the cabinet-level councils before it—never operated at the assistant secretary level nor was able to permeate the bureaucracy below, it never obtained the policy reach of the NSC.

President George Bush Sr. utilized all three models: multiple-advocacy structure and centralized and ad hoc mechanisms. Bush retained the EPC, but it became less effective, since the president used it less. OMB Director Richard Darman dominated domestic issues, often in contention with Chief of Staff John Sununu and Treasury Secretary Nicholas Brady. This situation is often criticized as an "ego game" in a closed process. On foreign economic policy, Bush utilized the EPC on trade issues with support of the USTR, the NSC, Treasury, and the State Department. In some cases "customized" interagency groups were formed to handle specific issues, such as the North American Free Trade Agreement (NAFTA), economic sanctions on Iraq, and aid to Central and Eastern Europe. These ad hoc groups were effective because they had a specific focus and were made up of experienced participants. Eventually, Bush merged the EPC into the Domestic Policy Council, creating the Policy Coordinating Group with a staff of only four, none of whom were cabinet members.

On the whole, U.S. policymakers found it very difficult to pursue a steady economic policy, and presidents failed to establish consistency in their organization of economic issues and the policymaking process. Foreign and domestic economics were sometimes integrated, sometimes kept distinct. Different interagency committees were created with short time spans, led by different officials with small staffs and various levels of clout. Clinton's initial view of the Bush White House largely reflected this larger reality: A highly organized NSC focused on a consistent and coherent foreign policy, and a highly divisive economic policy team offered competing advice and did not serve the president well.

THE PROBLEM OF PRESIDENTIAL ATTENTION AND KNOWLEDGE

Part of the problem in coordinating the foreign economic bureaucracy involves the lack of presidential attention to and knowledge of international economic affairs. Since the cold war, most presidents, and their closest foreign policy advisers, have been more knowledgeable and comfortable dealing with traditional political and military issues associated with national security policy. Paul Volcker, former chair of the Federal Reserve Board, has commented that American presidents "have not in my experience wanted to spend much time on the complexities of international finance."[19]

Most presidents and foreign policy advisers have not been well versed in the complexities of international economics. This has occurred primarily because, during the cold war, foreign economics was not considered "high" policy and, hence, did not require much presidential attention. Much of this was a function not only of the importance of national security policy and the need to contain the Soviet Union but also of America's unique position within the international political economy for at least two decades following World War II—while other industrial societies were trying to rebuild their war-destroyed economies, the U.S. economy prospered and dominated global trade and finance. In other words, as the United States became the central market and banker to the world, presidents, and their advisers, did not have to pay much attention to international economic affairs. This produced few individuals, whether in academia or among practitioners in or out of government, who were well versed in both national security and foreign economic policy, reinforcing what with time would increasingly become a problem for U.S. foreign policy.

Not surprisingly, the "low" priority of international economics during the cold war has left a strong legacy in the making of U.S. foreign policy: a foreign economic bureaucracy expanding in size and power but enjoying considerable freedom from supervision and control despite efforts to do so by different presidents. As I. M. Destler puts it, the net result has been a divided governmental policymaking process with a relatively centralized "security complex" and a decentralized "economic complex."[20] The overall result for the making of foreign economic policy, according to Harald Malmgren, a former deputy special representative for trade negotiations for the president, is that "widespread confusion exists as to who is responsible for what. Both policy and daily decisions seem to be aimed in several different directions simultaneously."[21] As Destler explains, "Decentralization is inevitable, not only of operational responsibility but of leadership and coordination responsibility as well."[22]

For certain policy areas, appropriate lead agencies are readily identifiable: the Fed and the Department of Treasury for monetary matters, USTR for most trade issues, the Department of Agriculture for food, the Department of Energy for issues within its sphere, and the Department of State for matters concerning assistance and many Third World issues. "But it is much harder, of course, to assure that [these agencies] will keep their parochialism in check. And no single department or cabinet member can exercise effective oversight of overall foreign economic policy."[23] Many of these agencies have also tended to be more accountable to Congress and economically oriented interest groups.

In order to promote greater policy coordination and coherence, a number of reforms and reorganization plans of the foreign economic policy–making process have been recommended. One example of this has been made by Stephen Cohen, in *The Making of United States International Economic Policy*, who proposed in 1988 the establishment of a Department of International Trade (or its equivalent), the creation of a permanent assistant to the president for international economic affairs with a small staff, and the creation of a cabinet-level Committee for International Economic Policy on a permanent basis with the president as chair.[24] Little came of this and other recommendations to better coordinate and centralize the making of U.S. foreign economic policy under the president, until the arrival of Bill Clinton as president and the creation of the National Economic Council.

CLINTON AND THE NATIONAL ECONOMIC COUNCIL

Although Bill Clinton has been accused of being a neophyte in the area of foreign policy, this is actually an oversimplification. There is no doubt that President Clinton began as a relative novice in the area of national security affairs and, like many presidents, was forced to experience much on-the-job training and learning. But unlike previous presidents, Clinton was deeply interested and knowledgeable about issues of economics, both domestic and international. As one Clinton adviser stated, "unlike his predecessors, he doesn't see the distinction between economics and politics or between the domestic economy and the international economy."[25] This meant that Clinton's attention, knowledge, and involvement in economic policy placed a premium on the need to better organize and coordinate the (foreign) economic bureaucracy. Hence, a new unit within the Executive Office of the Presidency—the National Economic Council—was born.

A significant change in the making of U.S. foreign economic policy was made under President Clinton. He created the **National Economic Council (NEC)** by executive order shortly after becoming president in 1993 in an attempt to coordinate and integrate economic policy—both domestic and foreign. The *functions of the new organization* were

1. To coordinate the economic policy–making process with respect to domestic and international economic issues,
2. To coordinate economic policy advice to the president,
3. To ensure that economic policy decisions and programs were consistent with the president's stated goals and ensure that those goals are being effectively pursued, and
4. To monitor implementation of the president's economic policy agenda.[26]

The NEC—like the National Security Council, after which it was modeled—is a formal mechanism led by a **special assistant to the president for economic affairs**—also known as the **national economic adviser**—and a small staff (of two or three dozen people). During his two terms of office, Bill Clinton relied on three na-

TABLE 9.7
NATIONAL ECONOMIC ADVISERS

NAME	YEAR	PRESIDENT	BACKGROUND
Robert Rubin	1993	Clinton	Law and Wall Street
Laura D. Tyson	1995	Clinton	Academia
Gene Sperling	1997	Clinton	Law and government
Lawrence Lindsey	2001	Bush Jr.	Academia
Stephen Friedman	2003	Bush Jr.	Wall Street

tional economic advisers to help him manage the bureaucracy and make economic policy at home and abroad. Along with the secretary of the treasury, the new national economic adviser clearly became one of the president's most prominent movers in the making of U.S. economic policy (see **table 9.7**).

The NEC is designed to function as an honest policy broker, coordinating the formation and implementation of policy by the major policymakers and the variety of executive agencies involved in economic policy. It has been described as a "low-profile but powerful institutional mechanism created to coordinate the Administration's Cabinet-level economic policy making. The goal was to do for economic policy what the National Security Council (NSC) has done for national security policy."[27]

ORIGINS

Clinton's NEC was not as innovative as he believed—his predecessors, especially Presidents Nixon and Ford, had also attempted to coordinate economic policy from within the White House. Despite previous presidential efforts and failures at coordination, Clinton was determined to try again. What he hoped to do was to recreate a mechanism that worked in much the same way as the National Security Council operated in foreign policy. In the post–cold war era, this notion seemed like an idea whose time had come. Although any attempt to track down the origins of an idea are somewhat futile, there are some interesting aspects in the development of the idea for an economic council.[28]

The notion bounced around Congress, universities, and think tanks for years before Clinton adopted it

as his own. In 1992 both Democrats and Republicans inside and outside Congress began calling for a similar council. The idea also germinated in New York governor Mario Cuomo's Commission on Trade and Competitiveness. In fact, there is an extensive Cuomo-NEC connection: NEC directors Laura D'Andrea Tyson and Robert Rubin had been members of the commission; Gene Sperling was a Cuomo aide and joined the Clinton campaign only after it became clear that Cuomo was not running. The commission's recommendation for an "Economic Security Council" was originally designed to emphasize international economic policy—a name that must have had some cachet when members of the commission discussed it with Clinton in the spring of 1992.

Around the same time, a bipartisan Commission on Government Renewal sponsored by the Carnegie Endowment for International Peace and the Institute for International Economics was developing a report titled "Memorandum to the President-Elect." Members of the commission included I. M. Destler, a prominent scholar in foreign economic policy, as well as a number of distinguished national security veterans, including: Admiral William Crowe, Frank Carlucci, Morton Halperin, and General Bobby Ray Inman. According to the report,

the combination of Cold War victory and deep economic difficulties allows—and indeed, demands—a shift of priority and resources away from national security as traditionally defined, toward the broader problems of making America competitive in a fiercely competitive world. . . . [T]he Economic Council and its staff would be your instrument for assuring that economic policy gets attention equal to traditional national security, working extremely closely with the NSC and its staff when international economic issues are under consideration, and with the domestic policy Council and its staff on domestic policy matters.[29]

In the end, however, it was Clinton's thoughts on economic policy making that translated the idea for the NEC into policy. Clinton picked up the idea for an economic council as not only a strategy for governing but a campaign issue. The notion first appeared in the Clinton-Gore campaign tract, *Putting People First*. Clinton wanted to create an "Economic Security Council, similar in status to the National Security Council, with responsibility for coordinating America's international economic policy."[30] The idea subsequently began to show up in campaign speeches such as one to the World Affairs Council in Los Angeles in August 1992. However, it wasn't espoused very often during the campaign, presumably because a proposal to create a new government agency wasn't particularly popular among the American electorate. Nevertheless, "It's the economy, stupid!" served as the dominant theme.

However, not everyone believed that Clinton's proposed council was a good idea. Herbert Stein, Nixon's CEA chair, described the Economic Security Council as "a dumb idea which probably won't hurt much. It is dumb to put the focus of economic policy on security." Security could imply a more protectionist stance toward imports that would alarm the United States' trading partners. Robert Reich, picked to head the economic transition, also decided that "economic security council" sounded too protectionist and advised a name change. Beryl Sprinkel, one of Reagan's economic advisers, called the idea of giving the NEC the same stature as the NSC troubling, particularly because of the implications for the treasury secretary, the nation's top economic policy spokesman.[31]

Editorials also questioned Clinton's plan. David Newsome, a former prominent foreign policy official, claimed in the *Christian Science Monitor* that the idea needed more study. "The president-elect," he further asserted,

> appears to envision a counterpart to the National Security Council (NSC) structure, presumably involving an assistant to the president for economic security affairs and a staff. If that

is what the new administration has in mind, it runs serious risks of complicating the policymaking machinery. Such a plan would establish a bureaucratic unit interposed between major cabinet officers, such as the secretaries of treasury and commerce, and the president. The president would risk being isolated from officials whom foreign representatives regard as responsible for major policy advice.[32]

That's exactly what President-elect Clinton had in mind, and it was up to his economic team to devise a mechanism that would work well and avoid the pitfalls highlighted above. After the election, economic policy was still in the forefront of Clinton's mind. The economic team was announced even before his team of national security advisers. But there was a tremendous amount of work to do even before the inauguration once it was decided to create an NEC.

The primary candidate to head the team was Harvard professor Robert Reich, the leader of the economic transition team and longtime friend of Clinton's. However, Reich sought a higher-profile post in which he would be freer to advocate policy. Clinton then turned to Wall Street financier Robert Rubin and asked him to "replicate on the economic side what George Bush had done on the foreign-policy side."[33] Clinton believed that Bush's foreign policy team had worked well but the economic team had been a disaster mainly because of constant bickering and backstabbing. Clinton chose Rubin to reassure Wall Street and because of his ability to create an atmosphere of collegiality. Clinton was very impressed with the way Rubin managed a group of smart, aggressive personalities as a partner of Goldman Sachs—Rubin's Wall Street firm. Rubin took the job only after Clinton assured him that the NEC's role would be taken seriously.

ROBERT RUBIN AND THE TRANSITION

Robert Rubin, the first national economic adviser, who subsequently became treasury secretary, was consequential in defining the initial role of the position and the council operations. He "conceived his role as honest broker, organizing options for the president, but he [was] not ... hesitant about articulating his own views" as well.[34] Rubin molded the NEC into the center of White House economic policy making. This was a major challenge because "other institutions had important process leadership roles too: the NSC, the Office of the US Special Trade Representative (USTR), the OMB, and most important of all for economic issues, the Department of Treasury. The NEC would have to negotiate a role for itself—and jurisdictional boundaries with each of them—or else fight with them."[35] For the most part the national economic adviser and the NEC were able to minimize conflict that its creation engendered with the economic bureaucracy while promoting a relatively open and collegial process, reflecting the teamwork and interaction that President Clinton preferred.[36]

Rubin began by carefully selecting the NEC's staff. As deputies, Rubin chose Gene Sperling, an economic adviser on the campaign, and W. Bowman Cutter, a former management consultant at OMB under Carter. Rubin also recruited Sylvia Matthews to serve as his chief of staff (though that was not her title). The remainder of the NEC staff—which included lawyers, political activists, professors, Congressional Budget Office analysts, Congressional aids, and former lobbyists—were recruited on the basis of collegiality, teamwork, analytic skills, and physical stamina. Together, this small group—in consultation with Clinton's economic principals—planned the NEC's jurisdiction and modus operandi. For example, they worked with Samuel "Sandy" Berger, deputy assistant to the president for national security affairs, on maintaining a joint international economics staff with the NSC—a strategy that had been worked out by Rubin and Anthony Lake, Clinton's national security adviser, over coffee in late 1992.

The difficulty of the group's mission cannot be overstated—especially given the time constraints (the NEC had to be up and working by the time Clinton was sworn in and have a major economic package prepared to present to Congress within a hundred days of the inauguration). The formation of the NEC posed not only ideological and organizational challenges but logistical challenges as well. As Rubin explained: "We had to define it, we had to create its acceptance within the government process, and then we had to staff it, all at the same time that we were working on the economic plan." Put another way, "when he [Rubin] was asked to set up the economic council, and superimpose it on an existing bureaucracy, it was as if he were being asked to land an alien spacecraft atop the White House

without shattering the fine china."[37] Forming a team that reflected Clinton's broad ideology but without "sharp elbows" or big egos was difficult enough; Rubin also faced the challenge of harnessing the numerous departments and agencies into the yoke of a new formal structure responsible for policy coordination.

As a newcomer, with no statutory status, no budget of its own, and a small staff, the NEC had little institutional clout. The challenge was establishing "a powerful but non-threatening position in the hierarchy of Cabinet officials, competing councils and agencies surrounding the president.[38] The NEC had to be powerful enough to enforce policy coordination without stepping on toes. And the most important toes belonged to the new administration's eminences, Treasury Secretary Lloyd Bentsen and Secretary of State Warren Christopher. The State Department was accustomed to policy coordination through the NSC and had steadily become less influential in the making of foreign economic policy. Treasury, however, was a different matter. Not only was Lloyd Bentsen regarded as one of the most prominent and powerful cabinet members, the Treasury Department had little experience with policy coordination and was considered the most resistant to NEC management.

Again, Rubin was especially well suited to the task. Rubin had an established, professional relationship with Bentsen, who held him in high regard. Clinton assured Bentsen that he would be the administration's chief spokesperson on the economy, and Rubin convinced Bentsen that his views would be adequately represented to the president. In the same way that Bentsen believed Rubin to be an agent of his policy preferences, the NEC largely succeeded because Rubin nurtured the view of the NEC as an honest broker of each agency's policy input. Although Clinton (on the advice of the first lady) considered the possibility of the NEC serving as sort of an economic think tank within the White House, this advice was considered impossible and unwise since it would only serve to create another, competing agency and would duplicate the role of the CEA and other bodies. The NEC would be effective only if it concentrated on vetting the policy proposals in a system where "almost 30 agencies involved in international economics rely largely upon ad hoc coordination of their overseas policies, [with the] initiative coming more from subordinate than top layers of government."[39] The intent was for the NEC to serve as a forum in which the economic policy bureaucracies could integrate disparate views into a single, coherent policy.

Still, the task of integrating a broad range of policy preferences from groups with a variety of bureaucratic, constituency, and political agendas—despite an underlying liberal market orientation—remained difficult. With over sixteen cabinet members belonging to the NEC and given the breadth of its mission, it could prove to be too unwieldy to efficiently manage both domestic and foreign economic policy. Yet the administration considered this process vitally important. According to Rubin: "Almost all issues have cross-agency ramifications, so you have to have some mechanism for getting the views of the different agencies, or you wind up with the President making a decision based on the perspective of one agency and not knowing what six other agencies might think about it. . . . You have to make sure that you are dealing with the President— and with everybody else in the economic team and in the Administration—in a totally neutral way . . . that you express the pluses and minuses, and then totally separate that from the expression of your opinion."[40]

This vision of the role and organization of the NEC was conveyed to President Clinton in January 1993. The NEC was already hard at work before Clinton signed Executive Order 12835 on January 25, 1993, officially establishing the White House body. Later, on March 24, 1993, Clinton issued a decision directive that formally established the NEC principals committee to serve as "a flexible instrument—a forum available for cabinet-level officials to meet to discuss and resolve issues not requiring the President's participation." The directive also established the deputies' group to serve as "the senior sub-cabinet interagency forum for consideration of policy issues affecting the national economy," to "review and monitor the work of the NEC interagency process," and to "focus significant attention on policy implementation."[41]

THE NEC IN OPERATION

The *NEC is structured very much like the NSC,* with two important exceptions: First, the NEC coordinates "domestic" as well as international economic policy (with two deputy assistants, one for international economic affairs and the other for domestic economic affairs); second, the NEC's staff is considerably smaller—a few

dozen members within the NEC versus well over one hundred within the NSC. The national economic adviser served "as Clinton's senior economic adviser— chairing senior staff meetings and conferring with the president privately."[42]

A "core group" of senior officials, or principals, met for the most prominent issues, usually led by the national economic adviser, with other interagency "working groups" made up of deputies and chaired by key NEC aides. As with national security policy making, foreign economic policy making consists of informal interaction among prominent officials and a more formal interagency process usually through the NEC (see **figure 9.2**).[43]

The NEC operated at various levels. Apart from the role of managing the process, the special assistant to the president for economic affairs was responsible for communicating the council's advice to the president. Rubin would brief the president on economic policy proposals generated by the NEC vetting process along with his own views. Rubin's communication would most often come in the form of a decision memo. Rubin prepared "exhaustive memos outlining differing points of view."[44] If the president planned to be involved in the policy debate, as Clinton liked to, Rubin would set an agenda, gather the NEC principals, and rehearse the discussion before the presidential meeting.

The principals committee was NEC's power base. Here Rubin could utilize his management skills while demonstrating his influence with the president. The principals usually discussed only urgent issues and proposals that were ready for an executive decision. At first, principals met every day, then every other week (often meetings were mixed with principals and deputies). At times, White House political and legislative aides were involved in meetings. In part they helped to ensure that the NEC wasn't leaving politics out of the process, but they were also necessary to make sure campaign promises were fulfilled.

Rubin and the NEC rose to prominence over the initial significant issue of formulating the new governmental budget. As the president's focus shifted to health care, the NEC became less important for more traditional domestic economic issues, such as over subsequent budget battles with a Republican Congress— especially after the 1994 Congressional elections and after Leon Panetta became chief of staff. Nevertheless,

FIGURE **9.2**
ORGANIZATIONAL STRUCTURE OF THE NEC
POLICYMAKING SYSTEM

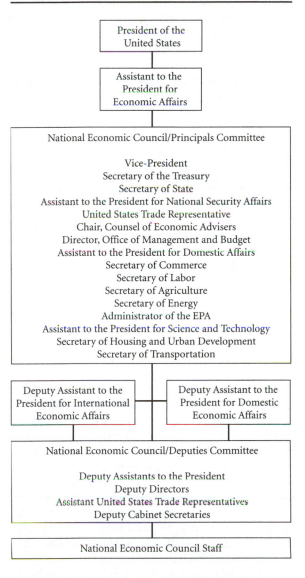

President of the
United States

Assistant to the
President for
Economic Affairs

National Economic Council/Principals Committee

Vice-President
Secretary of the Treasury
Secretary of State
Assistant to the President for National Security Affairs
United States Trade Representative
Chair, Counsel of Economic Advisers
Director, Office of Management and Budget
Assistant to the President for Domestic Affairs
Secretary of Commerce
Secretary of Labor
Secretary of Agriculture
Secretary of Energy
Administrator of the EPA
Assistant to the President for Science and Technology
Secretary of Housing and Urban Development
Secretary of Transportation

Deputy Assistant to the
President for International
Economic Affairs

Deputy Assistant to the
President for Domestic
Economic Affairs

National Economic Council/Deputies Committee

Deputy Assistants to the President
Deputy Directors
Assistant United States Trade Representatives
Deputy Cabinet Secretaries

National Economic Council Staff

three times a week to discuss policy. The March executive directive authorized a system of interagency working groups to be established at the deputies' direction. The NEC formed issue clusters, around international economic policy; regulatory policy, financial institutions, and community development; energy, environment, and natural resources; research-and-development and technology policy; defense conversion and reuse of military bases; and infrastructure and transportation. In contrast to previous attempts at policy coordination, much of the NEC's work was conducted at this level. The international economic policy cluster met weekly and worked closely with Deputy Assistant for International Economic Affairs Bo Cutter and, later, Daniel Tarullo.

The NEC was more structured in its management of foreign economic policy since there was an established group of bureaucratic agencies for foreign policy since World War II. The deputies' meeting was also more effective as the core group of officials from the NSC, State, Treasury, USTR's office, and Commerce worked on "building a policy community" and "bridging jurisdictions." Cutter ran deputies' meetings, often in conjunction with Berger. Because the foreign policy deputies "bonded," meetings were more freewheeling and involved much brainstorming.[45]

The NEC staff also played an important role. Rubin wanted the NEC to serve as a conduit for information to the White House for speeches and fact checking. The objective was to make the NEC "the place to go" for economic information. Sylvia Matthews played a crucial role as a sort of chief of staff to Rubin. She was responsible for oversight and management of the NEC staff. It was Matthews's job to ensure that all the right people in the bureaucracy were invited to the appropriate meetings, that the process worked smoothly, and that various study and decision memorandums were distributed to the appropriate staff.

"The early National Economic Council made its mark" I. M. Destler has argued, "through immersion in front-burner action issues: the budget, the North American Free Trade Agreement (NAFTA), the Uruguay Round, Japan."[46] Because the national economic adviser and the NEC became a significant force in coordinating myriad bureaucratic agencies and officials involved in economics and providing policy advice for the president, the scope of its activities expanded. "The NEC is playing a growing role in shaping

the principals committee was still used frequently for policy formulation relative to international trade and other foreign economic policy issues.

At the deputies committee level, the NEC was more consistent. The deputies committee met two or

the president's political messages, working with the White House's communications and political advisers on events and speeches designed to highlight Clinton's economic views and plans" Destler reported in 1996.[47] This continued under Laura Tyson and Gene Sperling for such issues as most favored nation (MFB) status for China. For other economic issues the NEC played a less prominent role, such as in the U.S. response to the Mexican peso crisis and the Asian financial crisis, where Treasury took the lead at a time when Rubin was treasury secretary.

As Destler has pointed out, the NEC system was not without problems: "Interagency coordination is extraordinarily difficult, particularly on economic issues, and particularly with a president who engages in a free-wheeling and not always predictable manner." And "even in its glory days, however, there were signs of trouble ahead. There were limits in substantive reach and difficulties in focusing very far ahead. . . . There was the sense of informality run rampant, particularly at the deputies level: meetings leading mainly to more meetings, without decisions taken or choices clarified or follow-up work assigned." Nevertheless, Destler concludes:

> President Clinton's National Economic Council started off strong, with Robert Rubin's exceptional adroitness joined to the president's priority agenda. The NEC recognized the primacy of informal relationships; it set out to show all the important players the benefits of working with and through its staff and its procedures. To a substantial degree, it made itself the central institution within its designated policy sphere. To a lesser but significant degree, it was an effective manager of policy.[48]

POLICYMAKING UNDER BUSH JR.

It is important to point out that these have been the formative years of what might very well be a powerful institutionalized presence of an NEC in the making of foreign policy. Much ultimately will depend on presidential interest in international economics and the future use of the NEC following Bill Clinton. As of this writing, President George W. Bush has decided to keep and rely on the National Economic Council as well as a national economic adviser.[49]

In economic policy, Bush originally appeared to be comfortable with Lawrence Lindsey heading the National Economic Council, which the new president has chosen to keep largely intact. Lindsey brings to the NEC years of experience as an academic and as a Washington political insider. Previously, Lindsey served as a member of the Federal Reserve Board of Governors, as a professor of economics at Harvard, and as a staff member on Reagan's Council of Economic Advisers. Although he was chosen to head the NEC over others in part because of his ability to explain complex economic issues to Bush in simple terms, he is also skilled in Washington politics and is close with Federal Reserve Chair Alan Greenspan.

For treasury secretary, Bush initially selected Paul O'Neil, former CEO of Alcoa. O'Neill has a reputation as a deficit hawk and has little experience in international economic policy making. Lindsey, in contrast, is a Reagan-style tax cutter and ardent free trader. Bush's insistence on sticking to the $1.6 trillion tax cut he proposed during the campaign and his willingness to go ahead with American participation in the Free Trade Agreement for the Americas (FTAA) is early evidence that Lindsey rather than O'Neill is the go-to guy in both domestic and foreign economic policy.

With respect to the nexus between security and economic issues, Bush enacted some major changes in the relationship between the National Security Council and National Economic Council in the policymaking process. In particular, Bush ordered Condoleezza Rice and Lawrence Lindsey to "share a foreign policy desk to more effectively integrate economics with security issues in America's post–cold war foreign policy objectives." Bush stated that the move was designed to make sure the economic people don't run off with foreign policy, and vice versa. He justified his moves by referring to the major role the Treasury Department had in the Clinton administration in setting foreign policy toward East Asia, Latin America, and Russia. "Globalization has altered the dynamics in the White House, as well as between the White House and the Treasury. We have to respond to that."[50]

In addition, Bush enlarged the joint NSC/NEC international economics staff, adding more foreign economics experts to make it more aware of the economic changes that have caused upheaval around the world and cutting the number of security officials in the of-fice. According to Rice, the staff would be physically lo-cated within the NSC structure, but would report both to her and to Lindsey through a newly created deputy assistant international economic policy adviser. Rice and Lindsey are directly responsible for the staff, which would deal with two sorts of issues, setting general in-ternational economic policy and coordinating White House responses to regional and international financial crises, similar to those that erupted in Mexico, East Asia, and Russia during the Clinton Administration. The staffs responsibility for responding to financial crises re-flects the Bush Administrations desire to develop more effective initial strategies in coordinating and managing what seem to be frequent occurrences among developing nations in the post–cold war world economy.

With the lackluster performance of the American economy, President Bush changed his major economic team following the 2002 congressional elections. Trea-sury Secretary O'Neil was replaced by Jack Snow; Na-tional Economic Adviser Lindsey was replaced by Stephen Friedman; and chairman of the Council on Economic Advisers, R. Glenn Hubbard was replaced by N. Gregory Mankiw. It remains unclear whether or not the shake-up of Bush's economic team will alter the policymaking process and, more importantly, the poli-cies of the administration.

This brief overview of the new Bush Administra-tion has produced both positive and negative results for policymaking in the post–cold war era. Several of Bush's staff changes and structural reforms are clearly steps in the right direction. Bush's move to create a joint desk for both the national economic adviser and national security adviser in the White House is a good sign that the new president shows no intention of re-segregating the domestic and foreign economic com-ponents of economic policymaking or to resist the merging of economics with security issues in post–cold war US foreign policy. For Rice, international eco-nomic issues are still not as integrated as they should be in the policymaking process. Nevertheless, the Bush administration's insistence on structural cooperation among the NEC and NSC is an acknowledgment that the role of economics in US foreign policy is impor-tant, making issues on the international economic agenda high policy priorities for policymakers in the Bush White House despite the emphasis on the war on terrorism.

What may not be so apparent for Bush and his foreign policy team is that the rise of economic issues to high policy status in the post–cold war will likely in-tensify the paradox of presidential power. As we dis-cussed, certain constraints on a post–cold war presi-dent are likely to increase especially in the area of economics due to a powerful bureaucracy, interest group influence, congressional assertiveness, and forces in the global environment.

Since September 11, Bush's concern with econom-ics has been superceded by highlighting the war on ter-rorism and re-invoking particular cold war themes. While the post-cold war world has afforded him with an opportunity to re-orient US national security policy, the war on terrorism, his call for a huge increase in the military establishment and intelligence community, as well as his promotion of a strategic missile defense sys-tem, has resulted in a foreign policy overwhelmingly based on the threat and use of coercion. During the cold war, the key to exercising strong presidential power after all rested on national security issues, in particular the use of military force. Bush's insistence on pursuing a global war on terrorism may be a reflection of his desire to invoke strong presidential leadership at a time and to minimize involvement in issue areas, such as economics, in which the president has difficulty monopolizing high policy status and governing foreign policy.

THE FUTURE OF THE NEC AND FOREIGN ECONOMICS

Overall, Destler found that the NEC system was a rela-tive success in helping the president manage the mak-ing of U.S. economic policy. *The NEC tended to work well, especially when four criteria were met:* (1) the issue was important to the president and the administration, (2) the issue was clearly within NEC jurisdiction, (3) the NEC had firm deadlines and action-forcing events that required central decisions, and (4) there was a natural lead operating agency.[51]

In sum, there have been consistent efforts to coor-dinate the foreign economic policy–making process since World War II, though they have met with at best mixed success and though they took a backseat to na-tional security policy making during the cold war. Under Clinton the president finally created and relied on a National Economic Council, indicating the continued and growing importance of foreign economics. Clearly, the creation and development of the NEC symbolizes the continued trend toward White House–centered policymaking in response to presidential efforts to better manage and govern foreign policy. Such centralization of the process through the NEC appears to becoming institutionalized and a permanent part of the policymaking landscape.

In the end, for Bush Jr. and his successors, much will depend on the political forces that underlie the relationship between security and economics in U.S. foreign policy making, the impact of U.S. foreign economic policy on the domestic economy, and on the cooperation between the cold war–era NSC and the post–cold war NEC. These complex and dynamic forces will determine the degree with which a post–cold war president will be able to exercise presidential leadership in a pluralistic policymaking environment well into the twenty-first century.

SUGGESTED SOURCES FOR MORE INFORMATION

Most studies of the politics of U.S. foreign policy focus on the national security bureaucracy. Little attention has been directed toward the foreign economic bureaucracy, until recently. An informative overview of U.S. foreign economic policy can be found in Joan Edelman Spero and Jeffrey A. Hart, *The Politics of International Economic Relations* (Belmont, CA: Wadsworth, 2002). An overview of the foreign economic bureaucracy and policy–making process is provided by Stephen D. Cohen, *The Making of United States International Economic Policy: Principles,*

Problems, and Proposals for Reform (New York: Praeger, 2000) and Harald B. Malmgren, "Managing Foreign Economic Policy," *Foreign Policy* 6 (spring 1972): 42–63. Karen Mingst provides a good discussion of the free market ethos in "Process and Policy in U.S. Commodities: The Impact of the Liberal Economic Paradigm," in William P. Avery and David Rapkin, eds., *America in a Changing World Political Economy* (New York: Longman, 1982), pp. 191–206. For an overview of presidential efforts to coordinate foreign economic policy making and the National Economic Council, see I. M. Destler, *The National Economic Council: A Work in Progress* (Washington, D.C.: Institute for International Economics, 1996), and Chris Dolan, "Striking a Balance: Presidential Power and the National Economic Council" (Ph.D. diss., University of South Carolina, 2001).

KEY TERMS

Alan Greenspan
Council on Economic Advisers
economic culture
export controls
Export-Import Bank (Eximbank)
Federal Reserve Board (the Fed)
free market ethos
National economic adviser
National Economic Council (NEC)
Office of the United States Trade Representative (USTR)
Office of Management and Budget (OMB)
open door policy
Robert Rubin
secretary of the treasury
Special assistant to the president for economic affairs
tourism
Treasury Department

$\mathcal{C}$HAPTER
10

. . . .

EXECUTIVE BRANCH POLICYMAKING
AND DECISIONMAKING THEORY

$\mathcal{M}$any people assume that foreign policy is made by the president and is based on some type of grand design. Yet as the previous chapters have indicated, far less purpose and grand design go on inside the White House and the executive branch than most people think. In the words of Fred Dutton, former White House adviser to President John Kennedy, "Washington isn't all that thought out. So much of it is improvisation. Too much rationality and planning can be attributed to it. Much of it is trying something, taking a pratfall, and then looking either bad or good when you do."[1] Usually in fact, as Charles Maechling, Jr., states, "the making and implementation of foreign policy is a collective process involving half a dozen agencies and hundreds of anonymous officials. In propagating the delusion of a master hand and only one tiller, both the executive branch and the news media have collaborated as if in a silent conspiracy."[2]

Now that we have examined the role of the president and the executive branch bureaucracy, including

the National Security Council, the State Department, the military establishment, the intelligence community, and foreign economic policy making and the NEC, it is important to fully understand the complex and dynamic nature of executive branch policymaking. Now that you have the substantive knowledge about the executive branch, it is time to think "theoretically." In order to do this we turn to **decisionmaking theory**—a body of knowledge developed by scholars to conceptualize, synthesize, and better understand the policymaking process within the executive branch. The fact is that all students of U.S. foreign policy, scholars, analysts, and "practitioners and policymakers need the benefit of conceptual frameworks."[3]

This chapter provides the necessary analytical perspective for understanding the complexity and dominant patterns that prevail in the policymaking process within the executive branch. This is done by discussing different stages of policymaking, describing four basic models of decisionmaking, highlighting two major policymaking levels, analyzing the critical role of individual personality and beliefs, and describing various situational tendencies in order to better understand the complex politics of U.S. foreign policy. But first let's briefly review what we have covered thus far before we begin to think theoretically.

To place the foreign policy process within the executive branch in proper perspective, it is important to *review the major post–World War II foreign policy patterns that have been discussed so far.* Seven key patterns stand out. First, World War II and the cold war resulted in the globalization of U.S. foreign policy. Second, following World War II the United States became the preeminent global actor, and American power reached its zenith during the cold war years. Third, World War II and the cold war resulted in the rise of presidential power in foreign policy. However, the Vietnam War, the breakdown of the Bretton Woods economic system, and Watergate all helped to restrict presidential power and were symptomatic of greater global and domestic complexity. Fourth, the National Security Council system has become increasingly powerful, gradually replacing the State Department as the tool for presidential management of national security policy. Fifth, since World War II there has been a rise in the national security bureaucracy, increasing the foreign policy role of elements such as the military establishment and the intelligence community. Sixth, bureaucratic agencies not devoted to traditional national security issues have become more visible and important since Vietnam, especially the foreign economic bureaucracy and the National Economic Council (NEC). Finally, all of these patterns together—especially the tremendous expansion in the size, scope, and complexity of the foreign policy bureaucracy—have greatly complicated presidential power and efforts to manage and control foreign policy within the executive branch, even in a post–cold war and post–September 11 environment. It is with this in mind that we examine executive branch policymaking and decisionmaking theory.

POLICYMAKING STAGES

Policymaking is a complex process that involves a number of different stages. Although any number of stages can be delineated, most scholars of foreign policy emphasize the involvement of at least *three general stages in the policymaking or decisionmaking process:*

1. Agenda setting,
2. Policy formulation, and
3. Policy implementation.[4]

The initial stage of policymaking is **agenda setting**. An issue must get the attention of governmental officials and organizations if policy is eventually to be produced. The second stage, **policy formulation**, is what most people think of when it comes to policymaking—the interaction of policymakers in arriving at a decision. Finally, in the **policy implementation** stage the decision is carried out by members of the government.

The distinction between agenda setting, policy formulation, and policy implementation is not as clearcut as described, for policymaking is usually a complex, political, and messy process. For example, once an issue is on the governmental agenda, its level of importance may change due to events at home or abroad. Issues and policies are not formulated solely at one point in time but often involve a series of decisions over time. Furthermore, the implementation of policy does not necessarily end the policymaking process for any one issue, for its success or failure often affects its future agenda status, which may produce changes in policy. In other words, the agenda-setting, policy formulation, and policy implementation stages affect each other and overlap throughout the entire policymaking process. Nevertheless, the three stages serve as useful analytical tools for making sense of the nature of policymaking within the executive branch.

DECISIONMAKING MODELS

Scholars of U.S. foreign policy have developed *four major theoretical models of how the policymaking process operates within the executive branch:* (1) rational actor, (2) groupthink, (3) governmental politics, and (4) organizational process. The rational actor, governmental politics, and organizational process models were developed and popularized by political scientist Graham Allison; groupthink was developed by psychologist Irving Janis.[5] These models provide four alternative understandings of or "lenses" into presidential power, the nature of the policymaking process within the executive branch, and the politics of U.S. foreign policy.

TABLE **10.1**
DECISIONMAKING MODELS

THE MODEL	DECISION STRUCTURE AND PROCESS	KEY EXPLANATORY CONCEPTS
RATIONAL ACTOR	Centralized	Presidential goals and beliefs
	Rational	
GROUPTHINK	Centralized	Beliefs of leader(s)
	Irrational	Personality of leader(s)
		Group norms and dynamics
GOVERNMENTAL POLITICS	Pluralistic	Policymaker beliefs and personality
	Political	Policymaker roles and power
ORGANIZATIONAL PROCESS	Decentralized	Organizational missions/functions
	Relatively autonomous bureaucratic dynamics	Organizational structures and roles
		Organizational subcultures
		Organizational programs and routines

We begin with the rational actor model because it involves the "ideal" process that most people assume takes place when they think of foreign policy making. Under this model, the president is in full control of U.S. foreign policy and arrives at decisions through a very rational process. The alternative three models are presented from the most centralized to the most decentralized: groupthink, then governmental politics, followed by the organizational process model. These three models describe a less rational, more political process in which the beliefs, personalities, and roles of officials are consequential in affecting the outcomes. Whereas groupthink portrays a centralized policymaking process under presidential control, governmental politics and organizational process portray a decentralized policymaking process with little control exercised by the president (**table 10.1** provides an overview of each model).

THE RATIONAL ACTOR IDEAL

On Tuesday, October 16, 1962, President John Kennedy was informed by the intelligence community that the Soviet Union was in the process of transporting and deploying medium- and intermediate-range ballistic missiles with nuclear warheads in Cuba that had the potential of striking substantial parts of the continental United States. This triggered what has become known as the **Cuban missile crisis,** and the president assembled his most trusted advisers to consider the American response. They included Attorney General Robert Kennedy, Secretary of State Dean Rusk, Secretary of Defense Robert McNamara, Director of Central Intelligence John McCone, Secretary of the Treasury Douglas Dillon, Special Assistant for National Security Affairs McGeorge Bundy, Special Counsel Theodore Sorensen, Undersecretary of State George Ball, Deputy Undersecretary of State U. Alexis Johnson, Assistant Secretary of State Edwin Martin, Soviet expert Llewellyn Thompson, Deputy Secretary of Defense Roswell Gilpatric, Assistant Secretary of Defense Paul Nitze, and Chairman of the Joint Chiefs of Staff Maxwell Taylor. For five days they met secretly and virtually round the clock, discussing and debating the foreign policy goals involved, the information available, and the possible policy options. Then on Saturday, October 20, President Kennedy decided to publicly blockade Cuba and privately offered Nikita Khrushchev, chairman of the Communist party of the Soviet Union, a political solution (withdrawal of Soviet missiles in Cuba for withdrawal of American missiles in Turkey and a U.S. pledge not to invade Cuba). By the following Sunday, October 28, the Soviet leader had agreed, and the Cuban missile crisis was history.[6]

As Graham Allison demonstrated in the *Essence of Decision: Explaining the Cuban Missile Crisis*, most people assume that the policymaking process operates according to what scholars have referred to as the **rational actor model.**[7] Most scholars have in fact concluded that the policymaking process that led to President Kennedy's decision closely approximated a rational process under presidential control, contributing to the prompt resolution of the crisis.[8]

This is the **ideal type or model** that is consistent with the formal organization charts that portray the government as extremely hierarchical. According to this conception, the executive branch operates according to a pyramid of authority. The president is on top and exercises power over foreign policy, using his staff within the Executive Office of the Presidency, such as the National Security Council (NSC), and his cabinet appointees for managing and coordinating the vast bureaucracy. Thus the president governs foreign policy, and the bureaucracy serves and responds to presidential interests—consistent with the popular image of policymaking.

This perspective assumes not only that the president is ultimately in charge but that the nature of the policymaking process tends to proceed in accordance with a rational or open process responsive to presidential beliefs and wishes. That is, once an issue gets on the governmental agenda, lots of information is provided by the bureaucracy and after extensively consulting his advisers, the president determines the foreign policy goals that he wants to achieve, considers a wide assortment of policy options and selects the policy alternative that promises to fulfill successfully his foreign policy goals. The president typically does not come to such a rational decision in isolation. He relies on formal policymaking channels (such as the NSC interagency process) for information and advice and informally consults governmental policymakers whom he has come to trust. The rational actor model also assumes that once the president makes a decision, the bureaucracy faithfully implements the policy in accordance with his wishes.

The rational actor model depicts an executive branch policymaking process that is rational and responsive to the president. This is consistent with the everyday language of foreign policy in which the public, journalists, and scholars typically use phrases such as the "United States government did this" or "the

president did that."[9] The rational actor model is applied regularly to explain not only U.S. foreign policy but also the foreign policies of other countries. For example, although considerable disagreement remains concerning why the Soviet Union invaded Afghanistan in 1979, popular agreement was that the decision was made within the Politburo by Leonid Brezhnev, general secretary of the Communist party, and that it was a function of rational design.

Thus the rational actor model, as its name suggests, sees foreign policy as a result of a policymaking process that is both centralized and rational. The policymaking process may in fact operate in a way that approximates the rational actor model. It is possible for the president to manage the policymaking process for those issues in which he has expressed the greatest interest. The policymaking process may also approximate a rational process in which a variety of goals, information and policy alternatives are considered by the president, but much depends on the president's beliefs and personality. As discussed in the chapters on presidential leadership and management, the dynamics of the policymaking process are heavily a function of the choices a president makes concerning his agenda, level of active involvement concerning issues and policymaking, executive-level appointments of staff and advisers, and organization of the policymaking process.

Presidential control and management may result from direct personal intervention by the president or, indirectly, through the involvement of his closest personal advisers, such as his chief of staff or the NSC adviser. A rational process may be imposed on the bureaucracy by the president, as occurred through Henry Kissinger and the NSC early in the Richard Nixon administration. In contrast, a rational process may occur because the president and his major foreign policy advisers enjoy a collegial relationship or considerable consensus in foreign policy views—conditions that characterized the early Jimmy Carter administration. Furthermore, presidential decisions may be implemented through established bureaucratic procedures or, as occurred under President Nixon, by having trusted advisers, such as Henry Kissinger and the NSC staff, take an operational role.

In sum, diplomatic history and foreign policy making are often explained in terms of a rational actor model. At times the policymaking process within the executive branch does in fact approximate this model, as occurred during the Cuban missile crisis. Nevertheless, the policymaking process often diverges from the centralized and rational process portrayed by the rational actor model.

GROUPTHINK

From 1964 to 1968 President Lyndon Johnson and a small group of advisers agreed to a number of decisions that were responsible for escalating American involvement in the Vietnam War. Once the initial decision was taken to rely on the use of force to defeat North Vietnamese aggression, there was no looking back. At each stage of the Vietnam War policymaking process, decisions centered on force levels and how much force should be used to maintain an independent South Vietnam. Information and policy alternatives that diverged from, or contradicted, the escalatory path were ignored or not well received within the policymaking group. This was primarily because President Johnson was accustomed to getting his way once he had made a decision. Through his strong personality, he dominated the policymaking process on Vietnam. Administration policymakers quickly learned that Johnson was committed to avoiding a loss of South Vietnam to communism. He did not want doubt or open discussion but loyalty and support for his Vietnam policy. Only the shock of the Tet Offensive and the collapse of the cold war consensus within government and in society forced Johnson to reconsider his policies.[10]

The Vietnam War policymaking process under President Johnson did not reflect the rational actor model. It reflected **groupthink,** a concept developed by Irving Janis as a result of his work in social psychology.[11] Janis found that the adage "Two minds are better than one" often is not borne out by the dynamics of small-group behavior. Instead, high cohesiveness and esprit de corps often develop among members of a group. This is true especially when members have similar backgrounds and beliefs, a strong leader emerges within the group, and the group faces a stressful situation. Under these circumstances, the group develops a strong concurrence-seeking tendency, and members tend to conform to group norms or decisions.

Groupthink describes a different policymaking process than is found in the rational actor model. On the one hand, the rational actor model and groupthink share a centralized policymaking structure under presidential control.[12] On the other hand, while the rational actor model depicts an open and rational process, a groupthink process is anything but rational. Instead of deliberating the relevant goals, searching for information, considering alternatives, and selecting the policy option that maximizes goals, groupthink often results in a nonrational process. *Symptoms of groupthink include* an overestimation of the competency and inherent morality of the group, a tendency to stereotype outgroups and rationalize decisions, and the tendency to pressure members toward uniformity (usually through self-censorship), providing the illusion of unanimity. Groupthink—having members of the group think alike—is often promoted and maintained because of a strong domineering leader within the group.

Janis predicts that the more a policymaking process takes the form of groupthink, the lower the probability that decisions will have a successful outcome. Failure results because the policymaking group is not open to new information and resists considering alternative policy options. These deficiencies prevent adjustments in policy to maximize the chances of success, as prescribed by the rational actor model. Under groupthink, the group is committed to a particular policy regardless of changes or developments. Groupthink characteristics help to explain the rigidity and ultimate failure of Johnson's Vietnam policy.

A similar situation occurred with the Reagan administration's Iranian initiative. Throughout 1985 and 1986, a number of decisions were made by President Ronald Reagan that led to selling arms to Iran in exchange for the release of American hostages held in the Middle East. Once it became public, the Iranian initiative led to an outcry against President Reagan and triggered the Iran-contra affair. The failure of the Iranian initiative, much more so then the contra initiative, appears to have been heavily a function of the groupthink process. While Reagan administration foreign policy officials fully supported and actively engaged in efforts to support the contras and overthrow the Nicaraguan Sandinistas, a major policy split developed within the administration over the Iranian initiative. During the initial policymaking meetings, Secretary of State George Shultz and Secretary of Defense Caspar Weinberger were strongly opposed to the Iranian initiative on both moral and practical grounds. In fact, on two different occasions Shultz and Weinberger believed they had convinced President Reagan to abandon the policy. However, Reagan was personally interested in the fate of the hostages, and the NSC adviser (first Robert McFarlane and then John Poindexter) and Director of Central Intelligence William Casey were strong advocates of the initiative. With President Reagan committed to the Iranian initiative, the policymaking circle narrowed to include only those who supported the initiative. Thus, dissenters within the administration were circumvented and a small group of likeminded individuals implemented U.S. foreign policy who were committed to the release of the hostages. Groupthink processes also explain the NSC's operational role in actually carrying out the Iranian initiative, keeping most of the government in the dark.[13]

The information on the Bush Sr. administration suggests that the policymaking process during the Persian Gulf crisis may have fallen victim to groupthink, led by George Bush, who was determined to respond strongly to Iraq's invasion of Kuwait. After the initial surprise, uncertainty, and undecidedness of President Bush and his advisers following the invasion on Thursday, August 2, 1990, a mere forty-eight hours later the president decided to make a major American commitment that resulted in sending over 100,000 American troops to Saudi Arabia and the Persian Gulf. The president apparently made the crucial decision on Saturday, August 4, at Camp David while consulting with a small circle of his closest advisers, a meeting in which there was little debate or discussion about alternative policies once the president's strong views were expressed. Instead, the meeting was devoted almost entirely to military options and how to get Saudi Arabia to approve. It was actively led by National Security Adviser Brent Scowcroft and, most vehemently, by President Bush. Hence, American underreaction before August 2 may have bred the president's initial surprise and subsequent strong stance.

The same situation prevailed when the president decided in late October to double American forces and abandon economic sanctions in favor of an offensive strategy, which was announced after the November elections. As Bob Woodward in *The Commanders* makes clear, the Joint Chiefs of Staff and in particular Chairman Colin Powell thought that such early reliance on the use of force and subsequent turn to a policy of brinksmanship were ill-advised, yet they were hesitant to challenge the civilian leadership.[14] As David

Halberstam observed in *War in a Time of Peace*, during the crisis "Bush had been the most hawkish member of his own administration, surprising a number of his closest advisers and the senior people in the Pentagon alike with his singular sense of purpose."[15]

If in fact the decisions to respond forcefully following the invasion and then to pursue a brinksmanship strategy to force Iraqi withdrawal were heavily conditioned by groupthink, this demonstrates that a groupthink process does not necessarily produce policies that lead to fiascoes, as Janis had predicted and many Americans had feared at the time.[16] Although President Bush failed to compel Iraq to withdraw from Kuwait, the resulting war ended in a military rout by the American and coalition forces.

A similar groupthink process appears to have prevailed following the attacks of September 11, 2001. Like his father, President George Bush Jr. wanted a strong reaction to the attacks. Unlike his father's situation, virtually all of President Bush's senior advisers also seemed to favor a relatively strong political and military reaction that quickly became a global war on terrorism from the very beginning. But President Bush Jr. was very much the driving force. According to Dan Balz and Bob Woodward of the *Washington Post*, within just thirteen hours after the attacks, President Bush met with his senior foreign policy aides and told them, "This is the time for self-defense. We have made the decision to punish whoever harbors terrorists, not just the perpetrators." Their job, the president said, "was to figure out how to do it." In other words, "the president and his advisers started America on the road to war that night without a map. They had only a vague sense of how to respond, based largely on the visceral reactions of the president." Bush Jr. says he remembered exactly what he thought after he heard of the attacks: "They had declared war on us, and I made up my mind at that moment that we were going to war." Not surprisingly, within 48 to 72 hours of September 11, more formal decisions were made and a general strategy was laid out to fight the war on terrorism, beginning with going after Al Queda in Afghanistan and then eventually going after Saddam Hussein and Iraq.[17]

As relayed by Bob Woodward in *Bush at War*, "Bush's leadership style bordered on the hurried. He wanted action, solutions. Once on a course, he directed his energy at forging on, rarely looking back, scoffing at—even ridiculing—doubts and anything less than

100 percent commitment. Careful reconsideration is a necessary part of any decision-making process." But this was not Bush's style. According to Woodward, the following was typical:

> When the meeting began in the White House Situation Room, Bush decided to let the meeting proceed with its routine presentations and updates before getting to the point. "I just want to make sure that all of us did agree on this plan, right?" he said after the reports. He looked around the table from face to face. There is an aspect of . . . urgency in Bush at such moments. He leans his head forward and holds it still, makes eye contact, maintains it, saying, in effect: You're on board, you're with me, right? Are we right, the president was asking. Are we still confident? He wanted a precise affirmation from each one [of his advisers]. . . . He was almost demanding they take an oath.

Unlike before September 11, George W. Bush dominated his meetings with his senior foreign policy advisers. National Security Adviser Rice "believed the president would tolerate debate, would listen, but anyone who wanted debate had to have a good argument, and preferably a solution or at least a proposed fix. It was clear that no one at the table had a better idea." According to Woodward, "In fact, the president had not really opened the door a crack for anyone to raise concerns or deal with any second thoughts. He was not really listening. He wanted to talk. He knew that he talked too much at times, just blowing off steam." Bush admitted "that is not a good habit at times. It is very important to create an environment in which people feel comfortable about speaking their minds."[18]

GOVERNMENTAL POLITICS

In a speech before the United Nations on May 20, 1968, the Russians signaled that they were interested in responding to the Johnson administration's overtures to reach an agreement on arms limitations. This was the beginning of the Strategic Arms Limitations Talks, known as **SALT I.** Although President Johnson wanted a U.S. SALT position ready by late summer, he refused to involve the White House in the policymaking process. Instead, he wanted to present the U.S.S.R. with a consensus SALT position that reflected bureaucratic concerns.

"Neither Johnson nor his staff would take part in bureaucracy's epic struggle to produce not just a simple, clear proposal, but one that would actually make a serious matter of SALT. In Johnson's day there was no Henry Kissinger to hold the bureaucracy in line and to force up presidential options, as distinct from the preferences of the various parts of the government. Unlike Nixon, Johnson—as everyone in government knew—wanted agreement, not options. This meant that the Joint Chiefs had to be on board."[19] Accordingly, the national security bureaucracy—the Defense Department, State Department, Arms Control and Disarmament Agency, and the Central Intelligence Agency—was left on its own to interact, bargain, and agree on a consensus SALT position.[20]

The formulation of the U.S. government's first SALT position resulted from a policymaking process that did not reflect rational actor or groupthink models. It reflected a policymaking process that Graham Allison, in *Essence of Decision*, has called governmental politics.[21] **Governmental politics** describes a policymaking process that is neither centralized under the president nor rational but rather is based on a pluralistic policymaking environment where power is diffused and the process revolves around political competition and compromise among the policymakers. This is a very common view of the nature of policymaking in the field of political science.

Under governmental politics, an issue is likely to trigger involvement of individuals from a variety of bureaucratic organizations, each differing in goals and objectives. However, no policymaker or organization is preponderant; the president (or the White House), if involved, is merely one participant, although his influence may be the most powerful. In this "pluralistic structure" within the policymaking process, different policymakers tend to provide information and advocate different policy alternatives. Given the competition and advocacy among the participants, none of whom can dominate the process, decisions emerge from "political bargaining, coalition building, and compromise." Nor does the policymaking process necessarily cease once a decision is made. Policymakers and bureaucratic organizations least satisfied by the decision may continue to "politic," that is, try to reverse or modify the decision and its implementation. Therefore, policymaking is a pluralistic and political process in which policymakers attempt to advance their personal, organizational, and national interests.

A governmental politics process is likely to prevail for agenda issues that are important enough to trigger the involvement of a number of policymakers and bureaucratic organizations but not important enough to engage the dominant interest and involvement of the president (or a personal adviser acting in the president's name). The process is *particularly useful for understanding the interagency process for a number of reasons*. First, the president and his closest advisers must be selective as to which issues to emphasize, leaving governmental politics to prevail for most other issues. President Johnson and his closest advisers were overwhelmed by the Vietnam War by 1968, and thus the bureaucracy dominated the SALT policymaking process.

Second, the president's management style may tend to reinforce the practice of governmental politics. President Reagan, for instance, downplayed the role of the NSC adviser and staff, preferring to delegate authority and remain removed from most foreign policy issues, as discussed in chapter 5. This management style intensified the political infighting among policymakers that tends to naturally occur in the foreign policy bureaucracy. As Hedrick Smith describes it in *The Power Game*, "the factional strife that plagued the making of Reagan's foreign policy will outlive Reagan—just as it preceded his presidency—because it lies deeply imbedded in our governmental system. Most of the skirmishes of the Reagan period ... fit a pattern of bureaucratic tribal warfare—institutional conflict fired by the pride, interests, loyalties, and jealousies of large bureaucratic clans, protecting their policy turf and using guile as well as argument to prevail in the battle over policy."[22]

Finally, even when the president, or his closest adviser, becomes heavily involved, he may be unable to dominate policymaking. Failure may occur because some of the participants may be quite formidable and the president remains uncommitted to any policy option. Such a situation characterized the Carter administration in its third year during the Iranian Revolution. While President Carter appeared to be uncertain as to what was in the best interests of the United States, NSC Adviser Zbigniew Brzezinski became a major advocate of using force in Iran and lobbied against the more moderate policy recommendations of Secretary of State Cyrus Vance.

Governmental politics often appeared to prevail within the Clinton administration. This was in part due to President Bill Clinton's general inattention to national security affairs, reinforced by his considerable uncertainty given his lack of national security experience and expertise. In addition, President Clinton had a very freewheeling management style that was long on debate and discussion and short on structure and consistency. Although overstated, it was often said that the last person whom President Clinton listened to often persuaded him to alter his thinking, making it very difficult for him to arrive at a final decision. This was most visibly illustrated by the Clinton administration's foreign policy-making process regarding such national security issues as Haiti, Bosnia, and Kosovo. President Clinton was on much firmer and comfortable ground when it came to foreign policy issues that closely reflected domestic and especially economic issues.[23]

In sum, governmental politics describes policymaking as extremely political. Unlike the rational actor model or groupthink, governmental politics describes the president as not ultimately controlling the policymaking process. Instead, policymaking is more pluralistic, involving a variety of policymakers and bureaucratic organizations, each exercising some political clout. The actual decisionmaking process is neither as rational as the rational actor model describes nor as conformist as groupthink. When no one actor is able to dominate the policymaking process, competitive politics usually prevail, and decisions become a function of bargaining, infighting, pulling and hauling, coalition building, and compromise.

ORGANIZATIONAL PROCESS

On January 28, 1986, the military's ability to place reconnaissance satellites in orbit and the National Aeronautics and Space Administration's (NASA's) space program came to an abrupt halt when the *Challenger* space shuttle exploded shortly after liftoff. Americans were shocked by the tragedy and tried to understand who was to blame for what went wrong. Governmental investigations were launched. Efforts to locate the responsible parties were based on the assumption that the government operated according to the rational actor model and that particular individuals were in charge. But this is not how the policymaking process for the space shuttle program operated. Nor do the policymaking models of groupthink or governmental politics enlighten us in this case.

To really understand what happened to the *Challenger* and why, one has to look at the organizational routines within the bureaucracies involved, principally NASA, the Department of Defense, and their corporate suppliers. NASA's major mission by the 1980s had become the space shuttle. Following repeated delays in the *Challenger*'s expected launch, NASA's mission and standard operating procedures resulted in a tendency to de-emphasize equipment deficiencies and overlook safety precautions to expedite the launch. The Defense Department was under pressure to replace aging military reconnaissance satellites with newer, more sophisticated versions. The major mission of Morton Thiokol, Inc., the manufacturer of the rocket boosters, was to make money and maintain its production schedule without damaging the overall reliability of the equipment (such as the O-rings) vital for the space shuttle launchings. Therefore, the power of the different bureaucratic missions and routines resulted in each of the organizational units, especially within NASA, ignoring warnings about equipment defects and deficiencies. This situation prevailed because all of the organizations involved had played their respective roles for years and enjoyed a string of successful shuttle launches. However, on the day the shuttle exploded, the flaws produced by the organizational routines and standard operating procedures came together, surpassing a critical threshold and resulting in tragedy.[24]

Who was to blame? No particular individual or set of individuals. Fault actually lay with a bureaucratic system of numerous organizations and with the structures and subcultures prevailing within those organizations. U.S. space policy and the *Challenger* tragedy were a function of the different behaviors produced by the organizations involved in the shuttle program. In *Essence of Decision* Graham Allison describes this situation as the **organizational process model** of policymaking.[25] This model emerged from the study of bureaucracy and organizational behavior that has prevailed within the fields of economics and public administration.

The organizational process model depicts a decentralized government in which the key actors are bureaucratic organizations rather than the president or a group of policymakers. Policymaking tends to be feudal, with most bureaucratic organizations relatively autonomous from the political leadership and each other. In this process, U.S. foreign policy consists of the sum of the various foreign policies produced by the organizations comprising the foreign policy bureaucracy. In other words, the bureaucracy has become so large and complex that it is an independent driving force behind policy, and the president, more often than not, is only the symbolic leader. As discussed in chapter 7, the United States does not have a single military under the centralized control of civilian leadership. Rather, it has four militaries, represented by each of the individual services and the overall decentralization of the Department of Defense.

A policymaking process dominated by the bureaucracy may not only prevent foreign policy coherence but produce contradictory policies as well. To use an example from the domestic policy arena, the Department of Health and Human Services has spent millions of dollars a year to convince Americans that smoking is dangerous while, simultaneously, the Department of Agriculture has spent millions of dollars a year to subsidize tobacco growers and, indirectly, the tobacco industry. In the area of foreign policy, this helps to explain why the Central Intelligence Agency's covert national security operations often involve individuals and groups within the criminal underworld, including those involved in the drug trade, even though the government has been fighting a long-standing war on drugs. These contradictions are one of the by-products of the president's limited ability to control the immense bureaucracy and promote a rational policymaking process throughout the executive branch.

Each bureaucracy develops its own organizational missions, occupational roles, and standard operating procedures. As discussed in chapter 5 and subsequent chapters, each bureaucracy is based on hierarchy, specialization, and routinization. These characteristics are reflected in the bureaucratic structures and subcultures that develop over time. Hence, organizational behavior tends to be "incremental" in nature, where members of organizations act very similarly from one day to the next. In other words, much of contemporary policymaking and U.S. foreign policy reflects bureaucratic momentum that has accumulated over the years.

An organizational process model is most helpful in understanding policy formulation for agenda issues that are not important enough to gain presidential attention. Much of the day-to-day policy set by the executive branch involves minor issues that are the domain of bureaucratic organizations. These issues do not move up the bureaucratic hierarchy or, if they do, are routinely rubber stamped by superiors. Such issues turn bureaucrats into policymakers by allowing them to make and implement policies usually in accordance with their organization's norms and routines.

For those issues that do gain the attention of high-level officials, policymakers are still dependent on the bureaucracy for information, policy alternatives, and policy implementation. These organizational programs and routines often constrain what policymakers can do in the future and determine how their decisions actually will be carried out. Intelligence assessments and military requirements of Iraq, for example, heavily influenced President Bush's decisions concerning troop levels and strategy that led to war following Iraq's invasion of Kuwait in the following ways: once the president had decided to send troops to Saudi Arabia, the military pushed for a large force of at least 100,000 troops to ensure they could repel an Iraqi attack should one occur; the lack of contingency plans for such an emergency forced the military to rely on its all-purpose general deployment plans and resulted in a swelling of the forces sent to the Persian Gulf to over 200,000; deployment of such a large force required mobilizing the reserves and the national guard; the military routine of a six-month rotation threatened the maintenance of such a large force abroad, and its abandonment threatened troop morale. All these bureaucratic imperatives forced and contributed to a presidential decision to abandon economic sanctions to compel a withdrawal, which would have required months to cripple Iraq, in favor of a strategy of brinksmanship based on the threat of war. In fact, military bureaucratic imperatives were such that the presidential decisions to commence war with a large-scale bombing campaign in mid-January followed by a ground campaign late in February were set in motion as early as late October. Ironically, at the time, General "Stormin' Norman" Schwarzkopf initially presented a traditional military plan for a direct frontal assault on the Iraqi forces in Kuwait (which was likely to produce thousands of American and allied casualties). He had to be prodded by his superiors to come up with the "left hook" offensive strategy that became so famous for overwhelming the Iraqi military.[26]

It is the implementation stage of policymaking that the organizational process model describes most powerfully. For example, although President Reagan made the decision to invade Grenada in 1983, the mili-

tary bureaucracy was responsible for the bungled operation that eventually succeeded in occupying the island. Likewise, that same military bureaucracy was responsible for the tremendous success of Operation Desert Storm once President Bush officially decided to go to war with Iraq in January 1991.

To use another example, presidents since Reagan have highlighted the importance of fighting a war on drugs. However, this war is being fought and implemented by the governmental bureaucracy. The point here is that the bureaucracy employs the programs, routines, and standard operating procedures for implementing presidential decisions (see **essay 10.1** on the American bureaucratic war on drugs).

The bureaucracy, especially the CIA, also appears to have played a crucial role in setting the policy agenda and options for what would become President Bush Jr.'s war on terrorism in response to the September 11 attacks. According to Balz and Woodward, on the morning of September 13, two days after the attack, President Bush Jr. met with his so-called war cabinet in the White House Situation Room. CIA Director George J. Tenet, a holdover from the Clinton administration, "and several other agency officials described in more detail the ideas Tenet had outlined the previous day. This was the second presentation in what became an increasingly detailed set of CIA proposals for expanding its war on terrorism." The CIA plan "called for bringing together expanded intelligence-gathering resources, covert action, sophisticated technology, agency paramilitary teams and opposition forces in Afghanistan. They would then be combined with U.S. military power and Special Forces into an elaborate and lethal package designed to destroy the shadowy terrorist networks."

Director of Central Intelligence (DCI) George J. Tenet had overseen the anti-terrorist plans that were developed in response to President Clinton's request after the 1998 bombings of the American embassies in Kenya and Tanzania. These were the plans that Tenet and the CIA put forth before President Bush Jr. and his administration. As Balz and Woodward report, "It was a memorable performance, and it had a huge effect on the president, according to his advisers. For two days Bush had expressed in the most direct way possible his determination to track down and destroy the terrorists responsible for the attacks of Sept. 11. Now, for the first time, he was being told without reservation that there

ESSAY 10.1
THE U.S. BUREAUCRATIC "WAR ON DRUGS"

Under President Ronald Reagan, a "war on drugs" was declared and became a relatively high priority within the U.S. government. Ever since, it has been a war fought abroad and at home, focusing on controlling the supply of narcotics at three levels of the global drug trade. According to Eva Bertram, Morris Blachman, Kenneth Sharpe, and Peter Andreas, in *Drug War Politics*, "First, U.S. antidrug agencies target drugs at the source by pressuring foreign governments to eliminate coca, poppy, and marijuana production (with eradication or crop-substitution programs) and to attack the refining facilities that convert the crops into heroin or cocaine." Second, "antidrug agencies target drugs at or en route to U.S. borders, using planes, boats, border patrols, and customs officers to interdict drug shipments." Finally, "drug-enforcement agents and local police go after drugs within the United States by trying to locate, arrest, and prosecute drug dealers and to seize drug supplies."

The drug war has created a rather extensive drug enforcement bureaucracy. Actually, "today's drug-enforcement bureaucracy began in 1914 as a small bureau in the Treasury Department (what became the current Bureau of Alcohol and Narcotics Control), charged with ensuring that only doctors and pharmacists sold cocaine and heroin-based drugs"—the first effort to limit the use of such drugs and narcotics. With the increasing illegalization of such drugs, the drug enforcement bureaucracy expanded. But as late as the 1960s the federal drug-control bureaucracy was a relatively small operation, with only a few hundred agents.

It was President Nixon who began to transform that operation into a sprawling **"narco enforcement complex."** By the 1980s, President Ronald Reagan requested over $30 million a year from Congress to control the production and transport of heroin, cocaine, and marijuana in Latin America, Southeast Asia, and Southwest Asia. Under President George Bush Sr., the war on drugs at home and abroad gained greater urgency, and more resources have been committed to international narcotics control efforts. By the late 1990s, under President Clinton, the total budget for domestic and international counternarcotic programs grew to almost $15 billion a year and now is increasing under President Bush Jr.'s war on terrorism.

A variety of agencies within the executive branch have become involved in narcotics control in what has become an extensive bureaucratic complex to fight the drug war. Traditional national security agencies and more domestically oriented agencies are involved in the drug war since it crosses domestic and foreign policy. As of 2002, agencies in the Departments of Justice, Treasury, and Defense are the most active and command the largest share of the nation's drug enforcement budget.

The Drug Enforcement Administration (DEA), within the Department of Justice, is the lead agency in the drug war, with a budget over $1 billion and more then three thousand special agents and over six thousand employees in more than 170 offices throughout the United States and in forty-eight foreign countries. Nevertheless, "at the Justice Department the DEA was by 1993 only one of fifteen agencies or programs involved in drug enforcement. . . . The FBI conducted investigations into organized trafficking groups. The Immigration and Naturalization Service detected and apprehended drug smugglers and illegal aliens at or near the border. The U.S. Marshals Service received funds for judicial security, prisoner transportation and detention, fugitive apprehension, and seized-assets management. The Bureau of Prisons provided custodial care for federal drug offenders and other inmates nationwide and constructed and maintained prison facilities."

At least seven agencies in the Treasury Department are involved in drug enforcement. The U.S. Customs Service, for example, is charged with interdicting and disrupting the illegal flow of drugs by air, sea, and land. Even the IRS is involved: Its role is "to identify and impede the transfer of drug-generated funds and to disrupt and dismantle—through select investigation, prosecution and asset forfeiture—the country's major narcotics and narcotics money-laundering organizations."

The Department of Defense receives the next highest share of the drug budget. "To carry out its drug war mission, the Pentagon created three new joint task forces. Fifty percent of the time of the North American Aerospace Defense Command, a command originally created to track incoming Soviet bombers and missiles, was redirected to targeting drug smugglers. The U.S. Southern Command (SOUTHCOM) in Panama was reorganized to fight the drug war in Latin America; its responsibilities included training local security forces for counternarcotics operations." The National Guard is also "involved in interdiction and eradication campaigns in all fifty-four U.S. states and territories; guardsmen searched cargo, patrolled borders, flew aerial surveillance, eradicated marijuana crops, and lent expertise and equipment to law-enforcement agencies."

"The reach of the narco-enforcement complex extends far beyond the Justice, Treasury, and Defense Departments." The State Department's Bureau of International Narcotics and Law Enforcement Affairs funds international law enforcement assistance and interdiction activities. The Agency for International Development provides assistance for crop-substitution programs. Within the Department of Transportation, the Coast Guard attempts to seize and disrupt drug smuggling on maritime routes, while the Federal Aviation Administration helps to identify "airborne drug smugglers by using radar, posting aircraft lookouts, and tracking the movement of suspected aircraft."

At the Department of the Interior, the Bureau of Land Management is involved in the eradication of illegal drugs grown on the approximately 270 million acres of public land under its control. The National Park Service and the Fish and Wildlife Service are also involved with fighting drug production and smuggling on the vast lands they control. At the Department of Agriculture, the Forest Service is engaged in the drug war with the 156 national forests and lands under its control—some 191 million acres. And the Agricultural Research Service develops herbicides to eradicate illegal drug crops, especially coca. And "beyond the executive branch bureaucracy, the vast system of federal, state, and local courts adds a further dimension to the complex."

Presidential efforts have been made over the years to coordinate and manage the war on drugs and the drug enforcement bureaucracy. A variety of interagency groups

have been established at different times under different presidents. In 1988 the Office of National Drug Control Policy was established to try to coordinate and add some coherence to the myriad of bureaucratic agencies—at last count, involving about fifty U.S. departments, agencies, and bureaus—that have become part of the war on drugs. The office is headed by the director of national drug control policy—the so-called "drug czar," appointed by the president with the advice and consent of the Senate, to oversee international and domestic drug programs.

The reality, nevertheless, is that the essential decentralization of the bureaucratic war on drugs continues to prevail. In some ways the creation of the Department of Homeland Security and the transfer of some of the above agencies to the new department (as discussed in chapter 8 on intelligence) has complicated an already incredibly bureaucratic complex. Nevertheless, the bureaucracy implements policy by developing programs in accordance with its organizational missions, structures, and subcultures. Therefore, although presidents have been successful in making the drug war an increasingly important "political" agenda item for the government and American society, the war is being fought from below by an extensive bureaucratic complex that is likely to expand with no end in sight.

SOURCES: Eva Bertram, Morris Blachman, Kenneth Sharpe, and Peter Andreas, *Drug War Politics: The Price of Denial* (Berkeley and Los Angeles: University of California Press, 1996); U.S. Congress, General Accounting Office, *Drug Control: Coordination of Intelligence Activities* (April 1993); U.S. Congress, General Accounting Office, *Drugs: International Efforts to Attack a Global Problem* (June 1993); U.S. Congress, General Accounting Office, *War on Drugs: Federal Assistance to State and Local Drug Enforcement* (April 1993).

was a way to do this, that he did not have to wait indefinitely, that the agency had a plan. . . . It was a detailed master plan for covert war in Afghanistan and a top-secret 'Worldwide Attack Matrix.'"[27]

As a final illustration of the powerful role of organizations, although the policymaking process in the Cuban missile crisis has been held up as a model of presidential control and rationality, it should be pointed out that a number of difficulties were experienced in the policymaking process due to problems involving bureaucratic programs and standard operating procedures. In the early phases of the policy formulation process, President Kennedy and some of his advis-

ers were leaning in favor of a "surgical air strike" to knock out the Soviet missiles in Cuba before they became operational. However, they were soon informed that the Air Force's operational plans for an air strike involved a massive bombing campaign throughout Cuba to complement a full-scale invasion. No matter how surgical the strike, Russian soldiers operating the missiles would die in the process. This knowledge was crucial in the decision by Kennedy and his advisers to rule out the air strike and opt for the blockade.

Once President Kennedy decided to offer Chairman Nikita Khrushchev a political solution while blockading Cuba as a demonstration of force, the Navy bureaucracy was responsible for "implementing the blockade." The Navy set up a blockade of warships around the island roughly five hundred miles from shore. At one point, a Soviet warship approached the blockade while President Kennedy was still waiting for a response from Khrushchev. To avoid a military confrontation and give Khrushchev more time to respond, Kennedy ordered the Navy to pull the blockade closer to Cuba. Yet the Navy never moved the blockade. At another point Secretary of Defense Robert McNamara, concerned with the delicate nature of the operations, confronted Admiral George Anderson, chief of naval operations. McNamara asked Anderson what he would do if he boarded a Soviet ship and the Soviet captain refused to answer questions about his cargo. Anderson, irritated at being interrogated, picked up the Manual of Naval Regulations and, waving it in McNamara's face, shouted, "It's all in there." To which McNamara replied, "I don't give a damn what John Paul Jones would have done. I want to know what you are going to do now." The face-off ended with Anderson commenting, "Now, Mr. Secretary, if you and your deputy will go back to your office, the Navy will run the blockade."[28]

Summary. To summarize briefly, four ways of making sense of the policymaking process have been presented. *Each model reaches a different conclusion about the decision-making structure and process:*

1. The rational actor model sees an open rational process under the centralized control of the president.
2. Groupthink depicts a centralized structure in which the process is irrational.
3. Governmental politics portrays a pluralistic structure in which the process consists of bargaining and compromise.
4. The organizational process model emphasizes an extremely decentralized structure in which the process is dominated by the norms and routines of organizations.

All four models also highlight different concepts to explain the policymaking process in U.S. foreign policy: the rational actor model emphasizes the beliefs of the president (and his closest advisers); groupthink focuses on the beliefs and personalities of the leaders within the group and the norms that prevail for the group; governmental politics emphasizes the varying beliefs, per-

sonalities, roles, and positions of power that policymakers occupy; and the organizational process model emphasizes organizational missions, bureaucratic structures and subcultures, roles, and standard operating procedures (review table 10.1).

The *four models have different implications for* **government learning** and for the possibilities of continuity and change in U.S. foreign policy.[29] The rational actor model suggests that presidents and other government officials are receptive to new information and readily adapt to changes in the environment in order to maximize the opportunity to promote appropriate and successful policies. In other words, such rationality provides optimism about the ability of governments to "learn" and change their foreign policy. This explains why the rational actor model is considered the ideal type and preferable way to arrive at decisions.[30]

The implications of groupthink, governmental politics, and organizational process, in contrast, are much more pessimistic about the government's ability to learn and change its foreign policy. These three models suggest that there are considerable psychological, social, political, and bureaucratic obstacles to governmental learning and that continuity and incrementalism are likely to prevail in U.S. foreign policy over time until crises and failure occur.[31] With these competing conceptions of the policymaking process within the executive branch, we turn to the policymaking patterns that are most likely to occur in the actual practice of U.S. foreign policy.

THE TWO GENERAL POLICYMAKING LEVELS

During the late 1970s and 1980s, the groupthink, governmental politics, and organizational process models gained popularity relative to the rational actor model as alternative and superior ways of understanding the policymaking process. Yet these three models were also criticized on a number of grounds. Analysts and scholars argued that it was not clear *when* these models actually explained policymaking; discussions of the models were often too rigid, for they specified a particular policymaking structure and process, thereby precluding the variety and complexity of political possibilities; and the models were treated in isolation from one another when, in fact, they overlapped and more than one model was often involved for any particular policy-making process. In other words, it was argued that these models oversimplified the political messiness and complexity of the policymaking process in U.S. foreign policy.[32]

This point has probably best been made in a volume entitled *Beyond Groupthink: Political Group Dynamics and Foreign Policy-Making*, edited by Paul 't Hart, Eric K. Stern, and Bengt Sundelius: "The central idea underlying this book and related works on the role of small groups in the policy-making process is that many aspects of foreign policy are shaped by small groups such as cabinets, committees, commissions, and cliques." The editors further argue that "in many crucial cases, the resulting policies cannot be predicted by parsimonious models of rational choice, nor can the behavior and outcomes of these policy-making groups be fully explained by meso-level decision-making models, such as Allison's paradigms of organizational and bureaucratic politics."[33] But the main focus of the book was to go "beyond groupthink" given its tremendous attention and popularity. As the editors state,

> It seems eminently reasonable, therefore, to treat groupthink as a contingent phenomenon, rather than as a general property of foreign policy decision making in high-level groups. Unfortunately, the very popularity of Janis's work has tended to obscure this simple conclusion. A cursory look at the standard textbooks on foreign policy-making will reveal that if they deal with small group decision making at all, the presentation is likely to be dominated by the groupthink phenomenon, inadvertently equating "group decision making" with "groupthink." This is a gross simplification, betraying the enormous variety of groups and group processes that play a part in foreign policy-making which, ironically had been recognized by early analysts not infatuated with the powerful groupthink heuristic.[34]

One particularly fascinating model is referred to as **newgroup syndrome**. Newgroup syndrome refers to that fact that "newly formed groups or groups subjected to drastic changes in membership or in mode of operation may be particularly susceptible to pathologies of group deliberation."[35] John F. Kennedy as a new

president and his newly appointed foreign policy advisers may have been particularly guilty of this syndrome in approving the Bay of Pigs operation, which was actually developed under the Eisenhower administration. It is possible that a type of newgroup system may have played a role in the Bush Administration's decision-making and groupthink-like process after President Bush Jr. appeared to have been radically transformed into a hands-on, war president in response to September 11. The newgroup model suggests that other decisionmaking dynamics may also occur. Ultimately, there needs to be a recognition of a certain amount of decisionmaking variety—"a multi-level approach" that highlights the interplay between individual, group, and institutional factors and takes into consideration complexity and context.

In sum, the four models provide valuable insights concerning some of the key patterns that prevail in policymaking, but as the critics suggest, the models tend to oversimplify the politics and complexity of the policy-making process. Although there are situations in which one of the four models may be particularly applicable, in order to maximize the strengths of the four models and incorporate the criticisms discussed above, it is probably useful to think in terms of *two general types or patterns for understanding policymaking within the executive branch:* (1) presidential politics and (2) bureaucratic politics.

PRESIDENTIAL POLITICS

Presidential politics operates when the president becomes interested and active in an issue, through direct personal involvement or indirectly when his staff and advisers act in his name. As discussed in chapter 5, presidents rely both on informal channels of communication with close advisers and a more formal process, usually under the supervision of the NSC (or NEC) adviser and staff. When an issue is of sufficient importance to gain the attention and interest of the president (or his surrogates), the policymaking process is also likely to involve other high-level policymakers from executive branch bureaucratic organizations and agencies. Such was the case, for example, during the Cuban missile crisis, in decisions leading to the escalation of the war in Vietnam, and during the Iran hostage crisis, the Persian Gulf crisis of 1990–1991, and the post-

September 11, 2001 terrorist attacks. Thus, presidential politics refers to **high-level policymaking** within the executive branch.

The notion of presidential politics makes it clear that the president's involvement is crucial. Presidential politics also indicates that the policymaking process is very political without precluding any possibilities about the particular dynamics of the process. A relatively open policymaking process may occur in which there is a broad search for information and policy views and alternatives are aired as suggested by the rational actor model. Alternatively, presidential politics may result in a relatively closed process more akin to groupthink. Other patterns may operate, as well, creating situations in which participants may be dissatisfied with presidential decisions and attempt to get them reversed or modified. In all cases, policymaking and politics are inseparable, for prominent individuals are involved, the issues affect the future of U.S. foreign policy, and the stakes are high. In the final analysis, how the politics of the policymaking process actually proceeds depends on the beliefs, personalities, and roles of the participants and the nature of their interaction.

BUREAUCRATIC POLITICS

Bureaucratic politics prevails when the president and his closest advisers remain relatively uninvolved or are unable to dominate the policymaking process. Under these circumstances, other policymakers and bureaucratic organizations become the key determinants of policymaking and the interagency process. This perspective is powerfully described by Charles Maechling, Jr.:

> The principal actors represent giant departments and agencies, each with its own constellation of vested interests and statutory responsibilities. Nearly all the actors are transients in space and time—whether plucked out of private life or promoted from the bureaucracy, they are usually newcomers to the immediate subject matter and prisoners of their position papers. Their latitude of action is always circumscribed by statutory restrictions, policy guidelines and prior decisions. Behind the confident facade that each actor presents to his colleagues and to the outside world lurks a morbid compulsion to protect himself from the unexpected, to make the weight of

one's agency count and to appear effective in the eyes of superiors—but with the gnawing realization that the options available are limited and the course of events uncontrollable.[36]

American foreign policy concerning Japan, for example, often is dominated by competing bureaucratic interests. According to Robert Pear in "Confusion Is Operative Word in U.S. Policy Toward Japan," "the State Department, the Pentagon, and the National Security Council emphasize Japan's value as a geopolitical and strategic asset and are seen by officials in other agencies as overly protective of Japan." The Department of Commerce and the Office of the United States Trade Representative usually "worry about the health of the American economy and favor a tougher attitude." The Department of the Treasury, the Office of Management and Budget, and the Council of Economic Advisers usually "adhere to free market principles and have generally opposed any government intervention to help American businesses compete with the Japanese."[37] Not surprisingly, the U.S. government is not able to pursue a coherent policy toward Japan because of the series of turf wars among federal agencies that limit communication and coordination, even with the existence now of the NEC. This illustration also demonstrates the difficulty of making foreign policy when national security and foreign economic interests intersect.

Such bureaucratic politics may reflect the bargaining, coalition building, and compromise described by the governmental politics model; or officials may pursue independent policies based on organizational routines as suggested by the organizational process model.[38] Other possibilities, however, cannot be ruled out. For example, bureaucratic and personal infighting could be so intense that compromise among the participants is not possible—instead, political winners and losers result. Regardless of the particular policymaking process, bureaucratic politics always involves a political process reflecting the interactions between the officials, organizations, and the political environment prevailing at the time. The beliefs, personalities, and roles of the individuals involved, often reflecting the bureaucratic structures and subcultures of their respective organizations, determine the nature of bureaucratic policymaking.

Since the president and his closest advisers are involved for only selective issues, bureaucratic politics tends to prevail for most issues in U.S. foreign policy. As Charles Maechling, Jr., states, "For every publicized decision [the president] makes, this second echelon of decision-makers makes a hundred equally important ones. And it is this steady stream of less conspicuous decisions, building on and interlocking with their predecessors, that fixes the direction and contours of foreign policy, just as effectively as the few spectacular decisions that are the result of conscious deliberation at the top."[39]

THE ROLE OF PERSONALITY AND BELIEFS

The important role of individual personality and beliefs needs to be highlighted in order to fully understand both presidential and bureaucratic politics and the particular decisionmaking dynamics involved. Reference to the importance of personality and beliefs for the politics of U.S. foreign policy has been made repeatedly throughout the book. Presidential politics is heavily a function of the personality and beliefs of the president and his closest advisers, for most of the other policymakers involved take their cues from him and, ultimately, the president makes the decision.

Bureaucratic politics are also heavily influenced by the personalities and beliefs of the individuals involved. The behavior of career officials, for instance, also is heavily influenced by the subcultures that dominate their bureaucracies, as discussed in the chapters above. It is also important to point out that the beliefs of government officials tend to reflect the beliefs that prevail throughout society, or key segments of society, as we will see later. For example, anticommunism, a national security ethos, and a free market ethos have been the foundation for the beliefs held by most officials in government since World War II.

In order to better understand the four decisionmaking models, as well as politics at both the presidential and bureaucratic levels, we need to better understand the role that personality and beliefs plays in policymaking. First, we will discuss the general patterns of belief shaped by individual cognition and images. This will be followed by a discussion of the impact of personality on policymaking, focusing on

the case of Lyndon Baines Johnson (LBJ) and the Vietnam War.

THE WORLD OF COGNITION AND IMAGES

It is relatively well-known, especially within the study of psychology, that people construct their world to a considerable extent. This helps to explain why people often disagree and see different realities. Walter Lippmann, one of America's most prominent and insightful journalists, stated in his 1922 classic *Public Opinion*: "We do not first see, and then define, we define first and then see." In other words, individuals tend to simplify reality and often are relatively closed minded toward new information. Such is the nature of human **cognition and perception**; that is, how people perceive and process the world around them.[40]

As John Steinbruner stated in *The Cybernetic Theory of Decision*, "The mind of man, for all its marvels, is a limited instrument." Given the complexity of the world and the limitations of the mind, the mind "constantly struggles to impose clear, coherent meaning on events."[41] In other words, as stated by Jack Snyder who applied a cognitive approach to the failure of deterrence during the Cuban missile crisis, "Cognitive theory argues that the mind craves certainty and will work to establish it even when it is unwarranted by objective conditions."[42] Therefore, Alexander George concludes:

> Every individual acquires during the course of development a set of beliefs and personal constructs about the physical and social environment. These beliefs provide him with a relatively coherent way of organizing and making sense of what would otherwise be a confusing and overwhelming array of signals and cues picked up from the environment from his senses.... These beliefs and constructs necessarily simplify and structure the external world.[43]

Human beings and human thought are not simply random and idiosyncratic. Humans are creatures of habit, and patterns exist in their images and thought processes. Basically, the mind imposes clarity and tries to make sense of reality through reliance on a few *common cognitive principles*. These include (1) the principle of cognitive structures of belief (that the human mind tends to consist of a vast assortment of beliefs that are organized and internally structured, especially around more central beliefs); (2) the principle of selective memory (that people tend to remember certain things better than others, especially the general picture or concept, and be loose with the details); (3) the principle of selective attention and perception (that, although the mind can perceive stable, significant features of the environment, it tends to be selective and incomplete in its attention); (4) the principle of causal inference (that people tend to make inferences about what happened and why based on their beliefs); and (5) the principle of cognitive stability (that the mind tends to keep internal belief relationships stable once formed, especially in the core structure of beliefs).

The two dominant theoretical approaches in cognitive psychology—cognitive consistency theory and schema theory—agree that central beliefs are most consequential but differ regarding the level of coherence and interconnectedness between beliefs. During the 1950s and 1960s it was popular to view the individual as a "consistency seeker"—motivated to maintain consistency and reduce discrepancies among beliefs. The assumption behind **cognitive consistency** is that "individuals do not merely subscribe to a random collection of beliefs" but make sense of the world by acquiring and maintaining "coherent systems of beliefs which are internally consistent."[44] Therefore, individuals attempt to avoid the acquisition of information that is inconsistent or incompatible with their belief systems, especially their central beliefs.[45]

A second generation of scholarship emerged in the 1970s describing a more complex cognitive process based on developments in social cognition and schema theory, viewing the individual as a "cognitive miser"— that is, the minds of individuals are limited in their capacity to process information, so they tend to rely on schemas, take shortcuts, and simplify. **Schemas** are mental constructs that represent different clumps of knowledge (or comprehension) about various facets of the environment. They necessarily simplify and structure the external environment, enabling individuals to absorb new information and intelligibly make sense of the world around them. The more complex and uncertain the environment, the more likely individuals will rely on schemas and cognitive heuristics—shortcuts in information processing—to make sense of the world and the situation at hand.[46]

How do images and cognition matter? How do they impact world politics? Through *common patterns of perception (and misperception).* Very simply, the mind has a tendency to

1. Categorize and stereotype,
2. Simplify causal inferences,
3. Use historical analogies.

As Robert Jervis stated in *Perception and Misperception in International Politics,* "perceptions of the world and of other actors diverge from reality in patterns that we can detect and for reasons that we can understand."

The human mind perceives the world and processes information by compartmentalizing and sorting things into categories. This necessarily simplifies and often leads to a certain amount of stereotyping. One common tendency in world politics, in this respect, is for the mind to form beliefs and schemas of the "other." The **enemy image**—according to which "we" are "good" and "they" are "bad" or "evil"—is about the most simpleminded image of all. Such is the image of the Soviet Union and communism that most Americans acquired during the cold war. Once formed, such an image of the enemy tends to be very rigid and resistant to change. For example, in a classic work Ole Holsti found that Secretary of State John Foster Dulles during the 1950s held an enemy image of the Soviet Union and resisted new information inconsistent with this image by engaging in a variety of psychological processes: discrediting (the information), searching (for other consistent information), reinterpreting (the information), differentiating (between different aspects of the information), engaging in wishful thinking, and refusing to think about it.[47]

In fact, it's not uncommon for conflict situations to result in **mirror images:** Each party holds an image that is diametrically opposite the other. In other words, each party has a positive and benevolent self-image while holding a negative and malevolent image of the enemy. As Ralph White found in *Nobody Wanted War,* an analysis of the two world wars and the Vietnam War, each party tends to hold a "diabolical enemy-image" and a "virile and moral self-image that becomes the source of mutual selective attention, absence of empathy (for the other), and insecurity." Such black-and-white thinking contributes to misperception, escalation, intervention, and war—or a cold war in the case of the United States and the Soviet Union.[48]

Given the mind's need for certainty and clarity and the tendency to categorize and stereotype, there will also be a corresponding tendency to simplify inferences about causality. As Jervis put it, "People want to be able to explain as much as possible of what goes on around them. To admit that a phenomenon cannot be explained, or at least cannot be explained without adding numerous and complex exceptions to our beliefs, is both psychologically uncomfortable and intellectually unsatisfying." *Four causal inferences likely to be simplified are particularly relevant to foreign policy:* (1) a tendency to overestimate or underestimate (internal) dispositional or (external) situational causes of behavior, (2) a tendency to overestimate or underestimate one's importance, (3) a tendency to overestimate the degree to which the behavior of others is planned and centralized, and (4) a tendency to overindulge in pessimistic and wishful thinking.[49]

Such simplifying tendencies heavily reinforce people's perceptions, especially in the case of enemy images. For example, it was virtually inconceivable in the minds of most Americans that the United States could "lose" the war in Vietnam, yet they could not allow South Vietnam to fall to communism given the devastating international and domestic consequences that they feared would result. In fact, American (especially civilian) policymakers constantly fluctuated between optimistic and pessimistic assessments in the early 1960s, immediately preceding the fateful decisions to militarily intervene and Americanize the war.

The third perceptual tendency is to use **historical analogies** in making sense of the present. "Previous international events provide the statesman with a range of imaginable situations and allow him to detect patterns and causal links that can help him understand his world," for "we cannot make sense out of our environment without assuming that, in some sense, the future will resemble the past," states Robert Jervis. But "a too narrow conception of the past and a failure to appreciate the impact of changed circumstances also result in 'the tyranny of the past' upon the imagination."[50]

Yuen Foong Khong found, in *Analogies at War: Korea, Munich, Dien Bien Phu, and the Vietnam Decisions,* of 1965 that the lessons policymakers drew from Munich, Dien Bien Phu, and most important, the Korean War had a powerful influence on the decision-making process under President Johnson regarding Vietnam. The use of these historical analogies helped to reinforce the enemy image and predispose the United States toward military intervention. It also helps to explain how the **domino theory** became a powerful metaphor in the minds of Americans—that the lessons of the past made clear that anything short of a policy of global containment would result in one country after another falling like dominoes to communist expansion.

The enemy image of the Soviet communism, and the cognitive dynamics behind it, was the basis of the consensus in the making of U.S. foreign policy during the cold war. It laid the foundation for the rise of the president and the national security state and American intervention (overt and covert) throughout the world. Such an enemy image revolving around Soviet communism would not survive the Vietnam War and the collapse of the Soviet Union, and obviously, other beliefs and images may now arise. But the enemy image of communism was a powerful cognitive force in the making of U.S. foreign policy following World War II and continues to have a powerful legacy, even as the United States enters the twenty-first century.

Such powerful enemy images appear to have heavily influenced members of the Bush Jr. administration, especially the president himself, as he has declared and conducted a global war on terrorism and has demanded the elimination of Saddam Hussein as Iraq's leader and the ultimate "axis of evil," preferably with international support but unilaterally if necessary. According to Balz and Woodward, "Bush fashioned a war of absolutes: good vs. evil, with us or against us. He brought a black-and-white mind-set" to the problem at hand.[51]

The cognitive approach and the cognitive patterns identified above have a profound effect on decision-making. Individuals and policymakers rarely formulate decisions through an open intellectual process where goals (and preferences) are clearly ordered, a strong search is made for relevant information, a variety of different alternatives are considered, and the option that maximizes benefits while minimizing costs is selected. Usually this is simply too demanding and too time-consuming a process for human beings and the human mind. This is the case not only for relatively simple and routine decisions—in which a simple, but powerful, cybernetic process of satisficing and incrementalism is much more likely—but especially under situations of complexity and uncertainty where the cognitive paradigm and cognitive predispositions become much more consequential. This increases the likelihood that not a rational actor model but group-think, governmental politics, organizational process, or other decisionmaking dynamics will prevail at the presidential and bureaucratic levels.

THE IMPACT OF PERSONALITY

In addition to the study of cognition and images, one must integrate the role of personality and motivation. Increasingly, an individual, including a policymaker, should be viewed as a **motivated tactician,** "a fully engaged thinker who has multiple cognitive strategies available and chooses among them based on goals, motives, and needs. Sometimes the motivated tactician chooses wisely, in the interests of adaptability and accuracy, and sometimes the motivated tactician chooses defensively, in the interests of speed or self-esteem."[52]

The role of **personality** and motivation was initially popularized by psychoanalytic theorists such as Sigmund Freud and Harold Lasswell and later culminated in *The Authoritarian Personality*, which argued that beliefs were dependent on ego-defensive needs. Developmental psychologists and other scholars such as Jean Piaget, Eric Erikson, and Abraham Maslow have emphasized that beliefs also fulfill individuals' more positive needs. The classic work highlighting the motivational foundation of political beliefs and behavior is *Woodrow Wilson and Colonel House: A Personality Study* by Alexander George and Juliette George, which distinguished between the "power-seeker" and "power-holder" in their personality study. In Wilson's efforts to gain power in order to overcome his low self-esteem from his childhood days, he conformed to the dominant beliefs of individuals who could significantly influence his rise. However, once Wilson successfully gained a position of power, he would demonstrate incredible rigidity and closed-mindedness after he took a stand.[53]

Ole Holsti also integrated the role of personality in examining John Foster Dulles's rigid enemy image of the Soviet Union, recognizing that "certain personality types can be more easily persuaded than others to change their attitudes." Individuals "also appear to differ in their tolerance for dissonance and tend to use different means to re-establish stable attitudes." Nevertheless, as Vamik Volkan explains, the "need to have

enemies and allies" appears to be quite powerful among the human species.[54]

The case of Lyndon Johnson, while not unique, demonstrates the impact of an individual's personality and beliefs on the foreign policy–making process and U.S. foreign policy. It demonstrates how prominent individuals are often driven and influenced by basic emotional needs—such as the need for love, for power and control, and to do good. According to Doris Kearns Goodwin, in *Lyndon Johnson and the American Dream*, one must delve into Johnson's childhood and personal development in the context of the times to understand the private man behind the public figure.[55]

Lyndon Johnson, the eldest of five children, was born in Stonewall, Blanco County, Texas, a small rural community, in 1908. His mother came from a family who had money, position, and respectability—her father was a lawyer, educator, and lay Baptist preacher. Lyndon's father came from the other side of the tracks—a small-time farmer, heavily involved in local Democratic politics, crude and vulgar, and a hard drinker. According to Goodwin, "the picture of Johnson's early life suggests a childhood torn between the irreconcilable demands of his mother—who hoped to find in his intellectual and cultural achievement a recompense of her dead father, unhappy marriage, and thwarted ambition—and those of his father—who considered intellect and culture unmanly pursuits."[56] In this environment, Lyndon did not feel loved for who he was and seemed unable to please his parents. The only time he felt comfortable and secure was with his grandfather, who would reminisce and romanticize about the glory days of the intrepid cowboy and the reformism of the Populist party. The situation worsened as Lyndon grew older, for when his grandfather died, he drew closer to his father, to the disapproval of his mother.

In order to overcome the terrible fear of rejection that resulted from his upbringing, Johnson developed, Goodwin argues, a desperate and insatiable need to be loved. His tremendous drive to "acquire power and achieve good works" was an attempt to fulfill this need. Given his background, Johnson's boundless energy was directed into politics, initially as a staff aide to a congressman, then as a participant in Franklin Roosevelt's New Deal, later as a member of the House of Representatives, then as a senator (becoming the youngest majority leader in history), and finally in the White

House, first as vice president and then president. The consummate political animal, Johnson lived and breathed politics, and bargained and compromised to make deals and policy. Yet, given his family and his rural Texan roots during the first half of the twentieth century, he also strived to achieve "great works," to help people as he understood them. This is best embodied in his commitment to eliminate poverty through his Great Society programs, which Goodwin argues acted as a vehicle to attract the admiration and love of Americans, fellow Texans, and ultimately, his parents.

His personality helps to explain his "particular management style" as president. Johnson could not bear to be alone and always had to be in control. He was constantly in motion, on the phone, with the radio or television always on around him. The Johnson White House revolved around his need for people to love, support, and be loyal to him. He often challenged his aides in acts of manhood in order for them to display this loyalty. Once Johnson made up his mind, he wanted consensus and support behind his position. As Johnson himself could so graphically state, "I don't want loyalty. I want *loyalty*. I want him to kiss my ass in Macy's window at high noon and tell me it smells like roses. I want his pecker in my pocket."[57]

Johnson was very thin-skinned, overly defensive, and sensitive to any criticism. Those who were skeptical or didn't go along received the famous "Johnson treatment—the use of friendship, intimacy, bargaining, horsetrading, gifts, and anything else it might take to get them on board. Continued criticism or disagreement represented disloyalty and those involved would eventually be completely frozen out of the power loop and Johnson's life." He was so sensitive to what was said about him, for example, that it was not unusual for him to watch the evening news on all three networks at the same time, all the while paying attention to how they reported 'his' presidency."

Johnson was primarily interested in and comfortable dealing with domestic issues and politics. Yet as president he was also responsible for U.S. foreign policy. "In dealing with foreign policy, however, he was insecure, fearful, his touch unsure. . . . As a result, his greatest anxiety—unlike his attitude toward domestic affairs—was to avoid making a serious error rather than to achieve great things."[58] Johnson tended to be heavily dependent on his advisers for information and understanding about world politics. His foreign policy

beliefs reflected the anticommunist consensus in U.S. foreign policy and the enemy image of the Soviet Union that prevailed during the 1950s and 1960s.

The experience of World War II and Korea—the need to avoid appeasement at all costs—made a far-reaching and decisive impression on Johnson, as it did for many of the cold war leadership. According to Goodwin, Johnson believed that "the way to prevent conflict was to stop aggressors at the start—the **lesson of Munich.** In every war, Johnson believed, the enemy is an alien force that 'invades' the allies' house. . . . America alone, our attitudes and behavior, were the key to war and peace. Nor was this mode of thought unique to Lyndon Johnson. On the contrary, it was deeply rooted in the American experience."[59] These beliefs were the foundation for the global policy of containment that, in failing to discriminate between different situations at different times, led Johnson to Americanize the war in Vietnam.

"The very qualities and experiences that had led to his political and legislative success," Goodwin argues, "were precisely those that now operated to destroy him." Whereas in domestic affairs Johnson was sophisticated and pragmatic, he operated as much more the "idealist and ideologue" in foreign affairs and for Vietnam. "In domestic affairs, particularly in the passage of legislation, he was used to grasping practical realities first and then adapting his goals to those realities. But his lack of intimate knowledge about foreign policy and Vietnam led him to rely, instead, on the goals and principles themselves, losing sight of the question of available means. . . . Faced with a situation he could not control and an adversary who was unwilling to bargain, Johnson would force him to bargain."[60]

Although Johnson delegated much authority in foreign policy, he was a domineering leader on those issues in which he was interested. With regard to the deteriorating situation in Vietnam, once the decision to escalate U.S. involvement was made early in his administration, the decision process was then closed. Future decisions never involved a serious consideration of de-escalation or withdrawal—the choices were always between more or less and different types of escalation as a means of finding light at the end of the tunnel. As David Halberstam concluded, "the Presidency is an awesome office, even with a mild inhabitant. It tends by its nature to inhibit dissent and opposition, and with a man like Johnson it was simply too much, too powerful an office occupied by too forceful a man."[61]

The advisers Johnson came to rely on, Walt Rostow and Dean Rusk, shared his anticommunist philosophy and belief in the "utility of force." When one of his advisers, Robert McNamara, came to reconsider and question the policies in Vietnam, he was shunned and eventually forced to resign. "The President's will, once expressed, was not challenged," states Goodwin. "Advisers began to anticipate his reactions before they said or did anything; self-deceptions multiplied in this hall of distorting mirrors. The more Johnson's energies turned to his critics, the more obsessed he became with the need to discredit his opponents, the less anyone tried to stop him."[62]

As the consensus behind Vietnam within his administration and the country began to break, a type of "siege mentality" developed, and the president began to insulate himself, finding comfort in his small group of loyal advisers. As the situation abroad and at home deteriorated, Johnson's moods increasingly oscillated, and critics were perceived as enemies. As Doris Kearns Goodwin explained it, only when many of his advisers and much of the country turned against the American war in Vietnam was Johnson able to realize the tragedy he faced. The Tet Offensive and the growing challenges by Eugene McCarthy and his arch rival Robert Kennedy in the presidential primaries were clear indicators that Johnson had lost control of his presidency and the country. Although he had risen to the top, the love and admiration he so needed to receive from the American people had been denied him, and he withdrew from public life.

Clearly, Johnson's personality had a profound effect on his management style and the decisionmaking process, at both the presidential and bureaucratic levels. Although it is a difficult concept and theoretical approach to capture, personality plays an important role, in a variety of different ways, in the decisionmaking process for all individuals and administrations.

It appears that President Bush Sr. personalized his conflict with General Noriega in a way that demonized his former ally and more fully rationalized the U.S. invasion of Panama (this is discussed more in chapter 17, on the importance of symbolic polities). However, in the 1991 Persian Gulf War regime change and the elimination of Saddam Hussein was never the goal of President Bush and his administration.

More recently, President Bush Jr. has acknowledged how the events of September 11, 2001, had a profound effect on him personally and gave him a new presidential focus and mission revolving around the threat of and war on terrorism. According to National Security Adviser Condoleezza Rice, "the president really had the sense here that this was an historic moment, that he had been cast into a historic moment." And Saddam Hussein and Iraq were constantly on his mind. According to Balz and Woodward, "As for Saddam Hussein, his father's nemesis, the president ended a debate that had gone on for six days. 'I believe Iraq was involved, but I'm not going to strike them now,' he said, adding, 'I don't have the evidence at this point.' Bush said that he wanted them [his advisers] to keep working on developing plans for military action in Iraq but indicated there would be plenty of time to do that."[63]

Bush Jr. appears to have very different personality characteristics from his father, especially visible after September 11. As explained by George W. Bush in an interview with Bob Woodward, "Reflecting on his own personality, he described himself at various points as 'fiery,' 'impatient,' 'a gut player' who liked to 'provoke' people around him and someone who likes to talk—perhaps too much—in meetings. He admitted that first lady Laura Bush had told him to tone down the 'tough guy' rhetoric on terrorism."[64]

Why did George W. Bush become transformed into a war president? Why did he become so obsessed on fighting a war on terrorism and in eliminating Saddam Hussein? Why, unlike his father, has he pursued the war on terrorism so aggressively and in such way as to antagonize so many U.S. allies and the international community, triggering dissent abroad and at home? Why was Bush Sr. more the pragmatist and the diplomat? Why is Bush Jr. more the moral crusader? Although difficult to answer, one must examine the background and upbringing of the individual to better understand their images and personality in order to better understand the policymaking process.

POLICYMAKING TENDENCIES UNDER DIFFERENT SITUATIONS

We have seen that one of two general policymaking patterns is likely to prevail within the executive branch—presidential politics or bureaucratic politics—and that personality and beliefs of individual leaders and policymakers play an important role on the dynamics of decisionmaking. However, much remains ambiguous.

When is each pattern likely to occur? What is the likely nature of the actual policy formulation and implementation process? The following are *broad generalizations about policymaking tendencies* that provide some initial answers to these questions, based on knowledge of foreign policy decision making.[65] Detailed information of what happened in a particular case is necessary for fully understanding the policymaking process (a difficult requirement to fulfill). These generalizations, therefore, provide a starting point for explaining and predicting how U.S. foreign policy tends to be made within the executive branch.

Agenda-Setting Patterns. Attention to agenda setting in the making of U.S. foreign policy has not received the attention that it deserves.[66] Nevertheless, *two generalizations involving the relationship between the importance of an issue and the policymaking process* seem to hold:

1. The greater the perceived importance of an issue, the more likely that it will attract presidential interest and involvement, resulting in presidential politics.
2. Conversely, the more insignificant and routine an issue is perceived to be, the greater the likelihood that the president will remain uninvolved, resulting in bureaucratic politics.

It is the nature of the issue that triggers the policymaking process and determines which officials and organizations become involved.[67]

Issues become part of the government's agenda in a variety of ways. First, issues get on the agenda as a result of initiatives taken by officials, including the president. Hedrick Smith points out in *The Power Game* the importance of defining and manipulating an issue to affect the "power loop"—that is, to affect which participants are involved and the circulation of information in order to control the policymaking process. "Those who are in control of policy, whether the President and his top advisers or bureaucrats buried in the bowels of government, will try desperately to keep the information loop small, no matter what the issue; those who are on the losing side internally will try to widen the circle."[68] The Strategic Defense Initiative, for example, was placed on government and public agendas by President Reagan during a speech to the nation so he could circumvent a skeptical and obstructionist foreign policy bureaucracy.

Second, issues that the government has considered important in the past tend to remain on the agenda. Continuing agenda status explains much governmental behavior, for the hundreds of issues that the bureaucracy considers daily are usually of this type. This also accounts for the difficulty presidents have managing the bureaucracy; so much of what the government does involves refining and implementing policies that were devised in the past. Many of these policies become so institutionalized and routinized that it allows careerists "to control policy by keeping the power loop small."[69]

Finally, issues are placed on the agenda as a result of domestic and international events. This is a common agenda-setting path. For example, crises such as the 1979 Soviet invasion of Afghanistan, the Iraqi invasion of Kuwait in 1990, and the September 11 terrorist attacks, usually go immediately to the top of the agenda and force policymakers to respond. The media often play a consequential role in agenda setting during such times. They are the vehicle by which most members of the executive branch are informed about developments throughout the world, within the domestic arena, and in government. The role of the media, discussed extensively in chapter 18, highlights the crucial importance of perceptions formed by people outside and inside the government, for this affects which issues acquire agenda status and the nature of the policymaking process within the executive branch.

Policy Formulation Patterns. For issues that are considered extremely important by the president, presidential politics is likely to prevail in the formulation of U.S. foreign policy. But what form is the policymaking process likely to take? *Two generalizations about presidential politics, based on the beliefs and personality of the president and his closest advisers, are warranted:*

1. The more strongly a president with a domineering personality holds beliefs about an issue, the more likely there will be a closed policymaking process.
2. Conversely, the less a president is committed about an issue and the less domineering his personality, the more likely an open policymaking process will result.

The beliefs and personality of the president, and the people who speak on his behalf, are major determinants of the actual nature of the policymaking process at the presidential level. Jimmy Carter, for example, usually was relatively open to information and advice, which often led to a more open policymaking process. As we have seen, Lyndon Johnson's strong, domineering personality and anticommunist beliefs, in contrast, made him a rigid decisionmaker who promoted groupthink in the policymaking process.

The intensity of an issue may also affect the dynamics of presidential politics. Different issues affect the government's agenda in different ways at different times—the relative importance of any single issue may fall anywhere in a range from extremely significant to very insignificant. Usually, only a few issues are able to dominate the government's agenda and presidential attention. Crises are times that catapult an issue onto the agenda and trigger intense presidential politics. Times of crisis, in fact, tend to produce considerable emotional and psychological stress on policymakers, often intensifying individual images and personalities, which often inhibit an open and rational decisionmaking process. (See **essay 10.2** for a discussion of the impact of crisis and stress on decision making.)

The above generalizations suggest that *considerable variation exists in the policymaking process.* Presidential politics rarely involves either a purely open or closed process in accordance with the rational actor model and groupthink. Instead, presidential politics usually contains elements that are both open and closed. Furthermore, for any particular issue, the policymaking process is sometimes more rational, sometimes less, depending on the dynamics. Ultimately, the nature of policymaking within presidential politics is a function of the beliefs, personalities, roles, and group dynamics of the policymakers involved in response to changes in the domestic and international environment.

Attempting to generalize about the nature of the policymaking process in the context of bureaucratic politics is very difficult given the possibilities. However, *two generalizations about bureaucratic politics* can be made concerning the relationship between the complexity of the process and the importance of an issue:

1. The less significant and more routine an issue, the fewer officials and organizations are involved.
2. Conversely, in the absence of presidential interest and involvement, the more significant and less routine an issue, the more officials and organizations are involved.

A minor issue is likely to attract the attention of only a small number of participants. Minor issues do not cross over many organizational jurisdictions, and the stakes are not high enough to concern many officials. Barnett Rubin's case study on the 1971 Janata Vimukti Peramuna (JVP) insurgency in Sri Lanka provides an excellent example of a **"localized" policymaking process.**[70] "Although it took place at a time when the Nixon-Kissinger National Security Council (NSC) system dominated American foreign policy," Rubin found, "the emergency was mainly handled within the State Department, where the regional bureau staff had the action." No agency opposed the leadership of the Bureau for Near East and South Asia Affairs (NEA). As a result, U.S. policy was formulated within NEA, at the country director level.[71] Other officials and agencies within the government did not perceive the issue to be of sufficient consequence to warrant participation.

More important issues will attract the attention of many more officials and bureaucratic organizations. This, for instance, occurred with regard to the formulation of a governmental policy for the Strategic Arms Limitation Talks under President Lyndon Johnson, as discussed previously. It is impossible, however, to predict which particular pattern will prevail in the policymaking process. The process could resemble Allison's governmental politics model, but it could also take many other forms. Since no policymaker (or organization) dominates the entire process, the beliefs, personalities, and roles of the participants, which ultimately determine the actual policymaking process, may produce endless combinations.

Policy Implementation Patterns. The implementation of policy presents the *clearest and most consistent patterns since the bureaucracy implements most governmental policy:*

1. Policy implementation tends to result in bureaucratic politics whenever particular organizations dominate the implementation process.
2. The less important the issue or the narrower the jurisdiction, the more likely that only one or a few organizations will be involved.
3. Presidents are most likely to be in control when they decide to take no action, thereby circumventing the need for bureaucratic implementation altogether.

ESSAY 10.2
CRISIS, STRESS, AND DECISIONMAKING

This chapter emphasizes the importance of the beliefs and personalities of policymakers, group dynamics and interaction, and bureaucratic norms and routines for understanding the policymaking process. Scholars have also found that the decision-making "context"—that is, the environment in which decisions are made—has an important influence on individual behavior and the policymaking process. Ole Holsti has reviewed the literature on the relationship between crisis, stress, and decisionmaking. He found that situations perceived to be crises produced individual stress and affected the nature of decisionmaking for individuals and policymaking groups.

Times of **stress** influence individual decisionmaking. *Two patterns, based on experimental work in psychology, were found.* On the one hand, Holsti found that low and moderate levels of stress were often conducive to rational decisionmaking, for individuals became more attentive and motivated to find a solution to the problem at hand. In some cases, high levels of stress may increase performance for elementary tasks over limited periods of time.

On the other hand, prolonged periods of high stress tend to result in defective decisionmaking, especially for tasks that are complex, ambiguous, and involve uncertainty. A foreign policy **crisis** (involving surprise, a threat to values, and little time to respond), Holsti's major concern, involves periods of high stress and decisions concerning such complex and ambiguous issues. During such crises, "lack of rest and diversion, combined with excessively long working hours, are likely to magnify the stresses in the situation."[A]

Holsti found that the preponderance of evidence from psychological experiments, psychological field research (for example, studies of individual behavior during natural disasters and combat), and historical studies of international crises indicated "that intense and protracted stress erodes rather than enhances the ability of individuals to cope with complex problems."[B] He found *a number of patterns associated with high stress and its impact on individual and group decision-making.* Specifically, high stress tends to:

1. Heighten the salience of time by distorting judgment, usually leading to a significant overestimation of how fast time is passing;

2. Reduce the size of the policymaking group;
3. Reduce tolerance for ambiguity and increase the likelihood to stereotype and rationalize;
4. Increase cognitive rigidity, reliance on familiar decision rules, and use of basic beliefs and metaphorical thinking;
5. Encourage random and selective search for information;
6. Produce concern for the present and immediate future;
7. Minimize communication with potential adversaries;
8. Increase use of ad hoc communication channels;
9. Limit the search and assessment of alternatives, often to one approach;
10. Increase the likelihood of a polarized choice, favoring positions of overcautiousness or greater risk taking;
11. Disrupt complex learning and the reexamination of decisions.

The stress produced by foreign policy crises, in other words, often contributes to poor policymaking performance and maladaptive behavior. Each of the eleven patterns mentioned above, with the exception of number 8, tends to contribute to a more closed decisionmaking process. Crises, therefore, may help trigger a groupthink policymaking process, especially if the group has a strong domineering leader.

It is important to emphasize, however, that stress does not guarantee defective decisionmaking but only increases the likelihood that rational decisionmaking will be constrained or inhibited. This is because "individuals appear to differ rather widely in the ability to tolerate stress, the threshold at which it begins to impair performance, and strategies for coping with various types of stress."[C] Ultimately, the policymaking process will be heavily affected by individual personality and perceptions (and misperceptions)—which are usually heightened during periods of crisis and high stress.

Although international crises usually inhibit rational decisionmaking, Holsti recognizes that "not all crises spin out of control owing to misperceptions, miscalculations, or

---

A. Ole R. Hosti, "Crisis Management," in Betty Glad, ed., *Psychological Dimensions of War* (Newberry Park, Calif.: Sage, 1990), p. 124.
B. Ibid.

C. Ibid., p. 127.

other cognitive malfunctions."[D] Therefore, "just as we cannot assume that 'good' processes will ensure high-quality decisions, we cannot assume that erratic processes will always result in low-quality decisions" or end up in fiascoes.[E] Nevertheless, theories of deterrence and compellence (and coercive diplomacy), which have been so central to great-power politics and U.S. foreign policy, "presuppose rational and predictable decision processes," and "scholars and policymakers tend to be sanguine about the ability of policymakers to be creative when the situation requires it."[F]

Therefore, it is important to understand that periods of intense crisis and stress may inhibit and overwhelm rationality during times when it is most needed.

SOURCES: Ole R. Hosti, "Crisis Management," in Betty Glad, ed., *Psychological Dimensions of War* (Newberry Park, Calif.: Sage, 1990), pp. 116–42; Ole R. Holsti, "Crisis, Stress and Decision-Making," *International Social Science Journal* 23 (1971): 53–67; Irving L. Janis and Leon Mann, *Decision Making: A Psychological Analysis of Conflict, Choice, and Commitment* (New York: Free Press, 1977); Richard Ned Lebow, *Between Peace and War: The Nature of International Crisis* (Baltimore: Johns Hopkins University Press, 1981); John R. O'Neal, "The Rationality of Decision Making During International Crises," *Polity* 20 (summer 1988): 598–622; and Jack L. Snyder, "Rationality at the Brink: The Role of Cognitive Processes in Failures of Deterrence," *World Politics* (April 1978): 344–65.

D. Ibid., p. 131.
E. Ibid., p. 127.
F. Ibid., p. 117.

Not only does bureaucratic politics tend to prevail, but the implementation process reflects the bureaucratic structures and subcultures of the organizations involved, thus resembling the organizational process model. Presidential politics may intrude occasionally, as with President Kennedy's efforts to influence policy implementation during the Cuban missile crisis. In some instances, presidential politics may be consequential, as was the case with Kissinger's use of back channels to the People's Republic of China and the Soviet Union under President Nixon. However, most presidential decisions that require implementation are dependent on the bureaucracy.

Much of the day-to-day policy routines made within the executive branch involve only a few persons from one or two organizations, involving such issues as military deployment decisions in the Department of Defense, issuing of visas and passports in the Department of State, or granting of food assistance in the Department of Agriculture. An excellent illustration of the power of bureaucracy and localized policy implementation is the role of the Immigration and Naturalization Service in immigration policy. Thus, the missions, structures and subcultures, and routines and standard operating procedures of the organizations involved are likely to prevail in accordance with the organizational process model for policy implementation.

As Morton Halperin puts it in *Bureaucratic Politics and Foreign Policy*, "At one extreme, if an action is a simple one capable of being carried out by a single individual in Washington without detailed technical ex-

pertise or training, presidential influence is likely to be overwhelming. To the degree that an action is a complicated one, requiring the cooperation of large numbers of people, many of them stationed outside of Washington, presidential influence on implementation fades."[72] Therefore, the most effective way a president can control the policy implementation stage is to decide against any action or a policy initiative, thereby circumventing the need for bureaucratic implementation altogether.

THE COMPLEX REALITY OF POLICYMAKING

We have examined the complexity of how policymaking operates within the executive branch. We have seen that policymaking involves three stages: agenda setting, policy formulation, and policy implementation. We reviewed four policymaking models and highlighted two general policymaking patterns—presidential politics and bureaucratic politics. We also discussed the important role that the personality and beliefs of leaders and policymakers has in decisionmaking. Finally, generalizations were proposed suggesting when presidential politics and bureaucratic politics are likely to occur and the nature of the policymaking process that is likely to result with each of these patterns. The reader should now have a fuller understanding of the president's power over the policymaking process, including the power of the bureaucracy and the difficulties he encounters in managing the executive branch.

The picture provided actually oversimplifies policymaking within the executive branch. First, the government does not consider one issue at a time but hundreds of foreign policy issues simultaneously. In other words, numerous policymaking processes operate within the executive branch at the same time. Presidential politics prevails for the more important issues, while bureaucratic politics guides the process for the remainder. Nor are agenda-setting, policy formation, and policy implementation processes clearly separated—they often overlap and impact on one another. Ultimately, policymaking efforts to address the dozens of issues involve the input of the beliefs, personalities, and bureaucratic roles of hundreds of individuals from numerous organizations throughout the executive branch. In other words, the president, his closest advisers, and bureaucratic officials and organizations throughout the executive branch are constantly initiating and responding to issues, participating in and influencing decisions, and implementing policies. These interactions and dynamic processes represent the complex politics of U.S. foreign policy as it occurs in the executive branch.

At the same time, it is important to point out that policymakers operate not in a political vacuum but in a large governmental, societal, and global context. This was a dominant theme that most of the early theorists of the U.S. policymaking process, including Paul Hammond, Roger Hilsman, Richard Neustadt, Warner Schilling, Glenn Snyder, and Richard Snyder, emphasized throughout their work.[73] As Samuel Huntington made clear in his study of the national security process from 1945 to 1960, *The Common Defense:* "If this book has any distinctive message, it is that military policy can only be understood as the responses of the government to conflicting pressures from its foreign and domestic environments. . . . Military policy cannot be separated from foreign policy, fiscal policy, and domestic policy. It is part of the warp and woof of American politics."[74] Or as stated by 't Hart, Stern, and Sundelius in *Beyond Groupthink*, this raises the agency-structure problem noted by international relations scholars by highlighting "the embedded nature of groups in broader organizational, political, and cultural constellations."[75]

Reflecting this concern expressed throughout this book, we now turn to the remainder of the government, beginning with the role of Congress, before integrating the role of society and domestic politics in the complex politics of U.S. foreign policy. And as with executive branch decisionmaking, we will explore additional theoretical perspectives—in particular, (1) interbranch politics and (2) domestic politics—in order to have a comprehensive understanding of the making of U.S. foreign policy.

SUGGESTED SOURCES FOR MORE INFORMATION

The nature of policymaking within the executive branch has received considerable attention, with an emphasis on national security affairs. Graham T. Allison's *Essence of Decision: Explaining the Cuban Missile Crisis* (Boston: Little, Brown, 1973) provides a classic comparative analysis of the rational actor, governmental politics, and organizational process models of decision making. Less conceptual, with greater emphasis on the reality of the bureaucratic political process, is Morton H. Halperin's *Bureaucratic Politics and Foreign Policy* (Washington, D.C.: Brookings Institution Press, 1974); Richard Holbrooke, "The Machine That Fails," *Foreign Policy* (winter 1970–71): 65–77; and Charles Maechling, Jr., "Foreign Policy-Makers: The Weakest Link?" *Virginia Quarterly Review* 52 (winter 1976): 1–23. Irving L. Janis describes the groupthink process in *Groupthink* (New York: Houghton Mifflin, 1982). Valuable critiques of the policymaking models and generalizations discussed above are offered by Stephen D. Krasner, "Are Bureaucracies Important? (Or Allison's Wonderland)," *Foreign Policy* 7 (summer 1972): 159–79; Jerel A. Rosati, "Developing a Systematic Decision-Making Framework: Bureaucratic Politics in Perspective" *World Politics* 33 (January 1981): 234–52; John R. O'Neal, "The Rationality of Decision Making During International Crises," *Polity* 20 (summer 1988): 598–622; and especially, Paul 't Hart, Eric K. Stern, and Bengt Sundelius, eds., *Beyond Groupthink: Political Group Dynamics and Foreign Policy-Making* (Ann Arbor: University of Michigan Press, 1997).

Excellent overviews of the general role of personality, beliefs, and interpersonal relations on the policymaking process can be found in Joseph H. de Rivera, *The Psychological Dimension of Foreign Policy* (Columbus, Ohio: Charles E. Merrill, 1968); William Freidman, "Woodrow

Wilson and Colonel House and Political Psychobiography," *Political Psychology* 15 (1994): 35–59; Alexander L. George, *Presidential Decisionmaking in Foreign Policy: The Effective Use of Information and Advice* (Boulder, Colo.: Westview Press, 1980); Robert Jervis, *Perception and Misperception in International Politics* (Princeton: Princeton University Press, 1976); Richard Ned Lebow, *Between Peace and War: The Nature of International Crisis* (Baltimore: Johns Hopkins University Press, 1981), and Jerel Rosati, "The Power of Human Cognition in the Study of World Politics," *International Studies Review* (fall 2000): 45–75, and "A Cognitive Approach to the Study of Foreign Policy," in Laura Neack, Patrick J. Haney, and Jeanne A. K. Hey, eds., *Foreign Policy Analysis: Continuity and Change in its Second Generation* (Englewood Cliffs, N.J.: Prentice-Hall, 1995), pp. 49–70.

More specifically, Doris Kearns (Goodwin) provides a fascinating psychological portrait of President Johnson and his impact on U.S. foreign policy in *Lyndon Johnson and the American Dream* (New York: Signet, 1976). Yuen Foong Khong highlights the importance of the beliefs of American leaders and the historical analogies used during the Vietnam War in *Analogies at War: Korea, Munich, Dien Bien Phu, and the Vietnam Decision of 1965* (Princeton: Princeton University Press, 1992). Jerel A. Rosati takes a broad psychological approach to explain presidential politics in the Jimmy Carter administration, examining the president's early foreign policy optimism and idealism, the disagreements that arose between Secretary of State Cyrus Vance and National Security Adviser Zbigniew Brzezinski, and the reinstatement of the containment policies of the cold war during Carter's final year in office in *The Carter Administration's Quest for Global Community: Beliefs and Their Impact on Behavior* (Columbia: University of South Carolina Press, 1987). For more of a prescriptive approach to maximize optimal decisionmaking, see Alexander L. George and Erick K. Stern, "Harnessing Conflict in Foreign Policy Making: From Devil's to Multiple Advocacy," *Presidential Studies Quarterly* (September 2001): 484–508.

KEY TERMS

agenda setting
bureaucratic politics
Challenger
cognition and perception
cognitive consistency
crisis
Cuban missile crisis
decisionmaking theory
domino theory
enemy image
governmental politics
Government learning
groupthink
high-level policymaking
historical analogies
ideal type or model
lesson of Munich
localized policymaking process
Lyndon Johnson
mirror images
motivated tactician
narco-enforcement complex
Newgroup syndrome
organizational process model
personality
policy formulation
policy implementation
presidential politics
rational actor model
SALT I
schemas
stress
war on drugs

CHAPTER
11

. . . .

CONGRESS AND INTERBRANCH POLITICS

Congress plays a significant, controversial, and often misunderstood role in the making of U.S. foreign policy. *This chapter will examine the following questions:* What is the constitutional foundation of Congress's power in foreign policy? What is the history of legislative-executive relations and what was the dominant pattern of interbranch politics before World War II? Why did congressional power decline during the cold war, and why did Congress reassert its authority in U.S. foreign policy after the Vietnam War? What have been the key institutional changes and characteristics of Congress since the Vietnam War and the end of the cold war? What are some of the general interbranch models and patterns? What is the contemporary nature of interbranch politics, especially with regard to war powers, advice and consent, the power of the purse and to make laws, and of oversight and investigation? What are the prospects for congressional reform and interbranch politics into the future? How has September 11 affected Congress? Addressing these questions about Congress and interbranch politics will provide considerable insight into the themes of continuity and change in the foreign policy–making process over time, the

constraints that presidents face in governing foreign policy, and the tensions that exist between the demands of national security and democracy.

THE CONSTITUTIONAL BASIS AND HISTORY OF INTERBRANCH POLITICS

The role of Congress in U.S. foreign policy has been frequently misunderstood. This is because it is usually assessed from the context of a partisan debate in which ideology and party play prominent roles. Since the Vietnam War, conservatives, often members of the Republican party, have tended to criticize congressional involvement in foreign policy, favoring greater exercise of presidential power in foreign policy making. They typically argue that the president has been supreme in the making of U.S. foreign policy throughout history and that this is consistent with the original intent of the Constitution. Liberals, in contrast, usually members of the Democratic party, tend to argue that the Constitution resulted in a sharing of foreign policy power between Congress and the president, and therefore both institutions have major roles to play.

Such partisan perceptions of the constitutional foundation of U.S. foreign policy have shaped the competing interpretations of important foreign policy issues, such as the Iran-contra affair. On the one hand, conservatives and Republicans have been most likely to see Iran-contra as no more than the exercise of poor judgment by the president and his administration. Liberals and Democrats, on the other hand, have been more likely to see the affair as a concerted presidential effort to circumvent the law and the constitutional role of Congress in foreign policy.[1] Similar partisan debates about congressional and presidential roles in the making of U.S. foreign policy became visible during the Persian Gulf crisis.

A particularly fascinating aspect of this debate is the reversal of these positions during the cold war years. Thirty years ago, liberal Democrats argued that the president was supreme in foreign policy, as intended by the Constitution. In contrast, conservatives argued that the Constitution required a vital and independent role for Congress in the foreign policy–making process. What could explain this reversal of views within thirty years?

The change in positions should not come as a surprise if one sees each view as a function of political partisanship rather than constitutional philosophy. On the one hand, liberal Democrats have championed the presidency since World War II, a time when they were more successful in influencing policymaking within the executive branch—beginning with the election of Franklin Roosevelt and continuing with the presidencies of Harry Truman, John F. Kennedy, and Lyndon Johnson. On the other hand, conservative influence was more likely to emanate within the institution of Congress. Conservative influence in the executive branch, however, grew after Vietnam—especially during the 1970s and 1980s—under the presidencies of Richard Nixon, Gerald Ford, Ronald Reagan, and George Bush Sr., while liberal influence was largely relegated to Congress. Therefore, conservatives and Republicans have been more likely to prefer a strong presidency. Liberals and Democrats, in contrast, tend to look more favorably toward the role of Congress, the institution with which they exercised greatest influence during the 1970s and 1980s.[2]

This partisan debate has been somewhat muddled with the collapse of the cold war; the likelihood of divided government, in which no one party controls both branches of government; the election and reelection of Democrat Bill Clinton as president; and then the election of Republican George Bush Jr. and the advent of his war on terrorism. Nevertheless, because of its overtly partisan and political nature, this debate sheds little light on the nature of interbranch politics in the making of U.S. foreign policy. What is required, instead, is *an examination and appraisal of the role of Congress in foreign policy in two areas:* (1) the constitutional foundation of the distribution of power within the national government and (2) the history of legislative-executive relations. Examining these two areas will provide the background for understanding the contemporary role of Congress in the making of U.S. foreign policy.

THE CONSTITUTIONAL FOUNDATION OF FOREIGN POLICY

What does the **Constitution** say about the distribution of power between the executive and legislative branches of government in the making of foreign policy? Before fully addressing this question, a number of points must be kept in mind. First, the document Americans refer to as the Constitution is actually the second constitution of the United States of America. The first constitution, the **Articles of Confederation,** lasted only from 1781 to 1788. It created a weak central government, leaving most governmental powers residing with the states. Second, the present Constitution is a short and ambiguous document. It is no more than a few pages long—one of the shortest written constitutions in the world (and far shorter than the average American state constitution). This means that the document consists of sweeping statements and generalizations, making it difficult to pinpoint the specific distribution of power in the government. Third, the Constitution is over two hundred years old. It was written for the eighteenth century, not for the twentieth or twenty-first centuries, although it has been remarkably adaptable to changing circumstances. Lastly, the final language of the Constitution was largely a function of political compromise. The fifty-five so-called "founding fathers" who devised the Constitution at the Philadelphia Convention had very different interests in mind. They seriously debated the document's purpose, content, and language; in fact, three founders refused to sign the final document.

Because the Constitution is a short, ambiguous, old document arrived at by negotiation and compromise, it is difficult to be definitive about the **"founders' intent."** It may be neither fair nor relevant to talk about the founders' intent, given the two hundred years that have passed since ratification. Still, the Constitution broadly defines the distribution of power in the government and provides the initial foundation for understanding legislative-executive relations in the making of foreign policy (see **appendix A** for those portions of the U.S. Constitution that pertain to foreign policy).[3]

As discussed in chapter 4, *Article II of the Constitution enumerates the powers of the president.* With regard to foreign policy, the president is the "commander in chief of the army and navy of the United States, and of the militia of the several States, when called into the actual service of the United States." Furthermore, Article II states, "He shall have power, by and with the advice and consent of the Senate, to make treaties, provided two-thirds of the Senators present concur; and he shall nominate, and by and with the advice and consent of the Senate, shall appoint ambassadors, other public ministers and consuls." The president "shall receive ambassadors and other public ministers; he shall take care that the laws be faithfully executed, and shall commission all the officers of the United States." Finally, the president has the power to veto legislation. In sum, the Constitution gives the president formidable powers in foreign policy, especially in the areas of treaties, appointments, and war.

Article I of the Constitution enumerates the powers of the legislative branch. Article I is three times as long as Article II. Among the important congressional powers, especially with respect to foreign policy, the Constitution stipulates that Congress shall "provide for the common Defense and general Welfare"; . . . regulate commerce with foreign nations, and among the several States, and with the Indian tribes; . . . define and punish piracies and felonies committed on the high seas, and offenses against the law of nations; . . . declare war, grant letters of marque and reprisal, and make rules concerning captures on land and water; . . . raise and support armies; . . . provide and maintain a navy; . . .

make rules for the government and regulation of the land and naval forces; [and] provide for calling forth the militia to execute the laws of the Union, suppress insurrections, and repel invasions." Finally, in addition to the Senate's advice and consent power, Congress shall have the power "to make all laws which shall be necessary and proper for carrying into execution the foregoing powers, and all other powers vested by this Constitution in the government of the United States, or in any department or officer thereof."

The Constitution clearly gives the Congress formidable powers in the area of foreign policy. Unlike most legislatures elsewhere in the world, especially in parliamentary systems of government, the U.S. Congress is an independent and powerful branch of government. In fact, most scholars of the Constitution have concluded that the founders intended and expected that the legislature to be the preeminent branch in the government. Nonetheless, the Constitution did not give power in the area of foreign policy solely to the Congress or to the president—power was distributed between the two branches of government.[4]

Americans have been raised to understand the distribution of power between Congress and the president as a separation of powers. But this concept does not accurately represent reality, for the Constitution did not create separate institutions with separate powers but **separate institutions sharing power**—which is what is meant by "checks and balances." While the Congress provides military funding and declares war, the president is the commander in chief. Congress may pass bills, but the president may veto them, and Congress may then override the veto. The president is able to make treaties and appointments, but the Senate must provide its advice and consent. In this way, the Constitution has produced a central government with separate institutions sharing powers. As students of the Constitution have indicated, the result was an **invitation to struggle,** which has fostered recurring conflicts between Congress and the president in the making of foreign policy throughout American history.

HISTORICAL PATTERNS IN LEGISLATIVE-EXECUTIVE RELATIONS

Given the sharing of power by separate institutions and the basic ambiguity of the Constitution, the distribution of foreign policy–making power between Congress and the president has fluctuated politically over time. There has been no single pattern in foreign policy making throughout American history. Neither Congress nor the president has always predominated in foreign policy. Legislative-executive relations and **interbranch politics** in foreign policy have been fluid and dynamic, fluctuating with changes in the political environment. Therefore, the key to understanding the history of legislative-executive relations is to see it in terms of the political interaction of these two governmental branches over time.

As Arthur Schlesinger, Jr., described it in *The Imperial Presidency*, the politics of legislative-executive relations in foreign policy has been characterized by a kind of **pendulum (or cyclical) effect** over the course of American history.[5] In times of national emergency, particularly war, power tends to flow toward the president and the executive branch. During times of peace—that is, when conflict has subsided—power tends to flow back to Congress. Yet while Congress tends to reassert its constitutional authority and power following war, increases in presidential power during periods of conflict tend to be so extensive that it seldom returns to prewar levels. Thus, the cyclical ebb and flow in legislative-executive relations in foreign policy has enabled the president to accumulate greater power over time.

The growth in power that the president and executive branch experience during periods of war was evident in the War of 1812, Mexican-American War, Civil War, Spanish-American War, and World Wars I and II. *Two major factors account for this expansion of presidential power.* First, in times of conflict the president's roles of commander in chief and chief executive give him control over the conduct of war. This fact is reinforced by the tendency of Congress to delegate extensive emergency powers to the president during wartime.[6] Second, periods of perceived national emergency are also times when most Americans in government and society turn to the president and rally behind him as the key authority for addressing the gravity of the situation. Referring back to the discussion of Richard Pious's work in chapter 4, periods of war and national emergency are times when the president can exercise prerogative government. That is, the president can push the Constitution to its extreme in the exercise of presidential power, with the likelihood of only minimal political backlash. This is exactly what occurred,

for example, under the administrations of Abraham Lincoln, Woodrow Wilson, and Franklin Roosevelt.

With the end of war and national emergency, the conditions that gave rise to the expansion of presidential power disappear. Periods of normalcy or relative stability result in congressional reassertion of power. Hence, the president experiences greater constraints on his ability to exercise power in foreign policy. Such cutbacks occurred after all of the major wars, but most noticeably following World War I. The Senate rejected the Treaty of Versailles that President Wilson negotiated in Paris and that included his grand design for a League of Nations. Also, during the interwar years, Congress passed legislation that increasingly affected the conduct of U.S. foreign policy and constrained presidential power, culminating in the neutrality legislation that tied the hands of President Franklin Roosevelt as World War II approached.

Even though postwar peace and relative stability increase congressional strength in legislative-executive foreign policy relations, the president's power nonetheless tends to experience net growth in comparison to prewar years. Thus, although the neutrality legislation certainly constrained Roosevelt's efforts to support Great Britain and the allies as World War II approached and during the early years of the war, President Roosevelt had the U.S. military participate in an "undeclared naval war" in the mid-Atlantic in support of the British about six months before the Japanese attack on Pearl Harbor legitimized full-scale American intervention in the war. Congressional reassertion also did not prevent presidents from pursuing an active foreign policy in areas deemed particularly important for U.S. national interests, such as Asia and Latin America. The interwar years, for example, were a time when American presidents routinely intervened militarily throughout the Caribbean and Central America, frequently relying on the use of American armed forces to exercise influence in the region.

The historical pattern is one in which presidents have accumulated more and more power in foreign policy over time as a result of war and national emergencies; at the same time, Congress has attempted, with only moderate success, to reassert its constitutional authority in foreign policy during times of peace. As a result, Congress has become increasingly unable to exercise preeminence in the making of foreign policy. Thus, times of war and national emergency are likely to be times of presidential preeminence, while times of peace are likely to result not in congressional ascendance but in political struggles between the legislative and executive branches over foreign policy. This cyclical pattern and the politics of legislative-executive relations was played out following World War II.

WORLD WAR II AND THE POSTWAR YEARS

American intervention in World War II in 1941 resulted in a major expansion of the national security bureaucracy and of presidential power in foreign policy. With the war's end in 1945, the U.S. government demobilized its military forces and reduced its global presence. At the same time, Congress began to reassert its authority in foreign policy. However, the jubilation of victory in World War II and peacetime hopes were quickly replaced by new fears and a new enemy—Soviet communism. Consequently, the post–World War II years never became a time of peace; the late 1940s, 1950s, and early 1960s were a time when most Americans perceived a major threat to their national security. For the first time in its history, the United States remobilized and remilitarized on a permanent peacetime basis to deter and contain what was believed to be a rising communist threat abroad.

Although the United States and the Soviet Union never engaged in a "hot war" (a direct military clash), the United States prepared for a direct military confrontation with the Soviet Union and engaged in a global cold war. This period of perceived national emergency resulted in renewed expansion of the national security bureaucracy and presidential power, restoring the president's preeminence in the making of U.S. foreign policy. The threat to national security was felt so intensely that a cold war consensus developed in America in support of the president's effort to fight communism. With the president receiving such widespread support, congressional reassertion over foreign policy was deferred during the cold war, to reappear only during the late 1960s with the growing dispute over the Vietnam War. Thus, *interbranch politics have gone through two general phases since the end of World War II:* (1) presidential preeminence and congressional acquiescence from the late 1940s to the mid-1960s,

when the cold war dominated U.S. foreign policy; and (2) congressional reassertion in foreign policy since the height of the Vietnam War in the late 1960s.

PRESIDENTIAL PREEMINENCE IN THE COLD WAR ERA

The president and the executive branch dominated the legislative branch in the making of foreign policy during the cold war years. At the same time, American politics and legislative-executive relations were much more complex than this simple generalization implies. Presidential preeminence neither occurred overnight nor dominated the entire history of the cold war years. *The congressional role in legislative-executive relations evolved through four phases or periods during the cold war:* (1) accommodation, from 1944 to 1950; (2) antagonism, from 1951 to 1955; (3) acquiescence, from 1955 to 1965; and (4) ambiguity, from 1966 to 1969.[7]

Congressional Accommodation, 1944 to 1950. What began as congressional assertion quickly became congressional accommodation in interbranch politics in the immediate postwar years. Tension between members of Congress and the president initially surfaced over the future of U.S. foreign policy. In response to the devastation suffered by Europe in the war, President Truman proposed the Marshall Plan to provide American assistance for European economic reconstruction. However, isolationist sentiment was still very strong among members of Congress, especially within the Republican party. Truman overcame congressional resistance to such an active American role abroad only by working closely with members of Congress and convincing them, and the American people, of the grave political instability that most European states faced from their economic situation and from the growing threat of Soviet communism. The Marshall Plan was eventually approved by Congress with considerable bipartisan support and symbolized an accommodationist relationship between the legislative and the executive branches.

During the immediate post–World War II years, most key decisions behind U.S. cold war and containment policies were a result of joint participation by the president and members of Congress. This was a period in which the evolving legislative-executive partnership approved of American participation in the United Nations, the International Bank for Reconstruction and Development (World Bank), the International Monetary Fund (IMF), and the General Agreement on Tariffs and Trade (GATT). It was also a time when the National Security Act of 1947 became law, foreign assistance to Greece and Turkey was approved in support of the Truman Doctrine, and the military was remobilized. Joint legislative-executive action supported a strong American global role, culminating in the **Senate approval of the North Atlantic Treaty Organization (NATO)** and the permanent stationing of American troops in Europe—a peacetime American military commitment unprecedented in the nation's history (recall that following World War I the Senate twice rejected the Treaty of Versailles and the United States becoming a member of the League of Nations).

Congressional Antagonism, 1951 to 1955. Although members of Congress and President Truman, followed by President Dwight Eisenhower, espoused a bipartisan approach to foreign policy, a growing segment of Congress was increasingly dissatisfied with U.S. foreign policy and global developments. Much of this frustration was experienced by more conservative members of Congress, especially within the Republican party. They saw a world in which the United States had won the war but was losing the peace. According to this view, events such as Soviet communist consolidation of power in Eastern Europe, the "fall" of Chiang Kai-shek and the Nationalists in China, and the North Korean attack on South Korea demonstrated that U.S. foreign policy was a failure and too weak to respond to the ever growing communist threat.

How could this happen? How could the United States win the war and emerge as the strongest country in the world yet fail to contain the expansion of communism? The answer was simple in the minds of many people—treason must be afoot. In other words, Americans were losing the war to communism abroad because communists, "fellow travelers" (that is, communist sympathizers), and liberal-leftists had penetrated the major institutions of American society, including the executive branch, and were aiding and abetting the enemy. Thus it was not enough to just contain communism abroad; one had to roll it back—an operation referred to as "rollback"—both abroad and at home.

This extremely pessimistic view had played a role in the politics of U.S. foreign policy since the end of World War II. However, it became much more prominent when the Republican party gained control of both chambers of Congress, first after the 1946 congressional elections and especially after the 1952 elections. Republican ascendance resulted in sweeping congressional investigations of communist threats at home, as well as growing political attacks against the Truman administration and the Democratic party.

"Republicans began referring to their congressional adversaries as members of 'the party of treason'—a slur that [Democratic leader Sam] Rayburn attributed to Nixon, and never forgave," according to William Manchester, in *The Glory and the Dream.* "Congressman Karl Mundt of South Dakota demanded that the President 'ferret out' those on the federal payroll 'whose Soviet leanings have contributed so greatly to the deplorable mess in our foreign policy.' Congressman Harold Velde of Illinois announced that Soviet spies were 'infesting the entire country,' like gypsy moths; Congressman Robert Rich of Pennsylvania charged that [Secretary of State] Dean Acheson was on Joseph Stalin's payroll." Manchester's narrative history provides a feel for the language and the nature of the times. "To [Senator William] Jenner of Indiana, every American whose advice to Chiang Kai-shek had failed to staunch the Red tide was, almost by definition, a criminal. Jenner called General [George] Marshall 'a front man for traitors,' a 'living lie' who had joined hands 'with this criminal crowd of traitors and Communist appeasers who, under the continuing influence of Mr. Truman and Mr. Acheson, are still selling America down the river.'"[8] It was in this political climate that Senator Joseph McCarthy of Wisconsin thrived and gave the conservative movement its name—McCarthyism. (See **essay 11.1** for more on Joseph McCarthy and McCarthyism.)

With the growing power of the Republican party and the rise of McCarthyism, U.S. foreign policy became an increasingly partisan political battleground, symbolized by the Truman-MacArthur controversy of 1951. President Truman fired General Douglas MacArthur as commander of the allied forces in Korea, charging him with insubordination and carelessly escalating the Korean conflict by triggering the military involvement of communist China (the People's Republic of China). President Truman represented a more moderate position in Korea,

ESSAY 11.1
JOSEPH MCCARTHY AND MCCARTHYISM

Journalist Richard H. Rovere begins his biography *Senator Joe McCarthy* by writing that "the late Joseph R. McCarthy, a United States Senator from Wisconsin, was in many ways the most gifted demagogue ever bred on these shores. No bolder seditionist ever moved among us—not any politician with a surer, swifter access to the dark places of the American mind."[A] McCarthy's political prominence was brief. His rise to power began in 1950, four years after he won a seat in the Senate. Within weeks, he became a major political figure known, loved, hated, and feared throughout the country and the world. By 1954 his career ended when the Senate passed a resolution of censure against him. He died a drunk three years later at age forty-eight. Yet, the impact of Joseph McCarthy and McCarthyism was immense.

Joseph McCarthy both reflected and promoted the anticommunist climate of the times. He embodied a political force—**McCarthyism**—that dominated American politics during the early 1950s and was instrumental in pushing the country and U.S. foreign policy to the political right. Joseph McCarthy and McCarthyism led to "the purge of thousands of government employees, educators, labor leaders, journalists, scientists, writers, and entertainers and, perhaps more important, the intimidation of hundreds of thousands more."[B]

Joseph McCarthy started out as a Democrat and made his first run for office in 1939 as a supporter of Franklin D. Roosevelt. He became a Republican and won election to the Senate in 1946 as "Tail Gunner Joe"—a war hero who never actually fought in the war. During his early years in the Senate, McCarthy was "known as a cheap politician of vulgar, flamboyant ways and a casual approach to the public interest."[C] One night in January 1950 in a small restaurant in Washington, D.C., while talking with three dinner companions about his Senate re-election possibilities, he discovered communism as an issue—not out of real concern for American national security but as an issue that would win him reelection.

He tested the issue in a speech he gave on February 9, 1950, in Wheeling, West Virginia, in which he claimed that the Department of State was full of communists and that he

and the secretary of state knew their names. To this day, nobody is sure whether he declared that there were 205, 81, 57, or "a lot" of communists; more important was the charge that communists "known to the secretary of state" were "still working and making policy." Although McCarthy was one of many politicians voicing the anticommunist theme, he gained the public spotlight like no other.

Following his Wheeling speech, he accused the Democratic administration of conniving with communists: "The Democratic label is now the property of men and women who have . . . bent to the whispered pleas from the lips of traitors."[D] He claimed that the Democratic years had been "twenty years of treason." The timing of the charges was impeccable. On January 21, Alger Hiss, a State Department official accused of being a communist, was convicted of perjury, and in June the communist government of North Korea invaded South Korea, vindicating and feeding the anticommunist hysteria that McCarthy represented.

Over the next four years, four different congressional committees conducted five major congressional investigations into the threat of communism and alleged treasonous behavior at home. Although congressional investigations of communism in different walks of American life had begun as early as 1938 with the creation of the House Committee on Un-American Activities, it was not until after World War II that such investigations began to gather momentum. The rise of McCarthy intensified this process and gave it renewed prominence in American politics. He used these committees as his bully pulpits for investigating the government and leveling accusations of communist infiltration in America.

McCarthy was a master of publicity and use of the media to give him power over his senatorial colleagues and throughout American politics. "He would say anything that came into his head and worry later, if at all, about defending what he had said."[E] For four years, he was the master of what Rovere called the "Multiple Untruth." The accusations got bolder and wilder with time. He let scarcely a day pass without demanding the resignation of Dean Acheson or the impeachment of Harry Truman. He relied on a secret network of extremely conservative individuals and groups, in government and throughout society, especially his allies J. Edgar Hoover and the FBI (re-

A. Richard H. Rovere, *Senator Joe McCarthy* (New York: World Publishing, 1959), p. 3.
B. Robert Griffith, *The Politics of Fear: Joseph R. McCarthy and the Senate* (New York: Hayden, 1987), p. xix.
C. Rovere, *Senator Joe McCarthy*, p. 6.
D. Ibid., p. 11.
E. Ibid., p. 46.

view essay 9.1) to feed him information for his accusations and investigations. In Rovere's words, McCarthy walked "with a heavy tread over large parts of the Constitution of the United States, and he cloaked his own gross figure in the sovereignty it asserts and the power it distributes. He usurped executive and judicial authority whenever the fancy struck him. It struck him often."[F]

McCarthy's popularity represented and intensified the rise of conservatism that was gathering national force. McCarthyism represented a diverse "coalition of the aggrieved," opposed to a variety of trends of the previous few decades: the growth of the left, including communism, liberalism, the New Deal, and the welfare state; American internationalism and Atlanticism (i.e., that Europe was more important then Asia); and Franklin Roosevelt and the Democratic party. "Into [McCarthyism] came large numbers of regular Republicans who had coolly decided that there was no longer any respectable way of unhorsing the Democratic majority and that only McCarthy's wild and conscienceless politics could do the job."[G] At his height, polls indicated that a majority of the American people had a "favorable opinion" of McCarthy and felt he was serving the country in useful ways. "It was a melancholy time," Rovere has observed, "and the Chief Justice of the United States was probably right when he said at the time that if the Bill of Rights was put to a vote, it would lose."[H]

Nothing was immune from attack by Joseph McCarthy. The United Nations, the State Department, the federal government, the Truman administration, the Democratic party, academia—even the Eisenhower administration after the 1952 elections—were all charged with being infested with communists and traitors who were selling the country down the river. The truth demanded congressional investigations, often led by McCarthy and his staff. "He was a great sophisticate in human relationships, as every demagogue must be. He knew a good deal about people's fears and anxieties, and he was a superb juggler of them. But he was himself numb to the sensations he produced in others. He could not comprehend true outrage, true indignation, true anything."[I]

In 1954 McCarthy finally went too far—he attacked and investigated the United States Army for being subversive. The investigation was initiated in order to prevent one of his staffers, David Schine, from being inducted into the Army. However, it quickly ballooned out of control. McCarthy was not crushed; instead, it was as if Americans finally began to tire of his outrageous and unscrupulous behavior. This turn of events gave his Senate colleagues the courage to vote to censure him. His quick political decline led to more drinking, charges of personal corruption, and death within three years.

There was great irony in the rise and decline of Joseph McCarthy. He was a pragmatist and cynic, a great believer in the promotion of Joseph McCarthy, "a political speculator, a prospector who drilled Communism and saw it come up a gusher."[J] Nevertheless, Joseph McCarthy and McCarthyism made their political mark on American history. According to Rovere, they "had enormous impact on American foreign policy at a time when that policy bore heavily on the course of world history, and American diplomacy might bear a different aspect today if McCarthy had never lived."[K]

SOURCES: Eric F. Goldman, *The Crucial Decade—and After: America, 1945–1960* (New York: Vintage, 1960); Richard M. Fried, *Nightmare in Red: The McCarthy Era in Perspective* (New York: Oxford University Press, 1990); Robert Griffith, *The Politics of Fear: Joseph R. McCarthy and the Senate* (New York: Hayden, 1987); Godfrey Hodgson, *America in Our Time* (New York: Vintage, 1976); William Manchester, *The Glory and the Dream: A Narrative History of America, 1932–1972* (New York: Bantam, 1973); and Richard H. Rovere, *Senator Joe McCarthy* (New York: World Publishing, 1959).

F. Ibid., p. 5.
G. Ibid., p. 21.
H. Ibid., p. 23.

I. Ibid., p. 60.
J. Ibid., p. 72.
K. Ibid., p. 5.

favoring the containment goal of restoring the original status quo of a divided yet peaceful Korean Peninsula. General MacArthur, a hero of the conservative right, represented the quest for victory, the rollback of communism in North Korea, and Korean reunification. This controversy eventually died down, but the Korean War had become the Democrats' and "Truman's War," and

foreign policy issues played a prominent role in the 1952 presidential election campaign between Democratic candidate Adlai Stevenson and Republican candidate Dwight Eisenhower.

With the election of Eisenhower as president, political attacks from the right did not stop. The administration's rhetoric, particularly from Secretary of State John

Foster Dulles, emphasized the need to roll back communism and liberate people from totalitarianism. Yet President Eisenhower basically continued the foreign policy of containment initiated by President Truman. Truman had started the effort to contain Soviet communism in Europe and, with the Korean War, extended it to Asia. Under Eisenhower, the containment policy was extended throughout the world and was further institutionalized within the U.S. government. Yet in the minds of the more conservative members of Congress, nothing had really changed, and the cold war was still being lost.

The peak of antagonism in legislative-executive relations came with the dispute over an attempt by Republican senator John W. Bricker to amend the Constitution in 1953. The **Bricker amendment** would have provided Congress with the responsibility and authority to approve all international agreements (in addition to treaties) entered into by the president; in effect, conservative (and isolationist) elements in Congress did not trust the president to act in the name of the U.S. government and the American people. After a year of intense debate, the Bricker amendment failed by a single vote (60–31) to achieve the necessary two-thirds majority. One scholar has concluded, "The Bricker Amendment both symbolized and brought to an end this period of antagonism in legislative-executive relations."[9]

Congressional Acquiescence, 1955 to 1965. With the decline of McCarthyism, the cold war consensus behind U.S. foreign policy and the containment strategy solidified. This period constituted the height of bipartisanship—mutual support behind the president, regardless of party affiliation, in the making of U.S. foreign policy.[10] The cold war consensus provided the basis for presidential support within Congress and throughout American society. Criticism of U.S. foreign policy tended to come from the political right, even though that political challenge had been largely defeated. Challenges to the U.S. containment policy that might have issued from liberals and the left were overwhelmed and silenced by the rise of McCarthyism, and this legacy of McCarthyism lived on during the 1950s and 1960s. Therefore, this period was the heyday of presidential power and the president's ability to exercise prerogative government in order to fight the cold war in the name of national security.

The president's foreign policies were rarely, if ever, seriously challenged during this time of congressional acquiescence. Congress rarely gave the president all that he wanted in important areas, such as defense and foreign assistance, but except for fine-tuning of presidential requests, the president usually proposed and Congress approved. During the cold war years, members of Congress acquiesced in and supported the growing independence and preeminence of the executive branch and the president in the making of U.S. foreign policy. In fact, most members of Congress preferred to remain uninformed, even of various intelligence activities conducted in the name of national security. Thus, the demands of national security took precedence over all other concerns, and Congress virtually abdicated its constitutional role in foreign policy. According to Frank Bax, "the chief function of Congress became the legitimizing of presidential decisions."[11]

David Halberstam explained Congress's increasing acquiescence in terms of "the fear of a democracy's vulnerability to a totalitarian aggressor, a belief that the speed of war had outstripped a democracy's capacity to debate it, an abiding guilt about what the Senate in a previous era had done to the League of Nations, a fear of taking on the President and looking soft on communism, and a belief that the President had genuine experts in foreign policy, that he had *all* the information. That, and a trust of the President as an extension of the nation."[12] Given this environment, the leadership promoted congressional acquiescence. Halberstam describes Sam Rayburn, Speaker of the House of Representatives during the late 1950s:

> He had, on most crucial issues, turned the House into an extension of the executive branch, making it an offering to the President. This was not a happenstance thing, it was very deliberate on his part. He talked often in great privacy about the limits of his own knowledge, the limits of the knowledge—indeed, the ignorance—of his colleagues. Their backgrounds were terribly narrow and he was appalled by the idea of getting involved in areas of national security.[13]

The cold war consensus and bipartisanship were so supportive of the president that, in many cases, foreign policy decisions were made without consulting Congress or getting its formal approval; at best, congressional leaders might be informed after the fact. As chapter 8, on intelligence, explains, a large foreign policy bureaucracy, permeated with a strong national security ethos, was in place by the late 1950s and responded to the president's bidding in fighting the cold war. Thus, the president no longer needed to work closely with members of Congress in the pursuit of foreign policy, especially with regard to the "high" policy of national security affairs. Whereas President Dwight Eisenhower and Secretary of State John Foster Dulles were much more concerned and active in interacting with Congress to promote and maintain bipartisanship, presidential supremacy and the assumption of congressional support reached its height under presidents Kennedy and Johnson.[14]

The fateful decisions to fully Americanize the Vietnam War were made under President Johnson within the executive branch. These vital decisions of war and peace were made with virtually no input from Congress (ironically, Johnson was a former Senate majority leader). From the president's perspective, the years of presidential preeminence in foreign policy since the 1940s and the strength of the cold war consensus made congressional input appear unnecessary. The cold war consensus prevented questions from being asked about whether the United States should or should not commit itself to defend South Vietnam from communism—this commitment was automatically assumed to be in the national interest. Rather, the questions always revolved only around how much American involvement it would take to contain communist aggression and prevent the downfall of an ally.

Consider congressional action following the Gulf of Tonkin incidents in August 1964. Rather than seriously debating the pros and cons of the resolution submitted by President Johnson to gain support for his actions, members of Congress rushed the **Gulf of Tonkin resolution** through—the vote was unanimous, 416–0, in the House of Representatives and 88–2 in the Senate. In effect, President Johnson was given what he considered to be a blank check for containing communism in Southeast Asia.

Ambiguity, 1966 to 1969. By 1966 members of Congress had become somewhat uneasy about U.S. foreign policy in Vietnam. More and more troops were pouring into Vietnam, but there still seemed to be no "light at the end of the tunnel." As a result, some members of Congress began to criticize the administration's overemphasis on the use of force in Vietnam; others became critical of the lack of restraint in the use of military force. Such criticism led to a series of congressional investigations of American policy in Vietnam, best symbolized by the hearings convened by the Senate Foreign Relations Committee under the chairmanship of J. William Fulbright.

Even with increasing congressional interest and concern expressed over the policy in Vietnam, nearly all members of Congress continued to support the president. By 1967 presidential decisions arrived at without any congressional input had resulted in over 550,000 American troops being committed to war in Vietnam. Yet Congress not only refused to oppose the war but continued to appropriate the necessary funds. The popular argument in support of U.S. foreign policy in Vietnam now stressed not only the need to contain the threat of communism but, with a major commitment of American troops now involved, the need to maintain U.S. prestige and credibility throughout the world and to support "American boys" who were risking their lives for their country.

The late 1960s thus represented a time of increasing ambiguity in legislative-executive relations. Given the incredible amount of American human and material resources committed to the conflict, members of Congress became uncomfortable with the lack of progress in the war effort in Vietnam. More and more members of Congress felt that they should be consulted by the president on crucial questions of war and peace. In June 1969 the Senate passed the National Commitments Resolution by a 76–19 vote, symbolizing this increasing congressional concern. Yet most members of Congress continued to support the war effort in Vietnam by providing continued funding (to support the troops). This increasing congressional ambiguity set the stage for the congressional reassertion in legislative-executive relations that has dominated the post–Vietnam War years.

CONGRESSIONAL REASSERTION SINCE VIETNAM

In the late 1960s, Congress began to reassert its constitutional authority in the making of U.S. foreign policy. The congressional role increasingly shifted from acquiescence to reassertion because the political environment abroad and at home was undergoing change.

Congressional behavior often reflects the times, for its members are among the most politically sensitive of elected officials. *The reassertion of congressional authority in foreign policy occurred for a number of complementary reasons, most of which had to do with the Vietnam War.*

First, the war was not going well. Over half a million American troops and $30 billion a year were not producing the light at the end of the tunnel that President Johnson and General Westmoreland were proclaiming. In fact, North Vietnam launched what became known as the Tet Offensive in early 1968. Although finally beaten back by the U.S. military, the North Vietnamese successfully contested most of South Vietnam for a short time, occupying major cities and even the American embassy in Saigon. Second, the lack of success in Vietnam, especially after the Tet Offensive, caused growing segments of the American public to question LBJ's handling of the war. Some Americans favored more escalation to win the war, but increasing numbers of Americans preferred withdrawal. This change was reinforced by a third factor: international pressures. U.S. policy in Vietnam was increasingly criticized by other countries, including the British, French, and other American allies in Europe. U.S. policymakers and Americans were finding the world increasingly hostile toward its containment policy.

A fourth reason was that the election of 1968 resulted in divided government in legislative-executive relations. The Republican candidate, Richard Nixon, defeated Democratic candidate Hubert Humphrey, Johnson's vice president, in an election in which dispute over the Vietnam War played a large role. Democratic defeat gave the Republicans control of the presidency, while the Democrats controlled the Congress. This event added a more partisan dimension to legislative-executive relations by escalating the influence of party politics. The impact of party politics was exacerbated by the fact that, unlike Eisenhower, Nixon had been perceived as extremely partisan throughout his political career. Finally and of great importance, a "secret plan" to end the war advocated by Henry Kissinger, President Nixon's national security adviser, included not only withdrawing American troops but escalating the levels of military conflict to achieve "peace with honor" before the troops left. Military escalation served to intensify all of the factors discussed above and accelerated and intensified congressional reassertion.

With the growing conflict over Vietnam during the late 1960s and early 1970s, the cold war consensus that had existed throughout the U.S. government and American society came unglued. This consensus had been the key to the rise of a large national security bureaucracy, to the enormous increases in presidential foreign policy power, to the cold war policies pursued by administrations from Truman to Johnson, and to congressional acquiescence in legislative-executive relations during cold war. With the consensus breaking apart over Vietnam, congressional acquiescence evolved increasingly into congressional reassertion.

Although Nixon and Kissinger were aware of this problem, they remained committed to many elements of previous cold war policies, particularly a belief in the utility of force. Thus they pursued a "two-track policy" in Vietnam, withdrawing American troops while escalating the level of American military involvement in an attempt to force a negotiated solution on North and South Vietnam that would allow the United States to walk away from the conflict. This strategy, particularly the Vietnamization program involving withdrawal of American troops, found public support, but the military escalation triggered more domestic political opposition that was reflected in Congress. The secret bombing of Cambodia (which was leaked to the press), the 1970 invasion of Cambodia, the 1971 invasion of Laos, the 1972 mining of the harbor of Haiphong in North Vietnam, and the stepped-up bombing of North Vietnam all intensified growing antiwar sentiment throughout the country and in Congress.

A classic struggle between the legislative and the executive branches ensued. Members of Congress, increasingly reflecting the change in views, as experienced by Senator J. William Fulbright (review essay 2.3), became more active in the making of U.S. foreign policy, demanding from the president and the executive branch more information, consultation, and participation in policymaking. In fact by 1973 Congress cut off all funding of direct American military involvement in the Vietnam War; and with the end of the war, congressional reassertion intensified. In 1973 the War Powers Act was passed over President Nixon's veto, shortly followed by the Budget and Impoundment Control Act of 1974—both symbolic of congressional reassertion.

President Nixon, however, resisted congressional reassertion every step of the way. He was still operating from cold war assumptions of presidential preeminence in legislative-executive relations. As Nixon and his supporters saw it, both congressional and societal oppositional forces were obstructing the president's constitutional authority to conduct foreign policy and the war in Vietnam. Given this view, it didn't take much for the president and his men to see the antiwar movement and other opposition forces, including the Democratic party, as the enemy and as subversive—not as American citizens who were exercising their constitutional rights. Given Nixon's presidential actions and the changing political environment, more and more people decided that an "imperial presidency" had arisen and that President Nixon had stepped well beyond the boundaries of the Constitution. It was President Nixon's inability, discussed in chapter 4, to adjust to changing times that led to the constitutional crisis of Watergate and his forced resignation in 1974 (review essay 4.2).

The end of the Vietnam War and the Watergate affair released a flood of congressional involvement in foreign policy. Members of Congress not only demanded a greater role in the policymaking process but became increasingly involved in the details of foreign policy making in a wide variety of areas. Since 1974 all presidents have had to face a more powerful Congress and have had greater difficulty in governing foreign policy. In fact, every president has faced major foreign policy setbacks as a result of congressional reassertion. This factor has contributed to the general perception of "failed" presidents since the Johnson presidency: Nixon experienced Watergate; the Nixon-Ford détente policies toward the Soviet Union were thwarted by congressional concern about Jewish immigration from the Soviet Union and a covert war in Angola; Carter could not get Senate approval of SALT II; and Reagan suffered from the Iran-contra affair. This pattern appears to have continued with the end of the cold war: George Bush Sr. lost reelection after the triumph in the Persian Gulf War, and Bill Clinton suffered from the Monica Lewinsky affair and impeachment efforts.

The history of legislative-executive relations demonstrates that *the greater Congress's success in reasserting its constitutional authority, the more constrained presidents are in governing foreign policy.* Presidential preeminence in foreign policy, the norm during World War II and most of the cold war, has become the exception rather than the rule since Vietnam.

Changes in the post–Vietnam political environment have resulted in the relative decline of presidential power in the making of foreign policy and the rise of congressional involvement.[15] With the end of the cold war, as discussed in chapter 4, presidents now have more opportunity for but also greater risks in exercising power in such a fluid political environment.

In sum, two major patterns have evolved in legislative-executive relations since World War II. Presidential preeminence and congressional acquiescence have prevailed during times of national emergency and war—that is, for the twenty-five-year period encompassing World War II and much of the cold war. This has been followed by congressional reassertion and independence during a period of peace—the post–Vietnam War and post–cold war years. Presidents like Nixon and Reagan, who have attempted to exercise power in foreign policy as if the cold war political environment still existed, have triggered constitutional crises. At the same time, presidents who do not attempt to exercise any prerogative government are likely to be highly constrained in their efforts to govern foreign policy, as presidents Bush Sr. and especially Clinton experienced relative to Somalia and the former Yugoslavia.

With the September 11, 2001, attacks on the World Trade Center towers in New York City and the Pentagon in Washington, D.C., the presidency of George Bush Jr., thus far, has been very successful in declaring a state of national emergency in order to exercise prerogative government and rally political support in Congress and throughout the country. But the key in the long term for presidential and congressional power will be whether the war on terrorism will be treated as a time of war or of peace (or some combination of the two). In sum, the years since Vietnam represent a frustrating time to be president, yet they are also an exciting period of much opportunity and uncertainty in interbranch politics in U.S. foreign policy.

MAJOR INSTITUTIONAL CHANGES

How is it that Congress as an institution has been able to reassert its authority since Vietnam? Very simply, Congress has changed as an institution. The contemporary

House of Representatives and Senate are different legislative bodies from those in the past. Although bureaucracies tend to be resistant to change, Congress is a relatively "dynamic" American political institution. This is not to say that Congress easily undergoes change but that Congress is more open to change than most bureaucratic institutions.

Historically, Congress has experienced long periods of continuity, but on occasion it has also experienced short periods of rapid change. This pattern exists because Congress is composed of a relatively small number of people, and its composition and interactions tend to be heavily affected by changes in the domestic political environment. The most obvious influence is that the 435 representatives and one hundred senators are elected by the people. Very simply, the events of the 1960s and early 1970s involving the civil rights movement, the Vietnam War, and Watergate affected the political environment in such a dramatic way that major institutional changes occurred in Congress. These events have been reinforced since 1989 with the collapse of the Soviet Union and communism in Eastern Europe and the terrorist attacks of September 11, 2001.

Numerous congressional reforms and changes took place in three key areas since the early 1970s: (1) membership, (2) institutional structure and process, and (3) staffing. These changes have been instrumental in promoting and maintaining congressional reassertion in the making of U.S. foreign policy. They have created more diverse, representative, decentralized, open, informed, and independent legislative bodies.[16]

MEMBERSHIP

Congress experienced a major turnover in its membership beginning in the 1970s. Changes occurred in region, party, and ideology. Throughout the cold war years of the 1950s and 1960s, both the House and Senate were dominated by southerners, members of the Democratic party, and political conservatives. This was because key positions within Congress were awarded on the basis of **seniority,** and **southern Democrats** usually had the greatest seniority. Since the Civil War the South had been a one-party region dominated by the Democratic party. Consequently, incumbent representatives or senators from the South never faced serious Republican challengers and were rarely challenged

within the Democratic party. Because this was not the case in other regions of the country, southern Democrats acquired a disproportionate amount of seniority and influence in Congress.

The situation changed during the early 1970s. By this time, many of the more powerful southern Democrats had either died in office or retired. They were replaced by younger members of Congress who still tended to be Democrats but were less conservative. This situation resulted in a new Democratic leadership that was much more liberal and much less southern. The rise of the new leadership was reinforced by the 1974 post–Vietnam War and post-Watergate congressional elections, in which Republicans faced major losses, resulting in a large influx of new liberal Democrats into Congress.

The new Democratic leadership, in coalition with the new members of Congress, took a more activist congressional role in U.S. foreign policy. The new leaders and members were much more critical of cold war policies. The Senate, for instance, moved from a pro- to an anti-involvement stance concerning the Vietnam War primarily because war supporters had been replaced by their opponents.[17] The liberal congressional leadership and membership were also critical of congressional passivity in foreign policy, which they felt had contributed to the growth of the imperial presidency. Consequently, they promoted a number of structural and procedural changes affecting the way Congress conducted its business.

Another change in congressional membership occurred during the late 1970s and early 1980s. Beginning in 1978, Republicans and conservative members of Congress became more influential, reflecting the rise of conservatism in the domestic environment. The 1980 election was particularly important in this respect. Not only did it put Ronald Reagan in the presidency, but Republicans picked up seats in the House and gained control of the Senate for the first time since 1954. The 1994 election reinforced and intensified this trend when the Republican party became the majority party within both houses of Congress for the first time since 1932—producing a new Republican leadership represented by Newt Gingrich.

The overall result of these changes has been a more diverse, representative, and politicized Congress that contained very active liberal and conservative members, and much greater party competitiveness between the Republicans and the Democrats for control of Congress. In fact, following the 2000 elections, the Republican party lost seats in both the House and the Senate but was able to maintain majority control until one of its members in the Senate switched to independent status in early 2001. This gave the Democratic party majority control in the Senate, fifty to forty-nine (with one new independent who often votes as a Democrat), while the Republican party maintained majority control in the House of Representatives, 223 to 211. In the 2002 elections Republicans regained slight majority control of the Senate (the importance of elections will be discussed in greater depth in chapter 15).

COMMITTEES AND PROCEDURES

Throughout the 1950s and 1960s, a small group of senior members of Congress, many of whom were southern Democrats, controlled the workings of Congress. Congress did most of its work within a **committee system,** whereby each committee had jurisdiction over certain policy issues and membership consisted of no more than two dozen members of the House or Senate from both parties (the ratio of Democratic to Republican committee members reflects the ratio of Democrats to Republicans in the entire chamber—which further reinforced the importance of election outcomes). The most influential members of Congress chaired the most important committees. Due to seniority, powerful committees were frequently dominated by older, more conservative members, who tended to be southern Democrats.

A small group of congressional "barons" thus enjoyed the real power within Congress. Most of the old House and Senate leaders were staunch cold warriors and were part of the cold war consensus that pervaded American government and society, thus accounting for the bipartisanship that prevailed in foreign policy. Such a situation also helps to explain why no civil rights legislation was passed by Congress until after the landslide Democratic victory in 1964. This election infused Congress with new blood, which was reinforced by the backing of a very strong legislative president—Lyndon Johnson.

The change in congressional membership during the 1970s also produced changes in the distribution and exercise of power within Congress. The new Demo-

cratic liberal leadership *changed the congressional committee rules of the game.* Power was stripped from committees and in particular from committee chairs. Every committee was now required to have multiple subcommittees, subdividing both issues and committee membership. Also, no committee member could be chair of more than one of its subcommittees, further dispersing the distribution of power. Thus, power has moved from committees and committee chairs to subcommittees and subcommittee chairs. The dynamics of each committee and subcommittee naturally are heavily dependent not only on its historical context, functions, structure, and subculture but also on the personalities and styles of its members, especially the chair (and to a lesser extent, the ranking minority member).

More committees (and subcommittees) also have gained jurisdiction over foreign policy issues. For example, new committees covering intelligence and the budget were created. Furthermore, while the Armed Services, Foreign Relations, and Intelligence committees of both chambers are actively involved in national security affairs, many other committees have become more active in foreign policy. This has been especially the case for other types of international issues, such as trade, finance, energy, transportation, communications, tourism, technology and space, immigration, and the environment—all of which have grown in importance in foreign policy. These changes have resulted in greater committee and congressional involvement in the making of U.S. foreign policy. (See **tables 11.1** and **11.2** for a listing of relevant committees and subcommittees, and notice the recent changes in majority party status and committee membership by party).

Congressional procedures were also changed. During the cold war, congressional barons generally exercised power behind the scenes, often holding committee hearings and votes behind closed doors. Congressional reforms during the 1970s resulted in a much more open and democratic process. Most formal committee activity is now open to the media and the public. Furthermore, changes have taken place in floor voting, which involves all members of Congress in each chamber. Voice votes (the option to vote as a group and thus remain unaccountable) have been mostly replaced by roll-call votes, in which each member must take an independent public stand on the issue.

The greater openness of congressional procedures does not mean that no informal interaction and

TABLE 11.1
MEMBERSHIP OF HOUSE COMMITTEES WITH JURISDICTION OVER FOREIGN POLICY

COMMITTEE (TOTAL SUBCOMMITTEES) RELEVANT SUBCOMMITTEES	103RD CONG. 1993–1994 DEMS./REPS.	104TH CONG. 1995–1996 DEMS./REPS.	106TH CONG. 1999–2000 DEMS./REPS.	107TH CONG. 2001–2002 DEMS./REPS.
Agriculture (5)	28/19	22/27	24/27	24/27
Specialty Crops & Foreign Agriculture Programs*	7/4	10/10	NC	8/9
Appropriations (13)	37/23	24/32	27/34	29/35
Commerce, Justice & State+	5/3	3/4	6/4	5/8
Foreign Operations & Export Financing+	7/4	4/8	5/7	5/8
Military Construction	7/4	4/6	5/7	5/8
Armed Services (5)	34/22	25/30	28/32	28/32
Military Installations & Facilities	12/8	8/9	8/9	8/10
Military Personnel	8/6	7/8	8/9	8/10
Military Procurement	NC	12/14	13/14	13/15
Military Readiness	9/6	9/10	10/11	10/12
Military Research and Development	12/8	11/13	13/14	13/15
Budget (0)	26/17	18/24	19/24	20/24
Education & the Workforce (5)+	28/15	19/24	22/27	22/27
21st-Century Competitiveness*	NC	NC	NC	9/11
Energy and Commerce (6)+	27/17	21/25	24/29	26/31
Commerce, Trade & Consumer Protection+	6/4	9/9	12/14	12/15
Telecommunications & the Internet+	13/8	11/12	12/14	14/17
Financial Services + (6)	30/20	22/27	27/32	32/37
International Monetary Policy & Trade+	13/10	8/9	11/13	13/14
Government Reform (8)	25/17	22/27	19/24	19/24
National Security, Veterans' Affairs & Intl. Relations+	6/4	7/7	6/9	9/11
International Relations+ (6)	18/27	19/23	23/26	23/26
Africa	5/3	5/6	4/5	4/5
East Asia & The Pacific+	5/4	6/7	10/11	7/8
Europe*	NC	NC	NC	8/10
International Operations & Human Rights	7/5	6/7	6/7	4/6
Middle East & South Asia*	NC	NC	NC	9/11
Western Hemisphere	5/4	6/5	7/8	5/6
Judiciary (5)	21/14	15/20	16/21	17/21
Immigration & Claims	5/4	5/6	5/7	5/7
Permanent Select Committee on Intelligence+ (3)	12/7	7/9	7/9	9/11
Human Intelligence, Analysis & Counterintelligence	NC	4/5	4/5	4/7
Intelligence Policy & National Security*	NC	NC	NC	4/6
Technical & Tactical Intelligence	NC	4/5	4/5	5/7
Resources (5)	28/15	20/25	24/28	25/28
Energy & Mineral Resources	8/6	6/7	8/8	8/9
Science (4)	33/22	23/27	22/25	22/25
Energy+	9/5	12/14	7/8	6/8
Environment, Technology and Standards+	17/12	5/6	9/10	9/10
Space & Aeronautics	15/9	10/11	13/14	10/12
Small Business (4)	27/18	19/22	17/19	17/19
Tax, Finance & Exports	5/4	5/6	4/4	7/8
Transportation & Infrastructure (6)	29/19	28/33	34/41	34/42
Aviation	20/13	12/13	22/26	20/24
Coast Guard & Maritime Transportation	14/9	4/4	3/3	4/5
Veterans' Affairs (3)	21/14	15/18	14/17	14/17
Ways and Means (6)	24/14	15/21	16/23	17/24
Trade	8/5	6/8	6/8	6/9
TOTAL Committees: 19 House Membership:	258/176	204/230	211/222	212/221

*Jurisdiction of committee or subcommittee is new or has changed over time.

+Title of committee or subcommittee has changed over time.

NC: No comparable committee or subcommittee exists.

The 2002 election outcome was 204/226. The distribution of seats in the 108th Cong (2003–2004) would be similar to the 104th Cong.

SOURCE: *The Almanac of American Politics*, Congressional Quarterly's *Politics in America*.

TABLE 11.2
MEMBERSHIP OF SENATE COMMITTEES WITH JURISDICTION OVER FOREIGN POLICY

COMMITTEE (TOTAL SUBCOMMITTEES) RELEVANT SUBCOMMITTEES	103RD CONG. 1993–1994 DEMS./REPS.	104TH CONG. 1995–1996 DEMS./REPS.	106TH CONG. 1999–2000 DEMS./REPS.	107TH CONG. 2001–2002 DEMS./REPS.
Agriculture, Nutrition and Forestry (4)	10/8	8/9	8/10	11/10
Marketing, Inspection & Product Promotion	5/5	4/4	3/3	5/5
Appropriations (13)	16/13	13/15	13/15	15/14
Commerce, Justice, State & Judiciary	5/5	5/5	5/5	6/6
Defense	9/8	8/8	8/8	9/9
Foreign Operations	6/6	6/6	6/6	7/7
Military Construction	3/3	3/3	3/3	4/4
Armed Services (6)	11/9	10/11	9/11	13/12
Airland Forcess	NC	6/6	4/4	6/6
Emerging Threats & Capabilities	NC	NC	4/4	6/6
Personnel	3/3	3/3	3/3	5/5
Readiness & Management Support	3/3	4/4	5/5	6/6
Seapower	NC	4/4	3/3	5/5
Strategic Forces	5/5	5/5	9/11	11/10
Banking, Housing & Urban Affairs (5)	11/8	7/9	9/11	11/10
International Trade & Finance	5/5	4/4	4/4	3/3
Budget (0)	12/9	10/12	10/12	12/11
Commerce, Science & Transportation (7)	11/9	9/10	9/11	12/11
Aviation	4/4	7/7	8/9	9/9
Communications	7/6	7/7	8/8	10/10
Consumer Affairs, Foreign Commerce & Tourism[+]	5/3	4/4	2/4	6/6
Manufacturing & Competitiveness	NC	NC	4/4	3/3
Oceans & Fisheries	4/7	3/3	3/3	5/5
Science, Technology & Space	4/4	4/4	4/4	7/7
Surface Transportation & Merchant Marine[+]	3/2	5/5	6/7	9/9
Energy & Natural Resources (4)	11/9	7/11	9/11	12/11
Environment & Public Works (4)	10/7	7/9	8/10	10/9
Clean Air, Wetlands, Private Property & Nuclear Safety	3/3	3/3	3/3	4/4
Finance (5)	11/9	9/11	9/11	11/10
International Trade	9/7	7/6	8/8	8/8
Foreign Relations (7)	11/8	8/10	8/10	10/9
African Affairs	2/2	2/2	2/2	3/3
East Asia & Pacific Affairs	3/3	4/4	4/4	4/4
European Affairs	3/3	4/4	4/4	4/4
International Economic Policy, Export & Trade Promotion	5/5	3/3	3/3	4/4
International Operations & Terrorism[+]	4/4	4/4	3/3	4/4
Near Eastern & South Asian Affairs	4/4	4/4	4/4	4/4
Western Hemisphere, Peace Corps, Narcotics Affairs[+]	3/3	3/3	3/3	4/4
Governmental Affairs (3)	8/5	7/8	7/9	9/8
International Security, Proliferation & Federal Services	2/2	NC	5/5	6/6
Intelligence (0)	9/8	8/9	8/9	9/8
Judiciary (6)	10/8	8/10	8/10	10/9
Immigration	1/1	3/3	3/3	5/5
Technology, Terrorism & Government Information	2/2	3/3	3/3	4/4
Veterans' Affairs (0)	7/5	4/8	5/7	8/7
TOTAL Committees: 20 Senate Membership:	57/43	48/52	45/55	50/49

*Jurisdiction of committee or subcommittee is new or has changed over time.

[+]Title of committee or subcommittee has changed over time.

NC: No comparable committee or subcommittee exists.

The 2002 election outcome was 47/51, The distribution of seats in the 108th Cong (2003–2004) would be similar to the 104th Cong.

SOURCE: The Almanac of American Politics, Congressional Quarterly's *Politics in America*.

bargaining occur behind the scenes. These continue for they have always been an essential element of politics. In fact, committee hearings and activities concerning issues, such as intelligence, that members of the executive branch define as grave matters of national security continue to be closed to the public. Nevertheless, congressional procedures are more open today than in the past (as reflected in C-Span television coverage of House and Senate hearings and proceedings in the two chambers).

Decentralization of power and more-public procedures also have affected the **legislative norms** governing congressional operations. It could be argued that a strong congressional subculture existed under the centralized, "old boy" leadership of the past. Structural and procedural changes have altered the norms of specialization and apprenticeship promoted by the old-boy network, particularly in the Senate. Nevertheless, legislative norms continue to prevail that affect formal and informal congressional behavior, despite the increase in partisanship and politicization. These include the importance of seniority (i.e., years one has been a member), reciprocity ("you scrub my back and I scrub your back"), public collegiality (despite partisan differences), and constituent casework (for the folks in the home district or state) for representatives and senators.[18]

Overall, these changes in committee structure and jurisdiction, procedures, and behavioral norms have provided the foundation for members of Congress to become more active in the making of foreign policy. Although many analysts argue that these changes allow for the possibility for a more informed public and greater democratic accountability, other observers argue that they have had detrimental effects as well, such as reinforcing congressional preoccupation with reelection, political posturing, and dependence on key interest groups.

STAFFING

During the cold war, members of Congress tended to have very small support staffs, giving the executive branch a decisive advantage in foreign policy making. The executive branch enjoyed a virtual monopoly of information, on which Congress was totally dependent. It is commonly argued that this dependence was rein-

forced by the tendency of most members of Congress to place their faith in the president and support his conduct of foreign policy. In either case, the lack of congressional support staff and information contributed to congressional acquiescence throughout the 1950s and 1960s.

An important source of power is control of information. Congressional reformers during the 1970s realized that this deficiency had to be addressed if Congress were to seriously reassert its authority in foreign policy. Consequently, **congressional staffs** *expanded tremendously during and after Vietnam*—for the individual member, the committee, and congressional support agencies. Individual representatives and senators began to enjoy the presence of large personal staffs, consisting of up to a few dozen individuals. Committee staffs of both the majority and minority parties, such as for the Senate Committee on Foreign Relations, also expanded tremendously in size. With the increase in staffing, members of Congress were no longer as dependent on the executive branch for information about foreign policy and world affairs.

Congress also increased the size of its support agencies and began using them consistently. The General Accounting Office, Congressional Research Service, and Congressional Budget Office are nonpartisan research agencies intended to support the members and committees of Congress. The **General Accounting Office (GAO),** the largest support agency, employing almost twenty thousand people, is the investigative arm of Congress and engages in oversight of the executive branch. The **Congressional Research Service (CRS),** with almost fifteen thousand people, provides research and analysis on issues of importance to congressional committees and individual members of Congress. Finally, the **Congressional Budget Office (CBO),** created in 1974 to provide financial and budgetary information and assessments, gives Congress an alternative to reliance on the executive's Office of Management and Budget.[19]

Clearly, members of Congress now have independent sources of information and are no longer as dependent on the executive branch. The personal, committee, and support agency staffs in Congress have expanded so quickly and become so large that we can now speak of the existence of a congressional bureaucracy that employs over fifty thousand people. Although adding to the bureaucracy, staff increases have contributed to congressional reassertion in foreign policy. These changes in congressional membership, committees and procedures, and support systems have produced a more independent, active, and influential body in the making of U.S. foreign policy.

GENERAL INTERBRANCH MODELS AND PATTERNS

To what extent is Congress a force to be reckoned with in the making of contemporary U.S. foreign policy? There is no consensus answer to this question. *Three models or schools of thought have evolved concerning the contemporary legislative-executive foreign policy relationship.*[20] One school still perceives **presidential dominance**—that the president remains the dominant actor. These scholars recognize Congress's assertion of greater authority in foreign policy but argue that this reassertion has constrained the president only minimally and that he has maintained his role as the major actor in foreign affairs.[21] A second school of thought believes that the contemporary legislative-executive relationship is one of **codetermination.** The argument is that Congress has successfully asserted its authority and has become a formidable force in the realm of foreign affairs—an equal actor with the executive branch.[22] The third school of thought argues that the pendulum has swung in favor of Congress in foreign affairs—that **congressional dominance** now prevails. Proponents emphasize that congressional constraints on the president have become so great that his ability to formulate and implement the nation's foreign policy has diminished considerably.[23]

All three models or schools of thought—presidential dominance, codetermination, and congressional dominance—paint an overly simplistic picture of the complex politics of legislative-executive relations. *No simple answer or single relationship prevails today between the legislative and executive branches in the making of U.S. foreign policy. Rather, a much more complex reality in legislative-executive relations has existed since the Vietnam War due to four important factors:*

1. the type of issue involved,
2. Congress's tendency to be a reactive body,
3. Congress's nature as the ultimate political institution, and
4. divided government as increasingly the norm.

First, the type of issue affects legislative-executive relations. On the one hand, the more an issue involves questions of war, the more likely it is that the president will continue to enjoy disproportionate influence in the making of policy for that issue. For example, Congress has attempted to reassert its authority over war powers but with only limited success. This is not to say that the president is as preeminent in the use of troops abroad as he was during the cold war years; the times have changed and the president faces more domestic constraints. However, he continues to exercise considerable power concerning the use of force abroad. On the other hand, the more an issue becomes divorced from the use of force, the more likely it is that Congress will play an active and influential role in the policymaking process. Thus, the type of issue on the political agenda is very important in determining the nature of interbranch politics.[24]

The second pattern to consider is that Congress tends to be a reactive body. The president usually initiates foreign policy, and the executive branch actually implement it. When Congress becomes involved in foreign policy, it tends to be in reaction to presidential initiatives and policies pursued by the executive branch. There are times when and issues for which Congress takes the initiative, but they are rare. Congress is reactive in another way as well. Not only is congressional action usually in response to executive action, but *congressional involvement in policy tends to be of a focused, specialized, and legalistic nature.* The president tends to set the policy agenda and frame the issues that Congress addresses, while Congress is more competent in influencing the specific features of a policy. Many scholars have long argued that Congress should focus on large policy questions and guidelines while leaving the details of policy to the executive branch. However, for better or worse, Congress is best equipped for manipulating policy details (it should be noted that most members of Congress have backgrounds in the legal profession).[25]

The third pattern to consider is that Congress is the ultimate political body within the U.S. government. Members of Congress are "political animals" who are preoccupied with their institutional status and power, their electoral security, and how they are perceived within and beyond the Washington beltway. They tend to be obsessed with reelection and are constantly soliciting funds from private contributors for reelection campaigns. A preoccupation with reelection also makes

ESSAY 11.2
NEWT GINGRICH, POLITICAL AMBITION, AND THE RISE AND DECLINE OF POWER

As a result of the election of 1994, Newt Gingrich became the first Republican Speaker of the House of Representatives in over forty years. After four decades of Democratic rule and being in the political wilderness for so long, the Republican party finally had the opportunity to exercise major political influence and to govern. And for Gingrich, he had finally achieved what he had been striving for throughout much of his life. He was on top of the "political world" in January of 1995. But within two years, Gingrich had fallen from political grace. He lost so much public support so quickly that he had become a political "pariah."

What happened to Gingrich and the so-called Republican revolution? As Garry Wills stated, "the villain in the piece was, as is usual in such cases, also the hero." Gingrich was undone by his own devices. He had the genius to invent the "congressional mandate," and the gullibility to believe in his own invention. A master of destructive techniques, he did not suspect that mere destruction destroys itself. Much of this had to do with Gingrich's **political ambition,** with his unrelenting quest for power and glory in the world of politics.

"Washington lies at the epicenter of power. All force collides here. In Washington resides the power to take money and spend money, the power to decide what people can do and what people cannot do, the power to make a nation strong or weak, the power to wage war or make peace." This is the political world of Washington, D.C., as described by journalist John Barry in *The Ambition and the Power*. It is not uncommon for individuals to strive to be on top of such a world, although it is very difficult to achieve as well as to maintain.

As explained by Barry, "By rising he exposed himself, made himself a target, and exposed his weaknesses. Now those weaknesses would be explored, probed, stressed, tested, to see if they could withstand the pressure. Perhaps his biggest weakness was ambition itself, an ambition dangerously close to hubris." In fact, "it was hubris, and the admixture of arrogance and innocence in him, to demand that others see the world his way," and to believe "that rules did not apply to him." Barry actually was describing the rise and fall of Jim Wright, the Democratic Speaker of the House during the eighties. Newt Gingrich was instrumental in bringing Wright down, leading to his eventual rise as Speaker of the House. But what Barry described about politics in Washington and about Jim Wright also pertained to Newt Gingrich.

When Gingrich took the podium for the first time as Speaker in 1995, Republicans chanted, "Newt. Newt. Newt." He had a forceful presence, constantly offering new ideas for the future of the country. With the landslide electoral victory producing a huge Republican triumph behind the "*Contract with America*," he was opposed to the president's and Democrats' agenda. He seemed to enjoy being confrontational. He encouraged partisan politics, while readily espousing his knowledge and thoughts. He loved the limelight and all the attention he was getting. For a while, he was so much in the spotlight that he declared himself more important then President Clinton.

But Gingrich's ambition and hubris—his exaggerated self-confidence to the point of arrogance—quickly got him into trouble and made him increasingly vulnerable politically. He was offered and agreed to a $4.5 million advance to write a book while Speaker of the House—a situation similar to the one that triggered the eventual fall of Jim Wright—thus creating a political controversy that eventually forced him to give up the advance. In fact, after serving as the driving force to get Jim Wright to resign as Speaker because of violation of ethics charges, Gingrich started to understand the proverb "What goes around, comes around." A two-year investigation by a panel of two Republicans and two Democrats found that Gingrich used tax-exempt charitable contributions to fund a televised college course that was deemed as a "recruiting vehicle," and he was fined $300,000. In addition, his confrontation with President Clinton peaked in the winter of 1996 in the fight over the budget, in which Gingrich and the Republicans forced the government to shut down for several days—a tactic that backfired with the public.

By this time, Gingrich's personality, leadership tactics, and behavior were increasingly self-destructive for him and for the Republicans. He was too much in the spotlight and overexposed, turning off many people. The public, as well as members of his own party, began to sour on Newt Gingrich. As Gary Wills commented, Gingrich became "the most unpopular politician on the national scene. Even those who disliked Gingrich had, heretofore, credited him with political shrewdness. Now they were wondering about that." The Republican's ability to dominate the agenda and influence politics that the 1994 election provided was being lost.

Gingrich's public approval declined so dramatically that members of his own party actually tried to overthrow him as Speaker. Although reelected as Speaker of the House in 1997, nine Republicans voted against him, and many other Republicans openly admitted that they voted for him only out of party loyalty (and because no better candidate was available). Within two years, Gingrich had seen his ambition, power, and glory run aground. His loss of political clout and public appeal made him a kind of lame duck Speaker.

Actually, the patterns of great victory and defeat have accompanied Gingrich throughout much of his political life. Gingrich has demonstrated little reluctance or remorse to do what is necessary to gain prominence and power until he pushes too hard and takes a fall. Once a member of the House without much influence, he fastened tightly when an opportunity came. He would come out hard and fast, conceding to no one—not even the president. Later, after political blunders, he would vanish, only to return with a newly waxed halo. After regaining his confidence and with a new strategy, he would offer an olive branch to his enemies and those he bruised along the way, only to shortly turn around and engage in hardball politics once again. Such a pattern has served him well, but in the incredibly visible arena of national politics it may be more difficult for people to for-

get, and maybe to forgive. Unlike Ronald Reagan and even Bill Clinton, who were seen as more personable and likable, Newt Gingrich's image was much more one of arrogance.

The political ambition, and quest for power and glory, is not unique to Newt Gingrich. In 2002, Republican Trent Lott was forced to resign as Senate Majority Leader in response to racist comments he made. Striving to get to the top is very much a part of the world of politics. Naturally, much of what transpires depends on the man and the times. And ultimately, what John Barry said of Jim Wright clearly applies to Newt Gingrich and others as well: He "had a brief, shining moment in the sun. He was alone, soaring above his colleagues, above the Congress, above the White House, his will his wings. He soared above the moment. For a moment."

SOURCES: John M. Barry, *The Ambition and the Power* (New York: Penguin, 1989); Lloyd Etheredge, "Hardball Politics: A Model," *Political Psychology* (spring 1979): 3–26; Newt Gingrich, *To Renew America* (New York: HarperCollins, 1995); Joan Didion, "The Teachings of Speaker Gingrich," *New York Review of Books* (August 10, 1995), pp. 10–13; Garry Wills, "What Happened to the Revolution," *New York Review of Books* (June 6, 1996), pp. 11–16; Hanna Rosin, "Newest Newt," *New Republic* (December 16, 1996), pp. 12–16.

them overly sensitive to public perceptions, political support, political trends, and their public images. If the public and their constituents are interested in an issue and have staked out a position, members of Congress tend to reflect the dominant public mood. If the public is uninterested, members of Congress have more freedom of action; yet they are constantly pressured by the president, executive agencies, congressional colleagues, special interest groups, and their constituents.[26]

No matter how politically conscious members of Congress may be, they must attempt to present a public image that depicts them as "above politics," motivated only by constituent and national interests. This is reinforced by the fact that the president is also extremely image conscious and politically oriented. Therefore, the particular nature of executive-legislative relations is often difficult to anticipate, and congressional behavior is influenced by political considerations, domestic political trends, and symbolic politics. For example, for all their talk about the human rights violations committed by Iraq during the 1980s, Congress rarely acted, and when it did, members' self-interested actions usually reinforced the Reagan and Bush Sr. administration's policies in sup-

port of Iraq (against Iran), hence contributing to Saddam Hussein's miscalculation of U.S. resolve and interests in the region leading to the Persian Gulf War of 1991.[27]

Also important, the Congress's political dynamics are also impacted by the personal agendas, leadership skills, and personalities of the members. The rise of Newt Gingrich as Speaker of the House in 1995 clearly demonstrates the role of politics and symbolism, ambition and power, and how quickly they can ebb and flow in the contemporary era (see **essay 11.2**).

Finally, divided government appears to have become endemic in American politics since the 1968 election. **Divided government** occurs when the Congress and presidency are controlled by different political parties, increasing the likelihood for interbranch disagreement and conflict. Such divided government has grown over time: From 1901 to 1944, divided government prevailed only 14 percent of the time (for six years); from 1945 to 1968, it prevailed 33 percent of the time (for eight years); but from 1969 to 2002, divided government increased dramatically to over 80 percent of the time—for twenty-eight years of the past thirty-four years (see **table 11.3** on party control of the presidency

TABLE 11.3

PARTY CONTROL OF THE PRESIDENCY AND CONGRESS IN THE TWENTIETH CENTURY

CONGRESS	YEARS	PRESIDENT	PARTY	SENATE D	SENATE R	SENATE OTHER	HOUSE D	HOUSE R	HOUSE OTHER
57th	1901–03	McKinley	R	32	56	2	153	198	5
		T. Roosevelt	R						
58th	1903–05	T. Roosevelt	R	33	57	—	178	207	—
59th	1905–07	T. Roosevelt	R	33	57	—	136	250	—
60th	1907–09	T. Roosevelt	R	31	61	—	164	222	—
61st	1909–11	Taft	R	32	61	—	172	219	—
62nd	1911–13	Taft	R	41	51	—	228*	162	1
63rd	1913–15	Wilson	D	51	44	1	290	127	18
64th	1915–17	Wilson	D	56	40	—	230	193	8
65th	1917–19	Wilson	D	53	42	—	210	216*	9
66th	1919–21	Wilson	D	47	49*	—	191	237*	7
67th	1921–23	Harding	R	37	59	—	132	300	1
68th	1923–25	Coolidge	R	43	51	2	207	225	3
69th	1925–27	Coolidge	R	39	56	1	183	247	5
70th	1927–29	Coolidge	R	46	49	1	195	237	3
71st	1929–31	Hoover	R	39	56	1	163	267	1
72d	1931–33	Hoover	R	47	48	1	220*	218	1
73d	1933–35	F. Roosevelt	D	60	35	1	313	117	5
74th	1935–37	F. Roosevelt	D	69	25	2	322	103	10
75th	1937–39	F. Roosevelt	D	76	16	4	333	89	13
76th	1939–41	F. Roosevelt	D	69	23	4	262	169	4
77th	1941–43	F. Roosevelt	D	66	28	2	267	162	6
78th	1943–45	F. Roosevelt	D	57	37	1	222	209	4
79th	1945–47	Truman	D	56	38	1	243	190	2
80th	1947–49	Truman	D	45	51*	—	188	246*	1
81st	1949–51	Truman	D	54	42	—	263	171	1
82d	1951–53	Truman	D	49	47	—	234	199	2
83d	1953–55	Eisenhower	R	47	48	1	213	221	1
84th	1955–57	Eisenhower	R	48*	47	1	232*	203	—
85th	1957–59	Eisenhower	R	49*	47	—	234*	201	—
86th	1959–61	Eisenhower	R	65*	35	—	283*	154	—
87th	1961–63	Kennedy	D	65	35	—	263	174	—
88th	1963–65	Kennedy	D	67	33	—	258	176	—
89th	1965–67	Johnson	D	68	32	—	295	140	—
		Johnson	D						
90th	1967–69	Johnson	D	64	36	—	248	187	—
91st	1969–71	Nixon	R	57*	43	—	243*	192	—
92d	1971–73	Nixon	R	54*	44	2	255*	180	—
93d	1973–75	Nixon	R	56*	42	2	243*	192	—
		Ford	R						
94th	1975–77	Ford	R	60*	37	2	291*	144	—
95th	1977–79	Carter	D	61	38	1	292	143	—
96th	1979–81	Carter	D	58	41	1	277	158	—
97th	1981–83	Reagan	R	46	53	1	243*	192	—
98th	1983–85	Reagan	R	45	55	—	269*	166	—
99th	1985–87	Reagan	R	47	53	—	253*	182	—
100th	1987–89	Reagan	R	54*	46	—	258*	177	—
101st	1989–91	Bush	R	55*	45	—	260*	175	—
102d	1991–93	Bush	R	56*	44	—	267*	167	1
103d	1993–95	Clinton	D	57	43	—	258	176	1
104th	1995–97	Clinton	D	48	52*	—	204	230	1
105th	1997–99	Clinton	D	45	55*	—	206	228*	1
106th	1999–01	Clinton	D	45	55*	—	211	222*	2
107th	2001–03	Bush	R	50*	49	1	212	221	2
108th	2003–05	Bush	R	46	51	1	203	226	1

*Chamber controlled by party other than that of the president.

NOTE: D, Democrat; R, Republican. Some seats were vacant or changed parties within a two-year Congress at times.

and Congress in the twentieth century). As James Sundquist recognized over a decade ago, "the country passed from a long era of party government, when either the Republican or the Democratic Party controlled both the presidency and the Congress almost all of the time, to an era when the government was divided between the parties most of the time."[28]

The existence of divided government is consequential because members of the party in opposition to the president can exercise greater control within Congress as a result of their majority status. This gives the opposition party the ability to dominate the organization of Congress—in leadership positions (such as Speaker of the House and Senate majority leader), as chairs of committees and subcommittees, and with majority representation on each and every committee and subcommittee (review tables 11.1 and 11.2 for the distribution of Republican and Democratic members over the last decade). Hence, President Bill Clinton, a Democrat, had to deal with a Congress that organizationally was dominated by Republicans. And President Bush Jr., despite strong initial political support for his war on terrorism, had to deal before the midterm elections with an even more complex situation in which the House had a Republican majority but the Senate had a Democratic majority. And unlike the fifties and sixties, which were times of bipartisanship and a cold war consensus—minimizing the impact of divided government in the making of foreign policy—divided government since Vietnam has been much more prone to promote conflict with the collapse of bipartisanship and the anticommunist consensus.[29]

In sum, the president tended to be predominant in the making of U.S. foreign policy during the cold war. However, there has been no simple trend in legislative-executive relations since Vietnam and the end of the cold war. Political scientist Bruce Jentleson found in a 1990 study that "'Pennsylvania Avenue diplomatic relations' on major issues of U.S. international diplomacy were characterized by four distinct patterns." First, on a number of regional issues—Nicaragua, South Africa, and arms sales to Saudi Arabia and other Arab states—there was outright "confrontation." Second, there was generalized "institutional competition" over much of the day-to-day conduct of diplomacy, such as foreign assistance. Third, on military aid to El Salvador and the leadership crisis in the Philippines, "constructive compromise" was eventually worked out.

Finally, for a number of issues—such as the use of force in Afghanistan and the Persian Gulf (to reflag Kuwait tankers) and relations with the Soviet Union and the People's Republic of China, especially late in the Bush Sr. administration—"bipartisan cooperation" prevailed.[30]

One could add that the Persian Gulf War under President Bush Sr., the Kosovo War under President Clinton, and the initial response to the September 11 terrorist attacks and President Bush's war on terrorism are all contemporary illustrations of bipartisan cooperation (and presidential dominance). But for other foreign policy issues, presidents Bush Sr., Clinton, and even Bush Jr. have had to face the other three patterns as well. Therefore, no one interbranch model prevails, and U.S. foreign policy is increasingly a function of diverse patterns in the complex politics of legislative-executive interaction.[31]

CONTEMPORARY INTERBRANCH POLITICS

To better understand congressional influence and legislative-executive relations in U.S. foreign policy, we will examine four general areas: (1) the war powers, (2) advice and consent, (3) the power to appropriate funds and to make laws, and (4) the power of oversight and investigation. These are not mutually exclusive categories. The Iran-contra affair, the 1991 Persian Gulf War, and the current war on terrorism, for example, have involved Congress in almost all of these areas. A brief examination of each area should help clarify questions concerning congressional influence and the president's ability to govern foreign policy.

THE WAR POWERS

The use of American armed forces abroad has been the factor most responsible for the growth of presidential power and the straining of relations between Congress and the president. Only Congress has the constitutional authority to declare war. Louis Henkin has summarized the constitutional foundation of the power to make war in his *Foreign Affairs and the Constitution:* "There is no evidence that the framers contemplated any significant independent role—or authority—for the President as the Commander in chief when there was no war."[32] Yet Congress has declared war just five times in American history, while presidents have committed military forces abroad in over two hundred instances. Therefore, as discussed above on the history of legislative-executive relations, the president's power over questions of war has grown remarkably over time, particularly during times of conflict.

Presidential power in the use of force reached its peak during World War II and continued during the cold war. For example, President Truman committed American troops to the Korean Peninsula in 1950 to defend against the North Korean invasion. Yet the Korean War was never officially declared by Congress. It was a presidential war; American involvement was initiated, formulated, approved, and implemented within the executive branch. Congress stayed in the background, remaining acquiescent and providing support. Throughout the cold war, the president directed American forces in a very similar fashion, intervening overtly and covertly around the globe.

Only after the bitter experience with the Vietnam War did Congress attempt to redress the imbalance. With the collapse of the cold war consensus, President Nixon's escalatory actions in Vietnam resulted in numerous antiwar proposals in Congress. Members were at first unable to obtain enough support to pass the resolutions. However, in the spring of 1973, they finally cut off all funding for direct American military intervention in Indochina, foreshadowing a major attempt by Congress to regain control of its lost war power.

Members of Congress had become frustrated with their ineffectual influence on American military involvement in Indochina and on the scope of U.S. foreign military commitments abroad during the cold war. Consequently, they overrode a veto by President Nixon and enacted a bill designed to limit the president's power to commit American armed forces abroad without congressional approval. The purpose of the War Powers Act was "to fulfill the intent of the framers of the Constitution of the United States and insure that the collective judgment of both the Congress and the President will apply to the introduction of United States Armed Forces" into conflict situations abroad.[33]

The **War Powers Act (WPA)** *attempted to redress the historical growth of presidential war-making power in three ways:* by requiring "presidential consultation" before troops are committed abroad; "presidential re-

porting" after troops are committed; and "congressional action" if American troops abroad become involved in a "situation of hostilities." In the latter situation, three outcomes were envisioned as possible: by doing nothing, Congress would force the president to withdraw the troops after ninety days; Congress could terminate the military intervention before ninety days; or it could extend the ninety-day deadline. (See **essay 11.3** for the specific requirements of the War Powers Act.) The WPA represented a major symbolic effort at congressional reassertion and complicates the president's ability to use force abroad, yet it has not fundamentally altered the president's preeminent position over the power to make war.[34]

How effective has the War Powers Act been in restoring joint legislative-executive possession of the war-making power? It appears that early pronouncements proclaiming a major redistribution of power in legislative-executive relations were exaggerated. Since 1973 the president has used U.S. armed forces abroad in numerous situations involving the War Powers Act. These have included military efforts to evacuate Americans abroad; the Mayaguez incident in Indochina; the Iran hostage rescue attempt; the placement of peacekeeping forces in Lebanon; military encounters with Libya; the reflagging of Kuwaiti tankers in the Persian Gulf; the invasions of Grenada and Panama; the deployment of over 500,000 American troops in the Persian Gulf, who eventually engaged in war; continual air combat with Iraq since that war; the use of military troops in Somalia, Haiti, and Bosnia; and the current military campaign in Afghanistan and against terrorism. In each case, the president initiated, formulated, and approved the use of military troops without congressional participation. The congressional role remained limited even after the commitment of troops, with Lebanon being the major exception and representing the height of congressional involvement under the War Powers Act. Thus, the record suggests that the WPA has had little impact on presidential preeminence over policy formulation and only limited influence on policy implementation involving the actual use of force abroad.

In reality, the War Powers Act has given the president great leeway to initiate, formulate, and approve the use of American armed force overseas. This is because the act does not actually require prior presidential consultation with Congress but rather consultation

ESSAY 11.3
REQUIREMENTS OF THE WAR POWERS ACT

The first requirement of the War Powers Act (WPA) is presidential consultation. During the cold war years, the president usually circumvented Congress entirely and informed members only after the decision to use force had been made. According to the War Powers Act, "the President in every possible instance shall consult with Congress before introducing United States Armed Forces" into situations of conflict abroad and "after such introduction shall consult regularly with the Congress until" they have been removed from such situations.[A] Congress intended that the president consult with them *before* a final decision was made.

The second requirement is presidential reporting. According to subsection 4(a) of the WPA, the president shall submit a report to Congress within forty-eight hours if, in the absence of a declaration of war, U.S. armed forces are introduced abroad *under the following three situations*:

1. "into hostilities or into situations where imminent involvement in hostilities is clearly indicated by the circumstances;"
2. "into the territory, airspace or waters of a foreign nation, while equipped for combat, except for deployments which relate solely to supply, replacement, repair, or training of such forces;"
3. "in numbers which substantially enlarge United States Armed Forces equipped for combat already located in a foreign nation."[B]

A report is required to describe the circumstances, the president's constitutional and legislative authority, and the estimated scope and duration of involvement. If U.S. armed forces remain in a situation of hostilities in accordance with subsection 4(a)(1), the president must continue to report to Congress at least every six months. The reporting requirement was intended to force the president to keep Congress informed *after* the decision to use troops abroad was taken.

The final requirement is congressional action. If U.S. armed forces are introduced into a situation of hostilities as stipulated in subsection 4(a)(1), the president must terminate their involvement within sixty days unless Congress extends the deadline. The president actually can extend the deadline for an additional thirty days, if deemed necessary for the safe withdrawal of American troops. This gives the president a total of ninety days before he must terminate the military commitment.[C] In this situation, three options are available to Congress. Congress may pass a "concurrent resolution" to terminate the military intervention earlier; this requires a simple majority in both chambers and is not subject to presidential veto. Second, Congress may pass a "joint resolution," signed by the president, to extend the deadline. Finally, Congress may do nothing, allowing the time limitation to take effect. Provisions for the time limitation and congressional involvement under subsection 4(a)(1) of the War Powers Act were the ultimate manifestation of congressional reassertion involving the power to make war.

A. U.S. Congress, House of Representatives, Committee on International Relations, *The War Powers Resolution: Relevant Documents, Correspondence, Reports,* Committee Print (94th Cong., 2nd sess., 1975), p. 1.
B. Ibid.

C. Actually, the president potentially has two additional days of leeway because the sixty-day period does not commence until the report is "submitted or required to be submitted." Therefore, this allows the president up to ninety-two days before the commitment must be terminated or before Congress must approve the activity.

SOURCE: U.S. Congress, House of Representatives, Committee on International Relations, *The War Powers Resolution: Relevant Documents, Correspondence, Reports,* Committee Print (94th Cong., 2nd sess., 1975).

only "in every possible instance." Not surprisingly, the president has never formally consulted Congress before arriving at a decision. In a few instances, a president has talked to members of Congress, informally and privately, about the use of force. However, the norm has been for the president to avoid official consultation and to inform members of Congress only after a decision (or the actual introduction of troops) has taken place.

At the same time, the War Powers Act does give Congress the potential to influence the president's decision to use troops abroad through the reporting requirement and its ability to terminate, modify, or approve military action if U.S. troops are committed. In this respect, the president must be cautious in deciding when, where, and how U.S. troops are to be committed. However, in situations since 1973 in which American troops have been committed abroad, especially for short periods of time, the congressional tendency has been to give the president a free hand.

Three factors account for presidential freedom when military action is taken. First is politics. The typical response to hostilities by most members of Congress and the public is to "rally round the flag" in support of the president. This was the case when American force was used in Grenada, Libya, Panama, and Somalia. Political support during the Persian Gulf crisis, as with Haiti and Bosnia, was more complex: rallying round the flag occurred with the initial deployment of American troops to the Persian Gulf following the Iraqi invasion of Kuwait in August; by November 1990 domestic support dwindled and became divided; then the public once again rallied behind the flag with President Bush's decision to go to war in January 1991. This rally-round-the-flag pattern is unlikely to change in the future, as reflected relative to President Bush Jr's war on terrorism following September 11, 2001. In fact, even with the increase of dissent at home and throughout the international community by 2003 concerning a war with Iraq, members of Congress have stayed overwhelmingly silent. Therefore, it appears doubtful that Congress would be willing to thwart such a major presidential initiative in its early phases—time is needed to demonstrate whether the military intervention is unsuccessful and counterproductive—bringing into play countervailing political forces critical of the president's policy.

Second, the lack of congressional will, reinforced by ambiguity in the language of the War Powers Act, has allowed the president to minimize the reporting requirements and avoid triggering congressional action. In many instances, the president has failed to submit any report at all, ignoring the act altogether. In those cases in which the president has submitted a report to Congress, he has avoided acknowledging that U.S. armed forces are involved in "a situation of hostilities," which would trigger the time limitation and congressional action (according to subsection 4[a][1]).[35] For example, the so-called peacekeeping military forces in Haiti and Bosnia (like the "humanitarian" forces in Somalia) were not officially considered to be involved in

"a situation of hostilities." This political strategy has been successful because most members of Congress are reluctant to force the president's hand, and since Vietnam the hostilities have tended to be short in duration.

The final reason the War Powers Act has had minimal impact on the president's use of force can be found in the role of the judiciary. In 1983 the U.S. Supreme Court ruled in *Immigration and Naturalization Service v. Chadha* that the "congressional veto," involving an immigration case, was unconstitutional because it violated the separation of powers. Although this was not a direct ruling on the congressional veto in the War Powers Act, the Supreme Court ruling, nevertheless, means that it may be unconstitutional for Congress to pass a concurrent resolution without the president's signature, preventing Congress from forcing the president to terminate the use of force abroad before the ninety-day deadline allowed in the War Powers Act.[36]

The War Powers Act poses the greatest potential for congressional involvement when a president commits American troops abroad to a situation of hostilities for an extended period, thus triggering the time limitation. This situation has occurred only with Lebanon in 1983, the Persian Gulf in 1991, the Somalia intervention in the early 1990s, Bosnia and Kosovo in 1999, and the anti-terrorist military campaigns, as in Afghanistan and Iraq. Yet only in Lebanon did it become a partial victory for Congress and the War Powers Act. The WPA played virtually no role whatsoever during the Persian Gulf, Somalia, and Bosnian conflicts, while Congress provided overwhelming political support for the war in Afghanistan and Iraq.

The first major test of the role of congressional action within the confines of the War Powers Act occurred when President Reagan deployed fifteen hundred American troops in Beirut from September 1982 to March 1984 to promote stability in Lebanon. When Reagan sent U.S. troops (along with British, French, and Italian troops) to Beirut, "he reported to Congress in accordance with the WPA. However, he also stated that there is no intention or expectation that U.S. Armed Forces will become involved in hostilities," thereby circumventing the time limitation and Congress's further participation.[37] As the conflict in Beirut escalated and American troops were fired upon, a major debate ensued between members of Congress and the president over what constituted a "situation of hostilities." The debate intensified and appeared to be leading toward a constitutional crisis over the war-making power. But a legislative-executive compromise was negotiated in which Congress agreed to activate subsection 4(a)(1), indicating a situation of hostilities, by passing a joint resolution that the president would acknowledge by signing; in return the president received congressional support to use military troops in Lebanon for up to eighteen months.

The Lebanese case appeared to be the first real victory for Congress in reasserting its authority over and participation in the policymaking process through the use of the WPA. However, the situation is more ambiguous than it appears, because the statement that accompanied the presidential signing of the congressional resolution did not acknowledge the legitimacy of the War Powers Act. The statement first discussed a number of disagreements with Congress's findings involving application of the WPA to Lebanon. President Reagan then proclaimed that "in signing this resolution . . . I do not and cannot cede any of the authority vested in me under the Constitution as President and as Commander in Chief of United States armed forces. Nor should my signing be viewed as any acknowledgment that the President's constitutional authority can be impermissibly infringed by statutes."[38] The president thus made an expedient political agreement with Congress over the use of troops in Lebanon yet continued to deny the legitimacy of the War Powers Act. President Reagan nevertheless was forced to bring the troops home after 256 soldiers died in their barracks in a terrorist bomb explosion, triggering a political outcry of growing domestic and congressional dissent.

From the president's perspective, it is unwise to acknowledge either the existence of a situation of hostilities or even the legitimacy of the War Powers Act, for it will limit his freedom of action and legitimize the constitutionality of the WPA. At the same time, presidents are hesitant to ignore the act altogether, because frustration among members of Congress might grow to the point that they pass new amendments to the War Powers Act strengthening Congress's legislative role. It is important to keep in mind that politics is extremely consequential in influencing the nature of the legislative-executive relationship and, in this case, the significance of the War Powers Act.

Unlike Lebanon, the Persian Gulf crisis offered virtually no role to the War Powers Act, even though over 500,000 American troops were committed to the region over a period of months and engaged in war. President Bush did report the troop commitment in accordance with the War Powers Act, and Congress did become actively involved in the policymaking process, eventually authorizing presidential use of force. But Congress became involved late in the crisis and, rather than relying on the War Powers Act, turned to its power of investigation and legislation as the source of its activity and authorization. Hence, the president's commitment of over half a million troops abroad and Congress's eventual endorsement of the president's brinksmanship strategy leading to war weakened the legitimacy and strength of the War Powers Act as a tool of congressional involvement in the making of U.S. foreign policy.[39]

In Somalia, as in Lebanon and the Persian Gulf crisis, presidents Bush and Clinton attempted to downplay and circumvent the War Powers Act, that is, until it became a prominent and controversial item on the national agenda after American troops were shot at and killed as the civil war intensified—forcing Clinton to bring the troops back home immediately. The signing of the Dayton Accords in 1995 among the relevant parties allowed President Clinton to send over twenty thousand American troops to Bosnia as part of a multilateral "peacekeeping" force while minimizing the role of the War Powers Act. Furthermore, when the United States and NATO allies stationed troops abroad and bombed Kosovo, Congress was quick to provide political support and military funding. The successful outcome of the Kosovo war insured congressional support and a limited role for the War Powers Act.[40]

The power of the president during a time of national emergency and the country's willingness, including Congress, to rally round the flag was revealed shortly after the terrorist attacks on the World Trade Center and the Pentagon on September 11, 2001. Within three days, on September 14, the House voted 420–1 and the Senate voted 98–0 in support of a resolution, initially submitted by President Bush Jr., "That the president is authorized to use all necessary and appropriate force against those nations, organizations or persons he determines planned, authorized, committed or aided the terrorist attacks that occurred on Sept. 11 or harbored such organizations or persons, in order to prevent any future acts of international terrorism against the United States by such nations, organizations or persons." According to the Washington Post, "The votes were remarkable for their gravity, urgency and absence of the partisan bickering that had prevailed in both chambers until the moment of the air assaults on New York and Washington."[41] Members quickly voted on the resolution with virtually no debate—a situation somewhat analogous to the 416–0 House vote and 88–2 Senate vote in favor of the Gulf of Tonkin resolution, which President Johnson presented to Congress in 1964.

As with the Persian Gulf War, authority for the joint resolution in support of the war on terrorism was based not on the War Powers Act but on Congress's spending and lawmaking powers (as will be discussed in greater depth below). As long as the war on terrorism appears to be succeeding, presidential policy will likely prevail and maintain political support. However, should the conflict escalate or appear to be making little progress, especially if American troops are taking fire and sustaining casualties, the situation is likely to become politicized throughout the country, and members of Congress are likely to take a more active and critical role, possibly reconsidering their earlier unconditional support and trying to reinvigorate the War Powers Act.

The War Powers Act also has limited teeth to constrain the president's ability to use force due to *what is not mentioned in the act*. The WPA applies only to the use of U.S. "armed forces" in a "situation of hostilities" or "in the territory of a foreign nation, while equipped for combat." These cases do not include the use of U.S. military troops as "advisers" abroad in noncombatant situations, "reconnaissance missions" over foreign territory involving military personnel if they are not equipped for combat, or U.S. "military training maneuvers" intended for political purposes. Most important, the War Powers Act does not apply to Americans engaged in "covert paramilitary action," for they are not officially U.S. armed forces. All of these activities were regularly used as part of the Reagan administration's Central American foreign policy to support the government of El Salvador and overthrow that of Nicaragua, and also are being used in President Bush Jr.'s war on terrorism.

In sum, the War Powers Act has given Congress the potential to play a more active role in the use of force abroad. However, members of Congress have been extremely cautious in challenging presidential initiatives in so vital a matter. The War Powers Act has been of major symbolic importance in promoting con-

gressional reassertion in foreign policy and has served as a model for other legislation. The act is indicative of a more reassertive Congress and a transformed political environment since Vietnam. While the president continues to be stronger than Congress with respect to war powers, he is nonetheless much more constrained and must be much more cautious today than in the cold war years. Even though Congress has been unable to exert great influence through the War Powers Act and some have called for its repeal, Congress has constrained the president's ability to use military force by other means, to be discussed below, such as through the power of legislation and investigations, as Presidents Nixon and Reagan learned.[42]

ADVICE ON AND CONSENT TO APPOINTMENTS AND TREATIES

The Senate has the constitutional authority to advise the president on and consent to his appointments and treaties. These are two areas in which senators possess power in foreign policy matters that members of the House of Representatives do not share, helping to account for the Senate's greater prestige and power within the Congress. Since World War II, however, members of the Senate have tended to be hesitant to exercise this power and challenge presidential foreign policy initiatives.[43]

With regard to **presidential appointments,** the nature of legislative-executive relations has not changed substantially since Vietnam. *Three patterns have prevailed.* First, the Senate has tended to rubber-stamp ambassadorships and presidential appointments to the executive branch. The Senate—particularly the Committee on Foreign Relations—holds hearings to examine the nominee's qualifications and views before deciding whether to approve the appointment. Appointments are considered first in committee, then by the entire Senate. These used to be relatively brief affairs, with the Senate merely going through the motions of providing advice and consent. However, not only have presidents taken longer to appoint personnel, as explained in chapter 5, but the Senate confirmation process has become more cumbersome and slower over the years, often taking months.[44]

A second pattern has evolved such that some appointments result in political and partisan struggles. It is not unusual for at least one major presidential appointment to draw a great deal of attention and political controversy during a president's term of office. For example, President Jimmy Carter's initial appointment as director of central intelligence was Theodore Sorenson. A White House aide and speechwriter for President Kennedy, Sorenson was heavily criticized by the political right and conservative members of Congress. When Sorenson was unable to gain majority support in the Committee on Foreign Relations, President Carter withdrew the nomination. President Bush Sr. suffered a similar fate when his nomination of John Tower as secretary of defense was denied by a Senate vote. The nomination of Robert Gates as director of central intelligence (DCI) by presidents Reagan and Bush Sr. also encountered obstacles over Iran-contra, as did President Clinton's appointment of his national security adviser, Anthony Lake, to be DCI.

Congressional impact can occur at different, and sometimes less visible, levels. Republican senator **Jesse Helms,** for example, of North Carolina was particularly active in the appointment process. As a member of the Committee on Foreign Relations, he held up and criticized many appointments made by presidents Reagan and Bush Sr., especially to the State Department, for holding insufficiently conservative views. With the 1994 Republican electoral triumph in Congress, Helms became chair of the Foreign Relations Committee until 2001 and became much more powerful and obstructionist, often successfully resisting President Clinton's appointments (he retired in 2003).

The third pattern involves the Senate's reluctance to provide advice and consent for a growing number of prominent positions within the White House and the Executive Office of the President (EOP). Individuals within these positions have been treated as the president's "personal staff," not as "officers." Such important positions as the national security adviser, national economic adviser, and director of the Office of Management and Budget, all located within the EOP, have not required Senate approval. This reinforces the historical trend toward presidential autonomy in appointing personnel, with occasional appointments becoming controversial.

With regard to the Senate's treaty power, the president continues to possess the dominant voice. A large number of overseas commitments have been made by the United States since the end of World War II through the use of international agreements. In fact, the U.S. government became party to over seven thousand agreements with other states between 1946 and 1974. Of these agreements, approximately 6 percent were formal treaties requiring Senate confirmation, while 87 percent were pursuant to congressional legislation. Roughly 7 percent were so-called **executive agreements,** consummated by the executive branch without congressional involvement. Together, these international agreements involved a wide range of cultural, technical, economic, diplomatic, and military issues. Most important, if an agreement entailed a significant military commitment, it was likely to take the form of an executive agreement.[45]

As with the war-making power, the treaty powers of Congress became dormant during the cold war. The growth of executive agreements has alarmed many members of Congress, who believed that agreements often represented significant policy decisions that were being made without congressional consultation. In response, *Congress has tried four techniques in attempting to restore its advice-and-consent role in the agreement-making process.* First, Congress has passed laws forcing the president to provide it with basic information when agreements are signed. Such legislation was considered a prerequisite for strengthening the congressional advice-and-consent role. Second, members of Congress have tried to force the president to submit executive agreements to the Senate as treaties. While, for example, the Senate forced President Nixon to submit the agreement to return Okinawa to Japan to the Senate as a treaty, this strategy has met with little overall success. Third, Congress has used the power of the purse in some cases, withholding funds necessary to implement executive agreements. This is a way for members of the House to become involved in the treaty power, as they did over the implementation of the Panama Canal treaties. Finally, Congress has tried to subject executive agreements to disapproval or approval, with limited success and the likelihood that such requirements may be unconstitutional.

Congress has made an effort to redress imbalances in the making of executive agreements, but the overall effect has been minimal. Nevertheless, these efforts are symbolic of Congress's reassertion of authority since the Vietnam War. The president must be sensitive to congressional concerns in negotiating executive agreements in order to avoid creating political controversies that might precipitate greater efforts by Congress to strengthen its role. This political caution is reinforced by the fact that international agreements in the form of treaties are subject to formal ratification by the Senate, with a two-thirds vote required for approval.

The Senate's role has been much more pronounced in the case formal **treaties**. Part of the reason is that treaties require more than a simple majority, which is not easy to acquire. This was clearly evident in the ratification process over the Panama Canal treaties. Senate skepticism and involvement, for example, were significant in extending the long, drawn-out negotiations that began during the early 1960s. In order to gain approval for the final treaties in 1978, which would return the canal to Panamanian control at the end of the century (or as opponents put it, "to give up our canal"), President Carter was forced to accept two controversial amendments that emphasized American security concerns to protect the canal. Treaty passage was so controversial that it contributed to the weakening of President Carter's ability to gain future political support on the Hill—a situation somewhat reminiscent of Woodrow Wilson's defeats to get Senate approval for the Treaty of Versailles following World War I, which included American involvement in the League of Nations. Another way Senate opposition can be exercised is simply by keeping treaties from ever coming to the floor for a final vote, which has been done repeatedly with international human rights covenants.[46]

Throughout the 1970s and 1980s, the Strategic Arms Limitation Talks (SALT) were the most prominent example of congressional participation and influence in the treaty-making process. The congressional debate over the Anti-Ballistic Missile (ABM) System, for example, was consequential in reducing the size of the strategic missile program, which contributed to the success of SALT I under President Nixon and its approval by Congress. Congress also played a crucial role in the treaty-making process for SALT II. Initially, members of the Senate were influential in persuading the executive branch to push for U.S. and Soviet strategic forces that were "essentially equivalent." Even with this guidance, the climate of opinion on SALT II following the Soviet invasion of Afghanistan in 1979 became so conservative and negative that President Carter withdrew the treaty from Senate consideration for fear of defeat in the final vote. This was a major political defeat for Carter, although American presidents continued to abide by the SALT II treaty subsequently.

The Senate has been very active in the area of foreign economics and trade policy, often through its treaty powers. Since the creation of the original Bretton Woods system during World War II, the trilateral countries—the industrialized democracies in North America, Europe, and Asia (and increasingly over time other countries of the world)—have gone through periodic negotiations since the creation of the original Bretton Woods system during World War II in an effort to arrive at common "rules of the game" for engaging in economic transactions as the world has changed and gotten more complex, especially involving trade. The most recent, Uruguay round of negotiations that began in the late seventies resulted in an international treaty that produced a more international, liberal trading regime and the creation of the World Trade Organization (WTO) to replace the GATT (review chapter 2). Another set of negotiations between Canada, Mexico, and the United States since the eighties produced the North American Free Trade Agreement (NAFTA).

In both cases, the Senate agreed to provide the executive branch and the president with what is referred to as **fast track authority** to negotiate such international economic agreements. Realizing that foreign economics inevitably involves domestic economics and, hence, would result in the Congress and the Senate micromanaging the negotiations and endlessly amending the final negotiated treaties (as it commonly does with domestic legislation), fast track legislation is a pragmatic effort to give the president a certain amount of freedom and leeway to negotiate for the United States, while giving the Senate the final choice to vote the entire final treaty package up or down. Despite being very controversial—raising concerns and passions about free trade and economic growth, the future of American jobs, labor and working conditions, environmental consequences—the WTO and NAFTA were ultimately passed by Congress under President Clinton.

President Clinton was unsuccessful, like presidents before them, in getting congressional support for additional fast track legislation for future international economic and trade agreements. Although Congress has been reluctant, President Bush Jr. finally succeeded in 2002 in getting compromised legislation giving him fast track authority. Nevertheless, Congress will remain heavily involved, in one way or another, in the making of U.S. foreign trade policy in the next round of international negotiations, for it reflects a diversity of interests—free and fair trade, strategic trade, and protectionism.[47]

In sum, the Senate tends to approve most presidential appointments with little difficulty, though some are controversial and can become a political liability for presidents. Also, while Congress lacks influence in the making of executive agreements, the Senate must approve all treaties. Therefore, even though the president is preeminent generally, there are plenty of times when Congress does play an influential advice-and-consent role. This is indicative of a Congress that has become more active in reasserting its role in foreign policy. And given the paradox of presidential power that has developed since Vietnam, it does not take many political controversies and failures to weaken the president's ability to govern, even in foreign policy.

THE POWER OF THE PURSE AND TO MAKE LAWS

Although Congress has been only somewhat successful in increasing either its war power or its advice-and-consent role relative to the president, it is still a force to be reckoned with, especially given its control of the purse and its ability to make laws. This has always been the greatest strength of the legislative branch, guaranteeing it a role in the policymaking process for most foreign policy issues. The tendency has been for the president and executive branch to develop legislation and submit it to Congress, which then approves, modifies, or rejects it. In this respect, Congress reacts to the president's political agenda. Yet the legislative process requires Congress to ultimately decide on the final laws and the appropriation of money. Congressional attempts to control policy by this means have intensified since the Vietnam War.[48]

Consider the example of congressional involvement in foreign assistance. As discussed in essay 6.1, the U.S. government provides roughly $15 billion annually of foreign assistance to countries around the world, the two largest recipients being Israel and Egypt. Since the beginning of the foreign-assistance program following World War II, congressional involvement and influence have always been considerable. As described by political scientist Barbara Hinckley in 1975, Congress's "general policy has been less aid, for less time, tied to more restraints, and more loans and fewer

grants, with loans repayable in American dollars."[49] Since the seventies, Congress's influence over foreign assistance has become even more pervasive.

Congressional involvement in foreign-assistance policy has often been used by members of Congress to influence U.S. foreign policy generally. For example, despite congressional failure to regain its claimed constitutional authority through the War Powers Act or the treaty-making process, Congress has been able to use its influence over foreign assistance to make occasional inroads on the war-making power. The first major effort along these lines involved the Vietnam War, in which Congress ended all U.S. military assistance to South Vietnam and Cambodia in February 1975, thereby accelerating the end of the war in April of that year.

Congress also has taken two other major actions intended to deter the president's ability to exercise war abroad. The first major effort occurred in the Angolan civil war. To American policymakers, the Soviet Union acted in an expansionist manner when it intervened in a civil war in Angola in 1975 following the abrupt departure of the Portuguese colonial presence. This Soviet action was seen as a threat to Kissinger's détente strategy. In response, the Ford administration increased its CIA-funneled covert military assistance to two pro-Western groups in Angola. The Soviet Union countered by increasing its support to a third Angolan group. However, American involvement soon became public. With fresh memories of the Vietnam War and CIA covert operations in mind, Congress refused an executive request for additional funding and barred all U.S. assistance for any activities directly or indirectly involving Angola. This marked a major triumph for congressional foreign policy action, for it thwarted an important presidential foreign policy initiative involving the use of force.

The other major policy action by Congress involved U.S. foreign policy toward Central America. It was through foreign-assistance laws that Congress influenced the Reagan administration's Central American policy, especially its efforts to conduct a covert war and overthrow the Nicaraguan government. During the early 1980s, Congress approved considerably less foreign assistance for El Salvador and the Nicaraguan contras than the administration requested. Eventually, the **Boland Amendments** were passed in 1984 and 1985, cutting off all American "direct and indirect" assistance to the contras during 1985 and 1986. President Reagan responded by circumventing congressional action and covertly supporting the contras.[50] When the public discovered this and the arms-for-hostages exchanges, the Iran-contra affair broke. The Iran-contra scandal constituted a major political crisis for President Reagan and the U.S. government because it involved constitutional questions concerning legislative versus executive authority to make foreign policy and war.

At times, Congress has taken the initiative through its power of the purse in setting the public agenda and steering foreign policy. For example, U.S. government concern with human rights is commonly attributed to the initiative taken by President Jimmy Carter, who was a major advocate of international human rights. However, U.S. support for human rights actually was initiated within Congress following Watergate and was manifested primarily through U.S. foreign-assistance policy. Foreign-assistance legislation was amended to prohibit security and developmental assistance to any country engaging in a consistent pattern of gross violations of internationally recognized human rights. These restrictions played an important role in influencing U.S. foreign policy in Central America and contributed to passage of the Boland Amendments. Likewise, Congress's threatened passage of the anti-apartheid bill over President Reagan's veto forced him to issue an executive order imposing sanctions on South Africa. Such human rights laws have repeatedly affected U.S. rhetoric and policies abroad, such as with Pakistan and China.

The terrorist attacks of September 11 initially increased congressional and bipartisan support for the president's foreign policy in general and anti-terrorist policies in particular. Congress was quick to pass a joint resolution in support of the war on terrorism, as discussed above; to support a $40 billion emergency appropriation to assist recovery operations, repair damaged facilities, strengthen internal security, and fight terrorism; to provide additional foreign assistance to countries supporting the anti-terrorism war, including Pakistan, whose authoritarian regime has a record of violating human rights and exploding a nuclear device in violation of the nuclear nonproliferation treaty and American foreign assistance laws; and passed an anti-terrorism bill—called the U.S. Patriot Act—that expands the government's ability to engage in domestic intelligence surveillance, detain suspects, and penetrate the banking and financial systems (the implications of this last bill for civil rights and liberties will be dis-

cussed in depth in chapter 14). Congress did scale back some of the sweeping anti-terrorism requests made by Attorney General John Ashcroft and President Bush Jr. and, to improve airport security, agreed to federalize all airport security personnel (whereas the president preferred to continue to subcontract to private employers under new federal guidelines).

Overall, the same patterns that have evolved with congressional involvement in foreign assistance also operate in other areas of foreign policy, such as national defense, trade, energy, immigration, and environmental policy. First, members of Congress have taken a renewed interest in foreign policy issues since Vietnam. Second, while the president usually initiates policy and proposes legislation, the Congress shapes it. Sometimes major presidential initiatives are rejected outright; more often they are modified or fine-tuned by Congress. Third, Congress occasionally takes the initiative or replaces a presidential initiative with one of its own. Fourth, the more an issue is divorced from national security affairs or the use of force, the greater the congressional attention, involvement, and influence. Where the cold-war legacy of presidential power over "high" national security policy remains strong, congressional activity in formally "low" foreign policy issues is reinforced by the fact that they resemble domestic policy issues for members of Congress—which is why they have been referred to as **intermestic issues.**[51] Congressional constituents, including the public and interest groups, are often interested in issues such as trade, energy, immigration, and the environment because of the direct impact of these areas on their lives.

The Legislative Process and Congressional Politics. How is it that members of Congress are able to exert the power of the purse and make laws that affect U.S. foreign policy? Very simply, through the **legislative process** and the nature of congressional politics, which are extremely complex and can be quite confusing. Although most Americans have been schooled on "how a bill becomes a law," this grossly simplifies the complexity and the politics of the legislative process. It is so complex that not even people who work on the Hill or study Congress can comprehend all the intricacies involved in the passage of legislation. Yet it is this complexity that allows individual members of Congress to play a vital role in the making of public policy. (See **essay 11.4** for a discussion of the complex reality of the legislative process.)

ESSAY 11.4
THE COMPLEX REALITY OF THE LEGISLATIVE PROCESS

Most Americans are schooled from an early age on how a bill becomes a law. After a bill is introduced in the House or the Senate, it is then introduced in the other house. It goes to the relevant committee with jurisdiction within each chamber; each committee holds hearings, amends, and votes on the bill. If the legislation survives the committees, it goes to the floor of the House and Senate for debate, more amendments, and a vote. After the floor vote, the legislation goes to a joint conference committee of senators and representatives to resolve the differences between the separate bills. Once the differences are ironed out, the bills go back to each chamber for a final vote, and then on to the president's desk for his signature or veto. A two-thirds vote in both the House and Senate is required to override a veto. This account does provide a crude overview, but it does not communicate the complexity of the legislative process through which Congress exercises its power to make laws and control the purse.

Once introduced in Congress, legislation is "farmed out" to committees. Committee jurisdiction is rarely clear-cut, and it is common for two or more committees within each chamber to consider the same legislation (in some cases, each committee involved will consider the entire bill; in other cases, only a part of the bill). For example, the 1988 trade bill was considered by ten committees in the Senate and twelve committees in the House (which explains the need for fast track presidential authority). Committee hearings, "markup" sessions, and votes on the bill do take place; yet before this occurs the bill usually is divided into parts and sent to subcommittees for hearings and markup. The entire package is then reassembled and considered by the full committee. For instance, the annual foreign assistance bill is always considered by the **Senate Committee on Foreign Relations** (and House Committee on International Relations), although it is initially submitted to seven subcommittees for consideration: African Affairs; East Asian and Pacific Affairs; European Affairs; International Economic Policy, Export and Trade Promotion; International Operations and Terrorism; Near Eastern and South Asian Affairs; and Western Hemispheric, Peace Corps, and Narcotics Affairs (see table 11.1 for House committees, table 11.2 for Senate committees).

If a bill gains majority approval within committee, it is passed on to the full House or Senate for consideration. The House of Representatives (the larger body) has strict procedures for considering a bill, while the Senate operates in much less rigid fashion. For example, the House

Rules Committee determines when the bill will be considered and under what conditions. In the Senate, bills automatically proceed to the floor. However, they can be "filibustered"—that is, a senator can take the floor and hold all other Senate bills hostage in an effort to have the targeted bill withdrawn from Senate consideration. A filibuster can be overcome only by a "cloture" vote of sixty senators. Another indication of the different operating styles of the two chambers is that in the House only "germane" amendments can be attached to bills. In contrast, any amendments can be attached to a Senate bill with a majority vote.

Considering the complex process and "hoops and ladders" that a bill must go through before final passage, one should better understand why only a small percentage of the few thousand bills introduced are ever passed. Moreover, those few dozen bills that are successful in becoming law look quite different from their initial form by the end of the process. In other words, it is easy to introduce legislation, but difficult to pass laws. This is due to the numerous stages in the process in both chambers of Congress at which the legislation can be amended or killed. This accounts for the fact that presidents are easily frustrated by Congress and must exercise strong leadership skills if they are to govern.

The legislative process is actually much more complex than portrayed above. Laws authorizing the expenditure of money by the government require that a money bill also be passed. In effect, many governmental policies require two legislative processes: an **authorization process** and an **appropriation process.** In other words, separate bills must be passed that *authorize* a governmental program and *appropriate* money for its implementation. This is in accordance with the constitutional provision in Article I that "no money shall be drawn from the treasury, but in consequence of appropriations made by law." Only the appropriations committees within the House and Senate deal with money appropriations; all other congressional committees are authorization committees. This explains why the appropriations committees are considered the most powerful committees in each chamber.

For example, the Senate Committee on Foreign Relations and the House Committee on International Relations authorize the president to provide foreign assistance to certain countries, stipulating certain "ceiling" amounts of money that can be spent in each country. However, they do not appropriate these funds. The president must also submit an appropriations bill to Congress. This separate legislation is considered by the two committees on appropriations (actually, first the subcommittees on foreign operations) and must proceed through another entire legislative process before the money is actually provided to the authorized program. Therefore, on the one hand, opponents of foreign assistance can derail presidential requests either in the authorization or appropriations process. The president, on the other hand, must be successful in both processes. Congress recently passed a law giving the president the "line item veto" for appropriation bills—that is, the ability to veto particular spending items, as distinguished from vetoing the entire bill. To further complicate things, the authorization and appropriations processes tend to occur almost simultaneously for the same issue, and Congress typically considers dozens of issues each year. While this may not be the most efficient way to conduct business, this is how Congress operates.

An additional factor complicates and confuses the legislative process even more. The U.S. government budget operates within a **fiscal year** that begins on October 1 and ends the last day of September. In other words, the 2004 fiscal-year budget starts in October of 2003 and ends in September of 2004. This means that Congress has only nine months from convening in January to pass the thirteen appropriations bills that fund the government's entire budget for the next fiscal year. Congress rarely passes all thirteen appropriations bills by October and thus must pass a **continuing resolution** allowing the government to expend funds and continue operating (usually at the previous year's funding level).

To place congressional appropriations in perspective, those bills are only one part and one year of a three-part, three-year **budgetary process** for the entire government. The executive branch prepares the 2004 budget, for example, during 2002 and the president submits it to Congress at the beginning of 2003. The budget then proceeds through the yearlong legislative process as thirteen appropriations bills and after eventual approval is spent by the government in fiscal year 2004. Another way to look at the process is that in 2002 the executive branch prepares the budget for the year 2004, fights for the 2003 budget before Congress, and spends the 2002 budget already approved by Congress. This is truly an immense undertaking; not only is it a three-year, overlapping process, but the U.S. government's annual budget is almost $2 trillion. Although Congress plays only one part in the overall budgetary process, it is a very consequential part.[A]

It is easy to be confused by the intricacies of the legislative and budgetary processes. As David Stockman, former director of the Office of Management and Budget under President Reagan, once said, "None of us really understands what's going on." Yet one need not comprehend all the specifics of the process but only identify the key patterns that prevail. In sum, Congress exerts considerable influence through its power to make laws and appropriate funds. This is done through an elaborate and complex political process involving the passage of legislation, authorization of specific programs, and appropriation of money for budgets operating in fiscal years.

SOURCES: Lewis A. Froman, Jr., *The Congressional Process: Strategies, Rules, and Procedures* (Boston: Little, Brown, 1967); Eric Redman, *The Dance of Legislation* (New York: Simon and Schuster, 1973); Hedrick Smith, *The Power Game: How Washington Works* (New York: Ballantine, 1996); David Stockman, *The Triumph of Politics: How the Reagan Revolution Failed* (New York: Harper and Row, 1986); and U.S. Congress, House of Representatives, *How Our Laws Are Made* (95th Cong., 1st sess., 1978).

A. Congress attempted to streamline its operations by passing the Budget and Impoundment Control Act in 1974, which added a budget committee in each chamber and the Congressional Budget Office. Congress is now better informed, strengthening its legislative involvement. However, it has also complicated things further by adding a toothless third layer—the budget resolution process—on top of the authorization and appropriation processes.

The legislative process is not only incredibly complex but also very political. Given the diffusion of power in Congress, congressional politics revolves around bargaining, **coalition building,** and compromise. Majority coalitions need to be constructed and maintained for every stage of the process if a bill is to survive and become law. Coalitions are formed through policy agreement, ideological affinity, personal relationships, persuasion, bargaining, horse-trading, coercion, or any tactic that is necessary depending upon the issue's perceived importance. Ultimately, compromise is the key to legislative success, for a majority of representatives and senators must reach an agreement in an institution in which power is quite decentralized. The political nature of the process is not unique to Congress, for as we saw in chapter 10, executive branch policymaking is also very political—this is the essence of policymaking, as we discussed in the very first chapter.

Congressional politics involves members who are motivated for different private and public reasons. As discussed above, members of Congress are political animals who are preoccupied with maintaining their institutional status and power as well as their electoral security, raising funds, and winning reelection. Senators and representatives also tend to be quite sensitive to the way power is exercised within Congress (and the beltway) and how their activities are perceived in public. Furthermore, congressional politics not only involves representatives and senators interacting but also includes efforts by the president, members of different executive departments and agencies, as well as social movements and interest groups (or special interests) to influence the legislative process. Thus, alliances and coalitions are made between representatives and senators within Congress and by members of Congress with other individuals and groups throughout the executive branch and society. At the same time, given the importance of their constituents and the public, members of Congress are preoccupied with how their actions will "play back in Peoria" and affect their reelection efforts. Much of the time this political process takes place with little public visibility, but sometimes it occurs under the media spotlight. Such is the nature of politics.[52]

The intricacies and complexity of the legislative process and congressional politics allow Congress as an institution to wield power in the making of U.S. foreign policy. Presidents have commonly complained that they have to deal with 535 politicized people who act as if they are all secretaries of state. Regardless of whether one is satisfied with the legislative process and the nature of congressional politics, these are the ingredients that constrain presidential power and affect legislative-executive relations.

THE POWER OF OVERSIGHT AND INVESTIGATION

Congress also has the power to oversee and investigate public policy matters. This includes Congress's constitutional right to ensure that the president "take care that the laws be faithfully executed." **Congressional oversight** to ensure that the president and executive branch implement policies in accordance with the letter and intent of legislation can powerfully restrain presidential power and the foreign policy bureaucracy. This right represents, in fact, the ultimate means by which Congress may exercise its constitutional role. For if sufficient abuse of power is determined by Congress, the president ultimately may be "removed from office on impeachment for, and on conviction of, treason, bribery, or other high crimes and misdemeanors."

Impeachment proceedings have occurred only three times in American history—twice since the Vietnam war. However, the power to investigate and engage in oversight has been a potent tool that Congress has exercised. *Since World War II, the use of congressional oversight and investigations in an effort to influence U.S. foreign policy has gone through three phases, sometimes challenging, at other times legitimizing, presidential power in U.S. foreign policy.*[53]

The first phase occurred during the late 1940s and early 1950s. Extremely conservative members of Congress became increasingly active in conducting congressional investigations to eradicate a supposed threat of communism in the United States. As discussed in essay 11.1, a number of congressional committees—including the House Committee on Un-American Activities and the Senate Committee on Internal Security—were active in investigating communist influence in government, academia and education, the media, Hollywood, and other walks of American life. The frequency of **internal security investigations** posed by communism and subversion is nothing less than staggering: four investigations during the 79th Congress (1945–1947); twenty-two during the Republican 80th Congress (1947–1949); twenty-four during the 81st Congress (1949–1951); thirty-four during the 82nd Congress (1951–1953); and fifty-one, an all-time high, during the Republican 83rd Congress (1953–1955).[54]

Although the gap was immense between the alleged communist threat at home and the small number of communists (usually former communists) that were found, the large number of well-publicized investigations led to the destruction and silencing of the American left. Likewise, liberals, the Truman administration, and Democrats were challenged, placed on the political defensive, and given notice that an anticommunist political assault could raise its head again in the future. The rise of McCarthyism, led by congressional investigations, pushed public opinion to the right and cemented the anticommunist consensus that drove U.S. foreign policy during the cold war.

The second phase of congressional oversight came subsequently, at the height of the cold war, when

Congress became relatively inactive in overseeing the president and the executive branch. Because this was a time of cold war consensus and bipartisanship in the making of U.S. foreign policy, the norm was congressional acquiescence in legislative-executive relations. The general attitude toward oversight of the national security bureaucracy at the time was expressed by Senator Leverett Saltonstall, the ranking Republican on the Armed Services Committee: "It is not a question of reluctance on the part of the CIA officials to speak to us. Instead, it is a question of our reluctance, if you will, to seek information and knowledge on subjects which I personally, as a member of Congress and as a citizen, would rather not have."[55] The few congressional hearings and investigations that did occur during the height of the cold war in the area of foreign policy were brief, intended more to legitimize than to investigate presidential foreign policy.

The third investigative phase began at the height of the Vietnam War and has continued to operate since. Congressional reassertion began with the investigation of the Vietnam War by the Senate Foreign Relations Committee—the **Fulbright hearings**. They helped trigger other congressional hearings and investigations into the exercise of presidential power and U.S. foreign policy. This has led to congressional efforts to reassert foreign policy-making power, such as passage of the War Powers Act, and has been an important means of acquiring information from the executive branch.

The ultimate manifestation of renewed congressional power came with the **Watergate hearings**—the congressional investigation of Nixon's presidential conduct. What began as an effort by members of Congress to reassert their constitutional authority in foreign policy eventually turned into a political challenge against a sitting president who was perceived as abusing the powers of his office. In effect, President Nixon's effort to fight the Vietnam War abroad and at home when the political environment that had legitimized and supported an imperial presidency was breaking down produced a full-blown constitutional crisis (review essay 4.2 on Watergate). The Watergate investigation by Congress eventually produced three impeachment counts by the House Judiciary Committee and forced President Nixon's resignation.

The Watergate episode reinforced congressional involvement in the making of U.S. foreign policy. Two detailed House and Senate investigations of the intelligence community and their role in U.S. foreign policy were undertaken by the Pike and Church committees in 1975. These investigations into U.S. foreign policy, more than any others, shocked most Americans. They revealed that the president and the executive branch were systematically involved in a variety of cloak-and-dagger operations, including foreign assassinations and blatant violations of American constitutional rights at home. As discussed in chapter 8, these investigations stimulated the creation of intelligence oversight committees within each chamber and triggered efforts at intelligence reform.

The mid-1970s, especially 1973 to 1975, may represent the height of congressional reassertion of its foreign policy power. Congressional investigations in this period involved getting the facts and achieving an understanding of what happened and why. However, they also represented partisan and political struggles between Democrats and Republicans, liberals and conservatives, members of the legislative and executive branches, supporters of the president and his opponents. Different people within Congress and the executive branch and outside government were involved for different reasons; yet they acted before the public spotlight as if they were above it all. Congressional reassertion and presidential resistance represented hardball politics of the highest order, for the stakes involved President Nixon's political future, the future of presidential power and legislative-executive relations in foreign policy and, in some respects, the future direction of American politics.

This was also the case with congressional involvement in the Iran-contra affair, which represented the second major legislative-executive struggle since Vietnam over foreign policy. The Reagan administration's efforts to covertly exchange arms for hostages with Iran and to fight a secret war to overthrow the Sandinista government in Nicaragua, in violation of the Boland Amendments passed by Congress prohibiting all "direct and indirect" governmental assistance to the contras, triggered a political crisis for President Reagan when they eventually became public. When his initial denials failed to quash the story, President Reagan himself appointed a presidential commission to investigate matters. The **Tower Commission**—consisting of John Tower, Brent Scowcroft, and Edmund Muskie—constituted another effort at political damage control as it was intended to buy time and soften criticism when the commission's report was released. Although the Tower Commission report concluded that the Iran-contra affair reflected flawed, not illegal, policy and resulted due to poor management style in the White House, the political storm grew nonetheless, triggering the congressional investigations.

In accordance with intelligence community preferences, the initial congressional investigations were performed by the intelligence committees, which were not known for aggressive oversight.[56] Intelligence committee investigations were held behind closed doors, respecting presidential claims that secrecy was necessary to preserve national security—a continuing legacy of the cold war era. However, when knowledge of the diversion of Iran arms sales funds to support the contras became public, a joint House and Senate congressional investigation could no longer be avoided.

For many Americans, the **Iran-contra hearings** by a joint congressional committee were interesting and entertaining. This was one of the few times that average citizens became actively interested in national politics, and figures like Oliver North became household names. While it was predominantly entertaining and of momentary interest for the public, Iran-contra involved a major constitutional crisis and political struggle.[57]

Once again, it was primarily the result of a president's efforts to exercise extraordinary power in order to conduct a war abroad in the name of national security in a post–cold war environment. As Elliot Abrams, former assistant secretary of state for inter-American affairs under President Reagan, described the conflict between Congress and the executive over U.S. foreign policy: "We were at war, we and the Democrats in Congress, or so we thought and they thought. . . . So when I was asked for information [on Central America] that might help them, might give them yet more ammunition, I tried to deny it to them. I tried to figure out how I could give them the least information possible" (review essay 8.2 on the secret Contra war).[58]

As with Watergate, the constitutional and political crisis that peaked during the Iran-contra hearings involved a major partisan and political struggle that affected the future of a president, his party, and the nature of legislative-executive relations in foreign policy. President Reagan and most of his staff understood that they were fighting for their political lives, which accounts for their efforts to minimize the negative political consequences through damage control. Members of

Congress were quite aware of the seriousness of the situation, and many chose sides accordingly, with most Republicans supporting the president and the Tower Commission view. In contrast, most Democrats were in the opposition camp, although they operated very cautiously since they were challenging a sitting president who was immensely popular. All those involved in this epic struggle remained sensitive to the need to play to the media and, ultimately, the public.

Considerable damaging information surfaced during the congressional inquiry concerning presidential abuse of power, particularly the circumvention of Congress and the public in pursuit of the covert contra war in Nicaragua. *The Report of the Congressional Committee Investigating the Iran-Contra Affair* ultimately found that "the common ingredients of the Iran and Contra policies were secrecy, deception, and disdain for the law. A small group of senior officials believed that they alone knew what was right."[59] Within the Reagan administration, the demands of national security had prevailed over the demands of democracy. Yet unlike Watergate, the Iran-Contra hearings did not result in impeachment proceedings, and President Reagan managed to survive the political storm. Also unlike the aftermath of Watergate and the CIA revelations, the congressional investigation treated Iran-contra as an aberration that did not result in any major efforts to strengthen the congressional role or reform the covert aspects of U.S. foreign policy.[60]

According to senators William Cohen and George Mitchell, the congressional committee wanted to avoid confronting the larger constitutional issues and the possibility of impeachment because of the difficulty of challenging such a popular sitting president and the fear of creating governmental paralysis in the making of foreign policy at a time when serious arms control negotiations with the Soviet Union were possible with the rise of Mikhail Gorbachev.[61] Therefore, according to Seymour Hersh in "The Iran-Contra Committees," the investigation was flawed from the beginning in a number of ways: the composition of the committee, the imposition of an unrealistic deadline for ending the investigation, the decision to permit the White House to review all internal documents for relevance before releasing them, failure to request other government sources of information, avoidance of certain topics of investigation altogether, the decision not to call forth relevant witnesses before private and public sessions, the immunity granted prematurely to key witnesses, and finally the intimidation of committee members in response to the aggressive testimony of Oliver North and Admiral John Poindexter.[62]

Despite considerable weaknesses and limitations in the congressional investigation of Iran-contra, the fact that the inquiry was held nonetheless is indicative of the reassertion of Congress in the post–Vietnam War era. Therefore, while President Reagan avoided "overshoot and collapse" (to use Richard Pious's term discussed in chapter 4), he did suffer considerable political "backlash" that damaged his professional reputation and public prestige. As a result, presidential power eroded and President Reagan became a lame duck near the end of his administration.

Both Watergate and Iran-contra entailed foreign policy and constitutional struggles over the power to make war illustrating the contradiction between the demands of national security and of democracy. This tension produced a political struggle between the legacy of the cold war—presidential preeminence over war and peace—and the political changes that have occurred since the Vietnam War, manifested by the reassertion of congressional power. Both crises resulted in the curtailment of presidential power by the power of congressional oversight and investigations.

Will other political and constitutional crises result from future legislative-executive conflicts over foreign policy? Certainly, an institutional structure remains in place that allows for such an occurrence. An immense and powerful national security bureaucracy continues to exist alongside a reassertive Congress. The contradictions between the demands of national security and those of democracy have not been resolved. Much will depend on each president and the nature of his administration and foreign policy, for the catalyst in both crises has involved major presidential commitments in the use of force. On the one hand, the collapse of the Soviet Union and of communism in Eastern Europe and the promise of the cold war's end has diminished the appeal of anticommunism as a justification for American military intervention abroad and may minimize the chances for a new legislative-executive crisis. On the other hand, the Persian Gulf War demonstrates that force remains a key instrument of presidential policy, and Congress's role remains an uncertain one, depending on the outcome of the conflict.

It is important to point out that the power of oversight and investigations allowed Congress to play an important role during the events preceding the Persian Gulf War. Congressional involvement in the Persian Gulf crisis went from initial passivity and support early on, to greater involvement and criticism as the crisis lengthened, and then to rallying round the flag when the war began. On the one hand, congressional passivity and support demonstrates the president's ability to dominate foreign policy during times of crisis involving the use of force. On the other hand, the period of congressional activism and criticism also demonstrates that the president faces a much more uncertain and inhospitable environment since Vietnam, even during a time of crisis involving the use of American troops abroad.

In response to Iraq's invasion of Kuwait on August 2, 1990, President Bush, after consulting with his closest advisers, decided to deploy over 100,000 American troops to defend Saudi Arabia from further Iraqi expansion. Although Congress remained uninvolved, these significant early decisions by the Bush administration were met with initial support by most members of Congress and the general population—the country rallied round the flag during a time of crisis. However, this supportive domestic environment changed once President Bush announced—following the November congressional elections—that he was doubling American troop strength to over 400,000 and moving from a defensive military strategy reliant on economic sanctions to an offensive strategy to force Iraq to withdraw from Kuwait.

As the crisis became prolonged and the threat of a bloody war appeared on the horizon, members of Congress and people throughout American society became increasingly uncertain and critical of Bush's resort to brinksmanship as the most sensible way to proceed. Relying on its power to investigate, Congress became active in the Persian Gulf crisis and increasingly critical of the president's policy of threatening the use of military force to persuade Iraq to withdraw without war. The Senate Armed Services Committee held hearings under Chairman Sam Nunn, one of the most respected members of Congress on questions of defense, in late November and December on the president's Gulf policy. Of the numerous individuals who testified during the **Nunn hearings,** including former secretaries of defense, chairmen of the Joint Chiefs of Staff, and other prominent officials, most expressed opposition to the Bush administration's change in policy away from reliance on economic sanctions to military force. Congress was thus acting as a forum by which presidential use of military force was being challenged during a foreign policy crisis in a way not seen since World War II. With divisions growing in Congress and throughout the country, along with President Bush's issuance of a January 15 ultimatum for Iraq to withdraw, the House and Senate debated and voted. It was a historic debate, and the final vote authorizing presidential use of force against Iraq, reflecting a divided country on the eve of war: 52–47 in favor in the Senate, 250–183 in favor in the House of Representatives.

Once President Bush took the country to war with Iraq on January 16, 1991, the Congress and the country again rallied behind the flag. Uncertainty and questions remained in the minds of many Americans and members of Congress about the costs of the war. But as the air war proceeded with little loss of American lives, followed by a ground war that fully routed the Iraqi military, most doubts were forgotten. Thus, the quick and decisive military victory squelched the doubts and criticisms of the Bush administration's handling of foreign policy in the Gulf and strengthened the president's ability to dominate policymaking during a crisis over the war-making power.

The rapidity with which the country and Congress became divided over the Persian Gulf policy, nevertheless, indicates that presidents do not automatically dominate crises and war making as they once did during the cold war years. While the Fulbright hearings occurred in 1966, during the height of the Vietnam War, *after* American troops had been fighting for some time, the Nunn hearings occurred *before* the war in the Persian Gulf began. Also, unlike the Gulf of Tonkin resolution, which was "unanimously" approved in 1964 with only two votes in opposition, the resolution authorizing presidential use of military force in the Persian Gulf in 1991 was a divided and close vote.

President Clinton experienced a number of congressional investigations during his term of office, though in a somewhat different fashion than discussed above. Committee investigations in both the House and the Senate were conducted into such matters as Whitewater and Clinton and Gore's 1996 presidential

campaign and fund-raising efforts, including the foreign policy impact of political contributions from the People's Republic of China to the Clinton-Gore campaign. Although most of the investigations had little to do with foreign policy per se, and regardless of the significance or truth of the allegations, they do impact the president's overall ability to govern and lead, including in the area of foreign policy. Like investigations of the past, discussed above, the Clinton investigations were heavily partisan as a result of divided government—led by Republican members of Congress after the 1994 elections to damage a sitting Democrat in the White House.

Ultimately, Clinton and the country went through and survived a yearlong crisis of governance over the Monica Lewinsky affair. Against the wishes of a majority of the American public (who opposed Clinton's personal behavior but deemed it to be more of a private matter), a Republican special prosecutor and Congress conducted numerous and intensive investigations of the Clintons, eventually resulting in the House of Representatives on December 18, 1998, voting, along highly partisan lines, four articles of impeachment for presidential abuse of power. Two of the articles of impeachment were considered and ultimately voted down in the Senate on February 12, 1999, also on a highly politicized and partisan vote (all Democrats voting against impeachment, almost all Republicans voting in favor).

The Watergate, Iran-contra, Persian Gulf War, and Monica Lewinsky hearings are testaments to the reassertion of congressional power and the greater uncertainty that presidents face since Vietnam in attempting to govern, especially in foreign policy. Congressional investigations and hearings can also affect U.S. foreign relations with countries abroad. This is best illustrated when members of the Bush Sr. administration testifying before Congress in 2000 may have contributed to the false impression that Saddam Hussein could invade Iraq without U.S. opposition and when the 1993 Republican-led Cox hearings in the House exaggerating charges of Chinese espionage damaged U.S.-Chinese relations. Such hearings and investigations can exacerbate relations, especially because foreign leaders and audiences do not understand the independent and often partisan nature of Congress within the U.S. government.

At the same time, Congress's initial response to the September 11 terrorist bombings demonstrates that Congress is also quite capable of rallying behind the president and the flag. And although reluctant to become involved in congressional hearings (including Democrats) *before* the war with Iraq, despite increasing dissent, this has not stopped Congress from investigating the Enron scandal or, as more information has surfaced, investigating the intelligence that existed and what the president and his foreign policy advisers knew before the September 11 terrorist attacks. But ultimately, although Congress agreed to a new Department of Homeland Security in 2002, serious reform of the FBI, the CIA and most of the intelligence community has not been pursued.

Whatever the outcome, since Vietnam presidents have experienced and can continue to expect a proliferation of executive branch activity on the Hill in response to greater congressional involvement and oversight. As Bruce Jentleson asserts, "The number of times the Secretary of State and top officials must come to Capitol Hill to testify, the number of reports that have to be written, the number of negotiating sessions that have to be held, the amount of congressional staff time invested, the days of floor debate taken up—all these come out of a finite stock of time and energy."[63]

PROSPECTS

Clearly, the years since Vietnam and the collapse of the cold war have produced a legislative branch more attentive and active in the making of U.S. foreign policy. Although Congress has been unsuccessful in fundamentally restricting presidential power and fully reasserting its own foreign policy power, the president nonetheless faces considerably greater congressional constraints than during the cold war. From the president's perspective, Congress is basically an obstructionist institution that prevents the country from achieving a coherent foreign policy that efficiently responds to the demands of national security. From the perspective of many members of Congress—depending on the president and his party identification—Congress is fulfilling its constitutional duties and acting as a check on presidential abuse of power. The argument is that a U.S. foreign policy that appears a little messy and inconsistent reflects the nature of American democracy.[64]

Regardless of one's sympathies in the continuing debate over the American national security and versus American democracy, this has been the nature of legislative-executive relations since Vietnam. This raises two important questions. First, what are the possibilities for reform in legislative-executive relations? Second, how might the complex politics of legislative-executive relations evolve in the future?

Legislative-Executive Reform? The reassertion of congressional power in interbranch politics has led to periodic calls for rationalizing the process. The reforms tend to revolve around the need to promote a more cooperative and efficient working relationship between the legislative and executive branches to overcome the divided government that appears to have become endemic in American politics. Some of the reforms emphasize the need to increase presidential power and the president's ability to govern, such as recommendations to limit the president to a single six-year term and to synchronize the terms of national office so that elections would be held for representatives every four years and senators every eight years, when presidential elections were held. Other reforms represent efforts to make members of Congress less responsive to special interests and more responsive to the general public, as reflected in the call for term limits for members of Congress. Reformers believe that changes such as these will strengthen the president's governing coalitions and allow more freedom of action. However, these recommendations do have problems. Constitutional amendments must be passed before they can become law—not an easy task. More important, a single presidential term of office eliminates the presidential accountability inherent in maintaining a reelection posture, a major strike against democracy in the name of greater efficiency.[65] And term limits do not guarantee that individual members will be more responsive to most of their constituents and the so-called general welfare.

Most of these reforms represent efforts to fine-tune the workings of legislative-executive relations and address the crisis of leadership discussed in chapter 4. Other reformers are more pessimistic about the stalemate in legislative-executive relations. They see the problem to be less a crisis of leadership—although leadership is important—than a crisis of governance. They argue that the paradox of presidential power is so severe today that a president can no longer form a government. This problem is most visible in the constant struggles and divisions in legislative-executive relations. This governmental gridlock represents larger patterns in society as well, such as weak political parties and strong interest groups. More pessimistic reformers advocate a radical restructuring of the Constitution, such as toward a parliamentary system of government along the lines of the English system.[66] They argue that this centralizes power under a strong chief executive while simultaneously maintaining strong democratic accountability. Regardless of one's view of such proposals, the obvious problem with them is the unlikelihood that the American public will choose to abandon a presidential system for a parliamentary one after more than two hundred years.

The Future? Aside from possibilities of reform, many observers question the ability of Congress to maintain a prolonged influence over foreign policy. They argue that Congress has excessive constraints that hamper its role as an effective and significant policy force. They point to the cyclical nature of legislative-executive foreign policy relations throughout American history. On these grounds, congressional reassertion is said to have peaked—a temporary phenomenon to be overwhelmed by the stronger pattern of presidential and executive dominance.[67] The reassertion of congressional authority and involvement since Vietnam, however, is unlikely to disappear in the foreseeable future, even though it may decline somewhat in response to the September 11 attacks and President Bush's war on terrorism.

Three principal elements support the continuation of an active, though sporadic, congressional role in the foreign policymaking process. First, Congress has experienced institutional changes that were instrumental in allowing its reassertion of influence in foreign policy. These changes are not temporary but have been institutionalized in a more bureaucratic environment. Furthermore, major membership turnover—which has the potential to alter Congress as an institution—is difficult to achieve in a short period of time given the high reelection rates of incumbents and the large number of "safe seats." Furthermore, the differences in the strength of each major party in each chamber is so small that the switch of only a few seats from one party to another following an election can produce different party control in the House and/or the Senate, creating considerable uncertainty for the future of divided government, presidential power, and majority coalitions. In this sense, the outcome of future congressional elections is both uncertain and likely to be potentially quite significant.

Second, changes in the domestic environment since the cold war have prompted and reinforced congressional activism in foreign affairs. The cold war consensus that fueled bipartisanship and the imperial presidency has been replaced by competing policy perspectives and greater diversity in domestic politics, which constrains presidential power while strengthening Congress's role in foreign policy. There is insufficient evidence that the September 11 attacks and the war on terrorism have produced a new foreign policy consensus to replace the anti-communist consensus of the cold war years. The importance of the domestic political setting in examining the role of the president, the foreign policy bureaucracy, and legislative-executive relations in the making of U.S. foreign policy will be examined in Part III.

Finally, changes in the international environment have affected the foreign policy agenda in ways that should ensure congressional involvement. The international system has become more complex since the 1950s, when most Americans saw the world divided between two superpowers and their opposing forces. A more complex international environment has provided the setting for America's failure in Vietnam and the shattering of the cold war consensus in domestic politics. This has been reinforced by the demise of the Soviet empire and the changes taking place in Eastern Europe. This has elevated what were once considered "low" policy issues, such as international economics, to the top of the contemporary foreign policy agenda—intermestic issues that members of Congress traditionally influence—even with the growing importance of terrorism as an issue.

Although institutional changes in Congress, changes in the domestic environment, and changes in the international environment and foreign policy agenda combine to ensure a prominent role for Congress in the future conduct of U.S. foreign policy, *a strong presidential role in foreign policy also will continue for the following reasons:* First, Congress has great difficulty coordinating its efforts, and this frequently makes its involvement ineffective and counterproductive for

U.S. foreign policy. Until Congress improves its collective leadership, which is unlikely, it will remain an institution that largely reacts to presidential initiatives. Second, congressional involvement in foreign policy has been reinforced by the existence of relatively weak presidents. Nixon became consumed with Watergate, Ford was a passive president, and Carter's naiveté quickly led to the alienation of Congress. Bush Sr. and Clinton were not particularly strong and successful post–cold war presidents. Nevertheless, the powers of the president remain formidable and can be revived under strong leadership, as Ronald Reagan demonstrated. Third, times of crisis tend to be moments of presidential dominance. The country tends to turn to the president during national emergencies, especially if they involve the use of American troops abroad, as was the case during the Persian Gulf War and following the September 11, 2001, terrorist attacks on New York and Washington, D.C. Finally, the growing complexity and demands of international politics upon American society and the governmental system will continue to require a strong presidency. Despite the end of the cold war, simple peace and prosperity are not at hand, and the United States remains the world's great power. This means that U.S. involvement and leadership in world affairs will, for better or worse, continue.

Ultimately, the president is the primary political figure capable of leading the government and the country in foreign policy. Yet the days of presidential supremacy in most areas of foreign policy are past; for a president to behave as if executive dominance prevails is to risk the type of political and constitutional crises that Nixon and Reagan experienced. Unless a global calamity occurs that creates the perception of a chronic state of national emergency for the United States, ushering in a new period of legislative-executive relations, considerable congressional involvement and influence will continue for the foreseeable future. This is likely to be the case even with the terrorist attacks on America and President Bush's war on terrorism.

SUGGESTED SOURCES FOR MORE INFORMATION

An abundance of literature on Congress and foreign policy is available. Arthur M. Schlesinger, Jr., in *The Imper-*

ial Presidency (Boston: Houghton Mifflin, 1989), provides an excellent historical overview of legislative-executive relations and the rise of presidential power from the constitutional foundations to Watergate, with a perspective on Iran-contra. An excellent analysis of the rise and impact of McCarthy and McCarthyism in Congress and U.S. foreign policy is provided by Robert Griffith in *The Politics of Fear: Joseph R. McCarthy and the Senate* (Amherst: University of Massachusetts Press, 1987). Louis Henkin provides a good summary assessment of the constitutional basis for the sharing of power in foreign affairs and its continued relevance for understanding contemporary legislative-executive relations in U.S. foreign policy in "Foreign Affairs and the Constitution," *Foreign Affairs* 66 (winter 1987–88): 284–310.

An extremely informative overview and discussion of the role of Congress in foreign policy since Vietnam is provided by Thomas M. Franck and Edward Weisband, *Foreign Policy by Congress* (New York: Oxford University Press, 1979), James M. Lindsay, *Congress and the Politics of U.S. Foreign Policy* (Baltimore: Johns Hopkins University Press, 1994), and Randall B. Ripley and James M Lindsay, eds., *Congress Resurgent: Foreign and Defense Policy on Capitol Hill* (Ann Arbor: University of Michigan Press, 1993). Thomas E. Mann provides an excellent overview of the contemporary legislative-executive relationship in foreign policy in "Making Foreign Policy: President and Congress," in Thomas E. Mann, ed., *A Question of Balance: The President, the Congress and Foreign Policy* (Washington, D.C.: Brookings Institution Press, 1990), pp. 1–34, as does James M. Scott in "Interbranch Rivalry and the Reagan Doctrine in Nicaragua," *Political Science Quarterly* (summer 1997): 237–60.

Good overviews of the way Congress operates as an institution are provided by Randall B. Ripley, *Congress: Process and Policy* (New York: W.W. Norton, 1988), and Lawrence C. Dodd and Bruce I. Oppenheimer, eds., *Congress Reconsidered* (Washington, D.C.: Congressional Quarterly Press, 2000). James L. Sundquist presents an excellent overview of the idea of party government and a theory of divided government in "The New Era of Coalition Government in the United States," *Political Science Quarterly* (1988): 613–35. An excellent and informative discussion of the actual workings of the legislative process and congressional politics can be found in John M. Barry, *The Ambition and the Power* (New York: Viking Penguin, 1989), and Hedrick Smith, *The Power Game: How Washington Works* (New York: Ballantine, 1996). Eric Alterman provides a fascinating portrayal of the institutional norms and expectations that exist throughout Congress in order for individuals to become effective by describing the evolution of Ron Dellums from radical outsider to "Ron Dellums: Radical Insider," in *World Policy Journal* (winter 1993–94): 35–46.

Michael Glennon provides a very good overview of the constitutional authority of the president, Congress, and the judiciary in the making of foreign policy during war, focusing on the relevancy of the War Powers Act, in "The Gulf War and the Constitution," *Foreign Affairs* (spring 1991): 84–101. Louis Fisher and David Gray Adler examine the legislative history of the WPA and come to a pessimistic conclusion in "The War Powers Resolution: Time to Say Goodbye," *Political Science Quarterly* (spring 1998): 1–20. Norman Ornstein and Thomas Donilon discuss how the process of nominating and confirming executive appointments has become cumbersome and slow in "The Confirmation Clog," *Foreign Affairs* (November–December 2000): 87–99.

In regards to interbranch politics and U.S. foreign policy toward Saddam Hussein and Iraq, Pamela Fessler chronicles the political dynamics of Congress during the 1980s, when most members were more interested in helping their constituents and promoting American business exports to Iraq, rather then exercise sanctions for human rights violations, thereby ultimately reinforcing the Reagan and Bush administrations' support of Saddam Hussein before he invaded Kuwait and triggered the Persian Gulf War in "Congress' Record on Saddam: Decade of Talk, Not Action," *Congressional Quarterly* (April 27, 1991), pp. 1068–77. See also Michael Dobbs, "When an Ally Becomes the Enemy: The U.S. Supplied Weapons to Iraq before 1990, Now it Denounces the Buildup," *Washington Post National Weekly* Edition (January 6–12, 2003), pp. 9–9–10, and Mark Hosenball, "The Odd Couple: How George Bush Helped Create Saddam Hussein," *The New Republic* (June 1, 1992), pp. 27–35.

KEY TERMS

Articles of Confederation
authorization and appropriation processes
Boland Amendments
Bricker amendment
budgetary process
coalition building
committee system
Congressional Budget Office (CBO)
congressional oversight
Congressional Research Service (CRS)
congressional staffs
Constitution
continuing resolution
divided government
executive agreements
fast track authority
fiscal year
founders' intent
Fulbright hearings
General Accounting Office (GAO)
Gulf of Tonkin resolution
Jesse Helms
impeachment proceedings
intelligence oversight committees
interbranch politics
intermestic issues
internal security investigations
invitation to struggle
Iran-contra hearings
legislative norms
legislative process
Joseph McCarthy
McCarthyism
Nunn hearings
pendulum (or cyclical) effect
political ambition
presidential appointments
presidential dominance versus congressional dominance
    versus codetermination
Senate approval of NATO
Senate Committee on Foreign Relations
seniority
separate institutions sharing power
southern Democrats
Tower Commission
treaties
War Powers Act
Watergate hearings

CHAPTER 12

. . . .

THE JUDICIARY, STATE GOVERNMENTS, AND THE WASHINGTON POLITICAL COMMUNITY

*W*hen discussing the government and foreign policy–making process, most observers focus on the role of the president, the bureaucracy, and Congress. These are the three key actors or sets of institutions directly involved in making foreign policy. To achieve a comprehensive understanding of governmental politics, however, it is also important to be aware of the remainder of the government and its place in foreign policy—which has too often been ignored in the study of U.S. foreign policy.

This chapter addresses the following questions: What role does the judiciary, especially at the federal level, play in U.S. foreign policy? To what extent do state and local governments play a role in foreign policy, and is this role likely to increase with the end of the cold war? And what exactly is the Washington political community, and how does it impact the politics of U.S. foreign policy? Addressing these questions will provide a more thorough understanding of continuity and change, presidential power, and the tensions between democracy and security in the complex politics of U.S. foreign policy.

THE JUDICIARY

The role of the judiciary has often been ignored in the study of U.S. foreign policy. Most scholars assume that **judicial restraint** has prevailed in foreign affairs and that, in the rare instance that the judiciary decides a case directly involving foreign policy, it usually reaffirms the status quo. This assumption of judicial restraint oversimplifies the complex reality of American history.[1]

HISTORICAL OVERVIEW

The judiciary has played a role in influencing U.S. foreign policy since the beginning of the country. The Constitution of the United States is quite explicit about judicial power in foreign affairs as prescribed in Article III, section 2:

> The judicial power shall extend to all cases, in law and equity, arising under this Constitution, the laws of the United States, and treaties made,

or which shall be made, under their authority;— to all cases affecting ambassadors, other public ministers and consuls; . . . to controversies . . . between a State, or the Citizens thereof, and foreign states, citizens or subjects.

In all cases affecting ambassadors, other public ministers and consuls, and those in which a State shall be party, the Supreme Court shall have original jurisdiction. In all the other cases before mentioned, the Supreme Court shall have appellate jurisdiction, both as to law and fact, with such exceptions, and under such regulations, as the Congress shall make.

Yet as discussed in chapter 11, the Constitution was ambiguous in specifying the powers of governmental institutions and the workings of the political system in the United States. Consequently, the judiciary has been crucial in deciding the parameters or boundaries of legitimate behavior for different actors within the political process. *The judiciary has been a significant force in interpreting the Constitution in two fundamental areas affecting foreign policy:* determining (1) the legitimate relationship between the state governments and the national government, and (2) the distribution of power within the national government.

The first major constitutional issue to confront the country concerned the question of federalism, that is, state versus national supremacy. The early power of the state governments clouded the nature of the powers of the national government. Because the Constitution had little to say about the distribution of power between the state governments and the national government, the judiciary helped fill an important void. Basing its decisions upon the Constitution and the concept of nation-state sovereignty, the Supreme Court usually ruled that the national government was supreme, especially concerning questions of war and peace. Since the first chief justice, **John Marshall,** the Supreme Court has rendered significant decisions concerning the nature of federalism that have had a major impact on foreign as well as domestic policy.

The second major constitutional issue involved the distribution of power within the national government. As discussed in chapter 11, a governmental arrangement of different institutions sharing power created major disputes between the legislature and the executive. As Louis Henkin has explained in *Foreign Affairs and the Constitution,* although "there is virtually

nothing related to foreign affairs that is beyond the constitutional powers of the federal government, . . . we are not told how the undifferentiated bundle of powers inherent in sovereignty is distributed among the federal branches."[2] The judiciary helped to fill the void. In foreign policy, the Supreme Court has tended to rule that the office of the president predominates, especially when the use of force abroad is involved.

By the twentieth century, major constitutional contention over federalism and the distribution of legislative-executive power gave way to a growing consensus that the national government was supreme and that the president was preeminent in foreign affairs. This perception was reinforced by America's participation in World Wars I and II. With these controversial questions apparently settled, the judiciary's activity and influence in foreign policy diminished. Hence, what most Americans take for granted today—that the national government and the president are supreme in foreign affairs, especially over questions of war and peace—was the product of long historical development in which the judiciary played a vital role, especially in the nineteenth century.

The mid-twentieth century probably represented the height of judicial restraint because of the rise of the cold war. Perceptions of a national emergency that were part of the cold war consensus propelled the president to the forefront of the foreign policymaking process, supported by the actions of Congress. As with other public and private institutions in American society, the judiciary during the cold war was hesitant to become involved in major issues of foreign policy. Moreover, when a federal court did decide a relevant case, it usually reaffirmed the political status quo. Judicial restraint and occasional involvement, in other words, served to legitimize the extraordinary powers of the president and the executive branch.[3]

THE POST—VIETNAM, POST—COLD WAR ERA

The height of the cold war is the period from which many Americans have based their view of the foreign policy-making process. It was an extraordinary time during which presidential supremacy and judicial restraint were the norm. Thus, the Supreme Court and the judiciary could be ignored, particularly if one was interested in understanding the sources of U.S. national security policy. The time since Vietnam, however, represents a movement away from the extraordinary years of the cold war. The breakdown of the cold war consensus not only resulted in the relative decline of presidential power and the reassertion of congressional authority in foreign policy but also allowed other governmental actors such as the judiciary to play a more active role.

Numerous contemporary legal cases suggest that the judiciary has become more active and influential in the area of foreign policy. In a 1983 decision, for example, the Supreme Court ruled in *Immigration and Naturalization Service v. Chadha* that the "legislative veto," here involving immigration, was unconstitutional because it violated the separation of powers. The veto was one of the major procedural techniques Congress used to assert its influence over executive branch decisions in a number of areas including foreign policy. The decision called into question Congress's ability to veto presidential decisions—that is, to pass a concurrent resolution without the president's signature—concerning, for example, the use of force abroad under the War Powers Act, sales of major weapons systems to foreign governments under the International Security Assistance and Arms Export Control Act, and the export of nuclear fuel and facilities to foreign countries under the Nonproliferation Act.[4]

In the same month as the *Chadha* decision, the Supreme Court ruled in *Capital Industries-EMI, Inc. v. Bennett* that the state of California may base its taxation on a corporation's worldwide income rather than on income earned solely within the state. This decision to allow a "unitary" system of taxation has important implications for the location of corporate headquarters and subsidiaries, thereby influencing America's international economic policy. (It is worth pointing out that this important Supreme Court decision about corporate taxation has been reaffirmed by the recently created World Trade Organization, which has ruled against U.S. tax laws allowing U.S. corporations to exempt their foreign revenues from U.S. taxation, arguing that this is an illegitimate form of government subsidization of foreign exports inconsistent with free trade. The ruling demonstrates the importance of the global context and international organizations.)[5]

Contemporary judicial decisions, in fact, have affected U.S. foreign policy in a wide variety of cases. These have included labor stoppages involving foreign trade, trade issues in violation of U.S. law, job discrimination in foreign multinational corporations operating in the United States, the rights of refugees and immigrants, foreign debt payments to private U.S. banks, nuclear proliferation, waste disposal and environmental degradation, libel suits against the press, and the release of classified government information.[6] Such cases are symbolic of a judiciary that has become more active and important in foreign policy.

As Louis Henkin suggested over thirty years ago:

> Common preoccupation with the Supreme Court in its role as the arbiter of the power of the political branches tends to conceal its other powers relevant to foreign policy.... [The courts] have not been wholly content to sit outside the growing field of foreign relations. The "infallibility" that comes from having final say on the meaning of the Constitution allows the courts to determine also what they may and will do in the exercise of their own judicial power, and they have been asserting it to play small parts—some old, some new—in regard to foreign relations.[7]

And since Vietnam and the end of the cold war, the judiciary has asserted itself to play a larger part in foreign relations.

This is not to say that the judiciary is as consequential as the legislature or the executive in influencing foreign policy. Rather, the judiciary has been more active and more influential since Vietnam than it was during the height of the cold war. Judicial decisions no longer simply reaffirm the status quo; rather, courts have become increasingly independent and now act as additional constraints on the president's ability to govern foreign policy.

The judiciary is most likely to play a significant role in issues divorced from political-military affairs, in what during the cold war was "low" foreign policy. The judiciary, particularly the Supreme Court, has been reluctant to decide controversial **"political questions"** with direct political-military implications, especially between the legislative and executive branches, usually preferring that the political system resolve these matters on its own. Nevertheless, the judiciary's power to resolve disputes involving the nature of the Constitution and the political process allows it to affect issues of foreign policy and play a growing role.[8]

Judicial activity in foreign policy tends to involve the resolution of disputes in three areas of the political process: between the national government and the state governments, the Congress and the presidency, and since World War II, the government and individuals. The first two areas have involved questions of traditional judicial involvement. In addition, the Supreme Court under **Chief Justice Earl Warren** in the 1960s extended and intensified the protection of the Bill of Rights to individuals (civil liberties and rights in the making of foreign policy will be examined in chapter 14). This action provided a foundation for greater judicial involvement and activism. Adjudication of these three types of disputes has resulted in increased direct judicial involvement in the policy–making process and, indirectly, in growing influence of the judiciary over policy areas such as international economics and immigration.

Although the judiciary may be most active and influential in issues considered low policy, such issues have become more important over the last few decades, and they do impact more traditional national security issues. The courts, for example, were used to prosecute members of the president's staff and administration for violating laws resulting from presidential abuse of power in the Watergate and Iran-contra affairs. With respect to Watergate, not only was President Richard Nixon forced to resign, but many of his advisers and members of the White House staff were found guilty and served prison terms (while over twenty business executives were convicted of giving illegal campaign contributions).

With respect to criminal prosecution in Iran-contra, four patterns predominated. First, a number of individuals carrying out the policies of the Reagan administration pleaded guilty or were convicted of violating laws related to the scandal. They included National Security Adviser Robert McFarlane, National Security Adviser John Poindexter, National Security Council staffer Oliver North, Assistant Secretary of State Elliott Abrams, courier Robert Owen, private fund-raisers Carl Channel and Richard Miller, arms merchant Richard Secord, financier Albert Hakim, and former officials of the Central Intelligence Agency (CIA) Thomas Clines, Alan Fiers, and Clair George. Second, most of the sentences were relatively light, involving probation, modest fines, and community service. In fact, President Bush Sr. pardoned six people on Christmas Eve of 1992: McFarlane, Abrams, Fiers, George,

former senior CIA official (indicted but not yet tried) Duane Clarridge, and (also indicted but not yet tried) Caspar Weinberger, secretary of defense under President Reagan. However, the lives of the individuals involved were completely disrupted by the congressional investigations and the public trials. Robert McFarlane became so distraught that at one point he tried to take his own life.[9]

Third, the trials demonstrated that the courts are not "above politics" or immune to ideology. For example, Colonel Oliver North appealed his four convictions in federal district court to a court of appeals. The appeals court ruled in a 2–1 decision to overturn one conviction and to send the other three convictions back to the district court to have the presiding judge determine if the trial proceedings were tainted by previous information disclosed during the congressional investigation of Iran-contra. The two appeals court judges in favor of the decision had been appointed by President Ronald Reagan, while the judge opposed was a Carter appointee. Furthermore, it was reported that one of the Reagan-appointed federal judges, Laurence H. Silberman, previously had been a longtime CIA agent who also was involved in the Iran-contra affair early on, thus resulting in a classic case of conflict of interest. Ultimately, the charges and convictions against Oliver North (and John Poindexter) were dismissed over the legal technicality that the judicial proceedings involved information derived from North's earlier "immune" testimony before Congress.[10]

Finally, the Iran-contra trials also demonstrated the continuing tension between the demands of national security and of democracy. A strong case by the government's special prosecutor Lawrence Walsh and the defendants' right to a fair trial required access to classified information, while the national security ethos required the primacy of government secrecy. "Thus," according to journalist Theodore Draper, "we have here a strange judicial proceeding brought in the name of the government but hamstrung by the same government."[11] Compromises were reached, such as President Reagan agreeing to testify, but the special prosecutor had to drop the most serious charges in most cases because of the secret classification of the evidence.[12] In other cases, such as that of Felix Rodriguez, former CIA station chief in Costa Rica, all charges were dismissed because the U.S. Justice Department blocked the release of classified information.[13]

Special Prosecutor Lawrence Walsh was furious with governmental blockage of information in the name of national security. In a report he sent to the House and Senate intelligence committees he stated:

> The Attorney General and the CIA not only frustrated the public development of this proof but did so in a manner that exasperated the district court and dragged out the resolution of this issue in unproductive litigation. . . . The administration's actions in *United States vs. Fernandez* and in the other Iran-Contra prosecutions underscore the need for objective standards to govern the release of classified information in criminal prosecutions. . . . This lack of objective standards can lead to the frustration of law enforcement.[14]

Walsh's preoccupation with legality and objective standards ignored the crucial role politics played throughout the Iran-contra episode, including the judicial proceedings. As Draper concluded in "Revelations of the North Trial,"

> So long as a few officials in the government can withhold documents, justice cannot be served. Once the defense demands the appearance in court of classified documents and the government decides to withhold them, the government—an interested party in these proceedings—has the power to determine the very nature of the trial.[15]

This was a similar problem, for example, in 2001 when the U.S. General Accounting Office on behalf of Congress sued Vice President Richard Cheney (who led the energy interagency task force) to release classified information that led to the Bush Jr administration's energy policy.

Due in part to the litigious nature of American society, *a relatively new development is the increasing numbers of individuals and organizations, both American and foreign, that are using U.S. courts to defend their rights under international law.* The plaintiffs range from Holocaust survivors to terrorist victims to the inhabitants of tropical rain forests; the defendants include multinational corporations, foreign officials, and even governments. This new trend toward lawsuits in American courts takes three basic forms: (1) suits against individuals for grave violations of international law, such as human rights, committed in the name of govern-

ments; (2) a growing body of litigation against foreign and multinational corporations for violating, for example, international law involving human rights and the environment (such as the Holocaust litigation against Swiss banks); and (3) suits against foreign governments to achieve justice for victims of terrorism and oppression. Although many of the cases have been rejected or have failed in court, many of the cases also have received considerable publicity and have contributed to the U.S. government negotiating settlements between the parties.

As Anne-Marie Slaughter and David Dosco state in "Plaintiff's Diplomacy": "When traditional diplomacy proves inadequate to the task of enforcing international law and justice, plaintiffs should be able to carve out new diplomatic channels, bypassing the uncertainty of political negotiations and compensating for the weakness of international tribunals by turning to effective national courts." That this development has occurred despite opposition from the U.S. executive branch in defense of traditional national sovereignty and immunity reflects the "continuing decentralization and democratization of foreign policy." But this also raises troubling foreign policy questions. "American courts today," Slaughter and Dosco argue, "are walking a fine line between expanding a transnational legal system capable of enforcing international law and engaging in a unilateral legal expansion" that may damage long-term U.S. interests. Moreover, continued American refusal to participate in and adhere to bodies like the International Criminal Court may create "the image of a country happy to haul foreign defendants into its own courts while stubbornly resisting even the remote possibility that its own citizens might be called to account." Clearly, "keeping U.S. courts open to legitimate claims based on violations of international law but closed to issues likely to damage the conduct of foreign policy and politicize the courts will not be easy" in the future (see essay 3.2 on international law and unilateralism).[16]

THE SUPREME COURT AND THE FUTURE

The role of the judiciary ultimately is heavily a function of Supreme Court actions. The Supreme Court is the most influential judicial body, for its behavior is fundamental in establishing legitimacy for judicial activism in all areas of public policy—both for lower federal courts (courts of appeals and district courts) and for all state courts.[17]

Supreme Court rulings represent the "law of the land"; their significance lies in the authority of the Supreme Court to undertake **judicial review,** determining the constitutionality of a law. Not only is the Supreme Court the ultimate arbiter of the Constitution and domestic law, it is also the major interpreter of international law for the United States, and its decisions occasionally result in additions to the body of international law.[18]

The future role of the judiciary—its level of involvement and the nature of its decisions—will be heavily affected by **presidential judicial appointments,** especially to the Supreme Court. When an opening on the Court appears, the president usually nominates, with the advice and consent of the Senate, someone who reflects his political beliefs. Therefore, presidential appointments affect the Court's ideological orientation as vacancies on the Court occur and as the political landscape evolves—a slow process involving long time lags since federal justices can remain on the bench for life.

Such a change in the ideological orientation is exactly what has happened to the Supreme Court over the past thirty years as a result of the Republican party's dominance of the presidency, which allowed Presidents Reagan and Bush Sr. to make a majority of appointments to the high court. Under **Chief Justice William Rehnquist,** the Supreme Court has increasingly reflected a more conservative orientation.[19]

The **Clarence Thomas confirmation hearings** demonstrated the political importance and partisan nature of the appointment and confirmation process. The testimony revolving around the charges of sexual harassment also was one of the few times that the significance of individual contacts and networking in Washington, D.C., was made painfully visible to the general public. During the administration of Bill Clinton—unlike the previous Democratic president, Jimmy Carter, who made no appointment—the opportunity arose to appoint two individuals more liberal in orientation and affect the ideological dynamics of the Supreme Court (see **table 12.1** on Supreme Court justices).

It is not exactly clear how these developments will affect Supreme Court and judicial decisions in the area of foreign policy. On the one hand, a more conservative Court may be more likely to exercise judicial restraint concerning so-called political questions and, when cases are reviewed, may be more likely to decide them in deference to the president over questions of war and peace. On the other hand, much uncertainty remains today, for many questions that bear on foreign

TABLE **12.1**
SUPREME COURT JUSTICES (IN ORDER OF SENIORITY)

NAME	YEAR OF BIRTH	PRIOR EXPERIENCE	APPOINTED BY	YEAR OF APPOINTMENT
William H. Rehnquist *Chief Justice*	1924	Assistant attorney general	Nixon*	1972
John Paul Stevens	1920	Federal judge	Ford	1975
Sandra Day O'Connor	1930	State judge	Reagan	1981
Antonin Scalia	1936	Law professor, federal judge	Reagan	1986
Anthony Kennedy	1936	Federal judge	Reagan	1988
David Souter	1939	Federal judge	Bush	1990
Clarence Thomas	1948	Federal judge	Bush	1991
Ruth Bader Ginsburg	1933	Federal judge	Clinton	1993
Stephen Breyer	1938	Federal judge	Clinton	1994

*Appointed chief justice by Reagan in 1986.

ESSAY 12.1
CURTISS-WRIGHT AND THE YOUNGSTOWN STEEL-SEIZURE CASE

Although the Constitution is ambiguous on the point, *two major judicial interpretations of the distribution of power between the executive, legislative, and judicial branches in foreign policy have prevailed since World War II*. The *Curtiss-Wright* case in 1936 concluded that the president was supreme in foreign policy making, and served to legitimize the extraordinary rise of presidential power during the cold war. The steel seizure case in 1952 concluded that foreign policy was produced by different governmental institutions that shared power and has come to serve as a more accurate barometer of the policymaking process that has evolved since the Vietnam War.

United States v. Curtiss-Wright Export Corp. has been cited by the president, and those who support presidential preeminence in foreign policy, as a major source of presidential power since World War II. The Supreme Court not only upheld a congressional grant of authority to the president to prevent the sale of arms to belligerents (which the Curtiss-Wright Corporation had violated in a war involving Bolivia and Paraguay) but ruled generally in favor of national governmental and presidential supremacy in foreign policy. The famous majority opinion by Justice George Sutherland was written in 1936 and legitimized in the most sweeping terms the president's implied constitutional authority to conduct foreign affairs, claiming that the president's "very delicate, plenary and exclusive power . . . as the sole organ of the federal government in the field of international relations . . . does not require as a basis for its exercise an act of Congress."[A]

In *Youngstown Sheet & Tube Co. v. Sawyer,* the Supreme Court in 1952 invalidated President Harry Truman's attempt to invoke national-security emergency powers during the Korean War to seize domestic steel mills that were under nationwide strike. The Supreme Court found that the president's steel seizure was not authorized by Congress. Thus, the president had violated Congress's lawmaking authority. The famous concurring opinion by Justice Robert Jackson described a more flexible relationship, in which separate institutions shared power: "Presidential powers are not fixed but fluctuate, depending on their disjunction or conjunction with those of Congress."[B]

Justice Jackson's opinion established a three-tiered hierarchy of legitimate presidential actions in terms of legislative-executive relations. First, "when the President acts pursuant to an express or implied authorization of Congress, his authority is at its maximum, for it includes all that he possesses in his own right plus all that Congress can delegate." Second, "when the President acts in absence of either a congressional grant or denial of authority, he can only rely upon his own independent powers, but there is a zone of twilight in which he and Congress may have concurrent authority, or in which its distribution is uncertain." The third level occurs "when the President takes measures incompatible with the express or implied will of Congress, his power is at its lowest ebb, for then he can rely only upon his own constitutional powers minus any constitutional powers of Congress over the matter."[C]

Thus, two very different perspectives, represented by these two important Supreme Court rulings, have developed as to the distribution of power over foreign policy. The *Curtiss-Wright* interpretation that the president is "the sole organ of the federal government" in the making of U.S. foreign policy legitimized the growth of presidential and executive branch power, congressional acquiescence, and judicial restraint during the cold war. Its legacy influenced presidential actions under Richard Nixon and Ronald Reagan, thereby triggering constitutional crises.

The steel seizure case, in contrast, is a more accurate reflector of the nature of legislative-executive relations in foreign policy since the Vietnam War. Congressional reassertion has constrained the president's ability to govern foreign policy, and the legislative-executive relationship has varied depending on the issue and other factors. The president is preeminent in some cases—reflecting Justice Jackson's first constitutional level, in which presidential authority is at its maximum. Yet many foreign policy issues are a function of joint participation—Justice Jackson's twilight zone of shared powers. Louis Henkin has observed, "Important foreign affairs powers lie in that twilight zone. Indeed, in few other respects is our constitutional system as troubled by uncertainty in principle and by conflict in practice between Congress and the Presi-

---

A. *United States v. Curtiss-Wright Export Corp.*, 299 U.S. 305 (1936).
B. *Youngstown Sheet & Tube Co. v. Sawyer*, 343 U.S. 579 (1952).

C. Ibid.

dent. The effect is to raise intractable issues of constitutional jurisprudence and constitutional politics."[D]

Therefore, Jackson's third level of interaction is particularly instructive: "when the President takes measures *incompatible with the express or implied will of Congress, his power is at its lowest ebb*" (my emphasis). This is the position in which both Presidents Nixon and Reagan found themselves with regard to Vietnam and Nicaragua, respectively. Rather than abstaining from acting or modifying their policy initiatives in accordance with congressional action, they circumvented Congress and triggered the Watergate and Iran-contra scandals.

The Jackson opinion in the steel seizure case also expressly rejected judicial restraint in foreign policy and national security affairs. Rather, Justice Jackson defined a pivotal role for the courts as arbiters of the nature of the legislative-executive relationship. Jackson argued that when challenges were made to the presi-

dent's sweeping claims of exclusive control over foreign affairs, the courts should not abstain but "must . . . scrutinize [those claims] with caution, for what is at stake is the equilibrium established by our constitutional system."[E] The contemporary era, in fact, has seen an increase in judicial involvement and influence in foreign policy, although the future remains unclear.

It is interesting to note that the height of the *Curtiss-Wright* case's influence was twenty years after the decision was rendered in 1936—a time when the president was far from the "sole organ" in foreign policy. Likewise, the steel seizure case's philosophy reflects the policymaking process since Vietnam, a generation after the original decision in 1952, a time when the president's power was almost supreme in foreign affairs. Thus, it may be only a matter of time before a new perspective arises, reflecting a different judicial ruling and offering a new interpretation of the role of the executive, the legislature, and the judiciary in the making of foreign policy.

D. Louis Henkin, "Foreign Affairs and the Constitution," *Foreign Affairs* 66 (winter 1987–88): 285.

E. Ibid.

SOURCES: Louis Henkin, *Foreign Affairs and the Constitution* (Mineola, N.Y.: Foundation Press, 1972); Harold Hongju Koh, "Why the President (Almost) Always Wins in Foreign Affairs: Lessons of the Iran-Contra Affair," *Yale Law Journal* 97 (June 1988): 1281–342; Harold Hongju Koh, *The National Security Constitution: Sharing Power After the Iran-Contra Affair* (New Haven, Conn.: Yale University Press, 1990); Gordon Silverstein, "Constitutional Interpretation and American Foreign Policy: What Congress and the Executive Can Learn from the Courts," in Paul E. Peterson, ed., *The President, the Congress, and the Making of Foreign Policy* (Norman: University of Oklahoma Press, 1994).

---

policy that come before the Court will involve foreign policy issues such as civil rights, economics, and immigration—areas in which ideology may not provide simple and straightforward answers. **Essay 12.1** provides a discussion of the two major competing judicial interpretations and their impact on the foreign policy–making process made in *United States v. Curtiss-Wright Export Corp.* and *Youngstown Sheet & Tube Co. v. Sawyer.*

It goes without saying that the judiciary had an indirect but profound effect on U.S. foreign policy through the controversial presidential election of 2000. Initially influenced by the Florida Supreme Court and ultimately decided by the U.S. Supreme Court, a vote of 5–4 stopped the Florida recount of the presidential votes, and Republican George Bush Jr. defeated Democrat Albert Gore in Florida, which gave Bush a majority of votes in the electoral college and made him president of the United States. As David Kaplan states in *The Accidental President*, "That wrenching decision pit-

ted the Court's five conservatives against its four liberals, producing vitriolic opinions not seen in a generation, in a case many thought the Court should not have taken in the first place."[20] It was also unprecedented in American history (except for the Hayes-Tilden presidential stalemate of 1876) and clearly represents another way the courts, although with great controversy, can impact the politics of U.S. foreign policy.

The outcome clearly demonstrates the significant role of ideology, personalities, and politics behind the black robes in the making of decisions. As reported in "The Truth Behind the Pillars," Supreme Court Justice Sandra Day O'Connor and her husband were at an election night party on November 7 with their friends. When the media called the state of Florida for Al Gore, she exclaimed "this is terrible" in public. "Moments later, with an air of obvious disgust, she rose to get a plate of food, leaving it to her husband to explain her somewhat uncharacteristic outburst." John O'Connor said "his wife was upset because they wanted to retire to Arizona, and a Gore win meant they'd have to wait another four years. O'Connor, the former Republican majority leader of the Arizona State Senate and a 1981 Ronald Reagan appointee, did not want a Democrat to name her successor. Two witnesses described this extraordinary scene."[21]

In fact, although the justices tried to defuse the controversy and publicly argue that the high court remained beyond partisanship, behind the scenes "the justices were stewing. In particular, the dissenters—Justices Stephen Breyer, Ruth Bader Ginsberg, David Souter and John Paul Stevens—couldn't believe what their conservative brethren had wrought." Given the magnitude of the decision and the hard feelings, "the amazing aspect of **Bush v. Gore** is that it just might've gone the other way. Justice Anthony Kennedy—the key swing vote, the man the Court's law clerks once dubbed 'Flipper' for his equivocations—had wavered, enough that Souter thought until the very end that he'd get him. If Kennedy could be flipped, the 5-to-4 ruling for Bush would become a 5-to-4 win for Gore."

A month later, the animosities within the Court finally spilled out when the American justices were playing host to special visitors from Russia—six judges. This was the fifth meeting between the two sets of judges at the Supreme Court—"an attempt by the most powerful tribunal in the world to impart some of its wisdom to a nascent system trying to figure out how constitutional law really worked in a democracy." But rather than discussing general topics, "some of the Russians wanted to know how *Bush v. Gore* had come to pass—how it was that somebody other than the electorate decided who ran the government. That was the kind of thing that gave Communism a bad name."

> Stephen Breyer, one of the dissenters and a Clinton appointee, was angry and launched into an attack on the decision, right in front of his colleagues. It was "the most outrageous, indefensible thing" the Court had ever done, he told the visiting judges. "We all agree to disagree, but this is different." . . . "However awkward or difficult" it might've been for Congress to resolve the presidency, Breyer had written, "Congress, being a political body, expresses the people's will far more accurately than does an unelected Court. And the people's will is what elections are about."

"O'Connor talked pedantically about the Electoral College," Kaplan reports, "which of course, had nothing to do with the Russians' curiosity. Rehnquist and Scalia—the intellectual firebrands on the Court's right flank—said almost nothing," leaving it up to Kennedy to explain the 5–4 ruling in which he was the critical vote. "'Sometimes you have to be responsible and step up to the plate,' Kennedy told the Russians. 'You have to take responsibility.' He prized order and stability. Chaos was the enemy." Congress wasn't even mentioned in the opinions of the Court's conservatives, even though Congress was "democratically elected, politically accountable, and specifically established by the Constitution as well as by federal statute, to finally determine a disputed presidential election." Kaplan concludes, "Nobody 'forced' Kennedy or four of his brethren to hear *Bush v. Gore.*" Ultimately, "the justices chose themselves."

In sum, since Vietnam there has been less judicial restraint and more judicial involvement in cases that affect U.S. foreign policy directly and indirectly. Judicial involvement is most likely to influence the policymaking process for issues that are more divorced from national security concerns. As Henkin has so appropriately concluded in his revised edition of *Foreign Affairs and the Constitution*:

> The role of the courts in foreign relations appears likely to remain modest, even more modest than its constitutional role generally. But it may yet become less modest if President and Congress are again tempted—as they were during the Cold War—to tread on important individual rights in the name of national security. Overall, the contribution of the courts to foreign policy and their impact on foreign relations are significant but not large. The Supreme Court in particular intervenes only infrequently and its foreign affairs cases are few and haphazard. The Court does not build and refine steadily case by case; it develops no expertise or experts; the Justices have no matured or clear philosophies; the precedents are flimsy and often reflect the spirit of another day. But though the courts have only a supporting part, it is indispensable and inevitable.[22]

Although the judiciary remains a peripheral institution in the making of U.S. foreign policy as compared to the executive and legislative branches, its involvement does complicate the policymaking process, especially for the president and his efforts to govern foreign policy. It is unclear as to how the events of September 11 will alter this, although they have clearly exacerbated the tension between national security and civil liberties. In the final analysis, the degree to which a more active judicial role is forthcoming depends on the political environment, the direction taken by the Supreme Court, and the judicial interpretation that guides its actions.

STATE AND LOCAL GOVERNMENTS

The role of state and local governments has received little attention in the study of U.S. foreign policy. However, due to the decline of the foreign policy consensus of the cold war, state and local governments have been playing a more active and visible role in U.S. foreign policy since Vietnam. As with the judiciary, state and local governments play a peripheral role and are most active on issues that are removed from national security affairs. Nonetheless, state and local governments have become increasingly involved in the complex politics of U.S. foreign policy.

State and local governments have become a part of the foreign policy political process for three principal reasons. First, the U.S. Constitution created a federal form of government. **Federalism** involves the sharing of sovereignty—the supreme authority to govern—between two sets of governments. Most countries have a unitary system of government, in which sovereignty resides with the national government alone. In the United States, however, sovereignty is shared between the central government—commonly referred to as the federal or national government by Americans—and the state governments. The creation of a federal governmental system is a function of America's early history, in which thirteen separate former colonies with strong state governments coexisted under the Articles of Confederation. Within a federal system, the state governments have certain rights and powers that the central government cannot restrict. This explains the existence of fifty-one constitutions in the United States—one for the central government and one for each of the fifty state governments. Although the Supreme Court has tended to rule in favor of the national government over state governments in disputes, state governments remain independent and retain significant sources of

power, allowing them to carve out areas of influence that impinge upon U.S. foreign policy.[23]

The second reason why state and local governments have impacted foreign policy is that the United States has a great deal of state and local government. The United States contains over eighty thousand different governmental bodies: one central government, fifty state governments, and a multitude of local governments that take the form of cities, townships, counties, school districts, and special districts (for fire protection, water service, and so on). Of the roughly seventeen million governmental bureaucrats in the United States, about 70 percent are employees of state and local governments. State and local governments spend over $1.6 trillion (of which almost one-third is provided by the federal government in the form of various grants for different purposes). The $1 trillion raised and spent by state and local governments represents roughly one-third of all governmental expenditures combined.[24] Clearly, the United States has much government below the central governmental level. There is a certain irony in the immense size of state and local government: Americans are very individualistic and cynical about large government, especially the federal government; yet most of the government is located at the local level and was created by the states. The sheer size and existence of state and local governments in the United States has made them a part of the complex politics of U.S. foreign policy.

Finally, state and local governments play a more active role in U.S. foreign policy due to increasing global interdependence. American society, including state and local communities, have become increasingly affected by international developments. Over two decades ago, Chadwick Alger documented the wide-ranging networks of interdependence that existed between Columbus, Ohio, and the rest of the world. As Alger has found throughout his work, "There is no doubt that the global context of cities is changing and that the self-conscious and organized responsiveness of people to these changes is growing."[25] John Hamilton, as well as other scholars, has described the growing connections between the smallest U.S. communities and the rest of the world in *Mainstreet America and the Third World.*[26]

IMPACT ON FOREIGN POLICY

The growth in the foreign policy activity of state and local government has impacted the making of U.S. foreign

TABLE 12.2
TOP FIFTY METROPOLITAN EXPORTERS

CITIES	EXPORTS ($BILLIONS)
1. Seattle–Bellevue–Everett, WA	32.4
2. San Jose, CA	28.3
3. Detroit, MI	28.0
4. New York, NY	24.5
5. Los Angeles–Long Beach, CA*	23.9
6. Chicago, IL	21.1
7. Houston, TX	19.0
8. Minneapolis–St. Paul, MN–WI	12.4
9. Miami, FL	11.9
10. Boston, MA–NH	10.4
11. Portland–Vancouver, OR–WA	9.4
12. Orange County, CA*	9.3
13. Philadelphia, PA–NJ	9.3
14. San Francisco, CA	9.0
15. San Diego, CA	9.0
16. Dallas, TX	8.1
17. El Paso, TX	7.8
18. Atlanta, GA	7.6
19. Phoenix–Mesa, AZ	7.5
20. Washington, DC–MD–VA–WV	7.2
21. Cincinnati, OH–KY–IN	6.8
22. Oakland, CA	6.7
23. Cleveland–Lorain–Elyria, OH	5.9
24. Newark, NJ	5.4
25. Indianapolis, IN	5.2
26. Austin–San Marcos, TX	4.9
27. Wilmington–Newark, DE–MD	4.9
28. St. Louis, MO–IL	4.9
29. Middlesex–Somerset–Hunterdon, NJ	4.9
30. Nassau–Suffolk, NY	4.7
31. Richmond–Petersburg, VA	4.6
32. Rochester, NY	4.4
33. Greensboro–Winston–Salem–High Point, NC	4.3
34. Bergen–Passaic, NJ	4.2

TABLE 12.2
(cont.)

CITIES	EXPORTS ($BILLIONS)
35. Fort Worth–Arlington, TX	4.0
36. Pittsburgh, PA	3.9
37. Hartford, CT	3.9
38. Milwaukee–Waukesha, WI	3.7
39. Greenville–Spartanburg–Anderson, SC	3.4
40. Kansas City, MO–KS	3.3
41. Grand Rapids–Muskegon–Holland, MI	3.3
42. Memphis, TN–AR–MS	3.1
43. Raleigh–Durham–Chapel Hill, NC	3.0
44. Charlotte–Gastonia–Rock Hill, NC-SC	2.8
45. Albuquerque, NM	2.7
46. Laredo, TX	2.7
47. Stamford–Norwalk, CT	2.6
48. Brownsville–Harlingen–San Benito, TX	2.6
49. New Orleans, LA	2.4
50. Tampa–St. Petersburg–Clearwater, FL	2.4

*Orange County is actually part of metropolitan Los Angeles.

SOURCE: U.S. Department of Commerce, 1999.

policy in two general ways. First, state and local government predominantly impacts non-security-oriented policy issues, the most obvious being trade and business investment. In the last few decades, state governments have become increasingly involved in foreign trade and investment, with state trade missions to foreign countries now routine affairs. As discussed in chapter 9, foreign imports into the United States exploded from $11.6 billion in 1955, to $55.3 billion in 1972, to $441 billion in 1988, to more than $1.4 trillion at the turn of the century. Likewise, American exports rose from $15.5 billion in 1955, to $49 billion in 1972, to $320 billion in 1988, to more then $1 trillion by the year 2000 (review table 9.1). Such a large and growing volume of international trade has major consequences for the economies of states and localities.

The Port of Los Angeles and the Port of Long Beach, for example, are the two busiest ports in the United States. Separately, they are the eighth and tenth busiest ports in the world. Together, they represent the third busiest port in the world (after Singapore and Hong Kong) and the largest final destination port in the world. In 2002, over 190 million metric tons and over 10 million container units valued at over $200 billion went through the Ports of Los Angeles and Long Beach, an increase of almost 200% since 1990. Ironically, they are geographically next to each other, but are administered by separate local port authorities and compete with each other as the port of choice for imports and exports.

Table 12.2 lists the top fifty metropolitan areas in the United States that are engaged in exports and are heavily impacted by international trade. Over $536 billion dollars in goods were exported by 253 cities, or Metropolitan Statistical Areas (MSAs). From 1993 to 1999, exports from the 253 metro areas increased by $172 billion. In 1999, ninety-three metro areas had export sales of $1 billion or more, representing over 70 percent of total U.S. merchandise exports. The metro areas that posted the largest percentage increases in export sales were almost exclusively small and midsized cities scattered throughout the United States.

Not surprisingly, state and city governments have gotten increasingly involved in matters of international economics. The competition between different locales throughout the country for foreign investment, such as for a Toyota or Sony plant, has become quite intense. Not only does this activity affect local economies, but state and local governments have increasingly played a direct role in international economics and indirectly affected U.S. foreign economic policy (see **essay 12.2** on the importance of foreign investment and trade for state governments).[27]

Immigration is another intermestic issue of great importance to the United States and many states. Anywhere from 700,000 to 1.5 million immigrants are legally admitted into the United States each year. More controversial has been the larger flow of "illegal" immigration into the United States. California, Texas, Florida, and New York have been most affected by large numbers of illegal immigrants. Over the last decade Florida has had to face huge waves of so-called "boat people" fleeing Cuba and Haiti—in the tens of thousands—in an effort to become refugees and enter the United States. The governor of Florida in response to the crises, and domestic concerns and politics, has been forced to declare states of emergency and become actively involved in U.S. immigration policy. Clearly, immigration flows and demographic changes have profound effects on the economies and governments of states and locales.

Second, state and local governments also play a role in directly affecting U.S. national security policy. With the rise of McCarthyism during the cold war, for instance, state government actions reinforced the politics of anticommunism that was prevailing in national politics. Over thirty states passed legislation, mirroring laws at the federal level, requiring public employees to take loyalty oaths and barring public employment to individuals engaged in subversive practices or involved in organizations on the U.S. attorney general's subversives list. Among those most affected were public school teachers—from elementary schools to universities—who were also prohibited from engaging in "seditious" classroom instruction. "Anti-radical legislation was not, of course, new to most states," according to historian Robert Griffith. "Yet what was remarkable about the great outpouring of the late forties was that

so many legislatures acted at the same time and in the same way." Municipalities likewise, among them Detroit and New York City, passed similar ordinances.[28] Clearly, cold war–era politics were pervasive at the national, state, and local levels, thus reinforcing and heightening the anticommunism of the times.

Since the post-Vietnam collapse of the anticommunist consensus, state and local governmental activity has affected U.S. national security policy in more diverse ways. During the early 1970s, for example, the Port Authority of New York, a local government, created a furor in U.S.-French-British relations when it denied clearance for the French-and-British-made SST (Super Sonic Transport) to land at Kennedy Airport because it violated local noise regulations. The French and the British could not understand why the president or the central government was unable to overrule the Port Authority of New York.

In the 1980s, state and local governments became important arenas for making the **nuclear freeze** and **anti-South-African-apartheid issues** of national concern. Grassroots efforts by local groups were successful in passing nuclear freeze resolutions by local governments and promoting divestment of government funds from American companies doing business with South Africa. States have also attempted to prevent the shipment of nuclear waste, such as from the federal nuclear weapons complex in Rocky Flats, Colorado, to other federal nuclear facilities—successfully in Idaho during the 1980s and with less success in South Carolina in 2002 (review essay 7.1 on America's nuclear weapons facilities). Sometimes these efforts at the state and local level catalyze social movements that influence governmental politics at the national level. Thus, grassroots efforts helped produce political controversy for the Reagan administration's arms-control policies and forced U.S. government economic sanctions against South Africa. The SST case also illustrates how so-called low foreign policy issues have a great impact on foreign policy relations in general, while the nuclear freeze and anti-apartheid movements dealt with matters of great national-security concern.[29]

STATE AND LOCAL STRATEGIES

Michael Shuman, in "Dateline Main Street: Local Foreign Policies," points out that the *foreign policy actions*

ESSAY 12.2
FOREIGN INVESTMENT AND EXPORTS, STATE GOVERNMENTS, AND THE COMPETITIVE SPIRIT

When foreign companies look to invest in America, states become aggressive in competing with each other through different development strategies and incentives packages. Foreign investment brings jobs and an influx of money for the local economy. Not surprisingly, state and local governments have become increasingly active in attempting to attract new foreign investment (from abroad as well as from outside the state). Such is the case not only for large states, like California and New York, but for small states as well. Clearly, the implications for local economies and politics, as well as the politics of U.S. foreign policy, loom large.

Foreign investment has grown enormously within the United States. Direct foreign investment in property, plant, and equipment in the United States surpassed $1 trillion by 2000 and employed over five million people. States offer big money to win foreign investment, and the trend has been to offer more and more incentives with time. For example, in the 1980s, Honda Corporation got a $16 million grant from the state of Ohio for a plant in Marysville. In the 1990s Kentucky had to agree to more than $125 million in perks for a Toyota Motor Corporation plant in Georgetown—it is estimated, in fact, that state and local governments will have paid as much as $350 million in incentives when all of the numbers are finalized.

Competition between states and locales have become, if anything, increasingly more fierce. The state of Tennessee had to offer the investors of a Japanese auto-parts plant highway improvements, new sewer lines, tax abatements, discounted utility rates, English language lessons, and driving lessons to win the plant. And the trend with most companies, especially Japanese-owned ones, is to know what the last investor got and use that as a starting point for negotiations. Some states have even attempted to get airlines to offer direct flights to Japan.

Similar incentives were given to BMW to build a plant in South Carolina—to invest a total of $800 million by 1998 and create over twenty-two hundred jobs. The tax incentives alone provided by the state of South Carolina and by local governments totaled over $200 million. The incentive package included $70 million for state and local tax breaks, $62 million for airport improvements, $37 million for land, $23 million for site improvements, and $10 million for training costs. A $100 million widening of the interstate highway was also to occur, most of it funded by the federal government. As the headline of Columbia's newspaper, *The State*, put it, "S.C.'s Incentive Deal for BMW Equals $100,000 per Job."

South Carolina economic development is a good illustration of the importance of these international economic activities for state and local governments. One of the most important governmental agencies is the South Carolina Department of Commerce, which actively attempts to attract foreign investment into the state (and promote exports abroad). Although the total value of foreign investment is not particularly large in comparison to other states—South Carolina has only three million people—it has a larger percentage of employees working for foreign-owned companies than any other state, after Hawaii. Since 1960 more than $20 billion of foreign corporate investment in manufacturing, distribution, and administrative headquarters have entered the state, producing more than ninety thousand jobs. And foreign investment has steadily grown, as **table 12.3** demonstrates.

In 1999 alone, 245 international firms invested over $2.7 billion in South Carolina and created about eight thousand new jobs. Michelin North America made the largest investment by an international firm, totaling $900 million in four South Carolina counties. Its expansion will create fourteen hundred new jobs. Investments by international businesses totaled over $16 billion from 1990 to 1999, four times more than that in the previous decade. New jobs from international companies grew by fifty thousand from 1990 to 1999, twice as much as the previous decade. Investments from new and expanding international companies often tend to have a ripple effect on the activities of other local companies. BMW, for example, engaged in subcontracting with at least fifteen other companies for supplies and parts.

South Carolina attracted foreign investment from twenty-three different countries by 1999, eight more than in 1996. Of this, the bulk of the foreign investment comes from France, Germany, Japan, Switzerland, and the United Kingdom. **Table 12.4** breaks down foreign investment by country within South Carolina in 1999.

South Carolina has become increasingly attractive to a widening range of high-tech, high value–added international companies, especially in the areas of metals and equipment, rubber and plastics, transportation, chemicals, and textile products. Although international companies

TABLE 12.3
INTERNATIONAL CAPITAL INVESTMENT ACTIVITY

SOUTH CAROLINA HISTORICAL TRENDS, 1960–1999

YEAR	EMPLOYMENT	INVESTMENT (THOUSANDS)
1999	7,993	$2,742,829
1998	7,532	$2,572,001
1997	5,977	$2,100,200
1996	4,981	$2,254,888
1995	6,307	$1,832,930
1994	4,089	$1,049,859
1993	3,376	$670,210
1992	5,085	$1,397,302
1991	2,043	$830,089
1990	2,424	$912,607
1989	3,503	$1,114,258
1988	3,162	$710,255
1987	5,226	$618,511
1986	1,819	$153,909
1985	2,228	$188,259
1984	1,225	$136,379
1983	1,164	$130,695
1982	965	$450,460
1981	2,716	$492,816
1980	1,347	$348,908
1979	3,988	$392,535
1978	2,719	$208,205
1977	3,825	$408,162
1976	2,260	$186,005
1975	275	$58,800
1974	3,005	$313,053
1973	3,713	$340,660
1972	705	$61,900
1971	290	$4,635
1970	940	$72,300
1969	610	$48,400
1968	2,525	$184,500
1967	350	$17,750
1966	2,582	$152,800
1965	2,200	$79,250
1964	510	$29,506
1963	825	$40,182

TABLE **12.3**
(*cont.*)

SOUTH CAROLINA HISTORICAL TRENDS, 1960–1999

YEAR	EMPLOYMENT	INVESTMENT (THOUSANDS)
1962	50	$485
1961	0	$500
1960	500	$32,083
Prior 1960	970	$79,560
Totals	**90,011**	**$20,675,807**

SOURCE: South Carolina Department of Commerce, 1999 *Annual Report.*

TABLE **12.4**
INTERNATIONAL CAPITAL INVESTMENT ACTIVITY IN SOUTH CAROLINA BY INVESTMENT LEVEL, 1999

COUNTRY	FIRMS	%	JOBS	%	INVESTMENT	%
France	28	11.4%	1,959	24.5%	1,041,624,378	38.0
Germany	54	22.0%	2,310	28.9%	527,290,279	19.2
Japan	29	11.8%	1,240	15.5%	463,512,729	16.9
Switzerland	20	8.2%	164	2.1%	248,742,097	9.1
United Kingdom	36	14.7%	514	6.4%	102,478,528	3.7
Belgium	7	2.9%	146	1.8%	79,730,586	2.9
Canada	16	6.5%	445	5.6%	73,068,321	2.7
Italy	9	3.7%	168	2.1%	53,221,082	1.9
Netherlands	9	3.7%	201	2.5%	43,281,852	1.6
China	2	0.8%	300	3.8%	30,010,000	1.1
Sweden	10	4.1%	220	2.8%	24,310,000	0.9
Bermuda	C	C	107	1.3%	11,946,000	0.4
Korea	C	C	82	1.0%	10,987,663	0.4
Kuwait	C	C	C	C	9,600,000	0.4
Australia	C	0.0%	21	0.3%	9,275,000	0.3
Denmark	4	1.6%	34	0.4%	5,205,710	0.2
Ireland	C	C	0	0.0%	3,345,000	0.1
Taiwan	1	0.4%	7	0.1%	2,200,000	0.1
Chile	1	0.4%	52	0.7%	1,500,000	0.1
Austria	C	0.0%	14	0.2%	715,000	0.0
Luxembourg	C	C	5	0.1%	650,000	0.0
Israel	C	C	2	0.0%	105,000	0.0
Singapore	1	0.4%	2	0.0%	30,000	0.0
Totals	**245**		**7,993**		**2,742,829,225**	

C indicates *confidential information* withheld at the request of the company.

SOURCE: South Carolina Department of Commerce, *1999 Annual Report.*

FIGURE 12.1
CAPITAL INVESTMENT OF INTERNATIONAL FIRMS IN SOUTH CAROLINA, 1999

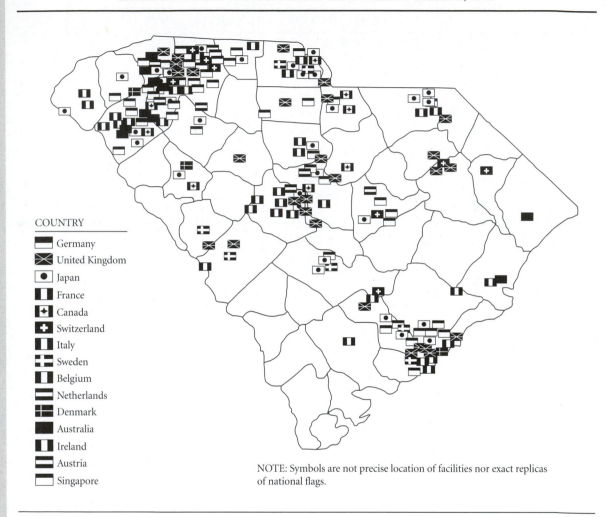

COUNTRY

Germany
United Kingdom
Japan
France
Canada
Switzerland
Italy
Sweden
Belgium
Netherlands
Denmark
Australia
Ireland
Austria
Singapore

NOTE: Symbols are not precise location of facilities nor exact replicas of national flags.

South Carolina Department of Commerce, *2000 Annual Report.*

have invested in plant and equipment throughout the state, most of the activity has been located near the three major metropolitan areas of Charleston, Columbia, and especially, Greenville-Spartanburg, as detailed in **figure 12.1**.

Clearly, for South Carolina as with many states, foreign investment is a major state and local strategy for promoting economic development. South Carolina has also been active in its trade promotion abroad. In 2000 South Carolina firms exported almost $8 billion of made-in-

South-Carolina products, up 50 percent from 1994, to over 170 countries (see **table 12.5** for major export markets abroad). Over thirteen hundred South Carolina manufacturers export abroad, representing 37 percent of total state manufacturers.

The state's Department of Commerce has a trade office in Munich for promoting markets in Europe, Africa, and the Middle East; a trade office in Tokyo; and a new trade office in Hong Kong, created in 1999 for trade pro-

TABLE **12.5**
SOUTH CAROLINA EXPORT MARKETS

RANK	COUNTRY	2000 ($THOUSANDS)	% CHANGE 1997–2000
1	Canada	2,230,499	37.6
2	Mexico	1,964,121	109.9
3	Germany	840,914	−1.6
4	Japan	400,343	46.6
5	United Kingdom	297,785	39.8
6	Belgium	202,482	82.8
7	France	139,091	28.8
8	Italy	103,139	4.1
9	Netherlands	93,053	−3.8
10	Brazil	89,165	1.7
11	Australia	89,150	6.2
12	Switzerland	86,798	271.6
13	El Salvador	86,786	267.3
14	South Korea	84,231	24.8
15	Honduras	83,041	39.8
16	Hong Kong	81,171	−21.2
17	Taiwan	77,342	−51.8
18	Thailand	62,466	260.8
19	China	61,012	32.8
20	Ireland	58,531	147.6
21	Malaysia	51,671	214.8
22	Singapore	48,786	9.1
23	Philippines	44,704	378.4
24	Peru	35,960	532.0
25	Argentina	32,301	−15.3
26	Jamaica	32,070	240.6
27	Dominican Republic	30,580	−39.1
28	United Arab Emirates	28,264	224.0
29	Spain	27,536	−22.3
30	Venezuela	25,287	−38.9
31	Chile	24,273	−8.8

(*cont.*)

TABLE 12.5
(*cont.*)

RANK	COUNTRY	2000 ($THOUSANDS)	% CHANGE 1997–2000
32	Guatemala	24,178	−2.4
33	Colombia	21,288	−21.0
34	Israel	19,062	−6.6
35	Saudi Arabia	18,026	−30.4
36	Sweden	15,134	6.5
37	New Zealand	14,614	−6.4
38	India	13,204	−54.9
39	South Africa	12,765	−16.0
40	Austria	12,577	−14.1
41	Turkey	10,681	−27.6
42	Denmark	10,211	29.3
43	Kuwait	8,334	0.4
44	Pakistan	7,698	−64.8
45	Costa Rica	6,500	−63.1
46	Panama	6,434	−37.6
47	Trinidad and Tobago	6,387	16.3
48	Poland	6,252	215.1
49	Indonesia	5,917	−83.3
Total	179	**7,817,552**	**20.7**

SOURCE: U.S. Department of Commerce, Bureau of Economic Analysis.

motion throughout Asia and the Pacific Rim countries. It also increased participation in international trade missions and trade shows, scheduling twenty trade events, up from just two the previous year. Locations included Israel, South Africa, Austria, Australia, South America, the Philippines, Poland, Japan, Germany, the Czech Republic, and the Slovak Republic.

Because of all the economic implications of foreign trade and investment, there is much room for political gain and controversy. Increased jobs and growing economies, whatever their source, tend to play well in state and local politics. The closing of plants and elimination of jobs, however—especially if they move abroad— can destroy a local community and produce popular re-

sentment. For example, in South Carolina, where international companies are newly investing, older businesses, such as textiles, have been closing their doors. Such is the complex politics of international trade and investment at the national, state, and local levels as the United States enters the twenty-first century.

SOURCES: Chris Burritt, "BMW Eases Boom and Bust of Textiles," *Atlanta Constitution* (April 14, 1996), sec. H, p. 9; Bill Powell, "War Between the States," *Newsweek* (May 30, 1988), pp. 44–45; Gerald F. Seib and John Harwood, "Foreign Competition Batters State's Textiles, but Fuji and BMW Provide Jobs," *Wall Street Journal* (Feb. 28, 1996), sec. A, p. 1; South Carolina Department of Commerce, *1999 Annual Report;* Betsy Teter, "S.C.'s Incentive Deal for BMW Equals $100,000 per Job," *The State* (September 27, 1992), pp. 1A, 11A.

by state and local governments fall into three rough categories: consciousness-raising measures, bilateral measures, and unilateral measures.[30] For example, "most local governments, whether they realize it or not, are involved in raising public consciousness on foreign affairs through education, research, and lobbying." According to Shuman, "virtually every municipality has international affairs–related curricula in its public schools, its adult education courses, and its museums and cultural centers."[31] Lobbying campaigns also have been used by local governments to promote the visibility of issues. Resolutions, as discussed above, were passed at the local level to promote the nuclear freeze and anti-apartheid issues.

In addition to consciousness-raising, state and local governments have negotiated thousands of bilateral agreements with foreign governments. The development of **sister cities** began to spread following World War II as a means to provide American humanitarian and cultural assistance. They have proliferated in the last three decades to sustain long-term, mutual relationships involving a diverse range of activities, including economic cooperation, student exchanges, heath care projects, cultural programs, municipal cooperation, and more. More than eight hundred American cities have formed over two thousand sister city relationships with over one thousand foreign cities, ranging across all fifty states and over 120 countries throughout the world. For example, there are over sixty U.S.-Italian, over two hundred U.S.-Japanese, over ninety U.S.-Chinese, and over forty U.S.-Taiwanese sister city relationships. Furthermore, there are four sister city relationships between the U.S. and Vietnam, and seven sister city relationships between the U.S. and Cuba. Sister Cities International (SCI), a nonprofit organization created in 1967, helps to coordinate sister city linkages and maintains a headquarters staff in Washington, D.C.[32] As discussed above, bilateral economic relationships have been actively pursued by state governments and agencies.

Finally, state and local governments have also taken unilateral initiatives—such as the use of policing, zoning, contracting, and investing powers—in addition to the initiatives involving trade and economic investment discussed above. These activities range from the creation of "nuclear free zones," to giving sanctuary to Central American refugees, to various measures to divest and restrict relations with South Africa and with companies doing business in South Africa. In fact, the impact of state and local governments continued after President George Bush Sr. lifted economic sanctions in September 1991 against South Africa following some progress in the dismantling of the legal policy of apartheid. Over twenty-five states, twenty counties, and eighty cities (plus many other public and private institutions), including big city governments such as Los Angeles, New York, and San Francisco, continued to impose sanctions until apartheid was completely abolished, thus contributing to very low levels of U.S.-South African trade.[33]

In a proactive initiative in response to the large influx of people from the Caribbean and Central America, the state of Florida in 1981 created the **Florida International Volunteer Corps**—a unique type of state-level "Peace Corps" to promote economic and political development throughout the region. The intent is for volunteers in a wide variety of professions and fields to provide short-term, small-scale, self-help technical assistance and training overseas in health, agriculture, social services, education, the environment, disaster management, and more. There are an estimated 150 volunteer missions currently each year, and there have been more than a thousand volunteer missions to twenty-five countries and territories in the Caribbean and Central American region since the corps's inception. The Florida International Volunteer Corps acts in partnership with its Caribbean neighbors, as well as the U.S. government (such as the Agency for International Development) and various international developmental organizations, on the assumption that Florida's future is interwoven with its Caribbean neighbors.[34]

In light of the September 11, 2001, terrorist attacks, states have become active in promoting anti-terrorism and homeland security measures. This new "emphasis on security," the *Christian Science Monitor* reported, "is bringing tougher state penalties for terrorism, better radio networks for police, and closer scrutiny of citizens—via everything from wiretapping to the renewal of a driver's license."[35] This has important implications for both U.S. national security policy and its inherent tension with civil rights and liberties in a democratic polity. It also means that not only must homeland security be financed and coordinated among the various federal departments and agencies, but it must also be financed and coordinated among state and local governments as well—a huge challenge facing the federal and state governments.

Overall, whether the role of state and local governments will become more influential remains to be seen. Judicial decisions have ruled in favor of national supremacy, limiting foreign policy actions by state and local governments.[36] Nevertheless, the political environment since Vietnam has given state and local governments greater flexibility for action. This is likely to be reinforced by changes in East-West relations with the end of the cold war, the increasing interdependence between America and the world, and the continuing revolution in global communications. For example, Governor Jim Hodges of South Carolina in his State of the State address on January 16, 2002, highlighted three themes, two of which directly involved foreign policy: homeland security; the state of the economy; including the importance of international trade and investment; and education. Clearly, although state and local governments remain peripheral foreign policy players for the most part, their involvement makes the politics of U.S. foreign policy an even messier and more complex process.

THE WASHINGTON POLITICAL COMMUNITY

The final governmental source of influence on the policymaking process that needs our attention is the Washington political community. The **annual Gridiron dinner** exemplifies this side of life in the nation's capital. "The annual spring dinner of the Gridiron Club, an elitist social club of sixty print journalists, is," Hedrick Smith writes, "one of the high tribal rites of Washington insiders. It is a gathering of political celebrities that combines snob appeal with Hollywood glitter." The Gridiron dinner brings together six hundred of the most powerful, best-known people in America at the Capitol Hilton hotel; every president since Benjamin Harrison has participated at least once. The Gridiron dinner is the scene of "Hollywood stars rubbing elbows with the captains of industry, the anchors of television, the publishers and other princes of the print press, the deans of the diplomatic corps, the elders of the Supreme Court, the movers and shakers of Congress, and the ranking echelons of the current administration."[37]

It's an evening of making fun of and roasting the nation's leaders. "For some politicians, the Gridiron has been a priceless forum for reshaping their images and reputations by showing a human side, an ability to laugh at themselves, which is the principal formula of success at the dinner." The beauty of it all is that there is no television coverage of the Gridiron dinner and virtually no press coverage—it's basically a private affair of the rich, powerful, and famous.[38]

Nancy Reagan used the Gridiron dinner in 1982 to improve her embittered image among the powerful guests whose opinions are so consequential in shaping the opinions of others. By the end of 1981, Nancy Reagan was receiving bad press about her wardrobe and lavish spending habits, such as the $209,000 she spent on new china for the White House. She was increasingly depicted as an uncaring, self-absorbed socialite—all of which was detracting from the president's program and popularity. Members of Nancy Reagan's and President Reagan's staffs sought ways to improve her public image and to show that she was a caring human being. One strategy was to get her involved in anti-drug work; another was to have her perform a vaudeville skit at the Gridiron dinner in which Nancy mocked herself.

On March 27, 1982, most guests at the annual Gridiron dinner were unaware of what was to transpire; even Ronald Reagan was in the dark. Late in the evening, Nancy Reagan excused herself from the table. Moments later she burst onto the stage dancing and singing the old tune "Secondhand Rose" recast as "Secondhand Clothes." "She was clad in an outlandish getup," Smith reports, "an aqua skirt with red and yellow flowers held together by safety pins, a floppy feathered hat, and a feathered boa." There was a moment of shock and deafening silence in the hall, but soon people jumped to their feet and applauded Nancy who was "unbelievably" mocking herself and her lavish style. For an exit, she tried to shatter a china plate on the stage (it didn't break) and the cheering crowd brought her back for an encore. "The affair remained unreported. Only the inner core of the Washington community had seen this side of Mrs. Reagan. But that community included most of the important journalists and politicians, and among this crucial audience, Mrs. Reagan's image had been remade in a few short minutes";[39] that is, until her involvement with astrology and her bitter relationship with Chief of Staff Donald Regan became public during President Reagan's second term.

In 1999 President Bill Clinton also took part in the 114-year-old tradition of the annual Gridiron dinner. "After the long and harrowing struggle to defeat impeachment," the *New York Times* reported, "President Clinton finally joined in the general laughter at his plight" when he sat through a satirical dinner that began with a brief note of homage to the good old days "when the Oval Office was used to raise money and the Lincoln bedroom was used for sex." "A wave of guffaws and applause greeted the president as he gingerly kidded himself" and was "lambasted in song and sketch through all the embarrassing—hilariously embarrassing—details of the sex-and-mendacity scandal that threatened his presidency." He was "serenaded with such song parodies as "Sex Is a Definition Thing" (to "Love Is a Many Splendored Thing") and had to hear a character posing as Vice President Al Gore wax jealous at how the scandal only improved Clinton's poll ratings. To the tune of "Embraceable You," the ersatz Gore sang woodenly, "Impeach me, so I can be popular, too. Impeach me, I can be sleazy for you." And Clinton had the last laugh "with the announcement of his White House memoir: 'My Story, and I'm Sticking to It.'"[40]

The annual Gridiron dinner is indicative of what Hedrick Smith, in *The Power Game: How Washington Works*, calls "life inside the beltway: the folkways of Washington."[41] A subculture and set of norms pervades Washington, D.C., and the national political community. President Jimmy Carter referred to Washington and "Washingtonians" as an island isolated from the rest of America. On the one hand, Washington, D.C., is a large and complex metropolitan area that includes northern Virginia and part of Maryland. Consisting of over four million people, most of whom are Americans from all walks of life, it is no different from many other urban areas in America. On the other hand, Washington is the seat of national government and attracts a large number of people in and out of government who are or become absorbed with politics.

The **Washington political community** comprises the "one hundred thousand or so whose life revolves around government, especially the few thousand at the peak who live and breathe politics."[42] It was to the Washington political community and its particular subculture to which Jimmy Carter referred. *At least eight characteristics pervade the Washington political community*: (1) a preoccupation with politics; (2) a

quest for power, status, and visibility; (3) networking; (4) pragmatism; (5) workaholism; (6) use of jargon; (7) a lonely existence; and (8) male predominance.[43]

Many of these characteristics that pervade the political world of Washington have been mentioned in previous chapters and essays (such as essay 11.2, "Newt Gingrich, Political Ambition, and the Quest for Power and Glory"). Examining these norms and folkways promotes a strong understanding of how the complex politics of U.S. foreign policy are played out at the nation's capital and in the higher echelons of power in American society.

First is the preoccupation with politics. For all its size, complexity, and cosmopolitan flavor, Washington is very much a "company town," dominated by a single employer, the federal government. The existence and growth of the federal government are the reason why Washington has grown and prospered as an urban area. The federal government has also attracted a large private sector filled with lawyers, lobbyists, policy analysts, and consultants. Governmental and national politics dominate the lives of the Washington political community and trickle down to affect local residents as well. It is a town where cab drivers regularly talk politics and where local television news shows begin their programs with national and international news. Politics is an all-day-and-night affair for the most politically active, and after-work hours are filled with cocktail parties and social functions that revolve around politics.

A second characteristic of the Washington political community is the quest for power, status, and visibility. "Power, of course, is the aphrodisiac—the special brand of federal power that is Washington's monopoly," Smith writes. The town attracts and rewards those who are the most ambitious and have the most powerful egos. Wrapped up in their own self-importance, people attempt to acquire and exercise power to demonstrate their importance to relevant others. Those who are new, young, and ambitious quickly learn the significance of position, status, and influence. Many catch **Potomac Fever**—the "incurable addiction of wielding power or feeling at the political center."[44]

Established figures are particularly preoccupied with placing themselves on public display and maintaining and promoting their status and influence. In the words of Elliot Richardson, who held four cabinet positions in the Nixon and Ford administrations, "Washington is really, when you come right down to it, a city of cocker spaniels. . . . It's a city of people who are more interested in being petted and admired than in rendering the exercise of power." Politicians, in particular, "love to be noticed, and they take their notices very seriously, assuming their own importance and grasping for daily confirmation in the attention of the press and television." Regardless of one's place within the Washington political community, "it is a self-selected group, ambitious and aggressive, marked by collective immodesty."[45]

Most prominent of all the social functions are probably the presidential state dinners. "State dinners are about elegance and refinement and haute cuisine, but mostly they are about politics. They are elaborately and painstakingly designed to stroke the large egos invited in without offending the large egos left out." This is all taken quite seriously. The "social secretary for JFK recalls being offered a $5000 bribe for an invitation." For President Bush Jr.'s first state dinner, honoring Mexican President Vicente Fox, Karl Rove, the senior adviser and assistant to the president, says he got "about 40 calls and e-mails fishing for an invite."[46]

For all its preoccupation with power, status, and visibility, the Washington political community actually is quite porous. Newcomers to Washington with prominent positions are readily accepted. "Indeed, Washington regularly takes in newcomers, absorbs them and makes them its own."[47] Young, ambitious types, wet behind the ears, can rise in position and influence if they are extremely résumé conscious and are ready to make new inroads within the Washington political community. The Washington political community is much larger and more permeable by outsiders today than it was forty years ago.

The third characteristic of the Washington political community is the crucial importance of **networking**. One quickly learns that the key to individual upward mobility is to extend one's network: to get to know other people, to become visible to others, and to be informed about what's going on. No matter how powerful and close to the center of things one gets, power is so diffused throughout the government and dispersed among so many groups and individuals, that maintaining and extending one's networks is the key to exercising power and influence. According to Hedrick Smith, "political alliances are vital not only for survival but to promote policies, to lobby former colleagues, or to play the more personal game of 'careers,' advancement up the ladder for the in-and-outers who ride the ebb and flow of partisan politics upward with each generation."[48]

Interacting and building coalitions with others is a crucial and necessary aspect of politics. Much of the interaction and the development of networks occurs informally and behind the scenes. Nothing is sinister about this activity; for the most part it reflects normal human interaction. Informal occasions, such as a cocktail party, a round of golf, or a beer at a local hangout, are likely to be the occasions when new ties are made and important business is conducted. Indicative of the preoccupation with networking in Washington is that upon leaving a social function with a spouse or friend, the first question is never, "Did you have a good time?" but "Who did you meet? What did you hear?"

Politicians and other members of the Washington political community also have a tendency to be pragmatic, which is consistent with the three first characteristics. To gain power and prestige, one must work with others. As the old adage says, "To get along one must go along." Few individuals can afford to make many enemies if they want to be politically successful and exercise influence. Some individuals and groups in Washington operate more ideologically. However, most Washingtonians quickly learn the value of political moderation, the need to compromise with adversaries, and the importance of not holding a grudge if they want to survive and prosper.

"Newcomers arrive full of idealism and energy only to discover what a tiny fragment of power they grasp." This fact reinforces the need to network and be pragmatic. The common problem is that pragmatism, and the other characteristics of the Washington community, pushes idealism and principles aside in the long run. In this respect, ideology and principle—at least the appearance of being principled and above politics—tend to be saved especially for the public and the folks back home. Nowhere is the gap between daily behavior and public pronouncements greater than among members of Congress. Thus, it should not be surprising that Washington can be a town of strange bedfellows, where "personal relationships often cut across party and ideological lines, so that conservative and liberal leopards who roar at each other in congressional debates play tennis on the weekends or joke together in the Capitol cloakrooms."[49]

A fifth characteristic is that Washington is a community of workaholics. "People coming into government from private life are shocked at the compulsive intensity and workaholic ethic of Washington." Sixty- and seventy-hour, six- and seven-day work weeks are common in and out of government; and this does not include the socializing after work where politicking and business continue. To "make it" and play an influential role, a degree of workaholism is required because of the increasing demands of the job, the incredible size of the government, the ever expanding size of the Washington political community, and the faster pace of modern lifestyles. Yet this is also the case because the more ambitious overachievers who get drawn to the top are people who have little difficulty working long hours. While some get burnt out and leave Washington altogether, others thrive in this environment. Among those who gain prominence "most stay in Washington and become lawyers, lobbyists, or consultants, because they've grown accustomed to Washington's ways and to thinking of themselves as movers and shakers, and no other place has quite the same excitement and allure."[50]

Washingtonians also communicate and interact in a language that is extremely jargonistic, a sixth characteristic. Much of the language is dry and formal because of many people's legal training and because of the bureaucratic nature of government that operates by laws, statutes, and regulations written in "legalese" and "bureaucratese." This is combined with a Washingtonian fondness for acronyms and other shorthand phrases. For example, the National Security Council is referred to as the "NSC," whereas the State Department goes by "State" or "Foggy Bottom." Where information is a source of power, language is often a sign of status, for it allows a Washingtonian quickly to know whether one is an outsider or an insider, and how much he or she is "in the know."

A seventh characteristic is that members of Washington's political community, especially those who have risen to the height of political power and prestige, live a rather lonely existence. The networks that one develops may be quite extensive, but most of the people are, at best, acquaintances. Everyone is perceived as being on the political make, interacting for a particular political purpose. "The competitiveness of the power game inhibits people from revealing the kind of personal vulnerability and doubts about life that are vital to forming close and sincere friendships. . . . The risk of inner self-revelation, which genuine intimacy requires, is too dangerous for most politicians and public officials."[51] Therefore, friendships are difficult to make and sustain.

Finally, Washington remains a man's town to this day. Women have progressed a great deal within Washington.[52] Women have made inroads into the Washington political community, many reaching highly visible and prominent positions; but most women in Washington fill secretarial and service positions. Although much has changed, as discussed in previous chapters, the more one examines high positions of power, prestige, and visibility, the more likely it is that one will find that the players are men.

CONTINUITY, CHANGE, AND POLITICS INSIDE THE BELTWAY

The Washington political community has always been around, yet it has experienced some change over time. Forty years ago, Washington was a smaller, sleepy, southern town with much less government, and politics was dominated by a small "old boy network." This has changed. Power has dispersed and the Washington community has grown in size. "'Washington used to be cozy,' observed Barbara Gamarekian, who worked in the Kennedy White House and later became a *New York Times* reporter. 'You could go to a party, a reception of a hundred people, and look around and say, 'Well, everybody's here—everybody who counts.' You can't do that anymore. The city has grown big and amorphous. There are so many social circles: the administration people, the corporate crowd, members of Congress, patrons of the arts, the old Kennedy-Johnson crowd, the Reagan Republicans, the Nixon-Ford Republicans. These circles bump up against each other now but it's not one cozy network anymore.'"[53]

The development of a dominant subculture among a select community of individuals is not unique to Washington. Such is the norm in all walks of life, whether in national government in Washington or local government elsewhere, in business and on Wall Street, within academia, in the entertainment world of Hollywood, or on Main Street U.S.A. The top of all professions and spheres of life tends to be dominated by a relatively small group of more active and involved individuals who operate according to an unwritten set of subcultural rules and norms. Yet the subculture pervading the Washington political community remains one of the great mysteries of American politics.

Bits and pieces of information about the Washington political community may be gleaned from the media. Yet most Americans are unaware of this subculture. When they visit Washington, they see the shining facades of the government buildings, the memorials, and the nice speeches that are part of the grand tours. More surprisingly, many academics, including political scientists, are unaware of the workings of the Washington political community or ignore its political importance. Whatever the case, *to ignore the Washington political community is to ignore an important ingredient* in understanding the complex politics of U.S. foreign policy.

The Washington political community describes the immediate political environment in which governmental policymaking in the executive branch and the Congress operates. As we will discuss in Part IV, it is the same political environment where, for example, interest groups from throughout society and the media also operate. Thus, the Washington political community is where much of domestic politics and governmental policymaking intersect, affecting agenda setting, policy formulation, and the implementation of policy.

Comprehending the nature of the Washington political community allows for a better understanding of how issues get on the political agenda, are dealt with, and disappear. While most of the hundreds of issues that the government deals with daily attract little attention, a few issues gain great national visibility, but rarely for more than a brief period. As Hedrick Smith notes, "Washington is a city mercurial in its moods, short in its attention span, and given to fetishes. Events flash and disappear like episodes in a soap opera, intensely important for a brief period and then quickly forgotten."[54] Subcultural rules and norms also explain why networking, coalition building, persuading, bargaining, and compromise are an integral part of politics within government and throughout the political community in the formulation and implementation of public policy.

The prevalence and power of life within the Washington political community account for the reason **politics inside the beltway** is different from politics as seen by the public from outside the beltway. It helps to explain why the politics of symbolism prevails when political issues are before the media spotlight and the public. Under these conditions, most people involved in the privileged Washington community present a public persona that is more principled, more idealistic, and more in accord with dominant American values than exists in reality. This has helped to create a gap between public expectations and political performance.

It also helps to explain why a president's professional reputation and public prestige, as discussed in chapter 4, are crucial ingredients in exercising leadership and governing. Presidents who have poorly understood the nature of the Washington political community, such as Jimmy Carter and his staff, have had great difficulty exercising power. Those who have understood the game better, such as Ronald Reagan and his staff, have been able to govern more successfully. In this respect, understanding the subculture of the Washington political community is one key to understanding the complex politics of U.S. foreign policy.

GOVERNMENTAL POLITICS IN PERSPECTIVE

We have now completed our overview of the government and the policymaking process as it affects U.S. foreign policy, the subject of Part III. Presidential power, the foreign policy bureaucracy, Congress, and the rest of government, including the Washington political community, have all been examined, along with the historical and global context in Part II. Together, they provide a picture of the three foreign policy themes addressed throughout this book: continuity and change, the president's ability to govern, and the tension between national security and democracy. Therefore, one should now have a better grasp of the complexity and the politics of the foreign policy process.

To fully understand how U.S. foreign policy is made, however, one must place governmental politics in perspective, for it is derived from and influences the larger domestic political environment. Thus, the next part of this book focuses on society and the role of domestic politics in influencing the government and the policymaking process. More specifically, we examine the public and its beliefs; civil rights, liberties, and political participation; electoral and group politics; and the media and the communications process in an effort to more fully understand the complex politics of U.S. foreign policy.

SUGGESTED SOURCES FOR MORE INFORMATION

The role of the Constitution and the judiciary in foreign affairs was once a popular scholarly topic, but the rise of presidential power during the cold war years diminished most of this interest, except among constitutional and legal scholars. Nor have the changes of the post–Vietnam War years or the constitutional crises of Watergate and Iran-contra rekindled much interest in the judicial role in foreign affairs. Nevertheless, a few important works on the Constitution and the judiciary are available. *Foreign Affairs and the Constitution* (Mineola, N.Y.: Foundation Press, first edition in 1972, revised in 1996) by Louis Henkin remains the definitive constitutional study of the distribution of power in the national government, federalism, and individual rights relative to foreign policy, including the role of the courts. Henkin also has published a series of thoughtful essays in *Constitutionalism, Democracy, and Foreign Affairs* (New York: Columbia University Press, 1990). A nice overview from a legal perspective is provided by Thomas M. Franck and Michael J. Glennon, in *Foreign Relations and National Security Law: Cases, Materials and Simulations* (St. Paul, Minn.: West, 1987). Harold Hongju Koh assesses the constitutional interpretations and judicial developments that contributed to the Iran-contra affair in *The National Security Constitution: Sharing Power After the Iran-Contra Affair* (New Haven: Yale University Press, 1990). The rise of litigation in American courts involving and impacting foreign policy is discussed by Anne-Marie Slaughter and David Bosco in "Plaintiff's Diplomacy," *Foreign Affairs* (September–October 2000): 102–16. David A. Kaplan provides a fascinating portrait of judicial politics in the 2000 presidential election in *The Accidental President* (New York: William Morrow, 2001).

While the role of state and local governments in foreign policy has historically attracted little attention, some scholarship has been generated over the last decade. Chadwick F. Alger discusses the changing global context of cities and its general impact on foreign policy in "The World Relations of Cities: Closing the Gap Between Social Science Paradigms and Everyday Human Experience," *International Studies Quarterly* 34 (December 1990): 493–518. Journalist John Maxwell Hamilton describes myriad connections between local American communities and the world in *Mainstreet America and the Third World* (Cabin John, Md.: Seven Locks Press, 1986). Informative overviews of the foreign policies of local governments can be found in Michael J. Shuman, "Dateline Main Street: Local Foreign Policies," *Foreign Policy* 65 (winter 1986–1987): 154–74; and Earl H. Fry, *The Expanding Role of State and Local Governments in U.S. Foreign Affairs* (New York: Council on Foreign Relations Press, 1998)

The nature and importance of the Washington political community has been almost completely ignored, especially by political scientists. Beyond the feel of the Washington subculture that one can derive from reading memoirs of political figures, Hedrick Smith provides an excellent portrayal of "Life Inside the Beltway: The Folkways of Washington" in *The Power Game* (New York: Ballantine, 1988), pp. 89–118, as does John M. Barry in *The Ambition and the Power: The Fall of Jim Wright, A True Story of Washington* (New York: Penguin, 1989).

KEY TERMS

annual Gridiron dinner
anti-South-African-apartheid issue
Bush v. Gore
federalism
Florida International Volunteer Corps
judicial restraint
judicial review
John Marshall
networking
nuclear freeze issue
old boy network
political questions
politics inside the beltway
Potomac Fever
presidential judicial appointments
Chief Justice William Rehnquist
sister cities
South Carolina economic development
Supreme Court
Clarence Thomas confirmation hearings
United States v. Curtis-Wright Export Corp.
Chief Justice Earl Warren
Washington political community
Youngstown Sheet & Tube Co. v. Sawyer

PART FOUR

. . . .

THE SOCIETY AND DOMESTIC POLITICS

Part IV examines how the larger society and domestic politics affect the government and the policymaking process. Chapter 13 discusses the role of the public and citizens' beliefs in foreign policy. Chapter 14 discusses the impact of national security on political participation and the exercise of civil liberties. Chapters 15 and 16 discuss the role of electoral and group politics. Chapter 17 discusses the role of the media and the communications process. Synthesizing these important characteristics about American society and domestic politics allows for a much more powerful understanding of the politics of U.S. foreign policy.

CHAPTER 13

. . . .

THE PUBLIC AND ITS BELIEFS

The role of the public in the foreign policy process is a most misunderstood, difficult, and important topic in the complex politics of U.S. foreign policy. It is misunderstood because observers tend to make sweeping generalizations, particularly in asserting the insignificance of the public and its beliefs in foreign policy. It is difficult because it is a complex topic involving different types of publics holding different kinds of beliefs that indirectly, as well as directly, affect the policymaking process. Finally, it may be the most important topic because the public—what the American people believe and how they behave—sets the social context and domestic political boundaries within which the government and the policymaking process must operate.

This chapter discusses the public's beliefs about the world and its general influence on foreign policy, while chapters 14, 15, and 16 concentrate on the public's direct participation in the political process by discussing civil rights and liberties, electoral politics, and group politics. More specifically, *this chapter addresses the following questions:* What is the traditional wisdom about the role of the public in the making of U.S. for-

eign policy? What are the differences among public opinion, political ideology, and political culture? How do each of these different types of beliefs held by the public impact the making of U.S. foreign policy? Examination of the public and its beliefs provides a crucial foundation for understanding continuity and change, presidential governance, and the tensions between national security and democracy in the making of U.S. foreign policy, including the present and the future in light of the September 11, 2001, terrorist attacks.

THE TRADITIONAL WISDOM

The common view held by most observers of American politics, as well as most Americans, is that the public plays a relatively insignificant role in the making of U.S. foreign policy. They posit that it does not matter what the public thinks about foreign policy issues, for it has little impact on the government and the policymaking process. Moreover, they say public indifference allows political leaders, especially the president, a great degree of freedom of action in foreign policy making.

Therefore, most observers of U.S. foreign policy focus on government policymakers and institutions in explaining how U.S. foreign policy is made, while ignoring the public and much of society.[1]

Why is the public portrayed as being relatively unimportant in the making of U.S. foreign policy? The traditional wisdom grows out of the height of the cold war and sees the public as uninterested and uninformed regarding foreign policy issues; "fickle" in its opinions, typically fluctuating day by day if not hour by hour; and responsive to political leadership especially during crises. A more cynical, critical perspective perceives a public that is easily manipulated by political elites. Regardless of the language or the political perspective, many observers of U.S. foreign policy hold the opinion, shared by much of the general public, that the public's impact is fleeting and usually unimportant in influencing policymakers.

This traditional view leads to a harsh conclusion about American democracy, and about the tension between the demands of national security and democratic practice. Americans pride themselves on having developed a democratic society based on a republican system of government in which political leaders are selected by the people and are responsive and accountable to the electorate. Yet if the public role is minimal and the public is extremely responsive to and easily manipulated by political leaders, then U.S. foreign policy making is not as democratic as it may seem. Many observers and policymakers throughout American history, in fact, have held an **elitist view of the public** and foreign policy making, arguing that policymakers should be distanced from the public. Those who hold this view tend to fear that the public is an ignorant, emotional "mob" that, when mobilized, often counteracts the cold, rational calculations of national interest that national security demands.[2]

As with any stereotype, this traditional picture of the public holds much truth. The majority of the public is uninformed, fickle, and responsive to established leaders. These characteristics often have given the president great flexibility in governing foreign policy and have allowed the demands of national security to prevail over the demands of democracy. However, the American public and its beliefs are more complex than this simple picture suggests. While the traditional wisdom concerning the insignificance of public opinion may help explain some of the politics of foreign policy

during the cold war, this view obscures a full understanding of the politics of U.S. foreign policy, especially since Vietnam and the end of the cold war.

A MORE COMPLEX AND CONSEQUENTIAL PUBLIC

Contrary to the traditional wisdom, in order to fully understand U.S. foreign policy during the cold war and since Vietnam, one must carefully examine the public and its role in domestic politics. "There is an American myth that politics stops at the water's edge, that the normal play of partisan competition and dissent gives way to unity in matters of foreign policy. This myth is unfounded but nevertheless potent." So states Leslie Gelb in *The Irony of Vietnam: The System Worked*, arguing that, when it came to U.S. foreign policy in Vietnam, "practical political imperatives against losing, as well as the shared foreign policy beliefs against losing, were very much on every President's mind"; in this sense the political system and democratic politics worked as intended.[3]

As Gelb argued as early as 1972, "academicians and public-opinion experts have helped to perpetuate the myth in their own way by 'demonstrating' that foreign policy simply is not a salient issue to the voter and that whatever the president says and does goes, [while] official silence on the subject prevails." But, according to Gelb, presidents have "known better. Citizens may not single out national security affairs as the basis for their votes—although war and peace issues often are so mentioned—but the security area inevitably plays an important part in determining their overall impression of how the President is doing his job. Moreover, communication leaders and 'elites' judge the President's performance with regard to foreign policy, and the mood which they convey to the public affects public appraisals of the man in the White House." Hence for Gelb, "American public opinion was the essential domino" affecting U.S. foreign policy in Vietnam. [4]

A growing number of observers of U.S. foreign policy, like Leslie Gelb, have challenged the simple traditional view that the role of the American public is inconsequential to the making of public policy, especially foreign policy. Over thirty years ago, when the traditional view of the American public was in vogue,

V. O. Key referred to the public as "a responsible electorate." Since the Vietnam War, a more positive portrayal and consequential interpretation has grown, as represented by Benjamin Page and Robert Shapiro's study, *The Rational Public*, Samuel Popkin's *The Reasoning Voter*, and Bruce Jentleson's "The Pretty Prudent Public."[5]

Unraveling the role of the public and its beliefs in the making of U.S. foreign policy is not a simple task, for as V. O. Key, Jr., found in *Public Opinion and American Democracy*, "the exploration of public attitudes is a pursuit of endless fascination—and frustration."[6] Nevertheless, *three major points indicate that the traditional view is simplistic and incomplete.* First, different types of publics exist: The most common breakdown is between the elite and mass publics. Second, members of the public hold different types of beliefs: The three that will be highlighted in this chapter are opinions, ideological beliefs, and cultural values. Finally, the public exercises influence through a number of different behaviors: directly through polls, through participation in electoral and group politics, and most indirectly, through **political socialization** (the informal process of human interaction by which Americans acquire their political beliefs from parents, schools, peers, etc.).

The traditional wisdom tends to focus predominantly on public opinion, that is, the level of influence that the opinions of the mass public have directly on policymakers, predominantly through the impact of polls. Yet the traditional view ignores the role of the elite public, political ideology and culture, and the other ways in which the public influences domestic politics and the governmental policymaking process. The public's overall role in U.S. foreign policy can be understood only in terms of the interaction of the different types of publics, beliefs, and behaviors. Chapter 14 focuses on the tensions between national security and the exercise of civil liberties and their impact on political participation, followed by a discussion of the public's role in electoral and group politics for foreign policy in chapters 15 and 16, and the role of the media in chapter 17. This chapter emphasizes the beliefs held by members of the public and, in doing so, discusses the role of different publics and the various ways they influence U.S. foreign policy.

Whereas the traditional view limits itself to the study of public opinion, it is vital to examine American political ideology and political culture to understand fully the role

of the public in the complex politics of U.S. foreign policy. American political culture sets the broad context within which the politics of U.S. foreign policy operates. The ideological beliefs of Americans further narrow what is possible and probable within domestic politics and the policymaking process. Finally, public opinion affects the foreign policy process as it fluctuates within the confines of American political culture and ideology. An examination of public opinion, political ideology, and political culture allows for a more comprehensive understanding of the role of the public in U.S. foreign policy. It demonstrates that the public's beliefs have experienced both continuity and change over time and that this is quite significant for understanding the president's ability to govern foreign policy and the evolving tension between national security and democracy during the cold war, since Vietnam, and into the present and future.

PUBLIC OPINION

Public opinion does play a role in the making of U.S. foreign policy. However, to assess its role one must be clear concerning the type of public most involved, the type of beliefs that opinions represent, and the type of influence most likely to be expressed. We begin with a discussion of the difference between elite and mass publics.

ELITE AND MASS PUBLICS

Typically, when people discuss the public they are referring to the mass of all Americans. It is easy to dismiss the public as an inconsequential actor in foreign policy at this level. The traditional wisdom, however, is misleading when it treats the public as a single, homogeneous entity. The United States is a complex and diverse society of over 280 million people. Certainly, not all Americans are inconsequential in American politics and the making of U.S. foreign policy. Therefore to better understand the role of the public, *it is important to recognize at least two basic types of publics:* (1) the elite public and (2) the mass public.[7]

The **elite public** *may be distilled further into two general groupings:* opinion leaders and the attentive public. **Opinion leaders** are "all members of the society who occupy positions which enable them regularly to transmit, either locally or nationally, opinions about any issue to unknown persons outside of their occupational field or about more than one class of issues to unknown professional colleagues."[8] National opinion leaders consist of people in various leadership positions throughout the country, such as major governmental and business leaders, well-known journalists, established professors and professionals, and other prominent individuals from different walks of life. Opinion leaders obviously constitute a very small percentage of people in American society, fluctuating depending upon each issue.

Opinion leaders generally are the people who are most informed about national and international affairs and whose ideas and views tend to be communicated broadly. This is not to say that the information and views they hold are correct; rather, it is that their understanding of the world tends to be more readily communicated to other members of society. In other words, opinion leaders tend to have great visibility in American society, and their views usually are considered more credible and legitimate by other members of society. This is what makes them opinion leaders, for their information and views carry weight and influence over what other people in society and government believe about the world.[9]

The **attentive public** includes people who are also relatively attentive and informed about national and international affairs but whose views are not as widely disseminated as those of opinion leaders. The size of the attentive public varies from issue to issue. For the most visible issues, the attentive public may be as large as one-fourth of the entire public. For most issues that do not receive wide media coverage, the attentive public may represent less than 10 percent of the population. As with opinion leaders, this represents a minority of the larger public, but it is an important minority. Members of the attentive public tend to be invisible at the national and community levels, but among their peers they may act as opinion leaders. Thus, it is often said that the attentive public acts as local mediators between opinion leaders and the mass public.

Most Americans are not part of the elite public but of the mass public. The **mass public** is the segment of the American population emphasized by the traditional wisdom. Although the number varies, at least two-thirds to three-fourths of Americans form the mass

public for most issues. Members of the mass public tend to have little interest in national and international affairs. Only those issues that make it to the front page of the newspaper and receive considerable media play gain the attention of the mass public, and then usually only briefly. Therefore, the mass public tends to be poorly informed about national and international affairs.

Because the mass public includes most Americans, there is obviously tremendous variation in the level of interest and information within this segment of the population. Some Americans, maybe as many as 20 percent, have virtually no interest in public affairs or limited access to information and have been labeled "chronic know-nothings." Other members of the mass public may be more attentive and better informed about foreign policy issues. Within this broad range are most Americans who generally demonstrate little interest but acquire some information about national and international affairs through upbringing, education, and the media.[10]

What accounts for the differing levels of interest and information about national and international affairs between the elite and the mass publics? Two key characteristics stand out: level of education and socioeconomic class.[11] The more educated an individual, the more likely that he or she will be interested in, and informed about, national and international affairs. There is no simple educational threshold beyond which a member of the mass public becomes a member of the elite public, for membership in these publics varies with the times and the individual. Sixty years ago a high school education (as well as experience in life) was likely to provide a stronger base of information than an undergraduate degree does today. Nowadays members of the elite public are likely to have acquired a graduate university degree or have been among the better undergraduate students, particularly if they attended a higher-quality educational institution and majored in the humanities, social sciences, or the arts.

The second important factor in differentiating among types of publics is socioeconomic class. Although Americans commonly think they are all members of one large middle-class, definite differences exist within American society in wealth, occupation, and status. Individuals raised in upper-middle-class or upper-class families and environments are the people most likely to become interested and informed about national and international affairs. Clearly, socioeconomic class and level of education are closely related. The higher the class background, the more likely one will go to college and pursue a graduate degree; moreover, the higher the level of education achieved, the more likely one will acquire more wealth, a professional occupation, and higher status within society. High levels of socioeconomic status and education not only reinforce each other and produce individuals with high levels of interest and information about national and international affairs but also help to provide the analytical and communication skills that tend to separate the elite public from the mass public.

MAJOR PATTERNS IN PUBLIC OPINION

Public opinion refers to the attitudes held by Americans generally toward specific issues and topics, expressed primarily through polls and periodically through voting. Hence, we are concerned predominantly with the role of the mass public. Public opinion includes views held by the elite public as well, but it represents no more than a small minority of Americans. *Three major patterns characterize American public opinion.* Generally, public opinion tends to be (1) inattentive, (2) uninformed, and (3) volatile. These traits support the traditional understanding of the nature of public opinion. However, this fact does not foreclose public opinion from influencing domestic politics and the policymaking process.[12]

First, public opinion represents views expressed by Americans who, for the most part, are inattentive—that is, they have little interest in national and international affairs. Most Americans are exposed to a great deal of information about national and international affairs through the mass media; and if they go beyond the mass media and visit a local library or bookstore (or the Internet), they would find that an incredible amount of information is readily available. However, few Americans take advantage of the available information because they are uninterested. This is illustrated simply by examining the circulation of the leading magazines in the country (see **table 13.1**). Only three of the fifty best-selling magazines—*Time, Newsweek,* and *U.S. News & World Report*—emphasize national and/or international affairs. Clearly, most Americans who try to acquire information beyond television, radio, and

the local newspaper by subscribing to magazines are interested in things other than politics: entertainment, travel, household, fashion, sex, sports and recreation, mechanics, family matters, and more.

This slight interest in national and international affairs produces and reinforces the second major pattern: Most Americans are relatively uninformed about national and international affairs. The mass public acquires little information about the political world and much of the information it does acquire tends to be simplistic and often inaccurate. For example, a poll was taken in 1964 to determine the level of information that Americans had about major events in Asia during a time when the United States had roughly twenty thousand troops in Vietnam and the Vietnam War was beginning to receive considerable media coverage. The poll revealed that 25 percent of all Americans had never heard of the war in Vietnam; 28 percent did not know that mainland China was communist; 29 percent were unaware that another Chinese government existed on the island of Taiwan; and 54 percent had never heard of Mao Tse-tung, chairman of the Communist party of the People's Republic of China. During the height of the cold war in the early 1960s, barely more than half of Americans polled could describe the meaning of cold war in a reasonably correct fashion. Surveys of American geographical knowledge at the time demonstrated that only 65 percent of people could point out England on a map of Europe and only 60 percent could show Brazil's position in South America, while less than one-third of the respondents could locate most other countries correctly.[13]

Little appears to have changed in terms of public information about international affairs. A survey in 1988 found that with regard to U.S. foreign policy in Central America—a salient national security issue when the Reagan administration's secret contra war was exposed during the Iran-contra episode—only half of all Americans knew that the Sandinistas and contras had been fighting. Furthermore, a majority of Americans incorrectly believed that the U.S. government was supporting the guerrillas in El Salvador and the government in Nicaragua. During the same year, one in three Americans could not name a single member of NATO, whereas—it's hard to believe—16 percent thought the Soviet Union was a member of the Western alliance. Americans also had difficulty identifying countries and regions on a world map, as was shown

TABLE **13.1**
CIRCULATION OF THE FIFTY LEADING U.S. MAGAZINES

MAGAZINE	CIRCULATION	MAGAZINE	CIRCULATION
1. Reader's Digest	12,589,919	26. O, the Oprah Magazine	2,066,440
2. TV Guide	10,383,083	27. Smithsonian	2,053,466
3. National Geographic Magazine	7,892,852	28. Parents	1,998,647
4. Better Homes and Gardens	7,662,981	29. Money	1,907,377
5. Family Circle	5,002,223	30. Ebony	1,757,066
6. Good Housekeeping	4,532,915	31. Field & Stream	1,754,163
7. Woman's Day	4,195,200	32. Star	1,669,923
8. Ladies' Home Journal	4,137,423	33. Country Living	1,662,499
9. McCall's	4,104,990	34. Men's Health	1,639,362
10. **Time**	4,064,815	35. Teen People	1,635,921
11. People Weekly	3,539,034	36. Woman's World	1,604,035
12. Sports Illustrated	3,208,918	37. Shape	1,578,161
13. **Newsweek**	3,141,578	38. In Style	1,578,062
14. Playboy	3,113,103	39. Golf Digest	1,567,604
15. Prevention	3,011,498	40. Popular Science	1,560,758
16. Cosmopolitan	2,651,192	41. Entertainment Weekly	1,518,689
17. Southern Living	2,539,153	42. First for Women	1,571,395
18. Martha Stewart Living	2,373,557	43. Parenting Magazine	1,459,669
19. Seventeen	2,372,269	44. Cooking Light	1,452,765
20. Maxim	2,307,737	45. American Rifleman	1,450,818
21. Redbook	2,304,273	46. Sunset	1,445,881
22. Glamour	2,177,589	47. Golf Magazine	1,403,074
23. **U.S. News & World Report**	2,100,014	48. Car and Driver	1,392,283
24. National Enquirer	2,081,623	49. Health	1,382,005
25. Teen	2,077,150	50. Outdoor Life	1,361,049

NOTE: Magazines that emphasize national and international news are boldfaced.

SOURCE: 2001 *The World Almanac and Book of Facts*, 2001.

when 75 percent of adult Americans polled were unable to locate the Persian Gulf, 50 percent could not identify Japan and South Africa, and 14 percent could not even correctly locate the United States. This is reinforced in the 1996 overview by Michael Carpini and Scott Keeter, *What Americans Know About Politics.*[14]

Although some knowledge may have increased for some areas with the Persian Gulf War, the Bosnian and Kosovo Wars, and the war in Afghanistan against the Taliban and Al Qaeda, at the same time, the collapse of the Soviet Union, the end of cold war, and the global war on terrorism probably increased much of the public's confusion about world politics and geography. According to a 2002 survey by the National Geographic Society of Americans between the ages of 18 to 24, one in ten could not locate the United States on a blank map of the world, only one in seven could place Iraq, one in four could find Saudi Arabia, and 30 percent could not locate the Pacific Ocean, the world's largest body of water. Overall, out of ten countries who were surveyed, young people from Sweden, Germany, and Italy did twice as well then young Americans who, along with Mexico, scored the worst. Knowledge of the U.S. was not good either. A majority of Americans were able to find only two of ten specific states on a map of the United States (only California and Texas). And only 25 percent knew the population figure for the United States from a multiple choice list.[15]

The low levels of attention, information, and understanding about national and international affairs among the American public are *relatively normal and quite understandable for most people.* In most countries, the mass public exhibits characteristics similar to Americans. One may argue whether Americans are more or less interested and informed than other people in industrialized countries (the same surveys have placed Americans near the bottom of the rankings, with eighteen-to-twenty-four-year-olds usually dead last). Nevertheless, the pattern remains the same—the mass public, whether in the United States or abroad, is minimally interested and poorly informed, especially in comparison to members of the elite public.

Low levels of political interest and information are also quite understandable if one examines the impact of everyday life. Most Americans, like people everywhere, face numerous daily demands and responsibilities that appear to have little to do with politics. While their lives are impacted by politics, it is often at a distance removed from the individual. The lives of most individuals revolve around work, family, household, and friends. With the increase of divorce and two-income families, adults lead ever busier and more demanding lives. Most want to relax and enjoy life during their leisure time, which is rarely spent reading, talking, or thinking about national and international affairs. Instead, American pastimes emphasize activities other than politics, such as sports or shopping.[16]

It would be a mistake, therefore, to conclude that the ignorance of most Americans is a function of stu-

pidity—a view often held by the more traditional and elitist perspectives of the mass public. Rather, it is primarily a function of the various pursuits and demands of everyday life, which are reinforced by the existence of few incentives in American society for people to become politically informed and active. As many observers have pointed out, a lack of knowledge and understanding about national and international affairs does not preclude the existence of intuition and common sense.[17]

It is also important to *place the low levels of interest and information in historical context, in which three trends appear to have evolved.* First, the level of interest and attention accorded to politics by most Americans has probably declined over the past decades. One hundred years ago politics and election campaigns were one of the few major forms of entertainment for many Americans; today, so many things compete with politics for people's attention—such as television, music, professional and college sports, Hollywood and movies, the shopping mall and mass consumerism—that a low level of political interest is only natural. Second, although the mass public tends to be poorly informed overall, Americans today are exposed to more information and are likely to have less simplistic images of the United States and the world than they held during periods such as the cold war. Much of this is due to rising enrollments in higher education over the last three decades and improved news coverage by the mass media. The final trend is that the size of the elite public has grown over time as a result of increases in higher education since the 1960s.[18]

Low levels of attention and information produce a third pattern in public opinion—its tendency to be volatile and to fluctuate over time. Since most Americans are uninterested and ill informed, their opinions about national and international issues tend to be very "soft" and open to change. Most Americans give little thought to most issues and are not committed to particular positions. Still, they have opinions and readily offer them when solicited by a public opinion poll. Secretary of State Dean Acheson once observed that most Americans do not feel it necessary to become informed before expressing an opinion. Not surprisingly, as an issue gets more media coverage, public attention increases for a while, members of the mass public acquire more information, and individual opinions change. Hence, opinion is volatile and fluctuates over time; and a **public opinion poll** is no more than a general snapshot of what the mass public may think at that brief moment.[19]

Such dramatic fluctuations in public opinion can be readily observed for most major events, such as presidential elections. As Americans acquire new information and images about the various candidates during the primaries and the general election, their opinions often change greatly in a very brief time. Nevertheless, the public's opinion of the candidates during the election process, however erratic, is instrumental in determining who becomes president of the United States. This is fairly typical of American politics and public opinion.

It is also important to point out that once the public pays some attention and acquires some information about an issue, usually through the media, it is not unusual that public opinion, though initially volatile, begins to harden. This was clearly the case experienced by President Clinton with the Monica Lewinsky affair. In the words of one journalist, "From the first headlines about Oval Office hanky-panky to the final impeachment vote, around two-thirds of the citizenry told pollsters that they disapproved of the Starr investigation and had no trouble distinguishing between the president's behavior as a man, which they deplored, and his performance as president, which they liked."[20] It was this eventual formation, differentiation, and stabilization of public opinion that made the political process so divided along party lines, saved Clinton from possible conviction on impeachment charges (since fellow Democrats in the House and Senate did not desert him), and allowed him to remain an active president until he left office.

IMPACT ON FOREIGN POLICY

These three public opinion pattern—inattentiveness, low levels of information, and the constancy of change—present problems for American democracy as discussed above. Democratic theorists have argued that democracy requires an informed and involved citizenry. However, most Americans are poorly informed about political affairs and do not participate in electoral or group politics. These patterns mean that the general public is not only open to being educated but vulnerable to manipulation by individuals and groups, especially through use of communications and the media, throughout society and the government. Overall, limited information and involvement, along with the potential for manipulation, has major implications for determining both the type of democracy the United States will have and the extent to which it exists. This will all be discussed to greater extent in this and subsequent chapters.

How does public opinion influence domestic politics and the policymaking process within foreign policy? In two ways: directly on policymakers within the government and much more indirectly by impacting the general domestic political process.

Direct and Immediate Impact. In terms of immediate and direct impact on policymakers within the government, *there are two contradictory consequences.*[21] The most obvious is that *inattentive, uninformed, and erratic public opinion gives policymakers great leeway in acting on most issues, for three reasons.* First, the content of public opinion serves as a poor guide for policymakers, especially given its fluctuating nature. Second, political leaders are often able to lead public opinion—that is, educate and manipulate the public—to support and follow their policies. Finally, during crisis periods, such as when troops are deployed abroad, the public tends to **rally round the flag** by supporting the president and his policies. The most visible illustrations of this phenomena were the huge spikes in public approval of presidential behavior for Bush Sr. following the success of the Persian Gulf War and Bush Jr. following the September 11 attacks.

As the traditional wisdom argues, public opinion rarely influences the government and the policymaking process in a direct and immediate way. In fact, public opinion often reinforces and strengthens presidential power because the president is the most visible and legitimate political figure in the United States, especially with respect to foreign policy. This is because the president and members of his administration are often successful in setting the agenda—that is, determining which issues are before the public and how they are discussed.

A second consequence, usually ignored by those who hold to the traditional wisdom, is that *for some issues, especially those that are most salient, public opinion may act as an immediate and direct constraint on political officials in the policymaking process for a number of reasons.*[22] First, elected officials are particularly sensitive to public opinion. No matter how inattentive, uninformed, and erratic public opinion is, the public votes political leaders in and out of office. As discussed in chapter 11, members of Congress are extremely sensitive to public opinion—at least within their own districts—because of their preoccupation with reelection. The same situation holds for the president. Within the White House, it is not uncommon to hear people say that "compared with analysts, Presidents and potential Presidents themselves see a close link between stands in foreign policy and the outcomes of presidential elections."[23] As we observed in chapter 4's discussion of presidential leadership, public prestige—that is, the perception of the president held by the general public—is an important element in exercising power. Whether a president tries to lead the public, to respond to public opinion, or to ignore public opinion—whatever the particular situation—he is likely to be greatly concerned with his overall level of public approval.

Second, if public feeling becomes intense concerning an issue, it severely constrains the choices available within the policymaking process. Following World War II until the late 1950s, for example, most Americans had to be convinced that the U.S. government should play an active internationalist role. Once the public was educated and led on the issue of anticommunism, however, American leaders began to feel constrained by public opinion, as cold war lessons—for instance, that the United States should never appease aggressors—were internalized by Americans. The result was that American policymakers had much leeway to deal with the Soviet Union and its allies during the cold war, but only if their policies took a hard-line approach. Policymakers, hence, were reluctant to appear soft toward communist governments. They could not recognize the People's Republic of China—the largest country in the world—during the 1950s and 1960s for fear that strong anticommunist sentiments among the public might be aroused. The last remnant of this anticommunist legacy in the present era is the constraints that it continues to place on policymakers' abilities to make foreign policy changes toward Fidel Castro and Cuba, even though the cold war has ended.

Third, public support for a policy may turn rapidly into public disapproval. Although the public tends to rally round the flag and the president during a crisis such as war, public support for presidential policies tends to dwindle over time. Studies, such as John Mueller's classic, *War, Presidents, and Public Opinion,* demonstrate that the longer a war lasts (and the greater the casualties), the more public support will erode. Lengthier wars produce greater numbers of American casualties and indicate that the war is going badly. Such events politicize the issue in American society and increase public disapproval of presidential policy. In other words, public support for the use of troops abroad has a limited threshold: quick and successful operations, as in Grenada, Panama, the Persian Gulf, and Kosovo maximize support; lengthy and unsuccessful conflicts, as in Korea, Vietnam, and Lebanon, bring public disapproval. The Iran hostage crisis in 1979 quickly rallied support behind President Jimmy Carter, but his inability to resolve the crisis by the end of 1980 produced strong public disapproval. Such public disapproval not only constrains presidential power but can lead to failed presidencies.[24]

Bruce Jentleson also found that public opinion "varies according to the *principal policy objective* for which force is used."[25] The tendency is for greater public support for the use of force in order to "contain" and "restrain" an aggressor state—such as in the Persian Gulf War—as opposed using force to "initiate" and "impose" internal political change within another state—such as within Nicaragua, Somalia, or Haiti. Obviously, many cases are likely to be, or be perceived as, somewhat mixed. Nevertheless, Jentleson concludes:

> The American public is less gun shy than during the Vietnam trauma period of the 1970s, but more cautious than during the Cold War consensus of the 1950s and 1960s. . . . Presidents who contemplate getting militarily involved in internal political conflicts—of which there may well be even more in the post–Cold War world than when bipolarity had its constraining effects—had better get in and out quickly and successfully. Otherwise, the public is strongly disposed to oppose the policy.[26]

Thus the public tends to discriminate over the use of force more than is commonly thought and is "pretty prudent." With the September 11, 2001, attacks, the war on terrorism at home and abroad, with all its complexity and uncertainty about policy objectives, may have complicated the impact of public opinion even further. This appears to be especially the case over whether the United States and the Bush Administration should go to war with Iraq and remove Saddam Hussein from power, with questions and dissent growing abroad and at home beginning in late 2002 and early 2003.

Finally, the collapse of the cold war consensus has made public opinion less responsive to the president (the cold war consensus is examined in the next section on political ideology). During the 1950s, most American leaders and members of the elite public shared a similar cold war view of the world that the mass public tended to follow. Since the Vietnam War, however, differing views of the world and U.S. foreign policy have arisen, leading to greater diversity and volatility in public opinion. As political scientist Thomas E. Mann points out, "There is little doubt that changes in public opinion about foreign policy were the root cause of the weakening of the President's leadership position and of the chronic conflict between the executive and legislative branches that began in the late 1960s."[27]

The continued prominence of the president gives him a distinct advantage in influencing public opinion, but the lack of a public consensus in support of presidential policies has made it much more difficult to shape foreign policy. On the one hand, the president has the potential for more leeway because the split in opinion allows him to promote different foreign policy orientations; on the other hand, disagreement over foreign policy makes it more difficult for the president to rally and maintain public support for particular policies. Opinion leaders with different foreign policy views now compete with each other for public support. This helps to explain why President Reagan was unsuccessful in persuading no more than 40 percent of Americans to support his anticommunist policies in Central America.[28]

In sum, the influence of public opinion on the foreign policy process is more complex than the traditional wisdom suggests. For many issues, public opinion has little, if any, immediate and direct impact on the policymaking process. However, for other issues high in salience, public opinion has an immediate and direct effect on policymakers within the government, including the president and members of Congress. The common denominators in these two contradictory patterns are (1) the level of salience and the politicization of issues and (2) the level of success or failure perceived among a public that tends to be very pragmatic and impatient.[29]

When the public feels things are going well in their lives and for the country and when few issues are salient and controversial, it tends to support the status quo and approve the president's performance. However, if the public perceives problems, such as a foreign policy fiasco or an economic recession, most people will want changes and the president's approval rating will drop. Public perception and satisfaction levels help to explain whether public opinion supports or constrains the president's ability to govern foreign policy. These contradictory public opinion patterns for foreign policy operated during the Persian Gulf crisis, affecting President Bush Sr. and the making of U.S. foreign policy. (See **essay 13.1** on public opinion and the Persian Gulf crisis.) The American response after September 11 attacks has increased public support for President Bush Jr. But the president's public approval has been declining, much remains to be done on the war on terrorism, and the future of public opinion is unclear and unpredictable.

Indirect and Longer-Term Influence. The foregoing discussion should help clarify the more indirect and longer-term influence of public opinion, which is *significant in three basic ways.* First, the public elects major governmental officials. It matters little how interested or informed most Americans are concerning foreign policy or whether their vote has anything to do with foreign policy issues. The fact remains that the public, especially the mass public, makes the final decision as to who becomes president and who runs Congress; it chooses the political leadership responsible for making U.S. foreign policy. Furthermore, with the collapse of a foreign policy consensus since the Vietnam War, the public's indirect impact on foreign policy through elections has increased, as different elected officials are now more likely to support different foreign policies.

Second, the ability of political leaders to influence the policymaking process during their tenure is heavily a function of their public prestige. As figure 4.2 in chapter 4 clearly illustrates, public approval of presidential performance over time not only fluctuates dramatically but also tends to move downward for each president. This accounts for the presidential life cycle, during which the president tends to enter office with highly favorable public opinion only to see it diminish with time, weakening his ability to govern.

ESSAY 13.1
PUBLIC OPINION AND THE PERSIAN GULF CRISIS

Public opinion fluctuated dramatically throughout the Persian Gulf crisis, illustrating the contradictory implications for American politics and presidential power in the making of U.S. foreign policy (see **figure 13.1**). *Three stages occurred*: public opinion was supportive during August and September, strengthening presidential power; became divided from October to early January, thus constraining presidential power; and after the war began, became supportive and reinforced presidential power once again.

Most Americans had little information about U.S. foreign policy toward Iraq and the Persian Gulf before August 2, 1990. Nevertheless, following President George Bush's decision to impose economic sanctions, send over 100,000 American troops to the region, and promote international support through the United Nations in response

to Iraq's invasion of Kuwait, the public rallied round the flag. By late August and September, President Bush's public approval ratings soared to historic levels of between 70 percent and 80 percent. Thus, before and immediately after the Iraqi invasion, public opinion had little impact on the policymaking process and, if anything, strengthened presidential power over foreign policy in the Persian Gulf.

Beginning in October, however, President Bush's approval ratings plummeted more than twenty points, bottoming around 50 percent, due to the disastrous budget negotiations between the president and Congress to reduce the growing federal deficits, the 1990 congressional and state elections, and President Bush's subsequent announcement that he was doubling the American military presence in the Persian Gulf to over 400,000 troops, re-

FIGURE 13.1
PRESIDENT BUSH SR.'S PUBLIC APPROVAL DURING THE PERSIAN GULF CRISIS

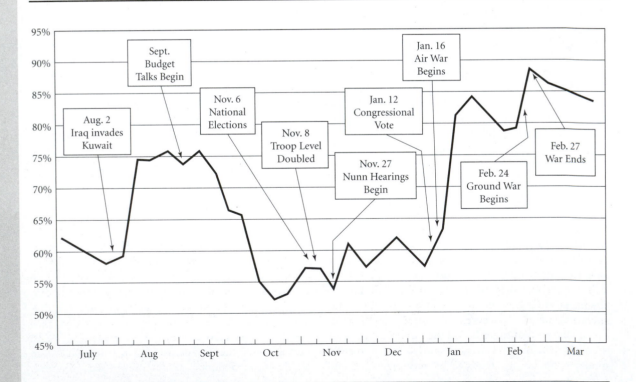

flecting a change from a defensive strategy to an offensive one to force Iraq to withdraw from Kuwait by taking it to the brink of war. What appeared to be solid public support for presidential policy in the Gulf quickly evaporated; public opinion was clearly divided by December over Bush's strategy and the consequences of an increasingly likely war (such as American casualties). It was the rise of a divided public and the drop in approval for the president's policies that acted as a catalyst for major congressional involvement—unprecedented in the heat of an international crisis—that resulted in hearings critical of presidential policy and a divided congressional vote authorizing the president to use force. Although Bush was ultimately successful in getting majority congressional support for his policy of brinksmanship, his ability to govern foreign policy was heavily challenged and badly constrained during this time as more and more members of the public criticized and questioned foreign policy developments.

Finally, after President Bush ordered American and allied troops into battle, American public opinion again rallied behind the flag, and this sentiment strengthened as the Iraqi military was overwhelmed with minimal loss of American life. Not surprisingly, the quickness and ease of the American allied military victory resulted in public approval ratings reaching new heights of over 80 percent for President Bush. Such public approval gave President Bush a new lease on governing foreign policy, so long as public opinion remained highly supportive.

A *fourth stage* in public opinion would have evolved if the Persian Gulf War had been prolonged and not gone well, resulting in the thousands of American casualties that many Americans feared. Under these conditions, public dissent and opposition would have increased, weakening presidential power and possibly producing another failed presidency. This did not happen during the Persian Gulf crisis; but since Vietnam it remains a distinct possibility in a future crisis, as so many other presidents have experienced.

It is important to point out that the three stages occurred during a foreign policy crisis involving the use of American troops, at a time when presidents historically dominate the political process until things go sour. This is indicative of the volatility of public opinion since Vietnam and the contradictory impact it has on the president's ability to govern foreign policy, even during a time of international crisis. As explained by Thomas E. Mann, "An administration that sails against the tide of public opinion

invites a more active congressional role; a President who succeeds in bringing foreign policy and public opinion into closer conformance—either by adjusting his policy or by reshaping public opinion—will be more successful in diffusing opposition on Capitol Hill."[A]

It appears that President Bush, and his closest advisers, was very sensitive to public opinion throughout the crisis. At one point, for example, political journalist Bob Woodward reported that Chairman of the Joint Chiefs of Staff Colin Powell urged President Bush to hold off on waging war and to rely instead on the international economic sanctions against Iraq, taking pains to explain that the sanctions option "has merit" and "will work" in time. The sanctions option, however, was dismissed by the president with the response, "I don't think that there's time politically for that strategy."[B] Likewise, Elizabeth Drew, in her "Letter from Washington" of January 25, 1991, reported that "it became known here not long ago that John Sununu, the president's chief of staff, was telling people that a short, successful war would be pure political gold for the president—would guarantee his reelection."[C] Unfortunately and unbelievably for Bush Sr., his high public approval dropped considerably following the war, and the public voted Bill Clinton in and Bush out in the 1992 presidential election.

Clearly, presidents take public opinion very seriously. Although the public tends to be uninterested, uninformed, and volatile concerning international affairs, public opinion nevertheless impacts the politics of U.S. foreign policy, posing considerable opportunities and risks for the president's ability to govern. Although President Bush Jr. rode high in public approval following the September 11 attacks—in sharp contrast to the pattern before the crisis—it will be very interesting to see to what extent it can be maintained over time and if he can avoid his father's fate if the crisis recedes into the background and new issues, such as the economy and federal budget deficits, gain public attention. Furthermore, given the rise of international and domestic dissent in 2003, President Bush Jr. may be betting his presidency on his apparent determination to go to war with Iraq and to overthrow Saddam Hussein.

A. Thomas E. Mann, "Making Foreign Policy: President and Congress," in Thomas E. Mann, ed., *A Question of Balance: The President, the Congress, and Foreign Policy* (Washington, D.C.: Brookings Institution Press, 1990), p. 11.
B. Bob Woodward, *The Commanders* (New York: Simon and Schuster, 1991), p. 42.
C. Elizabeth Drew, "Letter from Washington," *The New Yorker* (January 25, 1991), p. 83.

SOURCES: W. Lance Bennett and David L. Paletz, eds., *Taken by Storm: The Media, Public Opinion, and U.S. Foreign Policy in the Gulf War* (Chicago: University of Chicago Press, 1994); Larry Elowitz and John W. Spanier, "Korea and Vietnam: Limited War and the American Political System," *Orbis* (summer 1974): 510–34; Bruce W. Jentleson, "The Pretty Prudent Public: Post Post-Vietnam American Opinion on the Use of Military Force," *International Studies Quarterly* (1992): 49–74; John Mueller, *Policy and Opinion in the Gulf War* (Chicago: University of Chicago Press, 1994); John E. Mueller, *War, Presidents, and Public Opinion* (New York: John Wiley, 1973).

Finally, public opinion often sets the boundaries of legitimate political discourse and domestic politics, limiting the kinds of issues on the political agenda and decisions considered by policymakers. Although public opinion is erratic, it tends to fluctuate within a certain range of ideological and cultural beliefs that prevail in American society. It is to these more indirect and longer-term influences of the public to which we now turn by examining the role of, first, political ideology and then political culture.

POLITICAL IDEOLOGY AND FOREIGN POLICY ORIENTATIONS

A key to understanding how the public affects American politics and U.S. foreign policy is to examine the evolution of Americans' ideological views. **Political ideology** refers to beliefs about the preferred ends and means of a society (for example, liberty, equality, representative government, market-oriented economy). In this respect, we are also interested in the foreign policy orientations permeating American society—that is, how Americans see the world and the preferred role the United States should play in international relations. The ideological and **foreign policy orientations** prevailing in American society set the broad boundaries of legitimate political discourse and agenda setting within which public opinion operates to influence domestic politics and the policymaking process.

In reviewing the ideological and foreign policy orientations of Americans, *three points need to be kept in mind with respect to the types of publics involved, the nature of public beliefs, and their influence* on the politics of U.S. foreign policy. First, a discussion of ideological and foreign policy views must focus on the elite public and the extent to which it is supported by the mass public, because the elite public tends to have stronger, less moderate, and more influential ideological and foreign policy beliefs than the mass public. This is consistent with an important distinction that Godfrey Hodgson makes in *America in Our Time* between the **moral minority** (the elite public) and the **pragmatic majority** (the mass public).[30] During the cold war years, for example, it was popular to conclude that most Americans were not ideological, that the "end of

ideology" had arrived.[31] Clearly, if ideology refers to a set of values about the ends and means of a society, all people have ideological beliefs. As political scientist Robert Dahl pointed out over thirty years ago, "Americans are a highly ideological people. It is only that one does not ordinarily notice their ideology because they are, to an astonishing extent, all agreed on the same ideology."[32] What observers of American politics correctly pointed out is that the ideological beliefs of the mass public do not tend to be very sophisticated or consistent in comparison to the elite public; furthermore, most Americans correctly sense that they tend to be very pragmatic, reflecting more moderate and centrist ideological orientations. In other words, the mass public acts as a pragmatic majority, while the elite public often operates as the moral minority.

Second, the ideological and foreign policy orientations of Americans tend to be quite stable as compared to their expressions of public opinion. Ideological beliefs do not readily fluctuate; they tend to resist change. This is especially true among members of the elite public. Their ideological beliefs and foreign policy orientations are formed early in life through the process of political socialization and are based on considerable attention to national and international affairs. Therefore, opinion leaders and members of the attentive public tend to have more knowledge and greater emotional commitment to their views. The pragmatic majority, in contrast, tends to occupy more centrist positions while remaining more open and responsive to the ideological and foreign policy appeals of the elite public.

Third, ideology and foreign policy views are consequential in influencing the complex politics of U.S. foreign policy. *The ideological and foreign policy orientations in American society influence the foreign policy process in four ways:* They affect public opinion, influence the electoral process and voters' choices, affect the activity of groups and social movements in domestic politics, and are passed on to newer generations of Americans through the socialization process. In other words, the ideological and foreign policy views of Americans set the broad boundaries within which the complex politics of U.S. foreign policy operates.

A focus on ideology and foreign policy orientations enables one to understand how the national interest is defined in American society and government. Government leaders in power always argue that their policies promote the national interests of the United

States. However, the national interest is clearly a subjective concept, for different people define the national interest differently. Therefore, the national interest varies over time, and its character at any one point depends on which ideological beliefs and foreign policy views are prevalent within society and government.

The national interest and the making of U.S. foreign policy, in other words, are influenced heavily by the power of ideas—that is, the power of the ideological and foreign policy orientations held by the elite and mass publics. This has been a major theme running throughout this book in explaining continuity and change, presidential governance, and the tension between national security and democracy within the government and the policymaking process, and it sets the stage on which domestic politics impacts the making of U.S. foreign policy, as well. Thus, understanding the evolution of the ideological and foreign policy orientations of Americans throughout history is crucial for understanding how U.S. foreign policy is made.

The ideological and foreign policy orientations of Americans have gone through two major phases since the end of World War II. As Ole Holsti and James Rosenau make clear in *American Leadership in World Affairs*, the cold war years represented a time of foreign policy consensus throughout America, which was replaced by diverse and competing foreign policy views since Vietnam. Likewise, according to Godfrey Hodgson in *America in Our Time*, the cold war years were also a time of ideological consensus throughout America, which was replaced by ideological fragmentation as a result of Vietnam. In short, *two stages have characterized the ideological and foreign policy orientations of America in the post–World War II era:* (1) An ideological and foreign policy consensus prevailed during the cold war years; (2) an increase in ideological and foreign policy diversity has occurred since Vietnam.[33]

THE COLD WAR YEARS OF CONSENSUS

The cold war years led to the development of an **ideological and foreign policy consensus** throughout American society and government, an extraordinary time in American history. As Thomas Mann explains,

The bipartisan foreign policy consensus that prevailed for almost two decades after World War II was sustained by a leadership stratum that shared an internationalist and interventionist view of the U.S. role in world affairs, an attentive and educated group of citizens who followed and supported this leadership, and a poorly informed and largely inert mass public that tolerated official policy as long as it appeared to be working.[34]

This consensual view in American society fostered the rise of presidential power, the expansion of the foreign policy bureaucracy, the development of an acquiescent Congress, and the rise of a national security ethos and free market ethos in government and society. It also set the context for understanding the reinforcing role that public opinion and domestic politics played throughout the cold war years in the making of U.S. foreign policy.

The Rise of Foreign Policy Anticommunism. Holsti and Rosenau argue that most Americans in government and society shared a similar foreign policy orientation during the cold war years, which they call "cold war internationalism." Cold war internationalists saw a conflict-ridden, bipolar world that pitted the Soviet Union and communism against the United States and democracy. The Soviet Union was seen as an ambitious, aggressive, expansionist empire, leading a strong and patient group of communist allies toward a revolutionary goal: imposing a Moscow-dominated imperial system throughout the world. The United States, in contrast, was seen as the civilized and benevolent leader of democracy and prosperity throughout the so-called "free world." In a world where victory for one side was seen as defeat for the other, the assumed threat to American national security posed by the Soviet Union and communism became the predominant concern of American policymakers. It was this view of the world that laid the basis for the national security ethos to thrive during the cold war years. Therefore, U.S. foreign policy revolved around a strategy of containment of Soviet expansionism through the development, threat, and use of force around the world.

The anticommunist consensus did not develop overnight but evolved in three phases. First, a great debate took place over the future of U.S. foreign policy during the late 1940s in which the cold war internationalist perspective prevailed. Second, cold war internationalism and the policy of containment were challenged by the rise of McCarthyism and the political right during the early 1950s. Finally, an anticommunist consensus in U.S. foreign policy coalesced by the mid-1950s and reigned until the mid-1960s. These domestic patterns discussed below demonstrate the lead role of the elite public as well as the importance of mass public support, for it is the dynamic interaction between the two publics that determines which beliefs prevail in the making of U.S. foreign policy.[35]

Following the end of World War II, the natural inclination of most Americans was to revert to the **isolationist sentiment** prevalent before the war and support military withdrawal from most of the world. However, isolationist tendencies associated with the prewar period had been firmly discredited, especially among the elite public, with the bombing of Pearl Harbor and U.S. entry into World War II. Most American leaders realized that the United States had become too powerful to minimize its global involvement following the war. Increasingly vocal forces also publicized the potential threat posed by the Soviet Union and communism. Therefore, a **post–World War II great debate** took place among American leaders and intellectuals—that is, members of the elite public—about the world around them, the nature of the Soviet Union, and the proper foreign policy of the United States.

Some, like Henry Wallace, Franklin Roosevelt's former vice president and the 1948 presidential candidate on the Progressive party ticket, argued in support of the United Nations and the need to maintain a cooperative relationship with the Soviet Union through policies emphasizing spheres of influence and a type of détente. A few, like Walter Lippmann, one of America's most eminent journalists, emphasized a more realpolitik postwar approach toward Europe revolving around balance-of-power statecraft in which each great power would carve out traditional spheres of influence. Others, like George Kennan, a Sovietologist and important policymaker in Harry Truman's administration, asserted that the major threat was Soviet expansion in Europe and that the United States needed to contain the Soviet threat in Europe. Still others, like Paul Nitze, another important policymaker in the Truman administration, emphasized that the Soviet Union was a revolutionary state with designs to export communism aggressively worldwide and that the United States had no choice but to contain the Soviets militarily, not just in Europe but throughout the world.

In the late 1940s, individuals representing the two more pessimistic schools of foreign policy thought—European containment versus global containment—struggled for control of the Truman administration's foreign policy (see essay 2.2, on George Kennan). Truman himself was initially undecided about the nature of the Soviet Union and the appropriate U.S. response. With time he became increasingly skeptical of Soviet intentions. Relations were strained by difficulties over Poland and a divided Germany, the communist coup d'etat in Czechoslovakia, the "fall" of China, and the North Korean attack on South Korea. These events eventually convinced most members of the Truman administration, including the president, that the Soviet Union was indeed a revolutionary communist state attempting to achieve world domination. Therefore, they believed they had no choice but to assume leadership of what came to be referred to as the "free world" and stop—contain—communist aggression.

Not surprisingly, members of Congress and much of the public were reluctant to support such an activist international policy so soon after the country had fought a war (particularly since the Soviet Union was an ally). Yet there was an underlying anticommunist sentiment in U.S. society that could be traced to the Bolshevik Revolution in 1917 (see essay 8.1, on J. Edgar Hoover and the pursuit of security). Therefore, when the Truman administration responded to the post–World War II environment with proclamations like the Truman Doctrine, which committed the United States to assist Greece and Turkey in order to contain the communist threat, this produced growing public support for an overall policy of containment. The paramount lesson of World War II—that the appeasement of Adolf Hitler and fascism by England and France at Munich only produced more aggression—was applied to the contemporary situation: The United States must not appease Stalin and communism but must build up its military and contain communist aggression wherever it occurred.[36]

These events also propelled another segment of U.S. society to the forefront of politics—people who feared that the United States was losing the cold war because it was not doing enough to defeat communism. They believed that the United States not only was losing the cold war abroad, especially in Asia, but was threatened by subversion from within. Therefore, they argued that containment was not enough; a more aggressive policy was necessary that would roll back and eradicate communism. People who shared this view were most prominent within the Republican party, which had gained control of the Congress during the late 1940s and early 1950s. They attacked the policy of containment, as well as the Truman administration and its supporters, for losing the cold war (see essay 11.1, on Joseph McCarthy and McCarthyism).

McCarthyism was not successful in persuading either the Truman or Eisenhower administration to reorient its foreign policies beyond containment. However, *the challenge from the right had two lasting effects.* It reinforced perceptions held by U.S. policymakers and the American public that global communism was monolithic, controlled by the Soviet Union, and an ever present threat. Second, foreign policy views that were critical of the containment policy and argued for isolationism or a more realistic or cooperative policy (for example, as represented by Henry Wallace) lost all credibility and legitimacy during the cold war years. In short, a consensus developed within the United States during the 1950s that the world was divided between two hostile forces: communism led by the Soviet Union and democracy led by the United States. Despite disagreements over tactics (how much force? where should it be applied?), most Americans agreed on the source of the threat—communism—and the necessity of using force to forestall its expansion throughout the world.

The Rise of the Liberal-Conservative Ideological Consensus. The growing anticommunist foreign policy consensus reflected a larger set of ideological patterns which evolved in American society. During the cold war years, according to Godfrey Hodgson, "a strange hybrid, liberal conservatism, blanketed the scene and muffled debate."[37] *The two major aspects of the liberal-conservative consensus were,* first, belief in a democratic-capitalist political economy based on private enterprise and, second, the fear of communism. Thus, the foreign policy consensus behind containing the threat of Soviet communism abroad was part of a larger ideological consensus in American society.

Hodgson summarizes the basic tenets of the American **liberal-conservative consensus.** First, the American free enterprise system is democratic, creates abundance, and has a revolutionary potential for social justice. Second, the key to this potential is economic

growth based on private industry and governmental support, which allows the needs of all people to be met. Third, meeting popular needs will produce a more equal society in which conflict between social classes becomes unnecessary and obsolete and workers become members of the middle class. Fourth, social problems can be solved like industrial problems; the economy can be fine-tuned and the welfare state can eradicate poverty. Fifth, the main threat to this beneficent system is communism; therefore, the United States and its free world allies must fight a prolonged struggle against communism while promoting the American free enterprise system throughout the world. This was the ideological foundation for the national security and free market ethos that pervaded the minds of American policymakers.[38]

By the mid-1950s, most Americans within the mass and elite public were part of this liberal-conservative ideological consensus. This consensus became possible during the 1950s because most conservatives accepted the legitimacy of the limited welfare state created by the New Deal under Franklin Roosevelt, while most liberals adopted the anticommunist stance in vogue following World War II. Therefore, the liberal-conservative consensus represented neither liberalism nor conservatism but was a hybrid or amalgamation of the two ideologies.

Differences did exist among members of the consensus. Liberals were more favorable toward welfare and government intervention in the economy, while conservatives generally were opposed to such policies. Conservatives were more prone to rely on force to respond to instability in the Third World, while liberals were more sympathetic to the need to promote Third World economic and political development. However, such differences were overshadowed by agreement on the promise of the American private market system and the threat of communism. According to Hodgson, "Since the consensus had made converts on the Right as well as on the Left, only a handful of dissidents were excluded from the Big Tent: southern diehards, rural reactionaries, the more . . . paranoid fringes of the radical Right, and the divided remnants of the old, Marxist, Left."[39]

As with the foreign policy consensus, the liberal-conservative consensus did not develop overnight. *Beginning in the 1930s, American ideology went through three phases* that will be discussed below. First, the 1930s and 1940s witnessed the rise of liberalism and the political left and a corresponding decline of conservatism. Second, the late 1940s and 1950s resulted in the resurgence of conservatism and the political right. The more extreme conservative elements, represented by McCarthyism, were a powerful force even though they were ultimately unsuccessful in gaining political ascendance. Third, these two trends resulted in the formation of a liberal-conservative consensus by the mid-1950s that lasted throughout much of the 1960s.[40]

The United States experienced considerable change in ideological views from the 1920s to the 1940s. The Great Depression represented a momentous crisis in the lives of most Americans that politicized issues in society like no other event since the Civil War. Liberalism grew in popularity and became ascendant as Franklin Roosevelt passed the New Deal programs based upon activist government to pull the economy out of the Depression and provide welfare for the needy and impoverished. Conservatives, dominant before the Depression and representing many Americans afterwards, continued to believe in a laissez-faire approach to the economy based upon minimal government involvement and the magic of the marketplace. The economic collapse, massive unemployment, and impoverishment produced by the Depression also resulted in growing popularity for a third group of Americans advocating greater change, represented by socialists and American communists. Thus, politics became very divisive during the 1930s at the same time that the rise of domestic liberalism and greater government activity in the economy was accompanied by the growth of presidential power and the federal bureaucracy. Many conservatives, especially those with extreme views, accused Franklin Roosevelt of becoming a dictator and imposing socialism on Americans through his New Deal programs. Socialists and the left complained that New Deal policies were inadequate for addressing the mass poverty and inequality, for all they did was reform the capitalist system that was the fundamental source of the problems.

With the attack on Pearl Harbor, America's involvement in World War II temporarily united most of these competing ideological factions under the banner of liberalism against the common enemy of fascism. The isolationism behind U.S. foreign policy during the interwar years was overwhelmed by America's war effort. The decline of isolationism was accompanied by the growth of "liberal internationalism" in foreign policy,

whose advocates supported the establishment of a liberal international political economy—that is, a democratic-capitalist international order. A liberal world order would flourish through international cooperation, international law, and international organizations, such as the United Nations. Thus World War II not only represented a time of fear but also of great hope. In fact, the end of World War II was a triumph for the United States and liberalism, for the allies had won the war abroad and, with the war taking the United States out of the Great Depression, Americans were beginning to prosper at home once again.

With the war over, the middle and late 1940s witnessed the beginning of the cold war and a resurgence of conservatism in American society. Conservatives renewed their criticism of the New Deal, arguing that the restoration of economic prosperity no longer required the permanent intrusion of massive government in the economy. In foreign policy, conservatives initially promoted a "fortress America" strategy, emphasizing the need for isolationism abroad and military withdrawal, but this political stance was quickly discredited during the great foreign policy debate of the late 1940s. The issue of communism, however, began to surface and reinforced conservative concerns with the New Deal and perceptions of growing socialism at home. By the late 1940s and early 1950s, fear of communism both at home and abroad became the rallying cry of conservatism. McCarthyism represented the height of conservatism and its most extreme position during the cold war. Its proponents saw themselves as engaged in a battle for the future of America with its major ideological adversaries: liberalism and the left, Roosevelt's New Deal and Truman's Fair Deal policies at home, and the Democratic party's so-called appeasement policies of containment abroad.[41]

Although unsuccessful in gaining political ascendance in government and society, *conservatism and the political right were instrumental in pushing society to the right and providing conditions for the establishment of a liberal-conservative consensus*. First, most liberals became strong advocates of anticommunism and containment during the late 1940s and 1950s. "The lesson that Democrats drew was that never again could they afford to expose their foreign policy to the charge that it was soft on communism."[42] Second, conservatives increasingly accepted the notion of a limited welfare state in the domestic economy, especially during the

Eisenhower administration. Finally, liberals and the political left, who were critical of an aggressive U.S. policy of global containment abroad and believed in greater restructuring of American society at home, lost credibility and were silenced throughout the cold war.

Ideological anticommunism became the glue that bound the consensus among liberals, moderates, and conservatives, especially within the elite public. In the words of David Halberstam in *The Best and the Brightest*, "It was an ideological and bipartisan movement; it enjoyed the support of the press, of the churches, of Hollywood. There was stunningly little debate or sophistication of the levels of anti-communism. It was totally centrist and politically very safe; anything else was politically dangerous."[43] These ideological and foreign policy beliefs provided the foundation for the rise of the national security and free market ethos that prevailed in the minds of policymakers during the cold war years.

The ideological and foreign policy beliefs defined how Americans saw the world and limited the political choices available in the policymaking process. According to Hodgson, "The effect of McCarthyism has to be measured not only in individual careers destroyed but (more significantly for the nation as a whole) in assumptions unchallenged, in questions unasked, in problems ignored for a decade." Therefore, "until after 1965, when the Vietnam crisis broke in full force, there was no opposition to orthodox anti-communism from the Left in the Democratic Party, or none worth a President's consideration. Opposition from the Right was always a more real concern."[44] This domestic political situation prompted greater U.S. intervention in the Vietnam War and eventually led to a crumbling of the foreign policy and ideological consensus.

THE POST–VIETNAM LACK OF CONSENSUS

Events of the 1960s and early 1970s, such as the civil rights movement, the war on poverty, and Watergate, led many Americans to question the ideological and foreign policy beliefs that were the basis of the consensus during the cold war years. But the Vietnam War had the most traumatic impact on Americans, leading to the collapse of the ideological and foreign policy consensus that prevailed throughout the cold war.

These *events surrounding the collapse of consensus triggered two parallel and mutually reinforcing patterns.* First, American society became more ideologically diverse: The 1960s and early 1970s resulted in a resurgence of liberalism and the rise of the new left, while the late 1970s and 1980s witnessed the rise of conservatism and the political right. Second, the rise of ideological diversity also led to the development of competing foreign policy views or schools of thought. With the end of the cold war, these swings in the ideological and foreign policy orientations of Americans set the stage for the post–Vietnam War developments in domestic politics and governmental policymaking that have continued to the present day.

The Rise of Ideological Diversity. Throughout most of the 1950s and early 1960s, the American public—both elite and mass—tacitly supported increasing U.S. involvement in Southeast Asia. In reality, most Americans were unaware of what was happening in Vietnam, or even where it was located geographically. They were not interested in distant foreign policy ventures. Yet most Americans did not question the assumptions behind the ideological and foreign policy consensus that led to the nation's increasing involvement in Vietnam. Most Americans shared the belief that cold war policies were necessary to defend U.S. national security in Vietnam and promote democracy, freedom, and justice in the world. Therefore, if the president of the United States, supported by most leaders in government and society (the elite public), contended that Vietnam was vital to American interests and threatened by communism and that the free countries of Southeast Asia would fall if the threat was not contained, the American people stood behind him.[45]

The "failure" of Vietnam undermined many of these beliefs. Americans seemed to be dying for a lost cause—over 58,000 Americans died in Vietnam, with over 350,000 other Americans wounded. For what? The tragic loss of American lives and the failure in Vietnam led people to raise questions about U.S. foreign policy. Was Vietnam vital to U.S. national security? Was it an international war between the forces of communism and the forces of democratic capitalism, or was it a civil war between Vietnamese factions? Were American goals for and conduct in the war realistic? Were they just? Members of the mass public, on the one hand, came to critique the Vietnam War and U.S. foreign policy predominantly from a pragmatic perspective—they emphasized the limited importance of Vietnam and questioned U.S. failure to win the war. Members of the elite public, on the other hand, were more likely to debate the goals and the justice of U.S. foreign policy. The result was that American failure in Vietnam shattered the ideological and foreign policy consensus, turning the public increasingly against the war (see essay 2.3, on the evolution of Senator J. William Fulbright's views).

A massive antiwar movement developed during the 1960s, advocating U.S. withdrawal from the war. By the late 1960s, a substantial number of average Americans also had turned against the government and its policies in Vietnam; some wanted out through victory and military escalation, but most wanted out via withdrawal. For a while, the polarization between the antiwar movement and supporters of the war, between critics and supporters of mainstream society, appeared to verge on civil war. However, *polarization had given way to political fragmentation* by the 1970s. Thus, the ideological beliefs based on the liberal-conservative consensus that prevailed during the cold war years shattered, became polarized during the late 1960s and early 1970s, and fragmented during the post–Vietnam War years.

The events of the 1960s resulted in the growth of the political left in the United States and an alternative understanding of American society. Anticommunism and McCarthyism had silenced most liberals and leftists by the early 1950s. However, the new left entered the political scene in the late 1950s with the rise of the civil rights movement and grew dramatically as the Vietnam War intensified. Members of the new left and the counterculture dissented and rebelled against the liberal-conservative ideological and anticommunist consensus of mainstream society, which they held responsible for Vietnam (the new left will be discussed at greater length in chapter 16, on group politics and social movements).

The rise of the new left politicized society and pushed it in a more liberal direction. Liberalism once again began to emphasize the values of freedom and equality that had predominated throughout the 1930s and 1940s under Franklin Roosevelt, by rejecting the importance of anticommunism abroad and at home. Liberals were more likely to promote active governmental intervention in the economy and in support of needy individuals. Moreover, the Vietnam War and events of the 1960s prompted most liberals to become supportive of greater individualism in American life. Thus liberalism became quite distinct from conservatism in the post–Vietnam years.

At the same time, many Americans continued to hold a more conservative understanding of America and the world, emphasizing the threat of communism abroad and the importance of the private market at home—the same values that had once been the basis of the ideological consensus during the cold war. In fact, the late 1970s witnessed the resurgence of conservatism and the right, best associated with Ronald Reagan, in reaction to the perceived excesses of liberalism and the left during the 1960s and 1970s. Conservatives were particularly critical of the insufficient concern with the communist threat abroad and the moral decay they believed prevailed at home. These concerns account for not only the rise of conservatism but the growth of the ultraconservative and political right as well, including the religious fundamentalist right (which will also be discussed more in chapter 16).

Thus cold war dominance of the liberal-conservative consensus was superseded by greater ideological diversity. **Liberalism and conservatism** became increasingly distinct and competed for influence in American society and within the U.S. government. Furthermore, the growth of liberalism was accompanied by the rise of the new left, while the resurgence of conservatism was accompanied by the growing strength of the political right (see **essay 13.2**, on American liberalism and conservatism).

The Rise of Foreign Policy Diversity. Increasing ideological diversity paralleled the breakdown of the foreign policy consensus and the development of different foreign policy orientations and views. According to Holsti and Rosenau, *three major competing views in foreign policy have dominated the post–Vietnam War years*: cold war internationalism, post–cold war internationalism, and semi-isolationism. These three views are similar to the ones advanced by political analyst William Schneider, although he uses different labels to indicate their ideological home: conservative internationalism, liberal internationalism, and noninternationalism.[46]

To understand the complex politics of U.S. foreign policy in the post–Vietnam War period, it is important to know the general orientation of these three schools

ESSAY 13.2
AMERICAN LIBERALISM AND CONSERVATISM

Most Americans hold beliefs and values that are consistent with liberalism, conservatism, or some mixture of these two broad political ideologies. Yet there is considerable confusion, especially throughout the mass public, over what the terms liberalism and conservatism mean. Confusion is understandable given the common roots of liberalism and conservatism and their evolution through American history. Therefore, *in order to understand the similarities and differences between American liberalism and conservatism, at least five major points must be kept in mind.*

First, modern or twentieth- and twenty-first-century liberalism and conservatism in the United States share the same historical roots. They are both derived from **classical liberalism,** which developed in the seventeenth and eighteenth centuries in Europe. Liberalism arose in reaction to the order and inequality that characterized medieval society and feudalism under the aristocracy and the church. Classical liberals emphasized the importance of individual freedom in economic and political affairs through the promotion of democracy and capitalism and the separation of church and state. These classical liberal ideas, evident in the work of English philosopher John Locke, influenced many of the founding fathers and, hence, the Declaration of Independence and the two constitutions of the United States of America. As Alexis de Tocqueville recognized during the 1830s in his classic *Democracy in America*, the United States was a most liberal society, especially in comparison to Europe.

Second, classical liberalism has evolved over the course of American history into two modern derivatives developed during the twentieth century: **liberalism and conservatism**. Modern American liberalism and conservatism share a belief in individual freedom and a preference for a democratic-capitalistic political economy. However, the historical evolution of the American classical liberal tradition has also produced different interpretations of and splits on some issues. The first major dispute in this century concerned the role of the government in the economy. On the one hand, the Great Depression convinced many people—who became known as "liberals"—that the government should take a much more active role in regulating and steering the economy. Moreover, these liberals believed that the government should assist the unemployed and the poor, who were frequently victims of the failures and flaws of the market economy. On the

other hand, many people—who became known as "conservatives"—opposed such New Deal policies and preferred a more traditional, "laissez-faire," or minimal, governmental role in the economy, in which people would prosper through individual work and private charities would support the underprivileged.

The split over the government's role in the economy was the major difference between modern liberals and conservatives from the 1930s until the 1950s. During the 1950s, the cold war was a period of growing ideological consensus between liberals and conservatives because of a shared anticommunism and acceptance of a limited welfare state. The events of the 1960s shattered the consensus, producing new splits between conservatives and liberals.

Divisions over the political economy reemerged, while liberals and conservatives increasingly differed over foreign policy and social policy. Liberals criticized traditional cold war positions, while conservatives continued to adhere to cold war internationalism. For example, conservatives saw Vietnam as an honorable war lost through a failure of national will; in contrast, liberals tended to see Vietnam as a mistake and viewed the American use of force as counterproductive. Furthermore, while conservatives promoted traditional social norms and were concerned with maintaining social stability and order, liberals tended to favor greater individualism in social lifestyles. Therefore, modern American liberalism and conservatism have become increasingly distinct during the post–Vietnam War years, even though both sprang from the classical liberal, democratic-capitalistic tradition.

The third point to keep in mind when discussing American liberalism and conservatism is that each ideological orientation is made up of many variants. Differences exist among liberals and conservatives. These differences are not easy to identify, for they change over time and vary with the issue; nonetheless, they do exist. Liberalism consists of a broad coalition composed of a diverse set of people: "New Deal liberals" who favor more traditional forms of government intervention to support the economy and individuals; "neoliberals" who prefer a more cooperative relationship between government, business, and labor in order to reinvigorate the economy and increase American competitiveness abroad; "populist liberals" who place greater emphasis on reforming the American government and economy to respond to the needs of the poor, the disadvantaged, and working Americans; "social liberals" who are more concerned with individual lifestyle issues, as well as protecting the environment and human health; and others. Likewise, conservatism also consists of diverse elements: "market conservatives" who continue to emphasize unrestrained market forces as the key to economic growth and prosperity; "populist conservatives" who want more private involvement to supplement governmental support in responding to the needs of Americans; "neoconservatives"—usually former cold war liberals—who tend to emphasize threats to American security and international stability abroad; "social conservatives" who want certain norms and moral standards to prevail in society, such as school prayer and anti-abortion; and **"libertarians"** who emphasize individualism and limited government across all issues, including national security policy (making them both conservative or liberal depending on the issue).

Fourth, liberal and conservative ideological positions differ in elite and mass publics. Most members of the elite public tend to be more ideologically oriented—whether liberal or conservative—than members of the mass public. The mass public, in contrast, tends to be more centrist and moderate, reflecting beliefs and positions from both ideological orientations. This distinction between the elite and mass publics in terms of the nature and intensity of their ideological beliefs is consistent with Godfrey Hodgson's distinction in *America in Our Time* between the moral minority and the pragmatic majority.

Fifth, the growth of liberalism has been accompanied by the rise of the political left, while the ascendance of conservatism has been accompanied by growing strength in the political right. American liberalism and conservatism reflect a rather narrow range of ideological beliefs that have competed for power within American society over the last two centuries, especially when compared to the politics of European societies. For all their differences and variations, American liberalism and conservatism have much in common, although they have been challenged by other ideological traditions. The **political left** has a long tradition in the history of the United States, and there have been periods when it has grown in popularity

and influence: democratic socialism became popular before World War I, communism and pacifism grew during the 1920s and the Depression years, and the new left was prominent during the 1960s and 1970s. The **political right**, likewise, also has had a long history and has been able to attract support at different times, evident in the rise of McCarthyism during the cold war years and the prominence of the secular and fundamentalist-Christian right since Vietnam. Therefore, although small and often invisible to most Americans, the traditions of the left and right have played an active and sometimes important role in American politics.

This is a simple overview of the history and content of American liberal and conservative thought, but these five points should provide more clarity and understanding of these ideological positions. For example, it should be clear that the popular distinction that most Americans make between liberals as "pro-big government" and conservatives as "anti-big government" is inaccurate, for this difference depends on the issue and the times. For example, liberals usually prefer greater government involvement in the economy and conservatives less government intervention; however, conservatives usually prefer more government defense spending in support of national security, while liberals prefer less. Likewise, in the area of social policy, liberals emphasize active government in support of the rights of individuals, such as to prevent child abuse, while conservatives emphasize active government to promote certain moral standards, such as school prayer or the prevention of abortion. Regardless of the particular issue and the differences between liberalism and conservatism, however, most Americans have been part of a long (classical) liberal tradition throughout American history.

SOURCES: John Ehrman, *The Rise of Neoconservatism: Intellectuals and Foreign Affairs, 1945–1994* (New Haven: Yale University Press, 1995); Louis Hartz, *The Liberal Tradition in America* (New York: Harcourt Brace and World, 1955); Lawrence J. R. Herson, *The Politics of Ideas: Political Theory and American Public Policy* (Prospect Ill.: Waveland Press, 1984); Godfrey Hodgson, *America in Our Time* (New York: Vintage, 1976); and Jay Winik, "The Neoconservative Reconstruction," *Foreign Policy* 73 (winter 1988–89): 135–52.

of thought. At the same time, it is important to recognize that important differences or variants exist within each of these foreign policy orientations that reflect the broader ideological spectrum of American society. Finally, it is also important to keep in mind that some of the foreign policy beliefs held by Americans may be in a

process of undergoing change in light of the end of the cold war and the September 11, 2001, terrorist attacks.[47]

Many Americans, especially conservatives and those on the political right, continued to believe in **conservative internationalism** (or cold war internationalism) after Vietnam, especially during the 1970s and 1980s. In other words, they believed that the major global threat to the security of the United States and global order was communism directed by the Soviet Union, requiring a strong American military presence in much of the world. Yet disagreement among conservatives existed concerning the severity of the Soviet threat and the appropriate foreign policy strategy. Three variants of the conservative internationalist perspective prevailed during the eighties (see **table 13.2**).

More extreme conservatives (or "global crusaders") tended to see communism as monolithic and favored massive rearmament at home and a policy of aggressive rollback abroad—reminiscent of the policies advocated by McCarthy and the far right during the 1950s. Most conservatives (or "global containers"), recognizing that communism was no longer monolithic, focused on containing Soviet communism through a defense buildup

and a containment strategy—reminiscent of government policy during the cold war and the Reagan years. Finally, even more moderate conservatives (or "selective containers") did not emphasize Soviet communism but stressed the threat the Soviet Union posed to global stability and argued for a realpolitik or power-politics strategy of selective containment—a position promoted, for example, by Henry Kissinger under Presidents Nixon and Ford.

Other Americans, especially liberals and those on the political left, saw a much more complex and interdependent world in the 1970s and 1980s, composed of many important countries, global actors, and issues—a position that Schneider refers to as **liberal internationalism** (and Holsti and Rosenau refer to as post–cold war internationalism). In contrast to conservatives, liberals believed it was important to address not only the

TABLE 13.2
COLD WAR INTERNATIONALIST ORIENTATIONS

	GLOBAL CONTAINERS	GLOBAL CRUSADERS	SELECTIVE CONTAINERS
DEPICTION OF THE INTERNATIONAL SYSTEM	Bipolar	Bipolar but with unipolar tendencies	Bimultipolar
MAJOR ACTORS	U.S.—benevolent, defender of freedom, lacks will, militarily deficient	U.S.—morally superior, currently corrupted, militarily weak	U.S—strong but militarily deficient, naive at times about world
	U.S.S.R.—imperial, communist, totalitarian, militarily stronger	Communists—imperial, evil, militarily superior	U.S.S.R.—great power, opportunistic, expansionistic
MAJOR ISSUES	Cold war, superpower ideological struggle, terrorism, defense policy	Spread of international communism	Global balance of power, superpower rivalry, alliance politics
HISTORICAL LESSONS	WWII—need to reject appeasement; Vietnam—need to stand resolute	All post–WWII history illustrates U.S. foreign failures	WWI and WWII—need to maintain balance of power
PRESCRIPTION	Promote and protect freedom and democracy, global containment of Soviet communism, unilateral action if necessary	Promote freedom and capitalism, roll back communism, unilateral approach	Maintain order and stability, contain expansionism in vital areas, multilateral approach favored

SOURCE: Jerel Rosati and John Creed, "Extending the Three-Headed and Four-Headed Eagles: The Foreign Poplicy Orientations of American Elites During the 80s and 90s," *Political Psychology* (1997): 583–623.

East-West conflict, but West-West issues, involving re-lations between the United States and its allies, and North-South issues, focusing on the relationship be-tween industrialized nations and the Third World. Al-though there was general agreement that the cold war preoccupation with the Soviet threat and the use of force must be downplayed in order to promote global stability, peace, and prosperity, two variants of the lib-eral internationalist perspective existed (see **table 13.3**).

Most liberals (or "global reformers") tended to focus on promoting stability in U.S.-Soviet relations and advocate arms control and other confidence-building measures, while emphasizing the need for cooperative

economic relations between Europe, North America, and Asia to develop a liberal economic world order. They also tended to emphasize the importance of human rights, democracy, and the role of diplomacy in resolving disputes and conflict. More extreme views on the political left (or "global transformers") saw more global threats and inequalities and advocated greater arms control and global disarmament, supported greater efforts to redress Third World poverty and vio-lence, and were concerned with overcoming interna-tional environmental destruction.

Proponents of the third popular orientation of the 1970s and 1980s, spanning the political spectrum, recog-

TABLE 13.3
POST–COLD WAR INTERNATIONALIST AND SEMI-ISOLATIONIST ORIENTATIONS

	GLOBAL REFORMERS	GLOBAL TRANSFORMERS	SEMI-ISOLATIONISTS
DEPICTION OF THE INTERNATIONAL SYSTEM	Multipolar, interdependent	Multipolar, with U.S. prevalent	Generally multipolar, interdependent, chaotic
MAJOR ACTORS	U.S.—great power, in decline	U.S.—hegemonic power, in decline	Multitude of potentially important actors
	U.S.S.R.—strong military power, economically weak, opportunistic	U.S.S.R.—strong military power, largely weak and defensive in nature	U.S.—increasingly overcommitted
	Europe + Japan—growing economic powers	Third-World actors—often oppressed but offer hope	
	NICs—growing economic force		
MAJOR ISSUES	Superpower relations and arms race, regional conflicts, global economic stability, Third World development	Arms race, global expansionism, regional conflict, self-determination, global inequality	Arms race and other transnational problems, domestic issues
HISTORICAL LESSONS	Vietnam—example of decline in the utility of force	Vietnam—example of U.S. expansionism	Vietnam—U.S. global policy prone to failure
PRESCRIPTION	Maintain global order and stability, infuse justice, multilateralism	Restructure U.S. and international institutions to provide justice and dignity to world's people	Limited U.S. involvement in world affairs, only when vital interests at stake

SOURCE: Rosati and Creed, "Extending the Three-Headed and Four-Headed Eagles."

nized the increasing complexity of the world and the difficulty the United States had in affecting it and advocated a type of **noninternationalism** (or semi-isolationism, or a "selective engager" orientation—review table 13.3). Some noninternationalists argued that the United States needed to limit its involvement to those areas of the world where it really has vital interests—primarily Western Europe and Japan. Other noninternationalists believed that the United States should de-escalate its overseas military commitments and presence—in other words, "strategically disengage"—and concentrate on improving its international commercial and economic position. Whatever the particular position, noninternationalists were likely to believe that the highest priority of American society and the U.S. government should be to avoid entanglements abroad and address domestic issues and problems at home. Noninternationalists also tended to be more supportive of protecting American industry and jobs in the international political economy. Such a noninternationalist perspective was most prevalent among the mass public (in comparison to the elite public), among whom isolationist sentiment has historically been strong.[48]

What about the impact of the collapse of Soviet communism on the foreign policy orientations of Americans for the 1990s and beyond? As Norman Ornstein and Mark Schmitt ask, "How will the U.S. political system operate without anticommunism as its central organizing principle?"[49] The momentous events surrounding the end of the cold war, the collapse of communism in Eastern Europe, and the collapse of the Soviet Union raised the possibility of profound changes in American foreign policy orientations. Indeed, another great debate in the 1990s was generated over the nature of the world and the proper role of the United States abroad.

There has been a general recognition that, with the collapse of the Soviet Union and its Eastern European empire, the structure of the international system has changed—that the United States is the sole global power (or superpower) and is in a more advantageous position than before. But there is great debate about what this means. In fact, most American opinion leaders seem to be adapting and absorbing such a change within their prevailing foreign policy beliefs, maintaining much of the basic thrust of each of the foreign policy orientations outlined above.

The end of the cold war appears to have reaffirmed the beliefs of liberal internationalists that U.S. foreign policy needs to move beyond the cold war to "cooperative multilateralism" in order to address myriad issues in a complex and interdependent world. The same is true for semi-isolationists, who perceive that U.S. foreign policy should (and can) pursue strategic disengagement and greater independence in world politics. With the collapse of Soviet communism, one might expect to see some significant changes in conservative internationalist orientations. And while there has been some movement more toward a semi-isolationist and selective containment view, conservative internationalists, for the most part, continue to emphasize security threats to the United States and the stability of the world—but now in and from the Third World—and the need for American "primacy."[50]

The differences between conservative internationalists, liberal internationalists, and noninternationalists are particularly noticeable in national security affairs, as opposed to foreign economics. Since the collapse of the foreign policy consensus over the Vietnam War, Americans have differed over the nature of world politics and their prescriptions for a U.S. national security policy. Thus, where conservative internationalism once reigned supreme and provided the basis for the national security ethos of independence, secrecy, and realpolitik that prevailed among policymakers during the 1950s and 1960s (discussed in chapter 8), since Vietnam there have been fewer adherents of a strong national security ethos, and they must operate in a domestic political climate that, with the rise of liberal internationalism and semi-internationalism, is less receptive to such views.

The profound events, at least for Americans, of September 11 may have affected these foreign policy orientations and created even further uncertainty about the future. Despite the rallying round the flag and initial dramatic support behind President Bush Jr. and the U.S. war on terrorism, fragmentation of beliefs and ideological diversity are likely to continue among American elites and the American public. At the same time, it appears likely that the noninternationalist orientation probably will receive less support and sympathy in the area of national security affairs. This means that we are likely to see greater support for both liberal and conservative internationalism in the future, and possibly some mixture of the two. Furthermore, as long as anti-terrorism remains a high priority issue on the U.S. foreign policy agenda and in the minds of Americans, we may witness some degree of a resurgence of the conservative internationalist orientation, especially among the global containers, if the post–cold war concern with containing terrorism and Third World conflicts (and instability) replaces the cold war threat of communism. Certainly in the area of national security affairs, much remains uncertain and unpredictable for the future, with the potential for much change and disagreement in the foreign policy orientations of Americans about the nature of the world and the most appropriate foreign policy goals and means for the twenty-first century.

Foreign economic policy orientations and the free market ethos, discussed in chapter 9, have been much less affected by the Vietnam War and the collapse of the cold war consensus, as well as the collapse of the Soviet Union and the September 11 attacks. Internationalists still tend to sympathize with a free market ethos. Conservative internationalists are the strongest believers and advocates of an unregulated international political economy based on a free market (except for using coercion and embargoes, for example, against perceived enemies such as Cuba). Liberal internationalists, for the most part, also believe in a market-oriented international political economy, but argue for the need for more international multilateral cooperation, management, and regulation. Both conservative and liberal internationalists, for the most part, believe that U.S. foreign policy overall must support, for example, NAFTA, the World Trade Organization, and trade with China despite different views about its growing great power status. It is the noninternationalists who are the least receptive to the free market ethos and most willing to advocate **protectionism** for local industry and labor, especially for people who have been, are, or might in the future be directly affected.[51]

Therefore, the cold war consensus has collapsed, but the split in foreign policy beliefs is much greater in the area of national security than it is over foreign economics. This may undergo some change as the U.S. enters the twenty-first century and economic issues continue to rise to the forefront of U.S. foreign policy alongside national security issues. Together, the three broad foreign policy perspectives, and their variations, set the parameters of foreign policy thought and agenda-setting in the making of U.S. foreign policy. Members of the elite public tend to be more committed to some variant of conservative or liberal internationalism, but they usually are opposed to noninternationalism. Members of the mass public tend to be more moderate and pragmatic in their beliefs, demonstrating both liberal and conservative elements, and are more receptive to the noninternationalist orientation.[52]

This configuration of foreign policy beliefs among different types of publics has led to some major contradictions in public opinion. For example, although most Americans remain distrustful and skeptical of international communism, they also wanted more cooperative and peaceful relations with communist countries, such as the People's Republic of China. Likewise, most Americans continue to believe in a strong defense; however, they remain reluctant to support uses of force that may result in American troops dying abroad. Although these contradictory views are not easily resolved, they demonstrate that the legacies of both the cold war and Vietnam War—complicated by the collapse of the Soviet Union, the success of the Persian Gulf War, and the new war on terrorism—seem to have been absorbed by most Americans within their foreign policy beliefs as the United States moves into the twenty-first century. It also suggests that public opinion for the mass of Americans will remain relatively volatile depending on the level of public attention and information.

THE CONTINUAL SEARCH FOR CONSENSUS AND POLICY LEGITIMATION

The changes in ideological and foreign policy beliefs have important political implications for the foreign policy process. What is important to understand is that the movement from cold war consensus to post-Vietnam diversity has *widened the agenda of domestic politics and political discourse* in the making of U.S. foreign policy. Such changes in ideological and foreign policy beliefs cannot be understated, for the collapse of the cold war consensus has led to new era in which public opinion is more volatile, political participation has become more active and diverse, the media are more likely to act independently of the government, Congress has reasserted its authority, and the president's ability to govern foreign policy faces both greater constraints and opportunities. As Richard Melanson has concluded in *Reconstructing Consensus*, "In sum, a **fragmentation/swing model** has replaced that of cold war **followership model** as the most accurate depiction of foreign policy attitudes, . . . and its emergence has surely complicated the efforts of presidents to win and keep public support for their foreign policies."[53]

The diversity of ideological and foreign policy beliefs has led to some major fluctuations in public opinion. Whereas public opinion fluctuated within only a narrow range consistent with the liberal-conservative and cold war internationalist consensus during the cold war years, public opinion is now much more open to greater fluctuation, reflecting the breakdown of the cold war consensus. This is because, unlike the opinions of the elite public, which tend to reflect its members' commitment to a particular ideological and foreign policy view, members of the mass public tend to be more centrist (reflecting a mix of foreign policy orientations, and only a temporary mix at that) and more noninternationalist in their orientations. Therefore, members of the mass public, since they do not internalize the ideological views of the elite public, are more likely to change their opinion and be open to populist appeals: Sometimes they are responsive to a more conservative and cold war internationalist position while at other times they are more receptive to a liberal and post–cold war internationalist position (see **figure 13.2** for a visual comparison of the cold war versus the post-Vietnam War years).

The post–Vietnam War and cold war years of dissension have produced a much more complex and messy political process in which public opinion is much more volatile than during the cold war years of consensus. As William Schneider has pointed out, when a foreign policy issue gets on the political agenda and is framed in terms of security and "military strength," then the conservative internationalist orientation tends to win the political debate—such as immediately following the September 11 attacks. However, if it is framed in terms of "peace," then the liberal internationalist perspective tends to prevail. "Instead of elite consensus and mass followership, what emerged was an unstable system of competing coalitions in which the mass public swings left or right unpredictably in response to its current fears and concerns."[54] There are also times when an issue may trigger a strong semi-isolationist orientation among the public, such as over issues concerning jobs and the economy. Public opinion, therefore, tends to fluctuate dramatically depending on the political issues of the occasion and the

FIGURE **13.2**

COMPARING AMERICAN POLITICAL IDEOLOGY DURING THE COLD WAR AND SINCE VIETNAM

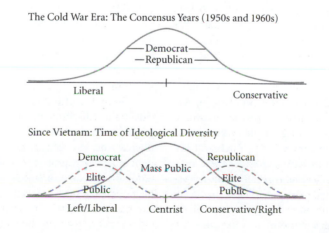

The Cold War Era: The Concensus Years (1950s and 1960s)

Democrat
Republican

Liberal   Conservative

Since Vietnam: Time of Ideological Diversity

Democrat   Republican
Elite   Mass Public   Elite
Public   Public

Left/Liberal   Centrist   Conservative/Right

success of different groups and leaders in communicating their positions. In this respect, it is important to maintain some historical context and recognize that liberal and conservative internationalism, as well as noninternationalism, all predate the cold war and will continue in a post–cold war international environment.

The fragmentation of public ideological and foreign policy beliefs gives a president great opportunities but also creates great risks. Unlike those in the 1950s, presidents now are no longer driven to pursue only an anticommunist containment policy. Yet it is unclear how far a president may go in pursuing any policy before losing public support. Presidents no longer come to office with automatic majorities behind their policies. No matter what the president and his advisers believe, a substantial number of Americans—in the mass public and especially the elite public—disagree, or are open to disagreement, with presidential policy. Hence, the continual presidential search for, and frustration in obtaining, consensus and **policy legitimation.**[55]

All post–Vietnam War presidents have discovered that most Americans expect presidential promises to be fulfilled, but the dissension since Vietnam makes it much more difficult for presidents to deliver. Presidents have found that, in addition to the reassertion of Congress, they face additional constraints on their ability to govern given the nature of civil rights and liberties, electoral politics, group politics, and the media and the communications process, as we will discuss in the next few chapters. All this is likely to continue in a post–cold war political environment. Therefore, differences in the ideological and foreign policy beliefs among the elite public, coupled with a pragmatic but volatile mass public, have provided a new set of domestic boundaries and possibilities for the making of U.S. foreign policy since Vietnam.[56]

Although the Bush Jr. administration is trying its political best to promote a new foreign policy (or national security) consensus around anti-terrorism, a new, strong, and consistent foreign policy consensus appears to be nowhere in the making. Much will depend on to what extent Americans consider their individual and country's security as threatened by terrorism in the long run. Even with the collapse of Soviet communism and the September 11 attacks, it is likely that the foreign policy orientations of Americans will continue to adapt to a post–cold war world. Where the end of the cold war appears to be reinforcing the beliefs of liberal internationalists and noninternationalists, conservative internationalists appear to be moving toward an emphasis on power politics and the need for international stability through American primacy, unilateral if necessary. Whatever the case, foreign policy thought is likely to remain highly diverse, especially among members of the elite public, and competitive, particularly for the support of the mass public.

POLITICAL CULTURE

In addition to the role of public opinion and political ideology, political culture plays a subtle but significant role in the making of U.S. foreign policy. **Political culture** refers to how people see themselves and their country relative to the rest of the world. Although American political culture includes a variety of important values, such as democracy and individualism, the focus in this section is on those cultural assumptions that Americans have about their country's role in the world. Not only does this suggest the existence of an **American national style,** but such nationalistic beliefs are particularly evident and powerful forces in the politics of U.S. foreign policy in times of crisis and war. As William Schneider observes, leadership and followership "can be founded only on intellectual and moral commitment to values and principles, to ideology in the truest sense of the word. In the United States it can be founded only on the values of liberty and equality, of freedom, that Americans have been extolling for two centuries or more."[57]

In considering political culture, a number of things must be kept in mind. First, we are most interested in the cultural and national values prevailing in the population; therefore, what the mass public believes plays a predominant role in determining America's national style. Second, cultural values also tend to be the most widely shared, resilient, and consistent set of beliefs held by individuals. Nationalistic views and feelings, in other words, strongly resist change, for people acquire them at a very young age. Finally, political culture and national style do not influence domestic politics and the policymaking process in an immediate or direct way, but by coloring how individuals see their country and its special place in the world. Because cultural and national values are socialized and deeply held, most people—within both the mass and elite publics—have a somewhat ethnocentric view of the world, thus affecting how foreign policy is made.

AMERICAN CULTURE AND NATIONAL STYLE

Throughout most of the 1960s and 1970s, American political culture and national style received little study, in part because of the difficulties involved in determining the key elements of a nation's cultural values or character. By the 1980s, however, numerous works had been produced highlighting the important role that American political culture and national style play in the making of U.S. foreign policy. These works tend to agree that most Americans are socialized to acquire a similar cultural outlook and that they developed a strong sense of nationalism by the twentieth century.[58]

Studies of American political culture typically portray Americans as a confident and optimistic people who have a special sense of destiny about the future of their country and its place in the world. In *Backfire*, for example, Loren Baritz argues that *three key characteristics describe how Americans see themselves* relative to the rest of the world: the notion of a "city on a hill," an idealistic and missionary spirit, and the invincibility of American technology. In other words, most Americans tend to believe inherently in (1) American innocence, (2) American benevolence, and (3) American exceptionalism.

Americans are raised to believe that the United States is innocent in world affairs as a people and a country. In other words, Americans do see themselves not as manipulative and aggressive but as a benign and defensive people and country. **American innocence** is consistent with the isolationist sentiments that have played such a dominant role in U.S. foreign policy, especially before the cold war.[59] According to this view, Americans have not been an outward-seeking people. Instead, they have been introspective and concerned with nation building and with serving as a "city on a hill" for other people and countries to emulate. Over the years, other countries and other ideologies have forced the United States to become actively involved in war and world politics. The German disregard of American neutrality forced the United States to fight in World War I, while the Japanese bombing of Pearl Harbor forced American entry into World War II. The September 11 attacks have reinforced this, with popular analogies to Pearl Harbor despite the fact the United States abroad and at home has been a target of terrorists for some time now. Thus, Americans tend to see themselves and their country as the innocent victims of the acts of others.

When the United States does become involved abroad, American behavior is perceived as benevolent. Such benevolence means that Americans do not become involved in war, for example, solely to defend themselves; rather, they enter wars in order to rid the world of evil and promote peace and freedom for all. As Americans have been taught at a very young age, World War I represented the "war to end all wars." European realpolitik would be replaced by American idealism, as embodied in President Woodrow Wilson's plan to create a League of Nations. In World War II, the United States and its allies were dedicated to ridding the world of fascism and constructing a world based on a liberal political and economic order as represented by the United Nations. In both wars, the United States saw itself as not only defending its national security but fighting for the principles of democracy, freedom, and justice for all. Likewise, the public goal of the war on terrorism is to rid the world of Osama bin Laden, Al Qaeda, and all terrorist networks.

Finally, Americans not only see themselves as innocent and benevolent but also have a strong sense of **American exceptionalism** as well. When Americans put their minds to something, they succeed in accomplishing their objectives. American history is perceived as one success story after another, from westward expansion to economic development to the rise of the United States as a global power. Much of this is seen as a function of American ingenuity and technological superiority over others. There is also an American sense of **manifest destiny**—a belief in the superiority of American culture and way of life and the need to Christianize and Americanize the world that goes back to the early nineteenth century.[60] In other words, American exceptionalism implies that God is on America's side and that America represents progress and the best social model for the future of the world. Thus, Americans have a high sense of optimism, that is, confidence about their ability to accomplish any task and faith in their future, "that Americans can do anything they desire, can build nations or rebuild societies, can speed progress, bring freedom and democracy to the world." In other words, James Oliver Robertson concludes,

"America, imperial America, is 'one giant step for mankind.'"[61]

The effects of these cultural and national values emphasizing American innocence, benevolence, and exceptionalism on American perceptions of the cold war are obvious. For most Americans, Soviet aggression forced the United States to take an active global leadership role, build up its military to contain aggression, and intervene throughout the world. Thus, Americans were innocent victims of Soviet aggression and needed to contain the threat. Moreover, the cold war was not just a classical struggle for power between two great powers but represented a messianic struggle between good and evil—the forces of democracy versus totalitarianism, capitalism versus communism, Christianity versus atheism. Thus, the globe was seen to be divided into two hostile blocs: the "evil" communist world led by the Soviet Union versus the "free world" led by the United States. In addition, the United States had not only rescued Western Europe through its generosity with the Marshall Plan but promoted liberal societies in Third World countries and assisted their nation-building efforts based on the American model. Americans, therefore, saw themselves not as imperialistic or even self-interested during the cold war but as an innocent society composed of benevolent and exceptional people who symbolized progress and a hopeful future for the world.[62]

Anders Stephanson, in *Manifest Destiny: American Expansion and the Empire of Right*, suggests a different interpretation—one much more consistent with America's historical past:

> In the 1840s, the spatial destination of destiny was clearly continental, a westward, horizontal movement; and the agent involved was the United States, separate and alone. In the 1890s the destination was diffusely conceived as a sphere of barbarism where the gradual struggle for civilization and race might occur on the way toward a final victory that was not that urgent; . . . and the agent, though still the United States, was often seen in combination with other Anglophones, even the "West" in general. In the cold war, however, every space could in principle be defined with instantaneous and razor-sharp distinction either as our side or theirs, or as an arena not yet won where destiny would be fought out right now; and the United

States was the global agent of freedom in lethal combat everywhere with a single, terrifying antagonist.[63]

Innocence, benevolence, and exceptionalism are not uniquely American beliefs but to some degree are common cultural and national values within all societies. Groups and societies often see themselves as a superior and chosen people. This is typical of all great powers in world history. For example, the French empire was justified in terms of *mission civilisatrice* (civilizing mission), and the British Empire reflected the "white man's burden" to uplift other people and civilize the world. As Godfrey Hodgson has observed, "All nations live by myths. Any nation is the sum of the consciousness of its people: the chaotic infinitude of the experience and perceptions of millions alive and dead."[64]

Although a strong sense of nationalism is not a uniquely American trait, what may be somewhat unique to the United States is the strong belief in **freedom (and liberty)**—the key value that unifies and defines Americans as Alexis de Tocqueville so aptly described it in his masterpiece, *Democracy in America,* in 1835.[65] This may help to explain why phrases like "the free world," "democracy," "the free market," and "free trade" seem to have been used with great regularity since World War II and resonate throughout the body politic. Furthermore, it is also commonly argued that, given America's short history, the rapid changes experienced with industrialization and modernization, and its ethnic diversity, American nationalism is as powerful a cultural force for most Americans as for any people throughout history. In the words of political analyst Richard Barnet, "All nations preach the ethic of national superiority but the United States has made a religion of it."[66]

FOREIGN POLICY IMPLICATIONS

American culture and national style have at least six important implications for U.S. foreign policy. First, America's national style contributes to the tendency of Americans to oversimplify, with a naive and rose-colored view, the history of the United States and its role in world affairs. Concepts such as "freedom," "democracy," "the free market," and "free trade" have become sacrosanct in the American mind and interwoven with the "United States of America." Westward expansion, for example, is fondly recalled in terms of the frontier spirit, individualism, and ruggedness represented by the farmer and gunslinger (reflected in numerous movies and stars, such as John Wayne), ignoring alternative interpretations that emphasize the ruthlessness of westward expansion and the taking of Native American and Mexican land and lives. In fact, the Mexican-American War was not a defensive war fought by the United States but a war started by President James Polk in support of territorial expansion. Such unattractive points of fact are commonly glossed over in the upbringing and education of most Americans at home, in school and American history textbooks, and throughout society, including much of the popular media.[67]

Much **popular folklore and myth** is accepted by Americans as fact and history. According to James Oliver Robertson, in *American Myth, American Reality*:

> Myths are the patterns—of behavior, of belief, and of perception—which people have in common. Myths are not deliberately, or necessarily consciously, fictitious. They provide good, "workable" ways by which the contradictions in a society, the contrasts and conflicts which normally arise among people, among ideals, among the confusing realities, are somehow reconciled, smoothed over, or at least made manageable and tolerable. . . . And they are passed on from one generation to another by an unconscious, nonrational process somewhat similar to the process by which language is transmitted.[68]

Myths help not only to unite a people and allow them to work together but also to produce simplistic and optimistic images, which makes it easy for Americans to ignore history and politics, thus reinforcing low levels of attention and information in public opinion.

American simplicity and naiveté contributed to the American response after the collapse of the Soviet Union and the cold war. According to Richard Betts, with the collapse of the Soviet Union and the cold war's end,

> the novelty of complete primacy may account for the thoughtless, indeed innocently arrogant way in which many Americans took its benefits for granted. Most who gave any thought to foreign policy came implicitly to regard the entire world after 1989 as they had regarded Western Europe and Japan during the past half-century: partners in principle but vassals in practice. The

United States would lead the civilized community of nations in the expansion and consolidation of a liberal world order.

Not only had the United States won the cold war, but it appeared that peace was at hand, and for some, it was "the end of history." However, "September 11 reminded those Americans with a rosy view that not all the world sees U.S. primacy as benign."[69] Such simple and naive images make it difficult for Americans to tolerate and accept historical facts or political realities that are inconsistent with their optimistic images and contributes to other consequences, discussed below.

Second, America's national style is responsible for the **moralization of foreign policy.** American leaders have often embodied a nationalist and idealistic yearning that has turned much of U.S. foreign policy into the equivalent of a moral crusade. This is probably best associated with the presidency of Woodrow Wilson and the coining of the term *Wilsonianism*. As summed up by Robert Nisbet, "From Wilson's day to ours the embedded purpose—sometimes articulated in words, more often not—of American foreign policy, under Democrats and Republics alike oftentimes, has boiled down to America-on-a-Permanent-Mission; a mission to make the rest of the world a little more like America the Beautiful."[70]

The moralization of foreign policy has been a major pattern throughout the twentieth century: Woodrow Wilson led the United States into World War I to "end all wars" and promote self-determination throughout the world; American cold war policies represented freedom against the forces of tyranny; President Carter's post–cold war foreign policy revolved around the promotion of human rights and democracy; President Reagan's reinstatement of the cold war was an effort to restore American greatness and battle the "evil empire"; President Bush Sr.'s touted the symbolic goal of a "new world order" during the Persian Gulf War; and President Bush Jr. has declared an effort to rid the world of all terrorists whether "dead or alive."

According to Howard Fineman, in "Bush [Jr.] and God," "Every president invokes God and asks his blessing. Every president promises, though not always in so many words, to lead according to moral principles rooted in biblical tradition. The English writer G.K. Chesterton called America a 'nation with the soul of a church,' and every president, at times, is the pastor in the bully pulpit. But it has taken a war, and the prospect of more, to highlight a central fact: this president—this presidency—is the most resolutely 'faith-based' in modern times, an enterprise founded, supported and guided by trust in the temporal and spiritual power of God." According to his closest friend, Commerce Secretary Don Evans, "It gives him a desire to serve others and a very clear sense of what is good and what is evil."[71]

Although he overstates the case, Nisbet argues that "the single most powerful cause of the present size and the worldwide deployment of the military establishment is the moralization of foreign policy and military ventures that has been deeply ingrained, especially in the minds of presidents, for a long time."[72] Furthermore, as Stanley Hoffmann has observed,

> There is a parallel here: like the ideological tenets of communism, American principles—those of a deeply Christian, liberal society, a kind of synthesis or smorgasbord of Locke, Paine, and Kant—are universal and equalitarian; all the nations of the world are seen capable of living in peace under law in an association of equals devoted to harmony. This mixture of universalism, legalism, and equalitarianism diverts Americans from any suggestion that their attempt to spread the gospel might be imperialistic or self-serving; what is being sought is the common good, in the best interest of all. But the proselytizing contradicts the stated purpose, the method clashes with the intended outcome.[73]

In the words of theologian Reinhold Niebuhr, "Moral pretensions and political parochialism are the two weaknesses of the life of a messianic nation."[74]

Third, this has resulted in major contradictions between principle and pragmatism. Despite its moralization, the actual conduct of U.S. foreign policy often involves the pragmatic pursuit of national interests heavily informed by a national security ethos that existed before, and has continued to exist since, the cold war. This means that policymakers engage in diplomacy, secrecy, bargaining, rewards, threats, force, and all of the other instruments associated with power politics in order to successfully promote their national interests as they define them. But such amoral and pragmatic behavior by the superpower, or great power, or hegemonic power of its day, as we discussed in chapter 8 on covert operations, is not consistent with notions of American innocence, benevolence, and exceptionalism, to the point that much of U.S. foreign policy has had to remain hidden and disguised from the public.

This contradiction has posed real problems for the leaders and makers of U.S. foreign policy, producing a kind of **American dualism,** the necessity to speak two different languages: the language of power and the language of peace and harmony. "Of course," states Stanley Hoffmann, "only a symbolic eagle can hold both the arrows and the olive branch easily at the same time."[75] Such contradictions between morality and pragmatism explains why the realpolitik foreign policy promoted by Henry Kissinger under Presidents Nixon and Ford was never well received by Americans—it was too amoral in nature. This also helps to explain why the economic (e.g., jobs and oil) and geopolitical (e.g., regional stability) explanations that President Bush Sr. relied on early in the Persian Gulf crisis largely failed to convince most Americans (until war broke out). Americans' unwillingness to recognize, and deal with, these contradictions between morality and pragmatism in foreign policy has been a topic of concern for quite some time for such thinkers as George Kennan, Hans Morgenthau, Reinhold Niebuhr, and Stanley Hoffmann.[76]

Fourth, American leaders often resort to overselling their policies in order to legitimate them with the public by simplifying them and infusing them with moral purpose in the process, further reinforcing American political culture and nationalism. It matters little whether political leaders themselves share these same cultural and nationalistic values—most do, some do not (at least in varying degrees). The fact is that the pragmatic majority is generally uninterested and uninformed about world affairs, and so political overstatement and oversell is deemed necessary to attract public attention and support, especially when foreign policy changes or the use of force is involved. This compels leaders to speak in terms of power and peace and to rely on the politics of symbolism to legitimize their policies (as discussed above and to a greater extent in chapter 17, on the media). Or in the words of William Schneider, "Foreign-policymakers must demonstrate not only that their policies work, but that they . . . express the values of major constituencies in American political life."[77]

To arouse public support, political leaders link issues to moral symbols and values with which most

Americans identify. To gain congressional support for military assistance to Greece and Turkey in 1947, Secretary of State Dean Acheson testified what was at stake through use of an analogy for what would become the domino theory, a "Soviet breakthrough [in the Near East] might open three continents to Soviet penetration. Like apples in a barrel infected by the corruption of one rotten one, the corruption of Greece would infect Iran and all to the East . . . Africa . . . Italy and France. . . . Not since Rome and Carthage had there been such a polarization of power on this earth." This made a huge impression on members of Congress and Senator Arthur Vandenberg, Republican Chairman of the Foreign Relations Committee, told senior Truman officials the only way to overcome post–World War II isolationist tendencies and to fully get Congressional and public support was to "scare the hell out of the American people" about the threat of communism to freedom, democracy, and the American way of life. Such was the language of the Truman Doctrine.[78]

This helps to explain the power of anticommunism in the making of foreign policy since World War II, as well as why Americans were told by President Reagan that the invasion of Grenada was for the humanitarian purpose of rescuing American students, and by the Bush Sr. administration that the Panama invasion was designed to help the Panamanian people by ridding them of the evil drug-trafficker Noriega. Realpolitik, power politics, and political reasons were mentioned only briefly or ignored entirely, for President Reagan was trying to rally public support. This also helps one to understand why President Bush in 1990 increasingly equated Saddam Hussein of Iraq with Adolf Hitler of Nazi Germany as the Persian Gulf crisis escalated—to justify the pursuit and exercise of American power abroad. Likewise, the war on terrorism is sold and legitimized for the American public as necessary to protect democracy, freedom, and the American way of life by exterminating terrorism, ultimately embodied by the most evil and omnipresent figure of first Osama bin Laden and then Saddam Hussein. Although such symbolism, moralization, and overselling often produces the desired political results, to what extent does it promote a highly informed and knowledgeable public to support a realistic and sophisticated foreign policy to respond to what in all likelihood is probably a pretty complex issue or situation?

Fifth, the moralization of and tendency to oversell foreign policy also often breed strong doses of American nationalism and intolerance abroad and at home. Nationalism is often a positive force, for it helps to promote a strong sense of community among members of society in support of a common effort—an essential quality in both war and peace. One of the major problems with a strong sense of nationalism, however, is that patriotism often turns into intolerance and **superpatriotism.** Such attitudes have the tendency to dehumanize adversaries and repress domestic criticism and dissent in the name of national security. Intolerance is particularly evident during periods of national emergency and war, when people feel threats to their values and to their country's security—such as after the September 11 attacks. Although such emotional responses are quite natural and understandable, strong doses of nationalism heighten the contradictions between the demands of national security and democracy at home, with profound implications for the exercise of individual civil rights and liberties, as will be discussed in depth in the next chapter.

A strong sense of nationalism also has made it difficult for Americans to accept criticism from abroad, including from the country's closest allies, thus reflecting deep-seated isolationist and unilateralist sentiments. As Hoffmann has argued, American foreign policy easily leads to "an activism that others see as imperialistic: for we expect them to join the consensus, we ignore the boundaries and differences between 'them' and 'us,' we prod them out of conviction that we act for their own good, and we do not take resistance gracefully."[79] This certainly seems to be the case concerning president Bush Jr's efforts to go to war with Iraq and overthrow Saddam Hussein. Americans have such a strong faith in American virtue and progress that it is difficult for them to understand, let alone accept, the value of alternative paths to economic and political development divorced from the American model. Or as was often asked after the September 11 attacks, how could the United States (and Americans) be so loved and so hated?

A final consequence of American culture and nationalism is their tendency to contribute to major swings in **public moods** or sentiments with respect to U.S. foreign policy. It is commonly argued that "twentieth-century exceptionalism has *fueled both interventionism and isolationism.*"[80] As Louis Hartz has stated in his classic *The Liberal Tradition: An Interpretation of American Political Thought Since the Revolution,* "Americas seem to oscillate between fleeing from the rest of the world and embracing it with too ardent a passion. An absolute national morality is inspired either to withdraw from 'alien' things or to transform them: it cannot live in comfort constantly by their side."[81]

Richard Barnet, in fact, has argued that "the internationalist versus isolationist debate is really an argument about little more than military strategy" abroad, in which both competing perspectives ultimately reflect an underlying sense of **unilateralism** among the mass public and in America's national style. Or as Stanley Hoffmann has stated, "Both quietism and activism are compensatory assertions of total independence."[82]

Major swings in public opinion have affected U.S. relations with both allies and enemies. This is easily seen in the cycles of U.S.-Russian relations. After the Bolshevik Revolution the United States invaded the Soviet Union during World War I and refused to recognize it until 1933; during World War II the Soviet Union under "Uncle Joe" Stalin became the patriotic ally of freedom against fascism; with the rise of the cold war, the Soviet Union represented a monolithic communist threat abroad and at home; the détente years from Nixon to Carter were a time of hope for a cooperative U.S.-Soviet relationship; under Reagan, cooperation was replaced by a new cold war to contain "the evil empire"; and with the collapse of communism Americans hailed Mikhail Gorbachev, Boris Yeltsin and Vladimir Putin as great leaders in a post–cold war future to be characterized by global peace and prosperity.

These dramatic swings in public moods and U.S. foreign policy have occurred with China, Japan, Germany, and other countries as well, while Americans have maintained a positive and moral self-image. Although American leaders initiated such foreign policy changes, public expectations and support were critical to their pursuit over time. This has often led the public mood to swing from one extreme to another due to the extraordinarily high levels of hope and fear aroused within American culture and politics. Hence, the high hopes and optimism of the immediate post–World War II years were replaced by disillusionment and fear during the cold war. The high hopes of the early post–cold war years have been replaced by the shock and anger of September 11 that has produced a new global war, but this time on terrorism. Such public mood swings, unfortunately, often do not reflect the complexity and messiness of world politics at the time, yet they heavily affect the formulation of U.S. foreign policy.

CONTINUITY, CHANGE, AND THE VIETNAM WAR

Most Americans share a common sense of what it is to be an American and this plays an important role in the politics of U.S. foreign policy. Obviously, there are subcultures within American society in which different cultural and national images prevail—some of which may not be composed of such positive views. Nevertheless, most Americans share a belief in the existence of American innocence, benevolence, and exceptionalism at home and abroad. These cultural beliefs were deeply engrained within most Americans by the turn of the twentieth century and the time of Woodrow Wilson, the apostle of freedom; self-determination; and the League of Nations.

The "great exception" in American history was the South, for it was the only region of the country that ever seriously attempted to secede from the Union, losing a devastating civil war fought mostly on its lands and experiencing military occupation and control following the war. By the beginning of the cold war, however, the differences between the South and the North in thought and in practice had diminished. With this great exception, the cultural assumptions of American innocence, benevolence, and exceptionalism seem to have grown stronger over time.

This sense of shared nationalism is especially noticeable during war. Thus, despite American fear and apprehension, World War II and the cold war were also times of hope and optimism in America. Most Americans believed that, after saving the world from the threat of fascism, the United States was innocently thrust onto the world stage to save the world from the tyranny of communism. Not only would the U.S. rearm and contain the national security threat, it would actively serve as a model, helping others to find the peace and prosperity that most Americans have experienced. In the minds of many Americans, especially American leaders, the post–World War II years represented the **American century** and the height of American innocence, benevolence, and, in particular, exceptionalism. Such a mindset helped to justify the pursuit and exercise of American power throughout the world in the name of responsibility for that world.[83]

As Godfrey Hodgson argues, the United States entered the 1960s in an Augustan mood: "united, confident, conscious of a historical mission, and mobilized for the great task of carrying it out." If Americans were anxious about danger from abroad, "it was because they saw their own society as so essentially just and benevolent that danger could come only from elsewhere. If they found international affairs frustrating, it was because they found it infuriating that foreigners could not always believe that their only ambition was a generous desire to share the abundance of American capitalism and the promise of American democracy with those less fortunate than themselves."[84]

Such a mood of American confidence and mission was best symbolized by **President John F. Kennedy's inaugural address** on January 20, 1961, when he declared:

> Let the word go forth from this time and place, to friend and foe alike, that the torch has been passed to a new generation of Americans—born in this country, tempered by war, disciplined by a hard and bitter peace, proud of our ancient heritage—and unwilling to witness or permit the slow undoing of those human rights to which this Nation has always been committed, and to which we are committed today at home and around the world. Let every nation know, whether it wishes us well or ill, that we shall pay any price, bear any burden, meet any hardship, support any friend, oppose any foe, in order to assure the survival and the success of liberty.

It was this sense of American confidence and exceptionalism—or what J. William Fulbright called "the arrogance of power—that ultimately led to war and tragedy in the jungles of Vietnam.[85]

The Vietnam War produced the first major assault on these optimistic assumptions central to American political culture and national style. The Great Depression of the 1930s had precipitated extreme criticism of the innocence and benevolence of American business and capitalism. In contrast, the events of the 1960s surrounding civil rights and the Vietnam War led many Americans to question the three assumptions in their entirety. How could the United States be innocent if Vietnam was not vital to American security? How could

policies that promoted activities such as the "needed to destroy cities in order to save them," carpet bombing and the use of napalm, and the My Lai massacre be justified as acts of American benevolence? How did American failure and withdrawal from the war fit with American exceptionalism? Clearly, Vietnam made clear that Americans were not willing to "pay any price" and "bear any burden." And, especially after Watergate, most members of the public came to lose their trust in public officials, the government, and the political process.[86]

The split between supporters and critics of the war was more than an ideological disagreement over U.S. foreign policy; it represented a fragmentation of American cultural and nationalistic beliefs. *The Vietnam War produced different lessons for different segments of the population.* Conservatives and the political right saw the Vietnam War as a just cause that was consistent with American innocence, benevolence, and exceptionalism—its failure was explained by the lack of will among the liberal establishment. Liberals and the political left believed that the Vietnam War was an example of the lack of sufficient innocence and benevolence in U.S. foreign policy and that the United States should not and could not impose its will on other people. The mass public emphasized more pragmatic lessons: American troops should be used only for the most vital of interests and for a good cause, where the war would be swift and involve minimal loss of American lives. Overall, the Vietnam War challenged the cultural assumptions that Americans held about themselves and their place in the world as no event had done before.

The rise of the so-called **Vietnam syndrome** and the negative images associated in the minds of many Americans with the failure of the Vietnam War, were reinforced by the events of the 1980s. American exceptionalism in particular was open to question given the sense of humiliation Americans felt concerning the 444-day Iran hostage crisis during the Carter presidency and the killing of 256 American marines in Lebanon under President Reagan, forcing their withdrawal from the region.

This mass feeling of national impotence on a world stage helps to explain why Americans seemed to express such jubilation with the great victory following the invasion of Grenada in 1983, for it followed immediately on the footsteps of the Lebanon fiasco and represented the first American military success abroad since Vietnam (even though the American military performance on the ground was abysmal; see essay 7.3). This was then followed by the successful invasion of Panama in 1989. But it was the impact of the Persian Gulf War that really was instrumental in renewing American faith in its cultural assumptions and national style. Although many questioned the vital interests at stake, most Americans saw the U.S. role in the Persian Gulf crisis as a just cause. Most important, Americans were able to restore their inherent faith in their exceptionalism with the triumphant and unexpected military rout of Iraq in the war, accounting for the sense of celebration that Americans felt toward the troops who returned from the Persian Gulf and President Bush's historically high public approval ratings following the war.

The Persian Gulf War, although it helped restore many of America's cultural assumptions, did not eliminate the memories and shadows of other crucial historical events that have deeply affected the minds of Americans, such as World War II, the Korean War, and most important, the Vietnam War. Although Americans continue to believe in their innocence, benevolence, and exceptionalism, this belief is colored by their understanding of the past and their hopes for the future. Conservatives and liberals possess strong nationalist sentiments and continue to believe in America, but in different ways. Conservatives and the right believe that American innocence, benevolence, and exceptionalism have prevailed throughout American history; in contrast, liberals and the left are more prone to see the good, the bad, and the ugly in American history, while still believing in the possibility of building an America where innocence, benevolence, and exceptionalism reign supreme. As Robertson has put it, "As a New World, many Americans believe their country to be the last, best hope of the world, a place of youth, of new beginnings, of booming. Even those who believe that America is, in reality, no such place of hope or virtue believe it somehow *ought to be*."[87]

Most members of the mass public, being more pragmatic and centrist, probably entertain both sets of feelings at different times—what they manifest depends upon the salience of the issues and how they are played out politically at the time. A kind of "pessimistic-optimistic dualism," in other words, operates among members of the mass public, since they share a certain cynicism about American politics while still maintaining an optimistic image of American innocence, benevolence, and exceptionalism. This helps to explain how

both liberal and conservative views—as embodied, for example, in President Carter's human rights policies and President Reagan's anticommunism—were initially attractive to most members of the public. It also explains why America's culture and national style will remain an integral part of the complex politics of U.S. foreign policy, as seen following the September 11 attacks. However, no matter how optimistic or hopeful, most Americans must continue to live in the shadow of the turbulent sixties and Vietnam.

SUMMARY: PATTERNS IN BELIEFS AND FOREIGN POLICY MAKING

In summary, the public's role in U.S. foreign policy making depends on three sets of beliefs, providing a more complex view of what makes the public consequential relative to the traditional wisdom. American political culture and national style set the broad context within which the politics of U.S. foreign policy transpire. Then the ideological and foreign policy beliefs of Americans further narrow what is possible and probable within domestic politics and the policymaking process. Finally, public opinion affects the foreign policy process as it fluctuates within the confines of American political culture and ideology. Together, the three sets of beliefs among the elite and mass publics are related and impact on one another, accounting for continuity and change in U.S. foreign policy since World War II.

The rise of a strong sense of American optimism and nationalism, of a foreign policy and ideological consensus, and of a responsive public opinion during the cold war led to increasing presidential power in foreign policy, an expanding national security bureaucracy, the development of a national security and free market ethos, and an acquiescent Congress and domestic environment. In this environment, the president and the executive branch dominated the making of U.S. foreign policy, while the demands of national security took precedence over the demands of democracy.

The challenges of Vietnam and the 1960s led Americans to question the assumptions of American innocence, benevolence, and exceptionalism; produced greater ideological and foreign policy diversity; and contributed to public opinion volatility. These developments led to a reassertive Congress and changes in the domestic environment, such as more diverse electoral politics, new and varied interest groups and social movements, and a more critical media—the topics of the next few chapters. Thus, presidents entering office now face a paradox of presidential power, making it very difficult to successfully govern contemporary foreign policy. Changes in political culture, political ideology, and public opinion since the height of the cold war have meant that the era of extraordinary presidential power in foreign policy has passed and tensions between national security and democracy have increased.

Presidents are still powerful, but they no longer automatically govern and dominate the making of U.S. foreign policy. Since Vietnam, presidents have been unable to promote or take advantage of a majoritarian coalition in society in support of their foreign policy because of the diversity of thought and the domestic political competition it has generated. President Johnson declined to run for reelection in 1968 over the Vietnam War once he lost the support of the American people. Nixon eventually was forced to resign in 1974 over the constitutional crisis of Watergate. Meanwhile, Nixon's détente policies, which continued under Ford, were attacked by both the left and right. Carter attempted to promote a post–cold war internationalist foreign policy but was placed on the political defensive by the right with the Iran hostage crisis and Soviet invasion of Afghanistan. Reagan entered office as a cold warrior, only to encounter liberal resistance that culminated in the Iran-contra affair and criticism from the right as he pursued arms control and a more open relationship with the Soviet Union.

What of the future? It is likely that presidents will continue to experience difficulty in governing foreign policy as long as efforts to establish a new consensus are overwhelmed by diversity of thought in American society. The contemporary domestic political environment is made particularly fluid by the dramatic changes taking place in Russia, Eastern Europe, the Middle East, and elsewhere. Presidents Bush Sr. and Clinton have had to navigate carefully through treacherous and unstable environments both at home and abroad. The successful military outcome in the Persian Gulf War temporarily strengthened President Bush's ability to govern, only to lose reelection in 1992. As Clinton learned all too well, in the post–cold war era presidents must operate in a domestic political climate where the diversity and volatility of the public and its beliefs create both considerable opportunities and uncertainties in politics, both at home and abroad. And only time will determine how long President Bush Jr. will be able to ride the wave of high public prestige in the wake of the September 11 attacks and be able to govern U.S. foreign policy.

With regard to public opinion, prolonged habits of interest, information, and thought about national and international affairs will not change overnight. Americans, especially members of the mass public, are likely to retain very short attention spans, as well as superficial knowledge and simplistic understandings of national and international affairs. These characteristics are reinforced by the fact that most Americans do not realize the extent to which national and international affairs directly and indirectly affect their daily lives, trends that are likely to grow as interdependence increases throughout the country and the world. Since Vietnam diversity of ideological and foreign policy beliefs is also likely to continue in the future. While anticommunism was the foundation of the ideological and foreign policy consensus during the cold war, the end of the cold war has given rise to a new great debate and may impact new interpretations of events. Whatever the case, one thing that can be predicted with great certainty is that the competing foreign policy orientations and the response of public opinion will reflect the moral foundation of American political culture and national style, which together will directly and indirectly impact the making of U.S. foreign policy into the future.

SUGGESTED SOURCES FOR MORE INFORMATION

Since the 1970s, there has been a proliferation of works studying the role of public opinion, political ideology, and political culture in U.S. foreign policy. Ole Holsti provides an excellent overview of the impact of public opinion on foreign policy, including the traditional wisdom and its critique, in "Public Opinion and Foreign Policy: Challenges to the Almond-Lippmann Consensus," *International Studies Quarterly* (1992): 439–66. James N. Rosenau's *Public Opinion and Foreign Policy* (New York: Random House, 1961) remains a classic in delineating the dynamics of opinion flows and influence among the different publics and for policymaking.

A good historical overview of the relationship between public opinion and U.S. foreign policy in American history is provided by Richard J. Barnet in *The Rockets' Red Glare, When America Goes to War: The Presidents and the People* (New York: Simon and Schuster, 1990). A more systematic analysis of the relationship is provided by Benjamin I. Page and Robert Y. Shapiro, *The Rational Public: Fifty Years of Trends in Americans' Policy Preferences* (Chicago: University of Chicago Press, 1992). An informative study of the impact of public opinion during war can be found in Larry Elowitz and John W. Spanier, "Korea and Vietnam: Limited War and the American Political System," *Orbis* (summer 1974): 510–34, and more recently in Bruce W. Jentleson, "The Pretty Prudent Public: Post Post-Vietnam American Opinion on the Use of Military Force," *International Studies Quarterly* (1992): 49–74, and Richard Sobel, *The Impact of Public Opinion on U.S. Foreign Policy Since Vietnam* (New York: Oxford University Press, 2001). For an excellent overview on polling and public opinion, see Barbara A. Bardes and Robert W. Oldendick, *Public Opinion: Measuring the American Mind* (Belmont, CA: Wadsworth, 2002).

One of the best overviews of ideology and culture in American society and its relevance for understanding American politics is presented by Godfrey Hodgson in *America in Our Time* (New York: Vintage, 1976). He offers an excellent history and analysis of the rise of the anticommunist and liberal-conservative ideological consensus after World War II and its decline due to the impact of the 1960s and the Vietnam War. A good analysis of the major competing schools of thought that arose after Vietnam is provided by Ole R. Holsti and James N. Rosenau, in *American Leadership in World Affairs: Vietnam and the Breakdown of Consensus* (Boston: Allen and Unwin, 1984); William Schneider, "Public Opinion," in Joseph S. Nye, Jr., ed., *The Making of America's Soviet Policy* (New Haven: Yale University Press, 1984), pp. 11–35; Barry R. Posen and Andrew L. Ross, "Competing Visions for U.S. Grand Strategy," *International Security* (winter 1996–97): 5–53; and Jerel Rosati and John Creed, "Extending the Three-Headed and Four-Headed Eagles: The Foreign Policy Orientations of American Elites During the 80s and 90s," *Political Psychology* 18 (1997): 583–623.

An excellent discussion of liberal thought during the cold war can be found in Richard H. Pells, *The Liberal Mind in a Conservative Age: American Intellectuals in the 1940s & 1950s* (New York: Harper and Row, 1985). Leslie H. Gelb, with Richard K. Betts, demonstrates how the anticommunist consensus affected the foreign policy–making process and led to greater U.S. intervention in Vietnam in *The Irony of Vietnam: The System Worked* (Washington, D.C.: Brookings Institution Press, 1979). Jerome L. Himmelstein analyzes the rise of conservatism, including the change following World War II from isolationism to interventionism, in *To the Right: The Transformation of American Conservatism* (Berkeley and Los Angeles: University of California Press, 1989), while George H. Nash describes the evolution of conservative intellectual thought into the post-Vietnam era in *The Conservative Intellectual Movement in America, Since 1945* (New York: Basic Books, 1976).

Tami R. Davis and Sean M. Lynn-Jones give a good overview of American political culture and its implications for U.S. foreign policy in "City Upon a Hill," *Foreign Policy* 66 (spring 1987): 3–19. Anders Stephanson provides a good overview of an important aspect of American exceptionalism in *Manifest Destiny: American Expansion and the Empire of Right* (New York: Hill and Wang, 1995). In an impressive study, Steven Twing demonstrates how American cultural myths and traditions colored the worldviews, identities, and decisionmaking styles of three policymakers—John Foster Dulles, Averell Harriman, and Robert McNamara—during the Cold War in *Myths, Models, and U.S. Foreign Policy: The Cultural Shaping of Three Cold Warriors* (Boulder, Colo.: Lynne Rienner, 1998). In a fascinating article, Howard Fineman demonstrates the importance of religion for George W. Bush and the war on terrorism in "Bush and God," *Newsweek* (March 10, 2003), pp. 22–30.

Paul Loeb provides a fascinating portrait of the political culture that developed around Hanford, Washington, with the growth of the nuclear weapons production complex and its implications for everyday life and the politics of U.S. foreign policy in *Nuclear Culture: Living and Working in the World's Largest Atomic Complex* (Philadelphia: New Society Publishers, 1987). And J. William Fulbright in *The Arrogance of Power* (New York: Vintage, 1966) describes the confidence and sense of exceptionalism that infuses the cultures of all great powers, including the United States at the height of the Vietnam War, and which may be relevant today given the nature of American power and the U.S. war on terrorism in the twenty-first century.

KEY TERMS

American century
American dualism
American exceptionalism
American innocence
American national style

attentive public

classical liberalism

conservative internationalism

elite public

elitist view of the public

foreign policy orientations

freedom (and liberty)

ideological and foreign policy consensus

isolationist sentiment

liberal–conservative consensus

liberalism and conservatism

libertarians

manifest destiny

mass public

moral minority and pragmatic majority

moralization of foreign policy

noninternationalism

opinion leaders

policy legitimation

political ideology

political left

political right

political socialization

popular folklore and myth

post–World War II great debate

President John F. Kennedy's inaugural address

protectionism

public moods

public opinion

public opinion poll

rally round the flag

superpatriotism

unilateralism

Vietnam syndrome

CHAPTER 14

. . . .

NATIONAL SECURITY VERSUS CIVIL LIBERTIES AND POLITICAL PARTICIPATION

*T*he September 11 tragedy and the war on terrorism have clearly demonstrated the tension between the demands of national security and those of democracy in the making of U.S. foreign policy. Democracy requires an open political process and high levels of civil rights and liberties for its citizens to politically participate. The demands of national security usually require a much less open political process with limitations on civil rights and liberties. The demands of democracy and of national security inherently have contradictory implications for political participation within a democratic society.

In addition to public opinion, the general public directly participates in the political process and influences the making of U.S. foreign policy in two basic ways. The public may participate in electoral politics, which is the focus of chapter 15, or in group politics, the focus of chapter 16. Both of these forms of political participation influence U.S. foreign policy making through their general impact on the domestic political environment and immediate impact on the policymak-

ing process. However, much depends on the impact of global and domestic developments on the exercise of democratic citizenship and civil liberties in American society.

In order to better understand the evolution of the beliefs of the public and political participation, as well as the implications for the future, we must briefly examine political participation and the exercise of civil liberties in American history, especially in relation to the ebb and flow of the politics of national security. More specifically, *this chapter addresses the following questions:* What is the contemporary nature of political participation? Who participates? What is the historical background of and development in the exercise of civil rights and liberties over two hundred years? In particular, what has been the relationship between the demands of national security and of democracy in the twentieth century, especially during World War I, World War II, the cold war, and the Vietnam War? What has been the impact of the end of the cold war and, most recently, the September 11 attacks on the exercise of civil liberties and political participation? A focus on the evolution of political participation and the exercise of civil liberties not only provides a richer understanding of the significance of the historical contradictions between the demands of national security and of democracy in the making of U.S. foreign policy but deepens an understanding of continuity and change in the politics of U.S. foreign policy and the president's ability to govern. It also provides the foundation for understanding the important role of both electoral and group politics on the making of U.S. foreign policy, the subjects of the next two chapters.

CONTEMPORARY POLITICAL PARTICIPATION

The public affects public policy through *the various ways that people participate in the political process.* People may vote; respond to a public opinion poll; write to their elected representatives; write letters to newspaper or magazine editors; give money for a cause; join an organization or group involved in politics; work for a political party, candidate, or issue; lobby; petition; demonstrate; or become involved in mass movements. In the next two chapters we will address *the two most common and important forms of active **political participation,*** which usually involve all of these activities: (1) electoral politics—that is, political participation in political parties and voting; and (2) group politics—that is, political participation in interest groups and social movements. In this chapter we will discuss who basically participates and why, and how civil rights and liberties have evolved over time—both impacting as well as being impacted by U.S. foreign policy.

It is often argued that most members of the public participate little, if at all, in the political process; that Americans are politically apathetic. There is much truth in this. Most Americans today do not hold **citizenship and civic duty** in as high regard as past Americans did. The events of the 1960s and 1970s, such as the Vietnam War and Watergate, produced a declining sense of **political efficacy and trust** in political officials—that is, a sense of powerlessness to affect change through the political process. Also, the common concerns of everyday life in modern America have pushed politics aside. The net result has been the rise of mass apathy (and cynicism) throughout American society, which raises some troubling questions about the nature of American democracy.[1]

This broad generalization about American political participation, nevertheless, oversimplifies as much as it enlightens. *Three predominant patterns actually characterize political participation in the United States.* First, most Americans participate infrequently in the political process, and when they do so, it is mainly through voting. Many Americans, in fact, have completely opted out of any form of political participation. Second, American participation in voting declined during the twentieth century, especially after World War II. Since the 1970s, no more than 50 percent of those eligible to vote have cast ballots in presidential general elections and much smaller percentages have voted in presidential primary elections, congressional elections, and state and local elections. Third, although only a minority of Americans participate in interest groups and mass movements, this form of participation actually has increased over time. The rise of interest group and mass movement participation is particularly noticeable if one compares the post-Vietnam War era to the cold war era. In sum, while most Americans do not participate in politics and fewer vote today than in the past, participation in interest groups and social movements has increased since Vietnam.[2]

Who participates? Members of the elite public tend to be more likely to vote, join interest groups, and become politically active than members of the mass public. As discussed in chapter 13, members of the elite public tend to be more interested and better informed about politics and also tend to have greater resources at their disposal—especially information and money—and a greater sense of political efficacy. Members of the mass public also participate; however, they do so less frequently than segments of the public who come from the higher socioeconomic classes and who have higher levels of education. Age is another important factor: Older people tend to vote more, younger people less. At the same time, younger people are more likely to become politically active in social movements and group politics than older people.

People participate both to further their own interests and the interests of their country. Interests fluctuate from person to person and depend on how people see the world, which is predominantly a function of their beliefs—that is, of political culture, political ideology, and public opinion (the topics of the previous chapter). While most people who participate do so through voting and, to a lesser extent, through joining groups and giving money, others are more politically "activist"— they give their time and become personally involved. To understand the contemporary nature of political participation and its future implications for foreign policy, it is necessary to provide some historical background to see how civil rights and liberties developed, as well as to focus on the significance of whether it is a time of war or peace.

HISTORICAL BACKGROUND AND DEVELOPMENT

Political participation is guaranteed, not under the Constitution of the United States as originally written, but within its first ten amendments. After delegates from the various states produced a new constitution in Philadelphia in 1787, a controversial ratification process ensued. It is worth remembering that "the vast majority of the Framers flatly repudiated the entire idea of a federal bill of rights, on philosophical as well as political grounds [as explained in *The Federalist Papers*]. And it is worth remembering that the father of the Bill of Rights [James Madison, although George Mason originally proposed it at the Philadelphia Convention, which rejected it] had to be dragged into fatherhood largely by forces outside his control."[3]

A Bill of Rights was promised to allay the fears widespread among Americans that the new Constitution would create too strong a central government that would restrict personal and state freedoms. Therefore, in order to guarantee approval by the states, ten amendments to the Constitution were eventually passed and took effect in 1791—three years after the Constitution was initially ratified. These ten amendments, which restrain the national government from limiting personal freedoms, have come to be known as the **Bill of Rights.**

According to the **First Amendment** of the Bill of Rights, "Congress shall make no law . . . abridging the freedom of speech, or of the press; or the right of the people peaceably to assemble, and to petition the government for a redress of grievances." Such civil rights and the exercise of such liberties were considered essential to prevent the majority from tyrannizing the

minority and to prevent minority factions from controlling the majority. These rights and liberties allowed people to participate and speak out without fear of persecution or political repression—a necessary core requirement of democratic politics.[4]

The **Declaration of Independence**, written by Thomas Jefferson and signed by many of America's founders in 1776, went so far as to argue "that whenever any form of government becomes destructive to these ends [life, liberty, and the pursuit of happiness], it is the right of the people to alter or to abolish it, and to institute new government." Hence, a democratic form of electoral and group politics requires the opportunity for its citizens to participate, engage in political dialogue and debate, and have the opportunity to criticize and change public policies.[5]

Although citizen participation and a broad exercise of civil liberties represented an "ideal" of the American revolution and the U.S. Constitution, the historical record has varied over time. *Three contradictory patterns in civil rights and liberties have predominated*: (1) Historically, many individuals have been denied full citizenship rights and suffered from discrimination. (2) Civil rights and liberties have expanded steadily over time. And (3) There have been times of contraction in the actual exercise of civil liberties, especially during and after war. These patterns in civil rights and the exercise of civil liberties impact American politics and the making of U.S. foreign policy, as will be discussed further below.[6]

First, the right to participate and exercise civil liberties—that is, American **civil rights**—was extremely limited throughout much of American history. At the country's founding, for example, only white males with property enjoyed the rights of full citizenship, such as voting. To keep things in historical perspective, we must recognize that these rights represented a revolutionary development, particularly given the despotic and aristocratic political systems then prevailing throughout Europe. Nevertheless, most Americans— the nonpropertied, women, ethnic minorities, Native Americans, and slaves—had few, if any, civil rights and liberties. Such legal disenfranchisement by federal and local governments, supported by the judiciary, has been encountered by many American citizens throughout the country's history.

Second, civil rights and liberties have expanded over the course of American history. Even though women and minorities were initially denied civil rights and liberties, they fought for them and were eventually successful. With the passage of the Nineteenth Amendment in 1920, for example, women finally won the right to vote. Blacks, however, had to go through a much greater ordeal before their rights, won through the Civil War and the passage of the Fourteenth Amendment, were finally guaranteed with passage of the Civil Rights Act of 1964 and Voting Rights Act of 1965. Today, all American citizens have the constitutional right to exercise the civil liberties stipulated in the First Amendment.

Yet it is important to understand that the expansion of civil rights was bitterly fought over and resisted by many forces. The extension of civil rights to some people and their denial to others was a function of the history of American politics. Most of the so-called "haves" who enjoyed civil rights, such as white males, resisted granting those rights to others. The "have-nots," therefore, had to challenge the politics of the status quo by speaking out, demanding their civil rights and liberties, and influencing the policymaking process in order to change the law. The successful expansion of civil rights and liberties, in other words, was accomplished at the price of considerable "blood, sweat, and tears": a "tradition of speech—and struggle to obtain the right to speak—did develop. Courageous, often rebellious Americans—including, most prominently, opponents of slavery and advocates of civil rights, women's rights and union's rights—fought for and shaped our system of free expression, often at considerable personal risk."[7]

Finally, while civil rights and liberties have expanded throughout history, there also have been times of contraction in the exercise of civil liberties. The freedom of Americans to exercise **civil liberties** and political participation, once they gained the right to do so, has varied over time. Historically, *large numbers of individuals have experienced political discrimination and have had great difficulty in exercising their civil liberties*, especially because of their class, gender, race (particularly new immigrants and minority ethnic groups), and their political beliefs (especially those who challenge government policy, established groups, and the status quo).

Times of contraction in the exercise of civil liberties tend to occur particularly in response to events that generate political instability and fear. Examples of such destabilizing events include the rise of industrialization

and efforts by American laborers to unionize, economic depressions and downturns, large waves of immigration to the states and most important, periods of national emergency and war.[8]

THE PREOCCUPATION WITH NATIONAL SECURITY VERSUS DEMOCRATIC LIBERTIES

Under conditions of war, civil liberties and political participation are often curtailed and violated in a systematic way by the government, usually with the active support of groups and people throughout society. This typically occurs because the demands of national security take precedence over the demands of democracy during war, when most segments of society tend to rally behind the president and the government in order to fight the enemy abroad. It is in the context of this political environment that the government's and, in particular, the president's ability to dominate the politics of U.S. foreign policy is maximized. This is because wars and national emergencies, in particular, tend to be times when little tolerance exists for individuals and groups that publicly criticize or challenge the government's foreign policy or the status quo within society.

The general American tendency toward conformity, as political scientist Seymour Martin Lipset wrote in 1963, "has been noted as a major aspect of American culture from Tocqueville in the 1830s to [David] Riesman [in *The Lonely Crowd*] in the 1950s."[9] In fact, times of perceived threats to national security are often accompanied by what historian Richard Hofstadter has called "the **paranoid style in American politics.**"[10] In other words, war often produces a preoccupation with internal threats to national security, and certain groups within society are targeted as security risks because of their ethnicity or political beliefs.

According to sociologist Robert Nisbet, "No nation in history has ever managed permanent war and a permanent military Leviathan at its heart and been able to maintain a truly representative character." He continues,

Is the United States somehow the divinely created exception to this ubiquitous fact of world history? Not, assuredly, if instead of a foreign policy based upon national security and finite objectives associated with this security, we indulge ourselves in a foreign policy with an "itch to intervene," and a purpose flowing out of the preposterous fantasy of a world recreated in the image and likeness of that city on a hill known as the United States of America.[11]

The net result is that the ability to politically participate and exercise civil liberties tends to be limited during periods of conflict because the government's war effort, combined with American nationalism and superpatriotism, tolerates little dissent and encourages political repression, as was briefly discussed in chapter 13 on American political ideology and culture. This is the underside of American history that is too often ignored, yet it is important to know in order to understand the evolution of political participation and the politics of U.S. foreign policy.

There were *three major periods in the twentieth century when the demands of national security prevailed over the demands of democracy and the exercise of civil liberties in domestic politics were severely curtailed:* (1) World War I, (2) World War II, and (3) The cold war. Each of these periods was accompanied by the supremacy of the president in the making of U.S. foreign policy.[12]

The years after the Vietnam War, however, were characterized by a decline in the demands of national security throughout American society, creating an uneasy tension between national security and democracy. This development led to a corresponding rise in the liberty of Americans to fully exercise their civil rights in electoral and group politics in order to influence the future of U.S. foreign policy. The net result is that presidents have had to operate in a political environment where they have had greater difficulty exercising power in the politics of U.S. foreign policy. The terrorist attacks of September 11, 2001, and the war on terrorism may, despite the end of the cold war, have again altered the tense dynamics between the demands of national security and democracy and the corresponding implications for exercising presidential power in foreign policy at the beginning of the twenty-first century.

WORLD WAR I

Civil liberties were heavily curtailed and circumscribed as a result of World War I. Strong antiwar sentiment existed as President Woodrow Wilson asked Congress to declare war on Germany. Convinced that he had done everything humanly possible to keep America out of the war, Woodrow Wilson demanded uncritical support. The government thus decided to clamp down on civil liberties, a move that was reinforced by intolerance and bigotry throughout much of the public. Not surprisingly, the power of President Wilson and the executive branch grew dramatically during the war.

The administration instituted one of the earliest modern and systematic uses of mass communications for propaganda purposes—that is, the **propaganda campaign** was intended to convince Americans that the United States was fighting "to make the world safe for democracy." On April 14, 1917, eight days after the formal declaration of war, President Wilson established the **Committee on Public Information (CPI)** to promote Allied war aims. The CPI consisted of the secretary of state, secretary of war, and secretary of the navy and was directed by a journalist from Denver, George Creel, who advised President Wilson that propaganda was more powerful than censorship in promoting public support. Throughout the war, the CPI distributed over seventy-five million pieces of printed material, including posters, pamphlets and books, as well as short movies. It also created seventy-five thousand "Four-Minute Men," who gave speeches throughout the country supporting food conservation and other issues important to the war economy. In the beginning, the CPI emphasized facts, but with time they promoted the exaggerated, cartoonish image of the "savage" Germans. The CPI geared their propaganda not only at Americans but also toward their enemies, especially Germans. They tried to prompt Germans to rebel, citing inflated figures of the size of U.S. forces, and a promise for peace.[13]

One of the main results of the propaganda office was the growth of major anti-German sentiment throughout the country. Much of this occurred because most of the press, and the public, accepted voluntary censorship and actively promoted the war effort. And with the fear of the **Germanic "Hun"** increasing, German Americans became the target of political attacks and hostility. Popular prejudices equated most anything German—names, language, culture—with disloyalty.

Members of the **Socialist party** and the political left also were targets of the narrowing and violation of civil liberties. This came at a time when the Socialist party, launched in 1901, was growing in popularity and making remarkable gains as a political force throughout American society. In 1912 Socialist party leader Eugene V. Debs received over 900,000 votes for president, about 6 percent of the total. "No fewer than 1,200 municipal officials—including fifty-six socialist mayors and many more aldermen and city councilmen—were elected, and there were now socialist police chiefs as well as state legislators."[14] In 1917, socialist candidates received 21 percent of the vote in New York City, 25 percent in Buffalo, 34 percent in Chicago, and 44 percent in Dayton, Ohio.

But the Socialist party and the left experienced rapid decline with the rise of political repression imposed by the government in the name of national security, which was reinforced by the rise of the progressive movement, represented by Woodrow Wilson and Theodore Roosevelt, as well as factional infighting among socialists and the left. In order to squash political dissent and opposition, the government ultimately passed the **Espionage Act** in 1917, forbidding any action that helped the enemy or interfered with the draft. This move was followed shortly by the **Sedition Act** of 1918, which virtually eliminated free speech in the United States. The Sedition Act forbade Americans to "utter, print, or publish disloyal, profane, scurrilous, or abusive language about the form of government, the Constitution, soldiers and sailors, the flag, or uniform of the armed forces . . . or by word or act oppose the cause of the United States."[15]

By the end of the war, as many as 200,000 Americans were accused or indicted for remarks heard in public; those found guilty were fined heavily or imprisoned. Eugene Debs, the Socialist party leader, received a twenty-year sentence in a federal prison for speaking out publicly against American participation in the war (and in 1920, while still in jail, he polled nearly one million votes for president).

With the Bolshevik Revolution in 1917, a wave of anti-Bolshevism and anti-radicalism hit the country. The U.S. government, led by the Justice Department and the Federal Bureau of Investigation (FBI), initiated a **Red Scare** campaign that completely destroyed socialist and other left-wing organizations. Numerous radicals and hundreds of innocent immigrants were deported to Russia, while thousands of U.S. citizens were incarcerated by the government without charge.

By the early 1920s, the FBI had secretly labeled a half million Americans as dangerous.

These government actions violated the civil rights and liberties of numerous people, many of whom were American citizens. Nevertheless, the actions were supported by nativist and conservative groups that promoted what was referred to as "100-percent Americanism." They saw eastern and southern European immigrants, the Jewish and Catholic religions, and different cultures and views as threats to their image of small-town, Protestant America. These discriminatory actions were reinforced by big business, which welcomed the influx of immigrants as a cheap source of labor but bitterly fought against the rise of unionization, liberal reform, and socialism. Thus, World War I was instrumental in the widespread violation and curtailment of civil rights and liberties that virtually destroyed the political left—pacifists as well as socialists, who had been the major challengers to the politics of the status quo (review essay 8.1, on J. Edgar Hoover and the pursuit of security).

WORLD WAR II

During World War II the government censored the press, and the FBI became more active in investigating fascist and communist subversive activity at home. The **Smith Act** was passed in 1940, making it illegal to advocate the overthrow of the U.S. government by force or to organize or belong to a group with such a goal. The House of Representatives' Un-American Activities Committee engaged in antiradical investigations that focused on the threat of communism. Yet overall, the civil liberties of Americans were curtailed to a lesser degree during World War II than during World War I.

Germans and the political left were not severely targeted by discriminatory and repressive measures. This may be explained in part by the assimilation of most German Americans, and other Europeans, within society (especially after World War I), the rise of liberalism under President Franklin Roosevelt, the fact that the Soviet Union was allied with the United States against fascism, and the existence of only minimal dissent in the face of the clear national security threat posed by the Axis powers.

Nevertheless, many American citizens and immigrants of European descent who were associated with the fascist countries were victims of wartime fears. This was especially the case for **Italian immigrants and Italian Americans:** Over 600,000 Italian citizens who were legal immigrants within the United States were classified as "enemy aliens" during the war and had to face travel restrictions and curfews; many Italians lost their jobs; about sixteen hundred Italian immigrants were interned, which cost them their livelihoods, possessions, and freedom; and about ten thousand Italian American citizens were forced to move from their houses in California coastal communities to inland homes. Italian cultural organizations, language schools, and newspapers were often closed. Italian Americans represented the largest group of foreign-born residents—over 5 million, of whom about 500,000 Italian American sons served in the U.S. armed forces. At Fort Missoula, Montana—an old frontier army post that served as one of the nation's largest internment camps—along with Italians, about eleven thousand Germans and German Americans as well as some Bulgarians, Czechs, Hungarians, and Romanians were interned during the war.[16]

A much graver situation, however, faced those Americans who were not of European heritage, especially following the attack on Pearl Harbor. The fear of enemy sabotage or a Japanese attack on the West Coast led to such hysteria among Americans that the U.S. government had the military collect all individuals of Japanese descent, most of whom were American citizens, and held them in concentration camps throughout the war. This was one of the most blatant examples of political repression in American history. Such was the power of the president and the government, with much societal support, during World War II. It was such a sad episode, in fact, that the American government eventually apologized to **Japanese Americans** and gave reparations to those (few) internees that survived forty years later. (See **essay 14.1** for more on the Japanese American internment, race, and the process of dehumanization.)

THE COLD WAR

Despite the end of World War II, the civil liberties of Americans were again attacked with the onset of the cold war. The strong anticommunist legacy in American history and the growth of McCarthyism as a politi-

cal force made communism an enemy to be feared and fought both abroad and at home. As discussed in earlier chapters, McCarthyism represented a broad political coalition of conservative and nativist groups throughout American society. Nothing was immune to their attack, for communists and un-Americanism seemed to be everywhere—within the Truman administration, the government, the Democratic party, in academia and local schools, in Hollywood and the media, and all other walks of life. The **anticommunist hysteria,** or Red Scare II, became so intense and the demands of national security so overwhelmed the demands of democracy, that even defending the constitutional rights and liberties of Americans was considered evidence of disloyalty—of aiding and abetting the enemy (review essay 11.1, on Joseph McCarthy and McCarthyism). The domestic politics of anticommunism curtailed the exercise of civil liberties and contributed to the liberal-conservative consensus that provided the foundation for the president's ability to exercise prerogative government in the making of U.S. foreign policy.

It is true that there were some individuals who engaged in espionage for the Soviet Union. It is also true that there were individuals who were members of the Communist Party, USA.[17] "Of course, not all Communists attacked their adversaries and only a handful received direct orders from Moscow. The rank and file included many who were engaged in work similar to that of other political activists—attending meetings, distributing leaflets, demonstrating, organizing workers" to promote equality, opportunity, and peace, especially within the United States.[18] Furthermore, communists and sympathizers of the Soviet Union were small in numbers. As discussed in chapter 13 on public opinion and ideology, the overwhelming number of Americans, both elites and masses, were liberals, conservatives, and centrists who formed the basis of the anticommunist consensus in the United States.

Nevertheless, under the warlike conditions of the cold war many Americans became paranoid and preoccupied with the threat of communism. Criticizing the status quo exposed one to charges of being "unpatriotic," "un-American" and "disloyal." Given this environment, it is easy to see why most liberals moderated their beliefs and behavior to become part of the liberal-conservative consensus. Most Americans learned to go along and "shut up" in public even if they did not fully

ESSAY 14.1
THE JAPANESE AMERICAN INTERNMENT

RACE AND THE PROCESS
OF DEHUMANIZATION

On February 19, 1942, President Franklin Roosevelt signed Executive Order 9066, authorizing the War Department to remove individuals of Japanese descent living within the continental United States to concentration camps in an effort to ensure the internal security of the country. Those affected had only forty-eight hours to dispose of their homes and businesses, had to forfeit all bank accounts and investments, and were permitted to take only personal belongings that could be carried in hand luggage. Over 110,000 individuals of Japanese descent, including men, women, and children—mostly American citizens—were rounded up and spent the next three years of their lives in eleven camps located in desolate locations throughout the western United States.

The Japanese Americans were particularly suspected of being un-American and maintaining allegiance to Japan, especially on the West Coast, most of them resided. General John L. De Witt, commander of the Western Defense Command, expressed the popular sentiment of the times: "A Jap's a Jap! It makes no difference whether he's an American or not." Although the constitutional rights of Japanese Americans were ruthlessly violated, the U.S. Supreme Court actually upheld the executive order in 1944 in *Korematsu v. United States*, thus reflecting the politics of the times and the preoccupation with national security over the demands of democracy.

Yet American fears and paranoia proved to be completely unfounded. The Japanese proved to be very patriotic Americans. The executive order did not apply to the Hawaiian Islands, where over 150,000 Japanese Americans remained free and where no charges of sabotage were ever reported. The Japanese were model citizens during their stay in the camps. In fact, over seventeen thousand Japanese Americans volunteered in the U.S. military to fight in the war, once they were allowed to join in 1944. No Japanese American soldier ever deserted the U.S. military, even though they were kept in segregated units. Their wartime exploits became legendary. For example, the 442nd Infantry was composed of Japanese Americans who fought in the Italian campaign and became one of the most highly decorated units in the war. Members of the unit received 3,000 Purple Hearts with 500 oak leaf clusters, 810 bronze stars, 342 silver stars, 47 distinguished service

crosses, and 17 Legion of Merit awards. After the war, Japanese Americans were released from the camps and given only $25 and transportation to make their way back into American society.

The American Civil Liberties Union would call it "the worst single wholesale violation of civil rights of American citizens in our history." How and why did this occur? The Japanese American internment demonstrates that even people who share a strong democratic tradition and philosophical commitment to civil liberties are vulnerable to fear and stereotypical thinking. "The wave of antipathy toward Japanese Americans which engulfed the Pacific Coast in the opening months of World War II had its origin far back in the history of California and the West. It was generated in the climate of indiscriminate antiforeignism which characterized the gold-rush period, and took definite shape during half a century of anti-Chinese activity, during which a hostile image of the 'Oriental' emerged that was subsequently shifted to the Japanese," especially following the attack on Pearl Harbor.[A]

According to John Dower, in *War Without Mercy: Race and Power in the Pacific War*, periods of war usually lead to strong nationalist feelings of self-righteousness, fueled by prejudices of "racial pride, arrogance, and rage on many sides" that dehumanize the enemy.[B] Not only does this unify national support for the war effort, it also makes it easier for people to wreak destruction and death on others. On the home front, it leads to hypervigilance against subversives and intolerance of dissent. The **dehumanization process** typically results in simplistic black-and-white views in terms of both one's self-image—as innocent, righteous, superior—and the "image of the enemy" or "others"—as aggressive, evil, inferior (as discussed in chapter 10 on cognition and images).

"The racist code words and imagery that accompanied the war in Asia were often exceedingly graphic and contemptuous" for all parties involved.[C] From the American perspective, the Japanese were portrayed as subhuman and cruel, repeatedly associated with images of apes and

A. Jacobus TenBroek, Edward N. Barnhart, and Floyd W. Matson, *Prejudice, War and the Constitution* (Berkeley and Los Angeles: University of California Press, 1954), p. 11.
B. John W. Dower, *War Without Mercy: Race and Power in the Pacific War* (New York: Pantheon, 1986), p. 4.
C. Ibid., p. 9.

vermin in order to convey these traits. Milder images depicted the Japanese as inferior to Westerners and Caucasians, primitive and childish at best, and mentally and emotionally deficient. "Cartoonists, songwriters, filmmakers, war correspondents, and the mass media in general all seized on these images—and so did the social scientists and Asia experts who ventured to analyze the Japanese 'national character' during the war." As Japanese wartime successes mounted early in the war, another stereotype took hold: the Japanese superman, possessed of uncanny discipline and military ferocity. "Subhuman, inhuman, lesser human, superhuman—all that was lacking in the perception of the Japanese enemy was a human like oneself."[D]

Thus, Japanese Americans became the major targets of fear and repression within the United States for they represented America's enemy, most Americans felt a need

D. Ibid.

to avenge the attack on Pearl Harbor, and the Japanese were racially and culturally different. Hence, World War II heightened a process of dehumanization in the United States that bred intolerance and repression, with Japanese Americans becoming the primary victims. Although most obvious during times of war, when the demands for national security and national unity are at their height, the process of dehumanization resulting in stereotypical pictures of the enemy tends to occur throughout government and society whenever individual rights and liberties are restricted.

SOURCES: John W. Dower, *War Without Mercy: Race and Power in the Pacific War* (New York: Pantheon, 1986); Audrie Girdner and Anne Loftis, *The Great Betrayal: The Evacuation of the Japanese-Americans During World War II* (New York: Macmillan, 1969); Peter Irons, *Justice at War: The Story of the Japanese-American Internment Cases* (New York: Oxford University Press, 1983); William Manchester, *The Glory and the Dream: A Narrative History of America, 1932–1972* (New York: Bantam, 1975); Jacobus Ten-Broek, Edward N. Barnhart, and Floyd W. Matson, *Prejudice, War and the Constitution* (Berkeley and Los Angeles: University of California Press, 1954); and Michi Weglyn, *Years of Infamy: The Untold Story of America's Concentration Camps* (New York: William Morrow, 1976).

agree with the dominant beliefs and institutions. This resignation also helps to explain why the cold war was a period of mass apathy and declining political participation. Clearly, it was a time of great conformity and intolerance in American politics, and these sentiments were driven largely by McCarthyism and the cold war politics of anticommunism. Those who did not conform to the anticommunist norm were often silenced by political repression or lost their legitimacy and credibility throughout society for their beliefs.

Government employees were compelled to take a loyalty oath; a secrecy system was erected to protect classified information; and personnel involved in national security affairs were given lie-detector tests and had their backgrounds investigated. It has been estimated that during the McCarthy era, of a total workforce of sixty-five million, thirteen million people were affected by loyalty and security programs. In the name of national security, the government even restricted Americans traveling to communist countries.[19]

All these actions were originally intended to protect U.S. national security and respond to congressional investigations of communism in government. However, the national security ethos that arose was quickly abused in order to keep information from the public domain and to maximize support throughout society for the

government's policies (review the discussion of the impact of intelligence activities on the practice of national security and democracy at the end of chapter 8).

Yet the real abuse during the cold war years involved attempts by the government and allied groups in society to weed out communists and stifle public dissent in the name of national security. Congressional committees engaged in one investigation after another in an effort to identify and destroy communist influence, and this directly affected people's lives and careers. The attorney general kept a list of hundreds of subversive organizations, making individuals vulnerable to charges of disloyalty if they were affiliated with any of these groups, even if they had been members before or during World War II—not during the cold war. Even the courts ruled in favor of national security over individual civil liberties, as in the 1951 case of *Dennis v. United States,* in which the U.S. Supreme Court ruled that advocating or teaching revolutionary philosophy constituted a crime.[20]

David Caute, in *The Great Fear: The Anti-Communist Purge Under Truman and Eisenhower,* documents how thousands of government employees, teachers, labor leaders, journalists, librarians, scientists, writers, and entertainers at national, state, and local levels—virtually all innocent of charges of disloyalty—lost jobs, careers, and reputations as a result of wild accusations and guilt by association. The most celebrated cases, for example, involved people in the movie business who were dismissed and "blacklisted," that is, unofficially but effectively barred from working in major Hollywood studios. Yet "every segment of society was involved. From General Motors, General Electric, and CBS to the *New York Times*, the New York City Board of Education, and the United Auto Workers."[21]

Even academia, with its commitment to academic freedom, failed to fight McCarthyism. Nearly one-half of the social science professors teaching in universities at the time expressed medium or high apprehension about possible adverse repercussions to them as a result of their political beliefs and activities. In fact, Ellen Schrecker, in *No Ivory Tower: McCarthyism and the Universities*, found that academia contributed to McCarthyism. "The dismissals, the blacklists, and above all the almost universal acceptance of the legitimacy of what the congressional committees and other official investigators were doing conferred respectability upon the most repressive elements of the anti-Communist crusade. In its collaboration with McCarthyism, the academic community behaved just like every other major institution in American life."[22]

As David Caute has shown, by 1949 twenty-two states required teachers to sign loyalty oaths as a condition of employment, twenty-one forbade "seditious" classroom instruction, and thirty-one considered membership in subversive organizations as defined by the Department of Justice a sufficient cause for dismissal. In California, twenty-eight public and private colleges, including Stanford University and the University of California at Berkeley, installed security officers—usually former FBI agents—to compile information on the political beliefs and affiliations of professors for state officials. Caute has calculated that, as a consequence of these anticommunist laws and practices, more than six hundred public school teachers and professors lost their jobs. Throughout the University of California system alone, twenty-six professors were dismissed who refused to sign the loyalty oath, thirty-seven others resigned in protest, forty-seven professors from other institutions turned down offers of appointment in California, and fifty-five courses from the university curriculum were eliminated.[23]

In *Compromised Campus: The Collaboration of Universities With the Intelligence Community*, Sigmund

Desmond demonstrates that university officials, including the presidents of Yale and Harvard, secretly cooperated with the FBI while publicly portraying their institutions as bastions of academic freedom.[24] Such draconian measures by the government and university administrators would trigger the "free speech movement" that began at the University of California at Berkeley in the early sixties and activate students on campuses throughout the nation, leading to the rise of the new left and antiwar movements (to be discussed in greater depth in chapter 16, on group politics).

Perhaps most important, McCarthyism had a chilling effect throughout society; millions of Americans were intimidated by these actions, for they sent clear messages to the public about what constituted proper political thought and behavior in American politics. As early as 1947 in response to the **House Un-American Activities Committee's investigation of the Hollywood Ten**—referring to the film makers and actors who initially refused to cooperate by naming names—Martha Gellhorn, a former leftist and one-time wife of Ernest Hemingway, sarcastically referred to it as "a little terror, calculated to frighten little people." But "it works"; under such pressure "a man can be well and truly destroyed." Her comments were prophetic. Someone "with a family will think many times before speaking his mind fearlessly and critically when there lies ahead the threat of an Un-Americans' investigation, a publicized branding, and his job gone." For if you could destroy the Hollywood Ten, "pretty soon you can ruin a painter and a teacher and a writer and a lawyer and an actor and a scientist; and presently you have made a silent place.[25]

During this time the FBI maintained a widespread network of informants to weed out subversives and covertly instituted **Operation Cointelpro** to target the Communist Party, USA. One of the "informants" was Ronald Reagan, who, while serving as the president of the Screen Actors Guild, was secretly reporting to the FBI on suspect members of the union he was elected to represent. Under Director J. Edgar Hoover this counterintelligence program soon broadened to include the civil rights movement and then the antiwar movement during the 1960s.[26]

The FBI ended up carrying out over 500,000 investigations of so-called subversives without a single court conviction and created files on over 1 million Americans. Hoover stated the goals of the activities of the "Disruption of the New Left" Internal Security Counter

Intelligence Program to the FBI's Albany, New York, office in the following manner:

> *The purpose of this program is to expose, disrupt, and otherwise neutralize the activities of the various new left organizations, their leadership and their adherents.* It is imperative that activities of those groups be followed on a continuous basis so we may take advantage of all opportunities for counter intelligence and also *inspire action where circumstances warrant. . . . We must frustrate every effort of these groups and individuals to consolidate their forces or to recruit new or youthful adherents. In every instance, consideration should be given to disrupting organized activity of these groups and no opportunity should be missed to capitalize on organizational or personal conflicts of their leadership* [emphasis in original].[27]

These steps, which inhibited Americans in exercising their liberties in accordance with the Constitution, were legitimate in the minds of Hoover and many American conservatives, for they believed that the civil rights movement and the new left, including people like Martin Luther King, Jr., and Students for a Democratic Society leader Tom Hayden, were too radical, too un-American, and too threatening to the status quo, if not downright communist directed.

More moderate political leaders, including cold war liberals such as Lyndon Johnson and Hubert Humphrey, tended to support these counterintelligence actions because they were unsure about the influence of communism, their governmental legitimacy and power were being challenged, and they were repulsed by such nonconformist political behavior—especially since they were accustomed to a relatively politically supportive and passive population when it came to foreign policy. As David Halberstam described LBJ's increasing "bunker" mentality in the White House by 1966: "Instead of leading, he was immobilized, surrounded, seeing critics everywhere. Critics became enemies; enemies became traitors."[28]

Although most Americans remained unaware of these covert actions at home, American nationalism promoted anticommunism and tolerated little dissent from the norm. This was, after all, the height of presidential power in exercising prerogative government in support of foreign policy in the name of national security. The right of political dissent and even a concern

for public health were not allowed to get in the way of the war on communism—such was the primacy of the national security ethos throughout government (see **essay 14.2** on the governmental drive for nuclear weaponry and its implications for public safety).

The politics of the cold war was serious business. Political instability was typically portrayed by supporters of the cold war and the Vietnam War as a function of communists or so-called "outside agitators" who were trying to stir up trouble. Cold war proponents simply could not understand that growing numbers of Americans were sincerely speaking out against them and their policies. Therefore, as was discussed briefly in chapter 8 on the intelligence community, the FBI's programs were complemented by similar covert counterintelligence activities conducted throughout the national security bureaucracy. The Central Intelligence Agency opened the mail of American citizens, kept over 1.5 million names on file, and infiltrated religious, media, and academic groups. The National Security Agency monitored cables sent overseas or received by Americans from 1947 to 1975. Army Intelligence investigated over 100,000 American citizens during the Vietnam War. The Internal Revenue Service allowed tax information to be misused by intelligence agencies for political purposes.

The U.S. government, moreover, worked closely with local leaders, relying on the police and the National Guard, to prevent demonstrations and officially restore law and order.[29] The criminal justice system, for example, was used to arrest, try, and in some cases, convict demonstrators as a means of preventing and deterring the exercise of their civil liberties, thus producing the equivalent of "political prisoners." These efforts to repress dissent resulted in dozens of Americans being fatally shot by the police and the militia during the turbulent years of the 1960s, including four students at Kent State University in Ohio and two students at Jackson State University in Mississippi. Finally, President Nixon attempted to take things into his own hands by allowing the "plumbers," operating out of the White House, to destroy Nixon's enemies and guarantee the reelection of the president, leading to the Watergate crisis.

In almost every such situation during the cold war years, the political dynamics were the same. Those who attempted to peacefully exercise their civil liberties through the political system and change the status quo from a liberal or left perspective were resisted by the government and its conservative allies in virtually all

ESSAY 14.2
NUCLEAR TESTING, DOWNWINDERS, AND HUMAN SAFETY

The Soviet Union detonated an atomic device in 1949, years earlier than most American scientists and political leaders had predicted. This event, combined with the rise of the cold war and growing fears of communism, resulted in an effort of maximum production and maximum secrecy in the United States to develop the hydrogen bomb and expand America's nuclear weapons stockpile. As part of the research and development of nuclear weapons, an above-ground **atomic testing program** was conducted by the Atomic Energy Commission from 1951 to 1958 at the Nevada Test Site, northwest of Las Vegas. Almost one hundred nuclear devices were tested above ground. Over 100,000 people who lived downwind from the Nevada Test Site felt the nuclear blasts and, more important, were exposed to the resulting radioactive fallout. These people were predominantly Mormons, very patriotic believers in God and country, who lived in small towns in Nevada and Utah.

When some of the so-called "downwinders" began to express concern about the fallout, the U.S. government—with the support of local political, business, and religious leaders—initiated a campaign to educate the public. Local citizens were told by the U.S. government that there was no need to worry because radioactive fallout is harmless (no more dangerous than medical X-rays) and that the atomic tests were a crucial component of efforts to safeguard the security of the United States. In 1955, before a new series of nuclear tests was to begin, a message from the Nevada Test Site manager appeared in an Atomic Energy Commission pamphlet given to schoolchildren and their parents:

> You are in a very real sense active participants in the Nation's atomic test program. You have been close observers of tests which have contributed greatly to building the defenses of our country and of the free world. . . . Some of you have been inconvenienced by our test operations. At times, some of you have been exposed to potential risk from flash, blast, or fallout. You have accepted the inconvenience or the risk without fuss, without alarm and without panic. Your cooperation has helped achieve an unusual record of safety. . . . I want you to know that each shot is justified by national or international security need and that none will be fired unless there is adequate assurance of public safety.

We are grateful for your continued cooperation and your understanding.[A]

Most residents, especially in the early years of the program, believed their government and acted accordingly. The following incident, as recalled by one resident when she was twelve years old, was far from unusual:

> I remember playing under the oleander tree, which is a wide-leaf tree, and the fallout was so thick that it was like snow. . . . [We] liked to play under the trees and shake this fallout onto our heads and our bodies, thinking that we were playing in the snow. I remember writing my name on the car because the fallout dust was so thick. Then I would go home and eat. If my mother caught me as a young child, I would wash my hands; if not, then I would eat with the fallout on my hands.[B]

By the late 1950s, many local citizens became increasingly skeptical of the U.S. government's bland assurances of their safety. Medical research, in fact, was indicating that radioactive fallout could be extremely harmful. The 1960s reinforced these concerns as an alarming increase in the number of leukemia patients was detected in the small communities that were downwind from the Nevada Test Site, particularly among the young (the most vulnerable). Feelings of great bitterness resulted. As expressed by one local citizen, "We trusted the government when they told us that it was safe and so we didn't take precautions that we might have otherwise done had they told us the methods to protect ourselves."[C]

The government's position didn't change: The nuclear tests were safe, and there was no proof that they were responsible for the cancers that were increasingly evident. Some local residents formed groups to fight for justice, for they considered themselves victims of the government's negligence. Little ground was gained over the next ten to fifteen years. In the late 1970s, after the impact of the Vietnam war, the Atomic Energy Commission was forced to release classified information. The information demonstrated that members of the Atomic Energy Commission and the

---

A. Howard Ball, *Justice Downwind: America's Atomic Testing Program in the 1950s* (New York: Oxford University Press, 1986), p. 73.
B. Ibid., p. 92.
C. Ibid., p. 93.

U.S. government had shown little interest in questions of safety during the nuclear testing program, "knowingly" lied about the harmlessness of radioactive fallout, and kept medical studies classified indicating the dangerous effects of low-level radiation in order to avoid adverse publicity.

This led to a lawsuit in 1979 by twenty-four down-winders against the U.S. government in U.S. district court. Although the law was written so as to favor the government, in 1984 the district judge found the government to have been negligent in the case of ten of the twenty-four plaintiffs and awarded $2.66 million to the survivors of the deceased. However, the victory was only temporary, for a federal court of appeals overturned the decision in favor of the U.S. government, and the U.S. Congress has failed to pass legislation compensating the victims of atomic testing from the Nevada Test Site. Other lawsuits by downwinders have suffered a similar fate.

The U.S. government's overwhelming preoccupation with national security while neglecting the safety and rights of its people was not confined to the Nevada Test Site case. In addition to the 100,000 civilians who lived downwind from the test site, islanders have been exposed to radioactive fallout from nuclear tests in the Pacific; military troops have been exposed to radioactive fallout while engaged in war exercises following nuclear tests in the Pacific and the Nevada Test Site; civilians have been exposed to dangerous bacteria as a result of the Army's germ warfare tests over populated areas; civilians were injected with radioactive substances in experiments to determine the effects of radiation; workers and local residents have been exposed to radiation from the government's nuclear weapons production facilities located throughout the country (as described in essay 7.1); miners and nearby residents have been exposed to radioactive material from uranium mines; Vietnam veterans (and countless local Vietnamese) have been exposed to dioxin in the chemical

defoliant Agent Orange; and military personnel and civilians are exposed to military toxic wastes while they work and live near toxic waste dumps on military bases.

Overall, it is estimated that millions of Americans, military and civilian, have been exposed to radioactive and toxic substances used by the U.S. government and the military in the name of national security. Since the Vietnam War, more information about threats to public health has come to light and efforts to redress these threats have grown. In each situation, the government response tends to be the same: The substances and facilities are claimed to be safe for humans, the release of relevant information is resisted, and any political or legal challenge that arises is fought. There have been some court settlements, and the U.S. government, usually through the Veterans Administration, has been forced to be somewhat more responsive. Estimates for environmental cleanup of the toxic waste and pollution at the nuclear weapons production facilities alone are in the hundreds of billions of dollars over the next generation. Clearly, with the rise of the cold war, the military establishment, and the national security ethos, a preoccupation with national security often prevailed over the safety and rights of American citizens.

SOURCES: Howard Ball, *Justice Downwind: America's Atomic Testing Program in the 1950s* (New York: Oxford University Press, 1986); Leonard A. Cole, *Clouds of Secrecy: The Army's Germ Warfare Tests Over Populated Areas* (Totowa, N.J.: Rowman and Littlefield, 1988); Michael D'Antonio, *Atomic Harvest: Hanford and the Lethal Toll of America's Nuclear Arsenal* (New York: Crown, 1993); Carole Gallagher, *American Ground Zero: The Secret Nuclear War* (Cambridge, Mass.: MIT Press, 1993); Clifford T. Honicker, "America's Radiation Victims: The Hidden Files," *New York Times Magazine* (November 19, 1989), pp. 38–41, 98–103, 120; Thomas H. Saffer and Orville E. Kelly, *Countdown Zero: GI Victims of U.S. Atomic Testing* (Middlesex, England: Penguin, 1982); U.S. Congress, General Accounting Office, *Nuclear Waste: DOE's Program to Prepare High-Level Radioactive Waste for Final Disposal* (November 1989); Eileen Welsome, *The Plutonium Files: America's Secret Medical Experiments in the Cold War* (New York: Random House, 1999).

levels of society. While both leaders and followers in the civil rights and antiwar movements confined themselves overwhelmingly to political acts of nonviolence and civil disobedience, the government was engaged in a massive campaign to limit and stifle the exercise of civil rights and liberties. Acts by the police to disrupt demonstrations often resulted in violence, radicalization, increased repression, and more violence until American society seemed to be at war with itself. Ultimately, these efforts to restrict and neutralize the civil rights and liberties of Americans failed to contain the

growth of massive political dissent against the Vietnam War during the 1960s and early 1970s.

THE POST–VIETNAM WAR RESURGENCE OF CIVIL LIBERTIES

Two major patterns involving civil liberties prevailed in the post–Vietnam years until the September 11, 2001, attacks. On one hand, the breakdown of the liberal-conservative and anticommunist consensus allowed Americans to exercise their civil liberties as never before. The civil rights and antiwar movements of the late 1950s and 1960s fundamentally challenged the conformity and passivity that prevailed during the height of the cold war and were highly responsible for expanding the world of group and participatory politics by the late sixties and seventies. The events surrounding civil rights and Vietnam produced greater ideological, electoral, and political diversity. Clearly, individuals and groups throughout American society have greater opportunities to exercise their civil liberties and participate in politics then previously. Furthermore, one of the offshoots of the social movements of the sixties and seventies is that, although participation in elections has decreased, more Americans actively participate in group politics than before.

On the other hand, some cold war patterns prevail in which threats to national security still take precedence over the ability of Americans to exercise their democratic rights. This continues to be the case because a large military and intelligence community continues to exist and engage in counterintelligence activities, a national security ethos still pervades the government and the military-industrial-scientific support infrastructure, and many Americans continue to have a conservative internationalist view of the world. Therefore, presidents have experienced a paradox of power in the post–Vietnam War political environment.

The Iran-contra affair demonstrates both of these patterns. Many of the Iran-contra activities of the Reagan administration involved efforts to stifle legitimate dissent to its policies. According to Robert Parry and Peter Kornbluh, in "Iran-Contra's Untold Story," "The White House deployed secretly funded private-sector surrogates to attack anti-contra [congressional] lawmakers through television and newspaper advertisements and to promote the contra cause through organizations with hidden funding ties to the administration. The FBI mounted intrusive and intimidating investigations of groups opposed to Reagan's Central American policies. . . . administration officials sought to manipulate criminal probes to protect their operations from exposure."[30]

Activities of the FBI that were part of its international terrorism counterintelligence program included the investigation of over eighteen thousand individuals

and thirteen hundred groups opposed to President Reagan's Central American policies, including the National Council of Churches, the Maryknoll Sisters, the United Automobile Workers, and the National Education Association, even though no criminal activity was ever uncovered. Of these, the U.S. General Accounting Office found that the FBI investigated 6,985 U.S. citizens and permanent resident aliens, that over 2,000 cases were selected simply because the individuals were from foreign countries that sponsored terrorism, and that the FBI "monitored First Amendment-type activities" in more than 2,000 other cases.[31]

Although these efforts to silence the exercise of civil rights and liberties occurred in the 1980s, this cold war and national security orientation operated in a post–Vietnam War domestic political environment, where such views and activities were much more likely to be exposed and criticized. Although Congress, the media, and the public were very slow to initially respond to the Reagan administration's involvement in Iran-contra, many of these activities nevertheless were eventually challenged, exposed, and stopped when the Iran-contra affair was moved onto the political agenda beginning in the fall of 1986. Such a political and constitutional crisis for President Reagan and the nation could have occurred only in a post–Vietnam War environment following the decline of the cold war. This also helps to explain the greater toleration for dissent and opposition experienced during the Persian Gulf crisis and war, even though some individuals were harassed for their beliefs and Arab Americans were placed under FBI surveillance.[32]

Thus contradictory patterns of continuity and change from the 1970s to the 1990s have created a new and uneasy tension between the demands of national security and those of democracy. With increasing numbers of Americans exercising their civil liberties, constraints on the president's ability to govern and potential opposition to his policies have grown. At the same time, if a president tries to limit dissent by violating civil rights and liberties in the name of national security, he risks political scandal, constitutional crisis, and disaster. Such was the fate of Richard Nixon with Watergate and Ronald Reagan with Iran-contra. Only in less intrusive ways can a president rely on the cold war patterns of the past in governing foreign policy, such as denying the public information through use of the secrecy system or involving the intelligence community in much more limited counterintelligence operations. By doing anything more, the president risks great political uncertainty, especially if the actions become public knowledge and find their way onto the political agenda.

It also means that the foreign policy bureaucracy is also more likely to be challenged in such a political environment. For example, in the late eighties the government tried to build the Special Isotope Separation Project, a plutonium purifying plant, at the Idaho National Engineering Laboratory. An important reason this site was chosen was because it was thought the plan would face little resistance in rural eastern Idaho. The Bush Sr. administration miscalculated, however, as a number of interest groups as well as local newspapers feverishly opposed the project. Despite the promise of jobs, the local population was swayed in opposition to the plutonium plant and the project was dropped, demonstrating that concern for public safety and civil liberties can prevail over the needs of national security, as least since Vietnam and the end of the cold war.[33]

The End of the Cold War: Placing the Tension in Perspective

With the collapse of the Soviet Union and communism in Eastern Europe, *the end of the cold war has had important implications for the exercise of civil liberties and the future of American politics.* First, Americans can rest assured that communism will likely have almost no appeal within the United States any longer. Therefore, Americans should have little reason to fear the threat of communism in the foreseeable future. Second, the decline of international communism means that anticommunism should fade as an important political issue (among liberals and especially conservatives), although the most extreme groups may continue to see the communist bogeyman on the march. In other words, where the threat of Bolshevism and communism was used throughout the twentieth century by conservatives and the political right to resist change and promote their policies, it should no longer have the symbolic value for uniting conservatives and attracting the support of Americans that it commanded in the past, especially during the red scares of World War I and the cold war years.[34]

The collapse of communism, in other words, has further expanded Americans' ability to exercise their civil liberties in American politics. Americans can choose to participate in electoral and group politics with little fear for their civil liberties, personal standing, and livelihood, especially in comparison to the cold war years. This suggests that ideological diversity will continue to increase among the mass and elite public, while new foreign policy issues may generate more political involvement in electoral politics, social movements, and interest groups. This is probably best illustrated by the existence of a divided public and country before the actual initiation of hostilities in the Persian Gulf War in 1991. It also suggests the need and potential for the reduction, and possible reform, of the immense national security bureaucracy and the prevalence of the national security ethos.[35]

It must be pointed out that, even with the decline of communism, international conflict and new issues—such as drugs—will continue to plague the world, bureaucratic institutions created to protect national security will continue to exist, and American nationalism will continue to promote conformity in response to crises. The **Wen Ho Lee case** during the late 1990s, at a time when China was often depicted as a growing regional power and a potential future threat to the United States, is an important reminder of this (see **essay 14.3** on the Lee case, nuclear espionage, politics, and racial profiling).

It appears that, as discussed in chapter 13 and earlier in this chapter about the "paranoid style of American politics," a **dualism of freedom and intolerance** with respect to the exercise of civil liberties has existed in the practice of American politics. On the one hand, American civil rights and liberties have steadily expanded throughout American history. In the post–Vietnam War era, Americans on the whole have become freer and more tolerant than during any previous period. This tolerance and freedom is much more in accordance with the ideals set down by the Declaration of Independence and the Constitution of the United States. On the other hand, there also have been periods of contraction in the exercise of civil liberties within the United States. Americans have been vulnerable to streaks of intolerance and discriminatory practices, usually accompanied by emotional appeals to Americanism and nationalism, especially during war. These contradictory patterns in the exercise of civil liberties

ESSAY 14.3
THE WEN HO LEE CASE: A CASE OF RACIAL PROFILING?

Until the 1990s, Wen Ho Lee was an obscure nuclear scientist who worked at the Los Alamos National Laboratory. He was accused of being a Chinese spy providing official secrets about nuclear weapons shortly after a March 8, 1999, *New York Times* article made it into a major story. He was indicted on December 10 on fifty-nine counts. On September 13, 2000, after 279 days behind bars in a solitary cell, shackled with leg irons, interrogated, and under a twenty-four-hour watch, Lee was released after pleading guilty to one count of mishandling classified information; the other fifty-eight charges were dropped.

The crime sounded alarming: China had stolen the design of America's advanced nuclear weapon. The suspect seemed suspicious enough: he was born in Taiwan, educated at Texas A&M, worked at Los Alamos, and had a history of contact with Chinese scientists. "What drove the Lee case was legitimate national security concerns—warped by politics," particularly the divisive politics of Washington.

It began in 1995, when an American agent in Asia was approached by a Chinese "walk-in" defector with a sensational intelligence coup—a seventy-four-page document purported to be the blueprint (seven years old) for modernizing China's nuclear weapons program, including a design similar to the W-88, the state-of-the-art thermonuclear warhead built for U.S. missile submarines. "It languished for several years, only to be revived in 1998 by a confluence of forces—a [Clinton] White House under siege of impeachment, festering accusations of Chinese money funneled to Democratic campaigns and a House panel that saw the W-88 case as the newest evidence of China's voracious appetite for American technology secrets." The so-called Cox Report—named for Republican Representative Chris Cox, the chair of the congressional committee investigating technology transfers to China—was sensationalized and the so-called spy scandal and China threat was widely reported by the American media.

Federal investigators made Dr. Lee their prime suspect "even though they had no evidence he had leaked weapons secrets." "Agents conducted 1,000 interviews over nine months, scouring the globe that Dr. Lee had leaked his secrets. The FBI carried out its largest computer forensic investigation ever. Investigators traced years of Dr. Lee's telephone calls." In fact, "investigators took fragmentary, often ambiguous evidence about Dr. Lee's be-

havior and Chinese atomic espionage and wove it into a greater case that eventually collapsed of its own light weight." The reality is that the "Federal Bureau of Investigation ignored the urging of a senior agent on the case to look beyond Dr. Lee. As a result, it failed to examine hundreds, if not thousands, of people outside Los Alamos" who may have had access to information about the W-88. Nevertheless, the government "brought a 59-count indictment and convinced a federal judge that he was so dangerous he had to be jailed without bail."

Ironically, Lee pleaded guilty to one charge about misuse of classified information, the same charge admitted by former deputy defense secretary and director of central intelligence under President Clinton John M. Deutch, who faced no such imprisonment or witch-hunt (and was pardoned by President Clinton after pleading guilty to a misdemeanor charge for keeping classified information on his home computers). Similar misuse of classified information is rather common. Upon the dismissal of the charges and Lee's release, U.S. District Judge James A. Parker, a conservative Reagan appointee, was infuriated for being "misled." He apologized to Dr. Lee for being treated as a dangerous spy, calling Lee's imprisonment "draconian" and "unfair." The judge excoriated "top decision-makers" at the Departments of Justice and Energy who, according to Parker, "embarrassed our entire nation and each of us who is a citizen in it."

Lee and his lawyers claimed he had been targeted for investigation because he was Chinese. Many critics and advocates of civil liberties further charged that the intelligence and law-enforcement agencies had engaged in a new form of racial profiling that they fear may grow in the future. In the end, "the spy hysteria . . . has taken a terrible toll on the life of one scientist and has cast suspicion over the entire community of Asian-American scientists." And this was before the September 11, 2001, attacks.

SOURCES: Michael Isikoff, "Into the Sunshine," *Newsweek* (September 2000), pp. 38–40; Matthew Purdy, "The Making of a Suspect: The Case of Wen Ho Lee," *New York Times* (February 4, 2001), www.nytimes.com; Matthew Purdy with James Sterngold, "The Prosecution Unravels: The Case of Wen Ho Lee," *New York Times* (February 5, 2001), www.nytimes.com; Robert Scheer, "No Defense: How the *New York Times* Convicted Wen Ho Lee," *Nation* (October 23, 2000), pp. 11–20; David A Vise and Vernon Loeb, "U.S. Probe of Former CIA Chief Expands; Earlier Instances of Mishandling Data Are Alleged," *Washington Post* (September 16, 2000), www.washingtonpost.com.

are reflected in the beliefs among both the mass and elite publics.[36]

J. William Fulbright, senator from Arkansas and the chairman of the Senate Foreign Relations Committee, was quite aware of this contradiction between Americans' belief in freedom, civil rights, and civil liberties, and at the same time, their low tolerance for criticism. As he stated in 1966 in *The Arrogance of Power*: "The discharge of the *duty* of dissent is handicapped in America by an unworthy tendency to fear serious criticism of our government. In the abstract we celebrate freedom of opinion as part of our patriotic liturgy; it is only when some Americans exercise it that other Americans are shocked." Nevertheless, Fulbright was the first significant public official to publicly criticize the war in Vietnam at the height of the Americanization of the war and the liberal-conservative anticommunist consensus. And his dissent was considered by most members of Congress, from both parties, and the Johnson administration, especially Lyndon Johnson, to be an unpatriotic act of disloyalty. Yet, Fulbright believed that

> to criticize one's country is to do it a service and pay it a compliment.... Criticism, in short, is more than a right; it is an act of patriotism, a higher form of patriotism, I believe, than the familiar rituals of national adulation.... And, in so doing, in the words of Albert Camus, "if at times we seemed to prefer justice to our country, this is because we simply wanted to love our country in justice, as we wanted to love her in truth and in hope."[37]

It was a courageous act by Fulbright because ultimately he would lose reelection, but he was also crucial in helping to legitimize the growing antiwar movement throughout the country.

This dualism is important for understanding continuity and change in the politics of U.S. foreign policy over the years. It is not mere coincidence that the height of presidential power in foreign policy occurred during a time when the demands of national security took precedence over the exercise of civil rights and liberties demanded by democratic practice. Likewise, as Americans have come to enjoy a greater ability to exercise their constitutional rights and liberties since the Vietnam War, it should not be surprising that domestic politics has constrained the president's ability to govern foreign policy and the bureaucracy's ability to act with abandon.

In sum, the cold war appears to be a historic artifact. Americans and foreigners alike should experience less repression and more civil liberties in the future politics of U.S. foreign policy. In other words, more and more people should feel free to exercise their speech, their beliefs, and their right to dissent—that is, unless the United States becomes involved in another war of global proportions. This takes us to the implications of the September 11 attacks and the Bush Jr. administration's war on terrorism.

Implications of the September 11 Attacks and War on Terrorism

Did the September 11 attacks create the equivalent of a new, permanent war or national emergency, reminiscent of World War I, World War II, or the cold war? To what extent should the demands of national security take precedence over individual rights and liberties in President Bush Jr.'s war on terrorism? To what extent will President Bush Jr.'s war presidency and war on terrorism resonate throughout the global and, in particular, the domestic political environment? To what extent should people fear for free speech and the right to dissent and look for a new paranoid style in American politics?

There is no doubt that in the short term the country has rallied round the flag in response to the terrorist attacks and their many victims. And there is also no doubt that President Bush Jr., and his war on terrorism, enjoys considerable political and public support, making the president very powerful once again in the making of foreign policy, especially involving security matters. Clearly, the attacks and the war on terrorism have substantially increased the legitimate concerns with the demands of national security not seen since the Vietnam War. However, especially as time has lapsed since September 11, 2001, and with the overthrow of the Taliban regime, the war on terrorism does not appear to be a new, permanent war or national emergency on a par with World War II or the cold war. Although the president is able to exercise considerable prerogative government with substantial support, presidential supremacy in foreign policy has not been fully achieved, and sensitivity to the demands of democracy and individual civil rights and liberties continues. Clearly, the tension between the demands of national security and of democracy have heightened and are visible, but the dynamics and balance between them remains unclear and needs time to play itself out.

The Bush administration has responded strongly to the September 11 attacks by emphasizing the priority of fighting a war on terrorism at home and abroad. The United States has sent troops (and covert agents) to Afghanistan to help overthrow the Taliban regime, destroy terrorist networks, and try to promote a new, friendly, and stable Afghan government. The administration has tried to build global support behind its initiatives while putting countries on notice that the United States might intervene if they pose a threat, especially Iraq, Iran, and North Korea. The CIA's role and use of covert and paramilitary operations, including the threat to overthrow foreign governments, have been renewed. Foreign assistance has increased, especially to friendly regimes in the Middle East such as Pakistan (regardless of their poor democratic and human rights records). As part of the war on terrorism, the military budget is expanding enormously, as is also the case for the intelligence community and other agencies (at both the federal and state levels) involved in anti-terrorism. A Department of Homeland Security has been created to try to coordinate the multitude of agencies involved in anti-terrorism within the executive branch. Immigration laws have tightened, along with airport security with the federalization of security personnel (against the wishes of President Bush, who wanted to keep airport security privatized).

The Bush administration quickly submitted an anti-terrorism bill known as the **USA Patriot Act** and it became law in October 2001. The statute is complicated, controversial and long—342 pages. Nevertheless, Congress acted quickly, given the post–September 11 political environment, voting overwhelmingly for its passage: 98 to 1 in the Senate and 356 to 66 in the House of Representatives. According to *The Washington Post*, "Molded by wartime politics and passed . . . in furious haste, the new anti-terrorism bill lays the foundation for a domestic intelligence-gathering system of unprecedented scale and technological prowess, according to both supporters and critics of the legislation."[38]

It also demonstrated how during times of national emergency the government can react quickly, maybe too quickly for there was little deliberation and the so-called democratic process failed to address numerous issues and constitutional questions. According to law professor Harry Tepker, "The push for quick passage avoided discussion of controversial measures. The truncated legislative process avoided real, needed debate of how to effectively improve the nation's ability not only to collect intelligence, but also to efficiently and wisely synthesize collected data into useful information. The absence of debates and hearings may also deprive the judiciary of a reliable legislative history when courts review the meaning and constitutionality of the act."[39]

The USA Patriot Act (which is an acronym for "Uniting and Strengthening America by Providing Appropriate Tools Required to Intercept and Obstruct Terrorism") increased penalties for acts of terrorism and harboring or financing terrorists or terrorist organizations. It expands the government's ability to conduct electronic surveillance, get subpoenas for e-mail, internet and telephone communications, acquire nationwide search warrants, detain immigrants without charges, and penetrate (and sanction) money-laundering banks. It also permits government officials to share grand jury information to thwart terrorism and relaxes the conditions under which judges may authorize intelligence wiretaps.

At the same time, concerns were expressed for the legitimate protection of civil rights and liberties, and the Bush administration did not get everything that it wanted. Despite the rallying round the flag, Congress remains ideologically diverse and politically divided, conditions that contributed to numerous compromises on the anti-terrorism bill. The law denies the administration the power to detain indefinitely immigrants suspected of involvement in terrorism—official charges must be made within seven days. The authority for expanded surveillance of computers and telephones expires after four years. Wiretaps, including roving wiretaps, and search warrants still require judicial approval (sometimes in special and more willing intelligence courts). The law denies the administration the power to use evidence gathered abroad (such as through foreign wiretaps) if it was obtained by methods considered unconstitutional in the United States.

The Bush administration also has taken a number of additional, unilateral initiatives, many of which have received increasing criticism at home and abroad, including allowing military trials for suspected terrorists;

suspending the right of detainees to have private conversations with their attorneys if the attorney general deems that they might pose a threat to the public; questioning thousands of people who have recently entered the United States who are from the Middle East; treating captured Taliban and Al Qaeda fighters as detainees, as opposed to prisoners of war (raising issues about human rights and international law reflecting interpretations about the Geneva Accords); detaining American citizens and foreigners for indefinite periods under laws not intended for this purpose (such as the "material witness" law); having prisoners and suspects taken out of the U.S. and American custody to "friendly" foreign countries so they can be interrogated and bypass American laws; exercising considerable secrecy and classifying more governmental information, including former presidential records and scientific studies—despite the Freedom of Information Act and Presidential Records Act; attempting to relax restrictions on the FBI's ability to spy on religious and political organizations that were imposed in the 1970s after the death of J. Edgar Hoover; allowing the CIA to engage in clandestine missions aimed at killing specified individuals despite executive orders issued in the 1970s and 1980s banning assassinations.

The anti-terrorism laws and Bush administration efforts have eroded efforts to protect the civil rights and liberties of people on American soil by expanding governmental powers, especially involving intelligence agencies and the military. For example, when Congress passed the National Security Act of 1947, the law distinguished between the "foreign" intelligence operations of the newly created CIA and the "domestic" intelligence and law enforcement operations of the FBI. Now this distinct separation has become increasingly blurred with the USA Patriot Act. Furthermore, the Bush administration has directed the Department of Justice and the Department of Defense to review the **Posse Comitatus Act** of 1887. The Posse Comitatus Act makes it a crime to use the military as a domestic police force in most circumstances. The act "was enacted after the Civil War in response to the perceived misuse of federal troops who were charged with domestic law enforcement in the South. But it has come to symbolize the separation of civilian affairs from military influence." Over the years, the law has been amended to allow the military to lend equipment to federal, state and local authorities; assist federal agencies in drug interdiction work; protect national parks; and execute quarantine and certain health laws. "Military leaders have generally supported the restrictions because their troops were not specifically trained [for domestic intelligence and enforcement] roles, and they worried that domestic tasks could lead to serious political problems. But in the aftermath of September 11, some Pentagon officials and military officers are beginning to realize that the law, as it stands, may slow or complicate their domestic defense missions," which are now part of the new Northern Command.[40]

All these actions are reinforced by the ambiguity and open-endedness of the USA Patriot Act. "The statute does not establish standards, limitations, or safeguards restricting disclosure or subsequent use of the 'foreign intelligence information,' but delegates to the attorney general the responsibility for establishing procedures for the disclosure of 'foreign intelligence information' originating from grand juries or wiretaps. Also critics fear that the Act's broad and ambiguous language allows the CIA and the intelligence community to again collect information about persons who have committed no crime, but who are involved in lawful, constitutionally-protected protests of American foreign policy."[41] For example, major political, legal, and constitutional issues are being raised about government efforts to gain access to individual library records and reading habits of individuals, and to acquire student records, emails, and computer files. Where high school, college and university administrators have been somewhat responsive to government requests, "librarians are having a harder time compromising. Library policies are typically designed to protect the privacy of their patrons, and librarians themselves have been staunch advocates of privacy rights."[42]

This is not the first time that schools and libraries have been targeted for surveillance. During the cold war the FBI set up the Library Awareness Program to monitor the reading habits of foreigners, particularly those from the Soviet Union, when public controversy ended it in 1987 (as briefly discussed in chapter 8 on intelligence). Many states "subsequently passed laws protecting library records. Libraries still adhere to this state law in criminal investigations. But in matters of surveillance and terrorist investigations, the Patriot Act supersedes any state law." And according to section 215 of the USA Patriot Act, "The Director of the Federal

Bureau of Investigation or a designee of the director may make an application for an order requiring the production of any tangible things (including books, records, papers, documents, and other items) for an investigation to protect against international terrorism or clandestine intelligence activities."[43]

Despite the compromised anti-terrorist legislation and some backtracking by the administration in response to the increasing vocal concerns about human rights, civil rights, and civil liberties—for American citizens, immigrants, and prisoners of war—the U.S. government has aggressively pursued the war on terrorism and has expanded its political powers. This has resulted in many unfortunate incidents and potential violations of civil rights and liberties for many Americans and immigrants. The understandable emotional reactions throughout the country, the manifestation of American nationalism (and superpatriotism?), and the overall rally-round-the-flag phenomenon have made many people, including American citizens, fearful to offer anything other then uncritical support, especially in the months immediately following the September 11 attacks.

Nowhere was the emotional reaction, political support, and potential intolerance clearer than in a *New York Times*/CBS News poll taken immediately after the attacks on September 13 and 14.[44] Eighty-five percent of Americans agreed that the United States should "take military action against whoever is responsible for the attacks." Sixty-four percent agreed "even if innocent people are killed." Sixty-three percent agreed "even if it means going to war with a nation that is harboring those responsible for the attacks." Most of this is quite understandable given the immense tragedy, the destruction of the World Trade Center towers (symbolic of New York and American capitalism), the damage to the Pentagon (symbolic of Washington, D.C., the U.S. government, and the military) and perhaps most important, the thousands of innocent victims. This is probably similar to how most people would respond within most societies if faced with comparable events.

But the response to one question is potentially ominous, for it indicates the incredible emotions triggered and the need for vengeance as well as for mourning: 58 percent agreed that the United States should take military action "even if it means many thousands of innocent civilians may be killed." The global war on terrorism is supposed to be about the prevention of at-

tacks and the protection of innocent civilians—in the United States certainly but also throughout the world. Such willingness to allow thousands of innocent civilians to be killed in retaliation for September 11 allows for the potential for considerable public intolerance and governmental abuse of the civil rights and liberties of individuals. In a very telling personal anecdote, after tiring of watching the repetitive news coverage of the September 11 attacks, my mother (born in Florence, Italy, raised under Mussolini, having to live under German and American occupation and bombings, who became a war bride and an American citizen) explained the American reaction (or overreaction) in a single sentence: "Americans do not know what it is to be bombed!"

One could see and feel the national sentiment, even on college and university campuses throughout the country, where so-called "academic freedom" and critical thinking are supposed to be protected and encouraged. Arab students in the U.S. went home by the hundreds, citing growing hostility. "Federal investigators have contacted administrators on more than 200 college campuses to collect information about students from Middle Eastern countries, the most sweeping canvass of the halls of academia since the cold war, the colleges say."[45] Not only do dissenters find colleges less tolerant, but professors who criticize the U.S. government or society find little tolerance for their views—and some have actually been fired. According to the *Chronicle of Higher Education*, "Assaults on foreign students are by far the most notorious offenses. But a more subtle form of attack has also emerged, as professors across the country have found their freedom to speak out hemmed in by incensed students, alumni, and university officials. . . . Emotions [are] so raw that people are struggling to think critically about what happened—and some administrators would prefer that professors not even try."[46] As a professor of international studies for over twenty years at a major public university, for the first time in my career, following the September 11 attacks, I felt that I had to walk a tightrope between trying to conduct a reasonable, intelligent, and informative discussion about the tragedy while not triggering a politically correct backlash.

The U.S. government and Bush administration have taken political advantage of this American sentiment and domestic environment. As of 2002, more than twelve hundred people have been detained in the

United States, although only a handful are believed to have ties to Al Qaeda. Over fifty-two hundred young male visitors from the Middle East who entered the country within the past two years have been interviewed. Altogether, the FBI is conducting more than 150 separate investigations into various groups in the United States. "The domestic targets include dozens of people who are under electronic surveillance through national security warrants, and others who are being watched by undercover agents attempting to learn more about their activities and associates." Over hundreds of thousands of tips have been received by the FBI and intelligence agencies (called officially Operation Tips). The CIA also has passed information on to foreign intelligence services, which have had more than hundreds of suspected terrorists arrested or detained abroad. Yet only one man has been charged by the U.S. government so far in connection with the September 11 plot.

Another controversial program is the effort to create the Information Awareness Office in the Pentagon to implement the "Total Information Awareness" project to develop a centralized grand database. According to conservative columnist William Safire, "In the name of combating terrorism, it would scoop up your lifetime paper trail—bank records, medical files, credit card purchases, academic records, etc.—and marry them to every nosy neighbor's gossip [under Operation Tips] to the FBI about you." This was made even more controversial by "entrusting this dangerous surveillance to one Admiral John Poindexter. He was convicted of five felony counts of lying to Congress about Iran-Contra, but the jury's verdict was overturned because Congress had immunized him." Clearly, many consider the Bush administration to be the most secretive since the cold war and unresponsive to Congress's and the public's right to be informed.[47]

Arab Americans, in particular, feel that they have to be particularly careful and are unfairly targeted as potential terrorists. As a *Newsweek* article entitled "What Price Security?" pointed out: "Here is why profiling is so alluring: of the suspected skyjackers responsible for upwards of 3,000 deaths on Sept. 11, 19 out of 19 were Arab. And here is why profiling is anathema to a just society: more than 3 million Arab-Americans live in the United States. Even if the government's worst fears are correct and 50 members of terrorist cells remain at large, that means that 99.99 percent of Arab-

Americans" are not connected to terrorism (see **table 14.1** for the demographics of Arab Americans and Muslims in America). What is particularly interesting, and surprising, concerning Arab American demographics is that despite the growth and increasing popularity of Islam in the United States, only 23 percent of Arab Americans are estimated to be of the Muslim faith—over 75 percent are Christians.[48]

The complexity of Islam and the Arab American community has rarely been sufficiently communicated and explained to the American people. This is in part because "the recent expansion of executive power in the legal fight against terrorism reflects a powerful conviction in the Bush Administration that it is fighting acts of war, not mere crimes, on American soil."[49] But as the months pass since September 11, as new revelations become publicized (such as the information that the intelligence community and the Bush administration had of the possibility of the terrorist attacks), as other issues compete for a place on the public agenda (such as the state of the economy), and as the president's public approval ratings tend to drop, the demands of national security are likely to diminish while the exercise of civil rights and civil liberties, including public dissent and critical information, are likely to increase.

Ultimately, much will depend on how the following questions are eventually addressed by the American political process: Will Bush Jr.'s war on terrorism, including with Iraq, resonate in the long run within the domestic political environment and especially among the American people? Will people feel it's a time of war and national emergency? If so, the result will likely be greater presidential power and greater ability to exercise prerogative government in the name of national security. Or will people feel that it is "war in a time of peace," with diminishing fears and concerns about the threat of terrorism. If so, the likelihood will be greater that the demands of democracy will resurface, making violations of civil rights and liberties more politically controversial and damaging.

The answers are unclear; the future remains uncertain. Much will depend on events and reactions, especially concerning the frequency and intensity of future terrorist attacks by foreigners on Americans and on American soil. Such uncertainty means that there will be an uneasy and changing tension and balance between the demands of national security and the demands of democracy. The future of many people's civil

TABLE 14.1
ARAB AMERICAN DEMOGRAPHICS, 2001

LARGEST ARAB AMERICAN COMMUNITIES

AREA	POPULATION
Los Angeles, CA	283,355
New York, NY	162,692
Northeastern, NJ	92,080
Chicago, IL	91,260
Washington, DC	69,350

MOSQUE AFFILIATION

	1994	2000
Total number of mosques	962	1,209
Muslims per mosque	485	1,625
Total affiliated Muslims	500,000	2 million

ARAB AMERICAN FAITHS

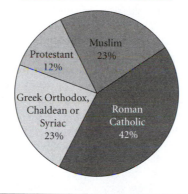

SOURCE: Newsweek (October 1, 2001).

rights and liberties hang in the balance, with important consequences for U.S. foreign policy and political participation, especially with respect to electoral and group politics—the topics of the next two chapters.

SUGGESTED SOURCES FOR MORE INFORMATION

The relationship between national security and the exercise of civil liberties and the study of political partici- pation have received considerable attention, although little of this work has been integrated in the traditional scholarship on U.S. foreign policy. A good overview of government efforts during the twentieth century to limit the exercise of civil liberties by Americans with respect to U.S. foreign policy can be found in Frank J. Donner, *The Age of Surveillance: The Aims and Methods of America's Political Intelligence System* (New York: Vintage, 1981). Richard Hofstadter provides provocative insights into the vulnerability of American political culture to intolerance and repression in *The Paranoid Style in American Politics and Other Essays* (New York: Knopf, 1965). An excellent discussion concerning the dynamics of dehumanizing the enemy in the context of World War II is provided by John W. Dower in *War Without Mercy: Race and Power in the Pacific War* (New York: Pantheon, 1986).

David Caute exhaustively documents the consequences of the politics of anticommunism on civil liberties during the cold war years in *The Great Fear: The Anti-Communist Purge Under Truman and Eisenhower* (New York: Simon and Schuster, 1978). The impact within higher education is well told by Ellen W. Schrecker in *No Ivory Tower: McCarthyism and the Universities* (New York: Oxford University Press, 1986). The role of the Truman administration in contributing to the politics of anticommunism is told by Richard M. Freeland in *The Truman Doctrine and the Origins of McCarthyism: Foreign Policy, Domestic Politics, and Internal Security, 1946–1948* (New York: Knopf, 1972). McCarthyism as an elite-led phenomena is further demonstrated by James L. Gibson, in "Political Intolerance and Political Repression During the McCarthy Red Scare," *American Political Science Review* 82 (June 1988): 511–29, and Michael Paul Rogin, *The Intellectuals and McCarthy: The Radical Specter* (Cambridge, Mass.: MIT Press, 1967).

David H. Bennett provides the historical context for understanding the politics of anticommunism embedded in the political right in *The Party of Fear: From Nativist Movements to the New Right in American History* (Chapel Hill: University of North Carolina Press, 1988). Herbert McClosky and Alida Brill discuss public beliefs about civil liberties since the Vietnam War in *Dimensions of Tolerance: What Americans Believe About Civil Liberties* (New York: Russell Sage Foundation, 1983). The implications of the end of the cold war for the exercise of civil liberties relative to the demands of national security are discussed by Morton H. Halperin and Jeanne M. Woods in "Ending the Cold War at Home," *Foreign Policy* 81 (Winter 1990–91): 128–43, and Kate Doyle in "The End of Secrecy: U.S. National Security and the Imperative for Openness," *World Policy Journal* (spring 1999): 34–51. For the implications of September 11, see Scott Carlson and Andrea L. Foster, "Colleges Fear Anti-Terrorism Could Turn Them Into Big Brother," *Chronicle of Higher Education* (March 1, 2002),

www.chronicle.com; Dan Cook, "Patriotism Perverted: September 11 and the Erosion of American Liberty," *Free Times* (July 3–9, 2002), www.free-times.com, and Jim McGee, "An Intelligence Giant in the Making; Anti-Terrorism Law Likely to Bring Domestic Apparatus of Unprecedented Scope," *The Washington Post* (November 4, 2001).

KEY TERMS

anticommunist hysteria
atomic testing program
Bill of Rights
citizenship and civic duty
civil liberties
civil rights
Committee on Public Information (CPI)
Declaration of Independence
dehumanization process
dualism of freedom and intolerance
Espionage Act of 1917
First Amendment
Germanic "Hun"
House Un-American Activities Committee's investigation of the Hollywood Ten
Italian immigrants and Italian Americans
Japanese Americans
Operation Cointelpro
paranoid style in American politics
political efficacy and trust
political participation
Posse Comitatus Act
propaganda campaign
racial profiling
Red Scare
Sedition Act of 1918
Smith Act
Socialist party
USA Patriot Act
Wen Ho Lee case

CHAPTER
15

. . . .

ELECTORAL POLITICS

The public participates in the political process and influences the making of U.S. foreign policy in two basic ways. The public may participate in electoral politics, which is the focus of this chapter, or in group politics, which is the focus of the next chapter. Both of these forms of political participation influence U.S. foreign policy making through their general impact on the domestic political environment and immediate impact on the policymaking process. But strangely, most students and scholars of U.S. foreign policy tend to ignore and downplay the role of electoral politics. But if one assumes that who is president is important and that members of Congress are also important in the making of foreign policy, then how one becomes president and a member of Congress (as well as a state and local official) is important, as well. Therefore, the importance of electoral politics.

Elections and campaign politics clearly affect continuity and change, presidential governance, and the tensions between national security and democracy in the making of U.S. foreign policy. The elections of 2000 should have made this more than obvious. Following the actual elections in November, the country and the world did not know who was the next president of the United States for weeks. Even though it remains unclear as to who actually won the presidency, the Supreme Court made a consequential decision in a 5–4 vote that determined the outcome. Republican George W. Bush, not Democrat Al Gore, would be the next president. The Republicans not only won the White House but maintained control of both chambers of Congress. But within a few months, a senator from Vermont would switch from the Republican party to Independent status, giving the Democrats 51–49 majority control and the United States divided government once again.

What difference did the election outcomes of 2000 make for U.S. foreign policy in a post–cold war world and following the September 11 bombings? Would some aspects of U.S. foreign policy have been different under a Gore presidency? Would a Republican-dominated Congress have made any difference? Probably, but we will never know how much, and we will never know for sure.

This chapter will discuss the following questions: Why are elections important and not to be ignored in the making of U.S. foreign policy? What is the nature of the American party system and electoral process? What have been the three dominant electoral patterns since the 1900s and their impact on foreign policy? And what is the contemporary nature of electoral and campaign politics? Hopefully, by the end of the chapter it will be clear that electoral politics does in fact play an important part in the politics of U.S. foreign policy.

THE ELECTION SURPRISE OF 1992

The presidential election of 1992 was an incredible surprise. In the words of David Halberstam, in *War in a Time of Peace*, "For a brief, glorious, almost Olympian moment it appeared that the presidency itself could serve as the campaign. Rarely had an American president seemed so sure of reelection. In the summer and fall of 1991, George Bush appeared to be politically invincible." In fact, "his personal approval ratings in the aftermath of the Persian Gulf War had reached 90 percent, unheard of for any sitting president, and even more remarkable for someone like Bush, a competent political insider whose charisma and capacity to inspire had in the past escaped most of his fellow citizens." As depicted by Halberstam, "The stunning success of the American units in the Persian Gulf War, the cool efficiency of their weapons and the almost immediate collapse of the Iraqi forces, had been savored by most Americans as more than a victory over an Arab nation about which they knew little and which had invaded a small, autocratic, oil-producing duchy about which they knew even less," especially after the tragedy and legacy of Vietnam and the humiliation of the Iranian hostage crisis.[1] In such a political environment, most potential Democratic candidates decided not to run for the nomination and challenge the sitting president.

But everything was not as clear at it seemed. "By the summer and fall of 1991, the polls had begun to show a potential vulnerability for Bush. His personal ratings still remained high, but there was a growing public restlessness about the direction of the economy and therefore of the country." In reality, "it was a war without real resonance. The actual land combat had lasted just four days, and it had been conducted by an elite professional army, thereby touching relatively few American homes. For much of the country it was a kind of virtual war, something few people were engaged in or had sacrificed for. Thus, like many things celebrated in the modern media, it was distant and oddly nonparticipatory; when it was over, it was over, leaving remarkably little trace."[2]

"Thus, a critical election year would begin with Americans bothered by the state of the economy and yearning for benefits from the end of the Cold War, and with George Bush under assault from a Democratic challenger for paying too much attention to foreign policy and too little to domestic policy."[3] So George Bush not only was challenged but defeated, and the next president of the United States was William Jefferson Clinton from the state of Arkansas.

POLITICAL PARTIES AND THE ELECTORAL PROCESS

According to the traditional wisdom concerning the role of the public, electoral politics can be dismissed in the making of U.S. foreign policy. This is consistent with the notion that "politics stops at the water's edge." But clearly, "foreign policy, like domestic policy, does not take place in a political vacuum."[4] Who gets elected, and the underlying electoral patterns that affect party politics, cannot be divorced from the politics of U.S. foreign policy. Certainly the presidential elections of 1992 and 2000 have made that pretty clear. Therefore, an examination of the electoral process is required to achieve a comprehensive understanding of the politics of U.S. foreign policy.

The electoral process directly involves political parties, candidates competing for governmental offices, and an electorate—that is, members of the public—choosing between party candidates through voting. The United States historically has had a **two-party system,** with the Democratic and Republican parties competing for political power. Each party represents a broad coalition of leaders, active participants, and regular party voters. These coalitions attempt to attract mass support for their parties by nominating appealing candidates for office and putting forth a program of attractive policy proposals, referred to as the "party platform."

Because of the U.S. federal system of government, there are fifty-one Democratic and fifty-one Republican parties—one in each state and one at the national level. The national organization is the nominal head of the party, but the overall party structure is decentralized, and the strongest party organizations are at the state level. As we focus on foreign policy, we are primarily interested in party and electoral politics at the national level, but activity at the state level does affect national politics as well.

In addition to the two major parties, the United States has a long tradition of **third parties.**[5] Though they tend to be relatively short-lived, third parties have affected electoral politics by presenting alternative programs and choices for the public and by influencing the leadership and programs of the two major parties. In fact, as Martin Wattenberg suggests, third-party candidates have become more prominent recently—indicative of the party changes and volatility of the public that have taken place since the 1960s:

> In the hundred years from 1864 to 1964 there were only three elections in which the presidential candidate of a minor party received more than 5 percent of the vote. Since then this threshold has been exceeded by George Wallace [in 1968], John Anderson [in 1980], and Ross Perot. Recently, for the first time ever, a third-party candidate—Perot—garnered more than 5 percent in two consecutive elections: 19 percent in 1992 and 8 percent in 1996.[6]

Furthermore, third-party candidates may draw votes away (assuming those voters would have gone to the polls anyway) from the major party candidates, impacting the presidential election outcome, as Ross Perot may have done for Clinton in 1992 and 1996 and Ralph Nader's 2 percent of the vote may have done for George Bush Jr. in 2000.

The Democratic and Republican parties, nevertheless, consistently have been the key to gaining political office. Therefore, political leaders such as the president are not only sensitive to electoral politics but attempt to influence it as well. Interest groups and social movements also attempt to influence electoral politics as a means of impacting society and the government.

Electoral politics influences the making of U.S. foreign policy in two major ways. First and most obviously, as discussed in earlier chapters, the outcomes of elections determine presidents and members of Congress. Because elected officials are significant policymakers and because they recruit personnel for critical positions

within the executive, legislative, and judicial branches of government, elections are an important source of influence. In the words of Robert Strauss, a prominent Democratic party leader over the years, "presidential campaigns are particularly important for foreign policy because of the pre-eminent role the eventual winner plays in guiding the country's fortunes abroad."[7] Once in office, elected officials also tend to remain very sensitive to domestic and electoral politics throughout their tenure, especially as election time approaches. Although traditional foreign policy and national security issues rarely are as prominent as domestic, especially economic, issues in affecting voter participation and choice, foreign policy, nevertheless, is "a prism through which voters judge the basic soundness of a candidate to govern the country."[8] And economic issues are increasingly recognized to be intermestic—having an international as well as a domestic side.

Second, the outcomes of elections also establish longer-term **electoral cycles** that influence domestic politics in society. Elections determine the relative power of the parties and the ideological predispositions of party leaders and the electorate and affect the general beliefs of the public, which are consequential for policymaking, as discussed. Both the immediate and longer-term effects of electoral politics impact and reinforce one another. Together, they tend to indirectly affect the governmental policymaking process by affecting the domestic politics of U.S. foreign policy.[9]

ELECTORAL PATTERNS OVER TIME

As with legislative-executive relations or public beliefs, the American two-party system has been dynamic, evolving through history. A brief overview of major electoral patterns over time allows for a better understanding of how domestic and electoral politics affect the governmental policymaking process in the making of U.S. foreign policy. *Party politics have progressed through three major stages or cycles during the twentieth century:* (1) The 1930s were a time of party realignment, in which the Democratic party became the majority party and the party of liberalism. (2) The cold war era was a time of bipartisanship in party politics, especially in foreign policy, where a liberal-conservative consensus prevailed. (3) The post–Vietnam War era has been a time of party dealignment, in which no majority party exists, the Democratic party tends to represent liberalism and the Republican party tends to represent conservatism, and both parties compete for an increasingly independent and apathetic voter.[10]

THE NEW DEAL REALIGNMENT

From the end of the Civil War until the Roaring Twenties, the Republican party was the majority party in American national politics. At the national level, this meant that a majority of representatives from the Senate and the House of Representatives tended to be Republican and Republican candidates were more successful than Democrats in gaining the presidency. At the state level, the Republican party also prevailed in parts of the country where there were strong two-party systems. Because of the Republican party's association with the abolition of slavery and support for Reconstruction, the Democratic party dominated the electoral process and politics only in the South.

The Republican party was in power under President Herbert Hoover when the Great Depression hit, following the 1929 stock market crash. Companies went bankrupt, individuals went broke, and as much as one-third of the workforce became unemployed. It was an economic disaster for the country and a time of great misery for large numbers of Americans. In these deteriorating conditions, the public turned against the Republican administration and its laissez-faire approach to the Depression. Thus, the **1932 election** victory of Democratic challenger Franklin Roosevelt reflected the loss of voter confidence in President Hoover and his policies. The public clearly opposed the status quo and supported the only viable alternative—Roosevelt and the Democratic party.

Unlike his predecessor, President Roosevelt instituted active government involvement in the economy designed to pull the country out of the Depression. Roosevelt's first hundred days in office produced the most active legislative agenda in American history. His administration attempted to create a "New Deal" through which most Americans could get back on their feet and take advantage of restored economic prosperity. New Deal policies were an invaluable aid to many Americans; however, they did not completely pull the country out of

the Depression—World War II accomplished that task. Nevertheless, for many Americans, especially the working class, the unemployed, and the poor, Roosevelt was a calm, reassuring, and hopeful voice about the future. Hence, Franklin Roosevelt and the Democratic party were rewarded with reelection in 1936, 1940, and 1944—an unprecedented four terms for an American president.

In the aftermath of the Great Depression, a political realignment occurred. **Realignment** refers here to a change in the majority and minority status of political parties.[11] Before the Great Depression, the Democratic party was the minority party. After the Depression, however, the Democratic party became the majority party under Franklin Roosevelt. Democrats won not only the presidency but also majority control in both houses of Congress from Republicans.

What happened was that a large number of established voters switched their allegiance or support from the Republican party to the Democratic party, while most new (usually younger) voters identified with the Democratic party. The Democratic party came to be seen as the party of hope and prosperity by most Americans, while the Republican party was seen as the party of the Depression. Thus, the **Democratic New Deal coalition** was born. The newfound strength of the Democratic party was reinforced by World War II, a second national emergency, in which President Roosevelt successfully led the allies to victory against Japan, Germany, and fascism. Thus, the economic war at home and the war abroad acted as catalysts for strong political leadership under Franklin Roosevelt and strong support for the Democratic party.

The Great Depression created major ideological splits, discussed in chapter 13, that we now associate with current-day liberalism and conservatism. The New Deal and the Democratic party came to symbolize a more active governmental role in avoiding depression, regulating the economy, and assisting the disadvantaged—the liberal position. The Republican party continued to emphasize reliance on the private market and a more laissez-faire governmental role within the political economy—the more conservative orientation. Thus, the rise of the Democratic party during the realigning era of the 1930s and early 1940s represented the rise of liberalism throughout American society and the policymaking process.

More important, given our concern with foreign policy, the election of Franklin Roosevelt and the ascendance of the Democratic party in national elections resulted in the rise of a liberal internationalist orientation in foreign affairs. Although isolationist sentiments favoring minimal political and military involvement in European politics and affairs were historically pervasive throughout the country, Franklin Roosevelt was an internationalist. Roosevelt approached world politics from a pragmatic perspective, yet he also represented the quest for global peace, cooperation, and prosperity symbolized by the principles of the Atlantic Charter and the formation of the United Nations (see chapter 2).

Hence, American involvement in World War II resulted in the beginning of the end of isolationism and the rise of a liberal internationalist perspective associated with Roosevelt and the Democratic party, while the Republican party remained the bastion of isolationist sentiment. This was a significant juncture in the history of U.S. foreign policy. In this respect, the election of Franklin Roosevelt and the ascendance of the Democratic party—in other words, electoral politics—deeply affected the making of U.S. foreign policy and contributed to the United States pursuing an active internationalist policy following the end of World War II.

THE PERIOD OF BIPARTISANSHIP

The New Deal realignment lasted through the 1950s and 1960s. Most members of the public continued to identify with the Democratic party and, throughout much of this time, Democrats controlled Congress and the presidency (as well as most statehouses and governorships). Following the war, however, a bitter fight erupted between Democratic and Republican leaders for national power and control of the government. The Democratic majority held, though only narrowly, and the conflict soon evolved into a bipartisan relationship between the two parties by the mid-1950s, resulting in the formation of a liberal-conservative ideological consensus during the height of the cold war. As will soon be discussed, even though the Democratic party remained the majority party, Democratic leaders worked closely with the Republican leadership, for the party no longer represented liberalism to the extent that it had during the 1930s and early 1940s, particularly in the area of foreign policy. Thus, electoral politics contributed to the rise and durability of the ideological and foreign policy consensus that laid the foundation for the making of U.S. foreign policy during the cold war.

On April 12, 1945, President Franklin Roosevelt died of a cerebral hemorrhage. The man who occupied the presidency for thirteen years and guided the United States through the Depression and World War II had fallen. Harry Truman, Roosevelt's vice president, was thrust into the presidency at a crucial time when he would be responsible for leading the country during the postwar years. Although Truman was not a part of Roosevelt's inner circle or privy to Roosevelt's postwar intentions, he would make decisions over the next few years that would be consequential in leading the United States into a cold war based on a policy of containment.

Would Roosevelt have taken the same course of action? Many have speculated that Roosevelt's foreign policy experience and liberal internationalism might have minimized the level of hostility that eventually arose between the United States and the Soviet Union. Yet we will never know, for Roosevelt's untimely death is one of many historic twists of fate. What we do know, however, is that the **selection of vice president**, Missouri Senator Harry Truman, was a compromise choice by Franklin Roosevelt to balance the presidential ticket in the 1944 elections. In fact, Harry Truman replaced Henry Wallace, Roosevelt's former vice president, who soon became the champion of liberal internationalism and cooperation with the Soviet Union during the postwar years. In this very subtle and roundabout way, electoral politics was instrumental in having Harry Truman occupy the White House in the critical postwar years.

With the death of Roosevelt, the restoration of economic prosperity, the end of World War II, and growing concern over the Soviet Union, the Democratic coalition became unstable and the party's control of government was vulnerable. A political counterattack was mounted during the **1946 elections** by conservatives and the Republican party—the party that was opposed to the New Deal at home and Roosevelt's and Truman's postwar internationalist policies abroad. Republican campaigners had a field day with the slogan, "Had enough?": "Got enough inflation? Got enough debt? Got enough strikes? Got enough communism?" Many of the electoral campaigns during this time took the form of "red-baiting"—accusing the opponent of being a communist, a fellow traveler, or just generally being "soft" on communism. A young man in California, for example, named Richard Nixon denounced his Democratic liberal opponent as a "lip service American" who consistently voted the Moscow line in Congress and who "fronted for un-American elements . . . by advocating increased federal control over the lives of people."[12] The outcome of the 1946 elections were important because the Republicans finally were successful in capturing control of Congress; among the victors were Richard Nixon and Joseph McCarthy.

The **1948 elections** looked like another impending disaster for the Democrats with the party splitting between Truman; the Dixiecrats, led by Strom Thurmond; and Henry Wallace, leading the progressive forces. Miraculously, Truman shocked the country with his surprise reelection victory over Republican Thomas Dewey, while the Democratic party regained majority control of Congress in 1948. Much of Truman's success in overcoming Henry Wallace and his liberal support was, as revealed in presidential aide Clark Clifford's famous election memo of 1947, "to identify and isolate him [Wallace] in the public mind with the communists."[13] Although successful, Truman's campaign strategy legitimized and intensified the politics of anticommunism that led to a Republican resurgence in 1952.

Red-baiting was most prominent and effective during the **1952 elections,** a banner year for the Republican party. Republicans were successful in gaining a narrow majority in Congress: 48 Republicans to 47 Democrats in the Senate; 221 Republicans to 213 Democrats in the House. But regardless of the size of their majority, it gave Republicans the ability to dominate the organization and workings of Congress. This was accomplished with an electoral change of just 1 seat in the Senate and 21 seats in the House in favor of the Republicans. (Before the election, the Democratic majority was 48 to 47 in the Senate and 234 to 199 in the House.) Yet, these electoral shifts in 1946 and, in particular, 1952 produced Republican ascendance in Congress that was consequential to the rise of the politics of anticommunism and McCarthyism. In this way, electoral politics had a major impact on foreign policy attitudes and behavior in the post–World War II era.

Nineteen fifty-two was also the year in which the Republican party was finally successful in capturing the presidency around the anti-Democratic themes of "Korea, communism, and corruption." Dwight Eisenhower charged the Democratic party and their presidential nominee, Adlai Stevenson, with bartering "away freedom in order to appease the Russian rulers."[14] He also selected Richard Nixon as his vice presidential running mate, to appease the political Right, who constantly attacked the Democratic party and their presidential nominee Adlai Stevenson as the bearer of "more Alger Hisses, more atomic spies, more crises."[15] At the same time, the victory of Eisenhower, a moderate conservative, played an important role in the development of a liberal-conservative ideological and foreign policy consensus by the mid-1950s.

The key to the consensus that transpired during the Eisenhower administration was that the political forces of liberalism and McCarthyism both declined as most Democrats became more conservative in their foreign policy views while most Republicans became more liberal in their political and economic views. Whereas McCarthyism succeeded in ravaging the Democratic party and Truman administration, its anticommunist attacks increasingly lost credibility with Republican ascendance and a popular World War II hero in the White House. Nevertheless, Democrats and liberals became more conservative because the cold war and the challenge of McCarthyism forced them to become ardent anticommunists. Conversely, with prosperity restored by Democratic leadership and New Deal policies, Republicans came to accept more governmental involvement in the economy and a limited welfare state. Hence, the election of Dwight Eisenhower, rather than sharpening Democratic-Republican differences, acted as a catalyst for a liberal-conservative consensus based on anticommunism and a limited welfare capitalist political economy.[16]

The growing ideological consensus produced considerable **bipartisanship** in party politics—following the previous intense partisanship between Republicans and Democrats. Bipartisanship existed predominantly in foreign policy, which further reinforced the cold war consensus in the making of U.S. foreign policy. Thus, where electoral politics were instrumental in the early postwar years in contributing to the rise of global containment, McCarthyism, and the formation of a foreign policy consensus, by the mid-1950s electoral politics acted to reinforce these trends into the late 1960s. Leaders from both parties were strong anticommunists who supported the containment policy and American reliance on the use of force abroad. Not surprisingly, candidates for political office nominated by both parties tended to have strong "anticommunist credentials." This was particularly the case in presidential elections, in which the consensus and bipartisan years produced American presidents who were strong cold warriors in one form or another.

The **1960 presidential election** illustrates how the liberal-conservative consensus permeated electoral politics. John F. Kennedy was the Democratic nominee and Richard M. Nixon was the Republican nominee for president. Kennedy was Irish Catholic, born to a wealthy and prominent New England family, and schooled at Harvard University. He was also handsome, polished, charismatic, and charming. Nixon was a Californian from a very modest background who became a lawyer and rose to the top of the political world. He was also a scrapper and political infighter, more comfortable with politics played behind closed doors. Yet these were differences of personality and style, not substance.

The first live television debates revealed that, although Kennedy was more impressive than Nixon, both were cold warriors. Each attempted to demonstrate that he was more anticommunist than the other. On domestic issues Kennedy may have been more liberal, or less conservative, than Nixon; on foreign policy issues, however, it was a choice between two similar variants of anticommunism and cold war policies. In *America in Our Time*, Godfrey Hodgson further elaborates upon the consensus nature of the 1960 race:

> The fact remains that they did share the same basic political assumptions: the primacy of foreign over domestic issues, the paramount importance of containing communism, the reign of consensus in domestic affairs, the need to assert the supremacy of the White House as the command post of a society mobilized to meet external danger. So did their staff and advisers. And so, too, did their running mates and closest rivals: Lyndon Johnson and Henry Cabot Lodge, Hubert Humphrey and Nelson Rockefeller, and everyone else who might conceivably have been nominated as a presidential candidate in that year by either the Democrats or by the Republicans.[17]

Such was the case throughout the 1950s and 1960s. Political campaigning between the candidates and between the parties was as intense as ever, but differences between the candidates' beliefs and policies were minimal, especially in the realm of foreign policy. There was much truth to the phrase, although over-

stated, that there wasn't "a dime's worth of difference" between the Democratic and Republican candidates—such as Adlai Stevenson and Dwight Eisenhower in 1952 and 1956, and Kennedy and Nixon in 1960—particularly in the area of foreign policy. There may have been choices between different personalities and parties, but there was not much difference between worldviews or programs. This ideological consensus and party bipartisanship that developed during the cold war helps to explain the rise of presidential power, an acquiescent Congress, and a compliant public in the making of U.S. foreign policy. Thus, electoral politics contributed to the development of a twenty-year period of foreign policy continuity in which cold war policies prevailed, from Harry Truman to Lyndon Johnson. It was a time in which differences between the parties did not mean much in foreign policy—three of the presidents were Democratic and one was Republican.

Only in the 1964 presidential election was there much difference; and, *once again, the political challenge came from the right*. Lyndon Johnson, who became president following the assassination of John F. Kennedy, represented the liberal-conservative consensus, while Republican nominee **Barry Goldwater** represented unabashed conservatism. Goldwater and the conservative right successfully gained control of the Republican party and argued for a more hard-line approach to contain and roll back communism, including a more aggressive stance in Vietnam. Although Goldwater lost in a landslide election (receiving less than 37 percent of the vote), he was the darling of the political right. More importantly, in the minds of established leaders within the Johnson administration and the Democratic party, the 1964 election also reinforced the importance of sensitivity to the political threat posed by the political right, and the comparative unimportance of the political left.

Lyndon Johnson, in particular, seemed forever preoccupied with the political threat posed by the right. Fear of the rise of the political right—as occurred after the so-called "fall" of China in 1949—is what motivated so many American political leaders like him to do what was necessary to prevent South Vietnam from falling to communism in the future. "I am not going to lose Vietnam," President Johnson said upon taking office. "I am not going to be the President who saw Southeast Asia go the way China went." As

David Halberstam explained how Lyndon Johnson saw his predicament in *The Best and the Brightest*:

> If he seemed weak as a President in dealing with Vietnam, he was sure it would undermine him politically. Hell, Truman and Acheson had lost China, and maybe it wasn't their fault, but they were blamed for it, and when it happened the Republicans in Congress were waiting and jumped on it, and Truman lost the Congress and then the country—it hadn't happened over domestic issues, remember that, he said, and Truman and Acheson were as strong anticommunists as anyone he knew. Well, he did not want the blame for losing Vietnam.[18]

In this way national and electoral politics reaffirmed the cold war consensus among most political leaders and the need for Democrats to avoid the charge of being soft on communism abroad.

THE POST—VIETNAM DEALIGNMENT ERA

The stable party alignment that began in the 1930s and lasted through the 1960s could not withstand the upheavals of the civil rights movement, the Vietnam War, Watergate, and other events of the times. *Three critical post–Vietnam developments occurred*:

1. The increase of independent voters created a movement toward party dealignment in which a majority party no longer existed;
2. A regional realignment occurred in the South that rejuvenated the Republican party; and
3. Bipartisanship collapsed and was replaced by greater ideological diversity between the Democratic and Republican parties.

These patterns have increasingly led to changes in party control of the executive and legislative branches over time and the rise of divided government, contributing to the politics of U.S. foreign policy that has come to predominate since the Vietnam War.[19]

First, there has been a large increase in independent voters producing party **dealignment**—as opposed to a party realignment—in which a majority party no longer exists. During the 1960s, 1970s, and 1980s, voters increasingly abandoned the Democratic party. However, they did not register Republican; instead,

most became "independent" of any party, and some dropped out of the electoral process entirely. While more people continued to register with the Democratic party than the Republican party, both became minority parties. **Independent voters** predominated, and overall voter turnout declined. Hence, the turmoil of the 1960s and early 1970s did not create a party realignment in which a new majority party emerged, as occurred during the 1930s; rather, what occurred was a process of party dealignment, in which party identification weakened and no majority party prevailed.[20]

The second important electoral development is that at the regional level a party **realignment in the South** has taken place. Until the 1960s, the South was dominated by the Democratic party, representing the party's more conservative wing. With the rise of the civil rights and anti–Vietnam War movements and increasing liberalism of the Democratic party, however, white southerners (especially males) began to turn their party allegiance and support away from the Democratic party. As James MacGregor Burns explains,

> Behind FDR's leadership the Democrats became much more of an urban, trade union, ethnic, and poor people's party, but . . . it retained its old and solid base in the white South. Truman's bold civil rights stance, Kennedy's Catholicism and growing commitment to civil rights, and LBJ's comprehensive civil rights program accelerated the reconstitution of the party. Blacks forsook their ancient allegiance to the Republican party of Lincoln and flocked to the Democratic party; white southern Democrats [moved] first toward third-party ventures and then toward their old partisan adversaries, the Republicans.[21]

This regional realignment over the years has produced two patterns. At the state and local levels, a two-party system was reborn in most parts of the South by the 1980s—the Republican party now became competitive with the Democratic party. A more important development, given our focus on foreign policy, occurred at the national level, where the South became a strong supporter of the Republican party, most visibly in presidential elections.[22]

This southern realignment at the presidential level first became noticeable during the Goldwater candidacy in 1964. Although Barry Goldwater was badly beaten by Lyndon Johnson, he received considerable support throughout the South. Since that time, the South has been crucial for every Republican presidential victory from Nixon to Bush Jr. The Republican advantage has been due to greater receptivity in the South to conservative "valence" issues, such as an emphasis on "anti–big government" at home and national security "strength" abroad.[23]

The critical role of southern realignment in presidential elections is due in part to the existence of the **electoral college.** The presidential candidate with the most votes within a state receives *all* the electors for that state (equal to the state's number of senators and representatives in Congress), and a majority of the electors then officially chooses the next president. A strong Republican South means that Republican presidential candidates have a strong hold on over one-fourth of the electors—representing more than half of those necessary for election—and require victories in only a few other states outside the South to win. This is obviously a major handicap for Democratic efforts to win the White House. Not surprisingly, the only Dem-

ocratic successes in the post–Vietnam War years have been southerners: Jimmy Carter, from Georgia, in 1976 and Bill Clinton, from Arkansas, in 1992 and 1996. If Al Gore from Tennessee—a border state—would have won a single state in the South (including Tennessee), he would have become president in 2001 (see the presidential electoral results for each state in **figure 15.1**).

Southern realignment took a longer time to impact the composition of Congress than it did the presidency, because both chambers were overwhelmingly Democratic by the 1970s and most constituents tend to reelect their representatives. This reflects the power of congressional incumbency—that members of Congress running for reelection are usually safe from potential challengers.[24] One reason for this is that the fund-raising gap between incumbents and challengers is greater than ever. A Federal Election Commission study found that in the final days of 1990 elections, for example, congressional incumbents had twenty times more money to spend than did their challengers: $120 million to $6 million. Of the 406 House members seeking

FIGURE **15.1**
2000 PRESIDENTIAL ELECTORAL VOTE BY STATE

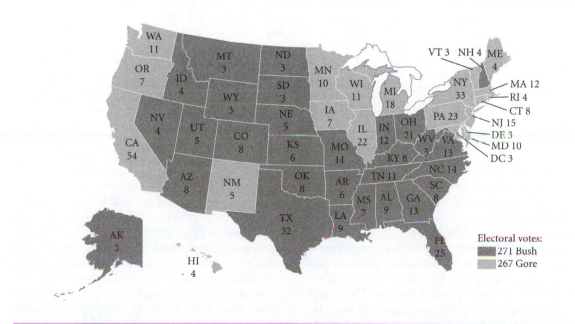

reelection, 178 were considered "financially unop-posed" because their challengers had raised less than $25,000.[25] Such spending gaps continue to the present day and will be discussed later in the chapter.

Nevertheless, Republican strength has grown in Congress. From 1981 to 1986, with Reagan in the White House, Republicans were the majority party in the Senate, while the House remained in Democratic hands. Although they subsequently lost control in 1984, with the 1994 congressional elections Republicans gained ascendancy in both the House and the Senate—despite a sitting Democratic president in the White House. Republicans are now able to benefit disproportionately from incumbency, although party dealignment does not guarantee their control of Congress in the future as was the case with the Democratic party previously.

A third critical development also transpired during this period: the liberal-conservative consensus collapsed, ending the period of bipartisanship and producing greater ideological differences and partisanship between the two parties, including over foreign policy. The initial assault on the consensus came from the rise of liberalism and the new left in the 1960s and early 1970s. The 1968 and 1972 presidential elections were particularly divisive over foreign policy, contributing to the collapse of the cold war consensus. In 1968 the entry of Eugene McCarthy and Robert Kennedy in the Democratic primaries as the "peace" candidates led to President Lyndon Johnson's withdrawal and a bitter nomination process in which Vice President Hubert Humphrey emerged victorious. In 1972 George McGovern captured the Democratic nomination by calling for America's quick withdrawal from Vietnam and the restoration of liberalism abroad and at home.

This was accompanied by the rise of conservatism and the far right with the election of Richard Nixon in 1968 and, more important, the rise of Ronald Reagan in the 1976 and 1980 elections. The political consequences have been that the Democratic party has come to reflect a more liberal ideology and a post–cold war internationalist perspective in foreign policy; in contrast, the Republican party has stood for more conservative policies, including a conservative internationalist approach in foreign policy. As political analyst William Schneider has found, the splits between liberal and conservative internationalists "have now acquired substantial influence within the major political parties."[26]

These ideological differences have occurred primarily among party leaders and activists—members of the elite public—so that "the polarization of elites has, to a considerable extent, been institutionalized within the party system."[27] Members of the mass public, in contrast, tend to reflect more moderate and mixed ideological positions and have become more politically apathetic. Therefore, as discussed in chapter 13, on the public, instead of the elite consensus, party bipartisanship, and mass followership of the cold war years, what has emerged since Vietnam has been considerable party partisanship reflecting "an unstable system of competing coalitions in which the mass public swings left or right unpredictably in response to its current fears and concerns."[28]

FOREIGN POLICY IMPLICATIONS

Given these changes and conditions, the outcomes of elections and selection of political leaders by the public have grown in importance. Who gets elected into Congress and the White House is more meaningful during a time of ideological diversity and party differences than in a time of consensus and bipartisanship. Therefore, it is somewhat ironic to note that, as voter turnout has declined, voter impact on American politics has increased. Electoral politics, in other words, may have become even more instrumental in affecting the making of U.S. foreign policy.

Presently, *the American voter is likely to be confronted with choices* between candidates that range across the liberal and conservative political spectrum. In contrast to the cold war years, when candidates sharing the same beliefs competed for party nominations and national offices, the ideological and foreign policy views of post–Vietnam War candidates differ in some meaningful ways, including their foreign policy orientations and programs.

Democratic nominees for president—George McGovern in 1972, Jimmy Carter in 1976 and 1980, Walter Mondale in 1984, Michael Dukakis in 1988, Bill Clinton in 1992 and 1996, and Al Gore in 2000—have tended to offer more liberal internationalist policies. Republican nominees have tended to hold more conservative internationalist views—Nixon in 1972, Gerald Ford in 1976, Ronald Reagan in 1980 and 1984, George Bush Sr. in 1988 and 1992, Bob Dole in 1996, and

George Bush Jr. in 2000. Thus, who gets elected makes a difference as to the direction the president intends to take the United States in world affairs, even if voter choice is not affected much by foreign policy issues.

Political scientists John Aldrich, John Sullivan, and Eugene Borgida provide a compelling study that counters the conventional wisdom that the time and effort presidential candidates spend campaigning on foreign and defense issues have negligible impact on voter behavior. In fact, they found that foreign policy issues have been prominent in the minds of voters in virtually all presidential elections since World War II and often are "as important as domestic issues in their impact on voting," especially when they perceive foreign policy differences between the candidates. Therefore, "candidates do not waltz before a blind audience. Ironically, it appears that the only blind audience has been a significant portion of the scholarly community."[29]

Who gets elected as president, and changes in who is president, make a difference for the general direction of U.S. foreign policy and the changes it has experienced over time, especially in comparison to the continuity that prevailed during the cold war. The election of Republican Richard Nixon in 1968 led to the pursuit of much more of a realpolitik and power politics approach in U.S. foreign policy toward the Soviet Union and the world. President Carter attempted to steer U.S. foreign policy away from the containment-oriented policies of the past toward a world order and human rights orientation following his 1976 election into the White House. With the election of Ronald Reagan in 1980 efforts were made to reinstate the policies of global containment reminiscent of the cold war past. The election of George Bush Sr. in 1988 softened much of the hard-line rhetoric and behavior associated with the Reagan administration, while emphasizing a realpolitik approach as U.S. foreign policy moved into a post–cold war era. Bill Clinton's election in 1992 and reelection in 1996 placed international economics and competitiveness on the top of the foreign policy agenda along with a more liberal, although pragmatic, internationalist orientation. George Bush Jr. as president following the disputed election of 2000 has resurrected a more conservative internationalist orientation and a war presidency following the September 11 attacks. As Ole Holsti and James Rosenau noted in *American Leadership in World Affairs*, "perhaps the only constancy in American foreign policy since the Vietnam War has been the conspicuous lack of constancy in its conduct."[30]

Electoral politics have also affected the membership of Congress as already discussed, thereby affecting legislative-executive relations in the making of foreign policy. The **post-Watergate congressional elections of 1974,** for example, resulted in major Democratic gains further strengthening their majority position—60 Democrats to 37 Republicans in the Senate (an increase of 4 seats), 291 Democrats to 144 Republicans in the House (an increase of 48 seats). Furthermore, many of the new Democrats represented strong liberal positions in the wake of the Vietnam War and Watergate. These electoral changes were instrumental in providing the basis for congressional resurgence in the making of U.S. foreign policy during the mid-1970s.[31]

The 1978 and 1980 elections resulted in a weakening of the Democratic majorities and brought an infusion of young Republican conservatives into Congress. In fact, beginning in 1980 the Republican party gained a narrow majority in the Senate for six years—the first time since 1954—producing important congressional support for President Reagan's early political success. And with the so-called **Republican revolution of 1994**—where every close congressional race was won by a Republican—the House and Senate reverted from Democratic to Republican control. Where Democrats once had a majority during the 103rd Congress of 1993–1994 (57 to 43 in the Senate and 258 to 176 in the House), the Republicans gained ascendancy beginning in the 104th Congress of 1995 (52 to 48 in the Senate and 230 to 204 in the House). The 2000 election narrowed the gap, with the Republicans having a slim (221 to 212) majority in the House and the slimmest of majority margins in the Senate (50 to 50, with the deciding vote cast by the Republican vice president Dick Cheney—until Vermont senator Jeffords switched from the Republican Party to Independent status, giving the Democratic party a slim 50 to 49 majority control of the Senate. But with the 2002 elections the Republicans gained two seats and control of the Senate (51 to 46) and picked up five seats to increase their margin in the House (226 to 203)—the first time since 1934 that the party of the incumbent president was able to win (as opposed to usually lose) more seats in both chambers of Congress.

In sum, the changes in congressional membership since Vietnam as a result of electoral politics have changed congressional membership, party control, and politicized Congress over the years, deeply affecting legislative-executive relations in foreign affairs. In fact, as discussed in the chapter on Congress, "divided government" has become increasingly the norm and has made it much more difficult for a president to govern, regardless of whether he is a Democrat or Republican. (Review table 11.3 for party control of the executive and legislature over time, including distribution of seats in the House of Representatives and the Senate.)

In addition to the importance of who gets elected, the rise of ideological diversity and political partisanship have *affected the political agenda and politicized foreign policy issues* in electoral politics. Unlike the cold war years, members of the opposition party, as well as factions within the same party, are more prone to question, criticize, and obstruct the president. These activities are more likely to damage the president's professional reputation, public prestige, and therefore, his ability to govern foreign policy.

Vietnam forced President Johnson to withdraw from the Democratic presidential race and helped to elect Republican Richard Nixon over the Democratic nominee, Vice President Hubert Humphrey. President Nixon's realpolitik policies were critiqued from the left for being too Soviet and containment oriented and from the right for not being sufficiently anticommunist. President Gerald Ford, who ascended to the presidency following Nixon's resignation over Watergate and tried to win the presidential nomination in the Republican party in 1976 against Ronald Reagan, faced an attack from the right that became so severe that the word *détente* was banished from the campaign. President Carter's foreign policy was increasingly attacked by conservatives, especially with the Iran hostage crisis and the Soviet invasion of Afghanistan, contributing to the election of Ronald Reagan in 1980. Yet President Reagan was placed on the political defensive by the left with the nuclear freeze and anti-apartheid movements and the Iran-contra affair, while his policies were attacked by the right once he began to pursue détente and arms control with the Soviet Union. In each case, the president was forced to moderate many of his initial policies over time in response to the politics of opposition.[32]

Thus far in the post–cold war world, foreign policy issues have not played as prominent a role in electoral politics. George Bush Sr. lost reelection despite his crushing triumph in the Persian Gulf War. And although international economics was important in Bill Clinton's presidential campaigns (and for Ross Perot's third-party campaign), especially in 1992, questions about the direction and state of the nation, with a domestic (as well as an intermestic) emphasis, dominated the 1992 and especially 1996 elections. Foreign policy issues were pretty much on the back-burner in the 2000 presidential election (though they may have contributed to Ralph Nader's third-party candidacy), although the September 11 terrorist attacks and Bush Jr.'s war on terrorism may have changed that. Hence, the role of foreign policy issues in electoral politics may be one of particular uncertainty and volatility as the United States enters the twenty-first century.

Overall, electoral patterns since Vietnam have produced contradictory outcomes. On the one hand, dealignment and greater ideological diversity have created greater party competition and choice for the American electorate at the national level. Although these trends maximize democratic politics, they also contribute to a lack of continuity in U.S. foreign policy as different parties and leaders with competing foreign policy views gain influence within the institutions of government. And dealignment and southern realignment have also increased the likelihood of divided government. This increases the likelihood of legislative-executive competition, partisanship, and policy conflict, which does not help promote strong presidents or coherent foreign policy over time.[33]

CONTEMPORARY ELECTORAL AND CAMPAIGN POLITICS

It is unclear which electoral patterns and political outcomes will prevail in the future. The rise of the independent voter, the large number of nonvoters, and the more moderate and pragmatic nature of the mass public allow for the possibility of different electoral outcomes at different times. The decline of anticommunism as an election issue—which had permeated electoral politics since the 1940s—as changes in the former Soviet Union and Eastern Europe continue, adds greater confusion to this picture. "As communism recedes," political analysts Norman Ornstein and Mark Schmitt ask, "American politics faces a strange new dilemma: How will the U.S. political system operate without anticommunism as its central organizing principle?"[34] To what extent will this damage the appeal of the Republican party, which has relied on anticommunism as a key issue throughout the 1970s and 1980s? What new issues will replace anticommunism with the end of the cold war? To what extent will the war on terrorism resonate among the American public? Which candidates and parties will benefit? Answers to these questions remain open, but much depends on the contemporary nature of electoral and campaign politics.

A number of key points about contemporary electoral politics and campaigning must be kept in mind to better understand possible political outcomes and their impact on the future of U.S. foreign policy.[35] First, party leaders have lost control of the **party nomination process** in the post–Vietnam War era. In the Democratic party, for example, Hubert Humphrey was the last presidential candidate selected by party leaders. With state primaries replacing party caucuses, the growing influence of professional political consultants, the need for large sums of money for campaigning, and the growing importance of the mass media, especially television, any individual may declare him- or herself a candidate and have a shot at winning the party nomination. Party outsiders—such as George McGovern in 1972, Jimmy Carter in 1976, Ronald Reagan in 1980, and Michael Dukakis in 1988—were able to capture control of their respective parties even though they were not the preferred choices of regular party leaders. The decline of party control over the election process has led to a corresponding rise of candidate-centered politics.[36]

Second, candidates attempting to gain party nominations and win office must be cognizant of key voting trends among the American public. Dealignment has resulted in *three voting participation patterns*: first, most Americans do not vote at all; second, roughly half of the eligible electorate vote in general elections, involving a presidential race; and third, considerably fewer people vote in national primary elections and general elections in which there is no presidential race. To understand this it is important to grasp the difference between **primary** and **general elections.** In other words, the elite public—the high participators—are extremely consequential in determining the outcome of primary elections—that is, who the nominees of the Democratic and Republican parties will be; whereas the mass public becomes more important in determining the outcome of general elections—deciding which of the two nominees becomes president (or a member of Congress). Furthermore, in general elections voters, such as independents, who are least likely to regularly

identify with the same party over time are the most consequential in determining which candidate receives majority support.[37]

As V. O. Key made clear in *The Responsible Electorate, the voting electorate consists of three general groups*: "standpatters," or those who regularly vote for the same party; "switchers," who vote for different parties at different times; and "new voters," who have never cast a ballot before or who previously opted out of the electoral process. Key also found that the electorate, especially switchers and new voters, often engage in what is called "retrospective voting," that is, voting for or against a candidate (and party) based on, first, a general evaluation of their performance (especially for the incumbent) rather than their programs for the future, and second, whether the times have been good or bad for them and the country. It was in this sense that Key believed in the existence of a "responsible" electorate.[38]

Third, the weakness of parties and the nature of the electorate affect general campaign strategies. Candidates usually make more "ideological appeals" during primary elections to gain the party nomination, when voter turnout is dominated by the elite public; in contrast, they make more moderate and popular appeals during the general election to win office, when the mass public is more likely to vote (reflecting the difference between the moral minority versus the pragmatic majority discussed in chapter 13). Although each party represents a broad coalition of individuals and groups, Republican standpatters are more conservative in their views, and Democratic standpatters are more liberal. Therefore, in primary elections candidates for the Republican nomination usually take more conservative positions to win the support of Republicans in primaries; likewise, candidates for the Democratic nomination take more liberal positions to win the support of Democrats. In the general election, in contrast, party nominees attempt to attract support from members of their own party, independent voters, and members of the opposition party. To use Key's terms, they attempt to retain the support of standpatters and attract the support of switchers and new voters. Thus, candidates tend to take "more moderate and popular" positions during the general election to maximize broad appeal and minimize opposition.

In the **1996 presidential election,** Bill Clinton, the Democratic incumbent, was much more successful in reflecting more moderate and popular positions for taking the country into the future, while portraying Bob Dole, the Republican candidate, as a man of the past. **Table 15.1** provides a picture of the electorate. Not surprisingly, Bill Clinton was quite successful in gaining the overwhelming support of those who identified themselves as Democrats and liberals, while Bob Dole obtained strong support from Republicans and conservatives—those most likely to be standpatters. But Bill Clinton's presidential campaign, in comparison to Dole's, was much more successful in appealing to and gaining the support of those most likely to switch their vote for a party and candidate with time—the independents and moderates. Clinton was also more successful in gaining the support of the younger, and usually newer, voters. The breakdown of the public vote in terms of gender, race, education, family income, and religion is also provided in the table.

Clearly, more of the public was sufficiently satisfied with Clinton as president in comparison to supporting a challenger and newcomer such as Bob Dole (or Ross Perot) for president. Although this may seem overstated, it is important to point out that Clinton is the first Democrat to be reelected as president since Franklin Roosevelt. And he is only the third president of either party since Roosevelt to have fully completed two terms of office. One analyst places Clinton's 1996 election and political skills in perspective in the following way:

> Successful politicians know how to play the cards they are dealt, and Clinton is the most successful Democratic politician of the postwar period. As a national candidate, he has no one in his own party to touch him; and although they may seem like the political equivalent of tomato cans now, the two Republicans he defeated (and defeated handily) were the most prominent and least ideologically compromised figures in their party. Clinton's style, a weird combination of compassion, self-centeredness, uplift, and indecisiveness, is a style that seems to suit a politically fractured, intellectually uninspired time.[39]

Unlike 1996, the **2000 presidential election** was particularly close. Al Gore and George Bush Jr. split the independent and moderate voters, as well as the younger and probably newer voters. George Bush's campaign strategy of "compassionate conservatism" was successful in making him appear more of a centrist, while Al Gore's campaign had difficulty in com-

municating any consistent message and Gore distanced himself from President Clinton and his successful economic record as well. George Bush did particularly well with the white male vote in comparison to Dole in 1996 and Gore in 2000. The third-party candidacy of Ralph Nader may also have hurt Gore and affected the outcome (the conventional wisdom is that if Nader had not run, those who voted for him would [assuming they had turned out] have probably voted for Gore, given their overwhelming liberal orientation). **Table 15.2** provides a demographic breakdown of the 2000 electorate and can be compared with table 15.1, on the 1996 presidential election. Ultimately, Al Gore won the popular vote, but the key question was who won the all-important (and usually symbolic) electoral college?

The election was so close and controversial that it came down to who won Florida—where Americans and the world for the first time in a long while were able to see the disputes and controversies, and claims and counterclaims, about the ballots, the votes, and the vote counting. That the national media initially called the state for Gore at 8 P.M., even though western Florida was in another time zone and people still had one hour to vote, did not help. Usually it is the United States, the so-called representatives of freedom and democracy, who judge the fairness of elections around the world. This time it appeared that the United States was undergoing its own type of "banana republic" election for who would be the next president. In Florida in particular there were major problems of being able to vote, confusing ballots, miscounting of the ballots, and political manipulation of the electoral process. This demonstrates that America's electoral process is far from being as efficient and fair as most Americans assumed given the different types of ballots, voting and vote counting procedures which vary from county to county and state to state due to the system of federalism (making national and uniform standards almost impossible).

After all the politics, the public relations efforts, and the legal maneuvering that occurred for weeks on all sides, the Supreme Court—rightfully or wrongfully—stepped in and made the crucial decision that made George Bush Jr. president. Even though efforts have been made to tabulate the votes, especially given the discrepancies and difficulties experienced predominantly but not solely in Florida, it still remains unclear who actually won the electoral college and therefore the presidential election. Ultimately, George Bush Jr.

was declared the victor and was sworn into office, Al Gore accepted the decision, and most Americans were able to put the controversial 2000 presidential election behind them—helping to restore legitimacy to the American governmental and electoral system.[40]

Fourth, larger and larger amounts of money are required to finance election campaigns—which takes us to the importance of campaign financing. As discussed in chapter 11, members of Congress are constantly fund-raising and running for reelection. Presidents who run for reelection and prospective presidential candidates start earlier and earlier to run, raise money, and build an organization. Given their positions of power and visibility, incumbents are particularly advantaged in this respect and are able to raise large campaign war chests to scare off and defeat challengers. The need for increasing amounts of money to run for office and re-election has been a problem in American politics for a long time and continues to be a controversial issue (see **essay 15.1** on money, campaigning, and politics).

Finally, given the nature of the electorate and general campaign strategies, **symbolic and negative campaigning** have been an integral part of electioneering. Most campaigns typically gloss over issues or information and emphasize personalities and symbolism, especially in the general election. Since candidates attempt to maximize their appeal by occupying the ideological center, campaigns often become battlegrounds over personal characteristics, leadership skills, experience, and any issue that happens to be on the political agenda. The key aim, however, is not to inform the electorate but to "market" the candidate to the electorate through use of the mass media. For example, given the legacies of the cold war and the Vietnam War, foreign policy issues that are identified with "nationalism" and "patriotism" tend to play into the hands of Republicans as opposed to Democrats, as was probably the case in the congressional elections of 2002 given the Republican's emphasis on the war on terrorism and the inability of Democrats to form a unified strategy in response.[41] Thus, campaigns emphasize symbolic appeals to the public in which the candidate is identified with values consistent with American political culture. Ronald Reagan was probably the most successful at this in recent decades.[42]

The importance of personalities and symbolism, a topic that will be further examined in chapter 17, on the media, also explains the emphasis on "negative" campaigning—attempts to set the agenda for the oppo-sition and put them on the defensive. Symbolic and negative campaigning is deemed necessary to get the attention of the mass public and motivate them to vote—if not for one's own candidate then at least against the opposing candidate. For example, in comparison to the inept handling of the Dukakis campaign, the 1988 Bush campaign team was masterful. Images of Willie Horton indicated the law and order theme; "Read my lips, no new taxes" was juxtaposed against Democratic spending; patriotism was demonstrated when Bush wrapped himself in the flag; and "Boston Harbor" depicted Dukakis's hypocrisy on environmentalism. These images and "sound-bite politics" did little to inform the electorate about what Bush or Dukakis would or could do as president, but they are the stuff of which virtually all present-day political campaigns are made.[43]

The 1992 presidential outcome was obviously less successful, despite Bush's triumph in the Persian Gulf War and Clinton's problems about his womanizing and Vietnam draft status, among others. Ultimately, Clinton's (as well as Ross Perot's) focus on "It's the economy, stupid" seemed to resonate. In the 1996 election, Bob Dole's campaign was poorly run in comparison to the workings of the Clinton campaign, as was Al Gore's poor campaign compared to George Bush Jr.'s.[44]

These campaign strategies make political sense when the goal is attracting mass support and winning elections; however, they also have *political consequences*. First, political campaigning often constrains presidential power by building up promises and expectations among the public that the president, in particular, simply cannot fulfill. While symbolic and negative campaign tactics may bolster a president's public prestige in the short term, in the long term public support is likely to wither, as the chapter 4 discussion of the presidential life cycle demonstrates. Making foreign policy statements and taking foreign policy stances in an effort to win election, furthermore, affects not only public expectations at home but the expectations and behavior of those abroad. Clinton was very critical of Bush's policies toward China and the breakup of Yugoslavia, for example, only to pretty much continue them once in office. George Bush Jr. emphasized a foreign policy of "humility" and very selective U.S. national interests abroad during the campaign, which did not reflect his administration's foreign policy behavior once in office, either before (such as over the spy plane incident with China) or especially after September 11.[45]

TABLE **15.1**
THE ELECTORAL VOTE OF 1996

	ALL VOTERS (%)	BILL CLINTON	BOB DOLE	ROSS PEROT
POPULAR VOTE (PERCENTAGE)		45,628,667 (49.2%)	37,869,435 (40.8%)	7,874,283 (8.5%)
ELECTORAL VOTES		379	156	0
PARTY IDENTIFICATION				
Democrat	39%	84%	10%	5%
Republican	29	13	80	6
Independent	16	43	35	17
POLITICAL IDEOLOGY				
Liberal	20%	78%	11%	7%
Moderate	47	57	33	9
Conservative	33	20	71	8
GENDER				
Male	48%	43%	46%	10%
Female	52	54	38	7
RACE				
White	83%	43%	46%	9%
African-American	10	84	12	4
Hispanic	5	72	21	6
Asian	1	43	48	8
Other	1	64	21	9
AGE				
18 to 29	17%	53%	34%	10%
30 to 44	33	48	41	9
45 to 59	26	48	41	9
60 or over	24	48	44	7
EDUCATION				
No high school	6%	59%	28%	11%
High school graduate	24	51	35	13
Some college	27	48	40	10
College graduate	26	44	46	8
Postgraduate	17	52	40	5
FAMILY INCOME				
Less than $15,000	11%	59%	28%	11%
$15,000 to $39,999	23	53	36	9
$40,000 to $59,999	27	48	40	10
$60,000 to $74,999	21	47	45	7
$75,000 to $100,000	9	44	48	7
$100,000 and up	9	38	54	6
RELIGION				
Protestant	38%	41%	50%	8%
Catholic	29	53	37	9
Other Christian	16	45	41	12
Jewish	3	78	16	3
No religion	7	59	23	13

SOURCE: CNN/Time All Politics, 1996.

TABLE **15.2**
THE ELECTORAL VOTE OF 2000

	ALL VOTERS (%)	GEORGE W. BUSH	AL GORE	RALPH NADER	PAT BUCHANAN
POPULAR VOTE (PERCENTAGE)		50,455,000 (47.9%)	50,992,000 (48.4%)	2,883,000 (2.7%)	449,000 (0.4%)
ELECTORAL VOTES		271	266	0	0
PARTY IDENTIFICATION					
Democrat	39%	11%	86%	2%	0%
Republican	35	91	8	1	0
Independent	27	47	45	6	1
POLITICAL IDEOLOGY					
Liberal	20%	13%	80%	6%	1%
Moderate	50	44	52	2	0
Conservative	29	81	17	1	0
GENDER					
Male	48%	53%	42%	3%	0%
Female	52	43	54	2	0
RACE					
White	81%	54%	42%	3%	0%
African-American	10	8	90	1	0
Hispanic	7	35	62	2	1
Asian	2	41	55	3	1
Other	1	39	55	4	0
AGE					
18 to 29	17%	46%	48%	5%	1%
30 to 44	33	49	48	2	0
45 to 59	28	49	48	2	1
60 and over	22	47	51	2	0
EDUCATION					
No high school	5%	38%	59%	1%	1%
High school graduate	21	49	48	1	1
Some college	32	51	45	3	0
College graduate	24	51	45	3	0
Postgraduate	18	44	52	3	0
FAMILY INCOME					
Less than $15,000	7%	37%	57%	4%	1%
$15,000 to $39,000	16	41	54	3	1
$40,000 to $59,999	24	47	49	2	0
$60,000 to $74,999	25	51	46	2	0
$75,000 to $100,000	13	45	52	2	0
$100,000 and up	15	54	43	2	0
RELIGION					
Protestant	54%	56%	42%	2%	0%
Catholic	26	47	50	2	1
Other Christian	6	28	62	7	1
Jewish	4	19	79	1	7
No religion	9	30	61	7	0

SOURCE: CNN.com; US Census Bureau.

ESSAY 15.1
MONEY, CAMPAIGNING, AND POLITICS

Following the reelection of Bill Clinton as president and Al Gore as vice president, controversy arose about whether the Clinton campaign was involved in illegal campaign contributions and fundraising. Questions were raised about the "overnights" and "coffees" provided to Clinton's friends and donors at the White House; about fund-raising calls made by Clinton and Gore from the White House; about all the "soft money" raised by the Democratic National Committee; about campaign contributions made by foreign governments, such as China, with the hope of influencing U.S. foreign policy. Such questions and charges of illegal and unethical behavior triggered congressional investigations led by Republicans, given their majority control, in both chambers and an investigation by the Department of Justice. The issue became so politicized that it produced a major partisan struggle between Republicans and Democrats, challenged the reputation of Clinton (which had never been impeccable) and Gore (which had been squeaky clean until then), and produced calls for further campaign financing reform that continues to the present.

Despite the Republican charges against the Democrats and the Clinton administration, money and elections and American politics have always been intertwined and of great importance. In fact, in the last few decades Republicans usually are more successful in raising money than Democrats (given their more pro-business orientation). But bottom line, people who run for office, especially at the national level, need money, and greater and greater amounts of it to run viable and successful campaigns. And not only are presidents, and prospective presidential candidates, preoccupied with elections, but so are virtually all members of Congress (as discussed in chapter 11). Hedrick Smith, in *The Power Game*, in fact, refers to members of Congress as being engaged in a "constant campaign" in which "money has been mother's milk to American politics." And campaign costs, especially as a result of expensive television ads, have skyrocketed over the years.

How much money was raised? In 1996, according to the Federal Election Commission, over $2 billion was "officially" raised (at just the federal level): over $450 million for the presidential race, over $300 million for Senate races, over $500 million for House races, and over $700 million raised by the Democratic and Republican parties (much of it so-called "soft money" that could be used for any of the elections). And this excludes the money provided to each major presidential candidate for the general election at public expense (over $62 million each for Clinton and Dole). Not only have the costs of running for president increased dramatically, but from the 1970s to the 1990s the cost of the average successful House campaign went from under $100,000 to almost $1 million, while the average successful Senate campaign went from a few hundred thousand dollars to over $5 million.

The need for larger amounts of money and the constant campaign have given members of Congress enormous advantages—reflecting the power of **congressional incumbency,** meaning that those running for reelection are usually safe from potential challengers. One reason for this is that the fund-raising gap between incumbents and challengers is greater than ever. A Federal Election Commission study found that in the final days of the 1990 elections, for example, congressional incumbents had twenty times more money to spend than did their challengers: $120 million to $6 million. Of the 406 House members seeking reelection, 178 were considered "financially unopposed" because their challengers had raised less than $25,000. In 1996, an incumbent in the House spent on average over $600,000, while a challenger spent over $200,000; in the Senate an incumbent spent on average over $5 million, while a challenger spent over $2 million. This helps to explain why usually around 90 percent of incumbents win reelection. And despite all the controversy over the Clinton campaign and Democratic party fundraising efforts, from 1995 to 1996 the Republican party raised some 60 percent more than the Democratic party—about $550 million to the Democrats' $330 million.

And the costs continue to increase. For example, the 2000 New York Senate race resulted in Democratic winner Hillary Rodham Clinton spending over $41 million dollars, while Republican Rick Lazio spent over $39 million. Numerous House races in 2000 involved individual campaigns in which over $2 million was spent (almost $7 million by one candidate in California alone). George Bush rejected public funding, and the spending limits that go with it, in his 2000 presidential primary race, raising and spending more than $100 million. In 2004 he is expected to reject public funding again (during the primaries and possibly even during the general election, for which the limit is $70 million per candidate) and raise even more.

Most of the money is raised from individuals and organizations—such as special interest groups and **PACs (political action committees,** usually formed by organized interest groups such as labor unions and corporations). Most of the money is spent on advertising, salaries for the campaign staff, mailing and polling, and not surprisingly, fund-raising (it takes money to get money). And all this despite laws supposedly reforming campaign financing enacted during the early and mid-1970s—limiting individual giving to no more then $1,000 per candidate per election; limiting PACs to no more then $5,000 per candidate per election; making taxpayer financing available for presidential candidates; and requiring candidates to disclose their finances.

Nevertheless, this change in the law just produced more concerted fund-raising efforts and new ways to find loopholes and overcome the new legal limits—such as giving so-called soft money to the national parties. While the amount of regulated "hard money"—money given directly to candidates—has slowly increased, the amount of unregulated and unlimited "soft money"—money given directly to political parties who can then use it for different races or however they see fit—has exploded: from about $250 million in 1996 to over $500 million in the year 2000.

Given all the flack about the Clinton administration's fund-raising, soft money, the buying of candidates, the Enron scandal, and so forth, Congress finally passed the **Campaign Finance Reform Act of 2002.** The new laws include the following provisions:

- Hard-money contributions from individuals are increased to $2,000 (from $1,000 before) to any presidential or congressional candidate, national political party, and political action committee, and increased to no more than $95,000 total to candidates (up to $37,500) and political parties and PACs (up to $57,500) in a two-year election cycle (from $50,000 before).
- Soft-money contributions from corporations, unions, PACs, and individuals to national parties are banned. Up to $10,000 can be given to state and local parties each year for "get out the vote" and "voter registration" efforts in federal elections.
- Corporations, unions, and nonprofit groups are prohibited from paying for broadcast advertisements if the ads refer to a specific candidate and run within sixty days of a general election or thirty

days before a primary election. Such ads could be paid for only with regulated hard money through political action committees.

Even with the new law, candidates from both parties will find ways to raise large sums of money legally and through current and new (and innovative) loopholes. There may also be some significant political consequences for the two parties. According to Michael Crowley, in "The Morning After," "The biggest problem for Democrats is the bill's virtual ban on soft money. In recent years the Democrats have reached near parity with Republicans in soft money.... What is certain is that Democrats still lag pitifully when it comes to 'hard money' donations.... And that's not about to change." And spending differences may impact electoral outcomes.

Despite public disgust and some reform, money appears to be embedded in the electoral and political process—a form of "legal" (and illegal) corruption with little end in sight. What journalist Edward Roeder stated in 1997 may still apply in the future: "The real scandal in fund-raising is larger, bipartisan and more obviously illegal. Both the national parties, all presidential candidates and most congressional candidates now routinely flout campaign finance law. And the supposed enforcer of that law, the Federal Election Commission, does nothing about it." In fact, the Federal Election Commission has made decisions that dilute the Campaign Finance Reform Act of 2002. Therefore, campaign finance reform may improve the process, but ultimately it will not eliminate the "mother's milk" of American politics.

SOURCES: Jill Abramson, "Lott, Champion Money-Raiser, Still Champions Rules of the Game," New York Times (October 13, 1997); Michael Barone and Richard E. Cohen, The Almanac of American Politics 2002 (Washington, D.C.: National Journal, 2002); Richard L. Berke, "In Fund-Raising Race, Incumbents Are Ahead," New York Times (November 5, 1990): Michael Crowley, "Mourning After," New Republic (March 4 & 11, 2002); Robert A. Rankin, "Campaign $1996," The State (March 6, 1997), pp. D1, D5; Edward Roeder, "Blank Check," New Republic (April 14, 1997), pp. 19–21; Hedrick Smith, The Power Game: How Washington Works (New York: Ballantine, 1988); "Strange Bedfellows," Newsweek (March 10, 1997), pp. 22–28; "With Friends Like These ...," Newsweek (March 17, 1997), pp. 17–23; R. A. Zaldivar, "Cash Lined Campaign Trail to Congress, White House," The State (January 19, 1997) pp. D1, D6.

Second, current political campaigning and electioneering methods are losing the interest of the American public. Many observers attribute the low voter turnouts to such things as difficult registration requirements, the demands of everyday life, and even general satisfaction with public policy. There is some truth to

these explanations, but the tremendous drop in public trust of government officials and decline in citizen political efficacy since the 1960s also suggests that there are too many elections, too much politicking and manipulation, and too few concrete results for people's lives. In other words, the public has acquired a high degree of cynicism about the nature of American politics, including party and electoral politics.[46]

If low voter turnout is explained by factors other than public satisfaction, it raises serious questions about the democratic nature of a political system in which only a minority of the citizenry participates in electoral politics. This general perception of the declining relevance of political parties and low participation in electoral politics also contributes to the growing importance of social movements and interest groups in the politics of U.S. foreign policy, the subject of the next chapter.

LIBERALISM, REALISM, AND THE ELECTION OF 2004?

In the post–cold war era, neither the Democratic nor Republican party has reflected a purely liberal internationalist or conservative (realist) internationalist worldview. The parties have reflected foreign policy orientations that are broadly similar and include elements of both liberal internationalism and realist/conservative internationalism. Both parties have championed democracy and free trade as ideal systems of government and commerce; both parties have made American national security and interests top priorities for any foreign policy; both parties emphasize American military strength as essential to national security and as an essential tool of diplomacy; and both parties prefer international cooperation to competition in the post–cold war era. There have been consistent differences, however, between the two parties in the degrees to which they are committed to these two orientations.

Under the leadership of former president Bill Clinton and vice president Al Gore, the Democratic party tended to more consistently reflect a liberal internationalist orientation through its support for globalization and international cooperation and institutions. The Democratic party has labeled its foreign policy orientation one of "Foreign Engagement," especially under President Clinton, as the way for the United States to achieve its broadest hopes for the world, not just its narrowest fears, and has emphasized the importance of the United States leading and promoting American ideals in an increasingly interdependent environment.

Under the leadership of President George Bush Sr., Senator Dole, and President George Bush Jr., the Re-

publican party has more consistently reflected a realist/conservative internationalist orientation in its unwavering commitment to American national security and interests. Though the Republican party is committed to active internationalism, it prefers the United States to take a leadership and, if necessary, more of a unilateral role. The Bush Jr. administration once in office labeled its current foreign policy orientation "New Realism," and President Bush Jr. has promised to be "a cold-eyed realist when it comes to this world [because] though the evil empire may have passed, evil still remains." The September 11 attacks certainly have reinforced and intensified such a view. Therefore, which parties and individuals are electorally successful in becoming members of Congress and, in particular, the winning the presidency does make a difference in U.S. foreign policy.[47]

As of 2002, President Bush Jr. was riding high in the polls and the war on terrorism has broad public support. But President Bush Jr. is also all too aware of what happened to his father in the presidential elections of 1992. The Bush team was well aware that his public approval was steadily dropping in 2003, with dissent increasing abroad and at home over a war with Iraq. He probably is also aware that Americans have limited attention spans and there is considerable time for American priorities and assessments to shift about, for example, to what extent the war on terrorism will resonate throughout the country; about the state of the economy and future direction of the country; about how George Bush Jr. is perceived over time, especially in comparison to future Democratic challengers.[48]

The centerpiece of the Bush administration since the tragedy of September 11 has been the war on terrorism and his has become the war presidency. At the same time, Bush is fully aware of the fate of his father. It will be interesting to see how the election of 2004 will play out when the Bush administration, in the words of David Halberstam, is engaged in a "war during a time of peace." The outcome will play an important role in the future politics of U.S. foreign policy.

SUGGESTED SOURCES FOR MORE INFORMATION

The study of party and electoral politics has received considerable attention by scholars and analysts of American politics, but the impact of these subjects on the politics of U.S. foreign policy generally has been ignored. Although most scholars of U.S. foreign policy traditionally have dismissed the role of electoral politics, over the last few years foreign policy specialists have begun to recognize the importance of electoral politics for fully understanding U.S. foreign policy. I. M. Destler, Leslie H. Gelb, and Anthony Lake, in *Our Own Worst Enemy: The Unmaking of American Foreign Policy* (New York: Simon and Schuster, 1984), particularly in chapter 1, provide a good overview of the impact of domestic politics and elections on U.S. foreign policy, as does Miroslav Nincic in "U.S. Soviet Policy and the Electoral Connection," *World Politics* 42 (April 1990): 370–96. John H. Aldrich, John L. Sullivan, and Eugene Borgida demonstrate that foreign policy issues are often as important as domestic issues in affecting voting in presidential elections in "Foreign Affairs and Issue Voting: Do Presidential Candidates 'Waltz' Before a Blind Audience?" *American Political Science Review* 83 (March 1989): 123–41. David Halberstam provides a fascinating portrayal of the politics of U.S. foreign policy and the role of electoral politics and electoral cycles in *War in a Time of Peace: Bush, Clinton, and the Generals* (New York: Scribner, 2001).

Martin P. Wattenberg provides a good overview of political participation and party politics in the electoral process over the last few decades in *The Decline of American Political Parties, 1952–1996* (Cambridge, Mass.: Harvard University Press, 1998). An excellent history and analysis of the rise and decline of the Democratic party since the 1930s can be found in James MacGregor Burns, *The Crosswinds of Freedom* (New York: Vintage, 1989) and Steve Fraser and Gary Gerstle, eds., *The Rise and Fall of the New Deal Order, 1930–1980* (Princeton: Princeton University Press, 1989). Earl Black and Merle Black, in *Politics and Society in the South* (Cambridge, Mass.: Harvard University Press, 1987), provide the most comprehensive understanding of political change and party realignment in the South. The contemporary electoral era is well depicted by Everett Carll Ladd in, "The 1996 Vote: The 'No Majority' Realignment Continues," *Political Science Quarterly* (spring 1997): 1–28.

The Responsible Electorate: Rationality in Presidential Voting, 1936–1960 (New York: Vintage, 1966), by V. O. Key, remains a classic on the electorate, as does Joe McGinniss on campaign strategies in *The Selling of the President, 1968* (New York: Pocket Books, 1969). For an excellent discussion of contemporary electoral and campaign politics, see Hedrick Smith, *The Power Game: How Washington*

Works (New York: Ballantine, 1988), especially chapters 18 and 19; the work of William Schneider, such as "The New Shape of American Politics," *Atlantic Monthly* (January 1987), pp. 39–54; and Anthony King, "Running Scared," *Atlantic Monthly* (January 1997), pp. 41–61. Kevin Phillips, the godfather of the Republican realignment strategy in the South, has written a provocative work on the future of electoral and domestic politics, predicting the resurgence of liberalism and the Democratic party before the rise of Bill Clinton, in *The Politics of the Rich and Poor: Wealth and the American Electorate in the Reagan Aftermath* (New York: Random House, 1990). And for the controversial 2000 presidential election, see The Washington Post, *Deadlock: The Inside Story of America's Closest Election* (New York: Public Affairs, 2001), and Robert S. Erikson, "The 2000 Presidential Election in Historical Perspective," *Political Science Quarterly* (spring 2001): 29–52.

KEY TERMS

bipartisanship
Campaign Finance Reform Act of 2002
congressional incumbency
dealignment
Democratic New Deal coalition
Electoral College
electoral cycles
Barry Goldwater
independent voters
political action committees (PACs)
party nomination process
primary versus general elections
post-Watergate congressional elections of 1974
realignment
realignment in the South
Republican revolution of 1994
selection of vice president
symbolic and negative campaigning
third parties
two-party system
1932 election
1946 election
1948 elections
1952 elections
1960 presidential election
1996 presidential election
2000 presidential election

$\mathscr{C}$HAPTER
16

. . . .

GROUP POLITICS

$\mathscr{G}$roup politics involves the role of social movements and interest groups in American politics. Political participation in group politics tends to be narrower than in electoral politics and occurs most frequently among members of the elite public. However, many Americans do participate in social movements and in thousands of widely varying groups, such as business, labor, consumer, environmental, religious, ethnic, civic, veterans, and national security groups. These *groups directly and indirectly affect the foreign policy–making process by* lobbying government, influencing electoral and domestic politics, participating in the policymaking process, providing sources of political recruitment for the government, and undertaking international activity.

In order to better understand how group politics influences U.S. foreign policy, *this chapter addresses the following questions:* What are the origins of groups and how do they develop in American politics? What was the nature of group politics during the cold war? What has happened to group politics since the Vietnam War, the end of the cold war, and the September 11 attacks? To what extent has there been a military-industrial complex throughout society and a foreign policy establishment at the top of society since World War II?

As we will see, continuity and change in the role of the public in group politics parallel the evolution of electoral politics, thus establishing the boundaries of political discourse and behavior within domestic politics and the policymaking process. In this way, group politics, like electoral politics, deeply affects the president's ability to govern foreign policy and the evolution of the tension between the demands of national security and democracy.

SOCIAL MOVEMENTS, GROUP ORIGINS AND DEVELOPMENT

Interest groups are organizations that possess an overriding concern with the political process and policy outcomes. They do not tend to be created randomly or continuously but often come in waves. In other words, large numbers of interest groups tend to form at certain times, usually in reaction to key events. For example, large numbers of interest groups formed during the 1930s in response to the Great Depression, during the 1940s and early 1950s in response to World War II and the cold war, and during the late 1960s and 1970s in response to events such as the Vietnam War. These time periods are often characterized by "negative" events—that is, events that hurt or are perceived to be counterproductive for people's lives. Such events activate people, many of whom previously may have been apathetic and politically passive.

Such periods of political instability and turmoil also usually produce **social movements**—large coalitions of individuals and groups that loosely unite around certain issues, usually in opposition to the status quo. Social movements involve thousands, sometimes millions, of people. They usually involve a change in the way people think about an issue, and these changes in attitudes usually remain even after the social movement fades. Although many of the people may not be part of any specific organized interest group, they nonetheless are motivated to be part of a social movement in order to influence the political system. Social movements also involve dozens, sometimes hundreds, of interest groups—older groups that have been around for a while and more recent groups that have arisen in reaction to the political climate of the times.[1]

Interest groups and social movements influence the domestic political environment and the governmental policymaking process in a number of ways. First and most well-known, groups usually "lobby" policymakers involved in the policy process. This is done by providing information and money, as well as mobilizing followers to provide support or cause political trouble. Second, the same techniques are used to influence domestic politics more generally, including the political agenda, public beliefs and behavior, and electoral politics. Third, members of some groups, especially those that are well established and have close relationships with government agencies and personnel, are consulted often by and actually participate with policymakers in the policy process. Fourth, well-established groups also tend to serve as important sources of political recruitment for official positions within government. As was discussed in chapter 5, major presidential appointees usually come from business, law, and academia. Finally, groups that are extremely active internationally, such as multinational corporations, affect U.S. foreign

policy and the policymaking process because of their visibility and activities abroad.

Social movements and groups tend to go through life cycles. Social movements tend to have a relatively short life span. Initially highly visible and potentially influential, they wither away as the issue dies due to either success or failure. Interest groups that survive tend to go through a longer life cycle. Groups in their formative stages tend to be more informally structured and nonbureaucratic. New interest groups, like the social movements of which they are often a part, also tend to be more purposive, as group leaders and members are motivated to accomplish certain goals. They also tend to be **challenging groups** in the sense that group leaders and followers are usually unhappy with things as they currently exist and are change oriented, challenging some aspect of the status quo, such as established groups. With time, interest groups tend to become more formal and less purposive. The activities of older groups tend to be much more bureaucratic and institutionalized. Members of older, **established groups** also tend to join for material and solidaristic (social) reasons—for example, in order to get certain services or to socialize with others. Older groups, especially those that are accepted or legitimate in society and have been somewhat successful in fulfilling their original purposive goals, also tend to be content with, and supportive of, the status quo.

In sum, *American group politics tends to go through different phases of political stability and instability.* During more stable periods, established groups and the status quo tend to dominate. Challenging groups exist, but they are often few in number, small in size and support, and invisible to most Americans. However, times of greater political instability produce considerable social movement activity and interest group expansion. During these periods, major political challenges of the status quo occur in which efforts are made to change the ideological beliefs and institutions that dominate society and the government. The forces supporting the status quo usually have a great advantage in resisting challenging groups, for the status quo tends to have considerable support throughout the government and much of society, at least initially among the mass public. Nevertheless, it is during these times that political changes have the greatest potential and likelihood of occurring.

Every political system, according to David Truman in *The Governmental Process,* "of course, tends to discriminate in favor of established groups of interests, and it may deny to new groups access to points of decision."[2] Established groups tend to support the status quo and thus promote continuity in the policy process. Challenging groups, in contrast, attempt to change domestic politics and the policymaking process. Therefore, in order to understand continuity and change, it is important to determine how successful new groups are in challenging more established groups and the dominant beliefs that exist throughout society and government. For James MacGregor Burns in *The Crosswinds of Freedom*, group politics and electoral politics have been intertwined throughout American history:

> Movements emerged out of economic stress and social tension and erupted in conflict, often violent. After a time they dominated political debate, overshadowed more traditional issues, cut across existing lines of party cleavage, polarized groups and parties. The immediate test of success was whether the movement could force one major party or both of them to embrace its cause. The test of long-run success was whether the movement left the whole party system altered and, even more, left the political landscape transformed.[3]

How successful are challenging groups at surviving, being accepted within society, and gaining their origi-

nal goals? Sociologist William Gamson performed an in-depth study of over fifty major challenging groups throughout American history. As **figure 16.1** shows, he found that only half of the challenging groups were able to survive and gain minimal acceptance within society. Furthermore, only half of the groups were successful in gaining at least some of their goals. Overall, while roughly 40 percent of the challenging groups were successful in both gaining some legitimacy and achieving some of their goals, 40 percent collapsed entirely. As Gamson concludes, "The central difference among political actors is captured by the idea of being inside or outside of the polity. Those who are inside are *members* whose interest is vested—that is, recognized as valid by other members. Those who are outside are challengers. They lack the basic prerogative of members—routine access to decisions that affect them."[4]

Many different factors account for these outcomes. However, one important element involves the salience of an issue upon the ability of groups to influence the political agenda. Challenging groups tend to have their greatest impact for those issues that have great salience and visibility in domestic politics. This occurs because issues that become politicized attract the attention of the elite and mass publics throughout society beyond the confines of government policymak-

FIGURE **16.1**
POLITICAL OUTCOMES FOR CHALLENGING GROUPS

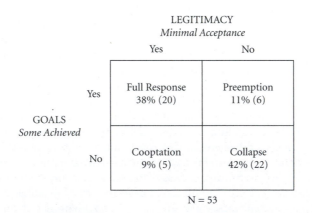

LEGITIMACY
Minimal Acceptance

		Yes	No
GOALS *Some Achieved*	Yes	Full Response 38% (20)	Preemption 11% (6)
	No	Cooptation 9% (5)	Collapse 42% (22)

N = 53

SOURCE: William A. Gamson, *The Strategy of Social Protest* (Homewood, Ill.: Dorsey Press, 1975), p. 37.

ers and established groups. However, for issues of low salience—the normal state of affairs for most issues—challenging groups are usually unable to overcome the lack of public attention and penetrate the web of relations that exists between government policymakers and established groups.

Clearly, group politics is demanding and rough. It tends to pit people from new and challenging social groups and movements against people from more established and status quo-oriented groups. Success for new and challenging groups is an uphill battle because more established groups tend to enjoy considerable support from much of society and the government. However, challenging groups that succeed in gaining legitimacy and promoting their goals are able to affect the public and their beliefs, political participation, domestic politics, and the governmental policymaking process. And as we will see, the rise of social movements and the evolution of group politics deeply influenced the making of U.S. foreign policy during the cold war and have continued to do so since the Vietnam War.

GROUP POLITICS DURING THE COLD WAR

Before World War II the group process played a vital role in domestic politics and the policy process of U.S. foreign policy making, especially with respect to issues of trade and protectionism. For most social movements and interest groups, however, foreign policy was usually secondary to domestic issues. Those few groups that were devoted exclusively to foreign policy rarely had much influence over the policymaking process. This situation permanently changed with American intervention in World War II and the rise of the cold war.

Two patterns evolved with respect to group activity during the 1940s and 1950s. First, new and established groups in American society became heavily involved in the foreign policy–making process. Second, most of these groups were overwhelmingly anticommunist and conservative in their foreign policy orientations. These patterns were promoted and reinforced by the rise of extremely conservative social movements at the time, represented by the forces of McCarthyism. *The results of these developments for group politics and the making of*

U.S. foreign policy were (1) the rise of foreign policy– and cold war–oriented groups, (2) the development of a military-industrial-scientific infrastructure, and (3) the rise of a foreign policy establishment.

These patterns in group politics during the cold war contributed to a domestic context that led to the rise of presidential power, the expansion of the foreign policy bureaucracy, an acquiescent Congress, a supportive public, and bipartisanship in party politics. Thus, a group process evolved during the 1940s and 1950s that became an important part of the anticommunist foreign policy consensus throughout society and enhanced the ability of the U.S. government under the leadership of the president to carry out its national security policies abroad. Groups and movements that challenged containment policies from the political left did exist during the cold war years. However, they were small in numbers and resources and constantly on the political defensive and remained primarily outside the realm of mainstream domestic politics.

FOREIGN POLICY AND COLD WAR–ORIENTED GROUPS

The 1940s and 1950s resulted in the *rise of numerous anticommunist groups that became active in the politics of U.S. foreign policy, including* (1) national security and public policy groups, (2) veterans and military support groups, (3) political and civic groups, (4) businesses and corporations, (5) labor unions, (6) religious groups, and (7) ethnic groups.

These groups directly and indirectly affected the foreign policy–making process by lobbying government, influencing electoral and domestic politics, participating in the policymaking process, providing sources of political recruitment for the government, and undertaking international activity. There were certainly differences in perceptions among leaders and members of these groups concerning the intensity of the Soviet communist threat and the particulars of U.S. national security policy; some were more anticommunist than others. However, all shared a general cold war internationalist orientation that formed the basis of a consensus in the making of U.S. foreign policy.[5]

National security and public policy groups became increasingly active and prominent in the making of U.S. foreign policy during World War II and the cold war.

These groups included the Carnegie Endowment for International Peace, Committee on the Present Danger, Council on Foreign Relations, Ford and Rockefeller foundations, Foreign Policy Research Institute, and the Rand Corporation. Membership and involvement in most of these groups were limited to proponents of American cold war policies, including select government officials (both current and former), business leaders, academics, journalists, and other opinion leaders within American society. The activities of these groups typically consisted of group seminars on important issues, involvement in policy research and proposals, and the publication and communication of members' work.

Not only did these activities affect the beliefs of the attentive and mass publics, but many of these groups became extremely important sources of ideas and personnel for the government during the cold war years. In this respect, it is important to remember that the foreign policy bureaucracy in government grew tremendously in size during the 1940s and 1950s, and many of its policymaking personnel were recruited from such groups.[6] (See **essay 16.1** for a discussion of the significant role the Council on Foreign Relations played in the postwar foreign policymaking process.)

Veterans and military support organizations were staunchly anticommunist supporters of American cold war policies and emphasized a large defense buildup and reliance on force. These organizations included the major veterans organizations, such as the American Legion and the Veterans of Foreign Wars, and military support organizations, such as the Navy League and the American Ordnance Association.

Broad-based political and civic organizations also became participants in the foreign policy consensus in American politics. Americans for Democratic Action, for example, was launched in the early 1950s by prominent American Democrats and liberals as a means to support the government's cold war policies. Such groups were highly visible, reinforcing the development of an anticommunist consensus throughout society and the government.

Business and labor groups were also part of the consensus supporting U.S. foreign policy. Business had long played a prominent role in American politics and government, especially since the rise of industrialization and the development of modern corporations. Much of this was because business leaders were regularly recruited into government policymaking positions by political leaders and because of the increasing scale

of activities of American business abroad, especially in Latin America. As historian William Appleman Williams has argued throughout his work, by the turn of the century U.S. foreign policy became increasingly supportive of a so-called "open door" policy for American business and investment abroad.[7]

Moreover, with World War II and the onset of the cold war, business groups such as the Chamber of Commerce, Committee for Economic Development, and the National Association of Manufacturers became strong supporters of the government's containment policy. Industry involvement in foreign policy was reinforced by the growing role of big business in defense production. As a result, a type of big business and government partnership developed in support of U.S. foreign policy during the cold war years. The symbiotic business-government relationship was best expressed by General Motors chairman Charles Wilson. When asked during his confirmation hearings on January 15, 1953, before the Senate Armed Services Committee whether he could make a decision as secretary of defense that would be adverse to the interests of General Motors, Wilson said, "For years I thought what was good for the country was good for General Motors and vice versa. The difference did not exist."[8]

Anticommunism accompanied the promotion of private enterprise at home and abroad. This was consistent with government efforts to contain communism and promote a liberal political and economic world order. As American banks and companies became increasingly multinationalized following World War II, they located in countries where there was a strong U.S. governmental presence abroad, such as in Latin America and Europe. One can debate whether the American "flag" led the American "dollar" abroad, or vice versa. Regardless, both business and government were driven to promote an open-door or free market ethos in U.S. foreign policy during the cold war years.

The **government-business relationship** was generally interactive and supportive: The increasing global presence of American government and the relocation of American multinational industry abroad led to greater mutual dependency between American business and government abroad. For example, U.S. governmental actions to assist postwar reconstruction of Western Europe through the Marshall Plan also relied on American private investment in the region; in addition, America's military and economy became increasingly dependent on continued access to oil by Ameri-

ESSAY 16.1
THE COUNCIL ON FOREIGN RELATIONS

The **Council on Foreign Relations (CFR)** was probably the single most important group involved in the making of U.S. foreign policy during the cold war. However, it exercised influence not by immediately affecting the policy-making process but by providing foreign policy ideas and personnel for government. In this respect, the Council on Foreign Relations served as a forum for bringing policy-makers and opinion leaders together and circulating ideas and policy proposals, which often played an important role in the foreign policy–making process.

The Council on Foreign Relations describes itself as "a nonprofit and nonpartisan membership organization dedicated to improved understanding of American foreign policy and international affairs." It was originally established in 1921 in New York City, shortly after World War I and the Senate's rejection of the Treaty of Versailles (and U.S. membership in the League of Nations), in order to promote American internationalism and involvement abroad.

The CFR's activities have revolved around three major areas. First, the council "strives to bring together experts within the Council membership and distinguished speakers from around the world for a forthright exchange of views that enlightens all participants." These meetings are generally restricted to CFR members and are off-the-record (not for public attribution). The second activity is the "Corporate Program" in which corporate executives— predominantly from prominent American companies— participate in discussions with council members and distinguished guests about the state of American business and its relationship to U.S. foreign policy. Finally, the council is very involved in communicating ideas and foreign policy views. This is done by furnishing policy studies on important contemporary issues to council members, government officials, and relevant policy experts. Most important, the Council on Foreign Relations publishes a quarterly journal, *Foreign Affairs*, which was the most influential policy journal in U.S. foreign policy during the 1950s and 1960s, for it was widely read by government officials and opinion leaders (and is still widely read today).

The Council on Foreign Relations caters to a rather narrow and exclusive audience by focusing on national opinion leaders. By its own description, the CFR is "composed of men and women with experience in matters of foreign policy who are leaders in academe, public service, business, and the media." Membership is achieved through a very selective process in which individuals are first nominated by a membership committee and then elected by the board of directors. During the cold war, membership in the Council on Foreign Relations represented the height of prestige and a sure route to participation in the making of U.S. foreign policy. In the political climate of the cold war, this meant that members tended to be part of the liberal-conservative ideological consensus and, thus, cold warriors in foreign policy.

Given the tremendous prestige of the Council on Foreign Relations, it not only provided a significant forum for generating ideas and policies for opinion leaders and government officials but was a significant source of political recruitment. Many important government positions throughout the foreign policy bureaucracy are often filled by presidential appointment of CFR members, including those at the secretary level and the national security adviser. As Robert Schulzinger concludes in his history of the Council on Foreign Relations, entitled *The Wise Men of Foreign Affairs*, its members filled the role of a "professional clergy" for the foreign policy community in and out of government. In fact, CFR membership was a clear indication of inclusion in the foreign policy establishment that arose during the cold war years and greatly influenced the making of U.S. foreign policy (discussed in greater detail later in this chapter).

SOURCES: Council on Foreign Relations, Annual Report, 1985–86 (New York: Council on Foreign Relations, 1986); J. Anthony Lukas, "The Council on Foreign Relations: Is It A Club? Seminar? Presidium? 'Invisible Government'?" *New York Times Magazine* (November 21, 1971); and Robert D. Schulzinger, *The Wise Men of Foreign Affairs: The History of the Council on Foreign Relations* (New York: Columbia University Press, 1984).

can petroleum companies, especially in the Middle East. As Michael Stoff concluded in *Oil, War and American National Security*, private corporations, not the government, "became the agents of national policy."[9] In turn, American multinational corporations expected the U.S. government to promote American private investment abroad and prevent nationalization by foreign governments.[10]

Organized labor was also a strong supporter of anticommunism at home and abroad. This fact may come as a surprise to many Americans given the popular impression of labor-management conflict and labor's pre–World War II history. Throughout the early part of the twentieth century, efforts by unions to organize, improve working conditions, and among the more radical unions, restructure the political economy were vehemently fought by business and government. It was not until after World War I and, in particular, the implementation of 1930s New Deal policies that the government officially recognized the right of workers to form unions. However, factors such as organized labor's growing legitimacy and moderation in goals, the postwar return of economic prosperity, Republican and McCarthyite attacks against New Deal policies and unionization, and the national security demands of World War II and the cold war produced unions that were much more comfortable and supportive of the status quo.

The **American Federation of Labor–Congress of Industrial Organizations (AFL-CIO),** the umbrella organization to which most American unions belonged during the 1950s, strongly supported the government's cold war policies at home and abroad. The AFL-CIO was active in the international labor movement through its International Confederation of Free Trade Unions, in particular in Europe, Asia, and Latin America. The AFL-CIO Institute for Free Labor Development was active, for example, in supporting anticommunist unionization and movements in Latin America (and often worked in conjunction with the CIA). Hence, while many American unions historically were the source of liberalism and the political left, they too became part of the anticommunist consensus during the cold war.[11]

Religious and ethnic groups also played prominent anticommunist roles during the cold war. Religious movements and groups have always played a powerful role throughout American history, dating back to the landing of the Pilgrims at Plymouth, Massachusetts. As Garry Wills argues in *Under God: Religion and American Politics,* "Religion has been at the center of our major political crises, which are always moral crises—the supporting and opposing of wars, of slavery, of corporate power, of civil rights, of sexual codes, of 'the West,' of American separatism and claims to empire."[12] Domestically, religion has been important because of the periodic occurrences of conservative Protestant revival movements, liberal social gospel

movements, and the rise of Catholicism in American society. This has been reinforced by the activities of Protestant **missionaries** abroad who attempted to Christianize foreigners, especially in Asia during the nineteenth and early twentieth centuries.[13]

Given this background, it is perhaps not surprising that religion played a prominent role in the rise of the anticommunist consensus during the post–World War II years. The Catholic church historically was extremely critical of communism and its atheistic views, rallying American Catholics behind the government's cold war policies. The late 1940s and early 1950s also witnessed the rise of Protestant fundamentalism against the secular trends of modern society, a movement that provided support for McCarthyism during the cold war years. Thus, American religion, even given its Christian diversity, reinforced the rise of anticommunism in society and the government.[14]

The United States is also a country of great ethnic diversity, and ethnic groups have actively influenced the making of U.S. foreign policy. For example, the Soviet Union's domination of Eastern Europe provoked a strong anticommunist response from ethnic groups with ties to the region. Polish Americans, reinforced by their Catholicism, were particularly vocal over the fate of Poland. Furthermore, they also represented a large bloc of potential voters in a number of key industrial states. This domestic political background helps to explain why Stalin's eventual consolidation of power in Poland was one of the important postwar developments during the late 1940s in hardening attitudes within the Truman administration and throughout society around the issue of anticommunism.

The rise of these various cold war–oriented groups laid the foundation for the development of the famed **China lobby,** or Taiwan lobby, that gained great prominence during the cold war years. The China lobby consisted primarily of Nationalist Chinese officials and Americans, including government officials, Protestant missionaries, China watchers and journalists, and American business leaders who were active in China before the 1949 revolution and interested in its future. The China lobby represented a broad coalition of diverse anticommunist groups, such as the American China Policy Association, the Committee to Defend America by Aiding Anti-Communist China, and the Committee for One Million (Against the Admission of Communist China Into the United Nations), that shared a common concern over the so-called "fall" of China and identified with the Nationalist Chinese government in Taiwan. Participants within the China lobby tended to emphasize the greater importance of Asia over Europe as a market, for national security reasons as symbolized by the Korean War, and for the future of Christianity. Members of the China lobby attacked the Truman administration for its Eurocentric and inadequate foreign policies, played a prominent role in the rise of McCarthyism, and helped forge an anticommunist consensus throughout society and the government during the cold war years.

The Committee for One Million, for example, was officially founded in 1953 by extremely conservative members of Congress and was very prominent and quite successful in lobbying congressional colleagues on China policy. One study conducted by the Congress's Congressional Research Service concluded that "the Committee's legitimation through direct, widespread, and explicit congressional participation in its creation and operation, over several decades, remains a remarkable event in the history of foreign policy lobbying in the Congress."[15] The rise of the China lobby, as embodied in organizations like the Committee for One Million, helps to explain why American presidents and their advisers were always more concerned about the political threat posed by the right than those on the left.

In sum, the prevalent social movements and groups during the cold war together helped to promote and reinforce the development of an anticommunist consensus throughout American society, in electoral and domestic politics, and in the governmental policymaking process. The prominence of these groups contributed to the rise of a powerful president in foreign policy, the expansion of the national security bureaucracy, and the development of an acquiescent and bipartisan Congress—all with strong public support throughout society and the domestic political environment.

Even American so-called "intellectuals," the traditional dissenters and critics of mainstream society, tended to join the anticommunist bandwagon. For example, the **Congress for Cultural Freedom**—an organization of prominent European and American writers and artists—took a strong anticommunist stand and tended to promote the American way of life in international forums (unbeknownst to most members, it was also heavily funded by the CIA).[16] Clearly, the cold war years were a time in which group politics formed a consensus behind a strong anticommunist foreign policy, and most challenging groups remained on the fringes of American politics.

THE MILITARY-INDUSTRIAL-SCIENTIFIC INFRASTRUCTURE

Before World War II, few institutions within the government or throughout American society were oriented toward foreign affairs and national security. World War II changed this situation dramatically and permanently. Almost overnight, the U.S. government redirected itself to waging a global war in which the military expanded enormously and civilian agencies grew to assist the president in fighting the conflict. This governmental effort, in turn, put the economy and society on a war footing to provide the necessary personnel, equipment, and services to achieve allied victory. Thus, a military-industrial-scientific infrastructure developed throughout society and government to support the war effort.

The national security infrastructure actually had its origins long before the 1940s, particularly during World War I when President Woodrow Wilson used the government to mobilize the country for war.[17] However, World War II and the cold war made this a permanent component of American society. Unlike the aftermath of previous wars in American history, the U.S. military demobilized for only a short time following World War II. With the rise of anticommunism, the United States once more expanded its resources in order to fight a global cold war. This not only resulted in the ascendance of the president in foreign policy and the growth of the foreign policy bureaucracy, but the military-industrial-scientific infrastructure continued to grow during the cold war years and became a permanent part of the American landscape. Thus, the development of the military-industrial-scientific infrastructure played a prominent role in defense politics and the making of U.S. foreign policy during the postwar years.

The **military-industrial complex** is actually a term popularized by President Dwight Eisenhower during his farewell address to the nation. His use of this term did not suggest that there existed a small collection of individuals within the military and private industry who conspired to dominate American national security policy against the wishes of the American people. Rather, Eisenhower understood that the military-industrial complex involved the existence of various segments of society with complementary interests that were mutually dependent on one another and together played a vital role in the politics of U.S. foreign policy. Eisenhower argued that such a complex of private and governmental bureaucratic institutions was an inevitable outcome of a society permanently mobilized for war, necessitated by the containment and deterrence policies.

Which organized segments of society comprise the military-industrial complex? *Four major elements exist:* (1) the military establishment within the executive branch, (2) industry and business, (3) Congress, and (4) academia and the scientific community. **Military-industrial-scientific infrastructure** (or national security infrastructure) is a more accurate term than *military-industrial complex.* The latter seems to conjure up simplistic conspiratorial notions and does not capture adequately the important role played by academia and the scientific community.[18]

Each of these organized segments had complementary interests: Members of the military establishment wanted weaponry and equipment to support containment; industry wanted to expand and make money; members of Congress wanted military bases and defense industry in their districts to provide jobs and votes; and scientists wanted the prestige and prominence that came with large grants and direct involvement in government. These complementary interests supported U.S. foreign policy throughout the 1940s and 1950s. They also developed into a complex web of mutually dependent and cooperative relationships between individuals and groups from these organized segments of society. Ultimately, the general public supported the development of a military-industrial-scientific infrastructure in the name of national security and because it was a key source of employment and prosperity.

As we discussed in chapter 7, the military establishment within the executive branch, especially the Department of Defense, grew enormously in size and scope as a result of World War II and the onset of the cold war. Demands for personnel, weaponry, and equipment were equally enormous. The government relied on its own production process, supervised by the Atomic Energy Commission and operated by private industry, for building nuclear weapons (review essay 7.1,

on the nuclear weapons production process). However, the military contracted out to private industry to meet its needs in virtually all other areas, from conventional weapons to uniforms to base construction.

Much of American industry became directly involved in equipping the military as a result of the cold war. This transformation began with U.S. entry into World War II, when the production of civilian materials and services changed to military production to defeat Germany and Japan. Large U.S. companies such as General Motors, Chrysler, McDonnell Douglas, and Boeing retooled their assembly lines to produce tanks and bombers rather than cars and commercial airplanes. With the rise of the cold war, these same companies continued working for the government and the Defense Department. By the 1950s, many Fortune 500 companies were **defense contractors** for the U.S. government. Some companies, such as General Dynamics and Rockwell International, became totally dependent on defense production; for other companies, such as General Electric, defense work was only a part of its business. Smaller, local businesses also became involved in defense work through the subcontracting of weapons systems or provision of services at local military bases. Taken together, defense-related industries provided millions of jobs for Americans, gaining the support of organized labor and workers in general. Thus, the permanent cold war economy and a close business-government partnership in defense politics was born.[19]

Congress helped to reinforce the networks of relationships that developed in defense politics. Members of Congress had to approve the defense programs and budget for the government. This role gave them considerable power, especially within the Armed Services and Appropriations committees. In return for political support, members of Congress were able to persuade the Pentagon and defense industry to build military bases and businesses in their states and districts. Not surprisingly, the military came to operate hundreds of bases located in every state, and major weapons systems were typically subcontracted out to dozens of businesses throughout the country. Although many basing and contracting decisions may have been made for sound national security and financial reasons, they also were made in order to win the political support of members of Congress. In this way, members of Congress were able to claim responsibility for economic growth and jobs back home, attracting local constituent support for their reelection.

Although it has typically been de-emphasized in discussions of the military-industrial complex, academia and the scientific community represent the final element in the military-industrial-scientific infrastructure. The ties between science and the government date back to the nineteenth century. However, the major drive to bring scientists together to work for the U.S. government began with the **Manhattan Project,** the effort to develop the atomic bomb during World War II.[20]

Since that time scientists in physics, chemistry, and other natural sciences have been employed by government, academia, and research and policy institutes to provide the know-how for designing weapons and turning ideas into reality. According to Stuart Leslie, "For better and for worse, the Cold War redefined American science. In the decade following the Second World War, the Department of Defense (DOD) became the biggest single patron of American science, predominantly in the physical sciences and engineering but important in many of the natural and social sciences as well."[21] Social scientists became heavily involved and provided many of the ideas which became the basis of U.S. national security policy during the cold war years, such as nuclear deterrence theory, the theory of limited war, counterinsurgency warfare, and Third World development strategies for nation building and modernization.[22]

The **militarization of research** was led by the more prominent universities, such as Yale University, Massachusetts Institute of Technology, Stanford University, and the University of California at Berkeley. The University of California, for example, operated the only two facilities responsible for designing nuclear weapons for the U.S. government, Lawrence Livermore Laboratory and Los Alamos Laboratory. Such institutions became heavily involved in conducting military research, received government defense money, and promoted a cold war orientation in their educational curriculum.

Scholarship in international relations proliferated and graduate programs in international studies grew to become a key source of recruitment and expertise for U.S. government foreign affairs personnel.[23] The president of the University of Michigan, for example, proudly declared in his annual report for 1958–1959 that "various areas of University teaching have recog-

nized the cold-war struggle and have reflected their concern in our teaching programs." He stressed the importance of new programs emphasizing area studies of Third World regions, such as South Asia and the Middle East. "The Soviet nation has seen with perfect clarity," the president triumphed, that "knowledge through research . . . is the secret of our greatness."[24]

The militarization of research raises serious questions about the purpose and nature of higher education. As Senator J. William Fulbright so forcefully reminded us a generation ago, "When the university turns away from its central purpose and makes itself an appendage to the Government, concerning itself with techniques rather than purposes, with expedients rather than ideas, dispensing conventional orthodoxy rather than new ideas, it is not only failing to meet its responsibilities to its students; it is betraying a public trust."[25] This is a fear that President Eisenhower voiced in his farewell address, as will be discussed below.

In sum, the 1940s and 1950s resulted in the formation of a large military-industrial-scientific infrastructure involving millions of people and the support of most segments of American society. Close and mutually supportive networks of relationships developed between the military establishment, industry, Congress, and the scientific community, particularly among more prominent groups and individuals. These relationships were reinforced by the development of a **revolving-door system** through which members of the military were hired by the defense industry upon retirement, defense industry leaders were appointed to important positions within the Department of Defense, and so on.[26]

The net result of these activities was that each organized segment of society could claim that its activities contributed to strengthening American national security while they were enmeshed in the politics of national defense:

> The influence of politics on national defense is so pervasive, so deeply embedded at every level, that it becomes difficult even to identify. Virtually every American is involved, directly or indirectly. Selfish political and economic interests in military affairs are often carefully wrapped in the American flag, and defended with the most elegant, sophisticated, and technically complex rationales. . . . Politics influences literally thousands of decisions that constantly must be made to create the treaties, strategies, forces, bases,

On January 17, 1961, President Dwight Eisenhower made his **farewell address** to the American people, imploring them to be knowledgeable citizens alert to the threats and opportunities that the United States faced both abroad and at home. It is in this speech that the term *military-industrial complex* was first used as Eisenhower warned Americans of the dangers it posed for the workings of democracy. Because he was retiring from public office, Eisenhower's farewell address may have represented a public airing of his most personal thoughts and feelings.

He began by discussing the importance of having a good working relationship between the president and the Congress, and then he turned "to share a few final thoughts" about U.S. foreign policy. Eisenhower pointed out that, although the twentieth century has produced major wars among the great nations, "America is today the strongest, the most influential, and the most productive nation in the world." At the same time, however, "we face a hostile ideology—global in scope, atheistic in character, ruthless in purpose, and insidious in method. Unhappily the danger it poses promises to be of indefinite duration. . . . But threats, new in kind or degree, constantly arise. I mention only two."

First, Eisenhower *warned of a permanent military-industrial complex.* "A vital element in keeping the peace is our military establishment. Our arms must be mighty, ready for instant action, so that no potential aggressor may be tempted to risk his own destruction." Yet as he pointed out, "our military organization today bears little relation to that known by any of my predecessors in peacetime, or indeed by the fighting men of World War II or Korea. Until the latest of our world conflicts, the United States had no armaments industry. American makers of plowshares could, with time and as required, make swords as well." But according to Eisenhower, "we can no longer risk emergency improvisation of national defense; we have been compelled to create a permanent armaments industry of vast proportions. Added to this, three and a half million men and women are directly engaged in the defense establishment. This conjunction of an immense military establishment and a large arms industry is 'new' in the American experience. The total influence—economic, political, even spiritual—is felt in every city, every State house, every office of the Federal government." Although Eisenhower recognized "the imperative need for this development," he also believed that Americans "must not fail to comprehend its grave implications. Our toil, resources and livelihood are all involved; so is the very structure of our society."

Eisenhower, therefore, emphasized the need for vigilance. "In the councils of government, we must guard against the acquisition of unwarranted influence, whether sought or unsought, by the military-industrial complex. The potential for the disastrous rise of misplaced power exists and will persist." Eisenhower continued, "We must never let the weight of this combination endanger our liberties or democratic processes. We should take nothing for granted. Only an alert and knowledgeable citizenry can compel the proper meshing of the huge industrial and military machinery of defense with our peaceful methods and goals, so that security and liberty may prosper together."

The second new threat that Eisenhower pointed to was the *role of technology, science, and academia and the rise of a scientific-technological elite.* "Akin to, and largely responsible for the sweeping changes in our industrial-military posture, has been the technological revolution during the recent decades. In this revolution, research has become central; it also becomes more formalized, complex, and costly. A steadily increasing share is conducted for, by, or at the direction of, the federal government." This technological revolution has changed the nature of academia and the conduct of science. As Eisenhower explained, "Today, the solitary inventor, tinkering in his shop, has been overshadowed by task forces of scientists in laboratories and testing fields. In the same fashion, the free university, historically the fountainhead of free ideas and scientific discovery, has experienced a revolution in the conduct of research." One of the consequences is that "partly because of the huge costs involved, a government contract becomes virtually a substitute for intellectual curiosity." Given these changes, Eisenhower warned that "the prospect of domination of the nation's scholars by federal employment, project allocations, and the power of money is ever present—and is gravely to be regarded. Yet, in holding scientific research and discovery in respect, as we should, we must also be alert to the equal and opposite danger that public policy could itself become the captive of a scientific-technological elite."

After cautioning Americans to remain knowledgeable and alert to the development of the military-industrial complex and the rise of a scientific-technological elite, Eisenhower ended his farewell address by stressing the need to ultimately overcome war, negotiate and compromise, and find peace among the peoples of the world. Progress in reducing the cold war was crucial in Eisenhower's thinking because the future of American society and democracy was ultimately at stake.

SOURCE: U.S. President Dwight D. Eisenhower, "Farewell Address," (January 17, 1961).

and weapons that collectively make up our national defense.[27]

The development of a national security infrastructure and the politics of national defense contributed not only to the development of the anticommunist consensus and a permanent large military establishment in support of the requirements of the containment strategy during the cold war era but also to waste, corruption, vested interests, and resistance to any challenges to the status quo. This also had a major impact in exacerbating the tensions between the demands of national security and the requirements of democracy. Eisenhower was aware of this possibility, and therefore in his farewell address to the country, he warned Americans to be "knowledgeable and alert" concerning the consequences of a military-industrial complex for the functioning of American democracy. (See **essay 16.2** on Eisenhower's farewell address about the military-industrial complex.)

THE FOREIGN POLICY ESTABLISHMENT

The cold war years also saw the rise of a foreign policy establishment. This was not a formal group of individuals per se but consisted of an informal network of like-minded individuals who shared an anticommunist consensus and served in high-level policymaking positions within the executive branch. In other words, the **foreign policy establishment** produced much of the high-level personnel and expertise that provided the basis of U.S. foreign policy throughout the cold war. Much has been written in the last three decades on the cold war–era foreign policy–making establishment. Its members have been referred to as the "best and the brightest," "national security managers," and the "wise men." Godfrey Hodgson, in "The Establishment," argues that *the foreign policy establishment can be defined by five characteristics: history, policy, aspiration, instinct, and technique.*[28]

First, the history of the foreign policy establishment dates to efforts by a small group of individuals associated with President Woodrow Wilson and his aide Colonel Edward M. House, to combat the rising tide of isolationism following Senate defeat of the League of Nations treaty in 1920. However, the crucial event in the formation of the foreign policy establishment was World War II. "It was the war which brought together *the three groups which make up the modern foreign policy establishment*: the internationally-minded lawyers,

bankers and executives of international corporations in New York; the government officials in Washington; and the academics."[29] They were initially recruited to staff the ever expanding national security bureaucracy and meet the war effort in the War Department, State Department, and Office of Strategic Services (OSS). It wasn't long before many of these people began to interact with each other and work together, forming working networks of relationships.

With the rise of anticommunism and increasing American global involvement following the war, many of the same people became involved in government efforts to fight the cold war through agencies like the National Security Council, Department of Defense, CIA, and others throughout the national security bureaucracy. According to Hodgson, "Each of the great decisions of American policy in the Truman years tied these same ties tighter. Bankers and professors took time off to work in the administration on the Marshall Plan, on NATO, or on rethinking strategic policy. A trickle of academics and lawyers began to go down to Washington as consultants, especially on these international programs."[30] Thus, the foreign policy–making establishment was born.

The foreign policy establishment should not be confused with the upper class, although "it may help you to rise in the establishment if you have inherited wealth, or family connections with powerful men in it, or an Ivy League education."[31] Most individuals who became members of the foreign policy–making establishment actually had upper-middle-class backgrounds. The **GI Bill** after World War II was particularly consequential in enabling young men of modest means to attend Harvard, Yale, or other prestigious universities where one could study law or international relations—key routes to foreign policy prominence. Nor should the foreign policy establishment be confused with a conspiracy by a small group of individuals to control the government. Rather, the foreign policy establishment consisted of hundreds of individuals of varying degrees of prominence who came to know each other (or of each other) and worked together through governmental service, work outside the government, and through social interaction.

Second, the policy emphases of the foreign policy establishment were anti-isolationism and anticommunism. "The American opponents of isolationism, to a man, felt that appeasement had been a disaster, and that the lesson to be drawn from the struggle against Fascism was that there were those in the world who could only be restrained by force."[32] This approach to foreign policy was heavily conditioned by a **realpolitik, or power politics, view** of the world in which states competed for power, threats to international stability and order came from unsatisfied and revolutionary great powers, and the threat and use of force were considered the most effective instrument of statecraft.[33]

Individuals of the establishment were particularly concerned with the threat of the Soviet Union and communist expansion, especially in Europe, but had little fear of domestic communism. At the same time, these characteristics distinguished them from the political right, such as the China lobby and McCarthyism, which was preoccupied with communist expansion not only throughout the world but at home as well. Nevertheless, such a power politics and anti-Soviet view of the world helps to account for the national security ethos that arose within government in the making of U.S. foreign policy.

Third, *the aspiration of the foreign policy establishment was quite simply the moral and political leadership of the world.* According to Hodgson, "the American establishment wanted to succeed Britain as the military and economic guarantor and moral leader of an enlightened, liberal, democratic, and capitalist world order."[34] Members of the establishment felt that the postwar years represented the "American century" and they relished exercising the unprecedented economic, military, and political power of the United States throughout the world. As previously discussed regarding political culture and national style in chapter 13, there was a strong sense of confidence and American exceptionalism that permeated American society. It is not by accident that America's foreign policy–making elite have been referred to as the "best and the brightest" and the "wise men."[35]

This reached its height under President John F. Kennedy and his "New Frontier" and through competition with the Soviet Union and Premier Nikita Khrushchev for the destiny of the world, a contest in which the United States was "committed to the cause of the new American empire, in bringing proof that our system was better than theirs." As David Halberstam stated, "They carried with them an exciting sense of American elitism, a sense that the best men had been summoned forth from the country to harness this dream to a new American nationalism, bringing a new, strong, dynamic spirit to our historic role in world affairs, not necessarily to bring the American dream to reality here at home, but to bring it to reality elsewhere in the world."[36]

Such an attitude exemplified what J. William Fulbright would shortly call an "arrogance of power."[37] Or

as theologian Reinhold Niebuhr stated during the 1950s, such an "illusion of American omnipotence is a natural mistake of a commercial community which knows that American hegemony is based upon our technical-economic power but does not understand the vast complexities of ethnic loyalties, of social forces in a decaying agrarian world, of the resentments which a mere display of military power creates among those who are not committed to us."[38]

Fourth, the establishment's instinct was for the political center. "The characteristic men of the establishment—Stimson, McCloy, Acheson, Rusk, Bundy—have always seen themselves as the men of judicious, pragmatic wisdom, avoiding ideology and steering the middle course between the Yahoos of the right and the impractical sentimentality of the left."[39] This reflected a long tradition going back to Teddy Roosevelt, of "an aristocracy come to power, convinced of its own disinterested quality, believing itself above both petty partisan interest and material greed." Hence, they "preferred to view their role as service."[40] And occupying the political center during the cold war years meant that the establishment represented the anticommunist consensus of the era while trying to avoid the wrath of the political right.

Finally, the establishment's technique was to operate out of public view and within the executive branch, especially the White House. Individuals of the foreign policy establishment were usually appointed by the president to policymaking positions within the foreign policy bureaucracy. They constantly revolved from government to the private world and back, continuing to interact informally and through membership in prominent foreign policy groups, most notably the Council on Foreign Relations (review essay 16.1). They virtually never ran for elective office. In fact, they tended to be distrustful and fearful of mass opinion, adhering to an elitist view of how U.S. foreign policy should be made, as discussed in chapter 13, on public opinion (for example, recall their opposition to isolationism, which was prevalent among the mass public before and immediately after World War II).

Thus, for Hodgson the foreign policy establishment consisted of "a self-recruiting group of men (virtually no women) who have shared a bipartisan philosophy towards, and have exercised practical influence on, the course of American defense and foreign policy."[41] This is not to assert that the foreign policy establishment was monolithic. Differences existed and considerable infighting over U.S. foreign policy took place. However, these were largely tactical differences existing within an overall anticommunist, realpolitik, and interventionist consensus. With regard to American policy toward Vietnam, for example, debates were limited to when and how to intervene: now or later? With advisers or troops? Therefore, "right up to 1965, the year of decision, the overwhelming consensus of the establishment accepted without moral or intellectual doubt that the war would have to be escalated—if the only alternative was losing it."[42]

By the 1950s, therefore, the foreign policy establishment represented an informal network of prominent individuals who shared the assumptions of the anticommunist consensus and exerted a great influence on the making of U.S. foreign policy. By constantly shifting between high-level positions in government and in the private world, they also provided a critical bridge between the president, the national security bureaucracy, and key groups and institutions throughout American society. Therefore, the rise of national security– and cold war–oriented groups, the development of a military-industrial-scientific infrastructure, and the growth of a foreign policy establishment dominated group politics at virtually all levels of society and were critical elements in the politics of U.S. foreign policy during the cold war years.

THE RISE OF MOVEMENTS OF THE LEFT AND THE RIGHT

Group politics changed considerably since Vietnam. The ideological and foreign policy consensus was challenged initially from the political left and then from the political right. In order to understand the collapse of the consensus and its implications for group politics and U.S. foreign policy, one must briefly discuss the rise of liberalism and the new left during the 1960s and early 1970s, embodied in the civil rights and antiwar movements, and the rise of conservative movements and the right during the 1970s and 1980s.

THE CIVIL RIGHTS AND ANTIWAR MOVEMENTS

The rise of liberalism and the new left began in the late 1950s with the **civil rights movement.** The movement began when groups such as the Southern Christian Leadership Conference (SCLC), under the leadership of Martin Luther King, Jr., and the Student Nonviolent Coordinating Committee (SNCC) and thousands of blacks demonstrated for civil rights in the South. Many white liberals, especially students from northern schools and groups such as Students for a Democratic Society (SDS), joined the fight for civil rights during the early 1960s as the movement expanded into the North to address issues of racism and poverty.[43]

The bulk of the civil rights movement represented a nonviolent liberal approach to reforming American society. However, the often violent resistance by more extreme segments of the public, established groups, and local governments in the North and the South embittered many of the protesters and radicalized them. This "politicization" and radicalizing process was reinforced by the lack of support for the movement from the Democratic party and the federal government under the leadership of John Kennedy and Lyndon Johnson. Thus, the civil rights movement was accompanied by the growth of black nationalism and black power, represented by Malcolm X and the Black Panthers.

Although the Civil Rights Act was passed in 1964 and Johnson initiated the war on poverty, these actions were perceived by many blacks as too little, too late. Black frustration and despair at local resistance, in fact, reached the boiling point, triggering riots in Los Angeles, Detroit, and other urban areas throughout the country. Therefore, what began as a liberal hope to bring black Americans into mainstream society ultimately ended with Americans bitterly divided, contributing to the collapse of the liberal-conservative ideological consensus.

A second issue, the Vietnam War, generated the **antiwar movement** during the mid-1960s. The antiwar movement represented a broad coalition of Americans united against escalation and continuation of the war. Many participants in this movement had been involved in, and heavily influenced by, the civil rights movement. The antiwar movement grew from a few dozen disparate groups during the early 1960s to represent a loose coalition of well over a thousand groups by the late 1960s. This coalition included a wide variety of groups, such as Quakers, pacifists, students, the old peace movement, Democrats, liberals, and the old left and new left. At its height, the antiwar movement was supported by a large segment of society and staged peaceful demonstrations involving millions of people throughout the country. Not only did over half a million men refuse to be drafted, but more and more soldiers went AWOL (absent without leave) and service people joined the peace marches as well.[44]

Like the civil rights movement, the antiwar movement represented the rise of challenging movements and groups reflecting the resurgence of liberalism and the ascendance of the new left. Furthermore, the Johnson administration's continuing escalation of the Vietnam War and the domestic resistance encountered by the antiwar movement embittered and radicalized some of the more active participants and groups. Radicalization led them to question the wisdom of working within the system and relying on nonviolence.[45] Thus, by the late 1960s *opposition to the war took many forms*:

> letters to congressmen and Presidents; advertisements in newspapers; signatures on petitions; vigils in town centers, at government buildings, installations, and other public places; lobbying congressmen; working to elect candidates sympathetic to the cause; tax refusal; draft refusal; desertion from the armed forces; nonviolent civil disobedience resulting in arrest, jailing, and court trials; nonviolent civil disobedience met by tear-gassing and/or violence from police and troops; legal mass marches and rallies of tens and hundreds of thousands of people; strikes on campus or at the workplace; draft board raids to destroy records—burning them or pouring blood on them; illegal, violent acts such as trashing, burning buildings or setting off bombs; suicide.[46]

Things culminated in 1968 as events fed one another: the Tet Offensive in Vietnam; Eugene McCarthy's strong showing in the New Hampshire Democratic primary relative to President Johnson; LBJ's withdrawal from the Democratic presidential nomination; Robert Kennedy's declaration for the Democratic presidential nomination on a platform favoring American de-escalation in Vietnam; the assassination of Martin Luther King, Jr.; urban riots; mass student demonstrations on campuses; and the assassination of Robert Kennedy after his victory in the California primary against Vice President Hubert Humphrey. It seemed like the country was being torn apart at the seams. For the antiwar movement it was a time of considerable hope and fear.

Then came Chicago and the **1968 Democratic National Convention.** While Hubert Humphrey was being nominated by the convention on a ticket supporting LBJ's Vietnam policies, a war was raging in the streets between the Chicago police, the Illinois National Guard, and the FBI against demonstrators opposed to the war and opposed to such Democratic leaders as Mayor Richard Daley and Hubert Humphrey. Events in Chicago further alienated and radicalized members of the antiwar movement, moving them away from the Democratic party and the workings of the political system. It also served to further splinter an unbelieving public that was watching the war at home on television. As a result, much of the public—the so-called "silent majority"—would turn against the demonstrators and toward Richard Nixon, the Republican presidential nominee.

The antiwar movement, the rise of liberalism, and the growth of the new left actually peaked in 1972, with the nomination of George McGovern as the Democratic presidential candidate. As with the rise of conservatism and the right during the late 1940s and early 1950s, the forces of liberalism and the new left were unable to fundamentally alter American society or capture control of the government. Nevertheless, the size and intensity of the antiwar movement politicized the issues surrounding the Vietnam War. The antiwar movement's pressures helped generate majority support in favor of American withdrawal and motivated President Nixon's "Vietnamization" program to bring American soldiers home and placate a war-weary public.[47]

The civil rights and antiwar movements also were responsible for *generating new social movements and politically active groups* in areas such as feminism, native American and Hispanic rights, gay rights, consumer rights (and Ralph Nader), and environmentalism.[48] Many women, for example, were active in the civil rights movement, the antiwar movement, and the new left. The experiences of these activist women were an important element in the mobilization of the modern women's movement.[49] The movements in favor of pro-choice, nuclear freeze, anti-apartheid, and human rights that arose in prominence after the 1970s are legacies of the civil rights and antiwar movements.[50] Overall, liberalism and the new left became active and influential forces in group and domestic politics since the 1960s. (See **essay 16.3** for a discussion of the American old and new left.)

ESSAY 16.3
THE OLD AND THE NEW LEFT

The 1960s resulted in the rise of the new left in American politics. But what is the new left? How does it differ from the old left? For most Americans, these political labels are confusing. Nevertheless, it is important to understand these ideological differences in order to comprehend the evolution of American politics and its impact on foreign policy (see essay 13.2 for the differences between American liberalism and conservatism).

The **old left** involves the period from the late nineteenth century until the 1950s, when American socialist thought and socialist groups dominated the political left in American politics. During the early twentieth century until the end of World War I, democratic socialism predominated among the political left. **Democratic socialists** envisioned a fully democratic society in which the economy was responsive to all its citizens. Adherents of democratic socialism were particularly critical of capitalism and big business, which they saw as the key sources of unemployment, poverty, and inequalities of wealth and political influence.

Although never representing more than a minority of Americans, democratic socialism did have a base of support within the mass public and grew in popularity during the 1910s. While business, established groups, and the government fought the rise of socialism, democratic socialists nevertheless had some success in fighting for the rights of workers and in gaining office in American politics. By 1912, in fact, the Socialist Party of America, led by Eugene Debs, received nearly a million votes in the presidential election and had elected over twelve hundred members to public office throughout the country. However, with American entry in World War I, democratic socialists and others on the political left declined in popularity as a result of the political conformity and repression imposed by the government and its supporters during and after the war.

With the success of the Bolshevik Revolution in 1917, **American communism** grew within the political left and began to overshadow democratic socialism. During the 1920s, the Soviet Union was often portrayed, especially by American communists, as a worker's paradise where the principles of Marxism were being implemented by the Soviet government and its citizens. This strong sense of identity with the Soviet Union was reinforced by the Great Depression, which devastated the American and European economies and impoverished large masses of people, as predicted by most critics of capitalism. As we have dis-

cussed in previous chapters, the mass public turned to more liberal and leftist solutions in pulling the country out of the depression. This period was the height of popularity and influence of the old left in American politics, for both American communism and noncommunist democratic socialism. American intellectuals were particularly attracted to Marxist thought and the American communist movement during the Great Depression.

With the success of New Deal policies and World War II, growing divisions between different socialist groups, and the rise of the cold war during the 1950s, the old left declined as a potent political force and fell victim to McCarthyism and the resurgence of conservatism and the political right. Yet the growth of the civil rights and anti–Vietnam War movements during the 1960s eventually produced a new left, which grew in popularity and influence in American politics.

A variety of different sources gave rise to the **new left**. Many leaders and activists of the new left were young students who were heavily influenced by their educational experiences, especially in college. While some were the children of socialist parents, known as "red diaper babies," most were the sons and daughters of Roosevelt, Truman, and Kennedy supporters who were instilled with a belief in modern American idealistic and liberal values. Yet when they compared their values and life experience to events occurring around them, such as the American war in Vietnam and the prevalence of segregation and racism in America, the contradictions between American ideals and reality politicized and radicalized them.

Whereas the old left was predominantly socialist in orientation, the new left was predominantly nonsocialist. The new left actually consisted of a variety of different groups and coalitions of individuals, some of whom were politically oriented, while others were more culturally oriented. Those within the new left who were *more politically oriented*, such as the Students for a Democratic Society (SDS), attempted to bring about political change at the local and national level through "participatory democracy" in order to make American society more democratic and just for its inhabitants. The young student activists were both influenced and joined by religious and secular groups that were motivated to address issues of civil rights, powerlessness and alienation, inequality, and poverty, thereby embodying a long historical tradition within the American political left. Religious influences, such as Quakers and

Jews, were reinforced by pacifist thought and groups, which represented another important historical tradition within the political left and provided a key element of the antiwar movement and the new left.

Those within the new left who were more culturally oriented emphasized the need to change American consciousness, beliefs, and ways of life in order to promote individual freedom throughout the country. They were critical of the conformity, rigidity, and "uptightness" of mainstream society and argued instead for greater individualism and emotional spontaneity in thought and lifestyle. They were influenced by the lifestyle of the "beats" during the 1950s and many turned to non-Western sources of thought, such as Buddhism and Hinduism. Not surprisingly, they were referred to as the **counterculture** because of their criticism of mainstream societal norms and lifestyles. Whatever was unacceptable within mainstream society was considered "in" within the counterculture: long hair, informal and flamboyant clothes, premarital sex, illegal drugs, rock music, and so on. Countercultural enclaves were carved out around the country, often near college campuses and in urban areas, such as the Haight-Ashbury district in San Francisco and Telegraph Avenue in Berkeley. The 1960s and 1970s also resulted in an increase of communal living, both in cities and in isolated rural areas.

The *growth of the new left achieved mixed success.* On one hand, the new left was unsuccessful in fundamentally changing American society and U.S. foreign policy in accordance with its values. Ultimately, the new left was too disparate, poorly organized, politically naive,

and unappealing—especially symbolically—to the mass public beyond the youth culture. On the other hand, the new left did contribute to the collapse of the anticommunist and liberal-conservative ideological consensus that dominated the cold war years, precipitating many of the changes in American politics that have occurred since Vietnam. Some of the values, lifestyles, and concerns of the new left (such as environmentalism) have become normal parts of contemporary mainstream society (although often commercialized by the market system). Furthermore, although most members of the new left have gotten older by now and live more mainstream lives, many continue to maintain a similar ideological (though much more pragmatic) orientation and continue to play important political roles through their jobs, as parents, and as citizens—a trend reflected in the proliferation of political activism and group activity in support of liberal and new left causes.

SOURCES: Milton Canton, *The Divided Left: American Radicalism 1900–1975* (New York: Hill and Wang, 1978); Albert Fried, ed., *Socialism in America: From the Shakers to the Third International* (New York: Columbia University Press, 1992); Godfrey Hodgson, *America in Our Time* (New York: Vintage, 1976); Maurice Isserman, *If I Had a Hammer . . . The Death of the Old Left and the Birth of the New Left* (New York: Basic Books, 1987); Kenneth Keniston, *Young Radicals: Notes on Committed Youth* (New York: Harcourt, Brace, and World, 1968); Harvey Klehr, *The Heyday of American Communism: The Depression Decade* (New York: Basic Books, 1984); Lawrence Lader, *Power of the Left: American Radical Movements Since 1946* (New York: W. W. Norton, 1979); Keith Melville, *Communes in the Counterculture: Origins, Theories, Styles of Life* (New York: William Morrow, 1972); and James Miller, *Democracy Is in the Streets: From Port Huron to the Siege of Chicago* (New York: Simon and Schuster, 1987).

THE RESURGENCE OF CONSERVATIVE MOVEMENTS AND THE RIGHT

The events and social movements of the 1960s also contributed to the resurgence of movements and groups reflecting conservatism and the **political right**. Conservatives and members of the political right were aghast over the loss of Vietnam to communism, the increasing power of the Soviet Union relative to the United States, the growth of government intervention in the economy and the welfare state represented by President Johnson's Great Society programs, the rise of individualism and sexual promiscuity, and the decline of law and order. Whereas the liberal and new left social movements prevalent during the 1960s had argued that American society and government policies were inconsistent with the moral and cultural values embod-

ied in the Declaration of Independence and the Constitution, conservatives believed that America was in a state of "moral decline" caused by the rise of liberalism and the left. Consequently, conservatives began to organize and become politically active. This activity was reinforced by the election of Nixon to the presidency, which enabled many conservatives to become members of the administration. Hence, social movements representing broad coalitions of conservative-oriented groups within society arose in support of anticommunism, private enterprise, and social issues such as school prayer and anti-abortion.[51]

As with the rise of liberalism and the new left, religious groups and forces played a prominent role in the rise of conservatism and the political right. The **Christian right** and religious fundamentalists, such as Jerry Falwell and Pat Robertson and other televangelists, took to the airwaves. They were dedicated to defeating "secular humanism" through the promotion of anti-communism and religious behavior throughout society. As with the growth of liberalism and the left, the rise of conservatism produced more extremist elements. For example, some religious fundamentalists wanted to change the United States into a theocracy—a religious state; and other groups on the far right attempted to promote change through violence.[52]

The influence of conservative social movements reached its height in the late 1970s and early 1980s, represented by the election of Ronald Reagan to the presidency. Overall, conservatives and the political right have become more influential throughout society and within government. The mass public also has tended to become more responsive to the symbolic and nationalist appeals of the Republican party, especially in the South. Conservatives, like the liberals before them, nevertheless have been unable to establish a new consensus behind their ideological view of the world.

GROUP POLITICS SINCE VIETNAM

In sum, the liberal-conservative ideological consensus that dominated the cold war years collapsed during the 1960s and 1970s and was replaced by greater ideological, electoral, and group competition in American politics. Particularly in foreign policy, the social movements that arose from the left and right shattered the anticommunist consensus. The breakdown of the foreign policy consensus *affected the post-Vietnam role of group politics in the making of U.S. foreign policy in three ways*, with two of the patterns representing change and one representing continuity: (1) The foreign policy establishment collapsed; (2) there was a proliferation of groups, ideological diversity, and political activism; and (3) at the same time, the military-industrial-scientific infrastructure continued to pervade society. Thus, some cold war patterns continued but were accompanied by new patterns of change. These patterns have for the most part continued into the post–cold war years and since September 11, 2001.

As David Truman states in *The Governmental Process*, "Any considerable increase in the types of such groups, or any major change in the nature of their in-

terrelationships will be reflected subsequently in the operation of the political system."[53] These changes in group politics had the contradictory impact during the post–Vietnam War and post–cold war years of providing the president with greater leeway to influence the direction of U.S. foreign policy while simultaneously posing greater domestic and democratic constraints on his ability to exercise power.

COLLAPSE OF THE FOREIGN POLICY ESTABLISHMENT

The last time individuals within the foreign policy establishment would operate with a consensus and act in unison was in March of 1968. The war in Vietnam was going badly and the country was being torn apart at home. As he had in the past, President Johnson convened a meeting of his major advisers and a group of senior policy advisers from outside the government, who were referred to as the "Wise Men." Johnson met with this collection of prominent individuals, representing members of the foreign policy establishment from as far back as the Truman administration, to decide what to do about U.S. policy in Vietnam. "Dean Acheson was there, and Arthur Dean, George Ball and McGeorge Bundy, Douglas Dillon, Robert Murphy and Cyrus Vance, all down from New York. The President's friend Abe Fortas, then a Supreme Court Justice, was there, and so were two legendary generals from World War II: Omar N. Bradley and Matthew B. Ridgeway." Others were present "by virtue of the office they held in the Administration: Dean Rusk, Clark Clifford, Richard Helms of the CIA, Walt Rostow, Nicholas Katzenbach, Henry Cabot Lodge, Paul Nitze, Averell Harriman, Arthur Goldberg and the older Bundy brother, Bill." In effect, the participants represented a who's who of the foreign policy establishment.[54]

These prominent individuals surprised President Johnson by telling him that they no longer supported further escalation of the war. As Godfrey Hodgson described their position, "Deeply discouraged by the way military victory was receding like a mirage into the future; impressed by the passionate opposition to the war they encountered in their children, their law partners, their banking correspondents, and their contacts of every kind across the country; aghast at what might happen to the threatened dollar on the world's exchanges;

faithful, finally, to its instinct for the center: the establishment made a characteristic decision not to put good money after bad."[55]

This signified the beginning of the end for the foreign policy establishment. By the early 1970s, the establishment was bitterly divided over Vietnam and the future of U.S. foreign policy. Walt Rostow and Dean Rusk, Johnson's national security adviser and secretary of state, continued to believe that the war was justified and that no major avoidable mistakes had been made in the way it was waged. Others, such as McGeorge Bundy, Kennedy's national security adviser, believed that the war was justified but that mistakes were made in its conduct. However, some members of the establishment, such as Clark Clifford, adviser to Truman and secretary of defense under Johnson, believed that the Vietnam War was a mistake. Others, like Paul Warnke and George Ball, high-level Johnson officials in the Defense and State departments, held not only that the Vietnam War was a mistake but that the pursuit of containment in a non-European context was misguided, as well. Finally, people like Daniel Ellsberg, a prominent Defense Department official, believed that containment and U.S. intervention throughout the world was not only inappropriate but a fundamentally unjust policy as well.

The consensus in foreign policy views of the establishment had collapsed and splintered, contributing to the ideological and foreign policy diversity that would permeate among the elite and mass publics. Thus, the foreign policy establishment not only contributed to American escalation in Vietnam but also shattered in the war's aftermath. These prominent individuals within American society would continue to receive attention and exercise influence, but they would no longer do so as a unified force in support of America's cold war policies. Instead, they would compete with each other for influence in the making of U.S. foreign policy by choosing sides in the group politics since Vietnam.[56]

EXPANSION OF GROUP POLITICS

The rise of social movements of the left and right led not only to the collapse of the anticommunist consensus and the foreign policy establishment but to the expansion of group politics as well. The events and movements of the 1960s and 1970s, fed by the weakening of American political parties discussed in the previous chapter, resulted in the proliferation of new and old groups in American politics, in increased ideological diversity and competition among groups, and in more individual political participation in social movements and group politics.[57]

During the 1970s and 1980s, liberal and left-leaning groups actively supported a U.S. foreign policy that promoted human rights and self-determination, arms control and disarmament, the eradication of Third World hunger and poverty, anti-apartheid and global environmentalism—a more liberal internationalist orientation to world politics. Conservative and right-wing groups emphasized expansion of Soviet power and communism, the need for a U.S. defense buildup, and support for Third World allies and market economies abroad—a more conservative internationalist orientation. Hence, the cold war consensus was replaced by considerable fragmentation and competition in group politics. This fragmentation prompted more Americans to actively attempt to influence American politics and U.S. foreign policy, attempts which have continued since the end of the cold war.

Established foreign policy groups such as the Carnegie Endowment for International Peace, Council on Foreign Relations, Foreign Policy Research Institute, and Rand Corporation continued to function and were complemented by new groups such as the Trilateral Commission. However, these centrist groups were now joined by more conservative groups, such as the American Enterprise Institute, Heritage Foundation, Hoover Institution, Center for Strategic and International Studies, a new Committee on the Present Danger, the Joseph Coors and John Scaife foundations, and the Heritage Foundation. In addition, more liberal groups increasingly became prominent and were formed, including the Arms Control Association, Brookings Institution, Center for Defense Information, Institute for Policy Studies, World Policy Institute, and Worldwatch Institute. These institutions also have been joined by those advocating a semi-isolationist orientation, such as the Cato Institute.

By the late 1960s and early 1970s, old think tanks began to grow and new ones were established, and were increasingly prone to take independent policy initiatives (as opposed to rely on contract work). Overall, of the nearly one hundred or so policy research groups, or

think tanks, in Washington, D.C. (some having fewer than a dozen employees, others employing up to 250), two-thirds were set up after 1970. "Every year, these institutes conduct thousands of conferences, luncheons, forums, and seminars, while publishing hundreds of books and innumerable pamphlets, reports, newsletters, backgrounders, and occasional essays. In addition, their members write scores of op-ed articles that appear in dozens of newspapers, and their most articulate fellows perform as commentators on radio and television news programs, often coast-to-coast."[58] Many of these individuals are recruited within the government depending on their ideological orientation and its overlap with the current administration (or member of Congress). The net result is that since Vietnam foreign policy expertise and personnel are no longer monopolized by a few old establishment groups, a development which reflects greater ideological diversity, among intellectuals as well (see **table 16.1** for a list of the most prominent groups or think tanks involved in foreign policy).[59]

Other types of groups involved in the politics of U.S. foreign policy were characterized by similar developments where new groups sprang up and groups representing different ideological positions became active. The older, conservative veterans associations, such as the Veterans of Foreign Wars and American Legion, were now accompanied by the more liberal Vietnam Veterans Association.

As the anticommunist and free trade consensus shattered in the aftermath of the Vietnam War and the Bretton Woods international economic system no longer functioned as originally intended, *labor and business (and governmental) interests increasingly splintered.* For instance, the AFL-CIO turned increasingly against free trade (such as the NAFTA negotiations) in order to protect American jobs as foreign economic competition increased. Within the business community, domestic-oriented companies began to push for protectionist measures by the government as large American multinational corporations (MNCs) became the champions of free trade. Furthermore, while an international business-government partnership characterized the cold war years, American MNCs began to dissociate themselves from the U.S. government, especially in light of Third World nationalism, the exposure of CIA activities abroad, and the powerful forces of globalization in the world political economy.[60]

Actually, it should not be surprising that government and business interests are sometimes mutually complementary and sometimes not. American businesses, especially those that are more export-oriented and major multinational corporations, are much more independent and have become much more globally oriented. This was also the case before the cold war consensus. The most blatant illustration of such independence, regardless of American governmental national interests, has been the documentation that demonstrates that a number of major American companies had close ties to Nazi Germany during the 1930s and the early part of World War II, until Hitler declared war on the United States. Such major companies as Ford, General Motors, Chase Manhattan Bank (known as Chase National Bank at the time), and IBM had significant German subsidiaries that played prominent roles in the revitalization of German industry and the Nazi war effort (including the Holocaust). Ford, in fact, continued to operate in Germany and Vichy France at least until August 1942—eight months after the United States entered the war. Even prestigious law firms, such as Sullivan and Cromwell (which was overseen by none other than John Foster Dulles), represented German companies until war with the United States broke out.[61]

Not surprisingly, *as business interests have multiplied, their presence in Washington, D.C., also has grown* substantially. Before World War II there weren't a dozen trade associations in town; by the 1960s, however, about one hundred corporations and one thousand trade associations maintained offices in Washington; and by the 1990s there were over thirteen hundred corporations and thirty-five hundred trade associations lobbying government and promoting their special interests. In fact, over eighty thousand people in Washington worked for trade associations alone.[62] These numbers have, if anything, increased. Thus, business interests continue to exert a heavy influence on governmental policies, but in a much more complex and contradictory fashion than that prevailing during the cold war.

For example, the bankruptcy in 2002 of energy giant Enron Corporation, headquartered in Houston, Texas—the largest bankruptcy in American history—resulted in a miniscandal for the administration of George Bush Jr. This was because the close ties that Bush and many of his advisers and appointees had with Enron (going back to his days as governor of Texas),

TABLE **16.1**
MAJOR FOREIGN POLICY THINK TANKS

NAME LOCATION	YEAR BEGAN	ISSUE ORIENTATION	IDEOLOGICAL ORIENTATION
Carnegie Endowment for International Peace Washington, D.C.	1910	Foreign	Liberal
Foreign Policy Association New York	1918	Foreign	Centrist
Hoover Institution Palo Alto, Calif.	1919	Domestic and foreign	Conservative
Council on Foreign Relations New York	1921	Foreign	Centrist
Brookings Institution Washington, D.C.	1927	Domestic and foreign	Liberal
American Enterprise Institution Washington, D.C.	1943	Domestic and foreign	Conservative
Rand Corporation Santa Monica, Calif.	1948	Domestic and foreign	Centrist
Aspen Institute Washington, D.C.	1951	Foreign	Liberal
Foreign Policy Research Institute Philadelphia	1955	Foreign	Conservative
Hudson Institute Indianapolis	1961	Domestic and foreign	Conservative
Center for Strategies & International Studies Washington, D.C.	1962	Foreign	Conservative
Institute for Policy Studies Washington, D.C.	1963	Domestic and foreign	Liberal
Center for Defense Information Washington, D.C.	1972	Foreign	Liberal
Trilateral Commission New York	1973	Domestic and foreign	Centrist
Heritage Foundation Washington, D.C.	1974	Domestic and foreign	Conservative
World Watch Institute Washington, D.C.	1974	Foreign	Liberal
Cato Institute Washington, D.C.	1977	Domestic and foreign	Noninternationalist
Institute for International Economics Washington, D.C.	1981	Foreign	Liberal
Carter Center Atlanta	1982	Domestic and foreign	Liberal
World Policy Institute New York	1983	Foreign	Liberal

the large campaign contributions given to Governor and President Bush, and their involvement with Enron officials until the bankruptcy. Furthermore, while upper-level management had huge salaries and cashed in their company stock (worth millions at the time), most employees not only lost their jobs but also their pensions. Enron chairman Kenneth Lay knew Bush so well that he got the nickname "Kenny Boy" from Bush and Lay served on Bush's presidential transition advisory team for the Energy Department. This is consistent with general information suggesting that major oil companies and oil executives may have heavily influenced the administration's official energy policy coordinated by Vice President Dick Cheney (a former CEO of Halliburton, a huge oil services company). Charges of conflicts of interest and unfair participation in the policymaking process have resulted in lawsuits filed by private groups and Congress to obtain information about the policymaking process from the executive branch, in selective release of information by the executive branch, and presidential claims of executive privilege that may ultimately have to be decided by the courts if a political resolution is not achieved.[63]

Religious and ethnic groups continued to play a prominent role in U.S. foreign policy. Conservative groups and the Christian right, such as the Moral Majority and fundamentalist organizations, became more active at the local, state, and federal levels. This activity was matched by more liberal groups, such as the National Council of Bishops and the Christic Institute. In the 1970s and 1980s, for instance, Catholic missions and lay workers in Latin America, along with Quakers and such groups as the World Council of Churches, provided a credible and legitimate voice of opposition to the Reagan administration's Central American policies, for they were respected on Capitol Hill for the accuracy of their data on human rights abuses.[64] Christian right groups have also been very active in American politics.

Although the old China lobby declined as a force—as evident in the establishment of diplomatic relations with the People's Republic of China in 1978—new ethnic groups grew in prominence. For example, Greek American groups promoted the American embargo of Turkey during the 1970s; African American groups played an important role in the anti-apartheid forces leading to U.S. sanctions against South Africa; and Cuban American groups remain very hostile to

Fidel Castro and any normalization in American-Cuban relations to the present day. Not only does ethnicity play a role in group politics, but politicians sometimes are very sensitive to the political clout of ethnic groups for electoral politics, especially in key states—such as the role of Cuban Americans in Florida elections.[65]

The so-called **Jewish lobby,** which includes a variety of individuals and groups, such as the American Israel Public Affairs Committee (AIPAC), is widely considered the most powerful of all the ethnic groups. It was not really powerful, well-organized, or connected until after the 1967 Arab-Israeli War. This lobby is credited with having gained the backing of members of Congress, as well as the president, to provide unwavering support and assistance to the state of Israel—to the tune of $3 billion of U.S. foreign assistance per year for the state of Israel and its six million citizens—as well as be the major provider of military weaponry. Consistent with interest group patterns, however, events in the Middle East during the last few decades have made Jewish Americans less than a cohesive and homogeneous force, and have brought about the development of an Arab lobby as well. The power of the Jewish lobby is a sensitive topic. "Jewish groups chafe at what they see as a conspiracy-theory view of legitimate political organizing." And in the words of Henry Hyde, Republican of Illinois and chair of the House International Relations Committee, "The pro-Israel lobby is not something members of Congress like to talk about very much." "Hyde says he constantly hears from pro-Israel groups on Mideast issues but not so much from Arab- or Muslim-American groups. Over the years, the House panel he now chairs has taken such a consistently pro-Israel stance it has been called 'the little Knesset.'"[66]

Senator Charles Schumer, Democratic of New York, describes three levels of Israeli political strength in the United States. "The most pro-Israeli group in America is the Congress. Next are the American people. The White House is least of the three because they have to deal with all of the Arab states and the variety of foreign policy factors at work."[67] Presidents nevertheless have usually been strong supporters of Israel, especially publicly, given the number of Jews in such critical states as California, New York, and Florida. Given this context, presidents have had to manage a difficult balancing act between supporting Israel and trying to act as a third party and evenhanded broker to help resolve the long-standing conflict in the Middle East between Israel and the Arabs. President Carter was the most successful in beginning the peace process with the Camp David Accords in 1978. President Bush Jr. has been the most pro-Israeli president in decades and has struggled as conflict has intensified between Israel and the Palestinians (and Arabs), especially after the September 11 attacks.[68]

In sum, the proliferation of groups and their increasing ideological diversity often makes life difficult for presidents, as even President Bush Sr. found out due to the group politics over the Persian Gulf crisis. After President Bush's announcement in early August 1990 that over 100,000 American troops were to be dispatched to the Persian Gulf, new and old political activists and peace groups already in place, going back to the Vietnam War and the nuclear freeze and anti-apartheid movements, were activated in opposition to the administration's military response and fear of another major war. Following the November elections, when Bush announced that he was doubling American troops to over 400,000 and was abandoning economic sanctions in favor of an offensive policy of brinksmanship to coerce Iraq to withdraw from Kuwait through the threat of war, the country splintered and the peace movement grew. New supporters were attracted from a cross-section of the country, many of whom before were politically passive, and the peace movement came to represent a sizable segment of the public. The growing crisis and likelihood of war also activated counter-demonstrations and a significant movement in support of the president's policies. Yet unlike that during the Vietnam War, the political debate was conducted with much greater civility and the participants were able to separate the politics of the crisis from support for the troops—the true American heroes and victims of war. Nevertheless, this politicized domestic environment was critical in escalating dissent and triggering congressional action. Ultimately, President Bush was successful in acquiring a majority vote in Congress in support of his policies, but the narrowness of his victory was symbolic of the fluidity of public opinion and group politics that have constrained the president's ability to govern since Vietnam.

The newest form of interest group gaining prominence in U.S. foreign policy has been consulting firms and foreign lobbies. **Consulting firms** representing dif-

ferent clients, corporations in particular, have proliferated since the 1970s. Henry Kissinger, for example, founded the consulting firm Kissinger Associates in 1982. For annual fees reported to start at $100,000, clients, which include some of the largest multinational corporations in the world, meet with Kissinger and his associates in his New York office overlooking Park Avenue in order to get information about world politics and gain access to policymakers around the world. Two of Kissinger's associates, Brent Scowcroft and Lawrence Eagleberger, subsequently became President Bush Sr.'s national security adviser and deputy secretary of state.[69]

Closely related to the rise of consulting firms is the growth of **foreign lobbies** through which foreign governments (and private interests) attempt to influence American domestic politics and the policymaking process. Foreign lobbies rely heavily on American expertise, such as in consulting, law, and advertising firms, and operate in a fashion similar to domestic pressure groups. In fact, foreign lobbies have existed throughout American history and often work closely with their domestic counterparts, such as ethnic groups. The Jewish lobby, for example, has always had strong ties with the state of Israel.[70]

Among the most prominent contemporary examples of the foreign lobby are Saudi Arabia and Japan. The Japan lobby is quite multifaceted, ranging from cultural organizations that try to promote favorable American attitudes toward Japan (such as the Japan Foundation) to professional economic organizations (such as the Japanese Economic Institute of America) and direct lobbying activities that represent Japanese business interests. Concerning the latter, according to journalist John Judis, "the Japanese alone have hired about 125 former government officials. These include two of the last three special trade representatives, three of the last four Democratic National Committee chairmen, and the last two Republican chairs."[71] South Africa alone, before the fall of apartheid, had sixteen American firms working for it in the 1980s as compared to five a decade prior.[72]

Such "Americans for hire" not only provide information and political access for foreign interests but also attempt to influence the political agenda and the general political environment. For example, "lobbyists for foreign firms often appear on television or are quoted as objective experts in the press without revealing that they have a vested interest in the opinions they express."[73] Yet, the activities of foreign lobbyists are actually routine practice today. It is estimated that over a thousand American firms or individuals represent foreign interests from all over the world.

It is not surprising, in this regard, that foreign governments would attempt to influence policymakers, including incumbent presidents such as Bill Clinton. In fact, in the case of China, according to Judis, "increasingly, many of our most distinguished and, in theory, disinterested, experts on U.S. China policy are selling their reputations and knowledge to clients with very particular business interests in China. Almost every prominent former government official who speaks out on this subject, regardless of party affiliation, has direct or indirect financial ties to China." For example, "Kissinger, Vance and Eagleburger each have business ties to China. Kissinger is the founder of a firm, Kissinger Associates, which helps its corporate clients secure business in China; Vance is a corporate lawyer who chaperones clients seeking outlets in China; and Eagleburger, once the president of Kissinger Associates, now works for a Washington law firm where he has also helped businessmen secure contracts in China."[74]

Obviously, the close ties between interest groups and the U.S. government (and foreign officials) raise important questions concerning personal and national **conflicts of interest** and ethical (and legal) behavior. These issues were illustrated clearly when Michael Deaver, deputy chief of staff and close friend to President Reagan, was convicted of perjury in federal court for lying about his lobbying activities in policy areas in which he was previously involved as a government official (an activity prohibited by law for just one year). Upon resigning from public office in 1985, Deaver immediately established his own consulting firm that represented domestic clients, such as Rockwell International, and foreign clients, such as the governments of Canada, South Korea, and Panama. In fact, a 1986 General Accounting Office study found seventy-six former high-level federal officials representing foreign interests from fifty-two countries after leaving office during the period from 1980 to 1985—probably a very strong contemporary trend.[75]

Such revolving-door behavior is not uncommon within the Washington political community, as discussed earlier in this chapter, and in the military establishment. During the 1990s Clark Clifford, former Truman adviser and secretary of defense under LBJ,

became probably the most prominent political player to have fallen victim to charges of ethical and legal violations.[76] Such a result is actually the exception to the rule, given the weakness of lobbying and conflict-of-interest laws and the normalcy of such political behavior (for example, review essay 15.1 on money, campaigning, and politics).

Kissinger Associates was, for example, also a part of the **U.S.-Iraq Business Forum** during the 1980s: a conglomerate of predominantly large American corporations—such as Amoco, Bell Helicopter, Caterpillar, General Motors, Mobil, Westinghouse, Xerox—responsible for increasing business and trade with the Iraqi regime, thus contributing to Saddam Hussein's buildup of his military into a regional threat. With its officers and staff based in Washington, D.C., the Iraqi Business Forum pressured the Reagan and Bush administrations to continue to provide government credits and loan guarantees to Iraq and oppose congressional sanctions, despite Iraq's terrible human rights record. Nevertheless, when Iraq invaded Kuwait in 1990, Henry Kissinger, speaking as a former national security adviser and secretary of state, was a leading proponent to expel Iraq with the use of force.[77]

All of these conflicts of interest, most of which are not well-known, raise all sorts of questions about the practice of American democracy. What Judis concludes about all the linkages between China and former (and current) government officials may speak to a larger truth:

Perhaps more important, the new China hands could have a corrosive effect on American democracy. In foreign policy debates, average Americans, as well as many of their political representatives, often defer to prominent former officials whom they believe speak disinterestedly for the national interest. When the public becomes aware that they are also speaking for the interests of their business clients, the cynicism about how important policy decisions are made will deepen. This, together with revelations about the Clinton Commerce Department and presidential campaign, and a growing anxiety about the role of money, especially foreign money, in American politics, could precipitate a crisis of political confidence.[78]

At a minimum, it will feed the apathy and cynicism that is all too prevalent among much of the public already.

Beyond attempting to influence domestic politics and government policymaking, the *international activities of private groups* affect the conduct and making of U.S. foreign policy. As Michael Doyle has demonstrated in *Empires*, throughout world history settlers, missionaries, merchants, and commercial companies, in addition to diplomats, soldiers, and officials—each with their own interests and mode of operation—have acted as **agents of foreign policy.**[79] Likewise, Emily Rosenberg has highlighted the important role such agents played during the expansion of U.S. foreign policy abroad from 1890 to World War II, especially those more economically and culturally oriented.[80] Such international activities by private groups are often quite pervasive and visible in foreign countries, especially smaller Third World countries, affecting how foreign elite and mass publics perceive and act toward the United States.

Most noticeable in this regard, as discussed above, have been the missionary activities of American religious organizations and the business activities of American multinational corporations. Missionary activities of American religious institutions remain quite active abroad, especially among more conservative Protestant churches and the (Mormon) Church of Latter Day Saints. The business activities of **American multinational corporations (MNCs)** abroad are also potentially quite pervasive. In fact, the gross sales of the largest American MNCs are greater than the gross national product (GNP) of most Third World countries (see **table 16.2**). To take just one illustration of an extremely well-known American company, McDonald's has over twelve thousand stores in the United States, and has more then eleven thousand stores in over one hundred countries throughout the world. McDonald's gross revenues from overseas are about the same as its gross revenues from the United States—about $20 billion in each case.[81] Thus, the mere presence of American religious groups and, in particular, big business abroad affects the politics of U.S. foreign policy.

But other types of private groups are active abroad, as well. Many private consulting firms and individuals, for instance, sell their services to foreign governments to provide advice on domestic and foreign policies. Such activity has become particularly noticeable in Eastern Europe with the end of the cold war, a region in which many American firms and individuals currently are instructing Eastern Europeans on the operation of democracies and market economies.

The international activities of **private voluntary organizations (PVOs),** such as CARE, Catholic Relief Services, and Lutheran World Relief—many of them religiously affiliated—have proliferated since Vietnam as well. Although they originated primarily as relief organizations during and immediately after World War II and focused most of their attention on the war-torn countries of Europe, over the past thirty years these and newer PVOs have diversified their activities and geographical focus to emphasize emergency and developmental assistance to Third World countries. In the 1980s, for example, over 125 U.S. PVOs received over $740 million from the United States Agency for International Development (AID) in support of their overseas work—a ten-fold increase since the 1960s.[82] Even private individuals, such as former President Jimmy Carter, through the Carter Center in Atlanta, have pursued their own foreign policy agendas abroad (which has increased Carter's public approval since he left the Oval Office and was eventually awarded the Nobel Peace Prize). It is through such international activities that private groups and individuals affect the making and conduct of U.S. foreign policy.

In sum, the post–Vietnam War and post–cold war years have been accompanied by the proliferation of interest group and social movement activity in foreign policy. Older, cold war–oriented groups have been joined by more liberal and more conservative groups. Ideologically motivated groups have been joined by hundreds of other groups representing specialized interests, including business, ethnic, and foreign interests. Such groups have flocked to Washington, D.C., which explains the explosion of lobbyists (365 officially registered in 1961, over 23,000 by the 1990s), lawyers (the District of Columbia Bar Association listed roughly 12,000 members in 1961 and over 45,000 in the 1990s), and journalists (1,500 were accredited to congressional press galleries in 1961, over 5,200 in the 1990s), whose numbers continue to grow.[83]

These social movements and interest groups *try to influence the political agenda and policymaking process in a variety of specific ways*: by gaining access to policymakers and participating in policymaking, having individuals appointed to governmental positions, providing information, contributing campaign funds and other money, actively campaigning, engaging in litigation, demonstrating, attracting media coverage, networking with other groups, and attempting to gain

TABLE **16.2**

REVENUES OF LARGEST U.S. CORPORATIONS RELATIVE TO VARIOUS COUNTRIES' GNP

CORPORATION (RANK)/ COUNTRY	REVENUES/GNP ($BILLIONS)	CORPORATION (RANK)/ COUNTRY	REVENUES/GNP ($BILLIONS)
United States	9,646	Venezuela	82
Japan	4,089	Malaysia	81
Germany	2,180	Egypt	79
France	1,465	Philippines	79
United Kingdom	1,264	Chile	74
Italy	1,157	Ireland	69
China	954	AT&T (9)	66
Brazil	768	Philip Morris (10)	63
Canada	581	Pakistan	62
Spain	555	Peru	61
India	427	J.P. Morgan (11)	60
South Korea	399	Bank of America (12)	57
Netherlands	389	New Zealand	55
Australia	387	Czech Republic	53
Mexico	368	SBC Communications (13)	51
Russia	332	Boeing* (14)	51
Argentina	290	Texaco (15)	51
Switzerland	284	Ukraine	49
Belgium	259	Duke Energy (16)	49
Sweden	227	Kroger (17)	48
Austria	217	Hewlett-Packard (18)	48
Exxon Mobil (1)	210	Chevron (19)	48
Turkey	201	State Farm (20)	47
Wal-Mart Store (2)	193	Bangladesh	47
General Motors* (3)	184	Hungary	46
Ford Motor* (4)	180	Ukraine	35
Denmark	175	Nigeria	33
Hong Kong	158	United Technologies* (59)	28
Norway	152	Lockheed Martin Corp* (77)	25
Poland	151	Honeywell International* (83)	24
Saudi Arabia	143	Guatemala	19
South Africa	137	Raytheon* (119)	17
Thailand	132	TRW* (122)	16
Indonesia	131	Syria	16
General Electric* (5)	130	Northrup Grumman* (151)	14
Finland	125	Bulgaria	12
Greece	123	General Dynamics* (166)	12
Citigroup (6)	111	Kenya	11
Portugal	106	Computer Sciences Corp* (181)	10
Iran	102	Panama	9
Columbia	101	Zimbabwe	6
Enron (7)	100	Honduras	5
Israel	97	Haiti	4
Singapore	96	Nicaragua	2
International Business Machines (8)	88	Central African Republic	1

*Major defense contractor

SOURCES: "500 Largest U.S. Corporations," *Fortune* (April 15, 2002); World Development Indicators Database (July 16, 2001).

general public support. The decline of the Soviet threat and the collapse of communism in Eastern Europe in a post–cold war global environment has accentuated these patterns in group politics.

As political scientist Chung-in Moon makes clear, groups typically engage in four general **lobbying strategies** in American politics:[84]

1. The access-to-power approach,
2. The technocratic approach,
3. The coalition-building approach, and
4. The grassroots mobilization approach.

In the access-to-power approach, interest groups use high-powered power brokers, law firms, public relations firms, and consultants to gain direct access to top policymakers within the government. The technocratic approach is another form of direct lobbying, in which groups retain lawyers and technical consultants who use their expertise and contacts to influence mid-level decisionmakers in government, the media, and other relevant groups in society. The other two lobbying strategies used by groups and social movements attempt to affect the policymaking process more indirectly by targeting electoral politics and domestic politics in general. The coalition-building approach emphasizes the formation of group alliances based on mutual interests in order to politicize issues, get issues on the political agenda, and place pressure on the government's policymaking process. Finally, the grassroots mobilization approach attempts to rally mass support in order to politicize issues, affect electoral and group politics, and increase public pressure on the policymaking process. As Hedrick Smith points out in *The Power Game*, the old game of **inside politics** within the Washington community has been supplemented by a new game of **outside politics** since Vietnam.[85]

Social movements and groups are politically active because of their potential impact on domestic politics and, more specifically, on the government's policymaking process. With respect to Congress, for example, a study by the Congressional Research Service found that:

Groups come to represent significant allies, or formidable opponents, when they are well organized; when they represent a sizable, well-educated, and middle- to upper-class constituency and when the positions they wish members of Congress to support are viewed as mainstream and respectable, entailing little or no political cost, and some political gains (e.g., support for Israel, Greece, Taiwan, Ireland, etc.); when the groups confront no significant internal counterlobbies in the private sector or can count on the neutral stance of much of the public when an opinion is yet unformed.[86]

As Smith explains, "to politicians, lobbyists, lawyers, journalists, staff aides, and high-level policymakers, access is bread and butter. . . . Without it, your case doesn't get heard; you can't be a player in the power game. Obviously that's why corporations, unions, and lobbyists of all sorts pay enormous fees for prestigious Washington lawyers or pump millions into campaigning. They are buying access, if not more."[87]

But outside politics has also been growing among groups. This has probably become most visible in the economic arena. Individuals and a variety of groups concerned with the detrimental effects of the globalization of market forces—such as on the environment, over jobs and poverty, and growing national and global inequality—have been building coalitions and engaging in grassroots mobilization against multinational corporations, Western governments, and international organizations, such as the IMF, the World Bank, and the World Trade Organization. This has resulted in major political demonstrations against economic and political leaders whenever they meet to discuss the international economy, as occurred in Seattle in 1999 and Washington, D.C., in 2000, as well as abroad in Italy in 2001, where violence broke out.[88]

Overall, the expansion of group politics allows one to better understand the making of U.S. foreign policy. One of the major implications of this, as Thomas E. Mann states in "Making Foreign Policy," is that "conflict between the President and Congress must be seen as a consequence of a broader set of developments affecting America's place in the world and domestic political interests and processes." The cold war consensus years in group politics have been replaced by group competition for public support and control of the government. Domestic politics have become more divisive, complex, and fluid. Therefore, Mann concludes, "it is no wonder that the President today occupies a less than dominant position in American foreign policy."[89]

CONTINUATION OF THE MILITARY-INDUSTRIAL-SCIENTIFIC INFRASTRUCTURE

Although the foreign policy establishment collapsed while groups proliferated and became more diverse, a massive military-industrial-scientific infrastructure still pervades the government and American society. *Four patterns have prevailed since Vietnam:*

1. The military establishment continues to require weaponry and other services, private industry manufactures and supplies weapons and material, Congress approves the programs and appropriates the funds that provide jobs and votes back home, and members of the scientific community still offer national security expertise and advice.

2. From the 1970s to the 1990s, in the absence of an anticommunist consensus, the institutions and activities of the military-industrial-scientific infrastructure no longer operated in a highly supportive domestic political environment and have been more likely to be challenged.

3. There has been a downsizing of the military, and therefore, the national security infrastructure has also been impacted since the collapse of the Soviet Union.

4. The September 11, 2001 terrorist attacks have resulted in a resurgence of an American military buildup and in the military-industrial-scientific infrastructure.

While defense spending has represented a smaller percentage of the federal government's budget and the domestic economy since Vietnam, and has been more open to criticism, the national security infrastructure remains huge and remains embedded in American society.[90] According to a *Los Angeles Times* analysis on the U.S. defense establishment during the 1970s and 1980s, "the jobs of one out of ten Americans depend directly or indirectly on defense spending. The Pentagon is the largest single purchaser of goods and services in the nation. Defense industries account for 10 percent of all U.S. manufacturing. In certain states, including California, defense-related employment is the largest single source of personal income. Defense employs more than 25 percent of all the nation's scientists and engineers."[91] Throughout the 1980s the federal government continued to devote the largest share of its budget to defense spending—roughly 30 percent. Defense prod-

ucts, such as arms, also accounted for over one-third of American exports abroad.

Many **local communities and economies** remain heavily dependent on defense spending. During the late 1980s, for example, the Pentagon spent over $5 billion in South Carolina, a state with roughly three million people and a gross domestic product of roughly $50 billion at the time. According to an article in *The State* newspaper entitled "Military Might: Military Installations Give Firepower to S.C. Economy," defense spending in the state primarily involved local defense firms, the Savannah River nuclear weapons plant, and military research and development (for example, at the major universities). Most important, defense spending supported the state's eight military bases through military and civilian payrolls, construction and related services, and materials equipment and supplies. According to the thinking of South Carolina state officials at the time, "military bases, in general, are relatively stable elements in South Carolina's economy, a virtually recession-proof 'industry' that provides steady employment and training in high-tech skills while bringing to their respective communities a civic-minded crew of service volunteers that often choose to retire in South Carolina."[92]

Defense Department domestic spending (which includes procurement contracts, payroll, military pensions, and grants) declined somewhat with the end of the cold war. Whereas the Pentagon used to spend about $5 billion in South Carolina, in 2000 the amount was about $3.5 billion. Nevertheless, Defense Department domestic spending is still quite sizable, totaling $238 billion in 2000: The top five states were California ($30 billion), Virginia ($25 billion), Texas ($21 billion), Florida ($13 billion), and Maryland ($9 billion). And this does not include domestic spending by other national security–oriented government agencies, such as the Department of Energy, NASA, and the Department of Justice (for example, Westinghouse, which runs the Savannah River plant, had $1.6 billion in government contracts in 2001).[93]

The **pork-barrel politics** of defense spending has become more sophisticated. For example, hundreds of private defense think tanks, lobbying offices, corporate government-relations offices, and law firms specializing in military contracts have sprung up around Washington, D.C., in order to lobby for defense spending and support the military establishment—known as

"Beltway Bandits." According to the Fairfax County Office of Economic Development, during the 1980s over 620 high-tech firms with forty-seven thousand employees, more than 70 percent of whom work on defense-sponsored projects, were located in the four northern Virginia cities closest to Washington.[94]

And the revolving-door system remains alive and well. As Gordon Adams documented in a definitive study of *The Iron Triangle*, "Our review of DOD data showed that 1,942 individuals (uniformed and civilian) moved between DOD/NASA and the eight [largest defense] companies between 1970 and 1979. Of these, 1,672 were hired by the companies, while 270 company employees went to work for DOD and NASA."[95] These types of developments have intensified the mutually supportive networks existing between members of the military establishment, Congress, and private industry at national and local levels.

As David Wood explains in the *Los Angeles Times*, "the story of the B-1 bomber provides a casebook example of how the military-industrial complex works, how the personal, professional, political and economic interests of thousands of individuals and institutions in government and the defense industries intertwine to influence what America does in the name of national security."[96] Since the late 1950s the Air Force had wanted a new bomber to replace the B-52. However, critics emphasized the B-1's cost, limited capabilities, and unclear mission. Not surprisingly, the bomber project was started and stopped half a dozen times during the 1960s and 1970s in response to the political dynamics of the times. Nevertheless, "the Air Force battled Presidents, Secretaries of Defense, and members of Congress for more than thirty years to build a new bomber."[97] For three years beginning in 1975, Air Force and Rockwell International officials planned, coordinated, and executed a major political campaign on behalf of the struggling **B-1 bomber** program, which was on the verge of cancellation. The company urged its 114,000 employees and holders of its thirty-five million shares of stock to write to their members of Congress. More than three thousand subcontractors and suppliers in forty-eight states were also asked to contact Congress concerning the economic impact B-1 production would have on their states and congressional districts.

Under President Reagan, Congress finally agreed to the full-scale production of one hundred B-1s at a cost of almost $500 million per plane. The Air Force and its supporters not only finally acquired the B-1 bomber but, to their delight, the B-2 "Stealth" bomber as well (at a cost of over $1 billion per plane). In *Wild Blue Yonder: Money, Politics, and the B-1 Bomber*, Nick Kotz concluded that over the years "the Air Force and its allies in science, industry, labor, and politics have relentlessly pursued their goals—and other groups have opposed them. On both sides, the motives of patriotism, financial gain, career ambition, political aggrandizement, and loyalty to an institution or idea were often so mixed that it is hard to tell what was narrow self-interest and what was concern for the national good."[98]

Once approval is given for its production, the geography and politics of production virtually guarantees the future of a weapons system such as the B-1 bomber. Although Rockwell International was awarded the $40 billion–plus contract, as many as fifty-two hundred subcontractors were involved in the forty-eight continental states. These subcontractors included most of the largest defense contractors, such as Boeing, TRW, Westinghouse, General Electric, Goodyear, Singer, Sperry, Bendix, Martin Marietta, Northrop, Litton, Westinghouse, IBM, and others. Unions such as the United Auto Workers and the Machinists were also involved. "Contract spreading" involved as many as 400 of the 435 congressional districts. For many Americans, this meant jobs—good-paying jobs. Thus, thousands of individuals and groups at the local and national level had a vested interest in providing support for B-1 production (see **figure 16.2** for the geographic contract spreading of the B-1 bomber).

The military-industrial-scientific infrastructure is so embedded in the U.S. government and American society that weapons systems and defense spending seem to acquire lives of their own. According to David Packard, deputy secretary of defense in the Nixon administration and chair of President Reagan's 1986 blue-ribbon commission on defense management, "There are strong perverse incentives for Congress, the military services, and defense contractors to play games with the budget to accommodate pet projects. Programs are kept alive to satisfy parochial, not national, interests and are introduced without realistic notions of future costs. In this environment, coherent long-range budget planning has become impossible."[99] Instead, the tendency is to produce what James Kurth in "Why We Buy the Weapons We Do" has called **"follow-on" and "bailout" imperatives** for weapons systems and major defense contractors in the weapons acquisition process.[100]

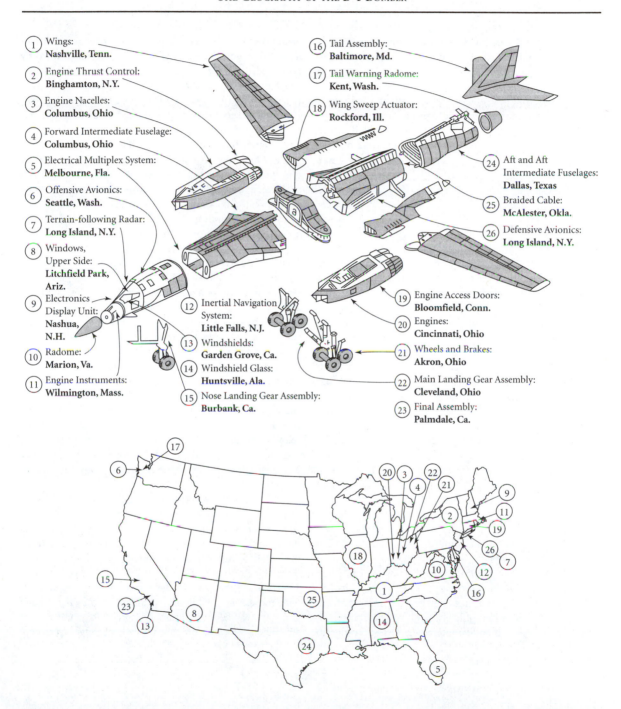

FIGURE **16.2**
THE GEOGRAPHY OF THE B-1 BOMBER

1 Wings: **Nashville, Tenn.**
2 Engine Thrust Control: **Binghamton, N.Y.**
3 Engine Nacelles: **Columbus, Ohio**
4 Forward Intermediate Fuselage: **Columbus, Ohio**
5 Electrical Multiplex System: **Melbourne, Fla.**
6 Offensive Avionics: **Seattle, Wash.**
7 Terrain-following Radar: **Long Island, N.Y.**
8 Windows, Upper Side: **Litchfield Park, Ariz.**
9 Electronics Display Unit: **Nashua, N.H.**
10 Radome: **Marion, Va.**
11 Engine Instruments: **Wilmington, Mass.**
12 Inertial Navigation System: **Little Falls, N.J.**
13 Windshields: **Garden Grove, Ca.**
14 Windshield Glass: **Huntsville, Ala.**
15 Nose Landing Gear Assembly: **Burbank, Ca.**
16 Tail Assembly: **Baltimore, Md.**
17 Tail Warning Radome: **Kent, Wash.**
18 Wing Sweep Actuator: **Rockford, Ill.**
19 Engine Access Doors: **Bloomfield, Conn.**
20 Engines: **Cincinnati, Ohio**
21 Wheels and Brakes: **Akron, Ohio**
22 Main Landing Gear Assembly: **Cleveland, Ohio**
23 Final Assembly: **Palmdale, Ca.**
24 Aft and Aft Intermediate Fuselages: **Dallas, Texas**
25 Braided Cable: **McAlester, Okla.**
26 Defensive Avionics: **Long Island, N.Y.**

SOURCE: Mickie Garrett, *Los Angeles Times.*

ESSAY 16.4
POLITICS AND CORRUPTION IN WEAPONS PROCUREMENT

During the late 1980s, the U.S. Department of Justice investigated hundreds of procurement fraud and bribery cases in which members of the defense industry had paid Pentagon insiders for documents, information, and competitive bidding advantages. Offices of the country's largest defense contractors and high-ranking former employees of the Department of Defense were raided by the Federal Bureau of Investigation. Indictments were handed down and dozens of individuals and over twenty-five companies—including Boeing, GTE Corporation, General Electric, General Motors, Northrup Corporation, and Raytheon pleaded guilty. For example, Unisys Corporation, one of the country's largest computer manufacturers, agreed in 1991 to pay $190 million to settle charges ranging from bribery and false claims to illegal campaign contributions and fraud. These cases represent the government's greatest effort thus far to crack down on fraud and corruption in the defense procurement process. Unfortunately, fraud and corruption have been endemic in defense procurement since the initial growth of the modern military establishment during the 1940s and 1950s.

The procurement of military airlift transport during the 1980s typifies this practice. The competition between the Boeing and Lockheed corporations, to the extent that competition is evident, demonstrates the mutually supportive relationships that develop between defense participants regardless of ethics or the law. In this case, the General Accounting Office (GAO), the investigative arm of the U.S. Congress, found that "an extensive and cooperative effort was made by officials of the air force, the Office of the Secretary of Defense, the Lockheed Corporation, and several other defense contractors and subcontractors during the period May 14, 1982, through July 22, 1982, to influence members of the House of Representatives, and later the House and Senate conferees, on the proposed $10 billion procurement of the C-5B aircraft."[A]

The GAO described a massive lobbying campaign that included over five hundred congressional visits "by air force, army, and marine officials, other congressmen, Lockheed Corporation officials, and representatives of other companies that had an interest in the C-5B program or did business with Lockheed or the Department of Defense."[B] A computerized "action plan" was maintained by Lockheed, listing, for example, businesses in 260 of the 435 House districts that would lose money and jobs if Boeing, rather than Lockheed, was awarded the contract.

High-level officials within the Department of Defense acknowledged that actions to promote the C-5B program were similar to those taken for other large weapons programs. One senior Air Force official, in fact, commented that the lobbying effort was "democracy in action."[C] The problem is that this type of corrupt behavior is not unusual, because most of it remains hidden, the laws are lax, investigations rarely produce indictments, and penalties are extremely light upon conviction. Therefore, few incentives exist to change the defense procurement process, especially if it stays off the public agenda.

In the case of the C-5B aircraft procurement program, private industry lobbying was legal. It was the "air force and OSD officials [who] violated Federal anti-lobbying laws by expending appropriated funds in the aiding and supporting of contractors to perform lobbying activities."[D] Yet the maximum penalty is a fine of not more than $500 or imprisonment for not more than one year, or both, and removal from office after notice and a hearing. According to the General Accounting Office, "no one has ever been successfully prosecuted under this statute."[E] Furthermore, federal contract law allowed Lockheed Corporation to be reimbursed by the U.S. government, and the American taxpayer, for its legitimate lobbying costs—in this case over $496,000 (Boeing was reimbursed for lobbying costs of $22,000).

Consider the severity of the penalties in the Justice Department cases. GTE Corporation pleaded guilty to one felony count involving the illegal use of Pentagon planning documents. In return, GTE had to undergo a fourteen-item plan of internal improvements to avoid suspension from U.S. government contracts and pay the government $580,000 for the cost of the inquiry. Boeing Company, with more than $3 billion in military contracts, pleaded guilty to two felony counts and agreed to pay a fine of $5 million—an amount that the federal judge overseeing

---

A. U.S. Congress, General Accounting Office, *Improper Lobbying Activities by the Department of Defense on the Proposed Procurement of the C-5B Aircraft* (September 29, 1982), p. 1.

B. Ibid., p. 10.
C. Ibid., p. 17.
D. Ibid., p. 23.
E. Ibid., p. 19.

the case questioned as being too light for a "very serious breach of security." Northrup Corporation, the manufacturer of the B-2 Stealth bomber, pleaded guilty to thirty-four counts involving failing to test parts for the Air Force's cruise missile and the Marine Corps's Harrier jet and was fined the maximum of $500,000 for each count for a total fine of $17 million. In return the Justice Department agreed to drop 141 other counts against Northrup and drop charges against two Northrup executives. Typically, however, the Department of Defense voluntarily pays the fines for the defense industry, as well. Lockheed Corporation somehow managed to avoid all indictments. And although members of Congress were involved, they were beyond investigation and prosecution because of political immunity.

Fraud and corruption in defense procurement demonstrates the difficulty of reconciling democratic practice and accountability with the existence of a large military establishment. However, these types of incestuous and corrupt governmental-private relationships are not unique to the military and the defense procurement process. A number of other scandals came to the public's attention since the early 1980s concerning the government and the private market. Corruption and scandal may be found wherever money, power, and prestige are highly valued, and these are certainly important attributes for the people and organizations involved in the military establishment and the U.S. defense process.

SOURCES: James Coates and Michael Kilian, *Heavy Losses: The Dangerous Decline of American Defense* (New York: Penguin, 1985), chapter 7; Steven Engelberg, "Boeing Expected to Plead Guilty in Pentagon Case," *New York Times* (November 7, 1989), pp. 1, 30; Molly Moore and Robert P. Howe, "Boeing Co. Is Guilty in Defense Case," *Washington Post* (November 14, 1987), pp. A1, A4; "Payoffs at the Pentagon," *Newsweek* (June 27, 1988), pp. 20–22; Eric Schmitt, "Guilty Plea by Unisys Is Expected," *New York Times* (September 6, 1991), pp. C1, C4; Richard W. Stevenson, "Northrup Inquiries Ended After Guilty Plea," *New York Times* (March 1, 1990), pp. C2; Richard W. Stevenson, "Many Caught but Few Punished for U.S. Military Contract Fraud," *New York Times* (November 12, 1990), pp. A1, A13; and U.S. Congress, General Accounting Office, *Improper Lobbying Activities by the Department of Defense on the Proposed Procurement of the C-5B Aircraft* (September 29, 1982).

The threat of the Soviet Union and communism was the major justification for over $10 trillion of defense spending from the fifties to the eighties. The collapse of the cold war consensus and end of the cold war, however, have made the operations of the military-industrial-scientific infrastructure more open to scrutiny, even with all their secrecy. As waste, corruption, and threats to human health have become common knowledge, national security infrastructure operations increasingly have been challenged. In this respect, the supportive political environment that existed during the cold war has been replaced by an environment in which groups increasingly fight over the legitimacy and consequences of the national security infrastructure (see **essay 16.4** on the politics and corruption of military procurement).

Nevertheless, according to the General Accounting Office, the dynamics of the weapons procurement process remains problematic at the beginning of the twentieth century. Procurement of a new weapons system is so laborious and lengthy—averaging at least eleven years from start to finish—that any sense of program continuity and personal accountability is nearly impossible to maintain. "This means that from drawing board to actual deployment, the average procurement project conceivably could outlast the involvement of four program managers, five program executive officers, eight service-acquisition executives, five chairmen of the Joint Chiefs, seven secretaries or undersecretaries of defense and three presidents." The GAO comptroller general recommended that "trying to reduce the acquisition cycle to no longer than five years from technology development to production (as many private companies do) and slowing the revolving door in key management positions might help reduce the number of major projects that are over budget, behind schedule and without focus."[101]

From the perspective of those dependent on the national security infrastructure for their livelihood, the end of the cold war represented a bad omen. The defense budget faced cuts and the military has been downsized. The major exception is American weapons export sales abroad (which are partially financed by the government) have actually increased to between $14 billion and 18 billion a year and represents 50 percent of the world's weapons exports at the turn of the century.[102]

This also has led to greater concentration of the defense industry, which has an impact not only on the politics of defense but on people and communities as well. For example, in 1997 Boeing Company (with $20 billion in revenues—about one-third of them military oriented) acquired McDonnell Douglas Corporation (with $15 billion in revenues—about two-thirds military oriented) in a $14 billion deal, the largest merger in the aerospace industry. Boeing Company replaced Lockheed Martin Corporation (which was formed in 1995 after a merger of Lockheed and Martin Marietta corporations) as the world's largest aerospace company and makes it the only manufacturer of commercial jets in the United States. Although Boeing had 145,000 employees and McDonnell Douglas had 64,000, located in various plants throughout the country, corporate mergers are usually accompanied by considerable streamlining and cutbacks, to minimize overlap and duplication and to cut costs. The impact for many employees, subcontractors, and communities is quite profound but is often not known for months, maybe even years. The same has been the case with the military base closures that occurred throughout the 1990s (see **essay 16.5** on the politics and economics of base closures).[103]

Such concentration raises serious questions about the future of defense politics. According to Lawrence Korb, former Assistant Secretary of Defense in the Reagan administration, in the 1990s "after 22 mergers, there will be only two mega-companies—Lockheed Martin and Boeing McDonnell Douglas—and three "major" companies, Hughes, Raytheon and Northrop." The likelihood of another megamerger among the remaining major companies in order to maintain competitiveness is pretty high. And, unbeknownst to most taxpayers, the federal government has contributed to such mergers and concentration by interpreting federal regulations in a way that allows defense companies to charge the Pentagon for the cost of carrying out these mergers. The previous "Lockheed [Corporation-]Martin [Marietta] merger alone is estimated to have cost the taxpayers $1.8 billion." The net result is a few megacompanies with "tremendous political clout." (review Table 16.2, which highlights which of the largest American multinational corporations are also engaged as defense contractors).[104]

How much is enough? Throughout the 1990s, emphasis was on a "peace dividend," cuts in defense spending and the need for reform. At the same time, the military triumph in the Persian Gulf War squelched some of the calls for further cuts. Ultimately, how much is enough is dependent on to what extent Americans feel that their country's national security is threatened (and how large a role they think the United States should play abroad). In this respect,

the September 11 attacks of 2001 and President Bush's global war on terrorism for the next few years will probably result in a substantial increase in defense spending and a resurgence of the military-industrial-scientific infrastructure.

Nevertheless, hard political choices continue to be required concerning the amount and importance of defense spending and the use of force abroad. These choices have serious consequences, not only for the government but for the economy, hundreds of local communities, and the livelihoods of thousands of individuals that have become dependent on the military-industrial-scientific infrastructure. These choices are not likely to get any easier as the United States continues to navigate the complex global environment of the twenty-first century.

GROUP POLITICS IN THE FUTURE

As we have seen, group politics, like electoral politics, has experienced considerable change, as well as some important continuities, from the cold war era to the present. Following World War II, the rise of foreign policy and cold war–oriented groups, of a military-industrial-scientific infrastructure, and of a foreign policy establishment provided a significant foundation and domestic context for the politics of anticommunism and the policy of containment that prevailed under presidential leadership. The rise of the civil rights, new left, and antiwar movements, however, challenged the dominance of presidential power, the liberal-conservative anticommunist consensus, and the national security ethos of the cold war years. Along with the subsequent rise of conservative movements and the right, the foreign policy establishment collapsed while there was a proliferation of new and old groups in American politics, increased ideological diversity and competition among groups, and more individual political participation in social movements and group politics. This contributed to a decline in presidential power in foreign policy since Vietnam while the military-industrial-scientific infrastructure continued to operate in a more inhospitable domestic environment. These post–Vietnam patterns have been both accentuated with the end of the cold war and with the September 11 attacks

ESSAY 16.5
THE POLITICS AND ECONOMICS OF BASE CLOSURES

As the cold war began to wane in the late 1980s, one could hear calls in Washington for a "peace dividend." In brief, this term described the expected budgetary windfalls from the closure and realignment of American military bases and facilities at home and abroad. Additionally, Pentagon planners asserted the need for such actions in order to utilize budget dollars for badly needed research and development, and the procurement of new weapons systems.

At the time, there were over nine hundred military bases and other military properties in every state of the Union (representing more than twenty-four million acres, equivalent to the territories of Connecticut, Massachusetts, New Hampshire, Rhode Island, Vermont, and two Delawares). The major drawback in closing a base is the loss of jobs and the economic effect on those communities that depended on the targeted bases for their livelihood. In locations where there is nothing on which to fall back (such as tourism), communities have found themselves left out in the cold. These economic impacts and the associated political costs for the elected representatives of the affected communities have produced a politicized climate of indecision concerning future rounds of closures.

In order to deal with the hard political decisions involved with base closings, Congress created an independent commission—the Base Realignment and Closure (BRAC) Commission. The commission was empowered to examine America's basing needs and propose which bases should close—which would go before Congress for a simple "up" or "down" vote. This way all the pork-barrel politics and amendments to save (or enhance) bases in one's district—so much a part of the normal legislative process—would be avoided and overcome (similar to fast track legislative trade authority given to the president periodically).

There have been five rounds of base closures. In the first round in 1988, the BRAC Commission compiled a list of sixteen major bases for closure with the aim of reaping budgetary savings from lower maintenance costs and in turn being able to use those savings in other areas. These bases were scattered all over the country, from California (particularly hard hit with four of the sixteen) to New Hampshire. In 1991 a second BRAC Commission list targeted twenty-six more major bases. In 1993 and 1995, twenty-eight and twenty-seven (respectively) more major bases were marked for closure for a total over the seven-year period of ninety-seven military bases (see **table 16.3**).

The pandemonium produced in the targeted communities was considerable. Populations that had relied for years upon the nearby bases for what in some instances was their main employer or customer (for various goods and services) were now faced with the prospect of their economic livelihoods being jeopardized. The location of the bases had direct bearing upon the potential survivability of the community after the closure. If the base was located in an area with other industry or commercial activity, then the impact of a base closure—though hard on the local economy—could still be weathered. However, if the base was the sole reason for there being a community, then the departure of the base and its associated jobs and customers would be devastating and turn the community into a virtual ghost town.

The example of the Charleston Naval Base and Shipyard is an interesting one in this respect. When it was announced in 1993 that the base would be closed, the eighty-nine hundred civilian and twenty-nine thousand military jobs were immediately in jeopardy. Although the city of, Charleston South Carolina, took in a fair amount of tourism dollars annually (and had a metropolitan population approaching half a million), the effect on the local economy of losing so many jobs and the residual income was still considerable. In fact, since 1993 there have been twenty-three thousand jobs lost in the area due to the base closure. Charleston, however, has responded creatively. The naval yard is coming back to life, with more than fifty businesses and federal agencies leasing old buildings and docks. Large-scale development of the base awaits the Navy selling the property and cleaning up the environmental pollution of nearly a century of operation. Furthermore, the mayor of Charleston has successfully emphasized tourism, especially of its expanding historic downtown. Therefore, although the economic demography has changed, Charleston has recovered considerably.

The secretary of defense, the Joint Chiefs of Staff, and the White House under both presidents Clinton and Bush Jr. believe, according to a Department of Defense report that "even after four previous rounds of BRAC, we still have more infrastructure than we need to support our forces." In fact, "the Department's excess infrastructure [estimated at 23 percent excess base capacity] is of a magnitude sufficient to justify two additional rounds of base closure." Naturally, such reports and statements trigger economic tremors felt all around the country. In localities

TABLE **16.3**

BASES APPROVED FOR CLOSURE

1988 COMMISSION
George AFB, CA
Mather AFB, CA
Norton AFB, CA
Presidio of San Francisco, CA
Chanute AFB, IL
Fort Sheridan, IL
Jefferson Proving Ground, IN
Lexington Army Depot, KY
Naval Station Lake Charles, LA
Army Material Tech Lab, MA
Pease AFB, NH
Naval Station Brooklyn, NY
Philadelphia Naval Hospital, PA
Naval Station, Galveston, TX
Fort Douglas, UT
Cameron Station, VA
1991 COMMISSION
Eaker AFB, AR
Williams AFB, AZ
Castle AFB, CA
Fort Ord, CA
Hunters Point Annex, CA
Moffett NAS, CA
Naval Station Long Beach, CA
NAV ElecSysEngrCrt, San Diego, CA
Sacramento Army Depot, CA
Lowry AFB, CO
Fort Benjamin Harrison, IN
Grissom AFB, IN
England AFB, LA
Fort Devens, MA
Loring AFB, ME
Wurtsmith AFB, MI
Richards-Gebaur ARS, MO
Rickenbacker AGB, OH
Naval Station Philadelphia, PA
Philadelphia Naval Shipyard, PA
Myrtle Beach AFB, SC
Bergstrom AFB, TX
Carswell AFB, TX
Chase Field NAS, TX
Naval Station Puget Sound, WA
1993 COMMISSION
Naval Station Mobile, AL
Mare Island Naval Shipyard, CA
MCAS El Toro, CA
Naval Airs Station Alameda, CA
Naval Aviation Depot Alameda, CA
Naval Hospital Oakland, CA
Naval Station Treasure Island, CA

Naval Training Center San Diego, CA
Naval Air Station Cecil Field, CA
Naval Aviation Depot Pensacola, FL
Homestead AFB, FL
Naval Training Center Orlando, FL
Naval Air Station Agana, Guam
Naval Air Station Barbers Point, HI
Naval Air Station Glenview, IL
O'Hare IAP ARS, IL
NESEC, St. Inigoes, MD
K.I. Sawyer AFB, MI
Naval Station Staten Island, NY
Plattsburg AFB, NY
Gentile Air Force Station, OH (DESC)
Newark AFB, OH
Defense Per. Support Center, PA
Charleston Naval Shipyard, SC
Naval Station Charleston, SC
Naval Air Station Dallas, TX
Naval Aviation Depot Norfolk, VA
Vint Hill Farms, VA
1995 COMMISSION
Naval Air Facility, Adak, AK
Fort McClellan, AL
Fort Chaffee, AR
Fleet Industrial SU. Center, Oakland, CA
Naval Shipyard, Long Beach, CA
McClellan AFB, CA
Oakland Army Base, CA
Ontario IAP Air Guard Station, CA
Fitzsimons Army Medical Center, CO
Ship Repair Facility, Guam
Savanna Army Depot Activitym, IL
Naval Air Warfare Center, Aircraft Division, IN
NAWC, Crane Division Detachment, Louisville, KY
Naval Air Station, South Weymoth, MA
Fort Holabird, MD
Fort Ritchie, MD
NSWC, Dahlgren Division Detachment, MD
Bayonne Military Ocean Terminal, NJ
Roslyn Air Guard Station, NY
Seneca Army Depot, NY
Fort Indiantown Gap, PA
NAWC, Aircraft Div., Warminster, PA
Defense Dist. Depot Memphis, TN
Bergstrom Air Reserve Base, TX
Resse AFB, TX
Defense Distribution Depot Ogden, UT
Fort Pickett, VA

TOTAL: 97 MAJOR CLOSURES

SOURCE: U.S. Department of Defense, *Major Base Closure Summary* (March 31, 1996).

such as Sumter, South Carolina, home of Shaw Air Force Base, the threat to the area's economic livelihood is quite real. The base there accounts for $500 million annually, or fully one-third of the community's economy. Shaw AFB is also Sumter's largest employer, providing jobs for 7,100 military and civilian personnel in a city of about 25,000 people.

It seems that after four rounds, the political costs of closing more bases for the elected representatives of these communities is increasing. Nevertheless, after delaying further cuts, in 2001 Congress did authorize another round of defense-based realignments and closures beginning in 2005. The signal from Capitol Hill remains unclear: more new closures, but also no new closures until the effects on local economies are further examined. The

latest GAO report concluded that "while some communities surrounding closed bases are faring better than others, most are continuing to recover from the initial economic impact of base closures." Yet with the rise in defense spending to fight the war on terrorism under President Bush, the economic futures of such places as Sumter, South Carolina, may be secure—at least in the short term.

SOURCES: Chris Burritt, "Charleston Still Struggling to Replace Old Economy," *The State* (June 1, 1997), p. A10; Lee Bandy, "Not Again: Sumter Steels Itself," *The State* (June 1, 1997), p. A1; Michell R. Davis, "South Carolina Girds for Base Closings," Knight-Ridder/Tribune News Service (August 29, 2001); Jerry Gray, "Senate Delays Military Base Closings," *New York Times* (July 10, 1997), p. 1; U.S. Department of Defense, *The Report of the Department of Defense on Base Realignment and Closure* (April 1998); U.S. General Accounting Office, *Military Base Closures: Progress in Completing Actions from Prior Realignments and Closures* (April 2002).

and the war on terrorism have an uncertain, unpredictable future.

SUGGESTED SOURCES FOR MORE INFORMATION

As with the study of political participation and electoral politics, most scholars of U.S. foreign policy traditionally have ignored and dismissed the role of group politics in the foreign policy process. However, changes in the foreign policy process since the Vietnam War have led to serious reconsideration of the role of group politics. A good general overview is *Interest Group Politics,* edited by Allan J. Cigler and Burdett A. Loomis (Washington, D.C.: Congressional Quarterly Press, 1995), and James Q. Wilson, *Political Organizations* (Princeton: Princeton University Press, 1995). William A. Gamson provides an excellent general and conceptual analysis of the nature of group politics in the United States, focusing on the opportunities and outcomes of challenging groups, in *The Strategy of Social Protest* (Homewood, Ill.: Dorsey Press, 1975).

I. M. Destler, Leslie H. Gelb, and Anthony Lake, in *Our Own Worst Enemy: The Unmaking of American Foreign Policy* (New York: Simon and Schuster, 1984), and Godfrey Hodgson, in *America in Our Time* (New York: Vintage, 1976), provide excellent overviews of the anticommunist consensus in group politics during the cold war years, the rise and collapse of the foreign policy establishment, and the expansion of group politics in the post–

Vietnam War era. For a fascinating portrayal of the foreign policy establishment, see David Halberstam, *The Best and the Brightest* (New York: Random House, 1969), and Walter Isaacson and Evan Thomas, *The Wise Men: Six Friends and the World They Made* (New York: Touchstone, 1986).

An excellent understanding of the rise, orientation, and evolution of the new left and the counterculture can be found in Maurice Isserman, *If I Had a Hammer . . . The Death of the Old Left and the Birth of the New Left* (New York: Basic Books, 1987); James Miller, *Democracy Is in the Streets: From Port Huron to the Siege of Chicago* (New York: Simon and Schuster); and Keith Melville, *Communes in the Counterculture: Origins, Theories, Styles of Life* (New York: William Morrow, 1972). Insightful analyses of the rise of the conservative movement can be found in Sidney Blumenthal, *The Rise of the Counter-Establishment: From Conservative Ideology to Political Power* (New York: Times Books, 1986), Jerome L. Himmelstein, *The Right: The Transformation of American Conservatism* (Berkeley and Los Angeles: University of California Press, 1991), and George H. Nash, *The Conservative Intellectual Movement in America* (New York: Basic Books, 1976).

Ross Y. Koen provides an informative account in *The China Lobby in American Politics* (New York: Harper and Row, 1974), while Lawrence P. Frank discusses the power of corporations and their relationship to government in foreign policy during the cold war in "The First Oil Regime," *World Politics* (July 1985): 586–98. For a good discussion of contemporary group politics, including the role of ethnic groups, consulting firms, and foreign lobbies, see Joe Conason, "The Iraq Lobby," *New Republic*

(October 1, 1990), pp. 14–17; Patrick J. Haney and Walt Vanderbush, "The Role of Ethnic Interest Groups in U.S. Foreign Policy: The Case of the Cuban American National Foundation," *International Studies Quarterly* 43 (1999): 341–61; John Judis, "The Pressure Elite: Inside the Narrow World of Advocacy Group Politics," *The American Prospect* (spring 1992), pp. 15–29, "The Contract With K Street," *New Republic* (December 4, 1995), pp. 18–25, and "Chinatown," *New Republic* (March 10, 1997), pp. 17–21.

A good conceptual discussion of general lobbying strategies can be found in the study by Chung-in Moon, "Complex Interdependence and Transnational Lobbying: South Korea in the United States," *International Studies Quarterly* 32 (March 1988): 67–89. A broad historical context for understanding the expansion of group politics and its implications for the workings of American democracy is addressed by David M. Ricci in *The Transformation of American Politics: The New Washington and the Rise of Think Tanks* (New Haven: Yale University Press, 1993). For grassroots lobbying about the international political economy and the environment see Susan Ariel Aaronson, *Taking Trade to the Streets: The Lost History of Public Efforts to Shape Globalization* (Ann Arbor: University of Michigan Press, 2002).

Nick Kotz, in *Wild Blue Yonder and the B-1 Bomber* (Princeton: Princeton University Press, 1988), and Patrick Tyler, in *Running Critical: The Silent War, Rickover, and General Dynamics* (New York: Harper and Row, 1986), provide a strong understanding of the military-industrial-scientific infrastructure and the politics of defense spending. Fred Kaplan, in *The Wizards of Armageddon* (New York: Touchstone, 1983), discusses the vital role played by prominent scientists and academics in devising the U.S. government's strategic policy with respect to deterrence and the fighting of nuclear war.

Key Terms

agents of foreign policy
American communism
American Federation of Labor–Congress of Industrial
　　Organizations (AFL-CIO)

American multinational corporations (MNCs)
antiwar movement
"Beltway Bandits"
B-1 bomber
challenging groups versus established groups
China lobby
Christian right
civil rights movement
conflicts of interest
Congress for Cultural Freedom
consulting firms
Council on Foreign Relations (CFR)
counterculture
defense contractors
democratic socialists
Eisenhower's farewell address
"follow-on" and "bail-out" imperatives
foreign lobbies
foreign policy establishment
GI Bill
government-business relationship
inside versus outside politics
interest groups
Jewish lobby
lobbying strategies
local communities and economies
Manhattan Project
militarization of research
military-industrial complex
military-industrial-scientific infrastructure
missionaries
oil, war and American National Security
old versus new left
political Right
pork-barrel politics
private voluntary organizations (PVOs)
realpolitik, or power politics, view
revolving door
social movements
think tanks
U.S.-Iraq Business Forum
1968 Democratic National Convention

CHAPTER 17

. . . .

THE MEDIA AND THE COMMUNICATIONS PROCESS

The mass media and the communications process have become very significant elements in the politics of U.S. foreign policy. Two factors account for this. First, as society and the global environment have grown in complexity and in importance in affecting the lives of Americans, people have developed a greater need for information about national and international affairs. Second, during the twentieth century a communications revolution occurred that makes it possible for the mass media to rapidly communicate information anywhere on the planet. The net result is that much of the information, knowledge, and images that individuals have of the world—whether the mass public, the elite public, or policymakers—come from the mass media.

This chapter examines the type of mediated reality that Americans tend to acquire through the American mass media and the communications process. It does this by *addressing the following questions:* What are the conventional images of the media and the complex reality of media impact? What is the nature of contemporary news media coverage? What are the characteristics

of the news business? What roles do American ideology, culture, and politics play on the news media? What are the implications for foreign policy coverage since World War II to the present, for public knowledge and democratic citizenship, and for the prevalence of symbolic politics? What role, if any, do the entertainment media play? And what role do the alternative media as well as the specialized foreign policy media have on the politics of U.S. foreign policy?

This chapter will shed light on many of the developments discussed concerning the making of U.S. foreign policy, such as the existence of the paradox of presidential power, the importance of agenda setting on the policymaking process, the role of public beliefs and political participation, and the significance of symbolism in American politics. In this respect, examining the role of the mass media and the communications process allows one to better understand the patterns of continuity and change, presidential governance, and tension between national security and democracy that have evolved over time.

THE CONVENTIONAL WISDOMS AND THE COMPLEX REALITY

Many people hold strong opinions about the role of the mass media and the news. No single conventional view predominates. Rather, *three competing views seem prevalent throughout American society.* Conservatives tend to argue that the media play a powerful role in American politics and that there is a liberal bias in the American news media. Liberals tend to agree that the media play a powerful role in American politics, but they believe that there is a conservative bias in the news media. Journalists, however, tend to argue that the power of the media has been overblown; the news media simply attempt to mirror reality, reporting events and the facts as they exist. In order to understand the media's role in the politics of U.S. foreign policy, we need to examine closely the news media and the communications process within American society.

Very simply, *all three views tend to be overly stereotypical and self-serving.* First, the news media are the major sources of information for Americans concerning national and international affairs; therefore, they occupy an important role in American politics. Second, because the news media are the major source of information, media coverage often affects agenda setting and the political agenda—that is, which issues gain (and do not gain) the attention of the public and policymakers. Third, news media coverage often affects the "climate of opinion" as well. In other words, the news media determine not only what issues Americans consider important but also how they think about those issues. Finally, because of the mass media's dominant role in the communication process, individuals and groups—government officials, national leaders, established groups, and challenging groups and social movements—compete for media attention and access in order to get their issues on the agenda and promote a favorable climate of opinion for their interests. In sum, as Shanto Iyengar and Donald R. Kinder demonstrate, and as is consistent with most media studies cited throughout this chapter, the news media provide "news that matters." Therefore, the media and the communications process affect the politics of U.S. foreign policy in ways that journalists tend to downplay, but in a much more complex fashion than either conservatives or liberals argue.[1]

The American public, both the mass and elite publics, has become dependent on the news media for information and understanding of national and international affairs. Clearly, a variety of different sources of information is available, as is obvious from a visit to any major urban newsstand or public library (or the internet). However, most Americans get their information from the **mainstream media:** the major newspapers, radio stations, and television stations available in their communities. The mass public, being relatively uninterested and uninformed about national and international affairs, tends to be most receptive to **headline news,** such as lead stories on the front page of the newspaper and, in particular, on television. The elite public follows the media's coverage of the news more closely and is most likely to go beyond the headlines and supplement its information beyond television and the local newspaper. In both cases, news coverage by the mainstream media directly affects the information and perceptions that Americans have of the world.[2]

In many ways, the news media coverage today is better than ever before. The mainstream media are more informative regarding national and international affairs. The quality of journalism has improved and become more professional. More public affairs programs are on television than in the past. Quality newspapers, such as the *New York Times* and the *Wall Street Journal,* are readily available in urban areas throughout the country. And the Internet has made much news readily accessible. In sum, members of the public who rely on the mainstream media can gain considerable information about national and international affairs if they are interested, especially if they already possess a good base of information.

At the same time, the mainstream media do not provide a comprehensive and complete picture of reality. The news media are highly selective with respect to which events are reported and how they are presented. Many public affairs programs provide soft (or "lite" as opposed to hard) news. Television news coverage is usually brief and simplistic, appealing to a mass public by emphasizing drama and the least common denominator. Little real investigative reporting is conducted by the mainstream media, while sources of information from alternative media outlets are ignored. Finally, much of the public typically has a short attention span and demonstrates little interest in becoming truly informed. Therefore, the net result of reliance on the mainstream media is often a simplistic understanding of reality; members of the mass public are as much confused as enlightened, while members of the elite public often lack the historical context to place the immediacy of the news in perspective.

CONTEMPORARY NEWS MEDIA COVERAGE

These contradictory patterns in American news media coverage and their implications for the foreign policy process can be better understood if we take a closer look at coverage of contemporary affairs. What do we know about *media coverage of contemporary national and international affairs*? For one thing, we know that the news media display considerable selective attention to the world around them. Most of the American media focus on local and national news, with little attention given to international news. Most studies examining media coverage have found that the percentage of news stories devoted to international affairs by major mainstream media organizations ranged from a low of 10 to a high of 40 percent (with the percentage declining over time), representing anywhere from five to fifteen international news stories daily.[3]

Media coverage of international affairs *varies to a considerable extent depending on the type of medium.* The print media, especially newspapers, usually cover more news stories and devote more space to each story than the electronic media. National news on television has a higher percentage of stories devoted to international affairs, but they are few in number. National television news programs broadcast an average of five to seven international stories (representing a total of seven to eleven minutes) out of fifteen to seventeen stories broadcast daily. At best, national news shown on a major television network, such as ABC, CBS, or NBC, provides only a brief digest of national and international events in less than twenty-five minutes—not much time to cover the world (the regular one-hour news show on CNN provides a longer version of similar coverage, while CNN *Headline News* provides a condensed version, as its title suggests).

International coverage by major newspapers represents a smaller percentage of their total news coverage, but newspapers tend to cover more international

stories overall. For example, the *New York Times*—considered the best daily American source of international news—averages only ten to fifteen international news stories per day. Overall, only a limited number of events and issues become news, especially in the media's coverage of the world beyond American shores. Or as H. D. Wu concluded after reviewing and synthesizing fifty-five different media studies of American international news coverage, "One cannot help but realize that the everyday representation of the world via news media is far from a direct reflection of global realities. International news is selected, sifted, edited and mostly discarded through a myriad of processes by the news organizations and professionals."[4]

Which international topics tend to be covered by the American media? Research has found that, in order to receive media coverage on television or in print, foreign news in general must be more consequential, especially for Americans; must involve people of higher status; and must entail more violence or disaster than national news. According to *Deciding What's News*, a 1979 study of CBS, NBC, *Newsweek*, and *Time* by Herbert Gans, *the following international topics tended to receive the most attention*:

1. American activities abroad (especially official visits),
2. Foreign events directly affecting the United States (involving especially national security and economic affairs),
3. East-West governmental relations,
4. Changes in heads of state (with a special interest in European royalty),
5. Dramatic political conflicts (such as wars, coups, revolutions, terrorism),
6. Natural disasters, and
7. Excesses of foreign dictators.[5]

Other, more recent studies have found similar results. Andrew Semmel, in "Foreign News in Four U.S. Elite Dailies," concluded that the American press "pays far greater attention to countries which are economically affluent, politically powerful and culturally similar to the United States."[6] Not only do issues in the developing world receive little attention; when they do get covered, they often entail more sensational items (military coups, wars, natural disasters, accidents, and crime). And not much has changed since the collapse of the Soviet Union and communism in Eastern Europe, with the exception that East-West governmental relations receive much less attention than they used to get.[7]

News coverage of events abroad by the U.S. media, in other words, tends to be American- and Western-centric (as opposed to being globally oriented), focuses on government officials (as opposed to nongovernmental groups and publics), highlights political and national security issues (as opposed to economic or environmental issues), and emphasizes so-called "negative" events such as conflict (as opposed to positive stories emphasizing cooperation). Mainstream media coverage of other countries (and global issues) not only tends to be simplistic and incomplete but often swings back and forth from more positive to more negative coverage. For example, reporting on China over the decades and years has often constantly shifted from "admiration to confrontation." Or as depicted in the title of one study of the media's post–September 11 coverage: "Forgotten Coverage of Afghan 'Freedom Fighters': The Villains of Today's News were Heroes in the '80s." Therefore, the news media not only provide selective coverage but emphasize a particular picture of reality that can easily change.[8]

This selective attention is reinforced during times of crisis, whether domestic or international, as will be discussed below. Crisis coverage is often so great that most other national and international news of consequence disappears entirely. Such was the case during the Bush Jr. administration for months following the September 11 attacks and the launching of the war on terrorism, followed by the Israeli-Palestinian conflict in the Middle East. Crisis coverage by the American news media also tends to be limited to events in which the United States is heavily involved or affected; little or no media coverage, for example, would be accorded a civil war in another country where the United States has little involvement, even though this may clearly be a crisis situation for the people and the region involved.

EXPLAINING NEWS MEDIA COVERAGE

Why does the mainstream media in the United States present information and portray reality in a way that is incomplete, selective, and particularistic? *Three general explanations account for the selectivity of news media*

coverage: (1) the world's complexity and ambiguity, (2) characteristics of the news business, and (3) the politics of the communications process. This has significant direct and indirect effects on the making of U.S. foreign policy.

MAKING SELECTIVE SENSE OF THE COMPLEXITY AND AMBIGUITY OF THE WORLD

To be fair, the American news media have no monopoly in selectivity in reporting about the world around us. This is inevitable, for the world is so complex that the media—even though it is not directly controlled by the government—must be selective in determining which items of significance are to be covered and how. Also, while American journalism has become more professional, the world has grown in complexity. A world of almost two hundred governments, thousands of nongovernmental groups, and over six billion people in constant interaction concerning hundreds of issues produces much potential news. Hence, the *New York Times*'s slogan—"All the News That's Fit to Print"—implies not only that the most significant news available has been covered but that decisions were made by people in selecting and determining what was "fit to print."[9]

The complexity and ambiguity of the world make selectivity of media coverage inevitable because different people will see different realities. People possess different beliefs about the world around them due to unique backgrounds and varying life experiences and interests. This is most obvious when people from different cultures and parts of the world are involved, but different perceptions of the same issue are also evident within the same culture. Therefore, decisions are made by the news media concerning which issues to cover and how these issues will be presented; and these decisions are consequential in affecting the kind of national and international reality readers, viewers, and listeners are likely to perceive.

The type of medium, as discussed above, also is important, for it affects not only the space available for news coverage but how the news is presented. While the print media, especially newspapers, usually cover more news stories and devote more space to each story than the electronic media, television news stories are unique because they are accompanied by video pictures that provide the viewer with a greater sense of immediacy—of "being there"—as opposed to words, further affecting viewers' perceptions. The **power of television** is particularly noticeable during crisis reporting, when issues and stories that are part of the crisis are highlighted and most vulnerable to being sensationalized. "Television is driven to dramatize the news, to give it plot, theme, and continuity to make it comprehensive to a mass audience. Television needs action and drama. It needs to boil down complexities. It needs identifiable characters. Hence the focus on personality, preferably one personality."[10] And the "tendency to present (and understand) politics in terms of demons and friends, good guys and bad guys."[11]

Overall, television news coverage tends to simplify reality the most for it tends to be more incomplete and provide less depth than the print media while, at the same time, its visual images make it more compelling and powerful. Television is, nevertheless, the major medium by which most Americans gain their information and understanding of national and international affairs. A Pew Research Center survey found that, within a few days after the September 11, 2001 attacks, nine in ten Americans said that they got most of their news from television, some of which was the local TV news. Half the respondents also said that they were reading newspapers more closely, and about a third were checking the Internet more often. A month later, Americans still relied predominantly on television, but increasingly looked to other news sources—especially newspapers, the Internet, and radio, but not magazines—for coverage of the war on terrorism both at home and abroad (see **table 17.1** for Americans' news sources of September 11).

Therefore, the media provide a **mediated reality.** This was cleverly portrayed in a simple political cartoon concerning the news media in which a young boy asked his father, "Dad, if a tree falls in the forest, and the media aren't there to cover it, has the tree really fallen?" The news media not only select but shape the way we see reality, oftentimes in storybook fashion. In other words, each news medium acts as a filter of reality for its audience—although some news sources do a better job than others.[12]

Conservative and liberal critics of the American media agree that the news media must select, simplify, and, consequently, distort reality. Most mainstream journalists, however, have difficulty acknowledging or admitting this, because it contradicts their belief that they are able to mirror reality. Perhaps most important, this admission would damage the news media's credibility with the American public as providers of information

TABLE 17.1
AMERICANS' NEWS SOURCES FOLLOWING THE SEPTEMBER 11, 2001, ATTACKS

NEWS SOURCE	MID-SEPTEMBER	MID-NOVEMBER
Cable News	45%	53%
Network TV News	30	17
Local TV News	17	18
Radio	14	19
Newspapers	11	34
Magazines	0	2
Internet	5	13
Other	3	3
Don't Know	3	1

The Question: "How have you been getting most of your news about terrorism? From television, newspapers, radio, magazines or Internet?" (Some respondents cited more than one.)

SOURCE: Michael Parks, "Foreign News: What's Next?" *Columbia Journalism Review* (January–February 2002): 54–55.

and the watchdog of government. The news media, nevertheless, can provide only a mediated reality, yet one that has an important impact on the politics of U.S. foreign policy.

CHARACTERISTICS OF THE NEWS BUSINESS

News media coverage is also affected by the history, functions, organization, and subculture of the mass media (as with any bureaucratic organization). In order to better understand the type of mediated reality the mainstream media tend to provide, we must examine *a number of important characteristics concerning the nature of the mass media and journalism in American society:* The media (1) have become concentrated, (2) are big business, (3) are very competitive, and (4) have become bureaucratic and professionalized.[13]

The Concentrated Media. The first important characteristic involves the increasing concentration of the mass media over the course of American history. Although thousands of independent media organizations once existed in a very competitive environment—especially in the print media—a few large media conglomerates now dominate the national and local markets. Of the fifteen hundred daily newspapers that existed in the 1990s, 99 percent were local monopolies, and fourteen corporations controlled most of the country's circulation. Independently owned newspapers, once dominant, have been replaced by large media chains, such as Gannett, which operates *USA Today* and over ninety other dailies (representing 10 percent of total circulation in the country); Knight-Ridder, which runs the *Philadelphia Inquirer*, *Miami Herald*, and over thirty other daily newspapers; the *New York Times*, which operates the *New York Times*, the *Boston Globe*, and over thirty other dailies (as well as twenty magazines and five television and two radio stations); and the *Chicago Tribune*, which merged with Times Mirror and owns the *Los Angeles Times*, the *Baltimore Sun* (four other regional newspapers, twenty-two television stations, four radio stations, and twenty magazines). A handful of firms control most of the magazine business, with Time, Inc., alone accounting for nearly 40 percent of magazine revenues. Most book publishers are controlled by fewer than a dozen companies.

The three broadcasting networks continue to enjoy more than two-thirds of the television audience, although it has been declining. This decline in viewership for the major networks is in part due to the existence of over twelve thousand cable systems, but each cable system operates local monopolies, and over half of all the cable systems are owned by four companies. Altogether, seven media corporations control the seeming diversity of channels and choice on television. And five companies own over three hundred radio stations throughout the country with a few basic formats.[14]

Overall, Ben Bagdikian, in *The Media Monopoly* found that concentration in the communications industry grew rapidly in the 1980s and 1990s, a time of numerous mergers:

> When the first edition of this book was published in 1983, fifty corporations dominated most of every mass medium and the biggest media merger in history was a $340 million deal. At that time, the strategy of most of the fifty biggest firms was to gain market domination in one medium—to have the largest market share solely in newspapers, for example, or in magazines, or broadcasting, or books, or movies, but not in all of them. By the time the second edition was published in 1987, the fifty companies had shrunk to twenty-nine. By the third edition in 1990, the twenty-nine had shrunk to twenty-three, by the fourth edition to fourteen. By the fifth edition in 1997, the biggest firms numbered ten and involved the $19 billion Disney-ABC deal, at the time the biggest media merger ever. But the "biggest" of 1983, worth $340 million, would give way seventeen years later to AOL Time Warner's $450 billion merged corporation, more than 1,000 times larger.

Today six firms dominate all American mass media and "those six have more communications power than all the combined fifty leading firms sixteen years earlier." "Each is a subsidiary of a larger parent firm, some of them basically operating in other industries. The six parent firms are General Electric, Viacom, Disney, Bertelsmann, Time Warner, and Murdoch's News Corporation. Bertelsmann is based in Germany and News Corp in Australia, the other four in the United States. All the parent firms are listed in *Fortune Magazine's* 1999 Global 5000 of the largest corporations in the world." According to Bagdikian, "Other giant firms in other industries clearly were on the prowl for new mass media in order to join the Big SIX—like Sony, a Japanese hardware firm; Seagram's, a Canadian liquor firm; and AT&T, a telephone company traditionally providing one-to-one (not mass) communication." As Michael Eisner, chairman and chief executive officer of Disney, put it succinctly, "It doesn't matter whether it comes in by cable, telephone lines, computer, or satellite. Everyone's going to have to deal with Disney," or as Bagdikian would put it, everyone has to deal with the few major media giants (see **figure 17.1** on the four largest corporate conglomerates involved in communications).[15]

Such concentration of the media has continued and resulted in a narrower, less diverse mediated reality presented to the general public. The Telecommunications Act of 1996, which was intended to promote greater competition (such as in long distance telephone service), had the unintended effect of making it easier to have mergers and greater concentration.

In the area of news, it could be argued that certain **national media**—sometimes referred to as the elite press—have developed and become the primary source of information on national and international affairs for the mainstream media in general and, consequently, for most Americans. The national media consist of the following organizations: ABC, NBC, CBS, Fox, CNN (Cable News Network), the *New York Times*, the *Washington Post*, the *Los Angeles Times*, Associated Press (AP), and United Press International (UPI); one could also include the *Wall Street Journal* for economic news as well as *Newsweek*—owned by the *Washington Post*—*Time*, and *U.S. News & World Report* for the attentive public. Other large urban media organizations, such as the *Boston Globe*, *Chicago Tribune*, *Miami Herald*, and *Philadelphia Inquirer*, are junior partners of the national media for they lack national reach beyond their regional market.

The national media, in addition to being the direct source of information for many people, also operate **wire services.** For example, the Associated Press, unknown to most Americans, is a significant part of the national media because it makes available a large number of news stories from its reporters throughout the world to other media organizations (at a cost) through its wire service. Not surprisingly, other major news media organizations have come to operate their own

wire services, such as the *New York Times* and the *Washington Post–Los Angeles Times* wire services, as well as the Knight-Ridder wire service. Through the wire services these national media organizations have become the basic source of national and international news for most television stations, radio stations, and newspapers in the country—the media through which most Americans acquire information about the world around them.

Most local newspapers, for example, rely on the national media for the source of their stories on national and international affairs; only the major urban newspapers can afford their own national and foreign correspondents. According to Stephen Hess in *International News and Foreign Correspondents*, three-quarters of the country's largest one hundred papers have no full-time foreign correspondents.[16]

A key consequence of the growing concentration of the media industry is greater concentration in news media coverage. While the existence of a dozen or so major news sources provides the appearance of considerable diversity, choice is much more limited at the local level. More importantly, the national media tend to present **homogeneous news coverage** rather than a diverse picture of the news and the world. Regardless of which of the national television news programs or newspapers one watches or reads, all of these sources usually select the same lead news item, cover the same stories, and provide similar information and interpretations—what some have referred to as "the CNN effect" given their more round-the-clock news coverage. Differences do exist, but they tend to be minor, concerning detail and nuance. Overall, the news and the basic pictures of reality presented by the national media tend to be amazingly similar.

The Media Business. One reason the news media have become concentrated and their coverage so homogenized is that the mass media have increasingly become a big business. Historically, the American press used to consist of small, independent operations that were usually quite partisan. Presses frequently were operated to make money and provide a living for those involved. In addition, many were financed by wealthy patrons who were more interested in providing news and political interpretation, even at a financial loss. With the rise of industrialization, urbanization, and mass society, however, the media

FIGURE 17.1
THE CONCENTRATED MEDIA

Janus Capital Corporation owns 6%
AOL/TIME WARNER
Revenues: $36.2 billion

MAGAZINES
More than 64, including the 3 bestselling: *Time, Life* and *People; MAD Magazine,* DC Comics (87.5% w/12.5% AT&T); IPC, leading consumer magazine publisher in Britain

MOVIES
Warner Bros., New Line and Fine Line Features (75% w/25% AT&T); library of MGM, RKO and pre-1950 Warner Bros. films; Warner Home Video (75% w/25% AT&T); theaters: UCI (50% w/50% Viacom); WF Cinema Holdings (50% w/50% Viacom)

MUSIC
More than 40 labels, including Warner Bros., Atlantic, Elektra, London-Sire and Rhino Records; manufactures, packages and distributes the company's CDs, tapes and DVDs, majority interest in Alternative Distribution Alliance; Quincy Jones Entertainment Co. (37.5% w/12.5% AT&T and 50% Quincy Jones); Columbia House (50% w/50% Sony); Music publisher Warner/Chappell

BOOKS
Warner Books; Little, Brown; Time-Life Books; Book-of-the-Month Club (50% w/50% Bertelsmann)

TELEVISION NETWORKS
WB (50% w/17% AT&T, 22% Tribune Co. and 11% WB officers), HBO and Cinemax, (75% w/25% AT&T), Comedy Central (37.5% w/12.5% AT&T and 50% Viacom), Court TV (37.5% w/12.5% AT&T and 50% Liberty), E! and Style (7.5% w/AT&T, Liberty, Disney and Comcast), TBS, TNT, Cartoon Network, Turner Classic Movies, CNN, Headline News, CNNfn and CNN/Sports Illustrated; TVKO (75% w/25% AT&T); Music Choice (w/Sony, EMI, AT&T and others); wholly and partially owned channels in Europe, Asia and South America

CABLE
Second-largest provider, with 12.8 million customers in wholly and partially owned systems (most with AT&T)

PRODUCTION
Warner Bros., Warner Bros. Animation, Telepictures, Castle Rock; library of 6,500 movies, 32,000 TV shows and 13,500 cartoons (all 75% w/25% AT&T) Other: TiVo 18% w/GE, Liberty, News Corp. and others; digital video recording

THEME PARKS
Warner Bros. Movie World Theme Park and hotel in Australia (w/AT&T and Village Roadshow)

INTERNET
America Online, CompuServe, Netscape, ICQ and AOL Instant Messenger; websites include MusicNet (20% w/20% Bertelsmann, 20% EMI and RealNetworks), digitalcity, moviefone, mapquest and music sites Spinner.com, Winamp and SHOUTcast; stakes in Amazon.com (2%), Dr. Koop (10%), RoadRunner cable modems (majority stake w/AT&T and Advance-Newhouse)

SPORTS
Atlanta Braves, Atlanta Hawks, Atlanta Thrashers, Goodwill Games, Phillips Arena

OTHER
Time Warner Telecom (37%), Warner Bros. Studio Stores (75% w/25% AT&T), licenses rights to DC Comics, Hanna-Barbera characters, other WB properties (75% w/25% AT&T); stake in Sportsline Radio

---

WALT DISNEY COMPANY
Revenues: $25.4 billion

MAGAZINES
US Weekly (50% w/Wenner Media), *Discover, Family Fun, Disney Adventures, ESPN The Magazine* (80% w/20% Hearst), *Talk* (50% w/50% Hearst)

RESORTS/THEMED ENTERTAINMENT
Disney World, Disneyland, Disney Cruise Line, Disney Vacation Club, Disneyland, Tokyo Disney (royalties on revenues), Disneyland Paris (39%), Hong Kong Disneyland (planned for 2005); ESPN Zone (80% w/Hearst)

BOOKS
Hyperion, Talk Miramax, Disney Children's Book Group, ESPN Books, ABC Daytime Press

TELEVISION NETWORKS
ABC; Disney Channel; Toon Disney; Soap Net; ESPN, ESPN2, ESPN Classic, ESPNEWS and ESPN Regional Television (all 80% w/20% Hearst); A&E, History and Biography channels (all 37.5% w/37.5% Hearst and 25% GE); Lifetime and Lifetime Movie Network (50% w/50% Hearst); E! and Style (40% w/40% Comcast, 10% Liberty, 7.5% AOL-TW and 2.5% AT&T), Fox Family Channel; Disney and ESPN channels in more than 140 countries, plus stakes in other channels

STATIONS
10 stations

PRODUCTION
Buena Vista, Touchstone, Walt Disney, IABC Entertainment, ABC News Productions, Saban

SPORTS
Mighty Ducks, Anaheim Angels

MOVIES
Walt Disney Pictures, Touchstone Pictures, Hollywood Pictures, Miramax Film Corp., Dimension, Buena Vista International

RADIO
Stations: 50; networks ABC Radio Network, Radio Disney, ESPN Radio (80% w/20% Hearst)

OTHER
Theatrical productions of *Beauty and the Beast, The Lion King, The Hunchback of Notre Dame* and *Aida;* New Amsterdam Theatre on Broadway; 741 stores and Disney catalogue; licenses characters for clothes, toys, etc., and for teaching aids; videos/films for schools; stakes in sites including NFL.com and Movies.com (50% w/News Corp.); markets cell art from Disney animated films; Celebration, Florida, a 4,900-acre town

FIGURE **17.1**
(*continued*)

MOVIES
Paramount Pictures, Nickelodeon Movies, MTV Films, BET Arabesque Films; Blockbuster (82%); about 1,800 screens in theaters in the US, Canada, Europe, Asia and South America through Famous Players, UCI (50% w/50% AOL-TW); WF Cinema Holdings (50% w/50% AOL-TW)

BOOKS
Simon & Schuster, Pocket Books, Scribner, The Free Press, Arabesque Books; divisions in Britain and Australia

INTERNET
MTVi (90% w/10% Liberty) includes MTV.com and VH1.com; Nickelodeon Online (w/AT&T); stakes also in iWon, Sportsline.com, MarketWatch.com, hollywood.com, storerunner.com, Thirdage.com and Webvan; web design

RADIO
184 Infinity radio stations; CBS Radio Network; Westwood One (18%) and Sportsline Radio (20% w/Reuters and AOL-TW)

National Amusements owns 68%
VIACOM, INC.
Revenues: $20 billion

TELEVISION NETWORKS
CBS, UPN, MTV, MTV2, VH1, Showtime, Nickelodeon, Noggin (50% w/Sesame Workshop), Nickelodeon GA3, TV Land, Comedy Central (50% w/37.5% AOL-TW and 12.5% AT&T), TNN, CMT, The Movie Channel, Sundance Channel (50% w/Vivendi and Robert Redford), FLIX, BET and BET on Jazz; stakes in channels throughout Europe, Africa, Asia and Russia

STATIONS
39, including two each in Philadelphia, Boston, Dallas and Detroit; operates 2 others.

PRODUCTION
CBS Enterprises (includes King World and CBS Broadcast International), Paramount, Spelling, Big Ticket, Viacom Productions, Nickelodeon Studios, MTV Productions, Nicktoons Animation; other TV: TiVo (w/AOL-TW, News Corp., Liberty and GE)

MAGAZINES
BET Weekend (w/*New York Daily News*), *Emerge, Heart & Soul, Nickelodeon Magazine*

THEME PARKS/ LIVE VENUE
Paramount theme parks in the US and Canada; Star Trek: The Experience at the Las Vegas Hilton; jazz restaurant in Las Vegas; theme-based restaurants and dance clubs in Largo, MD, Memphis and at Disney World; World Wrestling Federation Entertainment (3% w/3% GE and others); House of Blues Entertainment (w/that company)

OTHER
Exclusive advertising rights on buses, subways, trains, kiosks, billboards and other venues in New York, LA, Chicago, San Francisco, Philadelphia, Detroit, Houston, Atlanta and 82 other US cities and in cities in Mexico, Canada, Britain, Ireland and throughout Europe; BET Financial Services; BET Design Studio (w/G-III Apparel Group, Ltd.); licenses Viacom-owned properties and third-party clients including the US Postal Service, Jeep and Red Dog Beer; Famous Music holds copyright to more than 100,000 musical works

INTERNET
Includes stakes of 47% in Snap and NBC.com; CNBC.com (10%), Salon.com (10%), Autobytel.com Inc. (10%), and polo.com (50% w/Polo Ralph Lauren Media)

SPORTS/ LIVE VENUE
New York Knicks, New York Rangers, New York Liberty, New England Seawolves, Hartford Wolfpack, Madison Square Garden, management of Hartford Civic Center, New York Liberty (all 16% w/44% Cablevision and 40% News Corp.); Radio City Music Hall (16% w/44% Cablevision and 40% News Corp.), World Wrestling Federation Entertainment (3% w/3% Viacom and others)

GENERAL ELECTRIC
Revenues: $129.9 billion

OTHER
Aircraft engines; GE, Hotpoint and other appliances; light bulbs; operates 14 communications satellites; cars, computers, equipment for refineries, ammonia plants and nuclear reactors, MR and CT scanners, X-ray and ultrasound machines; health, accident and long-term-care insurance; investment and retirement plans, mortgages, home equity and commercial real estate loans, car loans, credit card application processing, sales authorization and collection services for retailers in 23 countries; owns stock in companies in retail, financial services, telecommunications, healthcare, food and beverages, cable and broadcasting industries; leases almost 1,000 aircraft, 190,000 railcars and about 1 million cars, trucks and tractor trailers

TELEVISION NETWORKS
NBC, CNBC, MSNBC (50% w/50% Microsoft), A&E, History and Biography channels (all 25% w/37.5% Disney and 37.5% Hearst); Snap TV (80%); AMC, Bravo, WE and Independent Film Channel (all w/Cablevision and MGM); Much Music (w/Cablevision); stakes in regional news, sports and entertainment channels with News Corp., AT&T and Cablevision; international channels include NBC and CNBC channels in Europe and Asia, Canal de Noticias NBC and TV Azteca (joint venture)

STATIONS
13 stations plus 32% stake in Paxson, owner of TV stations and PAX TV, a national programming network

PRODUCTION/PROGRAMMING
NBC Productions; Radio City Television, Bravo Original Programming, IFC Productions and Next Wave Films (16–26% w/Cablevision); Satellite DBS provider (13% w/37% Cablevision and 50% Loral); TiVo (w/AOL-TW, News Corp., Viacom and Liberty)

SOURCE: "The Big Ten" by *Nation* editors from the January 7, 2002 issue of *The Nation*. Reprinted with permission.

have become a big business where the bottom line—financial worth and profit—predominates. As economics has replaced politics as the basic source of motivation within the news business, "muckraking" journalism has declined and partisan viewpoints have been relegated to the editorial pages. Today, the major news media organizations are part of "large media corporations and conglomerates."[17]

NBC News, for example, is part of the National Broadcasting Corporation and was once owned by RCA. General Electric, one of the ten largest U.S. corporations (and a major defense contractor), with total revenues of over $130 billion today, purchased RCA during the 1980s for $6.3 billion and generated $3.64 billion in revenues from communications in 1988. CBS News, part of CBS, generated $2.8 billion in revenues during the same year; in 1995 it was purchased by Westinghouse. ABC News is part of the American Broadcasting Corporation, which was owned in 1988 by Capital Cities, Inc., with revenues from its communications business totaling $3.75 billion. In 1995 Walt Disney Pictures purchased Capital Cities/ABC for $19 billion. And in mid-1989 Time merged with Warner to form Time Warner at a cost of $450 billion, becoming the largest multimedia firm in the world. The news and communications process, in other words, has become big, and is becoming bigger, business.

The financial worth of these media organizations and their corporate ownership are reminders that the media field has become an arena open only to giant corporations and extremely wealthy individuals, as when Rupert Murdoch purchased Walter Annenberg's Triangle Publications for $3 billion in the 1980s. Murdoch's publishing empire has allowed, for example, Fox TV to eventually become a major electronic media player.

The growing emphasis on the need to remain financially solvent and, preferably, expand profits affects the resources available to media organizations and choices concerning the breadth and depth of news coverage. Most important, growing concern with generating revenue and maintaining profitability has led to the mass media's preoccupation with "maximizing its appeal to a large and broad audience," reinforcing the tendency to provide a selective and homogenized picture of national and international politics.

The Competitive Market Media. The third characteristic is that the news media are also very competitive, but in a narrow sense that reflects their concentrated and big-business orientation. The phrase used by one scholar to describe this situation is that the mass media are "rivals in conformity" for audiences and advertisers.[18] The news media, as in any business, attempt to increase their market share because their revenues are obtained through advertising (and sales of newspapers). Hence, a key concern of national media organizations is to present news in such a way that attracts, not alienates, audiences and advertisers—that, in other words, takes into consideration the beliefs of the mass and elite publics. This would include not alienating business in particular, since it is the major source of most media advertising. Therefore, the news business has its competitive elements, many of which have little to do with improving the quality of media coverage and which actually contribute to the homogenization of the news.

Television is probably the most competitive because the national networks compete for the same viewing audience (and the same national advertisers). Although advertising rates are lower for news than for entertainment programs, it still costs advertisers as much as $300,000 a minute for a commercial on one of the nightly network news shows (as opposed to around $2,000,000 for a thirty-second ad during the Super Bowl professional football championship game). Having a larger or smaller audience than one's network competitors means a difference of millions of dollars in what one can charge for advertising and millions of dollars in yearly revenues. As with any program on television, therefore, news programs are as heavily oriented toward maximizing a broad audience as they are toward informing the public. At the same time, the audience for the major networks has been declining, especially with the rise of cable TV.[19]

This competitiveness, ironically, tends to promote what might be called a "risk-avoidance approach" within the mass media. Rather than taking risks, the fear of losing viewers and offending corporate sponsors makes the media act with great caution in their programming. They usually prefer to emulate the news organization (or the entertainment shows) currently enjoying the greatest amount of success. This is especially true of television, whose news media executives, for example, have become increasingly attuned to the entertainment aspects of the news as a means of attracting the public's attention. As David Halberstam depicted television in general in *The Powers That Be:*

> The impulse to take risks in quality programming, to serve the national interest in public affairs, became weaker all the time. And the enormity of the new profits did not make the company stronger or more confident of itself. Ironically, as it became greedier, it became more nervous, more insecure. The race was getting faster and faster and the ice was getting thinner and thinner. . . . Now broadcasting was obsessed with the ratings.[20]

"Soft" public affairs programs that emphasize entertainment and personalities, such as *The Today Show* and "*20/20*," have proliferated. The television networks have also responded with tabloid shows such as *A Current Affair,* which reflects the popularity of tabloid magazines such as the *National Enquirer* and the *Star,* as well as more "news magazines" that try to do a little bit of everything, such as *Dateline* and *Prime Time Live* (which are much cheaper to make and more profitable then regular sitcoms and dramas). Even the nightly network news programs on television have tried numerous gimmicks, such as having the anchorperson report live from abroad or purchasing full-page ads in the *New York Times* to tell readers that they were first to predict who won the presidential election; such ploys are designed not to improve the quality of coverage but to increase popular appeal and viewership.[21]

The Monica Lewinsky story was in fact first broken not in the traditional media but on the Internet, in a 1:11 a.m., January 18, 1997, posting on *The Drudge Report.* As James O'Shea, deputy managing news editor for the *Chicago Tribune* said, "The days when you can decide not to print a story because it's not well enough sourced are long gone."[22]

Such competitive and popularly oriented attributes of the national media contribute to the selectivity, similarity, and sensationalism of news coverage discussed above. This is further reinforced by the fact that American journalism is also a competitive profession, especially among the national media. Journalists and the major media organizations are preoccupied with getting the story first and being the "number one" source of news. This concern with being the media leader tends to result in the phenomena of **pack jour-**nalism, in which journalists from different media organizations chase the same headline stories. Pack journalism is most noticeable, for instance, during crisis coverage or with the media's effort to cover presidential election campaigns, as depicted by Timothy Crouse in *The Boys on the Bus.* This tendency to congregate while in search of the same story is reinforced by the strong esprit de corps that develops among journalists. Thus, the competitiveness of the journalistic profession often results in pack journalism and great similarity in news coverage.[23]

At the same time, journalists are highly motivated, especially at the national level, to excel within their profession and to stand out from the pack. They compete for promotion and vie for more rewarding and prestigious assignments. Top journalists, in particular, are in great demand within the media business. Those most successful not only tend to become better journalists, they also command considerable fame, prestige, power, and fortune—strong factors motivating individual journalists. Television anchorpersons and journalists—such as Tom Brokaw, Peter Jennings, Ted Koppel, Dan Rather, Diane Sawyer, and Barbara Walters—have become well-known celebrities who enjoy annual salaries from $2 million to $15 million a year.[24] This success is typically accomplished as a result of operating within the routines and norms of the media business and journalistic profession.

The Media Bureaucracy and Professional Journalism. The fourth important characteristic of the national media, in addition to its concentration, big-business orientation, and competitiveness, is that it has become extremely bureaucratic and professionalized in the production of the news. National media organizations are large, complex bureaucratic enterprises involving thousands of people organized in terms of hierarchy, specialization, and routines. They are also heavily influenced by a media subculture based on certain norms and standards of professional journalism. This affects how the news media portray contemporary national and international affairs in terms of which issues, places, and events get covered (or do not get covered), how things are reported, which stories are finally run, and how they are presented to the public.

Much of the news is a function of the **beat system,** in which reporters are given responsibility for covering a particular issue or institution. Although journalists like to talk about the age of investigative reporting following the Vietnam War and Watergate, there are actually very few investigative reporters per se who make a concerted effort to uncover as many relevant sources and pieces of information as possible in putting a story together. Instead, "beat reporters" are assigned by their media organizations to cover established institutions, such as government and business, and rely on the authorities available as their basic source of information. The national media, for example, regularly assign political correspondents to cover the major institutions and agencies of the federal government, such as the White House, Pentagon, State Department, Congress, and Supreme Court.

The most prestigious beat is the White House. Whereas the entire White House press corps consisted of twenty-five reporters in 1945, over 2,000 people had regular White House press passes by the 1990s. But as explained in a study by Stephen Hess:

> While there are some 2,000 reporters accredited to the White House, the White House Press corps is the name given to about 60 reporters, the regulars, who have assigned seats at the press secretary's daily briefing, a desk in the press room, and who usually travel with the president. They include the wire services (AP, UPI, Reuters), each with 4 reporters; the TV networks (ABC, CBS, NBC, CNN), also with 3- and 4-person staffs. Some major newspapers (*The New York Times*, *The Washington Post*, *Wall Street Journal*, *Los Angeles Times*) and the weekly news magazines have 2 reporters. Smaller newspapers, magazines and newspaper chains cover the White House with a single fulltime reporter.[25]

Not surprisingly, much of the news is about what government officials from these institutions have said or done. In the *New York Times* or *Washington Post*, for instance, Leon Sigal, in *Reporters and Officials*, found that stories from regularly covered beats outnumbered offbeat stories two to one, including front-page headlines.[26] Such routinized news coverage means that news stories are also affected by the timing of events, because media organizations have deadlines for going to press and are less active over the weekend. Because so many journalists cover the same institutions and issues while operating under the same time constraints, the beat system also sets the stage for pack journalism.

International coverage, likewise, is heavily a function of the foreign correspondents, which developed during World War II and the cold war. They tend to be stationed in countries that are allied with the U.S. government and located in major cities. Of roughly seven hundred foreign correspondents, at least half are routinely stationed in Europe, while fewer than 10 percent are stationed in each of the three regions of Africa, Latin America, and the Middle East. Since the cold war, some media organizations actually have cut back on the number of their foreign bureaus and foreign correspondents. The only media organization with extensive global geographic coverage is the Associated Press, the largest American wire service (which submits stories that have to be selected and purchased by news media outlets). **Table 17.2** shows, as of September 1, 2001, the number of bureaus and the approximate number of correspondents for major American news organizations.

For example, in 1989 *Newsweek* had twenty-two full-time foreign correspondents located in fifteen bureaus abroad. Eleven correspondents were located in bureaus throughout the major cities of Europe (in London, Paris, Bonn-Berlin, Rome, Moscow, and Warsaw), six in Asia (in Tokyo, Beijing, Hong Kong, and Bangkok), only two in the Middle East (in Cairo and Jerusalem), two in Africa (in Nairobi and Johannesburg), and one in Latin America (in Mexico City). Over a decade later and well into a post–cold war world, *nothing* had changed—a similar number and **location of foreign correspondents** and bureaus! But by 2002, *Newsweek* was down to roughly sixteen foreign correspondents in eleven bureaus, overwhelmingly located in Europe and Asia. The television networks not only have relatively small numbers of full-time foreign correspondents but tend to base them in London and fly them from there to wherever the story is (as other media organizations do). Not surprisingly, given the distribution of the American news media, there is much more international news coverage of Europe (and Asia) than of the rest of the world.[27]

Editors and executives at the top of the bureaucratic hierarchy also play an important role, for they supervise and oversee the news production and **editorial process.** They make crucial decisions concerning which journalists are hired, what gets covered and by whom, which stories are published, the length and location of the stories, and their final presentation and wording. The importance of this is evident, for example, by studies that have found a much higher proportion of stories on the Third World in the AP and UPI wire services than appear in the American press.[28] Jour-

TABLE 17.2
FOREIGN CORRESPONDENTS AND BUREAUS OF
MAJOR MEDIA ORGANIZATIONS

(As of September 1, 2001)

ORGANIZATION	BUREAUS	CORRESPONDENTS
Associated Press	100	150
New York Times	26	40
Los Angeles Times	21	26
Washington Post	20	26
Knight Ridder	4	14
USA Today	4	4
Time	17	19
Newsweek	11	16
CNN	30	55
CBS	4	9
NBC	5	8
ABC	6	7
Fox	6	6

Regional papers with five or more bureaus: Chicago Tribune (10), Dallas News (5), Baltimore Sun (5), Boston Globe (5).

SOURCE: Michael Parks, "Foreign News: What's Next?," *Columbia Journalism Review* (January–February 2002), p. 53.

nalists of major news organizations who work in the field recognize that editors have certain idiosyncrasies and beliefs that make them more receptive to certain kinds of information and new angles than others. In this sense, a type of "self-censorship" actually occurs within the news process, as it does in all professions, given the incentives and disincentives built into the media bureaucracy and the journalistic profession.

Sometimes, in fact, conflicts of interest exist in which the content of news may be directly affected by personal, rather than journalistic, concerns. Editors and executives, for example, may intervene in the news production process to prevent or sanitize stories for purely self-interested reasons. The roles of political activist and reporter were clearly in conflict in 1980 when ABC reporter George Will secretly coached candidate Ronald Reagan for a presidential debate with Jimmy Carter, yet Will continued to cover the campaign for ABC News and the *Washington Post* as a neutral party.

Conflicts of interest also arise when individuals, in their role as policy experts, speak or are quoted by the news media on topics for which they also serve as private consultants to business firms or foreign countries involved in the issue at hand without any public acknowledgment (as discussed in the chapter on group politics). Naturally, these situations usually go unreported and remain hidden from the general public.[29]

The mediated reality that most Americans see and read is not only affected by the bureaucratic nature of the beat system and the editorial process; much of news media coverage is heavily affected by the subculture of the journalistic profession that prevails throughout the media organizations, as well. Journalists tend to be generalists, not specialists. As was briefly discussed in chapter 6 concerning foreign service officers, what a generalist gains in terms of breadth of information is offset by limited depth of knowledge and understanding relative to any particular issue or area. This is particularly a problem in international coverage because most foreign correspondents have limited language competency beyond English (or possibly Spanish and French for some) and face the additional constraint of government censorship in many countries. Therefore, foreign correspondents are often dependent for their information on local elites who speak English, which often limits access to a range of information and views.

This generalist orientation is reinforced by the professionalization of journalism. While media coverage was once quite partisan, the contemporary mainstream media take a nonpartisan approach in their news coverage, often referred to as **objective journalism** within the profession. Journalistic norms emphasize the importance of independence (acting free of "outside" political pressures), objectivity (presenting the facts without prejudice or distortion), and impartiality (avoiding partisanship and providing balance in representing without favor the views of contending parties.). On the one hand, this results in less personal bias affecting the selection and content of news coverage. On the other hand, such so-called objectivity in reporting usually results in a preoccupation with the immediacy of "news"—in other words, what is new and currently factual in a news story from establishment sources. Although informative, this allows others to influence the newsworthiness of stories, most stories tend to be accompanied by little historical background or context that would better inform the reader, and news stories come and go based on their timeliness, with little follow-up, producing little continuity in coverage over time. Most important, as we will see in the next section, the concept of objective journalism is a misnomer, for journalists do not operate in a political vacuum and they have political values that affect what they see and how they behave. Such nonpartisan journalism, in fact, is heavily affected by the political environment and plays a major role in the politics of U.S foreign policy.

CULTURE, IDEOLOGY, AND POLITICS IN THE COMMUNICATIONS PROCESS

The third general explanation that accounts for the selectivity and content of news media coverage, in addition to the complexity of the world and the characteristics of the news business, is the impact of the political environment on the communications process. *News coverage by the national media is heavily affected by the political environment in two fundamental ways.* First, journalistic perceptions of the world are shaped by the dominant political ideology and culture of American society. Second, the media are perceived as so important in affecting American politics that individuals and groups in and out of government actively attempt to influence and manipulate news media coverage. These factors not only reinforce the tendency of selective and homogenized news coverage but result in the national and mainstream media usually communicating a politically centrist understanding of reality to the American public.[30]

Ideology, Culture, and the Centrist Media. Journalists of the mainstream media tend to downplay and dispute the ideological basis of American reporting. They point out, quite correctly, that while the news media historically have been partisan, modern journalism is much more nonpartisan and professional. Although nonpartisan, American journalists nevertheless are not "value free." They hold cultural and ideological beliefs—as Americans they are socialized to see the world in terms of a liberal-conservative orientation. As Walter Lippmann, one of America's most prominent twentieth-century journalists, asserted in 1922, "We do not first see, and then define, we define first and then see."[31] This is inevitable and perfectly understandable because, as we discussed in chapter 13, liberalism and conservatism, or some blend of the two, are the basis of political thought for most Americans. Therefore, it would be more accurate to say that mainstream members of the mass media tend to operate from a nonpartisan tradition and cover the news from a centrist ideological perspective that ranges within a liberal-conservative understanding of the world.

This centrist ideological orientation obviously colors how journalists (including editors) see the world, what issues they believe are of consequence, why this is the case, and how these issues will be communicated to others. No matter how hard American journalists try to be objective, they are influenced by the values of democracy and capitalism they tend to hold dear. Viewpoints that are critical of this classical liberal orientation are rarely heard or communicated within the mainstream American media. The political consequences, as Doris Graber claims in *Mass Media and American Politics*, are that "the media usually support the political system and rarely question its fundamental tenets. They limit their criticism to what they perceive as perversions of fundamental social and political values."[32] The impact of culture and ideology is not unique to American journalism but affects media coverage in all countries. Nevertheless, the role of American culture and ideology deserve close attention in order to fully understand American news coverage and what is referred to as **framing,** especially within the mainstream media that operate under the guise of objective journalism.

Within this centrist ideological orientation, *news media coverage sometimes may be more liberal and at other times may be more conservative*—it ultimately depends on the issue, the times, and the political environment. The particular ideological slant of the coverage for any issue will normally reflect political thought prevalent throughout the mass and, in particular, elite public in American society at that time. As Stephen Hess argues in The *Washington Reporters*, "Washington news gathering, in other words, is an interaction among elites. One elite reports on another elite."[33] More specifically, the content of national media coverage tends to reflect the beliefs of the individuals within institutions and groups, in and out of government, that prevail in American politics. The communication of the news reflecting such beliefs subsequently affects the politics of U.S. foreign policy. Therefore, the news media and the political environment are part of an interactive process where more centrist views and positions tend to set the political agenda and influence the climate of opinion in domestic politics and the policy-making process.

As Herbert Gans explains, "It would be incorrect to say that the news is about elites per se or a single elite; rather, the news deals with those who hold the power within various national or societal strata, with the most powerful officials in the most powerful agencies, with the coalition of upper-class and upper-middle class people which dominates the socioeconomic hierarchy."[34] For instance, a study of the guests on ABC's *Nightline* from 1985 to 1988 found that over 89 percent were men, over 92 percent were white, and over 80 percent were professionals, corporate representatives, or government officials. In the area of foreign policy, the national media rely overwhelmingly on prominent current and former government officials as sources of information and for guests on public affairs programs, with the same faces—such as

Henry Kissinger—appearing time and time again. Similar results were found in a recent study for *The NewsHour with Jim Lehrer* on PBS, considered to be the most in-depth news show on TV.[35]

The news media, in other words, tend to practice **source journalism** as opposed to **investigative journalism.** "Very few newspaper stories are the result of reporters digging through files; poring over documents; or interviewing experts, dissenters, or ordinary people. The overwhelming majority of stories are based on official sources—on information provided by members of Congress, presidential aides, and other political insiders."[36] As Carl Bernstein has pointed out, this was the case during Watergate:

> America's news organizations assigned only fourteen of those 2,000 men and women [reporters working in Washington, D.C.] to cover the Watergate story on a full-time basis. And of those fourteen, only six were assigned to the story on what might be called an "investigative" basis, that is, to go beyond recording the obvious daily statements and court proceedings, and try to find out exactly what had happened.[37]

And according to Bernstein, not much has changed in post-Watergate journalism.

As Daniel Hallin concluded in *The Uncensored War: The Media and Vietnam*, the national media reflect the views of prominent leaders and government officials: When they agree, the news media reflect the consensus view (the sphere of consensus); when they disagree, the media reflect their level of diversity (the sphere of legitimate controversy). Topics and viewpoints that do not reflect prominent leaders and the political mainstream tend to be ignored, and not covered, by the national media (the sphere of illegitimate sources and views). In this respect, news media coverage of the world is heavily dependent and conditioned by the national politics that transpire at home (see **figure 17.2** on the political boundaries of national media coverage).[38]

This symbiotic relationship between the national media and the political environment ensures relatively centrist news coverage within an ideological spectrum occupied by most Americans, especially the most prominent opinion leaders. This produces coverage which sometimes is more liberal and other times more conservative. In the post–Vietnam War era, for example,

FIGURE **17.2**
THE POLITICAL BOUNDARIES OF NATIONAL MEDIA COVERAGE

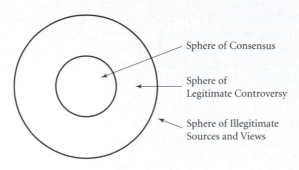

Sphere of Consensus

Sphere of
Legitimate Controversy

Sphere of Illegitimate
Sources and Views

Daniel Hallin, *The Uncensored War: The Media and Vietnam* (Berkeley and Los Angeles: University of California Press, 1986).

the rise of liberalism has resulted in civil rights coverage that often represent a more liberal viewpoint. On the other hand, economic issues tend to be covered from a more conservative perspective, especially since the resurgence of conservatism. To illustrate the point further, economic news in the mainstream media is equated with the coverage of business and finance (as reflected in the title of that separate section of the newspaper); however, coverage of labor and unions tends to be nonexistent except during a major strike where it is usually portrayed, through the eyes of government and business leaders, unsympathetically as a threat to the economy and law and order.[39]

Foreign policy coverage is much less consistent, for it reflects the greater ideological diversity that grew out of the breakdown of the cold war consensus. Sometimes foreign policy coverage is more supportive of the president and other times more critical; sometimes it is more liberal and other times more conservative. When the political forces of liberalism are on the rise throughout society, such as during the early and mid-1970s, news media coverage often leans to the liberal side. However, when the political forces of conservatism are ascendant, such as during the late 1970s and early 1980s, news media coverage often becomes more conservative.

During a foreign policy crisis, early coverage tends to be highly supportive of presidential policies, while later coverage is more likely to become diverse and critical. The cultural and ideological foundations of American journalism are also particularly noticeable. During such times American journalism is extremely vulnerable to becoming consumed by patriotic and nationalistic fervor. In fact, journalists often lose their nonpartisan nature and closely identify with the United States government and its policies; this is evident when journalists speak in terms of "we" and "they" as opposed to speaking in a more neutral language that distances them and their reporting from the parties and events, in accordance with the norms of objective journalism Typically, journalists act as a medium for promoting the president's views and policies and, thus, contribute to the phenomena of rallying round the flag. This was clearly evident, for example, in early coverage of the Iraqi invasion of Kuwait and the U.S. government's response under President George Bush Sr., and it occurred again following the start of the Persian Gulf War (see **essay 17.1** on crisis coverage).[40]

Sensationalist and nationalistic coverage was evident to a greater extent in the months following the September 11, 2001, attacks on the World Trade Center towers and the Pentagon. This was acknowledged in an article entitled "US Media Cowed by Patriotic Fever, Says CBS Star." The star was Dan Rather—the twenty year anchor for CBS News—interviewed in *The Guardian*, a British daily (that was not also reported within the American mainstream press). According to

ESSAY 17.1
CRISIS COVERAGE

Crisis coverage by the news media is extremely important in American politics because crises become major agenda items throughout the country, occupying the attention of policymakers and the general public alike. In order to fully understand the significance of crisis coverage, we must examine patterns in *news media coverage as they proceed through three general stages of coverage*: precrisis, crisis, and postcrisis. During crisis coverage, the resources of the media are heavily devoted to covering the key issue or event as the lead story. During precrisis and postcrisis coverage, however, the bureaucratic and routine nature of media politics prevails, in which any single issue typically receives little and uneven news coverage.

The **cycle in news media coverage** of an issue—from minimal coverage during routine times to maximum coverage during crisis and then back to minimal coverage after the crisis—deeply impacts the foreign policy process because it affects the understanding and images that people acquire of the issue involved. James Reston of the *New York Times* explained the reactive nature of media crisis coverage this way: "We are fascinated by events but not by the things that cause the events. We will send 500 correspondents to Vietnam after the war breaks out, and fill the front pages with their reports, meanwhile ignoring the rest of the world, but we will not send five reporters there when the danger of war is developing."[A] A study conducted for the State Department's Foreign Service Institute by A. Raphael, for example, found that the three television networks covered Iran an average of only five minutes each year from 1972 to 1977.[B] Yet with the fall of the shah of Iran and the taking of American diplomats, the Iran hostage crisis became the ultimate media event throughout 1979 and 1980 for 444 days. Once the international crisis was perceived to be over in Iran—or in Vietnam, Grenada, Panama, Haiti, Somalia, Kosovo, Afghanistan, and Iraq for example—there is little subsequent attention and follow-up by the media. It is the stark contrast between the media attention given to an issue during a crisis in comparison to the little attention devoted both before and after that allows crisis coverage to dramatically impact people and the politics of U.S. foreign policy.

Unlike the pre- and postcrisis phases, the news media reassign personnel and focus their attention on covering the lead story during crisis coverage. Crisis coverage, in fact, often results in what has been called "media diplomacy," where sometimes television in particular is used as an instrument of communication and negotiation by world leaders. Yet concentration on the lead story comes at the cost of curtailing coverage of most other national and international news. For example, American media coverage of the Persian Gulf conflict following Iraq's invasion of Kuwait in 1990 overshadowed all other news. Such major domestic and international issues as the savings and loan industry's insolvency and scandal, the government's growing federal debt, the collapse of communism in the Soviet Union and Eastern Europe, the reunification of Germany, and rapid developments in South Africa received little or no media attention throughout much of the crisis. Such overwhelming focus on the so-called lead story also appears to be the case with the post-September 11 coverage of the growing conflict and war with Iraq.

Most important, for all the information provided about a crisis, coverage is incomplete, inflated, and often "sensationalized," especially as a result of the immediacy and powerful images provided by television. Who can forget (for those who aren't too young) the image, for instance, of President Ronald Reagan being shot and pushed into the presidential limousine? Or the image of the World Trade Center towers in New York City being struck by the two airplanes and the ball of fire and smoke expanding from the buildings? Television stations began round-the-clock news coverage and, with little to report, repeatedly replayed tapes of Reagan being shot (or the towers being hit). In fact Frank Reynolds, ABC's news anchor, announced the death of Jim Brady, the White House press spokesman who was also shot—only to apologize later when it was learned that Brady actually survived the attack after all. This news blunder is but an extreme example of incomplete and unreliable media coverage that frequently characterizes times of crisis; and with the rise of CNN as part of the national media, round-the-clock coverage has become a more permanent feature of news coverage.

Crises, by definition, are periods of considerable uncertainty and fluidity. Yet crisis coverage is delivered as if it is comprehensive and accurate because of news media competition to get the story out first and gain the highest

A. James Reston, *Sketches in the Sand* (New York: Knopf, 1967), p. 195.
B. A. Raphael, "Media Coverage of the Hostage Negotiations—From Fact to Fiction," *Executive Seminars in National and International Affairs* (U.S. Department of State, Foreign Service Institute, 1981–1982).

audience, especially in television. This is reinforced by the media's preoccupation with reporting new and current developments. Furthermore, crisis coverage is usually accompanied by pack journalism, with most journalists pursuing the same story virtually in unison. During such frenzied searches for news, the news media become even more dependent on a few external sources of information—such as government officials—and thus are more vulnerable to being used or manipulated for political ends.

One of the most blatant examples of the president's ability to dominate and manipulate the news media occurred under President Lyndon Johnson. During the Tonkin Gulf crisis in the spring of 1965, government officials charged that American destroyers sustained two unprovoked attacks by North Vietnamese warships in international waters. This led to congressional passage of the Gulf of Tonkin resolution, with only two dissenting votes, which supported any presidential action taken in Vietnam and helped to legitimize the subsequent Americanization of the war. In fact, accounts now reveal that one of the two North Vietnamese attacks on American destroyers probably never took place and that the American ships were providing intelligence support for South Vietnamese covert military attacks of North Vietnam. Furthermore, the congressional resolution was actually prepared by the Johnson administration before both the Tonkin Gulf crisis and the 1964 presidential election. This suggests that President Johnson and his administration were able to use the Tonkin Gulf crisis to manipulate the media and maximize domestic political support in order to "get tough" and exercise greater force in Vietnam. In other words, "because of the secrecy and covert nature of the operation, because of administration lies, both the Congress and the public were seriously misled."[C]

What are *the implications of crisis coverage for presidential governance?* First, crisis coverage usually strengthens presidential foreign policy power in the short term. This is primarily because the president becomes the focus of news media attention and the executive branch becomes the major source of information for the media, allowing the president's perspective to dominate the communications process. Such was the case, for example, with President Johnson's Vietnam actions discussed above, for President Reagan with the Grenada invasion, for President George Bush Sr. in the Panama invasion and the conflict in the Persian Gulf, and for President Bush Jr. with the

war on terrorism. In fact, during the early phases of foreign policy crises, the American media are extremely responsive and vulnerable to becoming overwhelmed with patriotic and nationalistic fervor, typically acting as a medium that promotes the president's views and policies and contributing to a rally-round-the-flag phenomenon throughout the country.

A retired propagandist who spent much of his career with the United States Information Agency noted this nationalistic tendency with respect to media coverage of the Persian Gulf crisis and the initial movement of American troops to Saudi Arabia: "This is the old America we remember. Skipping Vietnam, this is the America our regular propaganda from the turn of the century was all about. It's very interesting to see these very up-to-date electronic media telling the old American story so successfully."[D] Kathleen Hall Jamieson of the Annenberg School of Communication at the University of Pennsylvania made the telling point about the Persian Gulf crisis that "in the early days, the coverage suggested to me that, if you didn't know our television wasn't state-owned, you would have thought it was."[E] At times, in fact, the fixation on communicating the latest tidbits of information provided by the U.S. government on American military troops and war battles by the media reflects what might be called **journalistic jingoism** (similar to the so-called "yellow" journalism at the turn of the century).

Second, sometimes crisis coverage may actually weaken presidential power. The most obvious examples involved presidents Richard Nixon, Ronald Reagan, and Bill Clinton, who each suffered significant political blows: one from Watergate, the other from Iran-contra, and the last from the Monica Lewinsky affair. In these cases the crises involved questions of presidential abuse of power and the president's credibility, forcing the news media to turn to other sources of information in covering the crisis. Such a crisis outcome is rare. The media is usually quite hesitant to report news that directly challenges a sitting president due to the rally-round-the-flag norm during a crisis, the public's positive identification with the office of the presidency, and the grave political stakes involved in being too critical of a president.

In this respect, it is important to point out that the national media were actually slow to cover Watergate and Iran-contra, even though bits and pieces of information

C. David Halberstam, *The Best and the Brightest* (New York: Random House, 1969), p. 412.

D. Gary Blonston, "In War of Words, Who Will Be on the Casualty List?" *The State,* Columbia, S.C. (August 27, 1990), p. 1A.
E. Ibid., 7A.

had been available and reported for some time. In fact, Watergate became a big story only due to the persistence of Carl Bernstein and Bob Woodward, relatively young reporters who were not originally assigned to a national beat (and unusual risk-taking by certain executives and editors of the *Washington Post*), while Iran-contra made headlines only after the story was broken by a small Lebanese newspaper.

Third, the longer the crisis endures, the more likely that news media coverage will weaken presidential power. Although Vietnam contributed to presidential power early on, it ended up being the principal cause of President Johnson's political fall. Likewise, the Iran hostage crisis initially boosted President Jimmy Carter's political fortunes but eventually led to increasing public questioning of his leadership as the crisis dragged on. President Bush began to experience this with the Persian Gulf crisis during the last two months before war broke out. Very simply, the longer a crisis continues, the greater the likelihood that domestic dissent will surface and intensify, both in

and out of government, and that the public will tire of policies that are not perceived as successful. Under these conditions, media coverage is likely to reflect the more critical aspects of the evolving political environment and to constrain the president's power to persuade others to support him and his policies. This leads to the question what will be the fate of media coverage of President Bush Jr's continual war on terrorism, initially after September 11, then the war in Afghanistan, the raising of domestic terrorism alerts, the war with Iraq, and new crises in the future?

SOURCES: Denise M. Bostdorff, *The Presidency and the Rhetoric of Foreign Crisis* (Columbia: University of South Carolina Press, 1993); Peter Braestrup, *Big Story: How the American Press and Television Reported and Interpreted the Crisis of Tet 1968 in Vietnam and Washington* (New Haven: Yale University Press, 1983); Joseph C. Goulden, *Truth is the First Casualty: The Gulf of Tonkin Affair—Illusion and Reality* (Chicago: Rand McNally, 1969); Brigitte Lebens Nacos, *The Press, Presidents, and Crises* (New York: Columbia University Press, 1990); Tom Rosentiel, "The Myth of CNN," *New Republic* (August 22 & 29, 1994), pp. 27–33.

---

the article, "In the weeks after September 11 Rather wore a Stars and Stripes pin in his lapel during his evening news show in an apparent display of total solidarity with the American cause. However, in an interview with BBC's [British Broadcasting Corporation] 'Newsnight,' he graphically described the pressures to conform that built up after the attacks, 'It starts with a feeling of patriotism within oneself. It carries through with a certain knowledge that the country as a whole—and for all the right reasons—felt and continues to feel this surge of patriotism within themselves. And one finds oneself saying: "I know the right question, but you know what? This is not exactly the right time to ask it."'"

According to *The Guardian* such a view is "astonishing" and demonstrates the problem of **self-censorship**. According to Rather,

> There has never been an American war, small or large, in which access has been so limited as this one. Limiting access, limiting information to cover the backsides of those who are in charge of the war, is extremely dangerous and cannot and should not be accepted. And I am sorry to say that, up to and including the moment of this interview [eight months after the attacks], that overwhelmingly it has been accepted by the

> American people. And the current administration revels in that, they relish that, and they take refuge in that.

Rather instead believes that "it's unpatriotic not to stand up, look them in the eye, and ask the questions they don't want to hear." But even such a prominent journalist and television anchor as Dan Rather has honestly admitted that he has felt the "fear" of "patriotism run amok" and has been unable to have the courage to ask the tough questions thus far.[41]

In sum, conservative groups who perceive a liberal bias and liberal groups who perceive a conservative bias both oversimplify the ideological nature of the news media. In fact, greater ideological diversity exists among journalists within the mainstream media than is suggested by either view. For example, whereas most reporters within the mainstream and national media tend to be moderate to liberal in orientation, editors and owners tend to be more conservative. Furthermore, one is more likely to find journalists who are extremely conservative and right wing as opposed to extremely liberal or left wing. Stephen Hess found that "the White House press corps might be characterized as liberal *and* considerably more conservative than it used to be."[42] Nevertheless, their personal beliefs are often moderated by their professional journalistic roles, for they must operate within the constraints of mainstream media that are concentrated, run like a business, competitive, and bureaucratic within a larger cultural and political environment. The net result is a tendency for the national media to present a homogenized view of the news, with coverage reflecting a more centrist ideological orientation.

The Media and Politics. In addition to the underlying role of American political culture and ideology and the distribution of power among different ideological forces in society, the news media are also directly affected by the political dynamics of the policymaking process and domestic politics. In fact, government officials and societal groups attempt to influence and manipulate the media's coverage of domestic and international affairs because they are aware of the power of the media, through their ability to influence the political agenda and the climate of opinion, to affect domestic politics and the policymaking process. They understand that the images communicated by the media, especially television, are powerful symbols that affect the public's political beliefs and behavior.

Politically active individuals and groups within government and throughout society compete with each other for access to the news media in an effort to promote their interests and causes. In other words, groups engage in **public relations (and propaganda) activities,** attempting to influence the media in order to promote a favorable image and response among the general public. According to David Truman in *The Governmental Process*, "one of the first results of the formal organization of any interest group is its embarking upon a program of propaganda, though rarely so labeled, designed to affect opinions concerning the interests and claims of the new group."[43]

Competing groups attempt to take advantage and manipulate the news business. For example, as Doris Graber observes, "public relations managers know the deadlines of important publications, such as the *New York Times, Wall Street Journal, Time, Newsweek,* and network television news. They schedule events and news releases so that stories arrive in gatekeepers' offices precisely when needed. If their releases are attractively presented and meet newsworthiness criteria, journalists find it hard to resist using them. . . . If news sources want to stifle publicity, they can announce the news just past the deadlines, preferably on weekends when few newscasts are scheduled."[44] Thus American politics is very much a competition between different individuals and groups in society and government for influence over ideas, images, and symbols throughout the mass communications process.

As discussed in the section above, established groups and institutions, such as government and business, tend to succeed more often than challenging groups in gaining access to the mainstream media and having their views communicated. David Truman maintains that "because propaganda must rest upon and use pre-existing attitudes, certain groups at any time enjoy special propaganda advantages."[45] Established groups are typically seen as more significant, newsworthy, and credible sources of information. Challenging groups—more critical of the president, big business, and the status quo in general—have greater difficulty in gaining access to the media, for they are treated as less mainstream, less credible, and less newsworthy sources of information. Although much depends on the politics of the times, the activities of challenging groups covered by the mainstream media are often depicted in a more negative light than the activities of more established groups and institutions.[46]

The institution most successful in gaining access to the news media and influencing their coverage is, in general, the government and, in particular, the presidency.[47] With the president considered the center of foreign policy activity, the national media, with their beat system and norms of objective journalism, have become heavily dependent on the government and especially the executive branch for much of their information concerning U.S. foreign policy and international affairs. As Bernard Cohen explained in his classic *The Press and Foreign Policy,* written in 1963, "the more 'neutral' the press is . . . the more easily it lends itself to the uses of others, and particularly to public officials whom reporters have come to regard as prime sources of news merely by virtue of their positions in government. This is unquestionably the case at the Presidential level."[48] In other words, as Daniel Hallin discovered in his study of media coverage of the Vietnam War, with the rise of so-called objective journalism, "journalists gave up the right to speak with a political voice of their own, and in turn they were granted a regular right of access to the inner councils of government, a right they had never enjoyed in the era of partisan journalism."[49]

Thus, the president, the top governmental official, has a unique advantage in gaining access to the news media and having them communicate his views and preferences to the American public, most visibly during the early stages of a foreign policy crisis. Whatever and whenever the president speaks or acts, it is newsworthy by definition. Also, with the rise of the paradox of presidential power since Vietnam, the president and government officials have become much more public relations conscious than ever before and strive to promote the kind of media coverage that strengthens their political position. It would not be an overstatement to say that all presidents have been preoccupied with their public images. President Lyndon Johnson, for example, was legendary for viewing all three television news networks at the same time to see how he and his policies were portrayed.

Not surprisingly, presidents have increasingly institutionalized and expanded their White House press and communications operations, beginning with Richard Nixon. This does not guarantee positive presidential coverage, as all presidents since Vietnam have found out. In fact, some presidents have troubled relations with the media and the White House press corps, as Bill Clinton quickly experienced. Nevertheless, the machinery allows presidents to *utilize a number of tools at their disposal to influence media coverage* of national and, in particular, international affairs. This would include taking advantage of the presidency's newsworthiness, credibility as a source of information, control of classified information, and contacts in all the media.[50]

Realizing that presidential acts are newsworthy, presidential appearances in public are often "staged" to maximize positive news coverage and communicate the desired information and message. This reflects a growing preoccupation with the creation and communication of what historian Daniel Boorstin called "pseudo-events."[51] According to David Gergen, a member of the White House staff to presidents Richard Nixon and Ronald Reagan and subsequent editor of *U.S. News & World Report,* "We had a rule in the Nixon operation that before any public event was put on his schedule, you had to know what the headline out of that event was going to be, what the picture was going to be, and what the lead paragraph would be. You had to think of it in those terms, and if you couldn't justify it, it didn't go on the [president's] schedule."[52] President Reagan's public appearances were also carefully staged and choreographed, down to where the president would

stand and what he would say. The Reagan presidency—which has been referred to as the "Teflon" presidency—in fact, was probably the most adept at using the mass media, in particular television coverage, to promote its agenda and a positive climate of opinion.

A second important advantage is that the government is routinely the source of much of the media's information. Part of this is a function of journalists' reliance on the beat system and their coverage of such institutions as the White House, the State Department, and the Pentagon. Under the beat system, government officials are able to control the release of information through press releases, briefings, and public statements. During foreign policy crises, the news media are almost exclusively dependent (or allow themselves to become almost exclusively dependent) on the executive branch for their information. For example, media reporting of the president's use of armed force in places such as Grenada, Panama, the Persian Gulf, Kosovo, and Afghanistan was totally dependent on the executive branch for information, especially early on, when the country rallied round the flag. Obviously, executive branch officials attempt to influence the political agenda and the climate of opinion by providing selective information to the news media that is intended to reinforce the government's policies and promote political support throughout the public and society.[53]

A third way that the executive branch controls information is to take advantage of the classification of information by denying the news media and the public access to information for national security reasons. Covert actions are therefore often an attractive option for the president, for they maximize the possibility of keeping information hidden from the news media and the public eye. Another favorite technique that government officials use to control the information flow to the news media is **leaks** of confidential and classified information to selective reporters. There are lots of ways that information can be leaked. Sometimes it is provided "off the record," in which case the individual (and sometimes the information) cannot be directly or indirectly mentioned but can still act as a guide for the journalist. Oftentimes, information is provided "on background," which means that the information can be used if it is attributed to an unnamed source vaguely identified as, for example, a "senior White House official."

As Hedrick Smith points out in *The Power Game,* "On Wall Street, passing insider information to others is an indictable offense. In Washington, it is the regular stuff of the power game."[54] Classified information is regularly leaked by "proponents" of a policy to gain its approval as well as by "opponents" designed to discredit policy. Oliver North, who vilified Congress during the Iran-contra hearings for leaking classified information, regularly leaked information in his efforts to win public support for Reagan's Central American policy. Although leaking is widespread throughout the Washington community, it tends to be more frequent within the executive branch, especially the closer one gets to the president.

Two of the more blatant governmental techniques used to manipulate the news media through information control have involved the use of systematic propaganda campaigns and censorship. The Pentagon, for example, spends millions of dollars each year for military bands and air shows throughout the country as part of a massive public relations campaign to promote strong public support for the military.[55] More ominous illustrations, however, have been documented. Members of the executive branch (such as the Reagan administration) orchestrated public relations campaigns using propaganda—that is, consciously distorting information and lying—and using disinformation (that is, knowingly manufacturing false information)—to use the media and rally public support for their foreign policy efforts (such as to destabilize Colonel Mu'ammar Gadhafi of Libya and overthrow the Sandinistas in Nicaragua in the 1980s).

Discussing the covert contra war in "Iran-Contra's Untold Story," Robert Parry and Peter Kornbluh assert that "to win this war at home the White House created a sophisticated apparatus that mixed propaganda with intimidation, consciously misleading the American people and at times trampling on the right to dissent." The administration's strategy was to distort the record by exaggerating the threat and abuses of the Sandinistas while hiding those of the contras. "To be sure, previous administrations have tried to impose their political wills on the news media, dissembling and lying when necessary to protect foreign-policy misadventures." But Parry and Kornbluh argue that the Reagan White House appears to be the first to have institutionalized the process. "Employing the scientific methods of modern public relations and the war-tested techniques of psychological operations, the administration built an unprecedented bureaucracy in the National Security Council and the State Department designed to keep the news media in line and to restrict conflicting information from reaching the American public."[56]

The Bush Jr. administration has attempted similar strategies to influence not only folks at home (including Hollywood) but also the views of foreigners abroad, especially in the Middle East so as to maximize support for the war on terrorism. After the September 11 attacks, the Pentagon created an Office of Strategic Influence, but was forced to shut it down in February 2002 because of the controversy about its propaganda orientation and its location within the military. In preparation for the war with Iraq, the administration has built a multimillion dollar communications complex in Qatar, where the Central Command is headquartered, so the military can brief journalists and have maximum control over media coverage.[57]

Along with propaganda, **censorship** has also been used by the government and its use during war has grown since the 1980s. One of the major "lessons" of the Vietnam War learned by many within the national security bureaucracy was the need to keep the news media under control. During the invasion of Grenada, for example, the Reagan administration censored the press by preventing journalists from accompanying soldiers on the ground. This made the media totally dependent on the administration's version of the invasion, which depicted it as a tremendous military success in support of a humanitarian cause while ignoring both the geopolitical reasons behind the invasion and the military foul-ups on the ground (review essay 7.5 on the Grenada operation.)

Given news media resistance to outright censorship, the government and mainstream media organizations have informally agreed to allow a small "pool of reporters" to represent all of the news media and accompany the military under strict guidelines when it intervenes abroad. Although many within the national media initially protested, they have nonetheless gone along with the restrictions, as occurred during the invasion of Panama and the Persian Gulf War, thereby providing the facade of an independent news media. Such censorship by the executive branch, and the national media's willingness to accept it, has resulted in the administration's views and interpretations of events becoming accepted and shared by most members of American society—a powerful advantage in the politics of U.S. foreign policy. (See **essay 17.2** on government censorship and the Persian Gulf War.)

ESSAY 17.2
Government Censorship, Propaganda, and the Persian Gulf War

Although the American national media pride themselves on being an independent, nonpartisan, and objective source of news, government censorship and manipulation of the news media was almost complete during the war in the 1991 Persian Gulf. As an article entitled "The Propaganda War" in *Newsweek* reported near the end of the war, "In theory, reporters in democratic societies work independent of propaganda. In practice they are treated during war as simply more pieces of military hardware to be deployed."[A] The result was that the government controlled the type of war that the American public saw in order to minimize dissent and maximize political support, which reinforces the old adage that "truth is the first casualty of war."

According to one assessment, "one casualty of the Gulf War appears to be the independent, itinerant war correspondent. The press pool system used in the Gulf encouraged the most docile sort of pack journalism" in which members of the national media competed in tandem for whatever censored information and video images that the White House and the Pentagon allowed them to communicate.[B] The public relations and propaganda strategy was fairly straightforward: "provide a lot of military briefings and high-tech videos to keep the press supplied with images and reports, impose strict censorship on everything you don't want covered (including images of people returning home in 'human-remains pouches'), overemphasize your successes and tell nothing of your failures. Most of all, keep the human dimension to a minimum."[C]

The Pentagon communicated through the news media to the American public a picture of an American military machine that was flawless in action. Television, for example, replayed again and again successful hits by American smart bombs that never seemed to miss their targets. The war seemed to be fought so efficiently and cleanly that it seemed more like a computer game than a war. As impressive as the air war was conducted by the United States and its allies, however, information released by the Department of Defense after completion of the war indicates that of the 88,000 tons of bombs dropped on Kuwait and Iraq only 7 percent were "precision-guided" munitions that approximated their targets 90 percent of the time, while over 90 percent were "dumb" conventional bombs that missed their target 75 percent of the time. This accurate portrait of the air war "contrasted sharply with the high-tech, never-miss image that the Pentagon carefully cultivated during the war."[D]

Although this was the most massive bombing and military campaign since the Vietnam War, Americans did not see any bloodshed during the war. American folks at home saw a "sanitized" war even though there were massive deaths, involving anywhere from 100,000 to 200,000 immediate casualties suffered by Iraqi military and especially civilians (with thousands more dying indirectly after hostilities ceased due to destruction of urban infrastructures). The Pentagon took the ultimate step to shield the American public from witnessing the costs of the Persian Gulf War: The honors ceremonies given to U.S. troops killed in action were, unlike previous wars, not open to the public and the press when their flag-draped coffins returned to the military's main East Coast mortuary at Dover Air Force Base in Delaware.[E]

Walter Cronkite, the granddaddy of television anchors for CBS News throughout the 1960s, concluded that "with an arrogance foreign to the democratic system, the U.S. military in Saudi Arabia is trampling on the American people's right to know."[F] Nevertheless, even though freedom of the press was heavily censored during the war and the government fed the public what has been referred to as "Iraq, the Movie," the American people seemed to like it that way. The public, typical of a national crisis and war, rallied round the troops and the president. Under these circumstances, the rise of American nationalism accepted government censorship while tolerating little dissent, as evidenced by treating the CNN broadcasts of Peter Arnett, the last American reporter in Iraq, as Iraqi propaganda.

Not surprisingly, given the political environment, members of the national media went along and allowed themselves to be managed completely by the government.

A. "The Propaganda War," *Newsweek* (February 25, 1991), p. 38.
B. Peter Schmeisser, "Shooting Pool," *New Republic* (March 18, 1991), p. 21.
C. Susan J. Douglas, "Camouflaging Reality with Faux News, Clever Decoys," *In These Times* (February 13–19, 1991), p. 20.

D. Barton Gellman, "U.S. Bombs Missed 70% of Time," *Washington Post* (March 16, 1991), p. A18.
E. Mark Thompson, "Pentagon Dictating Coverage of Conflict," *The State*, Columbia, S.C. (January 20, 1991), pp. 1A, 7A.
F. Walter Cronkite, "What Is There to Hide?" *Newsweek* (February 25, 1991), p. 43.

According to *New York Times* writer Tom Wicker, the press and television "to their discredit" did not "protest as effectively as they should have, or always made it clear as they could have, that much of what they conveyed—like the can't miss version of Air Force bombings—was not only controlled by the military but prettified for home consumption."[G]

If the war had been prolonged and not gone well, dissent probably would have increased within the mass and elite publics, increasing news media resistance to government censorship. Ultimately, however, the war was quick and went extraordinarily well, thereby allowing government censorship of the media to work to perfection. The White House and the Pentagon proved to be quite successful in using the national media to communicate the information and symbols by which the American public saw and would remember the Persian Gulf War. According to Michael Deaver, President Reagan's deputy chief of staff and communications chief, "The Department of Defense has done an excellent job of managing the news in

an almost classic way. There's plenty of access to some things and at least one visual a day. If you were going to hire a public relations firm to do the media relations for an international event, it couldn't be done any better than this is being done."[H] Such successful control and manipulation of the news media reinforced the lessons that the government learned from Vietnam, increasing the likelihood that it will revert to such censorship when war occurs in the future.

SOURCES: W. Lance Bennett and David L. Paletz, eds., *Taken By Storm: The Media, Public Opinion, and U.S. Foreign Policy in the Gulf War* (Chicago: University of Chicago Press, 1994); John J. Fialka, *Hotel Warriors: Covering the Gulf War* (Baltimore: Johns Hopkins University Press, 1992); Marie Gottschalk, "Operation Desert Cloud: The Media and the Gulf War," *World Policy Journal* (summer 1992): 449–86; John R. MacArthur, *Second Front: Censorship and Propaganda in the Gulf War* (New York: Hill and Wang, 1992); Micah L. Sifry and Christopher Cerf, eds., *The Gulf War Reader: History, Documents* (New York: Random House, 1991); and U.S. Congress, Senate, Committee on Governmental Affairs, Hearings, *Pentagon Rules on Media Access to the Persian Gulf War* (February 20, 1991).

G. Tom Wicker, "First Amendment a Casualty of War," *The State*, Columbia, S.C. (March 21, 1991), p. 14.

H. Alex S. Jones, "Process of News Reporting on Display," *New York Times* (February 15, 1991), p. A9.

Finally, government officials often promote favorable news media coverage by building upon their many contacts and personal relationships within the media. Henry Kissinger was a master, for example, at wooing the media in order to promote his foreign policy purposes. He was a constant source of information, often classified, anonymously provided to the media in general or to selective journalists, which they would then attribute to a "senior government official" (review essay 5.3 on Kissinger's ability to control the policymaking process). As Stanley Hoffmann pointed out long ago:

> The closeness to official Washington of the nation's leading columnists and reporters, writing for the main newspapers and television networks, is especially responsible for numbing the mass media's capacity to question and challenge. . . . Enjoying the confidence of the great usually kills the urge to investigate. Officials disarm these men by giving them the illusion of being admitted to the mysteries of decision-making, and by making them sympathize with their ordeals.[58]

The news media are open to such use and manipulation because journalists and editors have become dependent on government officials for information, many are ideological "kindred spirits" of these officials, and as members of the Washington community (as discussed in chapter 12), they are often driven to gain access and socialize with the famous and the powerful. Presidents regularly invite journalists to White House functions and often engage in informal interaction as a means of promoting good relations and positive images. And as journalist Walter Lippmann once wrote in his diary, "A writer on public affairs can't pretend to despise reputation, for reputation is not only flattering to the vanity, it is the only way of meeting the people you've got to know in order to understand the world."[59] Bob Woodward, the prominent journalist of Watergate fame, for example, "has never been a counter-establishment figure in the style of earlier muckrakers." If anything, his reporting and post-Watergate books "have been remarkable not for their criticism of the world of power, but for their access to it."[60]

In sum, three major patterns exist in the politics of the media. First, government-media relations are very much a symbiotic process. The nature of the news business and the political environment in American society have made the news media more dependent on the government, especially the president and the executive branch, whereas the president and government have become more dependent on the media. Second, the president and the executive branch have considerable advantages in promoting positive news media coverage, especially early in an administration, over issues of foreign policy and during crises, when presidential legitimacy and support are at their highest. Third, even with all its advantages, the presidency in the post–Vietnam War and post–cold war eras is unable to dominate and influence media coverage to the same extent it did during the cold war, even in the area of foreign policy.

In the contemporary political environment the paradox of presidential power has required that the president exert greater effort and sophistication in public relations at a time of greater uncertainty and difficulty in dominating the media—clearly evident throughout the Bush Sr. and Clinton years. The collapse of the cold war consensus, the rise of Congress, and the proliferation of groups have increased and widened the pool of credible sources of information that the news media may draw upon, which is most likely to occur when government leaders are divided on issues. Which raises the critical question of to what extent the September 11 attacks and President Bush Jr.'s war on terrorism have altered these patterns in the long term, as opposed to the short term. Ultimately, the politics of U.S. foreign policy since Vietnam involves different individuals and groups in competition for news media access and influence to affect domestic politics and the policymaking process.

IMPLICATIONS FOR THE POLICYICS OF U.S. FOREIGN POLICY

At least six conclusions about news media coverage can be drawn from the discussion above. First, most Americans are dependent on the news media, especially the national media, for information and understanding of national and international affairs. Second, the national media provide a considerable amount of information regarding national and international affairs. Third, coverage tends

to be selective and disjointed as stories come and go with little history or context provided. Fourth, the national media tend to provide a homogenized and centrist picture of national and international news—sometimes reflecting a more liberal orientation, sometimes a more conservative one—consistent with mainstream American political ideology and culture. Fifth, media coverage is influenced by politics and, at the same time, influences domestic politics and the policymaking process. Finally, these patterns are magnified during times of crisis, when certain issues are often inflated and sensationalized and certain actors and institutions are able to have a disproportionate influence on media coverage.

These patterns in news media coverage play an important role in the complex politics of U.S. foreign policy. In the words of Doris Graber in *Mass Media and American Politics*:

> The mass media are more than passive transmission agents for available information. Decisions made by media personnel determine what information becomes available to media audiences and what remains unavailable. By putting stories into perspective and interpreting them, media personnel assign meaning to the information and indicate the values by which it ought to be judged. News shaping is unavoidable because space is limited and because facts do not speak for themselves. Hence the media select and shape much of the raw material needed by political elites and the general public for thinking about the political world and planning political action.[61]

In this way the news media and the communications process affect continuity and change in the foreign policy process over time, the president's ability to govern U.S. foreign policy, and the tension between national security and democracy. The media's impact on these three themes can be seen by briefly examining their (1) post–World War II coverage, (2) consequences for public knowledge, and (3) role in the politics of symbolism that have come to pervade American society.

THE MEDIA AND U.S. FOREIGN POLICY SINCE WORLD WAR II

Since the beginning of World War II, there have been three broad patterns in news media coverage as it has related to the making of U.S. foreign policy: (1) During World War II, coverage by the American news media both reflected and reinforced the U.S. government's war effort. (2) During the cold war, news media coverage reflected and reinforced the anticommunist consensus prevailing in society and the government. And (3) since the Vietnam War, news media coverage has had a greater tendency to reflect diverse views and, consequently, become less consistently supportive of the government's foreign policy. These generalizations refer to general tendencies concerning coverage by the mainstream media most of the time.

World War II Coverage. Once the U.S. government declared war on Japan and entered World War II, the American mass media quickly acted as a medium to rally mass support behind the cause. As was discussed in chapter 14, times of war are also times of immense nationalism and narrowing of civil liberties, including free speech and free press. The U.S. government censored the media and conducted a domestic propaganda campaign of vast proportions in order to maximize public support and minimize dissent. Despite this censorship, most American journalists were repulsed by Japanese and German imperialism and saw it as their patriotic duty to defend and promote the American way of life.[62]

The media became the principal means by which pictures of the enemy were portrayed to the American public and acted as an important source for unifying the country against the Axis powers. The media depicted the allied countries as righteous defenders of democracy and freedom against the aggression and evil represented by Germany and Japan. This contributed, among other things, to a West Coast hysteria concerning Japanese sabotage and the internment of Japanese Americans in concentration camps during the war. (Review essay 14.1 on the World War II internment of Japanese Americans.)

American leaders also used the media to preach the value of Soviet-American friendship and continued cooperation following the war. The media popularized the Soviet Union as the great ally of the United States, frequently referring to Joseph Stalin as "Uncle Joe." Stalin, in fact, became *Time* magazine's "Man of the Year" in 1943. Americans, furthermore, were regularly told that Russians were becoming more like them. For instance, *Life* magazine announced in March 1943 that

the Russians were "one hell of a people" who "look like Americans, dress like Americans, and think like Americans." In April 1944 the *New York Times* went so far as to declare that it was not a misrepresentation "to say that Marxian thinking in Soviet Russia is out. The capitalist system, better described as the competitive system, is back."[63] Thus, the media not only played a prominent role during World War II in reflecting the views of the U.S. government and promoting American nationalism but also contributed to creating a set of unrealistic expectations about Soviet-American friendship that would haunt the postwar years.

Cold War Coverage. Immediately following World War II, the American news media began to reflect greater diversity of views, consistent with the great political debate raging over the future of U.S. foreign policy. However, with the rise of the cold war, media coverage again began to narrow and reflect the growing anticommunist political environment. The administrations of Harry Truman and Dwight Eisenhower communicated their fears of communism through the media to both educate the mass public and rally support for the containment policy. Such media coverage both reflected and contributed to the rise of the political right and anticommunism, further narrowing public debate.

A prime example of the active influence of the news media in the politics of anticommunism can be seen in the portrayal of American-Chinese relations after 1949: Taiwan, or the Republic of China, was the "real" China and ally of the United States, while the People's Republic of China was an illegitimate and expansionist communist state in alliance with Soviet communism. "Substantial elements of the press helped to promote the China lobby's line: Henry Luce, whose family had China ties, and his forceful wife, Claire, then had more influence over some of their publications than most major news publishers have today—especially *Life*." According to Russell Howe and Sarah Trott in *The Power Peddlers*, a "pro-Chiang policy was imposed on the *Washington Times-Herald*, the *Chicago Tribune*, and the Hearst press—notably the *New York Journal–American*, the *Los Angeles Examiner*, and the *San Francisco Examiner*." In addition, other publications put out the lobby line such as *Collier's*, the *Saturday Evening Post*, *Reader's Digest*, and *U.S. News & World Report*. Furthermore, "countless unsuspecting editors also printed China lobby copy, given free of charge to wire and feature services."[64]

As Edwin Bayley found in *Joe McCarthy and the Press*, charges of internal subversion were news and contributed to the rise of Senator Joseph McCarthy and McCarthyism.[65] Media coverage also eventually led to the downfall of Senator McCarthy. Nevertheless, by the mid-1950s an anticommunist consensus pervaded American society, including American journalism. There was no outright government censorship of the news media during the cold war (except for Korean War coverage)—there didn't need to be, for a consensus of thought clearly existed throughout American society. In other words, during the 1950s and most of the 1960s, anti-Soviet communist and pro-American democratic-capitalist perceptions colored how the world and U.S. foreign policy were seen and interpreted by the media to the American public.

In fact, as Carl Bernstein has reported, over four hundred American journalists occasionally worked closely for the CIA, and many carried out assignments (not always knowingly). This included major executives and reporters in the field from every major news organization in the country, as well as a few minor ones. As pointed out by the Senate Church committee investigation in 1975, such cozy relationships between the **media and the CIA** (and the intelligence community) raise serious concerns about the "potential, inherent in covert media operations, for manipulating or incidentally misleading the American public" and the "damage to the credibility and independence of a free press."[66] Such concerns about the integrity of a so-called free press gets to the heart of the contradictions that are endemic between the demands of national security and of democratic practice.

Although the media are credited with being critical of the Vietnam War, it is usually forgotten that, in their **Vietnam war coverage** during the late 1950s and early 1960s, the media dutifully communicated the government's position and promoted the Americanization of the Vietnam War. As David Halberstam observed in *The Powers That Be*, "The great heads of the media were anxious to be good and loyal citizens, and the working reporters had almost without question accepted the word of the White House on foreign policy. . . . The press corps might be congenitally skeptical in assessing the intentions and ambitions of domestic politicians, but it brought no such toughness of mind to the politics

of foreign policy."[67] Thus, the media contributed to the growth of presidential power in foreign affairs and the rise of a national security ethos in which the demands of national security often prevailed over the demands of democracy in response to the cold war.

Given the national emergencies represented by World War II and the cold war, it is understandable that the views dominating the executive branch pervaded the news media and became the orthodoxy by which Americans understood international politics and U.S. foreign policy. As a popular saying goes, "Winners write history." In other words, those individuals and groups most politically successful within government and throughout society are better able, through use of the media and the communications process, to define the popular or orthodox interpretation of the United States and the world—in this case, of the origins of the cold war in the postwar years. Therefore, most Americans, including journalists, came to believe that the cold war was caused by Soviet communist expansion to take over Europe and the world, which forced the United States to become active throughout the world, emphasizing containment and the use of force—which was consistent with the government's position during the cold war years.

Post–Vietnam War Coverage. Reflecting the breakdown of the anticommunist consensus, it was not until the mid- and late 1960s that the news media's coverage of the Vietnam War became more critical of the government. As Daniel Hallin found in *The Uncensored War*, media coverage of U.S. foreign policy in general and Vietnam policy in particular tended to reflect events occurring inside the government. As long as consensus prevailed within the government, media coverage reflected this consensus and supported government policy. It was only when dissent increased within the government—both in Congress and in the Johnson administration—that media coverage became more critical of the war and the government's policies.[68]

By the late 1960s and early 1970s, media coverage increasingly reflected the collapse of the anticommunist consensus in the government and society. The Watergate crisis, in fact, represented the height of a critical and cynical media independent of the administration and engaged in investigative reporting. Still, the American failure in the Vietnam War was one of the few times that the popular interpretation—that Vietnam did not represent a vital interest and that the war was a mistake—became inconsistent with the presidential view.

Today's news media retain some of the legacy of the Vietnam and Watergate experience. Clearly, since Vietnam the president no longer monopolizes media coverage as he did during World War II and the cold war. With the collapse of the anticommunist consensus, the media are more likely to represent a greater diversity of foreign policy thought, rely on more sources of information throughout society and in the policymaking process, and present news in a more critical and cynical fashion. This has contributed to the rise of Congress, the proliferation of group politics in the making of U.S. foreign policy, and the expansion of public affairs programs in the electronic media.

For example, on television, in addition to the existence of *60 Minutes,* public television aired *The MacNeil-Lehrer Report* in 1975, in 1980 ABC's *Nightline* went nightly and CNN was born, and a year later the Sunday morning news shows saw the addition of ABC's *This Week* with David Brinkley. The 1990s saw the creation of *Frontline* and *NOW* with Bill Moyers on PBS, and numerous news magazine, interview, and news programs were created on the major networks as well as on cable (easily found on C-Span, CNBC, and MSNBC). National Public Radio also created *All Things Considered, Morning Edition,* and *Weekend Edition* for news and newsmagazine-type coverage.

At the same time, there remains a strong cold war and realpolitik legacy among American journalists in their coverage of foreign policy and international affairs. This tendency is evidenced by the media's continued reliance on governmental sources of information, particularly the White House and the national security bureaucracy, and preoccupation with international conflict, especially the use of force. These contradictory patterns of continuity and change are reflected, for example, in the media coverage of the Iran-contra affair.

News media coverage of Iran-Contra and its political impact went through three general stages: sporadic coverage of Iran-contra from 1981 to 1986, in which the Ronald Reagan administration was able to keep most of its covert activities hidden; crisis coverage in 1986 and 1987, in which much of the covert foreign policy came to light and damaged the Reagan presidency; and minimal coverage following 1987, when the issue and its political impact faded. Whereas news

media coverage during the second stage was more reflective of the Vietnam legacy, coverage during the first and third stages was more reminiscent of the national security and realpolitik legacy in American journalism.

Throughout the 1980s, Central American policy was high on the foreign policy agenda for the Reagan administration, but most of the media coverage from 1981 to 1986 focused on the administration's overt foreign policy in Central America and legislative-executive battles over contra funding. There was some investigative reporting on the Reagan administration's covert contra war abroad and at home, but it was sporadic with little follow-up. In "Iran-Contra: Was the Press Any Match for All the President's Men?," Scott Armstrong observes that "exotic-sounding theories about an elaborate private arms network seemed to scare away" papers like the *New York Times, Wall Street Journal,* and *Washington Post.* The "press showed an ability to pick up pieces but less skill at putting them together.... There was no institutional memory. Breakthroughs by star reporters passed largely unnoticed by peers until months or years after they were first published or aired."[69]

On November 3, 1986, a small Lebanese newspaper, *al-Shiraa*—not the American news media—broke the story of the secret arms-for-hostages dealings between the United States and Iran in violation of the president's public proclamations against negotiating with terrorists. With these headline stories, the national media began "frenzied" coverage of President Reagan's denials, Attorney General Edwin Meese's announcement of the diversion of funds from Iranian arms sales to the contras, the Tower Commission report, and finally, the congressional hearings during the summer of 1987.

Although considerable information was revealed, the news media ultimately sensationalized and simplified the Iran-contra affair. In covering the congressional inquiry, discussed in chapter 11, efforts to acquire a full understanding of Iran-contra were lost in the search for "good guys" and "bad guys." According to Armstrong, reporters began to concentrate "on who was scoring more public relations points on any given day—the witnesses or the committee members and their counsel." The national media also became obsessed with "what did the president know of the diversion of monies from the Iran arms deal to the contras?" As described by Armstrong, "What had been an informed and effective corps of journalists, independently pursuing the story in the preceding months, mysteriously gravitated toward this one question."[70]

Following the congressional hearings and the publication of the committee's report, news media coverage of Iran-contra declined precipitously as the 1988 electoral race heated up, even though Vice President George Bush's role remained unclear. "While the North trial should have provided all the fuel that was necessary to keep the journalistic inquiry running, the press seemed to lose interest, perking up briefly only when some key Iran-contra players were nominated for high-level posts in the new administration."[71] Hence, Iran-contra became news media history.

Overall, much was revealed, much remained hidden, and larger questions were ignored. Most Americans, therefore, came away from the Iran-contra coverage with an interpretation consistent with either the more optimistic Tower Commission report, which emphasized the flawed policies of the Iran initiative, or the more pessimistic report published by the congressional inquiry, which emphasized a disregard for the law by a small group of administration officials. In both cases, however, the president was portrayed as having lost control of the ship of state and the covert operations as aberrations. Thus, the prime lesson was the need for competent and vigilant personnel in the White House and the executive branch. Yet neither Congress nor the national media sufficiently explored or communicated the full complexity and implications of Iran-contra (review essay 8.2). In conclusion, Armstrong and the handful of other journalists who attempted to investigate the story and present a comprehensive picture expressed their frustration at the halfhearted congressional investigation and stressed that "their strongest complaints were reserved for their peers—those editors and colleagues who treated the subject of constitutional violations as academic or, worse, as trivial, precisely because Congress had not responded with outrage."[72]

Iran-contra coverage demonstrated both the strengths and limitations of news media coverage as a source of information and understanding, which have had important implications for presidential governance since Vietnam. Although the president continues to enjoy great media visibility and influence, his policies and views are much less likely to dominate the news for an extended period of time, due to the decline of presidential power, rise of Congress, increase in ideological diversity, and proliferation of interest groups

and social movements. Because the pattern of media coverage since Vietnam is much more complex than during World War II and the cold war years, we can expect much greater uncertainty as to whether media coverage will strengthen the president or act as a constraint on the exercise of his power.

Sometimes news media coverage ends up being more supportive of the president, sometimes it is more critical—much depends on the nature of the issue, the political environment, and the times. This was the case not only with media coverage of Iran-contra but with coverage of the Persian Gulf crisis and war (as well as for other crises and wars). Early in the crisis, the cold war legacy prevailed as the bulk of the country rallied round the flag and the media acted as the bullhorn of the Bush Sr. administration's Persian Gulf policy. By the middle of the crisis, when dissension began to spread among the mass and elite publics symbolized by the Senate Armed Services Committee hearings and divisions in Congress, media coverage became more independent and open to critical views of presidential policy, a stance reminiscent of the latter stages of the Vietnam War. But with the start of the war, the media communicated the White House and military perspective while acquiescing in their censorship by the government. This cyclical pattern in media coverage was similar to the evolution of public opinion during the Persian Gulf crisis (as depicted in essay 17.1).

Likewise, for months following the September 11 attacks in 2001, the media and the country rallied behind President Bush Jr.'s war on terrorism. But by spring of 2002, questions and criticisms began to be raised about the Bush administration in response to its Middle East policy to the escalation of the Israeli-Palestinian conflict, how much was known within the government about the possibility of terrorist attacks before September 11, and President Bush's pursuit of a war with Iraq and Saddam Hussein. Therefore, the media act as a major source of both presidential power and also act to reinforce the paradox of presidential power, and none of this is easy to predict.

PUBLIC KNOWLEDGE AND DEMOCRATIC CITIZENSHIP

Because Americans are dependent on the media as their fundamental source of information concerning national and international affairs, the news media have a major impact on public knowledge and democratic citizenship in the politics of U.S. foreign policy. At best, most Americans acquire a simplistic awareness and familiarity of the world around them. This is because the mass public, as discussed in chapter 13, tends to be uninterested, inattentive, uninformed, and therefore, most receptive to media headlines. This simplistic awareness also is due to the public's tendency to be "overnewsed" and "underinformed" by the media: Issues appear one day and disappear the next, coverage jumps from one crisis to another, the emphasis is on the immediacy of news rather than history and context, the focus is on established institutions and government officials—especially the president—as opposed to the complexity of society and the world.

This problem is much more severe with respect to international news, for most Americans lack the context to make sense of the information and images being communicated to them about "foreign" places abroad. Not surprisingly, most members of the mass public often find events confusing and acquire only very simplistic images of the world. The net result is a mass public that bears little resemblance to the "alert and knowledgeable citizenry" called for by President Eisenhower in his farewell address. Instead, we see a mass public that is overwhelmingly uninterested and uninformed yet heavily dependent on the media. As a consequence, the nature of media coverage contributes to wild fluctuations in public opinion and swings in public mood, which affect both domestic politics and the policymaking process.[73]

If Eisenhower's alert and knowledgeable citizenry is to be found anywhere, it would most likely be among the elite public in American society. Yet, most members of the elite public also tend to rely heavily on the national media for their basic sources of information. They become informed but learn little history and acquire only a rather narrow range of ideological interpretations of national and international affairs. Furthermore, unless individuals are already knowledgeable about the world and make a concerted effort to use that knowledge when viewing or reading the media, media coverage, especially during crises, will likely determine not only what issues members of the elite public think about but how they go about examining those issues.[74]

The information and images communicated by the media, therefore, contributed to the rise of antifascism during World War II and anticommunism during the cold war among the mass and elite publics. This promoted a preoccupation with the demands of national security over the demands of democracy, and to the political conformity and passivity of most Americans even though the civil liberties of many citizens were being violated. Although post–Vietnam War media coverage has broadened and reflects a greater concern for the demands of democracy, it nonetheless continues to affect public knowledge and political participation. Crisis coverage by the mainstream media, for example, exerts a powerful influence over both elite and mass publics in terms of how they see and react to the world.

News media coverage of the Iran hostage crisis in 1979 and 1980, for instance, contributed to an increase in American nationalism, accompanied by a fear of Islam and intense hatred of the Ayatollah Khomeini and Iran. Yet even with massive reporting of the Iran hostage crisis, rarely was it communicated to the American people that their government (along with the British) was responsible for covertly overthrowing the nationalist leader of Iran in 1953 and imposing the shah on the Iranian people. Furthermore, continuous U.S. government support for the shah's regime over the years, even though he increasingly governed as a ruthless dictator, was downplayed. Consequently, it is not surprising that most Americans, within the mass and elite publics, had great difficulty understanding the predominant Iranian view of the U.S. government as the "Great Satan." Instead, they saw the United States as an innocent victim at the hands of the "crazed" Iranian government and people.[75] Not only did this affect the fate of President Jimmy Carter and his administration, but this intensely nationalistic and simplistic view of Arabs and Muslims (and the Middle East) shared by many Americans was triggered repeatedly, such as when it became public that the Reagan administration was trying to sell arms in exchange for American hostages with an unresponsive Iranian leadership; and most recently, following the September 11 terrorist attacks on American soil.

News media coverage of the electoral process provides another illustration of the powerful role played by the media in affecting public knowledge, democratic citizenship, and the outcomes of elections. On the one hand, interested and knowledgeable members of the public have access to a considerable amount of information concerning the candidates, the parties, and their policy positions. On the other hand, studies have demonstrated that the media emphasize "personal rather than professional qualities of the candidates and campaign events rather than substantive issues. Stories are chosen for their newsworthiness, not their educational value."[76] Overall, the media are overwhelmingly preoccupied with the "horse race" aspects of elections—that is, who is up, who is down, and why. This is especially true with respect to the presidency, the "Super Bowl" of news media coverage. Not only does this fail to promote a knowledgeable citizenry, but the television networks have demonstrated a disregard for the right to vote by their competitiveness to predict winners even before the polls close. Beginning in 1990, the networks informally agreed to wait at least until after the polls closed to predict winning candidates—but this was violated by all the major networks when they predicted the winner in the critical state of Florida (to Al Gore) in the 2000 presidential election at 8:00 Eastern Standard Time, even though Florida covers two time zones and many voters still had one hour to go to the polls.

In addition to the lack of depth of election coverage, the narrow breadth of news media coverage also impacts on public knowledge of candidates and participation in electoral politics. Most Americans believe, for example, that only two (or three) candidates compete for the presidency. True, only two "major" candidates, from the Democratic and Republican parties, actually have a viable chance to win election. However, fifteen official candidates and parties competed for the presidency in 1976; in 1980 there were twenty-one candidates and parties; and in 1974 sixteen candidates and parties entered the fray. This has continued to the present day, when there were sixteen candidates and parties in the 2000 presidential elections. Although third parties have little chance of winning, their efforts nonetheless have the potential to influence the major parties and American politics—as evidenced by the recent presidential campaigns of Ross Perot and Ralph Nader, thus indirectly impacting public policy and U.S. foreign policy (see **table 17.3** for an example of the presidential candidates in the 2000 election).

The numbers of candidates actually have grown over time: From 1920 to 1948 an average of seven to eight presidential candidates entered each election; from 1956 to 1972 the average was eleven; and since 1976 the average has been about seventeen presidential candidates. Most Americans, however, are unaware of this because the media cover only the campaigns of the two major parties. Rather than informing the public about the various candidates and parties running for office, thus allowing the public to choose in accordance with democratic practice, concentrated media coverage of the two major parties delegitimizes and marginalizes the other parties, reducing their potential political influence and, ultimately, narrowing the choice of presidential candidates for Americans down to two.

The best illustration of the power of the media in this respect is the independent presidential candidacy of John B. Anderson. In 1980, when Anderson broke from the Republican party and ran as an Independent, he received considerable media coverage and over 5,720,000 votes. In the 1984 campaign, he was totally ignored by the media and received only 1,486 votes.[77] Ross Perot also received much less media attention the second time he ran; not surprisingly his popular vote dropped from 1992 to 1996 by almost half. In the 2000 president election, longtime consumer advocate Ralph Nader and the Green Party were unable to get 5 percent of the vote—which would have allowed for future public funding like the major parties get—in part because of relatively limited (and often more critical) media coverage. Such media selectivity of the electoral process serves to reinforce the status quo in American politics and the making of U.S. foreign policy.

Therefore, while most Americans rely on the mainstream and national media for their information and understanding of the world around them, they should be sensitive to, and somewhat cynical about, the limits inherent in mainstream media coverage. In fact, much of the public probably realizes this at times, contributing to a certain "need-hate" relationship with the news media. Such tension between the public in general and the media may simply be unavoidable in today's world.[78]

Nevertheless, as Jerome Barron argues in *Freedom of the Press for Whom? The Right of Access to the Mass Media*, the mainstream media have fought for broad rights of free expression for themselves while denying much of the public access to media coverage. Timothy Cook, in *Making Laws and Making News*, concludes that the democratization of political news requires perspectives besides those provided by members of the Washington political community. In other words, a

TABLE **17.3**
2000 PRESIDENTIAL ELECTION RESULTS

CANDIDATE AND PARTY	POPULAR VOTES
George W. Bush, *Republican*	50,456,169
Al Gore, *Democratic*	50,996,116
Ralph Nader, *Green*	2,831,066
Pat Buchanan, *Reform*	447,798
Harry Browne, *Libertarian*	385,515
Howard Phillips, *Constitution*	96,907
John Hagelin, *Natural Law*	83,134
James Harris, *Socialist Workers*	7,408
L. Neil Smith, *Libertarian*	5,775
Monica Moorehead, *Workers World*	5,335
David McReynolds, *Socialist*	4,233
Cathy Brown, *Independent*	1,606
Denny Lane, *Grass Roots*	1,044
Randall Venson, *Independent*	535
Earl F. Dodge, *Prohibition*	208
Louie Youngkeit, *Independent*	161
None of the above	3,315

NOTE: The candidates listed above are those who appeared on ballots in at least one state.

SOURCE: *Washington Post* 2000 Presidential Election Results.

"multiperspectival" news is needed—"news that would include opinions of the public as well as those of officials, news about programs as they actually operate rather than as they are intended to work, and news that reflects a much greater variety of sources." Or as Bill Moyers, a former presidential aide to Lyndon Johnson and prominent journalist for first CBS and now PBS, has tried to communicate over the years, as reflected in a recent article: "Journalism & Democracy, On the Importance of Being a 'Public Nuisance.'"[79]

THE PREVALENCE OF SYMBOLIC POLITICS

Public knowledge and political participation are affected not only by the information communicated by the media but also by the **politics of symbolism** that pervades the political system and the mass media. Symbolism has been important in politics throughout history, especially given the role of American political culture as discussed in chapter 13. However, its presence today may be even more pervasive due to the rise of mass communications, particularly television.[80]

Symbolism is a powerful force in American politics because of the interaction of the media—which affects the information and images acquired by Americans, the political agenda, and the climate of opinion—and an overwhelmingly inattentive and uninformed public. Therefore, individuals and groups involved in American politics have increasingly attempted to use the media, especially television, to make symbolic appeals to the people in an attempt to gain their attention and support. Ultimately, the politics of symbolism seriously affects the political legitimacy of political actors and institutions, including the president and his ability to govern the country and make foreign policy.[81]

Power, for the president or any political actor, depends heavily on the illusion of power and the politics of symbolism. This was one of the key elements used by the Reagan presidency in overcoming the paradox of presidential power. In *The Power Game*, Hedrick Smith referred to the Reagan administration as the "Television Presidency." As he explained it, "Reagan is so natural onstage that, unlike most politicians, he creates the illusion of not being onstage." Furthermore, "Reagan has a political genius for selling his message—like the genius of Franklin Roosevelt. His secret is his mastery of political shorthand. He knows how to make ideas accessible and popular." Reagan and his administration have been the post-Vietnam masters of the sound bite and the politics of symbolism:

> Politicians and voters depend on labels, slogans, quick-stick, fast-fix clichés immediately recognizable to millions (though vaguely understood): Communists, welfare cheats, bureaucrats, New Right, New Deal, Star Wars, deficit spenders, supply-side, tax reform, evil empire. Reagan has a knack for coining phrases that tap into reservoirs of popular feeling—like his refrain to "get government off your back"—without having to explain what he means in policy terms, what his ideas will cost, or whom they will hurt. He is a master at using symbols that convey broad intention and leave him free to interpret their meaning.[82]

The politics of symbolism pervades American politics because perceptions of reality are as important as reality itself, especially given the limited interest of most Americans for national and international affairs. For example, the rise of the crisis of governance since the Vietnam War and the decline in public trust of government officials and the policymaking process have resulted in what Hedrick Smith calls the rise of **blame game politics.**[83] In other words, when the policymaking process becomes gridlocked, when policies fail, or when they are poorly received by the public, all government and private parties involved rush to disclaim any responsibility and blame others: The president blames Congress, members of Congress blame the president, Republicans blame Democrats, and Democrats blame

Republicans. Given this atmosphere, it has become fashionable for politicians to "run against Washington."

Elections are, in fact, the ultimate manifestation of media and symbolic politics. As Joe McGinniss demonstrated in 1968, the successful presidential campaign of Richard Nixon represented "the selling of the president."[84] Although the marketing of candidates, the use of symbolic appeals, and negative campaigning have been the hallmarks of election campaigns throughout American history, such efforts have become more systematic and pervasive with time. Today, as discussed in chapter 15, candidates rely heavily on marketing firms, political consultants, advertising and public relations campaigns, and most important, the power of television to attract voter attention and support—or at least turn voters against opposition candidates.[85]

This emphasis on marketing and symbolism has been reinforced by the media's coverage of elections, including presidential elections. For example, "an analysis of all week day evening network newscasts from Labor Day to Election Day in 1968 and 1988 reveals that the average 'sound bite' [on television] fell from 42 seconds in 1968 to only 9 seconds in 1988. Meanwhile the time the networks devoted to visuals of the candidates, unaccompanied by their words, increased by more than 300 percent."[86] Not much has changed now that the United States is in the twenty-first century.

While the politics of symbolism has become more pervasive with time, everyone involved nonetheless makes a concerted effort to appear to be "above politics." This is because politicians want to appear principled and statesmanlike, journalists are steeped in a culture of objective reporting, and the public expects politics in the United States, in comparison to politics in other countries and domains, to be more consistent with American political culture and thus "less political"—that is, more moral and clean. As Timothy Wirth, a Democratic congressman from Colorado, commented while preparing a video news release for the local media back home, "You have to get over the embarrassment of doing [public relations] and feeling it's hokey."[87] After all, as Hedrick Smith would say, it's all part of "the power game."

The politics of symbolism is particularly prominent in U.S. foreign policy. The Bush Sr. administration's depiction of General Manuel Noriega is a classic example of the politics of symbolism as the administration used the news media to rally the American public in support of the invasion of Panama in December of 1989. According to an article in the *Los Angeles Times*, American military officials, "in a procession of news conferences, guided tours and press releases, released unsavory material—much of which has been accepted by American reporters on the scene—to emphasize that Noriega was too base ever to have merited legitimate leadership and too evil to be allowed to go on unbridled." Through this public relations campaign, Americans learned that Noriega was a narcoterrorist who "wore red underwear to ward off the evil eye, practiced voodoo with vats of blood and animal entrails, kept a witch's diary in the same room with his favorite pornography and a portrait of Adolf Hitler, cavorted with his mistress in the mirror-walled bedroom of a luxurious yacht, and loutishly ignored the well-being of his wife while warning only his mistress that the American invasion was on its way."[88]

As the authors of this article observe, these official actions resemble "classic war propaganda" in which an enemy country is personified as the devil. (Review essay 17.1, on pictures of the enemy, the dehumanization process and the Japanese-American internment). Who was the target of the public relations campaign? The American people, since their support is crucial to the president's ability to govern. Therefore, administration officials utilized powerful symbols that would elicit a negative emotional reaction at the mere thought of Noriega. However, as we saw in chapter 8, U.S. relations with Noriega had a more complex and longer history than most Americans realize: Noriega had been on the Central Intelligence Agency (CIA) payroll since 1960, providing intelligence information and cooperation. Even though Noriega was involved in drug trafficking since 1971, he continued on the CIA payroll and was reportedly paid over $100,000 a year in 1976, when Bush was director of central intelligence, and $200,000 when William Casey became the DCI under President Reagan. He also had helped the Reagan administration support the contras with guns, money, and training in its covert war against the Sandinistas. Obviously, these facts were not shared with the American people by administration officials—it would not have been "smart" politics—and they were correspondingly downplayed or ignored by the mainstream media. Ultimately this strategy worked—the politics of symbolism orchestrated by the Bush administration was successful in manipulating the media and rallying

public support behind the invasion, making an ally into an enemy.

This pattern of using the art of persuasion and the politics of symbolism to mobilize the support of the public is not unique to the Panama invasion but *occurs whenever the U.S. government has relied on the use of force abroad*. Throughout the cold war, military intervention abroad was sold as essential in order to eradicate the threat of communism. Daniel Hallin, in *The Uncensored War*, found that:

> television coverage of Vietnam dehumanized the enemy, drained him of all recognizable emotions and motives and thus banished him not only from the political sphere, but from human society itself. The North Vietnamese and Vietcong were "fanatical," "suicidal," "savage," "halfcrazed." They were lower than mere criminals (there is usually some "human interest" angle in crime reporting): they were vermin. Television reports routinely referred to areas controlled by the NLF [National Liberation Front] as "Communist infested" or "Vietcong infested."[89]

In the post–cold war global environment new pictures of the enemy have to be highlighted and sold to the public. Hence, Saddam Hussein of Iraq ultimately was portrayed not as a communist threat (or a threat to cheap oil or American geopolitical interests in the Middle East) by the Bush Sr. administration following his invasion of Kuwait but as an aggressor in the vein of Adolf Hitler and Nazi Germany—despite the close relationship that existed between the United States and Saddam Hussein under both the Reagan and Bush Sr. Administrations before (as will be discussed further below). Such politics of symbolism are more important to the president since Vietnam than ever before because of the uncertainty of presidential control of the media and the need to overcome the paradox of presidential power.

The September 11 terrorist attacks on the United States, as tragic as they were, gave the Bush Jr. administration the opportunity to declare a war on terrorism and to communicate classic stereotypical images of the enemy, best illustrated by President Bush Jr.'s State of the Union address on January 29, 2002—better known as his "Axis of Evil" speech. The speech promoted and reinforced evil and negative images of the enemy—

which are automatically conjured up in the minds of most Americans at the mere mention of the names Osama bin Laden or Saddam Hussein or the countries of Iraq, Iran, and North Korea.

President Bush's call to war, patriotism, duty, and American innocence and exceptionalism was somewhat reminiscent of John F. Kennedy's inaugural address of 1961 over forty years ago:

> All nations should know: America will do what is necessary to ensure our nation's security. . . . Our war on terror is well begun, but it is only begun. This campaign may not be finished on our watch, yet it must be and it will be waged on our watch. . . . History has called America and our allies to action, and it is both our responsibility and our privilege to fight freedom's fight. . . . We want to be a nation that serves goals larger than self. We have been offered a unique opportunity, and we must not let this moment pass. My call tonight is for every American to commit at least two years—4,000 hours—over the rest of your lifetime to the service of your neighbors and your nation. . . . We have a great opportunity during this time of war to lead the world toward the values that will bring lasting peace. . . . No nation owns these aspirations, and no nation is exempt from them. We have no intention of imposing our culture, but America will always stand firm for the nonnegotiable demands of human dignity: the rule of law, limits on the power of the state, respect for women, private property, free speech, equal justice and religious tolerance. . . .

The speech ended with the following: "Steadfast in our purpose, we now press on. We have known freedom's price. We have shown freedom's power. And in this great conflict, my fellow Americans, we will see freedom's victory."

Virtually the entire speech revolved around foreign policy and the war on terrorism. Bush highlighted three major themes—according to the language of the speech: "national security," "homeland security," and "economic security." Clearly, the president was trying, for the most part successfully, to rally the country behind his presidency in declaring a war on terrorism in response to the national crisis triggered by September 11. Which leads us to one of the key political questions that may impact the future politics of U.S. foreign policy: To what extent will such nefarious images of terrorists (and terrorism) as the new enemy resonate in the twenty-first century in comparison to images of communists (and communism) following World War II?

THE ENTERTAINMENT MEDIA

While the foregoing focuses on the influence of the news media on American politics, the role of the **entertainment media** must also be considered. The news, after all, is only a small part of mass media offerings. The mass media's basic orientation is to entertain people: through television, radio, movies, novels, and more. Americans respond voraciously; most Americans are much more interested in being entertained than in being informed about public affairs and, thus, devote a considerable amount of attention to the entertainment media, especially television. Given the importance of entertainment programming—accompanied by a considerable amount of advertising—for the mass media and the general public, the entertainment media may have an indirect and subtle effect on American political beliefs and behavior. If anything, *the entertainment media appear to reinforce the consequences of the news media on American politics and U.S. foreign policy discussed above.*[90]

First, the entertainment media reinforce the pattern of public knowledge and democratic citizenship that prevails for most Americans. For example, watching and listening to entertainment shows (with an occasional newsbreak) on television on a daily basis contributes to a public that is uninterested and uninformed concerning national and international affairs. Not only does a preference for entertainment lower the priority for information about the world, the contents of the programs themselves often promote simplistic and stereotypical images of the world. As Todd Gitlin observes in *Inside Prime Time*, "what comes across the small screen amounts to an entertaining version of the world."[91] Therefore, it should not be surprising that entertainment often is substituted for information.

A study by George Gerbner and the Annenberg School of Communications, for example, found that perceptions of reality concerning American sex roles, age, race, work, health, and crime by "heavy viewers" of television (those who watch more than four hours a day, representing about one-third of the population) closely reflected the misrepresentations and biases of the world found on entertainment television.[92] If entertainment viewing affects Americans' perceptions of their own country, imagine the effect it may have on the image that Americans acquire of the rest of the world. For example, how are Arabs and Muslims commonly depicted? Who do Americans typically believe are terrorists? According to Gerbner, "no other medium reaches into every home or has a comparable, cradle-to-grave influence over what a society learns about itself."[93]

Second, the content and images of the entertainment media reflect the political environment of the times, reinforcing the evolution of news coverage. During World War II, for example, **Hollywood movies**— one of the major forms of mass entertainment—were overwhelmingly patriotic in nature, depicting the United States as the "land of the free and the home of the brave."[94] In war movies, Americans tended to be portrayed as innocent victims of aggression by ruthless and evil heathens, such as the Nazis and the Japanese. Some of this was a function of an industry that allowed itself to be censored in the name of national security. As explained by Clayton Koppes and Gregory Black in *Hollywood Goes to War*:

> During the war the government, convinced that movies had extraordinary power to mobilize public opinion for war, carried out an intensive, unprecedented effort to mold the content of Hollywood feature films. Officials of the Office of War Information, the government's propaganda agency, issued a constantly updated manual instructing the studios in how to assist the war effort, sat in on story conferences with Hollywood's top brass, reviewed the screenplays of every major studio (except the recalcitrant Paramount), pressured the movie makers to change scripts and even scrap pictures when they found objectionable material, and sometimes wrote dialogue for key speeches.[95]

This pattern continued into the cold war years. Although government censorship was lifted, its legacy remained with the rise of McCarthyism, the blacklists, and the anticommunist consensus throughout society. "Enemies changed, with wrenching suddenness," ob-

served John Dower in *War Without Mercy*, "but the concept of 'the enemy' remained impressively impervious to drastic alteration, and in its peculiar way provided psychological continuity and stability from the world war to the cold war."[96] Hence, as J. Fred MacDonald describes in *Television and the Red Menace: The Video Road to Vietnam*, the entertainment media during the cold war years became filled with dehumanized images of the communist bogeyman and the totalitarian threat to the United States and the so-called free world.[97]

Such images reinforced and contributed to the anticommunist consensus throughout American society. It was not until the 1960s that this cold war image of America was finally challenged within the entertainment media, most noticeably by the youth culture and, in part, through the growing popularity of *rock music*—another form of entertainment media (see **essay 17.3** on the politics of rock 'n' roll).

With the eventual collapse of the anticommunist and ideological consensus following the Vietnam War, the topics and images in the entertainment media—in movies and television dramas, comedies and docudramas—pertaining to national and international affairs began to reflect the greater diversity of the times. John Wayne's *Green Berets*, for example, reflecting the classic cold warrior view of an overconfident America (inevitably) containing the threat of communism in Vietnam, gave way to interpretations and impressions of the Vietnam War ranging from *Rambo* to *Apocalypse Now* to *Platoon* to *Born on the Fourth of July* (as well as the movie and television hit *M*A*S*H*, despite its Korean War context).[98]

With the exception of the Vietnam War, and the occasional James Bond and *Star Wars* movie, war and spy movies were no longer a major genre during the 1970s through the 1990s. But Hollywood occasionally produced successful movies with powerful political messages, such as *Norma Rae* (with Sallie Fields), on working conditions and unionization; *Silkwood* (with Meryl Streep and Sher) and *Erin Brokovitz* (with Julia Roberts), on corporations and environmental pollution; and *The Insider* (with Al Pacino and Russell Crowe), on the failure of *60 Minutes* and Mike Wallace to broadcast a segment on the spiking of cigarettes by the tobacco industry because of the corporate dynamics and political pressures on CBS. There has also been the rise of independent films that are often much more

ESSAY 17.3
THE POLITICS OF ROCK MUSIC

Rock music first became popular with American youth during the 1950s. The roots of what initially became known as "rock 'n' roll" are found in country music, gospel, and most important, the blues, which was quite prevalent throughout the black community. Most American adults were initially repulsed by the growing popularity of rock 'n' roll among youths in mainstream, middle America. The electricity and sensuality of the music, symbolized by Elvis Presley shaking his hips in the 1950s and the long-haired (for the time) Beatles singing "I Want to Hold Your Hand" to screaming fans in the early 1960s, was seen as a major source of juvenile delinquency, as depicted in the movie *Rebel Without a Cause*, resulting in efforts to censor the music.

What was happening, as Tom Wolfe pointed out in *The Kandy Kolored Tangerine Flake Streamline Baby*, was that "increasing American affluence" provided adolescent youth with the means to develop their own popular culture for the first time in the history of the world. One of the places to which American youth turned was rock 'n' roll. Changes in technology, culture, and politics during the 1960s affected the development of rock music. Rock 'n' roll became more sophisticated and refined due to technological improvements such as the development of full-length (vinyl) albums, FM radio (in addition to AM), and stereo sound (although many young people may find it hard to believe given their world of CDs, DVDs, the Internet, and so on). Rock 'n' roll also became more experimental and eclectic with time, as indicated by the development of different genres, such as the "Motown sound" of the Supremes and the Temptations; the "folk rock" of Bob Dylan, Simon and Garfunkel, and Joan Baez; the "British rock" of the Beatles and the Rolling Stones; and the "hard rock" of Jefferson Airplane and Jimi Hendrix.

By the mid-1960s, rock 'n' roll had become increasingly popular, particularly due to the incredible popularity of the "Fab Four"—John, Paul, George, and Ringo. Thus, the so-called "golden age of rock music" was born, representing a wide diversity of music and artists. Most important, given our interest in the politics of U.S. foreign policy, rock music became increasingly political in both content and style.

With the rise of the civil rights and antiwar movements, rock music began to reflect the values and beliefs of the new left and, in particular, the counterculture. The *lyrics of songs* increasingly dealt with American injustices at home and abroad and argued for the need to replace war and hatred with peace and love. This was symbolized, for example, by such songs as Bob Dylan's "Blowin' in the Wind," Neil Young's "Southern Man," Graham Nash's "Chicago," Peter, Paul and Mary's "If I Had a Hammer" (written by Pete Seeger), and John Lennon's "Imagine." American exceptionalism during the cold war and the Vietnam War were commonly caricatured by such songs as "With God on Our Side" by Dylan, "Back in the U.S.S.R." by the Beatles, and "I Feel Like I'm Fixin' to Die" by Country Joe and the Fish. In "The Music of Protest," Robert Rosenstone asserts that, in addition to the traditional concerns of war and injustice, the music of youth "worried about such things as the impact of technology on man, the confused state of American sexual practices, and the repressive nature of supposedly democratic institutions."[A] And stylistically, rock concerts—the sound, clothes, hair, drugs, and camaraderie—came to represent an alternative approach to mainstream culture.

Bob Dylan's "The Times They Are A-Changin'," written in 1963, in many ways became the anthem for the growing generation gap:

Come mothers and fathers throughout the land
And don't criticize what you can't understand.
Your sons and daughters are beyond your command.
There's a battle outside and it's ragin'.
It'll soon shake your windows and rattle your walls . . .
For the times they are a-changin'.

At the same time, the Rolling Stones' "Street Fighting Man," the Doors' "Five to One," the Beatles' "Revolution," and the Youngbloods' "Get Together" were indicative of growing internal differences within the 1960s movements over goals and strategies for change. Differences notwithstanding, the rock music of the time represented a consensus in protest against the status quo. Moreover, it symbolized hope for a rejuvenated America that was best illustrated by Jimi Hendrix's eerie guitar solo of the American national anthem at the Woodstock concert in 1969.

The **youth culture** of American young people increasingly revolved around peer interaction and the popularity

A. Robert A. Rosenstone, "'The Times They Are A-Changin': The Music of Protest," *The Annals* (March 1969), p. 131.
"The Times They Are A-Changin'" by Bob Dylan. Copyright © 1963, 1964 by Warner Bros. Music; Copyright renewed 1991, Special Rider Music. All rights reserved. International copyright secured. Reprinted by permission.

of rock music, acting as a major socializing force in the development of political beliefs and individual lifestyles, especially communicating the values and beliefs of the new left and the counterculture. As described by Godfrey Hodgson, in *America in Our Time*, "the promise that intoxicated initiates was that of a wider revolution of consciousness and culture, of which political revolution would come as a by-product."[B] According to one of the political bibles of the counterculture at the time, written by Charles Reich, rock music was part of a progress that would lead to the "greening of America."[C]

Rock music and the youth culture clearly helped to shatter the liberal-conservative ideological consensus that prevailed throughout the cold war and promoted other post–Vietnam War changes. However, reliance on rock music to "raise consciousness" and "change the world" also represented the height of political naiveté, such as ignoring more politically oriented activism and group politics as well as rock music's increasing commercialization by the entertainment business, that guaranteed only limited success at best. With the decline of the movements of the 1960s and the end of the Vietnam War, the golden age of rock came to a close. What was once an "alternative" music form became the dominant mainstream music—

and the classic rock (and now also part of "oldies" music)—of American society in general.

Today, rock includes many different forms of music that span a fifty-year period. While rock is less politically oriented than during the Vietnam War era, it has become more popular (as symbolized by MTV) and politically diverse than ever before. Some of the music continues to represent a liberal-left orientation, such as the songs of Bruce Springsteen and Tracy Chapman, "Live Aid" concerts, and rap music; however, some of the music represents a more conservative-right orientation, such as the rise of Christian rock. Most of all, rock music has become primarily big business—another story in the lives of the rich and famous—and increasingly commercialized—as epitomized by the advertising of Nike tennis shoes to the sound of the Beatles' "Revolution." Ultimately, rock music has become another form of mass entertainment and consumption, rocking 'n' rolling much of the American public (and people throughout the world) into the twenty-first century.

SOURCES: Simon Frith, *Sound Effects: Youth, Leisure, and the Politics of Rock 'n' Roll* (New York: Pantheon, 1981); Charlie Gillett, *The Sound of the City: The Rise of Rock and Roll* (New York: Pantheon, 1983); Don J. Hibbard with Carol Kaleialoha, *The Role of Rock* (Englewood Cliffs, N.J.: Prentice-Hall, 1983); Godfrey Hodgson, *America in Our Time* (New York: Vintage, 1976); Robert A. Rosenstone, "'The Times They Are A-Changin': The Music of Protest," *The Annals* (March 1969): 131–44; and Tom Wolfe, *The Kandy Kolored Tangerine Flake Streamline Baby* (New York: Pocket Books, 1965).

B. Godfrey Hodgson, *America in Our Time* (New York: Vintage, 1976), p. 336.
C. Charles A. Reich, *The Greening of America* (New York: Random House, 1970).

---

about real life and are thought provoking (best represented by Miramax productions), as well as the rise of independent film festivals (including Sundance and Cannes). And *West Wing* is probably the best dramatic show on TV in a long time to both be entertaining and to accurately reflect the world of politics.

But the bulk of American films (and TV shows), especially from major Hollywood studios, tends to continue to focus on entertainment and maximizing the box office, usually by developing action-oriented, thriller/mystery-oriented, and romance/comedy-oriented films. Since the September 11 attacks, there appear to be a renewed emphasis and popularity of war and spy movies and television shows not seen since the cold war. But it is important to remember that these shows remain entertainment oriented. Therefore, given the levels of public interest and information, the entertainment media since Vietnam are likely to reflect, reinforce, as well as pro-

mote the beliefs, stereotypical views, and simplistic images of national and international affairs held by most Americans.[99]

Finally, the prevalence of the entertainment media in the lives of most Americans reinforces the politics of symbolism. As Daniel Boorstin argued over thirty years ago, "The making of the illusions which flood our experience has become the business of America."[100] Many of the entertainment media, especially movies and television, deal with the world of symbols and make-believe. Although Paddy Chayefsky overstates the nature of the entertainment industry in his 1976 screenplay (and movie) *Network*, he nonetheless provides some important insights when he has the protagonist—a former news anchorman—shout out through the television:

> Television is not the truth! Television is a goddamned amusement park, that's what television

is! Television is a circus, a carnival, a traveling troupe of acrobats and storytellers, singers and dancers, jugglers, sideshow freaks, lion-tamers and football players! We are in the boredom-killing business. . . . No matter how much trouble the hero is in, don't worry: just look at your watch—at the end of the hour he's going to win. We'll tell you any shit you want to hear! We deal in illusion, man![101]

Not only is interest in the news and knowledge of the world overwhelmed by the growth of mass entertainment, but constant **advertising and mass marketing** has inculcated a consumption and materialistic ethic in most Americans. One study found that an average U.S. family is exposed to as many as sixteen hundred ads a day.[102] Nowhere is advertising more noticeable than through the power of television where, on average, Americans spend one and a half years of their lives watching television commercials alone. In the words of J. Fred MacDonald in *One Nation Under Television*, "TV has operated as a commercial billboard, rudely invading the privacy of every American with its pitches for dog food, clothing, Buicks, fast-food chains, and even candidates for the presidency of the United States. Still, the audience has never ceased to remain fascinated with the splashy spectacle."[103] Much of this applies to Hollywood movies as well. In movie theaters, ads are being shown along with previews. And the promotion of blockbuster movies by Hollywood studios, perhaps best illustrated by the *Star Wars* series, involves major mass marketing of both movies and products associated with the movies.[104]

As Ernest Calkins explained as far back as 1930 in his classic book on advertising, *Modern Publicity*, "The purpose is to make the customer discontented with his old type of fountain pen, kitchen utensil, bathroom, or motor car, because it is old-fashioned, out-of-date. The technical term for this idea is obsoletism. We no longer wait for things to wear out. We displace them with others that are not more effective but more attractive."[105] Not only does this create insecurity and impatience for a new product that individuals believe will fulfill their needs, it contributes to a public opinion that has a short attention span, is impatient with history and failure, and is very receptive to the politics of symbolism. Therefore, it naturally follows that candidates are mar-

keted and sold to the public as an AT&T commercial or a box of Tide. And it becomes more understandable why Ronald Reagan's Hollywood and acting experience served him so well as governor and president, for he excelled in symbolic appeals and made Americans feel good about themselves and their country.

There is one other impact of the entertainment media that is often overlooked—its impact on the images that foreigners have of Americans and the United States. Most countries and peoples in the world are highly dependent on foreign imports of entertainment media, especially television and movies. Many American television shows are broadcast all over the world and are often among the most popular shows. American movies dominate the world market. In fact, most American movies today gross more money from foreign viewership then they do from American viewership and sales (from 30 percent in 1980 to over 50 percent in 2000). *Star Wars: Episode I—The Phantom Menace* (1999) grossed almost $1 billion, with about 55 percent coming from overseas sales. *Titanic* (1997) may be the most successful of all, grossing over $1.8 billion worldwide, with over $1.2 billion coming from overseas. This means that what other people see on TV and in movies, much of which is American, may affect their images of the United States and contribute to simplistic and incomplete images of the America's complexity. The American media, after all, are huge multinational corporations in an age of increasing globalization.[106]

According to Michael Medved, "The vast majority of people in Pakistan or Peru, Poland or Papua New Guinea, may never visit the United States or ever meet an American face to face, but they inevitably encounter images of L.A. and New York in the movies, television programs and popular songs exported everywhere by the American entertainment industry."[107] Adventure and action movies and TV shows with good guys versus bad guys are popular not only in the United States but everywhere else and are relatively easily to follow (regardless of dubbing and language problems). They also tend to communicate spectacular American feats of power and technology through special effects that may have some basis in reality but are usually dramatic simplifications, as reflected in Tom Clancy's *Patriot Games* or *Mission Impossible* (the list is endless). This helps to promote and reinforce the simplistic, distorted, and naive images that foreigners are likely to have of the United States and the politics of its foreign policy.

For example, when I was a visiting scholar in Beijing, China, in 1999 and the U.S. government (supposedly) accidentally bombed the Chinese embassy in Belgrade during the Kosovo war, most Chinese people, including elites (such as graduate students and faculty), sincerely believed that it could not have been an accident.[108] Time and again, the common statement that I heard from almost everyone was that the U.S. government's technology was simply too good and superior to allow for such a mistake—so it had to be done on purpose to punish a growing China. It may be that too many Chinese have watched too many American movies, which are the most popular in China. Such is the potential power of the entertainment media, not only on Americans but for other people who comprise America's global context for understanding the politics of U.S. foreign policy.

THE ALTERNATIVE MEDIA

Although most Americans rely on the mainstream media for information about the world, alternative sources of information are available. **Alternative media** simply refers to those media outlets—such as television and radio programs, books, and magazines—that tend to address more varied issues, provide additional information, and offer interpretations beyond those available in the mainstream media. According to Lauren Kessler in *The Dissident Press: Alternative Journalism in American History,* "If we look only at the popular press, we will get little feeling for the richness, complexity, and conflict that have always been a part of American society. For historically the conventional press has spoken to and for the homogeneous middle."[109]

Throughout American history, alternative media have existed. In fact, the alternative media may have had greater visibility and influence for more Americans before the rise of the mass media and mass society during the twentieth century. Nevertheless, numerous and diverse alternative media have proliferated since Vietnam, although Americans are generally so dependent on the national media that the alternative media remain relatively invisible and unknown.

There are *alternative sources on television.* Some of the public affairs programs, such as *Frontline* and *NOW* with Bill Moyers on the Public Broadcasting System (PBS), tend to provide information from a more liberal orientation. Another basically liberal program, *60 Minutes* (the granddaddy of newsmagazines) can also be considered an alternative news source because its stories, although broadcast on CBS, tend to be ignored by other journalists within the national news media. However, most alternative public affairs programs on television are not on the network stations and tend to be more conservative in orientation. For example, PBS airs weekly programs hosted by editors of the extremely conservative *National Review* magazine, such as *Firing Line, The McLaughlin Group,* and *One on One.* PBS also broadcasts economic public affairs programs that reflect business interests such as *Wall Street Week, Adam Smith's Money World,* and the *Nightly Business Report.* The tendency of PBS to favor more conservative public affairs programs is mirrored throughout cable television as well. In fact, not only is conservative fundamentalism regularly aired Sunday morning on many television stations, but Pat Robertson and the 700 Club run their own national television station known as the Family Channel.

Radio has become an increasing alternative source of programming and information for more Americans over the last few decades (in part because broadcasting costs and infrastructure are relatively low). This would include the rise of public radio, such as National Public Radio (NPR), university radio stations, progressive and community radio, and Christian broadcasting. Probably of greatest visibility since the 1980s has been the rise of "talk radio," best symbolized by Rush Limbaugh. Community radio has also grown, of which the best known is *Pacifica,* which provides alternative programs for radio stations and also represents a network of radio stations (including Berkeley, Los Angeles, New York, Washington, D.C., and Houston). Overall, hundreds of radio stations representing considerable diversity exist across the country, although choice and diversity fluctuate dramatically depending on one's particular location.[110]

It is in the print media that diversity most proliferates. An *alternative and underground print press* has always existed, especially in large urban cities. During the

1960s and 1970s, for example, the rise of the new left was accompanied by the development of a "free press." Today, New York's *Village Voice*, San Francisco's *SF Weekly*, and Los Angeles's *LA Weekly* are among the most prominent of the free press (while the Phoenix-based *New Times, Inc.* is the largest chain of alternative newspapers organized as a private, for-profit corporation). *The Washington Times*, in contrast, reflects the rise of the right. Most cities often have free weekly newspapers that emphasize entertainment information around town but usually also include news and alternative commentary.

Small publishing houses and large publishing firms also produce thousands of books a year, ranging from the far right to the far left. Hundreds of newsletters also are produced by a variety of private individuals and groups, each with a topic or cause to promote (as discussed in the chapter on group politics). Such diversity is reflected in the variety of journals and magazines that compete for political influence and the attention of the elite public, probably the most visible and national of the alternative press. These would range from the *American Spectator, Commentary, Human Events, National Review, New American, Policy Review,* and *Public Interest* on the right, to the more centrist *New Republic*, to the *American Prospect, Dissent, In These Times, Mother Jones, Nation, New York Review of Books, Progressive,* and *Utne Reader* on the left.[111]

The alternative media have four important functions in American politics. First, the alternative media are often a major source of information for the most intellectually and politically active individuals throughout society. Second, information and interpretations arising within the alternative media occasionally affect news coverage by the mainstream media. Third, the variety of alternative media available reflects the ideological diversity and complexity of life in American society. Finally, the alternative media also serve as valuable sources of information and interpretations for improving one's understanding, thus supplementing the selective attention of the mainstream media's news coverage of the world.

While the national media, for instance, tend to rally round the flag early in a crisis and communicate the presidential view to the American public, the alternative media often provide information and interpretations that furnish valuable insights. Initial mainstream coverage of the Persian Gulf crisis in 1990, for example, reflected the presidential view that Iraqi president **Saddam Hussein and Iraq** was a threat to American vital interests, thus justifying an immediate and tough American response involving thousands of armed troops in the region. Hussein was portrayed by Bush administration officials and the American media as a ruthless tyrant, comparable to Hitler, who gassed his own people and has the ability to engage in chemical, biological, and possibly nuclear warfare. As has been the case throughout the history of U.S. foreign policy, events behind the Persian Gulf crisis were much more complex than the simple picture portrayed through the inflated rhetoric communicated by the Bush Sr. administration through the national media (and was subsequently portrayed by the Bush Jr. administration). It is to the alternative media that one must often turn to obtain a fuller picture, especially while it is an ongoing issue.

What the Bush administration and the media ignored in their Persian Gulf crisis coverage was the history and origins of the crisis. A one-hour special on *Frontline* entitled "The Arming of Iraq" (aired in early September on the same day as President Bush addressed the country before a joint session of Congress concerning the crisis) demonstrated the close relationship that had developed between the United States and Iraq during the 1980s. According to Mark Hosenball, in "The Odd Couple," From the early 1980s "until only days before diplomatic relations ruptured, the United States was one of Saddam's principal financial backers. The massive financial aid, comprising billions of dollars' worth of loan guarantees, continued long after it became apparent that Saddam was building an ambitious, menacing military machine.... Ultimately, the secret policy of building up Iraq economically and militarily had a far more disastrous result: the Reagan and Bush administrations helped arm Iraq for a war it fought against the United States."[112]

The Reagan and Bush administrations actively supported President Hussein during the Iran-Iraq war by taking Iraq off the State Department's terrorist list, providing military battlefield intelligence to Iraq, ignoring Hussein's use of chemical weapons on Iranians during the war and on Kurds within Iraq, and ignoring Iraq's military build-up on the border with Kuwait. In fact, just before the invasion the official position by the

Bush Administration, the State Department (in a briefing to Congress), and the Ambassador to Iraq (in a meeting with Saddam Hussein) was that the U.S. wanted to maintain good relations with Iraq and had "no official position" on Iraq's claim on Kuwait. Why? Because after the overthrow of the Shah in 1979 and the rise of Islamic fundamentalism, Iran was seen as the main enemy and Iraq and Saddam Hussein was now seen as a potential friend and ally—right up to the day they invaded Kuwait.

Furthermore, Western corporations—in particular, German, French, British, and American—had received their governments' approval to provide the equipment and personnel that allowed Hussein to build chemical, biological, and nuclear weapons capabilities. Much of the equipment, although officially provided for civilian use, was essential for weapons production as well. According to an unclassified government document, from 1985 to the invasion of August 2, 1990, the Departments of Commerce, State, Energy, and Defense approved 771 licenses by American companies to export $1.5 billion worth of high-technological goods to Iraq; of 1,133 license applications only 39 (3 percent) were rejected by the government.[113]

According to an October 1990 article in the *New Republic*, "Before the current crisis erupted, dozens of major U.S. and multinational corporations— nearly all of them members of a little-known trade association called the U.S.-Iraq Business Forum—eagerly supplied the Hussein regime with everything from rice to computers to helicopters, and anticipated that Hussein would spend billions more."[114] Annual sales to Iraq grew from about $400 million in 1985 to $1.5 billion in 1989. The forum's membership, as discussed in chapter 16, included more than fifty companies, including Amoco, Mobil, Occidental Petroleum, Westinghouse, Xerox, Bell Helicopter, Caterpillar, General Motors, and the First City Bancorporation of Texas. In some cases, "the companies seeking Iraq's petrodollars arranged for U.S. taxpayers to assume the risk of doing business with Hussein through commodity credits and loan guarantees underwritten by the federal government," such as through the Department of Agriculture's Commodity Credit Corporation and the U.S. Export-Import Bank.[115] In addition, consulting firms were involved, such as Kissinger Associates, which represented sev-

eral corporations, domestic and foreign, that had won large contracts from Iraq in the past few years, such as Coca-Cola, Volvo (Swedish), and the Yugoslav construction giant Energoprojekt.

Yet once American policymakers decided to respond massively after the invasion and portray Hussein as the Hitler of the Middle East, this history was avoided by the Bush administration and all but ignored by the mainstream media. As Hosenball concludes, "For nearly a decade Saddam Hussein played George Bush and his inner circle for suckers," and he continued to rule Iraq after the war. "The seeming failure to learn from, or even properly debate, the evidence of failed U.S. policy in Iraq hardly bodes well for the future."[116]

Another one of the biggest stories of the 1980s involving the Iran hostage crisis was completely ignored by the national and mainstream media. The story involved fear among the Reagan campaign team during the presidential elections that the Carter administration's efforts to negotiate with the Iranian government to release the American hostages would result in an "October surprise" and reelection victory for President Carter in what was a close and uncertain presidential race to the end. Under the direction of campaign manager William Casey, Reagan's soon-to-be director of central intelligence and architect of the Iran-contra covert actions, Reagan campaign personnel secretly opened up channels and negotiated with Iranian leaders to prevent the release of the American hostages until after the election in return for shipment of American spare parts and arms to Iran that they badly needed in their war with Iraq (similar to Richard Nixon's campaign team's efforts to sabotage negotiations between President Johnson and the Vietnamese as the 1968 election approached). The evidence is quite strong that negotiations were pursued; whether an actual deal was struck between the Reagan team and the Iranians is much more uncertain. It is interesting to point out that the American hostages, in fact, were not released by Iran until minutes after Ronald Reagan took the presidential oath of office and Israeli's first arms shipments to Iran with the Reagan administration's approval began in February 1981.

The key point, however, is that the national media did not report or even investigate a potentially significant story about the presidential election, U.S. foreign policy, and the origins of Iran-contra that had circulated since the election. The normal inclination of people, supported by governmental denials, was to dismiss the notion of an "October surprise" as rumor and a fanciful conspiracy theory. Investigation and reporting of the October surprise since the election, however, was conducted by the alternative media, such as *In These Times* and *The Nation*, which were heavily responsible for uncovering much of the story.[117] Yet it was not until eleven years later that the October surprise story was reported in the national media, and then only in the editorial section of the *New York Times* by Gary Sick, an established member of President Carter's NSC responsible for the Middle East, and in a *Frontline* show entitled "Election Held Hostage."[118]

As these illustrations demonstrate, one must acquire information from a variety of sources in order to obtain a comprehensive understanding of reality. Clearly, considerable information on national and international affairs is provided by the mainstream news media. However, given the media coverage patterns discussed in this chapter, it is important that mainstream media be supplemented by additional information and interpretations available only in the alternative news media. While difficult, it is possible for individuals to become "alert and knowledgeable" citizens, by relying on a variety of mainstream and alternative sources of information.

AN ALTERNATIVE MEDIUM: THE INTERNET?

One medium that has made it possible for people to access a multitude of mainstream and alternative sources is the Internet (or the World Wide Web). The popularity, affordability, and increasing technological capabilities of the personal computer (PC) has been revolutionary in the last two decades, especially for the world of communications. Through the Internet, people can be in direct contact with an amazing number and assortment of information sources and views (with varying degrees of reliability and credibility).

What many people do not fully realize is that the Internet is a function of the cold war. The Internet has

its origins in the late 1950s and early 1960s, when the U.S. government was trying to address how U.S. authorities could successfully communicate after a nuclear war. Postnuclear America needed a command-and-control network, linked from state to state, city to city, and base to base (and country to country). And so under the leadership of the Department of Defense's Advanced Research Project (ARPA), the RAND Corporation, University of California at Los Angeles (UCLA), and Massachusetts Institute of Technology (MIT), along with the National Physical Laboratory in England, kicked around the idea of creating a network with no central authority. By the late 1960s this developed into a small network of computers that could transfer data over transmission lines—named ARPANET after its Pentagon sponsor. Quickly, the main traffic on ARPANET became news and personal messages (what would be called e-mails). ARPANET grew tremendously during the 1970s since the network was public domain and the basic technology was decentralized (if not in fact anarchic), and more and more individuals and organizations with computers began to participate and form complexes of networks, which came to be known as the **Internet**.

The network continued to expand through the 1980s, to the point that ARPANET formally expired in 1989, a victim of its overwhelming success. Ever since, the Internet's pace of growth and the myriad activities that can be performed have been nothing less than spectacular if not ferocious. Users in virtually every country of the world are now connected to the Internet. The number of computer hosts is in the millions and increasing rapidly. Hence, within thirty years, the Internet has grown from a cold war concept for controlling the tattered remains of a postnuclear society to the "information superhighway."[119]

Table 17.4 lists a number of valuable sources—mainstream and alternative—on the politics of United States foreign policy and their Internet addresses. It is important to point out that one needs to be careful about the credibility, reliability, and security of the sources, given the overwhelming mass of information available. To what extent such a new and alternative medium will impact the communications process and American politics remains a speculative but fascinating question as the United States enters the next millennium.

TABLE **17.4**
WEBSITES FOR VARIOUS GOVERNMENTAL, POLITICAL, AND MEDIA SOURCES

TYPE	SOURCE	WEB ADDRESS
EXECUTIVE OFFICE OF THE PRESIDENCY	White House	http://www.whitehouse.gov
	National Security Council	http://www.whitehouse.gov/nsc
	National Economic Council	http://www.whitehouse.gov/nec
	Office of Management and Budget	http://www.whitehouse.gov/omb
	Office of the U.S. Trade Representative	http://www.ustr.gov
DEPARTMENTS AND AGENCIES	Department of State	http://www.state.gov
	Department of Defense	http://www.defenselink.mil
	Department of Homeland Security	http://www.dhs.gov/dhspublic
	Department of Justice	http://www.usdoj.gov
	Secretary of Treasury	http://www.ustreas.gov
	Secretary of Commerce	http://www.doc.gov
	Department of Agriculture	http://www.usda.gov
	Department of Labor	http://www.dol.gov
	Department of Energy	http://www.energy.gov
	Central Intelligence Agency	http://www.cia.gov
	National Security Agency	http://www.nsa.gov
	Federal Bureau of Investigation	http://www.fbi.gov
	Agency for International Development	http://www.usaid.gov
INDEPENDENT AGENCIES	Peace Corps	http://www.peacecorps.gov
	Federal Reserve Board	http://www.federalreserve.gov
	Environmental Protection Agency	http://www.epa.gov
	International Trade Commission	http://www.usitc.gov
	Export-Import Bank	http://www.exim.gov
	Overseas Private Investment Corporation	http://www.opic.gov
	Trade and Development Agency	http://www.tda.gov
	NASA	http://www.nasa.gov
CONGRESS	U.S. Senate	http://www.senate.gov
	U.S. House of Representatives	http://www.house.gov
	Congressional Budget Office	http://www.cbo.gov
	General Accounting Office	http://www.gao.gov/
	Library of Congress	http://www.loc.gov
	Congressional Quarterly	http://www.cq.com
JUDICIARY	U.S. Supreme Court	http://www.supremecourtus.gov
STATE GOVERNMENTS	National Association of States	https://www.nascio.org/stateSearch/index.cf
PUBLIC OPINION	Polling results	http://www.pollingreport.com

TABLE **17.4**
(*continued*)

TYPE	SOURCE	WEB ADDRESS
PARTIES	Democratic National Committee	http://www.democrats.org
	Republican National Committee	http://www.rnc.org
	Constitution Party	http://www.ustaxpayers.org
	Democratic Socialists of America	http://www.dsausa.org
	Green Party of the United States	http://www.greenpartyus.org
	Greens/Green Party USA	http://www.greenparty.org
	Libertarian Party	http://www.lp.org
	Natural Law Party	http://www.natural-law.org
	The New Party	http://www.newparty.org
	Reform Party	http://www.reformparty.org
	Socialist Party U.S.A.	http://sp-usa.org
	Communist Party USA	http://www.cpusa.org
	3rd Party Central	http://www.3pc.net/index.html
	Third parties in general	http://www.politics1.com
TELEVISION	ABC	http://www.abc.com
	CBS	http://www.cbs.com
	NBC	http://www.nbc.com
	CNN	http://www.cnn.com
	PBS	http://www.pbs.org
	C-Span .	http://www.c-span.org
	MSNBC	http://www.msnbc.com
RADIO	NPR	http://www.npr.org
	BBC NEWS	http://news.bbc.co.uk
	Voice of America	http://www.voa.gov
NEWSPAPERS	*New York Times*	http://www.nytimes.com
	Washington Post	http://www.washingtonpost.com
	Los Angeles Times	http://www.latimes.com
	Christian Science Monitor	http://www.csmonitor.com
	Wall Street Journal	http://www.wsj.com
	International Herald Tribune	http://www.iht.com
	Associate Press	http://www.ap.org
	Agence France-Presse	http://www.afp.com/english/home
	Reuters	http://www.reuters.com
NEWSMAGAZINES	*In These Times*	http://www.inthesetimes.com
	Newsweek	http://www.newsweek.com

(*continued*)

TABLE **17.4**
(*continued*)

TYPE	SOURCE	WEB ADDRESS
NEWSMAGAZINES	*Time*	http://www.time.com
	U.S. News & World Report	http://www.usnews.com
	Economist	http://www.economist.com
	World Press Review	http://www.worldpress.org
MAGAZINES	*American Conservative*	http://www.amconmag.com/
	American Prospect	http://www.prospect.org
	American Spectator	http://www.spectator.org
	Atlantic Monthly	http://www.theatlantic.com
	Commentary	http://www.commentarymagazine.com
	Dissent	http://www.dissentmagazine.org
	Mother Jones	http://www.motherjones.com
	Nation	http://www.thenation.com
	National Review	http://www.nationalreview.com
	New Republic	http://www.thenewrepublic.com
	New York Times Review of Books	http://www.nybooks.com
	Progressive	http://www.progressive.org
	Reason	http://reason.com
	Utne Reader	http://www.utne.com
	Z Magazine	http://www.zmag.org
CITES FOR MULTIPLE SOURCES	Politics Navigator	http://www.nytimes.com/library/politics/polpoints.html
	Newslink	http://newslink.org
	American Journalism Review	http://216.167.28.193

THE SPECIALIZED FOREIGN POLICY MEDIA

There is one other important source of U.S. foreign policy information: the specialized media. Every profession—whether medicine, law, business, or international affairs—has spawned a specialized literature that communicates information to members of the professional community. With respect to U.S. foreign policy and international relations, various **foreign policy journals** are published containing articles that revolve around contemporary issues and policy recommenda-

tions written and read by government officials, journalists, policy analysts, and academics. As with the historical patterns discussed throughout this chapter (and on group politics), the foreign policy specialized media have expanded and become more diverse over time (see **table 17.5**).

During the cold war, there were only two foreign policy journals to speak of: *Foreign Affairs*, a publication of the Council on Foreign Relations, and *Orbis*. These journals were influential, especially *Foreign Affairs*, for they were read by individuals in and out of government who were involved in the policymaking process. They were important because the contents of the articles re-

TABLE 17.5
MAJOR CONTEMPORARY FOREIGN POLICY JOURNALS

NAME	YEAR BEGAN	AFFILIATION	FOREIGN POLICY ORIENTATION*	WEB ADDRESS
ORBIS	1957	Foreign Policy Research Institute	Conservative	http://www.fpri.org/orbis
THE NATIONAL INTEREST	1985	(unaffiliated)	Conservative/ centrist	http://www.nationalinterest.org
FOREIGN AFFAIRS	1922	Council on Foreign Relations	Centrist	http://www.foreignaffairs.org/
FOREIGN POLICY	1970	Carnegie Endowment	Liberal/Centrist	http://www.foreignpolicy.com/
INTERNATIONAL SECURITY	1976	Harvard University	Centrist	http://mitpress.mit.edu/ journals.tcl/
WASHINGTON QUARTERLY	1978	Center for Strategic and International Studies	Conservative	http://www.twq.com
WORLD POLICY JOURNAL	1983	World Policy Institute	Liberal	http://worldpolicy.org/ journal/index.html/

*Most of the journals publish more diverse viewpoints today beyond their predominant orientation.

flected and promoted the thinking of the foreign policy establishment and the realpolitik/anticommunist consensus dominating American government and society. With the shattering of the foreign policy establishment and the anticommunist consensus after the Vietnam War, however, new journals appeared that reflected the greater ideological diversity of foreign policy thought.

In 1970, when *Foreign Affairs* was reluctant to criticize the U.S. government's Vietnam policy, a group of regular contributors created a new, and more liberal, journal, *Foreign Policy*. Soon other foreign policy journals appeared: *International Security*, reflecting a more centrist perspective; *National Interest* and *Global Affairs*, emphasizing a more conservative perspective, and *World Policy Journal*, reflecting a more liberal perspective. Since Vietnam, therefore, there has been a more diverse foreign policy specialized media that affects the communications process and the politics of U.S. foreign policy.

A similar pattern has characterized the academic and scholarly journals, which emphasize a more theoretical, analytic, and systematic study of international relations. The most pertinent American scholarly journals that contribute to the study of the politics of

United States foreign policy would include: *Diplomatic History, International Studies Quarterly, International Studies Perspectives, International Studies Review, Political Psychology, Political Science Quarterly,* and *Presidential Studies Quarterly.*[120]

INFORMATION, IDEAS, SYMBOLS, AND POLITICS

As we have found, the mainstream news media do not simply mirror reality, nor are they consistently biased in one ideological orientation, as both liberals and conservatives contend. Instead, the mediated reality of national and international affairs that is communicated to most Americans tends to provide selective information and a particular understanding of reality because of the complexity of the world, the nature of the media business, and the role of politics in the communications process. Therefore, the national media's foreign affairs coverage is both informative and narrow: It tends to present homogenized news and a centrist ideological understanding that reflects the prevailing political environment in government and society. These patterns in news media coverage, reinforced by the entertainment media, have heavily affected the foreign policy process throughout history, influenced public knowledge and democratic citizenship, and contributed to the politics of symbolism. The alternative media and the specialized media have also played a role, especially among those more active in politics and foreign policy. These sources serve as valuable supplements to the mainstream media, enabling individuals to acquire a greater breadth and depth of understanding about national and international affairs.

In a democratic society it is through the media and the communications process that the political competition over ideas and symbols is played out to a great extent. In this respect, *the media and the communications process are consequential throughout society and the politics of U.S. foreign policy for they fulfill three very important functions*: They are the basic source of information for people about world events, they interpret the meaning of those events for people, and they socialize individuals into their dominant cultural settings.[121] Therefore, the media affect the political agenda and the climate of opinion around the policymaking process for they act as the eyes through which people see and define the world. This explains why the media and the communications process have become a political battleground for access and influence between competing groups and interests within government and throughout society. Together, the mainstream, alternative, and specialized media occupy a critical role in the communication of information, ideas, and symbols to the mass and elite publics, affecting continuity and change, the president's ability to govern, and the tension between national security and democracy in the politics of U.S. foreign policy. If anything, given the pace of technological change, the communications process and the role of information, ideas, and symbols will grow in importance in domestic and world politics as we enter the twenty-first century.

RECOMMENDED MEDIA SOURCES FOR CONTEMPORARY ISSUES

The following print media are among the most significant and useful American "mainstream" sources for

becoming "alert and knowledgeable" with regard to national and international affairs. The *New York Times* is probably the single best daily source of news on national and international affairs. The *Washington Post* also provides strong political coverage, especially of the U.S. government, and is read religiously throughout the Washington political community. (The *International Herald Tribune*—consisting of both *New York Times* and *Washington Post* articles—has been available outside of the United States for years but can now be found in the United States.) The *Christian Science Monitor* also provides good overviews of national and international coverage. The *Wall Street Journal* is the best source of national and international economic news. *Newsweek* and *Time* are two newsmagazines that provide good summaries of the week's major events. *National Journal* is a superb source for following government policy and politics and *Congressional Quarterly* is excellent for following Congress.

On television, in addition to the nightly national news programs on ABC, CBS, NBC, and CNN, the *NewsHour with Jim Lehrer* (PBS), *Nightline* (ABC), *The News with Brian Williams* (MSNBC, CNBC), *Meet the Press* (NBC), and *This Week* (ABC) are some of the more interesting public affairs news and talk shows. Although not well-known to the general public, National Public Radio (NPR) provides excellent news coverage with *Morning Edition* (weekday mornings), *Weekend Edition* (weekend mornings), and *All Things Considered* (weekday evenings). These mainstream sources of news not only provide valuable information about national and international affairs but also indicate what government officials and national leaders are thinking.

There are also many good "alternative" sources of information and knowledge, from varying perspectives, to supplement the mainstream media. On television, *60 Minutes* (and "*60 Minutes II*") on CBS and *Frontline* and *NOW* on PBS are excellent sources of information based on investigative reporting.

Most of the alternative media, however, are print sources. The *New Republic* is an excellent weekly opinion magazine of both short articles and book review essays representing an ideological hodgepodge of liberalism and conservatism. From a liberal-left perspective, the *American Prospect* and *Dissent* are quarterly intellectual journals of articles and book reviews; *Mother Jones* is an investigative monthly; the *New York Review of Books* provides a wide-ranging biweekly source of book review essays and intellectual commentary; *In These Times* is an excellent weekly source of news and analysis of politics and culture, with the *Nation* and the *Progressive* providing greater political commentary and book reviews; and the *Utne Reader* (subtitled The Best of the Alternative Press) is a good bimonthly collection of news and general articles from diverse sources. From a conservative-right perspective, the *American Spectator* is a monthly intellectual journal of articles and book reviews; *Commentary* is a good monthly source of commentary and articles; the *National Review* is a biweekly source of information and opinion; *Reason* is a monthly journal of libertarian thought, and *American Conservative* is a new journal of conservative and semi-isolationist thought.

The following foreign policy journals are published quarterly and are particularly informative (listed from a more liberal to a more conservative international orientation): *World Policy Journal, Foreign Affairs*, and *The National Interest*. *Foreign Policy* has become a monthly journal and is an excellent source of a variety of views and information (American and non-American) with a new, livelier format.

Clearly, this is only a selective overview of *predominantly American* sources for acquiring information and knowledge. Tables 17.4 and 17.5 list their Internet addresses (and many of these sources have links to other sources). You can go to many of the Websites of the sources listed above and sign up so that emails containing their contents can be regularly sent to you. Beyond these Websites, a great place to begin to find a multitude of sources on the Internet is the "Politics Navigator" section of the *New York Times* (www.nytimes.com/library/politics/polpoints.html; if you have never used this Website, you will first have to register—it's free and quick).

Other television, radio, and print sources are available, including fictional accounts, such as novels and movies, that provide valuable information and interpretations. For example, the *West Wing* (NBC) is an excellent television show that provides a good feel for the politics and the role of the White House staff in particular around the presidency.

Non-American media sources are particularly valuable for providing broader global coverage and differing perspectives on the U.S. Among the many excellent non-American sources would be the *Economist* (www.economist.com) from England, a superb weekly magazine for global affairs; "The World," produced by the British Broadcasting Corporation, for radio coverage of world events on NPR; and *World Press Review* (www.worldpress.org), an extremely informative overview of news and different perspectives from a variety of sources, especially print, throughout the world and translated into English.

SUGGESTED SOURCES FOR MORE INFORMATION

Throughout the 1960s and 1970s, the study of the media in American politics was largely ignored by social scientists, especially in political science. Since then, the situation has changed dramatically, demonstrating a renewed interest in the role of the media in American society and U.S. foreign policy. The best general overviews of the news media are supplied by W. Lance Bennett, *News: The Politics of Illusion* (New York: Longman, 2001); Leonard Downie, Jr. and Robert G. Kaiser, *The News About the News: American Journalism in* Peril (New York: Vintage, 2003); Doris Graber *Mass Media and American Politics* (Washington, D.C.: Congressional Quarterly Press, 2001), Abbas Malek, ed., *News Media and Foreign Relations: A Multifaceted Perspective* (Norwood, N.J.: Ablex Publishing, 1999), and Gary Woodward, *Perspectives on American Political Media* (Boston: Allyn and Bacon, 1997). Stephen Hess provides an excellent overview of the media's international coverage in *International News and Foreign Correspondents* (Washington, D.C.,: Brookings Institution Press, 1996).

Shanto Iyengar and Donald R. Kinder demonstrate the influence of the news media on politics in *News That Matters: Television and American Opinion* (Chicago: University of Chicago Press, 1987). Daniel C. Hallin provides an excellent discussion of major patterns of foreign affairs media coverage and media-government relations in *The Uncensored War: The Media and Vietnam* (Berkeley and Los Angeles: University of California Press, 1986). Informative descriptions of the Reagan administration's efforts to dominate the communications process and the politics of symbolism are provided by Robert Parry and Peter Kornbluh, "Iran-Contra's Untold Story," *Foreign Policy* (fall 1988): 3–30, and Hedrick Smith, *The Power Game: How Washington Works* (New York: Ballantine, 1988), chapter 12. Marie Gottschalk provides a disturbing picture of media coverage of the Persian Gulf War that was submissive to the Pentagon and the Bush administration in "Operation Desert Cloud: The Media and the Gulf War," *World Policy Journal* (summer 1992): 449–86; an excellent overview and analyses also can be found in *Taken By Storm: The Media, Public Opinion, and U.S. Foreign Policy in the Gulf War* (Chicago: University of Chicago Press, 1994), edited by W. Lance Bennett and David L. Paletz.

David Halberstam, in *The Powers That Be* (New York: Knopf, 1979), gives a very informative narrative history of the growth and power of the national media.

Ronald Steel provides an excellent history of one of America's most prominent twentieth century journalists in *Walter Lippmann and the American Century* (New York: Vintage, 1980). Joe McGinniss's *The Selling of the President 1968* (New York: Pocket Books, 1969) remains a classic statement on presidential campaigning and the use of the mass media, as does Timothy Crouse's *The Boys on the Bus* (New York: Ballantine, 1972)—a fascinating look at pack journalism and political reporting during the 1972 presidential election.

For an excellent analysis of the role of the entertainment industry and film in American politics during war, see *Hollywood Goes to War: How Politics, Profits, and Propaganda Shaped World War II Movies,* by Clayton Koppes and Gregory Black (New York: Free Press, 1987), as well as Noral Sayre on the cold war years in "Assaulting Hollywood," *World Policy Journal* (winter 1995–96): 51–60. For a interesting analysis of the impact of the contemporary entertainment industry, see Michael Medved, "That's Entertainment? Hollywood's Contribution to Anti-Americanism Abroad," *The National Interest* (Summer 2002), pp. 5–14. Walter Hixson discusses the role of popular fiction in "Red Storm Rising: Tom Clancy Novels and the Cult of National Security," *Diplomatic History* (fall 1993): 599–613. A penetrating and lively look behind the scenes of the three television networks and the entertainment business can be found in *Inside Prime Time* (New York: Pantheon, 1983), by Todd Gitlin.

For the alternative media's coverage of the arming of Saddam Hussein and Iraq by the United States and the West, see "The Arming of Iraq," *Frontline* (September 11, 1990) and Mark Hosenball, "The Odd Couple: How George Bush helped create Saddam Hussein," *The New Republic* (June 1, 1992), p. 27–35, as well as the more current piece by Michael Dobbs, "When an Ally Becomes the Enemy" *The Washington Post National Weekly* Edition (January 6–12, 2003), pp. 9–10.

KEY TERMS

advertising and mass marketing
alternative media
beat system
blame game politics
censorship
cycle in news media coverage
editorial process
entertainment media
foreign policy journals
framing
headline news
Hollywood movies
homogeneous news coverage
Internet
journalistic jingoism
mainstream media
leaks
location of foreign correspondents
media and the CIA
mediated reality
national media
news media coverage
objective journalism
pack journalism
politics of symbolism
power of television
public relations (and propaganda) activities
Saddam Hussein and Iraq
selective attention
self-censorship
source versus investigative journalism
Vietnam War coverage
wire services
youth culture

PART FIVE

. . . .

CONCLUSION

Part V provides an overall synthesis and conclusion about the politics of U.S. foreign policy. Chapter 18 provides the conceptual tools for making sense of the overall politics of U.S. foreign policy and provides a summary of the major patterns discussed throughout the book, the nature and likelihood of foreign policy change, and its implications for the future politics of U.S. foreign policy.

CHAPTER
18

. . . .

SUMMARIZING THE MAJOR PATTERNS, THE NATURE OF CHANGE, AND THE FUTURE POLITICS OF U.S. FOREIGN POLICY

This chapter provides a summary of the major patterns discussed throughout the book and the conceptual tools necessary for making sense of the overall politics of U.S. foreign policy. In Part II, we examined the historical and global context of U.S. foreign policy. In Part III, we looked at the government and the policymaking process by focusing on the president, the National Security Council (NSC), the foreign policy bureaucracy, decisionmaking within the executive branch, and Congress. In Part IV, we examined the role of society and domestic politics, concentrating on the public and their beliefs, the exercise of civil liberties, electoral politics, group politics, and the mass media and communications process. Here, we integrate these differing perspectives and separate elements to afford a better understanding of how the foreign policy process operates in its entirety.

This final chapter addresses the following questions: What conceptual models help us make sense of the relationship between government and society, and the overall politics of U.S. foreign policy? What have been the basic patterns discussed throughout the book in order to determine which of the models best fits and explain the politics of U.S. foreign policy since World War II? What are the dynamics of foreign policy change given the interplay of all three perspectives—the context, the state, and society? Finally, what might be the implications for the future of the politics of U.S. foreign policy? This **synthesis** allows us to understand more fully the dominant themes, or questions, raised at the beginning of the book (and discussed throughout) concerning continuity and change, the president's ability to govern, and the tension between the demands of national security and of democracy in the making of U.S. foreign policy.

COMPETING THEORETICAL MODELS

Most students of United States politics agree that a **republican model** of democracy does not accurately reflect the workings of the American political system. In a republican polity, power is exercised on a daily basis by government officials who are elected and held accountable by a "sovereign" public: That is, the public exercises the ultimate power of majority rule. By the twentieth century, most scholars realized that this understanding of American politics was much too simplistic. This was probably communicated most forcefully by the writings of journalist Walter Lippmann in *Public Opinion* and *The Phantom Public*.[1]

Instead, *three competing interpretations or conceptual models have been developed to explain how the overall political process operates throughout society and the government (or state)*: (1) pluralism, (2) elitism, and (3) hyperpluralism. Each model provides a different understanding of the distribution of power and beliefs that exist throughout society and the government.[2]

Although each model should be considered an "ideal type," intellectual battles have raged over which of the models best captures the basic workings of American politics. When applied to the making of U.S. foreign policy, each model provides a unique understanding of the foreign policy process. Therefore, each model provides a different interpretation of the nature of American governance and democracy (see **table 18.1** for an overview).[3]

PLURALISM

Beginning in the 1940s, many American scholars and analysts saw a country in which democratic practice bore little resemblance to the republican ideal. Instead, they perceived a situation in which power was dispersed among numerous groups throughout society, with each competing for control of the government. According to Arnold Rose, in *The Power Structure*, **pluralism** "conceives of a society consisting of many elites, each relatively small numerically and operating in different spheres of life, and of the bulk of the population classifiable into organized groups and publics as well as masses."[4] Under this conception, power is dispersed among different groups throughout society and the government. Pluralism, therefore, is a type of competing-group politics, in which various groups (and elites) representing different goals and beliefs compete for influence throughout society and the government.

Robert Dahl was one of the most popular proponents of pluralism in American politics during the 1950s and 1960s. In *Pluralist Democracy in America*, he stipulated that "the fundamental axiom in the theory and practice of American pluralism is this: instead of a single center of sovereign power there must be multiple centers of power, none of which is or can be wholly sovereign."[5] Pluralism did not argue for the existence of a republican form of democratic politics. However, pluralists did argue that the decentralization of power among groups with competing goals represented a different form of democratic practice. Virtually all Americans were part of this democratic practice because of their membership in different groups. Moreover, even if they did not participate, their beliefs were represented by different organized interests throughout society. Therefore, as Dahl stated, pluralist politics "will help to tame power, to secure the consent of all, and to settle conflicts peacefully."[6] Thus pluralists maintained that "pluralist democracy" existed within the United States.

TABLE 18.1
MODELS OF THE STATE AND SOCIETY

THE MODEL	POWER	VIEWS	IMPLICATIONS FOR POLITICAL CHANGE
PLURALISM	Diffused	Diverse	Incrementalism
ELITISM	Concentrated	Shared	Status quo oriented
HYPERPLURALISM	Decentralized overall Concentrated networks for each issue	Diverse overall Shared for each issue	Status quo oriented

The empirical argument underlying pluralism also contained a normative or partisan element. Pluralists tended to see a world in which democratic practice had been challenged by the rise of totalitarianism in the twentieth century. They feared that the economic and social changes confronting people in modern societies contributed to the rise of fascism on the right and communism on the left—best exemplified at the time by the fall of the Weimar Republic in Germany and the rise to power of Adolf Hitler and the Third Reich. Therefore, pluralism was seen as a means to prevent the collapse of democracy stimulated by the rise of mass society, mass communications, and charismatic leadership.[7]

William Kornhauser laid out the argument in *The Politics of Mass Society*. "The central argument of this study is that insofar as a society is a 'mass society' it will be vulnerable to political movements destructive of liberal-democratic institutions; while insofar as a society is 'pluralist' the institutions will be strong."[8] Hence, the mass or "atomized society invites the totalitarian movement."[9] Likewise, Robert Nisbet in *The Quest for Community* argued that "there must be in any stable culture, in any civilization that prizes its integrity, functionally significant and psychologically meaningful groups and associations lying intermediate to the individual and the larger values and purposes of his society."[10]

A pluralistic political system, it was argued, based on the prevalence of competing groups (and elites) representing diverse views decreased the likelihood of major change. As Robert Dahl stated, pluralism "encourages incremental change, it discourages comprehensive change."[11] This was important to most pluralists, because the rise of mass society promoted too much freedom and too much potential for change with too little order. "Consequently," stated Dahl, "no part of the people, such as a majority, ought to be absolutely sovereign."[12] Competing groups representing diverse interests created the barriers between national leaders and the mass public that pluralists believed were essential to prevent the rise of authoritarianism. Therefore, proponents of pluralist democracy argued that it provided a balance between the demands of freedom and order.

ELITISM

Disputing the pluralist interpretation, some scholars and intellectuals began to seriously question the democratic nature of American society. They did not see a republican system characterized by dispersal of power among a public that elected and held the key leaders accountable. Nor did they see the essence of American politics in a pluralistic light. Instead, they saw a policy-making process in terms of **elitism**: one in which power was concentrated among elites who represented a small segment of the society, shared similar values and beliefs, and dominated the political and policy-making process.

Actually, *two somewhat different versions or proponents of elitism* existed: (1) those who saw class elitism and (2) those who saw institutional elitism.[13] The "class elitist" perspective emphasized class differences and the disproportionate amount of power that resided with the upper class in American society and government. The "institutional elitist" perspective emphasized how elites, not necessarily from the upper class, occupied and dominated positions of power within key institutions throughout society and government. Regardless of whether the focus was on the prevailing class or the prevailing institutions, the general public exercised little real influence within a governmental-societal political system that was essentially elitist in nature. As E. E. Schattschneider wrote in *The Semi-Sovereign People* in 1960, "The flaw in the pluralist heaven is that the heavenly chorus sings with a strong upper-class accent. Probably about 90 percent of the people cannot get into the pressure [group] system."[14] Instead of pluralist democracy, therefore, many concluded that elitism actually prevailed throughout American society.

In the mid-1950s, an elitist interpretation was popularized by C. Wright Mills in *The Power Elite*.[15] He argued that behind the facade of pluralistic politics a disproportionate amount of power lay with *the leaders of three key sets of institutions*: business, the military establishment, and the federal bureaucracy. Furthermore, these national leaders shared the same general beliefs as a result of common socioeconomic backgrounds, similar socialization experiences, and professional interaction. Not only did the general public exercise little influence over these institutions, but the institutions tended to respond to the wishes of national leaders.

Therefore, for Mills *American politics consisted of a three-tiered system of power*: a large, apathetic mass society at the bottom, a limited pluralist politics involving organized interests active in government and society at the middle levels of power (such as within the legislative process), and an elitist politics dominated by top government officials, military leaders, and corporate executives operating within the confines of a narrow ideological consensus at the highest levels of power. Hence, his response to pluralist claims was

> that on the bottom level there has come into being a mass-like society which has little resemblance to the image of a society in which voluntary associations and class publics hold the keys to power. The top of the American system of power is much more unified and much more powerful, the bottom is much more fragmented, and in truth, impotent, than is generally supposed by those who are distracted by the middling units of power which neither express such will as exists at the bottom nor determine the decisions at the top.[16]

In effect, pluralist politics actually operated within a narrow set of parameters determined by the elitist structure of society. Power, in other words, was ultimately exercised from the top down, with only a small cross section of elites dominating domestic politics and policymaking for the most significant issues, especially at the national level, throughout society and the government.

In addition to describing the nature of American politics, elitism also contained a normative or partisan dimension. Most proponents of elitist interpretations of American politics believed in democracy and the principles embodied in the American Constitution. However, they also believed that, with the rise of big business, big government, and mass (urban) society since the Civil War, American democracy had slowly been transformed into an elitist system. As Mills put it, "The history of modern society may readily be understood as the story of the enlargement and the centralization of the means of power—in economic, in political, and in military institutions."[17]

Therefore, elitists argued that major change had to occur in the elitist system that arose before American democracy could be restored. They tended to emphasize the development of countervailing power as a prerequisite for such change and to stress that members of the public had to become more interested and active in politics if they were to begin exercising the influence that predicated democratic practice. Despite their hopes, it was realized that it would be very difficult to change a system that was fundamentally elitist and status quo oriented.

THE GREAT DEBATE

During the late 1950s and early 1960s, elitists and pluralists fought intellectual and scholarly battles over the nature of politics in American society. Studies were done by elitists demonstrating that American politics was elitist at both the local and national levels. Similarly, contrasting studies performed by pluralists supported the existence of pluralist politics at the local and national levels as well.[18]

Ultimately, however, the great debate between elitists and pluralists was not resolved on the basis of evidence, for reasonable people could differ. Instead, it was determined by the evolution of American politics. Very simply, the pluralist interpretation prevailed by the early 1960s because most members of the elite public, including American academics and intellectuals, believed that the United States was in fact democratic in nature. Pluralism clearly became the most popular and powerful interpretation of American politics at the time.[19]

The rise of pluralist thought is understandable if one recalls the evolution of American ideology during the cold war era discussed throughout the book, for it reflected the formation of the liberal-conservative consensus in American society. People not included in the liberal-conservative consensus, whether on the right or left, were more likely to conclude that American politics was basically elitist. However, this elitist interpretation was limited to certain circles that remained largely outside the political mainstream and, therefore, invisible to most Americans.

HYPERPLURALISM, IRON TRIANGLES, AND ISSUE NETWORKS

During the late 1960s and 1970s, pluralism was again openly challenged. The collapse of the liberal-conservative consensus, along with the rise of the left and the right, renewed the pluralist-elitist debate to some extent.[20] During this time a third interpretation of American democracy also gained popularity, sometimes referred to as **hyperpluralism** by students of American politics. Pluralists emphasize the diffusion of power and diversity of thought characterizing the competition between groups in society and government on any single issue. Elitists emphasize the concentration of power and shared beliefs among a small segment of society that dominate politics with respect to the most important issues. Hyperpluralism blends the two models together, making it both similar to and distinct from pluralism and elitism.[21]

Hyperpluralists emphasize the rise of bureaucratic institutions and groups throughout government and society and the close ties established between them over issues of public policy. Therefore, a particular issue tends to produce a distinct network of interactive and mutually supportive ties between specific individuals (or elites) and groups throughout society and government that dominate the politics of that issue. The existence of a military-industrial-scientific infrastructure in defense policy is often cited as a classic example of hyperpluralist politics. This hyperpluralist view of American politics was popularized by Grant McConnell's *Private Power and American Democracy* and Theodore Lowi's *The End of Liberalism*.[22] Scholars have subsequently referred to the development of hyperpluralist **networks** of interaction throughout society and government as "iron triangles," "subgovernments," "issue networks" and "policy networks."[23]

Hyperpluralism borrows elements from both pluralism and elitism. Looking at American politics from a distance (or macro perspective), the existence of numerous issue networks dominating hundreds of different issues appears pluralist. Rather than competing for political access and influence, however, groups tend to establish networks of mutually reinforcing relationships that dominate access and influence in their particular area of interest. Issue networks develop among established governmental and private groups that, through their political access and influence, are able to keep challenging groups outside the power loop. Taking a close look (or micro perspective) at any single issue, therefore, the dominance of an issue network leads to concentration of power and is, in fact, quite elitist for that issue. Overall, however, *different policy issues result in the dominance of different subgovernments or issue networks*—the same coalition of individuals (or elites) and groups do not always dominate, in contrast to the elitist interpretation described above.

Hyperpluralism, in other words, is an exaggerated or perverted form of pluralism in which American politics is not merely decentralized and pluralistic; rather, the system is so decentralized around single issues that little room is left for the exercise of democratic practice and the prospects for change are slim.[24] This is because the individuals and groups comprising the issue networks that dominate society and government have both vested interests and the power to protect and promote the status quo. In other words, the federal government, including the executive branch, is not only weak but ineffective in responding to change. Yet, as hyperpluralists point out, change in the politics of hyperpluralism can occur. However, it is infrequent and usually results from outside efforts to open up the informal networks that control the placement of issues on the public agenda.

THE MAKING OF FOREIGN POLICY SINCE WORLD WAR II

To what extent do these competing conceptual models reflect the foreign policy process since World War II? Since that war, *two sets of conventional wisdom have prevailed during different periods about the making of U.S. foreign policy*: (1) During the cold war, the prevailing interpretation of the foreign policy process approximated the pluralist interpretation; and (2) Since the end of the Vietnam War, the dominant interpretation has been that the foreign policy process tended to be more elitist during the cold war years but has become more pluralist since Vietnam.

After briefly reviewing these two leading interpretations of the nature of the foreign policy process, we will discuss some important facets that have not been sufficiently explored by either conventional wisdom, such as the role of hyperpluralist politics. Overall, a summary analysis through use of the conceptual models will allow for a better understanding of continuity and change, presidential governance, and the tension between national security and democracy that have characterized the foreign policy process since World War II.

PLURALISM AND THE COLD WAR YEARS

During the cold war, the prevalent interpretation viewed the making of U.S. foreign policy as rather pluralist in nature. This was reflected in the work of foreign policy scholars and analysts such as Gabriel Almond, Paul Hammond, Samuel Huntington, Warner Schilling, and Glenn Snyder.[25] The most popular and powerful statement of this interpretation was Roger Hilsman's *To Move A Nation: The Politics of Foreign Policy in the Administration of John F. Kennedy*.[26]

"In its broadest meaning," states Hilsman, "politics concerns the activities and relationships of groups of people as groups."[27] *The group process shares three characteristics.* First, the political process includes the presence of competing groups or factions. Second, "politics implies a diversity of goals and values that must be reconciled."[28] Third, the relative power of the different groups prevents the same groups from dominating the policymaking process time after time. Hence, the politics of U.S. foreign policy is essentially pluralist in nature. "The fact that policy is made through a political process of conflict and consensus-building accounts for much of the untidiness and turmoil on the Washington scene. The issues are important; there are rival policies for dealing with them; and the rival policies are sponsored by different groups of advocates competing for the approval or support of a variety of different constituencies."[29]

Therefore, policymaking for Hilsman involves a political process of conflict, compromise, and incrementalism due to the multiplicity of actors attempting to reconcile competing goals. A nation, hence, is moved as a result of "the interaction of the President, the Congress, the press, and special interests" and "the rivalries of the great Executive departments, State, Defense, and the Central Intelligence Agency, as they clash in the actual making of policy."[30]

The implications of such a political and messy policymaking process is that "over some of this at certain times, the President may merely preside—if it is a matter of slight interest to him and has little impact on his position. But if *he* is an advocate or if the outcome affects *his* position and power, then the President, too, must engage in the politics of policy-making. In the field of foreign affairs, the President's power is immense. . . . But he, too, must build a consensus for his policy if it is to succeed." This means that "he must bring along enough of the different factions in Congress to forestall revolt, and he must contend for the support of wider constituencies, the press, interest groups, and 'attentive publics.' Even within the Executive Branch itself, his policy will not succeed merely at his command, and he must build co-operation and support, obtain approval from some, acquiescence

from others, and enthusiasm from enough to carry it to completion."[31] Hence, for Hilsman the making of U.S. foreign policy during the cold war was basically in accordance with pluralist politics.

Although Hilsman portrays the politics of U.S. foreign policy in pluralist terms, *upon close examination it is a very restricted or limited form of pluralism for three basic reasons.* First, competing groups are not found throughout society but predominantly within the government. Second, in most cases, members of the executive branch have a disproportionate amount of influence within the policymaking process. Third, the mass public plays virtually no role in the policymaking process at all. Each of these points is briefly considered below.

As Hilsman sees it, the policymaking process consists of a *series of "three concentric circles"*: an innermost circle of the president, his chief advisers, and his major appointments throughout the executive branch; a middle circle of the other departments, agencies, and layers of personnel within the executive branch; and an outermost circle consisting of "Congress, the press, interest groups, and—inevitably—the 'attentive publics.'"[32] The first two of these concentric circles involve policymaking solely within the executive branch. Hilsman maintains that some matters never go beyond the innermost circle, "but even here the process is political—the 'closed politics' of highly secret decision-making." However, "the longer a policy debate goes on, no matter how delicate the issue is, the more people will become involved until eventually the debate spills over into the public arena."[33]

While this may represent pluralist politics, it is a type of pluralism that is often limited to only a narrow range of government officials and groups located predominantly within the executive branch. According to this interpretation, Congress, the press, interest groups, and the attentive publics play a peripheral role, becoming involved only when issues become politicized beyond the executive branch. Even when this occurs, the influence of Congress tends to be "indirect or limit-setting rather than direct or initiative-taking. In domestic policy, Congress occasionally can take the initiative and force a new policy according to its tastes, but rarely in foreign policy. In foreign policy, the Executive calls the tune . . . it is the Executive who sets the framework in which policies are discussed, who defines the problems we will essay as a government and the alternatives from which we choose the courses of action to meet them."[34] Hence, for Hilsman pluralist foreign policymaking is largely a function of executive branch activity, with only a peripheral role for the outermost circle—more in accord with the model of governmental politics discussed in chapter 10.

Finally, the outermost circle also seems to exclude any role for the mass public—the bulk of the American people. Hilsman never discusses the mass public—only attentive publics—in terms of the influence or constraints that they place on domestic politics and the policymaking process. Instead, the public is indirectly referred to solely as a political target for different groups in their efforts to gain widespread support. For Hilsman, this leads to an inevitable oversimplification of foreign policy debates and the overselling of policies. As he explains, "If the debate is taking place in front of a variety of audiences whose attention is easily diverted, then the alternatives must be very clear-cut, simple, and dramatic and the arguments painted in colors that are both bold and bright."[35] Thus, a foreign policy process that virtually excludes most Americans raises serious questions concerning the extent to which the political system is democratic and pluralist.

In sum, the pluralist interpretation of U.S. foreign policymaking presented in Hilsman's work prevailed during the cold war era. However, it was a pluralistic political process largely dominated by the executive branch; Congress, the press, interest groups, and attentive publics were on the periphery and only occasionally involved when issues became politicized; and there was little role for the mass public. Therefore, the president and the executive branch tended to dominate a political process in which the demands of national security took precedence over the demands of democracy. This general interpretation described such a limited form of pluralism in politics as practiced—very similar to Graham Allison's governmental politics—that the growth in popularity of a different overall interpretation of the foreign policy process during the post–Vietnam War era is hardly surprising.

FROM ELITISM TO PLURALISM SINCE VIETNAM

Beginning in the 1970s, scholars and analysts of U.S. foreign policy developed a new interpretation concerning the making of U.S. foreign policy: During the cold war, the political process tended to be elitist; since Vietnam it became increasingly pluralist. This growing consensus concerning the politics of U.S. foreign policy is represented by such works as Richard Barnet's *Roots of War*, Destler, Gelb and Lake's *Our Own Worst Enemy*, John Donovan's *The Cold-Warriors*, Gelb and Bett's *The Irony of Vietnam*, David Halberstam's *The Best and the Brightest*, Godfrey Hodgson's *America in Our Time*, Isaacson and Thomas' *The Wise Men*, and Hedrick Smith's *The Power Game*.[36] This interpretation is also consistent with the basic understanding of the post–World War II foreign policy process provided by this book.

It is not really a case of disagreement over the particulars of Hilsman's analysis of the foreign policymaking process during the cold war. In fact, there is a great deal of shared understanding concerning the power of the president and the executive branch in a political process in which national security requirements took precedence over the demands of democracy. *The key dispute involves a different interpretation and conclusion concerning the overall political process:* that the foreign policy process during the cold war was, in fact, more elitist in nature, as opposed to pluralist. In other words, the argument is that, while the politics of any particular decision appears under close inspection to resemble a pluralistic process, the overall general political process was in fact relatively elitist in nature.

An elitist interpretation of the cold war years tends to place great weight on the concentration of power and thought that existed throughout society and government in the making of U.S. foreign policy. The focus is not only on the "immediate" politics of U.S. foreign policy but on the general "setting" and domestic context that molds and constrains the making of U.S. foreign policy. In other words, whereas Hilsman emphasizes the direct (and immediate) influence of the innermost and middle circles—the executive branch—beyond all other concerns, a more elitist interpretation is concerned with both the **direct influence** enjoyed by the innermost and middle circles on day-to-day policy as well as the **indirect** (and underlying and contextual) **influence** that the outermost circle has in terms of the constraints on policy and the limits it sets on the political process.[37] In this respect, the pluralist interpretation completely underemphasizes the crucial development and impact of the foreign policy establishment and the ideological consensus on the communications process, electoral and group politics, and the governmental pol-icymaking process.

Very simply, during the cold war, power became increasingly concentrated within the executive branch—especially in the White House and the national security bureaucracy—and in its linkages to key private groups, especially more prominent corporations, foreign policy groups such as the Council on Foreign Relations, and academic institutions. Furthermore, the politics that permeated society and government operated within a strong liberal-conservative ideological consensus, resulting in considerable bipartisanship among the most politically active supported by a largely apathetic and compliant mass public. Thus, in order to understand the foreign policy process during the cold war era, it is important to recognize that power was relatively concentrated and that a consensus of thought reigned supreme throughout society and the government.

The position that the foreign policy process tended to be elitist during the cold war years is consistent with the major patterns discussed in this book. *To briefly summarize, the dominant patterns that prevailed during the cold war years were the following*:

- Growth of American power
- Growth of presidential power
- Ascent of the NSC system
- Expansion of the national security bureaucracy
- Rise of the national security ethos
- Development of an acquiescent Congress (and courts)
- Existence of a Washington political community
- Rise of a liberal-conservative and anticommunist consensus
- Development of bipartisanship in electoral politics
- Prevalence of cold war–oriented groups and movements
- Growth of a foreign policy establishment
- Development of a military-industrial-scientific infrastructure
- Existence of mass apathy and a decline in the exercise of civil liberties
- Development of a nonpartisan and but cold war–oriented mass media

The cold war years, hence, represented a period when the presidency and the executive branch dominated the foreign policy process at the height of American power, with the involvement and support of mainstream

groups and institutions throughout society and government, held together by a foreign policy consensus that pervaded the elite and mass public.

One can debate *the extent of presidential and executive branch power* as a result of these patterns in the making of U.S. foreign policy. However, the cold war years were clearly the height of presidential power in U.S. foreign policy, when the president faced the fewest constraints within government and throughout society. The development of the foreign policy bureaucracy, military-industrial-scientific infrastructure, cold war–oriented groups, and foreign policy establishment further provided the support and means by which to pursue and implement a cold war policy. The rise of the foreign policy establishment and the military-industrial-scientific infrastructure, in particular, were consequential in the formation of significant ties and networks that developed between society and government in support of a cold war foreign policy. All of these developments were held together by the rise of a cold war consensus in which most Americans—throughout the mass and elite publics—came to believe that a national emergency existed due to the threat posed by Soviet communism. This promoted an acquiescent Congress, supportive mass media, and responsive public. Altogether, these elitist patterns produced the phenomenon of the "two presidencies," allowing the president and the national security bureaucracy to exercise "prerogative government" in foreign policy abroad and at home in the name of national security.

One can also debate *how much, or how little, democratic practice existed* in the politics of U.S. foreign policy during the cold war. Yet widespread fear of the Soviet Union and communism, symbolized by McCarthyism at its height, clearly meant that the demands of national security took precedence over the demands of democracy in the two decades following the end of the Second World War. Consequently, the development of a national security ethos limited the availability of information to the public; Democratic and Republican candidates for national office were cold warriors and offered voters little political choice; political participation declined, with little room allowed for the exercise of political dissent; and the rise of bureaucracy—in the executive branch and the private sector—minimized political accountability. Therefore, the existence of powerful groups in the government and throughout society operating under a cold war consensus considerably narrowed democratic practice within mainstream American politics.

To what extent, for example, was the mass public manipulated or educated? *Was the public responsive to national leaders, or were they a constraint on foreign policy leadership?* Answers to these questions are consequential in determining the extent of elitism within the politics of U.S. foreign policy during the cold war. Contradictory patterns are evident, depending on different publics and the times. Whereas the public for the most part may have been manipulated and responsive to national leaders, especially during the late 1940s and early 1950s, when cold war policies were devised and sold (consistent with the followership model discussed in chapter 13, on the public), the belief in anticommunism, once acquired by the public, served as a future constraint on domestic politics and the policymaking process. Therefore, it is with some irony that the more elitist interpretation, in comparison to the pluralist interpretation discussed above, actually allows for a greater role for the mass public in the politics of U.S. foreign policy.

Such an elitist interpretation suggests the following three patterns. First, that the height of presidential power was reached during the cold war years, especially from the mid-1950s to the mid-1960s. Second, the demands of national security took precedence over the demands of democracy. Finally, elitism notwithstanding, the politics of U.S. foreign policy was quite complex, as this book has attempted to demonstrate throughout. Together, the politics of U.S. foreign policy were mutually reinforcing with, and provided political support in government and throughout society for, American cold war policy abroad and decisions that led, for example, to the Americanization of the war in Vietnam. That war contributed to the political turbulence of the late 1960s and early 1970s that produced important changes in the complex politics of U.S. foreign policy. American intervention in the Vietnam War, therefore, represented the height and decline of elitism in the making of U.S. foreign policy.

The argument that the foreign policy process became more pluralist since Vietnam is also consistent with the major patterns discussed within the book. *To briefly summarize, the dominant patterns that have prevailed since the Vietnam War have been the following:*

- (Relative) decline of American power
- Decline of presidential power
- Rise of the foreign economic bureaucracy and "low" policy
- Reassertion of Congress
- Greater involvement of the judiciary and state and local governments
- Opening up of the Washington political community
- Shattering of the liberal-conservative cold war consensus and its replacement by greater ideological diversity
- Collapse of bipartisan electoral politics and the rise of divided government
- Collapse of the foreign policy establishment
- Proliferation of diverse social movements and groups
- Expansion in the exercise of civil liberties
- Rise of objective journalism and a centrist and potentially more independent mass media

Ultimately, the rise of pluralism has led to a decline in the president's ability to govern foreign policy and an increase in democratic practice relative to the demands of national security. This has been reinforced by the collapse of the Soviet Union and the cold war.

Since the late 1960s, *presidents have faced greater obstacles and constraints* than during the cold war years. The two-presidencies scenario—weak in domestic policy, strong in foreign policy—has been replaced by the post-cold war presidency thesis based upon a paradox of presidential power, which requires the exercise of strong presidential leadership to govern, even in the making of U.S. foreign policy. The crisis of governance facing most post–Vietnam War presidents, however, is so severe that a president has great difficulty fulfilling the high expectations created among the public and, consequently, is prone to experience failure. Most important, a president can no longer exercise prerogative government with virtual impunity, as occurred during the cold war years. To do so is to risk "overshoot and collapse" or "political backlash"—as President Richard Nixon experienced with the Watergate affair and President Ronald Reagan suffered with Iran-contra.

Presidents have greater difficulty governing U.S. foreign policy because *the political process has become more democratic* since the 1960s. In this respect, it is important to understand that the demands of national security and democracy are contradictory and have different implications for the ability of the president to govern foreign policy. While the demands of national security took precedence during the cold war, the political process since Vietnam has become more responsive to the demands of democracy. The public has greater access to information, a choice between more liberal and conservative presidential candidates, and increased opportunities to actively participate (reflecting more the fragmentation/swing model discussed in chapter 13). Furthermore, the separation of powers has been renewed, diversity in ideological and foreign policy thought has grown, and group politics have diversified and proliferated.

This is not to say that no elitist elements remain. The president and the executive branch retain significant advantages in the politics of U.S. foreign policy due to the legacy of the cold war and the cloak of the national security ethos, especially during crises. Furthermore, political competition among members of the elite public is heavily circumscribed by ideological thought that reflects the liberal-conservative political spectrum. In the short term, the September 11 terrorist attacks and President Bush Jr.'s war on terrorism have increased presidential power in national security affairs and the demands of national security relative to democracy. But the key question is what are the long-term consequences? Overall, the politics of U.S. foreign policy has evolved from a more elitist form of politics during the cold war to a more pluralist form during the post–Vietnam War and post–Cold War eras, although the future remains uncertain.

Therefore, presidents have less support and face considerably stronger constraints in exercising prerogative government in the name of national security since Vietnam. During the 1950s, for example, the effort to fight a covert war to overthrow communism in Central America would not have led to the constitutional and political crisis that President Reagan faced with the Iran-contra scandal; instead, the president would have been able to secretly pursue such a policy with widespread support and little opposition, as President Dwight Eisenhower did in Guatemala in 1954. In other words, whereas elitist politics considerably strengthened presidential power during the cold war era, the rise of pluralist politics has weakened the president's ability to govern foreign policy since the Vietnam War, at least until the September 11, 2001, attacks (**see essay 18.1** for the implications of democracy for international peace and war).

CONTINUITY IN HYPERPLURALIST POLITICS AND AN APOLITICAL MASS PUBLIC

The complex politics of U.S. foreign policy not only has experienced change but also has been characterized by continuity since the 1960s. *Continuity has occurred relative to two very important facets of the foreign policy process*:

1. The hyperpluralist politics of national security policy and
2. The continuing withdrawal or apathy of much of the mass public from politics.

These are two very important dimensions that are often ignored or downplayed by those who conclude that the political process has become more pluralist since the Vietnam War.

Since World War II and the cold war, foreign policy has become increasingly bureaucratic, which has led to the development of extensive networks between individuals and groups within the executive branch, Congress, and the private sector. Hyperpluralist politics is most visible in the development of defense politics during the cold war and its continuation since Vietnam, reinforced by September 11 despite the collapse of the cold war. Therefore, *important elements of hyperpluralism within the foreign policy process continues to exist to this day*, as discussed throughout the book:

- A large national security bureaucracy,
- A national security ethos,
- The Washington political community,
- The military-industrial-scientific infrastructure,
- The existence of cold war-oriented groups, and
- The existence of conservative internationalism among a segment of the public.

It is important to point out, however, that hyperpluralism is not limited to national security politics. In fact, wherever established groups and bureaucracies have arisen throughout society and government, issue networks have formed and, subsequently, resisted changes to the status quo.

Such hyperpluralist politics *both strengthen and weaken presidential power*. For example, the existence of a large national security bureaucracy and military-industrial-scientific support infrastructure strengthens the power of a president who wants to pursue more of

ESSAY 18.1
ARE DEMOCRACIES AND THE UNITED STATES PACIFIC?

What is the likelihood of war breaking out between the United States and one of the other industrialized democracies, such as France, Great Britain, or Japan? Or the likelihood of war along the U.S.-Canadian border—the longest, unmilitarized border in the world? Today, wars among such countries seem inconceivable. And yet each of these countries participated in the Persian Gulf War against Iraq. Not surprisingly, scholars have begun to theorize that a "zone of peace" develops among liberal, democratic states: that although democracies may be as likely to wage war toward other kinds of states, democracies do not fight other democracies.

The existence of a democratic peace was most powerfully espoused by the German philosopher Immanuel Kant in 1795. Kant's *Perpetual Peace* predicted expanding pacification in international politics as more and more states developed into liberal democracies. Perpetual peace would be established when states accepted three "definitive articles": (1) the adoption of a constitutional republic, (2) the making of agreements among liberal democracies creating a pacific union, and (3) the creation of cosmopolitan law establishing norms of "universal hospitality," allowing for high levels of international trade. Kant realized, however, that democratic states were prone to conflict and war relative to nonliberal states.

Many of Kant's ideas were reflected in Woodrow Wilson's hopes for the world after World War I, as espoused in his "Fourteen Points," especially the formation of a League of Nations and a liberal international political economic order. Although the world was once again swept up in international war, the liberal democracies allied together against fascism during World War II and communism during the cold war. Recently, this pattern of democracies not waging war against other democracies has been increasingly noticed by students of international affairs and been labeled the **democratic peace theory**.

Although there may be much truth to the existence of a democratic peace, the *causes* are very much open to debate. One major line of thought is that policymakers are "constrained" by the limits on executive power found in democratic political systems. Policymakers depend on domestic support and are reluctant to embark on unpopular foreign policies because it could quickly cost them political support and, ultimately, their jobs. This may also make it difficult for democratic states to quickly launch surprise attacks. Maintaining domestic support may also be more difficult to sustain if a conflict lasts longer than expected, if the goals are not clear or important, or if the numbers of casualties mount—witness Korea and Vietnam, versus the Persian Gulf War, in U.S. foreign policy. Another hallmark of democratic societies is the peaceful succession of political leaders, a problem that continues to plague nondemocratic states. A more cultural argument is that stable democracies develop established norms and expectations on resolving disputes with each other—norms in which violence is not an acceptable option.

As convincing as the democratic peace seems, there are plenty of critics. "Realists," in particular, claim that democracies act no differently than other states in an anarchical, self-help, international system—that democracies are just as prone to conflict and war as any state. After all, it is the pursuit of national power and national interests, not regime type, that determines war or peace. The United States, for example, has had a long history of supporting authoritarian regimes in the name of national security and political stability. Other critics emphasize the role of political stability, economic growth and wealth, alliances, nuclear weapons, and international institutions for furthering the goal of international peace, especially among democracies.

In fact, many students of foreign policy have traditionally argued that the constraints on democratic leaders actually make democratic states more unpredictable and dangerous in the international arena, because not only may democracies be slow to react to aggression but once engaged in war they often overreact and embark on moral crusades to unrealistically fight "wars to end all wars." This has been a common criticism of U.S. foreign policy throughout much of the twentieth century.

To what extent has U.S. foreign policy been pacific towards other democratic states? In the twentieth century, the empirical record appears to be quite strong in support of the democratic peace. The United States has been engaged in a number of wars and has relied on the (threat and) use of force extensively, but not toward other democratic states. The focus, however, has been on overt war; not much attention has been devoted to analyzing the role of "covert war." As was discussed in some depth in chapter 8, on intelligence, while the U.S. government attempted to deter Soviet expansion through the threat of nuclear war and conventional war, it relied heavily on covert political and paramilitary intervention to fight communism throughout the globe.

The record relative to covert war is not as clear-cut as with overt war. *Two cases, in particular, stand out* where the United States engaged in a covert war against democratic states: Guatemala and Chile. In 1954 in Guatemala, the U.S. government overthrew an uncooperative democratically elected president of a country that was in the formative stages of democracy in favor of a friendly military dictator. Chile, which had a much longer democratic tradition since its independence in the early nineteenth century (though periodically interrupted by authoritarian rule), had been operating as an established democracy since the early 1960s. However, with the election of Salvador Allende in 1970, the Nixon administration led a covert campaign to destabilize the Chilean economy and persuade the Chilean military to stage a coup, which came in 1973 and installed Augusto Pinochet as the dictator of Chile for the next sixteen years. It may be that covert war and action may be a way for liberal democracies to overcome many of the democratic constraints and obstacles to the use of force discussed above.

And what about *war "turned inward"* toward a country's own democratic citizens? With the rise of the cold war, a preoccupation with national security and secrecy also bred distrust of democracy and constitutional rights within the United States. As discussed in chapter 8 and chapter 14, the fear of communism was so great that the president and the intelligence community saw domestic dissent as an internal threat and acted to repress it. Domestic covert operations included the CIA's Operation Chaos, the FBI's Operation Cointelpro, and large spying operations by the NSA and army intelligence. In other words, a wide-ranging set of domestic covert operations were performed that broke the law and violated the civil rights and liberties of American citizens in the name of the protection of American democracy. The cold war clearly was a time when the demands of national security took precedence over the demands of democracy, when the president was able to exercise prerogative government, and when elitist politics dominated the making of U.S. foreign policy—suggesting that the United States became

something of a **garrison state** (although not everyone would agree, such as Friedberg in *In the Shadow of the Garrison State*).

Ultimately, this type of unconstitutional and undemocratic behavior by the early 1970s led to the tragedy of Watergate and the resignation of President Nixon. Clearly, the existence and nature of democratic states is not a simple open-and-shut case. But Bush's new war on terrorism has raised new concerns about governmental abuses of individual civil rights and liberties.

Despite the criticisms, many Americans and American policymakers believe and act as if democracies are more pacific and that expanding liberal democracy is important not only to the spread of American values but also to the enhancement of international peace and stability. Such an approach to U.S. foreign policy, popularized under Woodrow Wilson, has played a role under most presidents to the present day, certainly at the rhetorical level but also for actual policy. President Clinton's "policy of enlargement" was very consistent with the twentieth century tradition in U.S. foreign policy to promote political and economic development in a liberal democratic direction. President Bush Jr., in contrast, appears to have highlighted the difference between those who support the United States (friends) and those who don't (foes) in his war on terrorism, regardless of the nature of the regimes. To what extent liberal enlargement may (and should) become the guiding principle of U.S. foreign policy in a post–cold war world is a question that Americans must wrestle with for the foreseeable future.

SOURCES: Michael E. Brown, Sean M. Lynn-Jones, and Steven E. Miller, eds., *Debating the Democratic Peace* (Cambridge, Mass.: MIT Press, 1997); Michael Doyle, "Liberalism and World Politics," *American Political Science Review* 80 (December 1986): 1151–69; David P. Forsythe, "Democracy, War, and Covert Action," *Journal of Peace Research* 29 (November 1992): 385–95; Aaron L. Friedberg, *In the Shadow of the Garrison State: America's Anti-Statism and Its Cold War Grand Strategy* (Princeton, N.J.: Princeton University Press, 2000); Joe D. Hagan, "Domestic Political Systems and War Proneness," *Mershon International Studies Review* 38 (October 1994): 183–207; Harold Lasswell, *The Garrison State*, edited by Jay Stanley (New Brunswick, N.J.: Transaction Books, 1996).

a foreign policy reminiscent of the cold war, much as President Bush is doing with his war on terrorism. At the same time, however, presidential policies remain heavily affected by what the bureaucracy is able and willing to implement. Furthermore, should a president want to pursue a post–cold war foreign policy, hyperpluralist politics act as a major constraint on new pol-

icy initiatives. Regardless, the need to manage and circumvent the bureaucracy is one of the main reasons why most presidents have increasingly come to rely on a closed policymaking process revolving around a small circle of advisers who are White House centered.

Hyperpluralist politics also has *implications for the tension between national security and democracy* that exists in American politics. The existence of a huge national security bureaucracy and support infrastructure means that a strong constituency continues to exist throughout society and the government that remains sympathetic to the demands of national security. In other words, a national security ethos of independence, secrecy, and realpolitik continues to affect domestic politics and, in particular, pervade the governmental policymaking process. This is likely to increase and be reinforced by the September 11, 2001, attacks and Bush's war on terrorism. Therefore, the rise of pluralism and the continuation of hyperpluralism since Vietnam have increased the political contradictions and tensions between the demands of national security and democracy.

One other important trend of continuity concerns the role of the mass public in the politics of U.S. foreign policy. *The patterns of continuity prevalent among the mass public that we have discussed throughout the book are as follows*:

- An uninformed, uninterested, and erratic public opinion;
- A strong sense of political culture and nationalism;
- Decline in political participation, especially in electoral politics; and
- The prevalence of the politics of symbolism.

These patterns indicate that there has been a continual process in which a large segment of the public has basically withdrawn from American politics. Such mass apathy has added considerable uncertainty to the president's ability to govern and the contradictions between national security and democracy since Vietnam and the end of the cold war.

This continuity in the role of the mass public during a time when there is no consensus throughout society and government *adds considerable uncertainty to the president's ability to govern foreign policy.* On the one hand, the mass public's opinions and cultural beliefs, reflecting the split in elite beliefs, reinforces the dominant patterns that prevail since Vietnam. At the same time, because most of the public tends to be tuned out of politics, there is a likelihood of greater mood swings—which can strengthen or weaken the president depending on their direction. Clearly, there has been a huge nationalistic mood swing in support of the president and the war on terrorism since September 11. How long this nationalistic mood swing continues is a critical question. Ultimately, the political apathy of much of the mass public at a time of great foreign policy disagreement and competition is a source of great uncertainty and potential instability in the future politics of U.S. foreign policy.

This has important *implications for the practice of democracy* in American politics. Although the rise of pluralism has resulted in greater democracy and a more responsive political system, the prevalence of a predominantly apolitical mass public is a poor omen for the future of democratic politics. It is shocking how little information many Americans possess concerning national and international affairs. Furthermore, public cynicism toward politics appears to have grown. The political result has been a continual decline in mass participation in the electoral process, for example, and a mass public that has become increasingly vulnerable to the politics of symbolism. All of this is a far cry from the "alert and knowledgeable" citizenry that President Eisenhower called for and democratic practice demands. In other words, the increase in democratic politics since the Vietnam War has been paradoxically accompanied by the bulk of the American public tuning out of politics altogether. Not surprisingly, some contemporary political analysts have resurrected fears commonly espoused by pluralists during the 1950s concerning the decline of democracy and the rise of authoritarianism in American society. Certainly, the demands for national security have strongly resurfaced in the wake of September 11.

COMPLEXITY IN THE CONTEMPORARY POLITICS OF U.S. FOREIGN POLICY

In sum, the politics of U.S. foreign policy are too complex for any single model of the political process to capture for much depends on the time and the issues of concern. Overall, the complex politics of U.S. foreign policy has experienced continuity and change since World War II: A more elitist form of politics dominated the cold war years; after the Vietnam War, elitism was replaced by a more pluralist form of politics; politics during the cold war was also characterized by the rise of hyperpluralism in defense politics and a mass public that remained beyond politics altogether, which continued into the post–Vietnam era.

With the collapse of the Soviet Union and the end of the cold war, these post–Vietnam patterns have continued and intensified. Therefore, the cold war years represented the height of the president's ability to govern foreign policy, a time when the demands of national security prevailed over the demands of democracy. In contrast, the years after Vietnam represented a decline in presidential power due to growing contradictions between the growth of democracy and the persistence of national security demands. This has been somewhat counteracted by the September 11 attacks, but the long-term consequences remain quite uncertain in such a volatile global, domestic, and political environment.

Conceptually, it is interesting to note that more and more scholars have come to recognize the growing "convergence" between elitist and pluralist interpretations of American politics that have evolved since the Vietnam War. Whereas the competing conceptual models of government-society relations in American politics that were developed during the cold war were often incomplete and simplistic—and therefore divergent—each of these models has become much more sophisticated with time, thus capturing a greater amount of the complexity and dynamics of American politics—producing greater overlap. Therefore, even though like-minded scholars and analysts tend to communicate among themselves in their own language, often being insensitive to work developed from competing perspectives, pluralist and elitist studies of American politics have become much less incompatible with each other and much more complementary in the post–Vietnam War era.

Much depends, as Pat McGowan and Steve Walker point out in "Radical and Conventional Models of U.S. Foreign Economic Policy Making," on the question and the level of generality that one is addressing: "On the one hand, if one is interested in delineating the outer parameters of change in American policy, an [elitist] perspective identifies the constraints that limit the range of variation and provides insights into the deeper structural changes that appear to be required in order to reshape U.S. foreign economic policy. If, on the other hand, the analyst is interested in short-run, incremental changes in U.S. foreign economic policy, then the [pluralist] perspective sensitizes him to the immediate surface causes of these fluctuations."[38]

The rise of pluralism, accompanied by the continuity of hyperpluralist politics and an apolitical mass public, that has come to dominate the politics of U.S. foreign policy was quite evident during the Persian Gulf crisis of 1990–1991. Following Iraq's invasion of Kuwait on August 2, 1990, President Bush was able to exercise prerogative government by sending a massive force of American troops to the Persian Gulf to defend Saudi Arabia. The political response throughout the rest of the government and most of society—Congress, the public, and the media—was to rally round the flag. With President George Bush's announcement in early November, however, that American forces would increase from 200,000 to over 400,000 personnel and take a new, offensive military posture to force Iraq out of Kuwait, the domestic political climate changed dramatically, reflecting its more pluralist form. Dissent began to appear in Congress, among former government officials, in group politics, and in public opinion, increasingly communicated by the mass media. Within a three-month period, in other words, the president went from exercising extraordinary power during a foreign policy crisis to experiencing a crisis of governance that would determine the political fate of his presidency. Such contrasting political patterns occurred once again when the country rallied round the flag following President Bush's decision to go to war on January 16, 1991.

The Persian Gulf crisis also illustrates the contradictions in the making of U.S. foreign policy between the demands for national security—emphasized by President Bush—and the demands of democracy—emphasized by those who dissented from the president's policy. At the same time, the outcome of the crisis also strengthened the networks of individuals and groups in government and throughout society that were resisting cutting the military establishment in light of the collapse of communism in the Soviet Union and Eastern Europe. Such effects directly reflect the complexity and contradictions of the contemporary nature of the foreign policy process within the United States. It is important to understand that the foreign policy process is actually more complex and messy than this summary analysis suggests, because the **role of chance** or *"fortune"* (and unintended consequences) in the unfolding of politics has been ignored, often leading to a false sense of clarity about the making of U.S. foreign policy due to the benefit of hindsight.[39]

FOREIGN POLICY CHANGE

What will the future entail? Why do some patterns remain the same over time? When does **foreign policy change** occur? This is an area that has received only sporadic attention despite its importance, especially with the United States having just entered the twenty-first century. Nevertheless, tentative generalizations can be derived from the work that has been done on the study of political change.[40]

Although political systems can proceed down different historical paths, certain patterns of continuity and change tend to prevail in the politics of U.S. foreign policy. Very simply, American politics normally tends to resist change but is interrupted occasionally by political crises that stimulate change. **Incremental change**—that is, little change over a period of time—tends to be the prevailing norm during times of high political legitimacy and stability—a period of equilibrium in the political system. **Major change** tends to be infrequent and often abrupt, usually triggered by major crises indicative of failed policies and the rise of political instability—a time of disequilibrium in the political system. Discussion of patterns of incremental and major change have been described by scholars such as

Frank Baumgartner, Kjell Goldmann, Samuel Huntington, Charles Hermann, Kal Holsti, Theodore Lowi, Arthur Schlesinger Jr., and James Rosenau, as well as Jerel Rosati, Joe Hagan and Martin Sampson.[41]

As described by David Truman in *The Governmental Process*, "The moving pattern of a complex society such as the one in which we live is one of changes and disturbances in the habitual subpatterns of interaction, followed by a return to the previous state of equilibrium or, if the disturbances are intense or prolonged, by the emergence of new groups" that establish "a new balance, a new adjustment in the habitual interactions of individuals."[42] In other words, American politics tends to evolve from periods of political stability in which continuity (and incrementalism) prevails to periods of political instability and transition in which change is most likely. These **cyclical patterns of continuity and change** are consistent with those found in this book on the politics of U.S. foreign policy (see **figure 18.1** for an overview).[43]

Why does **status quo politics** tend to prevail? Very simply, all political systems, whether pluralist, elitist, or hyperpluralist in nature, tend to resist change. This situation prevails because established groups and institutions throughout government and society engage in

FIGURE **18.1**
CYCLES OF FOREIGN POLICY CONTINUITY AND CHANGE

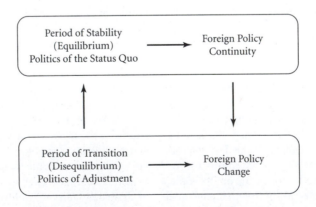

Jerel A. Rosati, "Cycles in Foreign Policy Restructuring: The Politics of Continuity and Change in U.S. Foreign Policy," in Jerel A. Rosati, Joe D. Hagan, and Martin W. Sampson, eds., *Foreign Policy Restructuring: How Governments Respond to Global Change* (Columbia: University of South Carolina Press, 1994), p. 227.

politics to promote their interests and protect the status quo from challenging groups and ideas. This influence is usually reinforced by the support of the mass public. Although predominantly apolitical, they support mainstream institutions and beliefs, ultimately providing the political system with its legitimacy and political stability. According to V. O. Key, Jr., in *Politics, Parties, and Pressure Groups*,

> The system—the established way of doing things—constitutes a powerful brake on political change. Those who agitate for a new order invariably encounter the resistance of the old order which exists, in considerable degree at least, in the revered values more or less firmly anchored in group life. These patterns of behavior, traditional modes of action, group norms, or social equilibria—the concept employed in their description may not matter—possess a powerful capacity for their own perpetuation and resist movements that would disturb them.[44]

In other words, all political systems with an established set of institutions and beliefs in place throughout the society and government resist change, although with varying degrees of rigidity and success. The implication is that change, if it occurs at all, tends to be incremental in nature.

Although continuity and incrementalism tend to be the norm, major change periodically occurs throughout society and the government. The **politics of change and adjustment** is most likely to prevail over the politics of the status quo during times of crisis and political instability, when the legitimacy of the political leadership is most likely to be questioned by members of society. This eventually occurs because of the growing gap that develops between the incrementalist policies of the government and the inevitable change experienced throughout the global environment and society. As the politics of the status quo continues to prevail and governmental policies fail to adjust to new developments in the international and domestic environment, the contradictions grow, increasing the likelihood of policy failure abroad and the growth of internal opposition at home.

As Stanley Hoffmann stated, "When rigidity leads to failure—but only then—the policy becomes unstuck and sudden reversals become possible."[45] Should these contradictory developments continue and intensify with time, governmental policy becomes increasingly maladaptive. Eventually, this may lead to major political crises at home that politicize members of society to challenge the legitimacy of the policies and the beliefs held by the individuals and groups that dominate society and the state.

The key to understanding the dynamics of foreign policy, in other words, is the interaction of the state, the society, and the global environment (or context) that produces a political process that usually reinforces governmental resistance to change and the maintenance of foreign policy continuity; sometimes, however, it produces contradictions to the status quo that contribute to foreign policy change. Whatever the causes, public policies that were once considered successful are now increasingly seen as failures and counterproductive. During such periods of political instability, greater numbers of people are likely to question and criticize the status quo, more new issues are placed on the political agenda, challenging groups and ideas gain strength, and the dominant groups and beliefs throughout society and government have less success dominating politics. Therefore, times of major crisis and political instability are often transitional periods that *may* produce major political change (see **figure 18.2** for an overview).

The making of U.S. foreign policy has followed this evolutionary pattern in which the politics of the status quo tends to be superseded by the politics of transition, producing change and a new politics of the status quo. The political crises faced by the United States in association with World War II, the rise of American power, and the development of the cold war triggered a number of significant changes in government and society, resulting in the more elitist political patterns of U.S. foreign policy during the cold war years that we have identified in this book. These patterns in the foreign policy process prevailed throughout the 1950s and early 1960s until the political crises and instability of the late 1960s and early 1970s, especially over U.S. foreign policy in the Vietnam War, triggered additional political changes in government and society in a more pluralist direction that have prevailed since Vietnam. At the same time, the hyperpluralism of defense politics and the political apathy among the mass public are continuing legacies of the cold war. Thus, the politics of U.S. foreign policy has experienced

FIGURE **18.2**

THE DYNAMICS OF FOREIGN POLICY CHANGE

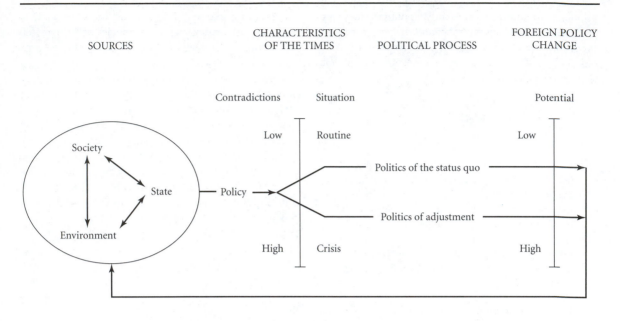

Jerel A. Rosati, "Cycles in Foreign Policy Restructuring: The Politics of Continuity and Change in U.S. Foreign Policy," in Jerel A. Rosati, Joe D. Hagan, and Martin W. Sampson, eds., *Foreign Policy Restructuring: How Governments Respond to Global Change* (Columbia: University of South Carolina Press, 1994), p. 237.

continuity and change over time, with significant implications for both the president's ability to govern and for the contradictory tension between the demands of national security and of democracy as the United States moves into the twenty-first century.

This leads to the following questions: Will the September 11 attacks and the war on terrorism be perceived as a time of real and permanent crisis and national emergency? How long and how much will the war on terrorism resonate in the American political system? To what extent can President Bush Jr. and other individuals successfully exercise political leadership in support of the war on terrorism? The more answers to these questions are in the affirmative, the more likely that these events and policies will produce foreign policy change and a new foreign policy era. The more the answers are negative, the more likely that the future politics of U.S. foreign policy will be one of relative stability accompanied by incremental change.

THE FUTURE POLITICS OF U.S. FOREIGN POLICY

Clearly, the end of the cold war and the evolving post–cold war global environment *have contradictory implications for the future politics of U.S. foreign policy.* The end of the cold war has created increasing global complexity, posing both greater opportunities and constraints for the evolution and exercise of American power. The collapse of communism, the decline of the Soviet Union, and the rise of new issues on the political agenda suggest the likelihood of more foreign policy change heading away from cold war policies of the past, further weakening the president's ability to govern foreign policy and increasing the demands of democracy. Yet the continued existence of instability and conflict throughout the world, although on a smaller scale than a potential U.S.-Soviet war, reinforces the likelihood of an active United States presence in the world and the continued exercise of presidential power in the name of national security. Certainly this appears to be the case thus far in response to the September 11, 2001, attacks and the war on terrorism.

It was the sense of national emergency associated with the cold war during the fifties and sixties, after all, that was the ultimate source of presidential power and American global leadership following World War II. Clearly, such a sense of national emergency tremendously declined following Vietnam, reinforced by the end of the cold war. The perception of a cold war was replaced with the perception of a time of relative peace abroad in the minds of most Americans. This means that the fragmented and pluralist political environment that has prevailed since Vietnam—resulting in a paradox of presidential power and a strong tension between national security and democracy—may likely continue in the twenty-first century, posing greater foreign policy opportunities and political risks for presidents and American leadership abroad.

Such continuity in the politics of U.S. foreign policy is most open to change and adjustment in response to new global and internal developments that prevail in the post–cold war era, especially if they are accompanied by political crises. The question now is to what extent the crisis of September 11, the war on terrorism, and other possible terrorist attacks will trigger a sense of national emergency in which Americans feel constantly and deeply threatened. Will this be perceived as another time of war, or as war in a time of relative peace?

There is no doubt that the United States will continue to have a powerful international presence given its relative power and its legacy of global leadership since World War II. There is also little doubt that the future leadership role of the United States in the world will be influenced by who is president as a result of the dynamics of American politics. Presidents can affect the general direction of U.S. foreign policy within the legitimate parameters of foreign policy orientations and constraints that prevail throughout American society. Certainly, the Bush administration's decision to launch a global war on terrorism and to become a war presidency is significant. But much will depend on the image that Americans have of the president's policies and of their relative success, at home and abroad—a

function of the fate of events and the strength of presidential leadership. And much will depend on the president's ability to manage and harness the huge bureaucracy that has developed over the years.

Although the boundaries or parameters of the future politics of U.S. foreign policy have been suggested, one cannot specify how politics will actually play out and affect U.S. foreign policy. Given the complexity and contradictions, one must honestly acknowledge considerable uncertainty and ignorance about more specific dynamics and their long-term impact in the formulation and conduct of U.S. foreign policy into the twenty-first century. Therefore, *answers to the questions below concerning the future of American foreign policy remain open to the workings of history:*

- What opportunities and constraints will the United States face as it navigates the twenty-first century?
- What will be the impact of the end of the cold war and the rise of new conflicts and threats, such as terrorism?
- Will American power experience relative decline or renewal in world politics?
- Will American politics continue to operate in a more pluralist fashion or will it undergo significant change?
- What is the future of the post–cold war presidency thesis and the paradox of presidential power in foreign policy?
- How will the tension between the demands of national security and democracy evolve?
- Will a new consensus in foreign policy beliefs emerge in society and government, or will fragmentation in foreign policy thought continue to prevail?
- What is the future of a more conservative internationalist orientation that emphasizes the significance of more traditional national security issues of global conflict and order, a power politics approach to foreign affairs, and the necessity of American primacy abroad?
- What is the future of a more liberal internationalist orientation that emphasizes the need to address a wide variety of issues in a world of great complexity, that the utility of force has become more costly, and the importance of American leadership and multilateralism abroad?
- Or, what is the future of a noninternationalist orientation that highlights the need for U.S. political

and military disengagement from much of the world and a turning inward to focus on domestic issues?

- Will the free trade ethos continue to prevail, or will the American response to changes in the international political economy result in movement toward multilateral managerialism, economic revitalization, or economic nationalism?
- Will economic and other issues continue to be important or be superceded by issues of national security?
- To what extent will "new" beliefs in the foreign policy orientations of Americans and America's approach to the world rise to prominence?
- How will the actual institutions and mechanisms that have arisen for making and implementing foreign policy be effected?

Clearly, although much continuity may prevail, the future may also be accompanied by considerable foreign policy change. Events and their political impact will be very important. Much will depend on the forces that underlie the politics of the status quo relative to forces in support of change (or different types of change) over time. Ultimately, it is the dynamic and unpredictable interaction of the government, the society, and the environment that will determine the complexity and direction of the future politics of United States foreign policy as the country navigates the twenty-first century.

SUGGESTED SOURCES FOR MORE INFORMATION

The study of pluralism, elitism, and hyperpluralism has produced a rich literature, although not much of it has been directly applied to the making of U.S. foreign policy. For a general discussion of pluralism and its significance for democratic practice, classic statements can be found in William Kornhauser, *The Politics of Mass Society* (New York: Free Press, 1956), and Robert A. Nisbet, *The Quest for Community* (New York: Oxford University Press, 1953). Roger Hilsman, in *To Move a Nation: The Politics of Foreign Policy in the Administration of John F. Kennedy* (New York: Delta, 1964), especially chapters 1 and 35, provides the best example of the pluralist perspective applied to the making of U.S. foreign policy for the cold war years.

For a general discussion of elitism, the classic statement is provided by C. Wright Mills in *The Power Elite* (London: Oxford University Press, 1956). A more contemporary account with a greater emphasis on the concept of class can be found in Ralph Miliband, *The State in Capitalist Society: The Analysis of the Western System of Power* (London: Quartet Books, 1969). For an elitist perspective on the politics of U.S. foreign policy during the cold war era, excellent accounts are provided by Richard Barnet in *Roots of War: Men and Institutions Behind U.S. Foreign Policy* (New York: Penguin, 1972); Leslie H. Gelb with Richard K. Betts, *The Irony of Vietnam: The System Worked* (Washington, D.C.: Brookings Institution Press, 1979); David Halberstam in *The Best and the Brightest* (New York: Random House, 1972); and Walter Isaacson and Evan Thomas in *The Wise Men: Six Friends and the World They Made* (New York: Touchstone, 1986). For an overview of all these competing models and a somewhat different elitist "business conflict" model, see David Gibbs, *The Political Economy of Third World Intervention: Mines, Money, and U.S. Policy in the Congo Crisis* (Chicago: University of Chicago Press, 1991).

Godfrey Hodgson, in *America in Our Time* (New York: Vintage, 1976), provides an impressive overview of the evolution of American politics since World War II in terms of movement from elitism to pluralism. Likewise, I. M. Destler, Leslie H. Gelb, and Anthony Lake, in *Our Own Worst Enemy: The Unmaking of American Foreign Policy* (New York: Simon and Schuster, 1984), and Hedrick Smith, in *The Power Game* (New York: Ballantine, 1988), emphasize the rise of pluralist politics after the Vietnam War. The classic statements on hyperpluralism remain Grant McConnell, *Private Power and American Democracy* (New York: Vintage, 1966), Theodore J. Lowi, *The End of Liberalism: Ideology, Policy, and the Crisis of Public Authority* (New York: W. W. Norton, 1969), and Hugh Heclo, "Issue Networks and the Executive Establishment," in Anthony King, ed., *The New American Political System* (Washington, D.C.: American Enterprise Institute, 1978), pp. 87–124.

An informative and provocative analysis of the dynamics of continuity and change in American politics can be found in Samuel P. Huntington, *American Politics: The Politics of Disharmony* (Cambridge, Mass.: Harvard University Press, 1981). More theoretical discussions that specifically address the dynamics of foreign policy change are provided by Charles F. Hermann in "Changing Course: When Governments Choose to Redirect Foreign Policy," *International Studies Quarterly* 34 (March 1990), pp. 3–21, and Jerel A. Rosati, Joe D. Hagan, and Martin W. Sampson, eds., *Foreign Policy Restructuring: How Governments Respond to Global Change* (Columbia: University of South Carolina Press, 1994).

Much more difficult to find are works that provide an in-depth analysis of developments within American government and society and their implications for the future of U.S. foreign policy. Good overviews can be found in Randall B. Ripley and James M. Lindsay, eds., *U.S. Foreign Policy After the Cold War* (Pittsburgh: University of Pittsburgh Press, 1997), and James M. Scott, ed., *After the End: Making U.S. Foreign Policy in the Post–Cold War Environment* (Durham, N.C.: Duke University Press, 1998). Jerel Rosati also addresses the political implications of the end of the cold war on presidential power and U.S. leadership abroad in "United States Leadership Into the Next Millennium: A Question of Politics," *International Journal* (spring 1997): 297–315.

KEY TERMS

cyclical patterns of continuity and change
democratic peace theory
direct and indirect influence
elitism
foreign policy change
garrison state
hyperpluralism
incremental change versus major change
networks
politics of change and adjustment
pluralism
republican model
role of chance
status quo politics
synthesis

NOTES

CHAPTER 1

1. On the concept of foreign policy, see Chuck F. Hermann, "Foreign Policy Behavior: That Which Is to Be Explained," in Maurice A. East, Stephen A. Salmore, and Charles F. Hermann, eds., *Why Nations Act* (Beverly Hills: Sage, 1978), pp. 25–47, and James N. Rosenau, "The Study of Foreign Policy," in James N. Rosenau, Gavin Boyd, and Kenneth W. Thompson, eds., *World Politics* (New York: Free Press, 1976), pp. 15–35. Although the concept of foreign policy is defined in reference to governments and, in particular, the United States in this book, it can also be argued that nonstate and nongovernmental actors can be said to have foreign policies, as well (such as individuals or groups, as will be discussed in chapter 16).

2. Roger Hilsman, *To Move a Nation: The Politics of Foreign Policy in the Administration of John F. Kennedy* (New York: Delta, 1964), p. 5.

3. Charles Maechling, Jr., "Foreign Policy-Makers: The Weakest Link?" *Virginia Quarterly Review* 52 (winter 1976): 1.

4. Hilsman, *To Move a Nation*, pp. 4, 5.

5. This definition is from Harold D. Lasswell, *Politics: Who Gets What, When, and How* (New York: McGraw-Hill, 1938). The next two definitions that follow were developed by the author.

6. Hedrick Smith, *The Power Game: How Washington Works* (New York: Ballantine, 1988), p. xvi.

7. See Charles A. Beard, *The Idea of National Interest: An Analytical Study in American Foreign Policy* (New York: Macmillan, 1934), and James N. Rosenau, "The National Interest," in James N. Rosenau, *The Scientific Study of Foreign Policy* (London: Frances Pinter, 1980), pp. 283–93.

8. See Gabriel A. Almond, *The American People and Foreign Policy* (New York: Harcourt Brace, 1950; reprint, New York: Praeger, 1960); Roger Hilsman, *To Move a Nation;* Stanley Hoffmann, *Gulliver's Troubles, or the Setting of American Foreign Policy* (New York: McGraw-Hill, 1968); Samuel P. Huntington, *The Common Defense: Strategic Programs in National Politics* (New York: Columbia University Press, 1961); Charles E. Lindblom, pp. 79–88; "The Science of 'Muddling' Through," *Public Administration Review* 19 (spring 1959); David Braybrooke, *A Strategy of Decision* (Glencoe, Ill.: Free Press, 1963); Richard A. Neustadt, *Presidential Power: The Politics of Leadership* (New York: John Wiley, 1960); Warner R. Schilling, Paul T. Hammond, and Glenn H. Snyder, *Strategy, Politics and Defense Budgets* (New York: Columbia University Press, 1962); and Richard C. Snyder, "A Decision-Making Approach to the Study of Political Phenomena," in R. Young, ed., *Approaches to the Study of Politics* (Evanston, Ill.: Northwestern University Press, 1958), pp. 3–37. On this first wave of policymaking theorists, see Graham Allison, *Essence of Decision: Explaining the Cuban Missile Crisis* (Boston: Little, Brown, 1971), chapter 5, and Robert Art, "Bureaucratic Politics and American Foreign Policy: A Critique," *Policy Sciences* 4 (1973): 467–90.

9. I. M. Destler, Leslie H. Gelb, and Anthony Lake, *Our Own Worst Enemy: The Unmaking of American Foreign Policy* (New York: Simon and Schuster, 1984), p. 20.

10. Smith, *The Power Game*, p. xvi.

11. Ibid., p. xx.

12. Alexander L. George, *Bridging the Gap: Theory and Practice in Foreign Policy* (Washington, D.C., U.S. Institute of Peace, 1993), p. 3. See also Dale R. Herspring, "Practitioners and Political Scientists," *PS: Political Science & Politics* (September 1992): 554–58; for historical perspective, see Stanley Hoffmann, "An American Social Science: International Relations," *Daedalus* 106 (1977): 41–60.

13. Typical examples of primary source documentation include government documents, memoirs, and private papers of individuals.

14. Burton M. Sapin, *The Making of United States Foreign Policy* (New York: Praeger, 1966), p. 1.

15. The conceptual framework revolving around the three perspectives is similar to the "frame of reference" originally suggested by Richard Snyder in his pathbreaking work on decisionmakers and the decisionmaking process operating in an organizational context and affected by various elements of the internal and external setting. See Richard C. Snyder, H. W. Bruck, and Burton Sapin, eds., *Foreign Policy Decision-Making* (Glencoe, Ill.: Free Press, 1962), pp. 14–185. For a similar but more contemporary framework based on systemic, society-centered, and state-centered explanations of contemporary U.S. foreign economic policy, see G. John Ikenberry, David A. Lake, and Michael Mastanduno, eds., "The State and American Foreign Economic Policy," *International Organization* 42 (winter 1988), special issue. For another contemporary effort to bridge the micro-macro problem, see Walter Carlsnaes, "The Agency-Structure Problem in Foreign Policy Analysis," *International Studies Quarterly* 36 (1992): 245–70.

CHAPTER 2

1. A. J. Bacevich, "Charles Beard, Properly Understood," *National Interest* (spring 1994): 75.

2. Albert K. Weinberg, "The Historical Meaning of the American Doctrine of Isolation," *American Political Science Review* 34 (June 1940): 539.

3. Although many of the cases might be considered "minor" incidents, especially from a twenty-first-century perspective, they all involved the "official" use of United States armed forces, involved conflicts with other states, and reflected American interests in much of the world.

4. Gregory H. Nobles, *American Frontiers: Cultural Encounters and Continental Conquest* (New York: Hill and Wang, 1997), p. 54.

5. Ibid., p. 63.

6. See also Fred Anderson, *The Crucible of War: The Seven Years' War and the Fate of Empire in British North America, 1754–1766* (New York: Knopf, 2000). Ian K. Steele, *Warpaths: Invasions of North America* (New York: Oxford University Press, 1994). For a more global perspective, see Eric Wolfe, *Europe and the People Without History* (Berkeley: University of California Press, 1982).

7. Nobles, *American Frontiers*, p. 91.

8. Barbara W. Tuchman, *The First Salute: A View of the American Revolution* (New York: Ballantine, 1988).

9. For a standard orthodox overview of U.S. diplomatic history, see Thomas A. Bailey, *A Diplomatic History of the American People* (Englewood Cliffs, N.J.: Prentice Hall, 1980), and Samuel Flagg Bemis, *A Diplomatic History of the United States* (New York: Holt, Rinehart, and Winston, 1965). For more critical, revisionist accounts, see Walter LaFeber, *The American Age: U.S. Foreign Policy at Home and Abroad Since 1750* (New York: W. W. Norton, 1989), and Thomas G. Paterson, J. Garry Clifford, and Kenneth J. Hagan, *American Foreign Policy, A History* (Lexington, Mass.: D. C. Heath, 1983). Richard W. Van Alstyne, in *The Rising American Empire* (Chicago: Quadrangle Books, 1965), emphasizes the important role of nationalism and expansionism in the history of U.S. foreign policy. An annotated bibliography to the literature is provided by Richard Dean Burns, ed., *Guide to American Foreign Relations Since 1700* (Santa Barbara, Calif.: ABC-Clio, 1983), and Gerald K. Haines and J. Samuel Walker, eds., *American Foreign Relations: A Historiographical Review* (Westport, Conn.: Greenwood Press, 1981).

10. LaFeber, *The American Age*, pp. 11–12.

11. Ibid., p. 12. See also William Earl Weeks, *Building the Continental Empire: American Expansion from the Revolution to the Civil War* (Chicago: Ivan R. Dee, 1996).

12. Nobles, *American Frontiers*, pp. x–xi.

13. Ibid., pp. 93, 94.

14. LaFeber, *The American Age*, p. 10.

15. James M. McPherson, "Big Little Big Horn," *The New Republic* (July 29, 1996), p. 40. But as pointed out by Nobles (*American Frontiers*, pp. 12–13), developments were rather complex. "Euro-Americans [such as the English, French, and later Americans] fought among themselves for control of the continent, and they often enlisted Indian allies to help them defeat fellow Europeans. . . . By the same token, the natives the Europeans lumped together as Indians were in reality a remarkably diverse people encompassing many different cultural and tribal groups. They had different belief systems, different ways of life, and different relationships with Europeans. Like Europeans, they could

be honorable allies or vicious enemies, equally capable of creating beauty and committing atrocity."

16. Nobles, *American Frontiers*, pp. 242, 120.

17. Ibid., p. 15.

18. Richard W. Van Alstyne, *The Rising American Empire* (New York: W. W. Norton, 1974), p. v.

19. Bailey, "America's Emergence as a World Power," pp. 9, 3.

20. Jefferson to Monroe, quoted in Van Alstyne, *The Rising American Empire*, p. 87.

21. Van Alstyne, *The Rising American Empire*, p. 100.

22. Ibid., p. 170.

23. Alfred E. Eckes, Jr., *Opening America's Market: U.S. Foreign Trade Policy Since 1776* (Chapel Hill: University of North Carolina, 1995), p. 1.

24. Ibid., p. 23. For a historical overview, see also Charles P. Kindleberger, "U.S. Foreign Economic Policy, 1776–1976," *Foreign Affairs* (January 1977), pp. 395–417.

25. Van Alstyne, *The Rising American Empire*, p. 126.

26. Richard W. Van Alstyne, *The American Empire: Its Historical Pattern and Evolution* (London: Historical Association, General Series Pamphlet no. 43, 1960), p. 10.

27. Weeks, *Building the Continental Empire*, p. 61. See also Reginald Horseman, *Race and Manifest Destiny* (Cambridge, Mass.: Harvard University Press, 1981); Frederick Merk, *Manifest Destiny and Mission in American History* (New York: Vintage, 1963); Anders Stephanson, *Manifest Destiny: American Expansion and the Empire of Right* (New York: Hill and Wang, 1995).

28. Seward quoted in Van Alstyne, *The Rising American Empire*, p. 146. See also Stephanson, *Manifest Destiny: American Expansion and the Empire of Right*.

29. Van Alstyne, *The Rising American Empire*, p. 166.

30. Ibid., p. 125. See also Emily S. Rosenberg, *Spreading the American Dream: American Economic and Cultural Expansion, 1890–1945* (New York: Hill and Wang, 1982).

31. According to Van Alstyne (*The Rising American Empire*, p. 185), "There has never been a satisfactory explanation as to why this attack took place. The direct order to attack was given, February 25, 1898, by Theodore Roosevelt, who was temporarily occupying the Secretary of the Navy's chair in Washington. This was ten days after the mysterious sinking of the battleship *Maine* in Havana harbour, but nearly two months before the start of hostilities." See also J. Rogers Hollingsworth, ed., *American Expansion in the Late Nineteenth Century: Colonialist or Anticolonialist?* (New York: Holt, Rinehart, and Winston, 1968).

32. See, for example, William Appleman Williams, *The Tragedy of American Diplomacy* (New York: Norton, 1988).

33. William I. Cohen, *Empire Without Tears: America's Foreign Relations, 1921–1933* (New York: Knopf, 1987), p. xii.

34. Cohen, *Empire Without Tears*, p. 54.

35. Ibid., p. 28.

36. Ibid., p. 41.

37. Ibid., xii.

38. The original agreement at Bretton Woods called for the creation of an International Trade Organization (ITO). But due to the opposition of the U.S. Congress, the GATT was

subsequently created in its place. See Richard N. Gardner, *Sterling-Dollar Diplomacy in Current Perspective: The Origins and the Prospects of Our International Economic Order* (New York: Columbia University Press, 1980), and G. John Ikenberry, "A World Economy Restored: Expert Consensus and the Anglo-American Post-War Settlement," *International Organization* 46 (winter 1992): 289–321.

39. A good overview of the literature is provided by Mark A. Stoler, "World War II Diplomacy in Historical Writing: Prelude to Cold War," in Gerald K. Haines and J. Samuel Walker, eds., *American Foreign Relations: A Historiographical Review* (Westport, Conn.: Greenwood Press, 1981), pp. 187–206. See also Robert Dallek, *Franklin Roosevelt and American Foreign Policy, 1932–1945* (Oxford: Oxford University Press, 1979), and John Lewis Gaddis, *The United States and the Origins of the Cold War, 1941–1947* (New York: Columbia University Press, 1972).

40. For standard orthodox accounts of the development of U.S. foreign policy since World War II, see Stephen E. Ambrose and Douglas Brinkley, *Rise to Globalism: American Foreign Policy Since 1938* (Middlesex, England: Penguin Books, 1997); Seyom Brown, *The Faces of Power: Constancy and Change in United States Foreign Policy from Truman to Clinton* (New York: Columbia University Press, 1994); John Lewis Gaddis, *Strategies of Containment: A Critical Appraisal of Postwar American National Security Policy* (Oxford: Oxford University Press, 1982); and Steven W. Hook and John Spanier, *American Foreign Policy Since World War II* (Washington: Congressional Quarterly Press, 2000). For more critical and revisionist accounts, which often integrate economic motives, see Richard J. Barnet, *The Alliance: America-Europe-Japan, Makers of the Postwar World* (New York: Simon and Schuster, 1983); Walter LaFeber, *America, Russia, and the Cold War 1948–1996* (New York: McGraw-Hill, 1997); and James A. Nathan and James K. Oliver, *United States Foreign Policy and World Order* (Glenview, Ill.: Scott, Foresman, 1989).

41. The origins and development of the cold war are a topic of unending interest to scholars. Richard A. Melanson, *Writing History and Making Policy: The Cold War, Vietnam, and Revisionism* (Lanham, Md.: University Press of America, 1983), and J. Samuel Walker, "Historians and Cold War Origins: The New Consensus," in Gerald K. Haines and J. Samuel Walker, eds., *American Foreign Relations: A Historiographical Review* (Westport, Conn.: Greenwood Press, 1981), pp. 207–36, provide excellent literature reviews of the origins of the cold war. They cover the orthodox interpretation that the Soviets caused the cold war, revisionist accounts emphasizing the U.S. role in contributing to the cold war, and postrevisionism, an increasingly popular interpretation that combines orthodox and especially revisionist explanations. Daniel Yergin, a postrevisionist, has written an excellent book, *Shattered Peace: The Origins of the Cold War and the National Security State* (Boston: Houghton Mifflin, 1983), explaining the rise of American cold war beliefs and the national security state in terms of the bureaucratic and domestic politics that dominated the times. See also Melvyn P. Leffler, *A Preponderance of Power: National Security, the Truman Administration, and the Cold War* (Stanford, Calif.: Stanford University Press, 1992).

42. Godfrey Hodgson, *America in Our Time* (New York: Vintage, 1976), p. 32.

43. On the assumptions behind deterrence theory and the global strategy of containment, see Gaddis, *Strategies of Containment;* Alexander L. George and Richard Smoke, *Deterrence in American Foreign Policy: Theory and Practice* (New York: Columbia University Press, 1974); and Bruce W. Jentleson, "American Commitments in the Third World: Theory vs. Practice," *International Organization* 41 (autumn 1987): 667–704. See also Michael Mastanduno, "Strategies of Economic Containment: U.S. Trade Relations with the Soviet Union," *World Politics* 37 (July 1985): 503–31.

44. See, for example, Robert Kuttner, *The End of Laissez-Faire: National Purpose and the Global Economy After the Cold War* (New York: Knopf, 1991); Joan Edelman Spero, *The Politics of International Economic Relations* (New York: St. Martin's Press, 1997).

45. See Yergin, *Shattered Peace,* especially chapter 12. One of the consequences of the distinction between high and low policy is that most scholars of U.S. foreign policy and world politics since World War II, including those cited above, tend to emphasize American national security policy. This has begun to change recently as foreign and international economics have become more prominent. Clearly, it is necessary to integrate both national security and foreign economic policy in order to arrive at a more comprehensive understanding of U.S. foreign policy. This book attempts to integrate both aspects and will discuss both areas of the foreign policy process, though I too am guilty of spending more time on national security issues.

46. See, e.g., Stanley Hoffmann, *Primacy or World Order: American Foreign Policy Since the Cold War* (New York: McGraw-Hill, 1978).

47. See, e.g., Jerel A. Rosati, "Jimmy Carter, A Man Before His Time? The Emergence and Collapse of the First Post–Cold War Presidency," *Presidential Studies Quarterly* 23 (summer 1993): pp. 459–76; Jerel A. Rosati, *The Carter Administration's Quest for Global Community: Beliefs and Their Impact on Behavior* (Columbia: University of South Carolina Press, 1987); and Gaddis Smith, *Morality, Reason, and Power: American Diplomacy in the Carter Years* (New York: Hill and Wang, 1986).

48. Although memoirs, biographies, and articles have been written, few major works have been produced on the Reagan administration's foreign policy. For an insightful analysis of Reagan's foreign policy in the context of the post–Vietnam War years, see Terry L. Deibel, "Reagan's Mixed Legacy," *Foreign Policy* 75 (summer 1989): 34–55; Kenneth A. Oye, "Constrained Confidence and the Evolution of Reagan's Foreign Policy," in Kenneth A. Oye, Robert J. Lieber, and Donald Rothchild, *Eagle Resurgent? The Reagan Era in American Foreign Policy* (Boston: Little, Brown, 1987), pp. 3–39.

49. Charles W. Kegley, Jr., "The Bush Administration and the Future of American Foreign Policy: Pragmatism, or Procrastination?" *Presidential Studies Quarterly* 19 (fall 1989): 730.

50. David Halberstam, War *in a Time of Peace: Bush, Clinton, and the Generals* (New York: Scribner, 2001), pp. 59, 73.

51. Terry L. Deibel, "Bush's Foreign Policy: Mastery and Inaction," Foreign Policy 84 (Fall 1991), p. 3.

52. For an overview of the Clinton administration's initial foreign policy orientation, see, for example, Anthony Lake, "From Containment to Enlargement," U.S. Department of State Dispatch 4:39 (September 27, 1993), pp. 658–64; Owen Harries, "My So-Called Foreign Policy," The New Republic (October 10, 1994), pp. 44–46.; and A National Security Strategy of Engagement and Enlargement (Washington, D.C.: U.S. Government Printing Office, July 1994).

53. See Mark Danner, "Marooned in the Cold War: America, the Alliance, and the Quest for a Vanished World," World Policy Journal (fall 1997): 1–23; Christopher Layne, "From Preponderance to Offshore Balancing: America's Future Grand Strategy," International Security 22 (summer 1997): 86–124; Jerel Rosati, "United States Leadership Into the Next Millennium: A Question of Politics," International Journal (spring 1997): 297–315; Benjamin Schwarz, "The Vision Thing: Sustaining the Unsustainable," World Policy Journal (winter 1994–95): 101–21.

54. Halberstam, War in a Time of Peace, p. 494. See also Condoleezza Rice, "Promoting the National Interest," Foreign Affairs (January–February 2000): 45–62.

55. Rice quoted in Nicholas Lemann, "The Next World Order: The Bush Administration May Have a Brand-New Doctrine of Power," The New Yorker (April 1, 2002), p. 44.

56. Michael Hirsh, "Bush and the World," Foreign Affairs (September–October 2002): 18.

57. Ibid., p. 19.

CHAPTER 3

1. For a general discussion of the underlying impact of the global environment on foreign policy, see Peter Gourevitch, "The Second Image Reversed: The International Sources of Domestic Politics," International Organization 32 (autumn 1978): 881–912; Robert Gilpin, War and Change in World Politics (Cambridge, England: Cambridge University Press, 1981); David A. Lake, Power, Protection, and Free Trade: International Sources of U.S. Commercial Strategy, 1887–1939 (Ithaca, N.Y.: Cornell University Press, 1988); Edward L. Morse, Foreign Policy and Interdependence in Gaullist France (Princeton, N.J.: Princeton University Press, 1973); Robert C. North and Nazli Choucri, "Population, Technology, and Resources in the Future International System," Journal of International Affairs 25 (1971): 224–37; Immanuel Wallerstein, The Capitalist World-Economy (London: Cambridge University Press, 1979); and Kenneth N. Waltz, Man, the State, and War: A Theoretical Analysis (New York: Columbia University Press, 1954).

2. For a general discussion of the immediate impact of international phenomena on foreign policy, see Charles F. Hermann, "International Crises as a Situational Variable," in James N. Rosenau, ed., International Politics and Foreign Policy (New York: Free Press, 1969), pp. 409–21; Richard Ned Lebow, Between

Peace and War: The Nature of International Crisis (Baltimore: John Hopkins University Press, 1981); Arthur A. Stein and Bruce M. Russett, "Evaluating War: Outcomes and Consequences," in Ted R. Gurr, ed., Handbook of Political Conflict: Theory and Research (New York: Free Press, 1980), pp. 399–422; John A. Vasquez, "Domestic Contention on Critical Foreign Policy Issues: The Case of the United States," International Organization 39 (autumn 1985): 643–66; and John A. Vasquez and Richard W. Mansbach, "The Issue Cycle: Conceptualizing Long-Term Global Political Change," International Organization 37 (1983): 257–79.

3. Harold and Margaret Sprout, The Ecological Perspective on Human Affairs (Princeton: Princeton University Press, 1965), p. 11.

4. For an overview of the evolution of Europe, the Soviet Union, and the United States in world politics, see Geoffrey Barraclough, An Introduction to Contemporary History (Middlesex, England: Penguin, 1964); Eric Hobsbawm, The Age of Extremes: A History of the World, 1914–1991 (New York: Vintage, 1994); Torbjorn L. Knutsen, A History of International Relations Theory (Manchester, England: Manchester University Press, 1997); Paul Kennedy, The Rise and Fall of the Great Powers: Economic Change and Military Conflict from 1500 to 2000 (New York: Random House, 1987).

5. See chapter 2 for sources on the origins of the cold war. See also Morris J. Blachman and Donald J. Puchala, "When Empires Meet: The Long Peace in Long-Term Perspective," in Charles W. Kegley Jr., ed., The Long Postwar Peace (New York: Harper Collins, 1991), pp. 177–201.

6. See, for example, R. Harrison Wagner, "What Was Bipolarity?" International Organization 47 (winter 1993): 77–106.

7. Godfrey Hodgson, America in Our Time (New York: Vintage, 1976), p. 19.

8. See, e.g., Simon Bromley, American Hegemony and World Oil: The Industry, the State System, and the World Economy (University Park, Pa.: Pennsylvania State University Press, 1991), and Daniel Yergin, The Prize: The Epic Quest for Oil, Money, and Power (New York: Simon and Schuster, 1991).

9. For a discussion of American hegemony, see Gilpin, War and Change in World Politics; Kennedy, The Rise and Fall of Great Powers; and George Modelski, "The Long Cycle of Global Politics," Comparative Studies in Society and History 20 (April 1978). pp. 214–35. To place this in a broader context, see Donald J. Puchala, "The History of the Future of International Relations," Ethics & International Affairs 8 (1994): 177–202, and "International Encounters of Another Kind," Global Society 11 (1997): 5–29.

10. See, for example, G. John Ikenberry, "Rethinking the Origins of American Hegemony," Political Science Quarterly 104 (fall 1989): 375–400. See also Stephen Gill, American Hegemony and the Trilateral Commission (Cambridge, England: Cambridge University Press, 1990).

11. For an overview of the rise of global pluralism and interdependence, see Seyom Brown, New Forces, Old Forces, and the Future of World Politics (New York: Addison-Wesley, 1997); Thomas L. Friedman, The Lexus and the Olive Tree: Understanding Globalization (New York: Knopf, 2000); Robert O. Keohane and Joseph S. Nye, Jr., Power and Interdependence: World Politics

in Transition (Glenview, Ill.: Scott, Foresman, 1989); Lynn H. Miller, *Global Order: Values and Power in International Politics* (Boulder, Colo.: Westview Press, 1985); Morse, *Foreign Policy and Interdependence;* Kenneth A. Oye, "Beyond Postwar Order and New World Order: American Foreign Policy in Transition," in Kenneth A. Oye, Robert J. Lieber, and Donald Rothchild, eds., *Eagle in a New World: American Grand Strategy in the Post–Cold War Era* (New York: Harper Collins, 1993), pp. 3–33; Joan Edelman Spero, *The Politics of International Economic Relations* (New York: St. Martin's Press, 1997), and Daniel Yergin and Joseph Stanislaw, *The Commanding Heights: The Battle Between Government and the Marketplace That Is Remaking the Modern World* (New York: Simon and Schuster, 1998). For a more critical, Third World perspective, see Paul Harrison, *Inside the Third World* (New York: Penguin, 1993), and Helen Epstein, "Time of Indifference," *New York Review of Books* (April 12, 2001), pp. 33–38.

12. David Morris, "Circumstances Shine on Reagan," *St. Paul Pioneer Press and Dispatch* (July 18, 1988), p. 13A.

13. Stephen D. Krasner, "American Policy and Global Economic Stability," in William P. Avery and David P. Rapkin, eds., *America in a Changing World Political Economy* (New York: Longman, 1982), p. 38.

14. See, for example, Robert Kuttner, *The End of Laissez-Faire: National Purpose and the Global Economy After the Cold War* (New York: Knopf, 1991), and Robert B. Reich, *The Work of Nations: Preparing Ourselves for 21st-Century Capitalism* (New York: Knopf, 1991).

15. Lawrence E. Grinter, "Bargaining Between Saigon and Washington: Dilemmas of Linkage Politics During War," *Orbis* (fall 1974): 837–65.

16. John E. Mueller, "The Search for the 'Breaking Point' in Vietnam: The Statistics of a Deadly Quarrel," *International Studies Quarterly* 24 (December 1980): 497–519.

17. Richard E. Feinberg, *The Intemperate Zone: The Third World Challenge to U.S. Foreign Policy* (New York: W. W. Norton, 1983), p. 34.

18. For an overview of future global prospects and their implications for U.S. foreign policy, see Daniel Bell, "The Future World Disorder," *Foreign Policy* 27 (summer 1977): 109–35; Brown, *New Forces, Old Forces;* James M. Goldgeier and Michael McFaul, "A Tale of Two Worlds: Core and Periphery in the Post-Cold War Era," *International Organization* 46 (spring 1992): 467–91; Paul Kennedy, *Preparing for the Twenty-First Century* (New York: Random House, 1993); Robert Kuttner, *The End of Laissez-Faire;* Michael Howard, "Cold War, Chill Peace," *World Policy Journal* (winter 1993–94): 27–34; William Pfaff, "Redefining World Power," *Foreign Affairs* 70 (America and the World 1990–91): 34–48; John J. Mearsheimer, "Why We Will Soon Miss the Cold War," *Atlantic Monthly* (August 1990): 35–50; John Mueller, *Retreat from Doomsday: The Obsolescence of Major War* (New York: Basic Books, 1989); Nicholas X. Rizopoulos, ed., *Sea-Changes: American Foreign Policy in a World Transformed* (New York: Council on Foreign Relations Press, 1990); Richard Rosecrance, "The Rise of the Virtual State," *Foreign Affairs* (July–August 1996): 45–61.

19. Kennedy, *Rise and Fall of the Great Powers,* p. xv.

20. Ibid., pp. xv–xvi.

21. Ibid., p. 158.

22. Ibid., pp. 514–15.

23. For a less pessimistic view, see Paul Kennedy, "The Next American Century?" *World Policy Journal* (spring 1999), pp. 52–58.

24. Kennedy, *Rise and Fall of the Great Powers,* pp. 533–34, 5.

25. Samuel P. Huntington, "The U.S.—Decline or Renewal?," *Foreign Affairs* (winter 1988–89): 76–96; Samuel P. Huntington, *The Clash of Civilizations and the Remaking of World Order* (New York: Simon and Schuster, 1996); Joseph S. Nye, Jr., *Bound to Lead: The Changing Nature of American Power* (New York: Basic Books, 1990). See also Joseph S. Nye, Jr., "Soft Power," *Foreign Policy* 80 (fall 1990), pp. 153–71; Joseph S. Nye, Jr., "The Changing Nature of World Power," *Political Science Quarterly* 105 (summer 1990), pp. 177–92.

26. Henry R. Nau, *The Myth of America's Decline: Leading the World Economy into the 1990s* (New York: Oxford University Press, 1990), and Richard Rosecrance, *America's Economic Resurgence: A Bold New Strategy* (New York: Harper and Row, 1990). See also Bruce Russett, "The Mysterious Case of Vanishing Hegemony; or, Is Mark Twain Really Dead?," *International Organization* 39 (spring 1985): 207–32.

27. Michael Cox, "September 11th and U.S. Hegemony–Or Will the 21st Century Be American Too?," *International Studies Perspective* (February 2002), pp. 60, 63.

28. Emily Eakin, "All Roads Lead to D.C.," *New York Times* (April 7, 2002).

29. See, for example, Lincoln Bloomfield, "Planning Foreign Policy: Can It Be Done?" *Political Science Quarterly* 93 (fall 1978), pp. 369–92.

30. Torbjorn L, Knutsen, *The Rise and Fall of World Orders* (Manchester, England: Manchester University Press, 1999), pp. 272, 67.

31. Richard K. Betts, "The Soft Underbelly of American Primacy: Tactical Advantages of Terror," *Political Science Quarterly* (spring 2002), pp. 33, 20.

32. Reinhold Niebuhr, "The Foreign Policy of American Conservatism and Liberalism," in *Christian Realism and Political Problems* (New York: Scribner, 1953), p 64; Edward Said, *Orientalism* (New York: Random House, 1978), p. 43; Donald Puchala, "International Encounters of Another Kind," *Global Society* (1997): 5–29, and "Colonization and Cultural Resistance; Egypt and Iran After Alexander," *Global Society* (2002): 7–30.

33. Knutsen, *Rise and Fall of World Orders*, p. 215.

34. J. William Fulbright, *The Arrogance of Power* (New York: Vintage, 1966), p. 9.

CHAPTER 4

1. Stanley Hoffmann, *Gulliver's Troubles, or the Setting of American Foreign Policy* (New York: McGraw-Hill, 1968), p. 289. See also Harold M. Barger, "Suspending Disbelief: The President

in Pre-College Textbooks," *Presidential Studies Quarterly* (winter 1990): 55–70, and Amy Carter and Ryan L. Teten, "Assessing Changing Views of the President: Revisiting Greenstein's *Children and Politics*," *Presidential Studies Quarterly* (September 2002): 453–62.

2. The classic statement on presidential roles is Clinton Rossiter, *The American Presidency* (New York: Harcourt, Brace, Jovanovich, 1960).

3. The civil service was originally created during the 1890s to protect governmental employees from presidential abuse through firing and hiring in order to provide political patronage to presidential supporters—a very common practice at the time.

4. For a general discussion of the paradox of presidential power, see Thomas E. Cronin, *The State of the Presidency* (Boston: Little, Brown, 1975); Godfrey Hodgson, *All Things to All Men: The False Promise of the Modern American Presidency* (New York: Touchstone, 1980); Richard E. Neustadt, *Presidential Power: The Politics of Leadership* (New York: John Wiley, 1960); Richard Pious, *The American Presidency* (New York: Basic Books, 1979); and Hedrick Smith, *The Power Game* (New York: Ballantine, 1988).

5. John F. Kennedy, foreword to Theodore C. Sorensen, *Decision-Making in the White House: The Olive Branch or the Arrows* (New York: Columbia University Press, 1963), p. xii.

6. Harry Truman quoted in, in Hedrick Smith, *The Power Game* (New York: Ballantine, 1988), p. 14.

7. See Dorothy Buckton James, *The Contemporary Presidency* (New York: Pegasus, 1974), chapter 1.

8. On the concept of issue area in foreign policy, see Matthew Evangelista, "Issue Area and Foreign Policy Revisited," *International Organization* 43 (winter 1989): 147–71, and William C. Potter, "Issue Area and Foreign Policy Analysis," *International Organization* 34 (summer 1980).

9. For a general discussion of the presidential life cycle and the crisis of governance, see James MacGregor Burns, The *Power to Lead: The Crisis of the American Presidency* (New York: Simon and Schuster, 1984); John E. Chubb and Paul E. Peterson, eds., *Can the Government Govern?* (Washington, D.C.: Brookings Institution Press, 1989); Stephen D. Hess, *Organizing the Presidency* (Washington, D.C.: Brookings Institution Press, 1976); Hodgson, *All Things to All Men;* Samuel P. Huntington, *American Politics: The Promise of Disharmony* (Cambridge, Mass.: Harvard University Press, 1981); Theodore J. Lowi, *The Personal President: Power Invested, Promise Unfulfilled* (Ithaca, N.Y.: Cornell University Press, 1985); Pious, *The American Presidency;* Smith, *The Power Game;* and James L Sundquist, "The Crisis of Competence in Our National Government," *Political Science Quarterly* 95 (summer 1980): 183–208.

10. Why the term honeymoon? With the election of a new president, as well as a House of Representatives and a Senate composed at least partly of new members, it is as if the president and Congress have become married in their joint effort to govern. So as with any honeymooners, the president and members of Congress go out of their way to be nice to each other, usually resulting in a great deal of early legislative success for the president.

11. David Halberstam, *The Best and Brightest* (New York: Random House, 1969), pp. 424–25.

12. See, for example, Paul Brzce, "The Structure of Presidential Approval: Constraints Within and Across Presidencies," *Journal of Politics* 53 (November 1991): 993–1017; Robine F. Marra, Charles W. Ostrom, Jr., and Dennis M. Simon, "Foreign Policy and Presidential Popularity: Creating Windows of Opportunity in the Perpetual Election," *Journal of Conflict Resolution* 34 (December 1990): 588–623; and John E. Mueller, "Presidential Popularity from Truman to Johnson," *American Political Science Review* 64 (1970): 18–34.

13. Lyndon B. Johnson quoted in Smith, *The Power Game,* p. 333.

14. See, for example, Richard A. Brody, *Assessing the President: The Media, Elite Opinion, and Public Support* (Stanford: Stanford University Press, 1991).

15. Halberstam, *The Best and the Brightest,* pp. 64–65.

16. For a conceptual discussion of the domestic and international sources of the modern crisis of governance, see Michel Crozier, Samuel P. Huntington, and Joji Watanuki, *The Crisis of Democracy* (New York: New York University Press, 1975); Edward L. Morse, *Foreign Policy and Interdependence in Gaullist France* (Princeton: Princeton University Press, 1973); and Harold and Margaret Sprout, "The Dilemma of Rising Demands and Insufficient Resources," *World Politics* 20 (1968): 660–93. The paradox of presidential power and the crisis of governance are not unique to the present time but have been a staple of American history. See James MacGregor Burns, *The Deadlock of Democracy: Four-Party Politics in America* (Englewood Cliffs, N.J.: Prentice-Hall, 1963); Huntington, *American Politics;* and Arthur Schlesinger, Jr., *The Imperial Presidency* (New York, Houghton Mifflin, 1989). On divided government, see Michael Laver and Kenneth A. Shepsle, "Divided Government: America Is Not 'Exceptional,'" *Governance* 4 (July 1991): 250–69.

17. Schlesinger, *The Imperial Presidency.*

18. Aaron Wildavsky, "The Two Presidencies Thesis," *Transaction* 4 (1966): 7–14. For a general assessment, see Steven A. Shull, ed., *The Two Presidencies: A Quarter Century Assessment* (Chicago: Nelson-Hall, 1991).

19. See, for example, Godfrey Hodgson, *America in Our Time* (New York: Vintage, 1976), chapter 5, and J. Richard Piper, "Situational Constitutionalism and Presidential Power: The Rise and Fall of the Liberal Model of Presidential Government," *Presidential Studies Quarterly* 24 (1994): 577–94.

20. See, for example, Hodgson, *America in Our Time;* Ernst R. May, "The U.S. Government, a Legacy of the Cold War," *Diplomatic History* 16 (spring 1992): 269–77; and Daniel Yergin, *Shattered Peace: The Origins of the Cold War and the National Security State* (Boston: Houghton Mifflin, 1983).

21. For a superb discussion of the impediments on presidential power in foreign policy during the cold war years, see Roger Hilsman, *To Move a Nation: The Politics of Foreign Policy in the Administration of John F. Kennedy* (New York: Delta, 1964), and Hoffmann, *Gulliver's Troubles.*

22. See Bayless Manning, "The Congress, The Executive, and Intermestic Affairs: Three Proposals," *Foreign Affairs* 55 (1977): 306–22.

23. See Duane M. Oldfield and Aaron Wildavsky, "Reconsidering the Two Presidencies," *Society* (July–August 1989): 54–59; Brandon C. Prins and Bryan W. Marshall, "Congressional Support of the President: A Comparison of Foreign, Defense, and Domestic Policy Making during and after the Cold War," *Presidential Studies Quarterly* (December 2001), pp. 660–78; Scot Schraufnagel and Stephen M. Shellman, "The Two Presidencies, 1984–98: A Replication and Extension," *Presidential Studies Quarterly* (December 2001), pp. 699–707; and Shull, *The Two Presidencies.* For a general discussion of the paradox of presidential power in foreign affairs, see also I. M. Destler, Leslie H. Gelb, and Anthony Lake, *Our Own Worst Enemy: The Unmaking of American Foreign Policy* (New York: Simon and Schuster, 1984), and Thomas E. Mann, "Making Foreign Policy: President and Congress," in Thomas E. Mann, ed., *A Question of Balance: The President, The Congress and Foreign Policy* (Washington, D.C.: Brookings Institution Press, 1990), pp. 1–34.

24. For a discussion of the importance of presidential leadership, see James MacGregor Burns, *Presidential Government: The Crucible of Leadership* (New York: Avon, 1965); Erwin Hargrove, *Jimmy Carter as President: Leadership and the Politics of the Public Good* (Baton Rouge: Louisiana State University Press, 1988); Barbara Kellerman, *The Political Presidency: Practice of Leadership* (New York: Oxford University Press, 1984); Lowi, *The Personal President;* Stephen Skowronek, *The Politics Presidents Make: Leadership from John Adams to George Bush* (Cambridge, Mass.: Harvard University Press, 1993). For a general overview of the significance and basis of leadership in political affairs, see James MacGregor Burns, *Leadership* (New York: Harper Torchbooks, 1978).

25. Richard E. Neustadt, *Presidential Power: The Politics of Leadership* (New York: John Wiley, 1960). Since its initial publication, it has been periodically revised with additional reflections on more current presidents.

26. Smith, *The Power Game,* p. 56.

27. See, for example, James David Barber, *The Presidential Character: Predicting Performance in the White House* (Englewood Cliffs, N.J.: Prentice-Hall, 1972); Erwin C. Hargrove, *The Power of the Modern Presidency* (New York: Knopf, 1974), chapter 2; and Doris Kearns, *Lyndon Johnson and the American Dream* (New York: New American Library, 1976).

28. George E. Reedy, *The Twilight of the Presidency* (New York: New American Library, 1970), p. 197.

29. Richard M. Pious, *The American Presidency* (New York: Basic Books, 1979), p. 47. See also Daniel P. Franklin, *Extraordinary Measures: The Exercise of Prerogative Powers in the United States* (Pittsburgh: University of Pittsburgh Press, 1991).

30. See, for example, James MacGregor Burns, *The Crosswinds of Freedom* (New York: Vintage, 1989), and William E. Leuchtenburg, *In the Shadow of FDR: From Harry Truman to Ronald Reagan* (Ithaca, N.Y.: Cornell University Press, 1985).

31. See Schlesinger, *The Imperial Presidency,* and Reedy, *The Twilight of the Presidency.*

32. Vietnamization was the American strategy of withdrawing American ground forces from Vietnam while training, equipping, and supporting the South Vietnamese army to carry the burden of fighting the war, as it did during the Eisenhower administration.

33. Although the House Judiciary Committee voted three counts of impeachment against President Nixon, the Senate never voted whether to convict Nixon on any of the counts for which he resigned from office.

34. See John Whiteclay Chambers II, "Jimmy Carter's Public Policy Ex-Presidency," *Political Science Quarterly* (fall 1998): 405–25; Mark J. Rozell, "Carter Rehabilitated," *Presidential Studies Quarterly* 5 (spring 1993): 317–30.

35. See Glenn P. Hastedt and Anthony J. Eksterowicz, "Presidential Leadership in the Post Cold War Era," *Presidential Studies Quarterly;* Jerel A. Rosati, "United States Leadership Into the Next Millennium: A Question of Politics," *International Journal* (spring 1997): 297–315.

36. See Jerel A. Rosati, "The Domestic Environment," in Peter A. Schraeder, ed., *Intervention Into the 1990s: United States Foreign Policy in the Third World* (Boulder, Colo.: Lynne Rienner, 1992), pp. 175–91, and Rosati, "United States Leadership Into the Next Millennium."

37. Destler, Lake, and Gelb, *Our Own Worst Enemy,* p. 13.

38. Alexander L. George, "Domestic Constraints on Regime Change in U.S. Foreign Policy: The Need for Policy Legitimacy," in Ole R. Holsti, Randolph Siverson, and Alexander L. George, eds., *Change in the International System* (Boulder, Colo.: Westview Press, 1980), p. 236.

39. For an overview of the Clinton administration's initial foreign policy orientation, see, for example, Anthony Lake, "From Containment to Enlargement," U.S. Department of State Dispatch 4:39 (September 27, 1993): 658–64; Owen Harries, "My So-Called Foreign Policy," *The New Republic* (October 10, 1994), 44–46; *A National Security Strategy of Engagement and Enlargement* (Washington, D.C.: U.S. Government Printing Office, July 1994).

40. See Jeffrey E. Cohen, "The Polls: Change and Stability in Public Assessments of Personal Traits: Bill Clinton, 1993–99," *Presidential Studies Quarterly* (December 2001): 733–41.

41. Jack H. Watson, Jr., "The Clinton White House," *Presidential Studies Quarterly* (1993): 431.

42. Fred I. Greenstein, "The Presidential Leadership Style of Bill Clinton: An Early Appraisal," *Political Science Quarterly* 108 (winter 1993–94): 592. See also Fred I. Greenstein, "The Two Leadership Styles of William Jefferson Clinton," *Political Psychology* 15 (June 1994): 351–62.

43. See James Carney and John F. Dickerson, "Inside the Mind of the CEO President," *Time* (August 5, 2002); Michael Duffy, "Better Late Than Never," *Time* (April 15, 2002); Glenn Kessler, "Swell of Foreign Support Goes Flat," *Washington Post* (August 31, 2002); Ryan Lizza, "White House Watch: World Away," *The New Republic* (July 22, 2002); Karen DeYoung and Walter Pincus, "Crises Strain Bush Policies," *Washington Post* (April 21, 2002).

CHAPTER 5

1. For a general overview of the federal bureaucracy, see Hugh Heclo, *A Government of Strangers: Executive Politics in Washington* (Washington, D.C.: Brookings, 1977); Harold Seidman, *Politics, Position and Power: The Dynamics of Federal Organization* (New York: Oxford University Press, 1980); and James Q. Wilson, *Bureaucracy: What Government Agencies Do and Why They Do It* (New York: Basic Books, 1989). Especially for a focus of the importance of size, see Richard Holbrooke, "The Machine That Fails," *Foreign Policy* (winter 1970–71), 65–77.

2. Edward Morse, *Foreign Policy and Interdependence,* chapters 1–2.

3. Raymond F. Hopkins, "Global Management Networks: The Internationalization of Domestic Bureaucracies," *International Social Science Journal* 30 (1978): 31–45. See also the special issue of *International Organization* (winter 1992) for a related discussion of "epistemic communities" in international networks.

4. Morse, *Foreign Policy and Interdependence,* p. 37.

5. Charles Maechling, Jr., "Foreign Policy-Makers: The Weakest Link?" *Virginia Quarterly Review* 52 (winter 1976): 6.

6. Ibid., p. 2.

7. For an overview of presidential management of the executive branch, see, for example, George C. Edwards III and Stephen J. Wayne, *Presidential Leadership: Politics and Policy Making* (New York: St. Martin's Press, 1990), and Richard M. Pious, *The American Presidency* (New York: Basic Books, 1996). For a focus on the making of U.S. foreign policy, especially in the post–cold war era, see Randall B. Ripley and James M. Lindsay, eds., *U.S. Foreign Policy After the Cold War* (Pittsburgh: University of Pittsburgh Press, 1997), and James M. Scott, ed., *After the End: Making U.S. Foreign Policy in the Post–Cold War Environment* (Durham, N.C.: Duke University Press, 1998).

8. See John P. Burke, "Lessons from Past Presidential Transitions: Organization, Management, and Decision Making," *Presidential Studies Quarterly* (March 2001): 5–24.

9. William B. Quandt, *Peace Process: American Diplomacy and the Arab-Israeli Conflict Since 1967* (Berkeley and Los Angeles: University of California Press, 1996).

10. See David B. Cohen, Chris J. Dolan, and Jerel Rosati, "A Place at the Table: The Emerging Roles of the White House Chief of Staff," *Congress & the Presidency* (Autumn 2002); Charles E. Walcott, Shirley Anne Warshaw, and Stephen J. Wayne, "The Chief of Staff," *Presidential Studies Quarterly* (September 2001): 464–89.

11. See, for example, Bradley H. Patterson and James P. Pfiffner, "The White House Office of Presidential Personnel," *Presidential Studies Quarterly* (September 2001): 415–38.

12. Douglas Jehl, "High-Level Grumbing Over Pace of Appointments," *New York Times* (February 25, 1993), p. A8; David E. Rosenbaum, "80% of Senior Positions Under Bush Still Empty," *New York Times* (May 13, 1989), p. 9.

13. David Halberstam, *The Best and the Brightest* (New York: Random House, 1969), p. 456.

14. See, for example, Alexander L. George, *Presidential Decisionmaking in Foreign Policy: The Effective Use of Information and Advice* (Boulder, Colo.: Westview Press, 1980).

15. See, for example, I. M. Destler, *Presidents, Bureaucrats, and Foreign Policy* (Princeton: Princeton University Press, 1972).

16. For an overview of the National Security Council, see I. M. Destler, "National Security Advice to U.S. Presidents: Some Lessons from Thirty Years," *World Politics* (January 1977): 143–76; Karl F. Inderfurth and Lock K. Johnson, eds., *Decisions of the Highest Order: Perspectives on the National Security Council* (Pacific Grove, Calif.: Brooks/Cole, 1988); Mark M. Lowenthal, *The National Security Council: Organizational History* (Washington, D.C.: Congressional Research Service, June 27, 1978); Kevin V. Mulcahy and Harold F. Kendrick, "The National Security Adviser: A Presidential Perspective," in Colin Campbell and Margaret Jane Wyszomirsky, eds. *Executive Leadership in Anglo-American Systems* (Pittsburgh: University of Pittsburgh Press, 1991), pp. 259–79; and United States Senate, Committee on Foreign Relations, *The National Security Adviser: Role and Accountability,* Hearings (96th Cong., 2nd sess., April 17, 1980).

17. Actually, according to the original National Security Act, the president could designate the secretaries of the executive departments, the chairman of the Munitions Board, and the chairman of the Research and Development Board to participate "from time to time." Other individuals could not be designated by the president to participate in the National Security Council "until the advice and consent of the Senate has been given" (United States, *The National Security Act of 1947,* Public Law 253 [80th Cong. 1st sess., July 26, 1947]).

18. I. M. Destler, Leslie H. Gelb, and Anthony Lake, *Our Own Worst Enemy: The Unmaking of American Foreign Policy* (New York: Simon and Schuster, 1984). See also William P. Bundy, "The National Security Process: Plus Ca Change?" *International Security* (winter 1982–1983): 94–109; I. M. Destler, *Presidents, Bureaucrats, and Foreign Policy;* I. M. Destler, "The Rise of the National Security Assistant, 1961–1981," in Charles W. Kegley, Jr., and Eugene R. Wittkopf, eds., *Perspectives on American Foreign Policy: Selected Readings* (New York: St. Martin's Press, 1983), pp. 260–81.

19. Destler, Gelb, and Leak, *Our Own Worst Enemy,* p. 172.

20. Maechling, "Foreign Policy-Makers," p. 3.

21. For an overview of the foreign policy process under presidents Nixon and Ford, see Seymour H. Hersh, *The Price of Power: Kissinger in the Nixon White House* (New York: Summit Books, 1983); Marvin Kalb and Bernard Kalb, *Kissinger* (New York: Dell, 1974); Henry Kissinger, *White House Years* (Boston: Little, Brown, 1979); Roger Morris, *Uncertain Greatness: Henry Kissinger and American Foreign Policy* (New York: Harper and Row, 1977); and John Newhouse, *Cold Dawn: The Story of SALT* (New York: Holt, Rinehart and Winston, 1973).

22. For an overview of the Carter administration's foreign policy process, see Zbigniew Brzezinski, *Power and Principle: Memoirs of the National Security Adviser, 1977–1981* (New York: Farrar, Straus and Giroux, 1983); Hamilton Jordan, *Crisis: The Last Year of the Carter Presidency* (New York: G. P. Putnam's

Sons, 1982); Alexander Moens, *Foreign Policy Under Carter: Testing Multiple Advocacy Decision Making* (Boulder, Colo.: Westview Press, 1990); Jerel A. Rosati, *The Carter Administration's Quest for Global Community: Beliefs and Their Impact on Behavior* (Columbia: University of South Carolina Press, 1987); and Cyrus Vance, *Hard Choices: Critical Years in America's Foreign Policy* (New York: Simon and Schuster, 1983).

23. Resignations based on principle have become quite rare in U.S. government service. The last principled resignation by a secretary of state occurred under Woodrow Wilson. William Jennings Bryan resigned over the administration's response to the sinking of the *Lusitania,* and Robert Lansing, Bryan's replacement, resigned because of policy differences with Wilson over the Versailles Treaty.

24. For an overview of the foreign policy process under President Reagan, see Alexander Haig, *Caveat: Realism, Reagan, and Foreign Policy* (New York: Macmillan, 1984); Hedrick Smith, *The Power Game: How Washington Works* (New York: Ballantine, 1988); and Tower Commission (President's Special Review Board), *The Tower Commission Report* (New York: Bantam, 1987).

25. Clark, first appointed deputy secretary of state and then national security adviser, had virtually no knowledge about foreign policy and world affairs but was a close friend and long-time confidant of Ronald Reagan. During the Senate confirmation hearings, for example, Clark was unable to recognize the names of many important foreign leaders.

26. With William Clark's resignation as national security adviser and appointment as secretary of the interior in 1983, Chief of Staff James Baker attempted to have President Reagan select him as national security adviser, with Michael Deaver becoming the chief of staff. The Baker-Deaver plan was vehemently opposed by Clark and Secretary of Defense Weinberger, who preferred United Nations Ambassador Jeane Kirkpatrick for the NSC job and set off a political storm in the Reagan administration. Eventually, Robert McFarlane, Clark's more moderate deputy, became the compromise choice for the position of national security adviser. See Smith, *The Power Game*, pp. 317–21.

27. For an overview of the foreign policy process in the Bush administration, see, for example, Kevin V. Mulcahy, "The Bush Administration and National Security Policy-Making: A Preliminary Assessment," *Governance* (April 1991): 207–20.

28. Terry L. Deibel, "Bush's Foreign Policy: Mastery and Inaction," *Foreign Policy* 84 (fall 1991): 5.

29. Christopher quoted in Thomas Friedman and Elaine Sciolino, "Clinton and Foreign Issues; Spasms of Attention," *New York Times* (March 22, 1993), p. A3. For an overview of the Clinton foreign policy strategy, see Vincent A. Auger, "The National Security Council System After the Cold War," in Ripley and Lindsay, *U.S. Foreign Policy After the Cold War*, pp. 42–73; Jacob Heibrunn, "Lake Inferior," *The New Republic* (September 20 and 27, 1993), pp. 29–35; Jacob Heilbrum, "Mr. Nice Guy: Sandy Berger's Sunny Foreign Policy," *The New Republic* (April 13, 1999); Bob Woodward, *The Agenda: Inside the Clinton White House* (Simon and Schuster, 1994).

30. David Halberstam, *War in a Time of Peace: Bush, Clinton, and the Generals* (New York: Scribner, 2001), p. 193.

31. See Richard L. Berke and David E. Sanger, "Some in Administration Grumble as Aide's Role Seems to Expand," *New York Times* (May 17, 2002); Howard Fineman and Martha Brant, "This is Our Life Now," *Newsweek* (December 3, 2001); Larence F. Kaplan, "Torpedo Boat: How Bush Turned on Arafat," *The New Republic* (February 18, 2002); Alan Sipress, "Policy Divide Thwarts Powell in Mideast Effort," *Washington Post* (April 29, 2002); Evan Thomas, "Chemistry in the War Cabinet," *Newsweek* (January 28, 2002); Evan Thomas, "He Has Saddam in His Sights," *Newsweek* (March 4, 2002); Karen DeYoung and Steven Mufson, "Leaner, Less Visible NSC Taking Shape," *Washington Post* (February 10, 2001).

32. Bob Woodward, *Bush At War* (New York: Simon and Schuster, 2002).

CHAPTER 6

1. For a general overview of bureaucracy, see Morton H. Halperin, *Bureaucratic Politics and Foreign Policy* (Washington, D.C.: Brookings Institution Press, 1974); Hugh Heclo, *A Government of Strangers: Executive Politics in Washington* (Washington, D.C.: Brookings Institution Press, 1977); Harold Seidman, *Politics, Position and Power: The Dynamics of Federal Organization* (New York: Oxford University Press, 1980); and James Q. Wilson, *Bureaucracy: What Government Agencies Do and Why They Do It* (New York: Basic Books, 1989).

2. For an overview of the State Department, see John Franklin Campbell, *The Foreign Affairs Fudge Factory* (New York: Basic Books, 1971); Anthony Lake, *Somoza Falling* (Boston: Houghton Mifflin, 1989); Barry Rubin, *Secrets of State: The State Department and the Struggle Over U.S. Foreign Policy* (New York: Oxford University Press, 1985); and Burton M. Sapin, *The Making of United States Foreign Policy* (New York: Praeger, 1966).

3. Tim Zimmerman, "Twilight of the Diplomats," *U.S. News & World Report* (January 27, 1997), pp. 48–50.

4. U.S. Department of State, "Department Commemorates 200th Anniversary," *Update* (September–October 1989); U.S. *Statistical Abstract of the United States* (Washington, D.C.: U.S. Government Printing Office, 1997).

5. For an overview, see Robert Hopkins Miller, *Inside an Embassy: The Political Role of Diplomats Abroad* (Washington, D.C.: Congressional Quarterly Press, 1992), and U.S. Congress, General Accounting Office, *State Department: Survey of Administrative Issues Affecting Embassies* (July 1993).

6. See Dick Kirschten, "Rescuing AID," *National Journal* (October 2, 1993): 2369–72; U.S. Congress, Congressional Budget Office, *The Role of Foreign Aid in Development* (May 1997); U.S. Congress, Congressional Research Service, *Foreign Assistance: A Profile of the Agency for International Development* (April 1992); U.S. Agency for International Development, *USAID's Strategies for Sustainable Development* (August 2, 1997).

7. For an overview, see Kim Andrew Elliott, "Too Many Voices of America," *Foreign Policy* 77 (winter 1989–90): 113–31; Richard N. Gardner, "Selling America in the Marketplace of Ideas," *New York Times Magazine* (March 20, 1983), pp. 44, 58–61; Allen C. Hansen, *U.S. Information Agency: Public Diplomacy in the Computer Age* (New York: Praeger, 1984); Sig Mickelson, *America's Other Voice: The Story of Radio Free Europe and Radio Liberty* (New York: Praeger, 1983); and John Spicer Nichols, "Wasting the Propaganda Dollar," *Foreign Policy* 56 (fall 1984): 129–40.

8. For an overview, see Gardner, "Selling America in the Marketplace of Ideas," and Hansen, *U.S. Information Agency.*

9. U.S. Congress, General Accounting Office, *Exchange Programs: Inventory of International Educational, Cultural, and Training Programs* (June 1993); United States Information Agency, *U.S. Government International Exchange and Training Activities* (1990).

10. Howard LaFranchi, "In PR War, US Gets Ready to Turn Up Volume," *Christian Science Monitor* (November 1, 2001), www.csmonitor.com; U.S. Congress, General Accounting Office, *TV Martí: Costs and Compliance with Broadcast Standards and International Agreements* (May 1992); U.S. Congress, General Accounting Office, *Voice of America: Management Actions Needed to Adjust to a Changing Environment* (July 1992).

11. Gardner, "Selling America," p. 44.

12. See Elaine Sciolino, "Friends as Ambassadors: How Many Is Too Many?" *New York Times* (November 7, 1989), pp. 1, 6; and U.S. Congress, Senate, Committee on Foreign Relations, *The Ambassador in U.S. Foreign Policy: Changing Patterns in Roles, Selection, and Designations* (97th Cong., 1st sess., July 1981).

13. See, for example, Halperin, *Bureaucratic Politics and Foreign Policy;* Hugh Heclo, "The In-and-Outer System," *Political Science Quarterly* (spring 1988): 37–56; and Bert A. Rockman, "America's Department of State: Irregular and Regular Syndromes of Policy Making," *American Political Science Review* (December 1981): 911–27.

14. Wilson, *Bureaucracy*, p. 91. See also Andrew M. Scott, "The Department of State: Formal Organization and Informal Culture," *International Studies Quarterly* (March 1969): 1–18; and the classic by William Whyte, *The Organization Man* (New York: Simon and Schuster, 1956).

15. See Duncan Clarke, "Why State Can't Lead," *Foreign Policy* (spring 1987): 128–42; I. M. Destler, *Presidents, Bureaucrats, and Foreign Policy* (Princeton: Princeton University Press, 1972); Robert Pringle, "Creeping Irrelevance at Foggy Bottom," *Foreign Policy* 29 (fall 1977): 128–39; Rockman, "America's Department of State"; Rubin, *Secrets of State;* Scott, "The Department of State"; and U.S. Department of State, *Diplomacy for the 70's: A Program of Management Reform for the Department of State* (December 1970). For an informal perspective from a junior officer in the foreign service, see Harry Crosby (a pseudonym), "Too At Home Abroad: Swilling Beer, Licking Boots, and Ignoring the Natives with One of Jim Baker's Finest," *Washington Monthly* (September 1991), pp. 16–20.

16. For a more in-depth discussion, see Martin Weil, *A Pretty Good Club* (New York: W. W. Norton, 1978).

17. See, for example, Robert D. Kaplan, *The Arabists: The Romance of an American Elite* (New York: Free Press, 1994).

18. See, for example, B. Drummond Ayres, Jr., "A New Breed of Diplomat," *New York Times Magazine* (September 11, 1983), pp. 66–67, 70–73, 105, and William I. Bacchus, *Staffing for Foreign Affairs: Personnel Systems for the 1980's and 1990's* (Princeton: Princeton University Press, 1983).

19. The example of Somalia was drawn from the author's personal experience. I was there as part of a USIA grant that funded a University of South Carolina–Somali National University Linkage Program, intended to develop an international studies curriculum and program within Somalia. The American governmental presence consisted of over one hundred official personnel, primarily from the Agency for International Development, but also from the Defense Department, State Department, and USIA (and the covert CIA). Only one American spoke Somali—the everyday language of the people. A young female foreign service information officer with USIA became fluent in Somali and developed a special relationship with many of the Somali people. Near the end of her three-year tour, she requested to stay in Somalia so she could put her language and Somali expertise to use. The State Department and USIA declined her request and posted her to the highly prestigious London embassy. See also John W. Tuthill, "What Can Be Done at Foggy Bottom: Operation Topsy," *Foreign Policy* 8 (fall 1972): 62–85.

20. David Halberstam, *The Best and the Brightest* (New York: Random House, 1969), p. 390.

21. See Halberstam, *The Best and the Brightest;* E. J. Kahn, Jr., *The China Hands: America's Foreign Service Officers and What Befell Them* (New York: Viking Press, 1972); Robert P. Newman, *Owen Lattimore and the "Loss" of China* (Berkeley and Los Angeles: University of California, 1992).

22. In Destler, *Presidents, Bureaucrats, and Foreign Policy,* p. 154, and Halberstam, *The Best and the Brightest*, p. 299.

23. For an overview of this perspective, see note 15.

24. John Owens, "The U.S. Foreign Service: An Institution in Crisis," *Mediterranean Quarterly* (summer 1991): 27–50. For a more optimistic view, see Strobe Talbott, "Globalization and Diplomacy: A Practitioner's Perspective," *Foreign Policy* (fall 1997): 69–83.

25. U.S. Department of State, *State 2000: A New Model for Managing Foreign Affairs* (December 1992), pp. 79–80.

CHAPTER 7

1. For a comprehensive historical overview, see Allan R. Millett and Peter Maslowski, *For the Common Defense: A Military History of the United States of America* (New York: Free Press, 1985); Geoffrey Perret, *A Country Made by War: From the Revolution to Vietnam—The Story of America's Rise to Power* (New York: Vintage, 1990).

2. U.S. House of Representatives, Committee on International Relations, *Background Information on the Use of U.S. Armed*

Forces in Foreign Countries, Committee Print (94th Cong., 1st sess., 1975), pp. 58–66.

3. U.S. Senate, Committee on Foreign Relations, *United States Foreign Policy Objectives and Overseas Military Installations,* Committee Print (96th Cong. 1st sess., 1989).

4. Carl E. Vuono, "Desert Storm and the Future of Conventional Forces," *Foreign Affairs* (spring 1991): 55.

5. *Statistical Abstract of the United States: 2001* (Washington, D.C.: U.S. Government Printing Office, 2001); U.S. Office of Assistant Secretary of Defense, *Military Strength Figures* (March 31, 2002).

6. See, for example, U.S. Congress, Congressional Budget Office, *The Costs and Benefits of Retail Activities at Military Bases* (October 1997).

7. Barry M. Blechman and Stephen S. Kaplan, *Force Without War: U.S. Armed Forces as a Political Instrument* (Washington, D.C.: Brookings Institution Press, 1978).

8. See James Coates and Michael Kilian, *Heavy Losses: The Dangerous Decline of American Defense* (New York: Penguin, 1985); Edward N. Luttwak, *The Pentagon and the Art of War* (New York: Simon and Schuster, 1985); and Mark Perry, *Four Stars* (Boston: Houghton Mifflin, 1989)

9. The commandant of the Marine Corps was not added to the JCS until 1958, when the National Security Act was amended; the vice chair was added in 1987 with the Goldwater-Nichols Act.

10. See, for example, Perry, *Four Stars.*

11. David C. Jones, "What's Wrong With Our Defense Establishment," *New York Times Magazine* (November 7, 1982), p. 79. See also Lawrence J. Korb, "The Budget Process in the Department of Defense, 1947–1977: The Strengths and Weaknesses of Three Systems," *Public Administration Review* (July–August 1977): 334–46.

12. For the modern origins of the different functions of the services and interservice rivalry, see Morton H. Halperin and David Halperin, "The Key West Key," *Foreign Policy* 53 (winter 1983–1984): 114–30.

13. Hadley, Arthur T. "Military Coup: The Reform that Worked." *The New Republic.* Jan 18, 1988 v198, n3 pgs. 17–20.

14. See Richard K. Betts, *Soldiers, Statesmen, and Cold War Crises* (Cambridge, Mass.: Harvard University Press, 1977), pp. 128–34.

15. See also, Larry Berman, *Lyndon Johnson's War: The Road to Stalemate in Vietnam* (New York: W.W. Norton, 1989).

16. Jones, "What's Wrong With Our Defense Establishment."

17. Harry G. Summers, Jr., *On Strategy: A Critical Analysis of the Vietnam War* (Novato, Calif.: Presidio, 1982).

18. Andrew F. Krepinevich, Jr., *The Army and Vietnam* (Baltimore: Johns Hopkins University Press, 1986), p. 171. See also D. Michael Shafer, *Deadly Paradigms: The Failure of U.S. Counterinsurgency Policy* (Princeton: Princeton University Press, 1988).

19. Mark Clodfelter, *The Limits of Air Power: The American Bombing of North Vietnam* (New York: Free Press, 1989).

20. Luttwak, *The Pentagon and the Art of War,* p. 17.

21. Peter J. Roman and David W. Tarr, "The Joint Chiefs of Staff: From Service Parochialism to Jointness," *Political Science Quarterly* (spring 1998): 91–122.

22. Ibid., pp. 99–102.

23. Ibid. p. 104.

24. Dana Priest, "The Proconsuls," *Washington Post,* three part series (September 28, 29, and 30, 2000).

25. Bernard E. Trainor, "Flaws in Panama Attack," *New York Times* (December 31, 1989), pp. 1, 6.

26. See "An Accident-Prone Army," *Newsweek* (November 5, 1990), p. 7, and Douglas Jehl and Bob Secter, "U.S., Noriega Both Found Invasion Surprises," *Los Angeles Times* (December 27, 1989), pp. A1, A6, A10.

27. Eliot A. Cohen, "After the Battle," *New Republic* (April 1, 1991), p. 22. See also Stephen Biddle, "Victory Misunderstood: What the Gulf War Tells Us About the Future of Conflict," *International Security* (fall 1996): 139–79; Gregg Easterbrook, "Operation Desert Shill," *New Republic* (September 30, 1991), pp. 32–42; U.S. House of Representatives, Committee on Armed Services, *Defense for a New Era: Lessons of the Persian Gulf War* (Washington, D.C.: U.S. Government Printing Office, 1992).

28. U.S. Congress, General Accounting Office, *National Guard: Peacetime Training Did Not Adequately Prepare Combat Brigades for Gulf War* (September 1991); U.S., Congress, General Accounting Office, *Operation Desert Shield: Problems Encountered by Activated Reservists* (September 1991).

29. See David Halberstam, *War in a Time of Peace: Bush, Clinton, and the Generals* (New York: Scribner, 2001).

30. See, Carl Kenneth Allard, Jr., *Command, Control and the Common Defense* (New Haven: Yale University Press, 1990); Betts, *Soldiers, Statesmen, and Cold War Crises;* Coates and Kilian, *Heavy Losses;* James Fallows, *National Defense* (New York: Vintage, 1981); Arthur T. Hadley, *The Straw Giant, Triumph and Failure: America's Armed Forces* (New York: Random House, 1986); Jones, "What's Wrong with Our Defense Establishment"; Luttwak, *The Pentagon and the Art of War;* Clark R. Mollenhoff, *The Pentagon* (New York: Pinnacle Books, 1967); and Adam Yarmolinsky, *The Military Establishment: Its Impacts on American Society* (New York: Harper and Row, 1971).

31. See U.S. Congress, General Accounting Office, *Department of Defense: Professional Military Education at the Four Intermediate Service Schools* (June 1991); U.S. Congress, General Accounting Office, *Department of Defense: Professional Military Education at the Three Senior Service Schools* (June 1991).

32. For a good overview of the role of technology and the rise of military managers in Western history, see Martin van Creveld, *Technology and War: From 2000 BC to the Present* (New York: Macmillan, 1989).

33. See also Vincent Davis, (Chapel Hill: University of North Carolina Press, 1967), and J. C. Wylie, *Military Strategy: A General Theory of Power Control* (New Brunswick, N.J.: Rutgers University Press, 1966).

34. See Halberstam, *War in a Time of Peace;* Samuel P. Huntington, *The Soldier and the State: The Theory and Politics of Civil-Military Relations* (Cambridge, Mass.: Harvard University Press, 1957); Richard H. Kohn, "Out of Control: The Crisis in Civil-Military Relations," *National Interest* (spring 1994): 3–17.

35. For an overview of the weapons acquisition process, see Jacob Goodwin, *Brotherhood of Arms: General Dynamics and the Business of Defending America* (New York: Times Books, 1985); William H. Gregory, *The Defense Procurement Mess* (Lexington, Mass.: Lexington Books, 1989); Nick Kotz, *Wild Blue Yonder and the B-1 Bomber* (Princeton: Princeton University Press, 1988); Patrick Tyler, *Running Critical: The Silent War, Rickover, and General Dynamics* (New York: Harper and Row, 1986); and U.S. Congress, General Accounting Office, *DOD Revolving Door* (September 1989).

36. "Producers Defend Costs of Military Parts," *The State*, Columbia, S.C. (September 26, 1984), p. 2A.

37. "Pentagon Efficiency Stressed," *The State*, Columbia, S.C. (February 11, 1988), p. 2A. See also Tim Weiner, *Blank Check: The Pentagon's Black Budget* (New York: Warner Books, 1990); U.S. Congress, General Accounting Office, *Financial Audit: Air Force Does Not Effectively Account for Billions of Dollars of Resources* (February 1990).

38. See, for example, A. Ernest Fitzgerald, *The Pentagonists: An Insider's View of Waste, Mismanagement, and Fraud in Defense Spending* (Boston: Houghton Mifflin, 1989), and Dina Rasor, *The Pentagon Underground* (New York: Times Books, 1985).

39. See Chris C. Demchak, *Military Organizations, Complex Machines: Modernization in the U.S. Armed Services* (Ithaca, N.Y.: Cornell University Press, 1991).

40. See, for example, "The Winds of Reform: Runaway Weapons Costs Prompt a New Look at Military Planning," *Time* (March 7, 1983), pp. 12–16, 23, 26–30; and U.S. Congress, General Accounting Office, *Weapon Performance: Operational Test and Evaluation Can Contribute More to Decisionmaking* (December 1986).

41. See U.S. Congress, General Accounting Office, *Operation Desert Storm: Early Performance Assessment of Bradley and Abrams* (January 1992).

42. See, for example, "A Case of Human Error," *Newsweek* (August 15, 1988) pp. 18–20; John Barry and Roger Charles, "Sea of Lies," *Newsweek* (July 13, 1992), pp. 29–39; and Wayne Biddle, "Testing Charade," *The Nation* (August 27–September 2, 1988), p. 153.

43. Carl von Clausewitz, *On War* (London: Penguin, 1832). See also Eliot A. Cohen, "The Mystique of U.S. Air Power," *Foreign Affairs* (January–February 1994): 109–24.

44. See Myra MacPherson, *Long Time Passing: Vietnam and the Haunted Generation* (New York: New American Library, 1984). Richard Severo and Lewis Milford, in *The Wages of War: When America's Soldiers Came Home—From Valley Forge to Vietnam* (New York: Simon and Schuster, 1989), demonstrate that the warm welcome and generous government benefits awarded to World War II veterans were "the exception" to the rule. In this respect, although the general climate may have been more divisive, Vietnam War veterans were treated as most veterans have been treated throughout American history.

45. See Douglas Kinnard, *The War Managers* (Hanover, N.H.: University Press of New England, 1977).

46. Betts, *Soldiers, Statesman, and Cold War Crises*.

47. For a discussion of the "machismo factor" in U.S. foreign policy, see, Paul M. Kattenburg, *The Vietnam Trauma in American Foreign Policy, 1945–75* (New Brunswick, N.J.: Transaction Books, 1980), pp. 73–75.

48. See Leslie H. Gelb, "Shultz, Pushing a Hard Line, Becomes Key Voice in Crises," *New York Times* (November 7, 1983): 1, 15; Halberstam, *War in a Time of Peace*; Elaine Sciolino, "Crowe vs. Abrams: Bitterness and Reagan Policies," *Washington Post* (October 23, 1989), p. 7; Bob Woodward, *The Commanders* (New York: Simon and Schuster, 1991).

49. Eliot A. Cohen, "Constraints on America's Conduct of Small Wars," *International Security* 9 (fall 1984): 165.

50. For a general discussion of the importance of size and history in creating governmental institutions that are highly resistant to changes in foreign policy, see Richard Holbrooke, "The Machine That Fails," *Foreign Policy* (winter 1970–71): 65–77.

51. See Janine A Davidson, "Doing More With Less? The Politics of Readiness and the United States' Use of Military Force in the Post–Cold War Era" (master's thesis, University of South Carolina, 2002).

52. *Statistical Abstract of the United States: 2001*; U.S. Office of the Assistant Secretary of Defense, *Military Strength Figures* (March 31, 2002).

53. See Robert L. Borosage, "Inventing the Threat: Clinton's Defense Budget," *World Policy Journal* (winter 1993–94): 7–15; Eliot A. Cohen, "Down the Hatch," *New Republic* (March 7, 1994), pp. 14–19. The official policy can be found in Colin L. Powell, "U.S. Forces: Challenges Ahead," *Foreign Affairs* (winter 1992–93): 32–45; and William S. Cohen, Secretary of Defense, *Report of the Quadrennial Defense Review* (May 1997).

54. Chairman of the Joint Chiefs of Staff, Guidance Message (April 2, 2002).

55. Stephen Biddle, "Afghanistan and the Future of Warfare," *Foreign Affairs* 82 (March/April 2003), pp. 32, 46.

CHAPTER 8

1. Richard K. Betts, "The Soft Underbelly of American Primacy: Tactical Advantages of Terror," *Political Science Quarterly* (spring 2002): 19–36.

2. See Rhodri Jeffreys-Jones, *The CIA and American Democracy* (New Haven: Yale University Press, 1989), p. 257.

3. For an overview, see Jeffreys-Jones, *CIA and American Democracy*; Loch Johnson, *America's Secret Power: The CIA in a Democratic Society* (New York: Oxford University Press, 1991); and Jeffrey Richelson, *The U.S. Intelligence Community* (Cambridge, Mass.: Ballinger, 1985). For an overview of the literature, see John Ferris, "Coming in from the Cold War: The Historiography of American Intelligence, 1945–1960," *Diplomatic History* (winter 1995): 87–115.

4. For an overview of the intelligence community, see Jeffreys-Jones, *CIA and American Democracy*; Johnson, *America's Secret Power*; and Richelson, *The U.S. Intelligence Community*.

5. See John Prados, "No Reform Here: A Blue-Ribbon Panel Proved Once Again That 'Intelligence Reform' is Something of an Oxymoron," *Bulletin of Atomic Scientists* (September–October 1996).

6. See Ronald Kessler, *The FBI: Inside the World's Most Powerful Law Enforcement Agency* (New York: Pocket Books, 1994).

7. John Ranelagh, *The Agency: The Rise and Decline of the CIA* (New York: Simon and Schuster, 1986), p. 27.

8. Nathan Miller, *Spying for America: The Hidden History of U.S. Intelligence* (New York: Paragon House, 1989). See also Charles D. Ameringer, *U.S. Foreign Intelligence: The Secret Side of American History* (Lexington, Mass.: Lexington Books, 1990).

9. See, for example, Johnson, *America's Secret Power,* p. 38, and David Wise and Thomas B. Ross, *The Invisible Government* (New York: Vintage, 1974), p. 4.

10. See Mark M. Lowenthal, *Intelligence: From Secrets to Policy* (Washington, D.C.: Congressional Quarterly Press, 1999), p. 32. See also, U.S. Director of Central Intelligence, *A Consumer's Guide to Intelligence* (July 2001).

11. See also Bruce D. Berkowitz and Allan E. Goodman, *Strategic Intelligence for American National Security* (Princeton: Princeton University Press, 1989); Stephen J. Flanagan, "Managing the Intelligence Community," *International Security* 10 (summer 1985): 58–95; Robert M. Gates, "The CIA and American Foreign Policy," *Foreign Affairs* (winter 1987–88): 215–30; and Johnson, *America's Secret Power.*

12. See Graham Allison, *Essence of Decision: Explaining the Cuban Missile Crisis.* (Boston: Little, Brown, 1971).

13. Ryan Lizza, "White House Watch: Big Deal," *The New Republic* (June 24, 2002), pp. 10–12.

14. Ellen Nakashima and Bradley Graham, "Direct Authority Called Key in Homeland Agency," *Washington Post* (September 27, 2001). See also Sydney J. Freedberg, Jr., "Shoring Up America, *National Journal* (October 20, 2001), pp. 3238–45.

15. Ranelagh, *The Agency,* p. 455.

16. Daniel Ellsberg, *Papers on the War* (New York: Simon and Schuster, 1972), p. 28.

17. Jeffreys-Jones, *CIA and American Democracy,* pp. 238–45.

18. See Melvin A. Goodman, "Ending the CIA's Cold War legacy," *Foreign Policy* (Spring 1997), pp. 128–143.

19. See Barton Gellman, "Terrorism Wasn't a Top Priority," *Washington Post National Weekly Edition* (January 14–20, 2002), pp. 11; James Risen, "In Hindsight, CIA Sees Flaws That Hindered Efforts on Terror," *New York Times* (October 7, 2001).

20. Betts, "The Soft Underbelly," p. 22.

21. See Roberta Wohlstetter, *Pearl Harbor: Warning and Decision* (Stanford, Calif.: Stanford University Press, 1962).

22. James Bamford, "Eyes to the Sky, Ears to the War, and Still Wanting," *New York Times* (September 8, 2002), Week in Review, p. 5.

23. See, for example, Richard K. Betts, "Analysis, War, and Decision: Why Intelligence Failures Are Inevitable," *World Politics* 31 (October 1978): 61–90; Willis C. Armstrong, William Leonhart, William McCaffrey, and Herbert C. Rothenberg, "The Hazards of Single-Outcome Forecasting," in H. Bradford Westerfield, ed., *Inside the CIA's Private World* (New Haven: Yale University Press, 1995).

24. See Gary Sick, *All Fall Down: America's Tragic Encounter With Iran* (New York: Penguin, 1985).

25. See Michael Wines, "C.I.A. Sidelines Its Gulf Cassandra," *New York Times* (January 24, 1991), p. A13; Michael Wines, "U.S. Says Bush Was Surprised by the Iraqi Strike," *New York Times* (August 5, 1990), p. 8; and Bob Woodward, *The Commanders* (New York: Simon and Schuster, 1991).

26. "The CIA Called It—But Nobody Listened," *Newsweek* (September 2, 1991), p. 44.

27. See Bruce D. Berkowitz and Jeffrey T. Richelson, "The CIA Vindicated," *National Interest* (fall 1995): 36–47, for a different perspective.

28. See Richard K. Betts, "Warning: Old Problems, New Agendas," *Parameters* (spring 1998): 26–35.

29. James Risen, "In Hindsight, CIA Sees Flaws That Hindered Efforts on Terror," *New York Times* (October 7, 2001). See also, Seymour M. Hersh, "What Went Wrong: The CIA and the Failure of American Intelligence," *The New Yorker* (October 8, 2001).

30. See also Michael Elliott, "How the U.S. Missed the Clues," *Time* (May 27, 2002), pp. 25–32; Michael Hirsh and Michael Isikoff, "What Went Wrong," *Newsweek* (May 27, 2002), pp. 28–35; Michael Isakoff and Daniel Lkaidman, "The Hijackers We Let Escape," *Newsweek* (June 10, 2002), pp. 20–28; Romesh Ratnesar and Michael Weisskopf, "How the FBI Blew the Case," *Time* (June 3, 2002), pp. 26–32.

31. Theodore Draper, "Is the CIA Necessary?" *New York Review of Books* (August 14, 1997), p. 18.

32. For an overview of the origins and organization of the CIA, see Jeffreys-Jones, *CIA and American Democracy;* Johnson, *America's Secret Power;* Thomas Powers, *The Man Who Kept the Secrets: Richard Helms and the CIA* (New York: Pocket Books, 1979); Ranelagh, *The Agency;* and Wise and Ross, *Invisible Government.*

33. See Burton Hersh, *The Old Boys: The American Elite and the Origins of the CIA* (New York: Scribner, 1992).

34. Theodore Shackley, *The Third Option: An American View of Counterinsurgency Operations* (New York: Dell, 1981).

35. See Jeffreys-Jones, *CIA and American Democracy;* Johnson, *America's Secret Power;* Jonathan Kwitny, *Endless Enemies: The Making of an Unfriendly World* (New York: Penguin, 1984); Powers, *Man Who Kept the Secrets;* John Prados, *President's Secret Wars: CIA and Pentagon Operations Since World War II* (New York: William Morrow, 1986); Ranelagh, *The Agency;* Wise and Ross, *The Invisible Government;* U.S. Senate, *Alleged Assassination Plots Involving Foreign Leaders,* Congressional Report (94th Cong., 1st sess., November 18, 1975); and U.S. Congress, Senate, *Final Report of the Select Committee to Study Governmental Operations with Respect to Intelligence Activities,* Books 1–6, Congressional Report (94th Cong., 2nd sess., April 14, 1976).

36. See Peter Grose, *Gentleman Spy: The Life of Allen Dulles* (Houghton Mifflin, 1995); Jacob Heilbrunn, "The Old Boy at War," *New Republic* (March 27, 1995), pp. 32–37.

37. Jeffreys-Jones, *CIA and American Democracy,* p. 41.

38. In interpreting the meaning of the act's phrase, the CIA's first general counsel, Lawrence Houston, concluded that "taken out of context and without knowledge of [the act's] history, these Sections could bear almost unlimited interpretation. In our opinion, however, either [propaganda or commando type] activity would be an unwarranted extension of the functions authorized" by the act. "We do not believe that there was any thought in the minds of Congress that the Central Intelligence Agency under this authority would take positive action for subversion and sabotage." Any such missions would necessitate going to Congress "for authority and funds." Such authority eventually was provided by passage of the Central Intelligence Act of 1949 (Jay Peterzell, "Legal and Constitutional Authority for Covert Operation," *First Principles* 10 [spring 1985]: 1–3). See also Jeffreys-Jones, *CIA and American Democracy,* chapter 3.

39. Harry Howe Ransom, "Strategic Intelligence and Intermestic Politics," in Charles W. Kegley, Jr., and Eugene R. Wittkopf, eds., *Perspectives on American Foreign Policy: Selected Readings* (New York: St. Martin's Press, 1983), p. 303.

40. U.S. Congress, Senate, *Final Report of the Select Committee to Study Governmental Operations with Respect to Intelligence Activities, Foreign and Military Intelligence,* Book I, Congressional Report (94th Cong., 2nd sess., April 14, 1976), p. 445.

41. Jeffreys-Jones, *CIA and American Democracy*, p. 51.

42. See James A. Bill, *The Eagle and the Lion: The Tragedy of American-Iranian Relations* (New Haven: Yale University Press, 1988), and Jonathan Kwitny, *Endless Enemies: The Making of an Unfriendly World* (New York: Penguin, 1984).

43. See Richard H. Immerman, *The CIA in Guatemala: The Foreign Policy of Intervention* (Austin: University of Texas Press, 1982), and Stephen Schlesinger and Stephen Kinzer, *Bitter Fruit: The Untold Story of the American Coup in Guatemala* (New York: Doubleday, 1982).

44. See Madelaine G. Kalb, *The Congo Cables: The Cold War in Africa from Eisenhower to Kennedy* (New York: Macmillan, 1981).

45. U.S. Department of State, *Foreign Relations of the United States, 1950,* vol. 2. p. 607.

46. Joel Bleifuss, "The First Stone," *In These Times* (July 4–17, 1990): 4. See also Peter Dale Scott, "The United States and the Overthrow of Sukarno, 1965–1967," *Pacific Affairs* and Joseph B. Smith, *Portrait of a Cold Warrior* (New York: Ballantine Books, 1976).

47. Joseph Albright and Marcia Kunstel, "CIA Tip Led to '62 Arrest of Mandela: Ex-Official Tells of U.S. 'Coup' to Aid S. Africa," *Atlanta Constitution* (June 10, 1990), p. A14.

48. See Peter Wyden, *Bay of Pigs: The Untold Story* (London, Jonathan Cape, 1979).

49. Jeffreys-Jones, *CIA and American Democracy,* p. 132.

50. U.S. Congress, Senate, *Final Report,* Book 1, *Foreign and Military Intelligence,* Congressional Report (94th Cong., 2nd sess., April 14, 1976), pp. 179–204. See also, for example, Robin W. Winks, *Cloak and Gown: Scholars in the Secret War* (New York: William Morrow, 1987).

51. Jeffreys-Jones, *CIA and American Democracy,* p. 167.

52. See John Stockwell, *In Search of Enemies: A CIA Story* (New York: W. W. Norton, 1978). During this time, the CIA may have politically intervened in Australian politics, leading to the fall of E. Gough Whitlam in 1975, the Labor party prime minister. See Denis Freney, *The CIA's Australian Connection* (Sydney: Denis Freney, 1977), and James A. Nathan, "Dateline Australia: America's Foreign Watergate," *Foreign Policy* 49 (winter 1982–83): 168–85.

53. Loch K. Johnson, "Covert Action and Accountability: Decision-Making for America's Secret Foreign Policy," *International Studies Quarterly* 33 (March 1989): 81–109.

54. Philip Taubman, "Casey and His CIA on the Rebound," *New York Times Magazine* (January 16, 1983), p. 21.

55. Jeffreys-Jones, *CIA and American Democracy,* p. 235.

56. Patrick E. Tyler, "U.S. Tracks Cuban Aid to Grenada," *Washington Post* (February 27, 1983), pp. A1, A11.

57. See, for example, Duncan L. Clarke and Edward L. Neveleff, "Secrecy, Foreign Intelligence, and Civil Liberties: Has the Pendulum Swung Too Far?" *Political Science Quarterly* 99 (fall 1984): 493–513, and Stansfield Turner and George Thibault, "Intelligence: The Right Rules," *Foreign Policy* 48 (fall 1982): 122–38.

58. See "Anatomy of a Fiasco," *Newsweek* (June 6, 1988), pp. 36–39; John Dinges, *Our Man In Panama: How General Noriega Used the United States and Made Millions in Drugs and Arms* (New York: Random House, 1990); "Drugs, Politics, and the Noriega Connection," *Frontline,* a PBS TV show (January 30, 1990); Stephen Engelberg with Susan F. Rasky, "White House, Noriega, and Battle in Congress," *New York Times* (October 25, 1989), p. 4; "Noriega's Surrender," *Newsweek* (January 15, 1990), pp. 14–18; "20-Plus Years of Service," *In These Times* (January 10–16, 1990), pp. 4–5; and Michael Wines, "U.S. Plans New Effort to Oust Noriega," *New York Times* (November 17, 1989), p. 3.

59. Ransom, "Strategic Intelligence and Intermestic Politics," pp. 299–319.

60. I thank my colleague, Paul Kattenburg, from whom I borrowed the term *ethos.* See Daniel Yergin, *Shattered Peace: The Origins of the Cold War and the National Security State* (Boston: Houghton Mifflin, 1976), especially chapter 8.

61. Actually, the army was the first to classify on an organized basis during World War I. Then in March 1940, President Franklin Roosevelt issued an executive order authorizing a military classification system. It was not, however, until September 1951 that the secrecy system was extended to civilian departments by executive order from President Harry Truman. See U.S. Congress, Committee on Foreign Relations, *Security Classification as a Problem in the Congressional Role in Foreign Policy* (92nd Cong., 1st sess., December 1971), and David Wise, *The Politics of Lying: Government Deception, Secrecy, and Power* (New York: Vintage, 1973), pp. 89–91.

62. U.S. Congress, Senate, 69th Cong., 1st sess., *Congressional Record* (June 24, 1963), p. 859.

63. Jeffreys-Jones, *CIA and American Democracy,* p. 83.

64. See Christopher Simpson, *Blowback: America's Recruitment of Nazis and Its Effects on the Cold War* (New York: Weidenfeld

and Nicolson, 1988), and U.S. Congress, General Accounting Office, *Nazis and Axis Collaborators Were Used to Further U.S. Anti-Communist Objectives in Europe—Some Immigrated to the United States* (June 28, 1985). See also John Gimbel, "Project Paperclip: German Scientists, American Policy, and the Cold War," *Diplomatic History* 14 (summer 1990): 343–65.

65. Jeffreys-Jones, *CIA and American Democracy*, p. 83.

66. U.S. Congress, Senate, *Final Report* (94th Cong., 2nd sess.), p. 9.

67. See Frank J. Donner, *The Age of Surveillance* (New York: Vintage Books, 1981); Robert J. Goldstein, *Political Repression in Modern America: From 1870 to the Present* (Cambridge, Mass.: Schenkman, 1977); Morton H. Halperin, Jerry J. Berman, Robert L. Borosage, and Christine M. Marvick, *The Lawless State: The Crimes of the U.S. Intelligence Agencies* (New York: Penguin, 1976); Joan M. Jensen, *Army Surveillance in America, 1775–1980* (New Haven: Yale University Press, 1992); Richard E. Morgan, *Domestic Intelligence: Monitoring Dissent in America* (Austin: University of Texas Press, 1980); Athan Theoharis, *Spying on Americans: Political Surveillance from Hoover to the Huston Plan* (Philadelphia: Temple University Press, 1978); U.S. Congress, Senate, *Final Report* (94th Cong., 2nd sess.); and Wise, The Politics of Lying.

68. See Ann Colins, *In the Sleep Room: The Story of the CIA Brainwashing Experiments in Canada* (Toronto: Lester and Orpen Dennys, 1990); Harvey Weinstein, *A Father, A Son and the CIA* (Toronto: James Lorimer, 1990); and U.S. Congress, *Final Report* (94th Cong., 2nd sess.), chapter 17.

69. See Anthony Lake, "Lying Around Washington," *Foreign Policy* 2 (spring 1971): 91–113.

70. See, for example, Theodore Draper, *A Very Thin Line: The Iran-Contra Affairs* (New York: Hill and Wang, 1991), and Kenneth E. Sharpe, "The Real Cause of Irangate," *Foreign Policy* 68 (fall 1987): 19–41.

71. Tim Weiner, *Blank Check: The Pentagon's Black Budget* (New York: Basic Books, 1990), pp. 5–6.

72. With respect to the contras, the committee report concluded that there was "substantial evidence of drug smuggling through the war zones on the part of individual contras, pilots who flew supplies, mercenaries who worked for the Contras, and Contra supporters throughout the region. There is also evidence on the record that U.S. officials involved in assisting the Contras knew that drug smugglers were exploiting the clandestine infrastructure established to support the war and that Contras were receiving assistance derived from drug traffickers" (U.S. Congress, Senate, Subcommittee on Terrorism, Narcotics and International Operations of the Committee on Foreign Relations, *Drugs, Law Enforcement and Foreign Policy*, Committee Print [100th Cong., 2nd sess., December 1989], pp. 120, 136). See also Jonathan Kwitny, *Crimes of Patriots: A True Tale of Dope, Dirty Money, and the CIA* (New York: W. W. Norton, 1987); Alfred W. McCoy, *The Politics of Heroin in Southeast Asia* (New York: Harper and Row, 1991); Peter Dale Scott and Jonathan Marshall, *Cocaine Politics: Drugs, Armies, and the CIA in Central America* (Berkeley and Los Angeles: University of California Press, 1991); and Jacqueline

Sharkey, "The Contra-Drug Trade Off," *Common Cause Magazine* (September–October 1988), pp. 23–33.

73. Steven Emerson, *Secret Warriors: Inside the Covert Military Operations of the Reagan Era* (New York: G. P. Putnam's Sons, 1988).

74. "Going After Dissidents," *Newsweek* (February 8, 1988), p. 29; "FBI Will Purge Files on Protester," *New York Times* (November 5, 1989), p. 17; U.S. Congress, General Accounting Office, *FBI Investigates Domestic Activities to Identify Terrorists* (September 1990).

75. David Johnston, "Documents Disclose FBI Investigations of Some Librarians," *New York Times* (November 7, 1989), p. 1; and Michael Wines, "Director of FBI Defends Checks Into Backgrounds of Librarians," *New York Times* (November 8, 1989), p. 12.

76. The official intelligence figures, normally hidden in the military budget, were accidentally published by Congress. See Hilsman, "Does the CIA Still Have a Role?" p. 105.

77. Thomas Powers, "The Trouble With the CIA," *New York Review of Books* (January 17, 2002), p. 31. See also Hersh, "What Went Wrong"; Massimo Calabrisi and Romesh Ratnesar, "Can We Stop the Next Attack?" *Time* (March 11, 2002), pp. 25–36.

78. See, for example, Draper, "Is the CIA Necessary?"; Tim Weiner, "The CIA's Most Important Mission: Itself," *New York Times Magazine* (December 10, 1995): 62–76, 80–82, 104–105.

79. Stansfield Turner, "Intelligence for a New World Order," *Foreign Affairs* (fall 1991): 150. See also Bruce D. Berkowitz, "Reform of the Intelligence Community," *Orbis* (fall 1996): 653–63; David L. Boren, "The Intelligence Community: How Crucial?" *Foreign Affairs* (summer 1992): 52–62; John Canham-Clyne, "Business as Usual: Iran-Contra and the National Security State," *World Policy Journal* (fall–winter 1992): 617–37; Dave McCurdy, "Glasnost for the CIA," *Foreign Affairs* (January–February 1994): 125–32; Roger Hilsman, "Does the CIA Still Have a Role?" *Foreign Affairs* (September–October 1995): 104–16; Loch K. Johnson, *Secret Agencies: U.S. Intelligence in a Hostile World* (New Haven: Yale University Press, 1996); Abram N. Skulsky and Gary J. Schmitt, "The Future of Intelligence," *National Interest* (winter 1994–95): 63–73.

80. Turner, "Intelligence for a New World Order," p. 150.

81. *Secrecy: Report of the Commission on Protecting and Reducing Government Secrecy* (Washington, D.C.: U.S. Government Printing Office, 1997). See also George Lardner, Jr., "A Cutback in Classified Information?" *Washington Post* (April 10, 1990), p. A21.

82. See Peter Andreas and Richard Price, "From War Fighting to Crime Fighting: Transforming the American National Security State," *International Studies Review* (fall 2001): 31–52; Johnson, *Secret Agencies;* Prados, "No Reform Here."

83. Gregory F. Treverton, "Intelligence Crisis," GovExec.com (November 1, 2001). See also Richard K. Betts, "Fixing Intelligence," *Foreign Affairs* (January–February 2002): 43–59; Grenville Byford, "The Wrong War," *Foreign Affairs* (July–August 2002): 34–43.

CHAPTER 9

1. For an overview of U.S. foreign economic policy, see Thomas A. Bailey, *A Diplomatic History of the American People* (Englewood Cliffs, N.J.: Prentice-Hall, 1980); Alfred E. Eckes, Jr., *Opening America's Market: U.S. Foreign Trade Since 1776* (Chapel Hill: University of North Carolina Press, 1995); Charles P. Kindleberger, "U.S. Foreign Economic Policy 1776–1976," *Foreign Affairs* (January 1977): 395–417; David A. Lake, *Power, Protection, and Free Trade: International Sources of U.S. Commercial Strategy, 1887–1939* (Ithaca: N.Y.: Cornell University Press, 1988); Walter LaFeber, *The American Age: U.S. Foreign Policy at Home and Abroad* (New York: W. W. Norton, 1989); Stefanie Ann Lenway, *The Politics of U.S. International Trade: Protection, Expansion and Escape* (Boston: Pittman, 1985); Emily S. Rosenberg, *Spreading the American Dream: American Economic and Cultural Expansion, 1890–1945* (New York: Hill and Wang, 1982); and William Appleman Williams, *The Tragedy of American Diplomacy* (New York: Delta, 1959).

2. Susan Ariel Aronson, *Trade and the American Dream: A Social History of Postwar Trade Policy* (Lexington: University Press of Kentucky, 1996). To understand the dissolution of the distinction between high and low politics in an increasingly interdependent age, see Edward L. Morse, *Foreign Policy and Interdependence in Gaullist France* (Princeton: Princeton University Press, 1973).

3. For an overview, see I. M. Destler, *American Trade Politics* (Brookings Institution Press, 1995); C. Roe Goddard, *U.S. Foreign Economic Policy and the Latin American Debt Issue* (Garland Publishers, 1993); Stephen D. Cohen, *The Making of United States International Economic Policy: Principles, Problems, and Proposals for Reform* (New York: Praeger, 1988, 2000); and United States, *United States Government Manual*.

4. U.S., Census Bureau, *Statistical Abstracts of the United States 2002.*

5. See William J. Long, *U.S. Export Control Policy: Executive Autonomy vs. Congressional Reform* (New York: Columbia University Press, 1989); Michael Mastanduno, *Economic Containment: CoCom and the Politics of East-West Trade* (Ithaca, N.Y.: Cornell University Press, 1992), and "Strategies of Economic Containment: U.S. Trade Relations with the Soviet Union," *World Politics* 37 (July 1985): 503–31; U.S. Congress, General Accounting Office, *Export Controls: Multilateral Efforts to Improve Enforcement* (May 1992).

6. See, for example, William Greider, *Secrets of the Temple: How the Federal Reserve Runs the Country* (New York: Simon and Schuster, 1987); I. M. Destler, *Dollar Politics: Exchange Rate Policymaking in the United States* (Washington, D.C.: Institute for International Economics, 1989).

7. U.S. Census Bureau, *Statistical Abstract of the United States.*

8. See, for example, James J. Emery and Michael C. Oppenheimer, *The U.S. Export-Import Bank* (Boulder, Colo.: Westview Press, 1983).

9. See Goddard, "The Politics of Market Maintenance," chapter 4; Louis Hartz, *The Liberal Tradition in America* (New York: Harcourt Brace and World, 1955); Lake, *Power, Protection, and Free Trade;* Judith Goldstein, "Ideas, Institutions, and American Trade Policy," *International Organization* 42 (winter 1988): 179–217; Karen Mingst, "Process and Policy in U.S. Commodities: The Impact of the Liberal Economic Paradigm," in William P. Avery and David Rapkin, eds., *America in a Changing World Political Economy* (New York: Longman, 1982), pp. 191–206; John S. Odell, *U.S. International Monetary Policy: Markets, Power, and Ideas as Sources of Change* (Princeton: Princeton University Press, 1982); and Robert Pastor, *Congress and the Politics of U.S. Foreign Economic Policy: 1929–1976* (Berkeley and Los Angeles: University of California Press, 1980). On the concept of economic culture, see Paul Egon Rohrlich, "Economic Culture and Foreign Policy: The Cognitive Analysis of Economic Policy Making," *International Organization* 41 (winter 1987): 61–92.

10. Herbert McClosky and John Zaller, *The American Ethos: Public Attitudes Toward Capitalism and Democracy* (Cambridge, Mass.: Harvard University Press, 1984). The study by Richard K. Herrmann, Philip E. Tetlock, and Matthew N. Diascro, "How Americans Think About Trade: Reconciling Conflicts Among Money, Power, and Principles," *International Studies Quarterly* 45 (2001), pp. 191–218, indicates that there is considerable complexity and variations among and between the elite and mass public.

11. Gerald L. Parsky quoted in Mingst, "Process and Policy in U.S. Commodities," p. 193.

12. Cohen, *Making of United States International Economic Policy* (1988), p. 159. For the roots of the open door policy, see Williams, *Tragedy of American Diplomacy.*

13. Goldstein, "Ideas, Institution, and American Trade Policy," p. 187.

14. See Cohen, *Making of United States International Economic Policy;* Destler, *American Trade Politics;* and Harald B. Malmgren, "Managing Foreign Economic Policy," *Foreign Policy* 6 (spring 1972): 42–63.

15. Terry L. Deibel, "Bush's Foreign Policy: Mastery and Inaction," *Foreign Policy* 84 (fall 1991): 15.

16. Hedrick Smith, *The Power Game: How Washington Works* (New York: Ballantine, 1988), p. 350.

17. John P. Leacacos, "The Nixon NSC: Kissinger's Apparat," *Foreign Policy* 5 (winter 1971–1972): 18.

18. See I. M. Destler, *The National Economic Council: A Work in Progress* (Washington, D.C.: Institute for International Economics, 1996); Chris Dolan, "Striking a Balance: Presidential Power and the National Economic Council" (Ph.D. diss., University of South Carolina, 2001); Malmgren, "Managing Foreign Economic Policy"; Kenneth I. Juster and Simon Lazarus, *Making Economic Policy: An Assessment of the National Economic Council* (Washington, D.C.: Brookings Institution Press, 1997); and U.S. Congress, General Accounting Office, *Export Promotion: Federal Programs Lack Organizational and Funding Cohesiveness* (January 1992).

19. Paul Volcker quoted in Goddard, *U.S. Foreign Economic Policy,* p. 176.

20. I. M. Destler, "A Government Divided: The Security Complex and the Economic Complex," in David A. Deese, ed.,

The New Politics of American Foreign Policy (New York: St. Martin's Press, 1994), pp. 132–47.

21. Malmgren, "Managing Foreign Economic Policy," p. 42.

22. I. M. Destler, *Making Foreign Economic Policy* (Washington, D.C.: Brookings Institution Press, 1983), p. 215.

23. Ibid.

24. Cohen, *Making of United States International Economic Policy* (1988 edition), chapter 12. See also Bruce Stokes, "Organizing to Trade," *Foreign Policy* (winter 1992–93): 36–52.

25. Bruce Stokes, "Elevating Economics," *National Journal* (March 13, 1993), p. 615.

26. Destler, *The National Economic Council*, p. 1.

27. Ben Wildavsky, "Under the Gun," *National Journal* (June 29, 1996), p. 1417.

28. See Destler, *National Economic Council*; Dolan, *Striking a Balance*; John B. Judis, "Old Master," *New Republic* (December 13, 1993); Juster and Lazarus, *Making Economic Policy*; Paul Starobin, "The Broker," *National Journal* (April 16, 1994), pp. 878–83.

29. Juster and Lazarus, *Making Economic Policy*, p. 8. The Carnegie report recommended three major policymaking committees, including a Domestic Policy Council.

30. Bill Clinton and Al Gore, Jr., *Putting People First: How We Can All Change America* (New York: Random House, 1992), pp. 131–132.

31. David R. Francis, "Views on Clinton's Economic Council," *Christian Science Monitor* (November 13, 1993), www.csmonitor.com

32. David D. Newsom, "Economic Council Needs More Study," *Christian Science Monitor* (November 25, 1992), www.csmonitor.com

33. "In Bob We Trust," *Economist*, (December 10, 1994), p. 28.

34. Judis, "Old Master," p. 21.

35. Destler, *National Economic Council*, p. 10.

36. See Destler, *National Economic Council*; Dolan, *Striking a Balance*; Fred Barnes, "Cabinet Losers," *New Republic* (February 28, 1994), pp. 22–29; Judis, "Old Master"; Juster and Lazarus, *Making Economic Policy*; Starobin, "The Broker."

37. Gwen Ifill, "The Economic Czar Behind the Economic Czars," *New York Times* (March 7, 1993), p. 22; Steven Greenhouse, "When Robert Rubin Talks," *New York Times* (July 25, 1993), section 3, p. 1.

38. Beth Belton, "Wall Streeter with a Heart Defies Stereotype," *USA Today* (March 3, 1993), section B, p. 6.

39. Henry Butterfield Ryan, "US Needs a Trade Czar," *Christian Science Monitor* (September 30, 1992), www.csmonitor.com

40. Robert Rubin quoted in Ifill, "Economic Czar," p. 22.

41. Juster and Lazarus, *Making Economic Policy*, p. 6.

42. Judis, "Old Master," p. 25.

43. See Destler, *National Economic Council*; Juster and Lazarus, *Making Economic Policy*.

44. Ifill, "Economic Czar," p. 22.

45. Destler, *National Economic Council*, p. 28.

46. Ibid., p. 29.

47. Ibid., p. 14, 18.

48. Ibid., pp. 40, 61.

49. For an overview, see Karen DeYoung and Steven Mufson, "Leaner, Less Visible NSC Taking Shape," *Washington Post* (February 10, 2001); Ryan Lizza, "White House Watch: Spokesmen," *New Republic* (January 18, 2001); David E. Sanger, "Bush Plans to Stress Effects of Economics on Security," *New York Times* (January 16, 2001); Rich Thomas and Keith Naughton, "Bush's Money Posse," *Newsweek* (January 15, 2001), pp. 19–22.

50. Bush Jr. quoted in Sanger, "Bush Plans to Stress Effects of Economics."

51. Destler, *National Economic Council*, p. 36.

CHAPTER 10

1. Fred Dutton quoted in Hedrick Smith, *The Power Game: How Washington Works* (New York: Ballantine, 1988), p. 56.

2. Charles Maechling, Jr., "Foreign Policy-Makers: The Weakest Link?" *Virginia Quarterly Review* 52 (winter 1976): 1–23.

3. Dale H. Herspring, "Practitioners and Political Scientists," *PS: Political Science & Politics* (September 1992), p. 554.

4. See James A. Robinson and R. Roger Majak, "The Theory of Decision-Making," in James C. Charlesworth, ed., *Contemporary Political Analysis* (New York: Free Press, 1967), pp. 175–88; and James A. Robinson and Richard C. Snyder, "Decision-Making in International Politics," in Herbert C. Kelman, ed., *International Behavior: A Social-Psychological Analysis* (New York: Holt, Rinehart and Winston, 1965), pp. 433–63.

5. Graham T. Allison, *Essence of Decision: Explaining the Cuban Missile Crisis* (Boston: Little, Brown, 1973); Irving L. Janis, *Groupthink* (New York: Houghton Mifflin, 1982).

6. See, for example, Allison, *Essence of Decision*. Much has been written on the events of the Cuban missile crisis since the 1973 edition, incorporating additional sources and perspectives. For a more comprehensive historical description involving all the major parties, see the new edition by Graham Allison and Philip Zelikow, *Essence of Decision: Explaining the Cuban Missile Crisis* (New York: Longman, 1999); Bruce J. Allyn, James G. Blight, and David A. Welch, "Essence of Revision: Moscow, Havana, and the Cuban Missile Crisis," *International Security* 14 (winter 1989–1990): 136–72; James G. Blight and David A. Welch, *On the Brink: Americans and Soviets Reexamine the Cuban Missile Crisis* (New York: Hill and Wang, 1989); and Raymond L. Garthoff, *Reflections on the Cuban Missile Crisis* (Washington, D.C.: Brookings Institution Press, 1989).

7. Allison, *Essence of Decision*. See also John D. Steinbruner, *The Cybernetic Theory of Decision* (Princeton: Princeton University Press, 1974).

8. Questions have been raised as to the extent to which President John Kennedy acted rationally. See Richard Ned Lebow, *Between Peace and War: The Nature of International Crisis* (Baltimore: Johns Hopkins University Press, 1981), chapter 8; James A.

Nathan, "The Missile Crisis: His Finest Hour Now," *World Politics* (January 1975): 256–81; and Jack L. Snyder, "Rationality at the Brink: The Role of Cognitive Processes in Failures of Deterrence," *World Politics* (April 1978): 344–65.

9. To save time and avoid complicating things, such shorthand phrases are necessary. These phrases, however, may be more than figures of speech, reflecting a set of assumptions about how people come to understand the world around them.

10. Janis, *Groupthink.*

11. Janis, *Groupthink.* See also Dean A. Minix, *Small Groups and Foreign Policy Decision-Making* (Lanham, Md.: University Press of America, 1978). David M. Barrett disagrees with the consensus position that Johnson's policymaking process reflected groupthink, resulting in the escalation of the war in Vietnam, in "The Mythology Surrounding Lyndon Johnson, His Advisers, and the 1965 Decision to Escalate the Vietnam War," *Political Science Quarterly* (winter 1988–89): 637–64.

12. It should be pointed out that it is possible for either rational actor or groupthink policymaking processes to occur below the presidential level, though this is not how the models are typically discussed.

13. See Smith, *The Power Game;* Tower Commission (President's Special Review Board), *The Tower Commission Report* (New York: Bantam, 1987); and Bob Woodward, *Veil: The Secret Wars of the CIA, 1981–1987* (New York: Simon and Schuster, 1987).

14. Bob Woodward, *The Commanders* (New York: Simon and Schuster, 1991). See also Maureen Dowd, "The Longest Week: How President Decided to Draw the Line," *New York Times* (August 9, 1990), p. 17A; Elizabeth Drew, "Letter From Washington," *New Yorker* (September 14, 1990), pp. 82–90, and (February 4, 1991), pp. 103–112; Thomas L. Friedman and Patrick E. Tyler, "From the First, U.S. Resolve to Fight," *New York Times* (March 3, 1991), pp. 1, 12; and "To the Brink of War," *Frontline,* PBS television (January 15, 1991); William H. Kincade, "On the Brink in the Gulf, Part I: Onset of the 'Classic' 1990 Crisis," *Security Studies* (winter 1992–93): 163–200, and "On the Brink in the Gulf, Part II: The Route to War," *Security Studies* (winter 1993–94): 295–329; Don Oberdorfer, "Missed Signals in the Middle East," *Washington Post Magazine* (March 17, 1991), pp. 19–23, 36–41; Jean Edward Smith, *George Bush's War* (New York: Henry Holt, 1992).

15. David Halberstam, *War in a Time of Peace: Bush, Clinton, and the Generals* (New York: Scribner, 2001), p. 69.

16. See, for example, Gregory M. Herek, Irving L. Janis, and Paul Huth, "Decision Making During International Crises: Is Quality of Process Related to Outcome?" *Journal of Conflict Resolution* 31 (June 1987): 203–26.

17. See Dan Balz and Bob Woodward, "Ten Days in September," *Washington Post* (eight-part special series, January 27–February 3, 2002). See also Michael Elliott, "They Had a Plan," *Time* (August 12, 2002), pp. 28–43; Howard Fineman and Martha Brant, "This Is Our Life Now," *Newsweek* (December 3, 2001), pp. 21–29; Evan Thomas, "Chemistry in the War Cabinet," *Newsweek* (January 28, 2002); Evan Thomas, "He Has Saddam in

His Sights," *Newsweek* (March 4, 2002); Evan Thomas, "The Quiet Power of Condi Rice," *Newsweek* (December 16, 2002), pp. 24–34; Bob Woodward, *Bush At War* (New York: Simon and Schuster, 2002).

18. Woodward, *Bush at War.*

19. John Newhouse, *Cold Dawn: The Story of SALT* (New York: Holt, Rinehart and Winston, 1973), p. 108.

20. See Newhouse, *Cold Dawn,* and Jerel A. Rosati, "Developing a Systematic Decision-Making Framework: Bureaucratic Politics in Perspective," *World Politics* 33 (January 1981): 234–52.

21. Allison, *Essence of Decision.* See also Morton H. Halperin, *Bureaucratic Politics and Foreign Policy* (Washington, D.C.: Brookings Institution Press, 1974), and Morton H. Halperin and Arnold Kanter, eds., *Readings in American Foreign Policy: A Bureaucratic Perspective* (Boston: Little, Brown, 1973).

22. Smith, *The Power Game,* p. 561.

23. See Halberstam, *War in a Time of Peace.*

24. See, for example, "A Fatal Error of Judgment," *Newsweek* (March 3, 1986), pp. 14–19.

25. See also Steinbruner, *Cybernetic Theory of Decision.*

26. Friedman and Tyler, "From the First," p. 12; Michael Massing, "The Way to War," *New York Review of Books* (March 28, 1991): 17–20, 22; and Woodward, *The Commanders.*

27. Balz and Woodward, "Ten Days in September." See also footnote 17.

28. Allison, *Essence of Decision,* pp. 131–32.

29. For a general discussion of the concept of government learning, see Lloyd S. Etheredge, *Can Governments Learn? American Foreign Policy and Central American Revolutions* (New York: Pergamon Press, 1985), and Jack S. Levy, "Learning and Foreign Policy: Sweeping a Conceptual Minefield," *International Organization* (spring 1994): 279–312.

30. Alexander L. George argues for a "multiple advocacy" approach in order to promote rational decisionmaking in "The Case for Multiple Advocacy in Making Foreign Policy," *American Political Science Review* 66 (1972): 751–85. See also, Alexander L. George and Erick K. Stern, "Harnessing Conflict in Foreign Policy Making: From Devil's to Multiple Advocacy," *Presidential Studies Quarterly* (September 2001): 484–508. James Nathan, in "The Missile Crisis: His Finest Hour," makes a compelling case that lessons from the Cuban missile crisis were overdrawn and overlearned by Kennedy administration officials and American policymakers. Furthermore, not everyone accepts the idea that a purely rational process is the optimal way to arrive at decisions. Miriam Steiner in a very interesting article argues in favor of a decisionmaking process that comprises both rationalistic and nonrationalistic dimensions in "The Search for Order in a Disorderly World: Worldviews and Prescriptive Decision Paradigms," *International Organization* 37 (summer 1983): 373–413.

31. See Robert Art, "Bureaucratic Politics and American Foreign Policy: A Critique," *Policy Sciences* 4 (1973): 467–90; Stephen D. Krasner, "Are Bureaucracies Important? (Or Allison Wonderland)," *Foreign Policy* 7 (summer 1972): 159–79; Jeanne Longley and Dean G. Pruitt, "Groupthink: A Critique of Janis's Theory," *Review of Personality and Social Psychology* 1 (1980):

74–93; Rosati, "Developing a Systematic Decision-Making Framework"; Snyder, "Rationality at the Brink"; and Steinbruner, *Cybernetic Theory of Decision.*

32. See Margaret G. Hermann and Charles F. Hermann, "Who Makes Foreign Policy Decisions and How: An Empirical Inquiry," *International Studies Quarterly* 33 (December 1989): 361–88; Rosati, "Developing a Systematic Decision-Making Framework"; and Peter J. Schraeder, "Bureaucratic Incrementalism, Crisis, and Change in U.S. Foreign Policy Toward Africa," in Jerel A. Rosati, Joe D. Hagan, and Martin W. Sampson III, eds., *Foreign Policy Restructuring: How Governments Respond to Global Change* (Columbia: University of South Carolina Press, 1994), pp. 111–37; "Whither the Study of Governmental Politics in Foreign Policymaking? A Symposium," *Mershon International Studies Review* 42 (1998), pp. 205–55.

33. Paul 't Hart, Eric K. Stern, and Bengt Sundelius, eds., *Beyond Groupthink: Political Group Dynamics and Foreign Policy-Making* (Ann Arbor: University of Michigan Press, 1997), p. 5.

34. Ibid., pp. 11–12. The early decision-making analysts alluded to are Richard C. Snyder, H. W. Bruck, and Burton Sapin and their *Foreign Policy Decision-Making: An Approach to the Study of International Politics* (New York: Free Press of Glencoe, 1962).

35. Erick K. Stern, "Probing the Plausibility of Newgroup Syndrome: Kennedy and the Bay of Pigs," in 't Hart, Stern, and Sundelius, editors, *Beyond Groupthink*, p. 154.

36. Maechling, "Foreign Policy-Makers," p. 18.

37. Robert Pear, "Confusion Is Operative Word in U.S. Policy Toward Japan," *New York Times* (March 20, 1989), p. 1. See also Stephen W. Twing, "The FSX Affair: Putting Bureaucratic Politics into Context" (Master's thesis, University of South Carolina, 1990).

38. At times, Allison has referred to a "bureaucratic politics model," which is a fusion of the governmental politics and organizational process models. See, in particular, Graham T. Allison and Morton H. Halperin, "Bureaucratic Politics: A Paradigm and Some Policy Implications," *World Politics* 24 (spring 1972): 40–79.

39. Maechling, "Foreign Policy-Makers," p. 3.

40. For a general discussion of beliefs on the foreign policymaking process, see Alexander L. George, *Presidential Decisionmaking in Foreign Policy: The Effective Use of Information and Advice* (Boulder, Colo.: Westview Press, 1980); Robert Jervis, *Perception and Misperception in International Politics* (Princeton: Princeton University Press, 1976); Jerel A. Rosati, "The Power of Human Cognition in the Study of World Politics," *International Studies Review* (fall 2000): 45–75; Jerel A. Rosati, "A Cognitive Approach to the Study of Foreign Policy," in Laura Neack, Patrick J. Haney, and Jeanne A. K. Hey, eds., *Foreign Policy Analysis: Continuity and Change in Its Second Generation* (Englewood Cliffs, N.J.: Prentice-Hall, 1995), pp. 49–70; and Steinbruner, *Cybernetic Theory of Decision.* See also Yuen Foong Khong, *Analogies at War: Korea, Munich, Dien Bien Phu, and the Vietnam Decision of 1965* (Princeton: Princeton University Press, 1992); Deborah Welch Larson, *Origins of Containment: A Psychological Explana-*

tion (Princeton: Princeton University Press, 1985); Jerel A. Rosati, "Continuity and Change in the Foreign Policy Beliefs of Political Leaders: Addressing the Controversy Over the Carter Administration," *Political Psychology* 9 (September 1988): 471–505; Jerel A. Rosati, *The Carter Administration's Quest for Global Community: Beliefs and Their Impact on Behavior* (Columbia: University of South Carolina Press, 1987); Jack L. Snyder, "Rationality at the Brink: The Role of Cognitive Processes in Failures of Deterrence," *World Politics* (April 1978): 344–65; and Stephen G. Walker, "The Interface Between Beliefs and Behavior: Henry Kissinger's Operational Code and the Vietnam War," *Journal of Conflict Resolution* 21 (March 1977): 129–68.

41. Steinbruner, *Cybernetic Theory of Decision*, pp. 12–13, 112.

42. Snyder, "Rationality At the Brink," p. 363.

43. George, *Presidential Decisionmaking*, p. 57.

44. Daryl J. Bem, *Beliefs, Attitudes, and Human Affairs* (Belmont, Calif.: Brooks/Cole, 1970), p. 13.

45. See Robert P. Abelson, Elliot Aronson, William J. McGuire, Theodore M. Newcomb, Milton J. Rosenberg, and Percy H. Tannenbaum, eds., *Theories of Cognitive Consistency: A Source Book* (Chicago: Rand McNally, 1968); Leon Festinger, *A Theory of Cognitive Dissonance* (Evanston, Ill.: Row-Peterson, 1957); Jervis, *Perception and Misperception in International Politics;* William J. McGuire, "The Nature of Attitudes and Attitude Change," in G. Lindzey and E. Aronson, eds., *Handbook of Social Psychology,* vol. 3, 2nd ed. (Chicago: Rand McNally, 1969), pp. 136–314; Stuart Oskamp, *Attitudes and Opinions* (Englewood Cliffs, N.J.: Prentice-Hall, 1977, 1994). This was reinforced by the literature at the time on "persuasive communications," which found that most individuals are indifferent to persuasive appeals, especially political propaganda—in fact, information typically gets interpreted in accordance with an individual's existing central beliefs and predispositions. See David O. Sears and R. E. Whitney, *Political Persuasion* (Morriston, N.J.: General Learning Press, 1973); and Christopher Simpson, *Science and Coercion: Communication Research and Psychological Warfare* (New York: Oxford University Press, 1994).

46. Alice H. Eagly and Shelly Chaiken, *The Psychology of Attitudes* (Dallas: Harcourt Brace Jovanovich, 1993); Fiske and Taylor, *Social Cognition;* Richard R. Lau and David O. Sears, eds., *Political Cognition* (Hillsdale, N.J.: Lawrence Erlbaum Associates, 1986); Hazel Markus and R.B. Zajonc, "The Cognitive Perspective in Social Psychology" in G. Lindzey and E. Aronson, eds., *Handbook of Social Psychology* vol. 2 (New York: Random House, 1985), pp. 139–230; Michael A. Milburn, *Persuasion and Politics: The Social Psychology of Public Opinion* (Pacific Grove, Calif.: Brooks/Cole, 1991).

47. Ole R. Holsti, "Cognitive Dynamics and Images of the Enemy: Dulles and Russia," in John C. Farrell and Asa P. Smith, eds., *Image and Reality in World Politics* (New York: Columbia University Press, 1967), pp. 16–39.

48. Ralph K. White, *Nobody Wanted War: Misperception in Vietnam and Other Wars* (Garden City, N.Y.: Doubleday, 1968).

49. Jervis, *Perception and Misperception.*

50. Ibid., p. 217.

51. See Balz and Woodward, "Ten Days in September." See also Glenn Kessler, "U.S. Decision on Iraq Has Puzzling Past," *Washington Post* (January 20, 2003); Evan Thomas, "Rumfield's War," *Newsweek* (December 16, 2002), pp. 20–27, as well as footnote 17.

52. Susan T. Fiske and Shelley E. Taylor, *Social Cognition* (New York: McGraw-Hill, 1999), p. 13.

53. Theodore W. Adorno, E. Frenkel-Brunswick, D. J. Levinson, and R. N. Sanford, *The Authoritarian Personality* (New York: Harper, 1950); Eric H. Erikson, *Childhood and Society* (New York: W. W. Norton, 1950); Sigmund Freud, *Civilization and Its Discontents* (London: Hogarth Press, 1930); Alexander L. George and Juliette L. George, *Woodrow Wilson and Colonel House: A Personality Study* (New York: Dover, 1956); Harold D. Lasswell, *Psychopathology and Politics* (Chicago: University of Chicago Press, 1930); Abraham Maslow, *Motivation and Personality* (New York: Harper and Row, 1954); Jean Piaget, *The Moral Judgement of the Child* (New York: Free Press, 1932).

54. Holsti, "Cognitive Dynamics and Images of the Enemy," p. 13; Vamik D. Volkan, *The Need to Have Enemies and Allies: From Clinical Practice to International Relationships* (Northvale, N.J.: Jason Aronson, 1988). For an overview of some of the literature on personality and foreign policy, see Geoffrey Cocks, "Contributions of Psychohistory to Understanding Politics," in Margaret P. Hermann, ed., *Political Psychology* (San Francisco: Jossey-Bass, 1986), pp. 139–66; Neta C. Crawford, "The Passion of World Politics: Propositions on Emotion and Emotional Relationships," *International Security* 24 (spring 2000): 116–56; William Freidman, "Woodrow Wilson and Colonel House and Political Psychobiography," *Political Psychology* 15 (1994): 35–59; Michael Link and Betty Glad, "Exploring the Psychopolitical Dynamics of Advisory Relations: The Carter Administration's 'Crisis of Confidence,'" *Political Psychology* 15 (1994): 461–80; Jerrold M. Post and Robert S. Robins, "The Captive King and His Captive Court: The Psychopolitical Dynamics of the Disabled Leader and His Inner Circle," *Political Psychology* 11 (1990): 331–51; Stanley A. Renshon, "After the Fall: The Clinton Presidency in Psychological Perspective, *Political Science Quarterly* (spring 2000): 41–65.

55. The original edition is under Doris Kearns, *Lyndon Johnson and the American Dream* (New York: New American Library, 1976); a 1991 printing is under Doris Kearns Goodwin (New York: St. Martin's Press). See also Robert Dallek, *Lone Star Rising: Lyndon Johnson and His Times, 1908–1960* (New York: Oxford University Press, 1991); David Halberstam, *The Best and the Brightest* (New York: Random House, 1969); Townsend Hoopes, *The Limits of Intervention: An Inside Account of How the Johnson Policy of Escalation in Vietnam was Reversed* (New York: David McKay, 1973); Herbert Y. Schandler, *The Unmaking of the President: Lyndon Johnson and Vietnam* (Princeton: Princeton University Press, 1977); and James C. Thomson, Jr., "How Could Vietnam Happen? An Autopsy," *Atlantic Monthly*.

56. Goodwin, *Lyndon Johnson and the American Dream,* p. 385.

57. Johnson quoted in Halberstam, *The Best and the Brightest,* p. 434.

58. Goodwin, *Lyndon Johnson and the American Dream,* p. 268.

59. Ibid., pp. 100–101 (boldfacing added).

60. Ibid., pp. 416, 415.

61. Halberstam, *The Best and the Brightest,* p. 456.

62. Goodwin, *Lyndon Johnson and the American Dream,* p. 418.

63. Balz and Woodward, "Ten Days in September," and Woodward, *Bush at War.* See also Howard Fineman, "Bush and God," *Newsweek* (March 10, 2003), pp. 22–30, as well as footnotes 17 and 51.

64. Woodward, *Bush at War.*

65. These generalizations are derived from much of the literature already cited but especially the following: Allison, *Essence of Decision;* Art, "Bureaucratic Politics and American Foreign Policy"; Joseph H. de Rivera, *The Psychological Dimension of Foreign Policy* (Columbus, Ohio: Charles E. Merrill, 1968); Etheredge, *Can Governments Learn?;* George, *Presidential Decisionmaking in Foreign Policy;* Halperin, *Bureaucratic Politics and Foreign Policy;* Charles F. Hermann, "Decision Structure and Process: Influences on Foreign Policy," in Maurice A. East, Stephen A. Salmore, and Charles F. Hermann, eds., *Why Nations Act* (Beverly Hills: Sage, 1978), pp. 49–68; Janis, *Groupthink;* Irving L. Janis and Leon Mann, *Decision Making: A Psychological Analysis of Conflict, Choice, and Commitment* (New York: Free Press, 1977); Jervis, *Perception and Misperception in International Politics;* Lebow, *Between Peace and War;* Rosati, "Developing a Decision-Making Framework"; Steinbruner, *Cybernetic Theory of Decision;* and 't Hart, Stern, and Sundelius, eds., *Beyond Groupthink.*

66. See Jerel Rosati, Ken Rogerson, and Richard Haeuber, "Agenda-Setting, World Affairs Organizations, and the Making of U.S. Foreign Policy" (unpublished manuscript, 1997). For an overview of the importance and impact of agenda setting, see John W. Kingdon, *Agendas, Alternatives, and Public Policies* (Boston: Little, Brown, 1984), and David A. Rochefort and Roger W. Cobb, "Problem Definition, Agenda Access, and Policy Choice," *Policy Studies Journal* 21 (1993): 56–71.

67. See, for example, Charles F. Hermann, "International Crisis as a Situational Variable," in James N. Rosenau, ed., *International Politics and Foreign Policy* (New York: Free Press, 1969), pp. 409–21; and Rosati, "Developing a Decision-Making Framework."

68. Smith, *The Power Game,* p. 83. On the general impact of the scope of conflict for political outcomes, see E. E. Schattschneider, *The Semisovereign People: A Realist's View of Democracy in America* (Hinsdale, Ill.: Dryden Press, 1960), chapter 1.

69. Smith, *The Power Game,* p. 80.

70. See Rosati, "Developing a Systematic Decision-Making Framework," for a discussion of localized decisionmaking.

71. Barnett Rubin, "The U.S. Response to the JVP Insurgency in Sri Lanka," *Commission on the Organization of the Government for the Conduct of Foreign Policy*, VII, Appendices (Washington, D.C.: U.S. Government Printing Office), p. 179.

72. Halperin, *Bureaucratic Politics and Foreign Policy,* p. 290.

73. Roger Hilsman, *To Move a Nation: The Politics of Foreign Policy in the Administration of John F. Kennedy* (New York: Delta, 1964): Richard E. Neustadt, *Presidential Power: The Politics of Leadership* (New York: John Wiley, 1960); Warner R. Schilling, Paul T. Hammond, and Glenn H. Snyder, *Strategy, Politics and Defense Budgets* (New York: Columbia University Press, 1962); and Snyder, Bruck, and Sapin, *Foreign Policy Decision-Making.* On this first wave of policymaking theorists, see Art, "Bureaucratic Politics and American Foreign Policy." Although Art criticized the so-called second wave of policymaking theorists, such as Graham Allison and Morton Halperin, for their narrow conceptualization of the policymaking process as limited to the executive branch, they did recognize the important role that domestic politics had on policymaking. See, for example, Halperin, *Bureaucratic Politics and Foreign Policy.*

74. Samuel P. Huntington, *The Common Defense: Strategic Programs in National Politics* (New York: Columbia University Press, 1961), pp. x, xi.

75. 't Hart, Stern, and Sundelius, *Beyond Groupthink,* p. 26.

CHAPTER 11

1. See U.S. Congress, *Report of the Congressional Committees Investigating the Iran-Contra Affair, with Supplemental, Minority, and Additional Views* (100th Cong., 1st sess., November 1987), and *The Tower Commission Report* (New York: Bantam, 1987). The Minority Report of the Committee and the *Tower Commission Report* reflect the more conservative view; the Majority Report of the Committee reflects the more liberal view.

2. See, for example, Godfrey Hodgson, *America in Our Time* (New York: Vintage, 1976), chapter 5; Richard J. Piper, "Presidential-Congressional Power Prescriptions in Conservative Political Thought Since 1933," *Presidential Studies Quarterly* (winter 1991): 35–54; and George Szamuely, "The Imperial Congress," *Commentary* (September 1987): 27–32.

3. See Jack N. Rakove, *Original Meanings: Politics and Ideas in the Making of the Constitution* (New York: Vintage, 1997).

4. The classic statement on this is Edward S. Corwin, *The President: Office and Powers, 1878–1957* (New York: New York University Press, 1957). See also Cecil V. Crabb, Jr., and Pat M. Holt, *Invitation to Struggle: Congress, the President and Foreign Policy* (Washington, D.C.: Congressional Quarterly Press, 1992); Michael J. Glennon, *Constitutional Diplomacy* (Princeton: Princeton University Press, 1991); Louis Henkin, "Foreign Affairs and the Constitution," *Foreign Affairs* 66 (winter 1987–88): 284–310; Louis Henkin, *Constitutionalism, Democracy, and Foreign Affairs* (New York: Columbia University Press, 1990); and Arthur Schlesinger, Jr., *The Imperial Presidency* (New York: Houghton Mifflin, 1989).

5. Schlesinger, *The Imperial Presidency.*

6. For an overview, see U.S. Congress, Senate, Special Committee on National Emergencies and Delegated Emergency Powers, *A Brief History of Emergency Powers in the United States* (93d Cong., 2nd sess., July 1974). This study concluded that "especially since the days of the 1933 economic emergency, it has been Congress' habit to delegate extensive emergency authority—which continues even when the emergency has passed—and not to set a terminating date" (p. v). By the early seventies, the president could make use of over 470 emergency power statutes in exercising power—most of which continue to exist today. See also Kenneth R. Mayer and Kevin Price, "Unilateral Presidential Powers: Significant Executive Orders, 1949–99," *Presidential Studies Quarterly* (June 2002): 367–86.

7. Frank R. Bax, "The Legislative-Executive Relationship in Foreign Policy: New Partnership or New Competition?" *Orbis* 20 (winter 1977): 881–904. See also John Rourke, *Congress and the Presidency in U.S. Foreign Policymaking: A Study of Interaction and Influence, 1945–1982* (Boulder, Colo.: Westview Press, 1983).

8. William Manchester, *The Glory and the Dream: A Narrative History of America, 1932–1972* (New York: Bantam, 1975), pp. 491–92.

9. Bax, "Legislative-Executive Relationship," p. 886. See also Natalie Hevener Kaufman and David Whiteman, "Opposition to Human Rights Treaties in the United States Senate: The Legacy of the Bricker Amendment," *Human Rights Quarterly* 10 (1988): 309–37; Cathal J. Nolan, "The Last Hurrah of Conservative Isolationism: Eisenhower, Congress, and the Bricker Amendment," *Presidential Studies Quarterly* (spring 1992): 337–49; and Duane Tananbaum, *The Bricker Amendment Controversy: A Test of Eisenhower's Political Leadership* (Ithaca, N.Y.: Cornell University Press, 1988).

10. See, for example, James M. McCormick and Eugene R. Wittkopf, "Bipartisanship, Partisanship, and Ideology in Congressional-Executive Foreign Policy Relations, 1947–1988," *Journal of Politics* 52 (November 1990): 1077–1100; and James Meernik, "Presidential Support in Congress: Conflict and Consensus on Foreign and Defense Policy," *Journal of Politics* (August 1993): 569–87.

11. Bax, "Legislative-Executive Relationship," p. 887.

12. David Halberstam, *The Powers That Be* (New York: Knopf, 1979), pp. 496–97.

13. Ibid., p. 248.

14. See Anna Kasten Nelson, "John Foster Dulles and the Bipartisan Congress," *Political Science Quarterly* 102 (spring 1987): 43–64.

15. An overview of congressional reassertion since Vietnam is provided by Barry M. Blechman, *The Politics of National Security: Congress and U.S. Defense Policy* (New York: Oxford University Press, 1990); Crabb and Holt, *Invitation to Struggle;* Thomas M. Franck and Edward Weisband, *Foreign Policy by Congress* (New York: Oxford University Press, 1979); Thomas E. Mann, ed., *A Question of Balance: The President, the Congress and Foreign Policy* (Washington, D.C.: Brookings Institution Press, 1990).

16. For an overview of these changes and their consequences, see Crabb and Holt, *Invitation to Struggle;* Lawrence C. Dodd and Bruce I. Oppenheimer, eds., *Congress Reconsidered* (Washington, D.C.: Congressional Quarterly Press, 2001); Franck

and Weisband, *Foreign Policy by Congress;* William J. Keefe, *The American Legislative Process* (Englewood Cliffs, N.J.: Prentice-Hall, 2000); James M. Lindsay, *Congress and the Politics of U.S. Foreign Policy* (Baltimore: Johns Hopkins University Press, 1994); Randall B. Ripley, *Congress: Process and Policy* (New York: W. W. Norton, 1988); Randall B. Ripley and James M. Lindsay, eds., *Congress Resurgent: Foreign and Defense Policy on Capitol Hill* (Ann Arbor: University of Michigan Press, 1997); Hedrick Smith, *The Power Game: How Washington Works* (New York: Ballantine, 1988).

17. See, for example, Paul Bernstein and William Freudenberg, "Ending the Vietnam War: Components of Change in Senate Voting on Vietnam War Bills," *American Journal of Sociology* 82 (1977): 991–1006, and Jerold E. Schneider, *Ideological Coalitions in Congress* (Westport, Conn.: Greenwood Press, 1979).

18. For a fascinating illustration, see Eric Alterman "Ron Dellums: Radical Insider," *World Policy Journal* (Winter 1993/94): 35–46.

19. See, for example, U.S. Congress, House of Representatives, Committee on Foreign Affairs, *Executive-Legislative Consultation on Foreign Policy: Strengthening Foreign Policy Information Sources for Congress,* Congress and Foreign Policy Series no. 4 (Washington, D.C.: U.S. Government Printing Office, February 1982). The Office of Technology Assessment (OTA), created in 1972, was the smallest support agency and the source of specialized knowledge concerning technology questions but was disbanded in the 1990s.

20. See Franck and Weisband, *Foreign Policy by Congress;* Robert A. Pastor, *Congress and the Politics of U.S. Foreign Economic Policy, 1929–1976* (Berkeley and Los Angeles: University of California Press, 1980); and Jerel A. Rosati, "Congressional Influence in American Foreign Policy: Addressing the Controversy," *Journal of Political and Military Sociology* 12 (fall 1984): 311–33.

21. See Morton Berkowitz, P. G. Bock, and Vincent J. Fuccillo, *The Politics of American Foreign Policy: The Social Context of Decisions* (Englewood Cliffs, N.J.: Prentice-Hall, 1977), and Paul E. Peterson, "The President's Dominance in Foreign Policy Making," *Political Science Quarterly* (summer 1994): 215–34.

22. See Crabb and Holt, *Invitation to Struggle;* Franck and Weisband, *Foreign Policy by Congress.*

23. See, for example, Lloyd N. Cutler, "To Form a Government," *Foreign Affairs* 59 (1980): 126–43; William D. Rogers, "Who's in Charge of Foreign Policy?" *New York Times Magazine* (September 9, 1979); and Szamuely, "The Imperial Congress."

24. See Rosati, "Congressional Influence in American Foreign Policy."

25. See, for example, James A. Robinson, *Congress and Foreign Policy-Making: A Study in Legislative Influence and Initiative* (Homewood, Ill.: Dorsey Press, 1967).

26. See Richard F. Fenno, Jr., *Home Style: House Members in Their Districts* (Boston: Little, Brown, 1978); Morris P. Fiorina, *Congress: Keystone of the Washington Establishment* (New Haven, Conn.: Yale University Press, 1977); John W. Kingdon, *Congressmen's Voting Decisions* (Ann Arbor: University of Michigan Press, 1989); David R. Mayhew, *Congress: The Electoral Connection*

(New York: Yale University Press, 1974); and Smith, *The Power Game.*

27. Pamela Fessler, "Congress' Record on Saddam: Decade of Talk, Not Action," *Congressional Quarterly* (April 27, 1991), pp. 1068–77.

28. James L. Sundquist, "Needed: A Political Theory for the New Era of Coalition Government in the United States," *Political Science Quarterly* (1988): 614.

29. See also Morris P. Fiorina, *Divided Government* (Boston: Allyn and Bacon, 1996); David R. Mayhew, *Divided We Govern* (New Haven: Yale University Press, 1991); Jeffrey S. Peake, "Coalition Building and Overcoming Legislative Gridlock in Foreign Policy, 1947–98," *Presidential Studies Quarterly* (March 2002): 67–83; Michael Smith, "Congress, the President, and the Use of Military Force: Cooperation or Conflict in the Post–Cold War Era?" *Presidential Studies Quarterly* (winter 1998); James A. Thurber, ed., *Divided Democracy: Cooperation and Conflict Between the President and Congress* (Washington, D.C.: Congressional Quarterly Press, 1991).

30. Bruce W. Jentleson, "American Diplomacy: Around the World and Along Pennsylvania Avenue," in Thomas E. Mann, ed., *A Question of Balance: The President, the Congress and Foreign Policy* (Washington, D.C.: Brookings Institution, 1990), p. 146.

31. See also Robert A. Pastor, *Congress and the Politics of U.S. Foreign Policy, 1929–1976* (Berkeley, Calif.: University of California Press, 1980); Brandon C. Prins and Bryan W. Marshall, "Congressional Support of the President: A Comparison of Foreign, Defense, and Domestic Policy Decision Making during and after the Cold War," *Presidential Studies Quarterly* (December 2001, pp. 660–678; Rosati, "Congressional Influence in American Foreign Policy"; and James M. Scott, "Interbranch Rivalry and the Reagan Doctrine in Nicaragua," *Political Science Quarterly* (Summer 1997), pp. 237–260.

32. Henkin, *Foreign Affairs and the Constitution,* p. 290. See also David Gray Adler, "The Constitution and Presidential Warmaking: The Enduring Debate," *Political Science Quarterly* 103 (spring 1988): 1–36, and Abraham D. Sofaer, *War, Foreign Affairs and Constitutional Power: The Origins* (Cambridge, Mass.: Ballinger, 1976).

33. U.S. Congress, House of Representatives, Committee on International Relations, *The War Powers Resolution: Relevant Documents, Correspondence, Reports,* Committee Print (94th Cong., 2nd sess., 1975), p. 1.

34. An overview of the legislative history that led to the passage of the War Powers Act and the act's impact through the early 1980s can be found in U.S. Congress, Senate, Committee on Foreign Affairs, *The War Powers Resolution,* Committee Print (Washington, D.C.: U.S. Government Printing Office, 1982).

35. Rarely has the president specifically cited subsection 4(a)(1) in a situation of hostilities. In one such case, the Mayaguez rescue attempt, the report was submitted after the forty-eight hours required by the WPA had elapsed and the military incident was over.

36. U.S., Supreme Court, *Immigration and Naturalization Service v. Chadha* 77 L Ed 2d 317 (June 23, 1983). It has also been

pointed out that the Supreme Court decision may ironically be detrimental to the president in the long run, for it will likely force Congress to pass less flexible legislation and become more involved in the details of policy. See, for example, I. M. Destler, "Dateline Washington: Life After the Veto," *Foreign Policy* 52 (fall 1983): 181–86.

37. U.S. House of Representatives, Committee on Foreign Affairs, *Use of U.S. Armed Forces in Lebanon, Communication from the President of the U.S.* (97th Cong., 2nd sess., 1982).

38. "Statement by Reagan on Resolution," *New York Times* (October 13, 1983) p. A7.

39. See Michael J. Glennon, "The Gulf War and the Constitution," *Foreign Affairs* (spring 1991): 84–101; James Nathan, "Salvaging the War Powers Resolution," *Presidential Studies Quarterly* (spring 1993): 235–68.

40. See Ryan C. Hendrickson, "War Powers, Bosnia, and the 104th Congress," *Political Science Quarterly* (summer 1998): 241–58.

41. John Lancaster and Helen Dewar," Congress Clears Use of Force, $40 Billion in Emergency Aid," *Washington Post* (September 15, 2001), p. A4.

42. See Louis Fisher and David Gray Adler, "The War Powers Resolution: Time to Say Goodbye," *Political Science Quarterly* (spring 1998): 1–20.

43. For an overview, see Franck and Weisband, *Foreign Policy by Congress,* chapter 6; Loch K. Johnson, *The Making of International Agreements; Congress Confronts the Executive* (New York: New York University Press, 1985); and U.S. Congress, Senate, Committee on Foreign Relations, *The Senate Role in Foreign Affairs Appointments,* Committee Print (97th Cong., 2nd sess., July 1982).

44. See Norman Ornstein and Thomas Donilon, "The Confirmation Clog," *Foreign Affairs* (November–December 2000): 87–99.

45. Loch Johnson and James M. McCormick, "Foreign Policy by Executive Fiat," *Foreign Policy* 38 (1977): 117–38. See also Johnson, *The Making of International Agreements,* and C. J. Stevens, "The Use and Control of Executive Agreements: Recent Congressional Initiatives," *Orbis* 20 (1977): 205–21.

46. See Natalie Hevener Kaufman, *Human Rights Treaties and the Senate: A History of Opposition* (Chapel Hill: University of North Carolina Press, 1990).

47. "Delegating Trade Policy," in I. M. Destler, *The President, The Congress, and The Making of Foreign Policy* (Norman: University of Oklahoma Press, 1994), pp. 228–45; Stanley D. Nollen and Dennis P. Quinn, "Free Trade, Fair Trade, Strategic Trade, and Protectionism in the U.S. Congress, 1987–88," *International Organization* (summer 1994): 491–525.

48. For an overview, see Franck and Weisband, *Foreign Policy by Congress.*

49. Barbara Hinckley, *Stability and Change in Congress* (New York: W. W. Norton, 1975), p. 75. Hinckley has since done some rethinking in *Less Than Meets the Eye: Foreign Policy Making and the Myth of the Assertive Congress* (Chicago: University of Chicago Press, 1994).

50. See, for example, Cynthia J. Arnson, *Crossroads: Congress, the Reagan Administration, and Central America* (New York: Pantheon, 1989).

51. See Bayless Manning, "The Congress, The Executive, and Intermestic Affairs: Three Proposals," *Foreign Affairs* 55 (1977): 306–32.

52. See John M. Barry, *The Ambition and the Power: The Fall of Jim Wright, A True Story of Washington* (New York: Viking Penguin, 1989); Ikwo Kabashima and Hideo Sato, "Local Context and Congressional Politics: Interest-Group Theory and Foreign-Policy Implications," *International Studies Quarterly* 30 (September 1986): 295–314; and Smith, *The Power Game.*

53. For an overview, see Joel D. Aberbach, *Keeping a Watchful Eye: The Politics of Congressional Oversight* (Washington, D.C.: Brookings Institution Press, 1990); Timothy M. Cole, "Congressional Investigation of American Foreign Policy: Iran-Contra in Perspective," *Congress and the Presidency* (spring 1994): 29–48; and Franck and Weisband, *Foreign Policy by Congress.*

54. Robert Griffith, "American Politics and the Origins of 'McCarthyism,'" in William H. Chafe and Harvard Sitkoff, ed., *A History of Our Time: Readings on Postwar America* (New York: Oxford University Press, 1991), p. 70.

55. Gregory F. Treverton, "Intelligence: Welcome to the American Government," in Thomas E. Mann, ed., *A Question of Balance: The President, the Congress and Foreign Policy* (Washington, D.C.: Brookings Institution Press, 1990), p. 74.

56. See Loch K. Johnson, "Covert Action and Accountability: Decision-Making for America's Secret Foreign Policy," *International Studies Quarterly* 33 (March 1989): 81–109.

57. See, for example, Harold Hongju Koh, *The National Security Constitution: Sharing Power After the Iran-Contra Affair* (New Haven: Yale University Press, 1990).

58. Elliott Abrams, *Undue Process: A Story of How Political Differences Are Turned into Crimes* (New York: Free Press, 1993), p. 223.

59. U.S. Congress, *Report of the Congressional Committees Investigating the Iran-Contra Affair,* p. 11. The minority report of the committee came to a conclusion similar to the Tower Commission's.

60. See, for example, Koh, *The National Security Constitution,* and Peter Kornbluh, "The Iran-Contra Scandal: A Postmortem," *World Policy Journal* 5 (winter 1987–88): 129–50.

61. William S. Cohen and George J. Mitchell, *Men of Zeal* (New York: Viking, 1988).

62. Seymour M. Hersh, "The Iran-Contra Committees: Did They Protect Reagan?" *New York Times Magazine* (April 29, 1990), pp. 46–47, 61, 64, 67, 70, 77–78. See also Peter Kornbluh, "The Iran-Contra Scandal: A Postmortem," *World Policy Journal* (winter 1987–88): 129–150.

63. Jentleson, "American Diplomacy," p. 171.

64. For an overview of the different political cultures within Congress versus the executive branch and how they affect interbranch foreign policy relations, see Stanley J. Heginbotham, "Dateline Washington: The Rules of the Game," *Foreign Policy* 53 (winter 1983–84): 157–72.

65. This has been true for a second presidential term since passage of the Twenty-Second Amendment in 1951, which has resulted in no electoral accountability during the second four years.

66. See, for example, Lloyd N. Cutler, "To Form a Government," *Foreign Affairs* 59 (fall 1980): 126–43.

67. See, for example, Lawrence C. Dodd, "Congress and the Quest for Power," in Dodd and Oppenheimer, eds., *Congress Reconsidered,* pp. 269–307, and Harvey G. Zeidenstein, "The Reassertion of Presidential Power: New Curbs on the President," *Political Science Quarterly* 93 (1978): 393–410.

CHAPTER 12

1. See Randall Walton Bland, *The Black Robe and the Bald Eagle: The Supreme Court and Foreign Policy of the United States: 1789–1961* (University Press of America, 1999); Thomas M. Franck and Michael J. Glennon, *Foreign Relations and National Security Law: Cases, Materials and Simulations* (St. Paul, Minn.: West, 1987); Michael J. Glennon, *Constitutional Diplomacy* (Princeton: Princeton University Press, 1991); Louis Henkin, *Foreign Affairs and the Constitution* (Mineola, N.Y.: Foundation Press, 1972 and 1996); Jerel A. Rosati, "A Neglected Actor in American Foreign Policy: The Role of the Judiciary," *International Studies Notes* 12 (fall 1985): 10–15; and Jean E. Smith, *The Constitution and American Foreign Policy* (St. Paul, Minn.: West, 1989).

2. Henkin, *Foreign Affairs and the Constitution,* p. 27.

3. See also Edward S. Corwin, *The President: Office and Powers* (New York: New York University Press, 1957); Clinton Rossiter with Richard P. Longaker, *The Supreme Court and the Commander in Chief* (Ithaca, N.Y.: Cornell University Press, 1976).

4. *Immigration and Naturalization Service v. Chadha,* 77 U.S. 317 (1983). See also U.S. Congress, Congressional Research Service, *Foreign Policy: Effect of the Supreme Court's Legislative Veto Decision,* Issue Brief IB83123 (September 6, 1983). These are only a few acts affecting foreign policy that contain a legislative veto; see U.S. Department of Justice, Office of Legal Counsel, *Compilation of Currently Effective Statutes that Contain Legislative Veto Provisions* (July 15, 1983).

5. *Capital Industries-EMI, Inc., v. Bennet,* 82 U.S. 688 (1983).

6. Rosati, "Neglected Actor in America," pp. 11–12.

7. Louis Henkin, "Constitutional Issues in Foreign Policy," *Journal of International Affairs* 23 (1969): 221.

8. See A. D. D'Amato and Robert M. O'Neil, *The Judiciary and Vietnam* (New York: St. Martin's Press, 1972); Louis Henkin, "Is There a 'Political Question' Doctrine?" *Yale Law Journal* 85 (April 1976): 597–695; and Howard E. Shuman and Walter R. Thomas, eds., *The Constitution and National Security* (Washington, D.C.: National Defense University Press, 1990).

9. See Bob Cohn, "Anatomy of a Pardon: Why Weinberger Walked," *Newsweek* (January 11, 1993), pp. 22–23.

10. Aaron Epstein, "Federal Appeals Panel Sets Aside North's Convictions," *The State,* Columbia, S.C. (July 12, 1990), pp. 1A, 4A; and Joel Bleifuss, "Decade of Deceit," *In These Times* (November 7–13, 1990), pp. 4–5. For a similar argument about the role of politics, but from a completely different perspective, see Elliot Abrams, *Undue Process: A Story of How Political Differences Are Turned Into Crimes* (New York: Free Press, 1993), and Gideon Rose, "When Presidents Break the Law," *The National Interest* (fall 1987): 50–63.

11. Theodore Draper, "Revelations of the North Trial," *New York Review of Books* (August 17, 1989), p. 55.

12. Ronald Reagan agreed to a taped interview while in office for the Oliver North trial and testified in person out of office in the trial of John Poindexter.

13. Doe Pichirallo, "Thornburgh Blocks Release of Secrets in Iran-Contra Trial," *Washington Post* (November 23, 1989), pp. A1, A12.

14. Special Prosecutor Walsh quoted in Bleifuss, "Decade of Deceit," p. 4.

15. Draper, "Revelations of the North Trial," p. 59. The National Security Agency traditionally has been the most secretive bureaucracy within the intelligence community and was the most obstructionist in opposing the release of classified information, even if it already existed in the public record. See George Lardner, Jr., "Uncompromising NSA Frustrated Prosecutors in Iran-Contra Case," *Washington Post* (March 19, 1990), pp. A1, A4.

16. Anne-Marie Slaughter and David Bosco, "Plaintiff's Diplomacy," *Foreign Affairs* (September–October 2000): 115.

17. In addition, at the federal level, there are the territorial courts, the United States Court of International Trade, the United States Court of Federal Claims, the United States Court of Appeals for the Armed Forces, and the United States Court of Veterans Appeals, which are described in the *U.S. Government Manual.*

18. For an overview of the Supreme Court and the judicial system, see Henry J. Abraham, *The Judiciary: The Supreme Court in the Governmental Process* (Boston: Allyn and Bacon, 1994), and Lawrence Baum, *The Supreme Court* (Washington, D.C.: Congressional Quarterly Press, 2000).

19. See, for example, David G. Savage, *Turning Right: The Making of the Rehnquist Supreme Court* (New York: John Wiley, 1992).

20. David A. Kaplan, *The Accidental President* (New York: William Morrow, 2001), excerpted in *Newsweek* (September 17, 2001), pp. 30–31.

21. Evan Thomas and Michael Isikoff, "The Truth Behind the Pillars," *Newsweek* (December 25, 2000), p. 46.

22. Henkin, *Foreign Affairs and the Constitution,* 2nd ed. (1996), pp. 148–49.

23. For some background, see Samuel H. Beer, *To Make a Nation: The Rediscovery of American Federalism* (Cambridge, Mass.: Harvard University Press, 1993).

24. U.S. Census Bureau, *United States Department of Commerce News* (2002).

25. Chadwick F. Alger, "The World Relations of Cities: Closing the Gap Between Social Science Paradigms and Everyday

Human Experience," *International Studies Quarterly* 34 (December 1990): 493–518. See also Chadwick F. Alger, "Columbus in the World: The World in Columbus," *International Associations* (1974): 393–405; "'Foreign' Policies of U.S. Publics," *International Studies Quarterly* 21 (June 1977): 277–318.

26. John Maxwell Hamilton, *Mainstreet America and the Third World* (Cabin John, Md.: Seven Locks Press, 1986). See also Earl H. Fry, *The Expanding Role of State and Local Governments in U.S. Foreign Affairs* (New York: Council on Foreign Relations Press, 1998); Earl H. Fry, "The United States of America," in Hans J. Michelmann and Panayotis Soldatos, eds., *Federalism and International Relations: The Role of Subnational Units* (Oxford: Oxford University Press, 1990), pp. 276–98; Terrence Guay, "Local Government and Global Politics: The Implications of Massachusetts' 'Burma Law,'" *Political Science Quarterly* 115 (fall 200): 353–76.

27. See also Douglas M. Brown and Earl H. Fry, eds., *States and Provinces in the International Economy* (Berkeley, Calif.: Institute of Governmental Studies Press, 1993); John M. Kline, *State Government Influence in U.S. International Economic Policy* (Lexington, Mass.: Lexington Books, 1983); Hugh O'Neill, "The Role of States in Trade Development," in Frank J. Macchiarola, ed., *International Trade: The Changing Role of the United States* (New York: Academy of Political Science, 1990), pp. 181–89.

28. Robert Griffith, "American Politics and the Origins of 'McCarthyism,'" in William H. Chafe and Harvard Sitkoff, eds., *A History of Our Time: Readings on Postwar America* (New York: Oxford University Press, 1991), p. 71. See also David Caute, *The Great Fear: The Anti-Communist Purge Under Truman and Eisenhower* (New York: Simon and Schuster, 1978).

29. See Janice Love, *The U.S. Anti-Apartheid Movement: Local Activism in Global Politics* (New York: Praeger, 1986).

30. Michael H. Shuman, "Dateline Main Street: Local Foreign Policies," *Foreign Policy* 65 (winter 1986–1987): 154–74. See also James O. Goldsborough, "California's Foreign Policy," *Foreign Affairs* (spring 1993): 88–96; Heidi H. Hobbs, *City Hall Goes Abroad: The Foreign Policy of Local Politics* (Thousand Oaks, Calif.: Sage, 1994); John M. Kline, "A New Federalism for United States Foreign Policy," *International Journal* (summer 1986): 507–38; Paul L. Knox and Peter J. Taylor, eds., *World Cities in a World System* (New York: Cambridge University Press, 1995). There is even a national journal, *Municipal Foreign Policies*.

31. Shuman, "Dateline Main Street," pp. 159–60.

32. Sister Cities International (www.sister-cities.org). See also Jeffrey Pasley, "Twisted Sisters," *New Republic* (June 22, 1987), pp. 14–18.

33. See Guay, "Local Government and Global Politics." 1. State of Florida, Florida International Volunteer Corps, brochures (1997, 2001).

34. Abraham McLaughlin, "Despite Budget Gaps, States Beef Up Security," *Christian Science Monitor* (January 14, 2002), www.csmonitor.com.

35. See, for example, Guay, "Local Government and Global Politics," and Michael H. Shuman, "Dateline Main Street."

36. Hedrick Smith, *The Power Game: How Washington Works* (New York: Ballantine, 1988), p. 388.

37. Ibid. There are other famous annual events when the nation's elites get together for an informal and private gathering, such as the Bohemian Grove in northern California. President Clinton had an annual Renaissance Weekend at Hilton Head, South Carolina. See Jacob Weisberg, "Clincest," *New Republic* (April 26, 1993), pp. 22–27.

38. Smith, *The Power Game*, pp. 391, 392.

39. "Clinton 'Singed but Not Burned' at Gridiron Dinner," *New York Times* (March 22, 1999).

40. Smith, *The Power Game*, chapter 6.

41. Ibid., p. 92.

42. For an overview, see the special issue on Washington, D.C., in *The New Republic* (July 9 and 16, 1977); John M. Barry, *The Ambition and the Power: The Fall of Jim Wright, A True Story of Washington* (New York: Penguin, 1989); Meg Greenfield, *Washington* (New York: Public Affairs, 2001); Nelson W. Polsby, "The Washington Community," in Thomas E. Mann and Norman J. Ornstein, eds., *The New Congress* (Washington: American Enterprise Institute for Public Policy Research, 1981); and Smith, *The Power Game,* chapter 6. Many of the observations that follow were also derived from my own experiences living and working in Washington from 1978 to 1982.

43. Smith, *The Power Game,* p. 91. See also Fred Barnes, "All the President's Perks," *New Republic* (September 2, 1991), pp. 22–25.

44. Smith, *The Power Game,* pp. 94–95 (quoting Abrams).

45. Martha Brant, "Making Dinner," *Newsweek* (September 17, 2001), p. 37.

46. Smith, *The Power Game*, p. 90.

47. Ibid., p. 99.

48. Ibid., pp. 90, 91.

49. Ibid., pp., 107, 91.

50. Ibid., p. 111.

51. See, for example, Edward P. Crapol, ed., *Women and American Foreign Policy: Lobbyists, Critics, and Insiders* (Scholarly Resources, 1992).

52. Gamarekian quoted in Smith, *The Power Game*, p. 28.

53. Ibid., p. 96.

CHAPTER 13

1. See Gabriel Almond, *The American People and Foreign Policy* (New York: Praeger, 1960); Bernard C. Cohen, *The Public's Impact on Foreign Policy* (Boston: Little, Brown, 1973); and Burtin Sapin, *The Making of United States Foreign Policy* (New York: Praeger, 1966).

2. For an overview and some historical context of the role of this paradoxical and elitist view, see Richard J. Barnet, *The Rockets' Red Glare, When America Goes to War: The Presidents and the People* (New York: Simon and Schuster, 1990); and Michael X. Delli Carpini and Scott Keeter, *What Americans Know About Politics and Why It Matters* (New Haven: Yale University Press, 1996). For classic statements representing this view, see Walter Lipp-

mann, *Public Opinion* (New York: Harcourt, Brace, 1922), *The Phantom Public* (New York: Macmillan, 1927), and *The Public Philosophy* (Boston: Little, Brown, 1955).

3. Leslie H. Gelb, with Richard K. Betts, *The Irony of Vietnam: The System Worked* (Washington, D.C.: Brookings Institution Press, 1979), p. 221.

4. Leslie H. Gelb, "The Essential Domino: American Politics and Vietnam," *Foreign Affairs* 50 (April 1972), pp. 461, 459.

5. V. O. Key, Jr., *The Responsible Electorate* (New York: Vintage, 1966); Benjamin I. Page and Robert Y. Shapiro, *The Rational Public: Fifty Years of Trends in Americans' Policy Preferences* (Chicago: University of Chicago Press, 1992); Samuel L. Popkin, *The Reasoning Voter: Communication and Persuasion in Presidential Campaigns* (Chicago: University of Chicago Press, 1991); Bruce W. Jentleson, "The Pretty Prudent Public: Post Post-Vietnam American Opinion on the Use of Military Force," *International Studies Quarterly* (1992): 49–74. The works of all these authors will be discussed and cited throughout the chapter. An excellent overview of the traditional view and its critique is provided by Ole R. Holsti, "Public Opinion and Foreign Policy: Challenges to the Almond-Lippmann Consensus," *International Studies Quarterly* (1992): 439–66. See also Ole R. Holsti, *Public Opinion and American Foreign Policy* (Ann Arbor: University of Michigan Press, 1996); Robert E. Lane, *Political Ideology: Why the American Common Man Believes What He Does* (New York: Free Press, 1962); Miroslav Nincic, *Democracy and Foreign Policy: The Fallacy of Political Realism* (New York: Columbia University Press, 1994); Philip J. Powlick, "The Sources of Public Opinion for American Foreign Policy Officials," *International Studies Quarterly* (December 1995): 427–51; and Robert Y. Shapiro and Benjamin I. Page, "Foreign Policy and the Rational Public," *Journal of Conflict Resolution* 32 (June 1988): 211–47. For a comparative perspective, see Thomas Risse-Kappen, "Public Opinion, Domestic Structure, and Foreign Policy in Liberal Democracies," *World Politics* 43 (July 1991): 479–12.

6. V. O. Key, Jr., *Public Opinion and American Democracy* (New York: Alfred A. Knopf, 1961).

7. See Almond, *The American People;* Carpini and Keeter, *What Americans Know about Politics;* Johan Galtung, "Foreign Policy as a Function of Social Position," *Journal of Peace Research* 2 (1965): 206–30; Barry B. Hughes, *The Domestic Context of American Foreign Policy* (San Francisco: W. H. Freeman, 1978); W. Russell Neuman, *The Paradox of Mass Politics: Knowledge and Opinion in the American Electorate* (Cambridge: Harvard University Press, 1986); and James N. Rosenau, *Public Opinion and Foreign Policy* (New York: Random House, 1961).

8. Rosenau, *Public Opinion,* p. 45.

9. See Richard A. Brody and Catherine R. Shapiro, "Policy Failure and Public Support: The Iran-Contra Affair and Public Assessment of President Reagan," *Political Behavior* 11 (1989): 353–69; Carol H. Weiss, "What America's Leaders Read," *Public Opinion Quarterly* 38 (spring 1974): 1–22.

10. See Herbert Hyman and Paul B. Sheatsley, "Some Reasons Why Information Campaigns Fail," *Public Opinion Quarterly* 11 (1947): 412–23, and Neuman, *The Paradox of Mass Politics.*

11. Other factors, such as age, ethnicity, gender, and region of the country, also play a role and must be kept in mind when discussing the American people. See, for example, Alexander De-Conde, *Ethnicity, Race, and American Foreign Policy: A History* (Boston: Northeastern University Press, 1994); David Fite, Marc Genest, and Clyde Wilcox, "Gender Differences in Foreign Policy Attitudes: A Longitudinal Analysis," *American Politics Quarterly* 18 (October 1990): 492–513; and Bruce M. Russett and Elizabeth C. Hanson, *Interest and Ideology: The Foreign Policy Beliefs of American Businessmen* (San Francisco: W. H. Freeman, 1975).

12. For an overview of the nature of public opinion, see Barnet, *The Rockets' Red Glare;* W. Lance Bennett, *Public Opinion in American Politics* (New York: Harcourt Brace Jovanovich, 1980); Harry Holloway with John George, *Public Opinion: Coalitions, Elites, and Masses* (New York: St. Martin's Press, 1986); Ralph B. Levering, *The Public and American Foreign Policy, 1918–1978* (New York: William Morrow, 1978); and Neuman, *The Paradox of Mass Politics.*

13. H. G. Erskine, "The Polls: The Informed Public," *Public Opinion Quarterly* 26 (1962): 669–77, and H. G. Erskine, "The Polls: Textbook Knowledge," *Public Opinion Quarterly* 27 (1963): 133–41.

14. See Carpini and Keeter, *What Americans Know About Politics;* "Lost on Planet Earth," *Newsweek* (August 8, 1988), p. 31, and "Test Reveals Americans' Knowledge of Geography Going Downhill," *The State,* Columbia, S.C. (November 9, 1989), p. 5A.

15. Paul Recer, "Geography Knowledge Lacking," *The State* (November 21, 2002), p. A4.

16. For a discussion of everyday life and its implications for American politics, see Robert D. Holsworth and J. Harry Wray, *American Politics and Everyday Life* (New York: Macmillan, 1987); Paul Loeb, *Nuclear Culture: Living and Working in the World's Largest Atomic Complex* (Philadelphia: New Society Publishers, 1987); and J. Anthony Lukas, *Common Ground: A Turbulent Decade in the Lives of American Families* (New York: Random House, 1985).

17. See Key, *Public Opinion and American Democracy;* Key, *The Responsible Electorate;* Page and Shapiro, *The Rational Public.*

18. See Michael X. Delli Carpini and Scott Keeter, "Stability and Change in the U.S. Public's Knowledge of Politics," *Public Opinion Quarterly* (winter 1991): 583–612. The trend toward greater levels of education may be offset by the increase in the high school dropout rate in inner cities, especially among the poor and minorities.

19. For an excellent overview on polling and public opinion, see Barbara A. Bardes and Robert W. Oldendick, *Public Opinion: Measuring the American Mind* (Belmont, CA: Wadsworth, 2002).

20. Katha Pollitt, "After Virtue," *The New Republic* (June 7, 1999), p. 42. See also Regina G. Lawrence and W. Lance Bennett, "Rethinking Media Politics and Public Opinion: Reactions to the Clinton-Lewinsky Scandal," *Political Science Quarterly* (fall 2001): 425–46.

21. See, for example, Douglas C. Foyle, "Public Opinion and Foreign Policy: Elite Beliefs as Mediating Variable," *International Studies Quarterly* (March 1997): 141–69; and Philip J. Powlick,

"The Attitudinal Bases for Responsiveness to Public Opinion Among American Foreign Policy Officials," *Journal of Conflict Resolution* 35 (December 1991): 611–41.

22. See Stanley Hoffmann, *Gulliver's Troubles, or the Setting of American Foreign Policy* (New York: McGraw-Hill, 1968), part III; Benjamin I. Page and Robert Y. Shapiro, "Effects of Public Opinion on Policy," *American Political Science Review* 77 (March 1983): 175–90; Risse-Kappen, "Public Opinion, Domestic Structure"; Bruce Russett, *Controlling the Sword: The Democratic Governance of National Security* (Cambridge, Mass.: Harvard University Press, 1990); Richard Sobel, *The Impact of Public Opinion on U.S. Foreign Policy Since Vietnam* (New York: Oxford, 2001).

23. Morton H. Halperin, *Bureaucratic Politics and Foreign Policy* (Washington, D.C.: Brookings Institution Press, 1974), p. 67.

24. John E. Mueller, *War, Presidents, and Public Opinion* (New York: John Wiley, 1973). See also Larry Elowitz and John W. Spanier, "Korea and Vietnam: Limited War and the American Political System," *Orbis* (summer 1974): 510–34; Matthew A. Baum, "The Constituent Foundations of the Rally-Round-the-Flag Phenomenon," *International Studies Quarterly* 46 (June 2002): 263–98.

25. Jentleson, "The Pretty Prudent Public." See also John R. O'Neal, Brad Lian, and James H. Joyner, Jr., "Are the American People 'Pretty Prudent'? Public Responses to U.S. Uses of Force, 1950–1988," *International Studies Quarterly* (June 1996): 261–80.

26. Jentleson, "The Pretty Prudent Public," p. 72.

27. Thomas E. Mann, "Making Foreign Policy: President and Congress," in Thomas E. Mann, ed., *A Question of Balance: The President, the Congress, and Foreign Policy* (Washington, D.C.: Brookings Institution, 1990), p. 11.

28. Bruce W. Jentleson, "American Diplomacy: Around the World and Along Pennsylvania Avenue," in Thomas E. Mann, ed., *A Question of Balance: The President, the Congress, and Foreign Policy* (Washington, D.C.: Brookings Institution Press, 1990), p. 185, and Barry Sussman, "On Central America, Reagan Is Consistently Unpersuasive," *Washington Post National Weekly Edition* (May 14, 1984), p. 37.

29. See, for example, Richard A. Brody, *Assessing the President: The Media, Elite Opinion, and Public Support* (Stanford: Stanford University Press, 1991); George C. Edwards, III, William Mitchell, and Reed Welch, "Explaining Presidential Approval: The Significance of Issue Salience," *American Journal of Political Science* 39 (February 1995): 108–34.

30. Godfrey Hodgson, *America in Our Time* (New York: Vintage, 1976). See also Cecil V. Crabb, Jr., *American Diplomacy and the Pragmatic Tradition* (Baton Rouge: Louisiana State University Press, 1989), and Lane, *Political Ideology.*

31. Intellectuals emphasized the lack of extreme views and ideological content in the beliefs of most Americans. See Daniel Bell, *The End of Ideology: On the Exhaustion of Political Ideas in the Fifties* (New York: Free Press, 1960), and Arthur Schlesinger, Jr., *The Vital Center: The Politics of Freedom* (New York: Houghton Mifflin, 1949). Social scientists emphasized that most Americans did not hold a consistent and logical set of intercon-nected beliefs that represented specific views, whether conservative or liberal. See Angus Campbell, Philip E. Converse, Warren E. Miller, and Donald E. Stokes, *The American Voter* (New York: John Wiley, 1964), and Philip E. Converse, "The Nature of Belief Systems in Mass Publics," in David Apter, ed., *Ideology and Discontent* (New York: Free Press, 1964), pp. 206–61. The work by Converse deeply affected the study of political science, as Gerald M. Pomper describes in "The Impact of 'The American Voter' on Political Science," *Political Science Quarterly* 93 (1978–79): 617–28. Most Americans also believe they are nonideological, meaning that they do not give much thought to politics and tend to take more pragmatic and centrist positions on most issues.

32. Robert A. Dahl, *Pluralist Democracy in the United States: Conflict and Consent* (Chicago: Rand McNally, 1967), p. 357.

33. Ole R. Holsti and James N. Rosenau, *American Leadership in World Affairs: Vietnam and the Breakdown of Consensus* (New York: Allen and Unwin, 1984), and Hodgson, *America in Our Time.*

34. Mann, "Making Foreign Policy," pp. 11–12.

35. See Eric F. Goldman, *The Crucial Decade—and After: America, 1945–1960* (New York: Random House, 1961); Hodgson, *America in Our Time;* Levering, *The Public and American Foreign Policy;* William Manchester, *The Glory and the Dream: A Narrative History of America, 1933–1972* (New York: John Wiley, 1972); Robert Endicott Osgood, *Ideals and Self-Interest in America's Foreign Relations: The Great Transformation of the Twentieth Century* (Chicago: University of Chicago Press, 1953); and Daniel Yergin, *Shattered Peace: The Origins of the Cold War and the National Security State* (New York: Houghton Mifflin, 1978).

36. See, for example, George H. Quester, "Origins of the Cold War: Some Clues from Public Opinion," *Political Science Quarterly* 93 (winter 1978–79): 647–64.

37. Hodgson, *America in Our Time,* p. 73.

38. Ibid., p. 76.

39. Ibid., p. 73. See also Ole R. Holsti, "The Study of International Politics Makes Strange Bedfellows: Theories of the Radical Right and the Radical Left," *American Political Science Review* 68 (March 1974): 217–52; John F. Diggins, "Four Theories in Search of a Reality: James Burnham, Soviet Communism, and the Cold War," *American Political Science Review* 70 (June 1976): 492–508.

40. See James MacGregor Burns, *The Crosswinds of Freedom* (New York: Vintage, 1989); Goldman, *The Crucial Decade;* Hodgson, *America in Our Time;* Manchester, *The Glory and the Dream;* and Richard H. Pells, *The Liberal Mind in a Conservative Age: American Intellectuals in the 1940s and 1950s* (New York: Harper and Row, 1985).

41. See also Jerome L. Himmelstein, *To the Right: The Transformation of American Conservatism* (Berkeley and Los Angeles: University of California Press, 1989).

42. Hodgson, *America in Our Time,* p. 46.

43. David Halberstam, *The Best and the Brightest* (New York: Random House, 1969), p. 108.

44. Hodgson, *America in Our Time,* pp. 45, 47.

45. See Gelb, *The Irony of Vietnam,* and Halberstam, *The Best and the Brightest.*

46. Holsti and Rosenau, *American Leadership in World Affairs;* William Schneider, "Conservatism, Not Interventionism: Trends in Foreign Policy Opinion, 1974–1982," in Kenneth A. Oye, Robert J. Lieber, and Donald Rothchild, eds., *Eagle Defiant: United States Foreign Policy in the 1980s* (Boston: Little, Brown, 1983), pp. 33–64; William Schneider, "Public Opinion," in Joseph S. Nye, Jr., ed., *The Making of America's Soviet Policy* (New Haven: Yale University Press, 1984), pp. 11–35; and William Schneider, "'Rambo' and Reality: Having It Both Ways," in Kenneth A. Oye, Robert J. Lieber, and Donald Rothchild, eds., *Eagle Resurgent? The Reagan Era in American Foreign Policy* (Boston: Little, Brown, 1987), pp. 41–72.

47. See Cecil V. Crabb, Jr., *Policy-Makers and Critics: Conflicting Theories of American Foreign Policy* (New York: Praeger, 1976); Barry R. Posen and Andrew L. Ross, "Competing Visions for U.S. Grand Strategy," *International Security* (winter 1996–97): 5–53; Jerel Rosati and John Creed, "Extending the Three-Headed and Four-Headed Eagles: The Foreign Policy Orientations of American Elites During the 80s and 90s," *Political Psychology* 18 (1997): 583–623; and Jerel Rosati, Michael W. Link, and John Creed, "A New Perspective on the Foreign Policy Views of American Opinion Leaders in the Cold War and Post–Cold War Eras," *Political Research Quarterly* 51 (June 1998): 461–479. Holsti and Rosenau have come to recognize that their original threefold schemas were not as mutually exclusive as they first thought. See Ole R. Holsti and James N. Rosenau, "The Structure of Foreign Policy Attitudes Among American Leaders," *Journal of Politics* 52 (February 1990): 94–125, and Holsti, *Public Opinion and American Foreign Policy.*

48. For a discussion of the strength of isolationist sentiment in the mass public, see Almond, *American People and Foreign Policy,* and Richard J. Barnet, *Roots of War: The Men and Institutions Behind U.S. Foreign Policy* (New York: Penguin, 1971), part III. For a slightly different take on the meaning of semi-isolationism for the mass public, see Steven Kull, "What the Public Knows That Washington Doesn't," *Foreign Policy* (winter 1995–96): 102–15; and Miroslav Nincic, "Domestic Costs, the U.S. Public, and the Isolationist Calculus," *International Studies Quarterly* 41 (December 1997): 593–610.

49. Norman J. Ornstein and Mark Schmitt, "Dateline Campaign '92: Post–Cold War Politics," *Foreign Policy* 79 (1990): 169.

50. See Charles William Maynes, "Contending Schools," *National Interest* (spring 2001): 49–58; Posen and Ross, "Competing Visions," Rosati and Creed, "Extending the Three-Headed and Four-Headed Eagles," and Rosati, Link, and Creed, "A New Perspective on the Foreign Policy Views of American Opinion Leaders."

51. William Schneider makes a distinction between "non-self-interested" issues—often national security issues—for which public support has dropped, and "self-regarding" issues—such as economic and other intermestic issues—which have gained public support. William Schneider, "The New Isolationism," in Robert J. Lieber, ed., *Eagle Adrift: American Foreign Policy at the End of the Century* (New York: Longman, 1997), pp. 26–38. See also Richard K. Herrmann, Philip E. Tetlock, and Matthew N. Di-

ascro, "How Americans Think About Trade: Reconciling Conflicts Among Money, Power, and Principles," *International Studies Quarterly* 45 (2001): 191–218.

52. See, for example, Eugene R. Wittkopf, "On the Foreign Policy Beliefs of the American People: A Critique and Some Evidence," *International Studies Quarterly* 30 (1986): 425–45, and Eugene R. Wittkopf, *Faces of Internationalism: Public Opinion and American Foreign Policy* (Durham, N.C.: Duke University Press, 1990). See also Sidney Blumenthal, "The Return of the Repressed: Anti-Internationalism and the American Right," *World Policy Journal* (Fall 1995): 1–13.

53. Richard A. Melanson, *Reconstructing Consensus: American Foreign Policy Since the Vietnam War* (New York: St. Martin's Press, 1990), p. 17.

54. Schneider, "'Rambo' and Reality," p. 51. See also James A. Stimson, *Public Opinion in America: Moods, Cycles, and Swings* (Boulder, Colo.: Westview Press, 1991).

55. See I. M. Destler, Leslie H. Gelb, and Anthony Lake, *Our Own Worst Enemy: The Unmaking of American Foreign Policy* (New York: Simon and Schuster, 1984); Alexander L. George, "Domestic Constraints on Regime Change in U.S. Foreign Policy: The Need for Policy Legitimacy," in Ole R. Holsti, Randolph Siverson, and Alexander L. George, eds., *Change in the International System* (Boulder, Colo.: Westview Press, 1980); Miroslav Nincic, "The United States, the Soviet Union, and the Politics of Opposites," *World Politics* 40 (July 1988): 452–75; Jerel A. Rosati, "United States Leadership Into the Next Millennium," *International Affairs* (spring 1997): 297–315; and Daniel Yankelovich, "Farewell to 'President Knows Best,'" *Foreign Affairs* (America and the World, 1978): 670–93.

56. See, for example, John E. Rielly, "Public Opinion: The Pulse of the '90s," *Foreign Policy* 82 (spring 1991): 79–96. For an extended discussion of the impact of the end of the cold war on opinion leaders in U.S. foreign policy, see Rosati and Creed, "Extending the Three-Headed and Four-Headed Eagles."

57. Schneider, "Public Opinion," p. 672. For a general discussion of political culture and the American ethos, see Gabriel A. Almond and Sidney Verba, *The Civic Culture: Political Attitudes and Democracy in Five Nations* (Princeton: Princeton University Press, 1963); Clifford Geertz, *The Interpretation of Cultures: Selected Essays* (New York: Basic Books, 1973); Herbert McClosky and John Zaller, *The American Ethos: Public Attitudes Toward Capitalism and Democracy* (Cambridge, Mass.: Harvard University Press, 1984). Two modern classics on American political culture are Louis Hartz, *The Liberal Tradition in America* (New York: Harcourt, Brace and World, 1955), and Richard Hofstadter, *The Age of Reform* (New York: Vintage, 1955). For an alternative interpretation from the perspective of minorities and women, see Rogers M. Smith, "Beyond Tocqueville, Myrdal, and Hartz: The Multiple Traditions in America" *American Political Science Review* (September 1993): 549–66. For an excellent overview of the study of political culture, see Lucian W. Pye, "Political Culture Revisited," *Political Psychology* (1991): 487–508.

58. See Loren Baritz, *Backfire: A History of How American Culture Led Us Into Vietnam and Made Us Fight the Way We Did*

(New York: William Morrow, 1985); Jack Citrin, Ernst B. Haas, and Christopher Muste, "Is American Nationalism Changing? Implications for Foreign Policy?", *International Studies Quarterly* (1994): 1–31; William W. Cobb, Jr. *The American Foundation Myth in Vietnam* (Lanham, Md.: University Press of America, 1998); T. R. Davis and S. M. Lynn-Jones, "City Upon a Hill," *Foreign Policy* 66 (spring 1987): 20–38; Hodgson, *America in Our Time*; Michael H. Hunt, *Ideology and U.S. Foreign Policy* (New Haven: Yale University Press, 1987); Richard J. Kerry, *The Star-Spangled Mirror: America's Image of Itself and the World* (Savage, Md.: Rowman and Littlefield, 1990); Roger S. Whitcomb, *The American Approach to Foreign Affairs: An Uncertain Tradition* (Westport, Conn.: Praeger, 1998). For an example of earlier works emphasizing the importance of American culture, see Almond, *American People and Foreign Policy*, chapter 3, and Hoffmann, *Gulliver's Troubles*.

59. See, for example, Selig Adler, *The Isolationist Impulse* (New York: Free Press, 1966); Almond, *American People and Foreign Policy*; and Barnet, *Roots of War*.

60. See Reginald Horseman, *Race and Manifest Destiny* (Cambridge, Mass.: Harvard University Press, 1981); Frederick Merk, *Manifest Destiny and Mission in American History* (New York: Vintage, 1963); Anders Stephanson, *Manifest Destiny: American Expansion and the Empire of Right* (New York: Hill and Wang, 1995); William Earl Weeks, *Building the Continental Empire: American Expansion from the Revolution to the Civil War* (Chicago: Ivan R. Dee, 1996).

61. James Oliver Robertson, *American Myth, American Reality* (New York: Hill and Wang, 1980), p. 349.

62. For an excellent overview of the literature on the origins of the cold war, including the orthodox interpretation, see Richard A. Melanson, *Writing History and Making Policy: The Cold War, Vietnam, and Revisionism* (Lanham, Md.: University Press of America, 1983).

63. Stephanson, *Manifest Destiny*, p. 125.

64. Hodgson, *America in Our Time*, pp. 3–4.

65. Alexis de Tocqueville, *Democracy in America* (New York: Vintage, 1945).

66. Barnet, Roots of War, p. 251. See also Michael Kammen, "The Problem of American Exceptionalism: A Reconsideration," *American Quarterly* (March 1993): 1–43; Joseph Lepgold and Timothy McKeown, "Is American Foreign Policy Exceptional? An Empirical Analysis," *Political Science Quarterly* (Fall 1995): 369–84; Byron E. Shafer, ed., *Is America Different: A New Look at American Exceptionalism* (New York: Oxford University Press, 1991).

67. See, for example, Alan Brinkley, "The Western Historians: Don't Fence Them In," *The New York Times Review of Books* (September 20, 1992): 1, 22–27; Patricia Nelson Limerick, *The Legacy of Conquest: The Unbroken Past of the American West* (New York: W.W. Norton, 1987); Richard Slotkin, *Gunfighter Nation: The Myth of the Frontier in Twentieth-Century America* (Atheneum, 1992). For an overview of the nature of historical textbooks in general used in American educational systems throughout the country, see Frances Fitzgerald, *America Revised: History Schoolbooks in the Twentieth Century* (Boston: Atlantic

Monthly Press, 1979); Alexander Stille, "The Betrayal of History," *The New York Review of Books* (June 11, 1998), pp. 15–20.

68. Robertson, *American Myth, American Reality*, p. xv.

69. Richard K. Betts, "The Soft Underbelly of American Primacy: Tactical Advantages of Terror," *Political Science Quarterly* (spring 2002), pp. 20, 33.

70. Robert Nisbet, *The Present Age: Progress and Anarchy in Modern America* (New York: Harper and Row, 1988), p. 32.

71. Howard Fineman, "Bush and God," *Newsweek* (March 10, 2003), p. 25.

72. Ibid., p. 29.

73. Hoffmann, *Gulliver's Troubles*, p. 194.

74. Reinhold Niebuhr and Alan Heimert, *A Nation So Conceived* (New York: Charles Scribner's Sons, 1963), p. 150.

75. Hoffmann, *Gulliver's Troubles*, p. 178. See also Donald W. White, *The American Century: The Rise and Decline of the United States as a World Power* (New Haven: Yale University Press, 1996).

76. See George F. Kennan, *American Diplomacy, 1900–1950* (New York: Mentor, 1951); Hans J. Morgenthau, *In Defense of the National Interest: A Critical Examination of American Foreign Policy* (New York: Knopf, 1952); and Reinhold Niebuhr, *The Children of Light and the Children of Darkness* (New York: Scribners, 1944), and *Moral Man and Immoral Society* (New York: Charles Scribner's Sons, 1932).

77. William Schneider, "Public Opinion," p. 33. See also Destler, *Our Own Worst Enemy*; George, "Domestic Constraints on Regime Change"; B. T. Trout, "Rhetoric Revisited: Political Legitimacy and the Cold War," *International Studies Quarterly* (1975): 251–84.

78. Yergin, *Shattered Peace*, pp. 281–82. See also Richard M. Freeland, *The Truman Doctrine and the Origins of McCarthyism: Foreign Policy, Domestic Politics, and Internal Security, 1946–1948* (New York: Knopf, 1972).

79. Hoffmann, *Gulliver's Troubles*, p. 195.

80. Davis and Lynn-Jones, "City Upon a Hill," p. 24. For a discussion of public moods and their impact on foreign policy, see Almond, *American People and Foreign Policy*; William R. Caspary, "The 'Mood Theory': A Study of Public Opinion and Foreign Policy," *American Political Science Review* (1970): 536–47; Frank L. Klingberg, "The Historical Alternation of Moods in American Foreign Policy," *World Politics* 4 (1952): 239–73; Michael Roskin, "From Pearl Harbor to Vietnam: Shifting Generational Paradigms and Foreign Policy," *Political Science Quarterly* 89 (fall 1974): 563–88; and Arthur Schlesinger, Jr., *The Cycles of American History* (Boston: Houghton Mifflin, 1986).

81. Hartz, *Liberal Tradition*, p. 286.

82. Barnet, *Roots of War*, p. 259; Hoffmann, *Gulliver's Troubles*, p. 191.

83. See also Christian G. Appy, ed., *Cold War Constructions: The Political Culture of United States Imperialism, 1945–1966* (Amherst: University of Massachusetts Press, 2000); Cobb, *The American Foundation Myth*; Ronald Steel, *Walter Lippmann and the American Century* (New York: Vintage, 1981); Stephen Twing, *Myths, Models, and U.S. Foreign Policy: The Cultural Shaping of

Three Cold Warriors (Boulder, Colo.: Lynne Rienner, 1998); White, *The American Century*.

84. Hodgson, *America in Our Time*, p. 12.

85. J. William Fulbright, *The Arrogance of Power* (New York: Vintage, 1966).

86. See, for example, Seymour Martin Lipset and William Schneider, "The Decline of Confidence in American Institutions," *Political Science Quarterly* 98 (fall 1983): 379–402.

87. Robertson, *American Myth, American Reality*, p. 348.

CHAPTER 14

1. See Michael X. Delli Carpini and Scott Keeter, *What Americans Know About Politics and Why It Matters* (New Haven: Yale University Press, 1996); E. J. Dionne, Jr., *Why Americans Hate Politics* (New York: Simon and Schuster, 1991); Herbert J. Gans, *Middle American Individualism: Political Participation and Liberal Democracy* (New York: Oxford University Press, 1988); Seymour Martin Lipset and William Schneider, "The Decline of Confidence in American Institutions," *Political Science Quarterly* (fall 1983): 379–402.

2. For an overview of political participation, see M. Margaret Conway, *Political Participation in the United States* (Washington, D.C.: Congressional Quarterly Press, 2000); W. Russell Neuman, *The Paradox of Mass Politics: Knowledge and Opinion in the American Electorate* (Cambridge, Mass.: Harvard University Press, 1986); Sidney Verba and Norman H. Nie, *Participation in America: Political Democracy and Social Equality* (Chicago: University of Chicago Press, 1972); and James Q. Wilson, *Political Organizations* (Princeton: Princeton University Press, 1995).

3. Sean Wilentz, "The Power of the Powerless: The Fierce and Forgotten Battle for the Bill of Rights," *New Republic* (December 23 & 30, 1991), p. 32. See also Gordon S. Wood, *The Radicalism of the American Revolution* (New York: Knopf, 1992).

4. For some valuable context, see David Lowenthal, *Possessed by the Past: The Heritage Crusade and the Spoils of History* (New York: Free Press, 1996); Pauline Maier, *American Scripture: Making the Declaration of Independence* (New York: Knopf, 1997).

5. As with various bills of rights, there were at least ninety different declarations of independence that Americans in the colonies (later states) and localities adopted between April and July of 1776, with many precedents in English history. See Maier, *American Scripture*.

6. For an overview, see James MacGregor Burns and Stewart Burns, *A People's Charter: The Pursuit of Rights in America* (New York: Knopf, 1991); Sara M. Evans, *Born for Liberty: A History of Women in America* (New York: Free Press, 1989); Leonard Dinnerstein, Roger L. Nichols, and David M. Reimers, *Natives and Strangers: Ethnic Groups and the Building of America* (New York: Oxford University Press, 1979); Alphonso Pinkney, *Black Americans* (Englewood Cliffs, N.J.: Prentice-Hall, 1969); and Howard Zinn, *A People's History of the United States* (New York: Harper and Row, 1980).

7. David Kairys, "The Evolution of Free Speech," *In These Times* (December 18–24, 1991), p. 12.

8. See, for example, John H. Broesamle, *Reform and Reaction in Twentieth Century American Politics* (Westport, Conn: Greenwood Press, 1990); James MacGregor Burns, *The Crosswinds of Freedom* (New York: Knopf, 1989); Arthur A. Stein and Bruce M. Russett, "Evaluating War: Outcomes and Consequences," in *Handbook of Political Conflict: Theory and Research*, edited by Ted R. Gurr (New York: Free Press, 1980), pp. 399–422.

9. Seymour Martin Lipset, *Political Man: The Social Bases of Politics* (Garden City, N.Y.: Anchor, 1968), p. 448. See also David Riesman, Nathan Glazer, and Reuel Denney, *The Lonely Crowd: A Study of the Changing American Character* (Garden City, N.Y.: Anchor, 1953).

10. Richard Hofstadter, *The Paranoid Style in American Politics and Other Essays* (New York: Knopf, 1965).

11. Robert Nisbet, *The Present Age: Progress and Anarchy in Modern America* (New York: Harper and Row, 1988), p. 39.

12. For an overview, see William H. Chafe, *The Unfinished Journey: America Since World War II* (New York: Oxford University Press, 1986); Frank J. Donner, *The Age of Surveillance* (New York: Vintage, 1981); Robert J. Goldstein, *Political Repression in Modern America: From 1870 to the Present* (Cambridge, Mass.: Schenkman, 1977); M. J. Heale, *American Anticommunism: Combating the Enemy Within, 1930–1970* (Baltimore: Johns Hopkins University Press, 1990); Michael Linfield, *Freedom Under Fire: U.S. Civil Liberties in Times of War* (Boston: South End Press, 1990); Richard Gid Powers, *Secrecy and Power: The Life of J. Edgar Hoover* (New York: Free Press, 1987); George Brown Tindall, *America: A Narrative History* (New York: W. W. Norton, 1988); and Zinn, *A People's History*.

13. Alan Brinkley, *The Unfinished Nation* (New York: McGraw Hill, 1993), p. 617; George B. Tindall, *America: A Narrative History* (New York: Norton, 1988), pp. 1003–5.

14. Milton Cantor, *The Divided Left: American Radicalism, 1900–1975* (New York: Hill and Wang, 1978), p. 31. See also James MacGregor Burns, *The Workshop of Democracy* (New York: Knopf, 1985), and Tindall, *America: A Narrative History*.

15. In Paul Goodman and Frank Otto Gatell, *USA: An American Record*, vol. 2 (Hinsdale, Ill.: Dryden Press, 1972), p. 380.

16. James Brooke, "After Silence, Italians Recall the Internment," *New York Times* (August 13, 1997), p. A8. See also Arnold Krammer, *Undue Process: The Untold Story of America's German Alien Internees* (Lanham, Md.: Rowman and Littlefield, 1997).

17. See, e.g., Harvey Klehr, John Earl Haynes, and Kyrill M. Anderson, *The Secret World of American Communism* (New Haven: Yale University Press, 1998).

18. Sam Tanenhaus, "Keeping the Faith," *New York Review of Books* (June 25, 1998), p. 48.

19. Ralph S. Brown, *Loyalty and Security* (New Haven: Yale University Press, 1958). See also Stephen J. Whitfield, *The Culture of the Cold War* (Baltimore: Johns Hopkins University Press, 1991).

20. See Stanley I. Kutler, *The American Inquisition: Justice and Injustice in the Cold War* (New York: Hill and Wang, 1982).

21. Ellen W. Schrecker, *No Ivory Tower: McCarthyism and the Universities* (New York: Oxford University Press, 1986), pp. 10–11. See also David Caute, *The Great Fear: The Anti-Communist Purge Under Truman and Eisenhower* (New York: Simon and Schuster, 1978); and Victor S. Navasky, *Naming Names* (New York: Penguin, 1980).

22. Schrecker, *No Ivory Tower,* p. 340. See also Lionel S. Lewis, *Cold War on Campus: A Study of the Politics of Organizational Control* (New Brunswick, N.J.: Transaction, 1988), and Paul Lazarsfeld and Wagner Thielens, Jr., *The Academic Mind* (Glencoe, Ill.: Free Press, 1958).

23. Caute, *The Great Fear,* pp. 406–24. See also David Caute, *The Fellow Travelers: A Postscript to the Enlightenment* (London: Weidenfeld and Nicolson, 1973).

24. Sigmund Desmond, *Compromised Campus: The Collaboration of Universities with the Intelligence Community, 1945–1955* (New York: Oxford University Press, 1992).

25. Martha Gellhorn, "Cry Shame . . . !" *New Republic* (October 6, 1947), p. 21.

26. See Gary Wills, *Reagan's America* (New York: Penguin, 1988), pp. 295–97; and James Kirkpatrick Davis, *Spying on America: The FBI's Domestic Counterintelligence Program* (New York: Praeger, 1992).

27. Cited in Tom Hayden, *Reunion: A Memoir* (New York: Collier, 1988), p. 283.

28. David Halberstam, *The Best and the Brightest* (New York: Random House, 1969), p. 623.

29. See Frank J. Donner, *Protectors of Privilege: Red Squads and Police Repression in Urban America* (Berkeley and Los Angeles: University of California Press, 1990).

30. Robert Parry and Peter Kornbluh, "Iran-Contra's Untold Story," *Foreign Policy* (fall 1988): 5.

31. U.S. Congress, General Accounting Office, *International Terrorism: FBI Investigates Domestic Activities to Identify Terrorists* (September 1990). See also Richard O. Curry, ed., *Freedom at Risk: Secrecy, Censorship, and Repression in the 1980s* (Philadelphia: Temple University Press, 1988).

32. See, for example, Lisa Belkin, "For Many Arab Americans, FBI Scrutiny Renews Fears," *New York Times* (January 12, 1991), p. 1A.

33. Keith Schneider, "Idaho Says No," *New York Times Magazine* (March 11, 1990), pp. 57–61.

34. Throughout twentieth-century American history, threats to the democratic exercise of civil rights and liberties have tended to come predominantly from the political right for two reasons: Conservatives and the right have traditionally been most intolerant of civil liberties and concerned with combating the threat of alien ideas, such as communism and socialism; and they have been powerful forces in government and have successfully generated political support throughout society by using the strong symbolic appeals of nationalism and Americanism. See David H. Bennett, *The Party of Fear: From Nativist Movements to the New Right in American History* (Chapel Hill: University of North Carolina Press, 1988); Michael Paul Rogin, *The Intellectuals and McCarthy: The Radical Specter* (Cambridge, Mass.: MIT Press, 1967); and Herbert McClosky and Alida Brill, *Dimensions of Tolerance: What Americans Believe About Civil Liberties* (New York: Russell Sage Foundation, 1983). It must be recognized, however, that the far right has no monopoly on intolerance and repression. Elements of the far left, such as Marxist-Leninist groups, are also quite dogmatic and authoritarian—although they have never had more than a minute following within American society and have never been influential within the government. Furthermore, liberals have been guilty of initiating violations of civil liberties, as with the internment of Japanese Americans under California Governor Earl Warren and President Franklin Roosevelt, and of feeding and appeasing the political right, such as the internal security measures instituted by the Truman administration following World War II that fanned the flames of anticommunism and McCarthyism during the cold war years. See also Richard M. Freeland, *The Truman Doctrine and the Origins of McCarthyism: Foreign Policy, Domestic Politics, and Internal Security, 1946–1948* (New York: Knopf, 1972); James L. Gibson, "Political Intolerance and Political Repression During the McCarthy Red Scare," *American Political Science Review* 82 (June 1988): 511–29; William Keller, *The Liberals and J. Edgar Hoover: Rise and Fall of a Domestic Intelligence State* (Princeton, N.J.: Princeton University Press, 1989); Coleman, *The Liberal Conspiracy;* and Richard H. Pells, *The Liberal Mind in a Conservative Age: American Intellectuals in the 1940s and 1950s* (New York: Harper and Row, 1965).

35. See Kate Doyle, "The End of Secrecy: U.S. National Security and the Imperative for Openness," *World Policy Journal* (spring 1999): 34–51; Morton H. Halperin and Jeanne M. Woods, "Ending the Cold War at Home," *Foreign Policy* 81 (winter 1990–91): 128–43.

36. See, for example, James L. Gibson, "The Political Consequences of Intolerance: Cultural Conformity and Political Freedom," *American Political Science Review* (June 1992): 338–56; McClosky and Brill, *Dimensions of Tolerance.*

37. J. William Fulbright, *The Arrogance of Power* (New York: Vintage, 1966), pp. 27, 25, 65.

38. Jim McGee, "An Intelligence Giant in the Making; Anti-Terrorism Law Likely to Bring Domestic Apparatus of Unprecedented Scope," *The Washington Post* (November 4, 2001).

39. Harry F. Tepker, "The USA Patriot Act," *Extensions* (Fall 2002), p. 10.

40 Eric Schmitt, "Military Role in U.S. Gains Favor," *The New York Times* (July 21, 2002), p. 16.

41. Tepker, "USA Patriot Act," pp. 11–12.

42. Scott Carlson and Andrea L. Foster, "Colleges Fear Anti-Terrorism Could Turn Them Into Big Brother," *Chronicle of Higher Education* (March 1, 2002), www.chroonicle.com

43. Carolina Bolado, "FBI Probes Records of Library Users," *The State* (June 29, 2002), p. B1.

44. Richard L. Berke and Janet Elder, "Strong Backing for Force Is Found in Poll," *New York Times* (September 16, 2001), pp. 1, 4.

45. Jacques Steinberg, "In Sweeping Campus Canvasses, U.S. Checks on Mideast Students," *New York Times* (November 12, 2001), www.nytimes.com

46. Robin Wilson and Ana Marie Cox, "Terrorist Attacks Put Academic Freedom to the Test," *Chronicle of Higher Education* (October 5, 2001), www.chronicle.com

47. Dan Eggen and Bob Woodward, "Casting a Wide Net for Al Qaeda," *Washington Post Weekly Edition* (January 7–15, 2002), p. 29; William Safire, "Congress Helps Repel the Privacy Invasion," *The New York Times* (February 13, 2003).

48. Sharon Begley, "What Price Security," *Newsweek* (October 1, 2001), p. 58.

49. Robin Toner, "Despite Some Concerns, Civil Liberties Are Taking a Back Seat," *New York Times* (November 18, 2001), www.nytimes.com

CHAPTER 15

1. David Halberstam, *War in a Time of Peace: Bush, Clinton, and the Generals* (New York: Scribner, 2001), pp. 9, 12.

2. Ibid, pp. 15, 16.

3. Ibid., p. 17.

4. Robert S. Strauss, "What's Right With U.S. Campaigns," *Foreign Policy* 55 (summer 1984): 4.

5. For an overview of the party system in the United States, see, for example, Paul Allen Beck, *Party Politics in America* (Boston: Addison-Wesley Longman, 2000); Fred I. Greenstein, *The American Party System and the American People* (Englewood Cliffs, N.J.: Prentice-Hall, 1963); and J. David Gillespie, *Politics at the Periphery: Third Parties in Two-Party America* (Columbia: University of South Carolina Press, 1993).

6. Martin P. Wattenberg, "The Crisis of Electoral Politics," *Atlantic Monthly* (May 1997), p. 119. See also Guy Molyneux and William Schneider, "Ross Is Boss," *Atlantic Monthly* (May 1993), pp. 84–96.

7. Strauss, "What's Right With U.S. Campaigns," p. 7.

8. William A. Galston and Christopher J. Makins, "Campaign '88 and Foreign Policy," *Foreign Policy* 71 (summer 1988): 4.

9. For an overview of the role of electoral politics in U.S. foreign policy, see I. M. Destler, Leslie H. Gelb, and Anthony Lake, *Our Own Worst Enemy: The Unmaking of American Foreign Policy* (New York: Simon and Schuster, 1984); Galston and Makins, "Campaign '88 and Foreign Policy"; Stephen Hess, "Foreign Policy and Presidential Campaigns," *Foreign Policy* 8 (fall 1972): 3–22; Ralph B. Levering, *The Public and American Foreign Policy, 1918–1978* (New York: William Morrow, 1978); Miroslav Nincic, "U.S. Soviet Policy and the Electoral Connection," *World Politics* 42 (April 1990): 370–96; and William B. Quandt, "The Electoral Cycle and the Conduct of Foreign Policy," *Political Science Quarterly* (Centennial Year, 1986): 825–37.

10. For a historical overview of major party and electoral patterns, see Walter Dean Burnham, *Critical Elections and the Mainsprings of American Politics* (New York: W. W. Norton, 1970); James MacGregor Burns, *The Crosswinds of Freedom* (New York: Vintage, 1989); Steve Fraser and Gary Gerstle, eds., *The Rise and Fall of the New Deal Order, 1930–1980* (Princeton: Princeton University Press, 1989); Everett Carll Ladd, *American Political Parties: Social Change and Political Response* (New York: W. W. Norton, 1970); James I. Sundquist, *Dynamics of the Party System: Alignment and Realignment of Political Parties in the U.S.* (Washington, D.C.: Brookings Institution Press, 1983).

11. For a good overview of the concept of realignment, see David G. Lawrence and Richard Fleisher, "Puzzles and Confusions: Political Realignment in the 1980s," *Political Science Quarterly* (spring 1987): 79–92.

12. William H. Chafe, *The Unfinished Journey: America Since World War II* (New York: Oxford University Press, 1991), p. 98.

13. Clark Clifford quoted in ibid., p. 103.

14. Robert A. Devine, *Foreign Policy and U.S. Presidential Elections: 1952–1960* (New York: New Viewpoints, 1974), p. 53.

15. William Manchester, *The Glory and the Dream: A Narrative History of America, 1932–1972* (New York: Bantam, 1973), p. 628.

16. This is the major theme of Eric F. Goldman, *The Crucial Decade—and After: America, 1945–1960* (New York: Random House, 1961).

17. Godfrey Hodgson, *America in Our Time* (New York: Vintage, 1976), pp. 73–74. See also Theodore H. White, *The Making of the President, 1960* (New York: Atheneum, 1961).

18. David Halberstam, *The Best and the Brightest* (New York: Random House, 1969), pp. 298, 425.

19. For an overview of these electoral patterns since the 1960s, see Everett Carll Ladd, "The Brittle Mandate: Electoral Dealignment and the 1980 Presidential Election," *Political Science Quarterly* (spring 1981): 1–25; Everett Carll Ladd, "On Mandates, Realignments, and the 1984 Presidential Election," *Political Science Quarterly* (spring 1985): 1–25; Everett Carll Ladd, "The 1988 Elections: Continuation of the Post-New Deal System," *Political Science Quarterly* (spring 1989): 1–18; Everett Carll Ladd, "The 1992 Vote for President Clinton: Another Brittle Mandate?" *Political Science Quarterly* (1993): 1–28; Everett Carll Ladd, "The 1996 Vote: The 'No Majority' Realignment Continues," *Political Science Quarterly* (spring 1997): 1–28; and Norman H. Nie, Sidney Verba, and John R. Petrocik, *The Changing American Voter* (Cambridge, Mass.: Harvard University Press, 1976); Martin P. Wattenberg, *The Decline of American Political Parties, 1952–1996* (Cambridge, Mass.: Harvard University Press, 1998).

20. See Byron E. Shafer, ed., *The End of Realignment? Interpreting American Electoral Eras* (Madison: University of Wisconsin Press, 1991); James L. Sundquist, "Needed: A Political Theory for the New Era of Coalition Government in the United States," *Political Science Quarterly* (1988): 613–35. See also Peter F. Nardulli, "The Concept of a Critical Realignment, Electoral Behavior, and Political Change," *American Political Science Review* (March 1995): 10–22.

21. Burns, *Crosswinds of Freedom*, pp. 656–57.

22. See Earl Black and Merle Black, *Politics and Society in the South* (Cambridge, Mass.: Harvard University Press, 1987), and

Kevin P. Phillips, *The Emerging Republican Majority* (New Rochelle, N.Y.: Arlington House, 1969).

23. See Rick Perlstein, *Before the Storm: Barry Goldwater and the Unmaking of the American Consensus* (New York: Hill and Wang, 2001).

24. To appreciate the politics involved behind the power of incumbency, see Hedrick Smith, *The Power Game: How Washington Works* (New York: Ballantine, 1988), chapter 7.

25. Richard L. Berke, "In Fund-Raising Race, Incumbents Are Ahead," *New York Times* (November 5, 1990), p. A11.

26. William Schneider, "'Rambo' and Reality: Having It Both Ways," in Kenneth A. Oye, Robert J. Lieber, and Donald Rothchild, eds., *Eagle Resurgent? The Reagan Era in American Foreign Policy* (Boston: Little, Brown, 1987), p. 46. See also Ole R. Holsti and James N. Rosenau, *American Leadership in World Affairs: Vietnam and the Breakdown of Consensus* (New York: Allen and Unwin, 1984), and James N. Rosenau, "U.S. Leadership in a Shrinking World: The Breakdown of Consensuses and the Emergence of Conflict Belief Systems," *World Politics* 35 (April 1983): 368–92.

27. William Schneider, "Public Opinion," in Joseph S. Nye, Jr., *The Making of America's Soviet Policy* (New Haven, Conn.: Yale University Press, 1984), pp. 13–14.

28. Schneider, "'Rambo' and Reality," p. 51. See also Marc J. Hetherington, "Resurgent Mass Partisanship: The Role of Elite Polarization," *American Political Science Review* 95 (September 2001,), pp. 619–31.

29. John H. Aldrich, John L. Sullivan, and Eugene Borgida, "Foreign Affairs and Issue Voting: Do Presidential Candidates 'Waltz' Before a Blind Audience?" *American Political Science Review* 83 (March 1989): 135. See also Miroslav Nincic and Barbara Hinckley, "Foreign Policy and the Evaluation of Presidential Candidates," *Journal of Conflict Resolution* (June 1991): 333–55; Benjamin I. Page and Robert Y. Shapiro, *The Rational Public: Fifty Years of Trends in Americans' Policy Preferences* (Chicago: University of Chicago Press, 1992), and Robert Y. Shapiro and Benjamin I. Page, "Foreign Policy and the Rational Public," *Journal of Conflict Resolution* 32 (June 1988): 211–47.

30. Holsti and Rosenau, *American Leadership in World Affairs*, p. 1. See chapter 2 for greater discussion of continuity and change in U.S. foreign policy since Vietnam.

31. See William Schneider, "JFK's Children: The Class of '74," *Atlantic Monthly* (March 1989), pp. 35–58.

32. See Miroslav Nincic, "The United States, The Soviet Union, and the Politics of Opposites," *World Politics* 40 (July 1988): 452–75; Jerel A. Rosati, "United States Leadership Into the Next Millennium," *International Affairs* (spring 1997): 297–315;

33. See, for example, Benjamin Ginsberg and Martin Shefter, *Politics by Other Means: The Declining Importance of Elections in America* (New York: Basic Books, 1990), Gary C. Jacobson, "A House and Senate Divided: The Clinton Legacy and the Congressional Elections of 2000," *Political Science Quarterly* 116 (2001): 5–27, and Smith, *The Power Game*, chapters 17 and 18.

34. Norman J. Ornstein and Mark Schmitt, "Dateline Campaign '92: Post–Cold War Politics," *Foreign Policy* 79 (Summer 1990): 169.

35. For an overview of the contemporary electoral process, particularly in presidential races, see Thomas Byrne Edsall with Mary D. Edsall, *Chain Reaction: The Impact of Race, Rights, and Taxes on American Politics* (New York: W.W. Norton, 1992); Thomas Byrne Edsall, "Willie Horton's Message," *New York Review of Books* (February 13, 1992): 7–11; William Schneider, "The New Shape of American Politics," *The Atlantic Monthly* (January 1987): 39–54; Smith, *The Power Game*, chapters 18 and 19; and Stephen J. Wayne, *The Road to the White House: The Politics of Presidential Elections* (New York: St. Martin's Press, 2001).

36. Martin P. Wattenberg, *The Rise of Candidate-Centered Politics: Presidential Elections of the 1980s* (Cambridge, Mass.: Harvard University Press, 1991).

37. In most primary elections, only registered party members—not independents—can cast a vote and usually only for a nominee from their party (although there is some variation among states). In general elections, all those registered—including independents—can vote for any party candidate.

38. V. O. Key, Jr., *The Responsible Electorate: Rationality in Presidential Voting, 1936–1960* (New York: Vintage, 1966). See also Richard A. Brody, *Assessing the President: The Media, Public Opinion, and Public Support* (Stanford: Stanford University Press, 1991); Morris P. Fiorina, *Retrospective Voting in American National Elections* (New Haven, Conn.: Yale University Press, 1981); Arthur H. Miller and Martin P. Wattenberg, "Throwing the Rascals Out: Policy and Performance Evaluations of Presidential Candidates, 1952–1980," *American Political Science Review* 79 (June 1985): 359–72; Samuel L. Popkin, *The Reasoning Voter: Communication and Persuasion in Presidential Campaigns* (Chicago: University of Chicago Press, 1991).

39. Louis Menand, "Inside the Billway," *New York Review of Books* (August 14, 1997), p. 4. For an overview of the election, see Thomas Omestad, "Foreign Policy and Campaign '96," *Foreign Policy* 105 (winter 1996–97): 37–54; Larry J. Sabato, ed., *Toward the Millennium: The Elections of 1996* (Boston: Allyn and Bacon, 1997).

40. See Robert S. Erikson, "The 2000 Presidential Election in Historical Perspective," *Political Science Quarterly* (spring 2001): 29–52; Gerald M. Pomper, "The 2000 Presidential Election: Why Gore Lost," *Political Science Quarterly* (summer 2001): 201–24; The Washington Post, *Deadlock: The Inside Story of America's Closest Election* (New York: PublicAffairs, 2001).

41. See Stephen Hess and Michael Nelson, "Foreign Policy: Dominance and Decisiveness in Presidential Elections," in Michael Nelson, ed., *The Elections of 1984* (Washington, D.C.: Congressional Quarterly Press, 1985), pp. 141–52; Howard Fineman, "How Bush Did It," *Newsweek* (November 18, 2002), pp. 29–38.

42. See, for example, Anthony King, "Running Scared," *Atlantic Monthly* (January 1997): 41–61; Joe McGinniss, *The Selling of the President, 1968* (New York: Pocket Books, 1969).

43. See Kathleen Hall Jamieson, *Dirty Politics: Deception, Distraction, and Democracy* (New York: Oxford University Press, 1992); Peter Goldman, Tom Mathews, and the Newsweek Special

Election Team, *The Quest for the Presidency, 1988* (New York: Touchstone, 1989), and Sidney Blumenthal, *Pledging Allegiance: The Last Campaign of the Cold War* (New York: HarperCollins, 1990).

44. See Newsweek, *Special Election Issue* (November 18, 1996); Bob Woodward, *The Choice* (New York: Simon and Schuster, 1996).

45. Robert Strauss provides a more optimistic discussion of contemporary elections and its impact on foreign policy in "What's Right With U.S. Campaigns."

46. See Everett Carll Ladd, *Where Have All the Voters Gone? The Fracturing of America's Political Parties* (New York: W. W. Norton, 1978); Richard M. Valelly, "Vanishing Voters," *The American Prospect* (spring 1990), pp. 140–50; and Wattenberg, *The Decline of American Political Parties.*

47. See Alexander P. Smith, "Idealism and Realism in United States Post–Cold War Foreign Policy Rhetoric" (Senior honors thesis, University of South Carolina, 2001).

48. See Erikson, "The 2000 Presidential Election in Historical Perspective."

CHAPTER 16

1. For an overview of social movements and interest groups see, for example, Jeffrey M. Berry and Margaret Loftus, *The Interest Group Society* (Glenview, Ill.: Scott, Foresman, 1997); Allan J. Cigler and Burdett A. Loomis, eds., *Interest Group Politics* (Washington, D.C., Congressional Quarterly Press, 1998); Ronald J. Hrebenar and Ruth K. Scott, *Interest Group Politics in America* (Englewood Cliffs, N.J.: Prentice-Hall, 1996); David B. Truman, *The Governmental Process: Political Interests and Public Opinion* (New York: Knopf, 1971); and James Q. Wilson, *Political Organizations* (Princeton: Princeton University Press, 1995). For a cross-national assessment of political oppositions to regimes and their effect on foreign policy, see Joe D. Hagan, "Regimes, Political Oppositions, and the Comparative Analysis of Foreign Policy," in Charles F. Hermann, Charles W. Kegley, Jr., and James N. Rosenau, eds., *New Directions in the Study of Foreign Policy* (Boston: Allen and Unwin, 1987), pp. 339–65.

2. Truman, *The Governmental Process,* p. xii.

3. James MacGregor Burns, *The Crosswinds of Freedom* (New York: Vintage, 1989), p. 656.

4. William A. Gamson, *The Strategy of Social Protest* (Homewood, Ill.: Dorsey Press, 1975), p. 140.

5. For a brief overview of group politics during this time, see Gabriel A. Almond, *The American People and Foreign Policy* (New York: Praeger, 1965), chapter 8.

6. See, for example, Colin S. Gray, "What RAND Hath Wrought," *Foreign Policy* 4 (fall 1971): 111–29, and Jerry W. Sanders, *Peddlers of Crisis: The Committee on the Present Danger and the Politics of Containment* (Boston: South End Press, 1983).

7. William Appleman Williams, *The Tragedy of American Diplomacy* (New York: Delta, 1962), and *The Roots of the Modern*

American Empire (New York: Random House, 1969). See also William I. Cohen, *Empire Without Tears: America's Foreign Relations, 1921–1933* (New York: Knopf, 1987); David A. Lake, *Power, Protection, and Free Trade: International Sources of U.S. Commercial Strategy, 1887–1939* (Ithaca, N.Y.: Cornell University Press, 1988).

8. U.S. Congress, Senate, *Nomination Hearings Before the Committee on Armed Services* (83rd Cong., 1st sess., 1953), p. 26.

9. Michael B. Stoff, *Oil, War and American Security: The Search for a National Policy on Foreign Oil, 1941–1947* (New Haven: Yale University Press, 1980), p. 208. See also Lawrence P. Frank, "The First Oil Regime," *World Politics* (July 1985): 586–98; G. John Ikenberry, *Reasons of State: Oil Politics and the Capacities of American Government* (Ithaca, N.Y.: Cornell University Press, 1988); Anthony Sampson, *The Seven Sisters: The Great Oil Companies and the World They Shaped* (New York: Bantam, 1975); Daniel Yergin, *The Prize: The Epic Quest for Oil, Money and Power* (New York: Simon and Schuster, 1990).

10. See Richard J. Barnet, *Roots of War: The Men and Institutions Behind U.S. Foreign Policy* (Baltimore: Penguin, 1971), chapters 6 and 7; Ron Chernow, *The House of Morgan: An American Banking Dynasty and the Rise of Modern Finance* (New York: Atlantic Monthly Press, 1990); Joanne Gowa, "Subsidizing American Corporate Expansion Abroad: Pitfalls in the Analysis of Public and Private Power," *World Politics* 37 (January 1985): 180–203; David Horowitz, *Corporations and the Cold War* (New York: Bertrand Russell Peace Foundation, 1969). On the other hand, Raymond A. Bauer, Ithiel de Sola Pool, and Lewis Anthony Dexter found that business pressure groups had limited success in directly influencing the specifics of U.S. trade policy in *American Business and Public Policy: The Politics of Foreign Trade* (New York: Atherton Press, 1964).

11. See Steve Fraser and Gary Gerstle, eds., *The Rise and Decline of the New Deal Order, 1930–1980* (Princeton: Princeton University Press, 1989); Rhodri Jeffreys-Jones, *The CIA and American Democracy* (New Haven, Conn.: Yale University Press, 1989); and Ronald Radosh, *American Labor and United States Foreign Policy: The Cold War in the Unions from Gompers to Lovestone* (New York: Vintage, 1970).

12. Garry Wills, *Under God: Religion and American Politics* (New York: Simon and Schuster, 1990), p. 25.

13. See James C. Thomson, Jr., Peter W. Stanley, and John Curtis Perry, *Sentimental Imperialists: The American Experience in East Asia* (New York: Harper and Row, 1981).

14. See A. James Reichley, *Religion in American Public Life* (Washington, D.C.: Brookings Institution, 1985); and Mark Silk, *Spiritual Politics: Religion and America Since World War II* (New York: Simon and Schuster, 1988).

15. U.S. Congress, House Committee on Foreign Affairs, "Foreign Policy Interest Groups as Information Sources," Executive-Legislative Consultation on Foreign Policy: Strengthening Foreign Policy Information Sources for Congress (Washington, D.C.: U.S. Government Printing Office, February 1982), p. 45. See also Stanley D. Bachrack, *The Committee of One Million: "China Lobby" Politics, 1953–1971* (New York: Columbia University Press, 1976), and Ross Y. Koen, *The China Lobby in American*

Politics (New York: Harper and Row, 1974). Ross Koen's book originally was intended for publication by Macmillan in 1960, but it was suppressed by the politics of the times and the opposition of the China lobby.

16. Peter Coleman, *The Liberal Conspiracy: The Congress for Cultural Freedom and the Struggle for the Mind of Postwar Europe* (New York: Free Press, 1989). See also Seymour Martin Lipset, *Political Man: The Social Bases of Politics* (Garden City, N.Y.: Anchor, 1963), chapter 10, and Richard H. Pells, *The Liberal Mind in a Conservative Age: American Intellectuals in the 1940s and 1950s* (New York: Harper and Row, 1985).

17. See, for example, Wayne Biddle, *Barons of the Sky: From Early Flight to Strategic Warfare, The Story of the American Aerospace Industry* (New York: Simon and Schuster, 1991); Geoffrey Perret, *A Country Made by War: From the Revolution to Vietnam—The Story of America's Rise to Power* (New York: Vintage, 1983); Ronald Schaffer, *America in the Great War: The Rise of the War Welfare State* (New York: Oxford University Press, 1991). For the national security infrastructure's development during and after World War II, see Daniel Yergin, *Shattered Peace: The Origins of the Cold War and the National Security State* (Boston: Houghton-Mifflin, 1978).

18. For an overview of the military-industrial-scientific infrastructure, see Adam Yarmolinsky, *The Military Establishment: Its Impacts on American Society* (New York: Harper and Row, 1971).

19. See also Seymour Melman, *Pentagon Capitalism* (New York: McGraw-Hill, 1970), and Richard J. Barnet, *The Permanent War Economy: American Capitalism in Decline* (New York: Touchstone, 1985).

20. See Richard Rhodes, *The Making of the Atomic Bomb* (New York: Simon and Schuster, 1986).

21. Stuart W. Leslie, *The Cold War and American Science: The Military-Industrial-Academic Complex at MIT and Stanford* (New York: Columbia University Press, 1994), p. 1.

22. See, for example, see Noam Chomsky, *American Power and the New Mandarins* (New York: Penguin, 1967); Gregg Herken, *Counsels of War* (New York: Oxford University Press, 1987); Fred Kaplan, *The Wizards of Armageddon* (New York: Touchstone, 1983); Michael E. Latham, *Modernization as Ideology: American Social Science and "Nation-Building" in the Kennedy Era* (Chapel Hill: University of North Carolina Press, 2000); Robert A. Packenham, *Liberal America and the Third World: Political Development Ideas in Foreign Aid and Social Science* (Princeton: Princeton University Press, 1973); Warner R. Schilling, "Scientists, Foreign Policy, and Politics," *American Political Science Review* (June 1962): 287–300; D. Michael Shafer, *Deadly Paradigms: The Failure of U.S. Counterinsurgency Policy* (Princeton: Princeton University Press, 1988); Christopher Simpson, *Science of Coercion: Communication Research and Psychological Warfare, 1945–1960* (New York: Oxford University Press, 1994); Bruce L. R. Smith, *American Science Policy Since World War II* (Washington, D.C.: Brookings Institution Press, 1990).

23. See Stanley Hoffmann, "An American Social Science: International Relations," *Daedalus* (1977): 41–60.

24. In James Miller, *Democracy Is in the Streets: From Port Huron to the Siege of Chicago* (New York: Simon and Schuster, 1987), p. 25.

25. J. William Fulbright, "The War and Its Effects: The Military-Industrial-Academic Complex," in Herbit I. Schiller, ed., *Super-State: Readings in the Military-Industrial Complex* (Urbana: University of Illinois Press, 1970), pp. 177–78.

26. See, for example, U.S. Congress, General Accounting Office, *DOD Revolving Door* (September 1989).

27. Nick Kotz, *Wild Blue Yonder and the B-1 Bomber* (Princeton: Princeton University Press, 1988), p. viii.

28. Godfrey Hodgson, "The Establishment," *Foreign Policy* 10 (spring 1973): 3–40. See also Kai Bird, *The Chairman: John J. McCloy and the Making of the American Establishment* (New York: Simon and Schuster, 1992); Barnet, *Roots of War;* Peter Grose, *Gentleman Spy: The Life of Allen Dulles* (Houghton Mifflin, 1995); David Halbertstam, *The Best and the Brightest* (New York: Random House, 1969); James G. Hershberg, *James B. Conant: Harvard to Hiroshima and the Making of the Nuclear Age* (New York: Knopf, 1994); Max Holland, "Citizen McCloy," *Wilson Quarterly* (Autumn 1991), pp. 22–42; Walter Isaacson and Evan Thomas, *The Wise Men: Six Friends and the World They Made* (New York: Touchstone, 1986); John B. Judis, "Twilight of the Gods," *Wilson Quarterly* (Autumn 1991), pp. 43–55.

29. Hodgson, "The Establishment," p. 8.

30. Ibid., p. 9.

31. Ibid., pp. 6–7.

32. Ibid., p. 9.

33. See E. H. Carr, *The Twenty Years Crisis, 1919–1939* (New York: Harper and Row, 1964); Hans J. Morgenthau, *Politics Among Nations: The Struggle for Power Peace* (New York: Knopf, 1978); and A. F. K. Organski, *World Politics* (New York: Knopf, 1958).

34. Hodgson, "The Establishment," p. 11.

35. Halberstam, *The Best and the Brightest;* Isaacson and Thomas, *The Wise Men.*

36. Halberstam, *The Best and the Brightest,* pp. 100, 41.

37. J. William Fulbright, The Arrogance of Power (New York: Vintage, 1966).

38. Reinhold Niebuhr, "The Foreign Policy of American Conservatism and Liberalism," in *Christian Realism and Political Problems* (New York, Scribner, 1953).

39. Hodgson, "The Establishment," p. 12.

40. Halberstam, *The Best and the Brightest,* p. 49. See also Godfrey Hodgson, *The Colonel: The Life and Wars of Henry Stimson, 1867–1959* (New York: Knopf, 1990); Edmund Morris, *The Rise of Theodore Roosevelt* (New York: Putnam, 1979).

41. Hodgson, "The Establishment," p. 13.

42. Ibid., pp. 16–17.

43. For an overview of the civil rights movement, see Taylor Branch, *Parting the Waters: America in the King Years, 1954–1963* (New York: Simon and Schuster, 1988), and David J. Garrow, *Bearing the Cross: Martin Luther King, Jr., and the Southern Christian Leadership Conference* (New York: Vintage, 1986).

44. See Charles De Benedetti, with Charles Chatfield, *An American Ordeal: The Antiwar Movement of the Vietnam Era*

(Syracuse, N.Y.: Syracuse University Press, 1990); Thomas Powers, *The War at Home: Vietnam and the American People, 1964–1968* (New York: Grossman, 1973); "Protest in the Sixties," *The Annals of the American Academy of Political and Social Science* (March 1969); and Nancy Zaroulis and Gerald Sullivan, *Who Spoke Up? American Protest Against the War in Vietnam, 1963–1975* (New York: Holt, Rinehart and Winston, 1984).

45. See John A. Vasquez, "A Learning Theory of the American Anti-Vietnam War Movement," *Journal of Peace Research* 13 (1976): 299–314.

46. Zaroulis and Sullivan, *Who Spoke Up?*, p. xi.

47. See, for example, Melvin Small, "Influencing the Decision Makers: The Vietnam Experience," *Journal of Peace Research* 24 (1987): 185–98.

48. See Burns, *The Crosswinds of Freedom;* Godfrey Hodgson, *America in Our Time* (New York: Vintage, 1976); and Ronald Inglehart, *Culture Shift in Advanced Industrial Society* (Princeton: Princeton University Press, 1990). For a general discussion, see Russell J. Dalton and Manfred Kuechler, eds., *Challenging the Political Order: New Social and Political Movements in Western Democracies* (New York: Oxford University Press, 1990).

49. See Sara Evans, *Personal Politics: The Roots of Women's Liberation in the Civil Rights Movement and the New Left* (New York: Vintage, 1979); Jo Freeman, *The Origins of the Women's Liberation Movement* (New York: David McKay, 1975); and Laura Woliver, "Feminism at the Grass Roots: The Recall of Judge Archie Simonson," *Frontiers* 11 (1990): 111–19.

50. See Barbara Epstein, *Political Protest and Cultural Revolution: Nonviolent Direct Action in the 1970s and 1980s* (Berkeley and Los Angeles: University of California Press, 1991); Paul Rogat Loeb, *Hope in Hard Times: America's Peace Movement and the Reagan Era* (Lexington, Mass.: Lexington Books, 1987); Steven Metz, "Anti-Apartheid Movement in American Politics," *Political Science Quarterly* 101 (1986): 379–96; David S. Meyer, *A "Winter of Discontent": The Nuclear Freeze and American Politics* (New York: Praeger, 1990); and Douglas C. Waller, *Congress and the Nuclear Freeze: An Inside Look at the Politics of a Mass Movement* (Amherst, Mass.: University of Massachusetts Press, 1987).

51. For an overview of the rise of conservatism and the political right in American politics, see Sidney Blumenthal, *The Rise of the Counter-Establishment: From Conservative Ideology to Political Power* (New York: Times Books, 1986); Alan Crawford, *Thunder on the Right: The "New Right" and the Politics of Resentment* (New York: Pantheon, 1980); Paul Gottfried and Thomas Fleming, *The Conservative Movement* (Boston: Twayne, 1988); Jerome L. Himmelstein, *The Right: The Transformation of American Conservatism* (Berkeley and Los Angeles: University of California Press, 1991); George H. Nash, *The Conservative Intellectual Movement in America* (New York: Basic Books, 1976); and Peter Steinfels, *The Neoconservatives: The Men Who Are Changing America's Politics* (New York: Simon and Schuster, 1979).

52. See, for example, Walter H. Capps, *The New Religious Right: Piety, Patriotism, and Politics* (Columbia, S.C.: University of South Carolina Press, 1990); James Coates, *Armed and Dangerous: The Rise of the Survivalist Right* (New York: Noonday Press,

1987); Carol Flake, *Redemptorama: Culture, Politics, and the New Evangelicalism* (New York: Penguin, 1984); Michael Lind, "Rev. Robertson's Grand International Conspiracy," *The New York Times Review of Books* (February 2, 1995): 21–25; Clyde Wilcox, *God's Warriors: The Christian Right in Twentieth-Century America* (Baltimore: Johns Hopkins University Press, 1991).

53. Truman, *The Governmental Process,* p. 52.

54. Hodgson, "The Establishment," pp. 23–24.

55. Ibid., p. 24.

56. For a more in-depth discussion of this process, see Daniel C. Hallin, *The Uncensored War: The Media and Vietnam* (Berkeley and Los Angeles: University of California Press, 1986). See also I. M. Destler, Leslie H. Gelb, and Anthony Lake, *Our Own Worst Enemy: The Unmaking of American Foreign Policy* (New York: Simon and Schuster, 1984), chapter 2; Isaacson and Thomas, *The Wise Men;* Judis, "Twilight of the Gods".

57. See Cigler and Loomis, *Interest Group Politics;* John B. Judis, "The Pressure Elite: Inside the Narrow World of Advocacy Group Politics," *The American Prospect* (Spring 1992), pp. 15–29.

58. David M. Ricci, *The Transformation of American Politics: The New Washington and the Rise of Think Tanks* (New Haven: Yale University Press, 1993), p. 208.

59. See also Destler, Lake, and Gelb, *Our Own Worst Enemy,* chapter 2; William J. Lanouette, "The Private Foundations with a Very Public Role," *National Journal* (February 17, 1979): 256–61; James G. McGann, "Academic to Ideologues: A Brief History of the Public Policy Research Industry," *Political Science and Politics* (December 1992): 733–40; James Allen Smith, *The Idea Brokers: Think Tanks and the Rise of the New Policy Elite* (New York: Free Press, 1991); and R. Kent Weaver, "The Changing World of Think Tanks," *Political Science and Politics* (September 1989): 563–78. For a description of the linkage and dynamics between private foreign policy groups and government, see Roger A. Coate, *Unilateralism, Ideology, and U.S. Foreign Policy: The U.S. In and Out of UNESCO* (Boulder, Colo.: Lynne Rienner, 1988), and Sanders, Peddlers of Crisis.

60. See Richard J. Barnet and Ronald E. Muller, *Global Reach: The Power of Multinational Corporations* (New York: Simon and Schuster, 1974); Benjamin J. Cohen, *In Whose Interest? International Banking and American Foreign Policy* (New Haven: Yale University Press, 1986); Jeffrey Garten, "Business and Foreign Policy," *Foreign Affairs* (May–June 1997): 67–79; Helen V. Milner, *Resisting Protectionism: Global Industries and the Politics of International Trade* (Princeton: Princeton University Press, 1989); Robert A. Reich, *The Work of Nations: Preparing Ourselves for 21st Century Capitalism* (New York: Knopf, 1991).

61. Edwin Black, *IBM and the Holocaust* (New York: Crown, 2001); Michael Hirsh, "Did U.S. Companies Cozy Up to the Nazis," *Newsweek* (December 14, 1998), p. 48; Ken Silverstein, "Ford and the Fuhrer," *Nation* (February 24, 2000), pp. 16.

62. John B. Judis, "K Street's Rise to Power of Special Interest to U.S.," *In These Times* (November 1–7, 1989): 7. See also his "The Contract with K Street," *The New Republic* (December 4, 1995): 18–25.

63. Howard Fineman and Michael Isikoff, "Lights Out: Enron's Failed Power Play," *Newsweek* (January 21, 2002),

pp. 15–18; Dana Milibank and Glenn Kessler, "Enron's Influence Reached Deep Into Administration," *New York Times* (January 18, 2002), p. A1; Don Van Natta, Jr., "Executive Order Followed Energy Industry Recommendation, Documents Show," *New York Times* (April 4, 2002). See also Howard Fineman, "Harkening Back to Texas," *Newsweek* (July 22, 2002), pp. 21–24, and Paul Krugman, "Steps to Wealth," *New York Times* (July 16, 2002), www.nytimes.com.

64. See Allen D. Hertzke, *Representing God in Washington: The Role of Religious Lobbies in the American Polity* (Knoxville: University of Tennessee Press, 1988); William Martin, "The Christian Right and American Foreign Policy," *Foreign Policy* (spring 1999): 66–80.

65. See Patrick J. Haney and Walt Vanderbush, "The Role of Ethnic Interest Groups in U.S. Foreign Policy: The Case of the Cuban American National Foundation," *International Studies Quarterly* 43 (1999): 341–61; Kenneth Longmyer, "Black American Demands," *Foreign Policy* 60 (fall 1985): 3–17; Bill Richardson, "Hispanic American Concerns," *Foreign Policy* 60 (fall 1985): 30–39; and U.S. Congress, "Foreign Policy Interest Groups," pp. 38–58.

66. John Diamond and Brianna B. Piec, " Thousands March in Support of Israel: Pro-Israel Lobby Remains Strong Force in D.C.," Knight Ridder/Tribune News Service (April 15, 2002).

67. Ibid.

68. See Mitchell Bard, "The Influence of Ethnic Interest Groups on American Middle East Policy," in Charles W. Kegley, Jr., and Eugene R. Wittkopf, ed., *The Domestic Sources of American Foreign Policy: Insights and Evidence* (New York: St. Martin's Press, 1988), pp. 57–69; David J. Sadd and G. Neal Lendenmann, "Arab American Grievances," *Foreign Policy* 60 (Fall 1985): 17–30; Smith, *The Power Game*, chapter 9.

69. Mark Feeney, "All the World's His Stage Revered or Reviled, Henry Kissinger Remains Diplomatic in Spotlight's Glare," *Boston Globe* (June 21, 2001); "The Kissinger Clique," *Newsweek* (March 27, 1989): 30–31; "Scowcroft, in Ethics Report, Tells of Consulting Ties to 70 Concerns," *New York Times* (March 15, 1989): 10; and Elaine Sciolino, "Eagleburger Won't Disclose Kissinger's Client List," *New York Times* (November 12, 1989): 17.

70. See Russell Warren Howe and Sarah Hays Trott, *The Power Peddlers: How Lobbyists Mold America's Foreign Policy* (New York: Doubleday, 1977).

71. Judis, "K Street's Rise to Power," p. 7. See also Pat Choate, *Agents of Influence: How Japan's Lobbyists in the United States Manipulate America's Political and Economic System* (New York: Knopf, 1991), Ronald J. Hrebenar and Clive S. Thomas, "The Japanese Lobby in Washington: How Different Is It?" in Allan J. Cigler and Burdett A. Loomis, eds., *Interest Group Politics* (Washington, D.C., Congressional Quarterly Press, 1995), and John B. Judis, "The Japanese Megaphone," *New Republic* (January 22, 1980), pp. 20–25.

72. See Barbara Bradley, "Lobbying for Foreign Interests Is Booming Business in Washington," *Christian Science Monitor* (February 5, 1986), p. 6; Steven Emerson, "The American House of Saud" (three-part series), *New Republic* (February 17, 1982),

pp. 18–25, (May 19, 1982), pp. 11–16, (June 16, 1992), pp. 18–23; Deborah M. Levy, "Advice for Sale," *Foreign Policy* 67 (summer 1987): 64–86; and Norman J. Ornstein, "Lobbying for Fun and Policy," *Foreign Policy* 28 (fall 1977): 156–65.

73. Judis, "K Street's Rise to Power," p. 7.

74. John B. Judis, "Chinatown," *New Republic* (March 10, 1997), pp. 17–18.

75. U.S. Congress, General Accounting Office, *Foreign Representation: Former High-Level Federal Officials Representing Foreign Interests* (July 1986). Lester W. Milbrath, however, in *The Washington Lobbyists* (Chicago: Rand McNally, 1963), emphasizes the limited amount of corruption and direct influence exercised by lobbyists on policymakers.

76. For his policymaking role from his perspective, see Clark Clifford with Richard Holbrooke, *Counsel to the President: A Memoir* (New York: Random House, 1991).

77. Joe Conason, "The Iraq Lobby," *New Republic* (October 1, 1990), pp. 14–17.

78. Judis, "Chinatown," p. 20.

79. Michael W. Doyle, Empires (Ithaca, N.Y.: Cornell University Press, 1986). See also Rosenberg.

80. Emily S. Rosenberg, *Spreading the American Dream: American Economic and Cultural Expansion, 1890–1945* (New York: Hill and Wang, 1992).

81. DeAnne Julius, "Foreign Investment and the Big Picture," *New York Times* (September 2, 1990), p. 13; Jolie Solomon and John McCormick, "A Really Big Mac," *Newsweek* (November 17, 1997), pp. 56–58.

82. Bruce H. Smith, "U.S. and Canadian PVOs as Transnational Development Institutions," in Robert F. Gorman, ed., *Private Voluntary Organizations as Agents of Development* (London: Westview Press, 1984), p. 116. See also J. Bruce Nichols, *The Uneasy Alliance: Religion, Refugee Work, and U.S. Foreign Policy* (New York: Oxford University Press, 1988).

83. Smith, *The Power Game*, p. 29.

84. Chung-in Moon, "Complex Interdependence and Transnational Lobbying: South Korea in the United States," *International Studies Quarterly* 32 (March 1988): 67–89.

85. Smith, *The Power Game*, chapter 9.

86. U.S. Congress, "Foreign Policy Interest Groups," p. 38. See also, for example, Thomas M. Franck and Edward Weisband, *Foreign Policy by Congress* (New York: Oxford University Press, 1979), chapter 8.

87. Smith, *The Power Game*, p. 71.

88. See Susan Ariel Aaronson, *Taking Trade to the Streets: The Lost History of Public Efforts to Shape Globalization* (Ann Arbor: University of Michigan Press, 2002; Kenneth Klee, "The Siege of Seattle," *Newsweek* (December 13, 1999), pp. 30–39.

89. Thomas E. Mann, "Making Foreign Policy: President and Congress," in Thomas E. Mann, ed., *A Question of Balance: The President, The Congress, and Foreign Policy* (Washington, D.C.: Brookings Institution Press, 1990), p. 16.

90. For an overview of the contemporary nature of the military-industrial-scientific infrastructure and defense politics, see Gordon Adams, *The Politics of Defense Contracting: The Iron Tri-*

angle (New Brunswick, N.J.: Transaction, 1982); Jacob Goodwin, *Brotherhood of Arms: General Dynamics and the Business of Defending America* (New York: Times Books, 1985); William H. Gregory, *The Defense Procurement Mess* (Lexington, Mass: Lexington Books, 1989); Kotz, *Wild Blue Yonder;* and Patrick Tyler, *Running Critical: The Silent War, Rickover, and General Dynamics* (New York: Harper and Row, 1986).

91. Rone Tempest, "U.S. Defense Establishment Wields a Pervasive Power," *Los Angeles Times* (July 10, 1983), part VI, p. 1.

92. Jan Tuten, "Military Might: Military Installations Give Firepower to S.C. Economy," *The State,* Columbia, S.C. (September 11, 1989), Business Section, pp. 10–12.

93. U.S. Census Bureau, *Statistical Abstract of the United States: 2001,* p. 326.

94. Rone Tempest, "Beltway Bandits Ring Washington," *Los Angeles Times* (July 10, 1983), part VI, p. 14.

95. Gordon Adams, *The Iron Triangle: The Politics of Defense Contracting* (New York: Council on Economic Priorities, 1981).

96. David Wood, "B-1 Symbolizes Power of Military-Industrial Complex," *Los Angeles Times* (July 10, 1983), part VI, pp. 8–9.

97. Kotz, *Wild Blue Yonder,* p. 22.

98. Ibid., p. 8.

99. Ibid., p. 239.

100. James R. Kurth, "Why We Buy the Weapons We Do," *Foreign Policy* (summer 1973), and James R. Kurth, "A Widening Gyre: The Logic of American Weapons Procurement," *Public Policy* 19 (summer 1971).

101. Sean Paige, "Projects Lose Way in Pentagon's Revolving Door," *Insight on the News* (May 29, 2000), p. 47.

102. "Armaments, Disarmament and International Security," *Stockholm International Peace Research Institute (SIPRI) Yearbook 2001* (London: Oxford University Press, 2001); International Institute for Strategic Studies, *The Military Balance 2001–2002* (London: Oxford University Press, 2001).

103. Adam Bryant, "Boeing Offering $13 Billion to Buy McDonnell Douglas, Last U.S. Commercial Rival," *New York Times* (December 16, 1996), pp. A1, D14.

104. Lawrence. J. Korb, "A Military Monopoly," *New York Times* (December 21, 1996), p. 25. For a less critical view, see John J. Dowdy, "Winners and Losers in the Arms Industry Downturn," *Foreign Policy* (summer 1997): 88–101; Eugene Gholz and Harvey M. Sapolsky, "Restructuring the U.S. Defense Industry," *International Security* (winter 1999–2000): 5–51.

CHAPTER 17

1. Shanto Iyengar and Donald R. Kinder, *News That Matters: Television and American Opinion* (Chicago: University of Chicago Press, 1987). See also W. Lance Bennett, *News: The Politics of Illusion* (New York: Longman, 2001); Richard A. Brody, *Assessing the President: The Media, Elite Opinion, and Public Support* (Stanford: Stanford University Press, 1991); Doris A. Graber,

Mass Media and American Politics (Washington, D.C.: Congressional Quarterly Press, 2001); Godfrey Hodgson, *America in Our Time* (New York: Vintage, 1976), chapter 7; Shanto Iyengar, *Is Anyone Responsible? How Television Frames Political Issues* (Chicago: University of Chicago Press, 1991); Abbas Malek, ed., *News Media and Foreign Relations: A Multifaceted Perspective* (Norwood, N.J.: Ablex Publishing, 1999); W. Russell Neuman, Marion R. Just, and Ann N. Crigler, *Common Knowledge: News and the Construction of Political Meaning* (Chicago: University of Chicago Press, 1992); Donald L. Shaw and Maxwell E. McCombs, *The Emergence of American Political Issues: The Agenda-Setting Function of the Press* (St. Paul, Minn.: West, 1978).

2. Carol H. Weiss, "What America's Leaders Read," *Public Opinion Quarterly* (spring 1974): 1–22.

3. See William C. Adams, ed., *Television Coverage of International Affairs* (Norwood, N.J.: Ablex, 1982); George Gerbner and George Marvanyi, "The Many Worlds of the World's Press," *Journal of Communications* 27 (winter 1971): 52–66; Graber, *Mass Media and American Politics;* James F. Larson, *Television's Window on the World* (Norwood, N.J.: Ablex, 1984); Hamid Mowlana, "World's Best-Informed Public?" *SAIS Review* 6 (winter-spring 1986): 177–88; Sophia Peterson, "International News Selection by the Elite Press: A Case Study," *Public Opinion Quarterly* 45 (summer 1981): 143–63; Gary C. Woodward, *Perspectives on American Political Media* (Boston: Allyn and Bacon, 1997).

4. H. D. Wu, "Investigating the Determinants of International News Flow: A Meta-Analysis," *Gazette* (1998): 507.

5. Herbert J. Gans, *Deciding What's News: A Study of CBS Evening News, NBC Nightly News, Newsweek and Time* (New York: Pantheon, 1979), pp. 31–38.

6. Andrew K. Semmel, "Foreign News in Four U.S. Elite Dailies: Some Comparisons," *Journalism Quarterly* 53 (1976): 736.

7. See, for example, Graber, *Mass Media and American Politics;* Stephen Hess, *International News and Foreign Correspondents* (Washington, D.C.: Brookings Institution Press, 1996); Mohamed Kirat and David Weaver, "Foreign News Coverage in Three Wire Services: A Study of AP, UPI, and the Nonaligned News Agencies Pool," *Gazette* 35 (spring 1985): 31–47; P. Norris, "The Restless Searchlight: Network News Framing of the Post–Cold War World," *Political Communication* (1995), pp. 357–70; W. James Potter, "News From Three Worlds in Prestige U.S. Newspapers," *Journalism Quarterly* 64 (spring 1987): 73–79, 276; Stephen Seplow, "Closer to Home," *American Journalism Review* (July/August 2002); Wu, "Determinants of International News Flow," pp. 493–512.

8. Edward Farmer, "From Admiration to Confrontation," *Media Studies Journal* (winter 1999): 136–45; David N. Gibbs, "Forgotten Coverage of Afghan 'Freedom Fighters': The Villains of Today's News were Heroes in the '80s," *Extra!* (January–February 2002), pp. 13–16. See also Tsan-Kuo Chang, *The Press and China Policy: The Illusion of Sino-American Relations, 1950–1984* (Norwood, N.J.: Ablex Publishing, 1992); Harold R. Isaacs, *Images of Asia: American Views of China and India* (Boston: MIT Press, 1958).

9. See, for example, J. Herbert Altschull, *Agents of Power: The Role of the News Media in Human Affairs* (New York: Longman, 1984).

10. Hedrick Smith, *The Power Game: How Washington Works* (New York: Ballantine, 1988), p. 395.

11. Stanley Hoffmann, *Gulliver's Troubles or the Setting of American Foreign Policy* (New York: McGraw-Hill, 1968), p. 311.

12. See, for example, Dan Nimmo and James E. Combs, *Mediated Political Realities* (New York: Longman, 1983).

13. For an overview of the nature and operations of the American media, see Robert M. Batscha, *Foreign Affairs News and the Broadcast Journalist* (New York: Praeger, 1975); Bernard C. Cohen, *The Press and Foreign Policy* (Princeton, N.J.: Princeton University Press, 1963); Edward Jay Epstein, *News From Nowhere: Television and the News* (New York: Vintage, 1973); Gans, *Deciding What's News;* Graber, *Mass Media and American Politics;* Stephen Hess, *The Washington Reporters* (Washington, D.C.: Brookings Institution Press, 1981); Leon V. Sigal, *Reporters and Officials: The Organization and Politics of Newsmaking* (Lexington, Mass.: D. C. Heath, 1973); Woodward, *Perspectives on American Political Media.*

14. Ben Bagdikian, *The Media Monopoly* (Boston: Beacon, 2000). See also Phillip H. Ault, "Mass Ownership Takes Over the Media," in Warren K. Agee, Phillip H. Ault, and Edwin Emery, eds., *Main Currents in Mass Communications* (New York: Harper and Row, 1986), pp. 168–73; John C. Busterna, "Trends in Daily Newspaper Ownership," *Journalism Quarterly* (winter 1988): 831–38; William Glaberson, "Times Co. Acquiring Boston Globe for $1.1 billion," *New York Times* (June 11, 1993), pp. A1, A4; "The Media Nation," *The Nation* (June 8, 1998), special edition; llan Sloan, "A Tale of Two Papers," *Newsweek* (March 27, 2000), pp. 48–49; Richard Turner, "An Ear for the CBS Eye," *Newsweek* (December 16, 1996), pp. 58–59.

15. Bagdikian, *The Media Monopoly* (Boston: Beacon, 2000), pp. xx-xxi.

16. Hess, *International News and Foreign Correspondents.*

17. See Bagdikian, Media Monopoly, and "Fifth Estate Fortunes: The Top 100 Top $38 Billion," *Broadcasting* (June 5, 1989), pp. 54–56; Bernard Roshco, *Newsmaking* (Chicago: University of Chicago Press, 1975).

18. Stanley K. Bigman, "Rivals in Conformity: A Study of Two Competing Dailies," *Journalism Quarterly* 25 (Autumn 1949): 127–31.

19. See Ken Auletta, *Three Blind Mice: How the Networks Lost Their Way* (New York,: Random House, 1991).

20. David Halberstam, *The Powers That Be* (New York: Alfred A. Knopf, 1979), p. 415.

21. See, for example, Joshua Gamson, "Incredible News," *American Prospect* (fall 1994): 28–35; Alex Kuczynski, "National Enquirer Is Out Front on Two Major Reports," *New York Times* (February 23, 2001); Larry Reibstein, "The Battle of the TV News Magazine Shows," *Newsweek* (April 11, 1994), pp. 61–65.

22. Joan Didion, "Clinton Agonistes," *New York Review of Books* (October 22, 1998), p. 18.

23. Timothy Crouse, *The Boys on the Bus* (New York: Ballantine, 1972). See also Larry Sabato, *Feeding Frenzy: How Attack Journalism Has Transformed American Politics* (New York: Free Press, 1991).

24. "A Star Is Rehired, Fabulously," *Newsweek* (February 28, 1994), p. 56.

25. Stephen Hess, "All the President's Reporters: A New Survey of the White House Press Corps," *Presidential Studies Quarterly* (spring 1992), p. 312. See also Smith, *The Power Game,* p. 29.

26. Leon V. Sigal, *Reporters and Officials: The Organization and Politics of Newsmaking* (Lexington, Mass.: Heath, 1973):, pp. 119–30. See also Leon V. Sigal, "Sources Make the News," in Robert Karl Manoff and Michael Schudson, eds., *Reading the News* (New York: Pantheon, 1987), pp. 9–37.

27. *Newsweek* (October 15, 1989; November 17, 1997). See also Hess, *International News and Foreign Correspondents;* John A. Lent, "Foreign News in American Media," *Journal of Communications* 27 (winter 1977); and Michael Parks, "Foreign News: What's Next?," *Columbia Journalism Review* (January–February 2002): 52–57.

28. See Gerbner and Marvanyi, "The Many Worlds of the World's Press"; Kirat and Weaver, "Foreign News Coverage in Three Wire Services"; Semmel, "Foreign News in Four U.S. Dailies"; and Wilhoit and Weaver, "Foreign News Coverage in Two U.S. Wire Services."

29. See, e.g., John B. Judis, "Chinatown," *New Republic* (March 10, 1997), pp. 17–20.

30. For an overview of the relationship between the political environment and the media, see Timothy E. Cook, *Making Laws and Making News: Media Strategies in the U.S. House of Representatives* (Washington, D.C.: Brookings Institution Press, 1989); Epstein, *News From Nowhere;* Gans, *Deciding What's News;* Graber, *Mass Media and American Politics;* Halberstam, *The Powers That Be;* Michael Parenti, *Inventing Reality: The Politics of the Mass Media* (New York: St. Martin's Press, 1977); and Sigal, *Reporters and Officials.*

31. Walter Lippmann quoted in Ronald Steel, *Walter Lippmann and the American Century* (New York: Vintage, 1980), p. 181.

32. Graber, *Mass Media and American Politics* (1989), p. 24.

33. Hess, *The Washington Reporters,* p. 118.

34. Gans, *Deciding What's News,* p. 62.

35. William Hoynes and David Croteau, "Are You on the Nightline Guestlist?" *Extra!* (January–February 1989), pp. 1–15, and "All the Usual Suspects: MacNeil/Lehrer and Nightline," *Extra!* (winter 1999). See also Marc Cooper and Lawrence C. Soley, "All the Right Sources," *Mother Jones* (February–March 1990): 20–27, 45–48; Dan Nimmo and James E. Combs, *The Political Pundits* (New York: Praeger, 1992); and Lawrence C. Soley, *The News Shapers: The Individuals Who Explain the News* (Minneapolis: School of Journalism and Mass Communication, University of Minnesota, 1989).

36. Walter Karp, "Who Decides What is News? (Hint: It's Not Journalists)," *Utne Reader* (November/December 1989): 61.

37. Carl Bernstein, "The Idiot Culture: Reflections of Post-Watergate Journalism," *New Republic* (June 8, 1992): 22.

38. Daniel C. Hallin, *The Uncensored War: The Media and Vietnam* (Berkeley and Los Angeles: University of California Press, 1986). See also Nicholas O. Berry, *Foreign Policy and the*

Press: An Analysis of The New York Times' Coverage of U.S. Foreign Policy (Westport, Conn.: Greenwood Press, 1990); Jonathan Mermin, "Television News and American Intervention in Somalia: The Myth of a Media-Driven Foreign Policy," *Political Science Quarterly* (fall 1997): 385–403.

39. See, for example, Jonathan Tasini, *Lost in the Margins: Labor and the Media,* (New York: Fairness and Accuracy in Reporting, 1990).

40. See, for example, Marie Gottschalk, "Operation Desert Cloud: The Media and the Gulf War," *World Policy Journal* (summer 1992): 449–86.

41. Matthew Engel, "US Media Cowed by Patriotic Fever, Says CBS Star," *The Guardian* (May 17, 2002), p. 4. See also, Neil Hickey, "Access Denied: Pentagon's War Reporting Rules Are Toughest Ever," *Columbia Journalism Review* (January–February 2002): 26–31.

42. Hess, "All the President's Reporters," p. 318.

43. David Truman, *The Governmental Process: Political Interests and Public Opinion* (New York: Knopf, 1971), p. 213.

44. Graber, *Mass Media and American Politics* (1989), p. 92. See also Lloyd N. Cutler, "Foreign Policy by Deadline," *Foreign Policy* (fall 1984): 113–28.

45. Graber, *Mass Media and American Politics* (1989), p. 260.

46. See, for example, Todd Gitlin, *The Whole World Is Watching: Mass Media in the Making and Unmaking of the New Left* (Berkeley, Calif.: University of California Press, 1981).

47. For an overview of governmental and presidential access to the media, see Gans, *Deciding What's News*; Michael Baruch Grossman and Martha Joynt Kumar, *Portraying the President: The White House and the News Media* (Baltimore: Johns Hopkins University Press, 1981); Charles Press and Kenneth Verburg, *American Politicians and Journalists* (Glenview, Ill.: Scott, Foresman, 1988); and Sigal, *Reporters and Officials.*

48. Cohen, *The Press and Foreign Policy,* p. 28.

49. Hallin, *The Uncensored War,* p. 8. See also Daniel Hallin, "The Media, the War in Vietnam, and Political Support: A Critique of the Thesis of an Oppositional Media," *Journal of Politics* 46 (1984): 13.

50. See James Bennet, "The Flack Pack: How Press Conferences Turn Serious Journalists into Shills," *Washington Monthly* (November 1991), pp. 18–28; Jonathan Chait, "Defense Secretary: The Peculiar Duplicity of Ari Fleischer," *The New Republic* (June 10, 2002), pp. 20–23; John Anthony Maltese, *Spin Control: The White House Office of Communications and the Management of Presidential News* (Chapel Hill: University of North Carolina Press, 1992).

51. Daniel J. Boorstin, *The Image: A Guide to Pseudo-Events in America* (New York: Atheneum, 1961).

52. Smith, *The Power Game,* p. 401.

53. See, for example, Juergen A. Heise, *Minimum Disclosure: How the Pentagon Manipulates the News* (New York: W. W. Norton, 1979).

54. Smith, *The Power Game,* p. 80. See also Morton H. Halperin, *Bureaucratic Politics and Foreign Policy* (Washington, D.C.: Brookings Institution Press, 1974), chapter 10.

55. See Michael J. Robinson, "Public Affairs Television and the Growth of Political Malaise: The Case of 'The Selling of the Pentagon,'" *American Political Science Review* (1976): 409–32.

56. Robert Parry and Peter Kornbluh, "Iran-Contra's Untold Story," *Foreign Policy* (fall 1988): 3, 16.

57. James Dao and Eric Schmitt, "Pentagon Readies Efforts to Sway Sentiment Abroad," *New York Times* (February 19, 2002); Michael R. Gordon, "U.S. Tries to Rally Public Support Overseas," *New York Times* (November 6, 2001); Thomas E. Ricks, "Rumsfeld Kills Pentagon Propaganda Unit," *Washington Post* (February 27, 2002); Sharon Waxman, "White House Looking to Enlist Hollywood in Terrorism War," *Washington Post* (October 20, 2001).

58. Hoffmann, *Gulliver's Troubles,* pp. 308–9.

59. Lippmann diary quoted in Steel, *Walter Lippmann and the American Century,* p. 67. See also Maureen Dowd, "President and the Press: A Clash of Two Obsessions," *New York Times* (February 21, 1990), p. A12.

60. Jason DeParle, "From Low-Level Aides to Power Wielders, Sources Shape Reporter's Books", *New York Times* (February 7, 1992), p. A7. See also Joan Didion, "The Deferential Spirit," *New York Review of Books* (September 19, 1996), pp. 14–19.

61. Graber, *Mass Media and American Politics* (1989), p. 29.

62. See George H. Roeder, Jr., *The Censored War: American Visual Experience During World War Two* (New Haven: Yale University Press, 1993); Michael S. Sweeney, *Secrets of Victory: The Office of Censorship and the American Press and Radio in World War II* (Chapel Hill: University of North Carolina Press, 2001).

63. Robert Dallek, *The American Style of Foreign Policy: Cultural Politics and Foreign Affairs* (New York: Knopf, 1983), p. 139.

64. Russell Warren Howe and Sarah Hays Trott, *The Power Peddlers: How Lobbyists Mold America's Foreign Policy* (Garden City, N.Y.: Doubleday, 1977), p. 30. See also James L. Baughman, *Henry R. Luce and the Rise of the American News Media* (New York: Macmillan, 1990).

65. Edwin R. Bayley, *Joe McCarthy and the Press* (Madison, Wis.: University of Wisconsin Press, 1981).

66. Carl Bernstein, "The CIA and the Media," *Rolling Stone* (October 1977); U.S. Congress, Senate, *Final Report of the Select Committee to Study Governmental Operations with Respect to Intelligence Activities,* Book 1, Congressional Report (94th Cong., 2nd sess., April 14, 1976), pp. 197–98.

67. Halberstam, *The Powers That Be,* pp. 446–47. See also James Aronson, *The Press and the Cold War* (Indianapolis: Bobbs-Merrill, 1970), and J. Fred MacDonald, *Television and the Red Menace: The Video Road to Vietnam* (New York: Praeger, 1985).

68. Hallin, *The Uncensored War.*

69. Scott Armstrong, "Iran-Contra: Was the Press Any Match for All the President's Men?" *Columbia Journalism Review* (May–June 1990): 28, 29. See also Robert Parry and Peter Kornbluh, "Iran-Contra's Untold Story," *Foreign Policy* (fall 1988): 3–30; and Bob Woodward, *Veil: The Secret Wars of the CIA, 1981–1987* (New York: Pocket Books, 1987).

70. Ibid., pp. 31, 30.

71. Ibid., p. 34.

72. Ibid.

73. On this topic, see William C. Adams, "Mass Media and Public Opinion About Foreign Affairs: A Typology of News Dynamics," *Political Communication and Persuasion* 4 (1987): 263–78; Doris A. Graber, *Processing the News: How People Tame the Information Tide* (New York: Longman, 1988); Doris A Graber, *Processing Politics: Learning From Television in the Internet Age* (Chicago: University of Chicago Press, 2001); Neuman, Just, and Crigler, *Common Knowledge.*

74. See, for example, Iyengar and Kinder, *News That Matters.*

75. See, for example, William A. Dorman and Mansour Farhang, *The U.S. Press and Iran: Foreign Policy and the Journalism of Deference* (Berkeley and Los Angeles: University of California Press, 1987).

76. Graber, *Mass Media and American Politics* (1989), p. 227. See also Thomas E. Patterson, *The Mass Media Election: How Americans Choose Their President* (New York: Praeger, 1980).

77. Richard M. Scammon and Alice V. McGillivray, eds., *America at the Polls: The Vote for President, 1968–1984* (Washington, D.C.: Congressional Quarterly Press, 1988), pp. 2, 3.

78. See James Fallows, "Why Americans Hate the Media," *Atlantic Monthly* (February 1996), pp. 45–64; and Judith Valente, "Do You Believe What Newspeople Tell You?" *Parade Magazine* (March 2, 1997), pp. 4–6.

79. Jerome Barron, *Freedom of the Press for Whom? The Right of Access to the Mass Media* (Bloomington: Indiana University Press, 1973); Cook, *Making Laws and Making News,* pp. 177–78; Bill Moyers, "Journalism & Democracy: On the Importance of Being a 'Public Nuisance,'" *The Nation* (May 7, 2001), pp. 11–17; Robert M. Entman, *Democracy Without Citizens: Media and the Decay of American Politics* (New York: Oxford University Press, 1989); and Gans, *Deciding What's News,* chapter 10.

80. See Denise M. Bostdorff, *The Presidency and the Rhetoric of Foreign Crisis* (Columbia: University of South Carolina Press, 1993); Murray Edelman, *The Symbolic Uses of Politics* (Urbana: University of Illinois Press, 1964); Michael Kazin, *The Populist Persuasion: An American History* (New York: Basic Books, 1995).

81. See B. Thomas Trout, "Rhetoric Revisited: Political Legitimation and the Cold War," *International Studies Quarterly* 19 (September 1975): 251–84.

82. Smith, *The Power Game,* pp. 418, 345–46, 346. See also Mark Hertsgaard, *On Bended Knee: The Press and the Reagan Presidency* (New York: Schocken Books, 1988).

83. Smith, *The Power Game,* chapter 17. See also R. Kent Weaver, "The Politics of Blame Avoidance," *Journal of Public Policy* 6 (October–December 1986): 371–98.

84. Joe McGinniss, *The Selling of the President 1968* (New York: Pocket Books, 1970).

85. See also Kathleen Hall Jamieson, *Dirty Politics: Deception, Distraction, and Democracy* (New York: Oxford University Press, 1992); and Darrell M. West, *Air Wars: Television Advertising in Election Campaigns, 1952–1992* (Washington, D.C.: Congressional Quarterly Press, 1993).

86. Kiku Adatto, "The Incredible Shrinking Sound Bite," *New Republic* (May 28, 1990), p. 20; Daniel C. Hallin, "Sound Bite News: Television Coverage of Elections, 1968–1988," *Journal of Communication* (Spring 1992): 5–24.

87. Timothy Wirth quoted in Smith, *The Power Game,* pp. 129–30.

88. Stanley Meisler and Thomas B. Rosensteil, "Epithets, Voodoo Reports Help U.S. Demean Noriega," *Los Angeles Times* (December 31, 1989), pp. A1, A12. See also George Klay Kieh, Jr., "Propaganda and United States Foreign Policy: The Case of Panama," *Political Communication* 7 (April–June 1990): 61–72.

89. Hallin, *The Uncensored War,* p. 158.

90. For an overview of the entertainment media, see Todd Gitlin, *Inside Prime Time* (New York: Pantheon, 1985); Walter L. Hixson, "Red Storm Rising: Tom Clancy Novels and the Cult of National Security," *Diplomatic History* (fall 1993): 599–613; J. Fred MacDonald, *One Nation Under Television: The Rise and Decline of Network TV* (New York: Pantheon, 1990); Michael Parenti, *Make-Believe Media: The Politics of Entertainment* (New York: St. Martin's Press, 1992); Sally Bedell Smith, *In All His Glory, The Life of William S. Paley: The Legendary Tycoon and His Brilliant Circle* (New York: Simon and Schuster, 1990); and Woodward, *Perspectives on American Political Media.*

91. Gitlin, *Inside Prime Time,* p. 203.

92. George Gerbner, Larry Gross, Michael Morgan, and Nancy Signorielli, "Charting the Mainstream: Television's Contributions to Political Orientations," *Journal of Communication* 32 (1982): 100–27; and "Life According to TV," *Newsweek* (December 6, 1982), pp. 136–40.

93. "Life According to TV," p. 140.

94. See, for example, Richard Slotkin, *Gunfighter Nation: The Myth of the Frontier in Twentieth-Century America* (New York: Atheneum, 1992).

95. Clayton R. Koppes and Gregory D. Black, *Hollywood Goes to War: How Politics, Profits, and Propaganda Shaped World War II Movies* (New York: Free Press, 1987), p. vii.

96. John W. Dower, *War Without Mercy: Race and Power in the Pacific War* (New York: Pantheon, 1986), p. 309.

97. MacDonald, *Television and the Red Menace.* See also Nora Sayre, *Running Time: Films of the Cold War* (New York: Dial Press, 1982); Stephen J. Whitfield, *The Culture of the Cold War* (Baltimore: Johns Hopkins University Press, 1991).

98. See, for example, Martha Bayles, "The Road to Rambo III: Hollywood's Visions of Vietnam," *New Republic* (July 18 and 25, 1988), pp. 30–35.

99. "Hollywood Goes to War," *Newsweek* (December 3, 2001), pp. 68–70. For a particularly critical review, see Richard Grenier, "Oliver Stone's JFK," *National Interest* (spring 1992), pp. 76–84.

100. Boorstin, *The Image,* p. 5.

101. Paddy Chayefsky, *Network* (New York: Pocket Books, 1976), p. 98.

102. Robert L. Heibroner, "Advertising as Agitprop," *Harper's* (January 1985), p. 72.

103. MacDonald, *One Nation Under Television,* p. ix.

104. David A. Kaplan, "The Selling of Star Wars," *Newsweek* (May 17, 1999), pp. 60–64; Louis Menand, "Billion-Dollar Baby," *New York Review of Books* (June 24, 1999), pp. 9–11.

105. Stuart Ewen, "Waste a Lot, Want a Lot: Our All-consuming Quest for Style," *Utne Reader* (September/October 1989): 84. See also William Leach, Land of Desire: *Merchants, Power and the Rise of a New American Culture* (New York: Pantheon, 1993), and Vance Packard, *The Hidden Persuaders* (New York: McKay, 1957).

106. See Edward S. Hermann and Robert W. McChesney, *Global Reach: The Missionaries of Global Capitalism* (New York: Continuum International Publishing, 1997); Michael Medved, "That's Entertainment? Hollywood's Contribution to Anti-Americanism Abroad," *The National Interest* (Summer 2002); Anthony Smith, *The Age of Behemoths: The Globalization of Mass Media Firms* (New York: Priority Press, 1991).

107. Medved, "That's Entertainment?," p. 5.

108. For alternative media accounts, see "Did the U.S. Deliberately Bomb the Chinese Embassy in Belgrade?" in Peter Phillips and Project Censored, eds., *Censored 2001* (New York: Seven Sotries Press, 2001), pp. 48–49.

109. Lauren Kessler, *The Dissident Press: Alternative Journalism in American History* (Beverley Hills, Calif.: Sage, 1984), p. 14. See also David Armstrong, *A Trumpet to Arms: Alternative Media in America* (Los Angeles: J. P. Tarcher, 1981).

110. See Thomas Byrne Edsall, "America's Sweetheart," *New York Review of Books* (October 6, 1994), pp. 6–10; Monika Bauerlein, "Radio Activity," *Utne Reader* (September–October 1992), pp. 110–12.

111. There are also a rash of alternative publications that are politically oriented and that target women, blacks, Hispanics, labor, environmental groups, and other more specialized audiences and interests. See David Armstrong, "Alternative, Inc.," *In These Times* (August 21, 1995), pp. 14–18; B. Katz and L. S. Katz, *Magazines for Libraries* (New York: R. R. Bowker, 1986); Lynette Lamb, "Parallel Worlds: Newsletters Provide Varied and Vital Alternative Information," *Utne Reader* (November–December 1992), pp. 111–14; J. Wanniski, *1992 Media Guide: A Critical Review of the Media* (Morristown, N.J.: Polyeconomics, 1992).

112. Mark Hosenball, "The Odd Couple: How George Bush helped create Saddam Hussein," *The New Republic* (June 1, 1992), p. 27. See also "The Arming of Iraq," *Frontline* (September 11, 1990); Michael Dobbs, "When an Ally Becomes the Enemy" *The Washington Post National Weekly Edition* (January 6–12, 2003), pp. 9–10; Judith Miller and Laurie Mylroie, *Saddam Hussein and the Crisis in the Gulf* (New York: Times Books, 1990); Kenneth R. Timmerman, *The Death Lobby: How the West Armed Iraq* (Boston: Houghton Mifflin, 1991).

113. Three hundred twenty-three (29 percent) applications were returned to the companies without action (without explanation in the report). U.S. Department of Commerce, *Fact Sheet on Export Licensing for Iraq* (undated).

114. Joe Conason, "The Iraq Lobby," *New Republic* (October 1, 1990), p. 14.

115. Ibid., 15.

116. Hosenball, "The Odd Couple," p. 35. Some of this information eventually seeped into the mainstream press, such as *Newsweek,* but it was two months after the invasion and limited to a brief article in the business section. More importantly, *Newsweek* failed to integrate this information into a larger article on the Gulf crisis in the same issue's international section. See "Should Iran Be a Lesson?" *Newsweek* (October 15, 1990), p. 58, and "Under the Boot," *Newsweek* (October 15, 1990), pp. 36–37. It needs to be pointed out that most members of Congress from both parties went along with the administration's policies and many members, in fact, actively promoted increased ties with Iraq so as to lead to greater exports from their states and districts. See Pamela Fessler, "Congress' Record on Saddam: Decade of Talk, Not Action," *Congressional Quarterly* (April 27, 1991), pp. 1068–77.

117. See, for example, Leslie Cockburn, *Out of Control: The Story of the Reagan Administration's Secret War in Nicaragua, the Illegal Arms Pipeline, and the Contra Drug Connection* (New York: Atlantic Monthly Press, 1987), and Barbara Honegger with Jim Naureckas, "Did Reagan Steal the 1980 Election?" *In These Times* (June 24–July 7, 1987), pp. 12–13.

118. "Election Held Hostage," *Frontline* (April 16, 1991), and Gary Sick, "The Election Story of the Decade," *New York Times* (April 15, 1991), p. 17.

119. Bruce Sterling, "Short History of the Internet," *Magazine of Fantasy and Science Fiction* (February 1993).

120. During the cold war, there were only two major American international relations journals—*International Organization* and *World Politics*—and two general political science journals—*Political Science Quarterly* and *American Political Science Review*. However, beginning in the 1960s, new political science and, more important, international relations journals were born, such as *Journal of Conflict Resolution, International Studies Quarterly,* and *International Interactions*. During the cold war, these journals represented primarily conventional and realpolitik perspectives on international relations (which became increasingly quantitative). Over the past decade, however, the scholarly journals have become receptive to a greater diversity of theoretical and systematic perspectives. Foreign policy practitioners and analysts generally find little of value in these more academic journals, limiting their immediate impact. Still, they often play a prominent role in the graduate education of individuals in political science and international studies programs across the country, many of whom go on to play relevant foreign policy roles in government and society. As John Maynard Keynes once observed, practical men and women are usually unconscious captives of conceptions created by "some academic scribbler of a few years back." See John Maynard Keynes, *The General Theory of Employment, Interest and Money* (London: Macmillan, 1957), p. 383.

121. Harold D. Lasswell, "The Structure and Function of Communication in Society," in Wilbur Schramm, ed., Mass Communications (Urbana, Ill.: University of Illinois Press, 1969), p. 103.

CHAPTER 18

1. See Walter Lippmann, *Public Opinion* (New York: Harcourt, Brace, 1922) and *The Phantom Public* (New York: Macmillan, 1927).

2. For an overview of state-societal relations and different theoretical approaches, see Douglas M. Fox, ed., *The Politics of U.S. Foreign Policy Making* (Pacific Palisades, Calif.: Goodyear, 1971); G. David Garson, *Group Theories of Politics* (Beverly Hills: Sage, 1978); Martin N. Marger, *Elites and Masses: An Introduction to Political Sociology* (Belmont, Calif.; Wadsworth, 1987); Joel S. Migdal, *Strong Societies and Weak States: State-Society Relations and State Capabilities in the Third World* (Princeton, N.J.: Princeton University Press, 1988); David Skidmore and Valerie M. Hudson, *The Limits of State Autonomy: Societal Groups and Foreign Policy Formulation* (Boulder, Colo.: Westview Press, 1993); Alfred Stepan, *The State and Society: Peru in Comparative Perspective* (Princeton: Princeton University Press, 1978).

3. The elitist, pluralist, and hyperpluralist models tend to assume the existence of a so-called "weak state," in American politics—that is, of a permeable or symbiotic government relative to society—as opposed to a "strong state" that is relatively independent of domestic politics and societal forces. Although the strong-state perspective dominates the (realist) study of international relations, it has become increasingly questioned, especially in the making of U.S. foreign policy. The terms *strong* and *weak states* actually are somewhat simplistic: An elitist perspective, for example, allows for a very powerful state to prevail in the area of foreign policy despite its societal interconnections and structural constraints. For a more traditional realist perspective on the making of U.S. foreign policy, see Stephen D. Krasner, *Defending the National Interest: Raw Materials Investments and U.S. Foreign Policy* (Princeton: Princeton University Press, 1978). For a more complex, "neorealist" understanding, see G. John Ikenberry, *Reasons of State: Oil Politics and the Capacities of American Government* (Ithaca, N.Y.: Cornell University Press, 1988); Peter J. Katzenstein, ed., *Between Power and Plenty: Foreign Economic Policies of Advanced Industrial States* (Madison: University of Wisconsin Press, 1978); David A. Lake, *Power, Protection, and Free Trade: International Sources of U.S. Commercial Strategy, 1887–1939* (Ithaca, N.Y.: Cornell University Press, 1988); Richard Rosecrance and Arthur A. Stein, eds., *The Domestic Bases of Grand Strategy* (Ithaca, N.Y.: Cornell University Press, 1993); Jack Snyder, *Myths of Empire: Domestic Politics and International Ambition* (Ithaca, N.Y.: Cornell University Press, 1991). This more complex understanding is more consistent with the early theorists of U.S. foreign policy—such as Gabriel Almond, Roger Hilsman, Stanley Hoffmann, Charles Lindblom, Richard Neustadt, and Richard Snyder—and those who followed in their paths, as discussed in chapter 1 and throughout this book, although this has rarely been acknowledged by neorealist authors.

4. Arnold H. Rose, *The Power Structure: Political Process in American Society* (New York: Oxford University Press, 1967), p. 5.

5. Robert A. Dahl, *Pluralist Democracy in the United States: Conflict and Consent* (Chicago: Rand McNally, 1967), p. 24.

6. Ibid.

7. For some intellectual background, see Neil McInnes, "Ortega and the Myth of the Mass," *National Interest* (summer 1996), pp. 78–88.

8. William Kornhauser, *The Politics of Mass Society* (New York: Free Press, 1956), p. 5.

9. Ibid., p. 16.

10. Robert A. Nisbet, *The Quest for Community: A Study in the Ethics of Order and Freedom* (New York: Oxford University Press, 1953).

11. Dahl, *Pluralist Democracy in America*, p. 298.

12. Ibid., p. 24.

13. For an overview and background, see T. B. Bottomore, *Elites and Society* (Penguin, 1966).

14. E. E. Schattschneider, *The Semi-Sovereign People: A Realist's View of Democracy in America* (New York: Holt, Rinehart and Winston, 1960), p. 35.

15. C. Wright Mills, *The Power Elite* (London: Oxford University Press, 1956).

16. Ibid.: 28–29.

17. C. Wright Mills, "The Structure of Power in American Society," in Pietro S. Nivola and David H. Rosenbloom, eds., *Classic Readings in American Politics* (New York: St. Martin's Press, 1986), p. 131.

18. For pluralist and elitist studies of American politics and an overview of the debate, see Peter Bachrach, ed., *Political Elites in a Democracy* (New York: Atherton Press, 1971); Robert A. Dahl, *Who Governs? Democracy and Power in an American City* (New Haven: Yale University Press, 1961); G. William Domhoff and Hoyt B. Ballard, eds., *C. Wright Mills and the Power Elite* (Boston: Beacon Press, 1968); Floyd Hunter, *Top Leadership U.S.A.* (Chapel Hill: University of North Carolina Press, 1959); Seymour Martin Lipset, *Political Man: The Social Bases of Politics* (New York: Doubleday, 1960); Nelson W. Polsby, *Community Power and Political Theory* (New Haven: Yale University Press, 1963).

19. For an overview of such intellectual thought during the cold war years, see Richard H. Pells, *The Liberal Mind in a Conservative Age: American Intellectuals in the 1940s and 1950s* (New York: Harper and Row, 1985).

20. See, for example, Robert A. Dahl, "Pluralism Revisited," *Comparative Politics* (1978): 191–203; Thomas R. Dye, *Who's Running America* (Englewood Cliffs, N.J.: Prentice-Hall, 1976); David Gibbs, *The Political Economy of Third World Intervention: Mines, Money, and U.S. Policy in the Congo Crisis* (Chicago: University of Chicago Press, 1991); Kenneth Prewitt and Alan Stone, *The Ruling Elites: Elite Theory, Power, and American Democracy* (New York: Harper and Row, 1973); and David M. Ricci, *The Tragedy of Political Science: Politics, Scholarship, and Democracy* (New Haven: Yale University Press, 1984), chapter 8. This also led to the rise of neo-Marxist and class analysis of American politics. See G. William Domhoff, *The Higher Circles: Governing Class in America* (New York: Vintage, 1970); G. William Domhoff, *The Powers That Be: Processes of Ruling Class Domination in America* (New York: Vintage, 1978); and Ralph Miliband, *The State in Capitalist Society: The Analysis of the Western System of Power* (London: Quartet Books, 1969). For a discussion of the more simplistic elitist interpretations of the far left and far right, see Gary Allen, *None Dare Call It Conspiracy* (Rossmoor, Calif.: Concord Press, 1976), and Ole R. Holsti, "The Study of International Politics Makes Strange Bedfellows: Theories of the Radical Right

and the Radical Left," *American Political Science Review* 68 (1974): 217–41. For a good overview of more sophisticated interpretations that have developed, see Clyde W. Barrow, *Critical Theories of the State: Marxist, Neo-Marxist, Post-Marxist* (Madison: University of Wisconsin Press, 1993).

21. Unlike the labels *pluralism* and *elitism,* there is no common label for this third interpretation or model of American politics. During the late 1960s and 1970s, *hyperpluralism* probably was more commonly used than any other single term in the study of American politics.

22. Theodore J. Lowi, *The End of Liberalism: Ideology, Policy, and the Crisis of Public Authority* (New York: W. W. Norton, 1969), and Grant McConnell, *Private Power and American Democracy* (New York: Vintage, 1966). See also Marc Pilisuk and Tom Hayden, "Is There a Military-Industrial Complex Which Prevents Peace?" in William C. Vocke, ed., *American Foreign Policy: An Analytical Approach* (New York: Free Press, 1976), pp. 215–28.

23. See, for example, Douglass Cater, *Power in Washington* (New York: Vintage, 1964); and Hugh Heclo, "Issue Networks and the Executive Establishment," in Anthony King, ed., *The New American Political System* (Washington, D.C.: American Enterprise Institute, 1978), pp. 87–124. For more contemporary overviews, see Michael M. Atkinson and William D. Coleman, "Policy Networks, Policy Communities and the Problems of Governance," *Governance: An International Journal of Policy and Administration* (April 1992): 154–80; Jeffrey M. Berry, *The Interest Group Society* (Glenview, Ill.: Scott, Foresman, 1989); David Knoke, *Political Networks: The Structural Perspective* (Cambridge: Cambridge University Press, 1990); and Barry Wellman and S. D. Berkowitz, eds., *Social Structures: A Network Approach* (New York: Cambridge University Press, 1988).

24. This is an interpretation with which Robert Dahl, for example, became increasingly sympathetic over time. See Robert A. Dahl, *Dilemmas of Pluralist Democracy: Autonomy vs. Control* (New Haven: Yale University Press, 1982), and John F. Manley, "Neo-Pluralism: A Class Analysis of Pluralism I and Pluralism II," *American Political Science Review* 77 (June 1983): 368–83.

25. Gabriel A. Almond, *The American People and Foreign Policy* (New York: Praeger, 1960); Samuel P. Huntington, *The Common Defense: Strategic Programs in National Politics* (New York: Columbia University Press, 1961); and Warner R. Schilling, Paul T. Hammond, and Glenn H. Snyder, *Strategy, Politics and Defense Budgets* (New York: Columbia University Press, 1962). See also Graham T. Allison, *Essence of Decision: Explaining the Cuban Missile Crisis* (Boston: Little, Brown, 1971), chapter 5; Stanley Hoffmann, *Gulliver's Troubles or the Setting of American Foreign Policy* (New York: McGraw-Hill, 1968); Theodore J. Lowi, "Making Democracy Safe for the World: National Politics and Foreign Policy," in James N. Rosenau, ed., *Domestic Sources of Foreign Policy* (New York: Free Press, 1967), pp. 295–331; Richard A. Neusdadt, *Presidential Power: The Politics of Leadership* (New York: John Wiley, 1960); and Burton M. Sapin, *The Making of United States Foreign Policy* (New York: Praeger, 1966).

26. Roger Hilsman, *To Move A Nation: The Politics of Foreign Policy in the Administration of John F. Kennedy* (New York: Delta, 1964).

27. Ibid., p. 552.
28. Ibid., p. 553.
29. Ibid., p. 544.
30. Ibid., p. 13.
31. Ibid., 561–62.
32. Ibid., p. 543.
33. Ibid., pp. 542, 543.
34. Ibid., p. 557.
35. Ibid., p. 546.

36. Richard Barnet, *Roots of War: Men and Institutions Behind U.S. Foreign Policy* (New York: Penguin, 1972); I. M. Destler, Leslie H. Gelb, and Anthony Lake, *Our Own Worst Enemy: The Unmaking of American Foreign Policy* (New York: Simon and Schuster, 1984); John C. Donovan, *The Cold-Warriors: A Policy-Making Elite* (Lexington, Mass.: D.C. Heath, 1974); Leslie H. Gelb with Richard K. Betts, *The Irony of Vietnam: The System Worked* (Washington, D.C.: Brookings Institution Press, 1979); David Halberstam, *The Best and the Brightest* (New York: Random House, 1972); Godfrey Hodgson, *America in Our Time* (New York: Vintage, 1976); Walter Isaacson and Evan Thomas, *The Wise Men: Six Friends and the World They Made* (New York: Touchstone, 1986); and Hedrick Smith, *The Power Game* (New York: Ballantine, 1988). Hedrick Smith provides a more general overview of the changes that have occurred throughout American politics in, along with Anthony King, ed., *The New American Political System* (Washington, D.C.: AEI Press, 1990). For a somewhat different but complementary perspective, see Mark Edward Rupert, "Producing Hegemony: State/Society Relations and the Politics of Productivity in the United States," *International Studies Quarterly* 34 (1990): 427–56.

37. For a general discussion of direct and indirect influence, see, for example, Peter Bachrach and Morton Baratz, "Two Faces of Power," *American Political Science Review* 56 (December 1962): 947–52.

38. Pat McGowan and Stephen G. Walker, "Radical and Conventional Models of U.S. Foreign Economic Policy Making," *World Politics* 33 (April 1981): 378.

39. See Niccolo Machiavelli, in *The Prince and The Discourses* (New York: Modern Library, 1950), on "fortune," and Carl Von Clausewitz, in *On War* (New York: Penguin, 1832), on the concept of "friction."

40. For an overview, see Jerel A. Rosati, Joe D. Hagan, and Martin W. Sampson, eds., *Foreign Policy Restructuring: How Governments Respond to Global Change* (Columbia: University of South Carolina Press, 1994), especially chapter 1, "The Study of Change in Foreign Policy."

41. On foreign policy change, in addition to the articles in Jerel A. Rosati, Joe D. Hagan, and Martin W. Sampson, eds., *Foreign Policy Restructuring: How Governments Respond to Global Change* (Columbia: University of South Carolina Press, 1994), see Kjell Goldmann, *Change and Stability in Foreign Policy: The Problems and Possibilities of* Détente (Princeton: Princeton University Press, 1988; K.J. Holsti, ed., *Why Nations Realign: Foreign Policy*

Restructuring in the Postwar World (London: Allen and Unwin, 1982); Charles F. Hermann, "Changing Course: When Governments Choose to Redirect Foreign Policy." *International Studies Quarterly* 34 (March 1990): 3–21; Samuel P. Huntington, *American Politics: The Politics of Disharmony* (Cambridge, Mass.: Harvard University Press, 1981); and Jerel A. Rosati, "Cycles in Foreign Policy Restructuring: The Politics of Continuity and Change in U.S. Foreign Policy," in Jerel A. Rosati, Joe D. Hagan, and Martin W. Sampson, eds., *Foreign Policy Restructuring: How Governments Respond to Global Change* (Columbia, S.C.: University of South Carolina Press, 1994): 221–61; and James N. Rosenau, *The Study of Political Adaptation* (New York: Nichols Publishing, 1981). On American political change, see John H. Broesamle, *Reform and Reaction in Twentieth Century American Politics* (Westport, Conn: Greenwood Press, 1990); Frank R. Baumgartner and Bryan D. Jones, *Agendas and Instability in American Politics* (Chicago: University of Chicago Press, 1993); James MacGregor Burns, *The Deadlock of Democracy: Four-Party Politics in America* (Englewood Cliffs, N.J.: Prentice-Hall, 1963); Steve Fraser and Gary Gerstle, editors, *The Rise and Fall of the New Deal Order, 1930–1980* (Princeton: Princeton University Press, 1989); Theodore J. Lowi, *The Politics of Disorder* (New York: Basic Books, 1971); Arthur M. Schlesinger, Jr., *Cycles of American History* (Boston: Houghton Mifflin, 1986); Schattschneider, *The Semisovereign People*; and James L. Sundquist, *Politics and Policy* (Washington, D.C.: Brookings, 1968).

42. David B. Truman, *The Governmental Process: Political Interests and Public Opinion* (New York: Knopf, 1951), p. 44.

43. For an overview, see Jerel A. Rosati, Joe D. Hagan, and Martin W. Sampson, eds., *Foreign Policy Restructuring: How Gov-*

ernments Respond to Global Change (Columbia, S.C.: University of South Carolina Press, 1994). On foreign policy change, see also Charles F. Hermann, "Changing Course: When Governments Choose to Redirect Foreign Policy." *International Studies Quarterly* 34 (March 1990): 3–21; Samuel P. Huntington, *American Politics: The Politics of Disharmony* (Cambridge, Mass.: Harvard University Press, 1981); and Jerel A. Rosati, "Cycles in Foreign Policy Restructuring: The Politics of Continuity and Change in U.S. Foreign Policy," in Jerel A. Rosati, Joe D. Hagan, and Martin W. Sampson, eds., *Foreign Policy Restructuring: How Governments Respond to Global Change* (Columbia, S.C.: University of South Carolina Press, 1994): 221–61. On American political change, see also John H. Broesamle, *Reform and Reaction in Twentieth Century American Politics* (Westport, Conn: Greenwood Press, 1990); Frank R. Baumgartner and Bryan D. Jones, *Agendas and Instability in American Politics* (Chicago: University of Chicago Press, 1993); James MacGregor Burns, *The Deadlock of Democracy: Four-Party Politics in America* (Englewood Cliffs, N.J.: Prentice-Hall, 1963); Steve Fraser and Gary Gerstle, editors, *The Rise and Fall of the New Deal Order, 1930–1980* (Princeton: Princeton University Press, 1989); Theodore J. Lowi, *The Politics of Disorder* (New York: Basic Books, 1971); Arthur M. Schlesinger, Jr., *Cycles of American History* (Boston: Houghton Mifflin, 1986); Schattschneider, *The Semisovereign People*; and James L. Sundquist, *Politics and Policy* (Washington, D.C.: Brookings, 1968).

44. V.O. Key, Jr., *Politics, Parties, and Pressure Groups* (New York: Thomas W. Crowell, 1964), p. 70.

45. Hoffmann, *Gulliver's Troubles*, p. 277.

APPENDIX A
THE U.S. CONSTITUTION
ABRIDGED, AS IT PERTAINS
TO U.S. FOREIGN POLICY

PREAMBLE

We the people of the United States, in order to form a more perfect union, establish justice, insure domestic tranquility, provide for the common defense, promote the general welfare, and secure the blessings of liberty to ourselves and our posterity, do ordain and establish this Constitution for the United States of America.

ARTICLE I
(THE LEGISLATIVE BRANCH)

Section 8 The Congress shall have power

To lay and collect taxes, duties, imposts, and excises, to pay the debts and provide for the common defense and general welfare of the United States; but all duties, imposts and excises shall be uniform throughout the United States;

To borrow money on the credit of the United States;

To regulate commerce with foreign nations, and among the several States, and with the Indian tribes;

To establish an uniform rule of naturalization, and uniform laws on the subject of bankruptcies throughout the United States;

To coin money, regulate the value thereof, and of foreign coin, and fix the standard of weights and measures;

To provide for the punishment of counterfeiting the securities and current coin of the United States;

To establish post offices and post roads;

To promote the progress of science and useful arts by securing for limited times to authors and inventors the exclusive right to their respective writings and discoveries;

To constitute tribunals inferior to the Supreme Court;

To define and punish piracies and felonies committed on the high seas, and offenses against the law of nations;

To declare war, grant letters of marque and reprisal, and make rules concerning captures on land and water;

To raise and support armies, but no appropriation of money to that use shall be for a longer term than two years;

To provide and maintain a navy;

To make rules for the government and regulation of the land and naval forces;

To provide for calling forth the militia to execute the laws of the Union, suppress insurrections, and repel invasions;

To provide for organizing, arming, and disciplining the militia, and for governing such part of them as may be employed in the service of the United States, reserving to the States respectively the appointment of the officers, and the authority of training the militia according to the discipline prescribed by Congress;

To exercise exclusive legislation in all cases whatsoever, over such district (not exceeding ten miles square) as may, be cession of particular States, and the acceptance of Congress, become the seat of government of the United States, and to exercise like authority over all places purchased by the consent of the legislature of the State, in which the same shall be, for erection of forts, magazines, arsenals, dockyards and other needful buildings;—and

To make all laws which shall be necessary and proper for carrying into execution the foregoing powers, and all other powers vested by this Constitution in the government of the United States, or in any department or officer thereof.

Section 10 No State shall enter into any treaty, alliance, or confederation; grant letters of marque and reprisal; coin money; emit bills of credit; make anything but gold and silver coin a tender in payment of debts; pass any bill of attainder, ex post facto law, or law impairing the obligation of contracts, or grant any title of nobility.

No State shall, without the consent of Congress, lay any imposts or duties on imports or exports, except what may be absolutely necessary for executing its inspection laws: and the net produce of all duties and imposts, laid by any State on imports or exports, shall be for the use of the treasury of the United States; and all such laws shall be subject to the revision and control of the Congress.

No State shall, without the consent of Congress, lay any duty of tonnage, keep troops or ships of war in time of peace, enter into any agreement or compact with another State, or with a foreign power, or engage in war, unless actually invaded, or in such imminent danger as will not admit of delay.

ARTICLE II
(THE EXECUTIVE BRANCH)

Section 2 The President shall be commander in chief of the army and navy of the United States, and of the militia of the several States, when called into the actual service of the United States; he may require the opinion, in writing, of the principal officer in each of the executive departments, upon any subject relating to the duties of their respective offices, and he shall have power to grant reprieves and pardons for offenses against the United States, except in cases of impeachment.

He shall have power, by and with the advice and consent of the Senate, to make treaties, provided two-thirds of the Senators present concur; and he shall nominate, and by and with the advice and consent of the Senate, shall appoint ambassadors, other public ministers and consuls, judges of the Supreme Court, and all other officers of the United States, whose ap-

pointments are not herein otherwise provided for, and which shall be established by law; but Congress may by law vest the appointment of such inferior officers, as they think proper, in the President alone, in the courts of law, or in the heads of departments.

The President shall have power to fill up all vacancies that may happen during the recess of the Senate, by granting commissions which shall expire at the end of their next session.

Section 3 He shall from time to time give to the Congress information of the state of the Union, and recommend to their consideration such measures as he shall judge necessary and expedient; he may, on extraordinary occasions, convene both houses, or either of them, and in case of disagreement between them, with respect to the time of adjournment, he may adjourn them to such time as he shall think proper; he shall receive ambassadors and other public ministers; he shall take care that the laws be faithfully executed, and shall commission all the officers of the United States.

ARTICLE III
(THE JUDICIAL BRANCH)

Section 2 The judicial power shall extend to all cases, in law and equity, arising under this Constitution, the laws of the United States, and treaties made, or which shall be made, under their authority;—to all cases affecting ambassadors, other public ministers and consuls;—to all cases of admiralty and maritime jurisdiction;—to controversies to which the United States shall be a party;—to controversies between two or more States;—*between a State and citizens of another State;*—between citizens of different States;—between citizens of the same State claiming lands under grants of different States, and between a State, or the citizens thereof, and foreign states, citizens or subjects.

In all cases affecting ambassadors, other public ministers and consuls, and those in which a State shall be party, the Supreme Court shall have original jurisdiction. In all the other cases before mentioned, the Supreme Court shall have appellate jurisdiction, both as to law and fact, which such exceptions, and under such regulations, as the Congress shall make.

APPENDIX B
INTERNET AND LIBRARY SEARCHES FOR INFORMATION

There are a variety of resources and information available (electronically and in print) at the library and on the Internet in order to conduct research and access lots of information. This is a very brief, but hopefully user friendly, guide on how to utilize electronic and print sources available on the Internet and most libraries in order to conduct research and update information on U.S. foreign policy. These are absolutely essential basic skills to learn and have for the future.

First, *a distinction must be made between a URL/Website address, an Internet search engine, and a database:*

1. A **URL/Website address** will take you to a specific site or source or organization on the Internet (e.g., the Website for an article from *The New York Times* begins *http://www.nytimes.com ...*, etc.). This is useful if you have a specific Website address and you know specifically where you want to go (see, e.g., Table 17.4).

2. An **Internet search engine** (e.g., yahoo and google are excellent places to begin) allows one to search for sources and information throughout the Internet. It usually allows for the broadest, most open-ended, but often time-consuming searches. You can access a search engine on the Internet by usually typing, for example, *www.yahoo.com* in the address area. After the yahoo homepage comes up, then you type the relevant topic, key words, title, or author in the search area. You should come up with lots of "hits" (or responses and links). You need to look them over to determine which are relevant to your concerns. You then left click the mouse on the link to access the Website and scan it to see if it provides helpful information. Always bookmark a valuable Website that you would like to go to again.

3. A **database** consists of a large set of information (such as references and articles in different newspapers, magazines, and/or journals) and is available in both electronic form (such as InfoTrac®

College Edition, *LexusNexus*) and in print form (such as *Public Affairs Information Service*) that is usually subscribed to by libraries (and other organizations).

Whereas the Internet is available to anybody who can connect, you must be authorized to have access to databases by, for example, being a member of a college or university (who subscribes to the database). Relevant information is found through searching within the electronic database by title, author, keywords, and subjects or by examining the printed index. Databases are probably the most efficient way to find references to relevant sources and information (and find full text articles). For example, InfoTrac College Edition, is an excellent database that covers, among other topics, international affairs, politics, and U.S. foreign policy with over 20 years worth of often "full-text articles" from nearly 4,000 scholarly, policy, and popular journals and magazines.

Second, what follows are *helpful hints as to which are some of the better databases to use to find different electronic and print sources* of information about international affairs and U.S. foreign policy:

- For American newspaper articles use *LexusNexus* and the General Magazine Index of InfoTrac College Edition (for an electronic version).
- For foreign newspaper articles use *LexusNexus* (for an electronic version).
- For popular magazine articles, such as *Newsweek* or *New Republic* or the *Economist,* use InfoTrac College Edition, *LexusNexus* (for an electronic version); *Public Affairs Information Service, Readers' Guide to Periodical Abstracts* (for the print version).
- For foreign policy-oriented journal articles, such as *Foreign Affairs, Foreign Policy* or *World Policy Journal,* use InfoTrac College Edition, (for an electronic version); *International Political Science Abstracts, Public Affairs Information Service, Social Science Abstracts* (for the print version).

- For academic journal articles, such as *American Political Science Review, Diplomatic History, Political Science Quarterly, International Security, International Studies Quarterly,* use InfoTrac College Edition, *Project MUSE* (for an electronic version) and *International Political Science Abstracts* (for the print version).
- For books, use your library catalogue system (for the print version), as well as *www.amazon.com* and *www.barnesandnoble.com* (for an electronic overview).
- For book reviews (of at least 250 words) use InfoTrac College Edition, *LexusNexus* (for an electronic version) and *Book Review Digest* (for the print version).

- For U.S. government documents, use *CIS (Congressional Universe), LexusNexus* (for an electronic version) and the library catalogue system (for the print version).
- For articles or documents from an IGO (International Governmental Organization) or a PVO/NGO (Private Voluntary or Non-Governmental Organization), use a search engine (for an electronic version).

If for some reason you are having difficulty finding any sources, especially electronically (because the helpful hints aren't working), then you will probably have to rely on search engines or engage in a more traditional search in a library.

INDEX

Index